edited and with an introduction by
Cary Nelson and Lawrence Grossberg

Marxism and the Interpretation of Culture

University of Illinois Press
Urbana and Chicago

Illini Books edition, 1988

© 1988 by the Board of Trustees of the University of Illinois
Manufactured in the United States of America
2 3 4 5 C P 5 4 3

This book is printed on acid-free paper.

Library of Congress Cataloging-in-Publication Data

Marxism and the interpretation of culture.

  Includes bibliographies and index.
  1. Communism and culture. 2. Philosophy, Marxist.
3. Europe—Intellectual life—20th century. 4. Marxist
criticism. 5. Communist aesthetics. 6. Humanities—
Methodology. 7. Social sciences—Methodology.
I. Nelson, Cary. II. Grossberg, Lawrence.
HX523.M3766 1988   306'.345   87-5981
ISBN 0-252-01108-2 (cloth: alk. paper)
ISBN 0-252-01401-4 (paper: alk. paper)

Contents

v

Marxism and the Interpretation of Culture grew out of a series of events organized by the Unit for Criticism and Interpretive Theory at the University of Illinois at Urbana-Champaign in the summer of 1983: a group of courses taught by several of the contributors (Anderson, Fields, Grossberg, Hall, Jameson, Lesage, Petrovíc, Schacht, Spivak) were attended by several hundred faculty members and students; the Marxist Literary Group held its annual meeting; and the summer culminated in a large international conference. For many of those who attended the conference, therefore, it was very much a culmination and working out of discussions and disputes that had not only a long prior history but also a very specific and extended interactive history that summer. During the following two years most of the papers were very heavily revised, in part as a result of the challenge of the whole summer's events. Several additional essays were solicited from people who were invited but could not attend the conference, and a few people who attended the conference but did not present papers submitted essays on their own.

We have retained from the conference itself only those commentaries and discussion sessions that suggest substantive critiques of a position, develop significantly the central issues of a particular essay, or provide interesting contrasts among positions. We have included the names of people asking questions or offering comments whenever they were willing to be identified; and we have cooperated with those who preferred to remain anonymous. We have also tried to follow people's wishes about such matters as whether or not to capitalize "Marxism." Finally, we should note that the editors assisted with the translation of the essays by Achugar, Balibar, Lefebvre, Mouffe, Negt, and Wang.

Neither the conference nor the book would have been possible without the help of a great many people. For advice, continuing assistance, and the benefit of their experience we give special thanks to Daniel Alpert, Nina Baym, David Bright, Theodore Brown, David Colley, Judith Edelstein, William Fierke, Joel Hersig, Roger Martin, Mark Netter, Gary North, William Plater, William Prokasy, Edward Sullivan, Patricia Wenzel, Richard Wentworth, and Linda Wilson. Jefferson Hendricks helped coordinate the conference, and many people worked long hours during it: Roberta Astroff, Steve Ater, Van Cagle, Meredith Cargill, Briankle Chang, K. C. Chen, Karen Cole, Jon Crane, John Duvall, Michael Greer, William May, Nelly Mitchell, Lisa Odell, Steve Olsen, David Riefman, Mary Robinson, Phillip Sellers, and Tim Vere. James Kavanaugh provided helpful advice on the Balibar translation. Karen Ford, Michael Greer, Marsha Bryant, Teresa Magnum, Gail Rost, and Anne Balsamo assisted us in assembling the final manuscript. The book was copyedited by Theresa L. Sears. Financial support within the University of Illinois at Urbana-Champaign came from the School of Humanities, the College of Liberal Arts and Sciences, the College of Communications, the Research Board, the George A. Miller Endowment Fund, International Programs and Services, the Office for Women's Resources and Services, the School of Social Sciences, the Center for Latin American and Caribbean Studies, the University Library, the Institute of Communications Research, the Religious Studies Program, and the Departments of Anthropology, English, French, Germanic Languages and Literatures, History, Philosophy, Political Science, Sociology, and Speech Communication; external support came from the National Endowment for the Humanities. The book was designed by David Colley.

Introduction:
The Territory of Marxism

The rather broad title of this book, *Marxism and the Interpretation of Culture,* signals our belief in an emerging change in the discursive formations of contemporary intellectual life, a change that cuts across the humanities and the social sciences. It suggests that the proper horizon for interpretive activity, whatever its object and whatever its disciplinary base, is the entire field of cultural practices, all of which give meaning, texture, and structure to human life. Moreover, the title situates Marxism at the center of such developments and thus suggests the need to transgress the line that has traditionally separated culture from social, economic, and political relations. Marxism, of course, has long been at least implicitly involved in breaking down the barriers between these domains, making each of necessity a site of interpretive activity—by politicizing interpretive and cultural practices, by looking at the economic determinations of cultural production, by radically historicizing our understanding of signifying practices—from political discourses to art, from beliefs to social practices, from the discourse of psychology to the discourse of economics—and, of course, by continuing to revise and enlarge a body of theory with multidisciplinary implications. It is nearly impossible, for example, to imagine that one can construct a well-informed Marxist analysis of literature without taking into account recent work in historiography, popular culture, theories of otherness and sexual difference, and analyses of the contemporary political scene. The essays gathered here clearly extend and complicate that tradition. And we hope that a further step is taken in collecting these diverse projects within one volume.

Indeed the very act of gathering these essays together challenges their self-sufficiency in ways some of the authors would, no doubt, be disinclined to allow. If the book undermines the traditional divisions between academic disciplines, it also, by its scope, by the juxtapositions it creates, of necessity calls many of the individual contributions into question. This book, then, is intended to be a collective intervention in the contested terrain it maps. Its identity depends both on the strengths of the individual essays and on the innumerable connections and disputations evoked when the essays are compared and contrasted. The structure of the book is designed to facilitate this process of making unfamiliar connections and to resist offering itself as its own alternative, stable map. In planning a con-

1

ference on this topic, we felt we had to recognize certain standard (but often marginalized) subject areas—popular culture, Latin America, feminism—so as to be certain that relevant constituencies were guaranteed a forum and a chance to work together; as a result, we adopted a dual strategy of both organizing separate sessions on these topics and placing related papers in other sessions. In organizing the book, we were able to encourage more diverse theoretical intersections. To read the book, we think, is to be drawn to reorganize both it and the domain of culture itself, for any point of entrance will lead one to risk losing control of the disciplinary terrain one considered a secure possession. Reading the book involves continually recognizing not only similarities and differences among the essays, relations that transgress traditional disciplines, but also multiple ways of structuring the book and thus of charting a path through the terrain in which the relations among power, signification, and history are defined and debated.

Thus, for example, to read Ross on the political implications of new writing practices is potentially to be encouraged to think of connections with Mouffe's analysis of how new social alliances are constituted. These issues in turn overlap with Anderson's and Petrović's rather different constructions of the connotations of revolutionary change. Their essays connect with Suvin's reconsideration of the representability of persons, a key issue in revolutionary art, with Moretti's critique of the politics of modernism, and with Reyes Matta's analysis of the role popular culture plays in radical change. And all of these essays are either explicitly or implicitly in dialogue with the volume's pervasive concern with the politics of theorizing within the contemporary social formation. Alternatively, to read Ross on commodification may lead one to think of connections with Laclau, Pêcheux, and Spivak on the discursive nature of power; with Lefebvre, Patton, and both Mattelarts on postmodernity and production; with Chambers and Frith on the meaning of popular resistance; and, more obviously, with Pfeil, Holland, Jameson, and Ryan. Yet the book also interrupts Ross's discourse with the feminist demands articulated by Mouffe, MacKinnon, Lesage, and Delphy, and with the more traditional sense of cultural politics in the essays by Reyes Matta, Achugar, and even Schacht and Negt. As every such pathway carries the reader into its own disciplinary and ideological articulations, reading itself becomes an effort to empower particular ways of constituting the discourses of Marxism, of foregrounding particular questions and answers. Our own interest is in multiplying these alternatives.

As little as twenty years ago it would have been impossible to imagine such a project and such a volume. Even as late as 1975, collections on Marxism and culture were limited to a predictable group of writers and interpretive frameworks.[1] Across a wide range of disciplines, culture was explained in terms of structures of power that were assumed as given and rarely questioned. Culture itself was always viewed as secondary and often as epiphenomenal. Marx and Engels themselves, of course, repeatedly had questioned the role of culture in politics and economics, just as they recognized the need to interpret literature and art politically and historically.[2] But their work here was very tentative and their suggestions often in conflict. Moreover, their accounts of the relations between culture and society were dependent on some of their most notoriously ambiguous concepts, such as ideology (a concept whose problematic history is recounted and newly challenged in this volume by Balibar and given subtle and reflective application by Hall and Spivak), intellectual labor, and base/superstructure. Later, the Communist party institutionalized Marxist theory in the form of Zhdanovism (the doctrine of socialist realism officially sanctioned by the Second and Third Internationals), and culture was reduced to a reflection of economic relations.[3] Since culture was considered to be totally determined by its class origin and mode of production, its politics seemed easy to define.

This sort of Marxism typically refused to grant cultural practices any specificity or to consider their active role in defining social relations and resisting political domination. Cultural forms were generally linked to specific classes. The dominant culture belonged to the dominant class and reflected both its interests and its interpretation of reality. When working-class culture that met the criteria of socialist realism could be found, it was celebrated as revolutionary. More frequently, the working class was seen as having accepted the ideas of the dominant class, ideas that represented the dominant position and thus distorted actual working-class living conditions. This theory dependably produced readings that revealed the economic content and class perspective disguised in culture's surface, formal characteristics.[4]

Yet this dismissal is itself overly reductive, for the theoretical orientation did yield powerful insights and did place the political and social significance of cultural production on the agenda of interpretive theory, successfully challenging the unthinking idealization of high art. Moreover, even the most notoriously reductive elements of traditional Marxism are difficult to dismiss easily. In fact, one might argue that reflection theories, however qualified and problematized, play a necessary and constitutive role, not only for all later and more sophisticated Marxisms, but also in all historically or politically grounded interpretation. Finally, the established canon of Marxist criticism provided the tradition against which an alternative tradition of Marxist cultural theorizing could be defined—not only, however, by way of correction, amplification, revision, or outright rejection, but also by way of an uneasy relation of derivation, potential return, and perhaps even occasional nostalgia for the security of its political interpretations. "Vulgar Marxism," that overdetermined and mythically hypostatized category, remains the anxiously regarded double of contemporary Marxist writing.

As it happens, an alternative tradition has existed for some time, but it remained, even as late as the 1950s, largely unknown. Antonio Gramsci's *Prison Notebooks,* central here to the essays by Hall, Laclau, West, Mouffe, and Golding, were unpublished.[5] Lukács's Hegelian reading of Marx, a reading he had repeatedly renounced, and his theory of reification, which argued against the simple class exploitation model, remained untranslated (*History and Class Consciousness,* first published in 1923, appeared in English only in 1971).[6] The work of Karl Korsch and Rosa Luxemburg was virtually unknown.[7] Also untranslated were the important 1930s debates between Lukács and Bloch and among Brecht, Benjamin, and Adorno.[8] And, of course, work by Marx and Engels, including the *Economic and Philosophical Manuscripts,* that later would prove influential remained unpublished.[9] Moreover, productive contradictions in work that at first seemed to provide a radical opening and then seemed more traditional and reductive, such as Lukács's attacks on the modern bourgeois novel, took some time to be carefully explored and recuperated in terms of their full com-

3

plexity.[10] While Lukács shifted critical attention to matters of form, and thus foregrounded the specificity of superstructural effects, he continued to read literary texts as if their class origin determined their representation of reality. The modern bourgeois novel was to be valued to the extent that it accurately depicted the fragmentation and lack of totalization at the heart of bourgeois reality. Unable to offer an alternative vision, the modern bourgeois novel failed the political test Lukács set for all literature.

In the end, however, it was not only the internal development of theory but also changes in the broader social formation that prompted the need for a more sophisticated Marxism. It is essential to realize that each generation is driven to theorize by the particular historical tendencies and events that confront it. In the twentieth century, as it happens, each generation has faced developments that have in some ways been parallel, such as the different stages of technological revolution; though always inflected differently, these developments have stimulated the appearance of related problematics at different points in the history of Marxist theory. If we keep in mind the economic, political, and social upheavals that accompanied the development of modernity, we will recognize that the major concerns of modern Western Marxism were formed in large part in response to the changing historical context of the Western capitalist nations. Thus the first major attempts to revise Marxism came between the two world wars, partly in response to the rise of fascism, the failure of the European working classes to organize in the name of a socialist revolution, Stalin's rise to power and the establishment of state communism in Russia, and, finally, the beginnings of the second industrial revolution, a revolution of technology and communication.

Interestingly, some of the historical pressures that these events produced have been repeated in structurally similar ways. One can trace the history of Marxist theorizing as, in part, a continuing response to a series of questions repeatedly prompted by historical events. One such question, at the heart of twentieth-century Marxism and debated throughout this volume, concerns the identity of the potentially revolutionary subject. In the 1930s Marxists faced the problem that the working classes did not in fact revolt in the way Marx had expected. After the Second World War a different but comparable issue arose—the need to understand the impact of mass culture on working-class lives (lives that were, for a time, no longer lived in poverty) and to confront the question of how the working class might retain the resistance that was at least a potential of class difference. Increasingly, Marxism, under what Ernest Mandel has called "late capitalism," has had to confront a quite unexpectedly different structure of class relations.[11] Thus, in the 1960s it became necessary to consider whether the potential revolutionary subject had actually been displaced, that, as events seemed to suggest, it was no longer to be found in the efforts of the working class to organize itself but in protest movements centered around blacks, distinctly privileged and middle-class college students, and women. As it happened, these movements had a number of specific successes. But the largely existential critiques they offered lacked an economic base, and the movements themselves failed not only to present an alternative organizational infrastructure but also to produce broad and pervasive political change. Their failure became the challenge for the theorists of the 1970s. A number of specific developments in Marxist theory, such as Lukács's understanding

4

of how class consciousness is different from class position, or the elaboration of subcultural theory in the 1970s, speak directly to these different social realities. Many of the essays that follow, including those by Hall, Balibar, Mouffe, and Negt, respond both directly and indirectly to this challenge.

A number of the writers included here were either active in or strongly influenced by another development of postwar society—the rise of the New Left, which gave the emerging theories of Western Marxism an organizational form. A loose, partly organized, partly fragmented configuration of varied political commitments and intellectual projects, the New Left helped establish the intellectual networks and shared urgencies that would later energize debate within Marxist theory. Beginning in England and in Europe as early as the mid-1950s (with much stronger links to Marxism than its American counterpart of the 1960s), the New Left challenged the ability of the inherited versions of Marxism (particularly as defined by the communist parties) to give adequate accounts of racism and imperialism on *either* side of the Iron Curtain. International events—from the Suez crisis to the Russian invasions of Hungary and Czechoslovakia—made idealizations of the major powers impossible. At the same time the violent history of Stalinism became more widely known and documented, putting still more distance between the New Left and those versions of Marxism aligned with the Soviet Union. Meanwhile, with the rise of mass culture and mass society and the development of a relatively affluent working class, the traditional Marxist construction of class difference, with its expectations of revolution, seemed increasingly inadequate. A consumption-oriented, technologically invested society demanded new models of class struggle and social change, imperatives apparent here in the essays by Hall, Negt, Petrović, Delphy, and Pêcheux.

Finally, like most major bodies of theory, Marxism has been gradually, but substantially, altered by the formal and linguistic self-consciousness that transformed modern art and culture, a transformation that eventually made it impossible to limit the notion of culture to a small body of privileged texts, objects, and discourses. Cultural theory has now expanded the category of culture well beyond "the best that has been thought and said," beyond the general forms of art, language, and entertainment, beyond the leisure (that is, nonlabor) activities of the general population.

Describing modernism's impact on Marxism would itself be a major project; but it is necessary, in this context, to point to a few of its key elements. Both in art and philosophy a foregrounding of issues of language promoted a broad concern with culture, symbolic forms, communication, and meaning. In philosophy, the appearance of logical positivism (with its concern for language and knowledge) and phenomenology (with its focus on meaning and consciousness) helped to energize major articulations of a critical humanism. The humanist (and often Hegelian) Marxism that emerged, ranging from Lukács to Korsch to the members of the Frankfurt school,[12] increasingly emphasized experience as a mediating term in the relations between social structures and individual lives. Other writers, such as Brecht, Benjamin, and Lefebvre were strongly influenced by artistic movements, while in Gramsci and Lefebvre one sees an increasing recognition of the need for historical and social specificity.[13] Then, in the work of a later generation of Marxist humanists (many of whose members, ironically, did not read the earlier Marxist humanists until after they had already begun

5

to define their positions)—including Jean-Paul Sartre and Henri Lefebvre in France; Raymond Williams, E. P. Thompson, and John Berger in England; and the Praxis group in Yugoslavia—human consciousness began to play a still more active and creative role in accounts of social life.[14]

Following on a critique begun, in fact, by Engels, this humanist Marxism typically attempted to rethink (or at least problematize) the unidirectional causality implicit in the base/superstructure model and often focused on questions of meaning, experience, and individuality as mediations. Furthermore, rejecting the traditional theories that locate the working class between false consciousness and revolution, it asked instead how human beings create meaningful social realities and emphasized discussions of culture and ideology as the site of domination and resistance. In this work from the 1950s and 1960s, culture as the officially sanctioned discourse of art and knowledge is explicitly brought into dialogue with more anthropological notions of culture—as whole ways of life, structures of experience, or symbolic systems.

Typically, this generation of Marxist humanists concentrated its efforts on conceptualizing the diverse field of culture and on describing and defining different cultural domains, thereby clearly establishing culture as a central political issue and interpretive problem, instead of glibly moving through it directly into economic production and class relations or confidently moving past it under the protection of an abstract philosophical discourse. Furthermore, this second rediscovery of Marxist humanism led critics to recognize that there are multiple cultures within the social formation. In many instances, this took the form of a concern with working-class cultures as continuing instances of difference from and even resistance to the dominant cultural practices of the ruling classes. In other cases, sometimes fueled by the negative views of the mass culture theorists, including those of the Frankfurt school, Marxists began to examine the forms of mass media and popular culture, seeing them as occasions for more complex relations of power and meaning than had heretofore been imagined.

As the implications of this second appearance of a humanist Marxism began to be recognized, it became clear that cultural analysis needed to be concerned with all the structural and meaning-producing activities by which human life is created and maintained. As this collection demonstrates, cultural theory is now as likely to study political categories (such as democracy), forms of political practice (such as alliances), and structures of domination (including otherness) and experience (such as subjectification) as it is to study art, history, philosophy, science, ethics, communicative codes, or technology. Cultural theory is involved with reexamining the concepts of class, social identity, class struggle, and revolution; it is committed to studying questions of pleasure, space, and time; it aims to understand the fabric of social experience and everyday life, even the foundations of the production and organization of power itself. Consequently, it is all but impossible to define the terrain of cultural theory by pointing to a finite set of object-domains or to the search for a limited set of interpretive tools. In fact, the current renaissance is, to some extent, predicated on the recognition that the constitution of the very category of "culture" (which is often opposed to something else—the economic, the social, or the natural) is itself already implicated within cultural processes.

6

In the middle and late 1960s (although it did not reach England and America until the late 1960s and the early 1970s), Marxism underwent a profound interchange with structuralism and semiotics, an interchange that marks the beginning of the third moment of Marxist revision and established the context within which the essays in this book were written, including the apparently humanistic essays by Schacht and Golding. While the second generation of humanist Marxists—who became known as cultural Marxists—placed the active human agent (understood both individually and socially) at the center of their theoretical perspective, it was the intersection of Marxism with structuralism and semiotics that gave the study of culture new momentum in the 1970s, both within Marxism and across a wide range of disciplines and theoretical perspectives. Of course, structuralism itself was not a static theory but an open-ended problematic built on its (at first implicit) critique of essentialism. As Saussure argued earlier, the meaning of a sign is not an intrinsic property of the signifier but rather a relationship defined by the differential relations into which the signifier is inserted.[15] And in his related critique of humanist Marxism, Louis Althusser argued, in a series of articles collected in *For Marx* (1965), that the human subject is itself a historical product, an ensemble of social relationships, not something essential and permanent.[16] Subjectivity is culturally determined; it is a function of the ideological practices by which certain subject positions become historically available. Furthermore, the social formation was reconceptualized as a structure of relatively autonomous levels of social practices, giving ideology a central and determining influence that could not merely be explained as the displaced trace of other forms of social practice. The overdetermination of any social practice by all the levels of the social formation meant that culture could not be reduced to the effects of economic relations, even if mediated through ideology. At the same time, across a wide range of fields, semiotics was offering an analytic vocabulary for the interpretation of signifying phenomena, while assigning such interpretations a certain independence from metaphysical issues of reality and psychological issues of intentionality.

As structuralism developed into poststructuralism—rejecting structuralism's unreflective claims to scientificity, crediting the semiotic and political nature of its own theorizing, recognizing that a more radically problematized human subject did have a place in textual production—it began to confront the implications these positions had for its own critical practice. While cultural Marxists did accept the ideological bases of their own theoretical and political positions, and consequently had begun to recognize the problematic, contingent nature of their own interpretive activities, it was poststructuralism that gave Marxists the vocabulary with which to begin theorizing their own determination.

Of course the contingent, variable nature of interpretation is also made apparent by the whole explosion of critical vocabularies in the past twenty-five years. If one were, today, to try to map the terrain of cultural theory, one would have to describe developments not only within Marxism but also within phenomenology and hermeneutics, structuralism and semiotics, psychoanalysis, feminism, deconstruction and poststructuralism, postmodernism, analytic philosophy (including speech act theory, pragmatics, and post-Wittgensteinian philosophy), as well as theoretical developments in sociology, anthropology, and narrative theory. The fairly recent self-reflexiveness about Marxist critical practice is thus a particularly overdetermined phenomenon, representing the belated extension into critical theory of the formal self-consciousness and the problematizing of meaning and signification long characteristic of modern art. In Marxism this move was certainly encouraged by more complex models of the fragmented social formation. And, of course, the poststructuralist revolution had strong implications for the kinds of knowledge Marxism traditionally claimed to possess. If the meaning of a text is not intrinsic to it but rather the product of a system of differences into which the text is articulated, then any text is open to multiple readings. Thus it is doubtful that one can, in fact, actually (and decisively) read the meaning and politics of a text or a practice simply by a straightforward encounter with the text itself or by mechanically applying some interpretive procedure. If meaning itself is overdetermined, the effects of any cultural practice (including criticism) can be both multiple and contradictory.

Critics sensitive to these arguments increasingly found themselves engaged in a problematic activity, one demanding attention to their own practices of consumption (use, appropriation) and to the contexts of their own intellectual production. Questioning the relationship between criticism and its object is especially difficult for any body of theory that, like Marxism, is committed to political critique and opposition. Yet this is part of Marxism's necessary (and paradoxical) burden in the contemporary theoretical scene, just as Marxism is also empowered to politicize epistemological doubt within other bodies of theory.

For Marxism in particular, reflections on the changing social formation have been a powerful force in the development of such theoretical positions. Many of the essays here—including those by Lefebvre, Patton, Jameson, Pfeil, Michèle Mattelart, Chambers, and Holland—in fact are concerned with theorizing in response to the specific structures of the contemporary social formation: the emergence of multinational capitalism as the dominant world economic structure; the rapid deployment of electronic media and the growth of both an information and a consumer-oriented economy; the fragmentation of the social formation and the proliferation of subcultures; the collapse of many traditional structures of authority; and even, finally, the explosion of critical methods that is part of the structure of contemporary academic life. These and other changes had important consequences, not only in the postcolonial world, where they undercut the apparent capacity for self-determination achieved in decolonialization, but, more powerfully, in the advanced capitalist societies themselves, where they suggest both the impossibility of any static representation of reality and the utility of localized theory and localized political resistance—though it is often Marxism's special task to defend its more general and enduring insights in the very face of these changes, as the essays by Anderson, Jameson, Negt, and Fields make clear.

Lefebvre, for example, argues that such new social conditions require new terms and concepts within Marxism, for capitalism has now filtered into the microstructures and organization of daily life. Responding to the increasing commodification of both experience and culture, including language, Ross reexamines the possibilities of an avant-garde, oppositional writing practice. Mouffe and West argue, respectively, that complex structures of resistance and domination require that Marxism radically expand

8

its theoretical and political base. Hall posits that the emergence of a hegemonic politics of the New Right demands a strategic theoretical and political realignment of the Left. MacKinnon and Patton, on the other hand, conclude that Marxism is finally inadequate in the face of the challenges of contemporary forms of power. Fields, however, responds by arguing that the variety of contemporary political struggles must be understood within the common systemic structures of capitalist oppression, while Negt attempts to open a space within those traditional categories for these new challenges.

In many of these essays, in fact, one can sense how more recent forms of political activity have also powerfully affected Marxist theory. The mass social movements of the 1960s, for example, were not organized by a "party," that is, by a central, hierarchical structure. The influential May 1968 university strike in Paris, supported by parts of the labor movement, was actually opposed by some of the formal leftist organizations. The strike apparently came from the bottom up; and to the traditional Left, it seemed in some ways indistinguishable from tendencies implicit in advanced capitalism itself. The populist potential of 1968, now symbolically linked with late 1960s political protests in America and broadly metaphorized in Marxist theory, has come in part to represent the need for a distinctly decentralized, self-critical, plural, and unpredictable notion of how Marxism should develop.

As Marxism has confronted its own claims to truth as a representation of reality, claims that are just as real for those who would deny Marxism the status of a "science," it has located itself at the center of current epistemological debates, which have now begun to confront the problematic nature and role of theorizing itself and the status of theoretical concepts. Aronowitz, for example, claims that Marxists have failed to challenge the status of science, the dominant culture of late capitalism, as a pure, uncontaminated form of knowledge. Unless we interrogate it as an ideological and socially constituted discourse, Marxism can have no independent basis for its explanatory powers. Repeatedly, in fact, these essays rewrite both the epistemology of Marxism and its basic concepts. Amariglio, Resnick, and Wolff conclude that if class can no longer designate a predefined and stable set of subjects, then the very categories of power in Marxism—such as domination, class struggle, ruling and ruled classes—have to be rethought. On the other hand, with a security uncommon in this book, Negt asserts that since the analysis of capital has been completed, Marxists should now turn to the remaining unresolved theoretical issues that presently block the formulation of a coherent position of critique—subjectivity, the proletariat, and ecology.

Negt's relative confidence, however, may be overshadowed by the radically problematized logic of Balibar's "Vacillation of Ideology." Simultaneously challenging Marxism's most basic claims while affirming their historical necessity, Balibar offers a history of the constitutive contradictions between ideology and the working class, a history that also represents an attempt to read his own situation as a leftist intellectual in France. If the working class is to play a revolutionary role in history, Balibar argues, then its relationship to the category of ideology must be rethought. And if ideology is only and always the dominant ideology, then the proletariat as potentially revolutionary subject stands outside ideology in the space of some other ideal knowledge. But this makes Marxism a theory of "mastery without slavery," which in turn makes the revolutionary act incomprehensible. On the other hand, if ideology is a worldview and, consequently, the proletariat must have its own ideology, then how is the proletariat to articulate its revolutionary struggle? The theoretical crisis of "ideology" and the crisis over whether the working class is to be the source of revolutionary struggle are historically one and the same. So Marxism must rethink the class identity of the workers' movement as the blind spot in its own politics in the history of capitalism. To do so is to deconstruct the process of the idealization of history.

None of these critiques of Marxism's own logic and historicity could exist, of course, without pressure and stimulation from other contemporary bodies of theory. Indeed many of the most productive developments within Marxism have come both from a more intricately responsive confrontation with positions opposed to Marxism's basic assumptions and from a mutually transforming dialogue with other views of culture and interpretation. Barrett, Eagleton, and Wang all, surprisingly, attempt to expand Marxist cultural theory by returning to consider more traditional questions of aesthetics and normative criticism. Marxism has become a place where competing theories work out their similarities and differences and articulate their challenges to one another. These differences are now frequently fought out within the space of a Marxist vocabulary, as disagreements over the problematics that should constitute a Marxist discourse.

As West's analysis of difference, Holland's and Pfeil's efforts to chart the psychodynamics of contemporary experience, Patton's and Chambers's postmodernism, Laclau's and Spivak's poststructuralism, and the book's pervasive engagement with feminism will all demonstrate, this almost forced dialogue of Marxism with other perspectives has had profound implications for Marxism itself, for the issues defining Marxism have come into question and have been reshaped as a result. Particularly important here have been Marxism's interactions with analyses of how power is exercised in terms of hierarchical structures of difference and otherness that are not reducible to the model of class exploitation. Marxism has had, as a result, to rethink its understanding of racism, sexism, and colonialism, a process that inevitably historicizes Marxism's earlier categories and concerns. Confronting its own historical status has meant also that Marxism has had to call into question basic assumptions about liberatory political practice—the role of the working class, the function of the intellectual, the determining nature of the mode of production, the place of the state apparatus—as it has attempted to adjudicate, if not always incorporate, the competing political claims of the various subordinate populations in late capitalism. As the organization of this book suggests, issues of sexual difference, in particular, cut across all the traditional categories of Marxist thought. The problematics of gender and the relations between Marxism and feminism are central here to the essays by MacKinnon, Mouffe, Delphy, Spivak, Pfeil, Lesage, and Franco.

Spivak's essay in particular demonstrates the complex heteroglossia of Marxism's engagement with other bodies of theory. Like Balibar, she works in part through rereadings of Marx, and, like Balibar again, she can be said to read historical realities from the instabilities of theoretical discourses themselves. By presenting a critique of Western theory that argues its cultural dependence on international economic exploitation, Spivak poses the question of whether the subaltern woman can speak for herself. She argues that our subject positions are constructed by the realities of global capitalism and imperialism. So, too, the political role of the Western intellectual is dependent on the construction of subjectivity at sites of enforced silence in the Third World. Spivak's corrective analysis proceeds by a Derridean reading of the colonial discourses surrounding the practice of suttee, or widow sacrifice.

As Marxism has been challenged and rewritten, both by its dialogue with other bodies of theory and by its effort to acknowledge the diverse political realities of the postwar world; as Marxism has attempted to find more sophisticated models of the relations between culture and power, more reflective understandings of its own position within these relations, and more politically insightful and relevant tools for the analysis of contemporary structures of power—so has it become a much more varied discourse. One can no longer speak of Marxism in isolation from other intellectual and political positions, nor apart from the wider exigencies of history, for Marxism is no longer a single coherent discursive and political practice. As readers of this book will discover, there are now an extraordinary number of Marxist positions, discourses, methods, and politics. In trying to decide which discourses are and are not Marxist, one looks, almost ludicrously, for an engagement with Marx's own work, though at the same time it is essential to note that an ability to *problematize* Marx's writings has been central to the whole renaissance in Marxist theory.

The struggle to decide which positions are and are not Marxist continues to animate Marxist discourse, as in the essays by Anderson, Jameson, Fields, MacKinnon, Delphy, and Patton. Where, for example, is the boundary to be drawn between deconstruction and Marxist cultural criticism, between postmodernism and a Marxist analysis of late capitalism, or between feminist and Marxist analyses of the social and economic oppression of women? In fact, can anyone attempting to write about the politics of culture in capitalism not, in some way, be caught up in the discourses of Marx and Marxism? As Foucault points out, privileging appeals to Marxism's founding discourses obscures the way Marxism, at least in his work, is a continuing (if implicit) context, albeit without the citations that might serve to normalize it for readers.[17] Marxism, like the historical realities it interrogates, cannot escape the critique of essentialism carried out by contemporary critical theory and manifested in the contemporary historical context. That critique does not refuse a practice, text, or event its own identity. But it does suggest that identity is unstable and never guaranteed in advance; identity is part of an event's contextual determinations, the articulation of its effects. By refusing to take its own categories for granted, contemporary Marxism has reappropriated the critical power of Marx's interpretive practice.

Thus one cannot, in light of the essays gathered here, easily set limits to Marxism's current concerns. Yet the effort to establish the core commitments of Marxism is a necessary part of its effort to maintain some unique influence in the field of interpretation. The problem for Marxism is thus twofold: on the one hand, to deterritorialize its own discourse in response to changing historical realities; and on the other hand, to reterritorialize itself in order to constitute that very response. Indeed, as the reader reorganizes this volume to suit his or her own interests and commitments—

deciding which patterns of alliance and opposition among the essays to credit—the territory of Marxism will thereby be redefined. Discursively, however, Marxism threatens to collapse into criticism with a political edge. And that political edge is necessarily reestablished in different political contexts, perhaps generalizable only as something like a commitment to revolutionary identification with the cause of the oppressed.

Just what will *count* as a revolutionary intervention is an issue that animates, defines, and challenges all the theoretical positions and cultural domains discussed in the book. One way of reading the book, in fact, is as a debate on that issue. For example, Franco deconstructs a series of semantic oppositions and equivalences centered around male authorship in the Latin American literary tradition, thereby showing how "women and indigenous people can take the production of meaning into their own hands." Destabilizing and altering cultural semiotics from an oppositional standpoint is also the theme of Reyes Matta's discussion of the Nuevo Canciones movement and of Frith's analysis of pop culture as resistance, in which he contrasts two views of subcultural resistance: the first sees politics determined by whether music, for example, is an authentic expression of an oppositional or marginalized culture; the second locates politics in the textual manipulation of signs within and against the continuous commodification of all meaning. Ryan, on the other hand, does not describe what people make of the texts they consume as much as he defines a theory that gives people an active role in political struggles within the consumption of cultural objects. Somewhat surprisingly, in an essay that combines his earlier humanism with a new poststructuralist play on the semiosis of "revolution," Petrović provides semantic evidence for the dispersion of the revolutionary impulse into different cultural domains. Lesage, however, argues that all revolutionary impulses fail if they are not now centered on the historical imperatives of sexism and racism. Anderson, finally, would cut short all this speculation—from Achugar's analysis of the potential of a revolutionary aesthetic to MacKinnon's concern with how our mental life has been colonized—stating firmly that revolution is *only* a specific, punctual, and convulsive event that radically transforms the political structures of a society.

Marxism is a territory that is, it would seem, paradoxically at once undergoing a renaissance of activity and a crisis of definition. There is a greater sense of the distance between our theoretical categories (even those of common sense in our daily lives) and the historical reality within which those categories must function. Yet, throughout this book there is an intellectual drive to deal with the disjunction between our need and our ability to intervene in our own historical reality. These essays offer a series of intersecting and competing discourses for that project.

Notes

1 For example, Berel Lang and Forrest Williams, eds., *Marxism and Art* (New York: David McKay Co., 1972); Maynard Solomon, ed., *Marxism and Art: Essays Classic and Contemporary* (New York: Alfred A. Knopf, 1973); and David Craig, ed., *Marxists on Literature: An Anthology* (Harmondsworth: Penguin Books, 1975).

2 Karl Marx and Frederick Engels, *On Literature and Art,* ed. Lee Baxandall and Stefan Morawski (New York: International General, 1974).

Grossberg and Nelson

3   See David Laing, *The Marxist Theory of Art: An Historical Survey* (Atlantic Highlands, N.J.: Humanities Press, 1978). For further discussions, see Mikhail Lifshitz, *The Philosophy of Art of Karl Marx*, trans. Ralph B. Winn (New York: The Critics Group, 1938; reprinted, London: Pluto Press, 1973); Henri Arvon, *Marxist Esthetics*, trans. Helen Lane (Ithaca: Cornell University Press, 1973). For overviews of the development of Western Marxism, see Perry Anderson, *Considerations on Western Marxism* (London: New Left Books, 1976); New Left Review, ed., *Western Marxism—A Critical Reader* (London: New Left Books, 1977); and Dick Howard and Karl E. Klare, eds., *The Unknown Dimension: European Marxism since Lenin* (New York: Basic Books, 1972).

4   See, for example, Christopher Caudwell, *Illusion and Reality: A Study of the Sources of Poetry* (1937; New York: New World, 1963); Ernst Fischer, *The Necessity of Art: A Marxist Approach*, trans. Anna Bostock (Baltimore: Penguin Books, 1963); and Georgi Plekhanov, *Art and Social Life*, trans. E. Fox and E. Hartley (Moscow: Progress Publishers, 1957).

5   Antonio Gramsci, *Selections from the Prison Notebooks*, ed. and trans. Quintin Hoare and Geoffrey Nowell Smith (New York: International Publishers, 1971).

6   Georg Lukács, *History and Class Consciousness: Studies in Marxist Dialectics*, trans. Rodney Livingstone (Cambridge: MIT Press, 1971).

7   Karl Korsch, *Marxism and Philosophy*, trans. Fred Halliday (New York: Monthly Review Press, 1970); Rosa Luxemburg, *Selected Political Writings*, ed. Dick Howard (New York: Monthly Review Press, 1971).

8   Ernst Bloch et al., *Aesthetics and Politics* (London: New Left Books, 1977).

9   Many of the developments in Western Marxism built on ideas that only became available with the eventual translation of *The Economic and Philosophic Manuscripts of 1844*, first published in German in 1932. See Karl Marx, *Early Writings*, ed. and trans. Tom B. Bottomore (London: Penguin, 1963).

10   See, for example, Georg Lukács, *The Historical Novel*, trans. H. and S. Mitchell (Boston: Beacon Press, 1963), and *Studies in European Realism*, trans. Edith Bone (New York: Grosset and Dunlap, 1964).

11   Ernest Mandel, *Late Capitalism*, trans. Joris De Bres (London: New Left Books, 1975).

12   Max Horkheimer and Theodor W. Adorno, *Dialectic of Enlightenment*, trans. John Cumming (New York: Herder and Herder, 1972). See also Andrew Arato and Eike Gebhardt, eds., *The Essential Frankfurt School Reader* (New York: Urizen Books, 1978).

13   Bertolt Brecht, *Brecht on Theatre: The Development of an Aesthetic*, ed. and trans. John Willett (London: Methuen, 1964); Walter Benjamin, *Illuminations: Essays and Reflections*, ed. Hannah Arendt (New York: Harcourt Brace and World, 1968); Henri Lefebvre, *Everyday Life in the Modern World*, trans. Sacha Rabinovitch (New Brunswick, N.J.: Transaction, 1984); Gramsci, *Selections from the Prison Notebooks*.

14   Jean-Paul Sartre, *Critique of Dialectical Reason*, trans. Alan Sheridan-Smith (London: New Left Books, 1976); John Berger, *Ways of Seeing* (Baltimore: Penguin Books, 1972); Raymond Williams, *The Long Revolution* (London: Chatto and Windus, 1961); E. P. Thompson, *The Making of the English Working Class* (New York: Random House, 1963); Gajo Petrović, *Marx in the Mid-Twentieth Century* (Garden City, N.Y.: Anchor Books, 1967).

15   Ferdinand de Saussure, *Course in General Linguistics*, trans. Roy Harris (La Salle, Ill.: Open Court, 1986).

16   Louis Althusser, *For Marx*, trans. Ben Brewster (New York: Vintage Books, 1970).

17   Michel Foucault, "Prison Talk," in *Power/Knowledge: Selected Interviews and Other Writings, 1972-1977*, ed. Colin Gordon (New York: Pantheon Books, 1980), p. 52

Cornel West

Marxist Theory and the Specificity of Afro-American Oppression

As racial conflicts intensify in Europe, North and South America, Asia, and, above all, South Africa, the racial problematic will become more urgent on the Marxist agenda. A neo-Gramscian perspective on the complexity of racism is imperative if even the beginning of a "war of position" is to be mounted. In fact, the future of Marxism may well depend upon the depths of the anti-racist dimension of this theoretical and practical "war of position."

Will this statement be susceptible of understanding? In Europe, the black man is the symbol of Evil. . . . As long as one cannot understand this fact, one is doomed to talk in circles about the "black problem."
Frantz Fanon
Black Skin, White Masks

The problem of the twentieth century is the problem of the color-line—the relation of the darker to the lighter races of men in Asia and Africa, in America and the islands of the sea.
W. E. B. Du Bois
The Souls of Black Folk

As we approach the later years of the twentieth century, Fanon's characteristic candor and Du Bois's ominous prophecy continue to challenge the Marxist tradition. Although I intend neither to define their meaning nor defend their veracity, I do wish to highlight their implicit interrogation of Marxism. Fanon's and Du Bois's challenge constitutes the germ of what I shall call the *racial problematic:* the theoretical investigation into the materiality of racist discourses, the ideological production of African subjects, and the concrete effects of and counterhegemonic responses to the European (and specifically white) supremacist logics operative in modern Western civilization.[1]

I understand the issue of the specificity of Afro-American oppression as a particular version of the racial problematic within the context of the emergence, development, and decline of U.S. capitalist society and culture. This problematic is, in many ways, similar to contemporary philosophical discussions of "difference" that flow from the genealogical inquiries of Michel Foucault and the deconstructive analyses of Jacques Derrida.[2] Yet this problematic differs in that it presupposes a neo-Gramscian framework, one in which extradiscursive formations such as modes of production and overdetermined, antagonistic class relations are viewed as indispensable. This neo-Gramscian framework attempts to shun the discursive reductionistic elements in the works of the ex-Marxist Foucault and sidestep the textual idealist tendencies in the perennially playful performances of Derrida. But this neo-Gramscian perspective welcomes their poststructuralist efforts to dismantle the logocentric and a priori aspects of the Marxist tradition. In other words, I accent the *demystifying moment* in their genealogical and deconstructive practices which attack hegemonic Western discourses that invoke universality, scientificity, and objectivity in order to hide cultural plurality, conceal the power-laden play of differences, and preserve hierarchical class, gender, racial, and sexual orientational relations.

This effort to put forward the racial problematic within a neo-Gramscian framework occupies new discursive space on the spectrum of philosophies of difference; it also enacts an untapped potentiality within the Marxist tradition. More important, this effort constitutes a sympathetic yet biting Marxist critique of poststructuralist philosophies of difference and a supportive yet piercing critique of the Marxist tradition from the viewpoint of an Afro-American neo-Gramscian. In short, the time has passed when the so-called race question, or Negro question, can be relegated to secondary or tertiary *theoretical* significance in bourgeois or Marxist discourses. Instead, to take seriously the multileveled oppression of African peoples is to raise crucial questions regarding the conditions for the possibility of the modern West, the nature of European conceptions of rationality, and even the limited character of Marxist formulations of counterhegemonic projects against multileveled oppression.

In order to more fully understand my neo-Gramscian conception of the specificity of Afro-American oppression, it is necessary to examine briefly the history of Marxist conceptions of Afro-American oppression. Any such history is itself a *political act*—an intervention into the present state of the Afro-American freedom struggle. My own crude interpretation and bold intervention bears the stamp of my neo-Gramscian stance, which takes on practical forms in an autonomist (not micropolitical) politics (e.g., the National Black United Front) and a prefigurative (not reformist) politics (e.g., the Democratic Socialists of America).[3]

I shall argue that there are four basic conceptions of Afro-American oppression in the Marxist tradition. The first conception subsumes Afro-American oppression under the general rubric of working-class exploitation. This viewpoint is logocentric in that it elides and eludes the specificity of Afro-American oppression outside the workplace; it is reductionistic in that it explains away rather than explains this specificity. This logocentric and reductionistic approach results from vulgar and sophisticated versions of economism. I understand economism to be those forms of Marxist theory that defend either simple monodeterminist or subtle multideterminist causal relations between an evolving economic base upon a reflecting and refracting ideological superstructure, thereby giving a priori status to class subjects and modes of production as privileged explanatory variables.

In regard to Afro-American oppression, economism and its concomitant logocentric and reductionistic approach holds that African people in the United States of America are not subjected to forms of oppression distinct from general working-class exploitation. Historically, this position was put forward by the major figures of the U.S. Socialist party (notwith-standing its more adequate yet forgotten 1903 resolution on the Negro question), especially Eugene Debs. In an influential series of articles, Debs argued that Afro-American oppression was solely a class problem and that any attention to its alleged specificity "apart from the general labor problem" would constitute racism in reverse.[4] He wrote, "we [the socialists] have nothing to do with it [the race question], for it is their [the capitalists'] fight. We have simply to open the eyes of as many Negroes as we can and do battle for emancipation from wage slavery, and when the working class have triumphed in the class struggle and stand forth economic as well as political free men, the race problem will disappear." In the meantime, Debs added, "we have nothing special to offer the Negro, and we cannot make separate appeals to all races. The Socialist Party is the party of the whole working class regardless of color."[5]

My aim is not simply to castigate the U.S. Socialist party or insinuate accusative charges of racism against Debs. Needless to say, the Socialist party had many distinguished black members and Debs had a long history of fighting racism. Rather, I am concerned with the fact that the Second International economism in the U.S. Socialist party lead to a logocentric and reductionistic approach to Afro-American oppression, thereby ignoring, or at best downplaying, strategies (as opposed to personal moral duties) to struggle against racism.

The second conception of Afro-American oppression in the Marxist tradition acknowledges the specificity of Afro-American oppression beyond general working-class exploitation, yet it defines this specificity in economistic terms. This conception is antireductionistic in character yet economistic in content. This viewpoint holds that African people in the United States of America are subjected to general working-class exploitation and specific working-class exploitation owing to racial discrimination at the workplace (at the levels of access to opportunities and relative wages received). In the U.S. Marxist past, this superexploitation thesis has been put forward by the Progressive Labor party in the late sixties and early seventies. Practically, this viewpoint accents struggle against racism yet circumscribes its concerns within an economistic orbit.

The third conception of Afro-American oppression in the Marxist tradition—the most influential, widely accepted, and hence unquestioned among Afro-American Marxists—holds the specificity of Afro-American oppression to be general working-class exploitation and national oppression; that is, it is antireductionistic and antieconomistic in character and nationalistic in content. This position claims that Afro-Americans constitute, or once constituted, an oppressed nation in the Black Belt South and an oppressed national minority in the rest of U.S. society.

There are numerous versions of the so-called Black Nation Thesis. Its classical version was put forward in the Sixth Congress of the Third International (1928), modified in its 1930 Resolution, and codified in Harry Haywood's *Negro Liberation* (1948). Subsequent versions have been put forward by the Socialist Workers party's George Breitman, the Communist Labor party's Nelson Peery, the Bolshevik League of the United States' Bob Avakian's Revolutionary Communist party, Amiri Baraka's U.S. League of Revolutionary Struggle, the Philadelphia Workers' Organizing Committee, and James Forman's recent book on *Self-Determination and the African-*

American People.[6] All of these versions adhere to Joseph V. Stalin's stipulative definition of a nation as set forth in his *Marxism and the National Question* (1913): "A nation is a historically constituted, stable community of people formed on the basis of a common language, territory, economic life, and psychological make-up manifested in a common culture."[7] This formulation, despite its brevity and crudity, incorporates a crucial cultural dimension that has had tremendous attractivenss to Afro-American Marxists. In fact, the Black Nation Thesis has been and remains hegemonic on the Black Marxist Left.

Since the Garvey movement in the early twenties—the first mass movement among Afro-Americans—the Black Left has been forced to take seriously the cultural dimension of the Afro-American freedom struggle. In this limited sense, Marcus Garvey's black nationalism made proto-Gramscians out of most Afro-American Marxists.[8] Yet the expression of this cultural concern among Afro-American Marxists has, for the most part, remained straitjacketed by the Black Nation Thesis. This thesis, indeed, has promoted and encouraged impressive struggles against racism in the U.S. communist movement. But with its ahistorical racial determination of a nation, its flaccid statistical determination of national boundaries, and its illusory distinct black national economy, the Black Nation Thesis continues to serve as an honest, yet misguided, attempt by Marxist-Leninists to repudiate reductionistic views on Afro-American oppression.[9] In short, it functions as a poor excuse for the absence of a sophisticated Marxist theory of the specificity of Afro-American oppression.

The fourth and last conception of Afro-American oppression in the Marxist tradition claims that the specificity of Afro-American oppression is that of general working-class exploitation and racial oppression. This conception is put forward, on the one hand, by the Socialist Workers party's Richard Kirk (alias R. S. Fraser in reply to George Breitman), who wrote:

> The Negro Question is a racial question: a matter of discrimination because of skin color, and that's all. . . .
> The dual nature of the Negro struggle arises from the fact that a *whole people* regardless of class distinction are the victims of discrimination. This problem of a whole people can be solved only through the proletarian revolution, under the leadership of the working class. The Negro struggle is therefore not the same as the class struggle, but in its independent character is allied to the working class. Because of the independent form of the Negro movement, it does not thereby become a national or separatist struggle, but draws its laws of development from its character as a racial struggle against segregation and discrimination.[10]

And on the other hand, Linda Burnham and Bob Wing wrote in *Line of March,*

> More specifically, the oppressed Black racial group in the U.S. is a unity of two interconnected but distinct

aspects: Black people are a racially oppressed section of the laboring masses, as well as a distinct racially oppressed people. Between these two, the principal defining aspect of the Black racial group is that of being a racially coerced section of labor in this country. This view stems from our analysis of the connection between racial oppression and U.S. capitalism. As we have emphasized, racial oppression and class oppression are qualitatively distinct social contradictions with their own dynamics and laws of development. But they are also interconnected. In our view, the nature of this interconnection is defined by the fact that capitalism gave rise to and ultimately determines the form and content of racial oppression. In particular, the ultimate *raison d'être* of racial oppression is the need of U.S. capital accumulation for a specially oppressed, coerced section of labor.[11]

This fourth conception of Afro-American oppression in the Marxist tradition has been motivated primarily by opposition to the predominant role of the Black Nation Thesis in the American and Afro-American Left. Hence, it has been promoted by breakaway Trotskyists such as the Spartacist League, the independent Marxist-Leninist trend Line of March, the Communist party of the United States of America after 1959, and leftists in academia such as Oliver C. Cox, James A. Geschwender, and Mario Barrera.[12] These contributions have been useful in regard to broadening the theoretical discourse of Afro-American oppression within Marxist circles.

My neo-Gramscian viewpoint requires a new conception of Afro-American oppression. I suggest that certain aspects of the preceding four conceptions are indispensable for an acceptable position, though all four are inadequate. A common feature is that their analyses remain on the macrostructural level; that is, they focus on the role and function of racism within and among institutions of production and government. Any acceptable conception of Afro-American oppression, indeed, must include macrostructural analysis, which highlights the changing yet persistent forms of class exploitation and political repression of Afro-Americans. In this regard, even narrow economistic Marxist analyses of Afro-American oppression are preferable to prevailing bourgeois perspectives, such as the Weberian liberalism of William Julius Wilson, the Friedmanian conservatism of Thomas Sowell, and the Parsonsian elitism of Martin Kilson.[13]

Building upon Stanley Aronowitz's seminal though brief treatment of race,[14] my neo-Gramscian viewpoint requires not only a macrostructural approach but also a broad genealogical investigation and a detailed microinstitutional (or localized) analysis. These three moments of a neo-Gramscian perspective consist of the following:

1. a genealogical inquiry into the discursive conditions for the possibility of the hegemonic European (i.e., white) supremacist logics operative in various epochs in the West and the counterhegemonic possibilities available;

2. a microinstitutional (or localized) analysis of the mechanisms that inscribe and sustain these logics in the everyday lives of Africans, including the hegemonic ideological production of African subjects, the constitution of alien and degrading normative cultural styles, aesthetic ideals, linguistic gestures, psychosexual identities, and the counterhegemonic possibilities available;

3. a macrostructural approach that accents modes of overdetermined class exploitation and political repression of African peoples and the counterhegemonic possibilities available.

The aim of the first moment is to examine *modes of European domination* of African peoples; that of the second moment, to probe into *forms of European subjugation* of African peoples; and that of the third moment, to focus on *types of European exploitation and repression* of African peoples. These moments of theoretical inquiry—always already traversed by male supremacist and heterosexual supremacist logics—overlap and crisscross in complex ways, yet each highlights a distinctive dimension of the multi-leveled oppression of Europeans over African peoples.[15]

These three moments constitute the specificity of the European oppression of African peoples *at the level of methodology;* that is, this neo-Gramscian viewpoint should capture the crucial features of such oppression anywhere in the world. Yet the specificity of the various manifestations of European oppression of African peoples in particular countries is constituted by *detailed historical analyses* that enact the three methodological moments. Needless to say, these concrete analyses must be ensconced in the particular culture, heritage, and economic history of the Africans and the nation of which the Africans are participants and victims.

Admittedly, this neo-Gramscian project is an ambitious one, yet the complexity of the oppression of African peoples demands it. Each of the three moments requires major volumes, possibly lifetime endeavors. Given the political urgency of our times, I shall briefly sketch the contours of each moment.

In regard to the first moment—the genealogical inquiry into the conditions for the possibility of the European (i.e., white) supremacist logics operative in the West—I suggest that there are three such basic discursive logics: Judeo-Christian, scientific, and psychosexual. The Judeo-Christian racist logic emanates from the biblical account of Ham looking upon and failing to cover his father Noah's nakedness and thereby receiving divine punishment in the form of blackening his progeny. Within this logic, black skin is a divine curse owing to disrespect for and rejection of paternal authority.[16] The scientific racist logic rests upon a modern philosophical discourse guided by Greek ocular metaphors, undergirded by Cartesian notions of the primacy of the subject and the preeminence of representation, and buttressed by Baconian ideas of observation, evidence, and confirmation that promote and encourage the activities of observing, comparing, measuring, and ordering physical characteristics of human bodies. Given the renewed appreciation and appropriation of classical antiquity, these activities were regulated by classical aesthetic and cultural norms. Within this logic, the notions of black ugliness, cultural deficiency, and intellectual inferiority are legitimated by the value-laden, yet prestigious, authority of

22

science.[17] The psychosexual racist logic arises from the phallic obsessions, Oedipal projections, and anal-sadistic orientations in European culture that endow African men and women with sexual prowess; view Africans as either cruel, revengeful fathers, frivolous, carefree children, or passive, long-suffering mothers; and identify Africans with dirt, odious smell, and feces. In short, Africans are associated with acts of bodily defecation, violation, and subordination. Within this logic, Africans are walking abstractions, inanimate things or invisible creatures.[18] For all three white supremacist logics, which operate simultaneously in the modern West, Africans personify degraded otherness, exemplify radical alterity, and embody alien difference.

The aim of neo-Gramscian genealogical inquiry is not simply to specify the discursive operations that constitute Africans as the excluded, marginal Other; it also is to show how white supremacist logics are guided by various hegemonic Western philosophies of identity that suppress difference, heterogeneity, and multiplicity. Since such discursive suppression impedes counterhegemonic practices, these philosophies of identity are not simply ideologies but rather modes of domination with their own irreducible dynamic and development. Similar to Derrida's own characterization of his work, this inquiry requires "a general determination of the conditions for the emergence and the limits of philosophy, of metaphysics, of everything that carries it on and that it carries on."[19] Unlike Derrida's, this inquiry is but one moment in our neo-Gramscian project, leading toward microinstitutional and macrostructural analyses of oppression. I suggest this first moment is an examination of modes of European domination of African peoples because it maps the discursive modalities—for hegemonic and counterhegemonic practices—circumscribed by white supremacist logics and thereby discloses the European discursive powers over African peoples.

The second moment—the microinstitutional (or localized) analysis—examines the articulation of the white supremacist logics within the everyday lives of Africans in particular historical contexts. It focuses on the effects upon African peoples of the binary oppositions of true/false, good/evil, pure/impure within the white supremacist logics. In the complex case of Africans in the United States of America, this analysis would include the production of colored and Negro subjects principally enacted by the ideological apparatus (and enforced by the repressive apparatus) in the South, the extraordinary and equivocal role and function of evangelical Protestant Christianity (especially the Separate Baptist and Methodist denominations),[20] and the blend of African and southern Anglo-Saxon Protestants and French Catholics from which emerged distinctive Afro-American cultural styles, linguistic gestures, and counterhegemonic practices. This analysis is, in many ways, similar to Foucault's "microphysics of power"—the specifying of the power relations within the crevices and interstices of what logocentric Marxists call the superstructure. Yet, unlike Foucault's, this analysis is but one moment in my neo-Gramscian project, whose regulative ideal is not mere antibourgeois revolt but rather antihierarchical socialist transformation.[21] I suggest that this second moment is a probe into forms of European subjugation of African peoples because it shows how the various white supremacist logics shape African self-identities, influence psychosexual sensibilities, and help set the context for distinctive Afro-American cultural styles, linguistic gestures, and modes of resistance.

The third moment—the macrostructural analysis—reveals the role and function of overdetermined class exploitation and political repression upon African peoples. This traditionally Marxist focus remains as a crucial moment in my neo-Gramscian perspective, yet the nature of this focus is modified. The neo-Gramscian rejection of the base/superstructure metaphors of economism (or logocentric Marxism) entails that it is no longer sufficient or desirable to privilege the mode of production and class subjects in an a priori manner and make causal claims (whether crude or refined) about racist ideology owing to simply economic factors. Instead, following Antonio Gramsci, the metaphor of a "historical bloc" replaces those of base/ superstructure. This new metaphor eschews the logocentric and a priori dimension of the old metaphors by radically historicizing them, thereby disclosing the complexity and heterogeneity suppressed by logocentric Marxism. Gramsci's rejection of vulgar economism is unequivocal: "The claim, presented as an essential postulate of historical materialism, that every fluctuation of politics and ideology can be presented and expounded as an immediate expression of the structure, must be contested in theory as primitive infantilism, and combated in practice with the authentic testimony of Marx, the author of concrete political and historical works."[22]

Gramsci's highly sophisticated investigations into the multivarious modalities of class domination serves as the springboard for my own neo-Gramscian perspective. Yet there are still significant logocentric and a priori elements in Gramsci's work, such as the primacy of class subjects and the bipolar class options for hegemony. Nevertheless, Gramsci's anti-reductionistic and antieconomistic metaphor "historical bloc" promotes a radically historical approach in which the economic, political, cultural, and ideological regions of a social formation are articulated and elaborated in the form of overdetermined and often contradictory class and nonclass processes.[23] Despite this rejection of forms of determinisms, this conception of social totality (or more specifically, the dynamics of particular social formations) does not result in a mere floating crap game in that, given a historical situation, *structural constraints* impose limits upon historically constituted agents, whereas *conjunctural opportunities* can be enacted by these agents. Given the historical process, many structural constraints can become conjunctural opportunities. Yet without some notion of historical structural constraints, my neo-Gramscian perspective slides into explanatory nihilism; namely, the refusal or inability to make explanatory commitments about history and society. Economism is preferable to such explanatory impotence, but fortunately Gramsci's metaphor "historical bloc" precludes such a choice.

The controversial issue of the relation between historical context and differential intertextuality, ideological closure, and infinite dissemination serves as the major bone of contention between Marxists and poststructuralists. My neo-Gramscian viewpoint resists explanatory nihilism; that is, despite immense theoretical difficulties and practical obstacles it does not give up on explaining and transforming history and society. There is no Marxist theory without some notion of operative though transient structural constraints in particular historical conjunctures, just as there is no Marxist praxis without some notion of conjunctural opportunities. Poststructuralisms rightly dismantle the logocentric and a priori aspects of Marxist theory, yet they wrongly textualize historical constraints and political praxis into mere endless chains of signifiers. To put this issue in Ernesto

Laclau's terms, the matter is not simply the impossibility of society and history but, more important, the specifying of the conditions for the possibility of the perennial process of this impossibility.[24] We must appeal to metaphors of society and history in order to account for the "impossibility" of society and history. Gramsci's metaphor of "historical bloc" performs this function. If appropriately employed, it precludes the logocentric economism of pre-Gramscian Marxisms and the labyrinthine abyss of poststructuralisms. Furthermore, my neo-Gramscian viewpoint rejects the remnant of class reductionism in Gramsci's work. In short, my neo-Gramscian perspective yields ideological yet differential closure—provisional structural constraints and engaged political praxis—but with no guarantees.

Therefore the macrostructural analysis of the role and function of overdetermined class exploitation and political repression from my neo-Gramscian perspective goes far beyond the aforementioned four macrostructural conceptions of Afro-American oppression in the Marxist tradition. This is so, in part, because it preserves the crucial structural feature—the complex interaction of economic, political, cultural, and ideological regions in social formations—of Marxist theory, yet it does not permit a priori privileging of the economic region within this structural feature. I suggest that this third moment is an investigation into the types of European exploitation and repression of African peoples because it highlights simultaneously the relations between African slaves and white slaveholders, African workers and white capitalists, African citizens and white rulers.

In conclusion, the contemporary crisis of Marxism results, in part, from extradiscursive terrains of contestation generated from racial, feminist, gay, lesbian, and ecological social movements—movements that are historically "new" only to ostrichlike logocentric Marxists whose sight has been confined to the workplace—and from discursive terrains of contestation initiated by Gilles Deleuze and deepened by Foucault and Derrida.[25] I use Deleuze, Foucault, and Derrida (as they prefer) not as proper names but rather as tropes signifying diverse discursive forces, including Frenchified Nietzschean and Heideggerian elements, which now bombard Marxist theories. In a sense, it is unfortunate that this fierce bombardment is a thoroughly French (and more specifically Parisian) assault. It is unfortunate principally because of the national baggage that accompanies the assaults—namely, distinctively French political cynicisms and intellectual dandyisms, alien to the seemingly incurable bourgeois optimism and intellectual inferiority complexes of North Americans in the United States, yet seductive to weary Marxist activists who have run up against walls of History and isolated Marxist intellectuals who often remain within walls of the bourgeois Academy, activists and intellectuals who have genuine antibourgeois sentiments yet possess no energizing emancipatory vision.

My neo-Gramscian conception of the multileveled oppression of Africans in the United States of America and elsewhere remains a rudimentary response to the contemporary crisis of Marxism. As racial conflicts intensify in Europe, South America, North America, Asia, and above all South Africa, the racial problematic will become more urgent on the Marxist agenda. And as the ruling classes in late capitalist societies fan and fuel the white supremacist logics deeply embedded in their cultures, a neo-Gramscian perspective on the complexity of racism is imperative if even the beginning of a "war of position" is to be mounted. In fact, the future of Marxism, at least among Afro-Americans, may well depend upon the depths of the antiracist dimension of this *theoretical* and *practical* "war of position."

Notes

1   In this definition, "materiality" simply denotes the multiple functions of power of racist practices over Africans; by "logics" I mean the battery of tropes, metaphors, notions, and concepts employed to justify and legitimate white supremacist practices. This racial problematic is related to but not identical with other possible investigative frameworks that focus on racist practices toward other peoples of color. I do believe this problematic is useful for such endeavors, yet I deliberately confine my major focus to peoples of African descent, especially Afro-Americans. Also, this problematic does not presuppose that a nostalgic undifferentiated unity or homogeneous universality will someday emerge among black, white, red, yellow, and brown peoples. Rather, it assumes the irreducibility of racial (that is, cultural) differences. The task is not to erase such differences but rather to ensure that such differences are not employed as grounds for buttressing hierarchical social relations and symbolic orders.

2   The major texts I have in mind of these two prolific and profound thinkers are Michel Foucault, *Discipline and Punish: The Birth of the Prison*, trans. Alan Sheridan (New York: Vintage, 1979); and Jacques Derrida, *Of Grammatology*, trans. Gayatri Chakravorty Spivak (Baltimore: Johns Hopkins University Press, 1976). For a brilliant critique and contrast of these two texts, see Edward W. Said, *The World, the Text, and the Critic* (Cambridge: Harvard University Press, 1983), pp. 118-225.

3   My political stance is *autonomistic* in that it is existentially anchored not simply in responses to class exploitation but more immediately in cultural degradation and political oppression— as is the National Black United Front led by Rev. Herbert Daughtry. Yet this autonomistic stance does not slide into mere micropolitics because it envisions and encourages links with those movements based primarily on class exploitation. My political stance is *prefigurative* in that it is, in principle, motivated by the fundamental transformation of U.S. capitalist civilization and manifested in working within an organization (the Democratic Socialists of America) whose moral aspirations and internal mechanisms prefigure the desirable socialist society—one that is radically democratic and libertarian. This prefigurative stance does not degenerate into reformism because, following Rosa Luxemburg's formulations in *Reform or Revolution* (1900), it supports reforms yet opposes illusions about reforms.

4   Eugene Debs, "The Negro in the Class Struggle" and "The Negro and His Nemesis," *International Socialist Review*, Nov. 1903, Jan. 1904.

5   Quoted from Philip S. Foner, *American Socialism and Black Americans* (Westport, Conn.: Greenwood Press, 1977). For a noteworthy response to Debs's disappearance thesis, see Manning Marable, "The Third Reconstruction: Black Nationalism and Race Relations after the Revolution," *Blackwater: Historical Studies in Race, Class Consciousness and Revolution* (Dayton, Ohio: Black Praxis Press, 1981), pp. 187-208. For the major work of this important Afro-American Marxist figure, see *How Capitalism Underdeveloped Black America: Problems in Race, Political Economy and Society* (Boston: South End Press, 1983).

6   George Breitman, "On the Negro Struggle, etc.," *Socialist Workers Party Discussion Bulletin*, Sept. 1954; Bolshevik League, *Liberation for the Black Nation* (Bronx, 1983); Nelson Peery, *The Negro National Colonial Question* (Chicago: Workers Press, 1978); Revolutionary Union, *National Liberation and Proletarian Revolution in the United States* (Chicago, 1972); Amiri Baraka, "Black Liberation and the Question of Nationality," *Unity*, 4:12 (1981), p. 6; Amiri Baraka, "Black Struggle in the 80's," *The Black Nation: Journal of Afro-American Thought*, 1:1 (1981), pp. 2-5; Philadelphia Workers' Organizing Committee, *Black Liberation Today: Against Dogmatism on the National Question* (Philadelphia, 1975); James Forman, *Self-Determination and the African-American People* (Seattle: Open Hand Publishing, 1981). To put it crudely, Breitman argues that Afro-Americans in the United States constitute an "embryonic nation"; Peery holds the "Negro Nation" to be a colony; Bob Avakian's Revolutionary Communist party claims that dispersed black communities constitute a "proletarian nation" of a new sort; Baraka, the Bolshevik League, and Forman argue for a Black Nation in the Black Belt South of the United States; and the Philadelphia Workers' Organizing Committee holds that there once was a Black Nation, but it dissolved in the fifties with vast industrialization, proletarianization, and urbanization of Afro-Americans.

7   Joseph V. Stalin, *Marxism and the National Question* (Moscow: Foreign Language Publishing House, 1954), p. 16.

8   This almost inescapable Gramscian perspective—the nearly unavoidable theoretical and prac-

tical confrontation with the problem of culture—has been a major preoccupation of the leading Marxist figures in developing nations. For brief samples of original third-world contributions to Marxist theory, see Mao Tse-tung, "Report on an Investigation of the Peasant Movement in Hunan," *Selected Works,* vol. 1 (Peking: Foreign Language Press, 1966), pp. 23-59; "On the Correct Handling of Contradictions among the People," *Four Essays on Philosophy* (Peking: Foreign Language Press, 1968), pp. 79-133. See also Jose Carlos Mariategui, "People and Myth," *The Morning Spirit* (1925); and "The Religious Factor," *Seven Essays of Interpretation of the Peruvian Reality* (1927). Unfortunately, most of Mariategui's works have not yet been translated into English. For noteworthy treatments of his thought and praxis, see Geraldine Skinner, "Jose Carlos Mariategui and the Emergence of the Peruvian Socialist Movement," *Science and Society,* 43:4 (1979-80), pp. 447-71; and Jesus Chavarria, *Jose Carlos Mariategui and the Rise of Modern Peru* (Albuquerque: University of New Mexico Press, 1979). See also Kwame Nkrumah, *Consciencism: Philosophy and Ideology for Decolonization* (New York: Monthly Review Press, 1970); Frantz Fanon, *The Wretched of the Earth,* trans. Constance Farrington (New York: Grove Press, 1964); Amilcar Cabral, "Presuppositions and Objectives of National Liberation in Relation to Social Structure" and "National Liberation and Culture," *Unity and Struggle: Speeches and Writings of Amilcar Cabral,* trans. Michael Wolfers (New York: Monthly Review Press, 1979), pp. 119-37, 138-54.

9   For the most thorough and convincing critique of the Black Nation Thesis, see Linda Burnham and Bob Wing, "Toward a Communist Analysis of Black Oppression and Black Liberation, Part I: Critique of the Black Nation Thesis," *Line of March: A Marxist-Leninist Journal of Rectification,* 2:1 (1981), pp. 21-88.

10   R. S. Fraser, "For the Materialist Conception of the Negro Struggle," in *What Strategy for Black Liberation? Trotskyism vs. Black Nationalism,* Marxist Bulletin 5, rev. ed., The Spartacist League, pp. 3, 16, reprinted from *Socialist Workers Party Discussion Bulletin,* A-30 (1955).

11   Linda Burnham and Bob Wing, "Toward a Communist Analysis of Black Oppression and Black Liberation, Part II: Theoretical and Historical Framework," *Line of March: A Marxist-Leninist Journal of Rectification,* 8 (1981), p. 48.

12   For the recent pronouncements of the Afro-American freedom struggle by the Communist party of the United States, see Henry Winston, *Class, Race and Black Liberation* (New York: International Publishers, 1977), and the resolution on the Afro-American struggle—Winston's *Struggle for Afro-American Liberation*—adopted by the party's Twenty-second National Convention in August 1979. See also Oliver C. Cox, *Caste, Class, and Race: A Study in Social Dynamics* (New York: Doubleday, 1948); James A. Geschwender, *Class, Race and Worker Insurgency: The League of Revolutionary Black Workers* (Cambridge: Cambridge University Press, 1977); Mario Barrera, *Race and Class in the Southwest: A Theory of Racial Inequality* (Notre Dame: University Press of Notre Dame, 1979). Although Barrera is primarily concerned with the racial problematic as it relates to Chicanos and Chicanas, his theoretical formulations are relevant to peoples of African descent in the United States of America.

13   William Julius Wilson, *The Declining Significance of Race: Blacks and Changing American Institutions* (Chicago: University of Chicago Press, 1978); Thomas Sowell, *Race and Economics* (New York: David McKay Co., 1975); Martin Kilson, "The Black Bourgeoisie Revisited: From E. Franklin Frazier to the Present," *Dissent* (Winter 1983), pp. 85-96. This latter essay is from Kilson's forthcoming book, *Neither Insiders nor Outsiders: Blacks in American Society.*

14   Stanley Aronowitz, *The Crisis in Historical Materialism: Class, Politics, and Culture in Marxist Theory* (New York: Praeger Publications, 1981), pp. 89-112.

15   These distinctions are necessary if we are to sharpen and refine the prevailing loose usage of domination, subjugation, exploitation, repression, and oppression. In my view, domination and subjugation are discursive affairs; the former relates to racial, sexual, ethnic, or national supremacist logics, whereas the latter involves the production of subjects and subjectivities within such logics. Exploitation and repression are extradiscursive affairs in that they result from social formations and institutions such as modes of production and state apparatuses. Domination, subjugation, exploitation, and repression constitute modes of oppression, which are distinguished for analytic purposes. Needless to say, they relate to each other in complex and concrete ways. These distinctions were prompted by Michel Foucault, "The Subject and Power," *Critical Inquiry,* 8:4 (1982), pp. 775-95.

16   Winthrop Jordan, *White Over Black: American Attitudes toward the Negro, 1550-1812* (New York: Norton, 1968), pp. 18-20, 36; Thomas F. Gossett, *Race: The History of an Idea in America* (Dallas: Southern Methodist University Press, 1965), pp. 3-31.

17   For a further elaboration of this logic, see Cornel West, "A Genealogy of Modern Racism," *Prophesy Deliverance! An Afro-American Revolutionary Christianity* (Philadelphia: Westminster Press, 1982), pp. 47-65. And for the metaphilosophical motivation for this inquiry, see Cornel West, "Philosophy, Politics and Power: An Afro-American Perspective," in *Philosophy Born of Struggle: Anthology of Afro-American Philosophy from 1917,* ed. Leonard Harris (Dubuque: Kendall/Hunt Publishing Co., 1983), pp. 51-59.

18   The best exposition of this logic remains Joel Kovel's *White Racism: A Psychohistory* (New York: Pantheon, 1970). For an interesting, yet less theoretical, treatment, see Calvin C. Hernton, *Sex and Racism in America* (New York: Grove Press, 1965).

19   Jacques Derrida, *Positions*, trans. Alan Bass (Chicago: University of Chicago Press, 1981), p. 51.

20   Primarily owing to parochial secular sensibilities, black and white Marxist thinkers—with exceptions such as Eugene Genovese in his magnum opus *Roll, Jordan, Roll: The World the Slaves Made* (New York: Random House, 1974), pp. 159-284, and Orlando Patterson's masterful *Slavery and Social Death: A Comparative Study* (Cambridge: Harvard University Press, 1982), pp. 66-76—have overlooked the tremendous impact of evangelical Protestantism on Afro-Americans in the United States, and especially the subtle ways in which Afro-Americans have employed their appropriation of this Protestantism for counterhegemonic aims. The major legacy of this appropriation is that present-day Afro-American resistance remains under the auspices of the small, yet quite visible, prophetic wing of the black church, as exemplified by Rev. Herbert Daughtry's chairmanship of the leftist National Black United Front and the African People's Christian Organization, by Rev. Joseph Lowery's presidency of the left-liberal Southern Christian Leadership Conference (founded by Rev. Martin Luther King, Jr.), by Rev. Benjamin Hooks's executive directorship of the liberal National Association for the Advancement of Colored People, and by Rev. Jesse Jackson's leadership of the liberal People United to Save Humanity. It is no historical, political, and existential accident that, as an oppositional African intellectual and activist in the United States, I teach in a Protestant seminary and write as an Afro-American neo-Gramscian Christian! For four noteworthy texts on the religious dimension of the racial problematic in the United States, see Albert Raboteau's superb *Slave Religion: The "Invisible Institution" in the Antebellum South* (New York: Oxford University Press, 1978); James Cone and Gayraud Wilmore's indispensable *Black Theology: A Documentary History, 1966-1979* (Maryknoll, N.Y.: Orbis Books, 1979); my own provocative work, *Prophesy Deliverance! An Afro-American Revolutionary Christianity* (Philadelphia: Westminster Press, 1982); and James Washington's brilliant hundred-page introduction to *Afro-American Protestant Spirituality* (New York: Paulist Press, 1984).

21   The seductive powers of Foucault must be resisted by leftist thinkers on two fronts: the trap of discursive reductionism, which posits the absolute (as opposed to relative) autonomy of discursive practices, and the trap of full-blown (as opposed to provisional) antitotalism, which promotes revolt yet precludes revolution. The Marxist path that incorporates Foucault's insights has been blazed by the grand pioneer of cultural studies, Stuart Hall. See especially his "Cultural Studies: Two Paradigms," *Media, Culture and Society*, 2(1980), pp. 57-72, and "The Rediscovery of 'Ideology': Return of the Repressed in Media Studies," in *Culture, Society and the Media*, ed. Michael Gurevitch, Tony Bennett, James Curran, and Janet Woollacott (New York: Methuen, 1982), pp. 56-90. For subtle elaborations of this perspective on untouched frontiers, see Hazel V. Carby, "Schooling in Babylon" and "White Woman Listen! Black Feminism and the Boundaries of Sisterhood," in *The Empire Strikes Back: Race and Racism in 70s Britain*, Center for Contemporary Cultural Studies (London: Hutchinson, 1982), pp. 183-211, 212-35.

22   Antonio Gramsci, *Selections from the Prison Notebooks*, ed. and trans. Quintin Hoare and Geoffrey Nowell Smith (New York: International Publishers, 1971), p. 407. For his formulations of a "historical bloc," note pp. 136ff., 365-66. For a useful treatment of this complex issue of the relation of base and superstructure, see Raymond Williams, *Marxism and Literature* (New York: Oxford University Press, 1977), pp. 75-89.

23   The best theoretical formulation I know of this Gramscian metaphor is found in Bob Jessop's superb work *The Capitalist State: Marxist Theories and Methods* (New York: New York University Press, 1982), pp. 211-59.

24   Ernesto Laclau, "The Impossibility of Society," *Canadian Journal of Political and Social Theory*, 7:12 (1983), pp. 21-24.

25   I consider the originary text of poststructuralism to be Gilles Deleuze's *Nietzsche and Philosophy*, published in 1962 and translated into English in 1983. This provocative and often persuasive attack on Hegel and dialectics from a Nietzschean viewpoint initiated and legitimated the now familiar poststructuralist assaults on totalizing frameworks, teleological narratives, homogeneous continuities in history, and recuperative, nostalgic strategies in interpretation. The rejection of ontology left Marxists with no grounds for theorizing, given their reliance on Hegelian dialectics. Since I agree with this rejection, the theoretical crisis of Marxism is, I believe, a serious one. Aronowitz's call—influenced by Adorno's philosophy of difference and Murray Bookchin's ecological perspective—for a new will to totality guided by ideals of workers' self-management, sexual and racial freedom, and the liberation of nature is noteworthy, as is Deleuze's and Guatarri's call—mediated by Spinoza and Nietzsche—for theoretical nomadism guided by a political metaphysics of desire. Both call for a new Marxist or materialist ethics, yet neither is forthcoming. The major alternative is to opt for a pragmatic viewpoint (informed by the work of Richard Rorty, Richard Bernstein, and others) in which dialectical modes of thinking become rhetorical strategies employed in intellectual, social, and existential warfare against dogmatic ways of thought, forms of oppression, and modes of despair. Such rhetorical Marxism or dialectical pragmatism (to use Max Eastman's term) preserves historically constituted human agency, accents the multileveled character of oppression, and demystifies poststructuralist strategies by circumscribing and thereby trivializing the radical skepticism that sustain them while accepting their powerful insights regarding the role of otherness and alterity in philosophies of identity, including most forms of dialectical thinking. Since energizing emancipatory visions are, to put it bluntly, religious visions, I see little alternative other than appropriating the subversive potential of Christianity and other religions.

Comment

Despite your efforts to escape logocentrism, you maintain the logocentric duality of black and white to describe the structure of a nation that is, on the contrary, clearly based on multiple dominations. To make the question of Afro-American problems central to Marxism may, for example, be to ignore Latinos and Indians. Though you acknowledge that we are sometimes dealing with quite specific subgroups, say Caribbean blacks, I wonder if there still may not be a problem in your project.

West

I believe there is a specificity to the various forms of the African experience that is distinct from that of other peoples of color. I was speaking to just that highly limited but crucial specificity. Of course, I do not want to reenact the very exclusion I would criticize in the dominant culture, and I do believe my framework could (and should) be enriched by analyses of the situations of other peoples of color. But it is important not to move too quickly to speak about a broad spectrum of peoples of color. On the other hand, you can't talk solely about specific oppressions without understanding the relations between the different oppressions of Latinos, Asians, indigenous peoples, etc. For example, in a discourse against slavery, one needs to distinguish between the oppression of indigenous peoples and the oppression of Africans. Finally, we need to recognize that oppression is manifested in different forms of discursive power.

Question

Many of us have started to study the history of black and white Hispanic people since they came to America. We have found that they begin a system of stratification that ironically replicates the existing black and white duality. When I ask black Latinos whether they are light or dark, most of them say they are light. It seems that every measure of color one takes on is simply a bourgeois tool of self-identification. If you study kinship structures and marital selection, you see again a stratification system inside the Latino community in which patterns of race relations around black and white begin to replicate themselves. How does one acknowledge the specific histories of these peoples while accounting for what is obviously a general structure for the reproduction of racial difference?

West

Understanding the function of racial differences raises the theoretical issue of the very play of difference itself. I do not have any Hegelian nostalgia for undifferentiated unities now or in the future. We are in a world of differences forever. That means we are talking about the irreducibility of differences in the racial sphere. Yet, historically, racial differences are always constituted as "scientific" by ideological discourses. I cannot envision, within the logics of the modern West, with its legacy of slavery, societies that do not have racial differences. Consequently, our social emancipatory visions and projects have to acknowledge the irreducibility of racial differences but fight against a translation of such differences into hierarchical social relations and symbolic orders. So we will not get beyond the play of differences and binary oppositions. The question is how we arrest the political and economic translation of such differences into hierarchical relations. That, to me, is the problematic. And I would say similar things about sexuality. I do not see an eschatological possibility of erasing these differences. To give an example: Frank Snowden's work on black antiquity suggests that if we could only get back to the way the Greeks interacted with the Ethiopians (when Heraclitis talked about how beautiful black women were), then we could get beyond these black/white prejudices. I can understand his motivations, but I think that is precisely the kind of nostalgia that must be resisted.

Cornel West

Question (Stanley Aronowitz)

Two recent texts suggest very different models of oppression and exploitation. Each proposes a mode of determination and makes a universal claim for it, which seems to contradict your strong bias toward historical specificity. In *Slavery and Social Death,* Orlando Patterson argues that the transhistorical development of slavery is based on the existence of a form of social domination that produces a category of otherness within the symbolic order. This form of social domination precedes economic exploitation and the labor process. This proposal almost turns Marxism on its head but still maintains the methodology of a primary contradiction (as Mao says). Class and race mediate this category of social domination; they are mechanisms by which the deratiocination process takes place. The second text is Barrington Moore's. Moore argues that there is no possibility for oppression to take place without consent. Thus the basis of revolt, if not revolution, is not a struggle against oppression and exploitation but the breaking of the contract between the oppressed and the oppressor, a contract fundamentally based on caste considerations. As long as people have a "contractual" place in the symbolic, social, and economic order, they are likely to reproduce their conditions of subordination. Can you comment on these two positions?

West

First, in regard to Patterson: his notion of modal alienation, in which a people born with no rights to predecessors (without a past) and with no right to progeny (without a future), is part of a discourse in which black people have no social ontology. Patterson is very ambiguous about the status of this view. If he believes this form of alienation is prior to social processes, then I think his position is unintelligible. If, however, he wants merely to accent the weight of that moment of alienation, then I am with him all the way. So for me the question is how modal alienation interacts with the various logics I have been talking about. Indeed, I think that is the direction Patterson himself takes. Patterson invokes Marx in arguing that slavery is a relation of domination. So Patterson views this as part of the Marxist project, and Perry Anderson and company published his essay in *New Left Review.*

Second, what Barrington Moore is attempting to get at is already clearly articulated by Ernest Becker: the relation between hegemony—the mobilization and reproduction of the consent of the oppressed to their domination, subjugation, exploitation, and repression—and the need for cosmic recognition, the horror of death. How are these issues manipulated, not in any crude sense by a ruling class, but so as to inscribe them within various modes of socialization which ensure that human beings consent to their domination? Unfortunately, Becker sees the horror of death in terms of Otto Rank's view of immortality—the need not to go in and out of this thing we call life without some kind of recognition, even if it's in a hierarchical order. But that's only *one* of its dimensions.

Question

Stanley suggested one way that an ontological category of otherness precedes social processes and structures oppression. Obviously feminism could say the same for the oppression of women by way of an already given category of otherness. Could you give us an example, within the contemporary black liberation movement, of how this needs instead to be read in terms of its precise historicity?

West

On a general level, I want to begin by saying that black feminists like Audre Lorde and others are the major figures that both the black Left and the American Left in general must come to terms with. Now I'll cite a specific historical context in answer to your question: consider the central role of the black church in black liberation. It is a radically patriarchal institution, even though its membership is 70 percent black women. Thus, the black feminist movement must in many ways be antichurch. Yet within the church itself there are black feminists who are struggling with the history of the doctrine and the various liberation theologies that come out of it. Nonetheless, this very specific history, with black men in leadership roles, provides many possibilities for polarization. It isn't simply that black men are in conflict with black women but that their relations are mediated by various institutions. So the issue of feminism within black liberation is always already traversed by class, by race, and by the institution of the black church. It's crisscrossed by class fractions as well. There is no doubt, for example, that gay life-styles will be much more acceptable among a black petit-bourgeois strata, because they interact with the larger culture and are not as affected by the patriarchal sensibilities of the black church. Yet most of these folks come out of the church, if not in one generation then two, so there are still internal struggles going on.

Question
I'd like to know your views on the growing struggle in South Africa. Can it be a mobilizing force for blacks in America?

West
I think that South Africa will continue to serve, in many ways, as a symbol of evil. It represents a massive concentration of white supremacist logic, inscribing this logic in institutions across the social spectrum. And it is no accident that the ruling classes in late-capitalist European societies repress information about this crypto-fascist society in the mass media. This repression will come back with a vengeance. Yet how one goes about mobilizing resistance to South Africa is a very difficult question. You are not only talking about the possibility of resistance by the armed forces in South Africa, of which about 22 percent are now of African descent; you are also talking about increasing black entrepreneurial interests in South Africa. You are talking about the rise of a diverse black trade union movement in South Africa that will have to define its own direction and its relation to the black petit bourgeoisie. These are all open-ended questions. The question for us will be whether the vocal opposition to the apartheid regime in South Africa can move toward an anticapitalist view and not remain simply, though importantly, antiracist.

Question
I'm interested in hearing your view of liberation theology—what it's trying to do, how it fits into Marxist theory, and its relevance to your project.

West
I believe it is important to understand the Christian viewpoint as a particular discursive formation, one that has had tremendous impact on people, particularly on the struggle for freedom among African peoples in the United States. That is not to say that there are not some crucial manipulative and reactionary elements in the black church. But if we take my neo-Gramscian framework seriously, we have to set aside all a priori enlightenment-informed, antireligious perspectives. We have to look at religion in very different ways, different even from that of the so-called master (small "m" for me), Karl Marx. That is important not only for Afro-American cases but also for understanding what is going on in Iran, in Nicaragua, in Chile. Although there are no acceptable nostalgic moves back to representational notions of God, God remains a very important signifying term. As Karl Barth understood, truth is always eschatological.

Question
Are you happy and hopeful about the black movement in this country?

West
I'm not happy with the black movement; I'm not happy with anyplace in the world. But I'm hopeful. The grounds of my hope are very complex because I'm a Christian and a whole lot of other things. Or at least I subscribe to that discourse in which God is a significant signifying term. I also subscribe to

Gramsci's optimism of the will. Yet as long as you are part of the struggle, pure hope becomes abstract because the actual historical process produces tremendous setbacks and certain small gains.

Stuart Hall
The Toad in the Garden:
Thatcherism among the Theorists

Until now, marxism has failed to renovate its own thinking sufficiently to explain how modern capitalism remains in being and sustains its hegemonic position in industrialized societies. Confronting and understanding Thatcherism may be the price we have to pay for a real advance in theoretical enlightenment within the Marxist problematic.

This paper is summary in several senses. First, in the course of the argument it summarizes a number of positions in the recent debate on ideology, without attempting to elaborate arguments or detail objections. Second, it represents a summary of my own, current provisional take, or position, on a number of those debates. Its structure is simple. We have been passing through a veritable deluge, in recent years, with respect to theorizing the domain of ideology. Much of this has taken the form of elaborate deconstructions of the classical marxist theory of ideology. The paper takes off from and reflects on this heightened period of theoretical contestation. However, this period of intense theorization has also engendered its opposite—a rigorous critique of the hyperabstraction and over-theoreticism that has characterized theoretical speculation since, roughly, the impact of structuralism in the early 1970s; and the charge that, in the pursuit of theory for its own sake, we have abandoned the problems of concrete historical analysis.

Edward Thompson's book, *The Poverty of Theory,* which mirrors in its very extremism the object it is criticizing (the project of Althusserianism), is only the latest, most prestigious example of this backlash. While I believe *The Poverty of Theory* to have been an ill-judged, intemperate enterprise, conducted by way of brilliant but crude polemic and caricature, where skillful argument and serious exemplification were the modes required, it clearly has a point.[1] It is possible—indeed, it had been widely attempted—to pile up one sophisticated speculative theoretical construction on top of another (meanwhile compounding the puns, usually on words already borrowed from the French, so that the whole results in the most barbarously hybrid language), without ever once touching ground and without reference to a single concrete case or historical example.

Therefore, instead of undertaking once more the line of pure theoretical critique and refutation, I have attempted in this paper—again in summary fashion—to refer *some* of the substantive emergent positions in the debate about ideology to the analysis of a concrete political problem, and specifically to the current political conjuncture in Britain, marked by the emergence of the New Right, the accession to power, first in the Conservative party and then in two successive governments, of Mrs. Thatcher and the political philosophy ("Thatcherism") she represents. The question I pose is simple. The purpose of theorizing is not to enhance one's intellectual or academic reputation but to enable us to grasp, understand, and explain—to produce a more adequate knowledge of—the historical world and its processes; and thereby to inform our practice so that we may transform it. If that is so, then which of the various positions in the current debate on ideology exhibits the greatest range, penetration, and explanatory power in terms of accounting for the rise of the New Right and the extraordinary political conjuncture to which it has led? Obviously, this cannot be answered in detail within the scope of a single paper, but a kind of exploratory test can be made, treating the issue in a summary fashion. And that is what is attempted here.

First, let me briefly and schematically characterize the political conjuncture in its more demonstrable aspects. The political character of the postwar period in Britain was defined by the "settlement" arrived at in the 1940s. Basically, a new kind of unwritten social contract emerged through which a bargain, a historic compromise, was struck between the different conflicting social interests in society. The Right—marginalizing their more reactionary and free-market elements—settled for the welfare state, comprehensive education, the Keynesian management of economic policy, and the commitment to full employment as the terms of peaceful compromise between capital and labor. In return, the Left accepted to work broadly within the terms of a modified capitalism and within the Western bloc sphere of strategic influence. Despite the many real differences of emphasis and a number of bitter political and industrial struggles which marked the political scene from time to time, the situation was characterized by a profound, underlying consensus or compromise on the fundamental social and economic framework within which conflicts were, for the moment, "settled" or contained.

It is possible for quite different actual political regimes to function in and dominate a historic compromise of that type. But, for a range of structural factors that cannot be entered into here, variants of social democracy (principally in the form of reformist Labour governments) came—with brief interludes—to dominate the British social formation in the 1960s and 1970s. This followed the immediate postwar period of "restoration," in which fundamental capitalist imperatives were restored to their rightful position under the aegis of Harold Macmillan's Conservative regime in the "affluent 1950s," within the framework of U.S. world hegemony and an expanding Atlanticism. By "dominate" I mean that Labour came, for the first time in British history, to look like an alternative majority party of government, not a temporary interloper; reformist goals and strategies tended to set the objectives for the political scene, even where the actual reality of implementation was extremely patchy. Above all, it was social democracy, not conservatism, that seemed best able to manage the new big-state/big-capital corporatist arrangements that developed as the basis of economic policy and planning in the period, both to harness the working classes to the corporatist bargains through the trade unions and, at the same time, discipline them through Labour's historic alliance with the unions. In the early 1960s, Harold Wilson made a bold attempt to consolidate this hegemony of social democracy by harnessing a number of different sectors within a broad alliance or historical bloc composed of "workers by hand and brain" (an unlikely social alliance, which stretched from the skilled white-coated machinist on the shop floor to the forward-looking company management team) and linking it with the "white heat" of the new technology behind a corporatist state. Had this attempt succeeded, it would have created the historical conditions for a long, settled period of reform capitalism under social democratic management.

The underlying conditions for this stabilization did not exist, however. The British economy and the whole industrial structure were too weak, too tied to a traditional worldwide imperial financial role, too unmodernized, "backward," and undercapitalized to generate the huge surpluses required both to sustain the capital accumulation and profitability processes *and* cream off enough to finance the welfare state, high wages, and improved conditions for the less well-off—the only terms on which the historic compromise could operate. As the world economic recession began to deepen, Britain—one of the oldest and now one of the weakest links in the capitalist chain—began to polarize under the conflicting pressures that had eroded the basis of the earlier settlement. Labor, obliged in a crisis to defend the system it had never intended to transform, was forced more and more into the role of disciplining its own working class. The internal contradictions inscribed in the historic compromise from its inception began to emerge—first, in the social and political upheavals of the 1960s, then in the countercultural social movements around the Vietnam War, and finally (during the Conservative interregnum of Edward Heath) in the industrial conflict and militancy of the early 1970s—and the social-democratic-dominated consensus that had stabilized the British political scene up to that point began to fracture and its legitimacy to evaporate. Both in the heartland of economic life—wages, production, strikes, industrial conflict, union militancy, and so on—and in the emergent arenas of social life—crime, permissiveness, race, moral and social values, traditional social roles and mores—the society declined into crisis. One phase of hegemony had disintegrated; the society entered that era of contestations, crises, and alarms that frequently accompanies the struggles for the formation of a new hegemonic stage.

This was the moment of the New Right. It did not, of course, materialize out of thin air. Ever since the disappearance, at the turn of the century, of the Liberal party as *the* alternative party of government and the rise of Labour in its place, many traditional free-market ideological elements had gravitated from their traditional liberal home to the Conservative party, finding within it at least a fundamental commitment to the free-enterprise system, the ethic of possessive individualism and rugged competition that afforded them ideological cover. These elements were combined with the more traditional, paternal, organic Tory tradition to compose the highly contradictory formation that modern conservatism became. But in the period of the postwar compromise, these neoliberal elements were decidedly pushed to the margins of the party. Let out on a tight leash at party conferences, they were permitted to air their recidivistic social doctrines (the hangem-and-flogem brigade) and to push a version of crude economic individualism and the petit-bourgeois ethic of competition against what they regarded as the too well bred Tory squirearchy. But the more fundamental forces dictating the political direction in the Conservative party were those

37

attempting to adapt conservatism to the conditions of life in which state welfare, widespread social assistance, state intervention of a limited kind in the operations of the free market, Keynesian demand management of the economy, trade union bargaining, corporatist management strategies, and big-state/big-capital combinations, were the order of the day.

It is true that, in the difficult years of Mr. Heath's government (1970-74), when the signs of crisis were clearly beginning to show, there were some significant departures moving the Conservatives closer to the neoliberal political pole. Law and order, the need for social discipline against the rising anarchic elements in society, a virulent racism directed against black immigrants—these volatile elements of the populist program were very much to the fore in the election of 1970. For a time, under Heath, the state-trade union bargaining links were broken, corporatism was buried, head-on confrontations with industrial militants and the unions were undertaken by the government, and attempts were made to break with the creeping elements of state capitalism that had become normal in British industry and to restore a more free-market, competitive economic regime. The period began with a runaway housing boom, a splurge of new banks of a distinctly shaky and shady variety, and widespread bankruptcies as industry tuned up for the more competitive climate of the European economic community. The period ended with British industry on a three-day week and the government brought down in a head-on collision with the miners' union. Many have interpreted, retrospectively, the popularity in this period of Mr. Enoch Powell, with his focus on race, nation, and the free market, and the strong law-and-order, competition-or-bust spirit of the early Heath period as vivid anticipations or rehearsals of Thatcherism.

Yet when Thatcherism finally emerged it was pitched against the "creeping corporatism" of *all* recent governments, including that of Mr. Heath. And it was led by distinguished converts—Sir Keith Joseph, the leading ideologue, and Mrs. Thatcher herself—who had been ministers in the Heath government but who now, Damascus-like, repudiated what they called the trend toward "state socialism," which they saw as built into a conjuncture dominated by social democracy, whatever the actual complexion of the government in power. Publicly, it was in the prelude period to the leadership stakes within the Conservative party that Joseph first emerged as the leading ideologue of an inner-party revolution, with a series of speeches in which the "new philosophy" was exposed. Joseph remains one of the key "organic intellectuals" of Thatcherism, but he alienated some crucial sections of the electorate by his high-handed manner and lack of the common touch. It was with his retirement, not from the ideological leadership of the bloc, but from the public political position of party leader, that Mrs. Thatcher emerged as the public figure best able to translate the high nostrums of monetarism and the gospel of the free market into the homespun idioms of the Tory householder.

Thatcherism thus won and transformed the Conservative party first, before setting about winning and transforming the country. I shall come back to what Gramsci would call this "organizational moment"—the "moment of party"—later. It is sufficient here to say that Thatcherism, though it owes much to and integrates key elements of traditional Toryism, is a radically distinct political and ideological force, radically different from older versions of conservatism that have dominated the party throughout the postwar period—or, rather, combining the different elements of conservatism in a radically distinctive and original way. It gained ascendancy first by contesting and defeating the old guard—the party guardians, the patricians—and the old doctrines. Its first historic mission was not to bend and subvert but to contest and disperse the social democratic corporatist consensus that had dominated the political scene since the end of the Second World War and to disorganize the common sense—the political taken-for-granted—of the British postwar political settlement. Its second historic mission was to reverse the dominant trends in British society. On matters of policy, this meant reversing the trend to state-subsidized welfare, breaking the curve of public spending and the public sector, restoring private enterprise and the imperatives of the free market and of free-market forces, rolling back the tide of state intervention, underpinning profitability, keeping wages in check, and breaking the power the working class had come to exercise in society, via the trade unions, in economic and political life.

What concerns us more specifically here are the reversals at which Thatcherism aimed in the area of social thought or the ideological domain. Its mission was to stem the anticapitalist tide it believed had been allowed to gather impetus during the 1960s—the view, to put it summarily, that no bright young person would be caught dead going into business—and also to crack the whole pattern of social expectations predicated on increased state support—or what was called, in the prophetic title of a pamphlet from the Centre for Policy Studies (of which more will be said later), "breaking the spell of the welfare state." The mission of Thatcherism was to reconstruct an alternative ideological bloc of a distinctively neoliberal, free-market, possessive individualist kind; to transform the underpinning ideologies of the Keynesian state and thus disorganize the power bloc, by now habituated to Keynesian recipes for dealing with crises in the economic life; and to break the incremental curve of working-class power and bargaining strength, reversing the balance of power and restoring the prerogatives of management, capital, and control. This was conceived on no narrow economistic basis. The aim was to reconstruct social life as a whole around a return to the old values—the philosophies of tradition, Englishness, respectability, patriarchalism, family, and nation. The most novel aspect of Thatcherism was indeed the very way in which it combined the new doctrines of the free market with some of the traditional emphases of organic Toryism. This contradictory structure of ideas, around which Thatcherism in its ascendancy managed to cohere the semblance of ideological unity, is best captured in the paradoxical slogan the political theorist Andrew Gamble coined on its behalf: "Free market *and* strong state."

Until its magical aura of invincibility began to depart, this formation had made enormous advances, without, of course, achieving universal success at any point in this historic venture. This judgment could be and has been contested; but it seems to me a claim, made tentatively in 1979 when I predicted successfully Thatcherism's quite unexpected victory in the election of that year, that has, if anything, been strengthened and confirmed rather than disproved by the passage of time. Of course, Thatcherism has never achieved absolute domination in electoral terms. The government retains the support of somewhat less than a majority of the British electorate—the scale of the 1983 victory was undoubtedly fictitiously magnified by the Falklands episode and by the split in the ranks opposite, between the Labour party and the newly formed Liberal Social Democratic Alliance. Quite rapidly in the wake of her second historic victory at the polls in 1983, Mrs. Thatcher has consistently run into difficulties, as some of the longer-term strategic failures (for example, a continuing level of unemployment of over three million) have come to compound her many tactical blunders and errors. No government is perfect; no politician in the parliamentary electoral system lasts forever.

On the other hand, taking the period of political contestation from the successful contest for the leadership of the party to the present, Thatcherism has become, qualitatively and without question, the *leading* political and ideological force. Even in the period of accident-prone government, the Labour party has only just managed, in crude electoral support terms, to come level in the opinion polls—a position not strong enough to reverse the overwhelming majority Thatcherism has secured in Parliament.

Even that is too crudely quantitative a measure. The fact is that Thatcherism has succeeded in reversing or putting into reverse gear many of the historic postwar trends. It has begun to dismantle and erode the terms of the unwritten social contract on which the social forces settled after the war. It has changed the currency of political thought and argument. Where previously social need had begun to establish its own imperatives against the laws of market forces, now questions of "value for money," the private right to dispose of one's own wealth, the equation between freedom and the free market, have become the terms of trade, not just of political debate in parliament, the press, the journals', and policy circles, but in the thought and language of everyday calculation. There has been a striking reversal of values: the aura that used to attach to the value of the public welfare now adheres to anything that is private—or can be privatized. A major ideological reversal is in progress in society at large; and the fact that it has not swept everything before it, and that there are many significant points or pockets of resistance (the national health service, for example, remains one), does not contradict the fact that, conceived not in terms of outright victory but more in terms of the mastery of an unequal equilibrium, Thatcherism has, in less than a decade, not only turned the tables but begun to reconstruct the social order.

One sign of this ideological success is the effective penetration into and dismantling of parts of the heartland, the mainstream, of the Labour party's social base. Substantial sections of the skilled and semiskilled industrial classes, a significant percentage of organized trade unionists, a large sector of the working-class urban vote, especially in the less deindustrialized parts of the country, and a majority of the unemployed—to name only some social categories—have gone over to Thatcherism in the last two elections, abandoning their traditional loyalty to Labour. Some of this movement may be temporary and may well revert. But for the absolutely critical decade in which Britain has absorbed the full impact of world capitalist recession, Thatcherism has, in these areas, positively won space. It set out to and has effectively become a populist political force, enlisting popular consent among significant sections of the dominated classes, successfully presenting itself as a force on the side of the people and moving into a commanding, or leading, position in society through a combination of the imposition of social discipline from above—an iron regime for Iron Times—and of populist mobilization from below—the combination I have elsewhere characterized

40

as "authoritarian populism" (to which I shall return later). Many of the trends and tendencies in postwar British society, which we came to assume were part and parcel of the very conditions of survival of British capitalism—big-state/big-capital corporatist strategies of management and the other corporatist features that late-capitalist economies seem to impose on the free play of market forces—are in the process of being either dismantled or reworked into new combinations.

Of course, ideology cannot function on its own; we should not mistake an ideological reading for an analysis of the conjuncture as a whole. Many things affirmed in Thatcherite ideology have not materialized in the so-called real world. The rate of inflation has been reduced and public expenditure cut, but the economy has not been revitalized nor unemployment reduced nor the money supply effectively constrained. Petit-bourgeois-type social values, for example—though powerfully articulated in the field of entrepreneurship, value for money, and the sacred character of the rates, as well as in the restoration of family values and the traditional roles for women—so far lack what might be called a "crudely material effect." Small businesses are rapidly being set up and almost as rapidly going to the wall. The claims in the economic arena are not that "monetarism works" but that "there is no alternative"—a sober, stoic, and longer-term gamble for support. Nevertheless, the ideological effectivity of Thatcherism in defining new contours in political language and calculation is striking, and not only at the fever-pitch high points, such as at the crest of the Falklands adventure. What is particularly significant for our purposes is Thatcherism's capacity to become popular, especially among those sectors of the society whose interests it cannot possibly be said to represent in any conventional sense of the term. This is the aspect of the phenomenon that, with respect to the various theories of ideology, most requires explanation.

Inadequate as it is, this must suffice as an account of the phenomenon to be explained. This account, however abbreviated, is not, of course, theoretically innocent. The description of the conjuncture is already ordered and organized by a set of concepts; it is not possible to give a theoretically neutral account. This points up the degree to which so-called concrete historical or empirical work is always inscribed by particular theories. Nevertheless, there are common features that different accounts would recognize at least as posing common problems requiring explanation to the different theoretical perspectives. (No prizes are awarded to the reader who identified the Gramscian concepts that have informed my reading of the conjuncture.)

Despite the above qualification, I think there is still enough ground for saying that the conjuncture I have just outlined is only partially and inadequately explained by the application of what we would call the "classic variant" of the marxist theory of ideology, such as we find in or derive from Marx and Engels's *German Ideology*. Whereas in that theory we would expect a broad coincidence or correspondence between "ruling class" and "ruling ideas," we find instead significant differences of ideological formation *within* the so-called dominant classes, with no perfect or consistent class symmetry in the way these ideological formations are distributed among classes. We have, indeed, been required to speak of an internal contestation

41

between one set of ruling ideas and another, and the partial displacement of one by the other. Similarly, the idea of the internal fractioning of the ideological universe of the dominant classes, or the suggestion that ideas may have to enter into a process of vigorous polemic and contestation in order to become the normative-normalized structure of conceptions through which a class "spontaneously" and authentically thinks or lives its relations to the world, are propositions equally foreign to classical marxism, at least in its more abstract and general form. (The concrete analysis of ideological formations in the *Eighteenth Brumaire* is quite a different question.) The conventional approach suggests that the dominant ideas are ascribed by and inscribed in the position a class holds in the structure of social relations and that the position of dominance is guaranteed elsewhere—by class location. It is not assumed that these ideas should positively have to win ascendancy (rather than being ascribed it) through a specific and contingent (in the sense of open-ended, not totally determined) process of ideological struggle.

In the classical perspective, Thatcherism would be understood as in no significant way different from traditional conservative ruling ideas. I have already noted that Thatcherism is a quite distinct, specific, and novel combination of ideological elements, distinct from other combinations through which the dominance of the English ruling classes has, historically, found expression. It is also the result of the positive reorganizing of certain key elements in the discourses of the Right—partly an effect of the *disorganizing* of a previously settled formation. Thatcherism, too, has emerged as the result of an extended ideological struggle *within* the ruling bloc. Traditionally, we would expect the bourgeoisie as a "whole" class, always already inscribed with "its" ideology, to go marching through history with monetarism imprinted (in Poulantzas's memorable phrase) "like a number plate on its back." We are looking here at a significant *shift* in thinking. Far from one whole unified class outlook being locked in permanent struggle with the class outlook of an opposing class, we are obliged to explain an ideology that has effectively penetrated, fractured, and fragmented the territory of the dominated classes, precipitating a rupture in their traditional discourses (laborism, reformism, welfarism, Keynesianism) and actively working on the discursive space, the occupancy or mastery of which alone enables it to become a leading popular ideological force.

The latter point is not, of course, historically novel. Between a quarter and a third of the British working class, however defined, has traditionally voted conservative in this century. Indeed, the most significant period in the reconstruction of modern conservatism prior to the advent of Thatcherism is the period from the closing decades of the nineteenth century to the early decades of the twentieth century when, faced with the emergence of mass democracy, the demise of the Liberal party and its replacement by Labour, conservatism was obliged to reconstitute itself as a mass political ideology capable of winning a majority in terms of electoral support. Some of the ideological elements currently being recast by Thatcherism are precisely the ones that coalesced into *modern* conservatism—nation before class, the organic unity of the English people, the coincidence between the "English genius" and traditionalism, the paternal duties the privileged owe to the lower orders, society as an orderly hierarchy of "powers," constitutionalism, and so on. In this way—from the absorption of the imperial theme by Disraeli, Chamberlain, and Saintsbury in the 1880s and 1890s, to the "great normalization" of the Baldwin era in the 1920s and 1930s—conservatism, against the odds, came to exert a powerful hegemony over key sectors of the popular classes, one it has not subsequently lost. Thatcherism thus poses for the classical marxist theory of ideology a long-standing problem of historical analysis, only in a new and challenging form.

The traditional escape clause for classical marxism, confronted with this historical fact, is the recourse to "false consciousness." The popular classes, we must suppose, have been ideologically duped by the dominant classes, using what *The German Ideology* calls their "monopoly over the means of mental production." The masses, therefore, have been temporarily ensnared, against their real material interests and position in the structure of social relations, to live their relation to their real conditions of material existence through an imposed but "false" structure of illusions. The traditional expectation on the Left, founded on this premise, would therefore be that, as real material factors begin once more to exert their effect, the cobwebs of illusion would be dispelled, "reality" would be transferred directly into working-class heads, the scales would fall from workers' eyes, and Minerva's Owl—the great denouement promised by the *Communist Manifesto*, as the socialization of labor progressively created the conditions for mass solidarity and enlightenment—would take wing at last (even if timed to arrive approximately 150 years late).

This explanation has to deal with the surprising fact that mass unemployment has taken a much longer time than predicted to percolate mass consciousness; the unemployed, who might have been expected to pierce the veil of illusion first, are still by no means automatic mass converts to laborism, let alone socialism; and the lessons that can be drawn from the fact of unemployment turn out to be less monolithic and predictable, less determined by strict material factors, more variable than supposed. The same fact can be read or made sense of in different ways, depending on the ideological perspective employed. Mass unemployment can be interpreted as a scandalous indictment of the system; or as a sign of Britain's underlying economic weakness about which mere governments—Left or Right—can do very little; or as acceptable because "there is no alternative" that is not more disastrous for the economy; or indeed—within the sociomasochistic perspective that sometimes appears to be a peculiarly strong feature of British ideology—as the required measure of suffering that guarantees the remedy will work eventually because it hurts so much (the Britain-is-best-when-backed-to-the-wall syndrome)! The logics of ideological inference turn out to be more multivariate, the automatic connection between material and ideal factors less determinate, than the classical theory would have us believe.

Is this a mere historical aberration—one of classical marxism's "little local difficulties"? Far from it. Within the gap opened up here between theoretical prediction and historico-empirical reality is inscribed, in essence, the whole dilemma of classical marxist theory in our time as a guide to political action; that is, its lack of adequate explanatory power about the concrete empirical development of consciousness and practice in the working classes of the advanced capitalist world—a gap neither Lukács's distinction between objective and empirical consciousness nor the more classical accounts of false consciousness have effectively bridged.

43

False consciousness had been—rightly—subjected to a rigorous epistemological critique. It assumes an empiricist relation of the subject to knowledge, namely, that the real world indelibly imprints its meanings and interests directly into our consciousness. We have only to look to discover its truths. And if we cannot see them, then it must be because there is a "cloud of unknowing" that obscures the unilateral truth of the real. The proposition—outside of the very rudimentary form of psychological sensationalism with which, in the name of materialism, it has occasionally been bolstered—does not contain any developed account of the actual mechanisms by which material factors ever and always reproduce their prescribed knowledge; or, more worryingly, of the mechanisms by which the transparency of the real could be obscured under conditions of false consciousness.

I add two somewhat more political critiques. It is a highly unstable theory about the world which has to assume that vast numbers of ordinary people, mentally equipped in much the same way as you or I, can simply be thoroughly and systematically duped into misrecognizing entirely where their real interests lie. Even less acceptable is the position that, whereas "they"—the masses—are the dupes of history, "we"—the privileged—are somehow without a trace of illusion and can see, transitively, right through into the truth, the essence, of a situation. Yet it is a fact that, though there are people willing enough to deploy the false consciousness explanation to account for the illusory behavior of others, there are very few who are ever willing to own up that *they* are themselves living in false consciousness! It seems to be (like corruption by pornography) a state always reserved for others. This resembles too palpably a self-excusing strategy to make much claim on our credulity as a serious explanation of a mass historical phenomenon.

This is by no means—as the deconstructionists would have us believe—a reason for throwing over altogether some of the insights of the classical marxist explanation. The social distribution of knowledge *is* skewed. And since the social institutions most directly implicated in its formation and transmission—the family/school/media triplet—are grounded in and structured by the class relations that surround them, the distribution of the available codes with which to decode or unscramble the meaning of events in the world, and the languages we use to construct interests, are bound to reflect the unequal relations of power that obtain in the area of symbolic production as in other spheres. Ruling or dominant conceptions of the world do not directly prescribe the mental content of the illusions that supposedly fill the heads of the dominated classes. But the circle of dominant ideas *does* accumulate the symbolic power to map or classify the world for others; its classifications do acquire not only the constraining power of dominance over other modes of thought but also the inertial authority of habit and instinct. It becomes the horizon of the taken-for-granted: what the world is and how it works, for all practical purposes. Ruling ideas may dominate other conceptions of the social world by setting the limit to what will appear as rational, reasonable, credible, indeed sayable or thinkable, within the given vocabularies of motive and action available to us. Their dominance lies precisely in the power they have to contain within their limits, to frame within their circumference of thought, the reasoning and calculation of other social groups. The "monopoly of the means of mental production"—or of the "cultural apparatuses," to use a more modern phrase—is not, of course, irrelevant to this acquisition over time of symbolic dominance vis-à-vis other, less coherent and comprehensive accounts of the world. Nor do they have literally to displace other ideas with illusions in order to acquire a hegemonic position over them. Ideologies may not be affixed, as organic entities, to their appropriate classes, but this does not mean that the production and transformation of ideology in society could proceed free of or outside the structuring lines of force of power and class.

Nor does it follow that interests—including material ones (whatever *they* are)—have no part in determining the play of ideas within which different groups figure out the world and their role and *allegiances* in it. The problem is that interests are not only not given as an objective feature of a structure of positions in a social system to which we are ascribed (and from which then dangle the appropriate forms of consciousness), but they change historically (Marx himself spoke of "new needs"). Class is not the only determinant of social interest (e.g., gender, race). More important, interests are themselves constructed, *constituted,* in and through the ideological process. What is more, social collectivities have more than one set of interests; and interests can be and frequently are contradictory, even mutually exclusive. Workers in a social system have both the interest of advancing and improving their position and advantages within it *and* of not losing their place. They are both dependent on *and* exploited by the capitalist system. Hence the lines of attachment and interdependence can run counter to and crosscut or interrupt the lines of solidarity and resistance between capital and labor. There is no prescriptive law as to which will always prevail. (Marx understood this actually contradictory basis to class consciousness better than subsequent marxists, with their predisposition to construct the pure, disembodied essence of the revolutionary proletarian as a substitute for their own distilled moral outrage).

It is therefore possible to hold both the proposition that material interests help to structure ideas and the proposition that position in the social structure has the tendency to influence the direction of social thought, without also arguing that material factors univocally determine ideology or that class position represents a guarantee that a class will have the appropriate forms of consciousness. What we know now is that there is no unitary logic of inference or deduction from one to the other. The logics of different ideological formations remain polyvocal, or as Volosinov would say of all discourse, "multiaccentual"; not infinitely open-ended, but essentially plural in character.

A somewhat modified position, then, would be that class interest, class position, and material factors are useful, even necessary, starting points in the analysis of any ideological formation. But they are *not sufficient—* because they are not sufficiently determinate—to account for the actual empirical disposition and movement of ideas in real historical societies. Thus, we would have to accept that, alongside the revolutionary political tradition in Britain (which has always, for historically specific reasons, been comparatively weak), the reformist tradition has always been well founded, embedded in a long tradition of historical evolution and social compromise; well articulated through a set of institutions deeply embedded in the culture of the dominated classes; and able, under certain historical conditions (those that have so far largely prevailed in British history), as effectively and plausibly to classify the world for working people and to make sense of certain courses of action and support, as other available traditions. This is not a matter of ideology alone. The structures that underpin a reformist definition of the world draw their roots from the us/them way of structuring the social divisions in society that both feed a corporate sense of class belongingness *and* are nourished by the cross-class-cutting lines of allegiance that, for example, knit conflicting classes and social groups into the larger, symbolic unity of the nation. What is required here is to understand how, *under different concrete conditions,* the perceptions and conceptions of the dominated classes can, equally cogently and plausibly, be organized, now into the reformist, now into the revolutionary discourse. Both are ways of organizing, discursively, not false but real, or (for the epistemologically squeamish) real enough, interests and experiences. Both impose on the same contradictory elements alternative inferential logics. And what can be said here of reformism—as indigenous a working-class ideology under certain historical conditions as the revolutionary logic—can and has also to be said and shown for Thatcherism. The first thing to ask about an "organic" ideology that, however unexpectedly, succeeds in organizing substantial sections of the masses and mobilizing them for political action, is not what is *false* about it but what about it is *true.* By "true" I do not mean universally correct as a law of the universe but "makes good sense," which—leaving science to one side—is usually quite enough for ideology.

The most cogent critique of some of the classical propositions of the marxist theory of ideology, such as we might find in *The German Ideology,* is to be found in the work of Althusser, especially the seminal "Ideological State Apparatuses" essay, which has stood in contemporary debate as the *locus classicus* of an alternative theorization. How does the phenomenon of Thatcherism stand in light of that argument?

Some of Althusser's key insights are positively confirmed; for example, the proposition that ideology is always materialized in concrete practices and rituals and operates through specific apparatuses. We have spoken of Thatcherism's extensive work of ideological transformations. But we have neglected to point out in detail how much this owes to the ways in which these new conceptions have been concretely materialized through the practices of state regulation in the apparatuses of the state—in education, in schooling, in family policy, in the administrative apparatuses of local and central government—and even more so in the specifically ideological apparatuses. I cannot enter here in detail into this matter, but it is extremely important, for example, to note the role of so-called private apparatuses, such as the Institute for Economic Affairs, which was set up in the dark days of the 1950s to advance the free-market, neoliberal cause. The IEA put many Thatcherite conceptions into public currency long before they were either fashionable *or* directly attached to any political party or faction, and it can now realistically claim to have played a leading role in constructing the new orthodoxy and to have "created the post-war focus for the demonstration that market analysis was indispensable for understanding and solving economic tasks and problems."[2] This institution was committed not only to advancing "the truths of classical political economy" but also to the validity of Adam Smith's philosophical view that "the instinct of man is to 'truck and barter in markets.' " One could say the same about the later formation of the Centre for Policy Studies by Sir Keith Joseph, which operated as the think tank that supported his U-turn into monetarism and directly harnessed the free-floating currents of free-market economic and social thinking—already making headway among leading economic journalists like Peter Jay and Samuel Brittan and among key state intellectuals in the economic departments—directly into the mainstream of the Conservative party. Or, to take another aspect, the remarkable way in which Thatcherism has gradually colonized the mass tabloid press (Britain is the most densely served mass newspaper-reading public in the world) so that the principal front-runners (excluding *The Mirror*)—*The Sun, The Mail, The Star, The Express*—vie with each other in the extremity of their vivid identifications with and glorification of Thatcherism as a philosophy and the symbolic person of Mrs. Thatcher herself.

In what free-marketeers regard as the dark days of Keynesian social democracy, the ascendancy over serious, informed, and popular mass opinion exerted through these apparatuses and agencies provided concrete rallying points for disabused anti-Keynesian intellectuals and points of condensation where alternative free-market, monetarist theoretical ideologies were concretely applied to one practical problem after another. In the period of the propaganda, between the succession of Mrs. Thatcher to the leadership of the Conservative party and the winning of the election in 1979, these organizations prepared the ground, were the trenches and fortifications, the advance outposts in civil society itself, from which the counteroffensive to the reigning consensus was launched; they were the base for the strategic regrouping of state intellectuals and academics, in the treasury, the common rooms, the think tanks and business schools from which the assault on the existing hegemony inside the power bloc was launched. And they were also the key sites—the popular press is strategic in *this* part of the process—in the translation of doctrine and philosophy into the terrain of practice and policy and the popular idiom of practical accomplishments. They helped to make the "intolerable" thinkable.

All of this represents a progressive ascendancy over the apparatuses of opinion formation in the society at a number of different strategic levels, and it is precisely where the Althusserian formation runs into difficulties. Althusser would argue that these are all ideological *state* apparatuses—regardless of what he considered the purely formal question of whether they belonged to the state or not. They are "state" by virtue of their function—the function, ascribed to the state, of sustaining the "reproduction of the social relations of production" in and through ideology. What is striking about Thatcherism is precisely its capacity to enter into struggle and win space *in civil society itself;* to use the trenches and fortifications of civil society as the means of forging a considerable ideological and intellectual *authority* outside the realm of the state proper and, indeed, *before*—as a necessary condition to—taking formal power *in* the state, as part of an internal contestation against key elements within the power bloc. (The hearts and minds the IEA set out to capture were not only informed public opinion generally but quite specifically key senior civil servants, subverted—as they saw it—by incorrect Keynesian nostrums.)

Is this merely a quibble? I think not. Despite the apparent similarities of phrasing (due in part to the fact that both Althusser's and my thinking on this point has been influenced by and reflects Gramsci), two fundamentally different processes are being described. The first (Althusser's

"Ideological State Apparatuses" essay) is the use of existing apparatuses to reproduce the already given ruling ideology; the second (mine) is the struggle and contestation for the space in which to construct an ideological hegemony. The fact is that a position of ideological authority and leadership—of intellectual and moral ascendancy—constructed by harnessing the lines of force and opinion in the apparently "free space" of civil society has a remarkable durability, depth, and staying power *because* the adhesion it wins among the people is not coerced, as it might be if the state were directly involved, but appears to be produced freely and spontaneously as the popular consent to power. The differences therefore touch what I regard as the key issue—the problem of explaining the popular consent to Thatcherism.

It is Althusser's functionalism that drives him to give an over-integrative account of ideological reproduction and to collapse the state/ civil society distinction as if it were without real or pertinent effects. Everything suggests that we must conceptualize the process by which the dominant ideology reproduces itself as a contradictory and contested one. Indeed, the term "reproduction," with its strong functionalist associations, carries quite the wrong connotations. The process must be conceptualized in terms of the continuous production and transformation of ideology; that is, in terms of the condensations Thatcherism has to some extent been able to effect, to bring about, to realize. And far from allowing us to collapse the distinction, this latter approach *requires* us to sustain the state/civil society distinction and not to conflate the two, since civil society is such a key site in the production of consensus. Althusser, of course, subsequently acknowledged the error of emphasis in the "Ideological State Apparatuses" essay (in an original footnote and in his "Notes on the ISA's" [1977], translated into English in *Economy and Society*): the "consensus effects of the ruling class"—its ideology—cannot be regarded "as a simple given fact, as a system of exactly defined institutions which would automatically duplicate the violent rule of the same class or which would have been installed by the clear political consciousness of this class of particular purposes defined by its function."[3] They succeed in establishing their hegemony "at the same time through an internal struggle to overcome the contradictions of the bourgeois class fractions and to produce unity within the bourgeoisie as ruling class." The unification of the ruling class "is always 'incomplete' and always 'has to be resumed.' " This goes some way toward correcting the functionalism of the original essay (though it still does not adequately tackle the state/ civil society distinction). But it cannot retrospectively correct the damaging theoretical effects Althusser's more functionalist way of conceptualizing the "reproduction" of ruling class consensus had on the main line of argument in his original essay and in those who have attempted to follow its protocols too strictly.

Althusser's essay, of course, contains not one but two related, yet distinct, ways of trying to secure the materialism of ideology without reductionism. It is the second formulation that provided the site of a very extensive reconstruction of classical marxist theories—the proposition, derived from Lacan, that ideology is material because it operates in and through the production of subjects. This question of ideology and the production of subjects has unrolled in the wake of Althusser's destruction of the integral, authorial individual subject, the subject origin of ideological discourse that is at the heart of traditional conceptions of ideology. His appeal to Lacan is the attempt—via Lacan's rereading of the psychoanalytic tradition in light of structuralism and Saussure—to fill the empty space created by the structuralist dethronement of the "I" of enunciation.

Now anyone who is genuinely interested in the production and mechanisms of ideology must be concerned with the question of the production of subjects and the unconscious categories that enable definite forms of subjectivity to arise. It is clear that the discourses of the New Right have been engaged precisely in this work of the production of new subject positions and the transformation of subjectivities. Of course, there might be an essential Thatcherite subject hiding or concealed in each of us, struggling to get out. But is seems more probable that Thatcherism has been able to constitute new subject positions from which its discourses about the world make sense, or to appropriate to itself existing, already formed interpellations. These have arisen through some process, central to the mechanism of ideology itself, by which new positions have interrupted and partially displaced older ones; or else new discourses have emerged that secure real points of identification. In many instances, such interpellations may already be in place. In other cases, rather than searching for the always already essentially reactionary working-class subject (to set against his/her opposite, the always already essentially revolutionary worker), we are driven to attend to the capacity of new political discourses to articulate themselves on and through the fractured, necessarily contradictory structures of formed subjectivities; to work on the ground of a formed common sense, or what Pêcheux and Henry call the "preconstructed"; and thus to interpellate already formed subjects in new discursive relations.

There is no space to demonstrate in detail how this reconstitution of subject positions is actually accomplished discursively, but it *can* be shown. For example, the whole discourse of Thatcherism combines ideological elements into a discursive chain in such a way that the logic or unity of the discourse depends on the subject addressed assuming a number of specific subject positions. The discourse can only be read or spoken unproblematically if it is enunciated from the imaginary position of knowledge of the self-reliant, self-interested, self-sufficient taxpayer—Possessive Individual Man (*sic*); or the "concerned patriot"; or the subject passionately attached to individual liberty and passionately opposed to the incursion of liberty that occurs through the state; or the respectable housewife; or the native Briton. Moreover, through the process Laclau has described as "condensed connotation," these imaginary positions, in the plenitude of their knowledgeable relation to knowledge, trigger off and connote one another in a chain of linked interpellations that *constitute* the Imaginary—the condition for the so-called unity, of the discourse, of the speaker to the spoken, as well as connecting one site of articulation with another: the liberty-loving citizen is *also* the worried parent, the respectable housewife, the careful manager of the household budget, the solid English citizen "proud to be British. . . ." The discourses of Thatcherism are constantly in this way formulating new subjectivities for the positions they are constructing, working through interpellation.

The question at issue is not whether this interpellative process is central to that through which ideology has its effects, but rather how we are to understand the process. In the Lacanian rereading of Freud, which is what Althusser was borrowing from and the source that has since provided

49

the principal site of subsequent theorization, these positionings are fundamentally secured through the resolution in infancy and early childhood of
some of the primary psychoanalytic processes—the Oedipus complex, primary narcissism, the mirror phase, and so on. These—in the now famous
formulations of discourse theory—are, at one and the same time, the primary mechanisms of the repression that becomes the basis of all apparently
stable subjective identifications; the points that establish the imaginary place
of knowledge in what then seems an empirically verifiable relation to the
world. They are the mechanism of entry into language itself, and thus into
Culture. And since these different aspects to the formation of subjectivities
are treated as identical or homologous, accomplished in the same series of
resolutions, they are also, finally, the entry into complicity with the law of
patriarchy, of the Father, or Althusser's "big S," Subject. These psychoanalytic processes are understood to provide the matrix of always unstable,
always contradictory locations or orientations with respect to meaning and
language, and hence with respect to ideology itself. Across this subjective
space—which is, of course, no longer unified but a place of constant displacement through the fracturing effects of repression—all subsequent discursive operations play.

Now it may be that, since the securing of sexual identity is, critically, the work that is done through these unconscious resolutions (Freud),
and the field of infant sexuality is clearly such a key domain in the formation
of subjectivity, there is little doubt of the critical importance of the processes
referred to above for the interpellation of gender—a factor not only of key
social and ideological importance in itself but one that becomes reinscribed
in or relayed through a wide variety of other domains, including, of course,
the political. Patriarchal positions are absolutely central, as points of condensed articulation, in the discourses of both middle-class, petit-bourgeois,
and working-class respectability—an apparently nonpolitical factor that has
the effect of stabilizing and securing to the Right a whole range of other
discourses. It does not, however, follow that the whole of the process of
discursive positioning can be read off from those primary positionings or
conceived largely as simply recapitulating the system, entry into which was
sealed forever with the original resolution of Oedipal identifications. The
entry into Language as such—and hence into Culture/Ideology—does begin
to occur at that stage in the formation of subjectivity itself. But there is all
the difference in the world between the capacity to use Language *as such*
and the appropriation and imaginary identity with particular *languages* and
their specific ideological and discursive universes. What Thatcherism poses
is the problem of understanding how already positioned subjects can be
effectively detached from their points of application and effectively *repositioned* by a new set of discourses. This is precisely a historically specific
level of application of the interpellative aspects of ideology that is *not* adequately resumed or explained by the transhistorical speculative generalities
of Lacanianism.

Lacanian psychoanalysis has been utilized, it seems, to explain
how it is we are formed as subjects and how we ever come to enter language,
meaning, representation. The problem before us is the rather different question of how subjects could be induced to begin to enunciate their relation
to the world in quite different meaning or representational systems. The
level of abstraction at which the theory is operating (even if it were correct)

is largely incommensurable with the nature of the object it is being wheeled in to explain.

Throughout, I have been speaking of ideology. But, of course, in many areas the problematic of ideology has itself been displaced into the analysis of the diversity of discursive practices and formations as such. This is directly connected with the influence of Foucault. A thorough assessment of the strengths and limits of Foucault's work is not possible within the scope of this essay, but one can make certain indications. From what has already been said, it will be seen that we do not in any way refuse the advances made by the development of the analysis of *the discursive*. No social practice exists outside of the domain of the semiotic—the practices and production of meaning. This necessarily modifies, in a radical way, the traditional material/ideal, base/superstructure dichotomies of classical marxist theories of ideology as well as their ascription of a dependent position to ideology in the ensemble of social practices. The positive positions taken in this paper are thus compatible with the general emphases (not necessarily the particular epistemological positions or other formulations) on discourse contained in, say, Foucault's *Archeology of Knowledge*—a text that, however full of interesting fluctuations, has been banished into a symptomatic silence by later "true Foucaultians." (What, for example, would the true disciples make now of Foucault's observation that discursive relations "must be distinguished from what we might call primary relations . . . which, independently of all discourse . . . may be described between institutions, techniques, social forms, etc. After all, we know very well that relations existed between the bourgeois family and the functioning of judicial authorities and categories in the nineteenth century that can be analyzed in their own right. . . ."[4] These "other relations" have since been wholly absorbed into that great nonessentialist Essence, that final Kierkegaardian trace in the Foucault episteme, The Body.)

Leaving the deep epistemological questions aside for now (Foucault's position then seemed closer to the realist philosophical position I myself adopt than to the full-blown, neo-Kantianism into which it has subsequently been drawn), many of Foucault's insights into the operations of the discursive deeply refresh and inform our understanding of how ideological formations work, even where he positively refuses the concept of ideology itself. Discursive formations (or ideological formations that operate through discursive regularities) "formulate" their own objects of knowledge and their own subjects; they have their own repertoire of concepts, are driven by their own logics, operate their own enunciative modality, constitute their own way of acknowledging what is true and excluding what is false within their own regime of truth. They establish through their regularities a "space of formation" in which certain statements can be enunciated; one constellation constantly interrupts, displaces, and rearranges another. This is at one with Foucault's project: to explain how it is that "one particular statement appeared rather than another."

It does not follow that social practices are only discourses. This would be to convert a polemical claim (i.e., the social exists within the semiotic; the ideological matters and has real effects) into an explanatory one—but with the effect of tipping the explanation from one one-sided emphasis to its opposite. I note that the same objection is recognized even by those, like Gary Wickham in a recent article in *Economy and Society*, whose project is to go beyond or to out-Foucault Foucault. Thus, I agree with Wickham when he writes: "I choose 'practices' [rather than discourses] because it seems less trapped in the reality side of the knowledge/reality distinction than 'discourses' is in the knowledge side." "By practices," he adds, "I mean more than institutionally constrained actions and I mean more than something which is outside of knowledge." (Presumably, he included those "more than" things in the definition.) "By practices here I [Wickham] mean common groupings of techniques and discourses"—an emphasis I much prefer.

More difficult to absorb or take into account are the extremes to which, in the search for a nonessentialist account, the "necessary noncorrespondence" of discursive practices has been driven. This seems to dissolve the real theoretical gains made by the recognition of difference, of plurality in discourse, of the nonessentialist, multiaccentual character of ideology—pushing them over the brink into the gospel of absolute diversity. Great insights have been achieved in Foucault's recent work on particular discursive formations (his work on the disciplinary archipelago in *Discipline and Punish* greatly outdistancing, in my judgment, the shaky historical generalizations of the more fashionable volumes on sexuality). But his work sometimes seems to appear to command allegiance for spurious and extrinsic reasons. Their specificity—law, medicine, psychiatry, sexuality—has reinforced the "return to the concrete," without quite having to acknowledge the claims of that old and rather unfashionable form of knowledge that used to be called History. And a permanently radical gloss is dubiously attached to it simply because it contains the magical terms "power," "resistance," and "plebeian."

Leave aside such oddities—for example, the fact that knowledge/power described as bypassing ideology is the problematic of ideology—and note instead that these gains are made at the cost of a radical *dispersal* of the notion of power, often achieved, so to speak, by reading Foucault through Derrida. (To make it more perplexing, Foucault sometimes seemed to read himself in that way!) It is one thing to speak of the switches and relays through which one discursive practice interrupts another—Thatcherism requires precisely such an analysis. It is quite another if they pass continually on different tracks, like trains in the night, on their way to an infinite plurality of destinations. An ascending analysis of power—"starting from its infinitesimal mechanisms," its "microphysics," is all very well. It subverts our tendency to treat power as an imposed system of coercive constraint from above. But the deep and difficult problem of the relation between the lateral powers in the sites of civil society and social relations and the vertical powers of, say, the state and political relationships (what was referred to earlier as the question of the "consent to power") is not tackled but sidestepped by distributing power "everywhere." The techniques and strategies of power thus become, in Foucault, highly specific, but at the expense of a concept of power that is generalized and essentialized. (The Body, as we have noted, and Resistance are other such false-concrete, nonessential Essences in Foucault's discourse.) This is, in fact, a very Durkheimean concept of power—that abstract force or collective conscience in society that constrains us all, or rather through which we endlessly constrain one another. And it leads to an equally generalized Durkheimean concept of social control—except

52

that it is now refashioned as discipline, which seems utterly without reference to any such point of condensation or articulation as *the state* (Foucault is highly ambiguous on this point, though his disciples are not).

As this analysis of Thatcherism clearly shows, the discursive relations of power cannot be constituted exclusively on the terrain of the state. They precisely crisscross the social body. There is no moment in which the powers that cohere in the state can ever exhaustively resume those that are dispersed through the plurality of practices in society. Nevertheless, the moment of the passage of power into the state and its condensation there into a definite system of rule is a critical historical moment, representing a distinct phase. Of course, no sovereign unity of discourse then unfolds: the moment of "state," like that of "party," is not a final one, as conceived in classical political theory. Thatcherism, as a discursive formation, has remained a plurality of discourses—about the family, the economy, national identity, morality, crime, law, women, human nature. But precisely a certain unity has been constituted out of this diversity. And there are different points of application through which, in turn, this constituted regime of truth has been secured to certain political positions. Unless, against the tendency to dispersal, these questions of articulation are also posed, the play of discourse becomes nothing but a high-level, advanced game for academic deconstructionists, a matter of intellectual diversion, as the complexity of one discourse after another is perpetually unraveled. To put the point more concretely: the particular ways in which Thatcherism has stitched together a contradictory juncture between the logics of the market and possessive individualism, on the one hand, and the logics of an organic conservatism, on the other, are highly amenable to a Foucaultian type of analysis, provided we understand that it is the contradictory unity so constructed and held that rules—not the rules of diversity alone. The problem with Foucault, to put it brusquely, is a conception of difference without a conception of articulation, that is, a conception of power without a conception of hegemony.

The question of hegemony brings us, of course, to Gramsci. Again, it is not possible within the scope of this paper to deal with Gramsci comprehensively, but it is possible to establish some indications as to the superiority of hegemony over other concepts in approaching the task of historical explanation and analysis. Hegemony points to a way of conceptualizing the emergence of Thatcherism in terms of the struggle to gain ascendancy over a whole social formation, to achieve positions of leadership in a number of different sites of social life at once, to achieve the commanding position on a broad strategic front. It entails the critical passage of a system of domination into the authority of a leading bloc, which is capable not only of organizing its own base through the construction of alliances between different sectors and social forces, but which has as a central feature of that process the construction and winning of popular consent to that authority among key sectors of the dominated classes themselves. The advantages of the concept of hegemony lay above all in the directness of its address (and not in a lopsided, false-consciousness way) to the central issue of *popular consent.*

Another advantage is the critique of essentialism implicit in all of Gramsci's formulations. Hegemony is *constructed,* through a complex series or process of struggle. It is not given, either in the existing structure of society or in the given class structure of a mode of production. It cannot be constructed once and for all, since the balance of social forces on which it rests is subject to continuing evolution and development, depending on how a variety of struggles are conducted. Hegemony, once achieved, must be constantly and ceaselessly renewed, reenacted. This implies a conception of the process of social reproduction as continuous and contradictory—the very opposite of a functional achievement. Central to this is the notion of various forms and intensities of struggle. It is the various outcomes of these struggles, not the reinscription in place of what already exists, that determines the nature of the unstable equilibrium on which the authority of a social bloc is founded and that also defines its weak or unstable points, the points of further unrolling and development. Typically, the Gramscian analysis of a conjuncture proceeds not from the invocation of the given "laws of economic development" but from an analysis of the "current relations of force." This, too, is not a once-and-for-all predetermined process: one must distinguish, Gramsci argued, "various moments or levels," "intervals of varying frequency," even, perhaps (the example is the French Revolution), "various revolutions" within an unfolding process. And the achievement of hegemony never has only one character, only a predominant tendency; it is always "destruction *and* reconstruction" (the latter "already under way in the very moment of destruction"), or what Gramsci elsewhere calls "revolution/restoration."[5]

The broadening of a system of domination into a wider social authority is thus, for Gramsci, tied in with the critique of economism. For Gramsci, the question of hegemony cannot be purely ideological, since it *must* have as its foundation the domination of a particular social bloc "in the decisive nucleus of economic activity." All those who therefore gloss Gramsci's concept of hegemony with the qualifying idea that it is ideological are doing a great disservice to his breadth of thought. Gramsci is deeply alive to the ethical, moral, intellectual, ideological, and cultural *dimensions* of the struggle for hegemony, but hegemony as a concept is not ethical or cultural alone. The culturalist reading of Gramsci has done profound damage. On the other hand, for Gramsci, hegemony cannot be economic alone, in either the first or the last instance, since it is by definition something that includes and transcends "the corporate limits of the purely economic class," something that must be able to "become the interests of other subordinating groups too," and can thus "gain the upperhand, propagate itself throughout society—bringing about not only the unity of economic and political aims, but also intellectual and moral unity, posing all questions around which the struggle rages, not on a corporate but on a 'universal plane' and thus creating the hegemony of a fundamental social group over a series of subordinate groups—the motor force of a universal expansion, of the development of all the 'national' energies."[6] This Gramsci equates with the "passage from the structure to the sphere of the complex superstructures," a process that for him is analytically irreversible.

Gramsci was, of course, writing in a coded way about the historical tasks of the revolutionary party and of the communist and workers' movements. (Note, however, the constant movement toward the national or universal level.) But his terms of analysis clearly have great analytic purchase on the analysis of Thatcherism. Nothing in our time (certainly nothing from the Left) so closely matches Gramsci's description of how, in a crisis, "the political forces which are struggling to conserve and defend the existing structure itself are making ... incessant and persistent efforts. ... These forces ... make imperative the accomplishment of certain historical tasks." The process of contestation and struggle "is developed in a series of ideological, religious, philosophical, political and juridical polemics whose concreteness can be estimated by the extent to which they are convincing and shift the previously existing disposition of social forces." The application could not be more precise.[7] So, at a narrower level, are Gramsci's passing remarks about laissez-faire, the doctrine to whose philosophical foundations neoliberalism aims to return. In the *Modern Prince*, Gramsci observes that *"laissez-faire*, too, is a form of state 'regulation,' introduced and maintained by legislative and coercive means," and that consequently *"laissez-faire* liberalism is a political program designed to change—so far as it is victorious—a state's leading personnel and to change the economic program of the state itself."[8]

Less well known than the essays from which the earlier passages were taken, but equally germane to this inquiry, are those that conceptualize the relationship between the broader processes of the struggle, which construct or transform hegemony, and the processes of ideology. Gramsci uses the term "ideology" in what may now seem a classical sense, as systems of ideas, but in a broad context: "on condition that the word is used in its highest sense of a conception of the world that is implicitly manifest in art, in law, in economic activity and in all manifestations of individual and collective life." He sees it also in terms of its historical functions: its role in "preserving the ideological unity of an entire social bloc"; of providing individuals and groups with their various "conceptions of the world," which influence and modify their actions; and, above all, as a means to "organize human masses and create the terrain on which men move, acquire consciousness of their position, struggle, etc." The role of "organic ideologies," those that seek to propagate themselves throughout society and create a new form of national-popular will for some immense historical task, is to intervene in the terrain of ordinary, contradictory, episodic common sense; to interrupt, renovate, and transform in a more systematic direction the practical consciousness of the masses, the given dispositions of their mental life. Common sense is itself a structure of popular ideology, a spontaneous conception of the world, reflecting the traces of previous systems of thought that have sedimented into everyday reasoning. Common sense, the "given ground and dispositions of a culture"—itself the complex result of previous struggles, reflecting previous forms of hegemony and earlier "unstable equilibria"—becomes the object that organic ideologies, which have evolved their own organic intellectual strata and passed through their moment of party, seek to refashion and transform.

The processes of ideology are conceived by Gramsci in different ways: as an "educative task"; as a "cultural battle to transform the popular mentality"; and, even more appositely, as a "struggle of political 'hegemonies' of opposing directions, first in the ethical field and then in that of the political proper."[9] Directly opposed to the monistic notion of "the dominant ideology," always already in place, Gramsci asks instead, "how it happens that in all periods, there co-exist many systems and currents of philosophical thought and how these currents are born, how they are diffused, and why in the process of diffusion they fracture along certain lines and in certain directions"? This is a conception of the field of ideologies in terms of conflicting, overlapping, or intersecting currents or formations. The key question—Foucault's, but in a decisively non-Foucaultian formulation—is their fracturing: What determines their lines of diffusion, their structuration, their differentiation, their rearticulation? Again, this is at the opposite extreme from the notion of whole class outlooks confronting the already formed whole class outlooks of another fundamental group. Dispensing with this last vestige of essentialism, Gramsci asserts, "what matters is the criticism to which such an ideological complex is subjected by the first representatives of the new historical phase—which makes possible a process of differentiation and change in the relative weight that the elements of the old ideologies used to possess. What was previously secondary and subordinate, or even incidental, is now taken to be primary—becomes the nucleus of a new ideological and theoretical complex. The old collective will dissolve into its contradictory elements since the subordinate ones develop socially."[10] The whole of Laclau's subsequent elaboration of articulation/disarticulation is contained in the nucleus of that thought.

Gramsci is not blind to the site of the problems modern theorists signify through references to "the subject," though he does not use the same terms. But he understands the contradictory formations of consciousness: for example, the split between the conception of the world which is "logically affirmed" and that which is "implicit in his mode of action"; the social character of subjectivity—"man is to be conceived as a historical bloc"—and its composite, fractured character—the "disjointed and episodic" character of common sense, the "stratified deposits" of popular philosophy, the "strangely composite" nature of personality, which contains "Stone Age elements and principles of a more advanced science, prejudices from all past phases of history at the local level and institutions of a future philosophy."[11] Each individual, Gramsci says, "is the synthesis not only of existing relations but of the history of these relations. He [or she] is a précis of all the past."

It should be clear from these selective references, and without further, more systematic exemplification: first, how far removed Gramsci is from the traditional or classical versions of the marxist conceptions of ideology; second, how much he anticipates—albeit in a language not yet reconstructed through loans from structuralism, discourse and linguistic theory, or psychoanalysis—many of the actual advances in theorizing these later developments have brought; third, how original some of his conceptions are—the rich concept of hegemony has absolutely no equivalent among the other theorists considered here (for example, Foucault's conceptions of power and resistance appear thin, undernourished abstractions); and fourth, how Gramsci is able both to promulgate a novel theorization of ideology by locating it within a broader set of historical and political processes and retain what the other alternative theorizations quite lack. I am referring to the final set of references—not the terminology and doctrinal content of classical marxism, but the *problematic* of marxism, which structures the whole of Gramsci's discourse and thought: the commitment to the project of socialist transformation that distinguished marxism as a living theory, an open-ended project of critical thought, without guarantees, from the many other academically closed discourses that presently struggle to hegemonize the intellectual world.

Stuart Hall

I end, therefore, with a paradox: a theory designed primarily to analyze capitalist social formations in order to point out strategic lessons for the socialist movement—Gramsci's—turns out to have the most to tell us about how to analyze one of the most historically reactionary and regressive hegemonic-seeking formations to appear in British society in this century. This may not be as gloomy a conclusion as it appears at first sight, since it has been, up until now, precisely marxism's failure to renovate adequately its own thinking to explain sufficiently how modern capitalism remains in being and sustains its hegemonic position in industrialized societies that has been so signally lacking. Understanding Thatcherism may be the price we have to pay for a real advance in theoretical enlightenment within the marxist problematic. Gramsci, at least, would have taken some pleasure from the unexpected nature of this next (last) dialectical twist.

Notes

1 Edward Thompson, *The Poverty of Theory* (New York: Monthly Review Press, 1978).

2 Institute for Economic Affairs, *The Emerging Consensus* (London: IEA, 1981).

3 Louis Althusser, "Notes on the ISA's," *Economy and Society* 12:4 (1983).

4 Michel Foucault, *The Archaeology of Knowledge* (New York: Pantheon, 1972), p. 45.

5 Antonio Gramsci, *Prison Notebooks: Selections*, trans. Quintin Hoare and Geoffrey N. Smith (New York: International Publishers, 1971), p. 168.

6 Gramsci, pp. 181-82.

7 Gramsci, p. 178.

8 Gramsci, p. 160.

9 Gramsci, "The Study of Philosophy," in *Prison Notebooks*.

10 Gramsci, p. 195.

11 Gramsci, p. 324.

Question

You seem to imply that there is a zero-sum game of political ideology in Britain; that the Right could only move ahead because the Left was weak. Is this a general claim or is it particular to Great Britain at this time?

Hall

I don't want to suggest it is a zero-sum game. I want to oppose the notion that the Right advances by, as it were, setting into place an already formulated whole conception of the world; or that it is only through its positive statements that it is able to become a pole of new articulations. The Right's success depends as much on its capacity to address precisely the contradictions that are already within the formations of the Left, to move effectively into positions of contestation. For example, the Right picked up the actual mixed and contradictory experience of ordinary people within the welfare state, and on the basis of that insertion into the vocabularies of the Left began to construct the discourses of antistatism. So, many positions on the Right are secured not by displacing but by disarticulating the discourse of the Left. Of course, the reasons why those discourses on the Left are in disrepair don't necessarily have to do with that process of contestation/opposition. There are a whole range of real historical tasks the Left did not and could not resolve within the limits of the program it adhered to. The Left in Britain is, in its own terms, very close to the end of one historical program, one whole kind of politics. So it's not simply a zero-sum game in the sense that the Right precipitates the crisis, but rather that the Right advances through occupying strategic territory within the terrain of the Left.

That is, therefore, the way I want to talk about the nature of ideological struggle. I don't think the ideological field is divided into elements of ideological discourses that have a necessary class connotation. In societies like ours, ideological contestation does not take place between fully formed, competing worldviews—theirs and ours. The field of ideology is not divided in that way. It's a field in which there are many different discourses and social forces in play at the same time. Contestation often has to do with the engagement around existing ideological symbols and slogans, winning them away from the connotative chains of association they have acquired, which build them into languages that seem to construct topics so that they deliver an answer that favors one end of the political spectrum. The language of nationhood, for example, is not a language we speak but a language that speaks us. So, in England, if you open your mouth and say "Britain," before you know where you are, you are off to the South Atlantic. Because there is no identity between one class and that nation, everybody has some investment in what Britain is about; it's their future; it's a place they live in; it has a real purchase for everyone. Everyone has some patriotic sentiments into which particular problems or projects can be inserted. People's social identity is going to depend on the way they negotiate themselves in relation to the nation. Consequently, I think the ideological struggle takes place precisely over what the nation means. What are the values associated with it and what are the excluded values? And what is the way in which those powerful symbols can be detached from their entanglement with one set of historical associations and rearticulated in a different direction? Now this is not only a question about what is happening in the field of discourse but also about the way in which social groups, social movements, or social classes come to locate themselves inside one or another ideological configuration—how they come to see themselves as authored, addressed, hailed by those statements.

Question

You seem to place very little importance on the systematic, coherent ideological statements, such as monetarist economics or the products of the Centre for Policy Studies. But isn't it necessary for ideological analysis to expose the weaknesses and contradictions in such positions?

Hall

It is perfectly true that much of the everyday monetarist economics the Thatcherites speak is not very internally consistent as a theoretical system, so theoretical economists can dismantle it in a moment. This lack of intellectual rigor doesn't make Thatcherism go away, partly because it operates elsewhere—in more commonsense ways, at the point where it connects with the ongoing, more episodic and contradictory common sense of people. It is at that level that monetarism has a kind of truth, a way of referencing the way real economic developments are constructed experientially. It has a way of placing into experience what people feel to be the errors and problems of the past. In this way, the theory connects with people's experience.

Remember Gramsci's argument that ideology has two domains—philosophy, or theoretical ideologies, and common sense—and that the relations between them are governed by politics. One has to investigate quite precisely how more elaborated theoretical ideologies fit, often very contradictorily, into people's actual local and immediate experience. I am therefore not arguing (as conservative pluralists did at a certain point) that the working class is "really" reactionary. The working class isn't "essentially" any one thing; like the rest of us, it's full of conservative feelings hiding behind a lot of radical language, and vice versa. Popular consciousness lies at the intersection of very fragmentary, contradictory discourses. Popular ideology is not consistent. The nature of systematic ideologies is precisely to begin to operate on common sense and to render common sense more consistent.

To take another example, I am interested in how grand theories of sovereignty, among people who have never read a word of Jefferson or Hobbes, nevertheless link with ideas of what is "right" about our country and where our country stops and where its boundaries symbolically should lie. The theoretical discourse of sovereignty sometimes clarifies popular conceptions of sovereignty, but when people move into action it's not because they have just read the Declaration of Independence. It's because some of those philosophically elaborated concepts have connected with a deeper groundwork of emotional loyalties and moral sentiments and bits of knowledge and so on. Symbolic identification—that is the real popular field on which those things are sorted out. In spite of the power of the media and of the central institutions and apparatuses of ideology, it's not possible simply to organize and deliver popular consciousness where it has to be delivered; it has a very complicated structure, and that is what provides for the politics of intervention—finding the appropriate cracks that just can't be filled in. Sometimes, precisely at moments of hegemony, those institutions begin to work so well on so many different sites that you despair of ever cracking it. But there is no permanent hegemony, only the struggle to construct and sustain it, which never ends.

Question

Can you clarify some of the ideas in your notion of ideological struggle, in particular the relation between language and ideology and the lack of guarantees in this relation? Is hegemony the attempt to produce such guarantees?

Hall

A fundamental insight of modern linguistics is that all language is multireferential, that there isn't a one-to-one relationship between the linguistic form and the object to which it intends to refer. It is, therefore, very difficult to argue that the material conditions in which people live can generate a single set of meanings, as if the concept of class always means just one thing. To put it another way, the appearance of social classes in relation to language is not that one class has ascribed to it a whole language, discontinuous from another. You can hear the different idioms of a language—class and gender, ethnicity and group, in the way people use the ideolects of language. But, broadly speaking, people in a single-language community can quite often understand one another across those boundaries. So the field of language is not strictly segmented by class but is obviously more open. Yet the semiotic systems of meaning are not, therefore, entirely disconnected from the social or class positions in which the speakers are placed. The play of power between different social groups is worked out *within* language, partly by the different ways in which shared terms are accentuated, or the ways in which shared terms are inserted into different discourses, as well as by different subcultural dialectics.

To give a concrete example, it's not the fact that some people are the democrats and other people are not that is important. The real problem is which meaning of democracy is actually in play. The struggle in this case is over the different meanings of the same word. Different meanings will share some common characteristics but differ in their connotations. In ideology, in the kind of struggle over languages that goes on, the struggle is to fill out the precise way in which my "popular democracy" differs from your "liberal democracy." It's exactly there, in the intersection of different connotations within the same linguistic sign, that the struggle takes place. And it *does* matter which becomes the dominant definition. It has real effects. Every time the word "democracy" is used, which of those two associations does it trigger? So you can't exempt the domain of meaning, language, representation from the play of social forces. But you cannnot think of it as being chopped up and ascribed in blocks to those forces, so that there is always a language those people speak and then there is our language. The linguistic or ideological domain is not structured in that way.

In that sense I am a revisionist. I accept the critique of the vulgar marxist theory of ideology in terms of reductionism. But I don't go so far as to say that, therefore, there are simply disparate, fragmented discursive chains, one after another, endlessly slipping past one another. I'm trying to *think* that relationship in a way that brings them back together, but *not* as a simple unity or identity. One can understand this project temporally. Marxism's temporal perspective suggests that the connections between the people, say, and the slogans that mobilize them are given in their class position or place in the mode of production. The same things that formed them as a class also formed their ideology.

From my perspective, it is only when you get the right people to speak the right language at the right time, to have the right identifications, that you can mobilize them behind a set of concrete slogans. So the class/ideology identity marxism *assumes* in the beginning is, for me, the end result, the product of politics. Politics must construct the meanings and deliver the group to the slogans, not assume that the group always "really" knew the slogans and always believed in them. They didn't! It's quite possible for a class to be mobilized behind other slogans. Can one develop a political practice that makes those slogans or those ways of defining the word make sense to that group at the right moment? That is what gives political practice a certain *necessary openness*. Somebody else might have a more effective politics and organize the class around some other slogan; then the connections get forged in a different way.

I no longer believe in the marxist notion of connections being "given" in the origins of the social formation. There *are* points where connections can be forged or radically transformed—hegemonic moments—where a wide variety of people in different social positions all find that a particular set of symbols or languages speaks their condition better than any other. This is the moment when people who are not at all, socially, Thatcherites or from the same class origins suddenly say, "Well, they aren't our kind of people, but she is talking a good deal of sense!" Mrs. Thatcher makes sense, but from a universe other than our own. That is a political moment of extraordinary complexity—when people you wouldn't think would find answers in Thatcherism, if you simply analyzed their class position, suddenly find her language more convincing, more resonant with their experience, than that of the welfare state or Keynesianism. This is the critical moment, when

masses of people are detached from their allegiance to a particular language they
have used to frame and define their experience and reattached to another language.
I still think this is why I was right when I predicted Thatch-
er's 1979 victory. I heard large numbers of people stop talking the language of
labourism, the welfare state, social democracy, and suddenly begin talking another
language of cost effectiveness, value for money, choice, freedom, etc. I heard people
responding to a set of different ideological concepts. You couldn't explain that by
a straight class analysis. You couldn't explain the fact that the majority of them
were unionized skilled and semiskilled workers who live in traditional labor, working-class communities, who appear to be fixed in their political loyalties by all the
processes that have kept the British political system stable. Yet here was a moment
when they just walked to another position altogether.

Indeed, Thatcherism gives you a better understanding of
what the struggle for hegemony is about than almost anything one has seen in the
politics of the Left. The Thatcherites were not the natural inheritors of something;
they had to engage in ideological struggle, to contest the opposition in their own
party, to construct their own position. They had to dismantle the particular sort of
social-democratic consensus that had been in place since the war. They had to unpack
the commitment to the welfare state and unravel a whole field of ideology that people
had come to take as perfectly obvious and unquestionable. They actually attacked
the groundwork of politics, not merely policy. They changed the frame, shifting the
basic forces in a fundamental way. And in order to do that they had to engage in a
powerful struggle on a whole series of fronts. The whole field of positions—the
position of women, the position of the family, the position of race, the position of
law and order—is a variety of different discourses that have been reconstructed by
the Thatcherite interventions in such a way as to construct new possible subject
positions. Then these new subject positions echo and reverberate off one another.
To give a rough example, there is a sense in which the Thatcherite project depends
on seeing the mother, who is trying to represent and understand the inability of her
child to get on in a competitive situation at school, as the same mother who is
concerned about women who go out to work and neglect their responsibility to the
family, the same as the woman who says to the miners, "You can't possibly go on
strike tomorrow because your wives and children don't have enough to live on."
These are all different positions, but the point where people begin to recognize
themselves in all of them is what I call the "point of articulation." By the notion
of hegemony I want to invoke precisely the capacity of a political formation to
intervene on all these different sites.

This way of defining hegemony is almost impossible to es-
tablish in English because of the distinction between reality and appearance. The
moment you say "appears," everyone hears "that's how it appears but it really is
something else." The notion that appearances are real is something that English finds
difficult, philosophically, to say. Similarly, it is difficult to establish a notion of
hegemony as something other than domination. As soon as you say "hegemony"
people see marching boots, rolling tanks, censorship, people being locked away. What
they cannot understand is the one thing we need to understand in societies like ours,
which is how people can be constrained while walking free; being utterly subject to
determinations that make you apparently free to say what you like. The problem
with liberal capitalism is the nature of the compulsion of a particular kind of freedom,
not the total denial of freedom. I don't mean to say that there aren't places in our
society where freedom is denied, just as I don't mean to say there aren't conspiracies.
But just as conspiracies don't explain history, so notions of direct coercion, social
control, and total domination, which is the way hegemony is customarily conceived,
are inadequate to explain the real negotations around power and language, control
and consent, on which hegemony depends.

Question
But where do these different hegemonic moments come from
and how are they effectively communicated?

Hall

One is describing a circuit of relations. Not all the moments in the circuit have equal power. There is unequal power at different points in the circuit. The power to initiate and formulate, for instance, is not decisive because you can't impose that formulation on everybody; but it does give you a first shot at the field—the power to formulate the question, to set the terms. Other definitions then have to respond to you; it's *your* definition that is being negotiated. The political apparatuses are effective precisely because of the monopolization of the power to formulate in our society. Think of how Star Wars came to be taken seriously. Thus, a greal deal happens when policies first begin to be visibly promulgated, even though they have a hidden prehistory.

Thatcherism has a prehistory, not only in popular discourse, but in previous elite and expert discourses as well—in the free-market doctrines of the Institute for Economic Affairs, for instance, which has been going since the late fifties. So you have to start the story somewhere, for convenience, say, 1975, when Sir Keith Joseph was going to run for prime minister but didn't make it, and Mrs. Thatcher took his place; that is how she came to power. And it is interesting why he didn't run and she did. Joseph was a more consistent, philosophical Thatcherite than Mrs. Thatcher. But he went to Birmingham, a large industrial city, and he made what were to be three keynote speeches. In one speech he referred to the problem of overpopulation of working-class families and the inability of working-class mothers to cope or to organize their lives. He was absolutely finished right there. If his project had been to continue the paternalistic version of Toryism, that would have been acceptable because the squire can tell mothers in the village how to bring up their children. But if you are going into the populist, libertarian variety of conservatism, that is the last thing you can do. Within a week it was decided that Joseph was not going to run. Then the question was Where are his votes going to? and Mrs. Thatcher came on. In that sense she is very much produced by a whole set of previous discourses, both popular and expert ones. Nevertheless, the moment when they are condensed in a single popular figure, and when that begins to get publicity in the media, when that is the only figure that gets talked about, and when it gets the highlight treatment of an election—which she dominated personally, and she had a personal victory in the Tory party, dispersing the old crew—that condensation adds a new dimension of power.

I want to give an account that is genuinely open at both ends but doesn't talk about a circuit as if it were equal at all points; everybody in the circuit does not have equal power. If you monopolize a piece of the mass media—the apparatus of cultural production—you have a certain kind of formative power. But it doesn't give you an absolute power. Yet we need to ask how such monopolies might be fought, for the fact is that the popular press in Britain is less varied than it used to be. There used to be a wider spectrum between, say, the tabloid *Daily Mirror* and the *Times*. Those intermediary papers have been squeezed out by increasing market polarization. So there are two or three quality newspapers at one end and then a mass of popular papers that all look alike. And increasingly those are monopolized by three or four multinational media corporations. So the actual room for openings in the existing structure of the media are very slim.

Now there has been a good deal of discussion over the last ten years about the possibility of starting a rival, not necessarily Labour, paper. There used to be two Labour papers: the *Mirror* supports Labour but is a multinational tabloid with a foot in both camps; the *Daily Herald* was quite committed to the Labour party and the cooperative movement, and it went out of business with still over a million readers. The argument has been that it is impossible for Labour to make any headway at all unless it enters the field of popular journalism and establishes an authentic, legitimate press of its own. The trouble now is that it is extremely difficult to capitalize such a venture. The costs of setting up a distribution network for a new national newspaper are very serious, and, though there has been

62

Stuart Hall

money on offer, there has not been enough. This absence is not countered by extensive internal political education. You could try to counter a national hegemony in the press by a great deal more education in the trade unions, and Labour party constituencies, and so on, which would build up informed public opinion able to challenge media definitions. But both the trade unions and the Labour party remain largely electorally rather than education-oriented. There is no counterinformation to bring to bear against the media's simplistic ways of constructing the news. So it is true that the whole structuring organization of the media makes it very difficult to compete. Even if you know what to say, you don't have the channels that allow you access to a wide slice of public opinion.

Question

How would you respond to the argument that you over-emphasize ideological elements and exclude both the economic and the political?

Hall

The moment you give the ideological dimension of the analysis its proper place, people invert the paradigm, accusing you of thinking that things work by ideology alone. Ideology is tremendously important, and it has its own specificity, its own kind of effects, its own mechanisms, but it doesn't operate outside the play of other determinations; it has social, political, economic conditions of existence. One has to take the question of the nucleus of economic activity seriously, as Gramsci said, even when using a hegemonic approach.

A comprehensive analysis of Thatcherism would be a collective research project using a whole range of skills, addressed to a range of different sites, including the economic. I am aware that I am cutting into this field from a particular dimension. But there is a difference between the research programs you define for the world and the more limited ones you engage in yourself. In any case, I don't think there is an either/or between economically and organizationally oriented work and ideological work. The question is how to understand the articulations between them, nonreductively. Moreover, while I don't believe that economics is the primary definer in the sense of the first instance, or that the economy stitches up the results in the end, it is possible to see where economic determinacy operates in structuring the ideological field of play at any one time. It's one of the structuring principles; it helps to set the constraints, the lines of tendency and force within which ideology operates. What it doesn't do is deliver the right answer, the correct, pregiven closure at the end.

That's why I am against determination in the last instance. But I do believe in provisional analysis. Wherever your research starts, you have to make some significant allowances in the direction of the dimensions you left out. So those doing economic analysis have to look at the ideological traditions that are at work, just as those analyzing ideological discourse or texts ought to look at the operation of those legal apparatuses, economic forces, etc., that are helping to establish the field they are looking at. That is because the object of analysis is the social formation, which is an ensemble of practices and relations; it is concrete because it has many determinations.

Question

Why, then, are there so few studies where the two elements are addressed, where one of them is not reduced to a skeleton?

Hall

It is difficult to do both. Practically, it means either that you have access to a wide range of analytic skills or that you have a well-differentiated research team. In your own work you accumulate certain insights that you can't match in other areas. I ask myself whether I should combine a sort of naive economic analysis with a highly sophisticated ideological one, and it doesn't seem to fit. In a more open intellectual climate we would take some risks like that. This is one of the arguments for more collective intellectual work. The Centre did try. *Policing the Crisis* did try to say something about a lot of areas we didn't know a lot about, individually, but that we didn't want, collectively, to leave off the agenda. And I think perhaps one should even be more risky than that—risk some generalizations. But the professionalization of intellectual life means the temptations are strong to play it safe.

Question
Could you say something about what you think the Left needs to be doing. Can the New Right be defeated?
Hall
If I knew that, I would be in business. But I *do* think one can begin to identify some weak spots, some contradictions, places where the discourses don't match up, or where there is a disparity between the promises and the delivery. There are lots of contradictions there, but they don't easily break in our direction or offer us big political opportunities; they require the constitution of an equally powerful, equally convincing alternative, all the way across the political terrain. The more hegemonic the Thatcherite alternative becomes, the more the Left must generate a whole alternative philosophy or conception of life or it will collapse. Otherwise, it simply can't match what the Right is offering, which is a hegemonic vision of life from birth to death. There is a Thatcherite way of being born, of rearing children, of going to hospitals, of being prosperous in business; there is an image for everyone and everything: how to bring up babies, how to teach, what you should wear to stand in front of the classroom. It's a hodgepodge of all kinds of different discourses; nevertheless, it does offer a set of positive social positionalities, which condense and connote one another. And the thing about the Left is that there is no such coherent alternative set. There is no way of being a teacher, to counter the Thatcherite style of being a teacher. All the Left has is a disarrayed, dispersed series of positionalities. Mounting a counteroffensive involves offering and setting in place alternative and equally powerful frames for life in the twenty-first century. I don't know whether the Labour party can be made to see that as its historical task.

Question
You have, on other occasions, stressed the key role of discourses of the nation in Thatcherism—for example, in the way the nation was mobilized for the Falklands war. But how does one decide whether the struggle over terms like "the nation" is possible to win? What is the strategic question one raises here? Can the Left engage in significant ideological struggles against Thatcherism around the nation, or is it so likely that the Left is going to lose that we had better find other issues?
Hall
You could make the same argument about law and order. You could argue that you cannot possibly engage with the issues that are concealed in the slogans of law and order because they always deliver results that are of a deeply conservative and reactionary kind. Then, one after another the domains of public argument are snatched away from you; you can't touch any of them because they all seem to be articulated, organized, and structured in such a way as to deliver a victory to the other side.

It is perfectly clear, historically, why the notion of the nation in Britain tends in that direction. Historically, the ideological terrain is tendentially articulated that way. But I still think that it is possible to begin to intervene on or engage the same terrain. The problem is that, as against the way the ideological terrain is historically articulated around the nation, it seems an abstract argument to ask ordinary people in the street, who are being appealed to powerfully in terms of the concrete experience of their sons sailing away on the Falklands task force, to reidentify, against the flag, with the Argentine people. It's totally outside their horizon. They've never heard of it; they have no living connections with it. The only way they know the Argentine is as the team that always beats us at football. There is not a lot of mileage in "We are one with the Argentines!" as a popular slogan.

I'm talking, then, about the kind of long groundwork or preparation that is necessary. Does any nation build solidarity with another nation when it doesn't know what it is? I suspect not. I suspect internationalism comes out of people having a sense of their own national, popular, or community identity, which allows them to build bridges to other people. After all, differences of national history, culture, and identity have to be recognized. The Argentines *do* have different interests from us. They do have a quite good claim to the Falklands, for example. So these are not easy contradictions to reconcile. But the building of solidarity has to come out of an actual, grounded sense of where *we* belong and fit into the world, a sense that is different from the old national-imperial one.

It is a very risky strategy, and I'm not recommending it. I recommend asking the questions so that the Left can actually begin to engage strategies within and around the languages of popular calculation, the languages of practical consciousness, the discourse in which the man-in-the-pub says, "I'm for the war," or "That hasn't anything to do with us." We really need to shift him and his wife and his family from "Of course let's get at the 'Argies'," at least to "This war is not our concern." I don't know that I could do it by saying, "Identify with the enemy, feel at one with them." I *have* to begin to talk the language in which popular calculation goes on, if I'm to appeal to any powerful counternotions that don't send people marching off into the sunset. Furthermore, the question of interests is always there, even though interests are themselves ideologically constructed. But that doesn't mean there aren't contrary interests, around which alternatives can be constructed that make sense to people. I can think of instances where the appeal to international solidarity does eventually overcome genuine differences. The Vietnam war, in the end, was such an example.

Comment

But it is clear that, historically, the British Empire no longer exists. Yet Thatcher seems to use it so centrally in her anticommunism.

Hall

I think the language of empire, and the wars that have been fought around it, still constitute a massive ideological repertoire in British history. The fact that the empire has been worn down doesn't tell you anything about how the vocabulary of the empire plays into present fears and anxieties about no longer being a powerful nation and so on. In fact, it still provides a lot of the discourses in which people construct what Britain's role in the world is. It is a living language, although it may refer to a real situation no longer historically pertinent. I think that those imperial traces invest the language of the holy war against communism. The holy war against communism is not, in England, a very popular language in its own terms. It could become popular precisely because it might mobilize traces of these other imperial languages one forgets. People *did* respond to Thatcher's self-construction as the "Iron Lady" and "telling the soviets where to go," but not in the same way as Reagan's "holy war." People *are* very terrified of Cruise and Pershing missiles.

There are, at the moment, counterpositionalities in popular languages that provoke powerful resistances. We could speak the language—the true language of the cold war—if we invested it with the energy that is associated with an older kind of war—Falklands-type wars—that place Britain in a much stronger, more leading position. But notions of sovereignty get in the way. Thus, notions of sovereignty aren't entirely reactionary. The question of national independence *is* an important question in the struggle against nuclear Atlanticism. People *do* have some sense of their rights in saying, "If we are going to be blown up it should be on our own decision and not because somebody else happens to be occupying 200 bases in our country." So even those concepts one thinks of as the pillars and underpinnings of a rather reactionary position are not entirely uncontradictory. They are not entirely without a certain popular counterpositional discursive force.

Question
Where can you possibly find the resources to struggle over the concept of "the nation"?

Hall
If the dialogue is constantly one that constructs the nation in the direction of Great Britain, the people will be interpellated only as subjects for war. But it's not necessarily the case that every way of being English is one that has to justify itself by waging war. There are a lot of associations in common popular traditions in England that are democratic. Cinema and TV in England are constantly representing the English civil war as one between the goodies and the badies, and the goodies are always Royalists; or all Puritans are systematically presented as dour Cromwellians, etc. But this is also the beginning of the English revolution, the beginning of popular movements secured at the price of cutting off the head of the king. It's the beginning of the parliamentary tradition, of the curtailment of absolute royal power. That is the English revolution—a bourgeois revolution that secured much wider popular support. There is no preordained reason why people who feel English shouldn't be English because of the English revolution rather than because of the Restoration. There *is* a popular content to English identity—the content of the struggle to make the nation into a popular nation rather than a nation of elites and kings. That is a struggle that goes on all the time. The offical language is, of course, wrapped up in the language of the crown, the royal navy, etc. But even that language is not uncontradictory. And there are constantly struggles to win some purchase for popular interpellations in an area that appears to be sewn up by alternative definitions.

Wherever you find popular struggles, the nation is always at issue. The field of national interpellations doesn't simply disappear because time and again one finds it inserted into a dominant discourse that is very reactionary. It does not cease to play an important part in countermovements. The antiwar, antiimperialist movement is one that has been sustained through a counterdefinition of nationhood.

But it is impossible to enter this argument without asking about the nature of popular memory in relation to language. After all, these terms are constructed out of some sense of what the history is, and there is always a struggle over popular historical memory. Contemporary questions always have a historical content—not necessarily the "real" content, but content as filtered and structured in the categories of popular memory. I don't want to suggest that the field of contestation is so open that you can construct any articulation you wish. Quite the reverse. But the only thing that would stem a tide like the Falklands one is some equally powerful set of counterimages, which would call up some different connotations in the popular memory. If you argue that nationalism has always been a difficult ideology to rearticulate because of the way Britain's history as an imperial formation has tendentially constructed the field, I would respect that answer. I disagree with the Laclau position that all discursive articulations are possible, but I *do* want to hear the argument gone through. To engage in that strategy, we will have to rethink and finally reject strategies based on the assumption that the great mass of people live permanently in false consciousness. I do not think it is possible to argue that a small number of people, who are themselves, of course, not in false consciousness—the Left—should address and mobilize large numbers of people who are. I don't think you will convince anyone by saying, "I'm sorry. I can see through you, but you can't see through yourself."

Comment
I'm concerned about your prioritizing "nation" to the exclusion of "class" and "race."

66

Hall

First, in relation to the discourses of popular conservatism, nation is an interpellation that directly crosscuts and neutralizes the interpellations of class. The way to construct the notion of the nation as composed of people linked into an organic unity is to say that what people share as a nation is larger and more inclusive than what divides them into classes. That, essentially, is how the super-imposition of nation over class was achieved by the Conservative party. And it has exactly that capacity to draw people together from different sectors of the population to suppress class differences and differences of class interest, etc., in order to unify them around shared common characteristics on a national basis, that made conservatism "popular."

It is important to emphasize that racism was already present, for instance, as the other, the unspoken of nation—for example, in the way the Falklands war was represented. When people said "Argies," it carried a highly racist connotation. It isn't just that these people are different, non-British; racism doesn't exist only in relation to blacks, but in relations to all foreigners. That is the imperialist connotation of "nation" in the British discourse. In the struggle to reach ordinary British people, the element of what they think of themselves in relation to other nations cannot be left out. If you leave that space empty it will constantly play the discourse against you. Those of us who do not belong to that nation also have to think about how we think about ourselves in relation to it.

And actually, there is a struggle, odd as it may sound, that blacks have had to wage in order to transpose the one-race notion of the nation that persists in the British discourse and give it a content that interpellates them; that is to say, that makes it refer to kids who are now born of black families who have lived in Britain for three generations, kids whose parents, for example, aren't Jamaican anymore. What are they? They are black British. So the question of racism does not take you outside the terrain of national identifications necessarily but is part of the struggle over the popular identifications present in the society. If the British are allowed to go on thinking of themselves only in terms of the great white British who have an imperial destiny, they will fix us all. Thus, we have to work on the ground in which people establish their national identity and associate it with a different range of understandings. Are the blacks Afro-Caribbeans? Are they black British? Are they West Indian immigrants? Etcetera. The question is one of the long-term stakes involved in the different interpellations. What is at issue is the positive content, for both the black and white sections of the population, of the discourses used. These don't foreclose the *other* struggles, which blacks conduct on another front, about their problematic insertion in the discourse of class.

Question

Given your emphasis on the struggles over identity, what does that imply about the Althusserian-Lacanian notion of the relationship between ideology and subjectivity? Do we discard the notion of the intimate connection between ideology and the concept of the subject?

Hall

Certainly, in traditional marxism, ideology has at its center the concept of the authorially centered, Western, epistemological "I": the author of the ideology is the person or group that speaks it, etc. So I regard the dismantling, or dethronement, by structuralism (structural linguistics, Lévi-Strauss, Althusser, and so on) of the already integrated "I" at the center of all ideological discourses as a major theoretical revolution. Obviously, then, there was a time when we tried to think the operation of discourse without any reference to subjectivity. Lévi-Strauss tells us that the mythmaker is just an empty narrative point of punctuation, spoken by the myth. But that is obviously inadequate. So we are beginning to get more sophisticated ways of trying to theorize subjectivity. I think the attempt to theorize the constitution of subject positions within ideological discourse, exclusively through psychoanalytic mechanisms (the Lacanian moment), is an important advance for understanding the establishment of *basic* orientations to language. I think that level lays down, again, certain tendential positionalities in relation to language. And those tendential positions are crucial in *some* domains. For instance, I think it is quite right that in the domain of sexuality a great deal happens at that stage. But what I am not prepared to say is that those primary psychoanalytic scenarios and resolutions contain the whole of the theory of ideology; or that once those mechanisms are in place, all that happens after that is the repetition of those same subject positions in a succession of later discursive formations. I don't think that is so; that is, I don't think we can replace economic determinism by a psychoanalytic reductionism. What is constituted are the fragmentary subject positions that are then open to a range of subsequent interpellations.

People with identities and relations to language already secured nevertheless can find themselves repositioned in new ideological configurations. I think Lacanianism is in danger of substituting a psychoanalytic essentialism for a class essentialism; and that, like class essentialism, precisely leaves out the actual play of negotiation, contradiction, interchange, etc. It leaves out the fact that ideologies have to *struggle* to recruit the same lived individuals for quite contradictory subject places in their discourses. I want to ask how people who already have an orientation to language nevertheless are constantly placed and replaced in relation to particular ideological discourses that hail and recruit them for a variety of positions.

I stand on the theoretical break that structuralism has made, but I refuse the new poststructuralist theoretical absolutism. I think there is something built into structuralism that, once it made the break, refuses to learn anything from what it has dethroned. You can see that in the language of many poststructuralist texts. A number of times Foucault says, "I'm interested not only in that, but also in that," and then only the "but also" is silenced. What happened to the "not only"? Everything in Foucault is periodized around the bourgeois revolution— ancien régime to modern—which is never itself theorized. Why do all the epistemes shift just then? Structuralism drives itself to detotalize everything, but it doesn't go back and recover the elements in the detotalized field, and I think that is an incorrect notion of theorizing. Theory is always what Marx did to Ricardo. Marx said, "He is the summit of bourgeois thought." Being that, Ricardo is clearly ideological. Where have I learned everything I know? Of course, from Ricardo. Where else can you go except to the cleverest man who ever thought that system of political economy?

You deconstruct a problematic, but the new problematic must retotalize the rational core of the paradigm it dethrones. Theory is a quite different thing from the leap from error to truth; it releases the problem from the terms in which the old problematic set it. But it doesn't abandon the problem. The problem has to be rethought in better, more adequate conceptual terms. I still think, then, that there is something about the complex interplay between subjectivity and objective social practice, etc., that needs work within the problematic of marxist structuralisms.

Question

Could you elaborate on your notion of theory? The way you were just talking, theory sounds like a kind of conversation with the past. Is this connected to the Centre's commitment to collective work?

Hall

I want to undermine the notion that theory consists of fully clarified concepts that are in a box in somebody's attic and one day you go up and open Pandora's box and let the truth out. I want to suggest that theorizing is a process—the operation of scientific concepts on the ground of theoretical ideologies—that always operates by deconstructing existing paradigms and at the same time snatching important insights from what it is tossing out. So it has a necessarily mixed nature. You recover things that stand in the wrong place in the old conceptual matrix but that nevertheless give you insights into aspects of society and culture you did not have before. You have to reposition them.

I do want to add as well a description of the contradictory and unformed exploratory nature of trying collectively as a group to develop a set of theorizations in a particular area. We need to disestablish a highly possessive, individualistic notion of what research and intellectual practice is about, which is the dominant notion in the humanities and, indeed, to some extent, in the social sciences. But I don't want to give an easy picture of the attempts to do collective work at the Centre—for example, the project to write collectively. I should tell you it's not easy; it's bloody hard. And unless you are feeling really strong, and unless you are not addicted to those well-wrought sentences of yours (which are bound to be the ones that nobody else likes; those are always the ones they want to rewrite, in their style, etc.), it's very difficult. I learned a lot about what practice means in this process. We tried to write and do research in a slightly more collective way than the dominant way—it wasn't a big shift you know; it wasn't like we were trying to take over the state or the telephone exchange or something. We just wanted to do intellectual work in a slightly different way, to make a small shift, to actually displace a dominant practice. The point is that when my favorite sentence was on the table and somebody said, "I just struck it out," that's when I learned what practice is. Practice is a hard taskmaster: harder to change in practice than appears in the head. I remember especially the way in which the practice would advance well for several weeks and then slip back; and people would say, "What does Raymond Williams do? Doesn't *he* just go away and write, by himself, what he wants to write, in a room? There is something to be said for *that* kind of individualism, too." And everyone would say, "There sure is!"

Question

It's interesting that you use Gramsci against the Althusserians, but Althusser himself uses Gramsci. How do you justify your reading of Gramsci in this context?

Hall

Gramsci is where I stopped in the headlong rush into structuralism and theoreticism. At a certain point I stumbled over Gramsci, and I said, "Here and no further!" Gramsci represented a kind of test of historical concreteness for me against the overtheoretical claims of structuralism. He wrote out of à particular historical configuration, a particular society. When I read him, I can see Gramsci's Italy; I can see north and south; I can see the problem the Italians have had in attempting to form a nation; I can see the absence that left in Italian life. You can see what Gramsci meant by saying that these are peoples who haven't yet become a nation; they have an aspiration for the national popular but it's never been constituted. You can see what Gramsci meant by saying that we all misunderstood fascism as an external force, as if it wasn't intrinsic to Italian political and cultural life. It was *in* the very field of play that the Left was engaged in. The people *they* won were the people *we* lost!

So Gramsci gave me an alternative to the antihistorical thrust of Althusserianism. I deeply resented Althusser's conflation of historicism with the historical. Historicism is a particular way of looking at history; but the historical is something quite different. That is the sense in which I use Gramsci as a kind of corrective. And I've gone on finding Gramsci extremely generative for me in two ways. One is just that sense of the historical concreteness of theory, of theorizing for particular cases. Althusser and Poulantzas thought that Gramsci was not properly theorized and that their task was to fully theorize him. But the moment you fully theorize Gramsci you lose what is most important about him, because the nature of his theorization is precisely its concreteness. If you ask me what is the object of my work, the object of the work is to always reproduce the concrete in thought—

not to generate another good theory, but to give a better theorized account of concrete historical reality. This is not an antitheoretical stance. I need theory in order do to this. But the goal is to understand the situation you started out with better than before.

I suppose the second thing that attracts me to Gramsci is precisely the un-fully theorized nature of his work. It enables me to appropriate him more easily. He doesn't dominate the concepts I borrow from him because his concepts aren't embedded in a full textual apparatus. It's very suggestive. There are *hints* about what he means by "the national popular," but there are no good texts on it; he never sat down and wrote it out. And therefore I have to *work* on it to see what he could have meant. So I find that Gramsci prevents me from becoming a disciple or a ventriloquist or a believer.

On the other hand, there is a danger in Gramsci. In spite of his attack on, say, class reductionism, there is no question that Gramsci regards class as the fundamental social dimension; whereas his notion of the politics of the war of positions, of the struggle for hegemony on many fronts, doesn't exclusively privilege one site but precisely asks you to attend to a whole range of social contradictions and movements. Nevertheless, one has to struggle, in a Gramscian framework, not to give class a kind of automatic place but to understand its massive historical constitution of the field of thought and action.

Comment (Paul Patton)

I'd like to take up your critical remark about Foucault. You said that Foucault describes transformations that historically occur in relations with other transformations that are described within a Marxist account. Foucault describes, for example, the emergence of the prison in terms of a quite coherent theoretical framework of techniques of power and the notion of disciplinary power. The story that he tells, as you point out, clearly intersects with the Marxist account of the development of the capitalist mode of production. And it's true that Foucault doesn't spell out, in any theoretical sense, any articulation between his story and a Marxist account. I wonder if you could say in more detail what you think is lacking.

Hall

Don't misunderstand the nature of my critique. I wasn't trying to rescue a sort of classical marxist historical account behind Foucault's back, although I *do* think that, in a funny way, his discourses are increasingly shadowed by precisely that. I suspect that it is read by large numbers of people only by their filling in the spaces, the silences. But that is not the main critique. Foucault's analyses begin to ask the key question of how to analyze the connection between different discursive formations in a nonreductionist way. But Foucault seems to me always to insist on the production of a further discursive diversity and to block the path to any conception of articulation. I agree that the problem is a real recovery of a genuine notion of difference, variation, diversity, nonreductionism, and that his critique of classical theories on these grounds is absolutely right. But I object to his theoretical proviso *against* recuperating complex notions of articulation.

A related problem with Foucalt's analysis is precisely the disjuncture he interposes between the power that belongs to sovereignty and the microphysics of power that operates in everyday life and practices. He seems to talk about them almost as if they were different and discontinuous modes of power. And he depresses the significance of the state as a contradictory instance of power. I think we need to examine the interchanges between what I call a macrohydraulics of power and a microphysics of power. The nature of power is a very complicated question, and Foucault is quite right to insist, against traditional notions, that power does not radiate from the sovereign or state or centralized instance of power *alone*. Power is multidimensional, a reciprocal interplay between centers of authority and practices, covering the relations and struggles of everyday life. One of the interesting things about our society is precisely that those centers of power are increasingly dispersed.

Stuart Hall

One of the main problems of seizing power in modern democracies is that you don't know where power (in the singular) lies. It is not in any one place. Foucault thinks that the nature of the power derived from the state is a rather useless issue; he is interested in the play of power at all the other intersections across a social body. Everybody has everybody else locked into power in some ways, as well as being the object of power. Oddly enough, this is a rather Durkheimian notion of social control dressed up in poststructuralist language. But I want to insist that there *are* centers that operate directly on the formation and constitution of discourse. The media are in that business. Political parties are in that business. When you set the terms in which the debate proceeds, that is an exercise of symbolic power. So I want to continue to question the radiation of power from the constituted centers of the state, parties, social groupings, and so on. Even then you've only just begun. Because the power didn't begin there; these apparatuses, including, by the way, organic intellectuals, operate to transform power that probably came from elsewhere. But within the framework of popular democracy they had to get it first in order to do anything with it. So power is already in circulation. But it circulates between constituted points of condensation. In that sense I do borrow the Foucaultian notion but refuse his absolute dispersion.

Question

Would you also say that power is creative in Foucault's sense, rather than negative?

Hall

Yes, I would certainly go along with that. It is powerful because it is positive. Think about the power to formulate terms: it is not only a prohibition but also a positive inducement to think about something in *this* way. To set those rules and promulgate a new way of conceptualizing, for example, how the economy works is a very positive instance. But I want to know about how that power gets supported, internalized, by those who appear to be its recipients, about how the conduits include them and are transformed by them, as well as about the centers from which it radiates.

Question

I am interested in how you deal with one position, a kind of undercurrent in what you have been saying, and that is Wilhelm Reich's question of ideology: What if the masses aren't just deluded but indeed desire, want, need their own oppression? How do you respond to that and how does that change our thinking about tactics?

Hall

My answer to that is not a very developed one. I know the position, but it is not one I've really tried to think my own position in relation to. But I don't believe people are *essentially* anything. I don't think that historically one can show the masses to be exclusively in love with power anymore than that they are outside the radii of power. The desire for power, the desire for domination is there. But what I am extremely dubious of is the attempt, especially in the moment of disillusionment (which I think is a moment Reich faces; it's a moment that Adorno faces; it's a moment that the Left has faced again and again), to avoid the troublesome problem of actually engaging with the analysis of a really contradictory field, of intervening in a real field of struggle, by simply assigning the people whom you hope to rescue permanently to one or the other of the poles. Everything we know about the way in which popular consciousness is formed historically suggests perfectly good reasons why people who have been systematically and structurally oppressed should be implicated in their oppression. It's inscribed in the nature of secondariness over any historical period of time in which you come to live with it and thus, indeed, to find pleasure in it. So it's not a denial of that dimension that Reich addresses. But the moment you collapse everything into that level, so as to say there is nothing

71

but their desire to escape from their freedom, that they are nothing but the dependency of the worker on the hand that feeds him or her, nothing but the implication of the slave with the master, you run a real risk of reductionism. You've won an insight the simple-minded Left often denies, namely, that those inconvenient things can exist. But you've also moved past the insight and gone over to what is, in fact, an inversion of the earlier position. Now, in place of the endless revolutionary potential of the proletariat, one has constructed the endlessly deceived, or endlessly authoritarian, masses. And I think when you go back to the actual conditions in which those situations appear in extreme form, such as fascism, you don't *need* a one-sided theory of that kind. You can see why those *were* the elements of popular consciousness that could be built on in certain historical situations; you can see why the irrational made rational sense at a certain moment; you can see why the collapse of alternative ways of understanding what was happening to them didn't connect in the same way. But you always see other oppositional elements as well.

This is not to undermine or deny the powerful subliminal force of unpleasant ideas. It's one of the things that in England we have had to do, and have had to insist on, and sometimes to insist on despite sounding very reactionary. For example, the problem of understanding working-class racism: we must avoid endlessly denying it and avoid as well the simple myth that racism really comes from above. We have had to insist that working people are deeply implicated in forms of racism, built on deep ideological foundations; and there are good reasons why that should be so. And you can't begin to operate in that field politically at all unless you accept that as a given fact of life.

So I don't want to deny the kinds of observations that Reich has made about extreme historical situations. What I object to is essentializing those observations, freezing the historical process, and assigning it to a set of permanent categories. When you look at the situation historically, it doesn't remain the same. One can see that there are always other tendencies. In relation to fascism, one of the most perplexing problems is precisely why fascism so obviously begins as an anticapitalist revolution. Now you don't explain that simply by talking about the built-in authoritarianism of the Germans or Italians. You also have to talk about the intrinsic appeal to a certain "radicalism of the masses" that nevertheless was articulated to very conventional slogans and politically reactionary positions. I don't think Reich's view gives you enough of a purchase, by itself, even on those situations that appear to have historically delivered very simple and stark results. I don't trust it.

Question

Given all that you have said, in what sense would you still describe yourself as a marxist? What, if anything, do you retain from Marx?

Hall

There are a lot of things in Marx that I choose to keep. I choose to keep the notion of classes; I choose to keep the notion of the capital/labor contradiction; I choose to keep the notion of social relations of production, etc.—I just don't want to think them reductively. That is the point. It's the reductionist understanding of the importance of economic relations that I am opposed to, not the categories themselves. And I quite deliberately talked about the working classes and about the level at which that is a pertinent level of abstraction.

My critique of marxism attempts to dethrone marxism from its guarantees, because I think that, as an ideological system, it has tried to construct its own guarantees. And I use the word "ideological" very deliberately. I think of marxism not as a framework for scientific analysis only but also as a way of helping you sleep well at night; it offers the guarantee that, although things don't look simple at the moment, they really are simple in the end. You can't see how the economy determines, but just have faith, it does determine in the last instance! The first clause wakes you up and the second puts you to sleep. It's okay, I can nod off tonight, because in the last instance, though not just yesterday or today or tomorrow or as far as I can see forward in history, but in the last instance, just before the last trumpet, as St. Peter comes to the door, he'll say, "The economy works."

I think those are very ideological guarantees. And as soon as you abandon that teleological structure under marxism, the whole classical edifice begins to rock. Now that isn't any news theoretically these days. Almost everybody of any note is in the business of rocking the marxist foundations. My question is, should we now admit that, since the guaranteed philosophical and epistemological underpinnings of the theory do not stand up, it is finished as a problematic? I want to try to account theoretically for what is still there, what needs to be retained.

Can one retheorize the theory in a nonreductionist way? I have tried to suggest some ways in which a modern, more discursive understanding of ideology, which mediates the link between ideas and social forces through language and representation, *can* accomplish that. That is the contemporary theoretical revolution: the notion that the arena or medium in which ideology functions is one of signification, representation, discursive practices. That is the intervening term that has changed the nature of the debate. I have tried to rethink some of the things that Marx was saying in that more discursive framework. My work, therefore, is in the very unfashionable mode of salvage work, of deconstruction/reconstruction—a dangerous enterprise in the age of deconstruction.

Henri Lefebvre
Toward a Leftist Cultural Politics: Remarks Occasioned by the Centenary of Marx's Death

Translated by David Reifman

It was only after the Second World War that capitalism succeeded in thoroughly penetrating the details of every-day life. We need new concepts in Marxism if it is to retain its capacity to help us both understand and transform this radically commodified contemporary world.

The topic of this book, Marxism and the interpretation of culture, which links interpretation to the political project of Marxism, suggests the distinct advantage of orienting oneself toward the future and of orienting critical knowledge toward this future so as to lay the foundations for it. At least in France, thoughts about the future are now often linked with a particular rallying cry, one diffused in France by the students in May 1968 and taken up not only by the workers but by the whole country: "Change life!" These were the events of May 1968: general strikes and a pervasive expectation of radical change. Since then, the Left has gained political momentum with this rallying cry, the only one that has resonated with the thinking of the French masses since Marx's "Workers of the world, unite!" Moreover, it accompanies the crisis of modernity and the difficulties of the technological transformation administered by capitalism.

This orientation to the project of "changing life" forces us to call into question many of our most basic concepts and tools. We have to start by inquiring, again, into the nature of Marxism and the crisis it confronts. We must also ask what must be changed and what has changed already. Here we will find it necessary to talk about the everyday and to ask how changes in the everyday have affected the situation of culture in the contemporary world. This will inevitably lead us back to reflect, however inadequately, on the general nature of culture and on its relation to the political project of Marxism, a project of changing life itself.

What Is Marxism?

One must first of all emphasize the diversity of the work that has been inspired by Marx's thinking. There is not *one* Marxism but rather many Marxist tendencies, schools, trends, and research projects. Marxism in France does not have the same orientation it has in Germany, Italy, the Soviet Union, or China. In France, after the French Revolution, after almost two centuries of democractic struggle, a certain Marxist thought has developed. But there are also other expressions of intellectual life in

France that one cannot disregard, such as surrealism, since they have intersected with Marxism. Moreover, one's personal history has some bearing on these intersections. As a friend of Tristan Tzara, the Dadaists, and the surrealists, I cannot think exactly like those who were friends of Thomas Mann.

Nonetheless, questions about Marxism's nature are unavoidable. For some, Marxism is defined through Marx's works. An apparently secondary, but in fact decisive, question arises: Which works? We know that one Marxist tendency, clustered around Althusser, rejects the works of Marx's youth as ideological and philosophical. Would Marxism be defined only through the works of his scientific maturity? Or rather through the last works, considering the writings on the Paris Commune as well as *The Critique of the Gotha Program* to be of primary importance? Thus, which Marx?

For others, Marxism is defined through the works of Marx *and* Engels. But between Marx and Engels there are notable differences, especially concerning the philosophy of nature, which was an essential consideration for Engels yet had only a subordinate importance for Marx. Thus, if one argues that Marx *and* Engels constitute Marxism, one is still left to decide which one is primary and which are the fundamental texts?

Still others declare the works of Marx, Engels, and Lenin as the central texts of Marxism. But we have had the opportunity to recall on several occasions that for a long time Stalin was promoted to the same rank as Marx, Engels, and Lenin. On the other hand, Leninism today seems somewhat fragile. It has strong points, such as the theory of unequal development, and weak points, such as the thesis according to which capitalism in the 1920s was supposed to stagnate and show itself incapable of the continued growth and development of its productive forces. What is left of Leninism today? Can we put Lenin's work on the same level as that of Marx and Engels?

Another position admits into Marxism all currents of thought stemming from Marx's works, in their diversity and plurality, including the opposition of dogmatism and relativism. But then the question of references arises. Do all these currents, all these works, refer equally to Marx? Where do we find the line of demarcation that separates so-called Marxist thought from thought that cannot be called Marxist? Furthermore, it has been noted that all contemporary thought, indeed, the entire twentieth century, is impregnated with Marxism, even the thought of those who fought it or who diverged from it, like Schumpeter and Keynes.

Finally, it can be admitted (and this is the thesis I support) that Marx's thinking constitutes a nucleus, an effervescent seed, the ferment of a conception of the world that develops without being able to avoid confrontation with entirely different works, like those of Freud or Nietzsche. This ferment in the modern world acts in and on this world by *contributing* to its transformation (it goes without saying that Marxist thought is not the only element of transformation). It is thus a matter of a deployment or a development through contradictions, in the course of which there are stagnations, retreats, and declines, but also innovations, additions of new concepts concurrent with the withering away of old ones.

According to this hypothesis, and going a little beyond it, it is necessary to emphasize here that Marxism always was and remains racked by internal as well as external contradictions: internal in its own development; external with what happens in the world. Is it necessary to recall the consolidation of the state in the twentieth century, whereas this theory of the modern state is not in Marx's works? Is it necessary to recall the development of the capitalist mode of production over the past century, something that did not enter in a definite manner into Marx's perspective? These contradictions have not brought about the death of Marxism but, on the contrary, the deployment of its theory. Because these contradictions have not brought about the withering away of the capitalist mode of production in the manner predicted, the project needs to introduce new concepts into the theory inspired by Marx. In order to understand the modern world, it is necessary not only to retain some of Marx's essential concepts but also to add new ones: the everyday, the urban, social time and space, the tendency toward a state-oriented mode of production. This last concept accounts for the role of the state in contemporary societies in which the state manages all aspects of these societies and simultaneously dominates them and perpetuates them. I emphasize that it does not designate something accomplished but rather a tendency toward a political form which cannot be reduced to traditional forms and which, from that point on, does not enter into Marx's analyses or those conceived subsequently.

In this way, Marx's thinking continues to become global, that is to say, to develop in a form commensurate with the current world situation in order to understand it and, of course, in order to shift it. Incontestably, something in Marxist thought persists. First and foremost is the imperturbable logic of the commodity; next, the analytic and critical understanding of relations of dependence, exploitation, and humiliation, not only of certain classes, but also of entire peoples. Peoples and countries are reduced to dependence and exploitation, such as so-called nonaligned or developing peoples, among which are the peoples of Latin America, Asia, and Africa. Time and again, in colloquia devoted to Marx, these people make their voices heard. Nonetheless, it is true that the lacunae in Marx's thinking have not been filled; rather, they have been artificially filled, notably by the practical reinforcement of the state in socialist countries.

In my opinion, then, Marxism is an instrument of research and discovery; it is valid only if one makes use of it. Marx's thinking cannot be conceived as a "pure" object of knowledge; it is not an object of epistemological reflection, even less a gadget that one deconstructs and reconstructs in a kind of intellectual game. It becomes useful in understanding what has come to pass in the modern world if one tries to orient and transform it; any other interpretation implies radical ignorance and leads Marxist thought to ruination. We must use it to discover what is new in the world. It is not a system or a dogma but a reference. Marxism is a method that, on the one hand, depends on a certain number of determined concepts but, on the other hand, is analytic and critical of a certain historical process of becoming. As a consequence of this movement, the real tends toward the possible while, at the same time, eliminating other potentialities, though the possible also comes up against the impossible, discernible only in the course of practical action. This attitude implies a triadic analysis of movement and becoming: reality/possibility/impossibility. Moreover, there is a strategic objective: to change the world. It is this imperative that leads us to introduce notions and ideas not found in Marx's thinking.

Does this imply that there is a crisis in Marxism? For the group of state-oriented and authoritarian Marxists, it cannot be a question of a crisis in Marxism. The crisis is someone else's problem. Furthermore, for these same people, all truth is to be found in Marx, in a repertoire that it is sufficient to know and to disclose. To these views, which retain more than a trace of (repudiated) dogmatism, are opposed those theories holding that Marxism is always in crisis (and has been since its beginnings). From the point of departure, the debate concerns the state; it unfolds between Lassalle, that is, state socialism, and Bakunin, who wants the immediate abolition of the state. Marx's thinking clears a path between them and is formulated through this conflict. Is it necessary to recall that Marx approved of the Paris Commune as the abolition of the existing state and the withering away of the state *tout court?* This affirmation is incompatible with socialism as it is constituted in Germany, as a movement and a party of the working class, beginning in the 1860s. This conflict surfaces in *The Critique of the Gotha Program,* a program that already contained virtually all state socialism. Stimulating but profound contradictions; thus, permanent crisis.

The Everyday

Since Marx's death more than a century ago, much has, of course, changed in the world. But many things have remained the same, most notably in terms of social relations. There has been progress and regression. In order to understand the changes, we need to supplement Marx's theories and vocabulary. The everyday is, of course, the concept I am most well known for adding to the vocabulary of Marxism.[1] The everyday is a kind of screen, in both senses of the word; it both shows and hides; it reveals both what has and has not changed.

What is the everyday? In appearance, it is the insignificant and the banal. It is what Hegel called "the prose of the world," nothing more modest. Before Marx, labor was considered unworthy of study, as before psychoanalysis and Freud, sex was considered unworthy of study. I think the same can be said of the everyday. As Hegel said, what is the most familiar is not for all that the best known. The *unrecognized,* that is, the everyday, still has some surprises in store for us. Indeed, as I was first rethinking the everyday, the surrealists were already attempting to conjure up ways to bring the extraordinary out of the ordinary.

Of course, the word "everyday" in English is not a perfect translation of *la quotidienne,* which really refers to repetition in daily life, to that which repeats itself consistently. Philosophers have had a tendency to avoid the *quotidienne,* to pull back from it. Since Plato and Aristotle, philosophy has put itself above the *quotidienne* and excluded it from consideration. For Plato it reflected public opinion (doxa), something vulgar; it was the contrary of the complete truth. This conception was constantly repeated in Western philosophy, even in Hegel. But Marx decentered this bias in philosophy and oriented it in the direction of *la quotidienne.* Marx himself, however, concentrated on labor, on work, on productive activity, an emphasis followed by many Marxists since then. But workers do not only have a life in the workplace, they have a social life, family life, political life; they have experiences outside the domain of labor. So my project was to continue correcting the work of classical philosophy, much as Marx did, but to reach dimensions of *la quotidienne* that he had not. (If one talks about philosophy and daily life, one has to note as well the intersection of literature and daily life, for it is also through literature that the idea of *la vie quotidienne* has entered into our reflections. Joyce, an Irish writer who had enormous influence in France, really established the idea of daily life in literature. *Ulysses* is twenty-four hours in the life of an ordinary man. Many writers call themselves existentialists, but in reality they are continuing Joyce's exploration of the everyday.)

The everyday has passed through three historical phases, three stages. The first, which was discounted and neglected by philosophy and by the philosophers, remained connected to nature for a long time, that is, connected to what is immediately given. The rhythms of life could be only poorly distinguished from the rhythms of nature: night and day, weeks and months, seasons and years. This everyday life was still impregnated with religion, and use value (in Marx's sense) still dominated. The machine was barely distinguishable from the tool. And the city could be only poorly distinguished from villages; it was a huge village, or an aggregate of villages. Capitalism during this period was busy constructing locomotives, ships, cannons, and so on, but it was not yet concerned with everyday life. This stage lasted in France until the middle of the twentieth century, until after the Second World War. But since the war there has been a huge wave of industrialization and urbanization. Exchange value prevails over use value. The commodity, the market, money, with their implacable logic, seize everyday life. The extension of capitalism goes all the way to the slightest details of ordinary life. And one can say that, at this point, production and the relations of production determine who is going to consume this production. Needs and the everyday are programmed; techniques enter into everyday life. It is extremely interesting to note that the huge multinational corporations are introduced into the economy *by* everyday life. They produce detergents, clothes, all the ordinary consumer goods. It is at this moment that technical revolution substitutes itself for social and political revolution, while capitalism seizes the ground that had escaped it in large part until then: everyday life. It is at this point that marketing assumes a role.

At the end of the Second World War the Left had great hope, but within a few years this hope had collapsed. Yet there was a grand movement in the areas of technology and urbanism, one that transformed many things. This epoch was marked by the development of a new class, the technocrats. This new group of people has come to share political power with the military and with heads of parties; it really has made the everyday become what it is. The technocrats manipulate; they program daily life through advertising and the media.

And now, the third stage: the everyday is not only programmed, but it is entirely mediated and mass-mediated. Marketing allows projections of up to ten years. The everyday is not only controlled, it is completely manipulated. It is managed and administered, in large part by multinational corporations that have colossal investments in it.

The everyday here becomes a social practice or, rather, the average *(la moyenne)* of social practice and the social practice of the middle classes *(les classes moyennes),* something that requires an understanding of an *infra*-everyday level and a *supra*-everyday level. The upper bourgeoisie lives in the supra-everyday. (Onassis directed his fleet of oil tankers from his yacht.) But hundreds of millions of poor people in the world aspire to everyday life. And this idea helps us analyze and better understand the modern world.

The everyday is a complex phenomenon. First, it is a modality of extending the capitalist mode of production. My analysis is thus an analysis of the mode of production in its actual application. There have been significant modifications in the capitalist mode of production, even in property relations. The operation of multinational corporations, for example, no longer presents us with the same mode of production Marx described, but it is still a capitalist mode of production. Before the Second World War the official Marxist position was that there could not be a continuing growth of productive forces within capitalism. Indeed, in Europe we did have economic stagnation until the Second World War. But it was obvious that in the United States there was a growth of productive forces that was not in conformity with Marxist arguments in Europe. Since Marx thought that capitalism was going to die, it was essential to determine how this mode of production had developed. Rosa Luxemburg first posed the question of why and how the capitalist mode of production was able to continue, which is one reason she has an important place in the history of Marxist thinking. She defined one solution to this problem, though not the definitive one. I have tried to continue this line of thought, to answer not only how capitalism survives but also how it is able to grow. I have noted that once the mode of production was established in an industry, it could integrate the industry. It integrated agriculture, it integrated the historical city, it integrated space, and it produced what I call *la vie quotidienne*.

Yet the everyday is not only a mode of production but also a modality of administering society. In both instances it refers to the predominance of the repetitive, of repetition in time. And this predominance of the repetitive is a way of life. It is a base of exploitation and of domination. But it is also a relation with the world and with human beings. The predominance of the repetitive masks and suppresses the fear of death, which is one of the profound reasons that the instituting of the everyday in the modern world succeeded: it dissimulates the tragic. This tragic period hides from itself the tragedy it lives. This is why the great fear of the future—the destruction of the planet—remains abstract for the overwhelming majority of people.

The everyday is ambiguous and contradictory. On the one hand, it provides satisfactions: it satisfies the very needs it produces. On the other hand, the everyday provokes a malaise, a profound dissatisfaction, an aspiration for something else. Presented in this way, the concept is not an object constructed according to certain epistemological rules. Nor is it apprehended by the deconstruction of reality. It is lived experience *(le vécu)* elevated to the status of a concept and to language. And this is done not to *accept* it but, on the contrary, to *change* it, for this everyday is modifiable and transformable, and its transformation must be an important part of a "project for society." A revolution cannot just change the political personnel or institutions; it must change *la vie quotidienne,* which has already been literally colonized by capitalism. I will come back to this point of a "project for society" shortly.

The Cultural

Before proceeding, I would like to make a few comments about culture. It is, first of all, necessary to recognize that this notion remains rather obscure and vague. In France, we have a minister of culture, though we hardly know what his responsibilities should be. Major conferences on culture have done nothing to clarify the situation. The word "culture" comes from the German, where it signifies civilization, that is, values, but now it is sliding toward designating cultural production, a movement that calls the notion of culture into question. What can Marxist thought contribute to the subject? Certain devout and often dogmatic Marxists oppose the concept of ideology to the notion of culture; they reproach culturalism for eliminating all of the content of this Marxist concept and notably for removing its critical impact. Indeed, it is true that certain culturalists do not hesitate to include in culture all forms of social life, from cooking to philosophy. None of this, however, contributes to clearing up the confusion that prevails around the term.

So, we do not know very well what we are dealing with. That is why, when I think about culture, I think also of certain verses from Lewis Carroll's *Hunting of the Snark*:

> *To seek it with thimbles, to seek it with care;*
> *To pursue it with forks and hope;*
> *To threaten its life with a railway-share;*
> *To charm it with smiles and soap . . .*

But there is also something serious about this unstable notion of culture. This is the notion of *cultural identity*. There are still groups, classes, and entire peoples who are seeking their cultural identity; indeed, the working class is still searching for its cultural identity. This gives some consistency to the somewhat vague notion of culture. Given these social and political realities, it would be regrettable if these struggles ended like *The Hunting of the Snark:*

> *In the midst of the word he was trying to say,*
> *In the midst of his laughter and glee,*
> *He had softly and suddenly vanished away—*
> *For the snark was a Boojum, you see.*

I hope that you allow a certain humor around these serious matters (a permissiveness that is not always allowable in France). In any case, it is certain that culture is no longer something easily definable and substantial, especially when one speaks of a country, a people, a region, or a city; indeed, culture is no more readily definable if one refers to a tradition or to cultural identity itself. The problem is especially intense for groups such as the Basques and the Palestinians. Whatever it may be, culture no longer has any relation to what was in other times the *cultivated being.*

It so happens that the word "culture" also evokes a magical image for me, that of Sleeping Beauty. She does not doze on flowers and on fragrant grass but on a thick mattress of texts, quotations, musical scores—and under a vast canopy of books, sociological, semiological, historical, and philosophical theses. Then one day the Prince comes; he awakens her and everything around the forest comes to life along with her—poets poetizing, musicians musicking, cooks cooking, lovers loving, and so on. Singers? Songs? Yes, they are a part of culture, yet they must not be considered in isolation but within an ensemble that also includes dance, music, cartoon strips, television, and so forth. Moreover, culture is not merely a static palimpsest of texts; it is lived, active, which is what the fable of the wakened princess suggests to me.

Rather than push these metaphors further, I will suggest instead what the situation of culture is now and how critical analysis should be oriented toward it. In what concerns me, I am far from neglecting recent innovations and inventions and what one calls modernity, even though this modernity is today challenged from all sides. The modernity from which we are emerging was neither the appearance of a new culture nor that of a new being. It was the appearance of new techniques, the time of a confrontation between traditional culture and innovation. But it was also the time of an accentuated conflict between the elite and the popular, without the capacity to resolve the conflict, a capacity that supposes new conditions. After a period in which the sign and abstraction reigned, our surrounding culture has slowly but forcefully begun reasserting its relation with the sensible, with the senses; indeed, the contemporary cultural ensemble reveals a new relation to the body. Around us a new kind of culture of the body is being born. Through their struggles, women have done a lot for this new culture of the body. After a long disappropriation, or rather an expropriation of this body (by morality, by puritanism), the reappropriation that is taking place is difficult and risky. It is used. It is taken back. Yet we are proceeding in this direction.

The new culture of the body is not constructed as a relation with primary nature but rather with a second nature. (I borrow these two terms from Marx, who did not develop them.) Primary nature includes the forest, the sea, the desert; second nature envelops the city and machines, but also the elaborated body, a "worked" body that is inseparable from its urban setting and its urban ornamentation. Second nature has the same elements as primary nature, but it is developed as the product of human work. This new culture has nothing in common with Marxism or philosophical materialism. Yet it is *material* because it reasserts and cultivates the body. And within this second nature the body can be represented and become an object of critical scrutiny. This new cultural ensemble is also apparent in the efforts—often modest and even pathetic—to break with the monotony of the everyday, to find spaces of freedom and *jouissance*. I notice around me, in France and elsewhere, a pursuit of "goods" that are not the products of the market and that have what one can call the grace of the gratuitous. As an example and a symbol, I take the ordinary willingness to find pleasure in beaches and in the expanses of water themselves, the lakes and oceans. As a consequence of the way these pursuits have restructured everyday life, we can no longer think about culture outside everydayness. While this new culture reasserts the body as its starting point, the everyday simultaneously seeks to represent what is human in abstract terms, as mind and soul. Already they confront each other and strive to connect themselves to each other, not without some confusion.

Aesthetics

If it is true that culture can no longer be conceived outside the everyday, this is also true of philosophy and art, which constitute the center of the cultural and define its axes. For many Marxists, it seems that art is only a distraction, a form of entertainment, at best a superstructural form or a simple means of political efficacy. It is necessary to remind these people that great works of art deeply touch, even disturb, the roots of human existence. The highest mission of art is not simply to express, even less to reflect, the real, nor to substitute fictions for it. These functions are reductive; while they may be part of the function of art, they do not define its highest level. The highest mission of art is to *metamorphose* the real. Practical actions, including techniques, modify the everyday; the artwork transfigures it.

By ignoring aesthetics, Marxists have left out the driving force behind much modern Marxist theory. Lukács, for example, is often spoken about, but in isolation, his works being separated from the context of the debates in which he was involved. For Lukács, modern art is only a product of bourgeois decadence, which began after Balzac and Tolstoy, with the exception of socialist realism (Lukács hardly knows anything besides the novel). Adorno, however, uncovers something new in art and especially in modern music: the negation of previous forms clears a path to new forms. This controversy was not always noticeable, but a dialogue unfolded within Marxism between different interpretations of something important, beginning with modernity, and in France with cubism and surrealism. Neglecting these questions has contributed to the sterilization of Marxist thought, to the weakening of its influence, that is, to what many call the crisis in Marxism.

Moreover, there are levels of art, and some works are at a higher level than others. Poetry, music, architecture, and especially theater once had the extraordinary power to transfigure banal reality and can possibly regain it. Modernity is inaugurated by the great but unfinished Nietzschean meditations on the tragic and on the Greek tragedies. When Marx wants to characterize the "new man," the "proletarian man," he calls him Promethean, inspired by Aeschylus. There is something singular in tragedy, whether Greek, Elizabethan, or seventeenth-century French. Tragedy metamorphoses the spectacle of suffering and of death into a paradoxical joy. Likewise, poetry allows the transfiguration of sexuality into love. (I am thinking of poets like Dante and Goethe.) As for architecture, in other times, as with cathedrals, it could transform the banality of the everyday into magnificence. This is the problem that many great contemporary architects pose to themselves. The paradox is that this aesthetic transfiguration enters in its way—by *culture*—into everyday life and the relations that make society. Practical changes and aesthetic transfigurations sometimes converge, in the great periods and the great civilizations—Greece, the Renaissance, the Enlightenment, and also in certain periods in the modern world.

Thus, it is necessary to take up again not only aesthetic theory but also the project according to which art succeeds in transfiguring practical reality, because it does not consist of a simple passive reflection of that reality. This thesis, which has been attributed to Marx, belongs more centrally to Lukács. Art metamorphoses reality and this metamorphosis returns to reality. Thus, the transformation of the world is not only a realization of philosophy but a realization of art. This development of the Marxist project would take into account the city as a work—everything that peoples and enriches urban space, with all that this implies. The city is a work of art and a practical realization of art. In this way, Marxist aesthetics would be taken up again, not merely as a theory of art, but as a practice that creates.

Culture and Questions of Marxist Theory

I would like to return to Marx's thinking, remembering that it remains a point of departure, not a point of arrival. Does it enter into culture? Yes. I do not mean only that it is appropriate to teach and read Marx in universities; nor that his work differs as much from the Gulag as Christ from Torquemada. Marx's thought enters into culture without having either the right or the claim to dominate it. I think one can conceive of Marxism's entry into culture by analogy with contemporary physics. There are still on earth, and even in France, people who believe that the sky is a dome, the firmament; they believe, as in Dante's and Saint Thomas's time, that this dome supports fixed stars above the trajectory of the planets and that celestial beings inhabit it. Nonetheless, one can claim that contemporary astronomy's conception of an infinity of time and space is a part of culture.

Obviously, conceptions enter into culture gradually, despite obstacles and objections. The same is true for certain ideas contributed by Freud or Marx. However, apart from what physics and astrophysics introduce into culture, there are specialists proceeding in this direction whose work pushes these concepts further. It is in this way that Marxist thought enters into culture without being absorbed by it—and without absorbing it. What comes from it? First of all, certain words: for example, "alienation," which is becoming almost as common as "repression" from psychoanalysis.[2] But what comes from Marx especially is the awareness of an important fact: it is not sufficient to appeal to God, to gods, or to the idea of justice to fight injustice and inequalities. This awareness and this knowledge spring, on the one hand, from a harsh experience of oppression and repression and, on the other hand, from Marxist thought. Is this not precisely the ethical and political aspect, absolutely legitimate as such, of what one calls *culture?*

Now I think it will be possible to examine some of the questions raised at the intersections between Marxism and contemporary culture.

Philosophy and Marxism

Some of Marx's well-known texts expressly state that philosophy is simply an ideology and that consequently it is necessary to abolish it, to replace it by a revolutionary science and practice. Other texts state that it is necessary to bring philosophy into being, that is to say, to bring, in a revolutionary manner, philosophy as a utopian project into the realization of a society that is at once true, good, and admirable. Is this a new project inspired from philosophy but abolishing it, or is it the realization of philosophical ideals, philosophers having interpreted the world instead of changing it? For some, there is a Marxist philosophy—their own; whereas for others, political practice has replaced philosophy. Here I would like to point out that Adorno begins *Negative Dialectics* with words that merit as much interpretation as Marx's formulation about the interpretation and the transformation of the world: "Philosophy continues because the moment of its realization was missed. . . ." What then remains of this immense movement of thought that goes from Heraclitus and Parmenides to Hegel, passing through Plato and Aristotle and so many others? What exactly is philosophy for Marx and in relation to Marxist thought? It is unfortunate that so few

84

contemporary discussions deal with this fundamental problem, as if it were either resolved or unsolvable.

The State

In Marx, as in Engels and Lenin, we find only indications about the state. For Marx, the state is a historical moment and not, as for Hegel, a realized God. This transitory moment will be brought to a withering away and to a surpassing of it. There would be many events to recall here, considering that the German working class, inspired by Lassallian state socialism, was defeated and a (provisional) state of unbelievably brutal power was constituted, the Hitlerian state. It would also be necessary to recall that, after the end of Stalinism, the infamous scientific and technical revolution turned up to fill the void, to be instituted in place of Marx's political and social revolution. This led to new political forms, since the state today has at its disposal, directly or indirectly, the resources of energy, information and communication technology, the relations of the national market with the world market. Whatever it may be in the contemporary world, an analysis of this triad of state/nation/classes is lacking in Marx's work. His critical analysis revolves primarily around class relations. The nation plays a rather secondary role in his thinking; he estimates that, beginning from the bourgeois period, the world market was going to go beyond national frameworks in such a way that the international working class would have only to put the finishing touches to this process in order to make the national state and the nation itself wither away. Since Marx, we have witnessed the appearance of the multinationals that dominate energy, the market, and information, but not without competition from the nation-states. It is therefore not sufficient to go back retrospectively to the neighborhood of 1930 in Germany, around 1956 with the end of Stalinism, around 1960 in Europe and in the world with the scientific and technical revolution. Today, it is advisable to introduce new elements into the critical analysis of the state and of the world.

Law (le droit)

According to Marx's predictions, civil law based on private property is destined to disappear. But is there such a thing as socialist law? Bourgeois law, in other terms the (Napoleonic) Civil Code, had and maintains a democratic aspect that has developed through time. The Civil Code in France has not remained immobile since its promulgation; workers' rights, union rights, women's rights have been added to it, even though this list is incomplete. But what about law in the socialist countries? Is there a legal system proper to each socialist country or, rather, a general formation of law in socialism? This is a critical question, for it concerns the status of individuals and groups in socialism.

Logic and Dialectics

What is logic according to Marxism? Would it be simply, according to one of Marx's formulations, the money of the human intellect? Or, according to another of Marx's formulations, would it be a less potent method of discovery than dialectics? What is its impact and what is its relation with dialectics? How does one think mathematics? The great modern effort to think mathematics is based on logic and tends to push dialectics out into the absurd. Now I believe that one can only conceptualize logic in relation to dialectics, and vice versa; only in this way can one move from formal to concrete identity, from logical principles to the processing of information. In the space between logic and information one passes through numerous intermediaries, including mathematics and even the codification of law, which claims to take logic as its authority. A triad can be brought in as an analytic framework of the becoming of thinking: formal logic/ dialectical logic/dialectics. This tends to substitute a more rigorous interpretation for dialectics as conceived first by Hegel, then by Marx (although he never specified his thinking on the question), then by Engels and Lenin. It is no longer a matter of the thesis/antithesis/synthesis dialectic, nor of dialectics in nature, nor of the affirmation/negation/negation-of-the-negation relationship. In this perspective, dialectics allows for the analysis of becoming, that is to say, of time, more or less connected to space, something that can only be conceived in three conflictual moments. This interpretation of Hegel and Marx can be supported by taking, as an exemplary case, music, the art of time, which can only be understood in relation to three notions: melody, harmony, and rhythm. In the same way we analyze the modern world by taking account of these three conflictual moments: the state/the nation/classes. We could multiply the cases of becoming that can only be seized through a dialectical triad initiated by Marx.

Information

Information is often spoken about; it is employed in an ordinary sense: to become informed—get information through the press, the radio, the TV. Today information is something entirely different. First, it is a mathematical quantity—a theory that is at once mathematical, physical, biological; that extends beyond these sciences and seems to be in full deployment. Information is an advanced technique, dominated by certain multinationals. It is also a commodity to be bought and sold, a product that is consumed (notably through the media) but is not a material object. It is, finally, a social practice, a way of communicating, with a usage and even a political application. Information processing can be located neither at the level of the base nor at the level of the superstructure in the usual sense, for it covers the whole of modern society, from the base to the superstructure. This is why it is necessary to have a Marxist and critical theory of information systems.

The Project

We have to elaborate a cultural project, but it must, these days, be connected to other elements of a qualitative development, one more and more distinct from quantitative growth, that is to say, purely and simply economic. It is a question, at least in Europe and France, of the extension of the activities that are deployed outside the spheres dominated by the commodity, its laws, and its logic.[3] It is a question of a slow but profound modification of the everyday—of a new usage of the body, of time and space, of sociability; something that implies a social and political project; more enhanced forms of democracy, such as direct democracy in cities; definition of a new citizenship; decentralization; participatory self-management (au-togestion); and so on—that is, a project for society that is at the same time

Henri Lefebvre

cultural, social, and political. Is this utopian? Yes, because utopian thought concerns what is and is not possible. All thinking that has to do with action has a utopian element. Ideals that stimulate action, such as liberty and happiness, must contain a utopian element. This is not a refutation of such ideals; it is, rather, a necessary condition of the project of changing life.

These considerations, these perspectives, and this project to change life can partly be found in Marx, but not entirely. They are implicit in Marx, in the sense of a renewed humanism. In terms borrowed from Hegel, Marx envisaged a total person of the future, being deployed as a body, as a relation between the senses, as thought. These investigations converge toward a supreme and final question that goes beyond classical philosophy. It is not a matter of understanding what the verb "to think" signifies, as Heidegger did, but of responding to the question, What remains to be thought now? Marx certainly thought the world in which he lived, but the modern world has not yet begun to think Marxism.

Thus, we need to rethink the nature of humankind. Human beings are not merely the theoretical essence they appear to be in many pre-Marxist, Marxist, or post-Marxist texts. To understand this in Marxist terms we need to reformulate the conflictual relations within the triad: nature/matter/human. If a person is first and foremost an earthly being and a human body, how do we relate the person to a representation of the world that includes the recent contributions of all the sciences, including cosmology, astrophysics, and microphysics? These types of knowledge extend from the infinitely small to the infinitely large. What, then, is the relationship of human beings to the world of which they continue to be a part? The paradox of Marx, which seems to escape most Marxists, is that human beings are their own self-creations: they create themselves. In sum, the number of conceptions of the world seem rather limited, and Marx introduces one into them. The other conceptions of the world take account either of the relationship of human beings with creative nature or of their relationship with some transcendence. Marx's thesis differs from these conceptions. The relationship of human beings to themselves is considered no longer as a temporal and spatial center of the universe but as a nucleus and center of self-creation. This includes, at the same time, a conception of the world and a project for life. Human beings are engaged in a perpetual adventure with its attendant risks. More deeply, however, they place themselves not only into question but also in play; they are perpetually at stake for themselves. Today this occurs dramatically: the risk of nuclear self-destruction accompanies self-creation.

1   I have elsewhere distinguished *la vie quotidienne* (daily life) from *le quotidien* (the everyday) from *la quotidiennete* (everydayness): "Let us simply say about daily life that it has always existed, but permeated with values, with myths. The word *everyday* designates the entry of this daily life into modernity: the everyday as an object of a programming *(d'une programmation)*, whose unfolding is imposed by the market, by the system of equivalences, by marketing and advertisements. As to the concept of 'everydayness,' it stresses the homogenous, the repetitive, the fragmentary in everyday life" (*Le Monde*, Sunday, Dec. I9, I982, pp. ix, x). I have also stated that "the everyday, in the modern world, has ceased to be a 'subject' (abundant in possible subjectivity) to become an 'object' (object of social organization)" (*La vie quotidienne ans le monde modern*, Paris: Gallinard "Idees," I968, p. II6).

2   The concept of alienation, in moving from Marxist thinking into culture, has lost much of its integrity and force. For example, young women have come to me to say they do not want any children because children represent self-alienation. I suggest that if you have a child against your will, that constitutes alienation. But it is different if you want the child. Alienation is determined not by the condition of women but by the action of will and desire.

3   The project described here begins with the question of how people live their everyday lives. It leaves unanswered those considerations that might result from looking especially at those whose incomes are well below the social average. How do the Northeastern Brazilians, the peasants of Upper Volta, the inhabitants of the Mexican *campamientos* survive? [Translator's note: This is an untranslatable play on words. The verb used, *sou-vivre*, does not actually exist in French. The verb for survive is *survivre* and Lefebvre is playing with the prefixes *sur-* (over) and *sou-*(under, as in underdevelopment).] Do they manage? But how? Is there not a parallel and underground economy being constructed in relation to ultramodern industry? It is not only a matter of turning one's attention to the way in which hundreds of millions of people manage to survive, but to know if this modern society—from the capitalist side—is not in the process of breaking up. A theoretical, practical, and political problem, as soon as one does not accept that the growth of production as well as of information is sufficient to conserve the unity of society.

Chantal Mouffe

Hegemony and New Political Subjects:
Toward a New Concept of Democracy

Translated by Stanley Gray

Contemporary social movements express antagonisms that emerged in response to the hegemonic formation fully installed in Western countries after 1945. The development of capitalism (the commodification of social life), increasing state intervention (bureaucratization), and the growing uniformity of social life (mass culture) have enlarged the scope of political struggle and extended the effect of the democratic revolution to the whole of social relations.

> It is incomprehensible that equality should
> not ultimately penetrate the political world as
> it has elsewhere. That men should be eter-
> nally unequal among themselves in one sin-
> gle respect and equal in others is inconceiva-
> ble; they will therefore one day attain
> equality in all respects.
> Alexis de Tocqueville
> Democracy in America

Despite Tocqueville's remarkable insight into the potential implications of the "democratic revolution," it is unlikely that he could have imagined its leading, today, to our questioning the totality of social relationships. He believed, in fact, as his reflections on women's equality testify, that the ineluctable drive toward equality must take into account certain real differences grounded in nature. It is precisely the permanent alterity based on such a conception of natural essences that is contested today by an important segment of the feminist movement. It is not merely that the democratic revolution has proven to be more radical than Tocqueville foresaw; the revolution has taken forms that no one could have anticipated because it attacks forms of inequality that did not previously exist. Clearly, ecological, antinuclear, and antibureaucratic struggles, along with all the other commonly labeled "new social movements"—I would prefer to call them "new democratic struggles"—should be understood as resistances to new types of oppression emerging in advanced capitalist societies. This is the thesis my essay will develop, and I shall try to answer the following questions: (1) What kind of antagonism do the new social movements express? (2) What is their link with the development of capitalism? (3) How should they be positioned in a socialist strategy? (4) What are the implications of these struggles for our conception of democracy?

Theoretical Positions

1. Within every society, each social agent is inscribed in a multiplicity of social relations—not only social relations of production

89

but also the social relations, among others, of sex, race, nationality, and vicinity. All these social relations determine positionalities or subject positions, and every social agent is therefore the locus of many subject positions and cannot be reduced to only one. Thus, someone inscribed in the relations of production as a worker is also a man or a woman, white or black, Catholic or Protestant, French or German, and so on. A person's subjectivity is not constructed only on the basis of his or her position in the relations of production. Furthermore, each social position, each subject position, is itself the locus of multiple possible constructions, according to the different discourses that can construct that position. Thus, the subjectivity of a given social agent is always precariously and provisionally fixed or, to use the Lacanian term, sutured at the intersection of various discourses.

I am consequently opposed to the class reductionism of classical Marxism, in which all social subjects are necessarily class subjects (each social class having its own ideological paradigm, and every antagonism ultimately reducible to a class antagonism). I affirm, instead, the existence in each individual of multiple subject positions corresponding both to the different social relations in which the individual is inserted and to the discourses that constitute these relations. There is no reason to privilege, a priori, a "class" position as the origin of the articulation of subjectivity. Furthermore, it is incorrect to attribute necessary paradigmatic forms to this class position. Consequently, a critique of the notion of "fundamental interests" is required, because this notion entails fixing necessary political and ideological forms within determined positions in the production process. But interests never exist prior to the discourses in which they are articulated and constituted; they cannot be the expression of already existing positions on the economic level.

2. I am opposed to the economic view of social evolution as governed by a single economic logic, the view that conceives the unity of a social formation as the result of "necessary effects" produced in ideological and political superstructures by the economic infrastructures. The distinction between infra- and superstructure needs to be questioned because it implies a conception of economy as a world of objects and relations that exist prior to any ideological and political conditions of existence. This view assumes that the economy is able to function on its own and follow its own logic, a logic absolutely independent of the relations it would allegedly determine. Instead, I shall defend a conception of society as a complex ensemble of heterogeneous social relations possessing their own dynamism. Not all such relations are reducible to social relations of production or to their ideological and political conditions of reproduction. The unity of a social formation is the product of political articulations, which are, in turn, the result of the social practices that produce a hegemonic formation.

3. By "hegemonic formation" I mean an ensemble of relatively stable social forms, the materialization of a social articulation in which different social relations react reciprocally either to provide each other with mutual conditions of existence, or at least to neutralize the potentially destructive effects of certain social relations on the reproduction of other such relations. A hegemonic formation is always centered around certain types of social relations. In capitalism, these are the relations of production, but this fact should not be explained as an effect of structure; it is, rather, that the centrality of production relations has been conferred by a hegemonic

90

policy. However, hegemony is never established conclusively. A constant struggle must create the conditions necessary to validate capital and its accumulation. This implies a set of practices that are not merely economic but political and cultural as well. Thus, the development of capitalism is subject to an incessant political struggle, periodically modifying those social forms through which social relations of production are assured their centrality. In the history of capitalism we can see the rhythm of successive hegemonic formations.

4. All social relations can become the locus of antagonism insofar as they are constructed as relations of subordination. Many different forms of subordination can become the origin of conflict and struggle. There exists, therefore, in society a multiplicity of potential antagonisms, and class antagonism is only one among many. It is not possible to reduce all those forms of subordination and struggle to the expression of a single logic located in the economy. Nor can this reduction be avoided by positing a complex mediation between social antagonisms and the economy. There are multiple forms of power in society that cannot be reduced to or deduced from one origin or source.

New Antagonisms and Hegemonic Formations

My thesis is that the new social movements express antagonisms that have emerged in response to the hegemonic formation that was fully installed in Western countries after World War II, a formation in crisis today. I say *fully* installed because the process did not begin at that time; these hegemonic forms were evolving, were being put into place since the beginning of this century. Thus, we also had social movements before the Second World War, but they really fully developed only after the war in response to a new social hegemonic formation.

The antagonisms that emerged after the war, however, have not derived from the imposition of forms of subordination that did not exist before. For instance, the struggles against racism and sexism resist forms of domination that existed not only before the new hegemonic formation but also before capitalism. We can see the emergence of those antagonisms in the context of the dissolution of all the social relations based on hierarchy, and that, of course, is linked to the development of capitalism, which destroys all those social relations and replaces them with commodity relations. So, it is with the development of capitalism that those forms of subordination can emerge as antagonisms. The relations may have existed previously, but they could not emerge as antagonisms before capitalism. Thus, we must be concerned with the structural transformations that have provided some of the objective conditions for the emergence of these new antagonisms. But you cannot automatically derive antagonism and struggle from the existence of these objective conditions—they are necessary but not sufficient—unless you assume people will necessarily struggle against subordination. Obviously I am against any such essentialist postulate. We need to ask under what conditions those relations of subordination could give birth to antagonisms, and what other conditions are needed for the emergence of struggles against these subordinations.

It is the hegemonic formation installed after the Second World War that, in fact, provides these conditions. We may characterize this formation as articulating: (a) a certain type of labor process based on the semiautomatic assembly line; (b) a certain type of state (the Keynesian interventionist state); and (c) new cultural forms that can be described as "mediating culture." The investiture of such a hegemonic formation involved a complex process, articulating a set of transformations, each of which derived from a different logic. It is impossible to derive any one of these from another in some automatic fashion, as in an economistic logic. In fact, the transformations of the labor process that led to Taylorization and finally to Fordism were governed by the need to destroy the autonomy that workers continued to exercise in the labor process and to end worker resistance to the valorization of capital. But the Fordist semiautomatic assembly line made possible a mass production for which, given the low salary level, there were insufficient outlets. Thus, the working class's mode of life had to change significantly in order to create the conditions necessary for accumulation to regain its ascendancy. However, the fact that certain conditions were necessary for the accumulation and reproduction of capitalist social relations to function in no way guaranteed that these conditions would come about. The solution was to use worker struggles, which were multiplying in response to the intensification of labor, to establish a connection between increased productivity and increased wages. But this required a state intervention with a double purpose: it was just as urgent to counter the capitalist's inclination to lower wages as it was to set up a political framework in which worker's demands could be made compatible with the reproduction of capitalism. This provides significant evidence that this new hegemonic formation resulted from a political intervention.

These changes in the labor process can also be defined as a transformation of an extensive regime of accumulation into an intensive regime of accumulation. The latter is characterized by the expansion of capitalist relations of production to the whole set of social activities, which are thereby subordinated to the logic of production for profit. A new mode of consumption has been created that expresses the domination of commodity relations over noncommodity relations. As a consequence, a profound transformation of the existing way of life has taken place. Western society has been transformed into a big marketplace where all the products of human labor have become commodities, where more and more needs must go through the market to be satisfied. Such a "commodification of social life" has destroyed a series of previous social relations and replaced them with commodity relations. This is what we know as the consumer society.

Today, it is not only through the sale of their labor power that individuals are submitted to the domination of capital but also through their participation in many other social relations. So many spheres of social life are now penetrated by capitalist relations that it is almost impossible to escape them. Culture, leisure, death, sex, everything is now a field of profit for capital. The destruction of the environment, the transformation of people into mere consumers—these are the results of that subordination of social life to the accumulation of capital. Those new forms of domination, of course, have been studied by many authors, but there has been a tendency, especially at the beginning of the sixties—you will remember Marcuse's *One Dimensional Man*—to believe that the power of capital was so overwhelming that no struggle, no resistance, could take place. Yet a few years later it became clear that those new forms of domination would not go unchallenged; they have given rise to many new antagonisms, which explains the widening of all forms of social conflict since the middle of the sixties. My thesis is that many of the new social movements are expressions of resistances against that commodification of social life and the new forms of subordination it has created.

But that is only one aspect of the problem; there is a second aspect that is extremely important. You remember that we have defined the new hegemonic formation not only in terms of Fordism but also in terms of the Keynesian welfare state. The new hegemonic formation has been characterized by growing state intervention in all aspects of social life, which is a key characteristic of the Keynesian state. The intervention of the state has led to a phenomenon of bureaucratization, which is also at the origin of new forms of subordination and resistance. It must be said that in many cases commodification and bureaucratization are articulated together, as when the state acts in favor of capital. Thus, while it might be difficult to distinguish between them, I think it is extremely important to do so and to analyze them as different systems of domination. There may be cases in which the state acts against the interests of capital to produce what Claus Offe has called "decommodification." At the same time, such interventions, because of their bureaucratic character, may produce new forms of subordination. This is the case, for example, when the state provides services in the fields of health, transportation, housing, and education.

A third aspect of the problem is that some new types of struggle must be seen as resistances to the growing uniformity of social life, a uniformity that is the result of the kind of mass culture imposed by the media. This imposition of a homogenized way of life, of a uniform cultural pattern, is being challenged by different groups that reaffirm their right to their difference, their specificity, be it through the exaltation of their regional identity or their specificity in the realm of fashion, music, or language.

The profound changes brought about by this construction of a new hegemonic formation gave rise to the resistances expressed in the new social movements. However, as I have said, one should not blame new forms of inequality for all the antagonisms that emerged in the sixties. Some, like the women's movement, concerned long-standing types of oppression that had not yet become antagonistic because they were located in a hierarchical society accepting certain inequalities as "natural."

Whether antagonism is produced by the commodification of all social needs, or by the intervention of state bureaucracy, or by cultural leveling and the destruction of traditional values (whether or not the latter are themselves oppressive)—what all these antagonisms have in common is that the problem is not caused by the individual's defined position in the production system; they are, therefore, not "class antagonisms." Obviously this does not mean that class antagonism has been eliminated. In fact, insofar as more and more areas of social life are converted into "services" provided by capitalism, the number of individuals subordinated to capitalist production relations increases. If you take the term "proletarian" in its strict sense, as a worker who sells his or her labor, it is quite legitimate to speak of a process of proletarianization. The fact that there are an increasing number of individuals who may suffer capitalist domination as a class does not signify a new form of subordination but rather the extension of an already existing one. What is new is the spread of social conflict to other areas and the politicization of all these social relations. When we recognize that we are dealing with resistances to forms of oppression developed by the postwar hegemonic formation, we begin to understand the importance of these struggles for a socialist program.

It is wrong, then, to affirm, as some do, that these movements emerged because of the crisis of the welfare state. No doubt that crisis exacerbated antagonisms, but it did not cause them; they are the expression of a triumphant hegemonic formation. It is, on the contrary, reasonable to suppose that the crisis was in part provoked by the growing resistance to the domination of society by capital and the state. Neoconservative theoreticians are, therefore, not wrong to insist on the problem of the ungovernability of Western countries, a problem they would solve by slowing down what they call the "democratic assault." To propose the crisis as the origin of the new social movements is, in addition, politically dangerous: it leads to thinking of them as irrational manifestations, as phenomena of social pathology. Thus, it obscures the important lessons these struggles provide for a reformulation of socialism.

New Antagonisms and Democratic Struggle

I have thus far limited my analysis to the transformations that have taken place in Western societies after World War II and to the resulting creation of new forms of subordination and inequality, which produced in turn the new social movements. But there is an entirely different aspect of the question that must now be developed. Pointing to the existence of inequalities is not sufficient to explain why they produce social unrest. If you reject, as I obviously do, the assumption that the essence of humankind is to struggle for equality and democracy, then there is an important problem to resolve. One must determine what conditions are necessary for specific forms of subordination to produce struggles that seek their abolishment. As I have said, the subordination of women is a very old phenomenon, which became the target of feminist struggles only when the social model based on hierarchy had collapsed. It is here that my opening reference to de Tocqueville is pertinent, for he was the first to grasp the importance of the democratic revolution on the symbolic level. As long as equality has not yet acquired (with the democratic revolution) its place of central significance in the social imagination of Western societies, struggles for this equality cannot exist. As soon as the principle of equality is admitted in one domain, however, the eventual questioning of all possible forms of inequality is an ineluctable consequence. Once begun, the democratic revolution has had, necessarily, to undermine all forms of power and domination, whatever they might be.

I would like to elaborate on the relationship between antagonism and struggle and to begin with the following thesis: An antagonism can emerge when a collective subject—of course, here I am interested in political antagonism at the level of the collective subject—that has been constructed in a specific way, to certain existing discourses, finds its subjectivity negated by other discourses or practices. That negation can happen in two basic ways. First, subjects constructed on the basis of certain rights can find themselves in a position in which those rights are denied by some practices or discourses. At that point there is a negation of subjectivity or identification, which can be the basis for an antagonism. I am not saying that this *necessarily* leads to an antagonism; it is a necessary but not sufficient condition.

The second form in which antagonism emerges corresponds to that expressed by feminism and the black movement. It is a situation in which subjects constructed in subordination by a set of discourses are, at the same time, interpellated as equal by other discourses. Here we have a contradictory interpellation. Like the first form, it is a negation of a particular subject position, but, unlike the first, it is the subjectivity-in-subordination that is negated, which opens the possibility for its deconstruction and challenging.

For example, consider the case of the suffragist movement, or, more generally, the question of why it is that, although women's subordination has existed for so long, only at the end of the nineteenth century and the beginning of the twentieth century did subordination give rise to a feminist movement. That has lead some Marxist feminists to say that there was no real women's subordination before; women's subordination is a consequence of capitalism and that is why feminism emerged under capitalism. I think this is wrong. Imagine the way women were constructed, as women, in the Middle Ages. All the possible discourses—the church, the family—constructed women as subordinate subjects. There was absolutely no possibility, no play, in those subject positions for women to call that subordination into question. But with the democratic revolutions of the nineteenth century the assertion that "all men are equal" appears for the first time. Obviously "men" is ambiguous because it refers to both men and women, so women found themselves contradictorily interpellated. As citizens women are equal, or at least interpellated as equal, but that equality is negated by their being women. (It is no coincidence that Mary Wollstonecraft, one of the important English feminists, was living with William Godwin, who was an important radical; this demonstrates the influence of radicalism on the emergence of the suffragist movement.) So that is what I understand by contradictory interpellation—the emergence of a section of equality at a point of new subjectivity, which contradicts the subordination in all other subject positions. That is what allows women to extend the democratic revolution, to question all their subordinate subject positions. The same analysis could be given for the emergence of the black liberation movement.

I should emphasize here the importance of actually existing discourse in the emergence and construction of antagonisms. Antagonisms are always discursively constructed; the forms they take depend on existing discourses and their hegemonic role at a given moment. Thus, different positions in sexual relations do not necessarily construct the concept of woman or femininity in different ways. It depends on the way the antagonism is constructed, and the enemy is defined by the existing discourses. We must also take into account the role of the democratic discourse that became predominant in the Western world with the "democratic revolution." I refer to the transformation, at the level of the symbolic, that deconstructed the theological-political-cosmological vision of the Middle Ages, a vision in which people were born into a specific place in a structured and hierarchical society for which the idea of equality did not exist.

People struggle for equality not because of some ontological postulate but because they have been constructed as subjects in a democratic tradition that puts those values at the center of social life. We can see the widening of social conflict as the extension of the democratic revolution into more and more spheres of social life, into more social relations. All positions that have been constructed as relations of domination/subordination will be deconstructed because of the subversive character of democratic discourse. Democratic discourse extends its field of influence from a starting point, the equality of citizens in a political democracy, to socialism, which extends equality to the level of the economy and then into other social relations, such as sexual, racial, generational, and regional. Democratic discourse questions all forms of inequality and subordination. That is why I propose to call those new social movements "new democratic struggles," because they are extensions of the democratic revolution to new forms of subordination. Democracy is our most subversive idea because it interrupts all existing discourses and practices of subordination.

Now I want to make a distinction between democratic antagonism and democratic struggle. Democratic antagonisms do not necessarily lead to democratic struggles. Democratic antagonism refers to resistance to subordination and inequality; democratic struggle is directed toward a wide democratization of social life. I am hinting here at the possibility that democratic antagonism can be articulated into different kinds of discourse, even into right-wing discourse, because antagonisms are polysemic. There is no one paradigmatic form in which resistance against domination is expressed. Its articulation depends on the discourses and relations of forces in the present struggle for hegemony.

Stuart Hall's analysis of Thatcherism enables us to understand the way popular consciousness can be articulated to the Right. Indeed, any democratic antagonism can be articulated in many different ways. Consider the case of unemployment. A worker who loses his or her job is in a situation—the first one described above—in which, having been defined on the basis of the right to have a job, he or she now finds that right denied. This can be the locus of an antagonism, although there are ways of reacting to unemployment that do not lead to any kind of struggle. The worker can commit suicide, drink enormously, or batter his or her spouse; there are many ways people react against that negation of their subjectivity. But consider now the more political forms that reaction can take. There is no reason to believe the unemployed person is going to construct an antagonism in which Thatcherism or capitalism is the enemy. In England, for example, the discourse of Thatcherism says, "You have lost your job because women are taking men's jobs." It constructs an antagonism in which feminism is the enemy. Or it can say, "You have lost your job because all those immigrants are taking the jobs of good English workers." Or it can say, "You have lost your job because the trade unions maintain such high wages that there are not enough jobs for the working class." In all these cases, democratic antagonism is articulated to the Right rather than giving birth to democratic struggle.

Only if the struggle of the unemployed is articulated with the struggle of blacks, of women, of all the oppressed, can we speak of the creation of a democratic struggle. As I have said, the ground for new struggles has been the production of new inequalities attributable to the postwar hegemonic formation. That the objective of these struggles is autonomy and not power has often been remarked. It would, in fact, be wrong to oppose radically the struggles of workers to the struggles of the new social movements; both are efforts to obtain new rights or to defend endangered ones. Their common element is thus a fundamental one.

Chantal Mouffe

Once we have abandoned the idea of a paradigmatic form, which the worker's struggles would be obliged to express, we cannot affirm that the essential aim of these struggles is the conquest of political power. What is needed is an examination of the different forms that democratic struggles for equality may take, according to the type of adversary they oppose and the strategy they imply. In the case of resistances that seek to defend existing rights against growing state intervention, it is obvious that the matter of autonomy will be more important than for those resistances that seek to obtain state action in order to redress inequalities originating in civil society. This does not change the fact that they are of the same nature by virtue of their common aim: the reduction of inequalities and of various forms of subordination. That the vast extension of social conflict we are living through is the work of the democratic revolution is better understood by the New Right than by the Left. This is why the Right strives to halt the progress of equality. Starting from different viewpoints, both neoliberal theoreticians of the market economy and those who are called, in the United States, "neoconservatives" are variously seeking to transform dominant ideological parameters so as to reduce the central role played in these by the idea of democracy, or else to redefine democracy in a restrictive way to reduce its subversive power.

For neoliberals like Hayek, the idea of democracy is subordinated to the idea of individual liberty, so that a defense of economic liberty and private property replaces a defense of equality as the privileged value in a liberal society. Naturally, Hayek does not attack democratic values frontally, but he does make them into an arm for the defense of individual liberty. It is clear that, in his thinking, should a conflict arise between the two, democracy should be sacrificed.

Another way to stop the democratic revolution is offered by the neoconservatives, whose objective is to redefine the notion of democracy itself so that it no longer centrally implies the pursuit of equality and the importance of political participation. Democracy is thus emptied of all of its substance, on the pretext that it is being defended against its excesses, which have led it to the edge of the egalitarian abyss.

To this purpose, Brzezinski, when he was director of the Trilateral Commission, proposed a plan to "increasingly separate the political systems from society and to begin to conceive of the two as separate entities." The idea was to remove as many decisions as possible from political control and to give their responsibility exclusively to experts. Such a measure seeks to depoliticize the most fundamental decisions, not only in the economic but also in the social and political spheres, in order to achieve, in the words of Huntington, "a greater degree of moderation in democracy."

The attempt is to transform the predominant shared meanings in contemporary democratic liberal societies in order to rearticulate them in a conservative direction, justifying inequality. If it succeeds, if the New Right's project manages to prevail, a great step backward will have been taken in the movement of the democratic revolution. We shall witness the establishment of a dualistic society, deeply divided between a sector of the privileged, those in a strong position to defend their rights, and a sector of all those who are excluded from the dominant system, whose demands cannot be recognized as legitimate because they will be inadmissible by definition.

It is extremely important to recognize that, in their antiegalitarian crusade, the various formations of the New Right are trying to take advantage of the new antagonisms born of commodification, bureaucratization, and the uniformization of society. Margaret Thatcher's success in Great Britain and Ronald Reagan's in the United States are unmistakable signs: the populist Right has been able to articulate a whole set of resistances countering the increase in state intervention and the destruction of traditional values and to express them in the language of neoliberalism. It is thus possible for the Right to exploit struggles that express resistance to the new forms of subordination stemming from the hegemonic formation of the Keynesian welfare state.

This is why it is both dangerous and mistaken to see a "privileged revolutionary subject" constituted in the new social movements, a subject who would take the place formerly occupied by the now fallen worker class. I think this is the current thinking represented by Alain Tourraine in France and by some of the people linked with the peace movement in Germany. They tend to see new social movements in a much too simplistic way. Like those of the workers, these struggles are not necessarily socialist or even progressive. Their articulation depends on discourses existing at a given moment and on the type of subject the resistances construct. They can, therefore, be as easily assimilated by the discourses of the anti–status quo Right as by those of the Left, or be simply absorbed into the dominant system, which thereby neutralizes them or even utilizes them for its own modernization.

It is, in fact, evident that we must give up the whole problematic of the privileged revolutionary subject, which, thanks to this or that characteristic, granted a priori by virtue of its position in social relations, was presumed to have some universal status and the historical mission of liberating society. On the contrary, if every antagonism is necessarily specific and limited, and there is no single source for all social antagonisms, then the transition to socialism will come about only through political construction articulating all the struggles against different forms of inequality. If, in certain cases, a particular group plays a central role in this transition, it is for reasons that have to do with its political capacity to effect this articulation in specific historical conditions, not for a priori ontological reasons. We must move beyond the sterile dichotomy opposing the working class to the social movements, a dichotomy that cannot in any case correspond to sociological separation, since the workers cannot be reduced to their class position and are inserted into other types of social relations that form other subject positions. We must recognize that the development of capitalism and of increasing state intervention has enlarged the scope of the political struggle and extended the effect of the democratic revolution to the whole of social relations. This opens the possibility of a war for position at all levels of society, which may, therefore, open up the way for a radical transformation.

The New Antagonisms and Socialism

This war for position is already underway, and it has hitherto been waged more effectively by the Right than by the Left. Yet the success of the New Right's current offensive is not definitive. Everything depends on the Left's ability to set up a true hegemonic counteroffensive to integrate current struggles into an overall socialist transformation. It must create what

98

Gramsci called an "expansive hegemony," a chain of equivalences between all the democratic demands to produce the collective will of all those people struggling against subordination. It must create an "organic ideology" that articulates all those movements together. Clearly, this project cannot limit itself to questioning the structural relations of capitalist production. It must also question the mode of development of those forces endemic to the rationale of capitalist production. Capitalism as a way of life is, in fact, responsible for the numerous forms of subordination and inequality attacked by new social movements.

The traditional socialist model, insofar as it accepts an assembly-line productivity of the Fordist type, cannot provide an alternative within the current social crisis and must be profoundly modified. We need an alternative to the logic that promotes the maximum production of material goods and the consequent incessant creation of new material needs, leading in turn to the progressive destruction of natural resources and the environment. A socialist program that does not include the ecological and anti-nuclear movements cannot hope to solve current problems. The same objection applies to a socialism tolerant of the disproportionate role given to the state. State intervention has, in fact, been proposed as a remedy for the capitalist anarchy. But with the triumph of the Keynesian state, the bourgeoisie has in large part realized this objective. Yet it is just this increase in state intervention that has given rise to the new struggles against the bureaucratization of social life. A program wishing to utilize this potential cannot, therefore, propose increased state intervention but must encourage increased self-determination and self-government for both individuals and citizens. This does not mean accepting the arguments of the New Right, or falling back into the trap of renewed privatization. The state ought to have charge of key sectors of the economy, including control of welfare services. But all these domains should be organized and controlled by workers and consumers rather than the bureaucratic apparatus. Otherwise, the potential of this antistate resistance will simply be used by the Right for its own ends.

As for the women's movement, it is apparent that it needs an even more thoroughgoing transformation. Such a transformation is not utopian. We are beginning to see how a society in which the development of science and technology is directed toward the liberation of the individual rather than toward his or her servitude could also bring about a true equality of the sexes. The consequences of automation—the reduction of the workday and the change in the very notion of work that implies—make possible a far-reaching transformation of everyday life and of the sexual division of labor that plays such an important role in women's subordination. But for this to occur, the Left would have to abandon its conservative attitude toward technological development and make an effort to bring these important changes under its control.

We hear, all too often, as a reaction to the apologists of postindustrial society, that we are still in a capitalist society and that nothing has changed. Though it is quite true that capitalism still prevails, many things have changed since Marx. We are, today, in the midst of an important restructuring. Whether the outcome will strengthen capitalism or move us ahead in the construction of a more democratic society depends on the ability of existing forces to articulate the struggles taking place for the creation of a new hegemonic formation.

What is specific to the present situation is the proliferation of democratic struggles. The struggle for equality is no longer limited to the political and economic arenas. Many new rights are being defined and demanded: those of women, of homosexuals, of various regional and ethnic minorities. All inequalities existing in our society are now at issue. To understand this profound transformation of the political field we must rethink and reformulate the notion of democracy itself, for the view we have inherited does not enable us to grasp the amplitude of the democratic revolution. To this end, it is not enough to improve upon the liberal parliamentary conception of democracy by creating a number of basic democratic forms through which citizens could participate in the management of public affairs, or workers in the management of industries. In addition to these traditional social subjects we must recognize the existence of others and their political characters: women and the various minorities also have a right to equality and to self-determination. If we wish to articulate all these democratic struggles, we must respect their specificity and their autonomy, which is to say that we must institutionalize a true pluralism, a *pluralism of subjects.*

A new conception of democracy also requires that we transcend a certain individualistic conception of rights and that we elaborate a central notion of *solidarity.* This can only be achieved if the rights of certain subjects are not defended to the detriment of the rights of other subjects. Now it is obvious that, in many cases, the rights of some entail the subordination of the rights of others. The defense of acquired rights is therefore a serious obstacle to the establishment of true equality for all. It is precisely here that one sees the line of demarcation separating the Left's articulation of the resistances of the new social movements from the utilization of these same by the New Right. Whereas the Left's program seeks to set up a system of equivalences among the greatest possible number of democratic demands and thus strives to reduce all inequalities, the Right's solution, as a form of populism, satisfies the needs of certain groups by creating new inequalities. This is why the politics of the latter, instead of extending democracy, necessarily widens an already deep social split between the privileged and the nonprivileged.

The progressive character of a struggle does not depend on its place of origin—we have said that all workers' struggles are not progressive—but rather on its link to other struggles. The longer the chain of equivalences set up between the defense of the rights of one group and those of other groups, the deeper will be the democratization process and the more difficult it will be to neutralize certain struggles or make them serve the ends of the Right. The concept of solidarity can be used to form such a chain of democratic equivalences. It is urgent that we establish this new democratic theory, with the concept of solidarity playing the central role, to counter the New Right's offensive in the field of political philosophy.

Faced with an effort like Hayek's to redefine freedom individualistically, what the Left needs is a postindividualist concept of freedom, for it is still over questions of freedom and equality that the decisive ideological battles are being waged. What is at stake is the redefinition of those fundamental notions; and it is the nature of these relations that will determine the kinds of political subjects who will emerge and the new hegemonic block that will take shape.

To combine equality and liberty successfully in a new vision of democracy, one that recognizes the multiplicity of social relations and their corresponding subject positions, requires that we achieve a task conceived at the beginning of the democratic revolution, one that defines the kind of politics required for the advent of modernity. If to speak of socialism still means anything, it should be to designate an extension of the democratic revolution to the entirety of social relations and the attainment of a *radical, libertarian, and plural democracy.* Our objective, in other words, is none other than the goal Tocqueville perceived as that of democratic peoples, that ultimate point where freedom and equality meet and fuse, where people "will be perfectly free because they are entirely equal, and where they will all be perfectly equal because they are entirely free."

Question

Could you elaborate on what it is about liberal democracy that needs to be redefined, and what a superseded or redefined liberal democracy of the Left would be like?

Mouffe

Let me reiterate what I said in the paper while elaborating a number of points. First, it is important to distinguish between democratic and liberal theory. What we know today as a single ideology—liberal democracy—is in fact the result of an articulation that took place during the nineteenth century. While many Marxists have assumed that democracy is in essence liberal, that there is no contradiction between the two, C. B. MacPherson has shown that the idea of democracy was articulated to that of liberalism only through struggle. That struggle created the organic ideology that is still, in some sense, dominant today—liberal democracy. The cost, of course, was that democracy was liberalized, though one can also say liberalism was democratized. In this way democratic ideology became linked with the defense of private property. Liberty came to mean the liberty to have your own property. I think we have to fight this restriction of the idea of democracy by rearticulating democracy with other important concepts to elaborate what I call a "radical, plural, and libertarian democracy."

Of course, we are also confronted by the neoconservative effort to sever the link between liberalism and democracy by redefining democracy as individual freedom. This is clearly a defense of private property, one that severs the link between democracy and political equality. If the idea of democracy as political equality has been incorporated and disarmed through its articulation with liberalism, it nevertheless remains potentially subversive. That is why the New Right is attempting to break with liberal democratic ideology by rearticulating liberalism without democracy, thereby transforming liberal democracy into liberal conservatism. I think the Left should also be trying to sever the link between liberalism and democracy, but in order to radicalize the concept of democracy. To do that we need to work at the level of political philosophy, to rearticulate ideas of equality and justice.

Finally, we need to consider what kind of institutions we would need in a radical democratic society. Left-wing Euro-communists have done some reflection here, proposing to augment representative democratic institutions with several forms of grass-roots democracy, both at the level of the workplace and at the level of the community. This is necessary but not enough, because it will not guarantee the inclusion of the wide range of democratic demands that must be represented in the expansive hegemony I have called for. For example, grass-roots democracy in a factory will not necessarily involve feminism or ecology. These questions clearly call for a new type of autogestion, a type of self-management that cannot be seen simply as laborers managing their own factory. We can perfectly well imagine a situation in which workers manage their factory without really taking care of the environment, without responding to the demands of women. To do so would involve rethinking what kinds of products we want to see produced by society. This new model of self-management would constitute a generalized, extended autogestion. This is the form of institution needed for a radical libertarian democracy to be implemented. It must be a democracy with a plurality of such institutions at different levels of the social formation.

Question

Could you elaborate on the concept of expansive hegemony and on how different demands would be related within the collective will?

Mouffe

First, as I read Gramsci, I don't think it is correct to see hegemony as the imposition of a class ideology on undergroups, as many have done.

Chantal Mouffe

What I've been defending is a view of hegemony as the articulation of demands coming from different groups to what Gramsci called a "hegemonic principle." But he distinguished two ways in which such demands can be articulated. One is through neutralization: you can take account of the demand of some group, not to transform society so as to resolve the antagonism it expresses, but only so as to impede the extension of that demand. That is what the New Right is doing when it takes account of some of the resistances against the new hegemonic system. It tries to neutralize demands by creating antagonisms that prevent the creation of a chain of equivalence between various democratic demands. That is how I understand hegemony by neutralization.

The opposite way demands are articulated is in what Gramsci called the "expansive hegemony." Rather than neutralize demands, an expansive hegemony links them with all other democratic struggles to establish a chain of equivalence. Of course, the wider the chain of equivalence, the wider the democratization of society, and the wider the collective will to be built on that basis. Then it would be unthinkable for workers to fight for their rights only and not, at the same time, for the rights of gays and women. It is important to reiterate that what makes a struggle democratic is not where it comes from but the way it is articulated with other democratic struggles. Yet such an expansive hegemony must respect the autonomy and specificity of the demands of different groups. It is not just a matter of saying that all those demands are implicit in the demands of the working class; that once the working class comes to power, racial, sexual, and gender contradictions will disappear.

Once we accept that there is no one privileged struggle, no single origin to all forms of domination, we must then avoid creating a hierarchy of struggles. Moreover, when we realize that most struggles are struggles to demand rights, we can recognize that in many cases rights have been acquired by creating inequalities with respect to other groups. The rights of some exist because others are in a subordinate position. That is certainly the case for the demands of the working class. The workers now have some rights by virtue of the oppression of blacks and women; the demand to give these oppressed groups their rights must mean that some of the rights of the workers must be abridged. Thus, any attempt to reduce inequalities among the working class requires the transformation of the subjectivity of the workers. And for that we need a new organic ideology that defines equality in a different way, not just on the basis of rights. In a sense, we need the elaboration of a postindividualist liberalism in which rights are defined not as a personal possession but as a form of solidarity among all oppressed groups. In calling this a form of liberalism I am suggesting that it is dangerous to do away with liberalism entirely, a danger reflected in the Soviet Union.

Question

Given your emphases on the need not to compromise the autonomy of various movements and on the plurality of discourses, how can you speak of a single collective will? Who could possibly interpret such a will?

Mouffe

I suppose you are right; "collective will" is a metaphor, and it is not necessarily a very good one! It was obviously a reference to Gramsci. In Gramsci the collective will is organized through the party on the basis of the hegemony of the proletariat. He believed that the working class necessarily provides the articulating principle for an expansive hegemony. To import that notion into my discourse creates a series of problems. Although I don't want to argue that the working class can *never* be the articulating principle—of course, in some circumstances it might be—I do want to argue that it won't *always* be. While it may, under certain historical conditions, develop the political capacity to represent the interests of others, we can also imagine that in other circumstances another social movement

103

can be the center. We can also imagine that there might not be any center; there is no reason why there should necessarily be a center of an expansive hegemony.

As a consequence, contrary to Gramsci, I do not believe that the party—and I am not thinking only of the Leninist party, but of any party—will necessarily be the agent of change. A party can be too authoritarian and too rigid to articulate all those different movements so as to maintain their autonomy. On the other hand, some people argue that once you question the necessary hegemony of the party and the working class, you are left with pure diversity; they go on to argue that there need not be any articulation of those struggles. But if you believe there must be an articulating principle, and it is not provided by the party, where will it be found? I think it is a mistake to look for one organization, *the* "good" organization. We need to think in terms of the articulations that must take place. Those forms of articulation will differ according to the country. For instance, I do not believe that trade unions can always play an important role. They can play an important role in France and Italy, but it is very unlikely that they can in England or Germany.

So there are no recipes. Intellectuals must abandon the idea that they have to tell the people how to organize, to design a blueprint for the "good" organization. All spontaneous revolutions—such as those in Hungary and Poland—have shown that people find their own form of organization. Each society must find its own way of articulating its different struggles together. And there will be different forms of articulation. So we can only use the Gramscian notion of a national collective will, or a popular national will, in a metaphoric way. Like Rousseau's concept of a general will, it can imply too much homogeneity.

Question

It seems to me that we are witnessing two different theoretical moves in Marxism today, with different political consequences. The first is a more traditional materialism and looks at the economic impact of and on discourse. But it apparently results in political pessimism. The second, which seems to be yours, privileges discourse as a way of transforming consciousness and agency. It gives a more optimistic political prognosis, but it fails to connect discourse to actual social groups and institutions. In that sense, it seems to be a new form of idealism. Could you comment on this?

Mouffe

I must say that I cannot accept the opposition between idealism and materialism—it doesn't pertain to my semantic world— and in that I think I follow Gramsci. One can show that materialism is idealist, because to think that there is only one principle of explanation, be it matter or ideas, is in fact the same problematic. In any case, I don't understand what you mean by describing me as idealist, especially since by discourse I understand not only speech and writing but also a series of social practices, so discourse is not just a question of ideas. That doesn't mean that the elaboration of a level of ideas is not important, which is why I made the point about political philosophy. Here, again, I follow Gramsci who said that philosophy, as ideology, permeates all levels of consciousness. Even common sense is informed by philosophy. Philosophy is where the categories of thought are elaborated, allowing us to speak about our experience. For example, many people who have never read anything about democratic theory nevertheless speak and act as political subjects on the basis of ideas elaborated by philosophers. That is why I insist on that level of analysis. But I am not saying this is all we need. We won't transform the world simply by writing the last word on equality. But it is important in constructing new political subjects, so it is one dimension of the struggle.

Catharine A. MacKinnon
Desire and Power: A Feminist Perspective

In my opinion, no feminism worthy of the name is *not* methodologically post-marxist. At the same time, we cannot talk about everyday life without understanding its division by gender, or about hegemony without understanding male dominance as a form of it.

This conference, however broad its inspiration, sophisticated its conception, competent its organization, and elaborate in what is called here "articulation," was not principally set up to maximize conferring. Conferring happens interstitially. Instead, those identified as speakers do what are called "talks"; however, we read them. They are called "works in progress"; however, many of them are quite "done." The audience responds with what are called "questions," many of which are in the form of statements. This event presents itself as a dialogue but operates through a linear series of speeches. We are presented as being engaged in a process, when in actuality we gather to produce a product. We are in a production-consumption cycle, the product being the book that will come out of all of this. The silence that comprises the audience's or the reader's half of the dialogue makes my half sound like one hand clapping. An ominous sound, I should think, for anyone trained on the Left. In partial, if entirely inadequate, response to these thoughts, I have, in revising my paper, interspersed questions I received both at the time of the conference and since, along with some partial responses. I have also retained the rhetorical style of an address to an audience. These expository choices are an attempt to make this paper more dialogic and open-textured, even if only marginally so.

One more thing about the politics of this project and my place in it. We purport to want to change things, but we talk in ways that no one understands. We know that discourses have fashions, that we're in the midst of a certain fashion now, and a few years later it will be another, and ten years ago it was different. We know better than to think that this is the pure onward progress of knowledge. We participate in these fashions, are swept along in them, but we don't set them. I'm particularly concerned that in talking thus fashionably about complicated realities—and I'm not saying that what we have said here is not central to real concerns—we often have highly coded conversations. Not only one-sided but coded. What conditions create access to the latest code book?

Sometimes I think to myself, MacKinnon, you write. Do you remember that the majority of the world's illiterates are women? *What are you doing?* I feel that powerfully when I think about what brings us all here—which is to make the changes we are talking about. When someone condemns someone else for the use of jargon, they tend to suppose that they themselves speak plain plate-glass. I'm not exempting myself from this criticism but saying that I see it as fundamental to developing a politics of language that will be deconstructive.

This essay comes in three parts. The first part is in argument form: I will state what I take to be feminism. I will take from and converse around my articles that appeared in *Signs*. I do take it upon myself to define feminism. I challenge everyone to do the same. I would like to open a discourse on what feminism means rather than on who we think we are to think that we can define what it means. In other words, I'd rather talk substance than relative postures of authority. I undertake this in critical awareness that each of our biographies limits the experience out of which we will make such a substantive definition, knowing that none of us individually has the direct experience of all women but that together we do, so that this theory must be collectively created. What we are here to do is to engage that process. Here and now. This is why the hierarchical structure of this conference is such a problem. What kind of theory does one create this way?

In the second part of this essay I will attempt to unpack and extend some of the implications from the initial compressed declarative argument. It will get more discursive. The implications of the initial argument for some central concerns in marxist theory, including the aspiration toward a unified theory of social inequality, are extended and directed principally to questions of method.

I will end with what I take to be some urgent questions on our agenda—not that there aren't urgent questions unanswered throughout; just to end with some things I do not yet, I think, adequately address. The posture of authority I take to do this comes because I agree with what I'm saying—which is not to shove it down your throats but to take responsibility for my own position.

In my view, sexuality is to feminism what work is to marxism. (Those of you who know my work will recognize this from the first *Signs* article.[1] I'm not assuming, though, that you do.) By sexuality is to feminism what work is to marxism, I mean that both focus on that which is most one's own, that which most makes one the being the theory addresses, that which is most taken away by that which the theory criticizes. You are made who you are to each theory by that which is taken away from you by the social relations each theory criticizes. In marxist theory we see society fundamentally constructed of the relations people form as they do and make those things that are needed to survive humanly. Work is the social process of shaping and transforming the material and social worlds, the process that creates people as social beings, as their interactions create value. It is that activity by which the theory comprehends how people become who they socially are. Class is the social structure of their work, production is its process, and capital is one congealed form. Control is its principal issue, that which is contested, that which we care about, that which Marx wrote about in an attempt to alter it.

Feminism has a parallel argument implicit in it. In my view— you will notice that I equate "in my view" with "feminism"—this argument is that the molding, direction, and expression of sexuality organizes society into two sexes, women and men. This division underlies the totality of social relations in a way that is as structural and pervasive as the place class occupies in marxist theory, although of course its structure and quality of pervasion are different. Sexuality is the social process that creates, organizes, expresses, and directs desire—desire here being parallel to value in marxist theory; not itself the same, but occupying an analogous theoretical location of being the quality that is taken for a natural essence or presocial impetus but is actually *created by* the social relations, the hierarchical relations, in question. This process creates the social beings we know as women and men as their relations create society. Like work to marxism, sexuality to feminism is socially constructed yet constructing. It is universal as activity yet always historically specific and jointly comprised of matter and mind. As the organized expropriation of the work of some for the use of others defines the class—workers—the organized expropriation of the sexuality of some for the use of others defines the sex—woman. Heterosexuality is its structure, gender is its social process, the family is a congealed form, sex roles are its qualities generalized to two social personae, and reproduction is a consequence. (Theorists sometimes forget that in order to reproduce one must first, usually, have had sex.) Control is gender's issue, also.

In this analysis, both marxism and feminism are theories of power and of its unequal distribution. They both provide accounts of how social arrangements of systematic disparity (by arrangement I don't mean to suggest it's equally chosen by all) are internally coherent and internally rational and pervasive yet unjust. Both theories are total theories. That is, they are both theories of the totality, of the whole thing, of a fundamental and critical underpinning of the whole they envision. The problem of the relation between marxism and feminism then becomes how both can be true at the same time. As the focus of my attempt to address this issue, I have taken the relationship between questions of power and questions of knowledge; that is, the relation between the political and the epistemological, as each theory conceives it. I will talk about the feminist theory of power and the feminist theory of knowledge and then move into their implications for an array of marxist methodological issues. I will then say what I think the relation between marxism and feminism is.

By political, I mean questions of power. The feminist theory of power is that sexuality is gendered as gender is sexualized. (This comes from the second *Signs* article.[2]) In other words, feminism is a theory of how the eroticization of dominance and submission creates gender, creates woman and man in the social form in which we know them to exist. Thus, the sex difference and the dominance-submission dynamic define each other. The erotic is what defines sex as an inequality, hence as a meaningful difference. This is, in my view, the social meaning of sexuality and the distinctly feminist account of gender inequality. The feminist theory of knowledge begins with the theory of the point of view of all women on social life. It takes as its point of departure the criticism that the male point of view on social life has constructed both social life and knowledge about it. In other words, the feminist theory of knowledge is inextricable from the feminist critique of male power because the male point of view has forced itself upon the world, and does force itself upon the world, as its way of knowing.

An epistemology is an answer to the question How do you know? What makes you think you know?—not exactly why should I believe you, but your account of why your reality is a true account. The content of the feminist theory of knowledge begins with its criticism of the male point of view by criticizing the posture that has been taken as the stance of "the knower" in Western political thought. It is the stance that Stanley Aronowitz refers to in the present collection, the neutral posture, which I will be calling "objectivity," that is, the nonsituated distanced standpoint. I'm claiming that this is the male standpoint, socially, and I'm going to try to say why. I will be arguing that the relationship between objectivity as the stance from which the world is known, and the world that is apprehended in this way, is the relationship of objectification. Objectivity is the epistemological stance of which objectification is the social process, of which male dominance is the politics, the acted out social practice; that is, to look at the world objectively is to objectify it. The act of control, of which what I have described is the epistemological level, is itself eroticized under male supremacy. To say women are sex objects is, in this way, sort of redundant. Sexualized objectification is what defines women as sexual and as woman under male supremacy.

I now want to develop some of the implications of this thesis. First, what gender is; then, what sexuality is; then, what kind of analysis this feminism is—in particular, why objectification is specifically male. Then I will digress slightly on the subject and object question. Then I will talk about the consequences of setting up a theory this way for questions of falsifiability and uncertainty, and about the verb "to be" in feminist discourse.

Gender here is a matter of dominance, not difference. Feminists have noticed that women and men are equally different but not equally powerful. Explaining the subordination of women to men, a political condition, has nothing to do with difference in any fundamental sense. Consequentially, it has a lot to do with difference, because the ideology of difference has been so central in its enforcement. Another way of putting this would be to say that there would be no such thing as what we know as the sex difference, much less would it be the social issue that it is or have the social meaning that it has, were it not for male dominance. Sometimes people say to me, "Does that mean you think there's no difference between women and men?" The only way I know how to answer that is, Of course there is. The difference is that men have power and women do not. I mean, simply, men are not socially supreme, women subordinate, by nature, and it is the fact that men are, nevertheless, socially supreme that constructs the sex difference as we know it. I mean to suggest that difference—in this I include *différance*—is a gender-based concept.

For those of you who think this is a lot of rhetoric, I want to specify the facts I have in reference. When I speak of male dominance, I mean as its content facts, from this culture. The facts have to do with the rate of rape and attempted rape of women, which is around 44 percent. If you ask a random group of women "Have you ever been raped, or been the victim of an attempted rape?" and do not include marital rape, that is the figure.[3] Women are victims of incest by their fathers at a rate of about one in ten; and sexual assault by other family members and friends, about a quarter to a third of all girls. This data, by the way, is predicated on believing women, a problem Freud had. You know that the theory of the unconscious was devised to explain how women come to invent experiences of childhood sexual abuse, because Freud did not believe, finally, that these

108

experiences could have happened. If you ask women if they've been sexually harassed in the last two years, about 15 percent report very serious and/or physical assaults; about 85 percent of all working women report sexual harassment at some time in their working lives. Battery of women by men in the family is running between a quarter and a third of all women. If you look at homicide data, between 60 and 70 percent of murdered women are killed by their husbands, lovers, or former lovers. The same is not true for murdered men. (Men also kill each other in great numbers.) Prostitution by women seems to run about 12 percent of current American society; by all reports it is women's best economic option—that is, it is the only thing, with modeling, for which women as a group are paid—by men—more than men. The pornography industry, an exemplary synthesis of the eroticization of dominance and submission with capitalism's profit motive, is put at eight billion dollars a year, with three to four times as many outlets as McDonald's restaurants.[4] To conceptualize this data as "the sex difference" acquiesces in, and obscures, the facts of male power it documents and suggests are systematic.

By the way, I use the word "male" as an adjective. My analysis of sex is social, not biological. This is not to exempt some men or valorize all women. It is to refer to the standpoint from which these acts I have documented are done, that which makes them invisible, which makes them glorious, which makes them glamorous, and which makes them normal. By "male," then, I refer to apologists for these data, to the approach that is integral to these acts, to the standard that has normalized these events to the extent that they define masculinity, to the male sex role, and to the way this approach has submerged its gender to become "the" standard. This is what I mean when I speak of the male perspective or male power. Not all men have equal access to male power, nor can they ever fully occupy a woman's standpoint. If they do, on occasion, they pay for it; although they can always reclaim male power, it is subject to being consciously disavowed. A woman can take the male point of view or exercise male power. Our access to it is not automatic; we're not born and raised to it. But we can aspire to it. Me, for instance, standing up here talking to you; socially, this is an exercise of male power. It's hierarchical, it's dominant, it's authoritative. You're listening, I'm talking; I'm active, you're passive; I'm expressing myself, you're taking notes. Women are supposed to be seen and not heard.

Question: Isn't the relationship between mother and child hierarchical and dominant?
C.M.: I don't think so, not quite in the same sense, no. Or at most it comes to have some hierarchical and dominant aspects under male supremacy. I disagree with the Chodorow-Dinnerstein[5] analysis as an explanation for male dominance. I think it is only within a context in which male power *exists*, once you already have it, that the relation between the mother and child can become one in which the mother is seen as powerful, such that it becomes a relation of horror, anxiety, betrayal, and—crucially—eroticism. I don't think this relation is *why* male supremacy exists.
Question: But isn't that the situation we are in—male dominance?
C.M.: It is its reality, yes. But I'm attempting to *explain* that reality. I find the mother/child relation, described as a relation of dominance, to be a

consequence of male supremacy, not its dynamic. Female mothering does not explain to me why hierarchy is eroticized or even why it is gendered. If hierarchy were not eroticized in male dominant sexuality, I do not think hierarchy would mean what it does, exist where it does, much less be attached to gender, hence to "mother," who remains a woman. I'm saying that I don't think female mothering is a *why* of male supremacy; although I do think women and children are linked in eroticized powerlessness under male supremacy. That is the level on which I disagree with that work—as explanation.

Question: What about female power?

C.M.: I think that is a contradiction in terms, socially speaking, and I think it will become clear why I think "female power" is a misnomer.

Now I want to speak to the question of what sexuality is, in this theory. I do not see sexuality as a transcultural container, as essential, as historically nonchanging, or as Eros. I define sexuality as whatever a given society eroticizes; that is, whatever sexual means in a particular society is what sexuality is. Sexuality is what sexuality means. This is a political hermeneutical view. Hermeneutics concerns matters of meaning. If sexuality is seen in this way, it is fundamentally social, fundamentally relational, and not a thing—which, by the way, does not mean it is not material, in a feminist sense of materiality. Because sexuality arises in relations under male dominance, women do not principally author its meanings. In the society we currently live in, the content that I want to claim for sexuality is the gaze that constructs women as objects for male pleasure. I draw on pornography for its form and content, for the gaze that eroticizes the despised, the demeaned, the accessible, the there-to-be-used, the servile, the childlike, the passive, and the animal. *That* is the content of the sexuality which defines gender female in this culture and visual "thingification" is its mode. Michèle Barrett asked earlier how we come to want that which is not in our interest. (This is a slight reformulation, but I think it is in the spirit of her question.) What I think is that sexual desire in women, at least in this culture, is socially constructed as that by which we come to want our own self-annihilation; that is, our subordination is eroticized in and as female—in fact, we get off on it, to a degree. This is our stake in this system that is not in our interest, our stake in this system that is killing us. I'm saying that femininity as we know it is how we come to want male dominance, which most emphatically is not in our interest. Such a critique of complicity, I would argue to Gayatri Spivak, does not come from an individualistic theory.

What *kind* of analysis such a feminism is, specifically by what standard it is accepted as valid, is largely a matter of the criteria one adopts for adequacy in a theory. If feminism is a critique of the objective standpoint as male, then we also disavow standard scientific norms as the adequacy criteria for our theory, because the objective standpoint we criticize is the posture of science. In other words, our critique of the objective standpoint as male is a critique of science as a specifically male approach to knowledge. With it, we reject male criteria for verification. We're not seeking truth in its female counterpart either, since that, too, is constructed by male power. We do not vaunt the subjective. We begin by seeking the truth of and in that which has constructed all this—that is, in gender.

110

Catharine A. MacKinnon

So why is objectivity as a stance specifically male? First of all, familiar to all of you, is social specificity, the particularity, the social situatedness of thought. Social situation is expressed through the concepts people construct to make sense of their situation. Either gender *is* one such social situation or it is not. If it is, then theories that are constructed by those with the social experience of men, most particularly by those who are not conscious that gender is a specific social circumstance, will be, at the least, open to being male theories. It would be difficult, it would take a lot of conscious effort, for them not to be. It is not (to repeat myself) that I have a biological theory of gender, so that every utterance out of a biologically gendered person's mouth is socially gendered in the same way. I'm saying that it is not foreign to us that social conditions shape thought as well as life. Gender either is or is not such a social condition. I'm claiming that it is.

Objectivity is a stance a subject takes. This is all very interesting on a verbal plane. Gayatri turned this question around; I'll turn it one more time. It is only a subject that gets to take the objective standpoint, the stance that is transparent to its object, the stance that is no stance. A subject is a self. An object is other to that self. Anyone who is the least bit attentive to gender since reading Simone de Beauvoir knows that it is men, socially, who are subjects; women, socially, who are other, objects. Thus, the one who has the social access to being the self that takes the stance that is allowed to be objective, that objective person who is a subject, is socially male. Further, we notice in language (as well as life) that the male tends to occupy both the neutral and the male position, which is another way of saying that the neutrality of objectivity and of maleness are coextensive linguistically, whereas women occupy the marked, the gendered, the different, the female position. Further—this is another expression of the sex-specificity of objectivity socially—women have been nature; that is, men have been knowers, mind, and women have been "to-be-known," matter, that which is to be controlled and subdued, to be acted upon. Of course, this is all a social order, for we live in society, not in the natural world.

In this context let me address the question of falsifiability. One consequence of women's rejection of science in its positivistic form is that we reject the head-counting theory of verification. Structural truths may, but may not, produce prevalent incidence. For example, to reply to a statement characterizing women's experience, "Not only women experience that," is to suggest that to be properly sex-specific something must be unique to one sex. Similarly, to say, "Not all women experience that," as if that contraindicates sex-specificity, is to suggest that to be sex-specific something must be true of 100 percent of the sex affected. Both of those are implicitly biological criteria for sex: unique and exclusive. Never mind that the biology of sex is not bipolar or exclusive. This is the way the biology of gender is ideologically conceived. Methodological assumptions have political consequences. One result of this implicitly biological notion of sex-specificity is that differences *among* women (notice differences again), such as, crucially, race and class, are seen to undercut the meaningfulness or even the reality of gender. If I say, "Such and so is true of women," and someone responds, "But it's not the same for all women," that is supposed to undercut the statement rather than point out features that *comprise* the sex-specificity of the thing. If gender is a social category, gender is what it socially means.

111

What that means is it either is or is not the case that all women, in particular ways, will be hit by the reality of gender, the totality of which will then comprise the meaning of gender as a social category. In other words, all it proves to say that something is not the same for all women is that it is not biological, not that it is not gendered. Similarly, to say that not only women experience something—for example, to suggest that the fact some men are raped makes rape not an act of male dominance when done to women—only suggests that the status of women is not biological. Men can be feminized too—and know they are when they are raped. The fact that sometimes whites have been slaves does not make black slavery not racist. That some non-Jews, such as gypsies and gays, were victims of the Holocaust does not mean the Holocast was not, or was less, anti-Semitic. We know something about the *content* of black slavery, that is, of white racism; we also know something about the *content* of the Holocaust, I trust, that makes it impossible to present isolated if significant counterexamples as if they undercut the specific meaning of the atrocities for the groups who were *defined* by their subjection to them. The fact that lots of white people are poor does not mean that the poverty of blacks has nothing to do with racism. It just means that social relations cannot be understood by analogy to chemical reactions or thermodynamics or even to quantum mechanics.

It has been suggested that men who experience similar feelings to those women articulate as women may be expressing ways in which being on the bottom of hierarchies can produce similar feelings in people. The declassed status of "student," for example, however temporary, makes a lot of men feel like most women feel most of the time. Except that the men tend to *feel* it, because they've fallen from something. There is nothing like femininity to dignify their indignity as their identity. Nor do women and men come to the status of "student" in the same way. Women have been silenced as women—told we are stupid because we are women, told that our thoughts are trivial because we are women, told that our experiences as woman are unspeakable, told that women can't speak the language of significance—then had our ideas appropriated by men, only to notice that those ideas have suddenly become worthy, even creative. Women have been excluded from education as women. This isn't to say that we're the only ones who've been excluded from education, but the specific history of that for us *as women* brings us to a structure like that of this conference, in which there's authoritative discourse emanating from the podium and silent receptivity in a mass; our history brings us to this in a way that specifically intimidates and has specific exclusionary resonances for us. To those of you who deny this, I claim the sex-specificity of that aspect of this experience.

The next thing I want to address is the methodological question of uncertainty. I want your thoughts on all of this, but in particular on this question. What I'm coming to think is that because men have power over women, women come to epistemological issues situated in a way that sheds a rather distinct light on the indeterminacy/determinacy question as men have agonized over it. Take the "Is there a reality and how do I know I'm right about it?" problem; the "Is there a there there?" business. How do we react in the face of Cartesian (updated as existential) doubt? Women know the world is out there. We know it because it hits us in the face. Literally. We are raped, battered, pornographed, defined by it by force, by a world that at least begins entirely outside us. No matter what we think about it, how we try to think it out of existence or into a different shape for us to inhabit, it remains real. Try it some time. It exists independent of our will. We can tell that it is there because no matter what we do we can't get out of it. Male power is for us, therefore *is,* this kind of fact.

The point of science, as I get it, has been to replace opinion with certainty, to replace religion and faith with the empirical hard stuff. Social science does this by analogy to the physical world: as things move, so society moves. Its laws of motion make society predictable, controllable—or try to. This analogy, by the way, has been very unexamined. The analogy between the social and the physical worlds that underlies the whole "science of society" project, which I'm here calling a specifically male project, has not been very deeply looked into to see whether it is applicable. Women's situation with respect to that project is that we have *been* that "world" for an implicitly male-centered social science. We come to this project as the *to be known about,* as part of that world to be transformed and controlled. Cartesian doubt, this anxiety about whether the world is really there independent of our will or of our representations—if I can doubt it maybe it doesn't exist—comes from the luxury of a position of power that entails the possibility of making the world as one thinks it to be—which is exactly the male standpoint. You can't tell the difference between what you think and the way the world is—or which came first—if your standpoint for thinking and being is socially powerful.

Consider the example of faking orgasms that Gayatri Spivak brought up. Men have anxiety that women fake orgasms. Take women's orgasms as an example of something about which one can have Cartesian doubt—"How do I know she's satisfied?" Now consider *why* women fake orgasms, rather than how it's too bad that men can't and therefore they're unequal to us. I would bet you that if we had the power they have, men would *learn.* What I'm saying is, men's power to *make* the world here is their power to make us make the world of their sexual interaction with us the way they want it. They want us to have orgasms; that proves that they're virile, potent, effective. We provide them that appearance, whether it's real for us or not. We even get into it. Our reality is that it is far less damaging and dangerous for us to do this, to accept a lifetime of simulated satisfaction, than to hold out for the real thing from them. For them, we are "world" to their knowledge of world. Their Cartesian doubt is entirely justified: it's because of their power to force the world to be their way that they're forever wondering what's really going on out there. Heisenberg's uncertainty principle expresses much the same situation in a slightly more aware key. If the way you know the world is this intervention, piercing the veil, making penetrating observations, incisive analyses . . . well, women's social powerlessness gives us the opposite problem. What we're forever wondering is whether there's anything *other* than the reality of the world men make; whether there is *any* sphere of the world that responds to our will, our thought. Women are awash in doubt, all right, but it never has the credibility of Descartes. It is our *reality,* even before our knowledge, that is in doubt. Thus, I think that the indeterminacy that arises in discourse theory, and in the social text, describes something that, as genders, we are unequally situated in. If you don't determine reality, its indeterminacy, its *un*fixity, is a good deal less apparent to you. Your world is *very determinate;* it is *all too fixed.* It *can't* just be any way at all.

Now I want to say something about the use of the verb "to be" in feminist theory. If the analysis I have given is right, to be realistic about sexuality socially is to see it from the male point of view. To be feminist is to do that with a critical awareness of what you are doing. This explains why feminist insights are often criticized for replicating male ideology, why feminists are called "condescending to women," when what we are doing is expressing and exposing how women are condescended to. Because male power has created, in reality, the world to which feminist insights, when they are accurate, refer, many of our statements will capture that reality, simply exposing it as specifically male for the first time. For example, men say all women are whores. We say men have the power to make this our fundamental condition. So feminism stresses the indistinguishability of prostitution, marriage, and sexual harassment. See, what a woman "is" is that which you have *made* women "be"; that "is" women, as men make women mean. They have the power to; they *do*—otherwise power means nothing. It's a very empirical "is." Men define women as sexual beings; feminism comprehends that femininity "is" sexual. Men see rape as intercourse; feminists say much intercourse "is" rape. Men say women desire degradation; feminists see female masochism as the ultimate success of male supremacy and marvel at its failures.

If male power makes the world as it "is," to theorize this reality requires its capture in order to subject it to critique, hence to change. Feminists say women are not individuals. To retort that we "are" will not make it so. It will obscure the need to *make change* so that it can be so. To the feminist charge that women "are" not equal, to retort, "Oh, you think women aren't equal to men," is to act as though *saying* we "are" will make it so. What it will do, instead, what it has done and is doing, is legitimize the vision that we already "are" equal, that *this,* life as we live it now, is equality for us. It acts as if the purpose of speech is to say what we want reality to be like as if it already is that way, as if that will help move reality to that place. This may be true in fiction but it won't work in theory. It suggests, instead, that if this is reality, nothing needs changing, that *this* is freedom, that we choose *this.* To me, this is about denial and the opposite of change.

Stanley Aronowitz talked pretty extensively about marxist method. I see two strains in marxist method; it is not monolithic. One is the more objectivist strain that purports to take the neutral position. The other, which I draw on, is more critical of the necessary situatedness of its own standpoint. The second one purports to capture as thought the flux of history and understands itself—this is more in Lukács's mode—as reflexive, as participating in an ongoing situation, trapped in it in a way, needing to be self-critical, and also having, by virtue of that involvement, some access to the truth of the situation. Feminism has widely been thought to contain tendencies of liberal feminism, radical feminism, and socialist feminism. Too often, socialist or marxist feminism has applied the objective strain in marxism to women and called that marxist feminism. Liberal feminism has applied the same objectivism that marxism shares with liberalism to women, resulting in liberalism applied to women that—especially on questions of sexuality—is markedly similar to the leftist view, because of the common maleness of the epistemological posture. At least some versions of radical feminism—not the biologcal but the socially based ones—are what I am calling feminism. This feminism is methodologically post-marxist. It is a move to resolve the relationship between marxism and feminism on the level of method. If women are analyzed as a social group, not in individualistic, naturalistic, idealistic, moralistic terms, nor in voluntaristic or harmonistic terms (namely, we're all really equal and socially we have a naturally harmonious relation between the genders at most in need of marginal reequilibration) . . . that is methodologically post-marxist. I've noticed that liberal views of sexuality—treating it in terms that are individual, natural, ideal, moral, and voluntaristic—seem to coexist remarkably well with many people's otherwise marxist views. And, in my opinion, no feminism worthy of the name is *not* methodologically post-marxist.

As an example of such a post-marxist feminism, I want to consider the often raised question of whether "all women" are oppressed by heterosexuality. The question is posed as if sexual practice is a matter of unconstructed choice. If heterosexuality is one gendered form of sexuality in a society where gender oppresses women through sex, sexuality and heterosexuality are essentially the same thing. This does not erase homosexuality, it merely means that sexuality in that form may be no less gendered. Either heterosexuality is the structure of the oppression of women or it is not. Most people see sexuality as individual, or biological, or voluntary—that is, they see it in terms of the myth structure that politically, formally is the liberal one. If you applied such an analysis to the issue of work—and I would like anyone who thinks that this is not a valid parallel here to target this peculiarly sensitive example—would you agree, as people say about heterosexuality, that a worker chooses to work? Does a worker even meaningfully choose his or her specific line or place of work? If working conditions improve, do you call that worker not oppressed? If you have comparatively good or easy or satisfying or well-paying work, if you even like your work, or have a good day at work, does that mean, from a marxist perspective, that you are not exploited? I would like those who think that one chooses heterosexuality under conditions that make it compulsory either to explain why it is not compulsory or to explain why the word choice can be meaningful here. And I would like you to address a question I think few here would apply to the workplace, to work, or to workers: whether a good fuck is any compensation for getting fucked. And why everyone knows what that means.

How to make change. Marxism teaches that exploitation and degradation somehow produce resistance and revolution. It's been hard to say why. What I've learned from women's experience with sexuality is that our exploitation and degradation also produce grateful complicity in exchange for survival. It produces self-loathing to the point of extinction of self, respect for which makes resistance conceivable. This makes the issue not why women acquiesce but why we ever do anything but. I would like us to see this as a particular question for explanation and for organization. A second urgent question has to do with class and with race. I would like to see the beginnings of a consideration of the interconnections between the theory of sexuality I have outlined and the forms of property possession and ownership *and* the eroticization of racial degradation. I think that may illuminate some issues of class and also some questions about race. A third urgent issue has to do with the relation of everything I've said to all forms of inequality. Am I describing only one form within a larger system, or is this *the* system, or is this too abstract a question?

115

What I do think is that none of our work can be done the way it has been done, if what I am saying is taken seriously. We cannot address aesthetics without considering pornography. We cannot think about sexuality and desire without considering the normalization of rape, and I do not mean rape as surplus repression. We cannot do or criticize science without talking about the masculinity of its premises. We cannot talk about everyday life without understanding its division by gender, or about hegemony without understanding male dominance as a form of it. We cannot talk about production without including not only its sex division but sexual harassment and prostitution (as well as housework) as underpinning the labor market. We cannot talk about the phallus in a way that obscures the penis. And we cannot talk about woman as signifier in a way that loses sight of woman as signified. We need systematically to understand, in order to criticize and change, rather than reproduce, the connection between the fact that the few have ruled and used the many in their own interest and for their own pleasure as well as profit—and that those few have been men.

Notes

Note: MacKinnon refers at several points to papers presented at the conference on Marxism and the Interpretation of Culture. Her reference to Michèle Barrett's argument, however, is not to Barrett's paper but to her response to Christine Delphy, which may be found on pp. 268–69. Though Stanley Aronowitz's and Stuart Hall's papers are considerably expanded, they still deal with the issues to which MacKinnon alludes.

1   Catharine A. MacKinnon, "Feminism, Marxism, Method and the State: An Agenda for Theory," *Signs* 7 (1982), pp. 515-44.

2   Catharine A. MacKinnon, "Feminism, Marxism, Method and the State: Toward Feminist Jurisprudence," *Signs* 8 (1983), pp. 635-58.

3   Diana E. H. Russell, *Sexual Exploitation* (Beverly Hills, Calif.: Sage Publications, 1984); Diana E. H. Russell and Nancy Howell, "The Prevalence of Rape in the United States Revisited," *Signs* 4 (1983), p. 688.

4   On incest: D. Finkelhor, *Child Sexual Abuse: Theory and Research* (New York: Free Press, 1984); J. Herman, *Father-Daughter Incest* (Cambridge: Harvard University Press, 1981); J. Renvoise, *Incest: A Family Pattern* (Boston: Routledge and Kegan Paul, 1982). On battery: R. and E. Dobash, *Violence against Wives* (New York: Free Press, 1979); L. Walker, *The Battered Woman* (New York: Harper, 1979); D. Russell, *Rape in Marriage* (New York: Macmillan, 1982). On prostitution: K. Barry, *Female Sexual Slavery* (Englewood Cliffs, N.J.: Prentice-Hall, 1979); P. Alexander, quoted in M. Griffin, "Wives, Hookers and the Law," *Student Lawyer*, Jan. 1982, p. 18. On pornography: J. Cook, "The X-Rated Economy," *Forbes*, 1978, p. 18; M. Langelan, "The Political Economy of Pornography," *Aegis*, 1981, pp. 5-17; A. Dworkin, *Pornography: Men Possessing Women* (New York: Putnam's, 1979); L. Lovelace and M. McGrady, *Ordeal* (Berkeley, Calif.: Berkeley Books, 1980). On murder: J. Boudouris, "Homicide and the Family," *Journal of Marriage and the Family*, 33 (1971), pp. 667-71; E. Gibson and S. Klein, *Murder 1957 to 1968* (London: HMSO, 1969); D. Molvihill, M. Tumin, and L. Curtis, *Crimes of Violence*, Eleventh Report of the National Commission on the Causes and Prevention of Violence, (Washington, D.C.: U.S. Government Printing Office, 1969); L. Bowker, "The Criminal Victimization of Women," *Victomology: An International Journal*, 4 (1979), pp. 371, 384.

5   N. Chodorow, *The Reproduction of Mothering: Psychoanalysis and the Sociology of Gender* (Berkeley: University of California Press, 1978); D. Dinnerstein, *The Mermaid and the Minotaur: Sexual Arrangements and Human Malaise* (New York: Harper, 1977).

Discussion

(At the conference, Gayatri Spivak's talk immediately preceded Catharine MacKinnon's. Spivak, MacKinnon, and Ellen Willis were all on stage during the discussion.)

Comment (Gayatri Spivak)

I would like to talk about the insistence, in the United States, on adjudicating freedom by rearranging the furniture or turning lecture sessions into town meetings. It is always Americans who pretend they can be free in a completely structured situation. I know this sounds somewhat mean, but I think there's an inherent meanness in that practice. In a way, it's an extremely aggressive practice, this declaration that one is now so free and easy.

What is really at issue is the need to recognize what the situation is in a ritual setting like this. As teachers and speakers (I have been both here), we are to some extent paid to perform. I am serious about my work but also about what I owe to you since you are here. So the relation of power is constantly undone in terms of service. Thus, there are other ways of thinking about well-articulated talks. To describe them as instances of male power is not only to forget that a lecture is an expression of an obligation to an audience but also to forget that the ideal of "rapping" with an audience has a history both in Ivy League institutions and in that very New Left that feminists have criticized as sexist.

I want to make clear that I don't question your goodwill, that what I am saying is as much a self-defense as a critique of your position. But I do think that history is stronger than benevolence and thus that there is a problem with authority that disguises itself as being permissive.

Comment (Ellen Willis)

Before I start, I want to say that actually men *can* fake orgasms; it's just that they usually don't have to. . . .

Catharine raised a whole complex of issues that are central to the debates now going on among feminists. I would like to address her idea of power and her definition of sex. Implicit in the system Catharine laid out is a view of male power and female powerlessness as absolute categories, even more absolute than if they were constituted by biology. The male point of view becomes so pervasive in this reality, which is entirely structured by gender, that even when it is taken up by a member of the oppressed class—women—its meaning is unchanged. Women can neither use it nor appropriate it for their own purposes. It remains male and it remains essentially an imposition on women. Furthermore, this view has underlying assumptions about biological maleness and femaleness, since it suggests, in a sense, that the biological female cannot authentically exercise power. Catharine herself has posed the basic problem with this system: it is a closed system in which the possibility for any kind of struggle or contestation seems nonexistent. It is another version of Marcuse's closed system in which capitalism is so pervasive in its ability to manipulate that any resistance is turned around and made part of the system; at best one has the opportunity for refusal. Yet even refusal would seem to contradict the closed system, since refusal implies the power to define one's own situation, to feel enough pain so as to invent the concept of feminism. Feminism suggests a power that is outside the closed gender system; it suggests, as well, that the structure of male dominance is only a dimension of reality, indeed, only a dimension of male/female relations. I would see feminism as struggling against, working to abolish, the dimension of reality that is male supremacy, but male supremacy does not dominate all human relations. In the feminist movement this totalizing view of power has led to a counterculture politics that is basically a politics of despair. Writing about

117

the situation of right-wing women, Andrea Dworkin argues that they realize there is no way out of this system of absolute male power and absolute female powerlessness. Feminists who hold out for change apparently don't see the gravity of women's situation; they have chosen to make an accommodation with that aspect of the male power structure that they think offers them the best deal. So the issue Catharine is raising has concrete consequences within the feminist movement and for feminist activism.

My own view is that power is not a monolithic system but a system of overlapping contradictions. Women have always struggled against their situation both individually and collectively. They have seized on contradictions in the system—demanding, for example, that the concept of human rights be applied to women—thereby using the discontinuities in the system to mobilize for their own power. And they have allied themselves with men when the ruling classes were seen to be oppressing them both.

This suggests a Marxist understanding of power exercised for the sake of particular interests, whereas the system Catharine has articulated—the system of absolute male power and absolute female powerlessness—implies a notion of power exercised for its own sake. Men get specific economic and social benefits from male supremacy, including having a class of people devoted to meeting their needs. Such interests also create a situation where the dominant class is dependent on the subordinate class for meeting its needs, which gives the subordinate class a certain opening wedge of power. Threatening to withhold meeting those needs, organizing to meet those needs in their own way, and finally opting for broader struggle. But if one has a notion of power exercised for its own sake, then this dialectic does not apply; there is only the closed system of absolutes. Catharine's view of feminism, indeed, requires a kind of metaphysics of power, of power exercised for the sheer pleasure of it; in effect, a conflation of power and eroticism.

This brings us to the issue of sex. I would agree that the manipulation and construction of our sexuality is central to the creation of gender. Yet I also think it cannot be subsumed under gender relations. The construction of sexuality underpins the entire culture's authoritarian relations; it influences the structures of class and race, of dominance and submission in general. Gender is a central example of this, but not the only one. Here, my difference with Catharine is illustrated by the fact that she talked about the eroticization of dominance and submission, whereas I would talk about the politicization of Eros. I do believe there is an erotic dimension that is bodily, physiological, and, in some sense, precultural. Sexual gratification is one element of eroticism, which includes the infant's intense bodily pleasure in eating. But I want to concentrate on sexuality, since it is the key political issue in feminist debates.

The political differences between our two positions are profound. If sex is simply a function of an all-pervasive male power, then there can be no meaningful female sexuality. Within this closed system a woman who feels desire and pleasure is really experiencing an abnegation of self. There seems to be a fundamental contradiction here. Is there such a thing as pleasure that is purely negative and imposed? I would argue that, despite contexts of powerlessness that are bound up with pleasure, pleasure nonetheless offers something like moments of self-affirmation or empowerment. This again contradicts the idea of absolute powerlessness. There is a moment of autonomy and empowerment in the demand that one's needs be gratified, in directly seizing pleasure. At the same time there is a moment of surrender—loss of ego control and surrender to one's feelings. In a hierarchical society these two elements are split and the moment of empowerment is confused and conflated with dominance. And surrender is confused and conflated with submission. This all comes to pass through the ways the culture manipulates one's sexuality, a process in which the relations between parents and children are as salient as those between men and women. In fact, our sexuality is constructed in the family and in the convergence of power relations between parents and children. These relations are often hierarchical and oppressive in ways that cannot be subsumed within male supremacy.

The division of eroticism—and the association of empowerment with dominance and of surrender with submission—occurs in both sexes, but there are differences in how this division is fantasized and acted out socially. Women often cannot overtly seek empowerment, even as men cannot overtly seek surrender, but both sexes covertly seek that to which they are not overtly entitled. Rape fantasies exemplify this pattern, to the extent that the man overtly identifies with the rapist but also, on some level, secretly identifies with the victim, while the woman may overtly identify with the victim but can also secretly identify with the rapist. None of this, of course, detracts at all from the fact that it is men who have the opportunity to act out dominance; men's confusion of empowerment and sexual pleasure with dominance wreaks great devastation on women. At the same time, however, it is important to realize that sex is not monolithic; it's a minefield of all these contradictions; it's an area of struggle. Sex is not entirely given over to oppression and thus women are not limited to refusing compliance. Every time women demand their own pleasure—despite the contradictions that may entail within heterosexuality—it is a moment of empowerment and liberation and a kind of wedge into struggle in other areas. In fact, the contradiction in male sexuality—the perversion of empowerment into dominance and the compulsion to repress the impulse to surrender—brings a real loss of pleasure. Forcing men to realize this provides another way into fighting male power generally.

Within the closed system of male power, heterosexuality simply becomes a scenario of dominance and submission, and sex and rape become indistinguishable. At that point, rape is hardly worth singling out as an issue. I see sexuality as a more complicated set of dynamics, as a contested terrain, not a static area of oppression. It involves the channeling of eroticism and all the culturally produced fantasies of dominance and submission. Yet there is also a utopian aspect to sexuality. Part of the heterosexual impulse, for example, has to do with the desire to transcend the antagonism between men and women. Men experience this but want to have it both ways—to maintain their power while transcending the antagonism, an impossibility. Women's sexuality has an undercurrent of hope—of getting men to give up their power. Even as a fantasy, it shows that part of women's sexuality is self-assertive rather than accommodating. The cultural fantasies of intercourse as merger and transcendence are just as real as the cultural fantasies of violation. Moreover, on some level the fantasies of merger prefigure political possibilities. This is not, however, intended to urge the virtues of individualism but rather to suggest what contradictions the women's liberation movement is working on.

MacKinnon

On the issue of my effort to open up the structure of the conference, let me say that I don't see what I did as even remotely adequate to the critique that I suggested. I don't pretend to have made us all free. I do think, however, that a certain kind of knowledge is created under certain conditions, and that this conference has reproduced those conditions. Those conditions include the maleness of the authority of the position that I'm in; but I don't imagine that, as a feminist, I'm going around making everyone free. I'm acknowledging how the structures we're living out right here and now are part of the cultural structures that are the topic of my talk. I don't pretend that I changed them.

Now, as to my concept of power. I don't think of power as something that floats freely, like some looming omnipresence, precultural or otherwise, and then takes specific forms. In other words, I don't think of power as something that just *is* and then becomes economic, racial, sexual, and finally individual. I think of power only as a socially constituted meaning, as existing only in its social forms. I use male power to refer to what men have appropriated and arrogated to themselves in a way that I take to be authoritative. If I don't speak of countering male power with female power it's because that suggests we are already equal. That's

119

why I resist using a term like "female power" at all; indeed, I rarely use "female" except to refer to biological issues. I guess I use "male" because I've so carefully given it a social meaning, not because I think it is biological. It isn't that women have no ways to resist, because obviously we do. But calling these resistances "power" is misleading because they're a form of powerlessness. The reason we don't exhibit "power" is because, whenever we do, we get pushed back into line in ways that are forcible, painful, and depriving.

Of course, subliminal to much of this discussion is the work of Andrea Dworkin, in particular *Pornography: Men Possessing Women* and *Right-Wing Women*. As to the critique that Dworkin's work promotes a politics of despair, I would suggest that the same critique would have to be made of Stuart Hall's analysis of Thatcherism. In other words, Dworkin's analysis of right-wing women is very similar to the one Stuart Hall made of people who choose Thatcherism; that is, they are, at least in part, under conditions where they choose survival over militancy. Yet it's difficult to understand the meaningfulness of the term "choice" under conditions of constraint. So, either these are conditions of constraint we're talking about or they're not. Either we operate under a condition where certain choices are hegemonically defined and other choices are blocked or we do not. I'm glad to hear Ellen Willis say, for example, that she thinks Eros is in some sense precultural, because I think that's implicit in much of the argument that stands against the argument I make, in which sexuality is cultural to the ground. It's a lot easier to see freedom of choice operative in your sexuality if the ground you're standing on is partly precultural as well as in part constrained by culture. Now I see these choices as operating within a closed system, not an absolute system, but one that is closed, rigid, and imposed. I don't *like* the reality of this system; neither the system nor my analysis of it give me pleasure.

In my overall project, what I would like to do is to redefine what it means to be human (a concept now dominated by maleness) so that it includes a revaluing of everything that women have always done but that has been relegated to femaleness or the feminine. In addition, I would like to work toward a transformation in the content of what being human refers to, so that it can be something to which women as well will want to aspire. A radical feminism involves not merely taking on those things that men have always done but instead transforming the content of those things in the light of women's experience.

Comment (Ellen Willis)

This may speak to part of the difference between us. I think feminism is in part about being able to do many of the things men have always done, which is to say that I think men have appropriated the majority of human activities and denied them to women. In appropriating them, they have in many ways also changed them and put them to oppressive ends. Nevertheless, there is one level where men have defined themselves as generic human beings, and women have been defined by what they aren't allowed to do. Part of what feminism is about is reappropriating the world and demanding to be allowed every human activity. This includes demanding to be able to express your violent impulses, demanding to be able to have economic power; this isn't ultimately what feminism is about (and it's a naive expression of that aspect of feminism), but there's an element of truth in that impulse. The ultimate reason why this kind of feminism can't win and doesn't make a movement is that women thereby risk becoming a kind of caricature of power. But it's not a question of maleness, since all these human activities—both oppressive and nonoppressive—are not inherently male. That's exactly the idea we're fighting.

Question

I would like to ask that you address the issue of homosexuality and place it in the context of your work.

Catharine A. MacKinnon

MacKinnon

The issue of choice is particularly relevant to issues of homosexuality. I cannot, for example, make a lot of sense out of what people call the choice of heterosexuality; it's like saying you *choose* to be a capitalist or a worker. I can understand the choice to be with a particular man who is engaged in a struggle against the dominant male sexuality. A choice that goes against the dominant culture is a real choice. A choice to be a lesbian, however, is different from a choice to be a gay man. For women to choose to affirm other women, both in terms of gender and sexuality, is very different from the choice to be a gay male. A choice to be a gay man can represent seeing through the way sex roles have made heterosexuality compulsory and thus be an affirmation of the feminist struggle. But it can also be an extension of the male bond, the ultimate conclusion of heterosexuality: men come first, men are better in every way, so why not also sexually? Yet some gay men may make this choice because they don't want to oppress women. In other words, so long as something in fact works against the structure of male supremacy and male dominance, I'm willing to countenance that the word "choice" begins to apply to it.

Comment (Ellen Willis)

I think the whole question of choice is complicated by the fact that we have a system that sets up overwhelming punishments for not being heterosexual, as well as certain rewards (even for women) for being heterosexual. If there's an institutionalized system in which the only "normal" masculine and feminine identity is heterosexual, not being heterosexual is not only to lose privilege but also to be an outcast in the culture. Given that, the choice to be homosexual is in some sense just as determined by the system. If we start with the assumption that attraction is pansexual, then both heterosexuality and exclusive homosexuality are artificial. If people blot out their heterosexual attraction in order to be able to rebel against an oppressive system, it's not a free and unstructured choice. At the same time, there are all kinds of systemic implications in being heterosexual. So it's difficult to talk about choice in either direction, though clearly the possiblity of refusal exists despite everything. I suppose the real question, and the one I want to ask Catharine, is what is your explanation of why, despite this system, people do refuse and do struggle politically?

MacKinnon

I have no explanation, though I do understand that women struggle. But I also know that we have never won.

Paul Patton
Marxism and Beyond: Strategies of Reterritorialization

Philosophy has traditionally been concerned to legislate, to draw lines of demarcation, and to establish hierarchies within discourse. The real alternative is not the position of the mythical Other of this state philosophy, the relativist for whom all distinction is impossible, but that of the nomad—not so much the member of a tribe as an activist in a movement, a militant on behalf of an avowedly partial perspective.

The principal intellectual effect of the protest movements that erupted in English-speaking countries during the 1960s and 1970s has been the revival of marxism. Since then, we have seen a vast amount of new research into marxism, and an avalanche of marxist social theory. More recently, however, marxism's hegemony over radical social thought and politics has begun to fall apart. The criticism of fundamental principles of historical materialism and the proliferation of alternatives have been such that one can properly speak of a "crisis" in leftist thought.[1] In addition to the familiar historical anomalies and failures to materialize, two novel sources of difficulty stand out.

The first has been the emergence of a range of specific-issue political movements whose ideals and aspirations fall outside of those traditionally encompassed by marxism. These include struggles against social government through techniques of individualization, by minority groups such as women, homosexuals, prisoners, and psychiatric patients. ("Minority" here does not mean numerically inferior but divergent from the norm.) These also include the struggles of racial minorities, ecological activists, peace and antinuclear groups. The fact that such movements cannot be defined in terms of class interests has led some to speak of a "crisis of identity" within the socialist movement.[2] At the same time, the strength of these movements in the advanced capitalist countries, and the importance of the issues they raise, has led others to question the adequacy of marxism as a guide to the present, much less the future.

The second source of difficulty has been the translation and assimilation of much poststructuralist French philosophy and social theory. This has been seen to provide not only substantive alternatives to the productivist perspective of marxism but also an explicit rejection of many of the assumptions and meta-theoretical principles that govern marxist discourse. For some, this *theoretical* confrontation is the central contemporary difficulty facing marxism. Thus, Alex Callinicos devotes the major part of his recent book, *Is There a Future for Marxism?*, to the refutation of "the 'nietzschean' challenge offered to marxism by Foucault and De-

123

leuze."[3] He acknowledges that the challenge proceeds on a philosophical plane as well as at the level of substantive social theory by charging these "anarcho-nietzscheans" with propagating a philosophy that denies the possibility of both objective knowledge and social emancipation.[4]

In addition to theorizing new objects of political concern (language, discourse, desire, and power), it is true that an important contribution of poststructuralist thought in general has been to politicize the question of styles of thought and rationality. Much of it is characterized by a rejection of the characteristic operations and values of the dominant forms of Western rationality: values such as unity, hierarchy, foundation, and transcendence. In part, this shift is evident in the different style in which the analysis of concrete objects such as forms of writing, desire, or power relations is carried out. In part, it is a matter of an explicit philosophical and methodological program. Deleuze and Guattari, for example, preface their sequel to *Anti-Oedipus* with an exposition of a rhizomatic model of organization which departs at every turn from the dichotomous and hierarchical tree structure that has dominated Western thought.[5]

It should not be thought that these questions of abstract theoretical principle are entirely remote from the concern with new political movements. In fact, these two sources of difficulty for marxism converge on the question of styles of theorizing and modes of argument. Any consideration of what is at issue in the polemics between marxists and feminists, ecologists or theorists of other forms of marginality leads directly to a concern with the principles and intellectual strategies that determine marxist responses. For example, since marxist feminism, by definition, cannot be a discourse that takes as its primary object the specific forms of female oppression, one feminist response has been to opt for an autonomous theory, a "conceptual separatism," that takes the oppression of women as its point of departure. Since it does not wish to deny the exploitation of wage labor, this response is immediately caught up in the "problem" of relativism: How can society be both capitalistic and patriarchal at once? Which term is primary? Thus, perceptive critics argue that a historical and materialist social theory that takes into account such autonomous analyses will have to adopt a different model of rationality.[6]

Nor should the political importance of these issues be underestimated. The style of rationality with which we operate will determine the range of intellectual strategies available to us, which in turn will set the limits of our political practice as intellectuals. The current debate concerning the future of marxism provides clear illustration of this. Among its chiefly marxist protagonists, the defense of orthodoxy takes a variety of forms. One is the resort to "unorthodox" readings of the canonical texts in the attempt to recover, or provide, alternative traditions within marxism that might better account for some of the anomalies. Jacoby, for example, concludes his *Dialectic of Defeat* with a call for a new "critical theory" to explain what he calls "class unconsciousness": the failure of revolutionary class consciousness to emerge. Such faith in the tradition appears unshakable. Another defense involves the appeal to the pseudo-neutrality of methodological criteria derived from the natural sciences. Callinicos deals with the problem of stalinism and the gulag in this manner, treating it as a potential refutation that must be explained in terms of basic marxist theory if it is not to encourage the search for alternative approaches. However, the preference for one explanatory strategy over another is not neutral. It is for political reasons rather than "objective" considerations of explanatory adequacy that one might prefer an account of the gulag in terms of the techniques of power it mobilizes, to one in terms of the relations of production that characterize the Soviet social formation.[7] These are the same sorts of reasons that lead us to prefer a power-oriented approach to those aspects of capitalist society that classical marxism tends to treat as secondary: the institutions of sexuality, mental health, education, and the family. Ultimately, the defense of orthodoxy refuses to take seriously the possibility that these new political concerns might call into question not only the goals of socialism but the forms of understanding of history on which these are founded.

It is this question of intellectual strategies in response to difference that forms the main concern of this paper. I will deal with only some of the strategies frequently employed in debates between marxist and non-marxist social theory, in particular with some of the forms of argument that tend to draw the theoretical and political perspectives of autonomous social movements back onto the discursive field of marxism. I shall attempt to name and criticize two of the more important of such theoretical obstacles to the emergence of a creative radical political culture: (1) the unitarian conception of knowledge and (2) the will to totality.

My primary examples of these strategies come from two of the "crisis of marxism" books already mentioned—those by Callinicos and Aronowitz. This is by no means to equate these books in other respects, since they take up diametrically opposed positions in response to this crisis. Moreover, they are only intended to serve as illustrations of forms of argument that are all too common elsewhere. Much of my argument is based on the intellectual strategies evident in the work of Deleuze, Foucault, and others. The conception of theory appropriate to this work is explicitly set out in various texts by Deleuze and Guattari, notably in *Rhizome*. I shall apply some deleuzean concepts to this question of what is an appropriate relation to marxism, in order to free the space in which it is posed rather than to provide an unequivocal answer, bearing in mind that these concepts are themselves only momentary staging points along lines of theoretical flight.

One way to approach the problem is to contrast Callinicos's conception of marxist theory, and the nature of his response to the work of Deleuze and Foucault, with the rather different attitude toward theory shared by those authors and with their own practical relationship to marxism. Callinicos defends a classical conception of classical marxist theory: it is no different from any other "scientific research program" and may be defined by a method and a set of core doctrines such as materialism, the determining role of the relations of production, the centrality of class struggle, and so on. His predominant attitude toward non-marxist theory is essentially reactive: the superiority of marxism must be asserted, along with the priority of the problems marxism addresses. Accordingly, his criticism is, for the most part, a practice of denunciation on the basis of fixed dichotomies. Where positions differ from those of marxism, they are denounced from the standpoint of the latter. In this manner, for example, the implicit denial of the prospect of social emancipation through a single revolutionary event is seen to lead either to a harmlesss academicism or to a reactionary pessimism.[8]

In fact, the relationship between the work of Foucault and Deleuze and marxism is more fluid than Callinicos allows. While they are not marxist theorists, neither are they critics of marxism who set out to refute its claims. The only criticism of marxism they practice is the active criticism that is the by-product of their own selective use of it. Foucault, for example, cites Marx in *Discipline and Punish* as a historian or historical source, although not as the founder of a discursive formation whose rules he seeks to be guided by. Deleuze and Guattari, on the other hand, take up Marx's account of primitive accumulation in *Anti-Oedipus,* in order to demonstrate the singular and contingent conjunction of deterritorialized flows that made capitalism possible: a deterritorialized flow of labor produced by rural enclosure and a deterritorialized flow of money able to be employed as capital. In a similar fashion, they incorporate into their own theory of the capitalist social machine a generalized version of the contradictory tendency Marx describes in relation to the rate of profit: capitalism is a system that constantly approaches its own limits while at the same time deferring them, overcoming them by their reproduction on a larger scale. The process is endless, since the limits are immanent to the system itself, determined by the same conditions that govern the expanded reproduction of capital. So, for Deleuze and Guattari, capitalism works by breaking down social codes and territorialities, replacing these with an "axiomatic system," the fundamental axiom of which is that everything be subject to the laws of market exchange. Deterritorialization on the one plane is accompanied by reterritorialization on the other.[9]

The question of their relationship to marxism is one that is only posed from outside the theoretical work of Foucault and Deleuze; within it, the question of marxism does not arise. At the level of intellectual strategy, it is the positivity of this approach that must be underscored. These authors deploy elements of marxist theory in the process of elaborating something else, a different form of intelligibility of social reality. In one direction, these expropriations of marxist analyses amount to a deterritorialization of fragments of the corpus. Deterritorialization is the operation characteristic of lines of flight; it is the movement by which one leaves a territory. As such, with rare exceptions, it is accompanied by a simultaneous movement of reterritorialization on some other domain, not necessarily continuous with the first. The intellectual strategy of deterritorialization itself obeys this law of double movement, for, in another direction, these marxist analyses are simultaneously reterritorialized on a new theoretical "plane of consistency," incorporated as functional elements of a new discursive apparatus. Thus, for example, the redescription in *Anti-Oedipus* of capitalism as an axiomatic of decoded flows occurs in the context of a general machine theory of desire, and specifically as part of an attempt to theorize certain abstract figures, or mega-machines, in terms of which social formations might be understood: the territorial machine of lineage and filiation, the despotic state machine of the primitive empires. . . . Similarly for Foucault, the analysis of the disciplinary techniques that formed part of the conditions of the specifically capitalist production process finds its theoretical surface not in the theory of capitalist production and exchange but in a projected "analytics" of micropower relations.

In one sense, the first movement is primary: the decison to leave, to quit the familiar theoretical territory, must be taken before anything else is possible. Ultimately, however, the second is more important, since the creation or occurrence of anything new requires the construction of an assemblage that makes it possible. In *Rhizome,* Deleuze and Guattari draw no distinction between their conception of a book and their understanding of desire. In either case it is a matter of assemblage. Their theory of desire is unequivocally constructivist: desires only exist insofar as they are assembled, insofar as the component parts are welded together into some sort of functional machine, be it emotional, political, or artistic. There is no desire outside of such a determinate assemblage. It requires a plane of consistency, or "body without organs," which has no prior existence but must be constructed along with the realization of the desire itself. So it is with books, which are also assemblages, collective assemblages of statements: "How can a book be a body without organs? There are several ways, according to the nature of the lines considered, their content or density, their possibility of convergence on a plane of consistency which would secure their selection."[10]

Deleuze and Guattari's theoretical practice, like their theory of desire, is constructionist rather than deconstructionist. The important thing is the construction of the body or plane on which a life may be led or an enterprise conducted. Deconstruction remains an essentially critical operation, devoted to the unsettling of certainty, the disruption of fixity of meaning, encouraging undecidability in the constructions of existing metaphysics. Denying the possibility of a fixed point from which to criticize, it can only gesture toward the possibility of another model of rationality. *Rhizome,* by contrast, may be read as a prolegomenon to an alternative metaphysics. It outlines both a style of thought and a range of concepts, necessarily inexact and mobile, with which they propose to conduct the analysis of a variety of domains which are themselves constructed in the process: rhizomatics, schizoanalysis, micropolitics, pragmatics. . . . This metaphysics of strata, assemblages, multiplicities, and lines is developed and deployed in *Mille Plateaux.*

In the latter sections of *Mille Plateaux,* the earlier project of defining the abstract machines that govern the functioning of social formations becomes centered on the specification of two figures, the state and nomadism. Very crudely, the opposition between these is the difference between an agent or force of territorialization and a force or movement of deterritorialization. The nomad is the figure of deterritorialization par excellence, inventor and realizer of a *machine de guerre* that is implacably hostile to the state. As a form of existence, nomadism is distinguished from the sedentary state form in a variety of ways: by its relationship to space, its internal articulation, and its system of affects. The state, on the other hand, is defined, above all, by its apparatuses of capture; that is, by its specific procedures for territorializing land, labor, and money. These are so many variations on the themes of rent, profit, and taxes; so many procedures for the entrapment of subjects.

My interest in mentioning this project here is not to take up its consequences for political analysis, which would be considerable, but to make use of its application to the question of intellectual strategies, for, Deleuze and Guattari suggest, there is also a *state form* of thought. There are forms of theoretical capture that define the limits of the rationally acceptable and preclude the possibility of different objects, let alone different styles of thought. The politics of theory is not only a matter of content but also a matter of form. Marxism has many of the appearances of a state form in the realm of theory. As a discursive assemblage, it is capable of alliance with some of the most powerful nondiscursive techniques of capture. This is the basis for Andre Glucksmann's impertinent question, How is it that a discourse ostensibly committed to human emancipation can function alongside a system of concentration camps?[11] In the different context of advanced capitalism, marxism's adoption of forms of theoretical capture provides the basis on which it can function as the "master discourse" of revolution, asserting and enforcing its ideological hegemony over the varieties of resistance to forms of subjection and domination. Finally, it is perhaps this participation in a state form of thought that explains why marxism has been able to accede to the position of "loyal opposition" to the dominant forms of knowledge within the academic and political institutions of the bourgeois society it condemns.[12]

It is clear, in any case, that marxism is inhabited by deeply rooted intellectual resistance to the idea of a nomadic social theory, pluralistic and deterritorialized. This is not just a matter of affective attachment to the tradition or the idea of being a marxist, although this certainly plays a part. There are also a number of theoretical figures that serve to block the enthusiasm for radical alternatives and maintain the preeminence of a certain style of marxist thought. These not only render impossible the kind of intellectual strategy in relation to marxism that is evident in the work of Deleuze and Foucault, but they determine the forms of intellectual response to any such novel approaches. In the remainder of this paper I want to analyze two of the principle apparatuses of intellectual capture prevalent within marxism.

Unitarian Epistemology

One of the ways in which marxism's position as the "master discourse" of human emancipation is maintained is by the tacit privileging of its own perspective in debates with others. Where they are not condemned for failing to respect marxist criteria or assumptions, the positions of feminists, black activists, or environmentalists are reinterpreted in marxist terms, their political and theoretical priorities reordered according to marxism's own causal hierarchy. From the standpoint of those who do not share the commitment to marxism, this is a completely circular process of argument. It is, nevertheless, a powerful technique for enforcing adherence to the faith, commonly deployed, for example, against feminists who take the social relations of patriarchy, rather than the social relations of capitalism, as their analytic point of departure. The possibility that both kinds of explanation together might enrich our understanding of society is not entertained: "For historical materialism, causal pluralism cannot be supported."[13]

The rationale for this exclusion of non-marxist perspectives does not lie in historical materialism so much as in a certain meta-theoretical assumption about knowledge. This is the idea that if a given theory provides knowledge of the social field, then no different set of concepts may also provide knowledge of that field, or if they can, it is only to the extent that they are consistent with the prior theory. Knowledge (or science) properly so-called is necessarily unique. Marxism has always tended to adopt unitarian views of knowledge and truth, whether of an empiricist or a historicist kind. Whether it is presented as an adequate representation of reality or as the authentic worldview of the class destined to universality, the effect is the same: to ensure that there is only *one* true science of history. In the recent history of marxism, Althusser stands out for his attempt to develop an epistemology that is neither empiricist nor historicist. Yet he still retains the idea that there is but a unique science of history, presented in the guise of a metaphor: there is only one continent of history and it was discovered by Marx. This is the basis for his hard-and-fast distinction between science and ideology, and for the particularly dogmatic form of criticism performed on the basis of that demarcation criterion.

So long as the uniqueness assumption is retained, however, quite different epistemological theories may underwrite the same type of criticism. For example, Callinicos defends a popperian conception of "objective knowledge," by which he means theoretical discourse that corresponds to reality. The true theory, on this view, is necessarily unique since it is defined by the univocal relation of correspondence supposed to obtain between it and reality. Callinicos's polemical responses to the theories of micropower and desire then illustrate the form of criticism. His judgments of the non-representationalist as well as non-marxist positions of Foucault and Deleuze are made from within the framework of his own representationalist and marxist assumptions, since his conception of theoretical debate is the familiar marxist one of struggle between two competing positions. The possibility of partial and limited claims is not admitted, nor is the idea of a plurality of truths. Since there can only be one truth, and since all claims are equally totalizing, the positions must be mutually exclusive. Debate as to their relative merits is thus ruled by the logic of exclusive disjunction: revolution *or* reform, relations of power *or* relations of production, and so on. Callinicos thus shares with many marxists a monoperspectivism that turns all theoretical difference into theoretical antagonism. Any attempt to theorize the social field in non-marxist terms is apt to be considered a threat, no matter how much it might otherwise owe to the work of Marx.

Deleuze and Foucault, by contrast, practice a perspectivism that occupies an altogether different epistemological space from that occupied by the defenders of objective knowledge. Theirs is a thoroughgoing relativism that allows for the plurality of truths. As a result, they view their own theories as necessarily limited in scope and not exclusive of alternatives. As Francois Ewald comments, "the rule of a perspective is that it not be unique, nor opposed to other perspectives. Every adoption of a perspective is inscribed in the relativity of its own point of view."[14] This leads to a quite different practice of criticism. Since it does not impose the demand for unity and consistency across the entire theoretical domain, it allows for the possibility of nonantagonistic theoretical difference. This does not mean that criticism becomes impossible, but it does show certain kinds of criticism to be futile, notably the kind that simply denounces one set of principles from the standpoint of another set.

To the extent that it is combined with a unitarian conception of knowledge, marxism is inhabited by an epistemological conservatism, unable to tolerate radical perspectives that are not based upon the determining role of the relations of production. This inhibits the proliferation of alternatives, excluding not only the perspectives of power and desire, but also the very idea of an autonomous feminist theory. However, historical materialism may be detached from this conception of knowledge and this practice of criticism. Aronowitz points to the work of Adorno, for example, as opposing the fundamental categories of Hegelian logic with the idea of a *negative* dialectic that would "insist on difference as an ineluctable feature of reality."[15] Moreover, Aronowitz himself argues for the rejection of marxism's monocausal conception of history in favor of a pluralistic approach that would allow for a multiplicity of determinations. Only such an open-ended conception, he argues, can enable us to take seriously the independence of those structures of determination that underlie the struggles of the autonomous social movements.[16] On this point, both Adorno's work and Aronowitz's own recommendations converge with the views of the post-structuralists. As well as a philosophical debt to Nietzsche, they share the rejection of the unitary and totalizing conception of knowledge.

The Position of the Totality

The second, powerful figure of reterritorialization that haunts marxism, and that may even affect those sympathetic to the movements beyond it, is the injunction to adopt the point of view of the totality. This will to totalize takes a variety of forms. Typically, it enjoins us to address society as a whole and is accompanied by a commitment to a unitary project of emancipation that may leave no room for the specific, limited concerns of "marginal" social movements. Alternatively, it may be applied to the dispersion of political subjects, calling for their recombination into a single, totalizing subject.

Thus, it is often argued that autonomous movements may have a limited effectivity, serving to put new forms of resistance onto political agendas or into public discourse, but that change in the social conditions that underlie oppression can occur only as the result of a global movement. *Revolutionary* social change, because it affects the interests of a variety of oppressed groups and must confront the power of ruling interests, requires the formation of a broadly based coalition. On this basis, Hilary Wainwright argues for a twofold process of totalization; first, there needs to be "a common program of political and social change, meeting the needs of all oppressed groups"; and second, these different sources of social strength need to be drawn together so as to pitch their combined "popular power against the existing state."[17]

The same will to totalize may be seen to operate in Aronowitz's discussion of the limits of historical materialism. Despite his overall sympathy for the concerns of the autonomous social movements, his discussion is conducted throughout on the assumption that these movements must, if they are to be effective, unite in a new "counterhegemonic bloc." Despite his willingness to abandon many of the core doctrines of historical materialism, he retains the ideal of a totalizing emancipatory project. The result is a political program that remains profoundly marxist in outlook, if not in doctrine: a new utopianism within which marxism remains the "moment of anti-capitalism in the general movement against all forms of domination and hierarchy."[18]

There are, however, good political reasons for rejecting the suggestion that the only finality that gives sense to these new social movements is their alliance in a counterhegemonic front. The major premise of the argument for this is demonstrably false: change in existing social relations does not have to be mediated by the totality. The conditions that sustain oppression can be altered piecemeal. The relationship of particular groups to the relations of production, if not the relations themselves, can be altered locally. For example, the campaign for land rights conducted by Australian aborigines in recent years, through legal and political channels as well as by direct action, has resulted in the restitution of land to aboriginal communities, enabling them to produce means of subsistence as well as commodities. Similarly, much recent feminist political activity can be seen as a guerilla campaign waged against various manifestations of the systematic oppression of women in male-dominated society, often with significant local results. For example, a Sydney group called Freedom for Women Behind Bars fought for several years for the release from prison of women who killed their husbands in response to domestic violence. They succeeded not only in having individual women released but in focusing public attention on this particularly brutal aspect of the social relations of patriarchy and in bringing about changes in the law.

There are many more examples, and they all show that immediate changes in the conditions of sexual, racial, and class domination are possible. Such changes are not only worthwhile in themselves, but they may also contribute in various ways to the larger process of breaking down existing forms of institutionalized oppression. It is never easy to predict where the fault-lines of a given conjuncture lie, or from where might come the lines of flight that destabilize an entire social system. Marxism has been notoriously unsuccessful in predicting the potential for global effectivity of such things as the student movement or antiwar protests. For all these reasons, we should perhaps argue not for moving beyond the fragments toward the global politics of a new alliance but for multiplying the fragmentary effects of such local campaigns.

The point here is not to deny that the perspective of the totality is an important vector of political calculation but to deny that it is the only one. Of course, the global balance of social forces is important; even groups such as those just mentioned must take account of it in their specific struggles. Not that the effectivity of these social movements should be limited to questions of legislation, state apparatuses of the social relations of production. Since feminist, ecological, and racial liberation movements only exist insofar as they assemble energies and desires directed at changing people's lives, they are capable of effects on many fronts: they may contribute to the creation of new aesthetic and cultural forms or to the development of new ethics that are inseparable from new forms of subjectivity. Whether or not such possibilities are realized may depend, for example, on the degree to which the political apparatus proper allows for the expression of these desires.[19] None of this, however, should mislead us into seeing politics only in global, molar terms. On the contrary, it demonstrates the no less important need to defend a space for more immediate, molecular forms of political action.

The privilege attached to the totalizing perspective also needs to be resisted on the level of theory, where it has analogous effects to those in

131

the domain of political judgment. To return to Aronowitz's discussion, the political project of a new alliance also informs his analysis of the theoretical perspectives implied by these movements. His account of their objectives is also directed at finding a level at which they are on common ground. Since marxism is no longer permitted the role of "master discourse" of counterhegemony, Aronowitz looks for some other objective basis for the desired unity. His solution is to follow Adorno and Horkheimer in seeking to ground patriarchy, racism, sexual oppression, and the destruction of the environment in the exploitative attitude toward nature, where this is taken to include both external nature and internal, human nature. Thus, he proposes as the theoretical basis for the new global political project the idea of a new relationship to nature.[20]

This attempt to make the domination of nature the archimedean point for social criticism remains unconvincing in several areas. For example, it relies on a repression hypothesis in regard to human sexual nature, which both Lacan and Foucault have given us reason to doubt. More important, however, it is the very project that should be questioned. This is a matter of elaborating a unified object of historical understanding and political struggle that would fulfill the same function as the "totality in thought" formerly provided by marxism. Ultimately, this amounts to a refusal to accept the possibility of difference and discontinuity at the heart of human history, and a corresponding refusal to allow that there can be irreducibly different theoretical perspectives, each in its own way critical of existing social reality. It is the refusal to accept, for example, that patriarchy may be a system of oppression quite distinct from that imposed by capital; one that may intersect with capital but cannot be subordinated to it or subsumed along with it under a more profound social pathology. The conception of theory appropriate to the independent aims of the new social movements is one that can allow conceptual autonomy to the objects of their contestation. Accepting the inevitability of difference requires a deterritorialized conception of the theoretical field, such that a plurality of theoretical objects is possible. This is what Deleuze has called a "nomadic conception of thought": the theoretical domain conceived as a milieu, rather than a territory, within which we may assemble and deploy whatever kinds of theoretical apparatus may prove useful, or necessary, to the enterprise in which we are engaged.

The refusal of difference in theory implies an assumption of homogeneity that is often nothing more than the effect of one perspective having adopted for itself the position of the totality. To the extent that marxism takes up this position, defining the object of all social theory, it imposes its own homogeneity and territoriality upon the entire domain of political analysis. Conceived of in this manner, marxism allows other accounts only to the extent that they can be recoded in marxism's own terms. Thus, it is often argued that Foucault's microphysics of power must be situated within the broader perspective of historical materialism, since, of the two, only the latter deals with society as a whole. It is suggested that it is a theoretical as well as a political weakness in Foucault's account that he does not relate history as understood in terms of power to the history of class struggle.[21] It is as though apparatuses and techniques of power can only be properly understood, or be proper objects of political contestation, to the extent that they can be located within a totalizing perspective.

The political aspect of this argument has already been dealt with above. At the level of theory, the objection is no more convincing. First, it begs the question against someone who eschews the totalizing position. The appeal to the social totality thus serves to privilege a particular kind of historical explanation, that of marxism. Second, Foucault's own explanation of the emergence of the prison as the dominant mode of punishment might just as well be taken as a refutation of the implicit claim that historical explanation must proceed by reference to a global theory. This explanation works by redescribing this event in the context of the social expansion of the techniques of disciplinary power. He defines the birth of the prison as an *event* in the terms of a rich conceptual and empirical apparatus constructed around the notion of micropower. This is the theoretical "plane of consistency" on which his account operates. No explanation does more than this, nor are there any ultimate standards of adequacy over and above the effects of intelligibility that are produced. There are, of course, as I suggested earlier, external reasons why we should prefer some kinds of explanation to others.

We need to distinguish between the universalizability of a perspective and the sense in which it may be called "totalizing." A political or theoretical perspective is universalizable to the extent that it can be applied to the whole range of social phenomena. Feminism, for example, is a universalizable perspective, applicable to all aspects of social policy: military strategy and foreign policy are no less legitimate objects of feminist concern than child-care, as a number of British women have recently demonstrated. Foucault's conception of the social field as an acentered domain of power relations is also universalizable in this sense. While it does not claim to exhaust the range of possible kinds of analysis, nor to exclude other perspectives, it may nevertheless be applied to all spheres of social activity. Similar remarks could be made about the deleuzean perspective based on desire: commerce, no less than the cinema, involves the assemblage and operation of desire.

A perspective is "of the totality" in a quite different sense to the extent that it purports to stand outside and oversee the different analyses of particular theories or to regulate the conflicting demands of particular social movements. Here, in the case of political perspectives, it is the social totality and its government that is at issue. The injunction to adopt a global view, even if it is initially only in respect of the conflicting needs of other oppressed groups, is ultimately the injunction to *govern* a multiplicity of interests. The position of the totality is the position of power, the perspective of the state whose duty it is to resolve conflicting interests, establish priorities, and institute hierarchies. This is undoubtedly an important function, even necessary in some situations. However, it expresses a different interest to that of a participant in a minority or specific-issue movement. This is why the injunction to adopt the position of the totality must be resisted from the point of view of these social movements; not because the position of the totality is in itself illegitimate, but simply because it is a different position. The specificity and irreducibility of the minority position have to be defended against all attempts to abolish that difference. This is hardly a novel assertion. In practice, autonomous movements do resist the pressure to be subsumed into larger strategic unities, as well as the demand to justify their concerns in terms of a totalizing theory. What lags behind is the theoretical recognition of the minority position, of the right to hold a limited and partial perspective.[22]

In the realm of theory, the position of the totality determines the typical perspective of the philosopher. Philosophy pretends to universality, even when its concerns are most particular, providing the theoretical foundations for existing orders of temporal power. To the extent that it has been historically constituted as a state form in thought, philosophy has been concerned to legislate, to draw lines of demarcation, and to establish hierarchies within discourse. The real alternative is not the position of the mythical Other of state philosophy, the relativist for whom all distinction is impossible and nothing is any better than anything else, but that of the nomad—not so much the member of a tribe as an activist in a movement, a militant on behalf of an avowedly partial perspective. Above all, it is the relation to theoretical space that is not the same.[23]

Marxism has a tendency to straddle these two positions, speaking now against the bourgeoisie as the representative of the economically exploited proletariat, now against the localized concerns of the autonomous movements from its own global, scientific perspective. The extent to which it currently adopts the latter position may be a measure of how much marxists aspire to the perspective of the state. Marxism, however, can survive the abandonment of the state perspective. It is, rather, the philosophical framework for certain forms of argument that would be lost. Detaching marxism from the position of the totality and the unitarian conception of knowledge would render inappropriate some of the discursive means by which marxists often defend the superiority of their approach over other perspectives. What would be gained is a deterritorialized conception of the theoretical field, a precondition for the acceptance of plurality and the practice of an intellectual nomadism. Such an attitude toward theory is already implicit in some of the positions that have been put to this conference. If, as Aronowitz suggests, there is no normal science, then we are left with a plurality of not necessarily competing, critical theories. If, as Laclau suggests, society is an impossible object, then there is no reason to expect that it could be encompassed within a single, closed theoretical system. We are left with an open-ended and pragmatic attitude, which need not deny the utility of marxist analyses in particular cases, but which does imply that the question of whether or not one remains marxist is of absolutely no importance.

Notes

1   See especially Stanley Aronowitz, *The Crisis in Historical Materialism* (New York: Praeger, 1981); Alex Callinicos, *Is There a Future for Marxism?* (London: Macmillan, 1982); Russell Jacoby, *Dialectic of Defeat* (Cambridge: Cambridge University Press, 1981). Barry Smart, *Foucault, Marxism and Critique* (London: Routledge and Kegan Paul, 1983), discusses much of this literature and the relationship of Foucault's work to contemporary marxism. There are also many articles on this theme, beginning with Althusser's address to the II Manifesto conference (1977), reprinted in *Power and Revolution in Societies* (London: Ink Links, 1979). Cf. P. Sweezy, "A Crisis in Marxian Theory," *Monthly Review*, 31:2 (1979); E. Altvater and O. Kallscheur, "Socialist Politics and the Crisis in Marxism," *The Socialist Register* (1979).

2   Ernesto Laclau and Chantal Mouffe, "Socialist Strategy—Where Next?" *Marxism Today*, 25:1 (1981).

Paul Patton

3   Callinicos, p. 3.

4   Callinicos, p. iii.

5   *Mille Plateaux* (Paris: Editions Minuit, 1980). The introduction, "Rhizome," appears in Deleuze and Guattari, *On the Line* (New York: Semiotext[e], 1983). An earlier version, published separately, is translated in *Ideology and Consciousness*, 8 (1981).

6   Notably Mia Campioni and Elizabeth Gross, "Love's Labours Lost: Marxism and Feminism," in *Beyond Marxism? Interventions after Marx*, ed. Judith Allen and Paul Patton (Sydney: Intervention Publications, 1983). A clear case for the methodological and political importance of an autonomous feminist theory was put forth by Christine Delphy in "Pour un feminism materialiste," in *L'Arc*, 61:6 (1975), an issue devoted to Simone de Beauvoir.

7   Callinicos, chap. 8.

8   Callinicos, pp. 160-62.

9   *Anti-Oedipus* (New York: Viking Press, 1977), pt. 3, secs. 9, 10. In *Mille Plateaux*, the authors insist on the nonmetaphorical character of this comparison: "It is the real characteristics of axiomatic systems which enable one to say that capitalism and current politics are literally a system of axioms" (pp. 576-77).

10   *On the Line*, p. 3; a slightly different rendering of the same passage is given in *Ideology and Consciousness*, 8, p. 50.

11   Andre Glucksmann, *La cuisiniere et le mangeur d'hommes* (Paris: Seuil, 1975).

12   See *The Left Academy*, ed. B. Ollman and E. Vernoff (New York: McGraw-Hill, 1982).

13   Gregor McLennan, *Marxism and the Methodologies of History* (London: New Left Books, 1981), p. 233. For examples of this kind of response to non-marxist feminism, see Michèle Barrett, *Women's Oppression Today* (London: New Left Books, 1980), and the discussion in Judith Allen, "Marxism and the Man Question: Some Implications of the Patriarchy Debate," in *Beyond Marxism? Interventions after Marx*.

14   Francois Ewald, "Anatomie et corps politiques," *Critique*, 343 (1975), p. 1246.

15   Aronowitz, p. 26.

16   Aronowitz, pp. 59-60.

17   Sheila Rowbotham, Lynne Segal, and Hilary Wainwright, *Beyond the Fragments: Feminism and the Making of Socialism* (London: Merlin Press, 1980), p. 5. A similar argument is developed in the concluding passages of the article by Laclau and Mouffe (see note 2).

18   Callinicos, p. 133.

19   Compare the explanation offered for the relative weakness of the autonomous social movements in France and the strength of the extrapolitical opposition in West Germany in A. Touraine, "State and Social Forces in Socialist France," *Telos*, 55 (1983). The vitality of the German "scene" is evident in *The German Issue*, 4:2 (1982).

20   In a more recent article, Aronowitz continues to campaign for a "social and cultural left" unified at the most general level by its challenge to "the capitalist domination of nature." The prospects for such a "social ecology" movement, however, are more circumspectly expressed. See Stanley Aronowitz, "Socialism and Beyond: Remaking the American Left, Pt. I," *Socialist Review*, 69 (1983).

21   Stuart Hall raised an objection of this kind in his opening night address to this conference, arguing for the importance of a global analysis of hegemony, where this is understood as the punctual alignment of social forces in a given conjuncture. It is not clear that he needed to do this, since pointing to specific connections between, say, the reconstitution of social relations such that late capitalism can survive in Britian and the reinforcement of patriarchy does not require any systematic homogeneity between these two objects. For a classic example of this kind of response to Foucault, see Nicos Poulantzas, *State, Power, Socialism* (London: New Left Books, 1980), pp. 67-68.

22   This is evident in Gerard Raulet, "The Agony of Marxism and the Victory of the Left," *Telos*, 55 (1983), where in the context of arguing for the need for a new political rationality as part of a process of resocialization, it is asserted that, "in contrast to the dominant modality of consensus which only gives us a pseudo-consensus, both unfree and manipulated, a new political culture is needed which will develop a totalizing strategy that takes differences as its starting point. This strategy must be a totalizing one because the new rationality—a non-reductive rationality—can no longer tolerate a purely dualistic mode of existence which juxtaposes technical rationality and traditional symbols" (p. 177).

23   An account of modern philosophy as a state form is given in Richard Rorty, *Philosophy and the Mirror of Nature* (Princeton: Princeton University Press, 1979). Paul Feyerabend, in a recent discussion of the relationship between theory and practice, distinguishes between

the position of participant and that of observer in relation to any well articulated practice, whether it be artistic, political, or ecclesiastical. In the philosophy of science, this distinction covers the difference between the philosopher and the practicing scientist. Much of the force of Feyerabend's attack on theories of scientific method rests upon his appeal to the position of participant. He is, of course, too kind to the philosophers in describing their position as merely that of observers who only want to know what is going on. See Paul Feyerabend, *Science in a Free Society* (London: New Left Books, 1978), pp. 18-19.

Discussion

Question (Peter Rose)

Don't you think we need a theoretical and strategic basis for creating linkages between different progressive movements? If they are left in constant isolation and nomadism, they are susceptible to various kinds of co-optation and differentiation that may not ultimately be progressive. In fact, without some common ground, what basis is there for judging a particular movement to be progressive?

Patton

I was not rejecting any attempt to find a common ground but rather the claim of certain totalizing perspectives to define the only possible form of coding for these new social movements. Certainly one of the consequences of the view of micropolitics that I alluded to as a political strategy would be to find and encourage productive and broadly effective connections between these movements. The example that I referred to in passing—the interest of certain British women in peace and antinuclear movements—seems to me a very good example of the connection between two specific concerns but one that doesn't require any particular global political framework.

Question (Michael Ryan)

I would like to pose three questions. First, it strikes me that you do an injustice to your own conceptual system when you make such a totalized monolith out of Marxism. There is no one thing called Marxism. There are just different attitudes toward the tradition. Callinicos represents a Euro-communist theorizing that many of us don't identify with. And this is not just a matter of naming, because it has to do with your disavowal of traditional economism. After all, these movements are related, and one of the moments of articulation is the economic. My second question concerns your use of "the nomadic," which strikes me as extremely romantic, and it has resonances with a masculine ideology of a culture of flight perhaps best captured in Kerouac. Finally, I wonder if there is not a stronger basis for the politics you are advocating, namely, that the molar is always molecular.

Patton

First, my characterization of marxism was quite intentionally polemical. And I tried to make that clear by suggesting that I was talking about certain figures, rhetorical figures, figures of thought that inhabit marxist discourse. In a sense, the central point of my paper wasn't concerned with marxist conceptions of politics but rather with the conception of theory within which particular political and theoretical prescriptions are offered and carried out. I was trying to unsettle that totalizing conception of theory, and that by no means excludes the possibility of other uses and of other kinds of marxist theory.

Second, my use of the metaphor of the nomad, like Deleuze and Guattari's use of the "schizo" (as in schizoanalysis) in *Anti-Oedipus,* is not an appeal to the real individuals or communities that are associated with the name. In both cases the term is used to create an abstract figure which can be juxtaposed to other figures. Thus, the schizo is opposed to the paranoid pole of desire; the nomad is opposed to the social organizational model of the state and sedentary forms of organization. So I don't think it is quite as much a romantic flight from the conditions of metropolitan culture as it might appear. You are also quite right to point out that the molecular and the nomadic cannot, in reality, be separated from the molar and the sedentary, from the state form. The importance of the distinction, however, is its ability to provide two clear-cut, identifiable, opposing poles for political organization, for conceptions of theory, even for an approach to literary texts, forms of collective assemblage of desire. It is that setting up of the two opposing poles that seems to me important for the recasting of the terms in which we think about the field of political analysis and other things.

Comment (Nancy Fraser)

I disagree on a number of points on the question of the relation of theory and practice. I want to defend a certain kind of totalizing theory by making a sharper distinction than you do between theory and practice. I do this not to defend traditional Marxism because, ironically, traditional Marxism too closely connects them in a way somewhat homologous with your position. Let me put it this way: You seem to want to argue directly from a style of theorizing to the kind of politics that follow from it. You claim that totalizing, monocausal, empirical theories somehow necessarily lead to Stalinist-Leninist centralized forms of political practice, and that if we stand back from such theoretical practices, we are guaranteed a democratic, pluralistic political practice. It seems to me that theory and practice don't have that kind of close connection. One way I might get at this is to raise a hypothetical question: What if it should turn out that some monocausal, empirical theory of society could actually have a real explanatory power in accounting for more phenomena than other available theories? You seem to say we can't choose that style of theorizing because the politics are bad. It is logically conceivable that such a theory might, in fact, be able to tell us things and that we would still have all kinds of political choices. Our political responses are not determined by the style of our theorizing in that close way. Let me put it another way: I think there are at least three kinds of critical theorizing that we need. First, an empirical, critical theory of what is happening in contemporary society, of where the tendencies for crisis are, of what the possibilities for change are. This should be as absolutely broad and as explanatorily powerful as we can make it. Second, we need the kind of normative political theory that Chantal Mouffe talked about: theorizing about what kinds of institutions we want to guarantee plurality and difference and nomadism and all those things you want—that is a political question. And finally, we need a critique of ideology of the sort that Deleuze, Foucault, and Derrida have been developing. In other words, I want to detotalize critical theory in order to argue that some parts should be as totalized as possible.

Patton

The question of the relationship between theory and practice is the important one, and it can be taken up in a variety of ways. I wasn't talking about the political consequences that flow from certain kinds of theory—the usual sense in which marxist discussions of the relationship are carried on. I was, rather, treating them, insofar as they can be treated as distinct domains, on the same plane and talking about a homology between a politics of theory and political practice. In that sense, what I am objecting to in a style of theorizing are the effects that it has on our ability to theorize. In particular, I am objecting to the way in which certain conceptions of the nature of theory impose limitations, close out the possibility of alternative theorizations. (One only has to look at the debates between marxists, marxist-feminists, and other kinds of feminists to see how it operates.) It is that politics of theory that was my concern.

And I agree with your plea for a certain kind of totality and the need for an understanding of society as a whole. The distinction I made between the two senses in which one can say that a perspective is totalizing was directed in part at that, since the kind of totalization I was objecting to was not the totalizing of a powerful, universalizable general theory (although it is a further question of how likely it is that we would ever find a theory that would apply to social phenomena in general). I was objecting to the view that if we have a powerful general theory like that, then there is no need to encourage alternatives; that, indeed, the fact of its being powerful and strongly explanatory should be taken as an argument against the elaboration of alternatives. In that sense, the politics of theory that I am defending is very close to the kind of epistemological pluralism that Feyerabend defends. And my response to your hypothetical question—What would we do if we had such a powerful theory?—would be the same as Feyerabend's: we should still encourage the search for alternatives because it is only on that basis that criticism is possible. Indeed, a society in which one dominant mode of explanation or theoretical form is imposed, taught, and funded for research is undemocratic in the realm of ideas.

A. Belden Fields

In Defense of Political Economy and Systemic Analysis: A Critique of Prevailing Theoretical Approaches to the New Social Movements

Both local resistances and new social movements must come to an understanding of the *systemic* impediments to their emancipatory projects. They must also build alliances with other groups if they are to work toward a more humane world.

Much of the writing done by contemporary theorists who consider themselves to be Marxist or neo-Marxist is a self-conscious reaction against either political economy as it has been traditionally understood or systemic analysis of any nature. The root of the reaction is twofold: (a) the proletariat has not served as an agency for change in the capitalist industrialized countries in which Marx anticipated the revolution; (b) where revolutions have taken place under the banner of Marxism, at least in the Eastern European context, party and state have assumed enormous power over individuals and the relations of production bear some striking similarities to those in the West. In both instances it is difficult for these theorists to find revolutionary subjects, the obvious precondition for basic change.

The theoretical dispute of the sixties between Marxist humanists and structural Marxists did not offer much in terms of theories of agency or the constitution of revolutionary subjects. The first school, appearing after the distribution of Marx's *1844 Manuscripts* in the West, was too abstractly philosophical. It sought to establish that Marx indeed had a vision of "man" that was something more than a reflection of the mode of production at any given historical juncture. The structuralist response, particularly from the pen of Louis Althusser, rejected any such essentialist notion; however, it appeared as abstract as the humanist formulation in that it left little room for a revolutionary subject. The subject in capitalist society was merely a product of ideology. The various structural levels—ideology, politics, economy—seemed rigidly fixed vis-à-vis individuals, the concept of overdetermination among structures notwithstanding. If the Marxist humanists appeared to be guilty of a kind of essentialist moralism, the reaction they produced in the form of Althusserian structuralism appeared to be characterized by a scientistic mode of exposition that left little more room for social change than the functionalist and cybernetic approaches offered by non-Marxist social scientists.

Then along came the "events" of 1968 in France! The world of Marxist and neo-Marxist theorizing would never be the same again. Acting subjects brought the productive, distributive, and service capabilities of a major Western capitalist nation to a halt for a substantial period of time. Moreover, after 1968, one saw in France an increasing radicalization and growth of groups that were confronting the state over a wide area of concerns.

I want to argue that the perceptions of what happened in 1968 and after in France were very selective. Some focused on the students rising up against the educational structures and the subsequent challenge to all kinds of hierarchical structures by those subjected to them. Others, particularly Marxist revolutionary groups in France, focused more on the participation of workers in the "events" and the subsequent increase in worker militancy. Indeed, if one only focuses on the student role, one is unlikely to appreciate fully the facts that between eight and nine million workers engaged in a general strike, many taking over their plants, and that even one of the labor "hierarchies," the Confédération Française Démocratique du Travail, was supportive of the actions of the students and workers.[1] If the students supplied the necessary catalyst for the workers, the workers supplied a shielding action that limited the regime's responsive possibilities.

Similarly, in the 1970s some focused on the proliferation of movements of nonworkers while others focused on the actions of workers. After 1968, worker militancy showed a marked increase over what it had been prior to the events of that year. Not only did the number of strike actions and working days lost increase, but there was also a qualitative escalation in tactics. Plant occupations and holding bosses hostage became a much more common occurrence. Moreover, two sectors of the working population that were among the most vulnerable now became among the most assertive: women workers and immigrant workers from North Africa, particularly the Algerians.

One finds the same kind of selective attentiveness in the United States. Some writers have been very attentive to the feminist movement, the environmental movement, the peace movement, the gay movement, and so on—in sum, to movements that are to a great extent middle-class movements. Relatively ignored have been the struggles of working people in the 1970s, such as the struggles of Farah pants workers, the struggles of farm workers, and the struggles of southern textile workers. Once again, these were struggles that involved primarily women and minority workers. Like many of the struggles in France, they were struggles at the site of production and indicated clear systemic linkages between the structures of capitalism, racism, and patriarchy.

The conceptualization of "new social movements," however, contained strong impulses to react against structuralism by deconstructing systemic analysis and to dichotomize between struggles of workers in which economic/material concerns are explicitly articulated and concerns of other largely middle-class groups that seem to have no material implications because they are not articulated. Since systemic analysis has been undercut, if the "discourse" of the actors is not a materialist or economic one, then there is no way to make the connection.

If the proletariat has failed the revolutionary challenge, some have argued, maybe the new force for basic change could now be the new social movements. After all, if the students could force the state to a stand-off in 1968, why could not a plurality of opposition groups force changes in the social and political sites of power? Perhaps it would not be a cen-

A. Belden Fields

tralized explosion beginning in the capital (e.g., Paris, the center of state sovereignty) this time. Perhaps it would be more amorphous, less noticeable to the nonparticipants, but much more enduring.

I have generalized enough. I now want to turn to four theorists who have, in one way or another and to a greater or lesser extent, contributed to what I regard as the unfortunate tendencies of deconstructing systemic analysis and avoiding the implications for political economy of many struggles that seem to be about something else.

Michel Foucault

Much of the subsequent writing regarding new social movements spins off from the thinking of Michel Foucault. Foucault was a teacher in the university system the students were revolting against. The revolt of 1968 was suggestive to Foucault in his attempt to challenge Althusser's structuralism and to offer a competing conception of power from which he criticized virtually all observable political action that was not spontaneous. I do not think it inaccurate to refer to Foucault's political orientation as anarchist.

Foucault's practical problem is an important one: in his words, "to imagine another system is to extend our participation in the present system."[2] The problem with utopian revolutionary theories, including Marxism, in Foucault's view, is that they seem inevitably to use the techniques of the present system (armies, parties, courts, etc.) in order to bring about social transformation. This frustrates the utopian project itself; witness the repressiveness of the Soviet Union. For Foucault, this cannot be fully explained either by the "backward" state of Russia when the revolution took place or by the personality of Stalin. The above, more basic theoretical problem was at work.

Foucault's resolution is to take a second look at the phenomenon of power. He penetrates through the almost exclusive focus on "state power," "sovereignty," and "legality." For Foucault, we need to consider power as something that is diffused throughout society, something that circulates, something about which it is often impossible to say that it circulates exclusively in so-and-so's hands.

Foucault directs us to the extremities, to the sites where power is exercised on people in concrete experiences. He seeks to break through the abstraction of the state and to reach down to the concrete level of human interaction where power is really and visibly exerted (e.g., the prison). The social interactions at these sites are informed by disciplinary knowledges that provide techniques (e.g., modern prisons are inspired by Bentham's scientific penology—the invention of the Panopticon—and by psychiatry—the prison psychiatrist). Schools, mental institutions, and so on, are decentered or regional areas in which control is exercised and conformity demanded—and obtained. Foucault's descriptions of such institutions remind one of Frederick Wiseman's films.

"Discourse" is defined by Foucault as "the group of statements that belong to a single system of formation."[3] An example would be psychiatric discourse. It is through discourse that disciplines articulate their knowledge; and there is an integral relationship between power and knowledge that no utopian scheme can overcome.[4] But not all domains are discursive. If systems of knowledge are examples of discursive formations, "institutions, political events, economic practices and processes" are con-

143

sidered by Foucault to be "nondiscursive domains."[5] The relationship between the discursive and the nondiscursive must be established by investigation.

Foucault's own resolution is less than satisfactory. On the one hand, he has us focusing on power as it is manipulated at the extremities by anonymous and changing agents. This power grew up piecemeal, as a result of new disciplinary advances and techniques; and it grew from the bottom up. No identifiable group or individual decided to implement it "so as to further their interests or facilitate their utilization of the social body."[6] *Local* conditions and *particular* needs shaped power in piecemeal fashion, "prior to any class strategy."[7]

On the other hand, Foucault tells us, these decentered regions of power with their own discourses and techniques do, indeed, serve the interests of capitalism: "power is exercised the way it is in order to maintain capitalist exploitation."[8] In one text he states: "One must . . . conduct an *ascending* analysis of power, starting, that is, from its infinitesimal mechanisms, which each have their own history, their own trajectory, their own techniques and tactics, and then see how these mechanisms of power have been—and continue to be—invested, colonized, utilized, involuted, transformed, displaced, extended, etc. by ever more general mechanisms and by forms of global domination."[9] In another text, Foucault pulls the ladder out from under us. He rejects "theory and all forms of general discourse. The need for theory is still part of the system we reject."[10] Analogous with the Maoist way of surrounding the cities from which power emanates by gaining control of the countryside, Foucault argues that we must engage "the system" "on all fronts—the university, the prisons, the domain of psychiatry—one after another since our forces are not strong enough for a simultaneous attack."[11] But we do this without any overarching or, in Foucault's word, "totalizing" theory.

How can we account for the larger and particularly nondiscursive structures Foucault admits exist? We do not have to, theoretically. "The system" does the work for us. In the face of this multifronted attack at the peripheries, "the system it opposes, as well as the power exercised through the system, supplies its unity."[12] Foucault's concern over utopian theories becoming perverted in action thus leads to a rejection of any kind of holistic systemic analysis, but it does so without denying that the system exists or that all power ultimately serves capitalism in the present epoch. The unity of the system will reveal itself—hence no general discourse and theory are necessary. Only regional theories are permitted, the force of which comes from regional, particular, and local popular knowledges of the people subjected to institutions and discourses of power. These knowledges are anti-sciences to be uncovered by genealogical research into the history of struggles. They are presently disguised within functionalist and systematizing theory; but, again in a way that resembles a Maoist formulation, this time the "mass-line," they can be resurrected.

More encouragement yet for the possibility of change. Foucault "suggests," as a hypothesis, that "there are no relations of power without resistances."[13] He later adds, however, that "what I have said here is not 'what I think,' but often rather what I wonder whether one couldn't think."[14] In fact, strategically, Foucault leaves us with very little to hold onto. He tells us that power is amorphous, a machine in which everyone is caught up. And he finds that "against these usurpations by the disciplinary mechanisms, against this ascent of a power that is tied to scientific knowledge, we find that there is no solid recourse available to us today."[15]

Foucault had contact with a group of French activists with a Maoist-anarchist orientation, La Gauche Prolétarienne.[16] They accepted the proposition that all power worked to the advantage of capitalism (and, they added, the state) and struggled beside any group that was willing to take on the state in a violent manner. By Foucault's logic they were correct in mounting the barricades along with small shopkeepers who were protesting taxes. However, they came under severe criticism from Sartre for not analyzing the nature of the antagonism and for not understanding that the struggle being waged was in no way progressive. In Sartre's view, the revolt was a resurrection of Poujadism, the right-wing populism that was strong in France in the 1950s. The problem is, if one cannot rise above the local sites of struggle, what evaluative criteria can one apply to such struggles? If all manifestations of power serve capitalism, it does not follow that all reaction against that power is progressive.

Foucault's only critical criterion appears to be nonreplication of the forms of the present system. Thus, when the French Maoists held "trials" for wealthy people who had abused working-class victims but had been acquitted by the courts, Foucault argued that by using the forms of the courtroom, the Maoists were in fact resurrecting the bourgeois court. He was critical of any action they took that resembled party, army, or judicial systems.[17] The proper forms, according to Foucault, remained "to be discovered."[18] This, of course, leaves us without the ability to theorize generally for fear of "totalizing"; it also leaves us without any indication of *how* to struggle even at the peripheries of the system of power.

Foucault encourages the regional struggle by *groupuscules* (small groups), but he assumes no responsibility—except a negatively critical one—for developing strategies consistent with his analysis. After all is said and done, one feels that perhaps one has reread Camus twenty-five years later, a Camus who has lived through the events of 1968 and is attempting to theorize its initial spontaneous success, its inspiration for the creation of all kinds of struggling, decentralized *groupuscules,* and its inability to change fundamentally the structure of French political economy. Foucault tells us not to even think about the latter!

Jürgen Habermas

In *Legitimation Crisis,* written in 1973, Jürgen Habermas thinks a lot about the latter. In this text, Habermas is concerned about how systems learn at two levels: the cognitive/technical and the moral/practical. The cognitive/technical seems to have a life of its own, much like Foucault's disciplinary or scientific knowledges which supply the techniques for the exercise of power. However, for Habermas the normative learning process Piaget analyzes in individuals is transposed onto society as a whole. The struggle in Habermas's theory is for a rational language, for a communicative competence that is essential for the development of normative criteria. Unlike Foucault, Habermas does not shirk from systems analysis because it has been used extensively by functionalists. But he tries to create a role for rational/critical human subjects who do not simply accept the validity of what present themselves as system imperatives.

Two crucial terms for Habermas are "system" and "life-world." Systems contain mechanisms that enable them to avoid or overcome crises, which occur "when members of a society experience structural alterations as critical for continued existence and feel their social identity threatened."[19] Life-world thematizes the "normative structures (values and institutions) of a society."[20] If the concept of "system" retains the notion of equilibrium ("steering," in Habermas's terminology) from functionalist systems theory and cybernetics, life-world permits a communal critique of system requisites by rational-moral beings who establish criteria through linguistic communication. The vision is almost an Enlightenment one of people establishing moral truths through language and of limiting the claims of systems and cognitive/technical knowledge on that basis. It is both more totalizing and more optimistic than Foucault's analysis. The individual subjects, however, are communicators rather than organizers and strugglers.[21]

Foucault engaged in communication with the French Maoists, but he did not actually develop a theory of social movements, only of the sites in which they ought to operate. It is clear, however, that he favored groups or *groupuscules* that worked in a decentered fashion and with decentered analyses over groups with holistic analyses and strategies. Thus, while the structuralist Althusser remained in the Communist party, Foucault would talk with and encourage the Maoist-anarchists but not the Marxist-Leninist-Maoists, Trotskyists, or the Communist party.

In the late seventies Habermas focused directly on opposition movements in an article entitled "New Social Movements," in which he attempts to distinguish between the "old politics" that had existed before the sixties and the "new politics" that had emerged as of his writing. His general characterization of the new politics is that it "entails problems of quality of life, equality, individual self-realization, and human rights."[22] Thus, the normative-critical capacity thematized by the life-world would seem to be called into play against the cognitive/technical claims of systems. Some of the other important characteristics of the new politics follow.

1. "The new politics are not sparked by *problems of distribution,* but concern the grammar of forms of life."[23]

2. They are "a colorful mixture of groups on the periphery ... removed from the 'productivist core' of performance in late capitalist societies, those who are more sensitive to the self-destructive consequences of the growth in complexity, or who are more seriously affected by them. The bond that unifies these heterogeneous groups is the critique of growth."[24]

3. With the exception of the feminist movement, where "the struggle against patriarchal oppression and for the realization of a promise that is deeply rooted in the acknowledged universalistic foundations of morality and legality lends feminism the impetus of an offensive movement, all other movements are defensive in character." They are "movements of resistance and retreat [and] seek to *stem* or block the formal, organized spheres of action in favor of communicative structures; they do not seek to conquer new territory."[25]

4. "A critique of growth based on *environmental and peace concerns* provides the common focus. ... What sparks the protest ... is the tangible destruction of the urban environment, the destruction of the countryside by bad residential planning, industrialization and pollution, health

impairments due to side effects of civilization-destruction, pharmaceutical practices, and so forth. These are developments that visibly attack the *organic foundations of the life-world* and make one drastically conscious of criteria of livability, of inflexible limits to the deprivation of sensual-aesthetic background needs."[26]

5. "Ascribed characteristics such as sex, age, skin color, even neighborhood and religion, contribute to the establishment and delimitation of communities, the creation of sub-culturally protected communications groups which further the search for personal and collective identity. High value is placed on the particular, the provincial, small social spaces, decentralized forms of interaction and nondifferentiated public spheres. This is all intended to promote the revitalization of buried possibilities for expression and communication. Resistance to reformist intervention also belongs here. Such intervention becomes its opposite because the means of implementation run counter to the declared, social-integrative objectives."[27]

6. "The new conflicts thus arise at the seam between system and life-world." They are a reaction to the "colonization" of the life-world by the "economic and political-administrative system of action" and to the "abstraction and neutralization process by virtue of which work and public opinion have been linked to media-directed interactions in modern societies."[28]

Sociologically, the people adhering to the new politics are young, middle-class, and well educated. Workers, entrepreneurs, and the professional middle class, according to Habermas, still support the older distributive-productive kind of politics with its fear of scarcity. The actual groupings that Habermas points to as being part of this complex of new social movements, at least in the German Federal Republic, are

> the anti-nuclear and environmental movement; the peace movement (encompassing the North-South conflict); the citizens' action movement; the alternative movement (which comprises urban scenarios with squatters and alternative projects as well as communities in the country); minorities (the elderly, homosexuals, disabled people, etc.); the psychological scene with support groups and youth sects; religious fundamentalism; the tax protest movement [which he later and confusedly admits must be separated out]; parent associations' school protest; resistance to "modernist reforms"; and . . . the women's movement. Furthermore independence movements struggling for regional, linguistic, cultural, or religious autonomy are also of international significance.[29]

Despite the differences that have been pointed out between Habermas and Foucault, Habermas's view of the new social movements owes a considerable debt to Foucault. In point 1, when Habermas talks about problems of distribution, he is referring to distribution of wealth and economic resources, something that concerns adherents of the old politics. The new social movements are not concerned with that, and there would be no argument with Foucault on this point. For Foucault, the concern is with the distribution of power, not of wealth in the old politics sense. Moreover, the grammar of forms of life that Habermas refers to relates to his concept of communicative groups and, although not very well spelled out, does not seem to differ fundamentally from Foucault's contestation over discourse at the various sites of the exercise of power.

In point 2 Habermas finishes off the concern over economics by arguing that productivity is a matter of concern only in a negative sense. As with Foucault, the groups operate on the periphery of society. What pulls them together is not a critique of capitalism as a system of production and distribution; rather, it is a critique of the qualitative effects of growth as such.

In point 3, the feminist movement excepted, Habermas presents these movements as purely defensive. They do not attempt to totalize or extend their influence beyond their specific area of interest. They are localized, defensive responses against the encroachment of systems with their imperatives and cognitive/technical language. Points 4 and 5 are further elaborations on this point. What is emphasized, and is consistent with Foucault, is the notion of decentralized forms of interaction.

Point 6 entails a difference from Foucault's view. The concept of a "seam" between system and life-world suggests that there are spaces in which the economic and political-administrative system of action has not penetrated. The view seems to be that there are little fortresses in which these groups or movements live that have not yet been contaminated by the larger system. These are islands of rational communication that are attempting to hold the exterior system at bay. For Foucault, power is totally permeating. No economic and political-administrative system is theorized in Foucault, but the ubiquitous exercise of power is somehow cumulatively at the service of capitalism.

In fact, the concept of a seam between system and life-world represents a considerable conceptual shift on the part of Habermas. In *Legitimation Crisis,* life-world is a conceptual way of thematizing the moral/practical capabilities of human beings. In "New Social Movements," life-world becomes a spatial metaphor, representing areas that are being defended against encroachment by exterior systems with a different and imperialistic logic and language.

In my view, neither Foucault nor Habermas is correct on this point, but Foucault is more correct than Habermas. No space is as free from the penetration of larger systems of dominance and subordination as Habermas suggests, and no battles are as purely defensive as Habermas seems to think: all will be forced to confront the dominant systems (which Foucault seems to simultaneously recognize and refuse to consider theoretically); and each emancipatory movement will be just as defensive/offensive as any other. The dichotomy, which is never theoretically justified anyway, between a universalistic, offensive feminist movement and defensive movements protecting their own territory must fall way.

Habermas seems to seek confirmation that his ideal speech situation is a real possibility in actual little islands of life that have resisted the encroachment of systems. He gives us much more optimism than Foucault does. But the dichotomy is just too idealistic. The systems are omnipresent, the specific battles have more in common than a critique of growth, and it is always a struggle for the social movements to keep the languages straight. This is no reason for pessimistic despair. It just means that the situation facing opposition or protest social movements in late-capitalist societies is more complex than the "small is beautiful" vision Habermas suggests.

Chantal Mouffe

While there are some similarities between Habermas and Mouffe (since she has contributed an essay to this volume, I need not recount her approach), one major difference is that in Mouffe's analysis the new social movements are not purely defensive—they really do threaten the system in its totality. Moreover, Mouffe adds the very important criterion of solidarity, which is lacking in the formulations of Foucault and Habermas. We have a much clearer notion of process here than in Habermas's rather static life-world (whether one views it as a concept of rational/normative capability or as spatial metaphor). Finally, Mouffe rightly argues against the clear opposition between the working class and the new social movements, which is particularly important in Habermas's distinction between the adherents of the new politics and the old politics, a distinction he borrows from the political scientist Ronald Inglehart.[30] In all of the above, Mouffe's thinking represents an advance over that of Habermas.

There are, however, problems in Mouffe's approach, the most glaring being the privileging of discourse. She does not define discourse in her essay and thus leaves herself open to the interpretation that discourse refers to language (this point was raised in the question-and-answer period that followed her presentation). She responded to the criticism that her formulation was idealist by saying: "I understand not only speech and writing, but also a series of social practices, so discourse is not just a question of ideas."[31] Clearly, Mouffe does not want to go to the extreme of Barry Hindess and Paul Hirst, for whom discourse refers only to theory, and thus language, and is divorced from any real objects in the world.

But what, precisely, is the definition of discourse? Since Mouffe does not provide a definition, can we gain any insight by looking at the writing of her sometimes collaborator Ernesto Laclau? In one of his articles, Laclau writes:

> By "discursive" I do not mean that which refers to "text" narrowly defined, but to the ensemble of the phenomena in and through which social production of meaning takes place, an ensemble which constitutes a society as such. The discursive is not, therefore, being conceived as a level or even as a dimension of the social, but rather as being co-extensive with the social as such. This means that the discursive does not constitute a superstructure (since it is the very condition of all social practice) or, more precisely, that all social practice constitutes itself as such insofar as it produces meaning. Because there is nothing specifically social which is constituted outside the discursive, it is clear that the non-discursive is not opposed to the discursive as if it were a matter of two separate levels. His-

149

tory and society are infinite text. . . . Economic practice should thus be considered as discourse.[32]

By this definition, all social practices are discursive. A bit later on in the same article, however, Laclau makes reference to the "non-discursive conditions in which antagonism emerges."[33] If we are truly considering the social world as an ensemble of social practices and relationships, and this is precisely the advantage that the Gramscian hegemonic approach is supposed to offer over the more static structural approach, then what are we to make of these "non-discursive conditions"?

The fact is that there are social and political interactions that are clearly physical and material, and one would really have to stretch the imagination to see them as discursive, which Laclau does. He sees peasants being driven off their lands as a discursive phenomenon. While there is always a message (threat, attempted intimidation) attached to severe material and physical punishment, does it really advance us to see everything as discourse—including driving peasants off the lands, forcing them to work on large plantations at low wages, torturing and killing them when they attempt to organize? This is a material and physical chain of events that is, indeed, designed to send messages, but for the final aim of preserving a certain mode of production and the set of privileges that attaches to it. I can sympathize with Mouffe's attempt to deny a clear cleavage between the ideal and the material, between idealism and materialism, between the base and the superstructure. But I do not see how calling everything that is social "discourse" clarifies that relationship, and I fear that we are back at the sort of privileging that is objectionable to her in the base/superstructure metaphor of traditional Marxism.

The discourse that Mouffe uses, and here I mean *language,* indeed can easily be interpreted as an idealistic one. She states: "[as] soon as the principle of equality was admitted in one domain . . . the eventual questioning of all possible forms of inequality was an ineluctable consequence. Once begun, the democratic revolution had, necessarily, to undermine all forms of power and domination, whatever they might be."[34] "All positions that have been constructed as relations of domination/subordination will be deconstructed because of the subversive character of democratic discourse."[35] These are statements that beg to be read as commitments to idealism. One is tempted to ask why, if that is not how we are supposed to read such statements, this formulation is any more enlightening than Lenin's emphasis on politics and his resurrection of ideology as an important aspect of the process of politics (as opposed to Marx's completely negative view of ideology as false mental commitments at the service of dominant systems).

Mouffe's almost deterministically progressive language, the fulfillment of Tocqueville's prediction with which she begins her essay, serves to hide one of her shrewder insights. I get the feeling that these new movements are all ineluctably (a favorite word) marching toward equality and democracy. One certainly gets that impression from Habermas's treatment as well, although he admits that sometimes tax revolts can be quite reactionary. That, however, seems to be the exception for Habermas. Mouffe, on the other hand, tells us specifically that, "like the workers, these struggles are not necessarily socialist or even progressive."[36] She furthermore suggests a criterion for the assessment of how progressive a movement is, that is, its link to other struggles.[37] This is an interesting insight that ought to help us judge, for example, among various manifestations of nationalism: those that assert rights to independence, self-respect, and cultural development but respect and support such assertions on the part of others as well, as opposed to nationalistic expressions that are chauvinistic and exclusive— that is, intrinsically hostile to both internationalism and other internal claims on people's allegiances. We could, using this text, avoid the "all third-world nationalism is revolutionary" versus "all nationalism is reactionary" dichotomy that has proved to be so fruitless as Marxists have attempted to come to grips with nationalism.

The language used in the first three-quarters of Mouffe's essay lulls us into an idealist, deterministic reading that is quite at odds with the fertility of the concluding section. I find it especially interesting that in that last section the word "discourse" does not appear once. It is replaced by words such as "struggle" and "solidarity" and the contention that "capitalism as a way of life is, in fact, responsible for the numerous forms of subordination and inequality attacked by new social movements."[38]

In sum, the absence of a definition of discourse and what appear to be two different approaches to this in Laclau's work (everything social is discourse versus the existence of nondiscursive conditions that give rise to antagonism) are confusing. The "everything is discourse" approach is either literally nonsensical (at least to this writer) or is bound to lead us to a retreat to the purely theoretical domain divorced from the world of concrete reality, a retreat that we find in Hindess and Hirst's *Mode of Production and Social Formation*,[39] that preserves the worst, scientist feature of Althusserian structuralism. On the other hand, if it is admitted that there are nondiscursive conditions that give rise to antagonism, then we need to specify those in terms of systemic effects and concrete human experience, interests, and relationships. We are then no longer justified in prioritizing discourse the way Mouffe does. But we cannot have it both ways.

Paul Patton

In some senses, the least delicate of the four approaches that I shall discuss is that of Paul Patton (his essay also appears in this volume). Patton begins with a healthy skepticism of *a* Marxism so caught up in an epistemological totalization that it cannot recognize difference or particularity. (At first, he seems to argue that skepticism is intrinsic to Marxism, but toward the end of the essay he takes the contrary position.) That, of course, is an old and correct charge against some theoreticians and self-professed practitioners both in the West and in the "socialist" countries. Foucault, Habermas, Mouffe, and this writer would all agree with Patton. However, he then draws upon Foucault's diffuse theory of power but, using Deleuze's concepts of territorialization, deterritorialization, and nomadic theory, pushes his analysis and conclusions to micrologic or decentered extremes.

Like Habermas, Patton views the new social movements as defensive. They represent the principle of deterritorialization. The state, on the other hand, represents the principle of territorialization. The state is totalizing; by nature, it practices a kind of internal imperialism; it is out to "capture" the new social movements, to destroy their difference. Marxism, at least as portrayed by Patton in its concrete texts and practices, is a totalizing discourse and thus must become complicit in the state's territorializing practices—hence Marxist theorists' complicity with state academic institutions in the West and Marxists' responsibility for statist conditions in the "socialist" countries.

Patton's resolution, however, is to present us with a view of new social movements that not only reflect difference but are totally separated and isolated from one another. He even rejects the possibility of broadly based coalitions because that degree of analytically and strategically putting together the complex of power would represent an unacceptable totalization which would threaten the autonomy of each of the parts.[40] Patton writes: "The injunction to accept a global view, even if it is initially only in respect of the conflicting needs of other oppressed groups, is ultimately the injunction to *govern* a multiplicity of interests."[41]

I would submit that Patton has failed to distinguish between "difference" and total "separateness" (the latter might go by the name "alienation"). Indeed, Mouffe's concept of solidarity has gone completely by the wayside. There is no sense, in Patton's analysis, of the need to *mediate* between legitimate self-interest and the interest and needs of others at the group level. One wonders how the individuals within such groups are supposed to have social sentiments strong enough to constitute the groups—unless the groups we are talking about are not emancipatory but are simply constituted to advance a narrow self-interest of relevance only to themselves. Are we then left with a reformulation of "interest group liberalism" or, perhaps, Nozick's individualistic, libertarian utopianism?[42]

Given Patton's apparently total rejection of utopianism, I am not sure that we could even get to Nozick's position. Again, in Patton's dichotomous either/or framework—either territorialization or deterritorialization; either micrologic or macrologic; either destruction of identity or total separateness—the point is missed that an emancipatory group must to a certain extent be utopian but can be utopian without attempting to go from the present to *"the* new socialist *man."* It can, indeed, be engaged in a project for the creation of a more humane world respecting "difference." But it cannot do this unless it transcends its own boundaries, or "territory," in two ways: (1) it comes to an understanding of the systemic impediments to its project, and (2) it reaches out to other groups and engages in mutual expressions of solidarity and strategic networking.

Just as in Habermas, women get singled out regarding the restriction against universalizability: "A political or theoretical perspective is universalizable to the extent that it can be applied to the whole range of social phenomena. Feminism, for example, is a universalizable perspective, applicable to all aspects of social policy: military strategy and foreign policy are no less legitimate objects of feminist concern than child-care, as a number of British women have recently demonstrated."[43]

Are women being used here merely as an example of a universalizability that can avoid the trap of totalizing? Or, as in Habermas, is there something really different about the struggle of women than the other new social movements? If the former is true, once we indicate how other movements (e.g., those of workers and minorities) have real stakes in military strategy and foreign policy—U.S. people of color being used disproportionately as troops against people of color in Vietnam, Grenada, and Central

America; U.S. workers losing jobs to Central American countries where wages and working conditions are poor and labor unrest dealt with by final means—are we not totalizing in the sense of coming to an understanding of the systemic dynamics of structures of oppression at both the national and international levels? Is that not precisely what this use of feminism as an example invites? On the other hand, if women are exceptional, as in Habermas's formulation, one can only, once again, ask why. The criteria are just not obvious.

Patton's major contention is that "change in existing social relations does not have to be mediated by the totality. The conditions that sustain oppression can be altered piecemeal. The relationship of particular groups to the relations of production, if not the relations themselves, can be altered locally."[44] Relations of production are singled out here because he is answering Marxists, who are particularly concerned with that, not because he seems to privilege these relations.

As proof of his contention that conditions can be altered piecemeal, Patton points to empirical examples of practice. He first tells us about a case of Australian aborigines using legal and political channels as well as direct action to gain back some of their lands for subsistence farming. He then goes on to say that much feminist activity also has had "significant local results,"[45] specifically referring to a group of women in Sydney who succeeded in gaining the release of women who had killed their spouses in response to violent abuse. According to Patton, these women also secured some changes in the laws and brought public attention to this aspect of patriarchal social relations.

All of this might be true. These groups might have won some victories at the local level. However, one can just as easily find counterexamples in Western societies, especially among the poor, where such purely local attempts did not work and, in some cases, led to very costly defeats.[46] Would Patton seriously argue that blacks in the United States should have pursued purely local strategies in the civil rights campaign of the sixties? Given the distribution of power in the local southern communities, that would have been suicide.

Specifically in regard to the aboriginal people, they may well be isolated and retain the potential for agricultural self-sufficiency. But Patton is not writing at the time of Rousseau. Subsistence farming, hunting, and gathering are not the dominant modes of production. If the land claims of the aboriginal people ever posed a serious threat to the dominant mode of production, no doubt they would stand little more chance of regaining those lands than the native Americans would of reclaiming the major cities and agricultural lands of the United States. Or, take another theoretical possibility, a purely local attempt on the part of peasants in El Salvador or Guatemala to regain their land rights. This might strike one as being a ludicrous extreme. However, Central American experiences are very instructive, particularly when one examines the success of the Nicaraguan revolution, which was based upon the dual thrusts of local, usually Christian-oriented base organizations *and* the centralized FSLN. The continuing dialectic involving the relationship between local groups (both supportive and oppositional groups) and the centralized, state machinery is the most interesting aspect of that revolution and differentiates it from the Cuban case, where the revolution was won by a single, military group and the base committees were creations of the central power after the revolution.

The example of feminism is of a different order from that of Australian aborigines or landless Central American peasants. Here we are talking about the system of patriarchy reinforced by a multitude of oppressive structures. But here, as well, most grass-roots groups operating at the local level see the necessity for (1) a systemic understanding of patriarchy on the order of a systemic understanding of capitalism and the links between patriarchy and capitalism (e.g., the "family" wage; the enormous profits of the pornography industry) and (2) political networking as the expression of an understanding that while local grass-roots work is crucial, it must be part of a national and international undertaking. Totally disconnected efforts are much more likely to be either frustrated or assimilated by the dominant structures than are efforts that are part of a larger social movement.

This adds complexity. One of the most difficult tasks facing the women's movement is to determine how the concerns of first-world women can be meshed with those of third-world women. But this has a reflexive heuristic value, as a reminder that first-world women are not homogeneous—there are black, Latina, native American, Asian-Pacific, and so on, women within the local contexts of North American first-world women. System complexity comes home to the locality, penetrates right into those neighborhoods of Chicago, New York, or Los Angeles. This is also true of workers (e.g., workers from France, Algeria, and Mali in a Renault factory in Paris). What does it mean to argue for a purely local action and strategy in this world so far from a homogeneous, aboriginal community? It means the opposite of putting things together, the opposite of understanding how oppressions relate to and reinforce each other. It not only means difference, for one can accommodate difference with a notion of mediation. No, it also means *fragmentation*. To whom is fragmentation of the oppressed useful?

Conclusion

One of the major advantages of a dialectical approach is its emphasis upon the concept of mediation of apparently contradictory social currents. When that concept of mediation is ignored, the way is paved for rigid dichotomizations and an opting for one side or the other. "Workerist" approaches and "new social movement" approaches as mutually exclusive options strike me as equally baseless. We ought not to turn away from the most dogmatic interpretations of the base/superstructure metaphor only to walk into another metaphoric trap that prioritizes language or discourse and constructs theory-proof roofs over local sites of contestation.

I would like to make two other observations. First, at least from the U.S. perspective, it is a bit late to be talking about new social movements in the way Habermas and Patton do, because imperialism has reached such an aggressive pitch in the policies of the overtly ideological Reagan administration. Particularly by its actions in Central America, its prioritization of the military and business sectors, and its cutbacks on domestic programs to aid the worst off, that administration has clearly demonstrated the distributive systemic stakes involved in imperialistic behavior and their relationship to the structures of capitalism, racism, and patriarchy at home. As opposed to the seventies, when imperialism took more subtle and less

A. Belden Fields

militaristic forms, an anti-imperialist movement has arisen whose function is to show the practical and theoretical implications of this phenomenon.[47]

Second, the thrust of micrologic analysis is toward a single-issue strategic approach, precisely the opposite of the above anti-imperialist approach. Within the U.S. context, the micrologic approach receives strong support from the "ideology of practicality." One of the major ways by which U.S. political culture has been rendered nonideological is precisely by the emphasis placed upon local, short-term results and the correlation of such "success" with micrologic strategies. Thus, Martin Luther King, Jr., was severely criticized for jeopardizing possible advances in civil rights when he criticized the war effort in Indochina. This micrologic approach frustrates systemic analyses which reveal dynamics in the political economy that are not otherwise obvious to those who think and act in purely compartmentalized terms. The kind of theorizing done by pluralists in the political science discipline has been a scientific discourse that reinforces compartmentalized thinking and delegitimizes systemic, political economy approaches by labeling them unscientific "ideologies."[48] It would be sad and ironic if the same tendency were to arise from the ranks of neo-Marxists today when the strategic stakes in the anti-imperialist struggle are at a more acute level.

Notes

1   The CFDT is the second largest labor confederation in France. It is characterized by a strong attachment to the concept of worker control over industry *(autogestion).*

2   Michel Foucault, "Revolutionary Action: 'Until Now,'" *Language, Counter-Memory, Practice,* trans. Donald Bouchard and Sherry Simon (Ithaca: Cornell University Press, 1977), p. 230.

3   Michel Foucault, *The Archaeology of Knowledge,* trans. A. M. Sheridan Smith (New York: Harper and Row, 1972), p. 107.

4   Michel Foucault, "Prison Talk," *Power/Knowledge,* trans. Colin Gordon et. al. (New York: Pantheon Books, 1972), p. 52.

5   Foucault, *The Archaeology of Knowledge,* p. 162.

6   Foucault, "The Eye of Power," *Power/Knowledge,* p. 159.

7   Foucault, *Power/Knowledge,* p. 159.

8   Foucault, "Intellectuals in Power," *Language, Counter-Memory, Practice,* p. 216.

9   Foucault, "Two Lectures," *Power/Knowledge,* p. 99.

10 Foucault, *Language, Counter-Memory, Practice,* p. 231.

11 Foucault, *Language, Counter-Memory, Practice,* p. 230.

12 Foucault, *Language, Counter-Memory, Practice,* p. 231.

13 Foucault, "Power and Strategies," *Power/Knowledge,* p. 142.

14 Foucault, *Power/Knowledge,* p. 145.

15 Foucault, *Power/Knowledge,* p. 107.

16 On La Gauche Prolétarienne see A. Belden Fields, "French Maoism," in Sohnya Sayres et al., eds., *The 60s without Apology* (Minneapolis: University of Minnesota Press, 1984), and Fields, *Trotskyism and Maoism: Theory and Practice in France and the United States* (New York: Praeger and Autonomedia, 1987).

17 Foucault, "On Popular Justice: A Discussion with Maoists," *Power/Knowledge,* p. 1.

18 Foucault, *Power/Knowledge,* p. 28.

19 Jürgen Habermas, *Legitimation Crisis,* trans. Thomas McCarthy (Boston: Beacon Press, 1973), p. 3.

20 Habermas, *Legitimation Crisis,* p. 4.

21   In this sense, I think that the theorizing of Anthony Giddens represents an advance over that of Habermas. Giddens takes care to introduce the "acting" subject into his theory of "structuration." See *Central Problems in Social Theory* (Berkeley and Los Angeles: University of California Press, 1979).

22   Jürgen Habermas, "New Social Movements," *Telos* 49 (1981), p. 33.

23   Habermas, "New Social Movements," p. 33.

24   Habermas, "New Social Movements," pp. 33-34.

25   Habermas, "New Social Movements," p. 34.

26   Habermas, "New Social Movements," p. 35.

27   Habermas, "New Social Movements," p. 35.

28   Habermas, "New Social Movements," p. 37.

29   Habermas, "New Social Movements," p. 34.

30   See Ronald Inglehart, "The Silent Revolution in Europe: Intergenerational Change in Post-Industrial Societies," *American Political Science Review* 65:4 (1971), pp. 991-1017, and *The Silent Revolution* (Princeton: Princeton University Press, 1977).

31   Chantal Mouffe, "Discussion," in this volume, p. 104.

32   Ernesto Laclau, "Populist Rupture and Discourse," *Screen Education*, no. 34 (1980), p. 89.

33   Laclau, p. 90.

34   Chantal Mouffe, "Hegemony and New Political Subjects: Toward a New Concept of Democracy," in this volume, p. 94.

35   Mouffe, "Hegemony and New Political Subjects," pp. 95–96.

36   Mouffe, "Hegemony and New Political Subjects," p. 98.

37   Mouffe, "Hegemony and New Political Subjects," p. 100.

38   Mouffe, "Hegemony and New Political Subjects," p. 99.

39   Barry Hindess and Paul Hirst, *Mode of Production and Social Formation: An Auto-critique of Pre-capitalist Modes of Production* (London: Macmillan, 1977).

40   Paul Patton, "Marxism and Beyond: Strategies of Reterritorialization," in this volume, p. 131.

41   Patton, p. 133.

42   See Robert Nozick, *Anarchy, State, and Utopia* (New York: Basic Books, 1974).

43   Patton, p. 133.

44   Patton, p. 131.

45   Patton, p. 131.

46   For a classic study of this see Michael Parenti, "Power and Pluralism: A View from the Bottom," in Marvin Surkin and Alan Wolfe, eds., *An End to Political Science* (New York: Basic Books, 1970), pp. 111-43.

47   I deal more explicitly with this in "U.S. Anti-imperialist Movements in Two Contexts: The War in Indochina and the Intervention in Central America," *Scandanavian Journal of Development Alternatives* 5:23 (1986), pp. 209-46.

48   See, for example, Nelson W. Polsby, *Community Power and Political Theory* (New Haven: Yale University Press, 1963), where class, elite, and stratification theories are attacked from an empirical, "scientific" perspective. This was written before there was even an explicitly Marxist body of literature in U.S. political science.

Étienne Balibar

The Vacillation of Ideology

Translated by Andrew Ross
and Constance Penley

The crisis of Marxism is shaped by the history of the way the class struggle has been organized in the context of the party; it is a history of contradictory relations between the "scientific" theory of historical materialism and actual proletarian political practice. Part of this history can be traced in the concept of ideology, which expresses not only a consistent antithesis between the dominant ideology and the revolutionary proletariat but also a continuous series of displacements—like that from the intellectuals to the masses.

I

Since there is a "crisis of Marxism" in the centenary of Marx's death, I would like to offer a schematic account of one of its most palpable elements, perhaps the most palpable of them all. I have had the occasion elsewhere, along with others and in their wake, to suggest that this crisis is much more profound and radical than is commonly acknowledged. It does not arise either from the relative exhaustion of a theory of history and social reality or from an initial error that led Marxists to stray from the paths of the intellectual, moral, and political progress of humanity. Nor does it arise from the perverse effects of a use of Marxism that would contradict its original aims, a use currently summed up in the phrase "actually existing socialism."

Crisis in Marxism or Crisis in Politics

Contrary to the facile alternative suggested by an all too hackneyed logic, the political and ideological uses of Marxist theory are no more logically implied in its original formulations than they are exterior to its meaning (or to its truth). In fact, the political and ideological uses of Marxism either produce or actually create its meaning; they maintain the historical process of its production, which already includes the texts of Marx, of Engels, his "close comrade in arms," and of their successors. From this point of view, Marxist discourse—taken in its totality as a scientific discourse *and* as an institutional form of political organization—starts out by pointing to the acute contradiction between the old and the new, between materialism and idealism, the effect of a revolutionary irruption as well as a conservative recuperation, if not a counterrevolutionary one in the strictest sense of the term. (By contrast, and of little importance, is the internal contradiction of the two aspects of the Hegelian system which Marxists have incessantly discussed, not so much to explain one of the sources of the constitution of Marxism as unconsciously to project the irreducible duality of their own thought upon it.)

Because the Marxist contradiction is internal, because it cannot be located between this or that part of the system but cuts across

159

each of its fundamental theses or concepts, because, finally, it keeps displacing its effects and its point of application, it is perfectly vain to imagine that one could get rid of that contradiction either by *purifying* Marxism of its "bad side," in order to deliver it into positivism, or by *refuting* it, in order to consign it to the trash can of history. Whether in the name of Marx or of Marxism-Leninism, scientific socialism, or anti-Marxism, the contradictions at stake here are, at present, strictly insurmountable; they never stop working our everyday existence, just as that existence never stops working them (and the rowdy proclamations of theories of totalitarianism are just one of the many symptoms of this).[1] The only possible way to carry out philosophical and political work today is by staying within the immediate boundaries of this internal/external crisis, closest to its sensitive areas.

The initial political and epistemological break in Marxism occurs when the terms of this contradiction are bound up, alongside the double positioning of the concepts of a science of history and the watchwords of a proletarian politics, within the unity of a "theoretical perspective based on a notion of class."

Thus, it is from the inside that the crisis of Marxism affects our current political situation. For unless we seek refuge in the illusion (cloaked in hypocrisy) of a political thought and practice that cuts the cost of the extremities of the class struggle and indefinitely defers the settling of accounts between social antagonisms (whether those of the economic crisis of capitalism, or those of the political crisis of socialism), unless we find the key to the good state and a healthy world economic order in the account books of technology or law, who would deny that the basic problems of all practical politics are still those at stake in the crisis of Marxism? Are there other ways of historically doing away with the recurring forms, old and new, of the exploitation and oppression of certain men and women by others than that of the revolutionary (not necessarily catastrophic) transformation of the determining social relations of social existence? And is there a revolutionary practice other than a collectively organized one in which "the masses make history," along with the permanent, built-in risk of a dual outcome (which, as experience shows, can be produced simultaneously): an effective liberation *and* the reproduction of a new "barbarism" whose technological sophistication scarcely disguises its ongoing primitivism?

If that is, indeed, the general problem, then the crisis of Marxism has nothing to do with the specific fate—specific, in accordance with the needs of a particular cause—of any single doctrine, nor even with that of historicist ideology and the nineteenth- and twentieth-century social utopias that are usually seen as its origin. In its most acute form the crisis of Marxism is the crisis of modern politics itself.

It is absurd, however, to try to generalize this "crisis" all in one go, as if its terms could be definitively established, for we would only end up with either a formalistic description or else a repetition of its symptoms, perpetually bringing together the false evidence of the immediate realities that contradict Marxist theory (the retreat of the workers' movement, the dissolution of the proletariat described by Marx and Lenin, the latent despotism and technocracy of socialist revolutions, the structural transformation of capitalism, the vitality of mass religious ideology that detracts from class consciousness, etc.) with the announcement of new acts of revolutionary faith.

160

Marxism's contradictions have no pure or simple existence; they only exist within a practico-theoretical *history*. To grasp them we must work out a detailed examination of this history, by addressing, simultaneously, the formulation of problems, the application of concepts, and mass social practice. Above all, this involves work on the transformations of the working-class movement, since it is specifically through the fusion of Marxist discourse with the practice of workers' organizations that each seems to have acquired, over the past century and more, a mutual trust in the other's consistency and continuity.

Such an analysis does not spring to hand; it is not well known; and it can no longer be got at simply by destroying classical illusions about the meaning and internal coherence of Marxism as a worldview. In principle, it still involves a considerable degree of the unknown—since there are only disparate elements of such a history of Marxism in existence today. However, it has no truck, a priori, with the unknowable or the esoteric.

I am offering only a small part of such an analysis, a very programmatic account of the history of the theory and even its origins. I want to discuss the position of *the concept of ideology in the Marxism of Marx and Engels* and its importance, not only for what it gives rise to, but ultimately for our present state of affairs. I will emphasize the *theoretical vacillation* that characterizes the concept of ideology, a vacillation that consistently manifests itself in terms of an eclipse, an antithetical deviation, or a displacement of the problematics.

A Double Birth for a Single Concept

Our starting point is marked by the odd distribution of the term "ideology" in Marx and Engels's texts themselves (in which language is the materialist site of the production of their concepts). Omnipresent in the writings of 1845-46, reduced to a few peripheral appearances in the period 1847-52, ideology is almost nowhere to be found after that until its fullblown restoration in the 1870s, chiefly from the *Anti-Dühring* on. In a sense, it is used there simply as a well-known philological fact; but if we look more closely, it can also be seen as the source of a false understanding played out in all contemporaneous discourses on Marxism, starting with its own discourse about itself.

The concept of ideology is clearly a decisive innovation and ensures Marxism's theoretical specificity.[2] Althusser sees its formulation as an unimpeachable sign of the break that engenders it. Yet it has actually been formulated *twice,* in disparate historical contexts and within problematics that precluded any immediate conflation: first, in *The German Ideology* by Marx and Engels (though mostly Marx), an unpublished text whose uneven yet insistent influence, brought to light by various rereadings and rediscoveries, can be traced throughout the entire history of Marxism; and second, in the group of historical and philosophical texts, mostly by Engels, designed to provide Marxism, for the first time, with the appearance of a system and to point out the ways in which that system could be applied. Writing these texts over two decades (initially under the supervision of Marx and then in the course of a systematic rereading of Marx's published and unpublished work), Engels at once *gave* historical materialism its name, *rediscovered* the term "ideology," and (temporarily) *covered over* the problems he was posing in the guise of an entirely coherent, indeed even positive, definition. This

161

second formulation is actually even more complex and contradictory, but it served to give the concept of ideology its initial outlines.

How can we fail to assign some symptomatic value to this twenty-year eclipse of the crucial term "ideology" following its debut (if we can call it that, since the text was not published) and extensive deployment in *The German Ideology?* Ideology almost vanished from the discourse of Marx and Engels. There are a few furtive appearances, particularly in polemical references from 1846 to 1852 to the "ideologues" of the bourgeoisie and the petit bourgeoisie (Proudhon et al.), then nothing more. There is no mention of ideology in the great political analyses of the conjuncture and relations of forces, such as *The Eighteenth Brumaire,* which Engels nonetheless took as the model of a materialist account of historical events. (In this subtle analysis of the political representation of social forces, all that is at stake is the question of "class in itself" and "class for itself.") Ideology does not appear in the preliminary work of *Capital* (notably the *Grundrisse*), nor even in the detailed critique of the economists (theories of surplus value). Here, again, it is simply a matter of the difference between classical economy and vulgar or apologetic economy.[3]

Above all, there is nothing about ideology in *Capital,* which, whether one likes it or not, is the cornerstone on which depends the solidity or fragility of the Marxist edifice. It can no doubt be argued that a good number of the theoretical apparatuses that figure in the classical analyses of ideology are well and truly present in *Capital:* those pertaining to commodity and money fetishism and, more generally, to the inverted relation Marx sets up between the deep sphere of production and the superficial sphere of exchange. Clearly these analyses, by dint of their object, ought to be part of the field of a theory of ideology (or of bourgeois ideology), either to explain the specific effects of ideology or to give an account of genesis. That only makes more conspicuous the absence of ideology in the theoretical space of *Capital* and generally within what is called the moment of *"Capital"* in the history of Marxism. Far from signifying the absence of any corresponding questions, this suggests a recognition that the question is not so simple that it can be inscribed, unequivocally, within any one theoretical statement.

I think it is worth considering this eclipse, not as an accident or an irrelevant terminological quirk, but as the sign of a difficulty, if not a fundamental contradiction. This hypothesis would be confirmed if we could find an instance where the definition of ideology is incompatible with the critique of political economy and where the description of fetishism can be inserted. Our hypothesis already has its counterproof: after *Capital,* the term "fetishism" *disappears in its turn* from the texts of Marx and Engels, in spite of its conceptual precision[4] and in spite of the organic place it occupies at the core of the development of "value-form" or in the explanation of the relation between the essence and the appearances of capitalist production, hence of the relation between wage exploitation, the consciousness assumed by the laborers themselves, and the discourse of the economists. In place of fetishism—but is it really in the same place?—a new term appears, one Engels salvaged from a forgotten manuscript, "ideology," whose meaning he (consciously?) transforms. This extraordinary shuffling of identities suggests that if the question of ideology is constitutive for historical materialism, then several relatively incompatible approaches are involved, each depending on different conditions, each of which has to be pursued in its turn. The study of these differences (which academia has completely obscured) then becomes a privileged means of access to the internal contradictions of the Marxist problematic.

Materialism and Criticism

Without going into the tricky details of the text of *The German Ideology,* I would like to point out a few of its noteworthy features in a way that will throw some light on the paradoxical nature of the concept of ideology. We can start with a double question: what makes Marx's materialism historical and what makes his conception of history materialist?

Marx's history is obviously not materialist simply because it purports to *eliminate the speculative* in order to constitute itself on an empirically verifiable causality. In principle, this elimination entails snatching history from the clutches of teleology, both in its religious forms (Providence, the meaning of history, Origins and Destinies) and in its philosophical forms (a periodization, governed by a principle of Human Progress—moral, juridical, spiritual, or logical); in short, this entails eliminating any identification of a Subject of history. In Marx, this critique coincides with the attack on an illusion that is also a fraud, one that makes the State the universal component of historical process and Man, as a universal abstraction, its proper subject. Yet this critique of speculation cannot be reduced to an empiricism or positivism (though general formulations point it this way, starting from the idea of a definitive departure from philosophy). Nor does it rely on a simple clarification of the economic process, of social labor, and of the needs and material interests of the classes. By itself such an analysis (of the "real bases" of history) can only return to the presuppositions common to both political economy and classical philosophical utilitarianism, whose individualist materialism itself also rests on an abstract hypothesis of human nature (and also, undoubtedly, on the perspective of the state, though less obviously so).

Despite what the term traditionally suggests, Marx's materialism can be contained neither within the definition of the matter of history nor within the application of a historical point of view (evolutionary, progressive, dialectical) with regard to matter.[5] It is presented as an *essentially derivative* position, as a critique of idealist (abstract, speculative, etc.) representations/illusions which mask over, mystify, and repress the determining reality of the labor of the individual and of social production. By virtue of its own labor, this critique alone can provide materialism with its specific content while also confirming that there is no universal materialism outside specific positions, conjunctures, or struggles.

Historical materialism is primarily an analysis (or a series of analyses) of the formation, the real production, of idealist representations of history and politics—in short, of *the process of idealization.* In *The German Ideology* this is the professed objective of a complex and incomplete construction centered on the role of the "division of manual and intellectual labor." Historical materialism is constituted when it can prove (and to the extent to which it *can* prove) that *the idealization of history is itself the necessary result of a specific history.* We can then see how the idea of a scientific critique (along with the equation, science = history) might be justified: because the movement of criticism that opens the analysis of these questions is itself just as much the result of "real historical relations" as are the idealities it addresses. As with science, the categories of history are manifest as problems in their own right (questions, as Marx puts it) rather than as explanations or autonomous responses.

Yet this is still not enough. We must come to terms with the force, or forces, that sanction the way the idealization of history imposes itself, not only on those who have an interest in it, but also on those for whom it mystifies the real and thereby calls a halt to the movement for liberation. On this point, someone like Stirner can only offer a tautology: the domination of ideas is the realm of ideas of domination (order, hierarchy, the sacred, etc.). What is the point of these ideas of democratic liberation (individual rights, political equality) if they are incarnated, in their turn, within the statist order (albeit a profane, nonhierarchical one) of the postrevolutionary bourgeoisie? In suggesting that every state makes use of religion and morality to impose its power, and that every discourse, when it begins to conflict with their *interests,* divides individuals, one from the other, Machiavelli and Hobbes do nothing to break out of this vicious circle; they only translate it into the language of a functionalist philosophy of power (the dominant ideas, whatever they are, are those serving the interests of the powerful; at best the powerful must believe in the ideas so that those they dominate do likewise). It is necessary to *determine the question historically,* to examine the nature of the "ideas of the ruling class" and the way they *become* the dominant ideas. Thus, the concept of ideology adds a third question to the preceding two. With respect to the other critiques of the speculative illusion (Kant, Feuerbach) or the necessity of appearances (Hegel), whether anthropological and ahistorical or historical and dialectical, Marx's originality lies in his overdetermining the question of the cause or necessity of idealities by questioning their mode of action, their power, or their subjugating effects.[6]

Considered in the light of this triple determination (the critique of teleology and speculative theory, the materialist origin of idealization, and the analysis of the effects of domination), the concept of ideology seems to be the correlative of a definition of the *real relations* that determine the historical process. In traditional philosophy such an invocation of the real and the empirical could only correspond to a recognition of error or illusion, an antithesis between idealism and realism. The materialist critique of ideology, for its part, corresponds to the analysis of *the real as a relation,* as a structure of practical relations. It corresponds to the discovery that the reality of the real is not a being identical to itself but is, in a sense, a specific abstraction the individual can only at first perceive as an abstraction twice-removed—speculative or, as Marx puts it, inverted and rendered autonomous. It is not individuals who *create* this abstraction, for they are themselves basically only relations or the product of relations. The whole science of history is virtually the distinction between these two antithetical abstractions, which is to say that it breaks up or deconstructs their identification. It is in this that the science of history is "concrete."

The Purely Proletarian Act

In rereading Marx's argument, however, it seems to be dominated by one forceful theoretical intervention, the abstraction of which is itself rather flimsy: an intervention that posits, against ideology, in the form of a force or antithetical instance, the very being of the proletariat, or, more precisely, the prophetic establishment *in the very place* occupied by the revolutionary proletariat of the discourse critiquing ideology. Thus, it is from this site, the real site of truth as well as the place from which the world is changed, that one can grasp the equivalence between the different types of idealization that constitute ideology: consciousness produced at a distance from the real, abstraction of the conditions of existence, inversion of their limitation (or their particularity) in a fictional universality, autonomization of intellectual labor, political idealism, and philosophico-religious speculation (of which German Hegelianism is the quintessential example). It is only from this site that we can *see* the fundamental equivalence between ideology and idealism, a correspondence that makes the idea of a materialist ideology or a materialist philosophy a contradiction in terms.

By that same token, however, materialism is defined as an absolutely positive term that gathers and unifies within itself all the antitheses of ideology/idealism: (real) life, (real) individuality, production (of conditions of existence), history, praxis, and, lastly, the revolutionary practice of the proletariat (or communism, not as the ideal future, but as the "real movement to do away with the existing state of things" without ever losing touch with production, its initial condition). The real movement of history is a developing labor of production (what philosophers call "alienation") accompanied by a developing production—or, better still, a productivity—of labor. The proletariat is thus a self-affirmation of production and a self-negation of labor, which is to say that the materialist instance is only seen to be a revolutionary practice when ideology in general can be identified with idealism. And this identification is only possible from the point of view of the proletariat.

Marx's argument thus comes full circle, and it is a strictly *philosophical* circle. Although his thesis—completely identifying material existence with practice and formally bound up within what he calls the "totality of productive forces"—is powerful and profound (if not wholly original), it nonetheless reconstitutes itself as philosophical at the very moment Marx claims to have abolished philosophy.

This circle is actually the result of adding a rupture (which radically divorces practice from abstract theory) to a denegation. The theoretical discourse announcing this divorce is not a true "discourse" in that it does not assume a theoretical position; it is, rather, the site of practice itself, or the self-articulation of practice (which presupposes, among other things, a notion of the absolute transparency of language—"the language of real life"). Moreover, it is the only discourse that, because of its obviousness, is held not by the intellectuals but by the proletariat itself, or at least in the name of the proletariat—the discourse of communism.[7]

This initial circle presents a major difficulty which *The German Ideology* copes with only by way of new denegations, precisely in reproducing the same circle for the proletariat itself. Consider two of its forms.

1. The self-consciousness of the proletariat is opposed to ideological illusion/inversion, but this consciousness must be both *unmediated* (conscious of its being, that is, its conditions of existence) and *produced* as a practical negation of the unmediated; to live up to this, the proletariat must transform and revolutionize itself. The proletariat is the prerequisite condition and the end result of its own revolutionary practice. Marx writes:

"In revolutionary activity, changing oneself and changing one's conditions (of existence) are the same thing."

2. The proletariat is first and foremost a class, the class antagonist of the bourgeoisie, and hence places its own interests above theirs. Put like this, however, the proletariat would, by definition, lack universality, or, more precisely, it would be caught up in turn within the mystifying and abstracting process that subsumes a "specific interest" into a "general interest." For the interests of the proletariat to tally with a real universality, with practice as such, those interests must cease to be class interests; and for that to happen, the proletariat itself must *cease to be a class,* must be a class/nonclass. Marx writes of "a class which has really rid itself of the old ways, and which stands in opposition to them at the same time." This is the surprising distinction made between the proletariat as a class and the proletariat as the masses. Only the masses are revolutionary, because they represent the disintegrating state of "society" *(la dissolution en acte de la "société")* as it exists, at the point when extreme exploitation has completely stripped the workers of all property and all inherited historical specificity, leaving them effectively naked. Marx presents us with this radical loss of individuality in the shape of a radical individualization. And revolution is nothing but this act itself, or the way history acts out this disintegration, which is its own product. But by the same rigorous logic, this means that there is no—or, at this point, there is no longer any—class struggle. Properly speaking, *the bourgeoisie is the only class in history;* before it there were only castes, orders, states *(Stände),* which were not yet real classes. As for the proletariat, once it matches its definition, it is no longer simply a class but the masses.

I will not discuss here the historical analyses that Marx uses to support this thesis; they are primarily generalizations, a hyperbolic extension of Adam Smith's ideas about the division of labor. In fact, they are derived from the politico-philosophical assumptions that define the proletariat. Yet we must emphasize the disastrous logical consequences of these analyses in the case of the relation between the (communist) proletariat and politics, two terms that are quite simply incompatible. The proletariat, by definition, is the negation of all politics identified with an ideological illusion/abstraction. Similarly, communism is the nonstate *(Staat),* a state of things *(Zustand)* in which all political mediation has, by definition, disappeared.

Because the proletariat is the actual negating (or the act of practical negation) of all ideology, there is no such thing as a proletarian ideology, or an ideology of the proletariat, just as we have seen that it would be absurd to talk about a materialist ideology. The proletariat is precisely the mass of concrete individuals, inasmuch as, and in accordance with their own conditions of existence, these individuals destroy all ideology (or ideological consciousness). That is why, as the *Manifesto* insists on repeating, the proletariat has no nationality or religion, no family or morality, no politico-juridical illusions; that is the absolute *"Illusionslosigkeit"* of the proletariat as such. This leads us, of course, to ask about the empirical working class *hic et nunc:* is it really so devoid of all ideological consciousness? The answer suggested by the text of *The German Ideology* is simple but completely tautological and speculative: such a working class would not (or not yet) be the revolutionary proletariat.[8]

166

Étienne Balibar

We should not, however, hasten to pass judgment on this construction, doing no more than condemning it for its idealist or speculative, if not mystical, character and thereby repeating Marx's attack on Hegelian and post-Hegelian philosophy. On the one hand, this construction includes the articulation of concepts that will be shown to be susceptible to a series of changes and modifications, ending with its very opposite: a historical analysis of the struggles of the proletarian classes as these struggles are determined by the successive configurations, created by capitalism, of the working class and the bourgeoisie. On the other hand, and most important by the very fact of its critical radicality, this formulation is likely, in a different context, to take on a new function and hence a new meaning. It will come to stand for something all the more pertinent to our reading of it, something more than a separation: an inevitable *contradiction* between the ideologies of the proletariat (whether spontaneous or imported; in fact, you never have one without the other) and revolutionary practice. The corollary is that *there always comes a time when "revolutionary ideologies" prove to be counterrevolutionary in practice,* a time when revolutions (if not *the* revolution, which is, by definition, a myth) come into conflict with revolutionary ideologies or ideologies of the proletariat and effectively destroy them—in other words, what Marx does not "think" but what we can think, by no means arbitrarily, in some of the concepts of *The German Ideology,* that which these concepts think today, namely, this intrinsically contradictory relation between revolution and ideology. Though this is not what Marx says in *The German Ideology,* it is a use we can make of his most radical philosophical theses, turned back on themselves and against the "dogmatic sleep" of Marxism. Could this retrospective reading salvage for us the most profound sense of what Marx understood at the time by the term "proletariat"? Is it not so much a class existence as an effective class struggle which, in propelling itself beyond its initial conditions, divides up ideology and thereby exposes it?

Domination without the Dominated?

Almost immediately the theses of *The German Ideology* posed some insoluble contradictions for Marx. One therefore understands why it was necessary for him to do away with this concept of ideology, if not with the problems it harbored.[9]

The first difficulty lay in the impossibility of inserting the discourse of political economy into the theoretical space as it was defined. It would not, in fact, fit into either the category of ideological abstraction (since its specific object was productive labor, analyzed as a relation; the division of labor and exchange) or into that of historical materialism or the science of history (because, to express the point of view of the bourgeoisie—Marx calls economists their "scientific representatives"—the discourse of political economics always erects a specific interest, that of private property, into the realization of human nature in general). This difficulty lies at the heart of *The German Ideology.* Indeed, it is from Adam Smith, Ferguson, and the Saint-Simonians that Marx draws the materialist categories of a periodization of civil society, a correspondence between the forms of property and the forms of the division of labor. All this becomes untenable when Marx, progressing from Smith to Ricardo, comes to grips with the Ricardian definition of value in order to extract socialist conclusions from it—in *The Poverty of Philosophy* and, implicitly, the *Manifesto.*

167

Far from clearing up this difficulty, Marx's extension of this critique to Ricardian economic principles (the definition of labor and value) only makes things worse. The critique of economic categories can no longer consist in the prior separation of the domain of the real from that of illusion but rather consists in the work of internally deconstructing each theoretical category. Such a critique involves separating the contradictory elements imbricated within the economic concepts in order to confront them with a practice that is not directly the revolutionary practice of the proletariat but is, rather, *the practice of capital* (with its own contradictions). Thus, one would have to be able to think both the objectivity of economic discourse and its bourgeois class character simultaneously; or even, contrary to the original definition, to think both *the real and the imaginary* within ideology. This is precisely what Marx tries to do in his analysis of fetishism, in attempting to demonstrate how the simultaneous birth of the "form of value" and the necessary illusions of commodity production is brought about, though he returns to a problematic of illusion inspired by Kant and Feuerbach.[10]

A second difficulty, however, may be more directly decisive. It arises from the radical antithesis between the autonomous action of the proletariat (absolutely creative because it is absolutely determined by its conditions of existence) and the abstract world of politics. One would think that by the time Marx (and Engels) wrote *The German Ideology* this difficulty could no longer be ignored, since at that very moment Marx was doing his utmost to bring about a reformation of communists from several countries within a single international organization, soon to become the League of Communists. If that is not practicing politics (and specifically against the states and their ruling classes), one wonders what is. The evidence of this difficulty in the text itself is a symptomatic lack of coherence, political theses that seem to be totally out of place, or equivocal statements for which several contradictory readings are possible.

Hence, these formulations no longer have anything to do with communism as a real movement of universal history but rather with real, living communists of the sort one meets *hic et nunc* (in Paris, for instance), communists we have to call to mind in order to explain this name we give to the real movement: "You can count on the fingers of one hand the few bourgeois communists that have surfaced since Babeuf's time who are not revolutionaries; everywhere the great mass of communists is revolutionary."

The differences are thereby set up between French (political) ideology and German (philosophical) ideology: the former is to the latter what history or practice in general is to ideology in general, namely, its antithesis, and thus its real criterion. Here, again, Marx takes up the old nostalgic notions of the young German radicals (going back at least to Fichte): "It is impossible to write history in Germany because *history does not happen here*." History happens in France; it happens politically. And it is because this political element is not purely illusory, or rather because all illusions are not equal, that the real differences between these ideologies offer a base for the concept of the revolutionary proletariat, as important, perhaps, as the reference to the bedrock assumption of material existence or production. Above all, these differences are the effect of a historically different relation to the state. They do not refer to an absolute action, with neither past nor future, but to a specific historical memory: the French had Danton and Robespierre, "the masses rising," Babeuf, Bonaparte; the Germans had only

168

Metternich and Wilhelm-Friedrich, who, at best, watched history pass by in the streets below.

The problem becomes more sharply defined in Marx's paradoxical formula of the dominant ideology. What does "ideology of the ruling class" mean? From one paragraph to the next, Marx gives us two answers, and it is from these that we can infer, not without ambiguity, the meaning of the question posed. This ambiguity is clearly reflected in the double semantic value of the term *"herrschend"*: is it the *dominance* of a body of representations or a discursive paradigm that typifies the epoch of its own, more or less undivided, "rule,"[11] or else the *domination* exercised (in a "repressive" manner, overtly or otherwise) by one body of representations over another, and, through this mediation, by one practice over another, by one way of life or thought over another? Both are correct, but to understand the causality at work we must look to another, more tricky ambiguity, one characterized by the fact that unraveling it, in every case, gives rise to an aporia.

We can construe the dominant ideology as a kind of "symbolic capital" of the ruling class itself, as the body of representations that expresses its relation to its *own* conditions and means of existence (for the bourgeoisie, for instance, commodity ownership, juridical equality, and political liberty), or at best as the expression of the relation of the average members of the ruling class to the conditions of domination common to their class (hence, the kind of universal values this domination assumes for each of them). How does this representation impose itself on individuals who do not have the same relation to the conditions of existence as do the ruling class (manual workers, for example)? Clearly it cannot be because it is forced on them by the material means (which includes the press and intellectual production in general) monopolized by the ruling class (a monopoly acquired through the mediation of their ideological servants—scribes and scholars of every ilk). Such a domination, however, remains necessarily exterior to the consciousness of the oppressed (without bringing in, as Marx did not, the irrationalist hypothesis of a "desire for submission"). This is why Marx writes that, for the proletariat, the representations of the dominant ideology—whether juridical, moral, patriotic, or otherwise—ultimately do not exist, or are purely fictional. But then the concept of ideology disintegrates, surviving only as a variation on the conspiracy theories of the "useful fictions" of power ("If God did not exist, they would have to invent him") of the sort put forward by the mechanistic rationalists of the eighteenth century.

Alternatively, we can construe ideological domination as the result (always already present, which is to say neither automatically nor eternally acquired) of a true ideological struggle, that is, as the domination of one ideological consciousness over another. From this point of view, what always corresponds to the constitution of a *dominant* ideology, in tendency at least, is the constitution of a *dominated* ideology, yoked to a process of repression but capable of subverting it. How do we interpret this conflicted birth? Do we pose the reciprocal confrontation, for example, of the representations of the relations members of the antagonistic classes have with their respective conditions of existence? Probably not. Rather, we pose against each other the representations of the relations individuals of antagonistic class have to the antagonism itself, that is, to the social relation that unites them while opposing them and to its derivative forms (property, division of labor, the state, etc.)—a relation they cannot, of course, live in the same manner but one that necessarily represents, for them as for others, the universal of a given epoch, which is their epoch, or the epoch of their antagonism.

This second interpretation is much more profound than the first. In fact, Marx's text points toward it. At any rate, we find its deferred trace in the resume of 1859 (the Preface to *A Contribution to the Critique of Political Economy*) in a reference to the "ideological forms through which men are made conscious of conflict, and draw it to a conclusion."

If we ourselves draw to its conclusion the logic brought into play here, we will obviously find ourselves in opposition to any thesis imputing an absolute lack of reality to the ideological world, and we will no longer understand the sense in which this world "lacks history," or the sense in which it "cannot exist" for the proletariat. Moreover, we will conclude that there are not only real differences in the ideological world but also contradictions, and that they clash with the contradictions of practice, contributing, in themselves, to "real life."

At this stage of Marx's problematic, however, this interpretation is no less aporetic than the one before; and in order to be able to bring it to conclusion, a dominated ideology would have to be placed in opposition to the dominant ideology—*which is exactly what Marx does not do,* except implicitly, in the emptiness or vacillation of the expression "dominated ideology." The whole of *The German Ideology* is precariously balanced on this concept of dominant ideology, for which there is no corresponding dominated ideology! It would be impossible to take this term literally without giving credence, finally, to the concept of a proletarian ideology and thus without questioning, again, the divorce of the proletariat from all ideology. And this means breaking up the whole constituent structure of materialism, the layers of correspondence between materiality, production, practice, history, and revolution.

Historical Materialism or Political Materialism

It is obvious that Marx has no solution to the problem. But he is hardly able to ignore it, since it is the essence of revolutionary politics. Ample confirmation of this is provided in the *Communist Manifesto,* written two years after *The German Ideology.* The *Manifesto* presents, more than ever, and crucially, with respect to the definition of revolutionary consciousness, the radical antithesis between such consciousness and all the forms of social consciousness that actually reflect the *past* history of former class oppressions: "The Communist revolution is the most radical rupture with traditional property relations; no wonder that its development involves the most radical rupture with traditional ideas." These ideas are none other than those of nationality, religion, family, liberty, culture, law, and so on, which used to make up the content of what Marx calls "ideology."

If the *Manifesto* refutes accusations of immorality and barbarism leveled at communism, the "specter which haunts Europe," it is clearly not to paint a better picture of proletarian morality, nor even proletarian culture, but rather to establish that the bases of morality and culture have already been destroyed by the rule of the propertied bourgeoisie.[12]

This essential de-ideologization, or, if you like, this a-ideological tendency of the proletariat, is consistent with the catastrophism of the theses in the *Manifesto* on class antagonism (the idea of "absolute impoverishment"; the bourgeoisie can no longer feed those who feed it), and with its universalism (the idea of crisis and of world revolution). It is consistent with the description of socialist and communist literature put forward in chapter 3, a remarkable outline for a class analysis of the anticapitalist ideologies but one strictly limited to the range of *nonproletarian* discourses, or discourses that express not the proletariat itself but rather the figure it cuts in the imaginary of other classes.[13]

Confronted with this imaginary, the discourse of the *Manifesto* is positioned, at once, by the critical relation it maintains with this imaginary and another radically different relation, since it looks not to the past but to the future of the movement, to the way this future is already at work in the present. This discourse, however, should be provided with an appropriate name and proof of existence other than the ideological. Otherwise, it will fall back into the vicious circle that would appear if the proletarian character of Marx and Engels's theses became an authority unto itself and if communism had no existence outside the publication of its manifesto! The name and the proof are combined in one phrase: "We do not here refer to that literature which, in every great modern revolution, has always given voice to the demands of the proletariat, such as the writings of Babeuf and others." Perhaps the whole trouble lies in the interpretation of "and others"! What irreducible *tendency* do the writings of Babeuf represent? And how is this tendency less ideological than that of the "systems of Saint-Simon, Fourier, Owen, *etc.*"?

The context of this question is quite clear. What distinguishes Babeuf's communism (and that of the Blanquistes) is simply that it is purely political, that it identifies itself with the practical revolutionary will against the systems, themselves identified with reformism.[14] In this, however, we have the full-blown contradiction of the *Manifesto*: how do we think a politics without political ideology, without a discourse on the state, or the future State, or the future of the state (were it to disappear)?

On this question the *Manifesto* strikes a markedly different note than *The German Ideology*. It uncovers, or recovers, a materialism other than that of history or even practice: *a materialism of politics*. Its analysis of the class struggle is articulated with the definition of a strategy.[15] The principal idea, with respect to the revolution, is no longer that of an act at once complete and instantaneous, although this image always haunts its catastrophic vision of the crisis of capitalism. Rather, it is a process, or a transition, that will bring about the change from a class society to a classless society, starting from social contradictions within their actual configurations. Henceforth, the very concept of practice changes its meaning; it has to include the moment of a direction, in the dual sense of the term—orientation and project, or program. The real movement of the revolution is no longer a radical *breakup* of bourgeois society, liberating the totality of the productive forces—or at least this is only its negative condition. Rather, it is a progressive construction, or *composition,* of forces, capable of joining together "the interests and immediate goals of the working class" with "the future of the movement," and capable of severing the constraints common to all of the "already established workers parties," transcending—but not ignoring—their national divisions and the limitations of their respective "class points of view."

It is clearly no longer a case of representing the revolutionary proletariat as situated beyond any existence as a class, in a mass of de-individualized individuals, as *The German Ideology* would have it. On the contrary, the concept of a class struggle must be extended to the revolutionary process itself in order to *think the revolution within the class struggle* (and not the class struggle within the imminence of revolution). Within the revolution, far from distinguishing itself from the bourgeoisie by ceasing to be a true class, the proletariat actually "constitutes itself as the ruling class" (by way of the "triumph of democracy"), which must lead dialectically to its own negation and the destruction of all class rule, including its own. It is hardly credible that the proletariat, acting in this process as a specific class, would not be both the bearer of an ideology proper and driven by the representations borne by that ideology. Thus, the proletariat is ultimately determined in its action, or in the strategic vicissitudes of its action, by these representations.

Does Marx pose this problem? Yes, if you take into account his reflection on the historical conditions in which the *bourgeois* class struggle inevitably had to educate politically the *proletarian* class struggle. And no, in the sense that none of the theses of the *Manifesto* correct, however modestly, the myth of a class consciousness as being radically exterior to ideology, nor do they give any idea of what a proletarian ideology might be. Since then, theoretical conflict can only be resolved (apparently) by breaking up the concept of ideology and abandoning its very use. Exit ideology, German or otherwise.[16]

II

In the first part of this study I have tried to show why the concept of ideology, set up in opposition to the philosophy of history, was obliged to disappear very quickly from Marx's problematic under the pressure of the very contradictions it established.[17] I have summarized those contradictions of an internal nature in demonstrating the ambiguity of the idea of domination implied in the notion of a dominant ideology. As for those of an external nature, I have linked these contradictions to the impossibility encountered in Marx's application of this concept to the classical political economy he was attacking. Above all, I have tried to point out the difficulties, for a materialism founded on the absolute antithesis of ideology and practice, of concretely thinking the problems and goals of a proletarian politics that began to take shape in 1848, around the experience of the European revolutions and their failures.

I shall now take the liberty of jumping over twenty years of history in order to consider the conditions of the revival of the concept of ideology in Marxism in the form given it by Engels. Again, we should speak of a vacillation, but in a different way, for it is no longer the case of a possible double reading of a single term. Rather, there is an unresolved theoretical (and linguistic) conflict signaled by the recourse to *two* concurrent terms, each of them assured of a long life: ideology and worldview. What does this conflict consist of? At what level of development does it surface in Engels's theoretical activities? And what can it teach us about the contradictory articulations of theory and politics?[18]

Two Concepts for One Problem?

These two terms make their debut in Engels's writing at the same time; the formulations of the *Anti-Dühring,* which employs them both, can be used as a point of reference. At the beginning of chapter 10, part 1, "Morality and Law—Freedom and Necessity," is the first definition of ideology: it comes from the opposition between the methodology of materialist thinking, which proceeds from the real to the conceptual, and that of idealist thought ("a priorist" and "axiomatic"), which inverts this process in order to pass (fictitiously) from the concept, or the abstraction, to the real which it spuriously purports to engender.[19] The definition, then, is purely epistemological. It implies, however, that if the effect of ideological discourse belongs to the order of knowledge (and of misunderstanding), its object, and its raison d'être, is social and political: ideological systems always result from the combination of a completely arbitrary element, which for Engels would be a result of the individual imagination, and an objective element constituted by preexisting social perspectives or conceptions *(Anschauungen)*, which express *(ausdruck)* real social relations. These perspectives are always already invested in a certain interest or position *("positiv oder negativ, bestätigend oder bakämpfand")*. We are thus led to believe that if the specific modality of the ideas of ideology is to appear in the form of "eternal truths," universal and ahistorical, then it is precisely because they represent a political value judgment, a sanctioning of the existing social order, which goes forth masked.

This interpretation is strengthened by the fact that the model for ideological discourse (ideologues and philosophers à la Dühring plagiarize their ideas from it, while vaunting their theoretical "originality") is the juridical discourse that turns on liberty, equality, justice, the rights and obligations of people, contractual relations, relations of violence, and so on. Engels returns here to a habitual theme of Marx's critique, one that joins the economic critique and the political critique in making juridical ideology the kernel of all bourgeois philosophical ideology.[20] Within this arrangement, the term "ideology" stands only for the misunderstanding, or the illusion, implied by these secondary characteristics. Ideology, by definition, does not admit of any historical effectivity, apart from its blocking knowledge and consciousness of the real movement; ideology is "pure" ideas.

Another term surfaces, however, alongside this critique: worldview. It is remarkable that Engels never gives it a general definition. Clearly it has been borrowed; in fact, it is an imported term. Even more than ideology, it is a word whose currency is widespread and riddled with allusions to the philosophical issues of Franco-German history.[21] But prior to the diffusion of Marxism, worldview had never figured as a systematic concept. In the *Anti-Dühring,* and simultaneously in a series of other articles, published or otherwise (particularly those exhumed between the wars under the title *Dialectics of Nature*), there is not only an attempt to counteract "ideology" (and idealism) with a "scientific" and "materialist worldview" but also the means of truly revealing it for what it is, the "communist worldview that we (will) represent, Marx and I, in quite a large number of domains" (which, taken literally, implies that *others* could represent it, too, in their own way, in other domains).

The goal of this project poses an immediate problem. In opposition to the idealism of bourgeois ideology which vindicates the existing order, the idea of a communist *and* materialist worldview constitutes itself within the critical recurrence of Marx's theory—a theory of exploitation and the state. It is the *fact* of this theory that sustains it. From then on, we find ourselves running counter to the theses of *The German Ideology*. Even when these terms and propositions are taken up again (or rediscovered), the point of reference (and the perspective on the structure and functions of ideology) has clearly been radically displaced—to the other end of the philosphical spectrum—from practice (and pure practice at that) to theory, or to historical materialism as a science of social production and class struggle.

One insistent theme, developed specifically in the fragments of *Dialectics of Nature,* conveniently maps out this reversal of perspective: a history of thought *(des Denkens),* the trajectory and principal stages of which Engels tries to chart. Whereas in *The German Ideology* thought has no history of its own, now the logic of this history gives its content to the materialist-communist worldview and allows the historical necessity of idealizations of ideology to be understood. In an ultrapositivist way, the Marx of *The German Ideology* denies philosophy any knowledge value and any historical positivity. Engels now takes the opposite position. If he is hesitant to qualify as philosophy (or materialist philosophy)[22] the communist worldview, whose kernel is the theory of history "discovered" by Marx, he nonetheless sees philosophy as a legitimate domain ("the laws and operations of thought"), and, above all, he describes the birth of the theory of history in terms of an essential relation to philosophy and its history. The materialist worldview is not, in this respect, a radical shift of ground, an absolute antithesis of all philosophy. If it succeeds in going beyond the categories of philosophical thought, then it is because it comes out of them, in the dual sense of an origin and an issue, or rather because it comes out of their contradictions. So there are contradictions in philosophy (and consequently in good dialectics. Even if philosophy is not itself *the* real, there is a reality in philosophy. Engels says as much in his later, improved reading of Hegel: all that is contradictory is real).

To put it another way, materialism, or *some* materialism (even in the form of its inversion and its denegation), is necessarily present within this history of thought in the form of an element always already constitutive of philosophy. The history of thought, of which philosophy is a kind of concentrate, is the struggle for and against materialism. In contrast to *The German Ideology,* for which only practice is materialist in the true sense, it is now necessary to posit that there is a theoretical materialism (well prior to historical materialism).

Let us not join those who have hastened to label this new discourse of Engels as regressive. Such a way of posing the problem of relations between theory and practice, or materialism, regardless of its own difficulties, is much less speculative than a way that directly identifies practice with reality in making it equivalent to the purely revolutionary act and establishes ideology (if not all theory) on the level of illusion or nonbeing. At least in this new arrangement a place (that of discourse?) is set aside for the confrontation between revolutionary practice and ideological domination, cutting across the opposition of worldviews and the interference between the history of thought and the history of class struggles. If materialism is a specific relation between theory and practice, one ought to be able to see it in theory itself.

As we will see, this modification is linked to new political conditions within the workers' movement. But it is also clear that it is ordained by the unimpeachable "fact" of Marx's production of a theory of class

174

struggle. The first concept of ideology ran up against the difficulty of thinking of the classical economic theory targeted by Marx's critical project at the beginning of the 1850s as a science, or even as a nonscience. The second concept of ideology and its antithesis, the worldview, constitutes an initial attempt to come to terms with the scientific consequences of this critique and its implications, as much in the field of theory (the identification of juridical and anthropological presuppositions of bourgeois economy) as in the practical field of proletarian revolution (the passage from the moral idealism of utopian socialism to the mass politics of scientific socialism, transcending the abstract alternatives of law and violence, or anarchism and state socialism, etc.).

A well-known term sums up this recasting of the Marxist problematic: dialectical materialism (or dialectical method). But does this ambivalent term (the later history of Marxism proves it)[23] not serve, again, to camouflage a forced resolution? Is the idea of a "history of thought," supporting this recourse to the dialectic, anything more than the result of confusing two separate processes that are not strictly complementary and inevitably tend to drift apart—namely, a (political) history of ideologies and a (theoretical) history of worldviews? In Engels himself the immediate breakup of this false identity is quite evident. The formulations I have just referred to are only the beginning of a contradictory development, or a dual divergence.

We must recall here the conditions that provided a proper time and space (over twenty years) for Engels's theoretical reflections, straddling the death of Marx. At the outset, following the Commune and the dissolution of the First International, the formation of workers' parties was on the agenda. Conditions developed within the struggle of tendencies against anticipated deviations, represented in anarchism, trade union syndicalism (apolitical), nationalist state socialism (Lassalle) or its liberal form (a juridical socialism we will hear more about; or, in France, "possibilism"). The struggle for a revolutionary socialism and the hegemony of Marxist theory—indeed, for control of the Social Democratic party—are effectively bound together. However, from the 1880s on (after Marx's death), the situation is reversed: already within German social democracy this hegemony has been officially attained (and the Program of Erfurt sanctions it). Volume 1 of *Capital,* reinstated by Engels himself within the more general historical framework set forth in the *Manifesto,* is recognized as the theory of the party, along with the interpretation of it put forward by the *Anti-Dühring.* While the first texts by Engels (and the last by Marx) are written to inaugurate and enforce Marxism, Engels's last are also written against it, because its mission, even though incomplete, has been too successful.[24] They are written as an attempt to rectify what, in the process of constituting a Marxist orthodoxy, appears from the start to be an idealization and an ideologization of theory, as disturbing in its critical form (neo-Kantian: Bernstein) as in its materialist form (Darwinian: Kautsky). As part of this realignment, could there not also be an element of self-criticism, more or less avowed, directed not only at Engels's own writing (since Bernstein and Kautsky insist they became Marxists by reading the *Anti-Dühring*) but also at the "perverse" effects of the (available) texts of Marx, along with their omissions or excesses?

These reflections also anticipate the character of the crisis of Marxism openly pronounced in the years immediately following Engels's death. They are inscribed, moreover, within the compass of the same practical contradictions, the same dislocations *(décalages)*. The contradictions: on the one hand, the growth of the Socialist party, the strengthening of its organization, and its trade union ties; on the other, its tendency to subordinate itself to the "rules of the game" of bourgeois politics, drawn up by the state, such that Engels fears Germany will repeat the English counterexample (a "bourgeoisification" of the proletariat that fails to explain the concept of the "workers' aristocracy"). The dislocations: between the theses freshly culled from *Capital* concerning the development of class relations in capitalist society and the consequences effectively borne out by the Great Depression of the 1870s (the emergence of a finance capital and the first signs of a social politics from the bourgeoisie, not easily reducible to the simple formula of a "class which has become redundant").[25]

This displacement (Engels literally changes his position toward Marxism, or, if you prefer, Marxism escapes him) is carried over into conceptual revivals. The splitting up of the pair ideology/worldview can be taken as a symptom of the crisis. These concepts are wont to shift around: arising out of an essentially epistemological problematic, they end up, in the 1890s, being formulated in an essentially historical and political way (one is tempted to say that they are now back where they started). Their symmetry falls apart; they run alongside each other, becoming partly interchangeable and, at the same time, partly incompatible.

The Failure of Engels's Epistemological Project

If Engels's first formulations, at the time of the *Anti-Dühring* and *Dialectics of Nature,* are heavily drawn toward the epistemological, this is not only a result of the theoretical "fact" represented by *Capital;* it is also the effect of the ideological environment. *Erkenntnistheoretisch,* the adjective Engels uses, is the very word that for neo-Kantians qualifies the problem of knowledge, which is not the case for *Weltanschauung* (or at least not yet).[26] In the *Anti-Dühring,* Engels sets out by opposing to philosophy a simple *Anschauung der Welt;* he then graduates to the idea of a *Weltanschauung* (or *Weltauffassung*), which takes into account the materialist aspect of philosophy, basing itself on a history of nature, of society, and of thought—a worldview that must be "scientific" as much in its form as in its content. This brings us back to the question of method, to a traditional opposition between a system of knowledge, phantasmically constructed, and systematic knowledge, proceeding indefinitely, beyond any closure (Engels's only originality here is to apply this distinction to Hegelian philosophy, thereby showing that the dialectic transforms theoretical thought on the condition that it transforms itself within this experimental proof). As for the content, it leads us back to the laws of "internal connections" between things, discovered by science, and to the general "law of evolution," which it eventually articulates for each specific domain (the examples of Laplace, Helmholtz, Darwin, and Marx). If philosophy as Engels practices it does not lay the foundations for these laws, then it reflects their analogy and their common antithesis to the metaphysics of nature (in this, Engels is clearly more Aristotelian than Kantian). The idea of the history of thought is thus established; it stands for the claim that, in history, "materialism" and "dialectic" reciprocally imply each other. Each is a means of developing the other.[27]

Engels's argument is obviously neither conclusive nor free of vacillation (particularly over the definition of philosophy). However, it is plainly not vulgar, and certainly not scientistic according to the criteria of contemporary discourse.[28] Its basic features would have to be put to a properly positivist test, whereby it could be seen that any significant agreements point, nonetheless, to an entirely different attitude toward tendencies, one that generally disavows a conception of the relation between theory and practice (and, consequently, the status of a "science of politics") in the positivist mode of a simple exteriority, as a prediction or application, implying the primacy of theory. A more delicate question is that of the relations between Engels's epistemological project and post-Darwinian "evolutionist" ideology. Whenever he characterizes the dialectical element of worldview, Engels always harkens back to the Darwinian example, the analogy between the discovery of a "historical law of nature" and Marx's own "natural law of history," as well as the analogy between these two discoveries, on the one hand, and the historicism of Hegel, on the other (they share the basic idea of process). More seriously, this same Engels, who openly challenges social Darwinism (in the often cited letter to Lavrov, for example, dated November 12, 1875), does not think twice about applying pseudo-Darwinian models of the "natural selection of ideas" to the history of Christianity and socialism (he was neither the first nor the last to take this path so well worn today).

We can observe in this the undeniable effects of the attraction exercised on Engels's thought by that of Haeckel—the first, it appears, to have used the phrase "struggle between two worldviews"—one monist, mechanist, even materialist; the other dualist, finalist, and spiritualist—in his *History of Natural Creation* (1868). If Engels does not employ the technique Haeckel made the cornerstone of his evolutionism,[29] the "fundamental law of biogenetics," or the "theory of the recapitulation of phylogeny by ontogeny" (could it be that he really thought it too "mechanistic"?), he nonetheless retains the idea of the principle of evolution as a passage from inferior to superior, in the sense of an increasing complexity, by shifts at levels of organization. Written into this law is the passage from natural to human history and the differentiation therein (from life to work, from work to language and consciousness). Hence, the linking of Darwin with Marx—one a theorist of the descent of humankind, the other a theorist of the necessity of the passage from capitalism to socialism—results in founding the latter upon the increasing mastery over nature (by way of science, social planning). So the proletariat is not only "heir to classical German philosophy," it is *heir to the full range of evolution,* in short, the Son of Man (not, of course, theological Man, but "natural" Darwinian Man).[30]

If we are obliged to take this tendency seriously—one well and truly present in Engels, which will be dominant for a good part of his posterity—it is because it goes hand in hand with a countertendency that is, perhaps paradoxically, manifest in the very way he rediscovers Hegel and reverts to his dialectic, itself surely "evolutionist" though irreducible to the model of biological evolutionism. The idea of history conceived as evolutionary law, though heavy with consequences, only temporarily provides Engels with the structure of his materialist dialectic—through its relation to a specific worldview or image: the fixed or mechanistic structure of natural science, the political philosophy, and the metaphysics of the seventeenth and eighteenth centuries. This critique, however, very quickly changes its tune. Having used the weapons of evolutionism against the fetish of fixity *(le fixisme)*, it directs the firepower of its Hegelian references (and occasionally Fourierist ones) against the transformation of evolutionism and, in its turn, into a metaphysics or a system. For Engels, the idea of evolutionary law never works alone; it is always accompanied by its opposite number, which defines the dialectic through contradiction. Evolutionism ignores this completely (including Darwin and, most of all, Haeckel). Contradiction, however, is not the "struggle to survive."

The importance of Hegel's thought, according to Engels, though he cannot establish its laws, lies in its positing the whole world (natural and social) as a process and wholly identifying this process with its intrinsic structure, the internal sequence of a set of contradictions. In Engels's sense, a dialectical law, holding sway within the material conditions specific to it and with which it interacts *(Wechselwirkung)*, does not express the continuity of a developing order or plan (belonging, implicitly, to a subject) but rather the moments of a contradiction or the phases of an antagonism. Here we must grasp as important the thesis that explicitly calls for the world to be thought of not as a "complex of things" but as a "complex of processes," that is, a complexity without a preexisting or final identity.

Though the results of this investigation were later to be presented as a "coherent" system, I do not think that it would be tenable; yet it must be judged in context. Ultimately, Engels can be seen here *playing off one teleology against another* (and under the circumstances, we should not be surprised by the political and theoretical ambiguity that results when, in the name of his dialectical explanation of the tendency toward socialism—the source for which is Marx's famous phrase about the "expropriation of the expropriators" as a "negation of a negation"—he finds himself cornered once more by the insoluble problem of a nonteleological conception of the end of the state, which would not be the end of history). However, if we want to accept, as a working hypothesis, the general inevitability of evolutionism as a nineteenth-century scientific ideology,[31] we will have to call attention to both the theoretical impasse caused by this recourse to Hegel in the constitution of a materialist worldview and the singular place it occupies, historically, between the official bourgeois evolutionism of the nineteenth century (notably, that which will inspire *Kulturkampf)* and the Darwinian Marxism of social democracy. Engels's efforts then take on the air of a long-awaited critique of evolutionism at the heart of the workers' movement and Marxism itself.

Engels, however, seems to have considered this untenable, an indication of which is the failure and abandonment of the theoretical projects whose fragments are collected in *Dialectics of Nature*. Our understanding of this stems from the paradox inherent in the idea of such a history of thought: indeed, the more Engels adds to his empiricist proclamations (e.g., all thought comes from experience, or social experience), the more it appears his history of thought is fundamentally autonomous, with its own preexisting logic, and consonant with a composite dialectical structure that does not come from experience but from the idealist tradition! As if by chance, this structure always falls back upon the Trinitarian model of the familiar adventures of the dialectic and posits materialism, hence the materialist and communist worldview, as the end of the process. And it happily falls in with Engels's own critique of Hegel, with respect to the system and the Absolute Spirit. Could communism-materialism not be another name for Absolute Spirit? How can one not ask oneself this question?[32]

Above all, Engels assumes that the materialist worldview is identical to the communist one. What justifies his identifying them? To say that the latter is the attainment of materialism, through Marx, as a science of the historical necessity of communism, only provides a mirror image of the question. It can be said that the communist worldview will necessarily be materialistic because it bases itself on extending the contemporary scientific method, culminating in the articulation of laws of evolution, to history and politics. But it can also be said that materialism, basically, stands for nothing other than this configuration of principles: communism + science = materialism. What seems to be missing here is a specifically political component, one both internal to the theory and necessarily implicated in its history.[33]

But where do we go to look for this lack—to the materialist side or the communist side? Which of these two terms suggests a class point of view, and who can thus *add* it to science *without* it being a "foreign addition"? In fact, two historical structures, fundamentally at odds with each other, layered one on top of the other, are at stake here. The first is that of the adventures of the dialectic, from its Greek origins to its completion in historical materialism. The second is that of the struggle between materialism and idealism throughout the history of thought. Each of these categories, considered alone, can be read in a perfectly idealistic way, as an expression of the *autonomy* of thought.

What would authorize another reading would be to understand each of these categories, and each in relation to the other, as expressing a political determination, the very instance of the class struggle. This would involve saying, on the one hand, that materialism in different historical epochs expresses resistance to the established order, the struggle of the oppressed and the exploited, in order to understand how the history of the dialectic, intersected by this struggle, ends up precisely in a theory of exploitation and the advent of communism. It would involve demonstrating, on the other hand (Engels occasionally suggests this, or do we foist this interpretation on him?), that the first form of the dialectic, the Greek one, is organically linked to the emergence of the class-state in the ancient city and that its ultimate form (representing, to some extent, its immanent self-criticism) is aimed at thinking the disintegration of that bond, the end of the state and its classes. Then we would have an explanation of how the relation between materialism and idealism is inverted before our eyes; how, for the first time, the struggle of the exploited ceases to assume the simple form of an endless resistance or rebellion, or of a stepping-stone toward a new order of domination; how, for the first time, the consciousness of the struggling class ceases to be idealistic (or utopian) and how the theory of this struggle can be identified with materialism, with the thinking of the real movement. However, for this interpretation, or the closest alternative, to lead us effectively away from any preestablished plan, we would need a complete history of the "class struggle within theory" and its necessary material conditions. The relationship between materialism and the class struggle would no longer seem naturally given or guaranteed; it would be produced as an encounter, fusion, or conflict within the determined conditions on which its modalities depend. But if Engels's assumption implicitly encompasses this historical problem, it also calls an immediate halt to any attempt at concrete analysis.

State, Masses, Ideology

If this analysis is correct, we are in a better position to judge the new definition of ideology that Engels puts forward in *Ludwig Feuerbach and the End of Classical German Philosophy* (1888). Engels's new definition is the result of ten years of trial and error, a process manifest in his rectification of and reaction against the nascent Marxism I have set out above.[34]

This detailed definition begins with the critique of the Hegelian dialectic, showing that the contradiction of materialism and idealism must be thought of as immanent. An idealism can itself be historical; one must, however, *distinguish idealism from the "ideological process" in general.* The ideological process (a formulation appearing in *Ludwig Feuerbach*) is more general than idealism, which is only a necessary, but derivative, effect of the ideological process within specific conditions:

> Some ideologies, even more refined, even more distant from their material and economic base, take the form of philosophy and religion. Here it is the correspondence of representations with their conditions of material existence which becomes increasingly complex, increasingly extenuated by the links in between. But it exists nonetheless.... once constituted, each ideology is developed on the base of given elements of representation and goes on to develop them. Otherwise it would not be an ideology; i.e., use ideas as autonomous entities that develop on their own and are subject solely to their own laws. That the conditions of the material existence of men, in whose minds this mental process takes place, determine its course in the last instance, remains for them a necessarily unconscious fact, or else all ideology would be at an end.

It is clear that ideology is a system of differences, a *chain of mediations.* The opposition of practice to ideology takes the form of a relation (the unconscious last instance) between two histories, one of which (that of secondary ideological elaborations) is inserted into the other (that of economics) by way of a materialist birth.

None of this would move us beyond a well-worn empiricism were it not for the way Engels attaches this definition to a new conception of the state. The birth of ideological forms is mediated essentially by the history of forms of the state apparatus ("the State is the foremost ideological power"). What we have again (as in *The German Ideology,* which Engels had just reread in manuscript, salvaged from the "nibbling rats") is at once a theory of the state and a theory of ideology. Yet their respective articulation has changed. In *The German Ideology,* ideology is formally anterior to the state, since it arises directly out of the division of labor at the base of the development of civil bourgeois society. In substance, however, it is no different from the state itself (which is to say, alienation): they are mirror images of the same critique of political illusion. Strictly speaking, the bourgeois state is itself only an ideological form, its material base being the division of intellectual and manual labor.

In *Ludwig Feuerbach,* there is a tendency to recognize a *real complexity of the state,* not only because it assumes both the general, productive functions of society and the coercive role of a class-state but also because it recapitulates or condenses all the historically anterior forms of domination (whereas the capitalist production relation actually effaces the past). This singular reality of the state apparatus in history raises the question of a (re)production of ideology by the state, or at least in strict complicity with the existence of the state, by means of those institutions that have a "statist" disposition (like the medieval Church). Only through this statist mediation is the relation to social antagonisms established, the result being the state, autonomized as a class apparatus. Only this internal relation to the state explains why the organization of ideology ultimately tends to manufacture dogmas or systems that ratify their own specific logic—if not their own axiomatics—giving them the illusory appearance of truth. In effect, no state is viable that does not suppress the contradiction in germ within every difference, in the unified interests of a dominant discourse. This relation, finally, enables the mapping of a topography of ideological regions (religious, juridical, moral, philosophical); it shows that in each social formation the articulation and hierarchy of these regions changes. When a new class becomes dominant and the state apparatus changes form, a new ideological form likewise becomes dominant, which means that it imposes its own logic on other forms after the fashion of its "enlightenment" (a metaphor inspired by Hegel). Thus, every revolt against the state, subject to this determining dominant system, necessarily starts as a heresy.

But this definition of ideological forms is not a given in itself. It fulfills a well-defined role—to resolve, in a materialist and scientific manner, the question of the historical movement *(geschichtliche Bewagung)* and its motor forces *(Treibkräfte),* otherwise known as the reciprocal problem of the reduction of an ideology to its material base.[35] Engels thus comes to terms with what, since Machiavelli and Hegel, has been a classical question, one that is typically ideological, namely, the relation between "individuality and the mass" (and even the relation between the individual, the masses, and the leaders: the repetition of the Napoleonic origins of the concept of *Führer).* Engels tries to solve this by combining two preexisting theoretical components: first, the whole gnosiological construction of the *inverted ideological image* as a means of explaining how, in people's minds, interests become ideas, then motives, and finally desires; second, the statistical construction of the *composition of individual wills,* which explains why people desire some determined outcome but end up with something altogether different. The conjuncture of these two components makes ideological forms the fundamental explanation of the *Rückwirkung* the process of reflexive determination *(action en retour)* by which the historical process defines itself. What is important here is not so much the fact that ideology acts reflexively *(agisse en retour)* upon its base but, more fundamentally, that ideology is, in its own right, *the median term of the historical process or of the image that society constructs of itself,* which forever generates its historicity.[36]

Whatever the validity or originality of Engels's constructions, they conclude with an irrefutable judgment: the concept of ideology can be both an instrument for the differential analysis of social formations and an organic component of the theory of history. It follows that the same concept, thus defined, can be tracked down and pinpointed theoretically within historical materialism. Yet this conclusion is tautological. In reality, there was no historical materialism beyond a critique of ideology *(The German Ideology)* and of political economy *(Capital)* until the time had come for raising the question of the relation between the economic, political, and ideological "instances." It is crucial that we recognize this problem as that of the historical relation between the masses and the state.

Historical materialism for Engels is neither the single concept of class struggle, nor even the correspondence of ideology with class relations, but the articulation of a series of concepts: class, state, masses, ideology. That the class struggle is the "motor of history" and that it is "the masses who make history" still does not represent a solution but, rather, the problem itself. In the conjuncture of what one can analyze as "the classes" (antagonism) and "the masses" (or mass movements), Engels attempts to define what should be understood as ideology: if the masses in their "being" are nothing other than a class—or, rather, do not exist as real individuals other than as individuals of specific classes—their mode of historical existence cannot be reduced to that of classes.

Just as Rousseau asked himself What makes a people a people? and answered by way of the contract and its distinctive ideality (or its symbolic form), Engels ponders What is it that constitutes the masses as the masses? and answers by way of ideology and its distinctive unconsciousness, linking it to a materialist birth in which the state represents the instance of the class struggle. On the political scene, where regimes come and go historically, the classes are not introduced in person, in the abstract, but as masses and mass movements, always already subject to the reflexive effect of ideology. It is this last moment that represents the concrete instance of politics.

In spite of what has just been suggested, however, it would be wrong to believe that the concept of ideology, defined in this way, actually enables Engels to solve the ongoing problem concerning the relation between the scientific theory of historical materialism and proletarian political practice, or the organization of the class struggle in the form of the party. This solution would only support, *hic et nunc,* a distinction between a revolutionary politics "leading to a great historical transformation" and a simple "tempest in a teapot," which applies to what the theoretical formulation of *Ludwig Feuerbach* always returns to in its reduction of the ideological makeup of the masses to the sum of individual variables *(une resultante des mobiles).* It also applies to two expressions that, within this problematic, are more impossible than ever: that of materialist ideology and proletarian ideology, since each implies the other and, if not the existence of a proletarian state, then at least the constitutive role played by the existing state in their formation. If there is an ideology of the proletariat, it is either a nonideology *(Illusionslosigkeit)* or the dominant ideology itself, surviving in the delayed consciousness or miraculously turned against the state which (re)produces it. Engels thus, on the one hand, has a principle for explaining the historical movement *in terms of ideology;* and on the other, he has a revolutionary force *devoid of ideology,* which, in this sense, is not a force.[37]

"Neither God, nor Caesar, nor Tribune"

One would think that it is in order to solve this problem from another angle that Engels embarks on a new attempt to define "worldview." The most interesting text from this point of view is probably the article he co-wrote with Kautsky in 1887, "Juridical Socialism," attacking the theses of Anton Menger.[38] Engels's argument rests on a comparison among the "three great world-views": medieval, bourgeois, and proletarian.

> The medieval world-view was essentially theological. . . . it is Catholicism which constitutes the unity of the Western European world, made up of developing peoples in a constant relation of reciprocity. This unification *(Zusammenfassung)* was not simply an ideal product *(ideell)*. It was an effective *(wirklich)* unification . . . thanks to the feudal, hierarchical organization of the Church. . . . It was the Church, with its feudal landed property, which constituted the real *(reale)* link between different nations, and which lent its religious consecration to the wordly order of the feudal State. The clergy, after all, were the only cultivated class of the period. It went without saying that all thought had for its origin and base *(Basis)*, the dogma of the Church. Law, natural science, and philosophy were each regulated in accordance with the content of the teachings of the Church.

Engels goes on to note that the power of the mercantile bourgeoisie was built out of the very substance of feudalism. The Reformation,

> in its theoretical aspect was no more than a series of efforts on the part of the bourgeoisie, urban plebeians, and peasants in revolt, to adapt the old theological world-view to the transformation of economic conditions and conditions of existence of the new classes. The banner of religion was waved for the last time in seventeenth-century England, but, scarcely fifty years later, the new world-view made its appearance in France in all of its purity as the *juridical world-view.* It was to become the classical bourgeois view. It was a lay version *(Verweltlichung)* of the theological view: in place of divine right was human right, in place of the Church was the State. Those economic and social relations that had been presented as creations of dogma and of the Church that sanctioned them were now represented as based on the law, and as a creation of the State.

This is explained, Engels argues, by a threefold activity: the universalizing of exchange, which requires fixed contractual form in accordance with state norms; free trade, which imposes the watchword of equality for all before the law; and the struggles of the bourgeoisie for political power, which, since the bourgeoisie is up against privilege, has to take the form of demands for its rights. All that, let us note, is very general but seems incontestable.

Against these two worldviews of the historical ruling classes, Engels posits the proletarian worldview, which is "in the process of taking over the world" through socialism, and the strengthening of the working-class movement (Lenin and Gramsci would say that it has a tendency to become hegemonic). This idea appears to differ from the outline of the history of ideology sketched out in *Ludwig Feuerbach* only by way of a substitution of terms. But the substitution is enough to do away with the obstacle that the concept of ideology encounters: it clears a space for the proletariat. We can now speak of a proletarian worldview that would be to the class struggle of the proletariat what the juridical worldview had been for the bourgeois class struggle: its weapon and its justification. We thereby move, it seems, away from an account of the reproduction of ideological dominations (in which, to be frank, they are all substantially the same, insofar as they legitimate the existing order) toward an account of transformation in which the relation to the state could be inverted. Thus, the conflict of worldviews, according to their content and the nature of the classes that hold them, would not be limited to adjusting the various configurations of a game of ideological regions (or discourses of domination, which buttress each other) but would overturn their effects.

Have we actually gotten any further? Perhaps not. In describing the "prolonged struggle" between two worldviews, bourgeois juridical and communist proletarian, as *the* form of the actual class struggle, Engels shows us that the latter has a necessary place in history. It is important that his demonstration is wholly based on the reaffirmation of the *existence of juridical ideology,* which is always stubbornly denied, even among the critics of the school of natural law. It is also symptomatic that this demonstration now has as its counterpart *the eclipse of the very term "ideology."* Engels seems to be in a quandary about defining *the proper content of the proletarian worldview* with a term comparable to "theological" and "juridical," which characterize its two precedents. He stubbornly agonizes over these difficulties, as is evident in the description he offers for the transition of the bourgeois worldview to the proletarian worldview. He condenses and clarifies the analysis of utopian socialism proposed in *Anti-Dühring* by identifying two stages. Socialist ideas first appear in a form itself juridical by turning against the bourgeoisie its own watchword and ideal of equality. Then they appear in a humanist and implicitly "moral" form that sanctions the critique of juridicalism but rejects all politics considered to be bourgeois (this corresponds very nicely to the themes of the early writings of Marx and Engels themselves). We can see what this transition actually leads to, with the experience of the revolutions and the growth of the workers' movement: *the recognition of the political nature of class struggle,* denied by all previous worldviews, for which politics is rather the suppression of class struggle (but not, of course, the classes themselves). Thus, it is not an a priori deduction but its very history that would provide us with the key to the unique "content" of the proletarian view, which would let us know another theory and another political practice.[39]

For all the worldviews, it always comes back to an idea of politics (or a political idea), "for all class struggle is political," as was already suggested in the *Manifesto* (what was earlier called a "materialism of politics"). However, in the case of feudalism and the bourgeoisie, politics appears in different forms and under different names (religious or juridical) that sublimate and disguise it. In a number of texts from the same period (preparatory to his work in *The Origin of the Family*), Engels uses a remarkable phrase to describe the process of displacement toward certain goals, of lateral objectives *(Nebenzwecke, Nebendinge)* "tangential" to the fundamental problem of class struggle. This suggests that politics, in its essence, is not juridical, contrary to what is always assumed, for the sake of argument, in the humanist works of his youth or in *The German Ideology.* The juridical is itself a political disguise, one of the means of sidetracking political activity that detours toward these *Nebenzwecke,* either fictional or real. What would characterize the proletarian worldview, to the extent of lifting statist constraints, would be the recognition of politics itself as a directly political form, without any displacement or diversion.

This argument only appears to be tautological, for the class struggle, in the last analysis, has a precise stake in it. Engels enters here into the whole consideration of communism, precipitated by the Commune, whose blueprint Marx has already provided (particularly in the *Critique of the Gotha Program*): *communism is a politics of labor,* not only as a struggle of workers aspiring to "government by the working class," but, more profoundly, as a redefinition and recomposition of politics starting from the very activity of labor, as a reciprocal transformation of politics by labor and labor by politics. This is what I have proposed elsewhere as the second concept of the "dictatorship of the proletariat" in Marx and Engels—a new form of politics, not a simple revolutionary strategy for seizing power.[40]

This reading of Engels's historical project assumes that we also might put an end to the ambiguity of the term "domination," present as much in the expression "dominant ideology" as in "dominant worldview." Until this point, paradoxically, Engels has always treated the proletarian worldview, that of the *exploited,* in a manner strictly parallel to that of the *exploiters* (apologists for slavery, serfdom, capitalism). In describing and historically placing this revolutionary worldview, he anticipates the fictional moment when it will, in turn, come to be dominant and "take over the world." Is it not just this anticipation that curtails any analysis of the organization of the class struggle corresponding to a proletarian worldview, precisely by constantly shuttling it back and forth between the statist analogy and its abstract antithesis, from the "party-state" to the "anti-state" party? Indeed, according to the logic of Engels's historical account, one would need to have an institution or an organization corresponding, on the part of the proletariat, to what the church or state had been in order to satisfy this function of theoretically developing the "class point of view" expressed by the worldview. To say that this institution is the "revolutionary party" (which Engels does not) would be to give a *name* to the process it suggests, that of an "affinity" or "correspondence" between what goes on in the mind of the proletariat during the class struggle and what Marx's mind produced: a materialist conception of history. But this would be to run the risk, as the anarchists point out, of perpetuating a political form that does not break with the historical inheritance of forms of domination.

Religion and "The Thought of the Masses"

Engels seeks to bring about this theoretical change by representing the masses not from above but from below, in the light of their own "convictions" (what he designates, in the preface to the English edition of *Socialism: Utopian and Scientific*, as a "creed," translated as *credo*). However, he is only able to do this in an indirect way, through a comparison between the history of socialism and that of Christianity. Let us reread, from this standpoint, one of his last texts, the "Contribution to the History of Primitive Christianity," from 1894 to 1895.[41] There he expresses satisfaction in discovering in Renan (of whom he has a rather low opinion) a comparison between the groups formed by the first Christians during the decadent Roman Empire and the modern "sections of the workers International," a comparison he intends to resurrect in order to shed light on the history of modern socialism by way of the Christian example. It is not enough to identify the base of political class unity with the revolt of the exploited, enslaved, or wage laborers; it remains to show how that base is produced out of the multiplicity of groups, sects, and rival organizations, and to describe the way in which, faced with exploitation, they represent to themselves salvation, the hopes and struggles that both unite them and perpetuate their divisions, which are properly the objects to be explained in examining revolutionary mass movements. As opposed to the Jacobin model, it is the Church or ("pre-Constantinian" Christianity) that here stands for, as is often the case in the German philosophical tradition, the antithesis of the statist imperium and the autonomous form of the organization of social consciousness.

"In fact," writes Engels,

> the struggle against a world which, from the outset, has the advantage of power, and the simultaneous struggle of the innovators among themselves, are common to both the primitive Christians and the socialists. The two great movements are not made by leaders and prophets—though there is no shortage of prophets in either—they are movements of the masses. And all mass movements necessarily begin in confusion because all "thought of the masses" *(Massendenken)* proceeds by way of contradictions, since it lacks clarity and coherence *(sich zuerst in Widersprüchen, Unklarheiten, Zusammenhangslosigkeit bewegt);* they are confused still, precisely on account of the role played by their prophets in the beginning.

And later:

> From where did the first Christians draw their recruits? Chiefly from "the worked and the over-worked," members of the lowest social echelons, as befits a revolutionary group.... There was absolutely no com-

mon path to liberation for so many diverse elements.
For each, paradise lost was behind them. . . . What was
the solution, the sanctuary, for these oppressed and
impoverished slaves? What was the common way out
(Ausweg) for these different human groups, with divergent and often opposing interests? There was certainly a need to find one, and it had to be one single
great revolutionary movement to embrace them all.
The solution exists, but not in this world. As things
stood, it could only be a religious solution. A new
world was discovered.

Early Christianity is truly a primitive communism.

These texts, the sheer extreme of Engels's speculations, are not
without their relevance, even a historical one; but they are clearly circular,
presupposing what they set out to demonstrate. What they no doubt proclaim, and in no uncertain terms, is that "the masses think," that *the proletarian worldview is nothing other than the thought of the masses,* whose
specific content (what we term the "politics of labor") is not the result of
a simple configuration of the class struggle but represents the conclusion to
a long history (and a properly historical memory). In this sense, this thinking
is not that of individuals; it is not the sum of individual psychologies (in-
terests/motives/desires). Does this show the influence of social psychology,
of the sort for which, at this time, certain reactionary theorists are drawing
up a program?[42] I say no, since we do not find in Engels any trace of the
two constitutive elements of such a psychology: neither the idea that the
constitutive process of the masses is its relation to a leader or an organizer
(meneur); nor the idea that the thought of the masses is, in the last analysis,
religious in the sense of a so-called elementary (archaic, primitive) religiosity
that makes a periodic return in human social behavior. Rather, we find the
reverse, the idea that religious conviction, with its own ambivalence, is a
given historical form of the thought of the masses. This means that the line
of demarcation could not be clearly drawn without constructing a concept
of the unconscious, one different from the notion of a shadow cast—epistemologically or biologically—by consciousness; one that would theoretically
reflect both the imaginary of salvation and the interpellation of individuals
(if necessary, by themselves) as bearers of the collective, institutional identity of the group, the social movement.

Engels's comparison never really breaks free from the positivist
antithesis between illusion and reality, even when it willingly takes to task
the most simplistic and dogmatic forms. Already, his insistence upon the
heritage of classical German philosophy and utopian socialism in historical
materialism is at odds with the congenital scientism of the workers' party.
But it always refers only to abstract intellectual productions. In making of
socialism not only an analogue of primitive Christianity but also the distant
result of its transformation—through the revolutionary mass movements of
the Middle Ages and the Renaissance, the peasant wars, the utopias of the
English Levellers and Diggers, the struggle of the Fourth Estate in the French
Revolution—Engels inscribes the ideological relation to history within the
very content of the proletarian worldview, or, if you will, within the mode
of production of mass consciousness. But he only does this in order to

confirm an evolutionist view of that history: in the end, sufficient cause for the transformation can always be found in the "real conditions" of liberation, that is, in the development of the productive forces and in the simplification or the radicalization of class antagonisms by capitalism. If real communism can grow out of imaginary communism, it is because these conditions force the proletariat today to leave illusion behind; it is because there actually exists a preestablished harmony between the impoverishment of the masses, the radical absence of property among wage workers, and the radical absence of illusions in Marxist theory. The political content of mass thinking remains suspended within this preestablished harmony, which is basically always that of a radical negativity and which requires all the pedagogical and organizational work of a party to bring it to the attention of the world.

III

The trajectory we have mapped, from the formulations of the young Marx to those of the later Engels, even if incomplete, helps to sketch the problematic of ideology within early Marxism. We have seen both an astonishing consistency, in the expression of an antithesis between the dominant ideology and the revolutionary proletariat, and an uninterrupted series of conceptual displacements, leading ultimately to a complete inversion of the initial positions: from practice to theory, from speculation to history, even from intellectuals (ideologues) to the masses (and their own thought). I think we have also provided some of the materials for a critique. What would the essential points of that critique be?[43]

Party Form and Class Identity

The theoretical problem of ideology has always been determined by the same practical problem: that of the constitution of a revolutionary force (or form). The constitutive role of the concept of ideology in historical materialism corresponds to the emergence of the workers' movement as a real force in the political field and to its polarizing effect there. Conversely, the revival of the concept of ideology in the discourse of the social sciences and of politics itself, even if it takes the form of a misappropriation, corresponds exactly to this polarizing effect. To begin with, the workers' movement is the "foreign body" of politics; as such, it has to be expelled. Later, when its inclusion within politics becomes an irreversible fact, it is the whole of politics—discourse and practice—organized around its inescapable presence. As for the theme of the "end of ideologies" (or the "end of worldviews"), whether in a pragmatic and decisionist form or in a hypercritical or skeptical form (designating the critique of dominant ideologies as ideological in itself), it also corresponds, for more than half a century, to the attempt to relativize this polarizing effect on the political field, and thus to the attempt to find a political structure that would be situated beyond or outside class struggles—and would therefore be more essential than class struggles.[44]

This confirms, then, that what is in question in the vicissitudes of this theoretical problem are the problems posed by the institution of the party form (*l'institution de la forme parti*) and the contradictions it harbors. The history of the workers' movement, from the 1840s on, is a dialectic of integration within and opposition to the party form. The workers' movement—and thus the existence of a working class as a political force—has never been able to constitute itself outside of the party form, no more than it has been able to confine itself to the party form. In fact, the party form contains an "impurity" or basic ambivalence that is responsible for its historical efficacy and necessity: it is not only the form in which the workers' movement resists assimilation into the dominant political model but also the form in which it is thereby admitted or introduced into that model, in order, eventually, to transform it, like the Trojan horse. That is why, when the crisis of the party form develops historically within the workers' movement (irreversible nowadays, even if its outcome is unclear), it is accompanied by a reconsideration of the Marxist (and anti-Marxist) discourse on ideology and a deconstruction of the very concept of dominant ideology. In part, this reconsideration also constitutes, if not a totally impracticable "return to the origins," at least a reactivation of the internal difficulties repressed in the constitutive moment of the concept. The history of the problem of ideology, including when it simply *repeats* the oscillations of the initial formulation, expresses in a privileged way the historical contradictions of the party form (I do not say it reflects or explains them).

The position of Marx and Engels, from this point of view, is very revealing. They already show a manifest tendency, as does the whole Marxist tradition thereafter, to formulate a concept in order to be able to think the class identity of the workers' movement and provide the working class with a practical recognition of its own historical identity. This tendency is inscribed from the start in the idea of a transformation from class *in* itself to class *for* itself. As opposed to the philosophical concept of class consciousness, the idea of a proletarian worldview describes this perspective and can furnish it with a practical name. If that becomes inseparable from the goal of constructing a party in such a way that the worldview of the proletariat realizes itself as the conception of the party, it is because the proletarian worldview only exists within the framework of a struggle against the dominant worldview (or ideology), dissociating itself from the latter by way of a periodically reaffirmed break. This is primarily because of the need to provide a historical continuity for the class identity, which is a result of this break. The continuity must go beyond the revolutionary conjunctures in which it is most conspicuous, both for itself and, above all, for the ruling class(es), conjunctures where the unity of the social body around a certain form of the state is shown to be a fiction, if it is not shattered altogether.[45]

From the catastrophism of 1840-50 to the evolutionism of the last period, the theoretical work of Marx and Engels is aimed at a steady distribution and accumulation, through a series of conjunctures, of the irruptive energy of revolutionary movements. It is aimed not only at transcending the slackening effects of the counterrevolutionary phases, those in which capitalism expands, but also at effectively anticipating the construction of new social relations. The base of this continuity is the industrial revolution itself; its matter is formed in the meeting of exploitation with class instinct and the proletarian revolt, but its form can only come out of organization.[46] Party organization and worldview crystallize a relation of forces, mediate an effective conquest of power and appropriation of knowledge without which it would be silly to believe that the masses could ever "make their own history." Under these circumstances class struggle within society can be carried to the limits of the system and beyond.

But is the position of Marx and Engels really as simple as this facile continuity suggests? The impossibility of talking about a proletarian ideology (as will be readily done later within the Socialist and Communist parties) and the oscillation between the concepts of ideology and worldview can be considered symptomatic. They redirect us toward the aporias also present, in the same period, within the definition of the party form. What remains unclear is the question of whether the conception of the party articulated by Marx and Engels, along with their definition of proletarian politics, ultimately represents nothing more than a critique of the different concurrent tendencies at the heart of the workers' movement (particularly the anarchist antistatist tendency and the statist tendency of post-Lassallean social democracy). The strength of the Marxist position is that it exposes the "fetishism of the State," as present in its abstract negations as in its fantasies of pragmatic utility, and that it therefore clears an autonomous space for the problem of the politics of the workers' movement. Its weakness is in only being able to manifest this theoretical autonomy by way of a permanent tactical compromise between those tendencies, or rather by way of a political "art" of struggle on several fronts, as a function of the conjunctures, at the very moment when the continuity of organization is being reasserted as a guarantee of the correctness of this theoretical autonomy.

The same aporia can be seen—but with paradoxically prolific consequences—in the difficulty Marx and Engels experience in occupying a stable position inside the organization, in what could be called the economy of the party form, as bearers of theoretical activity and scientific discovery concerning class struggle. Everything happens as if the unity of theoretical "core" and political "core," or the theoretical and strategic "direction" (a unity denounced on suspicion by the anarchists, as the "dictatorship" of Marx, thus providing ahead of time one of the elements of the future critique of Marxist totalitarianism), had never been able to exist without immediately breaking apart again. In the period of the First International, Marx was the strategic director of a very embryonic movement, but only as a mediator and arbiter of conflicts between tendencies in the organization, not as a theoretician of the mode of capitalist production. Any division thus takes effect, in a sense, within Marx, within his own subjectivity. In the period of social democracy, Marx and Engels were officially in charge of the party's theoretical direction but not, strictly speaking, of its political direction, which was in the hands of the "organic intellectuals" of the party apparatus with whom they found themselves in a constantly ambivalent relation, sometimes of conflict and sometimes of reciprocal advantage on the question of joining forces with the working masses. A series of well-known historical incidents illustrates this contradiction.

We can no longer believe nowadays that this represents only a historical delay, whether in the constitution of the working class as a collective intellectual or in the proletarianization of political apparatuses, since this contradiction is reproduced at each stage of the history of the workers' movement and Marxism. That is why, no doubt, the theory of the party form has never resolved the dilemmas of spontaneity and centralism, except in some of the intuitive critiques of Lenin, Gramsci, and Mao, at the time of its transformations, crises, and reworkings. In reality, the idea of the intellectual direction of class struggle can only be divided up, constantly, between the two discursive forms it must assume: program and theory. Each

190

is constituted as a way of engaging through thought the historical process in action, but each is constructed from different points of view or different conceptual rules of play. (Both are equally ways of responding to the demands of politics—if need be, by addressing them directly, but from different subjective positions).[47]

The fact that Marx and Engels (just as, in their own way, Lenin or Gramsci) are uncomfortable with the reduction of either of these positions to the other, always preserving a residual disparity between them—or covering it up under the pressure of circumstances—explains their resistance to the constitution of a political-theoretical dogma. In this context, the very idea of scientific socialism still possesses for them a critical connotation—and a democratic one in the strongest sense of the term. This is not an example of taking advantage of science to legitimize a managerial role, let alone the means of extending to a clique (or a caste) of Marxist intellectuals, disciples of the author of *Capital,* the theoretical sanction they need in order to establish a monopoly over political leadership. It is, rather, an attempt, in the spirit of the *Aufklärung,* to make available to the masses, or the base itself, the instruments of its historical orientation against the rule of leaders, prophets, and other bosses. In this way, the theoretical core would tend to be situated everywhere (as Pascal would have said), as a kind of noncenter. However, if the unity of theoretical thought (science, philosophy) and the thought of the masses is, indeed, the effect sought after by the proletarian worldview, it remains to this day the object of a postulate, that is, the more it remains empirically uncertain, the more it is affirmed as a unity of opposites.

Historicity without History

My proposal was to read as a symptom Marxism's conceptual oscillation between ideology and worldview, the symptom of a practical contradiction recurring throughout the history of the theory but also of a blockage in theory itself, one with a progressively more immediate effect on analyses of the state and the capitalist system. This blockage is quite evident (for us) in most of the texts by Marx and Engels that bear on the crisis, the wage form, syndicalism in its relations with proletarianization, and the difference between reform and revolution. Finally, what is at issue is the way *Capital* represents the historicity of the capitalist mode of production.

The striking fact about the theoretical forms I have described is that they never break free from either the metaphysical symmetry of truth (or being) and illusion (or unreality), or from the political symmetry of society and the state, even though the articulation of new definitions, and the passage from one term to the other, is always presented in terms of an attempt to transcend that symmetry. It could be that these two schema are intrinsically related and that the problems they pose may in fact be the same.[48]

Because the expressive relation between society (or, more precisely, mercantile society) and state (as the organ of the "general functions" of society *and* as the organization of the ruling class) finds itself under interrogation, we can say that there is a fundamental incompatibility between historical materialism and this representation of a social system as the superimposition of two spheres (economic and political, private and public, base and superstructure, society and state, etc.) that derive from philosophy and classical political economy. In the last analysis, it is the Marxist concept of class struggle that contradicts this representation, in rendering invalid any conception of history as the expression of society within the state or the symmetrical absorption of the state within society. The concept of ideology implies, in principle, the same critique. Finally, however, each new definition reproduces in its own way the same symmetry or dualism: it has only been displaced or formulated in a different way. The concept of class struggle is thereby buried again underneath the problematic of economy, political philosophy, and the classical philosophy of history. Paradoxically, the concept of critique nullifies the effect of theoretical rupture, or the epistemological break of historical materialism. Hence, the vacillation proper to the concept of ideology points toward and invites the theoretical vacillation in Marxism between the before and the after, the within and the beyond of a break with economic ideology and the bourgeois ideology of history that it denounces.

Engels's formulation in *Ludwig Feuerbach* (one could say the same about the analysis of commodity fetishism in *Capital*) points this out in a rather significant way. Against an economist representation of history in which the state is only the instrument of the ruling class in the class struggle, and the latter, in turn, the expression of a law of correspondence between relations of property and the development of productive forces, Engels sketches the analysis of a disparity or a dialectical game, characterized by the difference between the classes and the masses. In posing within the sphere of ideology the question of the constitution of the masses as "motor forces" of history, and defining the ideological process by way of its internal relation to the state, he introduces a germ of conceptualization that would carry us much further than the simple idea of a reflexive action of one sphere on the other. The masses, as Engels sees it, obviously exceed the sphere of the state, conceived as an apparatus of power, while determining its concrete forms. To specify this *internal* determination of the mode of ideological thought and of the state itself, it would be necessary either to advance to "a broadening of the concept of State," causing it to encroach structurally upon the sphere of society (this is Gramsci's method), or to try to think an "action at a distance," an "absent causality" of the state within the ideological process that characterizes the irreducible complexity of what is called the state (this is Althusser's method). The interest of the latter, of course, would be in supplementing Engels's insistence on the unconscious nature of the ideological process. The unconscious would precisely express this double instance, or double modality of the historical action of the ruling-class state, at once immediately manifest within its coercive and administrative apparatus and indirect and invisible in its effect on the ideology of the masses. This differential gap between consciousness and unconsciousness in the social and political struggle would thus designate the very materiality of ideology, its mode of historical action.

It is not difficult to see how the classical symmetry of society and state is lodged at the heart of this definition of ideology. It is represented there (very classically, for anyone who has read Hobbes and Hegel) by way of an account of the "birth" of ideology based on individual interests. That these interests are implicitly or explicitly defined as *class* interests, that they are determined by the material conditions of labor and the existence of

192

individuals, changes nothing; far from it, since this birth wholly reproduces the classical model of the formation of the "general interest" (or the "general will") arising from the concurrence of individual interests. As we have seen, this is the idea of the result or sum of variable forces *(resultantes des variables).* In other words, Engels's concept of ideology revives, by virtue of its theoretical form alone, if not its political content, the Hegelian conception of the upheaval of the state arising out of the contradictions of civil society: what Hegel christened "the cunning of reason."

In its form, the movement of the masses is to class antagonism in Engels what the state is to civil society in Hegel: its dialectical transcendence, or its active totalization. In both cases there is a *birth of historical individuality proceeding from the "infra-historical" individuality,* that of the economic classes and the empirical individuals they comprise. The very thesis (also a watchword) according to which "it is the masses who make history" therefore takes on a new light, as the equivalent of the role assigned by Hegel to the "great men" (and we must remember that on this point Engels felt it necessary to *reduce* the role of the "great men" to that of the masses). Engels's construction suggests that the masses are the *truly* "great men" (of the state) of history; in this sense, it inverts the ideological, statist theme that Hegelian philosophy has taken up. This inversion, however, preserves its Hegelian theoretical structure: both the masses and ideology function, respectively, like the "great men" and the "spirit of the people" in Hegel, namely, as the "spirit of the age" realizing itself. The trajectory in Engels (and Marx) that leads from class antagonism to communism through the action of the masses (or their historical individuation) exactly parallels, notwithstanding the difference in their contents, what in Hegel leads from civil society to freedom within the state, through transcending the concurrence that expresses the individuality of the "great men." The myth of the "great men" (Is it so original to the nineteenth century?) is replaced by a corresponding myth of the masses.[49]

Earlier on, I took up the paradox posed, on the one hand, by the dynamics of mass movement in the sphere of ideology and, on the other, by a revolutionary force without an ideology proper. One might add that it is the concept of the movement of history that is at stake here. Perhaps the paradox seems clearer now, for Engels's definition only had a temporary use; the distance between classes and masses, that is, between two modes of manifesting the same social reality (one passive, the other active; or one as the "effect," the other as the "cause" of the transformation of social relations) is in every case destined to collapse. In the historical movement of the proletariat, masses and classes ultimately come together again.

Engels's comparison of primitive Christianity with socialism has exactly the same consequences. On the one hand, there is the complexity and irreducible heterogeneity of the "worked and the overworked," who join forces in the imaginary hope of Christian salvation; and on the other, there is the homogeneity and preexisting unity of the modern proletariat, which alone constitutes the masses within bourgeois society. In the former case, the distance remains an irreducible one; in the latter, it collapses. Again, it is the thesis culled from the *Manifesto* (and projected onto the theory of *Capital,* according to the evidence of Marx) of a historical simplification of class antagonism that is responsible for this reduction. The ideology of the proletarian masses can be homogeneous with a directly political class consciousness and a scientific-materialist worldview *because* the modern form of exploitation is the tendency to establish a single "norm of existence" (*Lebensstandard,* says Engels), a "living wage" for everyone, and is the submission of the great mass of individuals to a process of proletarianization (and impoverishment) in which everyone becomes identical.

In this historical argument the theory of capitalist exploitation reveals its own internal impasse. Marxism stumbles on a paradoxical limitation—and it is a very serious one—of its representation of history, which can be illustrated in a number of ways.

Historical materialism is based on the discovery of the historicity of the capitalist mode of production and its corresponding economic categories: the relation between capital and wage labor is not "eternal"; produced historically, it must disappear under the effect of its internal contradictions. However, what Marx never really considers (nor, with any ease, do his successors)[50] is a history of capitalism in which the relation between capital and wage labor (hence the class struggle between the bourgeoisie and the proletariat, and the very composition of the classes) would take on new forms, still based on the accumulation of capital, commodity exchange, and the purchase of a labor force but qualitatively different from those that gave rise to the first industrial revolution. This failure is quite clear in *Capital* itself. Even if Marx does not provide any computable time frame for the development of the contradictions of capitalism, these are nonetheless considered fatal *in their immediate form,* that is, ultimately leading to the break with and the smashing of the system.

We are thus confronted with a theory that paradoxically affirms and denegates the historicity of capitalism. Although the class struggle is presented as the necessary effect of the relations of capitalist production, it nonetheless has no effect on them as long as no revolutionary transformation intervenes. It is always a case of all or nothing, of preserving capitalism identical to itself as long as it does not destroy it. This denegation, obviously related to the critique of reformism, is particularly evident in the analyses of syndicalism, aimed at showing that the economic working-class struggles only affect the regulation of norms of exploitation and change nothing of the relations of production. This paradox of a historicity without history is resolved precisely by the proposition of laws of evolution postulating the permanence of the system's structure.

There is a direct relation between this blockage and the difficulties we have encountered with the notion of dominant ideology. When Engels defines the bourgeois worldview by its *juridical* base, he invokes an argument borrowed from the history of the bourgeois struggles against feudalism which were carried out in the name of the law and in the dominant form of juridical discourse. He offers us no way of knowing whether this form stays the same indefinitely when the bourgeoisie becomes dominant and when the political problem becomes the struggle to maintain the exploitation of the working class. We can assume he thinks it does: for one, the general form of wage relations is always that of a contractual commodity exchange; and, second, the material instrument of the struggle is always the unmediated state, which is instituted as a guarantee of private property. These implicit arguments, however, harbor the same paradox of a historicity without history (or an essence of capitalism) as those regarding the relation of production itself. We certainly have two successive configurations for the

194

conflict between worldviews: first, the theological-feudal against the jurid-ical-bourgeois, then the juridical-bourgeois against the communist-prole-tarian. But the second of these has no effect on the contents of the juridical-bourgeois view, which remains true to its origins, for once and for all (as if the law functioned similarly against feudal privileges as against working-class demands). In other words, the existence of the proletariat and its struggle (that of the workers' movement) plays no role in the formation and transformation of the dominant ideology. Here, again, is the paradox of domination without the dominated I discussed in the first part of this study.

The same theoretical obstacle can be seen from the side of the proletariat. If the relation of production is a constant, the working class has no other history than that of extensions of proletarianization, of the kind identified with those of the salaried classes or "middle strata." Henceforth, the question of proletarian ideology is also represented in terms of all or nothing: a submission of the proletariat to the dominant ideology *or* a lib-eration from illusions, conscious or unconscious. Historically, there are working-class ideologies, bound up in different forms of exploitation, sites and conditions of existence, origins and mass cultural "traditions" (national, familial, religious), but these remain unthought and unthinkable. This is simply the result of a number of exceptions and delays; it has no theoretical relevance. Similarly, the fact that political organization, even when it is built with the aid of a scientific theory, produces mass ideological effects on the working class in providing them with a means of acknowledging their iden-tity and is beyond the range of historical analysis and criticism. The working class therefore becomes the blind spot of its own politics.[51]

The Mask of Politics

Let us then apply to Marx and Engels their own distinction be-tween method and system, in which method is not simply what remains of a system once it has been deprived of its conclusions or goals but rather what enters into contradiction with these conclusions and goals and, as a result—sooner or later—brings on a crisis in the system.[52] In the different theoretical forms we have encountered, the idea of a distance from the real has always been present, whether it takes the form of a doubling, an in-version, or a partitioning: the idea of a thinking that takes off at a tangent from the real, toward a lateral object *(Nebenobjekt),* and therefore deflects practice toward a fictive end, a *Nebenzweck.* It has always been clear that this deflecting (or metaphorical) operation has a political effect, in the sense of class struggle, but we have seen both Marx's and Engels's reluctance to define it as the distance of all politics from the real or as the distance from politics that would be the real itself.

We must look, then, at the way ideological dominations or world-views have been periodized. In the theological medieval form there would be an implied division of the instances of power (and consciousness, and representation or discourse): on the one side, the feudal state, the organi-zation of the ruling class of landed serf-owning gentry; on the other, the Church, at once caught within the feudal system and raised above it, there-fore capable of bestowing upon that system a guarantee of sacred authority. If religious (Christian) ideology's distance from the real is explained by this division, one can draw out its consequences: although the feudal state (mon-archy, empire) is explicitly represented as topmost in the hierarchy of rulers (the nobility), the Church is legally and effectively a community of *all* of the faithful, masters and slaves; while the state constitutes the world on behalf of the rulers, the Church, which draws its unity from its self-reference to a mystical beyond, is at the same time the organizer of everyone's everyday life, and of society.

What happens when a lay bourgeois ideology (a profane wisdom: *Weltweisheit,* as Hegel says) replaces this religious ideological apparatus? It seems that the division is reabsorbed. The Church, denounced as a "state within the state," does not disappear but loses its role of guaranteeing authority when the state stops organizing itself around a community of castes. The state then stands on its own, at once object (or means) and subject of the representations of the dominant ideology; it functions *directly* as an ideological power. Juridical ideology would thus be the direct expression of statist domination; but it can also be said that it is pure mystification in the service of this domination: an absolute transparence corresponds to absolute manipulation.

In fact, Engels's description, confirmed by Marx's analyses of the bourgeois state, suggests another reading: there is a new division and splitting of what, compared to its feudal past, seems quite simple. But this time the splitting is generated by the machine of the state, as a differentiation between state power and juridical order. This division repeats itself, in a way not entirely fictional, since it structures the practices, the distinction of the state, the "organization of the ruling class," and civil society, in which are inscribed all those relations of exchange that allow for the circulation of commodities and take the form of the contract. It also allows an ideal term (the law) to function as a guarantee of state power (and to appear as the lowest and uppermost limits of its empire): the division helps distinguish the political from the juridical, which would be situated above the political, expressing at the same time the community of its subjects. Finally, this division provides for the displacement or deflection of the goals of practice toward an ideal object (in the event of the "rule of ends" of law, the rule of the "rights of Man," liberty-equality-fraternity, etc.).

This entire process illustrates a *"law" of the transformation of ideological dominations,* a law of division-unity-division or (for unity is only a theoretical abstraction) a law of displacement, of the substitution of divisions. What actually designates the intermediate unity is the moment of transition in which the form of the state is seen as the real stake of a transformation, of a "seizure of power" (whatever the *duration* of this transformation; and this does not involve a measurable interval but, rather, the structural characteristic of a developing process). In practice, two transformations come together in this transition: the transformation of the form of the state by the class struggle, and the transformation of the dominant representations of domination (for example, the passage from sacred authority to juridical authority, from the Christian state to the constitutional state, from the clerical intellectual to the legal or scholarly intellectual). We can say this moment is eminently political when these transformations reveal their real stake (state power, the forms of its apparatus) in a theory and a historical mass practice. A theory of class struggle, or rather a concrete analysis of the forms class struggle takes in a determined historical transition, can show us, at any time, what its goals are. To describe the modality of the relation thus established between class struggle and its representation as political, we must use metaphors: let us say that it is in the *vacillation of ideology* that politics appears, but this time in the sense in which a form of ideological domination (theology, for example) must be negated in its power or in its capacity to represent the real, so that another (the juridical, for example) can take its place. We can also use another metaphor, the *twisting* of the relation between state and ideology, which must be undone so that the relation is twisted in the opposite direction, as a several-stranded rope twists one way and then the other under the effect of two forces.[53]

The bourgeoisie's accession to power (its transformation into a ruling class) is thus already represented as political (in forging the concept of the modern state). And this representation sustains its own materialism, one whose critical force is directed against theology: it involves destroying the idea inherent in everyday human life of a community of sin and salvation in order to replace it with the idea of an immanent social bond, woven here on earth into the exchange of commodities, the division of labor, contracts, government institutions, the constitution of the state and its various powers. Under these conditions, what are the representations thrown up by the struggle of a new class, the proletariat, against the bourgeois state? They take the form of a new materialism whose critical force is directed, this time, against the idealism proper to juridical ideology (against the ideological twisting of the real into the form of the law)—in effect, what can be called historical or dialectical materialism. These representations also introduce another concept of politics, which initially takes the form of the concept of another politics, irreducible to bourgeois politics: a politics of the masses, of labor, a communist politics. But can we not assume that this critique is accompanied by its own movement of ideological twisting? Or even that, if proletarian politics homogenizes what was present in the double form of the political and the juridical (in stripping bare the appeals and political stakes of the law), it is also accompanied by its own division?

To say that the unity of the political is divided afresh is to say that, in certain conditions, *politics itself can become the "mask" of politics:* it does not constitute a last term, a final solution to the enigma of class struggle (or history) but one of its forms, in which we still find symptoms of a distance from the real which has characterized the concept of ideology. What we must give up entirely is the idea of a "language of real life," this promised land of the philosophical critique envisaged in *The German Ideology,* whether one reads into the expression "language of real life" an impotent reduction of all language to the "life" it expresses, or whether we find the converse, the ideal of an originary language, absolutely "true" and nonmetaphoric. Politics, including that of the exploited class, since it is always both practice and language, or practice within language, must be what is masked over indefinitely and what is unmasked in its own words, or rather in the use made of them.[54]

It is not impossible to find Marx and Engels recognizing this situation, the practical state of things (but only the practical state). This is related, significantly, to their experiences of the dislocation *(décalage)* between the language of theory and the operations of the political party—hence the example of the episode of the *Critique of the Gotha Program,* whose result is as interesting as its origins. If Marx's critiques went unpublished, it was probably at the request of the party officials they might have offended, but it is also, as Engels tells us, because, within this conjuncture, *the workers read into the Program what was not there* (the affirmation of a class position), and, because of this, these critiques lost their "usefulness." But to read this position it would have to have been there, at least in the form of words that could take hold of a class practice; that is, it would have to have been in a conjunctural relation with the words or in the "line of demarcation" these words might trace out between the universes of discourse of a certain political conjuncture. Perhaps today we are less surprised by the possibility of such an equivocal reading, given that the history of revolutions in this century has shown how the words of religion or patriotism (even nationalism) can bear the class struggle and, at other times, how the words of the class struggle only support nationalism, if not religion.

Is this to say that, in the "sound and fury" of history, there is no practical difference but only successive forms of a perpetual illusion? On the contrary, it is clear that there are, precisely, differences, some of them irreducible. It is not because the judiciary appears, along with the antagonism between bourgeois and proletarian, in the form of a political mask that the bourgeois critique of religious ideology (which is made in its name) is entirely negated. What fails is its pretense to the ultimate truth of Man or History. Similarly, the fact that proletarian politics is divided and covered over again from the moment it acquires its own autonomy does not negate the difference between law and politics revealed by the critique of bourgeois juridical ideology. It simply signifies that this critique is also the moment of an incomplete process with no foreseeable end. From the point of view of this unfolding process, the succession of worldviews appears like a series of divisions and identifications of politics. But this figure—if it is not absolute—is no more unreal than the present process itself.

Let us take this further. Bourgeois ideology, by confusing in the same category of reason both juridical discourse and scientific discourse, has constructed a way of making one pass for the other and of therefore presenting science as a new form of the absolute. Conversely, the fact that proletarian politics is not based, in the last analysis, on reason but on the irreducibility of class antagonism can allow a recognition of the objectivity of scientific knowledge *within its limits,* extracted from the oscillation of "all or nothing" (subjectivism/objectivism, skepticism/speculation). Under these conditions, the fact that the concept of ideology in Marx or Engels is ultimately constituted by a denegation of the essentially metaphoric nature of language explains how a metaphysics of truth (or of the meaning of History) is built up around it. This does not, however, warrant substituting a generalized skepticism (through which other metaphysics might reappear) for the analysis or critique of ideologies. It is not a question of *substituting,* within a hyperbolic transcendence of worldviews, the metaphoricity of language for the identification of ideological differences, but of *inscribing* ideological effects as differential effects within the sphere of language.

If there is, again, a fresh division and a recovery of proletarian politics, inasmuch as it is given as politics pure and simple, what are its operative terms? First, it seems there is the same play of distinctions and confusions between economy and politics, one symptomatically present in the Saint Simonian formula taken up by Engels in *Anti-Dühring:* "to replace the government of men by the administration of things and the management of productive operations." This distinction/confusion can be equally read into the watchword "abolition of labor" in the works of the young Marx and in the later call for a (communist) politics of labor. It is striking that this distinction/confusion is to be found simultaneously in the two opposite tendencies between which the workers' movement constantly bounces back and forth, beginning with the model of the commune (or the Soviet model): either the workers' council (or the factory council), self-management associations, or state planning. Above all, however, this same distinction structures the way the workers' movement has practiced politics against the juridicalism of bourgeois politics: not in simply disavowing the juridical form but in distinguishing law from juridical ideology so as to avoid becoming a prisoner of the law through juridical ideology; to avoid "believing in the law" by "turning it round" and using it against the ruling class (either in forms of mass syndicalism or by way of universal suffrage). So, while the practice of the workers' movement has tended toward reformism, revolution has become its point of honor and its myth— what is believed in order not to believe in juridical ideology. And it is in this period—that of the first crisis of Marxism—that the ideologies of organization are constituted (still active in France today: Sorel against Lenin) to represent at times the union and at other times the party, one opposite the other, as *the* revolutionary form, the only one incompatible with the system (while the other remains inside it) and hence the sole bearer of the proletarian worldview. Both these representations, moreover, can seem Marxist, in the name of the critique of economism, by virtue of the struggle against "constitutional illusions," "parliamentary cretinism," or Jacobinism.

But what matters most here is the fact that the distinction/confusion between politics and economics, each exceeding the other while implying it, structures the workings of the bourgeois state in its relation to society. Economics has become the principal area of state intervention in social practice. In a contradictory way, it is also a constant hindrance to efficient decision making: what we call the crisis (all political discourse depends on how we assign a cause to it, or how we ascribe responsibility for it). Thus, transformation cannot be separated from the effects on the bourgeois state of the workers' movement as a mass movement. Nor can it be separated from the way in which, forcing the bourgeois state to reorganize itself as a function of its existence, the workers' movement has seen its own aims being displaced and finds itself displaced within the field of politics. The same words that used to denote a real political objective have now come, in a way, to mean a lateral or metaphorical objective, a *Nebensweck*. This is either because the struggle has already achieved this objective, albeit in an unrecognizable form, or because it can no longer be what it was, the conditions that made it thinkable and historically practicable having been destroyed by the class struggle.[55]

Behind the process of indefinite displacement of ideological forms lies the process of displacement of the conditions of class struggle. Both can be thought within the materialist notion of a permanent divergence of real history in relation to the trajectory and direction drawn up for each period by the sum or result of social conflicts in the sphere of discourse. It is remarkable that, in their critique of utopianism, but also in the aporia of their proletarian worldview, inasmuch as it has no specific content, or their proletarian ideology as a nonideology, Marx and Engels leave wide open and undetermined, a double possibility: either the myth of a definitive escape from ideology, corresponding to the myth of the end of history, or the concept of a "critique of politics" (which we can call materialism or communism), yet to be determined as a function of the ways in which politics itself masks its reality or its illusions.[56]

Of the "Truth" and the "Whole"

If the historical process (what we understand as history) never sticks to the path which, from its internal ideological tension, it seems to follow, then every simple representation of a result (or a salvation, even a worldly one) in the form of its anticipation or extrapolation is necessarily a lure, that of a *Nebenzweck*, even if it is the necessary form of practice. What is real is exactly that a transformation takes place in this form. It is a series that diverges without limit, not one that converges on an ideal limit. A bifurcation in an unforeseen form, it results from the instability of social relations.

The representation of historical convergence is one of the great common features of a philosophy of history which, in the modern age, goes from Leibniz to Teilhard de Chardin ("everything which rises must converge"). In Marx and Engels it is present in the lay form of the "negation of a negation," which manifests itself in two ways. Practially-historically, it subtends the extrapolation of the historical tendencies of capitalism that lead to its crisis (while history is, rather, a mutation of the form, or mechanism, of crises) and to the growth of the "objective conditions of revolution" (while history concerns revolutions that happen elsewhere, in places where these conditions are not met); but it leads also to the subjective conditions of revolution. Witness, in its echo of Marx's post-1848 expectations forty years earlier, Engels's forecast, which we can take to be the prototype for the evolutionist ideology of the party: "For the first time in history, a soundly knit workers party has appeared [in Germany] as a real political force. It is a force whose existence and mercurial rise are as incomprehensible and mysterious to governments and old ruling classes as the flow of the Christian tide was to the powers in decadent Rome. It increases and develops its forces as surely and inexorably as did Christianity before it, so much so that its rate of growth—and hence the moment of its ultimate triumph—can now be computed mathematically. Instead of suppressing it, the anti-socialist legislation has given it a boost" (letter from Engels to Kautsky, November 8, 1884).

Does this representation also subtend the epistemological notion of an absolute truth as an ongoing process of sublation or integration of relative truths (or relative errors)? In both cases, historical-political and epistemological, it is much the same positivist metaphysics (Hegelian or not) that is perpetuated in the heart of Marxism.

This metaphysics, if not suppressed (for it embraces every plan for organization except that one seeks to maintain a radical individualism or one that is anarchistic in principle), is at least counteracted by the simultaneous representation of the irreducibility of the antagonism and its nonteleological character (thereby incompatible with any expectation of a final solution). In the heat of the moment the reality of the historical process can be practically appropriated. Lenin clears up this point by defining historical materialism as the "concrete analysis of concrete situations" and by substituting a conception of the moment of absolute truth present in each relative truth *(Philosophical Papers)* for a conception of the absolute truth

200

as the progressive integration of relative truths. Taking this further, we can say that all truth is both a fact of and an effect of a conjuncture, in several senses.

Truth—or, rather, the true—is an effect of conjuncture, in that it contradicts the dominant forms or criteria of universality, that is, it embodies a *practical criticism of ideology,* and is therefore produced *within the context of ideology.* One can read in the same way Hegel's thesis that makes all truth the *aftereffect* of a negation through defining it by its essential recurrence *(Nachträglichkeit),* which is not exactly the glorification of a fait accompli, since that fait accompli presents itself in the very forms of the dominant ideology. The only certainty—but it is, at least, something—is that there is something in ideology incompatible with a certain practice of collective transformation (also with a certain form of social communication). We can call this current, critical certitude "truth" in the materialist sense. And inasmuch as it signals this practical effect—not stable or definitive, but irreducible—the concept of ideology is materialist and breaks free of the circle of dogmatism (originary or final truth) and skepticism (no truth, or truth as pure mystification, moral fiction, "loss of being," etc.). If the primary ideological effect is thus to change all knowledge (and also some nonknowledges) into an illusion of universality, the concept of ideology has its primary effect in the division of the concept of truth: between a concept that postulates its autonomy and one that acknowledges its practical dependence on the conjuncture; or to put it differently, between a concept that designates as truth the fantasy of a self-consciousness absolutely contemporaneous with itself and its conditions and a concept of truth as a process (or production) of knowledge, implying a noncoincidence, an irreducible noncontemporaneity of discourse and its conditions.

In the case of historical struggles, the truth is also an effect of conjuncture in that it is produced as a coming together, an exceptional condensation of the class struggle and the mass movement, inasmuch as these two realities are always relatively *heterogeneous.* No effect of knowledge (or truth) arises from what remains only mass movements, unified by an ideological faith and essentially defined—even when they weather well, or inspire a revolution, or smash the established order—as fluctuating forces, always ambivalently attracted to and repulsed by the state. Nor can truth arise from stabilized configurations of the class struggle, ones that nurture the dogmatism of the established order, or the "subaltern" dogmatism, as Gramsci put it with a vengeance, of the resistance of the oppressed organized in their trenches, each one characteristic, in effect, of what Gramsci also called the processes of "passive revolution." Indeed, one can ask whether these processes are not really the ordinary state of history inasmuch as it misunderstands itself.

What makes a break in knowledge (or some of its conditions) irrupt is the novelty of the conjunction of mass movements and class struggle, the days Lenin spoke of, following Marx, "during which the masses learn more than they would in years" (Days, however, can themselves be years if the problem is not chronological but structural. This would involve questioning the metaphor of a "crisis" subtending this formulation): whether, as Marx brilliantly analyzes for the nineteenth-century revolutions, the structure of class antagonism ends up by polarizing, displacing, and radicalizing the mass movements; or whether, above all, as Lenin, Gramsci, and Mao had a better opportunity to see, the mass movements (religious, nationalistic, "cultural" as in May 1968, or, tomorrow, perhaps pacifistic), constituted on the "surface" of the social formation (But what is "surface" and what is "depth"? Are we not to think these descriptive categories as intrinsically reversible?), determine a class struggle that remains hypothetical and provide it with its concrete content. I say "above all" because Marx and Engels probably did not envisage this reciprocity, in spite of their dialectic, and generally applied a reductionist conception to the class struggle, preventing them in the same movement from concretely developing the critical idea of a historical process *(procès)* whose causality would not express the destiny of a predestined subject (proletariat or other) but rather the contradictory articulation of the masses and the classes, never quite the same even "in the last instance." To parody Kant, it could be said that without the mass movements the class struggle is empty (which is to say, it remains full of dominant ideology). However, without the class struggle, the mass movements are blind (which is to say, they give rise to counterrevolution, even fascism, as much as revolution.) But there is no a priori correspondence between these two forms.[57]

   I would like to draw two further consequences from these hypotheses. The first is that the great theoretical lure in the history of Marxism has been constituted by the ever-developing and ever-aborting project of a theory of ideology. One can say that this project is grounded, for Marx and Engels, both in the dissatisfaction that provokes the constant vacillation of their concept of ideology and in the temptation to develop descriptions of the ideological inversion effect, which they put forward in terms of a coherent theory, articulated with the theory of capitalist exploitation, and so on. Neither Marx nor Engels, however, seems to have thought about constituting such a theory (unless, perhaps, it goes by the name "dialectic"); yet the constitutive instability of a founding concept is not exactly a theoretical lack. Rather, this project is the symptom of the *relation to Marx* maintained by Marxists and of the contradictions of that relation; it is, at the same time, the closed field of their confrontations or antithetical deviations. We should remember how this project is constituted (Bernstein is the first within the revisionist camp to formulate it in these terms, but, just as quickly, Plekhanov takes it up in the orthodox camp, opposing social psychology to the development of consciousness, the lesson of Taine to that of Kant, etc.) and what forms it later takes, right up to Sartre and Althusser, during what can be called the classical period of Marxism (the formation and dissolution of the parties of the Second and Third International, all with essentially the same common theoretical base). Sometimes this project is economistic, at others times antieconomistic. Paradoxically, it can be both at the same time (Lukács and, in general, all theorizing that tries to employ dialectically the commodity form against the mechanicalness, the evolutionism, or the reductionism of class).

   What I would like to emphasize here is that the idea of a theory of ideology has always functioned as an *ideal means of completing historical materialism,* of "filling up a hole" in its representation of the social totality, and thus as a means of *constituting historical materialism in totality,* as a system of explication that is generically consistent, at least according to its laws. Again, this ever-reviving project must be read as a kind of symptom: the necessity to complete the social whole—which is indeed the ambition, avowed or not, of all sociology and thus not of Marxism alone (other, ad hoc concepts arise from this point: mana, symbolic order, systemic restraint, etc.). This is finally to be able completely to localize the cause, in a given representation, in an outline of the structure of the social totality, whether in one of its parts, identified as the site of "determination in the last instance," or in the reciprocal play of all of its parts, that is, in their complexity or their *Wechselwirkung* together (even their hypercomplexity). And if the missing link must be designated "ideology," then it is because this term, turned against its initial use, comes to connote the imaginary correspondence between the practice of organization and theoretical knowledge in a program that would be formulated once and for all (that is, until it is fulfilled, until one can say "mission accomplished," even "transcended").[58] In this sense, the return of teleology to Marxism and the project of a theory of ideology (or a science of ideologies) seem to me always to be strictly correlative. One could even suggest that they always serve to compensate for the horizontal division that introduces class struggle into society, thereby preventing it from being represented as a whole—a compensation by way of another, more abstract unity, a principle of vertical totalization, if not material, at least theoretical or explanatory. The theory of ideology would then be symptomatic of the permanent unrest, maintaining with Marxism its own recognition of the class struggle!

I think that we can and should uphold the contrary: that the programs are never fulfilled, although they are sometimes adequate to their conjuncture (what Althusser suggests calling "practical accuracy," *le justesse pratique*); that the theory, or rather the concept, of ideology denotes no other object than that of the nontotalizable (or nonrepresentable within a given order) complexity of the historical process; and that historical materialism is incomplete in principle, not only in the temporal dimension (since it posits the relative unpredictability of the effects of determined causes), but also in its theoretical siting *(topique)*, since it requires the articulation of the class struggle in extramaterial concepts (for example, the unconscious, or sexuality).

Such a position seems to me to be consistent with the idea, argued above, of an effect of truth within the conjuncture. In political terms, this implies not the absolute separation or natural antagonism of knowledge and judgment, or organization, but the impossibility of a true fusion of theoretical and strategic functions (included, of course, under the weak form of a division of labor, with a provision for mutual services, whether the theorists propose that the "politicians" test the results of their analyses or else the "officials" hire the "organic intellectuals" to develop plans for them). If it is the meeting, or the conflict, between theory (or theories) and practices that gives rise to both knowledge and politics in the strong sense (the transformation of social relations), then it is certainly necessary, from time to time at least, that theory be produced outside the organization, which does not necessarily mean on another class base but according to other modalities and a different relation to discourse. It may even be that there are more opportunities—and not less—within this parallelism for the social division of labor to evolve and that theory (as a social activity) will increasingly cease to be a monopoly of individuals or of castes, a business for intellectuals—in short, for those Marx, in the beginning, calls "ideologues."

1 See Alain Badiou, *Théorie du sujet* (Paris: Seuil, 1982) and his presentation on January 17, 1983, at the Ecole Normale Supérieure (to appear in *Rejouer le politique, III*, Éditions Galilée).

2 I leave aside the very interesting question of Marx's retrieval of the term "ideology" from the French sensualist ideologues and the distortion it undergoes in the process.

3 In this schematic account there is one notable exception: the reference made in the preface of *A Contribution to the Critique of Political Economy* to the "ideological forms" identified with "social consciousness." This text is explicitly retrospective, alluding in particular to *The German Ideology*, whose persistent trace it carries. But its importance lies elsewhere. It teaches us nothing about ideology in any direct way, unless about its insistence within Marxism, even at the cost of the most outright conceptual indeterminacy (see the theme of "correspondence").

4 The classic French translation (Roy's) obscures the conceptual precision of fetishism in *Capital*. The recent publication, after a long delay, of J. P. Lefebvre's translation, by Editions Sociales, provides a definitive text for this question and others.

5 It is, however, important to note that the materialism of *The German Ideology* does not relate to the idea of matter, that it is a "materialism without matter," because it is nonsubstantial. See also the *Theses on Feuerbach*.

6 Marx is neither the first nor the last philosopher to take up the problem of the production of idealities, or the process of idealization, in this overdetermined form (see Spinoza before and Freud after). It is remarkable that these three intellectual efforts, clearly related but formulated within entirely different concepts, have actually surfaced independently and heterogeneously. Marx read Spinoza closely; but by way of an astonishing quid pro quo, inscribed within the tradition of the *Aufklärung*, and in his struggle against romantic pantheism, he has only seen in Spinoza an apology for rationalism and democracy. On this point see A. Matheron, "Le traité théologico-politique vu par le jeune Marx," *Cahiers Spinoza*, 1 (1977).

7 This identification of the place of theory with the place of practice must be given as already there. But it is, more accurately than my hasty presentation suggests, in the vein of a *tendency* that Marx seeks to define it after a fashion itself historical—a tendency toward the simultaneous breakup of manual labor and intellectual labor specifically, and hence their distance or *divergence*. See my study "Sur le concepte marxiste de la 'division du travail manuel et intellectuel' et la lutte de classes," in *Manuels et intellectuels dans le transition au socialisme*, ed. Jean Belkhir (Paris: Editions Anthropos, 1985).

8 Both Marx and Engels bear witness to the true answer: we have seen this proletariat radically stripped of ideology. See *The Condition of the Working Class in England:* "I discovered that you were much more than members of an insular nation who would only be English: I have affirmed that you were men. . . ."

9 It is tempting to explain, in addition to editorial rejections and the difficulties suffered in these troubled times through the insecurity of their personal situations, that Marx and Engels abandoned *The German Ideology* "to the nibbling critique of the mice."

10 I have tried to show elsewhere that this analysis, in spite of its dialectical power, and because it is offered in the form of a simple demonstration of the logic of commodities, had to become, for Marxism, a lasting obstacle to the analysis of economic ideology as the dominant ideology, or the economy of the state. And so it has, paradoxically, encouraged the "return" of the economic "repressed" in this economism, one repeated indefinitely ever since as the "return to the young Marx" (in *Ludwig Feuerbach and the End of Classical German Philosophy*).

11 I am thinking of a contemporary example, the "episteme" of Michel Foucault, and more generally of the universals of the culturalists.

12 Indeed, Marx, who is faithful on this point to his own German ideology, suggests that the proletariat alone can save the classical culture of humanity (Homer, Dante, Shakespeare) from its degeneration into bourgeois philistinism (see the 1857 introduction to the *Critique of Political Economy*).

13 It is an analysis that is in no way mechanistic. Preceding the Lenin of the articles on Tolstoy and the Mao of *Talks at the Yenan Forum*, it already implies the distinction (and the articulation) of existence (or origin) from class and class positions, hence the analysis of their conjunctures.

14 This is a reformism in which, it should be noted, Marx and Engels explicitly place the idea of the "transformation of the State as the simple administration of production."

15 Hence, the dominant model in Marx's thought regarding this strategy is that of a "permanent revolution" which offers the long-term transformation of bourgeois revolutions into proletarian revolutions and the short-term transformation of the radical democratic program into the communist program (because the polarization of the class struggle nullifies the petite bourgeoisie

Étienne Balibar

as an autonomous force). See Stanley Moore, *Three Tactics, the Background in Marx* (New York: Monthly Review Press, 1963) and my article, "Dictature du prolétariat," in *Dictionnaire critique du marxisme*, ed. G. Labica and G. Bensussan (Paris: P.U.F., 1982).

16   Another symptom of this disintegration is the generalization in the 1850s (when Marx was pondering the "immaturity" of the proletariat) of the conceptual pair class in itself/class for itself, which works symmetrically as much for the bourgeoisie as for the proletariat, the two "revolutionary classes" of history. But this is preceded, in the *Manifesto*, by a return to a "conspiracy" theory, a purely instrumentalist one, of the law as the will of the ruling class: "Your law is only the will of your class worked into the law, a will whose content is determined by the concrete conditions of existence of your class."

17   See *Raison Présente*, 66 (1983).

18   The first version of the following analyses took the form of a presentation on May 17, 1980, in the research seminar on the history of materialism led by Oliver Bloch at the Université de Paris I. I would like to thank G. Labica, B. Lacorra, Cl. Mainfoy, S. Mercier-Josa, M. Pêcheux, J. Texier, and E. Walter for observations that have been very useful to me in preparing this study.

19   Although the pairs abstract/concrete and thought/real are not strictly commutative, Engels's formulations on this are clearly more empirical than those of Marx in the 1857 introduction (unpublished) to the *Critique of Political Economy*, where it is the *scientific method*, inasmuch as it proceeds from the abstract to the "concrete of thought," that *seems* to engender the real, starting from the concept, and thus creates an idealistic illusion. In his critical reading of Hegel, Marx touches on the idea of the conditions and ideological effects inherent in scientific practice itself, but he does not use the term.

20   From the *Grundrisse* to the *Critique of the Gotha Program*, by way of books 1 and 3 of *Capital*, Marx presents a similar critical analysis of the categories "liberty" and "equality" as an internal reflection of production and commodity circulation, which produces (for example, in the chapter on commodity fetishism) a comparison between juridical and religious idealities (or abstractions) and a substitution of one for the other within history. However, what is never really clear in Marx is whether the law is itself ideological or whether it is better to make a distinction between law (property, contract, etc.) and juridical ideology (liberty and equality).

21   See the examples given in "Ideologie," in *Geschichtliche Grundbeariffe*, Brunner, Conze, and Koselleck, eds. (Stuttgart: Band 2, 1978).

22   The problem of terminology which Engels comes across here is far from idiosyncratic. At this same time, French positivists like Littré also posit a substitution of "worldview" for "philosophy" in order to designate the form in which, unconsciously and spontaneously, the positivist spirit becomes self-conscious and systematic (I owe this information to E. Coumet).

23   Remember that in this period Marx was the first to make a reference to the dialectic (and not only in materialism). See the postface to the second German edition of *Capital* (1872), where some of his formulations are rather close to the conclusions of the *Critique of Political Economy* published by Engels in 1859.

24   On the use of this term and on the ambivalence of the relations first Marx and then Engels have with it, see G. Hapt's detailed account, "Marxe il marxismo," in E. Hobsbawm et al., *Storia del marxismo* (Einaudi, vol. 1). On the crisis of Marxism, see R. Racinaro, *La crisi del marxismo* (Bari: De Donato, 1976); H. J. Steinberg, "Il partito e la formazione dell' ortodossie marxiste," in *Storia del marxismo*, vol. 2.
       The question of knowing whether the older Engels effected a change in point of view or still maintained, as Ch. Andler believes ("Fragment d'une étude sur la decomposition du marxisme," *Revue socialiste*, 1913), "two successive systems" has been the object of contemporary debates. See, lastly, the absorbing study of Oskar Negt, "Il marxismo e la teoria della rivoluzione nell'ultimo Engels," in *Storia del marxismo*, vol. 2. Although in complete agreement with the idea of a critical application of historical materialism to its own history (of the sort already performed by Korsch), and hence of a program of material analysis of the working class, I cannot agree with Negt that the latter ought to take the form of a "critique of the political economy of the force of labor," nor, a fortiori, of an "application of the law of value" to this critique. This would involve a special discussion, primarily about the meaning and the limits of validity for an identification of "force of labor" as a "commodity"—in short, about the reading of *Capital*.

25   See the essential article by Engels, "Notwendige und Überflüssige Gesellschaftsklassen," *Marx-Engels Werke*, vol. 21.

26   F. A. Langue's *Histoire du materialisme*, which represents the union between Marxist, neo-Kantian, and Darwinian circles, was published in 1866. O. Bloch's commentary on it clearly shows that while Engels rejects its epistemological theses, he does borrow a plan from it, or rather a historical project. It is with Dilthey, at the end of the century, as we know, that the term *Weltanschauung*, of Romantic origin (Schelling, Schleiermacher) becomes the

205

watchword of the philosophy of history and hermeneutics developed by the vitalist and sub-jectivist currents of neo-Kantianism against the rationalist currents (from Cohen to Cassirer).

27   The idea of a history of thought, understood in this way, obviously leads to several interpre-tations or programs of research: that of an empirical history of the sciences and their effects upon philosophy; that of a history of theories of the sort proposed by Althusser in *Reading Capital*, in reviving an expression of Hegel's; and, finally, that of a history of class struggle within theory, ultimately considered by the same Althusser as the proper terrain of philosophy (see *Lenin and Philosophy, Positions*) and which we will come across later on in taking up the difficulties of Engels's text.

28   The study by B. Kedrov, "Engels et ses prédécesseurs," *La classification des sciences*, vol. 1 (French translation of the 1977 Russian edition), is unfortunately flawed by his persistent desire to present Engels's thinking in terms of "the Marxist solution" to "the problem of the classification of the sciences." It seems, by contrast, that there are some original ideas to be found in the highly documented study by Sven Eric Liedman, *Motsatsernas Spel: The Philosophy of Engels and Nineteenth-Century Science* (Lund: Bo Cavefors Bokförlag, 1977), but I have only been able to consult a short resumé of it in English.

29   G. Canguilheim, G. Lapassado, J. Piquemal, J. Ulmann, "Du développement à l'évolution au XIXe siecle," *Thalès*, année 1960, special issue (Paris: P.U.F., 1962), is far and away the most rigorous study of the history and concepts of evolutionism before and after Darwin.

30   A striking illustration of this theme can be found in H. G. Wells, *A Short History of the World*, which tells the story of humanity starting from the formation of the solar system and ending with socialism.

31   See G. Canguilheim, *Ideologie et rationalité dans l'histoire des sciences de la vie* (Paris: Vrin, 1977). Canguilheim's work (see also *Thalès*) proves that it is impossible to discuss evolu-tionism as such; rather, we must speak of *evolutionisms* (Lamarck, Comte, Spenser, Darwin, Haeckel) according to their "constants" and their incompatibilities—what Foucault aptly char-acterizes as "points of heresy" in *The Order of Things*—and also the totally different effects produced by the inscription of evolutionist statements within theoretical/experimental or spec-ulative fields. The studies of Y. Conry and D. Lecourt, particularly those in *Raison Présente*, no. 66, seem to me to subscribe clearly to this point of view.

32   We can read Engels's "historical" account in the following way (see, e.g., particularly in *Dialectics of Nature*, the text entitled "Old Preface to the *Anti-Dühring*"): (1) Greek dialectic, (2) classical metaphysics, (3) modern dialectic; or this way: (1) the abstract unity of dialectic and ("physical") materialism, (2) the division of dialectic from materialism, (3) a new concrete unity of dialectic and (historical) materialism; or finally: (1) the unity of philosophy and the sciences (within the sphere of philosophy), (2) the division of philosophy (speculation) and the sciences (empiricism), (3) the new unity of philosophy and the sciences (within the sphere of the sciences).

33   Paradoxically, thought only avoids this autonomization when it is "false," a dialectical idea we could use to rectify the teleological conceptions of knowledge (in material terms, the "falsity" is the "truthful" element), but only on the condition that it no longer be presented in the form of a failure or an objection. Nonetheless, it is in *Anti-Dühring*, in response to the "eternal verities" of positivism (this critique is also made of Haeckel), that Engels comes to terms with the Hegelian critique of the "moral opposition between truth and error," that is, the critique of the classical metaphysical dualism of knowledge, preserved intact by positivism. It is only in this indirect manner that the practical and the political point of view are found to be represented.

34   See in particular "Bruno Bauer und das Urchistentum" (1882), in *Marx-Engels Werke*, vol. 19, which constructs a parallel between modern ideologies, those of the ancient world (philosophical and, above all, juridical), and those of the medieval world (theological and generally clerical). All these texts were first published in *Neue Zeit*, Kautsky's review and the bastion of orthodox Marxism.

35   This reduction is the grand proof, the unflaggingly repeated Marxist argument as it is practiced by Conrad Schmidt, Lafargue, or Kautsky. It involves, on the one hand, retracing the origin of the philosophical categories garnered by Engels (the distinction between simple causality and reciprocal action, first articulated by Kant) and, on the other, giving some idea of its afterlife (particularly in Gramsci and Sartre, who both consistently rework Engels's outline).

36   Let us judge the extent of this progress in relation to Marx's formulations in *Capital*, where it is the regulative intervention of the state (the legislation of the manufacturers) that is given as the "conscious reaction" of society to its own "organism."

37   Gramsci, from this point of view, is not mistaken in posing together the problem of proletarian hegemony and of the "crisis of the state" (ignored by Engels, if not by Lenin).

38   "Juristensozialismus," *Marx-Engels Werke*, vol. 21, p. 491. It is to the credit of Petter Schöttler, who gives us an illuminating analysis of it, to have brought to our attention the

importance of this text (see his study "Engels und Kautsky als Kritiker des Juristensozialismus," *Demokratis und Recht*, no. 1, 1980).

39   One constantly comes across this denegation of the existence of a juridical ideology, articulated from very different perspectives. One recent and very interesting example is in the
work of J. F. Lyotard, starting from his "pragmatic" analyses of the relations of communication
in advanced capitalism. See, for example, *Instructions païennes* (Paris: Galilée, 1977), pp.
55-56, "showing" that there is no bourgeois, juridical ideology because, generally speaking,
there is no dominant ideology within capitalism; capital would be, as such, *indifferent to
ideology* (to "semantics"), in contrast to archaic structures like the state, the party, the
Church, and so on. Similarly, he writes later (p. 76) that money, as a *medium* of communication, is outside of ideology, even juridical ideology. The most delicate position to discuss
would, of course, be that of juridical positivism (Kelsen), which explicitly distinguishes juridical
ideology and legal norms from natural law.

40   See my article "Dictature du proletariat," in *Dictionnaire critique du marxisme*, ed. G. Labice
and G. Bensussan (Paris: P.U.F., 1982). It is striking that, during this period, Engels is moved
to say something new about the ancient city (in *The Origin of the Family*) which clarifies the
"civic" sense of the idea of community present within the term "communism." In the ancient
city—note that its own worldview has not yet, in itself, been properly named—the citizens
directly and collectively pursue the common public interests without being "displaced" toward
the religious *Nebenzwecke* (albeit upon the repressed base of slavery), which clarifies the
ulterior motive behind the curiously Aristotelian phrase in *The Erfurt Program* (written against
the anarchists), according to which "the workers are political by nature." More than a nostalgic definition of politics, by way of the Greek example, it is a question of thinking the crux
of the proletarian worldview in reference to what, throughout the entire classical tradition,
symbolizes politics as such. Following upon the analysis of the Greek city as the first form,
in its contradictory development, of the fusion of politics and statism in the history of class
struggle, it is a way of showing that, in the transition to communism, the crucial stake of
struggle is the possibility of dissociating politics from statism by associating (or fusing) politics
with labor—two poles of a contradiction that cuts across all of history. See E. Balibar, C.
Luporini, A. Tosel, *Marx et sa critique de la politique* (Paris: Maspero, 1979).

41   "Zur Geschichte des Urchristentums" (1894-95), *Marx-Engels Werke*, vol. 22, p. 449; and
see Marx and Engels, *The Holy Family*.

42   The work of Gustave Le Bon, *The Psychology of Crowds*, which Freud discusses (for better
or worse?) in *Mass Psychology and the Analysis of the Ego*. Labriola and Plekhanov, in
particular, are very much taken up with the question of the relation between the theory of
ideology and social psychology.

43   Is such a retrospective critique, coming, by definition, "too late," not at once an oversimplified
and perfectly useless exercise? But suppose—as I suggest at the beginning of this study—
that the problems of current Marxism and its crisis are posed in a less linear fashion? This
might be a way out of the false dilemma of repetition and liquidation, neither of which change
anything.

44   See M. Heidegger's project to move out of the "doldrums" of the disputes around *Weltan-
schauungen* ("The Age of the World-View," 1938), establishing a distance from historicism
but particularly from a certain form of direct identification of the "destination" of humankind
and its mobilization. Read the interesting sixth issue of the review *Metamorfosi* (Turin, 1982),
"La decisione," with articles by C. Preve and M. Turchetto, among others.

45   In this respect it is difficult to see—unless we question the very idea of a class politics—how
the meaning of the party form in the workers' movement could not correspond to the development of a certain "schismatic spirit" within the working class. Not only does the constitutive role played by intellectuals over the entire history of the workers' movement not
present an obstacle, it largely contributes to the phenomenon of workerism. It is all the more
interesting to see Lenin (in *What Is to Be Done?*) defining the *proletarian* political party by
its capacity to intervene *in all classes* of society, that is, together, as a "unity of opposites."

46   Sorel says the organizing "myth." But, conversely, has every organization not its own working
myth? Gramsci, in particular, asks this question.

47   For the most elaborate thoughts on this, one should consult the recent work of Lecourt,
L'ordre et les jeux (Paris, 1981), chap. 4, and *La philosophie sans feinte* (Paris, 1982). In
a previous study ("Etat, parti, idéologie," in E. Balibar, C. Luporini, A. Tosel, *Marx et sa
critique de la politique* [Paris: Maspero, 1979]), I tried to relate this gap between "two
centers" that persist in Marx and Engels's analyses of the party to what Althusser calls the
"double inscription" of the theory of Marx within its own "topic": first, as the thought of
the historical *whole*, fictively exterior to its action *(procès);* and second, as the "ideological
form," inscribed and acting *within* this whole (and hence determined by it). But it was also
a case of demonstrating the limits of this representation, preventing the party from really
analyzing its own history, thereby falling far short of subsequent Marxist theorization.

48   See my article "Marx le joker," in *Rejouer le politique,* ed. Luc Ferry (Paris: Galilée, 1981).

49   See the study by S. Mercier-Josa, "Esprit du peuple et idéologie," *Pour lire Hegel and Marx* (Paris: Editions Sociales, 1980), p. 69.

50   This same difficulty does not rule out some interesting though puzzling conceptual creations: witness Engels's distinction between "revolution from above" and "revolution from below" (in relation to the way in which Napoleon III or Bismarck would have been "prevented" from making themselves the "testamentary executors" of the revolutions of 1848, after having surpressed them—which is also a way of explaining why the proletariat is prevented from acting *upon the base* of Bismarckian or Napoleonic society, even in its political forms, instead of "reviving" 1848, according to the model of "permanent revolution"). With his own notion of "passive revolution" (implicitly opposed to "active revolution" or to "revolutionary revolution"), Gramsci seems to be on the same track.

51   In this situation each word becomes a double-edged weapon. The notion of a "proletarian worldview" can act as the index of working-class ideologies (in the sense of practice, rather than opinions), irreducible to the dominant ideology. But it can also prevent all critical development of these ideologies in themselves—in the case of labor, family, or the state—to the extent that, according to the logic of speculative empiricism, it posits these ideologies as direct "representatives" of the universal (and through them the archetype of the worker). Conversely, it is not at all clear that the fact of speaking about working-class ideology, as Marx and Engels do not do, is enough to ruin the specular relation; "the worker" is a place within the action of capitalist labor. Under the guise of "giving power" (ideas or words) to the workers, such a notion perpetuates their position (even puts them back in it). It can thus be the instrument of a "new bourgeoisie" (including a "new bourgeoisie" of the party).

52   I try to use the very terms of Marx and Engels "out of the necessity to attack them," which seems to me to be one of the indispensable ways of determining what they think.

53   "Classical" political theory from Machiavelli to Hobbes and Rousseau (with its conformists and its heretics) is an admirable example—perhaps too much so—of this vacillation of ideology, from theology to the juridical, along with the moment of political recognition of the real state it contains. This moment, however, is never "pure" (even in Machiavelli), since the untwisting movement of theological recovering is always already also the twisting movement of the juridical recovering.

54   That politics is also its own mask is what prevents it from being based upon a concept or theory of "social ties," contractual or otherwise—no more so, of course, if it is defined as "alienation" from the originary social bond. Through his concept of the "social relations of production" and their history, Marx enters onto another terrain. However, inasmuch as the critique of ideology means, for him, foreseeing an end to ideology, an absolute transparency of social relations, or, if you will, a society in which individuals are at last contemporaries and thus the omnipotent creators of their own social relations, the problematic of the "social tie" is seen to be freshly inserted into all of his analyses.

55   This does not mean that proletarian ideology has become "dominant" in the modern state; but it undoubtedly has played a determining role in its transformations, both before and, even more, after the Soviet revolution, the lessons of which bourgeois capitalists have been assimilating and preaching against ever since. Every bourgeois, even capitalist, state, is today, in this sense, postrevolutionary. Negri is correct on this point; see *La classe ouvrière contre l'état* (Paris: Galilée, 1976). This is a better explanation of the fact that the crisis of the state—otherwise known as its restructuring—implies, on the part of the avant-garde ideologues of the ruling class, coming to terms with what they themselves call "proletarian ideology," or, rather, whatsoever of proletarian ideology has been incorporated into the bourgeois state. This is the meaning of neoliberalism, of antitotalitarian discourse, and so on.

56   In his book *Language, Semantics and Ideology,* trans. Harbans Nagpal (New York: St. Martins, 1982), Michel Pêcheux has shown the implications, as far as a discourse theory is concerned, of an ideological position (or better, within ideology); such a position can only be defined as the not inconsiderable sum (and this is different from a reciprocal neutralization) of the "dominant" worldview, and the proletarian class struggle, with no other support or point of reference than to this very struggle. The paradox that is central to his analyses is that of a subject who has to be able to pull himself out of the mess he or she has fallen into (the *"Munchhausen"* effect)—is this not, strictly speaking, the truth of any revolutionary practice?

57   A hint of this problem can be found in Marx, though in as contradictory a fashion as the relation to ideology, namely, in the hesitation often experienced in the use of the two terms "proletariat" and "working class" *(Arbeiterklasse).* The former, which carries all of the political weight of the *Manifesto,* is practically absent from *Capital,* particularly in its first edition, except specifically as an oblique reference back to the *Manifesto.* Moreover, if the term "proletariat" connotes the aggregate of the living conditions and reproduction of the working class (and not only its productive function), these are—in spite of the polemic against Malthusianism and the thesis of the "brazen law of wages"—at once standardized, and hence neutralized in their historical diversity and political relevance, within the concept of a tendency, inherent to the capitalist system, toward the minimal reproduction of the market labor force.

Naturally, the temptation to regard the object of historical materialism as a necessary and sufficient whole and to present it with its would-be missing link can take forms other than those of a theory of ideology. In particular, it can take the altogether different form of a theory of the state, which is hardly surprising when one begins to suspect that every historical form of the state has, as Marx put it, a double "base": both in the form of relations of production and that of ideological relations. It is striking that all of Althusser's theoretical work (from his initial definition of the overdetermination of historical causality to the introduction of the concept of ideological state apparatus) oscillates between two tendencies: one takes up again, albeit in a somewhat novel way, the Marxist project of a theory of ideology (or a theory of the state); the other explicitly considers the concept of ideology in terms of a constant excess, or deficiency, in relation to any totalization of social complexity or political practice, at the risk of crediting Marx with the very opposite of what he thought. Consequently, the work of Althusser, better than others, it seems to me, is able to *anticipate* the most significant features of the crisis of Marxism.

Oskar Negt

What Is a Revival of Marxism and Why Do We Need One Today?: Centennial Lecture Commemorating the Death of Karl Marx

Translated by Michael Palencia-Roth

The basic presupposition behind reconstituting a living dialogue with Marxist thought is the recognition of the *historical boundaries* of Marxist theory itself.

How is one to commemorate the centennial of Karl Marx's death? It is surely no ordinary anniversary, such as is due other great thinkers of the past.[1] One would speak quite differently, for example, in remembering Kant or Hegel, for however great their cultural significance has been for Europe, their theories do not have the sort of practical force that leads rebelling masses or social movements to use their categories as points of orientation. Yet, as proponents of academic theories that shaped philosophical schools and were transmitted by a philosophical education, they were in a position to influence the thinking of an entire generation of intellectuals—Marx and Engels as well as Lenin and Mao Tse-tung.

On the Dialectic of Truth-Content and Reality-Content

Kant's and Hegel's work is directed toward a concept of the completed world, one that, as Hegel says, philosophy paints in very somber colors. The entire substance of Marx's theory, conversely, is a lever for a movement toward social emancipation and a new society. This may sound very mechanical, but it is so only in the sense that conscious historical transformation inevitably requires the powers of material intervention— which is one reason why *theoretical* deduction is not an end in itself for this theory, despite the stringency of the thought process that characterizes its claim to truth.

Expressing it this way, though, risks a practical mis-understanding. If Marxist theory is to be confirmed principally in the trans-formation of objective conditions, then it does not require us to renounce an immanent truth-content. On the contrary, the problem that Marxist theory is concerned with is not *constricting* but *expanding* truth-content, an expansion based on doubling the presentation of the problem: grasping the true conditions (a grasping, however, that does not stop either during the process of understanding or upon its completion) and bursting these conditions (possible only when the power of the conceptual work, which feeds on the suprareferential consciousness, actually corresponds to the structure of these conditions).

That sounds very simple; in fact, the stipulation that historical praxis (not pragmatic-instrumental praxis) is a central criterion of truth for Marxism bears on a critical problem whose difficulties have produced many fluctuations in Marxist theory. These difficulties are especially clear today. When we speak about contemporary relationships to the theories of Marx and Engels, we realize we must consider the extremely stressful, contradictory, and tragic *history* of Marxism. What today circulates under the global, inclusive title "The Crisis of Marxism" reveals the inability of many intellectuals, who consider themselves leftists, to recognize Marxist theory in its substantive content as *historical fact*. The theory succumbs to the idealist prejudice that the validity of truth cannot be linked to the social origins of concepts and perceptions. Intellectuals are at pains to discover the class content and the origin in self-interest of all ideas that do *not* come from Marx and Engels. Yet, while applying the maxims of Marx's materialist conception of history to bourgeois society, they act as if the origins and history of Marxist thought are removed from historical mediation.

The consequence is that the dialectic inherent in Marxist thought—between truth-content and reality-content—will not be carried out in its determined ways; rather, it will be reduced to one of the two sides (according to specific perception-guiding interests). Those Marxist intellectuals who are unhappy with the structure of existing societies that base their self-understanding on Marx, who regard their structures as an inversion and moral corruption of Marxist positions, are inclined to turn their attention to the original truth-content of the theories of Marx and Engels. They sink into their work, constantly bringing to light new facets of its humanistic foundations, and from the reconstruction of the original history of this thought they gain the moral and speculative strength they need for political resistance work. Thus they sink into an attitude that does not allow itself to be intimidated by the normative power of facticity and to be led to the point where the *reality of error* enjoys greater esteem than the *unreality of truth*.

This kind of attitude, grounded in a moral and political integrity, is radically opposed to the attitude that considers Marxist thought essentially true wherever it is bound up with the reality of existing societies. Lenin's thesis that "Marxism is all-powerful because it is true" underlies such an immediate coupling of truth-content with reality-content; more precisely, it makes plain the reduction of truth-content to reality-content: what affirms itself as real cannot be untrue. In their interpretive discussions, these Marxist theorists behave toward Marx and Engels as though everything Marx and Engels say is, in a certain sense, explicable teleologically, that is, directed toward this reality. Thus they have no trouble elucidating those aspects of Marxism that legitimate this reality. The dialectic of truth-content and reality-content, a structural element of each epochal theory, has given way to a fundamentally positive attitude toward the existing postrevolutionary power relationships. The motivating center of materialist criticism is unexpectedly transformed into an element of counterrevolutionary decay. Just how much reality dominates possibility in these social orders is shown in the fact that the prevailing reality-concept is doubled, as though it needs the additional magical practice of fortification. They speak of a real, *existing* socialism as though there is an existing socialism that is unreal. Marxist thought is thus so pulled into the undertow of reality that the historical difference between the present and the past is sacrificed.

I consider the exclusive adherence to either position questionable because it cancels the immanent tension in the work of Marx and Engels on which its historical substance rests; in both cases it transforms a theory of historical materialism into an unhistorical, idealistic worldview. At the beginning of the 1960s Jürgen Habermas pointed to a similar cleavage in Marxism. He saw the separation of *natural law* from *revolution,* whose unity is constitutive for Marxist thought, internationally transformed and distributed for the production of ideology among enemy powers in the East-West conflict.

Truth Criterion and Anticipation

Marxism is an epochal theory containing all the instruments of self-criticism. Moreover, it does not need to give up its truth-content if it uses these critical means on itself. If, as has so often been said, Marxist thought represents a radical break in the history of European thought, then that is valid in a decisive way for the criterion of truth itself. Truth is traditionally an agreement between an object and the mental image of it. As Aristotle argues, *adequatio intellectus atque rei.* Nothing here is said about whether the object itself is true. Truth is a relationship of agreement between a concept or mental image and the state of affairs understood thereby. Hegel calls this a relationship of correctness, while whatever is true transcends mere agreement between the content of the conception and the object. For Hegel, a true state is not one understood correctly in a conceptual sense but one based on certain kinds of moral precepts and laws. According to traditional notions, even a theory that reflects a false reality correctly might be considered true.

According to our way of thinking, this moment of truth is always present when we undertake scientific investigations. Even so, it is only *one* moment. It is unthinkable that in our time we should give up all claim to grasping realities in their constellations of facts and thus restrict ourselves to presenting, as the only proof of truth, those perspectives and utopias that transcend this reality. Nevertheless, there is more to truth than the correspondence between categories and reality. It is precisely the *circumstantial* dialectic that sharpens theoretical consciousness and propels it to a critical movement of contiguous contraries so that the true sides of facts are not crushed in their finiteness or in their potentialities and so that manifest realities do not become unrealities, chimeras. Truth in this sense is no mere quality of the thinking Subject but a subjective-objective relation that cannot be determined independently of the structure of the object analyzed. Of course, the object itself has true and untrue components that also require the subjective activity of thought if they are to be grasped.

It is characteristic of Marxist thought that all its determining categories have this double structure. On the one hand, they designate reality in its sentient, graspable, and discoverable qualities. On the other hand, insofar as they also always indicate *better possibilities,* they point beyond the condition reality has attained. Reality and anticipation are thus inseparable from all Marxist concepts about the determining relationships of society.

When Marx speaks of class, he means the objective and subjective conditions of the masses. Whether the masses wish it or not, this implies the living conditions through which their individual life chances are assimilated at the same level. In the relationship of classes with one another, this structure gives rise to the battle cry for the transformation of the entire

213

society. But the whole conception of a class society receives its precise truth-content not in the confirmation that there are classes or that there must always be classes; it is confirmed, rather, in that this class society is to be abolished. That there are classes, and that the description of the conditions of these classes is accurate, still does not exhaust the truth-content of the concept of class. Perhaps one can formulate it paradoxically: the fact that there are classes contains in it the normative charge to abolish class society and to set up the freer condition of a classless society.

What I have said about the concept of class is valid in the same way for a series of other decisive categories. When Marx speaks of productive work, he persists in maintaining that this is a relationship between hired labor and capital, not a material element of work. The productive work is that which produces value and surplus value. It has always been a matter of controversy whether or not scholastic subtleties have since crept into this apparently restricted explanation. According to Marx, a piano player is not productive; the builder of pianos is. A clown who performs before me at home is engaged in unproductive work; the same clown who does the same act in a circus is engaged in productive work because he or she is in the service of an entrepreneur. Despite the fact that Marx here sees the restriction of productive work as a criticism of personal service activities within a feudal dependency, the concept of productive work points to a society in which no one would be excluded from work. Marx speaks of a "republic of work" in which science could be set free for the first time. Productive work—used in the narrow sense as hired labor—is linked with forced labor in a real way, not only in a metaphoric one; by the same token, productive labor refers to the possibility of the objectification of the individual through self-realization. "Productive work" and "human production" therefore belong together in the vision of the possible development of society, just as, in the existing reality, they are separated from one another.

A similar double structure lies in the concepts "division of labor" and "cooperation." The animal spirits, which are included in this cooperation and for which the capitalist pays nothing, comprise the underside of work relationships; they are determined by instinctive activities that exist as quite separate motivations for work. These types of work relationships depend on exactly this point of contact among human beings, among their social needs, in order to bring about an organized process of work. *Marxist categories are therefore at once relationships of correctness toward the social reality and implicit truth claims vis-à-vis that reality.*

The Praxis of Refutation in Marxist Thought and the *Memento Mori* of the Categories

What I have just explained touches on the question of how Marxist theory can be refuted. The fact that an analysis of this theory in terms of its logical consistency is not enough to establish its historical truth can be seen from the empirical hint that precisely these forms of refutation make up a host of good objections. What energy has been expended, in the hundred years since Marx's death, to overturn his work either logically or in a scientific-theoretical sense! There is probably no other theorist so many have tried to refute.

The forms of refutation inherent in Marxist thought are peculiar to his case. First, even when Marxist categories are used in a scientific way,

214

their object is not to make possible statements of eternal verities. Nor can it be said that the conditions designated by these categories are immutable. All Marxist concepts and perceptions carry within themselves a *memento mori* (literally, "Consider that you must die!"), a basic theme of self-negation. This self-negation does not occur because Marxism has failed to account fully for empirical conditions. As I have tried to show, that is only one side of Marxism.

Second, Marxist theory is neither a form of prophecy nor a series of statements contrary to fact. According to Karl Popper, a statement is scientifically real when it is *falsifiable* but not *falsified,* which means that a statement must be able to be examined according to empirical reality, and must survive this examination, but must not be refuted by it. Marxist categories also exist under the pressure of falsifiability. But the reality that could be falsified concerns a different structure. Let us suppose that a society might arise for which the Marxist concept of class is no longer completely applicable. The question would then be whether this picture of a classless society is merely an objective illusion that conceals everything we understand from the concept of class: exploitation, oppression, and alienation.

If one accepts Popper's concept of falsification, then, as applied to Marxist theory, it must be understood in the following way: a theoretical refutation is linked to a real change in relationships. A true refutation of Marxist theory would be, paradoxically, that the reality the theory tries to comprehend has become a completely different one (through the practically accomplished emancipation of men and women). Consequently, Marxist theory would be refuted only when the alienating conditions of life it describes no longer exist; human beings would have attained a condition in which they are freely able to lead a socially self-realized life. Then Marxist theory in its strict sense would be superfluous and a kind of pluralism might arise that many today already accept as an alternative to Marxism. This pluralism loses its concealing function of domination only if human beings coordinate their own activities freely and sensibly.

The Fundamental Conflict in the Contemporary Interpretation of Marxist Theory

If one starts from the thought that Marxist theory in its fundamental form is a historical theory, then a world-historical conflict follows which determines the developmental laws of Marxist thought in the contemporary world. If it is true that each mere repetition or varying interpretation of Marxism's original truth-content contradicts its essence—because unhistorical aspects thereby necessarily creep into the triangular relationship of past, present, and future—then it is simultaneously correct not to allow the historical development of Marxist thought to be assimilated into those systems that appeal to Marxism as a legitimizing facade for existing conditions.

The primary contradiction to which Marxist theory as a historical theory is open consists of the following: Marx's point of departure is that it is not the political power relationships of a society that hold it together at its core; rather, the social ensemble is founded on the capitalist form of the law of value, which regulates the form of production and exchange so that the state, at best, can take part in eliminating certain disparities. But the true power over reality lies in the production of goods, which is the foundation Marx relies on to ascertain whether or not a system is ripe for revolutionary transformations.

Historically, revolutions have taken place precisely in those countries where the law of value was *not* fully developed, where the production of goods had not yet saturated the ensemble of social relations. Consider the problem of social cohesion: in these lands the traditional means of production, the high concentration of capital in a few regions, and the different forms of communal property exist *simultaneously;* the despotic state is necessary to balance this explosive mixture of various *nonsimultaneous* forms of production and property. To be sure, there is a developed proletariat, small by modern industrial standards, but it is surrounded by an oppressive mass of small producers and farmers—a group whose existence and consciousness shows they have not been drawn into the modernizing process. *Marxist theory has not provided for the revolutionary transformation of these societies.* Toward the end of his life, Marx did not exclude such societies from this use of the theory, but he did see that revolutions in underdeveloped regions are necessarily dependent on revolutionary transformation in developed countries if they want to push through a program of social and political transformation *without bureaucratic deformation.*

Thus the contradiction: revolutions have occurred in places where the circumstances are not as Marx supposed necessary for revolutions to retain their emancipatory character; and revolutions have not occurred in places where the conditions for true revolutionary transformation are supposedly ripe. From the perspective of a moral worldview formulated in developed societies, one cannot argue that it would have been better that no revolutions should have taken place in such conditions or that revolution should wait until the conditions correspond to Marxist hypotheses. In such a view there is as well a blind, unhistorical element. If one assumes the true power of Marxism to be where Marxism has actually seized the masses, then one must also insist on taking literally the Marxist standards for revolutionary transformations.

Of course, Marxist theory does not depend on the rights won by workers in bourgeois societies being restricted to facilitate the industrialization and modernization of society. These rights have become precarious in all phases of bourgeois society, but they have never been done away with fully (if one disregards the travesties of capital in fascism). For Marx, it was unthinkable that the mechanisms of the merely representative democracies and their corresponding systems of bourgeois public spheres could be abolished without putting in their place much freer and more open forms of public spheres. His critique of the bourgeois public sphere is directed against its limitation; the sense of the critique consists in expanding, not abolishing, the freedom of speech, the freedom to form coalitions, and the right of assembly.

Historically, we now find ourselves facing a peculiar state of affairs. We seem to be forced to take back the Kantian critique of the ontological argument when we say that Marxist thought gained real power—something in addition to mere theory—wherever conditions for a true emancipation were not favorable. Insofar as these systems lack historical legitimacy and repeatedly have to confirm for themselves the power of reality, the result is an ideology in the classical sense, that is, a necessarily false consciousness. Kant says that "a hundred real thalers are not worth a bit more than a hundred imaginary ones." "To be" is apparently not a real predicate, that is, a concept of something that can be added to the concept of the thing—which is an objection to the ontological argument: existence must be added to the conception of God, to the notion of the totally consummate being. Thus it is said that the conception of God cannot be considered an *ens realissimum* unless existence is comprised in it.

That is the *theoretical* side of the refutation of the ontological argument. For the clever, practical bourgeois person—and Kant was one—the matter looks a bit different: "In my financial circumstances there is more to a hundred real thalers than to the idea of a hundred real thalers (that is, than to a hundred possible thalers). For the object is in reality contained in the idea not merely analytically but also synthetically (it is an idea determinant of my condition)." As the eleventh thesis on Feuerbach makes clear, Marxist theory is oriented toward practical change. In this regard it is not pointless to ask where Marxist theory has really changed the world, where something synthetic has been added. Naturally one can retreat to the trickle-down effect and say that many precepts of Marxist social theory have invaded modern intellectual disciplines and have become part of the real power of those disciplines, and yet one may not be able to name a single one of the precepts in question. That is one side of the history of Marx's influence he himself certainly had in mind. Basically, however, his skepticism about the transformative power of the intellectual disciplines alone was so great that, as he states in "The Class Struggles in France," he could imagine a truly and freely developing intellectual discipline, that is, a discipline in accord with its practical tasks of emancipation, only in a "republic of work," in a freely organized society.

"Criticism" and "partisanship" still belong together in Marx's work. According to him, partisanship is constituted by developing the scientific truth-content in the radical criticism of all that exists, that is, in the criticism that gets to the human root. A partisanship separated from this developed truth-content and in favor of socialism and the proletariat would be considered an ahistorical adventure. At the same time, however, the theoretical reconstruction of the laws determining the modern world, without their conditions coming to a head because of their capacity for change, is supposed to be a decisive partisanship, an extension of the blindness toward the historical powers of the past. The separation of partisanship from criticism is, however, an essential characteristic of Marxism's historical development. This separation reveals itself not only in the internal history of the Marxist science but also in the newly formed international class fronts. If so-called Western Marxism is designed to restore the wounded honor of a critically constituted truth-content of Marxist theory (this is clearest in the Frankfurt school, which therefore also labels *its* Marxism a critical theory), then the leading normative demand for a Marxist legitimation of Stalinism is oriented completely toward partisanship, that is, toward Marxism's thoughtless vow to defend the "Fatherland of Socialism."

Orthodoxy and Foreign Identification

It would require no particular effort to develop the dialectic between the power of reality and the truth-content of Marxist thought if this separation of partisanship from truth could have maintained its one-dimensional frontline positions. One might thereby be able to comfort oneself with the thought that, in industrially underdeveloped countries, revolutionary developments are established with the help of Marxist proposals for modernization, but that a socialist transformation of society does not have to come about because of it. Such a rectification, however, has proven impossible. Marxist thought, anchored in historical realities, has shaped and put its stamp on the entire Marxist discussion to such a decisive extent that, even in those countries for which Marxist theory was intended in its original form, no step can be taken in the recuperation of the origins of Marxist thought without at the same time being critical of "real, existing Socialism" and its consequences. *Equipped with the "imprimatur" of successful revolutions, Marxist thought has returned to the western European countries of its origin and here has become compressed into a new orthodoxy.* Consequently, the transformation of social realities in these countries has removed itself from precisely the spirited investigative look that is fundamental for the Marxist adaptation of reality.

There is another equivalent to the separation of partisanship from criticism: *the separation of the means of investigation from the modes of presentation.* Whoever does not follow Marxism literally in producing his or her own work is quickly suspected of revisionism. The literal-minded scholarship—and literal-mindedness is always characteristic of formal orthodoxies—has grown and completely oppresses the spirited modes of investigation that Marx himself used on the society of his time and that could have been the only means of comprehending the altered conditions of capitalism transformed by the socialist state.

It is not my task in these musings to go into detail on how one may speak, for example, of Russian and Chinese developments as social orders, each with its own idiosyncratic structure. In both societies, however, Marxism is, in a specific way, the product of the assimilation of Western rationalism to their dominant ways of thought and their long traditions of understanding nature and the world. To judge these forms of socialism according to Marx makes sense only if one recognizes at the same time the completely independent character of these social orders, which Rudolf Bahro quite properly characterizes as protosocialist. The claim to truth in these societies is not documented in Marxist theory; rather, it arises primarily out of the immanent logic of development of these countries. Only on this foundation can the true role of Marxist thought in the revolutionary processes of these countries be recognized.

In order to gain a new approach to Marx, we must free Marxist thought from the organizational contexts which, for more than half a century, have determined the political and cultural front lines in the class struggle: I am thinking here of the Third International. This embodied, since 1927 at the latest, the idea of "Socialism in a Country," which was supposed to present a bulwark against the fascist and bourgeois forms of domination and which understood itself to be the genuine heir to Marxist theory. The other connection that arose is not completely free from the reactions to these monopolizing, revolutionary thoughts. What represented itself after 1917 as the Second International of social democracy bears the imprint, on the one hand, of the transformational experiences of the capitalist system; on the other hand, it is also characterized by resistance to a form of socialism that made an appeal to Marx but that, given the reality of Russia's development, could not keep its promise of freedom. I do not consider it at all

218

too bold to maintain that social democracy would have died off long ago if it had not been for Stalinism. In fact, the Stalinist version of Marxism—which is merely a legitimating facade for domination—has done more to discredit socialism in the world than all the reactionary propaganda against Marxism taken together. (In a controversy between Lukács and Bloch, it is clear how these misunderstandings operated: for Lukács, even the worst socialism is better than the best capitalism; Bloch objects to that, correctly so, by saying that the worst socialism is no longer socialism and is therefore much more dangerous because it contributes to discrediting the socialist idea in the world.)

Today we find ourselves in a situation in which we must read Marx anew. Insofar as this challenge always arises in situations of social crisis, it is not new. When I say that we must study Marx anew I mean also that we must free ourselves from identifying with prior and sympathetic revolutions in other countries and with the modes of thought linked to them. Since the late 1960s this identification with alien interests has occurred frequently in different contexts, and the result has been that the spirited application of Marxist categories and incidents to the concrete conditions of the countries in question has been blocked. In the second half of the 1970s disillusionment concerning such identification with foreign interests arose because many admired products of social change either were destroyed or did not take the course the socialist intellectuals in this country had imagined.

A New Study of Marx Is Necessary

In light of these historical changes in Marxist theory, and in light of the dissension in which it presently finds itself, it seems impossible to propose a renewal of Marxist thought without acknowledging the theory to be substantially a historical one and without making evident the mechanism of its entanglement in history. Essential to this renewal is the recognition that the separation of theories and realities into distinct confines (the result of that monopolizing position of Marxist orthodoxy) cannot simply be canceled at one blow without being conscious of the reasons for these delimitations. Today, many who have become uncertain (but who nonetheless want things to remain as they were) are inclined to cover up the history of these separations by coupling Marx's work with other movements. What the modern sciences have produced—be it psychoanalysis, industrial sociology, or the theory of language—is linked to the categories and cognitive contexts of Marxism by means of an "and": Marxism *and* the natural sciences, Marxism *and* psychology, Marxism *and* ecology, and so on. Almost every new movement that appears today and is engaged in theoretical self-reflection produces such a new *and*.

These couplings are all attempts to complete the scientific, developmental history of Marxism by way of an exterior expansion, a history characterized by the separation of certain contents of experience, a history bourgeois sciences appropriated. The developmental history of Marxist thought has thereby been considered to have followed the normal laws of the history of a theory; but new theories and new realities have arisen. This shows, however, an insensitivity to the materialist conception of history; and the constitution of social reality, in the context of contradicting Marx's ideas, remains uncomprehended. Central to the development of Marxism is the question of why, in developing, it should have ignored or even suppressed many twentieth-century practical movements and theoretical analyses. Mere *"and* couplings," added subsequently, do no more than weave ideological threads about the web of an ahistorical reconstruction of Marx's work.

The basic presupposition behind reconstituting a living dialogue with Marxist thought—thereby investigating the history of Marxism's exclusions—is the recognition of the *historical boundaries* of Marxist theory itself. This recognition does not contain an objection to its truth-content. On the contrary, truth is constituted first of all through history. As Walter Benjamin put it, truth has a temporal core. Whoever thinks that perceptions are flawed because they have a genesis has fallen back into the ideological illusion of the bourgeois philosophy of origins. What Marx ascribes to Aristotle—namely, that he works within a historical boundary, without the truth-content of his theory thereby being diminished in the least—must be applicable to Marx as well.

Acknowledging the historical boundaries of Marxist thought makes it possible for us to analyze this epoch-making work from historical perspectives. One consequence is that we can escape the abstract alternative of either accepting as true everything that Marx thought and wrote or rejecting everything as false. The forceful character of this logic of alternatives has done much to facilitate anti-Marxist thought, which is, in large measure, a truth reaction in the scholastic mode. Since Marx's death, several phases of dried-up Marxist orthodoxy have alternated with phases of emotional anti-Marxism. Undergirded by the logic of abstract alternatives, the history of orthodox Marxism is compensated for by the shadowy world-understanding of renegades and dissidents.

In considering Marx historically, the point is to avoid judging him according to absolutist truth claims. In the global confrontation of whether or not everything in Marxist thought is true or false, the decisive question is not posed. Is not the point to determine, in detail, where in Marxist thought the agendas have been completed and where they have not? *The agenda of the analysis of capital has certainly been completed; incomplete is the agenda concerning the consitution of the Subject.* Everything that Marx said is correct, but he did not say everything that we need in order to comprehend the modern world. *Capital* does not have to be written yet again; and it certainly does not have to be recapitulated to the point of senselessness in terms of the old categorical relationships. If we distinguish complete from incomplete agendas, then we recognize simultaneously that Marx mainly undertook the scientific development of a field at the point at which an established science of it already existed. How could he speak scientifically about the constitution of the Subject when in his lifetime there was no psychology of internal development or of compulsive desires?

If one starts from the premise that Marx, in all modesty, saw his theory as fulfilling a dual function (as an introduction to research and an introduction to commerce), then one must be careful about asserting what authentic materialist thought consists of. We can certainly learn more about research by studying the way Marx analyzes theories and social relationships than by repeating the logic of his presentation, which owes a good deal to the tradition of grand bourgeois philosophy, that is, to the Kantian critique of pure reason and to Hegel's science of logic. As Marx himself emphasizes, dialectic is *the* form of thought that is active in matter—and it is active in such a way that it does not prescribe how matter acts in an external sense but rather how matter, in an effort to conceptualize itself, constitutes itself in its own movement. Hegel says that dialectic is pure observation, which is possible only through extreme effort, only through the work of the concept. When I speak of the "logic of research" having priority over the "logic of presentation," I do so in an authentically Marxist sense in order to be able to translate the completed results back into their modes of production; Marx himself proceeds in this way in his entire critique of political economy. It is not the products that are placed in relation to one another but rather the basic modes of production.

I will try to make clear in three problem areas those perspectives from which it is sensible (and possible) to speak of a revival of Marxism. Rather than include Marx's work in its entirety, I will work by examples that point to situations of particular importance today. Certainly I am not going to attempt, after the fact, to integrate everything that is historically new into the body of Marxist categories and perceptions. Since Marxist theory, in its essential content, is based on developed, bourgeois-capitalist countries, it makes sense first to discuss its truth-content so that its history (which is subject to the specific developmental conditions of those countries) is reconstructed without laying oneself open to the charge of partiality concerning those successful revolutions that also made an appeal to Marx. The fact that one works all too happily with borrowed realities has resulted in the development of a critical-productive relationship to Marxist thought according to one's own social conditions.

Above all, there is the question, asked repeatedly, about the constitution of the proletariat as the bearer of a historical mission of change. There have been many dismissals of the proletariat from the stage of history; however, the fact of the matter is—and one must always return to it—this point, even up to the present, has not gained a clear plausibility in everyone's eyes. The second problem is based on the history of the constitution of the Subject. Even the most orthodox representative of materialist psychology is becoming increasingly conscious that people do not think and behave according to conditioned reflexes or to patterns of images. If we take seriously the Marxist conception of humankind as the ensemble of social relations—Marx himself considers this ensemble to be an "inner community"—then it must be assumed that Marx believes the Subject has a complexity equal to or greater than that of the "exterior community," greater, that is, than the organically constructed structure of a highly developed social order. The third area concerns the altered relationship of work, the forces of production, and nature. What appears onstage today as an ecological question is not a specialized problem of social production or of the organization of social and communal living, not even in relation to nature. It concerns, rather, the specific character of the history of industrial civilization as a whole.

The Proletariat as Substance and the Proletarian Characteristics

The concern for the historical Subject in the history of Marxism has been given substance in such a way that it has completely suppressed research on proletarian subjects. We have failed to identify individual proletarian characteristics and to study how they are combined. The substantialization of the proletariat at the level of its historical-philosophical dimensions corresponds to the narrowing of vision with regard to the daily and (in a sense) worldly characteristics of individual proletariats; and it corresponds to the collective forms in which oppressed men and women conduct their battles for liberation. The view that a class, a group, or a rank could become the subject of history simply because of its existential condition or because of its higher social consciousness has always been questionable in any case. Certainly the alternative to the substantialization of the proletariat is not the dissolution of classes into merely individual entities consisting of the conditions of existence and of subjective attitudes.

In order to be able to find a new approach to research on the proletariat, one needs above all to adopt the way of seeing that Marx himself uses. When, in *Capital,* he starts with the notion of society as a gigantic collection of commodities, he also emphasizes that the single commodity is the cell-form of this whole and that the purpose of science is to decipher the inner dynamics of this cell-form. Marx is never content with determining synthetic wholes for which, in terms of politics and economics, he is able to identify only apparent movements. He focuses instead on the microscopic, on the "compressed particular," whose inner contradictory nature determines the true movement of the whole. This analytic approach is as valid for the analysis of commodities as it is for the political assessment of the entire condition of a society, such as Marx undertakes in the "Eighteenth Brumaire," in which he puts forward the constricted conditions of existence, the needs and characteristics of small landholders, as the exposed secret of patriotism and of the emperor's masquerade.

Now it is rather remarkable that Marx should display the analytic tools of the critique of the reification of consciousness and of behavior; and also that he should name the basic perversions of a society in which the production of commodities predominates. The fetishism of the commodity, which is the basis for the mechanism of all reification, of the personalizing of factual relationships as well as of the distortion of the process and its result so that the entire objective world takes on a ghostly objectivity—all this Marx applies to all the essential affairs of society (even if he does so often in hints of future research projects). *But he avoids applying this basic analysis of societal perversions to the proletariat itself.* This is all the more astounding because the cognitive methods he developed—aimed precisely at naming the manifold stumbling blocks to change—suggest that incisive research is also to be devoted to the subjects of this change. Marx acts as though the proletariat, because of its collective condition of misery, has the ability, concretely earned in practical battles, to unite itself in organizational terms and to bring the process of revolutionary upheaval to a successful conclusion. If, with regard to all other social contexts, Marx persists in microanalysis, then, concerning the proletariat, he is dealing essentially with a *synthetic whole.* Of course, Marxists can object that Marx himself in no way glorifies or gives substance to the proletariat. At various points in his work he emphasizes the need for the working class to educate itself for revolutionary emancipation.[2]

Marx was aware that under certain social conditions that allow—as they did in England—the proletariat to take part in the exploitation of the entire world, a worker aristocracy could arise in and alongside the working class. What he does not undertake, however, is the cell analysis of the characteristics, inclinations, and expectations of individual members of the proletariat insofar as these are societal characteristics and not merely individual or psychological ones. Whatever works to project the reifications of bourgeois society into the proletariat seems to Marx to be not constitutive of the collective process of emancipation and, on the contrary, to be easily surmountable. Thus, the fact of the nonanalysis of the proletariat, placed on a scientifically comparable level with the analysis of commodities, gives the proletariat the appearance of a substance making its way according to hard-and-fast historical rules.

The defective adaptation of the fetishism analysis to bourgeois society as a class object—an Object that tries to develop into a Subject through its battles with the will and with consciousness—is something that led both Marx and Engels (particularly in his later work) to a doubly faulty assessment: as they observed the quantitative growth of the working class and its organizations, and as they became aware of the undermining of the bases for legitimacy of the old class domination, they *overestimated* the revolutionary will of the working class and *underestimated* the capacities of the existing form of domination either to neutralize parts of this revolutionary will or to absorb it. In 1891, after the Erfurt Program had been accepted, Engels triumphantly asserted that "all the remains of Lassalle-ism have been destroyed. We have a completely Marxist agenda!"

As we know today, that was not totally false. The state-aided undertakings favored by Lassalle, which were supposed to place socialism on the path to a "system of acquired rights," gave way to the strong, sobering effect of a twelve-year ban on democratic socialism. This state, which Lassalle intended to be a reconciliation of the differences between prussianism and socialism in the interests of the working class, was established in reality only in the minds of a few pragmatists after the lifting of the socialist laws. But how the movement really fared does not become apparent in the platform of the party congress. Those who were trained to recognize Marxist formulas could easily discern the Marxist arguments in the theoretical, introductory part of the Erfurt Program. But even on the programmatic level, it was evident that, where the concern was with practical and short-term goals, the old *state orientation* of democratic socialism still existed; it was not at all broken by the experiences of being legally banned.

The contradiction between the *reality* and the *program* of the worker's movement goes back to its early history, which Marx and Engels lived through themselves, and in 1914 this contradiction became evident only by means of a historic pauper's oath. In the analysis of the bourgeois systems of economics and politics, Marx insists in detail upon the difference between public declarations and actual activities. In the history of the situation of the proletariat, continuous confusions between program and reality creep into Marx's and Engels's analyses.

These mistaken assessments also are manifest in the predictions Engels makes in his later work concerning the possible beginning of revolutionary upheaval. Shortly before his death, he declared that the revolution would probably come at the end of the (nineteenth) century, and it would be a good thing if the proletariat still had this time to prepare for the assumption of power. If the revolution were to come earlier, then the bourgeois intelligentsia—the teachers, the doctors, the engineers, and so on, whose help the proletariat would have to count on for the reconstruction of society—would be thoughtlessly betrayed. These classes would have to be brought into the process of the proletarianization of society so that, out of the loss of the bourgeois conditions of existence, they might learn to familiarize themselves with the perspectives of a new society.

How could Engels have arrived at such mistaken prognoses? He had such an unbelievable ability to predict the results of the constellation of armies and battles that he could foresee the debacle that befell the French army at Verdun, yet he allowed himself to be misled by the exuberance of idealism. In both the successful and the unsuccessful prognoses, it is certainly not a question of prophetic abilities in the usual sense. When Engels predicted the decisive battle between two contending armies, even though their plans still called for different marching orders, he did so by means of an infallible analysis of compelling material conditions. The immersion in details, the penetrating look into the contradictory nature of the military cell-organization, in clear distinction to strategic intentions that have merely been conceived—all this makes possible a caution concerning the material before him, material whose inner dynamics emerge because of an intense concentration on their conceptual work, material which is *not* subsumed to biased ideas from without. If the proletariat is not the object of such cell analyses, then it is not possible to make prognoses based on the proletarian contexts' own movements.

It was during the time of national socialism that Marxist thought first paid greater attention to the cell-characteristics of the proletariat and therefore to those individual proletariat interests linked to the existing system of domination. At that time people were forced to recognize that the quantitative power of worker organizations and the battle-preparedness of the working class were not enough to prevent its complete destruction. Also, the failure of the November Revolution and other European revolutionary attempts did not result in replacing the *substance* analysis of the proletariat with an *empirical* analysis. Here one must cite the researches into "family" and "prejudices" by the Frankfurt School for Social Research; these have been trailblazing in overcoming the notion that the powerful proletarian camp could maintain itself free from the destructive influences of the bourgeois environment. The proletarian family, rather than being simply the counterpart of the bourgeois family, reproduces its mechanisms. Authoritarian and authoritarian-dependent characters arise not only in bourgeois but also in proletarian families. Ethnocentric prejudices, the hatred of foreigners, the inclination to conceal the causes of crises and to expect Führer-like personalities to overcome them—these and other mechanisms of perversion, of the reification of behavior and of consciousness, also arise as ways of handling things in the working class. That does not mean that the susceptibility of workers to authoritarian developments is identical to that of the bourgeois class. But this difference is not based on existing dispositions; it is based, rather, on the ways these dispositions can be collectively bound and neutralized.

In his research on the behavior of blue- and white-collar workers in the prefascist period, Erich Fromm has developed an interesting thesis. The working class is not free of those prejudices and of that reified consciousness brought about by the capitalist production of commodities and their corresponding conditions of domination. However, as long as there exists an organizational support for workers, as long as unions and the

Communist and the Social Democratic parties can be preserved as historical organizations with certain traditions and perspectives on a change of circumstances and on the elimination of present misery—as long as all this occurs, the loyalty of the worker toward these organizations by and large will be preserved. It was not the workers who voted for Hitler in such great numbers; it was the dispossessed petite bourgeoisie, the authority-bound yea-sayers of the bourgeois classes, of the civil servant classes, of the white-collar classes, of the small-time producers, and so on. But national socialism is not founded on these classes exclusively; it is also capable of mobilizing overwhelming portions of the working class for its purposes. The Nazis were materialistic opportunists; they knew precisely that the destruction of worker organizations was the first step in mobilizing for their own purposes the behavior potential that had been kept in check by collective restraints. When these worker organizations were destroyed, the work force fell into the laps of the National Socialists, for them to deal with as they pleased. This explains why there were many attempts to resist collectively as long as these worker organizations still existed, and why this resistance was reduced to particular, single sacrifices when the collective resistance, supported by powerful organizations, ceased.

Although Marx and Engels had not placed this perspective of a dialectic proper to proletarian cell-characteristics and their organization at the center of their analysis, they did not exclude the possibility of a catastrophe, involving the entire society, that would signal the end of both the ruling and the oppressed classes. They were probably not able to imagine, however, that the working class, once reduced to a noncollective natural state of private exploitability, could take an active part in exploiting itself.

In light of the difficulty concerning these theoretical-historical and historical experiences, what are the consequences today of holding fast to class analysis and at the same time coming upon the reality of proletarian living conditions? It is not the single member of the proletariat who constitutes that cell-form to which one can return in order to make evident the political movements of fundamental forces. The individual is no synthetic whole whose organizing center consists of a stable identity. And the working class is not an oversized individual who participates in history according to homogeneous norms. As we discover the cell-forms in the individual proletarian characteristics of the workers, we are able simultaneously to see those bourgeois characteristics that bind the worker to the existing society. We must start from the methodological rule of thumb that *ambivalences and dual values are contained in each single characteristic of the worker.* The fact that workers belong to a class and are affiliated with it politically does not stamp them entirely; it concerns only certain characteristics. Their need to free themselves from oppression and from exploitation or to battle contemporary misery may lead them to organize into unions or to join a workers' party. Their entire livelihood is not necessarily loyally bound to these organizations; rather, they can be so involved—through other aspects of their circumstances—with the existing order of domination that only the politicization of these conditions can produce a total economy of attitudes, which grants them a certain independence from the continuing influences of the existing system of domination.

One of the fundamental mistakes of Marxist proletariat analyses is the assumption that workers who organize into unions and proletarian

225

parties are *exclusively proletarian in character.* I consider as proletarian those characteristics and forces, directed toward emancipation, which aim to break through the existing conditions of domination by means of pertinent opposition. If one proceeds in light of such an evaluation, then it is no longer self-evident that one sees proletarian characteristics only in the traditional working classes and acknowledges them only where there is a situation of need in terms of the material conditions of life. When people unite in order to fight against developments that threaten the fundamental grounds of human existence, they express such proletarian characteristics in the process of organizing their battles themselves. But even here we are speaking of parts rather than wholes. In this regard one can say that "proletarian characteristics" and "proletarian motives" come into play in bourgeois initiatives, in the women's liberation movement, in the antinuclear movement, in the student movement, even though all these initiatives and movements cannot be directly linked to the traditional notion of the industrial working class. The battle is not carried out with an eye toward transforming the entire society in terms of its existing system of domination and organizing it anew into another society. In actuality, the movement is focused on the detail, on the cell-form. But even the concentration on certain points to which emancipatory interests are tied gives rise to a decisive material lever, a concrete point of contact with objective reality, intended to effect a new organization of the remaining characteristics as well.

If one starts from the cellular organization of those characteristics that are linked to the process of emancipation or that depend on the existing system, then one presupposes also another concept of the organizing process and of organization. Traditionally, organizations have the tendency to challenge and to bind people on certain aspects of their interests and loyalties. One joins a party and pays the dues of loyalty for the protection expected from the party. By and large these organizations are not interested in politicizing whole persons, in loosening the non-emancipatory characteristics from their natural involvement with existing dependencies. Exacting loyalty as the main method of payment, however, has scant effectiveness in changing consciousness and behavior.

This traditional notion of organization, mainly influenced by the model of the ideal bourgeois association, is apparently partially responsible for the scant attention workers' organizations pay to the consciousness industry and the media. In their own consciousness and behavior, once they become aware of their true interests, workers are not empty vessels to be filled. Wherever the daily tabloid is the predominant workers' paper, that is where ideological material is continuously made palatable and where behavioral positions are actualized, all of which have precisely the function of *not* allowing workers to become aware of their immediate interests. Foucault located domination in the detail, in those arenas of movement that people have, in those times and places that determine their living conditions. Thus, it is not the system of domination by and large that hinders liberation; rather, it is the attachment we have for certain things, which often is so powerful that we make decisions that go against our own interests.

The whole person is the goal of liberation, not its point of departure. Of course, in a not exclusively metaphoric sense one can say that people, constituted as they are under the conditions of exploitation and oppression, still do not make up a true, synthetic unity. A synthetic unity would arise when the individual characteristics reach a stage of emancipation that allows them to be constituted in a way that gives them identity. That would presuppose that people's capacity to make sociability and solidarity their object has been developed enough for them to recognize themselves in objective reality. The negation of self-alienation proceeds along the same path as does self-alienation, according to Marx, and the negation of self-alienation can be accomplished only when the cell-forms of the Subject-Object relationship are being changed. Human significations arise only in order to beget the human objects of signification.

The Altered Position of the Subject in the Revolutionary Process

At a time when most people, whether willingly or not, were pulled into the undertow of class polarization, it was natural to consider the force of objective conditions as defining and limiting the arena of human action. In continuously reproaching Marx with misunderstanding himself objectively, people completely overlook the fact that this objectivity was not a question of cognitive judgment alone; rather, it was mediated by history. In cases where people are pulled into this class polarization, where they become merely the appendage of capital, Marx and Engels speak of societal natural laws. They do not do this to immortalize these natural laws but to make clear how little human will and consciousness actually intervene in historical processes.

If this superstructure of the objective in Marx's time is justified, then the as-it-were transcendental point of view—through which nineteenth-century life can be observed in light of the rapid development of capital—cannot be extended seamlessly to cover those circumstances in which capital predominates just as it did before and in which people's needs simultaneously grow in complexity and their forms of resistance become differentiated to an extent unimaginable by Marx. The anti-idealistic formula that the being of society determines consciousness and not vice versa is not a law that is independent of history.

The growth of the forces of production has not eliminated exploitation and oppression, but the *forms* in which they make their way are based on the consideration of the *dimensions of the Subject in domination* to a far higher extent in the developed capitalist social orders than they were in Marx's time. As long as one has grounds for the assumption that people have nothing to lose but their chains, one is able to deduce—from the want found in the objective situation—the motive for overcoming the existing situation. And one is able to rest assured that the pressure of circumstances will one day compel people to revolutionary activity, regardless of their ready excuse that *they* do not count. As soon as this close tie between motives for action and the objective situation no longer exists—because of the differences among systems of domination and because of the immense growth in society's wealth—the motives directed toward overcoming the present society become more complex as well.

Today we find ourselves in a situation in which a *revolutionary theory of action* is necessary. In this point as well the developmental history of Marxism has been determined by unfortunate separations. The utopia-prohibition of Marx and Engels has the worthwhile tendency of directing criticism toward conceptions that make the revolutionary will and the need for a free society the sole lever of change. In opposition to that, Marx and

Engels justifiably insist on the material basis of all constellations, which must be understood without illusions before successful historical action is possible. The strategic function of this utopia-prohibition is defined through the historical situation in which all opposition forces—regardless of the camp they are active in—have an overabundance of consciousness, ideas, and good intentions. Marx and Engels were aware that ideas alone could not accomplish anything against the compacted power of a capitalist class founded on material relationships.

Once the original profundities of Marx and Engels in relation to Subject and Object are declared to be eternal verities, many investigations and theories establish themselves next to Marxist historical science and occupy the lacunae in materialist analysis. Not all these theories conceive of themselves explicitly as answers to the loss of the Subject in Marxism. However, while Marxists staunchly repeat the microanalysis of the production of commodities and of capital, there develops (alongside and completely independent of the ideology of Marxist orthodoxy) a theory of the Subject that pursues the microperspective deep into the fundamental constitution of the individual. By contrast, Freudian psychoanalysis, with its discriminating way of interpreting the life of the psyche in terms of mere interests and needs, resembles the struggle of the concept, a struggle that Marx followed in investigating the total context of production and reproduction in social life. If, with his characteristic instinct for rooting out great scientific discoveries, Marx had learned of Freud's theory, he would probably have dealt with it as he had Hegel, for Freudian psychoanalysis is also bourgeois in its origin and is not written with the future proletariat in mind.

Marx constantly stresses that the value of categories and perceptions is not exhausted in their genesis. Even in Freudian psychoanalysis, Marx would have discovered the "rational kernel" he shelled out of Hegel's absolute idealism in order to be able to stand this theory right side up again.

The battle of orthodox Marxists against psychoanalysis proves itself increasingly to be Theater of the Absurd, and the categories of demarcation are more "police concepts" than those supposedly required by the matter at hand. That point is also valid for the history of science during the 1920s, where important Marxists like Wilhelm Reich were cut off from the communist movement because they put the notion of ambivalence in needs and interests—in sum, the daily conflicts of workers—at the center of their investigations. It was not only the rank-and-file party members who followed the mechanism of a psychological apparatus (a battle arena that includes repression, overcompensation, reality adjustment, and the superego as censor) but also the guiding spirits of this movement who could not adhere strictly to the catalog of duties for collective action, making amends thereby for all the damage to socialization suffered under bourgeois society. If people had noticed this, then they would not have so helplessly faced the collapse of the workers' movement and the torrential growth of fascism as if it had been a natural catastrophe. Let me make my critique polemically sharper: even burghers and functionaries of "real existing socialism" are stamped by categories like ego, superego, and ego-ideal, let alone the psychoses and neuroses that indicate a failure of socialization; they are stamped by their ability to adjust to reality and by their individual capacity for organizing spatial and temporal circumstances according to objective demands, especially by their entire behavior toward the Social Being. It is

pure fiction that people work only according to the rules of the neurophys-
iological system and that they are able to raise their interest and needs
straight up to the level of consciousness.

It is notorious that the battle against psychoanalysis runs along
a line—determined by archaic prejudice—which states that the messenger of
misfortune is its cause. Whoever refers to the complexity of the Subject, to
the manifold stumbling blocks that stand in the way of socialist, progressive
thought, will not be accepted as someone who is investigating the material
conditions of the alteration of the Subject. That person will be regarded,
rather, as a propagandist for bourgeois dissolution. Of course, the consequence of this prejudice is that *underneath* the official consciousness of these
social orders an ever stronger unconsciousness settles in, one that does not
get public expression and produces various forms of protest and attitudes
of escape.

This prejudice against subjectivity, however, has even deeper
systemic causes. At its foundation is obviously the conception that capital,
the economy—on the whole, the conditions commonly regarded as material—are the *hard* objects of science, whereas the psyche is made up of *soft
matter,* something malleable with no shape of its own. Today we know,
however, that people can die just as easily because of psychological problems
as they can because of an axe or material objects, things that injure them
physically. Historically as well, this mistake of considering objective reality
as worthy of theory and psychological reality as a question of sentiment has
always worked out unfortunately. For example: in the final analysis, the
collective wishful notions of many who felt their national honor compromised through the Treaty of Versailles had much greater material reality
than the Maginot Line, which was overrun in just a few days. It is a meaningful exaggeration to say that in this sense those realities of mass psychology, which, of course, are always anchored in individual psyches, can
be more objective than stone.

In the 1970s the entire history of the Third International repeated
itself under completely different assumptions in the form of the battle against
psychoanalysis. Those dimensions of the Marxist analysis of capital that
had been forgotten in the postwar period were again pushed into consciousness in obtrusive orthodoxy. The more analyses referred to capital, the more
scientific they appeared and the more emphatic was the exclusion of psy-
choanalytically oriented investigations. These analyses of capital joined forces
with an equally rigid concept of organization. It can commonly be said that
the greater the threat—because of those psychic energies that have been
forced into the subconscious—to that which the censuring court of the ego
has to do, the more decisive is the repression of psychoanalysis. Also, the
battle against psychoanalysis is always indicative of the fact that the Subject
takes great pains to keep its true needs hidden beneath its consciousness.

In this context, if one takes the concept of orthodoxy seriously,
then one has to endow it with new life. An orthodox Marxist is not one
who repeats Marxist terms as if one could unquestioningly apply this substantially historical theory arbitrarily to historical circumstances. An orthodox Marxist is, rather, one who can *adjudicate the dialectic between the
concept and the object.* Whatever Marx says about the constitution of the
Subject was not based on the developed science of psychology, which cor-
responded to the science of political economy then available. Concerning

the individual, he basically makes only statements of principle: about the individual being tied to the process of constituting bourgeois society and about the possibilities for emancipation. The *forms* in which the Social Being is transformed into the Subject, on the other hand, largely escaped the contemporary scientific knowledge of psychology. For this reason, Marx only formulates a research direction in relation to the Subject when he speaks of an ensemble of social relations or, better, when he speaks of the inner common being of men and women. That the outer common being, the society, is simply reflected in the Subject remained completely alien to Marx, for in the society itself one can already find constituents of the Subject. All exterior elements of society exist also within, but precisely in the form of subjective elements that are related according to their inner logic. If one considers Marx's statements about the individual and subjectivity to be the results of research processes corresponding to the level of knowledge of political economy, and one repeats these statements thanks to a specially formulated art of citation, then seeing things from the level of knowledge today, one would push Marx back to a prescientific level. Marx hints at a materialist theory of subjectivity, but he did not develop it as he did the theory of political economy; indeed, he could not. In order to accomplish that today, it is unavoidable that we end the compressed exclusion of psychoanalysis from the Marxist scientific context and at the same time take up those special investigations that are based on the real exploration of the Subject.

The Precarious Relationship of Work, the Forces of Production, and Nature

I come now to the third and final topic, namely, that a revival of Marxist thought is both necessary and meaningful. On the one hand, "revival" means a strict adherence to the content (not merely the vocabulary) of Marxist theory; on the other hand, it means carrying through unfulfilled agendas that are real research programs and that contribute to the orientation of the contemporary world. The most difficult point of such an unfulfilled agenda concerns the altered relationship between work, the forces of production, and nature.

Marx investigated the relationships of the logic of capital with unbelievable thoroughness, but he did not do the same with the underside of capital, which capital feeds on and which is generally the basis for the constitution of the object: the active work force. This is all the more astounding because active, or live, labor is the source of value and surplus value; it therefore constitutes that which finally also establishes the social context. *Strictly speaking, for Marx, we are born for the first time when we receive our first paycheck.* Of course, that is an exaggeration, for Marx knew that commodities cannot go to market all alone. Even here it is certainly not a question of principle, which criticism must take as its point of departure. It is, first, a problem of a differentiated scientific procedure; and, second, a problem of an unsystematically labeled direction of research.

"The determination of the value of the labor commodity contains a historical and moral element"—so writes Marx in the first volume of *Capital.* Only the determination of value? That matter aside, we have no systematic indication of Marx's cognitive interest in either element (that is, the moral or the historical element of the active work force) either within

230

or beside the question of the determination of value. If it is true that active labor is the determining source (but not the sole source) of societal wealth, even of value and surplus value, then it is incomprehensible to me how Marx could pay so little attention to—and use so few of his powers of discrimination on—the historical and social character of labor, for he did not otherwise hesitate to investigate even the most minute transaction in the context of capital when it concerned the *economy of dead labor.*

It is necessary—particularly in a centennial celebration of Marx—to break down the reifications of Marxist orthodoxies and, without thereby subscribing to the stupid mechanisms of delimitation, to revalidate provisional thinking and pose hypothetical questions. One of these hypothetical questions might be, Is it completely impossible that capital's power of reality, a power Marx wished to comprehend without illusions in order to destroy it, so fascinated Marx that he was incapable of perceiving the forms of resistance on the part of active labor *beyond* those of the proletariat, valorized as a collective Subject?

If it should prove true that a fascination with the power of capital—as Marx formulates it in the "Communist Manifesto"—is something that affected Marx himself, then a further question presents itself: Should not the underside of capital, a political economy of labor, be developed according to the present conditions in order for us to be able to grasp the historical effectiveness of capital at all? To do so would not constitute an abrogation of the mechanisms investigated in *Capital.* On the contrary, it would be the integration of this capitalistic legitimation into a political economy of labor as the science that is at the foundation of the entire process of the production and reproduction of society.

Nineteenth-century capital was fully integrated into the notion of social progress; nothing that existed beyond the capitalist context was able to avoid that progress. But under the developed conditions of capitalism the situation becomes increasingly absurd: the more capital develops, the less it is able to provide the active work force with conditions of realization. Even the old historically generic privilege of human beings to be the sole possessors (and users) of brains, muscles, and nerves has been threatened by modern machine systems. In these conditions, where is the active work force, the live labor? What are the new possibilities of realization for them when they fall out of the scheme of capital? How can one prevent unique historical skills from decaying because they can find no perspicuous activity or because they are pushed into the kinds of activity that serve the additional exploitation and degradation of men and women?

Today these are no longer just questions of the economics of crisis. They centrally concern the ways of people's lives, their relationships to one another and to nature. If one considers *Capital* to be the dominating viewpoint in the analysis, then of course one can develop notions that the bourgeois media, with its technologically improving consciousness industry, is about to use the labor that has been excluded from the productive work process to prevent people from becoming conscious of their new social situation; or that the bourgeois media is about to integrate the newly available labor forces into a proliferating apparatus of white-collar workers and civil servants in order to control, by means of a Big Brother state, the energy of protest. Capitalism has always been able to find areas of employment for the active work force in order to forestall the catastrophe or the revolution.

But in doing so it matters little which fantasy capitalism is able to develop in the interests of crisis management, something one surely should not underestimate; what is most threatening, however, is that the Left has allowed its own fantasy of change to be undermined by the crippling fascination with the possibilities of power in capitalism. The Left stares fixedly at the old concept of work and refuses to think of work as taking any form other than the subsistence labor defined by capital; everything beyond that the Left labels "play" or "leisure time." In relation to the underside of the analysis of capital, however, Marx himself has a very precise notion of work as one of the essential means of expression by which people discover their identities. While the Subject objectifies itself, the Object subjectifies itself: this Subject-Object dialectic is central for an emancipatory concept of work, without which even a liberation of science would not take shape.

People frequently reproach Marx and Engels for having a concept of progress which they, unreflectively, did not tie to the development of the forces of production. In fact, there are statements by Marx and Engels that confirm this. For example, Engels says: "steam engines, electricity and spinning wheels have been more revolutionary than the impact of Blanqui, Raspail and Barbes." Yes, more revolutionary in the destruction of old relationships(!)—in that productive forces like these still have determining, liberating functions. But the old relationships or conditions have already disintegrated, and the main thing now is to build a new society with themes oriented not toward the power of disintegration but rather toward the sociological fantasy of how a new, liberated society should look. Only then does the developmental logic of the forces of production lose its defining import. The function of capitalistic forces of production is to destroy traditional relationships; the importance Marx and Engels attributed to these forces of production may be one reason why their theories, elaborated in terms of classes emancipating themselves in traditional social orders, have been understood as theories of modernization.

However much Marx and Engels assign a deciding role in social development to the productive forces of the capitalist structure, they also understand that the plundering behavior of capital toward people and nature has a double meaning. Traditional dependencies are pulled into the undertow of commodity production, and the *objective* conditions of a possibly new organization of society arise. Marx was conscious that in this way the production disturbances of the ecological balance were linked inescapably to the tendencies immanent in the logic of capital. In the first volume of *Capital* he says that, with the steady growth of the urban population, piled together in large centers, capital production would both enlarge the historical force of society and disturb the metabolism between people and nature. (For example, we do not return to the soil those components used up as foodstuffs and clothing; the process of exchange is one-sided.) If urbanization, therefore, is linked to a concentration of the proletariat (which can thereby become a historically powerful force), the same process threatens the physical health of the urban worker and the spiritual life of the peasant. The capitalist transformation of the process of production appears to be the martyrdom of the producers, and labor seems to be a means of enslavement, of impoverishing the worker. The social combination of working processes becomes an organized oppression of individual spiritedness and freedom. Each increase in the soil's fruitfulness for a given period also speeds the ruin of its long-term fruitfulness. Marx summarizes his arguments on the relationship between people and nature in the following way: "the more a country like the United States of America, for example, bases its development on heavy industry, the quicker will be this process of destruction. Capitalist production accordingly develops the technology and combination of social production processes only at the same time that it undermines the well-springs of all wealth: the earth and the worker."

This dialectic of progress and destruction, developed at the intersection of city and country, points to a contextualized materialist analysis of ecology. The ecological problems cannot be separated from inclinations inherent in capital, but they also are not absorbed by them. Marx did not pursue this view further, since he hoped that the destruction of the worker and the soil would not come to pass because the proletariat would carry out the revolution. Marx venerates Justus von Liebig, who discovered artificial fertilizer, and he speaks in favor of using fertilizer as a means of increasing productivity. Evidently, Marx could not imagine the current social situation in which farmers complain that the soil only functions as a place where fruits are attached, that the only places where there is still life in the soil are the graveyards.

I am not concerned with cramming into the categories of Marxist thought all the social developments and protest movements that have appeared on the historical horizon. But it is a question of giving up—not without peril—theories that explain entire social contexts because individual events cannot be grasped any longer with these theories' cognitive means. As an epochal social theory, Marxist theory on the whole continues to explain much more than those compartmentalized bourgeois theories of empirical research, which can make clear highly focused, single phenomena, but which pay no attention to the main problem of theory construction, namely, context, concrete totality.

Whatever is valid for the qualitative workplace—and though this is intimated in Marx, it is not developed into a political economy of labor—is valid in a similar way for the concept of nature. Marx explicity discusses this concept in his early writings; but even in *Capital* and in the *Grundrisse* it is not entirely absent. In no way does it seem to be misguided to base a theory of ecology on Marx. It is in the third volume of *Capital* that Marx gives an almost poetic rendition of our relationship to nature. To be sure, the statement is hidden in economic stipulations on rent from the soil, formulated as a kind of *natural-law contract in the interests of succeeding generations:* "From the perspective of a higher economic social formation, a man's private ownership of part of the world appears to be just as unsavory a proposition as a man's private ownership of another man. Even a whole society, a nation, yea even all contemporary societies taken together, are not the owners of the earth; they are its occupants only, its beneficiaries and, as *boni patres familias* (as good family fathers), they have the responsibility of leaving behind an improved planet to succeeding generations." We have a natural-law duty to fashion the earth in such a way that we do not place a burden on the living conditions of future generations.

Accepting Marx's statement, one could link it effectively to today's fears about nuclear power. Even the argument that the creation of nuclear power plants both commits and endangers generations is linked to Marxist thought, and not only in a superficial sense. A generation that conducts itself like good parents must make the prudent handling of the earth the guiding principle of its behavior.

I now come to the end. No social emancipation movement can do without theory. Ruling classes limit themselves to using bits of legitimation as facades for their power. But the oppressed classes who wish to free themselves depend in their own battle for emancipation on fusing *utopia* and *knowledge*. When Marxism gives up the claim to a revolutionary theory of action, it degenerates into bourgeois academic posturing. The practical meaning of theory consists in the fact that it is impossible for emancipation movements to determine the conditions and limits of actions solely through practical experimentation. When men and women continuously run up against blank walls and have no idea why they are frustrated, the result is passivity and numbness because of failure. Freud defines thinking as a "trial act." That is also valid for the possible learning processes of historically active classes and groups, for there is no emancipation movement that can afford willingly to relinquish the social memory of the history of resistance and struggle.

I have already emphasized that it is not a matter of the reinstatement of a literal-minded orthodoxy. Marx does not investigate everything necessary for explaining the contemporary world. Each person who has to deal with modern conditions acquires an understanding of this world not only from reading Marx but also from reading Max Weber and other sociologists and philosophers. Nothing learned here is superfluous. What is missing from these theories, however, is the cohesive explanation that is linked by its perspective on emancipation movements. *Cohesiveness is the crucial criterion* for a theory that furnishes us with directions to help us find our way in the world and in our own lives. A spirited revival of Marxist thought would be an essential crystallization point for concrete, historical work in which today's emancipation movements might better be able to evaluate their social place and more effectively organize their generalizable processes of learning.

Notes

(Translator's note: I am grateful to Jochen Hoffman for his meticulous advice on the many problems this text presented.)

1   In an extemporaneous speech I lectured on the viewpoints presented here, first in a forum for adult education at the New Market Square, in Cologne (February 4, 1983) and then at the Social Academy in Dortmund (February 10, 1983). Subsequently, I worked these viewpoints into an essay and expanded on them considerably. Wherever possible, however, I have kept the lecture format.

2   The most famous instance is Marx's reckoning with the Willich-Schapper faction in a session of the central governing body of the Communist League on September 15, 1850: "In the place of critical observation the minority puts a dogmatic one, in the place of a materialist observation an idealist one. For you the driving-wheel of the revolution is not real conditions but the will alone. We tell the workers: you must experience fifteen, twenty, or fifty years of bourgeois wars and peasant battles, not only in order to change conditions but also in order to change yourselves and to prepare yourselves for political rule. You say, on the contrary: either we must come to power immediately or we will lie down and go to sleep."

Gajo Petrović
Philosophy and Revolution: Twenty Sheaves of Questions

Is not revolution the very essence of Being? And is not philosophy, then, necessarily, the thought of revolution—a new, higher kind of thought in which traditional philosophy is transcended and overthrown?

1. Must philosophy always be written exclusively in the form of dissertations, where everything is systematically explained, argued, and illustrated? Has not philosophy already appeared in the form of epic poems, novels, short stories, and plays; in the form of prose poetry, dialogues, letters, and books of travel? Has it not been shown that philosophy can be successfully expressed in the form of theses (Feuerbach, Marx) and even of sermons and commands (Nietzsche)? Might one, then, try to say something in the form of questions? Is the question *(pítanje)* not the form in which thought takes its nourishment *(pìtanje)?* Indeed, are not "philosophy" and "revolution" precisely the concepts that question everything else, and should they not, then, be able to bear the cutting edge of every question?

2. Is philosophy the thought of Being, or is it the thought of revolution? If it is the former, is it a thought that thinks Being, or is it a thought that is thought *by* Being? If philosophy is a thought that thinks Being, is this thought an ascertainment of what is, a search for what can be, or a prescribing of what must occur? Is its calling to stigmatize the harmful, extol the useful, show the way to the desirable, strengthen the belief in what is achievable, support the hope in what is not yet lost, or incite to what might be dangerous? Is it a neighbor or a stranger to Being, its shepherd or its hunter, its sower or its mower, its bodyguard or its concentration camp, its prophet *(porok)* or its vice *(porok)?* Is it a little of everything or nothing but a rigorous, inexorable thought, which, while thinking Being in its essence, rejects all these metaphoric descriptions as a kind of children's wear which is not fitting for its seriousness, so that to all questions about what or who it is, it replies with self-confidence that it is, in itself, the thought of Being, in person and without any further additions?

3. If Being is what philosophical thought thinks, what is that Being? If *what* is not the proper question, then *how* is it? Does it exist regardless of whether anybody thinks it? And is it distinguished primarily by the *way* in which it exists regardless of whether it is being thought? Does it experience its being thought as a pleasure or a discomfort, an enrichment or an impoverishment, an extollation or a humiliation, a perfection or a desecration? Does it laugh indifferently at that thought which exerts itself for it, not realizing that all its efforts remain idle? Or perhaps it is

Being itself which strives after thought because it feels that without thought it remains incomplete and insufficient, nameless and voiceless?

4. If philosophy is the thought that thinks Being, can it at the same time be the thought that is being thought *by* Being? Is not a person, as a philosopher, one who, by philosophizing, reflects on Being? Are not people a species with a particular being and philosophy one of their most special activities? Or perhaps people, while thinking Being, do not think as particular beings existing in one of the possible modes of Being but as *the* beings with an exceptional relationship to Being, comprising within themselves all possible forms of Being? And is philosophy only one among our many thoughts, or is it *the* thought which we, as people, think, the thought through which Being talks to itself?

5. If philosophy is the thought of Being, can it also be the thought of revolution? Is not revolution one particular social phenomenon that may be the subject matter of history, sociology, or political science but by no means also of philosophy? Are not the philosophers stepping over not only the fields of sociology and political science but also directly over politics and political struggles, if they try to say something about revolution? Is it really a mere accident that the concept of revolution did not acquire citizenship in respectable technical dictionaries and encyclopedias of philosophy? Can a philosopher as a philosopher (not to say as a citizen) be interested in revolution? Or is revolution perhaps such an important and specific phenomenon that philosophy, in addition to paying attention to many other interesting and important phenomena, must also pay some attention to this one that is so extolled and blamed, so exciting and frightful? If not, how could it be that a philosopher should not, out of professional duty, be concerned with the nature of revolution? What, then, is revolution?

6. Is every putsch, every change in the individuals or groups in power, already a revolution, or is a revolution only a change in which power passes over from one class to another? Is every transfer of power from one class to another necessarily a revolution, or is it only such a transfer of power that is accompanied by the construction of a new social order? Is every replacement of one social order by another a revolution, or is it only such a supersession by which a "lower" order is replaced by a "higher" one? Is every transformation of a lower order to a higher one a revolution, or does revolution in the full sense establish an essentially different, classless society, a really human society in which the self-alienation of people disappears and the relationships between people become really human?

7. Is revolution merely a change in this or that aspect of the social order, or is it a change of the whole social order in all of its aspects? Is revolution merely a change of the social order, or is it a change in people? Is it a change in some of our activities or is it a transformation of the whole person? Is it every human transformation or only a transformation through which we become fundamentally different? Is it merely a transformation of people, or is it a change in the "universe," the creation of a basically different type of Being, a free, creative Being, essentially different from every Being that is not human, inhuman, or not yet fully human?

8. Is revolution bound to people or are revolutions in nonhuman nature also possible? Should not big and sudden changes in nature be acknowledged as revolutions? Would we not, in this way, give an ontological foundation to revolutions in history? Do not revolutions in history remain

inexplicable if we deny revolutions in nature? Or perhaps, on the contrary, by denying revolutions in nonhuman nature we make it possible to understand revolutions in history and in nature in general. Are not people exactly, as beings of revolution, beings of nature who transcend their mere naturalness? Are not revolutions in history the only "natural" revolutions?

9. But are there really any revolutions in history? Is revolution merely a transition from one historical state to another, so that it is, like everything else, also *in* history, or is it a leap out of history, a step into eternity and timelessness? Can the locomotive engines of history be their own wagons? Can midwives of the new society help at their own birth? Is a revolution without certain presuppositions possible? Is a revolution possible without absolute, ahistorical criteria and without negating the historically given? Can the antihistorical character of revolution be incorporated into history as a kind of absurd detail, or is it the essential thing that makes history possible?

10. Is revolution an event in conformity with natural laws or is it a violation of laws and legality? Is revolution an expression of necessity, or is it a stepping over into the realm of freedom? Does revolution realize the possible or open up new possibilities? Is it a production of the planned or a spontaneous creation of the unexpected? Is not free creative activity the essential characteristic of revolution?

11. Are revolutions condensed fragments of social progress or are progress and revolution basically as different as the constant repetition of the improved old and the free creation of the qualitatively new, as the controlled increase of humanity measured in ounces, and the full blossom of humaneness that cannot be weighed? Are revolutions the basis of all progress? Is progress the best preparation for revolution? Can revolution be incorporated into progress? Can progress be combined with revolution? Or is progress, with its goals, methods, and roads, all of which have been determined in advance, of necessity opposed to the revolutionary vision with its unrestraint and openness for possibilities?

12. Is revolution without revolutionary organizations *possible?* Is revolution with pseudorevolutionary organizations possible? Does not revolution entail a self-organization that renders the free creativity of all individuals feasible? Does not organization tend to subordinate the action of all to common interests as conceived by chosen individuals? Is the organization the criterion for what is revolutionary, or is the revolutionary deed the criterion for the revolutionary character of any organization? Is real revolution possible only in the framework of institutions, or are institutions the tombs of revolution? Does a "responsible" revolution remain within prescribed limits, or is every revolution a pitiless criticism of everything existing and a bringing to life of the unseen? Is self-management one of the goals of revolution, or is every revolution self-activity and self-organization, self-creation and self-government?

13. Do revolutions suffer from illusions, or are "revolutionary illusions" truths feared by reactionary forces? Do revolutions lean to romanticism, or is "revolutionary romanticism" a living reality abhorred by counterrevolution? Are revolutions prone to destruction, or is revolution "destructive" because it does not want to take part in the construction and reconstruction of the exploitive social order? Do revolutions eat their children, or are they themselves eaten by counterrevolutions?

14. Are we allowed to speak about revolutions in the plural, or is only one, single Revolution possible? If small and "relative," "little" revolutions are possible, are they something peculiar, or are they revolutions only insofar as they participate in that single true, absolute and total Revolution?

15. Is the meaning and sense of revolution inside itself or in some later fruits it is supposed to bring, in a permanent condition it should establish? Can a revolution be victorious? Does not "victory" for a revolution mean its end, hence its defeat? What can follow after revolution if not counterrevolution? Is not the only possible true victory of revolution its further continuation? But can revolution be continued perpetually? Is not revolution exactly what is different from the customary, from that which lasts forever and repeats itself continuously?

16. Is revolution merely a transition from one form of Being to another, higher one—or perhaps a peculiar break, a leap, a "hole" in Being— or is it not only the highest form of Being but also Being in its fullness? Is not revolution the most developed form of creativity, the most authentic form of freedom? Is it not the field of open possibilities, the realm of the truly new? *Is not revolution the very "essence" of Being, Being in its essence?* And if revolution is Being itself, *is not philosophy as a thought of Being by that very fact* (and not in addition to it) *the thought of revolution?*

17. Can revolution get along without philosophy? Why should revolution not be able to manage without the thought of revolution? Is not revolution irrational, chaotic, immediate; is not thought rational, ordered, mediated? Is thought necessary to a volcanic eruption, especially if it is an eruption of humanity? But is revolution without thought really possible? Does revolution not presuppose conscious human will, commitment, and risk? Is it not led by a project of a possible future? Is not thoughtfulness the inner form of true spontaneity?

18. Can philosophy do without revolution? Why not? Were not many logics, methodologies, theories of knowledge, ontologies, ethics, and aesthetics elaborated without any help from revolution? Were not plenty of aporias and antinomies, subtleties and distinctions found and established without revolution? Is not that philosophy which associates itself with revolution a new one (not to say bent on innovations), hitherto unknown and unusual? Does it not represent a negation of all existing philosophy? However, must philosophy really be and remain always the same? Should it not deny itself if this is the condition for its becoming really thought? Is not the thought of revolution after all closer to great philosophies of the past than are the pseudoneutral scholastic disciplines that, at the highest technical level, engage in apologies for the existing order?

19. Can the thought of revolution merely think about revolution, without taking part in its realization? Does real thought only study, observe, and consider, or does it subvert the established, the antiquated, the consecrated, by opening up and creating the new and the not-yet-seen? To put it more briefly, is true philosophy merely the thought of revolution or is it the *thought-revolution* (thought as revolution)?

20. Are not general meditations about revolution only an obstacle for the concrete realization of revolution, or are these "abstract" musings perhaps a precondition for a true revolutionary attitude? Have revolutions failed thus far because there has been too much philosophizing about them

or because critical thought was suppressed? Have revolutions broken under the weight of philosophical books or under the pressure of economic interests and class privileges? Are the enemies of socialism those who exploit the workers or those who speak about that loudly? Are counterrevolutionaries those who live in magnificent palaces or those who refuse to be their court jesters?

Coda 1985: Introduction

The twenty sheaves of questions were written in 1968 and published in Serbocroatian and French the following year.[1] It may seem strange to publish now, in English, a text that was written that long ago. But the twenty sheaves of questions were not only a summary of my basic views at the time but also a program for their further elaboration, a program I still regard as both topical and not yet completed. In addition, I regard the "thinking of revolution," which I try to put forward in the sheaves, as the most promising interpretation of Marx, an interpretation that does not aim to remain an interpretation only. Of course, my own version of the thinking of revolution is not the only one. Indeed, there are at least two versions of that thinking which should be more widely known than they are—those developed by Milan Kangraga and Danko Grlic. But it is my own version I want to pursue here. First, I want to comment briefly on the basic meaning and structure of the sheaves. Then I want to discuss the relationship between the interpretation of Marx's thought contained in them (its interpretation as the thinking of revolution) and two other widespread interpretations of that thought (its interpretation as historical materialism and as philosophy of praxis).

A Few Remarks on the Twenty Sheaves of Questions

Though I discussed philosophy and revolution in the form of questions, I do not want to suggest this is the only proper way of doing either philosophy or the thinking of revolution. I regard this only as one possible way of writing philosophy—to be sure, one that is especially apt to stress the critical nature of philosophy, its capacity to bring everything into question.

It is not difficult to see that some of the questions are merely rhetorical. They more or less clearly suggest an answer; that is, they are really propositions in the guise of questions. But not all of them are of that type. Many are genuine questions, a challenge to thinking to find an answer, if it is possible to do so. Taken in isolation and regarded from the outside, those questions meant as genuine questions are not distinguishable from those meant only as disguised answers. Only in context is it possible to tell them apart.

The grouping of questions into sheaves was not made quite at random, so they should not be understood as heaps. Questions bound to one sheaf belong together: one should be careful not to untie them in such a way that those belonging together fall apart. Sheaves in the fields are always somehow ordered; those of which I speak now are numbered as well. These simplifying numbers serve as a warning that one should read the series in sequence. To understand them and to judge them one must have the patience to consider them one by one.

The first sheaf of questions is introductory. In the form of questions it considers the possibility of using that form for discussing philosophy

239

and revolution. This is essential, because if we deny this possibility, the remaining nineteen sheaves have little purpose. And if the first sheaf of questions represents a preliminary justification of the form of the whole text, then the last sheaf can be regarded as a subsequent and supplementary justification of its content (e.g., general meditations about revolution) in the form of a questioning refusal of some possible objections.

Sheaves 2 to 19 are concerned basically with one question, the one with which sheaf 2 begins: Is philosophy the thought of Being, or is it the thought of revolution? This question asks about philosophy—not about one or some of its qualities, but about what philosophy is (or rather can become). The question suggests we choose between "philosophy is the thought of Being" and "philosophy is the thought of revolution." Though it does not claim these are the only possible answers, in proposing to opt for one of the two it certainly gives them preference before others. Does the question exhibit some personal sympathy or affection for those two answers, or is it an intimation that those two important answers overshadow all others (though other answers may be important too)? Since the "or" seems exclusive, the question seems to demand that we commit ourselves to only one of the answers. Yet the demand need not be accepted. A question that is not posed properly may be rejected or corrected. This is exactly what happens to this question when we get to the sixteenth sheaf: *is not philosophy as a thought of Being by that very fact* (and not in addition to it) *the thought of revolution)?* And this is further improved by the concluding question of the nineteenth sheaf: is true philosophy merely the thought of revolution or is it the *thought-revolution* (thought as revolution)?

Does this mean the initial question of the second sheaf is a failure, or is it, despite its inadequacy, indispensable? Is it possible to understand the meaning and the scope of the "thesis" that philosophy exactly *as* the thought of Being can (and ought to) be at the same time the thought-revolution (thought as revolution) if one does not understand also the possibility of the opposite view that philosophy can (and must) be only one of the two, *either* the thought of Being *or* the thought of revolution?

The second question of the second sheaf assumes that we have opted for the first of the two basic possibilities (philosophy is a thought of Being), and it asks how this should be understood. The question suggests that the thesis about philosophy as the thought of Being can be understood in two basic ways: philosophy is the thought that thinks Being, and philosophy is a thought that is being thought by Being. By simplifying this a little, it would be possible to say, according to the first view, the thesis that philosophy is a thought of Being means that philosophy is the thinking that has Being for its subject matter or object; according to another view, it means that philosophy is a thinking that, as a function or an instrument, belongs to Being.

The thought that fancies itself a subject degrading Being to its object will hardly ever reach that object. The thought that considers itself a function or an instrument will hardly ever become an authentic thought. Thus, if I use here some traditional technical terminology (such as subject and object), it is not to justify the traditional conceptual framework but rather to become conscious of it in order to get out of it. But let us leave terminology aside and come back to the "thing itself."

240

If we assume that philosophy is a thought that thinks Being, we can regard this relationship from two sides: from the side of thought and from the side of Being. We can ask how this thought (subject) is related to Being (object) and, more specifically, how it succeeds in thinking Being; but we can also ask what is meant by Being and how Being (the object) is related to thinking (the subject).

The third question of the second sheaf, assuming that philosophy is the thought that thinks Being, sketches some possible attitudes of thought to Being. The three basic possibilities mentioned (stating the facts, discovering essential possibilities, and prescribing the norms) only roughly indicate the problematics. The remaining questions of the second sheaf investigate more complicated and specific relationships of thought to Being.

The whole third sheaf of questions remains within the conception of philosophy as the thought that thinks Being. Yet it is not concerned with the relationship of thought to Being but with Being itself and its relationship to thought. As it is not difficult to see, the last question decisively rejects the idea that Being is a mere object passively enduring the activity of the thinking subject. In this way we come to the fourth sheaf, which considers the idea that philosophy is thought by Being. It concludes by asking, Is philosophy only one among our many thoughts, or is it *the* thought that we, as people, think, the thought through which Being talks to itself?

This ends the preliminary examination of the possibility that philosophy is a thought of Being. In the fifth sheaf the consideration of the second basic possibility begins, the possiblility that philosophy is the thought of revolution. The preliminary consideration of that other possibility extends from sheaf 5 to sheaf 15, to be transformed in the next sheaf into a common examination of the two basic possibilities in their intrinsic connection or identity. Considering philosophy as the thought of Being—which by that very fact is not only the thought of revolution but also thought as revolution (sheaves 16 to 19)—is the very gist of the whole text.

But this is not my last word on the point. In a number of later publications I try to show that when philosophy becomes the thinking of revolution it is no longer philosophy in the old sense. The thinking of revolution is a new, higher type of thinking in which traditional philosophy is transcended and overcome (a little more about that below).

This is not to say that these sheaves of questions have lost their value. Sheaves 6 and 7, for example, suggest a certain concept that is of decisive importance for all subsequent sheaves and for the whole of my subsequent work. This is why I have tried to elaborate them in a "positive" way (also in the form of theses) in my paper "The Philosophical Concept of Revolution."[2] That paper touches also on some of the questions in other sheaves, as do my books *Philosophy and Revolution* and *The Thinking of Revolution.*[3] However, many of these questions have not been satisfactorily discussed so far. Thus, I still regard the sheaves as my basic task and my actual program.

In the twenty sheaves I mention Marx only once (in the first sheaf), as a thinker who wrote philosophy in the form of theses. But I make no claim that this small system of questions has something to do with Marx. As a matter of fact, it is more important for me to develop an adequate interpretation (or, rather, proper thinking) of revolution than to give an adequate interpretation of Marx. But justice requires me to say that the questions are inspired by Marx and that I regard their presentation of the thinking of revolution (as developed in works by friends and by myself) as the most adequate interpretation of Marx. This claim has to be supported, which is what I want to do at least partly in the next section.

Historical Materialism, Philosophy of Praxis, and Thinking of Revolution

In order to support the claim that the thinking of revolution is the relatively best (i.e., most adequate, truthful, or fruitful) interpretation of Marx, I want to say a few words about the relationship between historical materialism, philosophy of praxis, and the thinking of revolution. However, before I start discussing these three interpretations of Marx (let us call them that, though this description may be questionable, at least for the last of them), I want to indicate exactly why these interpretations have been chosen for a common consideration.

Marx has been interpreted in many different ways, not only as a historical materialist, a philosopher of praxis, and a thinker of revolution, but also, for example, as a dialectical materialist, a political economist, a critic of political economy, a political thinker, the founder of scientific sociology, and an ideologist of communism. So why are three interpretations chosen for consideration? The reason—not quite subjective and not simply objective—lies in the assumption that these are the interpretations that still have some chance to be taken seriously when claiming (1) that they most adequately show the basic meaning of Marx's thought, and (2) that they have some relevance for the topical problems of the contemporary world.

Some other interpretations of Marx, though still widespread, cannot be regarded as serious rivals to these three. Thus, the interpretation of Marx as a dialectical materialist was the official interpretation of his philosophy in some countries and in many communist parties (including Yugoslavia) in the 1950s and early 1960s. At that time, I was also writing essentially from that perspective.[4] Since then, no new variation of that conception has emerged (except, perhaps, Althusser's structuralist version of dialectical materialism, which has also pretty much gone out of fashion); thus there are no reasons to examine dialectical materialism anew.

Another interpretation I will not rexamine is one according to which Marx was primarily a political economist who founded the scientific study of the political economy of capitalism (for some he created the political economy of socialism as well). I would argue that it was shown long ago that Marx was not an economist but a critic of political economy. That is, in fact, an interpretation I *do* want to clarify here. Although alternative theories of political economy can be used to criticize one another, a critique of political economy as such can only be mounted from a viewpoint outside political economy. So we need to decide what Marx's standpoint was for *his* critique of political economy: historical materialism, philosophy of praxis, or the thinking of revolution? Or perhaps none of these.

Was Marx, then, a historical materialist? This interpretation of Marx's thought is one of the oldest and, at the same time, still one of the most widespread and vital. It owes its prestige and influence partly to its intrinsic merits and partly to the renown and influence of its author, Friedrich Engels, who expounded it in texts published when Marx was still alive (in "Karl Marx," in *Anti-Dühring,* and in *Socialism: Utopian and Scientific*)

242

and who repeated it concisely in his famous speech at Marx's graveside.[5] Of course, according to Engels, Marx's views cannot be reduced merely to historical materialism; we owe two major discoveries to Marx: the discovery of the "law of development of human history" (historical materialism) and the discovery of the "special law of motion governing the present-day capitalist mode of production and the bourgeois society" (surplus value). Marx also made a number of discoveries in different fields (allegedly even in mathematics). But Engels explicitly singled out historical materialism and the doctrine of surplus value as Marx's basic discoveries, historical materialism being the first and most important.

Engels's interpretaton of Marx as primarily a historical materialist and a political economist became, with small variations, dominant among the theoreticians of the Second International. While partly disagreeing about whether Marx's alleged rejection of every philosophy was good or bad, and whether some kind of philosophy might be helpful nevertheless, they mainly agreed that the true and mature Marx was not a philosopher but a historical materialist and economist. The important theoretician of the Second International who insisted that Marx had a philosophy called "dialectical materialism" was G. V. Plekhanov. Due to his disciple, Lenin, this view became obligatory in the Third International. Then it was dogmatized and canonized in Stalinism and compromised by inhuman practices, which demonstrates the philosophical fragility of dialectical materialism and its inadequacy to Marx. Since then, the main current of Western Marxism and Western Marxology has returned to the traditional conception of Marx as a historical materialist and a political economist. The view of Marx as a historical materialist has also been the starting point for some contemporary attempts at the reconstruction and renewal of Marx's thought, that is, its modernization and adaptation to the spirit of the time.[6]

Yet Engels inspired not only the interpretation of Marx as a historical materialist and economist, as developed in the Second International, but also the view of Marx as a dialectical materialist, as developed in the Third International. While he was glorifying Marx as the founder of historical materialism and the scientific political economy, and passing in silence Marx as a philosopher, Engels, in his polemics with Dühring, entered a general philosophical discussion and ventured a number of rather pretentious philosophical statements. Similarly, in the manuscripts published posthumously as *Dialectics of Nature,* Engels engaged in constructing a kind of a dialectical and materialist philosophy of nature. This suggests that he wanted to fill the philosophical gap he felt existed in Marx. Thus, it may be possible to say that the theoreticians of the Second International (or their majority), in their interpretations of Marx, followed Engels's explicit interpretation, while Plekhanov, Lenin, and the Third International followed (and tried to explicate) the implicit interpretation expressed in Engels's own theoretical efforts.

However, we are not interested here primarily in the historical adventures of historical materialism but in its value as an interpretation of Marx and as an answer to the question about history and humankind. In its narrow, vulgar, or dogmatic version, historical materialism is a theory about the absolute dominance of the economic factor in history (economic determinism). Since this theory has been convincingly criticized both by Engels and by many others, we may leave it aside. In its broader version, which we find in Engels and in many outstanding Marxists, historical materialism regards history as an interaction of different factors, in which the economic factor can be temporarily overpowered but comes through in the last analysis (or ultimately): "According to the materialist conception of history," wrote Engels in his famous letter to J. Bloch, "the *Ultimately* determining element in history is the production and reproduction of real life. More than this neither Marx nor I have ever asserted. . . . There is an interaction of all of these elements in which amid all the endless host of accidents . . . the economic movement finally asserts itself as necessary."[7]

In a number of papers I have criticized this broader version of historical materialism, especially its claim to be Marx's general theory of history (and the best theory of history overall). I have tried to show that historical materialism was not Marx's general theory of people and history but rather his critique of the self-alienated individual of class society ("man" as "economic animal") and of self-alienated human history (or, rather, prehistory). We are not as we are because we are, according to Marx, of necessity economic animals; we are self-alienated precisely because we remain on the level of economic animals. We are not, of necessity, split into mutually opposed spheres that relate in an external interaction; consequently, the economic sphere is not even necessarily ultimately the determining factor of history. On the contrary, as long as human history remains (even ultimately) determined by one of its spheres, we are still in the phase of prehistory, in the antechamber of true human history as the human creative being of praxis. True human history begins only when people begin to create and shape freely themselves and their human world.

At the time I was rethinking these issues, a number of Yugoslav (and non-Yugoslav) philosophers came to similar conclusions; thus the interpretation of Marx's thought as basically a philosophy of praxis developed and spread. This movement has produced detailed discussions of human freedom, creativity, alienation, and de-alienation, and it has developed the concepts of humanism and socialism in a new way. With the emergence of the philosophy of praxis the question about the relationship between historical materialism and the philosophy of praxis arose too. Some interpreters of Marx have come to think that the analysis of people as beings of praxis can be incorporated into the inherited theory of historical materialism as its partial enrichment or supplement. Others argue that the philosophy of praxis as a finally found, both adequate and fruitful interpretation of Marx can dispense with historical materialism.

In my opinion, the theory of historical materialism and the philosophy of praxis really can be connected, but only on the basis of the philosophy of praxis. In other words, the theory of historical materialism can be incorporated as a moment into the philosophy of praxis, but the philosophy of praxis cannot be incorporated into historical materialism. Historical materialism, or the materialist conception of history, as the phrase emphasizes, attempts to conceive history in a materialistic way. The materialistic character of historical materialism consists in that the determining role in history is attributed to a specific-material factor, the economic one. The decompositon of people into different factors, and the discovery of the ultimately determining material factor of historical development, is not something accidental but the very essence of historical materialism. Therefore, it is not clear how, except formally or nominally, the idea of a person as a total being and of free creativity as the essential quality of a person can be incorporated into it. Insofar as there is some talk of praxis within historical materialism, praxis can only be conceived as a human activity, or as a set of such activities (such as economic or political activity). In the same way, freedom is here of necessity interpreted as the known necessity (or as an activity based on the known necessity), and creativity as a multideterminated transformation (a transformation determined by material needs, material laws, etc.) of the given. Only terminology remains here from the philosophy of praxis. Within the conception of historical materialism, socialism cannot be imagined as an essentially new, integral form of our being (our human, free being) but merely as a new social and economic formation. Thus, the road to socialism cannot be understood as a free human deed but only as the predetermined, lawful development of socioeconomic organizations and institutions.

However, if the philosophy of praxis cannot be forced into the narrow limits of historical materialism, it is itself sufficiently broad to encompass historical materialism—as a special theory. In the philosophy of praxis we are conceived as free creative beings who shape ourselves and our world through our activities. But exactly *as* a free being one can alienate oneself from oneself, become a self-alienated, unfree being, an economic animal. Exactly because we alienate ourselves from ourselves, the theory of historical materialism can be partly justified and validated as an explanation and criticism of the self-alienated society. However, taken out of the whole philosophy of praxis and rendered independent, historical materialism can only describe the mechanism of economic determination and exploitation in the class society; it cannot even express the decisive thesis that this society and people are self-alienated, inhuman. Unsatisfactory as a general theory of society and of people, an independent historical materialism is not sufficient even for a full understanding of class society. Describing the facticity of that society as it is, it cannot adequately understand its historical limitation because it cannot conceive of an essentially different, not-self-alienated society.

Opting for the philosophy of praxis, some are inclined to retain for it the traditional name "historical materialism." This terminology can only be inadequate and confusing. How can we call a theory "historical materialism" if its central concept, the concept of praxis, transcends the distinction between the material and the spiritual? It is quite conceivable that in a *historical* materialism (or in a materialist conception of *history*) the metaphysical (or ontological) concept of matter need not be central. But in a *materialist* conception of history, some materialist concept, a concept of some material entity or activity, should nevertheless be central. However, praxis as conceived by Marx is not a material activity as opposed to a spiritual activity but is the structure of every human activity insofar as it is free.

If the interpretation of Marx's thought as a philosophy of praxis is deeper and more adequate to Marx's thought as a historical materialism, it does not mean that it is also the best possible interpretation of Marx. Or, more precisely, it perhaps is the relatively best interpretation of Marx (if we take the word "interpretation" strictly), but, just as Marx was not merely an interpreter of former thinkers, those who today want to think in his spirit and on his level cannot remain merely interpreters of his thought. More than any interpretation, that thinking is most faithful to Marx which does not remain only an interpretation—the *thinking of revolution*.

As is well known, the interpretation of Marx's thought as a philosophy of praxis has behind it a rather long history (or merely prehistory?): from the Italian Marxists A. Labriola and A. Gramsci, through early Lukács and Bloch, to H. Lefebvre and the Yugoslav praxis-philosophers. Precisely in that last group, it seems, the philosophy of praxis has been developed most fully and most consistently, so that here some of its difficulties and limitations have become best visible.

The journal *Praxis* was created as a forum for developing the philosophy of praxis. However, in the first issue the philosophy of praxis was already superseded, as can be seen in the editorial expressing the basic views of praxis-philosophers.[8] The editorial seems to testify that praxis-philosophers were already no longer merely praxis-philosophers, that they had become something else. It explains the need for the new journal in the following way: "Despite the abundance of journals, it seems to us that we do not have the one we wish: a philosophical journal which is not narrowly 'technical,' a philosophical journal which is not only philosophical, but also discusses the topical problems of Yugoslav socialism and of man and the contemporary world." And further: "In agreement with such views we want a journal that will not be philosophical in the sense in which philosophy is merely one special field, one scientific discipline, strictly separated from all the rest and from the everyday problems of man's life. We want a philosophical journal in the sense in which philosophy is the thought of revolution: a pitiless critique of everything existing, a humanistic vision of a truly human world and an inspiring force of revolutionary activity."

Praxis was not conceived as a vehicle for the philosophy of praxis but rather as a vehicle for the thinking of revolution. The central concern of praxis-philosophers has become not praxis but revolution (not in the usual sense!). To be sure, the sentence that follows immediately after the passage quoted above speaks in a different way: "The title *Praxis* has been chosen because praxis, that central concept of Marx's thought, most adequately expresses the sketched conception of philosophy." But this is obviously an inconsistency, or rather the original standpoint which here coexists with the new one.

Was this reformulation of the philosophy of praxis into the thinking of revolution an instance of progress or regression? Does the thinking of revolution reject the philosophy of praxis, or does it include it in itself? Or are these two mutually irrelevant conceptions that can coexist in a peaceful way?

If Marx's philosophy is really the thinking of revolution, and if revolution is its central concept, this does not mean that the concept of praxis should be eliminated from it. The conception according to which Marx's thinking is a philosophy of praxis is not simply false, it is insufficient insofar as it stops halfway. In that conception we are regarded as beings of praxis, and praxis as free creative activity. The highest form (and also the essence) of praxis for Marx is revolution, a radical negation of the self-alienated society and person, creation of a truly human community composed of free human beings. Such a concept of praxis is not, of course, the only one possible; there have been many different ones. Exactly for this reason the very phrase "thinking of revolution" has an advantage over the phrase "philosophy of praxis." But it is not only a matter of naming. Regardless of how we decide to name thought in the spirit of Marx, it is important to think what was, for him, also most important: the possibility of praxis as revolution.

However, the defect of the interpretation of Marx's thinking as the philosophy of praxis is not only in the name "praxis," nor (what is more important) in the hesitation to think praxis, in the spirit of Marx, as revolution, but is hidden in the name "philosophy." As is well known, Marx spoke about overcoming, superseding, and realizing philosophy. The leading theoreticians of the Second International interpreted this as a demand for a rejection of every philosophy. Opposed to such a positivist elimination of philosophy, Plekhanov and Lenin insisted that Marxism had a philosophy. Lenin, however, at the time strictly divided Marxism into three main parts: a philosophy, a political economy, and a politics. Not all advocates of Marx's philosophy have drawn such a sharp dividing line, but as a rule they more or less strictly divide Marxism into parts and discuss its problems within the limits they have drawn. Thus, revolution has been regarded as a social phenomenon, and the problems of revolution have been discussed within the limits of Marx's social and political theory. Philosophy has been reserved for a discussion of "more general" problems.

Viewing Marx's philosophy as the thinking of revolution means a radical break with this tradition and a revival of Marx's original insight, which brings philosophy and revolution together inseparably. In this new-old conception, philosophy does not live in a world of abstract generalities; it is concerned with the basic possibility (and reality) of our time, and this is revolution. On the other hand, revolution should not be conceived merely as a political or social phenomenon. The true revolution would radically change people and society, creating a new, higher mode of Being. As such, revolution cannot be understood if it is studied merely inside the social sciences or within some special philosophical discipline such as the philosophy of politics or social philosophy. The problem of revolution is the central problem of the central philosophical disciplines—ontology and philosophical anthropology. However, even this is not quite right. More precisely, the phenomenon of revolution can be adequately thought only by a philosophy that is not divided into philosophical disciplines and is not separated from social sciences and from social praxis. In other words, the phenomenon of revolution can be thought adequately only by a philosophy that is no longer philosophy in the traditional sense, by a philosophy that has become the thinking of revolution. This means that the formulation in the opening editorial of *Praxis* should be corrected: We do not want philosophy in that sense in which it is the thinking of revolution; we believe that traditional philosophy should be transcended by the thinking of revolution.

The last statement can be again misunderstood as a plea for a positivist elimination of philosophy. However, this does not follow from what was said. The thinking of revolution presupposes and incorporates philosophy (i.e., what was essential in it). Far from being *unphilosophical*, it is in many respects *more philosophical* than any previous philosophy. Exactly for that reason, it cannot remain *merely philosophical*.

247

Notes

1 The twenty sheaves of questions were originally prepared to be read on August 21, 1968, as part of the Fifth Session of the Korcula Summer School, which was devoted to "Marx and Revolution." However, early in the morning of that day the news spread that the troops of the Warsaw Pact had invaded Czechoslovakia. The work of the school was interrupted, the invasion was discussed, and an appeal to world public opinion and a number of telegrams (such as a protest telegram to Brezhnev) were issued. The appeal was first signed by Ernst Bloch; the signatures of Herbert Marcuse, Serge Mallet, Alfred Sohn-Rethel, Lucien Goldmann, Thomas Bottomore, Eugen Fink, Jürgen Habermas, and others followed. On August 22 the school resumed its work. Some of the papers that had been scheduled for the preceding day were squeezed into the remaining program, but I renounced reading mine. Thus, I first read my text at a Croatian Philosophical Society meeting in autumn 1968. It was published in the Belgrad *Student*, a paper that played an important role in the Yugoslav student rebellion of 1968, and then in the journal *Praxis*, nos. 1-2 (1969), which brought out the proceedings of the 1968 Korcula Summer School.

2 In M. Markovic and G. Petrović, eds., *Praxis: Yugoslav Essays in the Philosophy and Methodology of the Social Sciences*, Boston Studies in the Philosophy of Science, vol. 36, (Dordrecht, Boston, London: D. Reidel, 1979), pp. 151-64.

3 *Philosophie and revolution* (Reinbek bei Hamburg: Rowohlt, 1971); *Filosofia y revolution* (Mexico: Editorial Extemuoraneos, 1972); *Filozofija i revolucija* (Zagreb: Naprijed, 1973); *Misljenje revolucije* (Zagreb: Naprijed, 1978).

4 See my *Filozofija i marksizam* (Zagreb: Mladost, 1965), translated into English as *Marx in the Mid-Twentieth Century* (New York: Doubleday, 1967).

5 See K. Marx, F. Engels, *Werke* (Berlin, 1969), vol. 19, pp. 102-6, 209, 335-36.

6 Most important among those attempts is probably Habermas's reconstruction of historical materialism; see *Zur Rekostruktion des Historischen Materialismus* (Frankfurt: Suhrkamp, 1976). A number of interesting attempts in the same direction have been collected in: U. Jaeggi and A. Honneth, eds., *Theorien des historischen materialismus* (Frankfurt: Suhrkamp, 1976), and A. Honneth and U. Jaeggi, eds., *Arbeit, handlung, normativität: Theorien des historischen materialismus, 2* (Frankfurt: Suhrkamp, 1980).

7 Robert C. Tucker, ed., *The Marx-Engels Reader* (New York: W. W. Norton, 1972), p. 640-41.

8 "A quoi bon praxis," *Praxis: A Philosophical Journal* (International Edition), 1:1 (1965), pp. 3-7.

Ernesto Laclau
Metaphor and Social Antagonisms

> The order of society is only the unstable order of a system of differences that is always threatened from the outside. As an underlying mechanism that gives reasons for its partial processes, society never actually exists. Indeed, it is because no meaning is actually fixed that there is a space in which hegemonic struggle can take place.

One way of describing my project in this paper is that I want to continue the work of Max Black by extending the domain of metaphor from the area of science to that of social antagonisms. My argument will revolve around three basic concepts: hegemony, discourse, and antagonism.[1] I will present these three concepts against the background of the thesis that society is ultimately impossible.

Let me start by referring to a classic text in the history of marxism, one that contains, in nascent form, many of the problems I will analyze: Rosa Luxemburg's *Mass Strike, the Political Party and the Trade Unions.* But let me first say something about the moment in which her book was written. The book was part of a considerable discussion about the role of mass strikes in overcoming the capitalist system subsequent to their successful use during the first Russian revolution. But, in fact, the book was also at the center of a still larger discussion concerning what was then called, for the first time, the crisis of marxism, a phrase coined by Thomas Masaryk. This crisis was the result of a set of historical processes I can only briefly describe here. First, the great depression that had started in 1873 had come to an end toward 1896, and marxists began to realize that this was not the last crisis of capitalism. Second, with the boom that ensured the end of the depression and lasted until the beginning of the First World War, many of the old certitudes were put into question. Among these, one in particular created a problem in the image of the identity of the working class which had existed up to that moment. This was the increasing dissociation between economic and political struggle, or the polarization within socialist politics between trade unions and the party as the center of decision. This was perhaps the first moment in the history of socialism where one sees a breakup of the different positions of the class subject and, increasingly, a decentering of classes as a nucleus of socialist politics. Finally, from the moment of crisis on, the identity of the working class was perceived increasingly as split. It is the problem of this split identity that Rosa Luxemburg deals with in her book.

Luxemburg's answer to the problem of the unity of the working class involves what today we would call the "unfixing" of the meaning of any social event. She argues as follows: We are wrong in trying,

249

a priori, to determine or fix the meaning of the strike or the party as moments in a socialist transition because, in fact, the unity of the working class is not achieved in that way. Instead, the unity of the working class is the process of the revolution itself. Luxemburg describes Russia at the time as a country in which there was widespread repression and, as a consequence, an accumulation of unfulfilled democratic demands. Then, in one locality we have a strike of a particular fraction of workers around a very localized and particular issue. But in this climate of generalized repression, the meaning of this strike cannot simply rest there. Immediately, this strike begins to represent, for the whole population, a resistance against the regime. And immediately the meaning of this event is transformed into a political act. This, Luxemburg says, is the unity between political and ideological demands. It is not a unity that is given by any structure determinable a priori, but is constructed in this process of what today we would call the overdetermination of the meaning of a social event. The following year, another strike takes place in a different locality and about a different issue, not a union issue, but the same process of unity takes place. We see here that the unity of the class is precisely a symbolic unity. We have a symbol whenever the signified is more abundant than, or overflows, a given signifier. That is to say, we have a process of condensation. And in this process of condensation, the unity of a series of signifieds is created. If the unity of the class is created through this process of symbolic representation, the unity of the class itself is a symbolic event and belongs consequently to the order of the metaphor.

This is the most profound sense of the spontaneity of Rosa Luxemburg: the perception that there is a kind of unity between elements in a social formation which totally escapes the category of necessity that had so far dominated the discourse of the Second International. But at the very moment she gives a place to this opening, she also closes her discourse in an essentialist way. There is, after all, a problem with this way of presenting the unity of the class. Here, two discourses are producing contradictory effects in Luxemburg's text. If the class is united through the overdetermination of different struggles, why does the resulting entity have to be a class? Why could it not be some different type of social identity or social subject? Why does the necessary result have to be a class subject? Her answer is the traditional, rather uninteresting one: because of the necessary laws of capitalist development.

But if we withdraw the essentialist assumption, we immediately see, in a microcosm, many phenomena that are going to dominate the history of the twentieth century. In the countries of the Third World, this process of overdetermination of popular struggles creates social identities that are not essentially class identities. And in the case of the advanced capitalist countries, we also see that the dispersion of social struggles has created new forms of subjectivity which escape any kind of class identification. These developments introduce some gaps into the argument concerning the necessary laws of capitalist development as presented by the Second International.

The concept of hegemony emerged in the marxist tradition precisely as a concept destined to fill this gap. It emerged in the discussions of social democracy in Russia, discussions about the relationship between social classes and democratic tasks. For the old essentialist scheme, which was defended by the Mensheviks in the last moment, there is a necessary succession of stages. The argument was that the bourgeoisie was extremely weak in the Russian case and could not take up its own democratic task, so it had to be taken up by the proletariat. The problem was the significance of this relationship of "taking up" tasks that do not correspond to the class essence of the subject as posed by the Second International. What is the importance of this gap which had emerged in the chain of necessity? Within the Russian debates, Plekhanov argued that it was minimal and that the working class simply had to force the bourgeoisie to take up this task, while Trotsky argued that the gap was maximal and required a total transference of the democratic task to a new class subject in the process of the revolution. But in the discourse of all the participants in this debate, this gap was seen as an abnormal situation that subsequent capitalist development was going to supersede. That is to say, the necessary complement of the Russian revolution was going to be the European revolution and, in this sense, the gap which the concept of hegemony tried to cover had itself to be quickly superseded.

But, on the contrary, this gap became wider and wider. Thus, in the discourse of Leninism, this gap covers an entire historical space because the contradiction of the imperialist stage is such that there is no precise and necessary relation between the degree of economic development of a given country and its readiness for revolutionary process. Trotsky developed the consequences of this analysis when he argued that combined and uneven development is the historical law of our time. But then, do we not have to ask ourselves, if this unevenness is constitutive of all struggles, what exactly is normal development? The very idea of normal development has completely collapsed, and the identity and nature of political relations, once this category of necessity collapses, have to be put into question. This separation between those tasks that are essential to a class and those that are external to that class but have to be taken up by it creates a complex dialectic between interiority and exteriority. Once this class has taken up these democratic or popular tasks and enters into a complex system of political and social relations of a new type not predetermined by the class nature of the subject, this relation comes to be an integral part of the subjectivity of the class. Consequently, either the class ceases to be merely a class or, on the contrary, when viewed from the outside, the class is taking a purely instrumental and external relation with these tasks in order to ensure a succession of political effects.

Lenin made a rather eclectic attempt to solve this problem. Leninism, and the whole tradition of the Comintern, wanted to accept the complexity of the political scenarios in which working-class practices had to operate. These complex scenarios were not explained at all by the pure relation between the bourgeoisie and the proletariat, that is to say, by the struggle that was internal to the very identity of the class. On the other hand, Leninism wanted to maintain a pure class identity. Historical subjects were always classes. They attempted to fill this gap through the concept of the vanguard party which represented both the historical interests of the working class and a system of political calculation which, while maintaining the homogeneity of class subjects, engaged in very complicated political operations. These in turn gave rise to a totally militaristic political language. The essential definition of historical subjectivity as class remained as unquestioned as in Kautskyism. (I have elsewhere described Leninism as the surrealist moment of Kautskyism.)

The problem of the relation between the internal and external exists at many theoretical levels and has a long history in Western thought. It was a central element in Hegel's philosophy as well as in much of Anglo-Saxon philosophy. The debate between Bradley's idealism and Russell's logical atomism is, to a large extent, a discussion about the internal or external character of relations for certain series of given identities.

In Gramsci, we find a new turning point in this transformation of the dialectic between internal and external. In his concept of hegemony, he accepts the idea that many relations that do not have a class character in fact come to constitute the very identity of class subjects. There is no direct continuity between political subjectivity and classes in the economic sense. The dialectic between the internal and external has evolved to a new point. The concept of hegemony no longer involves the direction of elements whose identity remains the same through all of the processes, as in Lenin's argument. On the contrary, hegemony is a process of rearticulation, of the internalization through new articulations of something that was external. However, Gramsci still retains an element of essentialism because this process of the interiorization of the external always has to take place around a class core. While the class core remains very deeply buried below an ensemble of layers, it is this class core that we see dissolving today.

We can see not only that hegemony can take place whenever there is this process of the internalization of the external but also that there is no necessary core around which this internalization has to take place. In fact, what we are seeing today in advanced capitalist countries is a dispersion of positionalities of the subject, of the proliferation of struggles, none of which has an essence in itself; rather, each depends upon an ensemble of relations that need not be organized around a class core. From this, however, many problems emerge. First, if hegemony is no longer the hegemony of the class subject, whose hegemony is it? And second, what is involved in these hegemonic relations? What are the requirements for a relation to be hegemonic? How must we conceive of social links in order to be able to understand them as hegemonic ones? To address these questions, I need to move from the historical terrain to a set of more theoretical considerations.

I shall begin to answer these questions from a point, one among many possible starting points, within the trajectory of the Althusserian school. Althusser attempted to break with essentialist conceptions of social relations, and this break took place around the central concept of overdetermination. As this concept has been so frequently misunderstood as multiple causality, it is necessary to go back to its initial meaning in Althusserian analysis and to the precise constructive effects that this concept had to play within the field of marxist discursivity.

For Althusser, it was not a causal concept at all. The concept was taken from two existing disciplines: specifically, linguistics and psychoanalysis. In these disciplines it has an objective dialectical connotation, particularly in psychoanalysis; and since this objective connotation is related formally to the content it designates, Althusser's borrowing is neither arbitrary nor metaphorical. That is to say, for Althusser there was a specific logic involved in psychoanalytic relations which had to be incorporated into historical analysis. The concept of overdetermination in Freud only makes

252

sense within a symbolic world and involves the symbolic constitution of relations. Taking us back to the same point I drew earlier in my discussion of Luxemburg, Althusser initially uses the concept in his analysis of the Russian revolution. The deepest sense of the concept in Althusser's analysis is that any kind of social relation is constituted in a symbolic way. However, the full development of the concept, its full constructive effect, could not be reached because Althusser attempted to make it compatible with another element of his theoretical system, namely, the concept of determination in the last instance by the economic. The latter concept had a double effect, even if determination in the last instance never arrives, as Althusser insisted; it is there, producing some precise theoretical effects in his discourse. First, it says that there is one element, the economy, which, in whatever social formation we are speaking about, has to be defined separately from any kind of social relations. Otherwise, the concept of determination in the last instance would be meaningless. Second, it implies that society has an essence. Despite whatever mediating processes are involved, determination in the last instance defines the locus at which the particular effect—society— is created. And once we have accepted that society has an ultimate structure, that it is ultimately an intelligible and rational object, the concept of overdetermination can only circumscribe a field of contingent effects within a framework of necessity, which is the horizon of any possible social meaning.

Subsequently, in both France and England, there was a sustained deconstruction of the Althusserian discourse which led to the liquidation of the architecture of the whole Althusserian system. However, this project did not redefine or reestablish what overdetermination means; there was no way back to the concept of overdetermination. On the contrary, it involved a logistic attempt to show that there was really no connection at all between elements where one had supposed the existence of a necessary connection. This project was carried to its ultimate conclusion in the work of Hindess and Hirst in England, for example. They abandoned practically all the concepts of marxist theorization through a purely logical critique of the consistency of Althusserian connections. The problem with this position is not their surrendering of the language of marxism but rather that this is ultimately self-defeating. If you start by saying that there are no logical connections between two elements, then you have to ask about the internal connections within the elements themselves; and you will have to find there also that there are no necessary connections. The problem with this type of exercise is, simply put, that the structure of the social world is not the structure of a conceptual order. Here we can see an increasing polarization between an essentialism of the structure and an essentialism of the elements. That is to say, we are right back to the polemic between Bradley and Russell: either a logicism of the structure or a logical atomism.

The question is how we move outside this critical situation. I think the way out is to start by considering the very terrain on which these two extreme positions constructed their discourse, the terrain of a closed system. Either we have a closed system of identities (Russell, Leibnitz) or a closed system of the structure (Spinoza, Bradley, Plekhanov). But both positions accept that society as such is a closed system. If we abandon this assumption, many of the theoretical problems discussed here begin to dissolve. Why? Because if the system is not closed, then the meaning of each element of the system and of the system as such is constantly threatened from the outside. Both relations and identity are always in a precarious state because there are no signifieds that can be ultimately fixed. In other words, relations never succeed in totally absorbing the identity of every element. Each element has a surplus of meaning because it cannot be located in a closed system of difference. And at the same time, no identity is ever definitely and definitively acquired. Such a situation, in which there is a constant movement from the elements to the system but no ultimate systems or elements—these are finally metaphoric expressions—a structure in which meaning is constantly negotiated and constructed, is what I call "discourse."

The concept of discourse describes the ultimate nonfixity of anything existing in society. One must, of course, not reduce discourse to speech and writing but instead expand it to any kind of signifying relation. This concept of discourse is the terrain on which a concept of hegemony can be constructed. The closest use I find to the notion of discourse that I am proposing is in Derrida's "Structure, Sign and Play in the Discourses of the Human Sciences." There he links the notion of discourse to the dissolution of any transcendental signifier. He argues that when the transcendental signifier is recognized as an illusion, when all we have is the constant sliding of difference, everything becomes discourse because discourse is precisely the moment of nonfixity. In other words, discourse is not a mental act in the usual sense. Material things, external objects as such, also participate in discursive structures. This is not unlike Wittgenstein's concept of language games, which involves the constitution of a signifying order in which the materiality of the things themselves participates. Thus, the concept of discourse requires a radical reconsideration of the nature of the sign. To what extent do the two poles of langue—the paradigmatic and the syntagmatic—involve two incompatible logics? I shall come back to this question at the end of my argument.

Now let me return to the notion of hegemony. Society as a sutured space, as the underlying mechanism that gives reasons for or explains its own partial processes, does not exist, because if it did, meaning would be fixed in a variety of ways. Society is an ultimate impossibility, an impossible object; and it exists only as the attempt to constitute that impossible object or order. That is to say, the order of society is the unstable order of a system of differences which is always threatened from the outside. Neither the difference nor the space can be ultimately sutured. We can speak about the logic of the social, but we cannot speak of society as an ultimately rational and intelligible object. And the fact that we cannot speak of society in such a way is why we have to have a concept of hegemonic relations. Hegemonic relations depend upon the fact that the meaning of each element in a social system is not definitely fixed. If it were fixed, it would be impossible to rearticulate it in a different way, and thus rearticulation could only be thought under such categories as false consciousness.

If no meaning is ultimately fixed, conquered, mastered, then there is a space in which hegemonic struggle can take place. For example, I would say that the concept of hegemony is perfectly relevant to feminism because feminism can only exist in a hegemonic space. Consider the signifier "woman": what is its meaning? Taken in isolation it has no meaning; it must enter into a set of discursive relations to have some meaning. But, on the one hand, "woman" can enter into a relation of equivalence with family, subordination to men, and so on; and, on the other hand, "woman" can enter into discursive relations with "oppression," "black people," "gay people," and so on. The signifier "woman" in itself has no meaning. Consequently, its meaning in society is going to be given only by a hegemonic articulation. Here the Lacanian concept of *point de capiton,* the nodal point that partially fixes meaning, is profoundly relevant for a theory of hegemony.

Can one ever confront this movement of difference, this continuous deferral of the moment of reaching the transcendental signified? Are there certain experiences in which the vanity of the movement itself, the ultimate impossibility of any objectivity, manifests itself? Such a moment exists in society—it is the moment of antagonism. I shall argue briefly that, first, antagonistic relations are not objective relations and, second, that antagonisms take place outside rather than inside society because antagonism is what limits the societal effect. There have been many discussions about antagonism, from theories of conflict to marxist theories of contradiction, but most of these have taken for granted the meaning of what it is to be in an antagonistic relation and then they move immediately to speak about concrete antagonisms.

I can use the discussions of Lucio Colletti and the Della Volpean school to describe the problem of antagonism. Colletti poses the distinction between real opposition and contradiction, which he takes from Kant's discussion (in *The Critique of Pure Reason*) of Leibnitz's theory of contradiction. Briefly, a relation of real opposition is between two things, while a relation of contradiction is between propositions. A car crash is a real opposition, while asserting "I am A" and "I am not A" at the same time is a contradiction. Colletti argues that in a materialist perspective, which refuses to reduce the real to the concept, the concept of contradiction can play no function. We have to describe the entire ensemble of social antagonisms in terms of a theory of real opposition. But I do not think antagonistic relations are relations between things. A car crash is not an antagonistic relation; there is certainly no enmity between the two intervening entities. The concept of real opposition is either a metaphor from the physical world translated into the social world or vice versa, but clearly it is not useful to try to subsume the two types of relations under the same category.

Can we describe antagonisms, then, as contradictions? Given that we contradict each other constantly in social life, some people have concluded that contradiction does not necessarily involve any idealistic subordination of the real to the concept. For example, Jon Elser has argued that it is one thing to assert that the real is contradictory and another to assert that there are contradictions in reality; that is to say, there are situations in reality that can only be understood in terms of contradiction. However, even accepting the possibility of contradictions in reality, I do not think we can speak of antagonisms as contradictions. After all, somebody can have two absolutely contradictory beliefs but they cannot live this contradiction in antagonistic terms. Codes of law can be partially contradictory without this contradiction generating any kind of antagonism.

So how are we to explain antagonism? We might begin to rethink the question by asking what the categories of real opposition and logical contradiction have in common. The answer is that both are objective relations; they produce their effects within a system of differences. Alterna-

255

tively, I want to argue that antagonistic relations are not objective relations at all but involve the collapse of any possible objectivity.

In an antagonistic relation there is the peculiar possibility that the object, the entity that I am, is negated. On the one hand, I am something, a pure presence, logos, identity, and so on. On the other hand, this presence is precarious and vulnerable. The threat which the other represents transforms my own being into something questionable. But at the same time those who are antagonizing me are also not a full presence because their objective being is a symbol of my not being; and in this way, their objective being is overflowed by a meaning that fails to be fixed, to have a full presence. Thus, antagonism is neither a real opposition nor a logical contradiction. A real opposition is an objective relation between things; a contradiction is an equally objective relation between concepts. An antagonism is the experience of the limits of any possible objectivity, the way in which any objectivity reveals the partial and arbitrary character of its own objectification. To use a simile from linguistics, if the langue is a system of difference, then antagonism is the failure of difference. And in this sense antagonism locates itself in the limits of language and can only exist as a disruption of language, that is, as metaphor.

If you examine any sociological or historical account of concrete antagonisms, you will find that the account explains the conditions and the processes that made the antagonism possible but becomes silent in the face of having to explain the antagonistic relation as such. For instance, those who explain how landlords began to expel peasants from the land inevitably reach a point at which they commonly say, "And at this moment, *logically,* the peasants reacted." There is a gap in the text, and you, the reader of the account, must fill in the gap with your common sense, your experience, and so on. Antagonism is something that is showable but not sayable (using the Wittgensteinian distinction). Antagonism is the limit of the social, the witness of the ultimate impossibility of society, the moment at which the sense of precariousness reaches its highest level. Antagonism operates within a system of difference by collapsing differences. And differences are made to collapse by creating chains of equivalences. For instance, if I say that, from the point of view of the interests of the working classes, liberals, conservatives, and radicals are all the same, I have transformed three elements that were different into substitutes within a chain of equivalence. If difference exists only in the diachronic succession of the syntagmatic pole, equivalence exists at the paradigmatic pole. Equating differences reduces the possible differential places the system can have. This is why any antagonism always tends to disrupt a system of differential positionality and to simplify the social space.

Ultimately, antagonism can only operate in a world that is divided between two opposed camps, two paratactic successions of opposed equivalences. Why is this so? Because if we introduce a tertium quid, it immediately creates a precise location for each of what were previously two camps. And in this sense, antagonisms transform the two poles in objective relations. Antagonism only fully develops in a radically sharp opposition between two camps, with a frontier internal to the societal effect.

To conclude, I want to raise two sets of questions that place the concept of antagonism into the context of contemporary political struggles. First, to what extent does the fact that left-wing politics in advanced industrial societies is ceasing to be a politics of the frontier the result of the increasing difficulty of dividing the social space into two camps? In this sense, we are in a transition to a new type of society in which the plurality of antagonisms cannot create the politics of the frontier in the traditional sense in which left-wing politics has been understood. And second, does the proliferation of social spaces divided into two camps give us the way to accede to a new conception of politics in which the unity and homogeneity of the political world cannot be assumed?

Notes

1. The present essay was delivered orally at the conference that provided the basis for this volume. The full argument is developed in the first three chapters of Ernesto Laclau and Chantal Mouffe, *Hegemony and Socialist Strategy: Towards a Radical Democratic Politics* (London: New Left Books, 1985).

Christine Delphy

Patriarchy, Domestic Mode of Production, Gender, and Class

Translated by Diana Leonard

As classes, men and women are socially named, differentiated, and made pertinent through social practices. The patriarchal system which subordinates women to men in contemporary society is based in the economic relations of the domestic mode of production.

The analysis of patriarchy in our society that I have been developing for the last fifteen years has a history I would like to detail. I came to my use of the concept and to the model growing out of it by way of two projects whose theoretical concerns might seem unrelated. One project was to study the transmission of family property (patrimony), and the other was to reply to criticisms of the women's liberation movement that had come from the Left.

As it happened, when I started to do research on these two topics, I found that lack of relatedness was only apparent. This might have been predictable from the coherent commitment that had led me to these topics: I had wanted to work "on women," which is to say, for me, on women's oppression. Yet my director of studies at the time told me this was not possible, so I chose to study the inheritance of property instead, hoping eventually to get back to my initial interest by an indirect route. In my research I first discovered what a great quantity of goods change hands without passing through the market; instead, these goods were passed through the family, as gifts or "inheritance." I also discovered that the science of economics, which purports to concern itself with everything related to the exchange of goods in society, is in fact concerned with only *one* of the systems of production, circulation, and consumption of goods: the market.

At the time (between 1968 and 1970) I was also participating in the activities of one of the two groups that historically helped create the new feminist movement in France. I was very annoyed—and I was not alone, though like the hero of *Catch 22* I thought I was being personally got at!—by one of the men in this mixed group. He claimed that the oppression of women could not be as severe or as important as the oppression of the proletariat because although women were oppressed, they were not "exploited."

I was well aware that something was wrong with his position. In that group, at least, we recognized that women earned half as much as men and worked twice as hard, but apparently women's oppression nevertheless had, in theory, no economic dimension! While we knew at the time that housework existed, we saw it principally as a question of an unfair

259

division of boring tasks; and since we did not ask the relevant questions about the problem, not surprisingly we got no relevant answers. However, my work on patrimony—that is, on the economic aspects of the nonmarket sphere; or, to put it another way, on the nonmarket sphere of the economy—served to help me find and pose certain of these questions. Others, at the time, were also discovering the theoretical as well as the practical importance of housework, but they came to it by different routes and therefore arrived at rather different conclusions.

Analysis of gifts and the inheritance of property within the family allowed me to demystify the market. This prevented my getting caught in the classic trap of opposing exchange value and use value, an opposition that had lead the pioneers (Benston and Larguia), as well as those who came later, into a number of impasses, or, if you will, into a circular route from which they could find no way out. By showing that this opposition only makes sense if one adopts the viewpoint of the market, I was able to propose a theory in which nonmarket value, instead of being a *problem* in understanding housework, is one of the clues to elucidating the specific nature of housework. By taking this nonvalue as a constitutive element of housework, I was able to show that (a) housework's exclusion from the market was the cause, and not the consequence, of its not being paid for; (b) this exclusion involved not only housework, nor only particular types of work, but rather social *actors* as well, or, to be more precise, work done within certain social relations; and (c) in seeking to understand housework, it is a mistake to see it merely as a particular set of tasks, whether one is seeking to describe them or to explain them in terms of their "intrinsic usefulness." I have taken up all these points again in my recent work, but they were present, at least in germ, in "The Main Enemy."[1] From this time on I have been able to propose a theoretical rather than an empirical analysis of housework, which I see as a particular part of the much larger category of "domestic work," thanks to my initial creation of the concept of the "domestic mode of production."

Since 1970 I have also used the term "patriarchy," and in all my work I have tried to specify and delimit this word and to state precisely the relations between patriarchy and the domestic mode of production. I am still working on this. If I have used a fairly vague term, it has been so as to show from the start that I consider the oppression of women *to be a system*. But the question is, what are the system's components and how is it constituted? The notion has to be filled in, and this can only be done bit by bit.

I have, however, since entering the field, restricted the meaning I attach to the term "patriarchy." For many, it is synonymous with "the subordination of women." It carries this meaning for me, too, but with this qualification: I add the words "here and now." This makes a big difference. When I hear it said, as I often do, that "patriarchy has changed between the stone age and the present," I know that it is not "my" patriarchy that is being talked about. What I study is not an ahistoric concept that has wandered down through the centuries but something peculiar to contemporary industrial societies. I do not believe in the theory of survivals—and here I am in agreement with other Marxists. An institution that exists today cannot be explained by the fact that it existed in the past, even if this past is recent. I do not deny that certain elements of patriarchy today resemble elements of the patriarchy of one or two hundred years ago; what I deny is that this *continuance*—insofar as it really concerns the same thing—in itself constitutes an explanation.

Many people think that when they have found the point of origin of an institution in the past, they hold the key to its present existence. But they have, in fact, explained neither its present existence nor even its birth (its past appearance), for one must explain its existence at each and every moment by the context prevailing at that time; and its persistence today (if it really is persistence) must be explained by the present context. Some so-called historical explanations are in fact ahistorical, precisely because they do not take account of the given conditions of each period. This is not History but mere dating. History is precious if it is well conducted, if each period is examined in the same way as the present period. A science of the past worthy of the name cannot be anything other than a series of synchronic analyses.

The search for origins is a caricature of this falsely historical procedure and is one of the reasons why I have denounced it, and why I shall continue to denounce it each and every time it surfaces—which is, alas, all too frequently. (The other reason why I denounce the search for origins is because of its hidden naturalistic presuppositions.) But from the scientific point of view, it is as illegitimate to seek keys to the present situation in the nineteenth century as in the Stone Age.

Since 1970, then, I have been saying that patriarchy is the system of subordination of women to men in contemporary industrial societies, that this system has an economic base, and that this base is the domestic mode of production. It is hardly worth saying that these three ideas have been, and remain, highly controversial.

Like all modes of production, the domestic mode of production is also a mode of circulation and consumption of goods. While it is difficult, at least at first sight, to identify in the capitalist mode of production the form of consumption that distinguishes the dominant from the dominated, since consumption is mediated by wage, things are very different in the domestic mode. Here consumption is of primary importance and has this power to serve as a basis for making discriminations, for one of the essential differences between the two modes of production is that domestic production is not paid but rather maintained. In this mode, therefore, consumption is not separated from production, and the unequal sharing of goods is not mediated by money. Consumption in the family has to be studied if we want not only to be able to evaluate the quantitative exploitation of various members but also to understand what upkeep consists of and how it differs from a wage. Too many people today still "translate" upkeep into its monetary equivalent, as if a woman who receives a coat receives the value of the coat. In so doing they abolish the crucial distinction between a wage and retribution in kind, produced by the presence or absence of a monetary transaction. This distinction creates the difference between self-selected and forced consumption and is independent of the value of the goods consumed.

Every mode of production is also a mode of circulation. The mode of circulation peculiar to the domestic mode of production is the transmission of patrimony, which is regulated in part by the rules of inheritance but is not limited to them. It is an area that has been fairly well studied in some sectors of our society (e.g., farming) but completely ignored in others. Here we can also see, on the one hand, the difference between the abstract model and the concrete society and, on the other hand, the consequences of the fact that our social system (or more precisely the representation that has been made of it, i.e., the model of our social system) is composed of several subsystems.

The intergenerational circulation of goods is interesting in that it shows the mechanisms at work that produce complementary and antagonistic classes: the division between owners and nonowners of the means of production. The effect of the dispossession is clear in the agricultural world: those who do not inherit—women and younger siblings—work unpaid for their husbands and inheriting brothers. Domestic circulation (the rules of inheritance and succession) leads directly into patriarchal relations of production. But patrimonial transmission is equally important at another level in reconstituting, generation after generation, the capitalist mode of production. It not only creates possessors and nonpossessors within each family, but it also creates this division among families. This is the only aspect of patrimonial transmission that has really been studied to date. The former, the division into classes of a kin group, is passed over in silence by many sociologists and anthropologists, who pretend, against all the evidence—and in particular against all the evidence on the division of society into genders—that *all* the children in a family inherit equally the goods and status of the head of the family. But being the only effect of patrimonial transmission recognized by (traditional) sociology makes its reconstituting of capitalist classes no less real, and this is, indeed, one of the times when the domestic mode of production meets the capitalist mode and where they interpenetrate.

Depriving women of the means of production is not the only way in which women are dispossessed of direct access to their means of subsistence, if only because many families do not have any family property *not* to transmit to them. The same effect is produced by the systemic discrimination women face in the *wage*-labor market (let us for the moment call it the "dual labor" market). This too pushes women to enter domestic relations of production, mainly by getting married. The situation of women on the labor market has been well studied, and the only originality in my approach has been to invert the direction of the links usually established. While ordinarily it is seen as the family situation that influences the capacity of women to work outside, I have tried to show that it is the situation created for women on the labor market that constitutes an objective incentive to marry; hence, the labor market plays a role in the exploitation of women's domestic work.

How should this fact be conceptualized? How should we interpret its meaning with regard to the relations between patriarchy and the domestic mode of production? Can we talk of capitalist mechanisms serving the domestic mode of production, or must we speak of domestic mechanisms at work in the labor market? Whatever the reply—and the question will stay open for a long time—one thing is clear: whether it concerns patrimonial transmission (which assists, if not creates, relations of production other than those that are strictly domestic) or the capitalist labor market (which assists, if not creates, relations of production other than capitalist ones), the two systems are tightly linked and have a relationship of mutual aid and assistance. Moreover, the relations between patriarchy and the domestic mode of production are not simple relations of superposition. The domestic mode of production in places overruns patriarchy and in places is slighter. The same is true also of the capitalist mode of production: one of its institutions, the labor market, is in part ruled, or used, by patriarchy.

Thus, the domestic mode of production does not give a total account of even the economic dimension of women's subordination. And it does not account for other dimensions of this subordination, in particular the oppressions that are just as material as economic exploitation, including all the varieties of sexual violence. Some of these forms of violence can be attached to the appropriation of women's labor power. For example, C. Hennequin, E. deLesseps, and I attached them to the prohibition of abortion.[2] Since the bringing up of children is labor extorted from women, it could in fact be thought that men fear women will seek to escape from the labor of child-rearing, notably by limiting births, and that men therefore accord themselves the means to withdraw such control from women by prohibiting abortion. The constraint to be heterosexual and the "choice" within sexuality of practices that result in impregnation can also be seen as a means to withdraw control over fertility from women and give it to men. The same sort of reasoning has been applied to marital violence[3] and rape.[4] However, to be fair, the links so established are too abridged to be called full explanations. There remain whole sections of women's oppression that are only very partially, if at all, explained by my theory. This can be seen as a shortcoming, but not an involuntary one; rather, it is a consequence of certain refusals and choices of a methodological kind which I have made.

I distrust theories that seek from the outset to explain as a totality all the aspects of the oppression of women. The first, general reason I distrust them is that such theories themselves remain particular. In being too glued to their object, to its specificity, they become specific, unable to locate their object among other similar things (e.g., among other oppressions), because they do not possess the tools to make it comparable. However, the explanatory power of a theory (or a concept or a hypothesis) is tied to its capacity to discover what is common to several phenomena of the same order, and hence to its capacity to go beyond the phenomenal reality (i.e., what is immediately present) of each case. The idea that the raison d'être of things is to be found beyond their appearance, that it is "hidden," is part of scientific procedure (though it can, of course, be contested).

Thus, one of the objections that has been made to my use of the concepts "mode of production" and "class" has been that these concepts were created to describe other situations and that in using them I deny the specificity of our oppression. But analysis proceeds by a kind of logical "butchery." To understand a phenomenon, one begins by breaking it down into bits, which are later reassembled. Why? So that the bits will be the same for all instances of the phenomenon studied. (Here the phenomenon under study is the subordination of one group by another, the oppression of women being one instance.) The recompositions later obtained are then comparable. With a few concepts a geographer can describe any landscape. To understand is first to compare. This is how all sciences proceed, and it is how we proceed in everyday life: how you and I describe a person, a place, a situation to people who are not able to have direct experience of them.

But these nonspecific concepts are made not so much to describe things as to explain them. (Although all description requires a classification

263

and, hence, at the start is an explanation, all explanation is also a description insofar as it can itself be further explained.) This is the ambition of analysis. The bits into which a phenomenon is broken are also not those of immediate perception. The economic dimension, for instance, is not an "obvious" category for thinking about the family today, but then it was also not an obvious one for thinking about any phenomenon whatsoever a few centuries ago, even those our current language now calls "the economy."

It follows that when the bits are gathered together, the assemblages so obtained are in no way restitutions of the objects initially treated but rather models: images of what it is suggested are the realities underlying and causing the objects. The initial "objects" are also not themselves "pure" facts but rather the immediate perception of things, informed in a nonexplicit fashion by a certain view of the world (what Feyerabend referred to as "natural evidences"). Thus, it could be said, on the one hand, that the more a theory pretends to be "general" (its object), the more it has descriptive power and the less it has explanatory power; and, on the other hand, the more it is intended to account for immediate perception, precisely because to have a descriptive power it must stick to the "facts," the more it is ideological.

The other reason for my distrust of theories that wish to be "total" is that even when they do not aim to "cover" everything, they still aim to explain everything by a single "cause"; and when their concern is women's oppression, this thirst for a single cause generally leads straight into the arms of naturalism. Naturalism is a major sin of which we are not responsible since it is the indigenous theory—the rationalization—for oppression. Today it is applied to the oppression of women and people "of color," but it was also used to explain the oppression of the proletariat scarcely a century ago. It is not sufficiently recognized that the exploitation of the working class was justified, in the nineteenth century, by the "natural" (today one would say "genetic") inferiority of its members. And naturalism continues to infect our thought. This is most obvious in antifeminist thinking, but it is still present, in large measure, in feminism itself.

Feminists have been shouting for more than a decade whenever they hear it said that the subordination of women is caused by the inferiority of our natural capacities. But, at the same time, the vast majority continue to think that "we must take account of biology." Why exactly? No one knows. Science has thrown out, one after another, all the "biological explanations" of the oppression of proletarians and nonwhites, so it might be thought that this type of account would be discredited. This century has seen the collapse of such racist theories, even though one-quarter of primatologists keep trying to save them from annihilation. But the role that biology never merited historically it does not merit logically either. Why should we, in trying to explain the division of society into hierarchical groups, attach ourselves to the anatomy of the individuals who compose, or are thought to compose, these groups? The pertinence of the *question* (not to speak of the pertinence of the replies furnished) still remains to be demonstrated as far as I am concerned.

Naturalist "explanations" always choose the most convenient biology of the moment. In the last century it was the (feeble) muscles of women; in the 1950s it was the (deleterious) influence of our hormones on our moods; today it is the (bad) lateralization of our brains. Feminists are outraged by such "theories," but no one has yet explained to me how these theories differ fundamentally from the explanation in terms of women's ability to gestate which is so in favor today under the name of "reproduction."

One of the axioms, if not the fundamental axiom, of my approach is that women and men are *social* groups. I start from the incontestable fact that they are socially named, socially differentiated, and socially pertinent, and I question these social practices. How are they realized? What are they for? It may be (again, this remains to be proved) that women are (also) females and that men are (also) males, but it is women and men who interest me, not females and males. Even if one gives only minimal weight to the social construction of sexual difference, if one contents oneself with merely stating the pertinence of sex for society, then one is obliged to consider this pertinence as a social fact, which therefore requires an equally social explanation. (Just because Durkheim said it does not make this any less true.) This is why an important part of my work is devoted to denouncing approaches that seek a natural explanation for a social fact, and why I want to dislodge all approaches that implicitly bear the stamp of this reductionism.

A considerable theoretical step forward was taken ten years ago with the creation of the concept of "gender." The term is, however, unfortunately little used in French and not systematically used in English, with the result that we continue to get entangled by the different meanings of the word "sex" or are constrained to use paraphrases (e.g., "sexual divisions in society"). The concept of gender carries in one word both a recognition of the social dimension of the "sexual" dichotomy and the need to treat it as such, and its consequent detachment from the anatomical-biological aspect of sex. But it only partially detaches the social from the anatomical. If gender identifies a social construction, it is, however, not arbitrarily built on no matter what: it is constituted by anatomical sex, just as the beret is set on the head of the legendary Frenchman. And, since its creation, the concept of gender, far from taking wing, has seemed always to function in composite expressions such as "sex and gender" or "sex/gender"—the "and" or the slash serving to buttress rather than separate the two. When two words are always associated, they become redundant; when, in addition, the association is not reciprocal—when sex can happily dispense with gender—the optional addition of the second term seems but a cautious form of speech that lacks real meaning.

The concept of gender has thus not taken off as I would have wished, nor has it given rise to the theoretical development it carried in germ. Rather, gender now seems to be taken at its most minimal connotation. It is accepted that the "roles" of the sexes vary according to the society, but it is this *variability* that is taken to sum up the social aspect of sex. Gender is a content of which sex is the constraining container. The content may vary from society to society, but the container itself does not. Gayle Rubin, for example, maintains that sex inevitably gives birth to gender. In other words, the sexual dimorphism of the human species contains in itself not only the capacity but also the *necessity* of a social division. The very existence of genders—of different social positions for men and women (or, more correctly, for females or males)—is thus taken as given, as not requiring explanation. Only the content of these positions and their (eventual, according to Rubin) hierarchy are a matter for investigation. Those who, like me, took gender seriously find themselves, today, pretty isolated.

I give above my reasons for mistrusting "specific" explanations. They may, perhaps, not totally explain for readers my use of the term "class." Beyond responding to the needs of analysis as described above—though, perhaps, no better than another concept might (namely, breaking down an object—here the oppression of women—into small sections, or, more precisely, into nonspecific *dimensions*)—the concept of class has the advantage of being the only one I know that at least partially responds to the strict requirements of a social explanation. It is perhaps not totally satisfying, but it is the least unsatisfying of all the terms used to analyze oppression.

The term "groups" says nothing about their mode of constitution. It can be thought that the groups—the dominant and the dominated—each have an origin that is sui generis; that having already come into existence, they later enter into a relationship; and that this relationship, at a still later time, becomes characterized by domination. The concept of class, however, inverts this scheme. It implies that each group cannot be considered separately from the other because they are bound together by a relationship of domination; nor can they even be considered together but independent of this relationship. Characterizing this relationship as one of economic exploitation, the concept of class additionally puts social domination at the heart of the explanation of hierarchy. The motives—the material profit in the wide sense—attributed to this domination can be discussed, and even challenged or changed, without changing the fundamental scheme.

Class is a dichotomous concept and thus has its limitations. But we can also see how class applies to the exhaustive, hierarchical, and precisely dichotomous classifications that are internal to a given society, such as the classification into men *or* women (adult/child, white/nonwhite, etc.). The concept of class starts from the idea of social construction and specifies its implications. Groups are no longer sui generis, constituted before coming into relations with one another. On the contrary, it is their relationship that constitutes them as such. It is, therefore, a question of discovering the social practices, the social relations that, in constituting the division by gender, create the groups of gender (called "of sex").

I put forward the hypothesis that the domestic relations of production constitute one such class relationship. But this relation does not account for the whole of the "gender" system, and it also concerns other categorizations (e.g., by age). I would put forward as another hypothesis that other systems of relationship constitutive of gender divisions also exist—and these remain to be discovered. If we think of each of these systems as a circle, then gender division is the zone illuminated by the projection of these circles onto one another. Each system of relations, taken separately, is not specific, either of gender division or of another categorization. But these systems of relations do combine in various ways, each of which is unique. According to this hypothesis, it is the particular combination of several systems of relationships, of which none is specific, that gives singularity to the division.

Is it the specificity of this combination that is meant when we say that patriarchy is a system? Or does this combination, in addition to

266

being unique and noncontingent possess a *meaning?* And is it this meaning that makes patriarchy a system? Above all, *what* are the other systems that articulate with the domestic mode of production to form patriarchy? These are some of the questions I think we must pursue.

Notes

1   Originally published in 1970, "The Main Enemy" is reprinted in Christine Delphy, *Close to Home: A Materialist Analysis of Women's Oppression* (Amherst: University of Massachusetts Press, 1984).

2   C. Hennequin, E. Lesseps, and C. Delphy, "L'interdiction de l'avortement: Exploitation economique," *Partisans* (1970), no. 54-5.

3   J. Hanmer, "Violence and the Social Control of Women," in G. Littlejohn et al., eds., *Power and the State* (London: Croom Helm, 1978).

4   On the issue of rape, see the mimeographed paper "Patriarchal Justice and the Fear of Rape," issued by Féministes Revolutionnaires in 1976.

Comment (Michèle Barrett)

I want to make three comments on Christine's position which I think are particularly central for understanding the relation between Marxism and feminism. I don't want to dwell very long on any of them, since I have engaged them in a more detailed way elsewhere.

The first point concerns the question of gender. I think Christine is absolutely right that the analysis of gender has not taken off in the way that a lot of feminists hoped it would. But I think that is partly because there has been a theoretical debate about how we analyze gender. I might briefly characterize this debate along a continuum between two extreme positions. At one end (and I would locate Christine here) is a theory that sees gender as, in a sense, a Durkheimian social fact. What we are studying when we look at the acquisition of gender is the acquisition of a social identity that is already there. At the opposite pole is the theoretical view that there is no such fixed social category already there but, rather, that the meaning of gender—the meaning of femininity and masculinity—is constructed anew in every encounter. I would associate this view with discourse theory and the various kinds of feminist appropriations of discourse theory.

Neither of these poles is very satisfactory. The Durkheimian position doesn't explain social change, and I think that there has been a considerable amount of change in the meaning of gender. The discourse position doesn't explain persistence. If you insist that gender is created anew on every occasion, you can't explain how it is that familiar things keep popping up time and time again. So it seems to me that the more useful way to approach gender would be somewhere between these two extremes. And I think the failure of gender analysis to really take off is due to the way the debate has been defined already.

The second issue I want to raise involves the concept of class. While I agree to some extent with what Christine says, I think it is necessary to pose the difficulties of reconciling a Marxist and a feminist approach. Christine reconciles these through the concepts that she uses (e.g., patriarchy, domestic mode of production, and wage-labor). Clearly, one might use different concepts but still pose, in a very general way, the theoretical relationship between Marxism and feminism. I've argued in the past that this is an extremely difficult project and that, to put it crudely, the success of the project is not really assisted by simply using a Marxist concept of class in relation to gender. Christine acknowledges that it is not ideal but maintains that it is the least unsatisfying term with which to analyze oppression. But when we are trying to reconcile Marxist and feminist approaches, we must face the problem that Christine raises at the very beginning, which is the question of the distinction between exploitation and oppression. The real key to the debate is to describe how we might say that women are *exploited* rather than *oppressed* by men. The concept of class, as developed by Marx, does not simply register dichotomy; it is not simply a descriptive term that can be transferred onto other sets of relations—or, at least, it can only be transferred metaphorically. The question is crucial politically because it raises the question of the status of economic arguments and the status of exploitation as an economic category in political theory and political strategy. And it seems to me—I'll float this as a rather provocative point—that it doesn't help us in thinking about feminist questions to reproduce some of the difficulties associated with the concept of class that Marxism has plowed through with great pain and suffering.

My third point concerns the relations between political strategies and theoretical interpretations. I will give two examples. The first is the question of biology: whether feminism is, as it were, infected by naturalism as soon as it raises the question of biology. While I completely agree with Christine in principle, I think that a political difficulty remains because we are not in a situation where impeccable logic rules the world. We are in a situation where biologistic arguments absolutely hold the commanding heights of popular sentiments on the question of gender. We simply cannot afford the luxury of saying that biological or biologistic arguments should not be addressed by feminists. In fact, our arguments have too often been very unconvincing. There is a political imperative that demands more work here, more serious engagements with and refutations of pseudoscientific arguments, and more popular campaigning as well.

The other example I want to give is perhaps a bit more controversial: abortion. Of course, it's true that abortion is a feminist issue. But we will be in a lot of trouble politically if we rest there, because abortion is an issue that cannot really be posed exclusively in terms of the antagonism between men and women, or of male control over women. To pose it in that way is to deny the role of women in the antiabortion movement, and that is, in some ways, a rather patronizing approach. Nor is it politically helpful at this moment because it leaves the Right too much in control of popular ideologies. And it doesn't give due recognition to the complexity of women's experience. Instead, it tends to imply that women mistake their own interests, rather like the traditional Marxist view of the working class as misperceiving their own objective interests. Neither position really engages with the question—at the level of either experience or popular ideology—of why people want these things that we are, analytically, so critical of. The refusal to engage with the question of consent leads us into a victimology of women. Those of us who come from the other side of the Atlantic are very conscious of this because of the phenomenon of Thatcherism: that you cannot make do with a theoretical position in which you don't take seriously the "nonprogressive" needs, wants, and desires of people. Paradoxically, that leads me back to my first point, that we need to consider in a more nuanced, more complex way how gender is constructed and the political parameters of that process.

Can the Subaltern Speak?

An understanding of contemporary relations of power, and of the Western intellectual's role within them, requires an examination of the intersection of a theory of representation and the political economy of global capitalism. A theory of representation points, on the one hand, to the domain of ideology, meaning, and subjectivity, and, on the other hand, to the domain of politics, the state, and the law.

The original title of this paper was "Power, Desire, Interest."[1] Indeed, whatever power these meditations command may have been earned by a politically interested refusal to push to the limit the founding presuppositions of my desires, as far as they are within my grasp. This vulgar three-stroke formula, applied both to the most resolutely committed and to the most ironic discourse, keeps track of what Althusser so aptly named "philosophies of denegation."[2] I have invoked my positionality in this awkward way so as to accentuate the fact that calling the place of the investigator into question remains a meaningless piety in many recent critiques of the sovereign subject. Thus, although I will attempt to foreground the precariousness of my position throughout, I know such gestures can never suffice.

This paper will move, by a necessarily circuitous route, from a critique of current Western efforts to problematize the subject to the question of how the third-world subject is represented within Western discourse. Along the way, I will have occasion to suggest that a still more radical decentering of the subject is, in fact, implicit in both Marx and Derrida. And I will have recourse, perhaps surprisingly, to an argument that Western intellectual production is, in many ways, complicit with Western international economic interests. In the end, I will offer an alternative analysis of the relations between the discourses of the West and the possibility of speaking of (or for) the subaltern woman. I will draw my specific examples from the case of India, discussing at length the extraordinarily paradoxical status of the British abolition of widow sacrifice.

I

Some of the most radical criticism coming out of the West today is the result of an interested desire to conserve the subject of the West, or the West as Subject. The theory of pluralized "subject-effects" gives an illusion of undermining subjective sovereignty while often providing a cover for this subject of knowledge. Although the history of Europe as Subject is narrativized by the law, political economy, and ideology of the West, this concealed Subject pretends it has "no geo-political determina-

271

tions." The much-publicized critique of the sovereign subject thus actually inaugurates a Subject. I will argue for this conclusion by considering a text by two great practitioners of the critique: "Intellectuals and Power: A Conversation between Michel Foucault and Gilles Deleuze."[3]

I have chosen this friendly exchange between two activist philosophers of history because it undoes the opposition between authoritative theoretical production and the unguarded practice of conversation, enabling one to glimpse the track of ideology. The participants in this conversation emphasize the most important contributions of French poststructuralist theory: first, that the networks of power/desire/interest are so heterogeneous that their reduction to a coherent narrative is counterproductive—a persistent critique is needed; and second, that intellectuals must attempt to disclose and know the discourse of society's Other. Yet the two systematically ignore the question of ideology and their own implication in intellectual and economic history.

Although one of its chief presuppositions is the critique of the sovereign subject, the conversation between Foucault and Deleuze is framed by two monolithic and anonymous subjects-in-revolution: "A Maoist" (FD, 205) and "the workers' struggle" (FD, 217). Intellectuals, however, are named and differentiated; moreover, a Chinese Maoism is nowhere operative. Maoism here simply creates an aura of narrative specificity, which would be a harmless rhetorical banality were it not that the innocent appropriation of the proper name "Maoism" for the eccentric phenomenon of French intellectual "Maoism" and subsequent "New Philosophy" symptomatically renders "Asia" transparent.[4]

Deleuze's reference to the workers' struggle is equally problematic; it is obviously a genuflection: "We are unable to touch [power] in any point of its application without finding ourselves confronted by this diffuse mass, so that we are necessarily led ... to the desire to blow it up completely. Every partial revolutionary attack or defense is linked in this way to the workers' struggle" (FD, 217). The apparent banality signals a disavowal. The statement ignores the international division of labor, a gesture that often marks poststructuralist political theory.[5] The invocation of the workers' struggle is baleful in its very innocence; it is incapable of dealing with global capitalism: the subject-production of worker and unemployed within nation-state ideologies in its Center; the increasing subtraction of the working class in the Periphery from the realization of surplus value and thus from "humanistic" training in consumerism; and the large-scale presence of paracapitalist labor as well as the heterogeneous structural status of agriculture in the Periphery. Ignoring the international division of labor; rendering "Asia" (and on occasion "Africa") transparent (unless the subject is ostensibly the "Third World"); reestablishing the legal subject of socialized capital—these are problems as common to much poststructuralist as to structuralist theory. Why should such occlusions be sanctioned in precisely those intellectuals who are our best prophets of heterogeneity and the Other?

The link to the workers' struggle is located in the desire to blow up power at any point of its application. This site is apparently based on a simple valorization of any desire destructive of any power. Walter Benjamin comments on Baudelaire's comparable politics by way of quotations from Marx:

Marx continues in his description of the *conspirateurs de profession* as follows: ".... They have no other aim but the immediate one of overthrowing the existing government, and they profoundly despise the more theoretical enlightenment of the workers as to their class interests. Thus their anger—not proletarian but plebian—at the *habits noirs* (black coats), the more or less educated people who represent [*vertreten*] that side of the movement and of whom they can never become entirely independent, as they cannot of the official representatives [*Repräsentanten*] of the party." Baudelaire's political insights do not go fundamentally beyond the insights of these professional conspirators. ... He could perhaps have made Flaubert's statement, "Of all of politics I understand only one thing: the revolt," his own.[6]

The link to the workers' struggle is located, simply, in desire. Elsewhere, Deleuze and Guattari have attempted an alternative definition of desire, revising the one offered by psychoanalysis: "Desire does not lack anything; it does not lack its object. It is, rather, the subject that is lacking in desire, or desire that lacks a fixed subject; there is no fixed subject except by repression. Desire and its object are a unity: it is the machine, as a machine of a machine. Desire is machine, the object of desire also a connected machine, so that the product is lifted from the process of producing, and something detaches itself from producing to product and gives a leftover to the vagabond, nomad subject."[7]

This definition does not alter the specificity of the desiring subject (or leftover subject-effect) that attaches to specific instances of desire or to production of the desiring machine. Moreover, when the connection between desire and the subject is taken as irrelevant or merely reversed, the subject-effect that surreptitiously emerges is much like the generalized ideological subject of the theorist. This may be the legal subject of socialized capital, neither labor nor management, holding a "strong" passport, using a "strong" or "hard" currency, with supposedly unquestioned access to due process. It is certainly not the desiring subject as Other.

The failure of Deleuze and Guattari to consider the relations between desire, power, and subjectivity renders them incapable of articulating a theory of interests. In this context, their indifference to ideology (a theory of which is necessary for an understanding of interests) is striking but consistent. Foucault's commitment to "genealogical" speculation prevents him from locating, in "great names" like Marx and Freud, watersheds in some continuous stream of intellectual history.[8] This commitment has created an unfortunate resistance in Foucault's work to "mere" ideological critique. Western speculations on the ideological reproduction of social relations belong to that mainstream, and it is within this tradition that Althusser writes: "The reproduction of labour power requires not only a reproduction of its skills, but also at the same time, a reproduction of its submission to the ruling ideology for the workers, and a reproduction of the ability to manipulate the ruling ideology correctly for the agents of

273

itation and repression, so that they, too, will provide for the domi-
n of the ruling class 'in and by words' [*par la parole*]."[9]

When Foucault considers the pervasive heterogeneity of power,
he does not ignore the immense institutional heterogeneity that Althusser
here attempts to schematize. Similarly, in speaking of alliances and systems
of signs, the state and war-machines *(mille plateaux)*, Deleuze and Guattari
are opening up that very field. Foucault cannot, however, admit that a
developed theory of ideology recognizes its own material production in
institutionality, as well as in the "effective instruments for the formation
and accumulation of knowledge" (*PK*, 102). Because these philosophers
seem obliged to reject all arguments naming the concept of ideology as only
schematic rather than textual, they are equally obliged to produce a mechanically schematic opposition between interest and desire. Thus they align
themselves with bourgeois sociologists who fill the place of ideology with a
continuistic "unconscious" or a parasubjective "culture." The mechanical
relation between desire and interest is clear in such sentences as: "We never
desire against our interests, because interest always follows and finds itself
where desire has placed it" (*FD*, 215). An undifferentiated desire is the agent,
and power slips in to create the effects of desire: "power . . . produces positive
effects at the level of desire—and also at the level of knowledge" (*PK*, 59).

This parasubjective matrix, cross-hatched with heterogeneity,
ushers in the unnamed Subject, at least for those intellectual workers influenced by the new hegemony of desire. The race for "the last instance" is
now between economics and power. Because desire is tacitly defined on an
orthodox model, it is unitarily opposed to "being deceived." Ideology as
"false consciousness" (being deceived) has been called into question by
Althusser. Even Reich implied notions of collective will rather than a dichotomy of deception and undeceived desire: "We must accept the scream
of Reich: no, the masses were not deceived; at a particular moment, they
actually desired a fascist regime" (*FD*, 215).

These philosophers will not entertain the thought of constitutive
contradiction—that is where they admittedly part company from the Left.
In the name of desire, they reintroduce the undivided subject into the discourse of power. Foucault often seems to conflate "individual" and "subject";[10] and the impact on his own metaphors is perhaps intensified in his
followers. Because of the power of the word "power," Foucault admits to
using the "metaphor of the point which progressively irradiates its surroundings." Such slips become the rule rather than the exception in less
careful hands. And that radiating point, animating an effectively heliocentric
discourse, fills the empty place of the agent with the historical sun of theory,
the Subject of Europe.[11]

Foucault articulates another corollary of the disavowal of the role
of ideology in reproducing the social relations of production: an unquestioned valorization of the oppressed as subject, the "object being," as Deleuze admiringly remarks, "to establish conditions where the prisoners
themselves would be able to speak." Foucault adds that "the masses *know*
perfectly well, clearly"—once again the thematics of being undeceived—"they
know far better than [the intellectual] and they certainly say it very well"
(*FD*, 206, 207).

What happens to the critique of the sovereign subject in these
pronouncements? The limits of this representationalist realism are reached

274

with Deleuze: "Reality is what actually happens in a factory, in a school, in barracks, in a prison, in a police station" (*FD*, 212). This foreclosing of the necessity of the difficult task of counterhegemonic ideological production has not been salutary. It has helped positivist empiricism—the justifying foundation of advanced capitalist neocolonialism—to define its own arena as "concrete experience," "what actually happens." Indeed, the concrete experience that is the guarantor of the political appeal of prisoners, soldiers, and schoolchildren is disclosed through the concrete experience of the intellectual, the one who diagnoses the episteme.[12] Neither Deleuze nor Foucault seems aware that the intellectual within socialized capital, brandishing concrete experience, can help consolidate the international division of labor.

The unrecognized contradiction within a position that valorizes the concrete experience of the oppressed, while being so uncritical about the historical role of the intellectual, is maintained by a verbal slippage. Thus Deleuze makes this remarkable pronouncement: "A theory is like a box of tools. Nothing to do with the signifier" (*FD*, 208). Considering that the verbalism of the theoretical world and its access to any world defined against it as "practical" is irreducible, such a declaration helps only the intellectual anxious to prove that intellectual labor is just like manual labor. It is when signifiers are left to look after themselves that verbal slippages happen. The signifier "representation" is a case in point. In the same dismissive tone that severs theory's link to the signifier, Deleuze declares, "There is no more representation; there's nothing but action"—"action of theory and action of practice which relate to each other as relays and form networks" (*FD*, 206-7). Yet an important point is being made here: the production of theory is also a practice; the opposition between abstract "pure" theory and concrete "applied" practice is too quick and easy.[13]

If this is, indeed, Deleuze's argument, his articulation of it is problematic. Two senses of representation are being run together: representation as "speaking for," as in politics, and representation as "re-presentation," as in art or philosophy. Since theory is also only "action," the theoretician does not represent (speak for) the oppressed group. Indeed, the subject is not seen as a representative consciousness (one re-presenting reality adequately). These two senses of representation—within state formation and the law, on the one hand, and in subject-predication, on the other—are related but irreducibly discontinuous. To cover over the discontinuity with an analogy that is presented as a proof reflects again a paradoxical subject-privileging.[14] *Because* "the person who speaks and acts . . . is always a multiplicity," no "theorizing intellectual . . . [or] party or . . . union" can represent "those who act and struggle" (*FD*, 206). Are those who act and *struggle* mute, as opposed to those who act and *speak* (*FD*, 206)? These immense problems are buried in the differences between the "same" words: consciousness and conscience (both *conscience* in French), representation and re-presentation. The critique of ideological subject-constitution within state formations and systems of political economy can now be effaced, as can the active theoretical practice of the "transformation of consciousness." The banality of leftist intellectuals' lists of self-knowing, politically canny subalterns stands revealed; representing them, the intellectuals represent themselves as transparent.

If such a critique and such a project are not to be given up, the shifting distinctions between representation within the state and political economy, on the one hand, and within the theory of the Subject, on the other, must not be obliterated. Let us consider the play of *vertreten* ("represent" in the first sense) and *darstellen* ("re-present" in the second sense) in a famous passage in *The Eighteenth Brumaire of Louis Bonaparte*, where Marx touches on "class" as a descriptive and transformative concept in a manner somewhat more complex than Althusser's distinction between class instinct and class position would allow.

Marx's contention here is that the descriptive definition of a class can be a differential one—its cutting off and difference from all other classes: "in so far as millions of families live under economic conditions of existence that cut off their mode of life, their interest, and their formation from those of the other classes and place them in inimical confrontation *[feindlich gagenüberstellen]*, they form a class."[15] There is no such thing as a "class instinct" at work here. In fact, the collectivity of familial existence, which might be considered the arena of "instinct," is discontinuous with, though operated by, the differential isolation of classes. In this context, one far more pertinent to the France of the 1970s than it can be to the international periphery, the formation of a class is *artificial* and economic, and the economic agency or *interest* is impersonal because it is systematic and heterogeneous. This agency or interest is tied to the Hegelian critique of the individual subject, for it marks the subject's empty place in that process without a subject which is history and political economy. Here the capitalist is defined as "the conscious bearer *[Träger]* of the limitless movement of capital."[16] My point is that Marx is not working to create an undivided subject where desire and interest coincide. Class consciousness does not operate toward that goal. Both in the economic area (capitalist) and in the political (world-historical agent), Marx is obliged to construct models of a divided and dislocated subject whose parts are not continuous or coherent with each other. A celebrated passage like the description of capital as the Faustian monster brings this home vividly.[17]

The following passage, continuing the quotation from *The Eighteenth Brumaire,* is also working on the structural principle of a dispersed and dislocated class subject: the (absent collective) consciousness of the small peasant proprietor class finds its "bearer" in a "representative" who appears to work in another's interest. The word "representative" here is not *"darstellen"*; this sharpens the contrast Foucault and Deleuze slide over, the contrast, say, between a proxy and a portrait. There is, of course, a relationship between them, one that has received political and ideological exacerbation in the European tradition at least since the poet and the sophist, the actor and the orator, have both been seen as harmful. In the guise of a post-Marxist description of the scene of power, we thus encounter a much older debate: between representation or rhetoric as tropology and as persuasion. *Darstellen* belongs to the first constellation, *vertreten*—with stronger suggestions of substitution—to the second. Again, they are related, but running them together, especially in order to say that beyond both is where oppressed subjects speak, act, and know *for themselves,* leads to an essentialist, utopian politics.

Here is Marx's passage, using *"vertreten"* where the English use "represent," discussing a social "subject" whose consciousness and *Vertretung* (as much a substitution as a representation) are dislocated and incoherent: The small peasant proprietors "cannot represent themselves; they

276

must be represented. Their representative must appear simultaneously as their master, as an authority over them, as unrestricted governmental power that protects them from the other classes and sends them rain and sunshine from above. The political influence [in the place of the class interest, since there is no unified class subject] of the small peasant proprietors therefore finds its last expression [the implication of a chain of substitutions—*Vertretungen*—is strong here] in the executive force [*Exekutivgewalt*—less personal in German] subordinating society to itself."

Not only does such a model of social indirection—necessary gaps between the source of "influence" (in this case the small peasant proprietors), the "representative" (Louis Napoleon), and the historical-political phenomenon (executive control)—imply a critique of the subject as *individual* agent but a critique even of the subjectivity of a *collective* agency. The necessarily dislocated machine of history moves because "the identity of the *interests*" of these proprietors "fails to produce a feeling of community, national links, or a political organization." The event of representation as *Vertretung* (in the constellation of rhetoric-as-persuasion) behaves like a *Darstellung* (or rhetoric-as-trope), taking its place in the gap between the formation of a (descriptive) class and the nonformation of a (transformative) class: "In so far as millions of families live under economic conditions of existence that separate their mode of life . . . *they form a class.* In so far as . . . the identity of their interests fails to produce a feeling of community . . . *they do not form a class.*" The complicity of *Vertreten* and *Darstellen*, their identity-in-difference as the place of practice—since this complicity is precisely what Marxists must expose, as Marx does in *The Eighteenth Brumaire*—can only be appreciated if they are not conflated by a sleight of word.

It would be merely tendentious to argue that this textualizes Marx too much, making him inaccessible to the common "man," who, a victim of common sense, is so deeply placed in a heritage of positivism that Marx's irreducible emphasis on the work of the negative, on the necessity for de-fetishizing the concrete, is persistently wrested from him by the strongest adversary, "the historical tradition" in the air.[18] I have been trying to point out that the uncommon "man," the contemporary philosopher of practice, sometimes exhibits the same positivism.

The gravity of the problem is apparent if one agrees that the development of a transformative class "consciousness" from a descriptive class "position" is not in Marx a task engaging the ground level of consciousness. Class consciousness remains with the feeling of community that belongs to national links and political organizations, not to that other feeling of community whose structural model is the family. Although *not* identified with nature, the family here is constelled with what Marx calls "natural exchange," which is, philosophically speaking, a "placeholder" for use value.[19] "Natural exchange" is contrasted to "intercourse with society," where the word "intercourse" *(Verkehr)* is Marx's usual word for "commerce." This "intercourse" thus holds the place of the exchange leading to the production of surplus value, and it is in the area of this intercourse that the feeling of community leading to class agency must be developed. Full class agency (if there were such a thing) is not an ideological transformation of consciousness on the ground level, a desiring identity of the agents and their interest—the identity whose absence troubles Foucault and Deleuze. It is a contestatory *replacement* as well as an *appropriation* (a *supplementation*) of something that is "artificial" to begin with—"economic conditions of existence that separate their mode of life." Marx's formulations show a cautious respect for the nascent critique of individual and collective subjective agency. The projects of class consciousness and of the transformation of consciousness are discontinuous issues for him. Conversely, contemporary invocations of "libidinal economy" and desire as the determining interest, combined with the practical politics of the oppressed (under socialized capital) "speaking for themselves," restore the category of the sovereign subject within the theory that seems most to question it.

No doubt the exclusion of the family, albeit a family belonging to a specific class formation, is part of the masculine frame within which Marxism marks its birth.[20] Historically as well as in today's global political economy, the family's role in patriarchal social relations is so heterogeneous and contested that merely replacing the family in this problematic is not going to break the frame. Nor does the solution lie in the positivist inclusion of a monolithic collectivity of "women" in the list of the oppressed whose unfractured subjectivity allows them to speak for themselves against an equally monolithic "same system."

In the context of the development of a strategic, artificial, and second-level "consciousness," Marx uses the concept of the patronymic, always within the broader concept of representation as *Vertretung:* The small peasant proprietors "are therefore incapable of making their class interest valid in their proper name *[im eigenen Namen],* whether through a parliament or through a convention." The absence of the nonfamilial artificial collective proper name is supplied by the only proper name "historical tradition" can offer—the patronymic itself—the Name of the Father: "Historical tradition produced the French peasants' belief that a miracle would occur, that a man *named* Napoleon would restore all their glory. And an individual turned up"—the untranslatable *"es fand sich"* (there found itself an individual?) demolishes all questions of agency or the agent's connection with his interest—"who gave himself out to be that man" (this pretense is, by contrast, his only proper agency) "because he carried [*trägt*—the word used for the capitalist's relationship to capital] the Napoleonic Code, which commands" that "inquiry into paternity is forbidden." While Marx here seems to be working within a patriarchal metaphorics, one should note the textual subtlety of the passage. It is the Law of the Father (the Napoleonic Code) that paradoxically prohibits the search for the natural father. Thus, it is according to a strict observance of the historical Law of the Father that the formed yet unformed class's faith in the natural father is gainsaid.

I have dwelt so long on this passage in Marx because it spells out the inner dynamics of *Vertretung,* or representation in the political context. Representation in the economic context is *Darstellung,* the philosophical concept of representation as staging or, indeed, signification, which relates to the divided subject in an indirect way. The most obvious passage is well known: "In the exchange relationship *[Austauschverhältnis]* of commodities their exchange-value appeared to us totally independent of their use-value. But if we subtract their use-value from the product of labour, we obtain their value, as it was just determined [*bestimmt*]. The common element which represents itself [*sich darstellt*] in the exchange relation, or the exchange value of the commodity, is thus its value."[21]

278

According to Marx, under capitalism, value, as produced in necessary and surplus labor, is computed as the representation/sign of objectified labor (which is rigorously distinguished from human activity). Conversely, in the absence of a theory of exploitation as the extraction (production), appropriation, and realization of (surplus) value *as representation of labor power,* capitalist exploitation must be seen as a variety of domination (the mechanics of power as such). "The thrust of Marxism," Deleuze suggests, "was to determine the problem [that power is more diffuse than the structure of exploitation and state formation] essentially in terms of interests (power is held by a ruling class defined by its interests)" (*FD,* 214).

One cannot object to this minimalist summary of Marx's project, just as one cannot ignore that, in parts of the *Anti-Oedipus,* Deleuze and Guattari build their case on a brilliant if "poetic" grasp of Marx's *theory* of the money form. Yet we might consolidate our critique in the following way: the relationship between global capitalism (exploitation in economics) and nation-state alliances (domination in geopolitics) is so macrological that it cannot account for the micrological texture of power. To move toward such an accounting one must move toward theories of ideology—of subject formations that micrologically and often erratically operate the interests that congeal the macrologies. Such theories cannot afford to overlook the category of representation in its two senses. They must note how the staging of the world in representation—its scene of writing, its *Darstellung*—dissimulates the choice of and need for "heroes," paternal proxies, agents of power—*Vertretung.*

My view is that radical practice should attend to this double session of representations rather than reintroduce the individual subject through totalizing concepts of power and desire. It is also my view that, in keeping the area of class practice on a second level of abstraction, Marx was in effect keeping open the (Kantian and) Hegelian critique of the individual subject as agent.[22] This view does not oblige me to ignore that, by implicitly defining the family and the mother tongue as the ground level where culture and convention seem nature's own way of organizing "her" own subversion, Marx himself rehearses an ancient subterfuge.[23] In the context of poststructuralist claims to critical practice, this seems more recuperable than the clandestine restoration of subjective essentialism.

The reduction of Marx to a benevolent but dated figure most often serves the interest of launching a new theory of interpretation. In the Foucault-Deleuze conversation, the issue seems to be that there is no representation, no signifier (Is it to be presumed that the signifier has already been dispatched? There is, then, no sign-structure operating experience, and thus might one lay semiotics to rest?); theory is a relay of practice (thus laying problems of theoretical practice to rest) and the oppressed can know and speak for themselves. This reintroduces the constitutive subject on at least two levels: the Subject of desire and power as an irreducible methodological presupposition; and the self-proximate, if not self-identical, subject of the oppressed. Further, the intellectuals, who are neither of these S/ subjects, become transparent in the relay race, for they merely report on the nonrepresented subject and analyze (without analyzing) the workings of (the unnamed Subject irreducibly presupposed by) power and desire. The produced "transparency" marks the place of "interest"; it is maintained by

279

vehement denegation: "Now this role of referee, judge, and universal witness is one which I *absolutely refuse* to adopt." One responsibility of the critic might be to read and write so that the impossibility of such interested individualistic refusals of the institutional privileges of power bestowed on the subject is taken seriously. The refusal of the sign-system blocks the way to a developed theory of ideology. Here, too, the peculiar tone of denegation is heard. To Jacques-Alain Miller's suggestion that "the institution is itself discursive," Foucault responds, "Yes, if you like, but it doesn't much matter for my notion of the apparatus to be able to say that this is discursive and that isn't . . . given that my problem isn't a linguistic one" (*PK*, 198). Why this conflation of language and discourse from the master of discourse analysis?

Edward W. Said's critique of power in Foucault as a captivating and mystifying category that allows him "to obliterate the role of classes, the role of economics, the role of insurgency and rebellion," is most pertinent here.[24] I add to Said's analysis the notion of the surreptitious subject of power and desire marked by the transparency of the intellectual. Curiously enough, Paul Bové faults Said for emphasizing the importance of the intellectual, whereas "Foucault's project essentially is a challenge to the leading role of both hegemonic and oppositional intellectuals."[25] I have suggested that this "challenge" is deceptive precisely because it ignores what Said emphasizes—the critic's institutional responsibility.

This S/subject, curiously sewn together into a transparency by denegations, belongs to the exploiters' side of the international division of labor. It is impossible for contemporary French intellectuals to imagine the kind of Power and Desire that would inhabit the unnamed subject of the Other of Europe. It is not only that everything they read, critical or uncritical, is caught within the debate of the production of that Other, supporting or critiquing the constitution of the Subject as Europe. It is also that, in the constitution of that Other of Europe, great care was taken to obliterate the textual ingredients with which such a subject could cathect, could occupy (invest?) its itinerary—not only by ideological and scientific production, but also by the institution of the law. However reductionistic an economic analysis might seem, the French intellectuals forget at their peril that this entire overdetermined enterprise was in the interest of a dynamic economic situation requiring that interests, motives (desires), and power (of knowledge) be ruthlessly dislocated. To invoke that dislocation now as a radical discovery that should make us diagnose the economic (conditions of existence that separate out "classes" descriptively) as a piece of dated analytic machinery may well be to continue the work of that dislocation and unwittingly to help in securing "a new balance of hegemonic relations."[26] I shall return to this argument shortly. In the face of the possibility that the intellectual is complicit in the persistent constitution of Other as the Self's shadow, a possibility of political practice for the intellectual would be to put the economic "under erasure," to see the economic factor as irreducible as it reinscribes the social text, even as it is erased, however imperfectly, when it claims to be the final determinant or the transcendental signified.[27]

II

The clearest available example of such epistemic violence is the remotely orchestrated, far-flung, and heterogeneous project to constitute the

280

colonial subject as Other. This project is also the asymmetrical obliteration of the trace of that Other in its precarious Subject-ivity. It is well known that Foucault locates epistemic violence, a complete overhaul of the episteme, in the redefinition of sanity at the end of the European eighteenth century.[28] But what if that particular redefinition was only a part of the narrative of history in Europe as well as in the colonies? What if the two projects of epistemic overhaul worked as dislocated and unacknowledged parts of a vast two-handed engine? Perhaps it is no more than to ask that the subtext of the palimpsestic narrative of imperialism be recognized as "subjugated knowledge," "a whole set of knowledges that have been disqualified as inadequate to their task or insufficiently elaborated: naive knowledges, located low down on the hierarchy, beneath the required level of cognition or scientificity" (*PK*, 82).

This is not to describe "the way things really were" or to privilege the narrative of history as imperialism as the best version of history.[29] It is, rather, to offer an account of how an explanation and narrative of reality was established as the normative one. To elaborate on this, let us consider briefly the underpinnings of the British codification of Hindu Law.

First, a few disclaimers: In the United States the third-worldism currently afloat in humanistic disciplines is often openly ethnic. I was born in India and received my primary, secondary, and university education there, including two years of graduate work. My Indian example could thus be seen as a nostalgic investigation of the lost roots of my own identity. Yet even as I know that one cannot freely enter the thickets of "motivations," I would maintain that my chief project is to point out the positivist-idealist variety of such nostalgia. I turn to Indian material because, in the absence of advanced disciplinary training, that accident of birth and education has provided me with a *sense* of the historical canvas, a hold on some of the pertinent languages that are useful tools for a *bricoleur,* especially when armed with the Marxist skepticism of concrete experience as the final arbiter and a critique of disciplinary formations. Yet the Indian case cannot be taken as representative of all countries, nations, cultures, and the like that may be invoked as the Other of Europe as Self.

Here, then, is a schematic summary of the epistemic violence of the codification of Hindu Law. If it clarifies the notion of epistemic violence, my final discussion of widow-sacrifice may gain added significance.

At the end of the eighteenth century, Hindu law, insofar as it can be described as a unitary system, operated in terms of four texts that "staged" a four-part episteme defined by the subject's use of memory: *sruti* (the heard), *smriti* (the remembered), *sastra* (the learned-from-another), and *vyavahara* (the performed-in-exchange). The origins of what had been heard and what was remembered were not necessarily continuous or identical. Every invocation of *sruti* technically recited (or reopened) the event of originary "hearing" or revelation. The second two texts—the learned and the performed—were seen as dialectically continuous. Legal theorists and practitioners were not in any given case certain if this structure described the body of law or four ways of settling a dispute. The legitimation of the polymorphous structure of legal performance, "internally" noncoherent and open at both ends, through a binary vision, is the narrative of codification I offer as an example of epistemic violence.

The narrative of the stabilization and codification of Hindu law is less well known than the story of Indian education, so it might be well to start there.[30] Consider the often-quoted programmatic lines from Macaulay's infamous "Minute on Indian Education" (1835): "We must at present do our best to form a class who may be interpreters between us and the millions whom we govern; a class of persons, Indian in blood and colour but English in taste, in opinions, in morals, and in intellect. To that class we may leave it to refine the vernacular dialects of the country, to enrich those dialects with terms of science borrowed from the Western nomenclature, and to render them by degrees fit vehicles for conveying knowledge to the great mass of the population."[31] The education of colonial subjects complements their production in law. One effect of establishing a version of the British system was the development of an uneasy separation between disciplinary formation in Sanskrit studies and the native, now alternative tradition of Sanskrit "high culture." Within the former, the cultural explanations generated by authoritative scholars matched the epistemic violence of the legal project.

I locate here the founding of the Asiatic Society of Bengal in 1784, the Indian Institute at Oxford in 1883, and the analytic and taxonomic work of scholars like Arthur Macdonnell and Arthur Berriedale Keith, who were both colonial administrators and organizers of the matter of Sanskrit. From their confident utilitarian-hegemonic plans for students and scholars of Sanskrit, it is impossible to guess at either the aggressive repression of Sanskrit in the general educational framework or the increasing "feudalization" of the performative use of Sanskrit in the everyday life of Brahmanic-hegemonic India.[32] A version of history was gradually established in which the Brahmans were shown to have the same intentions as (thus providing the legitimation for) the codifying British: "In order to preserve Hindu society intact [the] successors [of the original Brahmans] had to reduce everything to writing and make them more and more rigid. And that is what has preserved Hindu society in spite of a succession of political upheavals and foreign invasions."[33] This is the 1925 verdict of Mahamahopadhyaya Haraprasad Shastri, learned Indian Sanskritist, a brilliant representative of the indigenous elite within colonial production, who was asked to write several chapters of a "History of Bengal" projected by the private secretary to the governor general of Bengal in 1916.[34] To signal the asymmetry in the relationship between authority and explanation (depending on the race-class of the authority), compare this 1928 remark by Edward Thompson, English intellectual: "Hinduism was what it seemed to be . . . It was a higher civilization that won [against it], both with Akbar and the English."[35] And add this, from a letter by an English soldier-scholar in the 1890s: "The study of Sanskrit, 'the language of the gods' has afforded me intense enjoyment during the last 25 years of my life in India, but it has not, I am thankful to say, led me, *as it has some,* to give up a hearty belief in our own grand religion."[36]

These authorities are *the very best* of the sources for the nonspecialist French intellectual's entry into the civilization of the Other.[37] I am, however, not referring to intellectuals and scholars of postcolonial production, like Shastri, when I say that the Other as Subject is inaccessible to Foucault and Deleuze. I am thinking of the general nonspecialist, nonacademic population across the class spectrum, for whom the episteme operates

282

its silent programming function. Without considering the map of exploitation, on what grid of "oppression" would they place this motley crew?

Let us now move to consider the margins (one can just as well say the silent, silenced center) of the circuit marked out by this epistemic violence, men and women among the illiterate peasantry, the tribals, the lowest strata of the urban subproletariat. According to Foucault and Deleuze (in the First World, under the standardization and regimentation of socialized capital, though they do not seem to recognize this) the oppressed, if given the chance (the problem of representation cannot be bypassed here), and on the way to solidarity through alliance politics (a Marxist thematic is at work here) *can speak and know their conditions.* We must now confront the following question: On the other side of the international division of labor from socialized capital, inside *and* outside the circuit of the epistemic violence of imperialist law and education supplementing an earlier economic text, *can the subaltern speak?*

Antonio Gramsci's work on the "subaltern classes" extends the class-position/class-consciousness argument isolated in *The Eighteenth Brumaire.* Perhaps because Gramsci criticizes the vanguardistic position of the Leninist intellectual, he is concerned with the intellectual's role in the subaltern's cultural and political movement into the hegemony. This movement must be made to determine the production of history as narrative (of truth). In texts such as "The Southern Question," Gramsci considers the movement of historical-political economy in Italy within what can be seen as an allegory of reading taken from or prefiguring an international division of labor.[38] Yet an account of the phased development of the subaltern is thrown out of joint when his cultural macrology is operated, however remotely, by the epistemic interference with legal and disciplinary definitions accompanying the imperialist project. When I move, at the end of this essay, to the question of woman as subaltern, I will suggest that the possibility of collectivity itself is persistently foreclosed through the manipulation of female agency.

The first part of my proposition—that the phased development of the subaltern is complicated by the imperialist project—is confronted by a collective of intellectuals who may be called the "Subaltern Studies" group.[39] They *must* ask, Can the subaltern speak? Here we are within Foucault's own discipline of history and with people who acknowledge his influence. Their project is to rethink Indian colonial historiography from the perspective of the discontinuous chain of peasant insurgencies during the colonial occupation. This is indeed the problem of "the permission to narrate" discussed by Said.[40] As Ranajit Guha argues,

> The historiography of Indian nationalism has for a long time been dominated by elitism—colonialist elitism and bourgeois-nationalist elitism . . . shar[ing] the prejudice that the making of the Indian nation and the development of the consciousness—nationalism—which confirmed this process were exclusively or predominantly elite achievements. In the colonialist and neo-colonialist historiographies these achievements are credited to British colonial rulers, administrators, policies, institutions, and culture; in the nationalist and

283

neo-nationalist writings—to Indian elite personalities, institutions, activities and ideas.[41]

Certain varieties of the Indian elite are at best native informants for first-world intellectuals interested in the voice of the Other. But one must nevertheless insist that the colonized subaltern *subject* is irretrievably heterogeneous.

Against the indigenous elite we may set what Guha calls "the *politics* of the people," both outside ("this was an *autonomous* domain, for it neither originated from elite politics nor did its existence depend on the latter") and inside ("it continued to operate vigorously in spite of [colonialism], adjusting itself to the conditions prevailing under the Raj and in many respects developing entirely new strains in both form and content") the circuit of colonial production.[42] I cannot entirely endorse this insistence on determinate vigor and full autonomy, for practical historiographic exigencies will not allow such endorsements to privilege subaltern consciousness. Against the possible charge that his approach is essentialist, Guha constructs a definition of the people (the place of that essence) that can be only an identity-in-differential. He proposes a dynamic stratification grid describing colonial social production at large. Even the third group on the list, the buffer group, as it were, between the people and the great macro-structural dominant groups, is itself defined as a place of in-betweenness, what Derrida has described as an *"antre"*:[43]

elite
1. Dominant foreign groups.
2. Dominant indigenous groups on the all-India level.
3. Dominant indigenous groups at the regional and local levels.
4. The terms "people" and "subaltern classes" have been used as synonymous throughout this note. The social groups and elements included in this category represent *the demographic difference between the total Indian population and all those whom we have described as the "elite."*

Consider the third item on this list—the *antre* of situational indeterminacy these careful historians presuppose as they grapple with the question, Can the subaltern speak? "*Taken as a whole and in the abstract* this ... category ... was *heterogeneous* in its composition and thanks to the uneven character of regional economic and social developments, *differed from area to area*. The same class or element which was dominant in one area ... could be among the dominated in another. This could and did create many ambiguities and contradictions in attitudes and alliances, especially among the lowest strata of the rural gentry, impoverished landlords, rich peasants and upper middle class peasants all of whom belonged, *ideally speaking*, to the category of people or subaltern classes."[44]

"The task of research" projected here is "to investigate, identify and measure the *specific* nature and degree of the *deviation* of [the] elements [constituting item 3] from the ideal and situate it historically." "Investigate, identify, and measure the specific": a program could hardly be more essen-

284

tialist and taxonomic. Yet a curious methodological imperative is at work. I have argued that, in the Foucault-Deleuze conversation, a postrepresentationalist vocabulary hides an essentialist agenda. In subaltern studies, because of the violence of imperialist epistemic, social, and disciplinary inscription, a project understood in essentialist terms must traffic in a radical textual practice of differences. The object of the group's investigation, in the case not even of the people as such but of the floating buffer zone of the regional elite-subaltern, is a *deviation* from an *ideal*—the people or subaltern—which is itself defined as a difference from the elite. It is toward this structure that the research is oriented, a predicament rather different from the self-diagnosed transparency of the first-world radical intellectual. What taxonomy can fix such a space? Whether or not they themselves perceive it—in fact Guha sees his definition of "the people" within the master-slave dialectic—their text articulates the difficult task of rewriting its own conditions of impossibility as the conditions of its possibility.

"At the regional and local levels [the dominant indigenous groups] ... if belonging to social strata hierarchically inferior to those of the dominant all-Indian groups *acted in the interests of the latter and not in conformity to interests corresponding truly to their own social being*." When these writers speak, in their essentializing language, of a gap between interest and action in the intermediate group, their conclusions are closer to Marx than to the self-conscious naivete of Deleuze's pronouncement on the issue. Guha, like Marx, speaks of interest in terms of the social rather than the libidinal being. The Name-of-the-Father imagery in *The Eighteenth Brumaire* can help to emphasize that, on the level of class or group action, "true correspondence to own being" is as artificial or social as the patronymic.

So much for the intermediate group marked in item 3. For the "true" subaltern group, whose identity is its difference, there is no unrepresentable subaltern subject that can know and speak itself; the intellectual's solution is not to abstain from representation. The problem is that the subject's itinerary has not been traced so as to offer an object of seduction to the representing intellectual. In the slightly dated language of the Indian group, the question becomes, How can we touch the consciousness of the people, even as we investigate their politics? With what voice-consciousness can the subaltern speak? Their project, after all, is to rewrite the development of the consciousness of the Indian nation. The planned discontinuity of imperialism rigorously distinguishes this project, however old-fashioned its articulation, from "rendering visible the medical and juridical mechanisms that surrounded the story [of Pierre Riviere]." Foucault is correct in suggesting that "to make visible the unseen can also mean a change of level, addressing oneself to a layer of material which had hitherto had no pertinence for history and which had not been recognized as having any moral, aesthetic or historical value." It is the slippage from rendering visible the mechanism to rendering vocal the individual, both avoiding "any kind of analysis of [the subject] whether psychological, psychoanalytical or linguistic," that is consistently troublesome (*PK*, 49-50).

The critique by Ajit K. Chaudhury, a West Bengali Marxist, of Guha's search for the subaltern consciousness can be seen as a moment of the production process that includes the subaltern. Chaudhury's perception that the Marxist view of the transformation of consciousness involves the (*knowledge*) of social relations seems to me, in principle, astute. Yet the heritage of the positivist ideology that has appropriated orthodox Marxism obliges him to add this rider: "This is not to belittle the importance of understanding peasants' consciousness or workers' consciousness *in its pure form*. This enriches our knowledge of the peasant and the worker and, possibly, throws light on how a particular mode takes on different forms in different regions, *which is considered a problem of second-order importance in classical Marxism*."[45]

This variety of "internationalist" Marxism, which believes in a pure, retrievable form of consciousness only to dismiss it, thus closing off what in Marx remain moments of productive bafflement, can at once be the object of Foucault's and Deleuze's rejection of Marxism *and* the source of the critical motivation of the Subaltern Studies group. All three are united in the assumption that there *is* a pure form of consciousness. On the French scene, there is a shuffling of signifiers: "the unconscious" or "the subject-in-oppression" clandestinely fills the space of "the pure form of consciousness." In orthodox "internationalist" intellectual Marxism, whether in the First World or the Third, the pure form of consciousness remains an idealistic bedrock which, dismissed as a second-order problem, often earns it the reputation of racism and sexism. In the Subaltern Studies group it needs development according to the unacknowledged terms of its own articulation.

For such an articulation, a developed theory of ideology can again be most useful. In a critique such as Chaudhury's, the association of "consciousness" with "knowledge" omits the crucial middle term of "ideological production": "Consciousness, according to Lenin, is associated with a *knowledge* of the interrelationships between different classes and groups; i.e., a knowledge of the materials that constitute society.... These definitions acquire a meaning only within the problematic within a definite knowledge object—to *understand* change in history, or specifically, change from one mode to another, *keeping the question of the specificity of a particular mode out of the focus*."[46]

Pierre Macherey provides the following formula for the interpretation of ideology: "What is important in a work is what it does not say. This is not the same as the careless notation 'what it refuses to say,' although that would in itself be interesting: a method might be built on it, with the task of *measuring silences*, whether acknowledged or unacknowledged. But rather this, what the work *cannot* say is important, because there the elaboration of the utterance is carried out, in a sort of journey to silence."[47] Macherey's ideas can be developed in directions he would be unlikely to follow. Even as he writes, ostensibly, of the literariness of the literature of European provenance, he articulates a method applicable to the social text of imperialism, somewhat against the grain of his own argument. Although the notion "what it refuses to say" might be careless for a literary work, something like a collective ideological *refusal* can be diagnosed for the codifying legal practice of imperialism. This would open the field for a political-economic and multidisciplinary ideological reinscription of the terrain. Because this is a "worlding of the world" on a second level of abstraction, a concept of refusal becomes plausible here. The archival, historiographic, disciplinary-critical, and, inevitably, interventionist work involved here is indeed a task of "measuring silences." This can be a description of "inves-

286

tigating, identifying, and measuring . . . the *deviation*" from an ideal that is irreducibly differential.

When we come to the concomitant question of the consciousness of the subaltern, the notion of what the work *cannot* say becomes important. In the semioses of the social text, elaborations of insurgency stand in the place of "the utterance." The sender—"the peasant"—is marked only as a pointer to an irretrievable consciousness. As for the receiver, we must ask who is "the real receiver" of an "insurgency?" The historian, transforming "insurgency" into "text for knowledge," is only one "receiver" of any collectively intended social act. With no possibility of nostalgia for that lost origin, the historian must suspend (as far as possible) the clamor of his or her own consciousness (or consciousness-effect, as operated by disciplinary training), so that the elaboration of the insurgency, packaged with an insurgent-consciousness, does not freeze into an "object of investigation," or, worse yet, a model for imitation. "The subject" implied by the texts of insurgency can only serve as a counterpossibility for the narrative sanctions granted to the colonial subject in the dominant groups. The postcolonial intellectuals learn that their privilege is their loss. In this they are a paradigm of the intellectuals.

It is well known that the notion of the feminine (rather than the subaltern of imperialism) has been used in a similar way within deconstructive criticism and within certain varieties of feminist criticism.[48] In the former case, a figure of "woman" is at issue, one whose minimal predication as indeterminate is already available to the phallocentric tradition. Subaltern historiography raises questions of method that would prevent it from using such a ruse. For the "figure" of woman, the relationship between woman and silence can be plotted by women themselves; race and class differences are subsumed under that charge. Subaltern historiography must confront the impossibility of such gestures. The narrow epistemic violence of imperialism gives us an imperfect allegory of the general violence that is the possibility of an episteme.[49]

Within the effaced itinerary of the subaltern subject, the track of sexual difference is doubly effaced. The question is not of female participation in insurgency, or the ground rules of the sexual division of labor, for both of which there is "evidence." It is, rather, that, both as object of colonialist historiography and as subject of insurgency, the ideological construction of gender keeps the male dominant. If, in the context of colonial production, the subaltern has no history and cannot speak, the subaltern as female is even more deeply in shadow.

The contemporary international division of labor is a displacement of the divided field of nineteenth-century territorial imperialism. Put simply, a group of countries, generally first-world, are in the position of investing capital; another group, generally third-world, provide the field for investment, both through the comprador indigenous capitalists and through their ill-protected and shifting labor force. In the interest of maintaining the circulation and growth of industrial capital (and of the concomitant task of administration within ninteenth-century territorial imperialism), transportation, law, and standardized education systems were developed—even as local industries were destroyed, land distribution was rearranged, and raw material was transferred to the colonizing country. With so-called decolonization, the growth of multinational capital, and the relief of the administrative charge, "development" does not now involve wholesale legislation and establishing educational *systems* in a comparable way. This impedes the growth of consumerism in the comprador countries. With modern telecommunications and the emergence of advanced capitalist economies at the two edges of Asia, maintaining the international division of labor serves to keep the supply of cheap labor in the comprador countries.

Human labor is not, of course, intrinsically "cheap" or "expensive." An absence of labor laws (or a discriminatory enforcement of them), a totalitarian state (often entailed by development and modernization in the periphery), and minimal subsistence requirements on the part of the worker will ensure it. To keep this crucial item intact, the urban proletariat in comprador countries must not be systematically trained in the ideology of consumerism (parading as the philosophy of a classless society) that, against all odds, prepares the ground for resistance through the coalition politics Foucault mentions (*FD,* 216). This separation from the ideology of consumerism is increasingly exacerbated by the proliferating phenomena of international subcontracting. "Under this strategy, manufacturers based in developed countries subcontract the most labor intensive stages of production, for example, sewing or assembly, to the Third World nations where labor is cheap. Once assembled, the multinational re-imports the goods— under generous tariff exemptions—to the developed country *instead of selling them to the local market.*" Here the link to training in consumerism is almost snapped. "While global recession has markedly slowed trade and investment worldwide since 1979, international subcontracting has boomed. . . . In these cases, multinationals are freer to resist militant workers, revolutionary upheavals, and even economic downturns."[50]

Class mobility is increasingly lethargic in the comprador theaters. Not surprisingly, some members of *indigenous dominant* groups in comprador countries, members of the local bourgeoisie, find the language of alliance politics attractive. Identifying with forms of resistance plausible in advanced capitalist countries is often of a piece with that elitist bent of bourgeois historiography described by Ranajit Guha.

Belief in the plausibility of global alliance politics is prevalent among women of dominant social groups interested in "international feminism" in the comprador countries. At the other end of the scale, those most separated from any possibility of an alliance among "women, prisoners, conscripted soldiers, hospital patients, and homosexuals" (*FD,* 216) are the females of the urban subproletariat. In their case, the denial and withholding of consumerism and the structure of exploitation is compounded by patriarchal social relations. On the other side of the international division of labor, the subject of exploitation cannot know and speak the text of female exploitation, even if the absurdity of the nonrepresenting intellectual making space for her to speak is achieved. The woman is doubly in shadow.

Yet even this does not encompass the heterogeneous Other. Outside (though not completely so) the circuit of the *international* division of labor, there are people whose consciousness we cannot grasp if we close off our benevolence by constructing a homogeneous Other referring only to our own place in the seat of the Same or the Self. Here are subsistence farmers, unorganized peasant labor, the tribals, and the communities of zero workers on the street or in the countryside. To confront them is not to represent

288

(vertreten) them but to learn to represent *(darstellen)* ourselves. This argument would take us into a critique of a disciplinary anthropology and the relationship between elementary pedagogy and disciplinary formation. It would also question the implicit demand, made by intellectuals who choose a "naturally articulate" subject of oppression, that such a subject come through history as a foreshortened mode-of-production narrative.

That Deleuze and Foucault ignore both the epistemic violence of imperialism and the international division of labor would matter less if they did not, in closing, touch on third-world issues. But in France it is impossible to ignore the problem of the *tiers monde,* the inhabitants of the erstwhile French African colonies. Deleuze limits his consideration of the Third World to these old local and regional indigenous elite who are, ideally, subaltern. In this context, references to the maintenance of the surplus army of labor fall into reverse-ethnic sentimentality. Since he is speaking of the heritage of nineteenth-century territorial imperialism, his reference is to the nation-state rather than the globalizing center: "French capitalism needs greatly a floating signifier of unemployment. In this perspective, we begin to see the unity of the forms of repression: restrictions on immigration, once it is acknowledged that the most difficult and thankless jobs go to immigrant workers; repression in the factories, because the French must reacquire the 'taste' for increasingly harder work; the struggle against youth and the repression of the educational system" (*FD,* 211-12). This is an acceptable analysis. Yet it shows again that the Third World can enter the resistance program of an alliance politics directed against a "*unified* repression" only when it is confined to the third-world groups that are directly accessible to the First World.[51] This benevolent first-world appropriation and reinscription of the Third World as an Other is the founding characteristic of much third-worldism in the U.S. human sciences today.

Foucault continues the critique of Marxism by invoking geographical discontinuity. The real mark of "geographical (geopolitical) discontinuity" is the international division of labor. But Foucault uses the term to distinguish between exploitation (extraction and appropriation of surplus value; read, the field of Marxist analysis) and domination ("power" studies) and to suggest the latter's greater potential for resistance based on alliance politics. He cannot acknowledge that such a monist and unified access to a conception of "power" (methodologically presupposing a Subject-of-power) is made possible by a certain stage in exploitation, for his vision of geographical discontinuity is geopolitically specific to the First World:

> This geographical discontinuity of which you speak might mean perhaps the following: as soon as we struggle against *exploitation,* the proletariat not only leads the struggle but also defines its targets, its methods, its places and its instruments; and to ally oneself with the proletariat is to consolidate with its positions, its ideology, it is to take up again the motives for their combat. This means total immersion [in the Marxist project]. But if it is against *power* that one struggles, then all those who acknowledge it as intolerable can begin the struggle wherever they find themselves and

in terms of their own activity (or passivity). In engaging in this struggle that is *their own,* whose objectives they clearly understand and whose methods they can determine, they enter into the revolutionary process. As allies of the proletariat, to be sure, because power is exercised the way it is in order to maintain capitalist exploitation. They genuinely serve the cause of the proletariat by fighting in those places where they find themselves oppressed. Women, prisoners, conscripted soldiers, hospital patients, and homosexuals have now begun a specific struggle against the particular form of power, the constraints and controls, that are exercised over them. (*FD,* 216)

This is an admirable program of localized resistance. Where possible, this model of resistance is not an alternative to, but can complement, macrological struggles along "Marxist" lines. Yet if its situation is universalized, it accommodates unacknowledged privileging of the subject. Without a theory of ideology, it can lead to a dangerous utopianism.

Foucault is a brilliant thinker of power-in-spacing, but the awareness of the topographical reinscription of imperialism does not inform his presuppositions. He is taken in by the restricted version of the West produced by that reinscription and thus helps to consolidate its effects. Notice the omission of the fact, in the following passage, that the new mechanism of power in the seventeenth and eighteenth centuries (the extraction of surplus value without extraeconomic coercion is its Marxist description) is secured *by means of* territorial imperialism—the Earth and its products— "elsewhere." The representation of sovereignty is crucial in those theaters: "In the seventeenth and eighteenth centuries, we have the production of an important phenomenon, the emergence, or rather the invention, of a new mechanism of power possessed of highly specific procedural techniques ... which is also, I believe, absolutely incompatible with the relations of sovereignty. This new mechanism of power is more dependent upon bodies and what they do than the Earth and its products" (*PK,* 104).

Because of a blind spot regarding the first wave of "geographical discontinuity," Foucault can remain impervious to its second wave in the middle decades of our own century, identifying it simply "with the collapse of Fascism and the decline of Stalinism" (*PK,* 87). Here is Mike Davis's alternative view: "It was rather the global logic of counter-revolutionary violence which created conditions for the peaceful economic interdependence of a chastened Atlantic imperialism under American leadership. ... It was multi-national military integration under the slogan of collective security against the USSR which preceded and quickened the interpenetration of the major capitalist economies, making possible the new era of commercial liberalism which flowered between 1958 and 1973."[52]

It is within the emergence of this "new mechanism of power" that we must read the fixation on national scenes, the resistance to economics, and the emphasis on concepts like power and desire that privilege micrology. Davis continues: "This quasi-absolutist centralization of strategic military power by the United States was to allow an enlightened and flexible subordinancy for its principal satraps. In particular, it proved highly accommodating to the residual imperialist pretensions of the French and British . . . with each keeping up a strident ideological mobilization against communism all the while." While taking precautions against such unitary notions as "France," it must be said that such unitary notions as "*the* workers' struggle," or such unitary pronouncements as "like power, resistance is multiple and can be integrated in global strategies" (*PK*, 142), seem interpretable by way of Davis's narrative. I am not suggesting, as does Paul Bové, that "for a displaced and homeless people [the Palestinians] assaulted militarily and culturally . . . a question [such as Foucault's 'to engage in politics . . . is to try to know with the greatest possible honesty whether the revolution is desirable'] is a foolish luxury of Western wealth."[53] I am suggesting, rather, that to buy a self-contained version of the West is to ignore its production by the imperialist project.

Sometimes it seems as if the very brilliance of Foucault's analysis of the centuries of European imperialism produces a miniature version of that heterogeneous phenomenon: management of space—but by doctors; development of administrations—but in asylums; considerations of the periphery—but in terms of the insane, prisoners, and children. The clinic, the asylum, the prison, the university—all seem to be screen-allegories that foreclose a reading of the broader narratives of imperialism. (One could open a similar discussion of the ferocious motif of "deterritorialization" in Deleuze and Guattari.) "One can perfectly well not talk about something because one doesn't know about it," Foucault might murmur (*PK*, 66). Yet we have already spoken of the sanctioned ignorance that every critic of imperialism must chart.

III

On the general level on which U.S. academics and students take "influence" from France, one encounters the following understanding: Foucault deals with real history, real politics, and real social problems; Derrida is inaccessible, esoteric, and textualistic. The reader is probably well acquainted with this received idea. "That [Derrida's] own work," Terry Eagleton writes, "has been grossly unhistorical, politically evasive and in practice oblivious to language as 'discourse' [language in function] is not to be denied."[54] Eagleton goes on to recommend Foucault's study of "discursive practices." Perry Anderson constructs a related history: "With Derrida, the self-cancellation of structuralism latent in the recourse to music or madness in Lévi-Strauss or Foucault is consummated. With no commitment to exploration of social realities at all, Derrida had little compunction in undoing the constructions of these two, convicting them both of a 'nostalgia of origins'—Rousseauesque or pre-Socratic, respectively—and asking what right either had to assume, on their own premises, the validity of their discourses."[55]

This paper is committed to the notion that, whether in defense of Derrida or not, a nostalgia for lost origins can be detrimental to the exploration of social realities within the critique of imperialism. Indeed, the brilliance of Anderson's misreading does not prevent him from seeing precisely the problem I emphasize in Foucault: "Foucault struck the characteristically prophetic note when he declared in 1966: 'Man is in the process of perishing as the being of language continues to shine ever more brightly upon our horizon.' But who is the 'we' to perceive or possess such a ho-

291

rizon?" Anderson does not see the encroachment of the unacknowledged Subject of the West in the later Foucault, a Subject that presides by disavowal. He sees Foucault's attitude in the usual way, as the disappearance of the knowing Subject as such; and he further sees in Derrida the final development of that tendency: "In the hollow of the pronoun [we] lies the aporia of the programme."[56] Consider, finally, Said's plangent aphorism, which betrays a profound misapprehension of the notion of "textuality": "Derrida's criticism moves us *into* the text, Foucault's *in* and *out*."[57]

I have tried to argue that the substantive concern for the politics of the oppressed which often accounts for Foucault's appeal can hide a privileging of the intellectual and of the "concrete" subject of oppression that, in fact, compounds the appeal. Conversely, though it is not my intention here to counter the specific view of Derrida promoted by these influential writers, I will discuss a few aspects of Derrida's work that retain a long-term usefulness for people outside the First World. This is not an apology. Derrida is hard to read; his real object of investigation is classical philosophy. Yet he is less dangerous when understood than the first-world intellectual masquerading as the absent nonrepresenter who lets the oppressed speak for themselves.

I will consider a chapter that Derrida composed twenty years ago: "Of Grammatology As a Positive Science" (*OG*, 74-93). In this chapter Derrida confronts the issue of whether "deconstruction" can lead to an adequate practice, whether critical or political. The question is how to keep the ethnocentric Subject from establishing itself by selectively defining an Other. This is not a program for the Subject as such; rather, it is a program for the benevolent *Western* intellectual. For those of us who feel that the "subject" has a history and that the task of the first-world subject of knowledge in our historical moment is to resist and critique "recognition" of the Third World through "assimilation," this specificity is crucial. In order to advance a factual rather than a pathetic critique of the European intellectual's ethnocentric impulse, Derrida admits that he cannot ask the "first" questions that must be answered to establish the grounds of his argument. He does not declare that grammatology can "rise above" (Frank Lentricchia's phrase) mere empiricism; for, like empiricism, it cannot ask first questions. Derrida thus aligns "grammatological" knowledge *with the same problems* as empirical investigation. "Deconstruction" is not, therefore, a new word for "ideological demystification." Like "empirical investigation ... tak[ing] shelter in the field of grammatological knowledge" obliges "operat[ing] through 'examples' " (*OG*, 75).

The examples Derrida lays out—to show the limits of grammatology as a positive science—come from the appropriate ideological self-justification of an imperialist project. In the European seventeenth century, he writes, there were three kinds of "prejudices" operating in histories of writing which constituted a "symptom of the crisis of European consciousness" (*OG*, 75): the "theological prejudice," the "Chinese prejudice," and the "hieroglyphist prejudice." The first can be indexed as: God wrote a primitive or natural script: Hebrew or Greek. The second: Chinese is a perfect *blueprint* for philosophical writing, but it is only a blueprint. True philosophical writing is "independen[t] with regard to history" (*OG*, 79) and will sublate Chinese into an easy-to-learn script that will supersede actual Chinese. The third: that Egyptian script is too sublime to be deciphered. The first prejudice preserves the "actuality" of Hebrew or Greek; the last two ("rational" and "mystical," respectively) collude to support the first, where the center of the logos is seen as the Judaeo-Christian God (the appropriation of the Hellenic Other through assimilation is an earlier story)—a "prejudice" still sustained in efforts to give the cartography of the Judaeo-Christian myth the status of geopolitical history:

> The concept of Chinese writing thus functioned as a sort of *European hallucination*. . . . This functioning obeyed a rigorous necessity. . . . It was not disturbed by the knowledge of Chinese script . . . which was then available. . . . A *"hieroglyphist prejudice"* had produced the same effect of *interested blindness*. Far from proceeding . . . from ethnocentric scorn, the occultation takes the form of an hyperbolical admiration. We have not finished demonstrating the necessity of this pattern. Our century is not free from it; each time that ethnocentrism is precipitately and ostentatiously reversed, some effort silently hides behind all the spectacular effects to *consolidate an inside* and to draw from it some domestic benefit. (*OG*, 80; Derrida italicizes only "hieroglyphist prejudice")

Derrida proceeds to offer two characteristic possibilities for solutions to the problem of the European Subject, which seeks to produce an Other that would consolidate an inside, its own subject status. What follows is an account of the complicity between writing, the opening of domestic and civil society, and the structures of desire, power, and capitalization. Derrida then discloses the vulnerability of his own desire to conserve something that is, paradoxically, both ineffable and nontranscendental. In critiquing the production of the colonial subject, this ineffable, nontranscendental ("historical") place is cathected by the subaltern subject.

Derrida closes the chapter by showing again that the project of grammatology is obliged to develop *within* the discourse of presence. It is not just a critique of presence but an awareness of the itinerary of the discourse of presence in one's *own* critique, a vigilance precisely against too great a claim for transparency. The word "writing" as the name of the object and model of grammatology is a practice "only within the *historical* closure, that is to say within the limits of science and philosophy" (*OG*, 93).

Derrida here makes Nietzschean, philosophical, and psychoanalytic, rather than specifically political, choices to suggest a critique of European ethnocentrism in the constitution of the Other. As a postcolonial intellectual, I am not troubled that he does not *lead* me (as Europeans inevitably seem to do) to the specific path that such a critique makes necessary. It is more important to me that, as a European philosopher, he articulates the *European* Subject's tendency to constitute the Other as marginal to ethnocentrism and locates *that* as the problem with all logocentric and therefore also all grammatological endeavors (since the main thesis of the chapter is the complicity between the two). *Not* a general problem, but a *European* problem. It is within the context of this ethnocentricism that he tries so desperately to demote the Subject of thinking or knowledge as to say that "*thought* is ... the blank part of the text" (*OG*, 93); that which is thought is, if blank, still *in the text* and must be consigned to the Other of history. That inaccessible blankness circumscribed by an interpretable text is what a postcolonial critic of imperialism would like to see developed within the European enclosure as *the* place of the production of theory. The postcolonial critics and intellectuals can attempt to displace their own production only by presupposing that *text-inscribed* blankness. To render thought or the thinking subject transparent or invisible seems, by contrast, to hide the relentless recognition of the Other by assimilation. It is in the interest of such cautions that Derrida does not invoke "letting the other(s) speak for himself" but rather invokes an "appeal" to or "call" to the "quite-other" (*tout-autre* as opposed to a self-consolidating other), of "rendering *delirious* that interior voice that is the voice of the other in us."[58]

Derrida calls the ethnocentrism of the European science of writing in the late seventeenth and early eighteenth centuries a symptom of the general crisis of European consciousness. It is, of course, part of a greater symptom, or perhaps the crisis itself, the slow turn from feudalism to capitalism via the first waves of capitalist imperialism. The itinerary of recognition through assimilation of the Other can be more interestingly traced, it seems to me, in the imperialist constitution of the colonial subject than in repeated incursions into psychoanalysis or the "figure" of woman, though the importance of these two interventions *within* deconstruction should not be minimized. Derrida has not moved (or perhaps cannot move) into that arena.

Whatever the reasons for this specific absence, what I find useful is the sustained and developing work on the *mechanics* of the constitution of the Other; we can use it to much greater analytic and interventionist advantage than invocations of the *authenticity* of the Other. On this level, what remains useful in Foucault is the mechanics of disciplinarization and institutionalization, the constitution, as it were, of the colonizer. Foucault does not relate it to any version, early or late, proto- or post-, of imperialism. They are of great usefulness to intellectuals concerned with the decay of the West. Their seduction for them, and fearfulness for us, is that they might allow the complicity of the investigating subject (male or female professional) to disguise itself in transparency.

IV

Can the subaltern speak? What must the elite do to watch out for the continuing construction of the subaltern? The question of "woman" seems most problematic in this context. Clearly, if you are poor, black, and female you get it in three ways. If, however, this formulation is moved from the first-world context into the postcolonial (which is not identical with the third-world) context, the description "black" or "of color" loses persuasive significance. The necessary stratification of colonial subject-constitution in the first phase of capitalist imperialism makes "color" useless as an emancipatory signifier. Confronted by the ferocious standardizing benevolence of most U.S. and Western European human-scientific radicalism (recognition by assimilation), the progressive though heterogeneous withdrawal of consumerism in the comprador periphery, and the exclusion of the margins of even the center-periphery articulation (the "true and differential subaltern"), the analogue of class-consciousness rather than race-consciousness in this area seems historically, disciplinarily, and practically forbidden by Right and Left alike. It is not just a question of a *double* displacement, as it is not simply the problem of finding a psychoanalytic allegory that can accommodate the third-world woman with the first.

The cautions I have just expressed are valid only if we are speaking of the subaltern woman's consciousness—or, more acceptably, subject. Reporting on, or better still, participating in, antisexist work among women of color or women in class oppression in the First World or the Third World is undeniably on the agenda. We should also welcome all the information retrieval in these silenced areas that is taking place in anthropology, political science, history, and sociology. Yet the assumption and construction of a consciousness or subject sustains such work and will, in the long run, cohere with the work of imperialist subject-constitution, mingling epistemic violence with the advancement of learning and civilization. And the subaltern woman will be as mute as ever.[59]

In so fraught a field, it is not easy to ask the question of the consciousness of the subaltern woman; it is thus all the more necessary to remind pragmatic radicals that such a question is not an idealist red herring. Though all feminist or antisexist projects cannot be reduced to this one, to ignore it is an unacknowledged political gesture that has a long history and collaborates with a masculine radicalism that renders the place of the investigator transparent. In seeking to learn to speak to (rather than listen to or speak for) the historically muted subject of the subaltern woman, the postcolonial intellectual *systematically* "unlearns" female privilege. This systematic unlearning involves learning to critique postcolonial discourse with the best tools it can provide and not simply substituting the lost figure of the colonized. Thus, to question the unquestioned muting of the subaltern woman even within the anti-imperialist project of subaltern studies is not, as Jonathan Culler suggests, to "produce difference by differing" or to "appeal . . . to a sexual identity defined as essential and privilege experiences associated with that identity."[60]

Culler's version of the feminist project is possible within what Elizabeth Fox-Genovese has called "the contribution of the bourgeois-democratic revolutions to the social and political individualism of women."[61] Many of us were obliged to understand the feminist project as Culler now describes it when we were still agitating as U.S. academics.[62] It was certainly a necessary stage in my own education in "unlearning" and has consolidated the belief that the mainstream project of Western feminism both continues and displaces the battle over the right to individualism between women and men in situations of upward class mobility. One suspects that the debate between U.S. feminism and European "theory" (as theory is generally represented by women from the United States or Britain) occupies a significant corner of that very terrain. I am generally sympathetic with the call to make U.S. feminism more "theoretical." It seems, however, that the problem of the muted subject of the subaltern woman, though not solved by an "essentialist" search for lost origins, cannot be served by the call for more theory in Anglo-America either.

That call is often given in the name of a critique of "positivism," which is seen here as identical with "essentialism." Yet Hegel, the modern inaugurator of "the work of the negative," was not a stranger to the notion of essences. For Marx, the curious persistence of essentialism within the dialectic was a profound and productive problem. Thus, the stringent binary opposition between positivism/essentialism (read, U.S.) and "theory" (read, French or Franco-German via Anglo-American) may be spurious. Apart from repressing the ambiguous complicity between essentialism and critiques of positivism (acknowledged by Derrida in "Of Grammatology As a Positive Science"), it also errs by implying that positivism is not a theory. This move allows the emergence of a proper name, a positive essence, Theory. Once again, the position of the investigator remains unquestioned. And, if this territorial debate turns toward the Third World, no change in the question of method is to be discerned. This debate cannot take into account that, in the case of the woman as subaltern, no ingredients for the constitution of the itinerary of the trace of a sexed subject can be gathered to locate the possibility of dissemination.

Yet I remain generally sympathetic in aligning feminism with the critique of positivism and the defetishization of the concrete. I am also far from averse to learning from the work of Western theorists, though I have learned to insist on marking their positionality as investigating subjects. Given these conditions, and as a literary critic, I tactically confronted the immense problem of the consciousness of the woman as subaltern. I reinvented the problem in a sentence and transformed it into the object of a simple semiosis. What does this sentence mean? The analogy here is between the ideological victimization of a Freud and the positionality of the postcolonial intellectual as investigating subject.

As Sarah Kofman has shown, the deep ambiguity of Freud's use of women as a scapegoat is a reaction-formation to an initial and continuing desire to give the hysteric a voice, to transform her into the *subject* of hysteria.[63] The masculine-imperialist ideological formation that shaped that desire into "the daughter's seduction" is part of the same formation that constructs the monolithic "third-world woman." As a postcolonial intellectual, I am influenced by that formation as well. Part of our "unlearning" project is to articulate that ideological formation—by *measuring* silences, if necessary—into the *object* of investigation. Thus, when confronted with the questions, Can the subaltern speak? and Can the subaltern (as woman) speak?, our efforts to give the subaltern a voice in history will be doubly open to the dangers run by Freud's discourse. As a product of these considerations, I have put together the sentence "White men are saving brown women from brown men" in a spirit not unlike the one to be encountered in Freud's investigations of the sentence "A child is being beaten."[64]

The use of Freud here does not imply an isomorphic analogy between subject-formation and the behavior of social collectives, a frequent practice, often accompanied by a reference to Reich, in the conversation between Deleuze and Foucault. So I am not suggesting that "White men are saving brown women from brown men" is a sentence indicating a *collective* fantasy symptomatic of a *collective* itinerary of sadomasochistic repression in a *collective* imperialist enterprise. There is a satisfying symmetry in such an allegory, but I would rather invite the reader to consider it a problem in "wild psychoanalysis" than a clinching solution.[65] Just as Freud's insistence on making the woman the scapegoat in "A child is being beaten" and elsewhere discloses his political interests, however imperfectly, so my insistence on imperialist subject-production as the occasion for this sentence discloses my politics.

Further, I am attempting to borrow the general methodological aura of Freud's strategy toward the sentence he constructed *as a sentence* out of the many similar substantive accounts his patients gave him. This does not mean I will offer a case of transference-in-analysis as an isomorphic model for the transaction between reader and text (my sentence). The analogy between transference and literary criticism or historiography is no more than a productive catachresis. To say that the subject is a text does not authorize the converse pronouncement: the verbal text is a subject.

I am fascinated, rather, by how Freud predicates a *history* of repression that produces the final sentence. It is a history with a double origin, one hidden in the amnesia of the infant, the other lodged in our archaic past, assuming by implication a preoriginary space where human and animal were not yet differentiated.[66] We are driven to impose a homologue of this Freudian strategy on the Marxist narrative to explain the ideological dissimulation of imperialist political economy and outline a history of repression that produces a sentence like the one I have sketched. This history also has a double origin, one hidden in the maneuverings behind the British abolition of widow sacrifice in 1829,[67] the other lodged in the classical and Vedic past of Hindu India, the *Rg-Veda* and the *Dharmasastra*. No doubt there is also an undifferentiated preoriginary space that supports this history.

The sentence I have constructed is one among many displacements describing the relationship between brown and white men (sometimes brown and white women worked in). It takes its place among some sentences of "hyperbolic admiration" or of pious guilt that Derrida speaks of in connection with the "hieroglyphist prejudice." The relationship between the imperialist subject and the subject of imperialism is at least ambiguous.

The Hindu widow ascends the pyre of the dead husband and immolates herself upon it. This is widow sacrifice. (The conventional transcription of the Sanskrit word for the widow would be *sati*. The early colonial British transcribed it *suttee*.) The rite was not practiced universally and was not caste- or class-fixed. The abolition of this rite by the British has been generally understood as a case of "White men saving brown women from brown men." White women—from the nineteenth-century British Missionary Registers to Mary Daly—have not produced an alternative understanding. Against this is the Indian nativist argument, a parody of the nostalgia for lost origins: "The women actually wanted to die."

The two sentences go a long way to legitimize each other. One never encounters the testimony of the women's voice-consciousness. Such a testimony would not be ideology-transcendent or "fully" subjective, of course, but it would have constituted the ingredients for producing a countersentence. As one goes down the grotesquely mistranscribed names of these women, the sacrificed widows, in the police reports included in the records of the East India Company, one cannot put together a "voice." The most one can sense is the immense heterogeneity breaking through even such a skeletal and ignorant account (castes, for example, are regularly described as tribes). Faced with the dialectically interlocking sentences that are constructible as "White men are saving brown women from brown men" and "The women wanted to die," the postcolonial woman intellectual asks the question of simple semiosis—What does this mean?—and begins to plot a history.

To mark the moment when not only a civil but a good society is born out of domestic confusion, singular events that break the letter of the law to instill its spirit are often invoked. The protection of women by men often provides such an event. If we remember that the British boasted of their absolute equity toward and noninterference with native custom/law, an invocation of this sanctioned transgression of the letter for the sake of the spirit may be read in J. M. Derrett's remark: "The very first legislation upon Hindu Law was carried through without the assent of a single Hindu." The legislation is not named here. The next sentence, where the measure is named, is equally interesting if one considers the implications of the survival of a colonially established "good" society after decolonization: "The recurrence of *sati* in independent India is probably an obscurantist revival which cannot long survive even in a very backward part of the country."[68]

Whether this observation is correct or not, what interests me is that the protection of woman (today the "third-world woman") becomes a signifier for the establishment of a *good* society which must, at such inaugurative moments, transgress mere legality, or equity of legal policy. In this particular case, the process also allowed the redefinition as a crime of what had been tolerated, known, or adulated as ritual. In other words, this one item in Hindu law jumped the frontier between the private and the public domain.

Although Foucault's *historical narrative,* focusing solely on Western Europe, sees merely a tolerance for the criminal antedating the development of criminology in the late eighteenth century (*PK,* 41), his *theoretical description* of the "episteme" is pertinent here: "The *episteme* is the 'apparatus' which makes possible the separation not of the true from the false, but of what may not be characterized as scientific" (*PK,* 197)—ritual as opposed to crime, the one fixed by superstition, the other by legal science.

The leap of *suttee* from private to public has a clear and complex relationship with the changeover from a mercantile and commercial to a territorial and administrative British presence; it can be followed in correspondence among the police stations, the lower and higher courts, the courts of directors, the prince regent's court, and the like. (It is interesting to note that, from the point of view of the native "colonial subject," also emergent from the feudalism-capitalism transition, *sati* is a signifier with the reverse social charge: "Groups rendered psychologically marginal by their exposure to Western impact . . . had come under pressure to demonstrate, to others as well as to themselves, their ritual purity and allegiance to traditional high culture. To many of them *sati* became an important proof of their conformity to older norms at a time when these norms had become shaky within."[69])

If this is the first historical origin of my sentence, it is evidently lost in the history of humankind as work, the story of capitalist expansion, the slow freeing of labor power as commodity, that narrative of the modes of production, the transition from feudalism via mercantilism to capitalism. Yet the precarious normativity of this narrative is sustained by the putatively changeless stopgap of the "Asiatic" mode of production, which steps in to sustain it whenever it might become apparent that the story of capital logic is the story of the West, that imperialism establishes the universality of the mode of production narrative, that to ignore the subaltern today is, willy-nilly, to continue the imperialist project. The origin of my sentence is thus lost in the shuffle between other, more powerful discourses. Given that the abolition of *sati* was in itself admirable, is it still possible to wonder if a perception of the origin of my sentence might contain interventionist possibilities?

Imperialism's image as the establisher of the good society is marked by the espousal of the woman as *object* of protection from her own kind. How should one examine the dissimulation of patriarchal strategy, which apparently grants the woman free choice as *subject?* In other words, how does one make the move from "Britain" to "Hinduism"? Even the attempt shows that imperialism is not identical with chromatism, or mere prejudice against people of color. To approach this question, I will touch briefly on the *Dharmaśāstra* (the sustaining scriptures) and the *Rg-Veda* (Praise Knowledge). They represent the archaic origin in my homology of Freud. Of course, my treatment is not exhaustive. My readings are, rather, an interested and inexpert examination, by a postcolonial woman, of the fabrication of repression, a constructed counternarrative of woman's consciousness, thus woman's being, thus woman's being good, thus the good woman's desire, thus woman's desire. Paradoxically, at the same time we witness the unfixed place of woman as a signifier in the inscription of the social individual.

The two moments in the *Dharmaśāstra* that I am interested in are the discourse on sanctioned suicides and the nature of the rites for the dead.[70] Framed in these two discourses, the self-immolation of widows seems an exception to the rule. The general scriptural doctrine is that suicide is reprehensible. Room is made, however, for certain forms of suicide which, as formulaic performance, lose the phenomenal identity of being suicide. The first category of sanctioned suicides arises out of *tatvajñāna,* or the knowledge of truth. Here the knowing subject comprehends the insubstantiality or mere phenomenality (which may be the same thing as nonphenomenality) of its identity. At a certain point in time, *tat tva* was interpreted as "that you," but even without that, *tatva* is thatness or quiddity. Thus, this enlightened self truly knows the "that"-ness of its identity. Its demolition of that identity is not *ātmaghāta* (a killing of the self). The paradox of knowing of the limits of knowledge is that the strongest assertion of agency, to negate the possibility of agency, cannot be an example of itself. Curiously enough, the self-*sacrifice* of gods is sanctioned by natural ecology, useful for the working of the economy of Nature and the Universe, rather than by self-knowledge. In this *logically* anterior stage, inhabited by gods rather than human beings, of this particular chain of displacements, suicide and sacrifice *(ātmaghāta* and *ātmadāna)* seem as little distinct as an "interior" (self-knowledge) and an "exterior" (ecology) sanction.

This philosophical space, however, does not accommodate the self-immolating woman. For her we look where room is made to sanction suicides that cannot claim truth-knowledge as a state that is, at any rate, easily verifiable and belongs in the area of *sruti* (what was heard) rather than *smirti* (what is remembered). This exception to the general rule about suicide annuls the phenomenal identity of self-immolation if performed in certain places rather than in a certain state of enlightenment. Thus, we move from an interior sanction (truth-knowledge) to an exterior one (place of pilgrimage). It is possible for a woman to perform *this* type of (non)suicide.[71]

299

Yet even this is not the *proper* place for the woman to annul the proper name of suicide through the destruction of her proper self. For her alone is sanctioned self-immolation on a dead spouse's pyre. (The few male examples cited in Hindu antiquity of self-immolation on another's pyre, being proofs of enthusiasm and devotion to a master or superior, reveal the structure of domination within the rite). This suicide that is not suicide may be read as a *simulacrum* of both truth-knowledge and piety of place. If the former, it is as if the knowledge *in a subject* of its own insubstantiality and mere phenomenality is dramatized so that the dead husband becomes the exteriorized *example* and *place* of the extinguished subject and the widow becomes the (non)agent who "acts it out." If the latter, it is as if the metonym for all sacred places is now that burning bed of wood, constructed by elaborate ritual, where the woman's subject, legally displaced from herself, is being consumed. It is in terms of this profound ideology of the displaced place of the female subject that the paradox of free choice comes into play. For the male subject, it is the felicity of the suicide, a felicity that will annul rather than establish its status as such, that is noted. For the female subject, a sanctioned self-immolation, even as it takes away the effect of "fall" *(pātaka)* attached to an unsanctioned suicide, brings praise for the act of choice on another register. By the inexorable ideological production of the sexed subject, such a death can be understood by the female subject as an *exceptional* signifier of her own desire, exceeding the general rule for a widow's conduct.

In certain periods and areas this exceptional rule became the general rule in a class-specific way. Ashis Nandy relates its marked prevalence in eighteenth- and early nineteenth-century Bengal to factors ranging from population control to communal misogyny.[72] Certainly its prevalence there in the previous centuries was because in Bengal, unlike elsewhere in India, widows could inherit property. Thus, what the British see as poor victimized women going to the slaughter is in fact an ideological battleground. As P. V. Kane, the great historian of the *Dharmaśāstra,* has correctly observed: "In Bengal, [the fact that] the widow of a sonless member even in a joint Hindu family is entitled to practically the same rights over joint family property which her deceased husband would have had . . . must have frequently induced the surviving members to get rid of the widow by appealing at a most distressing hour to her devotion to and love for her husband" (*HD* II.2, 635).

Yet benevolent and enlightened males were and are sympathetic with the "courage" of the woman's free choice in the matter. They thus accept the production of the sexed subaltern subject: "Modern India does not justify the practice of *sati,* but it is a warped mentality that rebukes modern Indians for expressing admiration and reverence for the cool and unfaltering courage of Indian women in becoming *satis* or performing the *jauhar* for cherishing their ideals of womanly conduct" (*HD* II.2, 636). What Jean-Francois Lyotard has termed the *"différend,"* the inacessibility of, or untranslatability from, one mode of discourse in a dispute to another, is vividly illustrated here.[73] As the discourse of what the British perceive as heathen ritual is sublated (but not, Lyotard would argue, translated) into what the British perceive as crime, one diagnosis of female free will is substituted for another.

300

Of course, the self-immolation of widows was not *invariable* ritual prescription. If, however, the widow does decide thus to exceed the letter of ritual, to turn back is a transgression for which a particular type of penance is prescribed.[74] With the local British police officer supervising the immolation, to be dissuaded after a decision was, by contrast, a mark of real free choice, a choice of freedom. The ambiguity of the position of the indigenous colonial elite is disclosed in the nationalistic romanticization of the purity, strength, and love of these self-sacrificing women. The two set pieces are Rabindranath Tagore's paean to the "self-renouncing paternal grandmothers of Bengal" and Ananda Coomaraswamy's eulogy of *suttee* as "this last proof of the perfect unity of body and soul."[75]

Obviously I am not advocating the killing of widows. I am suggesting that, within the two contending versions of freedom, the constitution of the female subject *in life* is the place of the *différend*. In the case of widow self-immolation, ritual is not being redefined as superstition but as *crime*. The gravity of *sati* was that it was ideologically cathected as "reward," just as the gravity of imperialism was that it was ideologically cathected as "social mission." Thompson's understanding of *sati* as "punishment" is thus far off the mark:

> It may seem unjust and illogical that the Moguls, who freely impaled and flayed alive, or nationals of Europe, whose countries had such ferocious penal codes and had known, scarcely a century before suttee began to shock the English conscience, orgies of witch-burning and religious persecution, should have felt as they did about suttee. But the differences seemed to them this— the victims of their cruelties were tortured by a law which considered them offenders, whereas the victims of suttee were punished for no offense but the physical weakness which had placed them at man's mercy. The rite seemed to prove a depravity and arrogance such as no other human offense had brought to light.[76]

All through the mid- and late-eighteenth century, in the spirit of the codification of the law, the British in India collaborated and consulted with learned Brahmans to judge whether *suttee* was legal by their homogenized version of Hindu law. The collaboration was often idiosyncratic, as in the case of the significance of being dissuaded. Sometimes, as in the general Sāstric prohibition against the immolation of widows with small children, the British collaboration seems confused.[77] In the beginning of the nineteenth century, the British authorities, and especially the British in England, repeatedly suggested that collaboration made it appear as if the British condoned this practice. When the law was finally written, the history of the long period of collaboration was effaced, and the language celebrated the noble Hindu who was against the bad Hindu, the latter given to savage atrocities:

> The practice of Suttee . . . is revolting to the feeling of human nature. . . . In many instances, acts of atrocity have been perpetrated, which have been shocking to

the Hindoos themselves. . . . Actuated by these considerations the Governor-General in Council, without intending to depart from one of the first and most important principles of the system of British Government in India that all classes of the people be secure in the observance of their religious usages, so long as that system can be adhered to without violation of the paramount dictates of justice and humanity, has deemed it right to establish the following rules. . . .) (*HD* II.2, 624-25)

That this was an alternative ideology of the graded sanctioning of suicide as exception, rather than its inscription as sin, was of course not understood. Perhaps *sati* should have been read with martyrdom, with the defunct husband standing in for the transcendental One; or with war, with the husband standing in for sovereign or state, for whose sake an intoxicating ideology of self-sacrifice can be mobilized. In actuality, it was categorized with murder, infanticide, and the lethal exposure of the very old. The dubious place of the free will of the constituted sexed subject as female was sucessfully effaced. There is no itinerary we can retrace here. Since the other sanctioned suicides did not involve the scene of this constitution, they entered neither the ideological battleground at the archaic origin—the tradition of the *Dharmasāstra*—nor the scene of the reinscription of ritual as crime—the British abolition. The only related transformation was Mahatma Gandhi's reinscription of the notion of *satyāgraha,* or hunger strike, as resistance. But this is not the place to discuss the details of that sea-change. I would merely invite the reader to compare the auras of widow sacrifice and Gandhian resistance. The root in the first part of *satyāgraha* and *sati* are the same.

Since the beginning of the Puranic era (ca. A.D. 400), learned Brahmans debated the doctrinal appropriateness of *sati* as of sanctioned suicides in sacred places in general. (This debate still continues in an academic way.) Sometimes the cast provenance of the practice was in question. The general law for widows, that they should observe *brahmacarya,* was, however, hardly ever debated. It is not enough to translate *brahmacarya* as "celibacy." It should be recognized that, of the four ages of being in Hindu (or Brahmanical) *regulative* psychobiography, *brahmacarya* is the social practice anterior to the kinship inscription of marriage. The man—widower or husband—graduates through *vānaprastha* (forest life) into the mature celibacy and renunciation of *samnyāsa* (laying aside).[78] The woman as wife is indispensable for *gārhasthya,* or householdership, and may accompany her husband into forest life. She has no access (according to Brahmanical sanction) to the final celibacy of asceticism, or *samnyāsa.* The woman as widow, by the general law of sacred doctrine, must regress to an anteriority transformed into stasis. The institutional evils attendant upon this law are well known; I am considering its asymmetrical effect on the ideological formation of the sexed subject. It is thus of much greater significance that there was no debate on this nonexceptional fate of widows—either among Hindus or between Hindus and British—than that the *exceptional* prescription of self-immolation was actively contended.[79] Here the possibility of

302

recovering a (sexually) subaltern subject is once again lost and overdetermined.

This legally programmed asymmetry in the status of the subject, which effectively defines the woman as object of *one* husband, obviously operates in the interest of the legally symmetrical subject-status of the male. The self-immolation of the widow thereby becomes the extreme case of the general law rather than an exception to it. It is not surprising, then, to read of heavenly rewards for the *sati,* where the quality of being the object of a unique possessor is emphasized by way of rivalry with other females, those ecstatic heavenly dancers, paragons of female beauty and male pleasure who sing her praise: "In heaven she, being soley devoted to her husband, and praised by groups of *apsarās* [heavenly dancers], sports with her husband as long as fourteen Indras rule" (*HD* II.2, 631).

The profound irony in locating the woman's free will in self-immolation is once again revealed in a verse accompanying the earlier passage: "As long as the woman [as wife: *stri*] does not burn herself in fire on the death of her husband, she is never released [*mucyate*] from her female body [*strisarīr*—i.e., in the cycle of births]." Even as it operates the most subtle general release from individual agency, the sanctioned suicide peculiar to woman draws its ideological strength by *identifying* individual agency with the supraindividual: kill yourself on your husband's pyre now, and you may kill your female body in the entire cycle of birth.

In a further twist of the paradox, this emphasis on free will establishes the peculiar misfortune of holding a female body. The word for the self that is actually burned is the standard word for spirit in the noblest sense *(ātman),* while the verb "release," through the root for salvation in the noblest sense *(muc → moska)* is in the passive *(mocyate),* and the word for that which is annulled in the cycle of birth is the everyday word for the body. The ideological message writes itself in the benevolent twentieth-century male historian's admiration: "The Jauhar [group self-immolation of aristocratic Rajput war-widows or imminent war-widows] practiced by the Rajput ladies of Chitor and other places for saving themselves from unspeakable atrocities at the hands of the victorious Moslems are too well known to need any lengthy notice" (*HD* II.2, 629).

Although *jauhar* is not, strictly speaking, an act of *sati,* and although I do not wish to speak for the sanctioned sexual violence of conquering male armies, "Moslem" or otherwise, female self-immolation in the face of it is a legitimation of rape as "natural" and works, in the long run, in the interest of unique genital possession of the female. The group rape perpetrated by the conquerors is a metonymic celebration of territorial acquisition. Just as the general law for widows was unquestioned, so this act of female heroism persists among the patriotic tales told to children, thus operating on the crudest level of ideological reproduction. It has also played a tremendous role, precisely as an overdetermined signifier, in acting out Hindu communalism. Simultaneously, the broader question of the constitution of the sexed subject is hidden by foregrounding the visible violence of *sati.* The task of recovering a (sexually) subaltern subject is lost in an institutional textuality at the archaic origin.

As I mentioned above, when the status of the legal subject as property-holder could be temporarily bestowed on the *female* relict, the self-immolation of widows was stringently enforced. Raghunandana, the late fifteenth-/sixteenth-century legalist whose interpretations are supposed to lend the greatest authority to such enforcement, takes as his text a curious passage from the *Rg-Veda,* the most ancient of the Hindu sacred texts, the first of the *Srutis.* In doing so, he is following a centuries-old tradition, commemorating a peculiar and transparent misreading at the very place of sanction. Here is the verse outlining certain steps within the rites for the dead. Even at a simple reading it is clear that it is "not addressed to widows at all, but to ladies of the deceased man's household whose husbands were living." Why then was it taken as authoritative? This, the unemphatic transposition of the dead for the living husband, is a different order of mystery at the archaic origin from the ones we have been discussing: "Let these whose husbands are worthy and are living enter the house with clarified butter in their eyes. Let these wives first step into the house, tearless, healthy, and well adorned" (*HD* II.2, 634). But this crucial transposition is not the only mistake here. The authority is lodged in a disputed passage and an alternate reading. In the second line, here translated "Let these wives first step into the house," the word for first is *agré.* Some have read it as *agné,* "O fire." As Kane makes clear, however, "even without this change Apararka and others rely for the practice of *Sati* on this verse" (*HD* IV.2, 199). Here is another screen around one origin of the history of the subaltern female subject. Is it a historical oneirocritique that one should perform on a statement such as: "Therefore it must be admitted that either the MSS are corrupt or Raghunandana committed an innocent slip" (*HD* II.2, 634)? It should be mentioned that the rest of the poem is either about that general law of *brahmacarya*-in-stasis for widows, to which *sati* is an exception, or about *niyoga*—"appointing a brother or any near kinsman to raise up issue to a deceased husband by marrying his widow."[80]

If P. V. Kane is the authority on the history of the *Dharmasāstra,* Mulla's *Principles of Hindu Law* is the practical guide. It is part of the historical text of what Freud calls "kettle logic" that we are unraveling here, that Mulla's textbook adduces, just as definitively, that the *Rg-Vedic* verse under consideration was proof that "remarriage of widows and divorce are recognized in some of the old texts."[81]

One cannot help but wonder about the role of the word *yonī.* In context, with the localizing adverb *agré* (in front), the word means "dwelling-place." But that does not efface its primary sense of "genital" (not yet perhaps specifically *female* genital). How can we take as the authority for the choice of a widow's self-immolation a passage celebrating the entry of adorned wives into a dwelling place invoked on this occasion by its *yonī*-name, so that the extracontextual icon is almost one of entry into civic production or birth? Paradoxically, the imagic relationship of vagina and fire lends a kind of strength to the authority-claim.[82] This paradox is strengthened by Raghunandana's modification of the verse so as to read, "Let them first ascend the *fluid* abode [or origin, with, of course, the *yonī*-name—*a rōhantu jalayōnimagné*], O fire [or of fire]." Why should one accept that this "probably mean[s] 'may fire be to them as cool as water' " (*HD* II.2, 634)? The fluid genital of fire, a corrupt phrasing, might figure a sexual indeterminancy providing a simulacrum for the intellectual indeterminacy of *tattvajnāna* (truth-knowledge).

I have written above of a constructed counternarrative of woman's consciousness, thus woman's being, thus woman's being good, thus the good woman's desire, thus woman's desire. This slippage can be seen in the fracture inscribed in the very word *sati,* the feminine form of *sat. Sat* transcends any gender-specific notion of masculinity and moves up not only into human but spiritual universality. It is the present participle of the verb "to be" and as such means not only being but the True, the Good, the Right. In the sacred texts it is essence, universal spirit. Even as a prefix it indicates appropriate, felicitous, fit. It is noble enough to have entered the most privileged discourse of modern Western philosophy: Heidegger's meditation on Being.[83] *Sati,* the feminine of this word, simply means "good wife."

It is now time to disclose that *sati* or *suttee* as the proper name of the rite of widow self-immolation commemorates a grammatical error on the part of the British, quite as the nomenclature "American Indian" commemorates a factual error on the part of Columbus. The word in the various Indian languages is "the burning of the *sati*" or the good wife, who thus escapes the regressive stasis of the widow in *brahmacrya.* This exemplifies the race-class-gender overdeterminations of the situation. It can perhaps be caught even when it is flattened out: white men, seeking to save brown women from brown men, impose upon those women a greater ideological constriction by absolutely identifying, *within discursive practice,* good-wifehood with self-immolation on the husband's pyre. On the other side of thus constituting the *object,* the abolition (or removal) of which will provide the occasion for establishing a good, as distinguished from merely civil, society, is the Hindu manipulation of female *subject*-constitution which I have tried to discuss.

(I have already mentioned Edward Thompson's *Suttee,* published in 1928. I cannot do justice here to this perfect specimen of the justification of imperialism as a civilizing mission. Nowhere in his book, written by someone who avowedly "loves India," is there any questioning of the "beneficial ruthlessness" of the British in India as motivated by territorial expansionism or management of industrial capital.[84] The problem with his book is, indeed, a problem of representation, the construction of a continuous and homogeneous "India" in terms of heads of state and British administrators, from the perspective of "a man of good sense" who would be the transparent voice of reasonable humanity. "India" can then be represented, in the other sense, by its imperial masters. The reason for referring to *suttee* here is Thompson's finessing of the word *sati* as "faithful" in the very first sentence of his book, an inaccurate translation which is nonetheless an English permit for the insertion of the female subject into twentieth-century discourse.[85])

Consider Thompson's praise for General Charles Hervey's appreciation of the problem of *sati:* "Hervey has a passage which brings out the pity of a system which looked only for prettiness and constancy in woman. He obtained the names of satis who had died on the pyres of Bikanir Rajas; they were such names as: 'Ray Queen, Sun-ray, Love's Delight, Garland, Virtue Found, Echo, Soft Eye, Comfort, Moonbeam, Love-lorn, Dear Heart, Eye-play, Arbour-born, Smile, Love-bud, Glad Omen, Mist-clad, or Cloud-sprung—the last a favourite name.' " Once again, imposing the upper-class Victorian's typical demands upon "his woman" (his preferred phrase), Thompson appropriates the Hindu woman as his to save against the "system." Bikaner is in Rajasthan; and any discussion of widow-burnings of

Rajasthan, especially within the ruling class, was intimately linked to the positive or negative construction of Hindu (or Aryan) communalism.

A look at the pathetically misspelled names of the *satis* of the artisanal, peasant, village-priestly, moneylender, clerical, and comparable social groups in Bengal, where *satis* were most common, would not have yielded such a harvest (Thompson's preferred adjective for Bengalis is "imbecilic"). Or perhaps it would. There is no more dangerous pastime than transposing proper names into common nouns, translating them, and using them as sociological evidence. I attempted to reconstruct the names on that list and began to feel Hervey-Thompson's arrogance. What, for instance, might "Comfort" have been? Was it "Shanti"? Readers are reminded of the last line of T. S. Eliot's *Waste Land*. There the word bears the mark of one kind of stereotyping of India—the grandeur of the ecumenical Upanishads. Or was it "Swasti"? Readers are reminded of the *swastika*, the Brahmanic ritual mark of domestic comfort (as in "God Bless Our Home") stereotyped into a criminal parody of Aryan hegemony. Between these two appropriations, where is our pretty and constant burnt widow? The aura of the names owes more to writers like Edward FitzGerald, the "translator" of the *Rubayyat of Omar Khayyam* who helped to construct a certain picture of the Oriental woman through the supposed "objectivity" of translation, than to sociological exactitude. (Said's *Orientalism*, 1978, remains the authoritative text here.) By this sort of reckoning, the translated proper names of a random collection of contemporary French philosophers or boards of directors of prestigious southern U.S. corporations would give evidence of a ferocious investment in an archangelic and hagiocentric theocracy. Such sleights of pen can be perpetuated on "common nouns" as well, but the proper name is most susceptible to the trick. And it is the British trick with *sati* that we are discussing. After such a taming of the subject, Thompson can write, under the heading "The Psychology of the *'Sati'*," "I had intended to try to examine this; but the truth is, it has ceased to seem a puzzle to me."[86]

Between patriarchy and imperialism, subject-constitution and object-formation, the figure of the woman disappears, not into a pristine nothingness, but into a violent shuttling which is the displaced figuration of the "third-world woman" caught between tradition and modernization. These considerations would revise every detail of judgments that seem valid for a history of sexuality in the West: "Such would be the property of repression, that which distinguishes it from the prohibitions maintained by simple penal law: repression functions well as a sentence to disappear, but also as an injunction to silence, affirmation of non-existence; and consequently states that of all this there is nothing to say, to see, to know."[87] The case of *suttee* as exemplum of the woman-in-imperialism would challenge and deconstruct this opposition between subject (law) and object-of-knowledge (repression) and mark the place of "disappearance" with something other than silence and nonexistence, a violent aporia between subject and object status.

Sati as a woman's proper name is in fairly widespread use in India today. Naming a female infant "a good wife" has its own proleptic irony, and the irony is all the greater because this sense of the common noun is not the primary operator in the proper name.[88] Behind the naming of the infant is *the* Sati of Hindu mythology, Durga in her manifestation as a good wife.[89] In part of the story, Sati—she is already called that—arrives

306

at her father's court uninvited, in the absence, even, of an invitation for her divine husband Siva. Her father starts to abuse Siva and Sati dies in pain. Siva arrives in a fury and dances over the universe with Sati's corpse on his shoulder. Visnu dismembers her body and bits are strewn over the earth. Around each such relic bit is a great place of pilgrimage.

Figures like the goddess Athena—"father's daughters self-professedly uncontaminated by the womb"—are useful for establishing women's ideological self-debasement, which is to be distinguished from a deconstructive attitude toward the essentialist subject. The story of the mythic Sati, reversing every narrateme of the rite, performs a similar function: the living husband avenges the wife's death, a transaction between great male gods fulfills the destruction of the female body and thus inscribes the earth as sacred geography. To see this as proof of the feminism of classical Hinduism or of Indian culture as goddess-centered and therefore feminist is as ideologically contaminated by nativism or reverse ethnocentrism as it was imperialist to erase the image of the luminous fighting Mother Durga and invest the proper noun Sati with no significance other than the ritual burning of the helpless widow as sacrificial offering who can then be saved. There is no space from which the sexed subaltern subject can speak.

If the oppressed under socialized capital have no necessarily unmediated access to "correct" resistance, can the ideology of *sati,* coming from the history of the periphery, be sublated into any model of interventionist practice? Since this essay operates on the notion that all such clearcut nostalgias for lost origins are suspect, especially as grounds for counterhegemonic ideological production, I must proceed by way of an example.[90]

(The example I offer here is not a plea for some violent Hindu sisterhood of self-destruction. The definition of the British Indian as Hindu in Hindu law is one of the marks of the ideological war of the British against the Islamic Mughal rulers of India; a significant skirmish in that as yet unfinished war was the division of the subcontinent. Moreover, in my view, individual examples of this sort are tragic failures as *models* of interventionist practice, since I question the production of models as such. On the other hand, as objects of discourse analysis for the non-self-abdicating intellectual, they can illuminate a section of the social text, in however haphazard a way.)

A young woman of sixteen or seventeen, Bhuvaneswari Bhaduri, hanged heself in her father's modest apartment in North Calcutta in 1926. The suicide was a puzzle since, as Bhuvaneswari was menstruating at the time, it was clearly not a case of illicit pregnancy. Nearly a decade later, it was discovered that she was a member of one of the many groups involved in the armed struggle for Indian independence. She had finally been entrusted with a political assassination. Unable to confront the task and yet aware of the practical need for trust, she killed herself.

Bhuvaneswari had known that her death would be diagnosed as the outcome of illegitimate passion. She had therefore waited for the onset of menstruation. While waiting, Bhuvanesari, the *brahmacārini* who was no doubt looking forward to good wifehood, perhaps rewrote the social text of *sati*-suicide in an interventionist way. (One tentative explanation of her inexplicable act had been a possible melancholia brought on by her brother-in-law's repeated taunts that she was too old to be not-yet-a-wife.) She generalized the sanctioned motive for female suicide by taking immense trouble to displace (not merely deny), in the physiological inscription of her body, its imprisonment within legitimate passion by a single male. In the immediate context, her act became absurd, a case of delirium rather than sanity. The displacing gesture—waiting for menstruation—is at first a reversal of the interdict against a menstruating widow's right to immolate herself; the unclean widow must wait, publicly, until the cleansing bath of the fourth day, when she is no longer menstruating, in order to claim her dubious privilege.

In this reading, Bhuvaneswari Bhaduri's suicide is an unemphatic, ad hoc, subaltern rewriting of the social text of *sati*-suicide as much as the hegemonic account of the blazing, fighting, familial Durga. The emergent dissenting possibilities of that hegemonic account of the fighting mother are well documented and popularly well remembered through the discourse of the male leaders and participants in the independence movement. The subaltern as female cannot be heard or read.

I know of Bhuvaneswari's life and death through family connections. Before investigating them more thoroughly, I asked a Bengali woman, a philosopher and Sanskritist whose early intellectual production is almost identical to mine, to start the process. Two responses: (a) Why, when her two sisters, Saileswari and Rāseswari, led such full and wonderful lives, are you interested in the hapless Bhuvaneswari? (b) I asked her nieces. It appears that it was a case of illicit love.

I have attempted to use and go beyond Derridean deconstruction, which I do not celebrate as feminism as such. However, in the context of the problematic I have addressed, I find his morphology much more painstaking and useful than Foucault's and Deleuze's immediate, substantive involvement with more "political" issues—the latter's invitation to "become woman"—which can make their influence more dangerous for the U.S. academic as enthusiastic radical. Derrida marks radical critique with the danger of appropriating the other by assimilation. He reads catachresis at the origin. He calls for a rewriting of the utopian structural impulse as "rendering delirious that interior voice that is the voice of the other in us." I must here acknowledge a long-term usefulness in Jacques Derrida which I seem no longer to find in the authors of *The History of Sexuality* and *Mille Plateaux*.[91]

The subaltern cannot speak. There is no virtue in global laundry lists with "woman" as a pious item. Representation has not withered away. The female intellectual as intellectual has a circumscribed task which she must not disown with a flourish.

Notes

1   I am grateful to Khachig Tololyan for a painstaking first reading of this essay.

2   Louis Althusser, *Lenin and Philosophy and Other Essays*, trans. Ben Brewster (New York: Monthly Review Press, 1971), p. 66.

3   Michel Foucault, *Language, Counter-Memory, Practice: Selected Essays and Interviews*, trans. Donald F. Bouchard and Sherry Simon (Ithaca: Cornell University Press, 1977), pp. 205-17 (hereafter cited as *FD*). I have modified the English version of this, as of other English translations, where faithfulness to the original seemed to demand it.

Gayatri Chakravorty Spivak

It is important to note that the greatest "influence" of Western European intellectuals upon U.S. professors and students happens through collections of essays rather than long books in translation. And, in those collections, it is understandably the more topical pieces that gain a greater currency. (Derrida's "Structure, Sign, and Play" is a case in point.) From the perspective of theoretical production and ideological reproduction, therefore, the conversation under consideration has not necessarily been superseded.

4   There is an implicit reference here to the post-1968 wave of Maoism in France. See Michel Foucault, "On Popular Justice: A Discussion with Maoists," *Power/Knowledge: Selected Interviews and Other Writings 1972-77,* trans. Colin Gordon et al. (New York: Pantheon), p. 134 (hereafter cited as *PK*). Explication of the reference strengthens my point by laying bare the mechanics of appropriation. The status of China in this discussion is exemplary. If Foucault persistently clears himself by saying "I know nothing about China," his interlocutors show toward China what Derrida calls the "Chinese prejudice."

5   This is part of a much broader symptom, as Eric Wolf discusses in *Europe and the People without History* (Berkeley: University of California Press, 1982).

6   Walter Benjamin, *Charles Baudelaire: A Lyric Poet in the Era of High Capitalism,* trans. Harry Zohn (London: Verso, 1983), p. 12.

7   Gilles Deleuze and Felix Guattari, *Anti-Oedipus: Capitalism and Schizophrenia,* trans. Richard Hurley et al. (New York: Viking Press, 1977), p. 26.

8   The exchange with Jacques-Alain Miller in *PK* ("The Confession of the Flesh") is revealing in this respect.

9   Althusser, *Lenin and Philosophy,* pp. 132-33.

10   For one example among many see *PK,* p. 98.

11   It is not surprising, then, that Foucault's work, early and late, is supported by too simple a notion of repression. Here the antagonist is Freud, not Marx. "I have the impression that [the notion of repression] is wholly inadequate to the analysis of the mechanisms and effects of power that it is so pervasively used to characterize today (*PK,* 92)." The delicacy and subtlety of Freud's suggestion—that under repression the phenomenal identity of affects is indeterminate because something unpleasant can be desired as pleasure, thus radically reinscribing the relationship between desire and "interest"—seems quite deflated here. For an elaboration of this notion of repression, see Jacques Derrida, *Of Grammatology,* trans. Gayatri Chakravorty Spivak (Baltimore: Johns Hopkins University Press, 1976), p. 88f. (hereafter cited as *OG*); and Derrida, *Limited inc.: abc,* trans. Samuel Weber, *Glyph* 2 (1977), p. 215.

12   Althusser's version of this particular situation may be too schematic, but it nevertheless seems more careful in its program than the argument under study. "Class *instinct,*" Althusser writes, "is subjective and spontaneous. Class *position* is objective and rational. To arrive at proletarian class positions, the class instinct of proletarians only needs to be *educated;* the class instinct of the petty bourgeoisie, *and hence of intellectuals,* has, on the contrary, to be *revolutionized*" (*Lenin and Philosophy,* p. 13).

13   Foucault's subsequent explanation (*PK,* 145) of this Deleuzian statement comes closer to Derrida's notion that theory cannot be an exhaustive taxonomy and is always formed by practice.

14   Cf. the surprisingly uncritical notions of representation entertained in *PK,* pp. 141, 188. My remarks concluding this paragraph, criticizing intellectuals' representations of subaltern groups, should be rigorously distinguished from a coalition politics that takes into account its framing within socialized capital and unites people not because they are oppressed but because they are exploited. This model works best within a parliamentary democracy, where representation is not only not banished but elaborately staged.

15   Karl Marx, *Surveys from Exile,* trans. David Fernbach (New York: Vintage Books, 1974), p. 239.

16   Karl Marx, *Captial: A Critique of Political Economy,* vol. 1, trans. Ben Fowkes (New York: Vantage Books, 1977), p. 254.

17   Marx, *Capital,* I, p. 302.

18   See the excellent short definition and discussion of common sense in Errol Lawrence, "Just Plain Common Sense: The 'Roots' of Racism," in Hazel V. Carby et al., *The Empire Strikes Back: Race and Racism in 70s Britain* (London: Hutchinson, 1982), p. 48.

19   "Use value" in Marx can be shown to be a "theoretical fiction"—as much of a potential oxymoron as "natural exchange." I have attempted to develop this in "Scattered Speculations on the Question of Value," a manuscript under consideration by *Diacritics.*

20   Derrida's "Linguistic Circle of Geneva," especially p. 143f., can provide a method for assessing the irreducible place of the family in Marx's morphology of class formation. In *Margins of Philosophy*, trans. Alan Bass (Chicago: University of Chicago Press, 1982).

21   Marx, *Capital*, I, p. 128.

22   I am aware that the relationship between Marxism and neo-Kantianism is a politically fraught one. I do not myself see how a continuous line can be established between Marx's own texts and the Kantian ethical moment. It does seem to me, however, that Marx's questioning of the individual as agent of history should be read in the context of the breaking up of the individual subject inaugurated by Kant's critique of Descartes.

23   Karl Marx, *Grundrisse: Foundations of the Critique of Political Economy*, trans. Martin Nicolaus (New York: Viking Press, 1973), pp. 162-63.

24   Edward W. Said, *The World, the Text, the Critic* (Cambridge: Harvard University Press, 1983), p. 243.

25   Paul Bové, "Intellectuals at War: Michel Foucault and the Analysis of Power," *Sub-Stance*, 36/37 (1983), p. 44.

26   Carby, *Empire*, p. 34.

27   This argument is developed further in Spivak, "Scattered Speculations." Once again, the *Anti-Oedipus* did not ignore the economic text, although the treatment was perhaps too allegorical. In this respect, the move from schizo- to rhyzo-analysis in *Mille plateaux* (Paris: Seuil, 1980) has not been salutary.

28   See Michel Foucault, *Madness and Civilization: A History of Insanity in the Age of Reason*, trans. Richard Howard (New York: Pantheon Books, 1965), pp. 251, 262, 269.

29   Although I consider Fredric Jameson's *Political Unconscious: Narrative as a Socially Symbolic Act* (Ithaca: Cornell University Press, 1981) to be a text of great critical weight, or perhaps *because* I do so, I would like my program here to be distinguished from one of restoring the relics of a privileged narrative: "It is in detecting the traces of that uninterrupted narrative, in restoring to the surface of the text the repressed and buried reality of this fundamental history, that the doctrine of a political unconscious finds its function and its necessity" (p. 20).

30   Among many available books, I cite Bruse Tiebout McCully, *English Education and the Origins of Indian Nationalism* (New York: Columbia University Press, 1940).

31   Thomas Babington Macaulay, *Speeches by Lord Macaulay: With His Minute on Indian Education*, ed. G. M. Young (Oxford: Oxford University Press, AMS Edition, 1979), p. 359.

32   Keith, one of the compilers of the *Vedic Index*, author of *Sanskrit Drama in Its Origin, Development, Theory, and Practice*, and the learned editor of the *Krsnayajurveda* for Harvard University Press, was also the editor of four volumes of *Selected Speeches and Documents of British Colonial Policy* (1763 to 1937), of *International Affairs* (1918 to 1937), and of the *British Dominions* (1918 to 1931). He wrote books on the sovereignty of British dominions and on the theory of state succession, with special reference to English and colonial law.

33   Mahamahopadhyaya Haraprasad Shastri, *A Descriptive Catalogue of Sanskrit Manuscripts in the Government Collection under the Care of the Asiatic Society of Bengal* (Calcutta: Asiatic Society of Bengal, 1925), vol. 3, p. viii.

34   Dinesachandra Sena, *Brhat Banga* (Calcutta: Calcutta University Press, 1925), vol. 1, p. 6.

35   Edward Thompson, *Suttee: A Historical and Philosophical Enquiry into the Hindu Rite of Widow-Burning* (London: George Allen and Unwin, 1928), pp. 130, 47.

36   Holograph letter (from G. A. Jacob to an unnamed correspondent) attached to inside front cover of the Sterling Memorial Library (Yale University) copy of Colonel G. A. Jacob, ed., *The Mahanarayana-Upanishad of the Atharva-Veda with the Dipika of Narayana* (Bombay: Government Central Books Department, 1888); italics mine. The dark invocation of the dangers of this learning by way of anonymous aberrants consolidates the asymmetry.

37   I have discussed this issue in greater detail with reference to Julia Kristeva's *About Chinese Women*, trans. Anita Barrows (London: Marion Boyars, 1977), in "French Feminism in an International Frame," *Yale French Studies*, 62 (1981).

38   Antonio Gramsci, "Some Aspects of the Southern Question," *Selections from Political Writing: 1921-1926*, trans. Quintin Hoare (New York: International Publishers, 1978). I am using "allegory of reading" in the sense developed by Paul de Man, *Allegories of Reading: Figural Language in Rousseau, Nietzsche, Rilke, and Proust* (New Haven: Yale University Press, 1979).

39   Their publications are: *Subaltern Studies I: Writing on South Asian History and Society*, ed. Ranajit Guha (Delhi: Oxford University Press, 1982); *Subaltern Studies II: Writings on South Asian History and Society*, ed. Ranajit Guha (Delhi: Oxford University Press, 1983); and Ranajit

Gayatri Chakravorty Spivak

Guha, *Elementary Aspects of Peasant Insurgency in Colonial India* (Delhi: Oxford University Press, 1983).

40   Edward W. Said, "Permission to Narrate," *London Review of Books* (Feb. 16, 1984).

41   Guha, *Studies*, I, p. 1.

42   Guha, *Studies*, I, p. 4.

43   Jacques Derrida, "The Double Session," *Dissemination*, trans. Barbara Johnson (Chicago: University of Chicago Press, 1981).

44   Guha, *Studies*, I, p. 8 (all but the first set of italics are the author's).

45   Ajit K. Chaudhury, "New Wave Social Science," *Frontier*, 16-24 (Jan. 28, 1984), p. 10 (italics are mine).

46   Chaudhury, "New Wave Social Science," p. 10.

47   Pierre Macherey, *A Theory of Literary Production*, trans. Geoffrey Wall (London: Routledge, 1978), p. 87.

48   I have discussed this issue in "Displacement and the Discourse of Woman," in Mark Krupnick, ed., *Displacement: Derrida and After* (Bloomington: Indiana University Press, 1983), and in "Love Me, Love My Ombre, Elle: Derrida's 'La carte postale,' " *Diacritics* 14, no. 4 (1984), pp. 19-36.

49   This violence in the general sense that is the possibility of an episteme is what Derrida calls "writing" in the general sense. The relationship between writing in the general sense and writing in the narrow sense (marks upon a surface) cannot be cleanly articulated. The task of grammatology (deconstruction) is to provide a notation upon this shifting relationship. In a certain way, then, the critique of imperialism is deconstruction as such.

50   "Contracting Poverty," *Multinational Monitor*, 4, no. 8 (Aug. 1983), p. 8. This report was contributed by John Cavanagh and Joy Hackel, who work on the International Corporations Project at the Institute for Policy Studies (italics are mine).

51   The mechanics of the invention of the Third World as signifier are susceptible to the type of analysis directed at the constitution of race as a signifier in Carby, *Empire*.

52   Mike Davis, "The Political Economy of Late-Imperial America," *New Left Review*, 143 (Jan.-Feb. 1984), p. 9.

53   Bové, "Intellectuals," p. 51.

54   Terry Eagleton, *Literary Theory: An Introduction* (Minneapolis: University of Minnesota Press, 1983), p. 205.

55   Perry Anderson, *In the Tracks of Historical Materialism* (London: Verso, 1983), p. 53.

56   Anderson, *In the Tracks*, p. 52.

57   Said, *The World*, p. 183.

58   Jacques Derrida, "Of an Apocalyptic Tone Recently Adapted in Philosophy," trans. John P. Leavy, Jr., in *Semia*, p. 71.

59   Even in such excellent texts of reportage and analysis as Gail Omvedt's *We Will Smash This Prison! Indian Women in Struggle* (London: Zed Press, 1980), the assumption that a group of Maharashtrian women in an urban proletarian situation, reacting to a radical white woman who had "thrown in her lot with the Indian destiny," is representative of "Indian women" or touches the question of "female consciousness in India" is not harmless when taken up within a first-world social formation where the proliferation of communication in an internationally hegemonic language makes alternative accounts and testimonies instantly accessible even to undergraduates.

        Norma Chinchilla's observation, made at a panel on "Third World Feminisms: Differences in Form and Content" (UCLA, Mar. 8, 1983), that antisexist work in the Indian context is not genuinely antisexist but antifeudal, is another case in point. This permits definitions of sexism to emerge only after a society has entered the capitalist mode of production, thus making capitalism and patriarchy conveniently continuous. It also invokes the vexed question of the role of the " 'Asiatic' mode of production" in sustaining the explanatory power of the normative narrativization of history through the account of modes of production, in however sophisticated a manner history is construed.

        The curious role of the proper name "Asia" in this matter does not remain confined to proof or disproof of the empirical existence of the actual mode (a problem that became the object of intense maneuvering within international communism) but remains crucial even in the work of such theoretical subtlety and importance as Barry Hindess and Paul Hirst's *Pre-Capitalist Modes of Production* (London: Routledge, 1975) and Fredric Jameson's *Political Unconscious*. Especially in Jameson, where the morphology of modes of production is rescued from all suspicion of historical determinism and anchored to a poststructuralist theory of the subject, the "Asiatic" mode of production, in its guise of "oriental despotism" as the concomitant state formation, still serves. It also plays a significant role in the transmogrified mode of production narrative in Deleuze and Guattari's *Anti-Oedipus*. In the Soviet debate, at a far remove, indeed, from these contemporary theoretical projects, the doctrinal sufficiency of the "Asiatic" mode of production was most often doubted by producing for it various versions and nomenclatures of feudal, slave, and communal modes of production. (The debate is presented in detail in Stephen F. Dunn, *The Fall and Rise of the Asiatic Mode of Production* [London: Routledge, 1982].) It would be interesting to relate this to the repression of the imperialist "moment" in most debates over the transition from feudalism to capitalism that have long exercised the Western Left. What is more important here is that an observation such as Chinchilla's represents a widespread hierarchization within third-world *feminism* (rather than Western Marxism), which situates it within the long-standing traffic with the imperialist concept-metaphor "Asia."

I should add that I have not yet read Madhu Kishwar and Ruth Vanita, eds., *In Search of Answers: Indian Women's Voices from Manushi* (London: Zed Books, 1984).

60   Jonathan Culler, *On Deconstruction: Theory and Criticism after Structuralism* (Ithaca: Cornell University Press, 1982), p. 48.

61   Elizabeth Fox-Genovese, "Placing Woman's History in History," *New Left Review*, 133 (May-June 1982), p. 21.

62   I have attempted to develop this idea in a somewhat autobiographical way in "Finding Feminist Readings: Dante-Yeats," in Ira Konigsberg, ed., *American Criticism in the Poststructuralist Age* (Ann Arbor: University of Michigan Press, 1981).

63   Sarah Kofman, *L'énigme de la femme: La femme dans les textes de Freud* (Paris: Galilée, 1980).

64   Sigmund Freud, " 'A Child Is Being Beaten': A Contribution to the Study of the Origin of Sexual Perversions," *The Standard Edition of the Complete Psychological Works of Sigmund Freud*, trans. James Strachey et al. (London: Hogarth Press, 1955), vol. 17.

65   Freud, "'Wild' Psycho-Analysis," *Standard Edition*, vol. 11.

66   Freud, "'A Child Is Being Beaten'," p. 188.

67   For a brilliant account of how the "reality" of widow-sacrifice was constituted or "textualized" during the colonial period, see Lata Mani, "The Production of Colonial Discourse: Sati in Early Nineteenth Century Bengal" (masters thesis, University of California at Santa Cruz, 1983). I profited from discussions with Ms. Mani at the inception of this project.

68   J. D. M. Derrett, *Hindu Law Past and Present: Being an Account of the Controversy Which Preceded the Enactment of the Hindu Code, and Text of the Code as Enacted, and Some Comments Thereon* (Calcutta: A. Mukherjee and Co., 1957), p. 46.

69   Ashis Nandy, "Sati: A Ninteenth Century Tale of Women, Violence and Protest," *Rammohun Roy and the Process of Modernization in India*, ed. V. C. Joshi (Delhi: Vikas Publishing House, 1975), p. 68.

70   The following account leans heavily on Pandurang Vaman Kane, *History of the Dharmasastra* (Poona: Bhandarkar Oriental Research Institute, 1963) (hereafter cited as *HD*, with volume, part, and page numbers).

71   Upendra Thakur, *The History of Suicide in India: An Introduction* (Delhi: Munshi Ram Manohar Lal, 1963), p. 9, has a useful list of Sanskrit primary sources on sacred places. This laboriously decent book betrays all the signs of the schizophrenia of the colonial subject, such as bourgeois nationalism, patriarchal communalism, and an "enlightened reasonableness."

72   Nandy, "Sati."

73   Jean-Francois Lyotard, *Le différend* (Paris: Minuit, 1984).

74   *HD*, II.2, p. 633. There are suggestions that this "prescribed penance" was far exceeded by social practice. In the passage below, published in 1938, notice the Hindu patristic assumptions about the freedom of female will at work in phrases like "courage" and "strength of character." The unexamined presuppositions of the passage might be that the complete objectification of the widow-concubine was just punishment for abdication of the right to courage, signifying subject status: "Some widows, however, had not the courage to go through the fiery ordeal; nor had they sufficient strength of mind and character to live up to the high ascetic ideal prescribed for them [*brahmacarya*]. It is sad to record that they were driven to lead the life of a concubine or *avarudda stri* [incarcerated wife]." A. S. Altekar, *The Position of Women in Hindu Civilization: From Prehistoric Times to the Present Day* (Delhi: Motilal Banarsidass, 1938), p. 156.

75   Quoted in Sena, *Brhat-Banga*, II, pp. 913-14.

76   Thompson, *Suttee*, p. 132.

77   Here, as well as for the Brahman debate over *sati*, see Mani, "Production," pp. 71f.

78   We are speaking here of the regulative norms of Brahmanism, rather than "things as they were." See Robert Lingat, *The Classical Law of India*, trans. J. D. M. Derrett (Berkeley: University of California Press, 1973), p. 46.

79   Both the vestigial possibility of widow remarriage in ancient India and the legal institution of widow remarriage in 1856 are transactions among men. Widow remarriage is very much an exception, perhaps because it left the program of subject-formation untouched. In all the "lore" of widow remarriage, it is the father and the husband who are applauded for their reformist courage and selflessness.

80   Sir Monier Monier-Williams, *Sanskrit-English Dictionary* (Oxford: Clarendon Press, 1899), p. 552. Historians are often impatient if modernists seem to be attempting to import "feministic" judgments into ancient patriarchies. The real question is, of course, why structures of patriarchal domination should be unquestioningly recorded. Historical sanctions for collective action toward social justice can only be developed if people outside of the discipline question standards of "objectivity" preserved as such by the hegemonic tradition. It does not seem inappropriate to notice that so "objective" an instrument as a dictionary can use the deeply sexist-partisan explanatory expression: "raise up issue to a deceased husband"!

81   Sunderlal T. Desai, *Mulla: Principles of Hindu Law* (Bombay: N. M. Tripathi, 1982), p. 184.

82   I am grateful to Professor Alison Finley of Trinity College (Hartford, Conn.) for discussing the passage with me. Professor Finley is an expert on the *Rg-Veda*. I hasten to add that she would find my readings as irresponsibly "literary-critical" as the ancient historian would find it "modernist" (see note 80).

83   Martin Heidegger, *An Introduction to Metaphysics*, trans. Ralph Manheim (New York: Doubleday Anchor, 1961), p. 58.

84   Thompson, *Suttee*, p. 37.

85   Thompson, *Suttee*, p. 15. For the status of the proper name as "mark," see Derrida, "Taking Chances."

86   Thompson, *Suttee*, p. 137.

87   Michel Foucault, *The History of Sexuality*, trans. Robert Hurley (New York: Vintage Books, 1980), vol. 1, p. 4.

88   The fact that the word was also used as a form of address for a well-born woman ("lady") complicates matters.

89   It should be remembered that this account does not exhaust her many manifestations within the pantheon.

90   A position against nostalgia as a basis of counterhegemonic ideological production does not endorse its negative use. Within the complexity of contemporary political economy, it would, for example, be highly questionable to urge that the current Indian working-class crime of burning brides who bring insufficient dowries and of subsequently disguising the murder as suicide is either a *use* or *abuse* of the tradition of *sati*-suicide. The most that can be claimed is that it is a displacement on a chain of semiosis with the female subject as signifier, which would lead us back into the narrative we have been unraveling. Clearly, one must work to stop the crime of bride burning *in every way*. If, however, that work is accomplished by unexamined nostalgia or its opposite, it will assist actively in the substitution of race/ethnos or sheer genitalism as a signifier in the place of the female subject.

91   I had not read Peter Dews, "Power and Subjectivity in Foucault," *New Left Review*, 144 (1984), until I finished this essay. I look forward to his book on the same topic. There are many points in common between his critique and mine. However, as far as I can tell from the brief essay, he writes from a perspective uncritical of critical theory and the intersubjective norm that can all too easily exchange "individual" for "subject" in its situating of the "epistemic subject." Dews's reading of the connection between "Marxist tradition" and the "autonomous subject" is not mine. Further, his account of "the *impasse* of the second phase of poststructuralism as a whole" is vitiated by his nonconsideration of Derrida, who has been against the privileging of language from his earliest work, the "Introduction" in Edmund Husserl, *The Origin of Geometry*, trans. John Leavy (Stony Brook, N.Y.: Nicolas Hays, 1978). What sets his excellent analysis quite apart from my concerns is, of course, that the Subject within whose History he places Foucault's work is the Subject of the European tradition (pp. 87, 94).

313

Perry Anderson

Modernity and Revolution

"Revolution" is a term with a precise meaning: the political overthrow from below of one state order and its replacement by another. Nothing is to be gained by diluting it across time or extending it over every department of social space.

The relation between modernity and revolution has been a focus of intellectual debate and political passion for at least six or seven decades. It already has a long history, in other words. It so happens, however, that in 1983 a book appeared that reopened the debate with such renewed passion and such undeniable power that no contemporary reflection on modernity and revolution could avoid trying to come to terms with it. The book to which I refer is Marshall Berman's *All That Is Solid Melts into Air*. My remarks will focus—very briefly—on the structure of Berman's argument and how it provides us with a persuasive theory capable of conjoining the notions of modernity and revolution. I will start by reconstructing, in compressed form, the main lines of his book and then proceed to some comments on their validity. Any such reconstruction sacrifices the imaginative sweep, the breadth of cultural sympathy, and the force of textual intelligence that is integral to *All That Is Solid Melts into Air*. These qualities will surely, over time, make this work a classic in its field. Although a proper appreciation of the book exceeds our business today, it must be said at the outset that a stripped-down analysis of the general case is in no way equivalent to an adequate evaluation of the importance and attraction of the work as a whole.

Modernism, Modernity, Modernization

Berman's essential argument begins as follows:

> There is a mode of vital experience—experience of space and time, of the self and others, of life's possibilities and perils—that is shared by men and women all over the world today. I will call this body of experience "modernity." To be modern is to find ourselves in an environment that promises us adventure, power, joy, growth, transformation of ourselves and the world— and, at the same time, that threatens to destroy everything we have, everything we know, everything we are. Modern environments and experiences cut across all boundaries of geography and ethnicity, of class and nationality, of religion and ideology: in this sense, modernity can be said to unite all mankind. But it is

317

a paradoxical unity, a unity of disunity: it pours us all into a maelstrom of perpetual disintegration and renewal, of struggle and contradiction, of ambiguity and anguish. To be modern is to be part of a universe in which, as Marx said, "All that is solid melts into air."[1]

What generates this maelstrom? For Berman it is a host of social processes: he lists scientific discoveries, industrial upheavals, demographic transformations, urban expansions, nation-states, mass movements—all propelled, in the last instance, by the "ever-expanding, drastically fluctuating" capitalist *world market*. These processes he calls, for convenient shorthand, "socioeconomic modernization." Out of the experience born of modernization, in turn, has emerged what Berman describes as the "amazing variety of visions and ideas that aim to make men and women the subjects as well as the objects of modernization, to give them the power to change the world that is changing them, to make their way through the maelstrom and make it their own"—visions and values that have come to be loosely grouped together under the name of "modernism."

The ambition of his book, then, is to reveal the "dialectics of modern*ization* and modern*ism*."[2] Between these two lies the key middle term of "modern*ity*"—neither economic process nor cultural vision but the *historical experience* mediating one to the other. What constitutes the nature of the linkage between them? Essentially, for Berman, it is *development*, which is really the central concept of his book and the source of most of its paradoxes—some of them lucidly and convincingly explored, others less seen.

In *All That Is Solid Melts into Air*, "development" means two things simultaneously. On the one hand, it refers to the gigantic objective transformations of society unleashed by the advent of the capitalist world market: that is, essentially but not exclusively *economic* development. On the other hand, it refers to the momentous subjective transformations of individual life and personality which occur under their impact: everything that is contained within the notion of *self*-development as a heightening of human powers and a widening of human experience. For Berman the combination of these two, under the compulsive beat of the world market, necessarily spells a dramatic tension within the individuals who undergo development in both senses. On the one hand, capitalism—in Marx's unforgettable phrase of the *Manifesto*, which forms the leitmotif of Berman's book—tears down every ancestral confinement and feudal restriction, social immobility and claustral tradition, in an immense clearing operation of cultural and customary debris across the globe. To that process corresponds a tremendous emancipation of the possibility and sensibility of the individual self, now increasingly released from the fixed social status and rigid role hierarchy of the precapitalist past, with its narrow morality and cramped imaginative range. On the other hand, as Marx emphasized, the very same onrush of capitalist economic development also generates a brutally alienated and atomized society, riven by callous economic exploitation and cold social indifference, destructive of every cultural or political value whose potential it has itself brought into being. Likewise, on the psychological plane, self-development in these conditions could only mean a profound disorientation and insecurity, frustration and despair, *concomitant with*—

318

indeed, inseparable from—the sense of enlargement and exhilaration, the new capacities and feelings, liberated at the same time. Berman writes, "This atmosphere of agitation and turbulence, psychic dizziness and drunkenness, expansion of experiential possibilities and destruction of moral boundaries and personal bonds, self-enlargement and self-derangement, phantoms in the street and in the soul—is the atmosphere in which modern sensibility is born."[3]

That sensibility dates, in its initial manifestations, from the advent of the world market itself—1500 or thereabouts. But in its first phase, which for Berman runs to about 1790, it lacks any common vocabulary. A second phase then extends across the nineteenth century, and it is here that the experience of modernity is translated into the various classical visions of modern*ism,* which Berman defines essentially by their firm ability to grasp both sides of the contradictions of capitalist development—at once celebrating and denouncing its unprecedented transformations of the material and spiritual world without ever converting these attitudes into static or immutable antitheses. Goethe is prototypical of the new vision in his *Faust,* which Berman, in a magnificent chapter, analyzes as a tragedy of the developer in this dual sense—unbinding the self in binding back the sea. Marx in the *Manifesto* and Baudelaire in his prose poems on Paris are shown as cousins in the same discovery of modernity—one prolonged, in the peculiar conditions of forced modernization from above in a backward society, in the long literary tradition of St. Petersburg, from Pushkin and Gogol to Dostoevsky and Mandelstam.

Berman argues that a condition of the sensibility so created was a more or less unified public still possessing a memory of what it was like to live in a premodern world. In the twentieth century, however, that public simultaneously expanded and fragmented into incommensurable segments. Therewith, the dialectical tension of the classical experience of modernity underwent a critical transformation. While modernist *art* registered more triumphs than ever before—the twentieth century, Berman says in an unguarded phrase, "may well be the most brilliantly creative in the history of the world"[4]—this art has ceased to connect with or inform any common life: as Berman puts it, "we don't know how to use our modernism."[5] The result has been a drastic polarization in modern *thought* about the experience of modernity itself, flattening out its essentially ambiguous or dialectical character. On the one hand, from Weber to Ortega, Eliot to Tate, Leavis to Marcuse, twentieth-century modernity has been relentlessly condemned as an iron cage of conformity and mediocrity, a spiritual wilderness of populations bleached of any organic community or vital autonomy. On the other hand, against these visions of cultural despair, in another tradition stretching from Marinetti to Le Corbusier, Buckminster Fuller to Marshall McLuhan, not to speak of outright apologists of capitalist "modernization theory" itself, modernity has been fulsomely touted as the last word in sensory excitement and universal satisfaction, in which a machine-built civilization itself guarantees aesthetic thrills and social felicities.

What each side has in common here is a simple identification of modernity with technology itself—radically excluding the people who produce and are produced by it. As Berman writes: "Our nineteenth-century thinkers were simultaneously enthusiasts and enemies of modern life, wrestling inexhaustibly with its ambiguities and contradictions; their self-ironies and inner tensions were a primary source of their creative power. Their twentieth-century successors have lurched far more toward rigid polarities and flat totalizations. Modernity is either embraced with a blind and uncritical enthusiasm, or else condemned with a neo-Olympian remoteness and contempt; in either case it is conceived as a closed monolith, incapable of being shaped or changed by modern men. Open visions of life have been supplanted by closed ones, Both/And by Either/Or."[6] The purpose of Berman's book is to help restore our sense of modernity by reappropriating the classical visions of it. "It may turn out, then, that going back can be a way to go forward: that remembering the modernisms of the nineteenth century can give us the vision and courage to create the modernisms of the twenty-first. This act of remembering can help us bring modernism back to its roots, so that it can nourish and renew itself, to confront the adventures and dangers that lie ahead."[7]

Such is the general thrust of *All That Is Solid Melts into Air.* The book also contains a very important subtext, which must be noted. Berman's title and organizing theme come from *The Communist Manifesto,* and his chapter on Marx is one of the most interesting in the book. It ends, however, by suggesting that Marx's own analysis of the dynamic of modernity ultimately undermines the very prospect of the communist future he thought it would lead to, for if the essence of liberation from bourgeois society would be for the first time a truly unlimited development of the individual—the limits of capital, with all its deformities, now being struck away—what could guarantee either the harmony of the individuals so emancipated or the stability of any society composed of them?

> Even if the workers do build a successful communist movement, and even if that movement generates a successful revolution, how amid the flood tides of modern life, will they ever manage to build a solid communist society? What is to prevent the social forces that melt capitalism from melting communism as well? If all new relationships become obsolete before they can ossify, how can solidarity, fraternity and mutual aid be kept alive? A communist government might try to dam the flood by imposing radical restrictions, not merely on economic activity and enterprise (every socialist government has done this, along with every capitalist welfare state), but on personal, cultural and political expression. But insofar as such a policy succeeded, wouldn't it betray the Marxist aim of free development for each and all?[8]

Yet, Berman argues,

> if a triumphant communism should someday flow through the floodgates that free trade opens up, who knows what dreadful impulses might flow along with it, or in its wake, or impacted inside? It is easy to imagine how a society committed to the free development of each and all might develop its own dis-

tinctive varieties of nihilism. Indeed, a communist nihilism might turn out to be far more explosive and disintegrative than its bourgeois precursor—though also more daring and original—because while capitalism cuts the infinite possibilities of modern life with the limits of the bottom line, Marx's communism might launch the liberated self into immense unknown human spaces with no limits at all.[9]

Berman thus concludes: "Ironically, then, we can see Marx's dialectic of modernity re-enacting the fate of the society it describes, generating energies and ideas that melt it down into its own air."

The Need for Periodization

Berman's argument, as I have said, is an original and arresting one. It is presented with great literary skill and verve, uniting a generous political stance with a warm, intellectual enthusiasm for its subject: the notions of both the modern and the revolutionary, it might be said, emerge morally redeemed in his pages. Indeed, for Berman, modern*ism* is profoundly revolutionary. As the dust jacket proclaims: "Contrary to conventional belief, the modernist revolution is *not* over."

This book, written from the Left, deserves the widest discussion and scrutiny of the Left. Such discussion must start by looking at Berman's key terms, "modernization" and "modernism," and then at the linkage between them through the two-headed notion of "development." If we do this, the first thing that must strike us is that while Berman has grasped with unequaled force of imagination one critical dimension of Marx's vision of history in *The Communist Manifesto,* he omits or overlooks another dimension that is no less critical for Marx and is complementary to the first. Capital accumulation and the ceaseless expansion of the commodity form through the market is, for Marx, a universal dissolvent of the old social world, which he legitimately presents as a process of "constant revolutionizing of production, uninterrupted disturbance, everlasting uncertainty and agitation." The adjectives "constant," "uninterrupted," and "everlasting" denote a *homogeneous* historical time in which each moment is perpetually different from every other moment by virtue of being *next,* but—by the same token—each moment is eternally the *same* as an interchangeable unit in a process of infinite recurrence. Extrapolated from the totality of Marx's theory of capitalist development, this emphasis very quickly and easily yields the paradigm of modernization proper—an anti-Marxist theory, of course, politically. For our purposes, however, the relevant point is that the idea of modernization involves a conception of fundamentally *planar* development—a continuous-flow process in which there is no real differentiation of one conjuncture of epoch from another, save in terms of the mere chronological succession of old and new, earlier and later, categories themselves subject to unceasing permutation of positions in one direction as time goes by and the later becomes earlier, the newer older. Such is, of course, an accurate account of the temporality of the market and of the commodities that circulate across it.

But Marx's own conception of the historical time of the capitalist mode of production as a whole was quite distinct from this: it was of a complex and *differential* temporality in which episodes or eras were discontinuous from each other and heterogeneous within themselves. The most obvious way in which this differential temporality enters into the very construction of Marx's model of capitalism is, of course, at the level of the *class order* generated by it. By and large, it can be said that classes as such scarcely figure in Berman's account. The one significant exception is a fine discussion of the extent to which the bourgeoisie has always failed to conform to the free-trade absolutism postulated by Marx in the *Manifesto,* but this has few repercussions in the architecture of Berman's book as a whole, in which there is very little between *economy,* on the one hand, and *psychology,* on the other, save for the *culture* of modernism that links the two. Society as such is effectively missing.

If we look at Marx's account of that society, what we find is something very different from any process of planar development. Rather, the trajectory of the bourgeois order is curvilinear: it traces not a straight line ploughing endlessly forward, or a circle expanding infinitely outward, but a marked parabola. Bourgeois society knows an ascent, a stabilization, and a descent. In the very passages of the *Grundrisse* that contain the most lyrical and unconditional affirmations of the unity of economic development and individual development, which is the pivot of Berman's argument, Marx writes of "the point of flowering" of the basis of the capitalist mode of production as "the point at which it can be united with the highest development of productive forces, and thus also of the richest development of the individual." He also stipulates expressly: "It is nevertheless still this basis, this plant in flower, and therefore it fades after flowering and as a consequence of flowering. . . . As soon as this point has been reached, any further development takes the form of a decline."[10] In other words, the history of capitalism must be *periodized,* and its determinate *trajectory* reconstructed, if we are to have any sober understanding of what capitalist "development" actually means. The concept of modernization occludes the very possibility of that.

The Multiplicity of Modernisms

Let us now revert to Berman's complementary term "modernism." Although this postdates "modernization," in the sense that it signals the arrival of a coherent vocabulary for an experience of modernity that preceded it, once in place, modernism too knows no internal principle of variation—it simply keeps on reproducing itself. It is very significant that Berman has to claim that the *art* of modernism has flourished, is flourishing, as never before in the twentieth century, even while protesting at the trends of *thought* that prevent us from adequately incorporating this art into our lives.

There are a number of obvious difficulties with such a position. The first is that modernism, as a specific set of aesthetic forms, is generally dated precisely *from* the twentieth century, is indeed typically construed by way of contrast with realist and other classical forms of the nineteenth, eighteenth, or earlier centuries. Virtually all of the actual literary texts analyzed so well by Berman—whether Goethe or Baudelaire, Pushkin or Dostoevsky—precede modernism proper in this usual sense of the word (the only exceptions are fictions by Bely and Mandelstam, which precisely are twentieth-century artifacts). In other words, by more conventional criteria

322

modernism too needs to be framed within some more differential conception of historical time.

A second, related point is that once modernism is treated in this way, it is striking how uneven its distribution actually is, geographically. Even within the European or Western world generally, there are major areas that scarcely have generated any modernist momentum. My own country, England, the pioneer of capitalist industrialization and master of the world market for a century, is a major case in point: beachhead for Eliot or Pound, offshore to Joyce, it produced no virtually significant native movement of a modernist type in the first decades of this century—unlike Germany or Italy, France or Russia, Holland or America. It is no accident that England should be the great absentee from Berman's conspectus in *All That Is Solid Melts into Air*. The space of modernism, too, is thus differential.

A third objection to Berman's reading of modernism as a whole is that it establishes no distinctions either between very contrasted aesthetic tendencies or within the range of aesthetic practices that comprise the arts themselves. But in fact it is the protean variety of relations to capitalist modernity that is most striking in the broad grouping of movements typically assembled under the common rubric "modernism." Symbolism, expressionism, cubism, futurism or constructivism, surrealism—there were perhaps five or six *decisive* currents of "modernism" in the early decades of the century from which nearly everything thereafter was a derivation or mutant. The antithetical nature of the doctrines and practices peculiar to these would suffice in itself, one would have thought, to preclude the possibility that there could have been any one characteristic *Stimmung* defining the classical modernist bearing toward modernity. Much of the art produced from within this range of positions already contained the makings of those very polarities decried by Berman in contemporary or subsequent theorizations of modern culture as a whole. German expressionism and Italian futurism, in their respectively contrasted tonalities, form a stark instance.

A final difficulty with Berman's account is that it is unable, from within its own terms of reference, to provide any explanation of the divarication it deplores between the art and thought, practice and theory, of modernity in the twentieth century. Here, indeed, time divides in his argument, in a significant way: something like a *decline* has occurred, intellectually, which his book seeks to *reverse* with a return to the classical spirit of modernism as a whole, informing art and thought alike. But that decline remains unintelligible within his schema, once modernization is itself conceived as a linear process of prolongation and expansion, which necessarily carries with it a constant renewal of the sources of modernist art.

The Sociopolitical Conjuncture

An alternative way to understand the origins and adventures of modernism is to look more closely at the differential historical temporality in which it was inscribed. There is one famous way of doing this, within the Marxist tradition: the route taken by Lukács, who read off a direct equation between the change of political posture of European capital after the revolutions of 1848 and the fate of the cultural forms produced by or within the ambit of the bourgeoisie as a social class. After the mid-nineteenth century, for Lukács, the bourgeoisie becomes purely reactionary—abandoning its conflict against the nobility, on a continental scale, for all-out struggle against the proletariat. Therewith it enters into a phase of ideological decadence, whose initial aesthetic expression is predominantly naturalistic but eventually issues into early twentieth-century modernism.

This schema is widely decried on the Left today. In fact, in Lukács's work, it often has yielded rather acute local analyses in the field of philosophy proper: *The Destruction of Reason* is a far from negligible book, however marred by its postscript. On the other hand, in the field of literature—Lukács's other main area of application—the schema proved relatively sterile. It is striking that there is no Lukácsian exploration of any modernist work of art comparable in detail or depth to his treatment of the structure of ideas in Schelling or Schopenhauer, Kierkegaard or Nietzsche; by contrast, Joyce or Kafka—to take two of Lukács's literary *bêtes noires*—are scarcely more than invoked and never are studied in their own right. The basic error of Lukács's optic here is its *evolutionism*, that is, time differs from one epoch to another, but *within* each epoch all sectors of social reality move in synchrony with each other, such that decline at one level must be reflected in descent at every other. The result is a plainly overgeneralized notion of "decadence"—one, of course, enormously affected, it can be said in extenuation, by the spectacle of the collapse of German society and most of its established culture, in which Lukács had himself been formed, into nazism.

If neither Berman's perennialism nor Lukács's evolutionism provide satisfactory accounts of modernism, then what is the alternative? The hypothesis I will briefly suggest here is that we should look rather for a *conjunctural* explanation of the set of aesthetic practices and doctrines subsequently grouped together as "modernist." Such an explanation would involve the intersection of different historical temporalities, to compose a typically overdetermined configuration. What were these temporalities? In my view, "modernism" can best be understood as a cultural force field "triangulated" by three decisive coordinates. The first of these is something Berman perhaps hints at in one passage but situates too far back in time, failing to capture it with sufficient precision: the codification of a highly formalized *academicism* in the visual and other arts, which itself was institutionalized within official regimes of states and society still massively pervaded, often dominated, by aristocratic or landowning classes that were in one sense economically "superseded," no doubt, but in others were still setting the political and cultural tone in country after country of pre-First World War Europe. The connections between these two phenomena are graphically sketched in Arno Mayer's recent and fundamental work, *The Persistence of the Old Regime,*[11] whose central theme is the extent to which European society down to 1914 was still dominated by agrarian or aristocratic (the two were not necessarily identical, as the case of France makes clear) ruling classes, in economies in which modern heavy industry still constituted a surprisingly small sector of the labor force or pattern of output.

The second coordinate is then a logical complement of the first: the still incipient, hence essentially *novel,* emergence within these societies of the key technologies or inventions of the second industrial revolution; that is, telephone, radio, automobile, aircraft, and so on. Mass consumption industries based on the new technologies had not yet been implanted anywhere in Europe, where clothing, food, and furniture remained overwhelmingly the largest final-goods sectors in employment and turnover down to 1914.

The third coordinate of the modernist conjuncture, I would argue, is the imaginative proximity of social revolution. The extent of hope or apprehension that the prospect of such revolution arouses varies widely, but over most of Europe it was "in the air" during the Belle Époque itself. The reason, again, is straightforward enough: forms of dynastic ancien régime, as Mayer calls them, did persist—imperial monarchies in Russia, Germany, and Austria, a precarious royal order in Italy; even the United Kingdom was threatened with regional disintegration and civil war in the years before the First World War. In no European state was bourgeois democracy completed as a form or the labor movement integrated or co-opted as a force. The possible revolutionary outcomes of a downfall of the old order were thus still profoundly ambiguous. Would a new order be more unalloyedly and radically capitalist, or would it be socialist? The Russian Revolution of 1905-7, which focused the attention of all Europe, was emblematic of this ambiguity, an upheaval at once and inseparably bourgeois and proletarian.

What was the contribution of each of these coordinates to the emergence of the force field defining modernism? Briefly, I think, the following: the persistence of the anciens régimes, and the academicism concomitant with them, provided a critical range of cultural values *against which* insurgent forms of art could measure themselves but also *in terms of which* they could partly articulate themselves. Without the common adversary of official academicism, the wide range of new aesthetic practices have little or no unity: their tension with the established or consecrated canons is constitutive of their definition as such. At the same time, however, the old order, precisely in its still partially aristocratic coloration, has afforded a set of available codes and resources from which the ravages of the market as an organizing principle of culture and society—uniformly detested by every species of modernism—could also be resisted. The classical stocks of high culture still preserved—even if deformed and deadened—in late nineteenth-century academicism could be redeemed and released against the old order, as also against the commercial spirit of the age, as many of these movements saw it. The relationship of imagists like Pound to Edwardian conventions or Roman lyric poetry alike, of the later Eliot to Dante or the metaphysicals, is typical of one side of this situation; the ironic proximity of Proust or Musil to the French or Austrian aristocracies is typical of the other side.

At the same time, for a different kind of "modernist" sensibility, the energies and attractions of a new machine age were a powerful imaginative stimulus, one reflected, patently enough, in Parisian cubism, Italian futurism, or Russian constructivism. The condition of this interest, however, was the abstraction of techniques and artifacts from the social relations of production that were generating them. In no case was capitalism as such ever exalted by any brand of "modernism." But such extrapolation was precisely rendered possible by the sheer incipience of the still unforeseeable socioeconomic pattern that was later to consolidate so inexorably around them. It was not obvious where the new devices and inventions were going to lead. Hence the, so to speak, ambidextrous celebration of them from Right and Left alike—Marinetti or Mayakovsky. Finally, the haze of social revolution drifting across the horizon of this epoch gave it much of its apocalyptic light for those currents of modernism most unremittingly and violently radical in their rejection of the social order as a whole, of which the most significant was certainly German expressionism. European modernism in the first years of this century thus flowered in the space between a still usable classical past, a still indeterminate technical present, and a still unpredictable political future. Or, put another way, it arose at the intersection between a semi-aristocratic ruling order, a semi-industrialized capitalist economy, and a semi-emergent, or semi-insurgent, labor movement.

The First World War, when it came, altered all of these coordinates, but it did not eliminate any of them; for another twenty years they lived on in a kind of hectic afterlife. Politically, of course, the dynastic states of Eastern and Central Europe disappeared. But the Junker class retained great power in postwar Germany; the agrarian-based Radical party continued to dominate the Third Republic in France, without much break in tone; in Britain, the more aristocratic of the two traditional parties, the Conservatives, virtually wiped out their more bourgeois rivals, the Liberals, and went on to dominate the whole interwar epoch. Socially, a distinctive upper-class mode of life persisted right down to the end of the 1930s, whose hallmark—setting it off completely from the existence of the rich after the Second World War—was the normalcy of servants. This was the last true leisure class in metropolitan history. England, where such continuity was strongest, was to produce the greatest fictional representation of that world in Anthony Powell's *Dance to the Music of Time,* a nonmodernist remembrance from the subsequent epoch. Economically, mass production industries based on the new technological inventions of the early twentieth century achieved some foothold in two countries only—Germany in the Weimar period, and England in the late 1930s. But in neither case was there any general or wholesale implantation of what Gramsci was to call "Fordism," on the lines of what had by then existed for two decades in the United States. Europe was still over a generation behind America in the structure of its civilian industry and pattern of consumption on the eve of the Second World War. Finally, the prospect of revolution was now more proximate and tangible than it had ever been—a prospect that had triumphantly materialized in Russia, touched Hungary, Italy, and Germany with its wing just after the First World War, and was to take on a new and dramatic immediacy in Spain at the end of this period.

It is within this space, prolonging in its own way an earlier ground, that generically "modernist" forms of art continued to show great vitality. Quite apart from the literary masterpieces published in these years but essentially nurtured in earlier ones, Brechtian theater was one memorable product purely of the interwar conjuncture, in Germany. Another was the first real emergence of architectural modernism as a movement, with the Bauhaus. A third was the appearance of what was, in fact, the last of the great doctrines of the European avant-garde—surrealism, in France.

The West's Season Ends

It was the Second World War that destroyed all three of the historical coordinates I have discussed and therewith cut off the vitality of modernism. After 1945, the old semiaristocratic or agrarian order and its appurtenances were finished, in every country. Bourgeois democracy was finally universalized. With that, certain critical links with a precapitalist past were snapped. At the same time, Fordism arrived in force. Mass production and consumption transformed the West European economies along North American lines. There could no longer be the smallest doubt as to what kind of society this technology would consolidate: an oppressively stable, monolithically industrial, capitalist civilization was now in place.

In a wonderful passage of his book *Marxism and Form,* Fredric Jameson admirably captures what this meant for the avant-grade traditions that had once treasured the novelties of the 1920s or 1930s for their oneiric, destabilizing potential: "The Surrealist image," he remarks, was "a convulsive effort to split open the commodity forms of the objective universe by striking them against each other with immense force."[12] But the condition of its success was that

> these objects—the places of objective chance or of preternatural revelation—are immediately identifiable as the products of a not yet fully industrialized and systematized economy. This is to say, that the human origins of the products of this period—their relationship to the work from which they issued—have not yet been fully concealed; in their production they still show traces of an artisanal organization of labor while their distribution is still assured by a network of small shopkeepers. . . . What prepares these products to receive the investment of psychic energy characteristic of their use by Surrealism is precisely the half-sketched, uneffaced mark of human labor; they are still frozen gesture, not yet completely separated from subjectivity, and remain therefore potentially as mysterious and as expressive as the human body itself.[13]

Jameson goes on to say:

> We need only exchange, for that environment of small workshops and store counters, for the *marché aux puces* and the stalls in the streets, the gasoline stations along American superhighways, the glossy photographs in the magazines, or the cellophane paradise of an American drugstore, in order to realize that the objects of Surrealism are gone without a trace. Henceforth, in what we may call post-industrial capitalism, the products with which we are furnished are utterly without depth: their plastic content is totally incapable of serving as a conductor of psychic energy. All libidinal investment in such objects is precluded from the outset, and we may well ask ourselves, if it is true that our object universe is henceforth unable to yield any "symbol apt at stirring human sensibility," whether we are not here in the presence of a cultural transformation of signal proportions, a historical break of an unexpectedly radical kind.[14]

327

Finally the image or hope of revolution faded away in the West. The onset of the Cold War, and the Sovietization of Eastern Europe, cancelled any realistic prospect of a socialist overthrow of advanced capitalism for a whole historical period. The ambiguity of aristocracy, the absurdity of academicism, the gaiety of the first cars or movies, the palpability of a socialist alternative, were all now gone. In their place there now reigned a routinized, bureaucratized economy of universal commodity production, in which "mass consumption" and "mass culture" had become virtually interchangeable terms.

The postwar avant-gardes were to be essentially defined against this quite new backdrop. It is not necessary to judge them from a Lukácsian tribunal to note the obvious: little of the literature, painting, music, or architecture of this period can stand comparison with that of the antecedent epoch. Reflecting on what he calls "the extraordinary concentration of literary masterpieces around the First World War," Franco Moretti in his recent book *Signs Taken for Wonders* writes: "extraordinary because of its quantity, as even the roughest list shows (Joyce and Valery, Rilke and Kafka, Svevo and Proust, Hofmannsthal and Musil, Apollinaire, Mayakovsky), but even more than extraordinary because that abundance of works (as is by now clear, after more than half a century) constituted the last *literary season* of Western culture. Within a few years European literature gave its utmost and seemed on the verge of opening new and boundless horizons: instead it died. A few isolated icebergs, and many imitators; but nothing comparable to the past."[15] There would be some exaggeration in generalizing this judgment to the other arts, but not, alas, all that much. Individual writers or painters, architects or musicians, of course produced significant work after the Second World War, but the heights of the first two or three decades of the century were rarely or never reached again. Indeed, no new aesthetic movements of collective importance, operative across more than one art form, emerged after surrealism. In painting or sculpture alone, specialized schools and slogans succeeded each other ever more rapidly, but after the moment of abstract expressionism—the last genuine avant-garde of the West— these were now largely a function of a gallery system necessitating regular output of new styles as materials for seasonal commercial display, along the lines of haute couture: an economic pattern corresponding to the *non*reproducible character of "original" works in these particular fields.

It was now, however, when all that had created the classical art of the early twentieth century was dead, that the ideology and cult of mod-ern*ism* was born. The conception itself is scarcely older than the 1950s, as a widespread currency. What it betokens is the pervasive collapse of the tension between the institutions and mechanisms of advanced capitalism and the practices and programs of advanced art, as the one annexed the other as its occasional decoration or diversion, or philanthropic *point d'honneur*. The few exceptions of the period suggest the power of the rule. The cinema of Jean-Luc Godard, in the 1960s, is perhaps the most salient case in point. As the Fourth Republic belatedly passed into the Fifth, and rural and provincial France was suddenly transformed by a Gaullist industrialization appropriating the newest international technologies, something like a brief afterglow of the earlier conjuncture that had produced the classical innovatory art of the century flared into life again. Godard's cinema was marked in its own way by all three of the coordinates described earlier.

Suffused with quotation and allusion to a high cultural past, Eliot-style; equivocal celebrant of the automobile and the airport, the camera and the carbine, Leger-style; expectant of revolutionary tempests from the East, Nizan-style.

The upheaval of May-June 1968 in France was the validating historical terminus of this art form. Regis Debray was to describe the experience of that year sarcastically, after the event, as a voyage to China that, like Columbus's, discovered only America—more especially, landing in California[16]—that is, a social and cultural turbulence that mistook itself for a French version of the Cultural Revolution, when in fact it signified no more than the arrival of a long-overdue permissive consumerism in France. But it was precisely this ambiguity—an *openness* of horizon, where the shapes of the future could alternatively assume the shifting forms of either a new type of capitalism or the eruption of socialism—that was constitutive of so much of the original sensibility of what had come to be called "modernism." Not surprisingly, it did not survive the Pompidou consolidation that succeeded, in Godard's cinema or anywhere else. What marks the typical situation of the contemporary artist in the West, it might be said, is, on the contrary, the closure of horizons: without an appropriable past, or imaginable future, in an interminably recurrent present.

This is not true, manifestly, of the Third World. It is significant that so many of Berman's examples of what he reckons to be the great modernist achievements of our time should be taken from Latin American literature. In the Third World generally, a kind of shadow configuration of what once prevailed in the First World does exist today. Precapitalist oligarchies of various kinds, mostly of a landowning character, abound; capitalist development in these regions is typically far more rapid and dynamic, where it does occur, than in the metropolitan zones, yet it is infinitely less stabilized or consolidated; socialist revolution haunts these societies as a permanent possibility, one already realized in countries close to home—Cuba or Nicaragua, Angola or Vietnam. These are the conditions that have produced the genuine masterpieces of recent years that conform to Berman's categories: novels like Gabriel Garcia Marquez's *One Hundred Years of Solitude* and Salman Rushdie's *Midnight's Children,* from Colombia and India, or films like Yilmiz Guney's *Yol,* from Turkey. However, works such as these are not timeless expressions of an ever-expanding process of modernization but emerge in quite delimited constellations, in societies still at definite historical crossroads. The Third World furnishes no fountain of eternal youth to modernism.

The Limits of Self-Development

So far, we have looked at two of Berman's organizing concepts—modernization and modernism. Let us now consider the mediating term that links them: modernity. That, it will be remembered, is defined as the *experience* undergone within modernization that give rises to modernism. What is this experience? For Berman, it is essentially a subjective process of unlimited self-development, as traditional barriers of custom or role disintegrate—an experience necessarily lived at once as emancipation and ordeal, elation and despair, frightening and exhilarating. It is the momentum of this ceaselessly ongoing rush toward the uncharted frontiers of the psyche that assures the world-historical continuity of modernism; but it is also the momentum that appears to undermine in advance any prospect of moral or institutional stabilization under communism; indeed, perhaps, to disallow the cultural cohesion necessary for communism to exist at all, rendering it something like a contradiction in terms. What should we make of this argument?

To understand it we need to ask, Where does Berman's vision of a completely unbounded dynamic of self-development come from? His first book, *The Politics of Authenticity,* which contains two studies—one of Montesquieu and the other of Rousseau—provides the answer. Essentially, this idea derives from what the subtitle of the book rightly designates the "radical individualism" of Rousseau's concept of humanity. Berman's analysis of the logical trajectory of Rousseau's thought, as it sought to contend with the contradictory consequences of this conception across successive works, is a tour de force. But for our purposes the crucial point is that Berman demonstrates the presence of the same paradox he ascribes to Marx within Rousseau: if unlimited self-development is the goal of all, how will community ever be possible? For Rousseau the answer is, in words that Berman quotes: "The love of man derives from love of oneself"—"Extend self-love to others and it is transformed into virtue."[17] Berman comments: "It was the road of self-expansion, not of self-repression, that led to the palace of virtue. . . . As each man learned to express and enlarge himself, his capacity for identification with other men would expand, his sympathy and empathy with them would deepen."[18]

The schema here is clear enough: *first* the individual develops the self, *then* the self can enter into relations of mutual satisfaction with others—relations based on identification *with* the self. The difficulties this presumption encounters once Rousseau tries to move—in his language—from the "man" to the "citizen," in the construction of a free community, are then brilliantly explored by Berman. What is striking, however, is that Berman nowhere himself disowns the starting point of the dilemmas he demonstrates. On the contrary, he concludes by arguing: "The programs of nineteenth-century socialism and anarchism, of the twentieth-century welfare state and the contemporary New Left, can all be seen as further developments of the structure of thought whose foundations Montesquieu and Rousseau laid down. What these very different movements share is a way of defining the crucial political task at hand: to make modern liberal society keep the promises it has made, to reform it—or revolutionize it—in order to realize the ideals of modern liberalism itself. The agenda for radical liberalism which Montesquieu and Rousseau brought up two centuries ago is still pending today."[19] Likewise, in *All That Is Solid Melts into Air,* Berman can refer to "the depth of the individualism that underlies Marx's communism"[20]—a depth which, he quite consistently goes on to note, must formally include the possibility of a radical nihilism.

If we look back, however, at Marx's actual texts, we find a very different conception of human reality at work. For Marx, the self is not *prior to* but *constituted by* its relations with others, from the outset: women and men are *social* individuals whose sociality is not subsequent to but contemporaneous with their individuality. Marx wrote, after all, that "only in community with others has each individual the means of cultivating his gifts in all directions: only in the community, therefore, is personal freedom possible."[21] Berman cites the sentence but apparently without seeing its

330

consequences. If the development of the self is inherently imbricated in relations with others, its development could never be an *unlimited* dynamic in the monadological sense conjured up by Berman, for the coexistence of others would always *be such a limit,* without which *development itself could not occur.* Berman's postulate is thus, for Marx, a contradiction in terms.

Another way of saying this is that Berman has failed—with many others, of course—to see that Marx possesses a conception of *human nature* that rules out the kind of infinite ontological plasticity he assumes himself. That may seem a scandalous statement, given the reactionary cast of so many standard ideas of what human nature is. But it is the sober philological truth, as even a cursory inspection of Marx's work makes clear and Norman Geras's *Marx and Human Nature—Refutation of a Legend* makes irrefutable.[22] That nature, for Marx, includes a set of primary needs, powers, and dispositions—what he calls in the *Grundrisse,* in the famous passages on human possibility under feudalism, capitalism, and communism, *Bedurfnisse, Fahigkeiten, Krafte, Anlagen*—all of them capable of enlargement and development but not of erasure or replacement. The vision of an unhinged, nihilistic drive of the self toward a completely unbounded development is thus a chimera. Rather, the genuine "free development of each" *can only* be realized if it proceeds in respect of the "free development of all," given the common nature of what it is to be human. In the very pages of the *Grundrisse* on which Berman leans, Marx speaks without the slightest equivocation of "the full development of human control over the forces of nature—including those of his own nature"; of "the absolute elaboration *(Herausarbeiten)* of his creative dispositions," in which "the universality of the individual . . . is the universality of his real and ideal relationships."[23] The cohesion and stability Berman wonders whether communism could ever display lies, for Marx, in the very human nature it would finally emancipate, one far from any mere cataract of formless desires. For all its exuberance, Berman's version of Marx, in its virtually exclusive emphasis on the release of the self, comes uncomfortably close—radical and decent though its accents are—to the assumptions of the culture of narcissism.

The Present Impasse

To conclude, then, where does this leave revolution? Berman is quite consistent here. For him, as for so many other socialists today, the notion of revolution is distended in duration. In effect, capitalism already brings us constant upheaval in our conditions of life and in that sense is—as he puts it—a "permanent revolution," one that obliges "modern men and women" to "learn to yearn for change: not merely to be open to changes in their personal and social lives, but positively to demand them, actively to seek them out and carry them through. They must learn not to long nostalgically for the 'fixed, fast-frozen relationships' of the real or fantasized past, but to delight in mobility, to thrive on renewal, to look forward to future development in their conditions of life and relations with their fellow men."[24] The advent of socialism would not halt or check this process but on the contrary would immensely accelerate and generalize it. The echoes of 1960s' radicalism are unmistakable here. Attraction to such notions has proved very widespread, but they are not, in fact, compatible either with the theory of historical materialism, strictly understood, or with the record of history itself, however theorized.

"Revolution" is a term with a precise meaning: the political overthrow from below of one state order and its replacement by another. Nothing is to be gained by diluting it across time or extending it over every department of social space. In the first case, it becomes indistinguishable from mere reform—simple change, no matter how gradual or piecemeal—as in the ideology of latter-day Eurocommunism or cognate versions of Social Democracy; in the second case, it dwindles to a mere metaphor, one that can be reduced to no more than supposed psychological or moral conversions, as in the ideology of Maoism, with its proclamation of a "Cultural Revolution." Against these slack devaluations of the term, with all their political consequences, it is necessary to insist that revolution is a *punctual* and not a permanent process; that is, a revolution is an episode of convulsive political transformation, compressed in time and concentrated in target, with a determinate beginning—when the old state apparatus is still intact—and a finite end—when that apparatus is decisively broken and a new one erected in its stead. What would be distinctive about a socialist revolution that created a genuine postcapitalist democracy is that the new state would be truly transitional toward the practicable limits of its own self-dissolution into the associated life of society as a whole.

In the advanced capitalist world today, it is the seeming absence of any such prospect as a proximate or even distant horizon—the lack, apparently, of any conjecturable alternative to the imperial status quo of a consumer capitalism—that blocks the likelihood of any profound cultural renovation comparable to the great Age of Aesthetic Discoveries in the first third of the twentieth century. Gramsci's words still hold: "The crisis consists precisely in the fact that the old is dying and the new cannot be born; in this interregnum a great variety of morbid symptoms appears."[25] It is legitimate to ask, Could anything be said in advance as to what the new might be? One thing, I think, might be predicted. Modern*ism* as a notion is the emptiest of all cultural categories. Unlike Gothic, Renaissance, Baroque, Mannerist, Romantic, or Neoclassical, it designates no describable object in its own right at all: it is completely lacking in positive content. In fact, as we have seen, what is concealed beneath the label "modernism" is a wide variety of very diverse—indeed, incompatible—aesthetic practices: symbolism, constructivism, expressionism, surrealism. These -isms, which spell out specific programs, were unified post hoc in a portmanteau concept whose only referent is the blank passage of time itself. There is no other aesthetic marker so vacant or vitiated, for what once was modern is soon obsolete. The futility of the term "modernism," and its attendant ideology, can be seen all too clearly from current attempts to cling to its wreckage and yet swim with the tide still further beyond it, in the coinage "postmodernism"—one void chasing another, in a serial regression of self-congratulatory chronology.

If we ask ourselves what revolution (understood as a punctual and irreparable break with the order of capital) would have to do with modernism (understood as this flux of temporal vanities), the answer is, it would surely end it, for a genuine socialist culture would be one that did not insatiably seek the new, defined simply as what comes *later*, itself to be rapidly consigned to the detritus of the old, but rather one that multiplied the different, in a far greater *variety* of concurrent styles and practices than had ever existed before—a diversity founded on the far greater plurality and

Perry Anderson

complexity of possible ways of living that any free community of equals, no longer divided by class, race, or gender, would create. In other words, the axes of aesthetic life would, in this respect, run horizontally, not vertically. The calendar would cease to tyrannize, or organize, consciousness of art. The vocation of a socialist revolution, in that sense, would be neither to prolong nor fulfill modernity but to abolish it.

Notes

Perry Anderson's "Modernity and Revolution" was first presented at the conference on Marxism and the Interpretation of Culture. It was subsequently published in *New Left Review* and is reprinted here with their permission.

1   Marshall Berman, *All That Is Solid Melts into Air* (New York: Simon and Schuster, 1983), p. 15.

2   Berman, *All That Is Solid*, p. 16.

3   Berman, *All That Is Solid*, p. 18.

4   Berman, *All That Is Solid*, p. 24.

5   Berman, *All That Is Solid*, p. 24.

6   Berman, *All That Is Solid*, p. 24.

7   Berman, *All That Is Solid*, p. 36.

8   Berman, *All That Is Solid*, p. 104.

9   Berman, *All That Is Solid*, p. 114.

10   Karl Marx, *Grundrisse der Kritik der Politischen Okonomie* (Frankfurt, 1967), p. 439.

11   Arno Mayer, *The Persistence of the Old Regime* (New York: Pantheon, 1982), pp. 189-273.

12   Fredric Jameson, *Marxism and Form* (Princeton: Princeton University Press, 1971), p. 96.

13   Jameson, pp. 103-4.

14   Jameson, p. 105.

15   Franco Moretti, *Signs Taken for Wonders* (New York: Schocken, 1983), p. 209.

16   Regis Debray, "A Modest Contribution to the Rites and Ceremonies of the Tenth Anniversary," *New Left Review* 115 (1979), pp. 45-65.

17   Marshall Berman, *The Politics of Authenticity* (New York: Atheneum, 1970), p. 181.

18   Berman, *Politics*, p. 181.

19   Berman, *Politics*, p. 317.

20   Berman, *All That Is Solid*, p. 128.

21   Karl Marx and Friedrich Engels, *The German Ideology* (New York: International Publishers Co., 1970), p. 83; cited by Berman, *Politics*, p. 97.

22   Norman Geras, *Marx and Human Nature* (New York: Schocken, 1983).

23   Marx, *Grundrisse*, pp. 387, 440.

24   Berman, *All That Is Solid*, pp. 95-96.

25   Antonio Gramsci, *Selections from the Prison Notebooks*, eds. Quintin Hoare and Geoffrey Nowell-Smith (New York: International Publishers Co., 1971), p. 276.

333

Question
What do you mean by human nature?

Anderson
Marx never really fully articulates his concept of human nature. But there are innumerable passages of his work we can use to bring out the contours of and assumptions behind his implicit conception of human nature. That conception clearly has a biological origin, in the sense that the human physiognomic structure is that of a specific animal species. This endows us with certain potentials, obvious psychological needs, physical powers, and certain dispositions as well—the latter a word he uses quite a lot. On the other hand, the course of human history immensely enlarges, elaborates, and complicates that primary physiological basis, so that human nature is an indissoluble compound of the biological and the social. The fact that the biological is always coded in social terms does not mean that it can be simply absorbed by the social. We cannot simply say that human nature is the ensemble of social relations at any one given moment. The biological basis sets certain determinate limits to what kinds of change any given historical variation can impose. Indeed, it is only because human nature has a determinable core of meaning that we can speak of human emancipation at all. Were it not for that core, we would have no markers at all, no criteria for talking of liberation, emancipation, or of a better society.

Comment (Gajo Petrović)
I understand Marx to say that the essence of human nature is that we don't have a nature in the sense in which all other beings have one. For Marx the possibility of being free is what, if you like, constitutes human nature. But this is a negation of "nature" in any ordinary sense of the word, since it doesn't imply an essence or a set of fixed qualities. I would say that what is specific to human beings is their structure of being—praxis or freedom.

Anderson
Of course, for Marx human nature isn't fixed. Gajo is quite correct on this point, but it doesn't mean that its principles of variation are unlimited. We can't imagine human beings who don't have certain physiological necessities of an elementary sort: food, shelter, relationships with others, and so on. So in a sense those are constants throughout human history, but they are coded in and elaborated by the changing social forms of human society. These two positions aren't incompatible.

Comment
The fact of a biological substrate is what a lot of the debate about modernism and postmodernism is all about. As I understand Berman, the end of the road for modernism was its attempt to describe, to create, to represent in many forms of art precisely the field of energies and the structure of human nature that would provide the ground for its liberating project. But modernism kept running into the dead end of fascism. While I share many of your attitudes toward modernism and postmodernism, I think you undervalue the postmodernist project; it is a useful corrective to many of those premature claims for closure that modernist art and sociology initiated. Berman's fear is that the malleability of human nature, its ability to be saturated by many sociosymbolic codes, does not in itself solve the value problem. Your discussion of the problems of a revolutionary communism that too quickly totalizes itself does not necessarily suggest how communism is to define the ethical principles that will enable it to avoid falling into traditional structures of victimization (antisemitism, the Gulag). For Berman, the benefit of the capitalist order is the limit it sets on such ethical transgressions, limits it so far has not broken.

334

Perry Anderson

Anderson

I don't entirely disagree, but I think Berman greatly over-states the degree of human malleabilility. His assumption is empirically just not so. Thus the frightening scenario he conjures up is not one we should be overly worried about. There are many other more serious problems than those of a kind of communism that capsizes over into generalized nihilism. I think that particular worry is a fairy story.

Question

You set out in a very impressive way the conjunctural conditions for modernism as it distinguishes itself from an older realist discourse. And you mention Lukács, who, although acutely conscious of this transformation, is unable to grasp the spirit of modernist literature. But you repeat Lukács's gesture, it seems to me, in the way you dismiss postmodernism. Why do you refuse a dialectical assessment of what succeeds modernism if, as you say, modernism is over after the Second World War?

Anderson

There are two differences. Lukács has a homogeneous and evolutionary conception of historical phases. Once capitalism enters into what, for him, is a period of historical decline after 1848, then everything has to go into decline. That's not a position I would subscribe to. Capitalism today remains both an immensely dynamic and a stable economic force; at the same time it is manifest that its political powers of innovation or renewal are bankrupt. You have only to look at the quality of its world leaders. Compare them with the generation of Roosevelt, Churchill, and de Gaulle. It's obvious that changes have occurred and, from the point of view of the loyal bourgeoisie, not for the better. The economic and the political don't necessarily go in tandem.

Now, as far as aesthetic practices since the war are concerned, it's not that all works of art since then are negligible. I can think of some you could describe as great. Rather, my point is that, if we look at the whole panorama, it is difficult to see anything that stands comparison with the creative years of the early part of this century. If people want to contest that, the onus of proof would be on them to come up with some names similar to the ones Franco Moretti cited in literature. The point about postmodernism is that I don't take it to be an aesthetic practice at all. I think it is a doctrine, a very tenuous doctrine indeed, built on the back of something that is also enormously tenuous, namely, modernism. What strikes me about it is the absence of those positive aesthetic programs we identify with the great moments of symbolism, expressionism, futurism, constructivism, and surrealism. All of these words denote quite specific aesthetic biases, practices, and emphases. Postmodernism is simply a reference of a purely temporal sort; it has no determinate content. And today I don't think we can find aesthetic programs operative across more than one art form of the sort we find in the modernist epoch. That's what strikes me most forcibly and makes me very wary of the notion of postmodernism.

Finally, I would insist on the possibility of identifying great individual works of art. I would deny the nihilist position of excluding the possibility of anything of significance emerging today. But I do react strongly against a complete historical relativism, one that simply assumes that any one historical age necessarily produces as good art or as much art as another historical age. Nobody in his or her right mind has ever claimed that the art of the dark ages is equivalent to the art of classical Greece. I'm not saying we're in a dark age now—we aren't—but I do think you cannot just level out historical epochs on the presumption that there is a constant fund of human creativity that is always going to find equivalent expression.

Question

You offer a utopian vision for the postrevolutionary world. Not that you are offering it in recompense for all the costs of the revolution—no one would pretend that a revolution is made for art—but you speak nevertheless about the proliferation of art in the postrevolutionary period. Could you offer us an explanation, comparable to the triangulation you described for the period of the late nineteenth/early twentieth century, that would provide us a material basis for understanding why art might flourish in the postrevolutionary period? Then perhaps you could comment on whether our historical experience of socialist revolutions supports your claim.

Anderson

If you look back at all the utopias—from William Morris's to Marcuse's—in nearly all of them, even in the utopian socialists, there is a great emphasis on simplicity; and simplicity usually implies uniformity as well. The whole utopian tradition, in effect, assumes that a free and equal society would be transparent. My presumption, on the contrary, is that a socialist society would be a far more complicated one than what we have today. It seems perfectly clear that if you actually had a socialist society in which production, power, and culture were genuinely democratized, you would have an enormous multiplication of different ways of living. People would choose how to live, and it is perfectly obvious that people have different temperaments, gifts, and values. These differences are suppressed and compressed within very narrow limits by the capitalist market and the inequalities of bourgeois society.

The simple monolithicity of capitalist private property controlling all the means of production would be broken down into a great variety of different forms of social control of the economy and of wealth. The political system would be enormously more complicated. You wouldn't just have elections every five years of a more or less symbolic sort—elections of a powerless parliament or a too-powerful president with a permanent bureaucracy. You would have multiple electoral mechanisms.

The number of people who can create art in our society, who can find any sort of aesthetic self-expression, is a fraction of what would be possible if society were democratic in this more radical socialist sense. You would get something like what existed in the epoch of high modernism. The really interesting thing about that period is not the completely confected and bogus notion of modernism. What is interesting is how many quite different and incompatible but concurrent aesthetic programs and practices there were. That is the richness of the period from 1900 to 1930. I think that richness would be reproduced on a much larger scale if you didn't have the particular triangulation of the early twentieth century—a declining aristocratic order, an incipient bourgeois technology, and the prospect of social revolution. After a revolution that installed a postcapitalist socialist democracy, you would have the material basis for a much richer social and cultural life.

Question

You seem to argue for a concept of revolution as a single transformative event. Do you see no value in a view of revolution as a more gradual social process?

Anderson

I think the notion of revolution should be valued and upheld, but also limited; the two operations necessarily go together. Marx's theory of historical materialism is more than simply a sociology of revolution. While it includes a program for socialist revolution, that is not its totality. The totality of history is not merely the history of revolutions. Nor is the history of socialism the totality of the history of revolutions. To retain the utility of the concept of revolution you have to set some kind of boundaries. This doesn't depreciate the importance of the long-term social, economic, and cultural transformations that must occur in any postrevolutionary society. But there is an enormous danger, as twentieth-century political history has shown, in a demagogic extension of the notion of revolution beyond the

336

period when one state is overthrown and replaced by another. We saw that very clearly in China in the 1960s, just as we saw it in the Soviet Union in the 1930s, which are not dissimilar experiences. So it's necessary to be both hard and sober about revolution.

Question (Cornel West)
I would like to go back to the charge that your position is a repetition of Lukács's evolutionism. Given the papers at this conference that have trashed classical versions of Marxism, it is important to note that you represent a highly refined version of classical Marxism. Indeed, when you specify the three coordinates of the conjuncture, you still start with the economic and the political. The ideological and the cultural are reflected and refracted by those first two dominant and determinant coordinates. If that is so, then your ritualistic gesture to overdetermination is a mask for an economism, for a classical logocentric view. In many ways this is a breath of fresh air, given a certain discourse analysis. Nonetheless, one wants to know, how do your views differ from Lukacs's evolutionism?

Anderson
What you are calling classical Marxism is not something I'm particularly ashamed of; actually, I think it's a kind of common sense. Culture has material conditions of possibility, and it's important to look at those rather than become simply bemused or bewitched by the genuine magnificence of modernist works of art. In my analysis I did emphasize some cultural determinants as well. For example, if one is going to look at the range of practices we now call modernism, we have to look at the bogey of realism as well. The real enemy at the time the modernist movements crystallized was academicism, not realism.

Finally, my position is not evolutionistic. I've suggested that the conjuncture that produced modernism can recur at other times and at other points across the globe. Berman is right to see a lot of third-world contemporary fiction as having some of the vitality of the original modernist forms.

Question
If the only masterpieces are now coming out of the Third World (and the only hope for revolution is in the Third World), is any significant art being produced in modern Western capitalist societies that furthers the analysis of revolution?

Anderson
I'm not certain that the function of art is to further the analysis of social developments in an instrumental sense. But it wouldn't be difficult to cite major works of art that have come out of first- or second-world experiences. They are not necessarily modernist or postmodernist. I regard Solzhenitsyn's *First Circle* as a very great novel, although much of the rest of his work is inferior. The other example, cited in my paper, is the highly conservative, multivolume novel by Anthony Powell, *A Dance to the Music of Time;* this is the most important piece of postwar fiction in the English language for the metropolitan world. I'm confident it will be looked back on as a very great work, although it's not modernist in any strict sense.

Question
Could you comment on the ostensible antimodernism of nazism? Because it was actually nazism, not World War II, that wiped out Wiemar culture.

Anderson
I don't think nazism by itself destroyed those creative impulses. Don't forget that Brecht's masterpieces were actually produced well after the triumph of German fascism. The question of the attitude of successive political regimes of the thirties to various forms of avant-garde art is rather complex. One

would have to explore the reasons why nazism was implacably hostile to anything other than the most sterile neoacademic art, whereas Italian fascism was not. Right down to the end, Italian fascism maintained a fondness for certain avant-garde and modernist art. It's not the case, for instance, that all Italian architecture of the period is bad. We would also have to discuss the attitude of the Soviet regime institutionalized under Stalin and the way it wiped out an extraordinarily rich and experimental cultural life.

Comment (Doug DiBianco)
I'm concerned with the privileging of the first thirty years of the century as the key years of artistic accomplishment. While I would agree that people like Proust, Rilke, or Stravinsky produced great works, the rest of the century includes equally important work. It seems to me that these works are all films. I would include directors from Renoir to Sembene, from Bunuel to Pasolini, from Mitzougoushi to Bresson. I would list Ozu's *An Autumn Afternoon,* Hawks's *Rio Bravo,* and Waters's *Pink Flamingoes,* and many others.

Anderson
Well, I like the movies, too. But to be honest, I don't find the resources within me, seriously, to compare *Rio Bravo* to *Remembrance of Things Past.* It's just a different order of achievement.

Franco Moretti
The Spell of Indecision

Marxists have too often interpreted the aesthetic field of modernism by emphasizing the oppositional politics of irony and ambiguity. But it is not clear that these are, in themselves, subversive. They may also be the basic principles of capitalism's hegemony. Marxism has to recover a critical relationship to culture if it is not to surrender all claims to history and responsibility.

In the past two decades the dominant attitude toward modernism within Marxist criticism has completely changed. In essence, Marxist readings of avant-garde literature are increasingly based on interpretive theories—Russian formalism, Bakhtin's work, theories of the "open" text, deconstructionism—which, in one way or another, belong to modernism itself. This sudden loss of distance has inevitably given way to a sort of interpretive vicious circle; but what seems to me even more significant is the transformation that has occurred in the field of values and value judgments. From this point of view, recent Marxist criticism is really little more than a left-wing "Apology for Modernism."

We need only think of such pioneering Marxist work in the field of modern art as that of Benjamin and Adorno, and the extent of this cultural transformation (or reversal) becomes immediately evident. Benjamin and Adorno associated "fragmentary" texts with melancholy, pain, defenselessness, and loss of hope. Today, these same texts, along with the whole aesthetic field they evoke, would suggest the far more exhilarating concepts of semantic freedom, detotalization, and productive heterogeneity. In the deliberate obscurity of modern literature, Benjamin and Adorno saw the sign of an impending threat; now this obscurity is taken rather as a promise of free interpretive play. For them, the key novelist of the modern world was, quite clearly, Franz Kafka; today, just as clearly, he has been replaced by James Joyce, whose work is just as great, but certainly less urgent and uncanny.

By and large, I agree with critical emphasis on the antitragic or nontragic elements of modernism. What does not convince me at all, however, is the widespread idea that what we may call the dominant "ironic" mode of modernist literature is subversive of the modern bourgeois worldview. There is no doubt that "open" texts contradict and subvert organicistic beliefs, but it remains to be seen whether, as is now widely and uncritically assumed, in the past century the hegemonic frame of mind has not in fact abandoned organicism and replaced it with openness and irony. I will try to show that such is indeed the case and that, although I consider irony an indispensable component of any critical, democratic, and progressive culture, there is a dark side to its modernist version with which we

339

are not familiar enough and which may be even more relevant to Marxist culture than those elements given greater attention in the recent past.

Let us start with a small classic of the modernist imagination, one which, I believe, we owe to Lautréamont: an umbrella and a sewing machine meeting on an anatomical table. Dada, surrealism, Pound, Eliot, and several others have produced countless variations on this basic model and its attendant aesthetic, one which, to be sure, ironically negates any idea of "totality" and any hierarchy of meanings, leaving the field free for a virtually unlimited interpretive play.

Fine—and yet is this really such a subversive image? It would seem that Lautréamont's dream was shared, not only by fellow poets, but also by the owners of the first department stores as well. Describing their windows, D'Avenel wrote in 1894 that "the most dissimilar objects lend each other mutual support when they are placed next to each other." "Why should they be?" wonders Richard Sennett, to whom I owe the quotation; he replies: "The use character of the object was temporarily suspended. It became 'stimulating,' one wanted to buy it, because it became temporarily an unexpected thing; it became strange."[1]

A common object transformed into something unexpected and strange: is this not precisely the disautomatization of the way we perceive everyday things advocated by that crucial modernist principle—*ostranenie*—of Russian formalism? Likewise, is it not also the basic technique of modern advertising, which took off shortly after the golden age of avant-garde movements and whose task is to endow commodities with a surprising and pleasant aesthetic aura?

These are just local affinities, so I will try to broaden the field of inquiry a little. At the turn of the century, Georg Simmel wrote an essay on "The Metropolis and Mental Life" in which he maintained that the main psychological problem of the city dweller lies in "the swift and continuous shift of external stimuli . . . the rapid telescoping of changing images . . . the unexpectedness of violent stimuli."[2] In Simmel's metropolis, which is a typically modernist text, stimuli can be dangerous—can be shocks, as Benjamin puts it when writing about Baudelaire. One has to protect oneself from them. But at the same time one cannot do that simply by being blind to them, because they are the best the modern world has to offer and suggest: objects to be owned, social roles to be played, fascinating situations to be experienced.

One has then to see and not to see, to accept and to disavow at the same time. It is a contradictory predicament, and in order to make us "feel at home" in the bourgeois metropolis—a feeling that is bound to be very near the core of what we call the "hegemonic worldview"—both external stimuli and subjective perception have to possess rather peculiar attributes, which, once more, turn out to be barely distinguishable from those usually associated with literary modernism. As for the stimulus, it has to be "evocative" more than "meaningful"; it must possess as little determinacy as possible and therefore be open to, or better still produce, such a plurality of associations that everybody can "find something" in it. It must, in other words, center around that key word of modernism: ambiguity. By contrast, what must develop on the side of the subject is the idea that this galaxy of associations is valuable *as such,* not as a starting point from which to move toward a definite choice—whether the choice is of a specific object, in advertising, or a semantic choice, in the reading of a poem—but as a "field of possibilities" whose charm lies precisely in its growing irreducibility to the field of "actuality."

This is an aesthetic-ironic attitude whose best definition still lies in an old formula—"willing suspension of disbelief"—which shows how much of the modernist imagination—where nothing is unbelievable—has its source in romantic irony. And romantic irony—observed one of its sharpest critics, Carl Schmitt, in *Politische Romantik*—is a frame of mind that sees in any event no more than an "occasion" for free intellectual and emotional play, for a mental and subjective deconstruction of the world as it is. Devoted to the category of "possibility," romantic irony is therefore incapable and even hostile to whatever resembles a decision. But decision—leaving aside Schmitt's reactionary development of this concept—is inseparable from praxis and history. Decisions have to be made all the time; even, paradoxically, in order to ensure the existence of that realm of possibility and indecision to which romanticism and modernism have attached such a central meaning. In order to come to terms with this paradoxical coexistence of tension and indecision, modern literature has developed one of its most powerful metaphors, of which I shall now briefly sketch three different stages.

Let us start with the first chapter of Balzac's *La peau de chagrin.* The hero has just lost his last francs at *roulette,* and tonight he is going to drown himself in the Seine. In the meantime, he wanders through an old curiosity shop, though it is really much more than that—let us say it is something midway between the Louvre and the Bon Marché. He is bewitched by the heterogeneous, almost surrealistic collection of objects that surround him. His imagination flares up in a perfect romantic reverie, when all of a sudden his dream comes true, thanks to that metaphor I have announced: the pact with the Devil. The Devil is a highly popular character with all oppositional cultures, so I will not attempt to criticize him/her but will simply point out the price of the pact: "And what shall be my counter-service therefore?" asks Goethe's Faust. Mephisto replies: "The time is long: thou need'st not now insist."[3] The time *is* long. Over a century later, Thomas Mann's Mephisto echoes this line: "We sell time. . . . that's the best thing we have to offer . . ." (*Doktor Faustus,* chap. 25).

We sell time and, in fact, buy it too. What happens is that Faust and Mephisto, so to speak, exchange times: to Faust, the unlimited possibilities of the future; to Mephisto, not eternity (Faust's soul, in the end, will go to Heaven) but the present. The line I have just quoted—"The time is long: thou need'st not now insist"—does not defer Faust's payment but enacts it. Precisely by not worrying "for the present," Faust ends up by surrendering it completely to Mephisto.

In Goethe, therefore, time splits: there is Faust's time, devoted to explorations and experiments, always fully and splendidly in view, and Mephisto's time, more often than not invisible but devoted precisely to those ruthless actions that are necessary in order to realize Faust's desire and visions, but of which Faust himself would prefer to feel innocent. "I grudge thee not the pleasure / Of lying to thyself in moderate measure" (vv. 3297-98) is Mephisto's sarcastic and truthful reply to Faust's disavowals in the crucial scene of the Gretchen tragedy (and a similar exchange takes place again in the episode of Philemon and Baucis).

One major psychological result of the pact is therefore a growing sense of irresponsibility on Faust's part. The enjoyment of "all treasures of the earth" is severed, although not completely, from the awareness of what is necessary to their production: "Before chaste ears one may not name straight out / What chaste hearts cannot do without" (vv. 3295-96). It is clear that the issue of decision, here, has not been erased but rather entrusted to someone who, being the Devil, will act in a totally unscrupulous way. Decision has not been eliminated; that cannot be. It has become even more cruel, and precisely because Faust leaves it to Mephisto, but it has also become less visible; and it is almost possible not to feel its weight.

In our second text, Flaubert's *L'education sentimentale,* Mephisto has become a hidden devil. Frederic Moreau already enjoys the gifts traditionally offered by Mephisto—youth, beauty, and money—without having to sign any contract. A wealthy old uncle dies, and that is it; there is really no responsibility on Frederic's part. The distribution of this social power is the product of an entirely autonomous mechanism that is also, for the same reason, utterly unpredictable. The course of history is no longer contradictory and cruel (as in Goethe) but rather inscrutable and erratic. Potentially, it is even more catastrophic, but it has also become so remote that Frederic can see it—and does see it, in the first days of the 1848 revolution—simply as a show to be contemplated.

This aesthetic attitude toward life and history is the key to another novelty of Flaubert's work. Here money ceases to be the medium through which desire is satisfied, as Marx pointed out was the case with Goethe's Mephisto. In *L'education sentimentale* money is desirable because it allows not satisfaction but its postponement. Now that he is rich, Frederic can finally indulge in his dreams as dreams. Since he knows that he can realize them whenever he wishes, there is no need actually to do so now: "And indeed there will be time / . . . / And time yet for a hundred indecisions, / And for a hundred visions and revisions. . . ."

Frederic's life is really a monument to ironic indecision—so much so that he manages to remain undefined even in those crucial years between 1848 and 1851 when everybody had to take sides. And you probably can recall the last page of the novel: "the best thing we have had," says an aged Frederic to his lifelong friend Deslauries, is that flight from the brothel, in early adolescence, when "the sight of so many women, all at his disposal" had paralyzed Frederic's capacity for decision. The best thing we can have is an experience that has not taken place and therefore can be reexperienced in a totally unconstrained and subjective way. The romantic charm of indecision has found its most adequate temporal expression: no longer Faust's violent desire for the future, but *daydreaming,* which can freely renegotiate between and manage past, present, and future alike. The split between two different times and two parallel lives has gone a step further.

Daydreaming is the kernel of Bloom's "stream of consciousness" in *Ulysses,* which is the third text. Stream of consciousness, we know, does not deal with consciousness but with what is usually called the "preconscious," which contains the countless "possible selves" of each individual, what he/she would like to be or to have been but—for whatever reason—is not. From this point of view, Bloom's daydreaming completes the separation

342

between "objective" and "public" time, and its "subjective" and "private" version. The latter, it goes without saying, is by now considered the most interesting of the two; life as "actuality" has become far less meaningful than that parallel form, life as "possibility."

But Joyce's more significant and typically modernist innovation lies in the fact that he has managed to break down the connection between "possibility" and "anxiety." This connection was still strong in Goethe (in the interplay of "streben" and "Sorge" in *Faust*), in Kierkegaard, and in that great and pained exploration of the logic of a possible second life that was the nineteenth-century novel of adultery (of which Flaubert was, predictably, a master). In *Ulysses,* adultery has become a harmless pastime, and even the most extreme experiments of its modernist imagination may well produce stupefaction, but they no longer evoke anything threatening.

How did this disconnection between "possibility" and "anxiety" come to pass? The remarkable weakening of guilt feelings that has occurred in our century is certainly part of the answer, but perhaps something else has been at work too. The "possibilities" of a "second" life produced anxiety because they constituted a challenge to what was "real" and forced everybody to rethink his/her own "first" life. Imagination, so to speak, was taken quite seriously: to the extent that it was a promise, it was also a threat. This implied a great deal of discomfort and stiffness—and also of anxiety and guilt—but precisely because the products of the imagination were a source for inspiration and transformation of man's and woman's "first" and "actual" life.

It is this feedback that has ceased to work in our century. Modernist imagination has become immensely more ironic, free, and surprising than it was in the past—but at the price of leaving our "first" life wholly bereft of these qualities. From this point of view, modernism appears once more as a crucial component of that great symbolic transformation that has taken place in contemporary Western societies: the meaning of life is sought no more in the realm of public life, politics, and work; instead, it has migrated into the world of consumption and private life. This second sphere has become incredibly more promising, exciting, and free, and it is within its boundaries that we can indulge in our unending daydreams. But they are symmetrical; and more than that, they owe their very existence to the bored and blind indifference of our public life. Daydreams—even the most subversive ones—really have no interest in changing the world because their essence lies in running parallel to it, and since the world is merely an "occasion" for their deployment, it may just as well remain as it is. Romanticism, observed Carl Schmitt, managed to coexist with all sorts of political regimes and beliefs. This is even more true of modernism, whose unbelievable range of political choices can be explained only by its basic political indifference.

There is a complicity between modernist irony and indifference to history, and we find one of its most perfect expressions in Joyce's rhetorical choice to rewrite what is practically the same passage in two or more different styles, a device that is emphasized in several chapters of *Ulysses* and present as well in the text as a whole. Almost never "motivated" (with the personality of the speaker, for instance), this technique is put in front of the reader as a breathtaking exercise in literary competence and, I should add, in literary irony, since the root of irony lies precisely in being able to see something from more than one point of view.

Still, this rhetorical choice has a rather evident consequence on our perception of time and history. The status of history in *Ulysses* is, as you know, intrinsically rather low; to put it plainly, very little happens in the book. But more than that, the multiplicity of styles forces our attention *away* from whatever happens and focuses it entirely on the various ways in which events can be seen. To use narratology's standard terms, Joyce radicalized the narrative tendency that aimed at overdeveloping the level of "discourse" at the expense of the "story." What is really meaningful is not what happens, the logic of events and decisions, but rather our un-motivated—that is, free—subjective reactions to it. And in order for our reactions to be fully unconstrained, the story should exert as little pressure as possible; if the story stands still in eternal repetition—as in *Finnegan's Wake*—so much the better.

Novels, of course, can stop stories, but not history, and the forms with which we picture historical moments to ourselves are crucial for the fashioning of our identity. Once avant-garde literature abandoned plot, the void was inevitably filled by a parallel literary system—mass literature—which, just as inevitably, has acquired an ever increasing relevance. The appeal of mass literature is that "it tells stories," and we all need stories; if instead of *Buddenbrook* we get *The Carpetbaggers,* then Harold Robbins it is. This certainly represents no progressive development in our perception of history, but it is nonetheless a fact that, in this century, narrative forms capable of dealing with the great structures and transformations of social life more often than not have belonged to the various genres of mass literature and, more broadly, mass culture.

I believe that Marxist criticism has not only unduly underesti-mated the relevance of mass culture in our century but has also been blind to its systematic connection with avant-garde experiences. If the study of modernism must be a study of modern cultures and its role in history—and not just of a chosen section of it—we must realize that the silence of mod-ernism is as meaningful as its words and that it has also been covered by other, quite different voices. And, finally, what a century of modernism teaches us is that irony, extraordinary cultural achievement though it is, has to recover some kind of problematic relationship with responsibility and decision, or else it will have to surrender history altogether.

Notes

1   Richard Sennett, *The Fall of the Public Man* (New York: Random House, 1976), p. 144.

2   Georg Simmel, "The Metropolis and Mental Life," *On Individuality and Social Forms: Selected Writings* (Chicago: University of Chicago Press, 1971), p. 325.

3   J. W. Goethe, *Faust,* trans. Bayard Taylor (London: Sphere Books, 1969), vv. 1649-50.

Franco Moretti

Comment (Colin MacCabe)

Much as I respect your ability to restate a traditional Marxist case, I find it difficult to contain my anger at the way those who invoke "comrade history" never pay much attention to particular histories. I'd like to focus on a couple of your examples from Joyce. You argue that the treatment of adultery in *Ulysses* represents a decline from its treatment in the bourgeois novel of the nineteenth century. In the nineteenth-century novel, you claim, adultery at least was seen as a major problem; it typically focused the difference between two possible lives. I want to suggest that your position ignores the way adultery functioned throughout the nineteenth century and ignores, as well, the way Joyce produces it in *Ulysses*. Within the novel adultery is linked with art, as when Stephen has a vision of himself as the great artist, as Shakespeare, in the moment in which his and Bloom's faces congeal in the mirror, underneath the antlers of the cuckold. I think Joyce is suggesting that that kind of serious art, with its commitment to absolute meaning, is inextricably linked to the concerns of the cuckold, to the man's desire to control his seed. So I think your reading slights the text.

The second point I want to make is about the whole notion of public life and the way in which Joyce's texts are considered to back away from an interest in and concern with public life. Once again, it is important to reflect on the actual history in which Joyce's text was issued in 1922, in exactly the same year as the Irish Free State gained independence. It is difficult to imagine—and I am sure that Joyce could not imagine it—a public life in a state in which the national liberation movement was linked to a totally reactionary church. This left someone like Yeats in 1928 and 1929 having to speak in the senate as divorce was outlawed, indeed as a whole series of reactionary measures went through. (Even now the Irish state is going to enshrine abortion in its constitution.) Once we supply that historical context, we can understand why Joyce felt that there was no public voice for him in Ireland. He made that very clear in a whole series of writings very early on in Trieste and then in the novels. This in turn reflects back on a general problem in Marxist ethics. It seems to me that what Franco was saying is that one of the things we have to think very seriously about—and perhaps this is one of the times when we have to think very seriously about it—is what one does when public positions cannot be taken.

Moretti

Although adultery occupies a large section of the text, it has ceased to be a highly meaningful and potentially tragic event in the lives of the characters. Adultery did function that way in the nineteenth-century European novel, but it no longer does in *Ulysses*. My effort, then, was to explain how the concept of adultery was dissociated from the idea of anxiety. This seems to me one of the strangest psychocultural events of our century.

As for the issue of public life, I would not want to say that public life is good in itself, that any public position is worthy simply because it is public. But to be more specific, consider the history of the genre to which *Ulysses* belongs, the history of the novel. For two and one-half centuries the novel has been a sustained effort to fix the meaning of an individual's life in its connection with public events, with history, macro-history, if you wish. Now, I would maintain that *Ulysses* tends to break down this connection in a very radical way. You object by recalling the conditions of Irish public life and you end up by asking what one should do when public positions are impossible. Well, a hundred years before Joyce wrote *Ulysses,* Stendhal faced this problem in writing *The Red and the Black,* which is the story of a young man who believes in certain values that are no longer publicly tenable. Stendhal dealt with the problem of the untenability of a public voice in a particular historical context. *Ulysses* does not confront this problem. In *Ulysses* the weight is placed on subjective dreaming, and public life seems less important as a result. I suppose we need a shootout on *Ulysses;* we've been disagreeing for years.

345

Question (Darko Suvin)

I would like to take a position halfway between Franco Moretti and Colin McCabe. The way to deal with an important process such as modernism is dialectically, to identify its contradictions and the dominant moment within them. This is also a problem of deciding what is the true canon of modernism. Marxists have too often accepted the canon of bourgeois theoreticians which moves from Kafka to Joyce. The proper canon of modernism would be the one significant for us today. What is the dominant contradiction in *this* canon? It is the tension between those who tried to have their work intervene in history and those who despaired of it, the tension between Brecht and Joyce. We also need to consider the place of mass literature *within* modernism.

Moretti

"Modernism" is a portmanteau word that perhaps should not be used too often. But I don't think I would classify Brecht as a modernist—perhaps the young Brecht, but then several of the problems I have identified in other modernists might also apply to the young Brecht. I certainly would not include *Saint Joan,* the *Lehrstucke,* or *The Measures Taken* within modernism. I just cannot think of a meaningful category that could include, say, surrealism, *Ulysses,* and something by Brecht. I can't think of what the common attributes of such a concept could be. The objects are too dissimilar.

Comment

You maintain the reflection theory of culture when you deny the conflictual status of modernism and assert its complete harmony with the goals of capitalism in the age of the big department store. And then, by way of an essentialist and moralistic invocation, you argue that our need for stories is fulfilled by mass literature once modernism abandons plot. Finally, your call for a modernist irony connected with decision is based on no ground that I can identify except voluntarism.

Moretti

When I say we all need stories, that is not a moralistic invocation; it is a statement of fact. We all need to have stories in our heads, plots that give meaning. But the main question concerned irony and decision. You object that there is no ground for my reconnection of irony and decision, that it is ultimately voluntaristic. You are absolutely right. It is a choice we have to make. I'm not saying No to modernism—it is certainly a great cultural development. The point is that it has a reverse side, one I have been trying to elucidate. And I wonder whether this great development, which is modernist irony, can be put to use by combining it with other values. I have proposed that irony be joined with decision. But I am not at all sure it is a connection that can be worked out. While at present I don't see any ground for their combination, it would be a pity if it proves impossible, because either way you lose something that could be very important for human culture.

346

Fredric Jameson
Cognitive Mapping

> Without a conception of the social totality (and the pos-
> sibility of transforming a whole social system), no prop-
> erly socialist politics is possible. It involves trying to
> imagine how a society without hierarchy, a society that
> has also repudiated the economic mechanisms of the
> market, can possibly cohere.

I am addressing a subject about which I know nothing
whatsoever, except for the fact that it does not exist. The description of a
new aesthetic, or the call for it, or its prediction—these things are generally
done by practicing artists whose manifestos articulate the originality they
hope for in their own work, or by critics who think they already have before
their eyes the stirrings and emergences of the radically new. Unfortunately,
I can claim neither of those positions, and since I am not even sure how
to imagine the kind of art I want to propose here, let alone affirm its possibility, it may well be wondered what kind of an operation this will be, to
produce the concept of something we cannot imagine.

Perhaps all this is a kind of blind, in that something
else will really be at stake. I have found myself obliged, in arguing an aesthetic of cognitive mapping, to plot a substantial detour through the great
themes and shibboleths of post-Marxism, so that to me it does seem possible
that the aesthetic here may be little more than a pretext for debating those
theoretical and political issues. So be it. In any case, during this Marxist
conference I have frequently had the feeling that I am one of the few Marxists
left. I take it I have a certain responsibility to restate what seem to me to
be a few self-evident truths, but which you may see as quaint survivals of
a religious, millenarian, salvational form of belief.

In any case, I want to forestall the misapprehension
that the aesthetic I plan to outline is intended to displace and to supercede
a whole range of other, already extant or possible and conceivable aesthetics
of a different kind. Art has always done a great many different things, and
had a great many distinct and incommensurable functions: let it continue
to do all that—which it will, in any case, even in Utopia. But the very
pluralism of the aesthetic suggests that there should be nothing particularly
repressive in the attempt to remind ourselves and to revive experimentally
one traditional function of the aesthetic that has in our time been peculiarly
neglected and marginalized, if not interdicted altogether.

"To teach, to move, to delight": of these traditional
formulations of the uses of the work of art, the first has virtually been
eclipsed from contemporary criticism and theory. Yet the pedagogical function of a work of art seems in various forms to have been an inescapable
parameter of any conceivable Marxist aesthetic, if of few others; and it is

347

the great historical merit of the work of Darko Suvin to repeatedly insist on a more contemporary formulation of this aesthetic value, in the suggestive slogan of the *cognitive,* which I have made my own today. Behind Suvin's work, of course, there stands the immense, yet now partially institutionalized and reified, example of Brecht himself, to whom any cognitive aesthetic in our time must necessarily pay homage. And perhaps it is no longer the theater but the poetry of Brecht that is for us still the irrefutable demonstration that cognitive art need not raise any of the old fears about the contamination of the aesthetic by propaganda or the instrumentalization of cultural play and production by the message or the extra-aesthetic (basely practical) impulse. Brecht's is a poetry of thinking and reflection; yet no one who has been stunned by the sculptural density of Brecht's language, by the stark simplicity with which a contemplative distance from historical events is here powerfully condensed into the ancient forms of folk wisdom and the proverb, in sentences as compact as peasants' wooden spoons and bowls, will any longer question the proposition that in his poetry at least— so exceptionally in the whole history of contemporary culture—the cognitive becomes in and of itself the immediate source of profound aesthetic delight.

I mention Brecht to forestall yet another misunderstanding, that it will in any sense be a question here of the return to some older aesthetic, even that of Brecht. And this is perhaps the moment to warn you that I tend to use the charged word "representation" in a different way than it has consistently been used in poststructuralist or post-Marxist theory: namely, as the synonym of some bad ideological and organic realism or mirage of realistic unification. For me "representation" is, rather, the synonym of "figuration" itself, irrespective of the latter's historical and ideological form. I assume, therefore, in what follows, that all forms of aesthetic production consist in one way or another in the struggle with and for representation— and this whether they are perspectival or trompe l'oeil illusions or the most reflexive and diacritical, iconoclastic or form-breaking modernisms. So, at least in my language, the call for new kinds of representation is not meant to imply the return to Balzac or Brecht; nor is it intended as some valorization of content over form—yet another archaic distinction I still feel is indispensable and about which I will have more to say shortly.

In the project for a spatial analysis of culture that I have been engaged in sketching for the teaching institute that preceded this conference, I have tried to suggest that the three historical stages of capital have each generated a type of space unique to it, even though these three stages of capitalist space are obviously far more profoundly interrelated than are the spaces of other modes of production. The three types of space I have in mind are all the result of discontinuous expansions or quantum leaps in the enlargement of capital, in the latter's penetration and colonization of hitherto uncommodified areas. You will therefore note in passing that a certain unifying and totalizing force is presupposed here—although it is not the Hegelian Absolute Spirit, nor the party, nor Stalin, but simply capital itself; and it is on the strength of such a view that a radical Jesuit friend of mine once publicly accused me of monotheism. It is at least certain that the notion of capital stands or falls with the notion of some unified logic of this social system itself, that is to say, in the stigmatized language I will come back to later, that both are irrecoverably totalizing concepts.

I have tried to describe the first kind of space of classical or market capitalism in terms of a logic of the grid, a reorganization of some older sacred and heterogeneous space into geometrical and Cartesian homogeneity, a space of infinite equivalence and extension of which you can find a kind of dramatic or emblematic shorthand representation in Foucault's book on prisons. The example, however, requires the warning that a Marxian view of such space grounds it in Taylorization and the labor process rather than in that shadowy and mythical Foucault entity called "power." The emergence of this kind of space will probably not involve problems of figuration so acute as those we will confront in the later stages of capitalism, since here, for the moment, we witness that familiar process long generally associated with the Enlightenment, namely, the desacralization of the world, the decoding and secularization of the older forms of the sacred or the transcendent, the slow colonization of use value by exchange value, the "realistic" demystification of the older kinds of transcendent narratives in novels like *Don Quixote,* the standardization of both subject and object, the denaturalization of desire and its ultimate displacement by commodification or, in other words, "success," and so on.

The problems of figuration that concern us will only become visible in the next stage, the passage from market to monopoly capital, or what Lenin called the "stage of imperialism"; and they may be conveyed by way of a growing contradiction between lived experience and structure, or between a phenomenological description of the life of an individual and a more properly structural model of the conditions of existence of that experience. Too rapidly we can say that, while in older societies and perhaps even in the early stages of market capital, the immediate and limited experience of individuals is still able to encompass and coincide with the true economic and social form that governs that experience, in the next moment these two levels drift ever further apart and really begin to constitute themselves into that opposition the classical dialectic describes as *Wesen* and *Erscheinung,* essence and appearance, structure and lived experience.

At this point the phenomenological experience of the individual subject—traditionally, the supreme raw materials of the work of art—becomes limited to a tiny corner of the social world, a fixed-camera view of a certain section of London or the countryside or whatever. But the truth of that experience no longer coincides with the place in which it takes place. The truth of that limited daily experience of London lies, rather, in India or Jamaica or Hong Kong; it is bound up with the whole colonial system of the British Empire that determines the very quality of the individual's subjective life. Yet those structural coordinates are no longer accessible to immediate lived experience and are often not even conceptualizable for most people.

There comes into being, then, a situation in which we can say that if individual experience is authentic, then it cannot be true; and that if a scientific or cognitive model of the same content is true, then it escapes individual experience. It is evident that this new situation poses tremendous and crippling problems for a work of art; and I have argued that it is as an attempt to square this circle and to invent new and elaborate formal strategies for overcoming this dilemma that modernism or, perhaps better, the various modernisms as such emerge: in forms that inscribe a new sense of the absent global colonial system on the very syntax of poetic language itself, a new play of absence and presence that at its most simplified will be haunted by the erotic and be tattooed with foreign place names, and at its most intense will involve the invention of remarkable new languages and forms.

At this point I want to introduce another concept that is basic to my argument, that I call the "play of figuration." This is an essentially allegorical concept that supposes the obvious, namely, that these new and enormous global realities are inaccessible to any individual subject or consciousness—not even to Hegel, let alone Cecil Rhodes or Queen Victoria—which is to say that those fundamental realities are somehow ultimately unrepresentable or, to use the Althusserian phrase, are something like an absent cause, one that can never emerge into the presence of perception. Yet this absent cause can find figures through which to express itself in distorted and symbolic ways: indeed, one of our basic tasks as critics of literature is to track down and make conceptually available the ultimate realities and experiences designated by those figures, which the reading mind inevitably tends to reify and to read as primary contents in their own right.

Since we have evoked the modernist moment and its relationship to the great new global colonial network, I will give a fairly simple but specialized example of a kind of figure specific to this historical situation. Everyone knows how, toward the end of the nineteenth century, a wide range of writers began to invent forms to express what I will call "monadic relativism." In Gide and Conrad, in Fernando Pessoa, in Pirandello, in Ford, and to a lesser extent in Henry James, even very obliquely in Proust, what we begin to see is the sense that each consciousness is a closed world, so that a representation of the social totality now must take the (impossible) form of a coexistence of those sealed subjective worlds and their peculiar interaction, which is in reality a passage of ships in the night, a centrifugal movement of lines and planes that can never intersect. The literary value that emerges from this new formal practice is called "irony"; and its philosophical ideology often takes the form of a vulgar appropriation of Einstein's theory of relativity. In this context, what I want to suggest is that these forms, whose content is generally that of privatized middle-class life, nonetheless stand as symptoms and distorted expressions of the penetration even of middle-class lived experience by this strange new global relativity of the colonial network. The one is then the figure, however deformed and symbolically rewritten, of the latter; and I take it that this figural process will remain central in all later attempts to restructure the form of the work of art to accommodate content that must radically resist and escape artistic figuration.

If this is so for the age of imperialism, how much more must it hold for our own moment, the moment of the multinational network, or what Mandel calls "late capitalism," a moment in which not merely the older city but even the nation-state itself has ceased to play a central functional and formal role in a process that has in a new quantum leap of capital prodigiously expanded beyond them, leaving them behind as ruined and archaic remains of earlier stages in the development of this mode of production.

At this point I realize that the persuasiveness of my demonstration depends on your having some fairly vivid perceptual sense of what is unique and original in postmodernist space—something I have been trying to convey in my course, but for which it is more difficult here to substitute a shortcut. Briefly, I want to suggest that the new space involves the suppression of distance (in the sense of Benjamin's aura) and the relentless saturation of any remaining voids and empty places, to the point where the postmodern body—whether wandering through a postmodern hotel, locked into rock sound by means of headphones, or undergoing the multiple shocks and bombardments of the Vietnam War as Michael Herr conveys it to us—is now exposed to a perceptual barrage of immediacy from which all sheltering layers and intervening mediations have been removed. There are, of course, many other features of this space one would ideally want to comment on—most notably, Lefebvre's concept of abstract space as what is simultaneously homogeneous and fragmented—but I think that the peculiar disorientation of the saturated space I have just mentioned will be the most useful guiding thread.

You should understand that I take such spatial peculiarities of postmodernism as symptoms and expressions of a new and historically original dilemma, one that involves our insertion as individual subjects into a multidimensional set of radically discontinuous realities, whose frames range from the still surviving spaces of bourgeois private life all the way to the unimaginable decentering of global capital itself. Not even Einsteinian relativity, or the multiple subjective worlds of the older modernists, is capable of giving any kind of adequate figuration to this process, which in lived experience makes itself felt by the so-called death of the subject, or, more exactly, the fragmented and schizophrenic decentering and dispersion of this last (which can no longer even serve the function of the Jamesian reverberator or "point of view"). And although you may not have realized it, I am talking about practical politics here: since the crisis of socialist internationalism, and the enormous strategic and tactical difficulties of coordinating local and grassroots or neighborhood political actions with national or international ones, such urgent political dilemmas are all immediately functions of the enormously complex new international space I have in mind.

Let me here insert an illustration, in the form of a brief account of a book that is, I think, not known to many of you but in my opinion of the greatest importance and suggestiveness for problems of space and politics. The book is nonfiction, a historical narrative of the single most significant political experience of the American 1960s: *Detroit: I Do Mind Dying*, by Marvin Surkin and Dan Georgakis. (I think we have now come to be sophisticated enough to understand that aesthetic, formal, and narrative analyses have implications that far transcend those objects marked as fiction or as literature.) *Detroit* is a study of the rise and fall of the League of Black Revolutionary Workers in that city in the late 1960s.[1] The political formation in question was able to conquer power in the workplace, particularly in the automobile factories; it drove a substantial wedge into the media and informational monopoly of the city by way of a student newspaper; it elected judges; and finally it came within a hair's breadth of electing the mayor and taking over the city power apparatus. This was, of course, a remarkable political achievement, characterized by an exceedingly sophisticated sense of the need for a multilevel strategy for revolution that involved initiatives on the distinct social levels of the labor process, the media and culture, the juridical apparatus, and electoral politics.

351

Yet it is equally clear—and far clearer in virtual triumphs of this kind than in the earlier stages of neighborhood politics—that such strategy is bound and shackled to the city form itself. Indeed, one of the enormous strengths of the superstate and its federal constitution lies in the evident discontinuities between city, state, and federal power: if you cannot make socialism in one country, how much more derisory, then, are the prospects for socialism in one city in the United States today? Indeed, our foreign visitors may not be aware that there exist in this country four or five socialist communes, near one of which, in Santa Cruz, California, I lived until recently; no one would want to belittle these local successes, but it seems probable that few of us think of them as the first decisive step toward the transition to socialism.

If you cannot build socialism in one city, then suppose you conquer a whole series of large key urban centers in succession. This is what the League of Black Revolutionary Workers began to think about; that is to say, they began to feel that their movement was a political model and ought to be generalizable. The problem that arises is spatial: how to develop a *national* political movement on the basis of a *city* strategy and politics. At any rate, the leadership of the League began to spread the word in other cities and traveled to Italy and Sweden to study workers' strategies there and to explain their own model; reciprocally, out-of-town politicos came to Detroit to investigate the new strategies. At this point it ought to be clear that we are in the middle of the problem of representation, not the least of it being signaled by the appearance of that ominous American word "leadership." In a more general way, however, these trips were more than networking, making contacts, spreading information: they raised the problem of how to represent a unique local model and experience to people in other situations. So it was logical for the League to make a film of their experience, and a very fine and exciting film it is.

Spatial discontinuities, however, are more devious and dialectical, and they are not overcome in any of the most obvious ways. For example, they returned on the Detroit experience as some ultimate limit before which it collapsed. What happened was that the jet-setting militants of the League had become media stars; not only were they becoming alienated from their local constituencies, but, worse than that, nobody stayed home to mind the store. Having acceded to a larger spatial plane, the base vanished under them; and with this the most successful social revolutionary experiment of that rich political decade in the United States came to a sadly undramatic end. I do not want to say that it left no traces behind, since a number of local gains remain, and in any case every rich political experiment continues to feed the tradition in underground ways. Most ironic in our context, however, is the very success of their failure: the representation—the model of this complex spatial dialectic—triumphantly survives in the form of a film and a book, but in the process of becoming an image and a spectacle, the referent seems to have disappeared, as so many people from Debord to Baudrillard always warned us it would.

Yet this very example may serve to illustrate the proposition that successful spatial representation today need not be some uplifting socialist-realist drama of revolutionary triumph but may be equally inscribed in a narrative of defeat, which sometimes, even more effectively, causes the whole architectonic of postmodern global space to rise up in ghostly profile behind itself, as some ultimate dialectical barrier or invisible limit. This example also may have given a little more meaning to the slogan of cognitive mapping to which I now turn.

I am tempted to describe the way I understand this concept as something of a synthesis between Althusser and Kevin Lynch—a formulation that, to be sure, does not tell you much unless you know that Lynch is the author of a classic work, *The Image of the City,* which in its turn spawned the whole low-level subdiscipline that today takes the phrase "cognitive mapping" as its own designation.[2] Lynch's problematic remains locked within the limits of phenomenology, and his book can no doubt be subjected to many criticisms on its own terms (not the least of which is the absence of any conception of political agency or historical process). My use of the book will be emblematic, since the mental map of city space explored by Lynch can be extrapolated to that mental map of the social and global totality we all carry around in our heads in variously garbled forms. Drawing on the downtowns of Boston, Jersey City, and Los Angeles, and by means of interviews and questionnaires in which subjects we asked to draw their city context from memory, Lynch suggests that urban alienation is directly proportional to the mental unmapability of local cityscapes. A city like Boston, then, with its monumental perspectives, its markers and monuments, its combination of grand but simple spatial forms, including dramatic boundaries such as the Charles River, not only allows people to have, in their imaginations, a generally successful and continuous location to the rest of the city, but in addition gives them something of the freedom and aesthetic gratification of traditional city form.

I have always been struck by the way in which Lynch's conception of city experience—the dialectic between the here and now of immediate perception and the imaginative or imaginary sense of the city as an absent totality—presents something like a spatial analogue of Althusser's great formulation of ideology itself, as "the Imaginary representation of the subject's relationship to his or her Real conditions of existence." Whatever its defects and problems, this positive conception of ideology as a necessary function in any form of social life has the great merit of stressing the gap between the local positioning of the individual subject and the totality of class structures in which he or she is situated, a gap between phenomenological perception and a reality that transcends all individual thinking or experience; but this ideology, as such, attempts to span or coordinate, to map, by means of conscious and unconscious representations. The conception of cognitive mapping proposed here therefore involves an extrapolation of Lynch's spatial analysis to the realm of social structure, that is to say, in our historical moment, to the totality of class relations on a global (or should I say multinational) scale. The secondary premise is also maintained, namely, that the incapacity to map socially is as crippling to political experience as the analogous incapacity to map spatially is for urban experience. It follows that an aesthetic of cognitive mapping in this sense is an integral part of any socialist political project.

In what has preceded I have infringed so many of the taboos and shibboleths of a faddish post-Marxism that it becomes necessary to discuss them more openly and directly before proceeding. They include the proposition that class no longer exists (a proposition that might be clarified by the simple distinction between class as an element in small-scale models of

353

society, class consciousness as a cultural event, and class analysis as a mental operation); the idea that this society is no longer motored by production but rather reproduction (including science and technology)—an idea that, in the midst of a virtually completely built environment, one is tempted to greet with laughter; and, finally, the repudiation of representation and the stigmatization of the concept of totality and of the project of totalizing thought. Practically, this last needs to be sorted into several different propositions—in particular, one having to do with capitalism and one having to do with socialism or communism. The French *nouveaux philosophes* said it most succinctly, without realizing that they were reproducing or reinventing the hoariest American ideological slogans of the cold war: totalizing thought is totalitarian thought; a direct line runs from Hegel's Absolute Spirit to Stalin's Gulag.

As a matter of self-indulgence, I will open a brief theoretical parenthesis here, particularly since Althusser has been mentioned. We have already experienced a dramatic and instructive melt-down of the Althusserian reactor in the work of Barry Hindess and Paul Hirst, who quite consequently observe the incompatibility of the Althusserian attempt to secure semiautonomy for the various levels of social life, and the more desperate effort of the same philosopher to retain the old orthodox notion of an "ultimately determining instance" in the form of what he calls "structural totality." Quite logically and consequently, then, Hindess and Hirst simply remove the offending mechanism, whereupon the Althusserian edifice collapses into a rubble of autonomous instances without any necessary relationship to each other whatsoever—at which point it follows that one can no longer talk about or draw practical political consequences from any conception of social structure; that is to say, the very conceptions of something called capitalism and something called socialism or communism fall of their own weight into the ash can of History. (This last, of course, then vanishes in a puff of smoke, since by the same token nothing like History as a total process can any longer be conceptually entertained.) All I wanted to point out in this high theoretical context is that the baleful equation between a philosophical conception of totality and a political practice of totalitarianism is itself a particularly ripe example of what Althusser calls "expressive causality," namely, the collapsing of two semiautonomous (or, now, downright autonomous) levels into one another. Such an equation, then, is possible for unreconstructed Hegelians but is quite incompatible with the basic positions of any honest post-Althusserian post-Marxism.

To close the parenthesis, all of this can be said in more earthly terms. The conception of capital is admittedly a totalizing or systemic concept: no one has ever seen or met the thing itself; it is either the result of scientific reduction (and it should be obvious that scientific thinking always reduces the multiplicity of the real to a small-scale model) or the mark of an imaginary and ideological vision. But let us be serious: anyone who believes that the profit motive and the logic of capital accumulation are not the fundamental laws of this world, who believes that these do not set absolute barriers and limits to social changes and transformations undertaken in it—such a person is living in an alternative universe; or, to put it more politely, in this universe such a person—assuming he or she is progressive—is doomed to social democracy, with its now abundantly documented treadmill of failures and capitulations. Because if capital does not exist, then clearly socialism does not exist either. I am far from suggesting that no politics at all is possible in this new post-Marxian Nietzschean world of micropolitics—that is observably untrue. But I do want to argue that without a conception of the social totality (and the possibility of transforming a whole social system), no properly socialist politics is possible.

About socialism itself we must raise more troubling and unsolved dilemmas that involve the notion of community or the collective. Some of the dilemmas are very familiar, such as the contradiction between self-management on the local level and planning on the global scale; or the problems raised by the abolition of the market, not to mention the abolition of the commodity form itself. I have found even more stimulating and problematical the following propositions about the very nature of society itself: it has been affirmed that, with one signal exception (capitalism itself, which is organized around an economic mechanism), there has never existed a cohesive form of human society that was not based on some form of transcendence or religion. Without brute force, which is never but a momentary solution, people cannot in this vein be asked to live cooperatively and to renounce the omnivorous desires of the id without some appeal to religious belief or transcendent values, something absolutely incompatible with any conceivable socialist society. The result is that these last achieve their own momentary coherence only under seige circumstances, in the wartime enthusiasm and group effort provoked by the great blockades. In other words, without the nontranscendent economic mechanism of capital, all appeals to moral incentives (as in Che) or to the primacy of the political (as in Maoism) must fatally exhaust themselves in a brief time, leaving only the twin alternatives of a return to capitalism or the construction of this or that modern form of "oriental despotism." You are certainly welcome to believe this prognosis, provided you understand that in such a case any socialist politics is strictly a mirage and a waste of time, which one might better spend adjusting and reforming an eternal capitalist landscape as far as the eye can see.

In reality this dilemma is, to my mind, the most urgent task that confronts Marxism today. I have said before that the so-called crisis in Marxism is not a crisis in Marxist science, which has never been richer, but rather a crisis in Marxist ideology. If ideology—to give it a somewhat different definition—is a vision of the future that grips the masses, we have to admit that, save in a few ongoing collective experiments, such as those in Cuba and in Yugoslavia, no Marxist or Socialist party or movement anywhere has the slightest conception of what socialism or communism as a social system ought to be and can be expected to look like. That vision will not be purely economic, although the Marxist economists are as deficient as the rest of us in their failure to address this Utopian problem in any serious way. It is, as well, supremely social and cultural, involving the task of trying to imagine how a society without hierarchy, a society of free people, a society that has at once repudiated the economic mechanisms of the market, can possibly cohere. Historically, all forms of hierarchy have always been based ultimately on gender hierarchy and on the building block of the family unit, which makes it clear that this is the true juncture between a feminist problematic and a Marxist one—not an antagonistic juncture, but the moment at which the feminist project and the Marxist and socialist project meet and face the same dilemma: how to imagine Utopia.

Returning to the beginning of this lengthy excursus, it seems unlikely that anyone who repudiates the concept of totality can have anything useful to say to us on this matter, since for such persons it is clear that the totalizing vision of socialism will not compute and is a false problem within the random and undecidable world of microgroups. Or perhaps another possibility suggests itself, namely, that our dissatisfaction with the concept of totality is not a thought in its own right but rather a significant symptom, a function of the increasing difficulties in thinking of such a set of interrelationships in a complicated society. This would seem, at least, to be the implication of the remark of the Team X architect Aldo van Eyck, when, in 1966, he issued his version of the death of modernism thesis: "We know nothing of vast multiplicity—we cannot come to terms with it—not as architects or planners or anybody else." To which he added, and the sequel can easily be extrapolated from architecture to social change itself: "But if society has no form—how can architects build its counterform?"[3]

You will be relieved to know that at this point we can return both to my own conclusion and to the problem of aesthetic representation and cognitive mapping, which was the pretext of this essay. The project of cognitive mapping obviously stands or falls with the conception of some (unrepresentable, imaginary) global social totality that was to have been mapped. I have spoken of form and content, and this final distinction will allow me at least to say something about an aesthetic, of which I have observed that I am, myself, absolutely incapable of guessing or imagining its form. That postmodernism gives us hints and examples of such cognitive mapping on the level of content is, I believe, demonstrable.

I have spoken elsewhere of the turn toward a thematics of mechanical reproduction, of the way in which the autoreferentiality of much of postmodernist art takes the form of a play with reproductive technology—film, tapes, video, computers, and the like—which is, to my mind, a degraded figure of the great multinational space that remains to be cognitively mapped. Fully as striking on another level is the omnipresence of the theme of paranoia as it expresses itself in a seemingly inexhaustible production of conspiracy plots of the most elaborate kinds. Conspiracy, one is tempted to say, is the poor person's cognitive mapping in the postmodern age; it is a degraded figure of the total logic of late capital, a desperate attempt to represent the latter's system, whose failure is marked by its slippage into sheer theme and content.

Achieved cognitive mapping will be a matter of form, and I hope I have shown how it will be an integral part of a socialist politics, although its own possibility may well be dependent on some prior political opening, which its task would then be to enlarge culturally. Still, even if we cannot imagine the productions of such an aesthetic, there may, nonetheless, as with the very idea of Utopia itself, be something positive in the attempt to keep alive the possibility of imagining such a thing.

Notes

1 Dan Georgakis and Marvin Surkin, *Detroit: I Do Mind Dying, A Study in Urban Revolution* (New York: St. Martin's Press, 1975).

Fredric Jameson

2   Kevin Lynch, *The Image of the City* (Cambridge: MIT Press, 1960).

3   Quoted in Kenneth Frampton, *Modern Architecture: A Critical History* (New York: Oxford University Press, 1980), pp. 276-77.

Question (Nancy Fraser)

First, I want to say something, for the record, about the implicit political gesture built into your presentation of the question of totality, which seemed to me rather irresponsible, given that there have been many discussions of the issue and that many nuanced positions have been expressed. You essentially conflated many differences and subtle positions on this question. But I do have a more constructive question to ask, because I am also sympathetic to a certain kind of totalizing thought, namely, a critical social science that would be as total and explanatorily powerful as possible. Thus, I wonder why you assume that cognitive mapping is the task of the aesthetic? Why wouldn't that be a task for critical social science? Or are two different kinds of tasks conflated in your paper?

Jameson

The question of the role of the aesthetic as opposed to that of the social sciences in explorations of the structure of the world system corresponds, for me, to the orthodox distinction (which I still vaguely use in a somewhat different way) between science and ideology. My point is that we have this split between ideology in the Althusserian sense—that is, how you map your relation as an individual subject to the social and economic organization of global capitalism—and the discourse of science, which I understand to be a discourse (which is ultimately impossible) without a subject. In this ideal discourse, like a mathematical equation, you model the real independent of its relations to individual subjects, including your own. Now I think that you can teach people how this or that view of the world is to be thought or conceptualized, but the real problem is that it is increasingly hard for people to put that together with their own experience as individual psychological subjects, in daily life. The social sciences can rarely do that, and when they try (as in ethnomethodology), they do it only by a mutation in the discourse of social science, or they do it at the moment that a social science becomes an ideology; but then we are back into the aesthetic. Aesthetics is something that addresses individual experience rather than something that conceptualizes the real in a more abstract way.

Question

Your paper suggests that cognitive mapping is an avenue by which we might proceed at this point in time. Is this a tactical or a strategic choice? If it is tactical, then how do you conceive the question of strategy? And if it is strategic, what do you consider the problem of tactics today? The reason I raise such a question is that there seem to be opportunities now to create an interconnected culture that might allow real political problems to be discussed. If that's true, the question of strategy and tactics seems central.

Jameson

That's an important question. I would answer it by trying to connect my suggestion with Stuart Hall's paper, in which he talked about the strategic possibilities of delegitimizing an existing discourse at a particular historical conjuncture. While I haven't used it, the language of discourse theory is certainly appropriate here (along with my own more dialectical language). My comrade and collaborator Stanley Aronowitz has observed that whatever the Left is in this country today, it has to begin by sorting out what the priorities really are. He takes the position that our essential function for the moment is pedagogical in the largest sense; it involves the conquest of legitimacy in this country for socialist discourse. In other words, since the sixties, everybody knows that there is a socialist discourse. In the TV serials there's always a radical; that has become a social type, or, more accurately, a stereotype. So while people know that a socialist discourse exists, it is not a legitimate discourse in this society. Thus no one takes seriously the idea that socialism, and the social reorganization it proposes, is the answer to our problems. Stuart Hall showed us the negative side of this struggle as the moment in which a

Fredric Jameson

hegemonic social democratic discourse finds its content withdrawn from it so that, finally, those things that used to be legitimate are no longer legitimate and nobody believes in them. Our task, I think, is the opposite of that and has to do with the legitimation of the discourses of socialism in such a way that they do become realistic and serious alternatives for people. It's in the context of that general project that my more limited aesthetic project finds its place.

Question (Darko Suvin)

First of all, I would like to say, also for the record, that I agree with your refusal to equate totality with totalitarianism. I want to remind people of the strange origins of the connotations of the word "totalitarianism." They arose after the war, propagated by the Congress of Cultural Freedom, which was associated with such names as Stephen Spender and Irving Kristol and with journals such as *Encounter,* funded by the CIA as it turns out. This is admittedly not a conclusive argument; even people funded by the CIA can come up with intelligent ideas now and then. But it should make us wary of such an equation. So I think your rebuttal is well taken and not at all irresponsible.

Now to my question. I have a major problem with this idea of postmodernism, even though your elaboration of it is more sophisticated than Ihab Hassan's. I would like to try to suggest a way out of this problem. Rather than thinking of your three stages of capitalism—which I gather are coextensive with realism, modernism, and postmodernism—as closed, Hegelian world-historical monads subsequent to each other in time, so that at some point (around 1910 or 1960) one begins and the other ends, couldn't we think of capitalism as a whole (beginning whenever you wish), and then a series of movements (such as realism, modernism, postmodernism) that have become hegemonic in a given subphase of capitalism but that do not necessarily disappear. After all, most literature and painting today is still realistic (e.g., Arthur Hailey). In other words, we have shifting hegemonies, although I think it is still a question of how one proves that a shift of such major dimensions (e.g., the shift associated with the names Picasso, Einstein, Eisenstein, and Lenin) really occurred in the 1960s. But in that case, postmodernism could emerge as a style, even become hegemonic in the United States and Western Europe, but not in India and Africa, and then lose its dominant position without our having to shift into a new episteme and a new world-historical monad. And you would have a subtler interplay between a simultaneously coexisting realism, modernism, and post-modernism, on various levels of art and literature.

Jameson

The questions of periodization, coexistence, and so on, are difficult and complex. Obviously, when I talk about such periods they are not sealed monads that begin and end at easily identifiable moments (beginning in 1857 and ending in 1913, or beginning in 1947 or 1958, etc.). And there are certainly survivals and overlaps. I would, however, like to say something about the problem people have with the concept of postmodernism. For me, the term suggests two connected things: that we are in a different stage of capital, and that there have been a number of significant cultural modifications (e.g., the end of the avant-garde, the end of the great auteur or genius, the disappearance of the utopian impulse of modernism—about which I think Perry Anderson was both eloquent and extremely suggestive). It's a matter of coordinating those cultural changes with the notion that artists today have to respond to the new globally defined concrete situation of late capitalism. That is why it doesn't bother me too much when friends and colleagues like Darko Suvin or Perry Anderson or Henri Lefebvre find this concept of postmodernism suspicious. Because whatever Perry Anderson, for example, thinks of the utility of the period term—postmodernism—his paper demonstrates that something really fundamental did change after 1945 and that the conditions of existence of modernism were no longer present. So we are in something else.

Now the relative merit of competing terms—postmodernism or high modernism—is another matter. The task is to describe that qualitatively different culture. By the same token, I trust that people who have some discursive stake in other terms, such as totality or its refusal, do not take my remarks on the subject too narrowly. For example, I consider the work of Chantal Mouffe and Ernesto Laclau an extremely important contribution to thinking about a future socialist politics. I think one has to avoid fighting over empty slogans.

Comment (Cornel West)

The question of totality signals an important theoretical struggle with practical implications. I'm not so sure that the differences between your position and Perry Anderson's, and those put forward by Stanley Aronowitz, Chantal Mouffe, Ernesto Laclau, and a host of others can be so easily reconciled. And it seems to me that if we continue to formulate the question in the way that you formulate it, we are on a crash course, because I think that holding on to the conception of totality that you invoke ultimately leads toward a Leninist or Leninist-like politics that is basically sectarian, that may be symptomatic of a pessimism (though that is a question). If we opt for the position that Mouffe, Laclau, Aronowitz, and others are suggesting, the results are radically anti-Leninist as well as radically critical of a particular conception of totality. It is important to remember that nobody here has defended a flat, dispersive politics. Nobody here has defended a reactionary politics like that of the *nouveaux philosophes*. Rather, their critiques of totality are enabling ones; they are critiques of a totality that is solely a regulative ideal we never achieve, never reach. And if that is the case, I really don't see the kind of reconciliation that you are talking about. I think you were very comradely in your ritualistic gestures to Chantal and Ernesto and others, but I am not so sure that we are as close as you think. Now that means we're still comrades within the Left in the broad sense, but these are significant differences and tendencies within the Left, and I didn't want to end the discussion with a vague Hegelian reconciliation of things when what I see is very significant and healthy struggle.

Jameson

I don't understand how the politics I am proposing is repressive, since I don't think I have yet even proposed a politics, any more than I have really proposed an aesthetics. Both of those seem to be all in the future. Let me try to respond by expanding on the distinction that came up in the second question, the notion of tactics versus strategy. It is not a question of substituting a total class/party politics for the politics of new social movements. That would be both ridiculous and self-defeating. The question is how to think those local struggles, involving specific and often different groups, within some common project that is called, for want of a better word, socialism. Why must these two things go together? Because without some notion of a *total* transformation of society and without the sense that the immediate project is a figure for that total transformation, so that everybody has a stake in that particular struggle, the success of any local struggle is doomed, limited to reform. And then it will lose its impetus, as any number of issue movements have done. Yet an abstract politics that only talks socialism on some global level is doomed to the sterility of sectarian politics. I am trying to suggest a way in which these things always take place at two levels: as an embattled struggle of a group, but also as a figure for an entire systemic transformation. And I don't see how anything substantial can be achieved without that kind of dual thinking at every moment in all of those struggles.

Andrew Ross

The New Sentence and the Commodity Form: Recent American Writing

The proposition that language is not *about* the world but is *in* the world itself has had as many serious political and epistemological ramifications in recent years as Marx's famous thesis on Feuerbach, which it both resembles and, perhaps, supersedes. Yet the problem of the intellectual's weary anxiety about co-option persists: How do we tell the real thing from its simulation? The point is, there is no "real thing." Writers have been saying it, and Marxism will have to speak to it.

We imagine that there is a gap between the world of our private fantasies & the possibilities of meaningful action & so it becomes easy to talk & talk on what is lacking, to discourse on end, & yet feel impotent. "What's to do." But this gap is a measure not so much of desires or depression or impotence but of ourselves. It has been the continual failure of Marxist aesthetics to insist that this gap is simply another illusory part of our commodity lives. It is at the root of our collectivity.
Charles Bernstein
"Three or Four Things I Know about Him"

The train ceaselessly reinvents the station.
Barrett Watten
1-10

Of all the "casualties" sustained by American writing in the volatile cross fire of political imperatives that prevailed in the thirties, George Oppen's case is, perhaps, the most exemplary. Barely though successfully launched as a poet in New York, and too much of a formalist to sustain his convictions, artistically, in that time and place, he shunned the available alternatives like the *New Masses,* stopped writing in 1932, and dropped out of literary circles for over twenty-five years, at first organizing the unemployed and then living in itinerant "exile" in California and Mexico. In her autobiography, his wife, Mary, describes their return from a trip to France as "the momentous winter of 1932 . . . when we began to see and understand what was happening."[1] For Oppen himself, forty-five years later, the imperative of that year was still painfully clear (though italicized, which is to say mediated): *"we wanted to know if we were any good / out there"* ("Disasters," *Primitive*). Here is the poet on trial again, and in Oppen's case somehow called on to *explain* where the politically irresponsible, like Pound, had long since been pardoned for their "aesthetic" crimes. Indeed, Oppen

361

recalls a meeting with Hugh Kenner in which the poet attempted to explain at length what populism had meant for a writer in the thirties, at which point Kenner interrupted: "In brief, it took you twenty-five years to write the next poem."[2]

For most of us, Kenner's "in brief" would seem much too flimsy, logically or otherwise, to bear the heavy moral weight of his remark. And under other circumstances one might be tempted to demonstrate how normative such logical moves are in the "official" literary histories of modern poetry, where Kenner's work has held more than a little sway.[3] As it is, my interests here are primarily descriptive rather than polemical, and are therefore more concerned with Oppen's dilemma than with Kenner's. "In brief," I shall be pointing to some of the ways in which recent American writing has approached that dilemma a half-century later and found that it is no dilemma at all. Clearly, it is not the mere fact of the passage of a half-century, Oppen's term of disgrace twice over, that has made the difference. And for some writers on the Left, the burden of history has actually only increased, forcing their hand further, as it were, into the awkward and consuming habits of the protest poem, or·else the thankless perpetuation of right-thinking sentiments. On the contrary, we can point above all else to concrete developments in Marxist theory during this period that have enabled writers to face the full brunt of political commitment in terms of their own cultural practice, rather than in the service of some external cause or party line, no matter how loosely drawn. This, of course, is not to deny that a new field of activity is not also a field of conflict, perhaps even more irreconcilable than ever. What is clear, nonetheless, is that Oppen's dilemma can no longer be found *in the same place:* "There are situations," he writes, "which cannot honorably be met by art, and surely no one need fiddle precisely at the moment that the house next door is burning"—Brecht is under fire here! Regardless of whether we might agree with Oppen that it is not a question of aesthetics, or "bad fiddling," his final opinion—that "the question can only be whether one intends, at a given time, to write poetry or not"—would have to be regarded today as a superannuated one.[4]

Oppen's dilemma, however, is a product of modernist culture, the very model of crisis culture, because it is wholly consumed by its contradictions; even the debates of the day about Marxist aesthetics—Bloch versus Lukács, Lukács versus Brecht, Benjamin versus Adorno—are *perfectly* antagonistic, while the artist is generally perceived as a binary or double agent: "In Pound I am confronted by the tragic double of our day. He is the demonstration of our duality. In language and form, he is forward, as much the revolutionary as Lenin. But in social, economic, and political action he is as retrogressive as the Czar."[5] In modernism, the "political" and the "aesthetic" struggle for sovereignty over every last inch of cultural soil, both within and beyond the limits of language—and also nationality. The radicalism of Hugh MacDiarmid, for example—to "aye be whaur / Extremes meet"—which lures him into an impossible dual allegiance to communism and Scottish nationalism, is always spliced by another set of linguistic oppositions: between the oral subversiveness of Scots and the assimilative power of English. Whereas MacDiarmid lives out this heady mix, Joyce, confronted with a similar set of options, collapses all contradictions onto the page and creates an international politics of the signifier.

362

It is Pound, however, whose instrumentalism is most complete and who can thus strip the most heterogeneous experience of conflict into Confucian-cum-Imagist forms: "When I gather chestnuts on the hills of Rapallo I step outside the capitalist system."[6] And it is Pound whose work, ironically enough, offers the clearest manifestations of the kind of thinking classed as "economist" and "historicist," tendencies that have recently fallen into disrepute within Marxism itself.[7] Of course, Pound has his own notions about economic determinism (it so blatantly serves his own didactic ends), while the "homogeneous time" of his historicism appeals unambiguously to an *aesthetic* termination of history, the fascist form of the inevitability theory of revolutionary Marxism. In this, however, Pound is much more than the archetypal American tourist, a mobile commodity form like Baudelaire's *flaneur* or Enzensberger's "tourist of the revolution," "exchanged" and "used" in support of an external logic of social and economic relations.[8] Pound's difference, after all, lies in his overt subjectivism, or what Charles Olson called "the beak of his EGO," the willful, controlling impulse to organize any field of available materials.[9]

The struggle against that subjectivist impulse is a dominant feature of the political development of modernism, and it takes the form of a movement toward objectivism. As much as anything else, this movement helps determine the style of the aesthetic manifestos of the Popular Front: Breton's "surrealistic situation of the object," for example, or Francis Ponge's more quiescent *Le parti pris des choses*. Oppen's own debt to this commitment is historically marked by his association, at the end of the twenties, with the Objectivist poets—Louis Zukofsky, Charles Reznikoff, William Carlos Williams, and Carl Rakosi (who also gave up his literary career and became a social worker). The content-oriented regional populism of Carl Sandburg, Vachel Lindsay, and Edgar Lee Masters was already thriving at the time. What distinguished the Objectivists, however, was their emphasis on form and technique as a conscious activity of intellectual labor, their concerns with particulars and everyday life, and their common appeal to moral (not representational, which is to say traditionally realist) imperatives of sincerity, authenticity, and conviction: "An Objective . . . Desire for what is objectively perfect, inextricably the direction of historic and contemporary particulars."[10] The objectification of the poem is also an act of demystification, for it determines the poem's existence in an everyday world of particulars, as opposed to the universalistic, hieratic realm of symbolist correspondences.

To scan the direction of American poetry since the thirties, it would seem that the lesson of the Objectivists' stand against mystification has had little impact. In the dense outcropping of "academic" poetry that accompanied New Criticism, a genteel taste for the wrangling of the Metaphysical Poets (among them Karl Shapiro, Delmore Schwartz, the Agrarians, J. V. Cunningham, etc.) quickly degenerated into an full-blown "personality" cult that glorified the orneriness or eccentricity of the poet's private genius, a cult (Theodore Roethke, John Berryman) that moves from the braggadocio of decadent bodily consumption to the celebration of nervous breakdown and finally suicide. Geoffrey Thurley describes these paeans to the reified self as a "symptom of [mid-century] affluence," but perhaps he is closer to the mark in his depiction of the campus poet of the fifties as a "class eunuch."[11]

The radical tradition, by contrast, monumentally represented in Donald Allen and Warren Tallman's 1960 anthology *The New American Poetry*, is generally characterized by its dominant anti-intellectualism. Assuming the unbridled Renaissance air of the sixties, many of the poets represented in that anthology espoused the kind of political romanticism that appealed to arcane and mystificatory images of "bardic" power—shamanism, orality, Orientalism, Americanism. "Hot" lives were valued over and above the problematic of language and form. The theatricalization of nonconformity and anticonventionality displaced the necessity of responding to the familiar, numbing strangeness or automatism of everyday life. Above all, in most of the work of the Beats and the Black Mountaineers, modernity—urban, technological, and massively commodifed—is either passed over entirely for some preindustrial cause or else pilloried for its dark Satanic birthright in Capital (if Vietnam was a *crise de conscience* for many of these writers, it was more often than not cast in the same technological-voodoo drama—Ginsberg's *Wichita Vortex Sutra* is the best example and is quite symptomatic); only the New York school stood by its acceptance of modern life, even if that acceptance often took the form of an undiscriminating optimism (a Forster-like faith in personal friendship), the other side of the utopian coin. And as for the figures who fell outside of these movements—Robert Bly, James Wright, Adrienne Rich, Robert Lowell, and so on—their "topical" discussion of political questions reaffirmed the polite, social role of poetry as a recognized and largely innocuous liberal organ.

Clearly, then (and we cannot say *in spite of* the Objectivists, if only on account of their relative obscurity until recently), these transcendental categories of "poet" and "poem" are dying hard. Aside from the subjectivist/objectivist debate, however, it is, of course, the question of language itself that has increasingly come to occupy the forefront of discussion about cultural autonomy with respect to modern writing. As a nostrum for Oppen's empirical defection from language, the counterexample of Zukofsky's "survivalism" has been revalued in recent years. Eschewing not only the International but every shred of activism in an age of the *engagé*, Zukofsky's alternative insistence on the value of intellectual labor comes to a focus in his perception that history is to be found in language: in utterance, measure, pitch, sound, particularity, and general craftsmanship.

There is a theoretical and practical clarity about Zukofsky' long poem *A*—"the words are my life"—which is almost Leninist (the stance is a studied one[12]) in its balanced, intellectual inspiration. The debt to determinism and necessity runs high throughout his work: in the objective, universal design of things—Bach's perception that "the order which rules music is the same order that controls the placing of the stars"; in the determined, or positioned, voice of the artist—"He who creates / Is a mode of these inertial systems" ("A"-6); and even in the compositional principle he calls the "Aleatorical Indeterminate," by which the linguistic play so boldly asserted in his poetry is everywhere subject to the necessity of strict musical codes. *A* is not a "Marxist" poem (it has been described as "an epic of the class struggle"[13]), if that means, for example, "telling the story" of surplus value. Nor, as Eisenstein sought to do in his films, does it attempt to embody a formal, dialectical *method* to relay affect and information, the twin components of the art of agit-prop. On the contrary, Zukofsky's example turns on the desire to fully *compose* his personal experience of historical change over the space of forty years of American politics. More important, however, it involves something like an honest or respectful encounter with language as a given medium, where other American writers have imposed their theoretical will on the medium, forcing it to comply with other, more "natural" processes (Pound's ideographism, Olson's projectivism, the Beat rap, etc.).

Consequently, it is Zukofsky, not only as anti-iconoclast but also as linguistic technocrat, who has been adopted as one of the chief precursors of the "language" poetry movement that has made a powerful impact on American writing in the last five or six years. In effect, the work that has been characterized as language writing falls outside the more familiar tendencies I have touched on so far. In its political claims it exhibits little or no "partyness," at least wherever we can speak of political content; and in its ideological bearing it is rigorously opposed to the dominant anti-intellectualism of radical American writing. Much of this essay will be devoted to discussing the consequences of this new hardheadedness in cultural and social matters. I shall, of course, be concerned with describing some of the more common features of the language movement, or at least those that make a special appeal to discursive attention. The dangers of this should be self-evident, however, for there is no excuse for commodifying, yet again, the "aesthetic" line of a new school. Indeed, many of the writers involved have been intent on guarding their work, in various ways, against this inevitable form of recognition by the culture industry, for there is a much larger social project at stake, of which this "guarding against" can be interpreted as both an internal symptom and a form of oppositional activity.

Let us assume that this double interpretation is not the result of a traditional double-bind (the "natural" dilemma of the poet confronted with an imperfect and uncomprehending world) but rather a contradiction that can be analyzed at a number of levels—political, economic, and ideological—and in conjunction with some estimate of the complex social standing of the arts in America today. Within the context of this larger analysis, we can pose the following question: In an age in which the established roles of an avant-garde no longer exist, or have been stripped of all progressive meanings (an age in which the countercultural gestures have all been played out, and the traditional refuge of "poetic license" or "art for art's sake" is no longer politically desirable), how does the old necessity of producing some kind of oppositional response *come into conflict with* the new necessity of recognizing or coming to terms with a massive commodification of experience governed by a rationality that increasingly insists that all culture now is mass, or popular, culture? In addition, we shall want to ask what form this conflict will assume; to what extent its terrain will be almost wholly technocratic—the rejection of appeals to organicism, natural or social totalities, utopianism—and to what extent it will still find room for the classic fetishism, for example, of Mayakofsky's revolutionary proviso—"the other foot was still running along a side-street."[14]

Before discussing in greater detail the work produced by the language poets, it would be useful to consider very briefly some of the developments in Western Marxist theory that have made it possible for writers now to present their work as politically sufficient in itself. Clearly, the broadest shift in emphasis has been in the relative autonomization of the notion of ideology. Freed from the orthodox economic insistence on its secondary superstructural role as an illusory or "false" consciousness, determined at every turn by the relations of production, ideological practices have increasingly assumed the full significance of their "specific effectivity," which Marx had barely acknowledged in his fitful discussions of aesthetics.[15] As a result, the unitary world-picture of "society" as a mechanistic structure built on a materialist base has been replaced by more multideterminate analyses, like Althusser's "social formation," which recognizes the "specific effectivity" of human practices lived out in each of three regions: the economic, political, and ideological.

This transformation, of course—from the causal dominance of the mode of production to a less mechanistic model—is not the mere consequence of a "barren" pursuit of theoretical sophistication (at a certain stage in Althusser's own thinking, "theory," in the opinion of some of his critics, took on more than its fair share of autonomy);[16] on the contrary, it is a real response to the cumulative need, from the failure of the Western proletarian revolutions onward, to account for the survival and growth of capitalism. Various theories of mediation were therefore necessary as modifications of an earlier reflectionist thinking: Lenin's role for the Party as vanguardist, Lukács's account of the reification of human relations, Gramsci's notion of hegemony, and so on. In addition to developing more efficient explanations for the constitutions of social structures, Marxist theorists also pursued ways of accounting for capitalism's maintenance of social relations as an effective medium for extending and reproducing its ideological dominance. It is at this point that cultural practices come to be recognized as a specific area of political conflict and change, and therefore as a material praxis in their own right, available for oppositional activity. In short, the theoretical conditions for a *cultural* revolution were now fully present, and ideology became the privileged terrain of analysis in Western Marxism, "sounded," as Perry Anderson puts it, "by thinker after thinker with an imagination and precision that historical materialism had never deployed here before."[17]

For the most part, the materialist analysis of ideological relations has based itself on various extensions of Marx's discussion of commodity fetishism. For Lukács, there was no doubt that commodification was "the central structural problem of capitalist society in all of its aspects."[18] In other words, the commodity character of a capitalist mode of production based on an abstract system of exchange is just as much a social as an economic effect. Consequently, social relations are reified and "veiled" to the material producer, a set of circumstances that is then made to appear "natural."

To say that this analytic concept of reification (focused primarily, for Lukács, on the alienated "plight" of the humanist individual) can be generalized to explain the universalization of capital's ideological dominance, is to make room for later theories of consumer society saturation like Baudrillard's, which describe the "no-win" option presented by late capitalism. A further extension of this thinking has in fact resulted in the various forms of post-Marxism (promulgated by the Gulag question), which turn on resistance to the rationality of Marxist discourse itself, now perceived by some as a repressive, totalizing project with little tolerance for its dissidents, theoretical or otherwise. Without the time to properly describe these developments, it would be useful to preserve the shift in strategic logic that they demonstrate; a shift from the humanist insistence on the priority of delivering the individual from the alienated situation of commodity existence, to the emphasis on the priority of analyzing the rationality of systematic discourses, whether the discourse of reification or the discourse of Marxist totalities. Such a distinction may only be meaningful if seen in terms of a certain history of Marxist thinking; and, therefore, it may be reductive to employ it as a way of delineating the differences between forms of resistance that are possible today. Nonetheless, it does seem to put into question some of the more popular conceptual ways of talking about oppositional practice—and I am thinking in particular of the sixties debate about working inside/outside or for/against the system. Clearly, it is this metaphor of inside/outside that has had to be rethought, for there is no more of a position "outside" ideology and commodification than there is a place "outside" language.

The contradictions involved in developing such a position, however, can be seen in the work of the Frankfurt school. Committed to the study of the nonmechanistic specificity of culture, their analysis of the "culture industry" as a development in the universalization of the commodity form established, for the first time, the importance of examining the significance of mass, or popular, culture. Few would deny, however, that mass culture per se has a monolithically negative value for both Adorno and Horkheimer; and for Marcuse, the distinction between negative *material* (popular) culture and positive *intellectual* (high) culture is strictly observed in his theoretical practice. Modernist "art," in effect, was seen as a refusal of the one-dimensional permeation of mass culture, and therefore regarded as a subversive force, a way of keeping one's head above the floodwaters. The same kind of nostalgic proviso is evident in Adorno and Horkheimer's lingering faith in what lies behind the "rationalization" of the world (Weber's term), a faith in the Enlightenment pursuit of rational self-interest that has merely been "irrationally" organized, in advanced capitalism, into the perverted form of *instrumental reason* (or technological rationality), geared to subsuming and incorporating all oppositional forms into standardized and bureaucratic systems. The rationality of the commodity system, then, is real, but it is not the real rationality of human purpose (which exists nonetheless—as in the classic proposition of Freudian fetishism).

If the Frankfurt critique has less relevance today than twenty years ago, then perhaps this is indeed a consequence of the increasingly systematic dominance of technological rationality and the related erosion of oppositional circumstances; more than ever, perhaps, co-option is a problem of totalitarian proportions. There is, however, another theoretical perspective that bears on this question, and it is one that stems from a renegade product of the Frankfurt school: Benjamin's studied belief in the *positive* use of certain aspects of the technocratic apparatus, especially the radical potential of mechanical reproduction. For Benjamin, there is no "other" order of human relations behind the commodity system, no unalienated realm of objectivity that is somehow more "real" than the reified present. His claim for the mass cultural apparatuses in an age of mechanical reproduction is that they usurp the authority of the art cult of originality and authenticity, replacing it with a new set of relations to the object—less stable, less institutionalized, and much more secular—relations, in short, that are themselves closer to the conditions for reproducibility and thus lend themselves to the radical project of a "functioning transformation" of mass culture. In Benjamin's critique, art is stripped of its higher rank and put to work as a technocratic force in its own right, rather than mourned as a lost comrade.

More recent theorists in this vein have not, generally, been willing to share Benjamin's technological optimism. In the French tradition we have seen the Situationists promote an exclusive faith in the liberation of the individual from the alienation of the "spectacle"—their epistemological model for *all* modern social relations. And Baudrillard has produced the most exhaustive critique of the one-dimensional code of consumer society. His particular analysis of the logic of consumption is worth examining here because it asserts that there is no longer any counterhegemonic, or positivistic, value to be found in the traditional Marxist options of "real" production or "concrete" labor; the positing of use value as the materialist underside of exchange value is no longer viable in a commodity system that presents its medium of exchange as a "nonreflecting surface." [19]

Baudrillard's working metaphor (and it is much more than a metaphor or model) for this instant readability of the whole system is "the smooth operational surface of communication,"[20] for it is not just the commodity object itself but the whole system of objects, or its *meaning,* that is consumed at every turn. Baudrillard therefore extends Marx's critique of political economy to a critique of the economy of signification, which semiotics has provided as an analytic code for explaning all systems, and finds the same logic of exploitation and domination at work there. To put it crudely, signifier and signified correspond to exchange value and use value. Within the free circulation of a commodity system, however, the signifier is always exchanged like a sign, offering itself as *full* value, in the absence of a signified. As a result, both codes, that of signification and of commodity, are seen to rest on the "abstract equation of all values."[21] All meanings are equal, and therefore the illusion of democratic choice is perpetuated, yet again, for the consumer.

One of the possible cultural uses to be made of Baudrillard's analysis of the "code of general equivalence" is its contribution to a critique of a modernism bound to the politics of the signifier. In this respect, the easy lure of the polysemic served up for reader and critic alike—the right to produce an infinity of meanings out of any particular text—would only serve to reproduce the polyvalence of the system itself. All meanings, again, are equal and thus can be exchanged without endangering the abstract logic of the system. If the modernism of Mallarmé and Joyce, brought to culmination in the poetics of Tel Quel, has largely been perceived as an attack on the rationalism of the Cartesian subject, then it can also be interpreted, now, as a way of helplessly reproducing the *rationality* of commodification that has everywhere incorporated the liberationary strategies of modernism. Such are the rapidly changing ethics of political literacy.

In its most general terms, then, we can characterize the recent cultural withdrawal from modernism as a shift from the critique of *rationalism* to a critique of *universalism* (or, rather, the rationality of universalization). For writers, this has meant modifying the traditional militancy against what Marcuse calls the "operationalism" or "functionalization" of language—the instrumental identification of "things and their functions"[22]— and taking up instead either of two alternatives (which are not mutually exclusive): first, the less glamorous task of adopting wholesale the terms or conditions of this "functionalizing" process, thereby feigning complicity in order to foreground and reveal the working codes of any institutional discourse (a practice that has its relevance, as I shall argue, to the language poet's project but is primarily associated with the Image Scavenger photographers—Barbara Kruger, Richard Prince, Sherrie Levine, Cindy Sherman, etc.); and second, the maverick use of transcultural pastiche—a consciously undoctored infusion of high and mass culture—in order to counteract the purity value of Literature for the culture industry (Kathy Acker's fearless experiments with popular fiction are a striking example).

In the context of American writing under consideration here, it is problematic to speak of values, structures, or traditions inherited from a modernist avant-garde. Moreover, it has often been pointed out that the political thrust of the historical avant-garde (notwithstanding its own "failure," a fact that cannot simply be explained away by pointing to its suppression at the hands of fascism and Stalinism), in its crusade to dissolve the institution of "autonomous" art, failed to carry over into a postwar intellectual and artistic milieu that was itself to be brutally depoliticized by the McCarthy era. More often than not, however, this essentially nostalgic perspective has served neoconservative interests as much as it has benefited the American cultural Left. Indeed, the current, lively debate over the conceptual validity of the term "avant-garde" is also a struggle for the political soul of postmodernism. Is postmodernism an ahistorical free-for-all in which supply-side critical theory rubs shoulders with the panstylistic mercenaries of the culture industry? Or is it still committed to attacking the power to define cultural meanings exercised by the ideological apparatuses of this same culture industry, a critique of similar proportions to that of the historical avant-garde but mounted on different terms and in accord with different strategies?[23]

Without wishing to complicate this debate needlessly, it is important to recognize, again, that there are different social, economic, and ideological elements involved in the cultural makeup of any radical or "avant-garde" art practice, and therefore it is often quite reductive to speak of an avant-garde "tradition," as if it were an imprimatur to which new groups can have equal historical and geographical access. The very least we can say is that all avant-garde practices work in oppositional proximity to their specific institutional discourses: art—the gallery and the museum; writing—the trade publishing houses; theater—Broadway; film—Hollywood; music—concert halls; and for all of these, the various review circuits, the academy, and, ultimately, their place in cultural histories.

Unlike other "language"-oriented groups elsewhere (Tel Quel in France, Gruppo 63 in Italy, even the Noigandres circle in Brazil), there exists no *centralized* social, political, and ideological role for an avant-garde among American writers. The ideological thrust of the Beats, for example, such as it was, came closest to national attention purely on account of its media impact as an easily aestheticized life-style. Instead of a centralized avant-garde, then, there are what Ron Silliman has called "networks" and "scenes," distinguished by their specific social organizations—the Objectivists, Black Mountain—who depend on contact through correspondence and thus generally manifest a much more homogeneous *aesthetic* than those writers who belong to a scene—Bolinas, St. Marks, Naropa/Boulder, North

Beach—randomly composed of more community elements.[24] Moreover, the situation whereby different groups constantly vie for some kind of temporary dominance over the national scene is *not* a simple effect of what is habitually passed off as the "natural" decenteredness of American life. On the contrary, this phenomenon of the "poetry wars" is largely determined by the exclusive practices of a publishing industry that consistently ensures that the most progressive writing is denied widespread distribution, unlike the practices in other countries where the avant-garde often enjoys a traditionally accepted, if not prominent, place on major publisher's lists and where there is a ritually acknowledged line of succession to that privileged place. As Jed Rasula puts it, "in terms of the critical apparatus that dominates the review media, 'American poetry' consists only of that portion of poets published with a university press or a New York trade publisher's imprimatur."[25] Of course, as little as 3 percent of all American poetry is published by these presses, while over 90 percent of the contents of any single anthology oriented toward the lucrative college course reading list market is likely to be drawn from those collections with the well-known poetry imprimaturs[26]— Atheneum, Viking, Norton, Random House, Penguin, Wesleyan, Yale.

Inasmuch as one can speak of a commodity market in poetry, the evidence of the small-press revolution of the last few decades (based on developments in offset printing technology and supported by extensive NEA subsidization), with its thin web of distribution outlets nationwide, has had little impact on the dominant patterns of distribution and consumption; after almost fifty years, New Directions, a pioneer, is still a marginal figure in terms of its review drawing power, while other reliable houses like Black Sparrow, The Figures, Jargon, and even City Lights, have a commercial credit that is negligible in proportion to the radical influence of the writers they publish. This last observation, of course, invites conclusive judgments about the extracommercial *value* of certain writers, an evaluative path I have no intention of pursuing here. Suffice it to say that Poetry published by the major presses is generally, as one might expect, more easily "consumed" than less well distributed writing; to give just one example, the John Ashbery published now by Viking/Penguin is easier to "read" (an activity that has too many social, economic, and ideological determinations for it to have purely cognitive effects) than the John Ashbery of, say, the Ecco Press, from the seventies.

Where, then, do the language poets fit into this global pattern? As a group, they are organized around two specific "scenes" in the Bay Area and the urban New York area respectively, with some "network" elements (though by no means homogeneous or noncontradictory) existing between the two. Predominantly white, baby-boom, middle-class, and heterosexual,[27] with a prominent role claimed by women, both scenes have displayed a commitment to investigating the aesthetic and ideological components of a group practice: there are, for example, no manifesto or leading figures to point to, for in many respects it is the idea of the Poet within an authorial tradition that is in question: "the individual . . . needs to be defined not as a single isolated Romantic individual but as a methodological practice learned in active collective work with other's reading and writing. . . . It is to bring back a visceral understanding of the collective nature of consciousness that I suggest the things I do. The centrality of the inscription of the individual cannot be subverted. The nature of that inscription is 'our' investigation."[28]

Andrew Ross

In contrast, then, to the inherited structure of the writers' group or community as an instrumental support for a more coherently propagated "voice," here is an integrated community, urban, residential, and largely nonbohemian, intent on generating productive resistance through collective practice to the commodification of such a "voice." In terms of publication and distribution, a series of ongoing poetics debates and presentations of new work have appeared in journals created as specific group outlets over the last ten years: *This, Roof, Tottel's, Qu, A Hundred Posters, miam, Hills, L=A=N=G=U=A=G=E*, and *Poetics Journal,* as well as the respective presses of This, Segue, Tuumba, Roof, and The Figures. As important, however, has been the use of other discourses, not just to support the marginal distribution of the poetry, but also to critique, again, the transcendental Poet who only writes or speaks *pure poetry:* the notorious espousal of theory-oriented discourse, the highly successful and exotic Poet's Theater, and the gradual displacement of the poetry reading by the specific cultural form of the "talk"—public presentations that range, in their incorporation of "marked" elements, from the discursive edges of performance art to the more inflexible margins of the formal lecture[29] (again, however, it is important to point to the economic and political determinations of this seemingly "autonomous" form of cultural discourse).[30] There remains a precarious but effective distinction between putting these formations to work as a way of better propagating an "aesthetic" line or message and employing them as a means of analyzing the construction of a collective, social experiment in writing: the full recognition that "poetry gets shaped—informed and transformed—by the social relations of publication, readership, correspondence, readings, etc. (or historically seen, the 'tradition'), and indeed, that poetry community(ies) are not a secondary phenomenon to writing but a primary one."[31]

On an intermediate level, somewhere between the commodity form of the "book" itself and the question of the commodification of language, there have been numerous recent attempts to reinterpret material forms of resistance to the transparent activity of reading. One can point to Hannah Weiner and Johanna Drucker's respective experiments with typographic variation; the extraordinary rhythmical density of David Melnick's *zaum* poems (after the Cubo-futurist manner of Khlebnikov and Kruchemyk); the graphic exploration of space and page in the work of Peter Inman and Robert Grenier; the sometime asyntactic field poetry of Clark Coolidge, Bernadette Mayer, and Bruce Andrews; and, on a different level, the fragile performance-oriented "monologues" of Steve Benson. It is important to distinguish these individual projects, on the one hand, from the specific epistemological claims of the (now largely defunct) concrete poetry movement, claims that were essentially related to problems of *visual* perception, whereas most of these writers are engaged with problems of *cognitive* perception; and, on the other hand, with the more general ethos of the modernist emphasis on the autonomy and materiality (early and late modernism, respectively) of the word. Indeed, for the sake of polemical convenience, we might contrast the so-called modernist Revolution of the Word, more often than not a reassertion of the divinity of the Word, with Shklovsky's "Resurrection of the Word": "The aim of Futurism is the resurrection of things—the return to man of the sensation of the world."[32] Rather than eschew the world for a better idea of it, the aim of much of

371

language writing, in agreement with Shklovsky's proposition, would be to return us to the world in different ways, through a series of cognitive-perceptual shocks.

In a synthesis that is, of course, much more than a synthesis of these two slogans, we are confronted now with the more universal question of Jameson's "Prison-House of Language." (Lyn Hejinian puts it baldly: where once one sought a vocabulary for ideas, now one seeks ideas for vocabularies."[33]) The proposition that language is not *about* the world but is *in* the world itself has had as many serious political and epistemological ramifications in recent years as Marx's famous thesis on Feuerbach, which it both resembles and, perhaps, supersedes: "The philosophers have only interpreted the world in various ways. The point, however, is to change it." Language is no longer merely "practical consciousness," as Marx put it in *The German Ideology;* it is also seen as the "constructive" fabric of social reality. To ignore the need to respond consciously to that process of linguistic mediation and construction is to effectively renounce any hope of partial understanding, let alone control, of that social reality. Such a response, moreover, for writers as much as anyone, involves the acknowledgment of the extent to which dominant political codes, the system of capital and the traces of its history, are on "display" in the language we use. Responding, then, to the *givenness* of language is also to respond politically to the instrumentality of these codes and the way in which they effortlessly circulate the "natural" meanings of ideological life according to Baudrillard's golden commodity rule of "general equivalence."

One of the dominant impulses of modern American writers has been to act *on* language rather than *within* it. As a result, modernist American poetry has consisted, in its radical element, of a series of attempts to force language to conform to some theoretical ideal—the natural, kinetic flux of organic processes—or to reproduce certain ideological qualities of "American" discourse—spontaneity, directness, sincerity, heroism, authenticity—as a way of capturing the "raw" American, as opposed to the "cooked" European voice. Whatever genuinely liberating value "free verse" had for the early modernists, the history of its development as a writing medium in America is also the history of a remarkable complicity with a system that fosters and markets the lived illusion of the "free" as its chief set of ideological meanings. From the various restagings of serious Whitmanesque thunder to the inimitable kitsch nonchalance of Frank O'Hara's "just free that's all, never argue with the movies,"[34] writers have failed to actively recognize that the celebration of liberationary formal means is *the* specific form of American political internment. Behind the lure of autonomism is the cunning of automatism.

In their critique of this same automatism—the universalization of perceptual habits that sustains and is sustained by the commodity system—various language writers have responded to the need for certain historical projects. Ron Silliman has sketched out a rough "history of referentiality" dating from the impact of the emergence of capitalism on the arts and tracing the subsequent fetishization of the instrumentalist conception of language.[35] Charles Bernstein has been involved in examining, historically, the increasing standardization of expository writing as a process that sacrifices method for universal forms: "As a mode, contemporary expository writing edges close to being merely a *style* of decorous thinking, rigidified

372

and formalized to a point severed from its historical relation to method in Descartes and Bacon. It is no longer an enactment of thinking or reasoning but a representation (or simplification) of an eighteenth-century ideal of reasoning. And yet the hegemony of its practice is rarely questioned outside of certain poetic and philosophic contexts."[36]

In looking for historical models of opposition to this contemporary plain style, much of Barrett Watten's work has been devoted to following through the consequences of the Russian formalist emphasis on defamiliarization: the willful use of grammatical "devices" that counterpoint rhythmical insistence with unexpected semantic shifts, as a means of renovating the reader's perception.[37] Watten's aim is to explore not only the cognitive but also the social effects of a limited kind of syntactical activity. But this is not to revive the old homology between formal and social disjunction. On the contrary, what is foregrounded by these experiments with parallelism, subordination, and other grammatical elements is the *language system* itself and its otherwise transparent methods of circulating meaning (while the easy Luddism of smashing this system of language relations is replaced by the practice of constructing new relations within the system). In this respect, Hejinian's comment on the book jacket of Silliman's *Tjanting* is symptomatic: "The reader recognizes every word." First, there is no poetic arcane, and thus the writing can acknowledge the rhythmic requirements of everyday life. (Watten says, "It is possible, in fact, to read this book on the bus.") Second, beyond this fresh appeal to a realism there is also an appeal to fresh perception, not as an end pursued in itself, but through a recognition of the *universality* ("every word") of language relations and our complicity with their "hegemonic" ways.

The net result is a claim for the importance of writing that attempts to *expose our patterns of consumption at the commodity level of meaning.* Clearly, this is no celebration of the utopian reader, free to produce meanings at will, in response to the open invitation of canonical poststructuralism. Nor is it the celebration of a liberationary, utopian language, like the surrealists' discourse of contradictions. The construction of a future, utopian or otherwise, lies instead in a technologically planned present, or more properly, in the *shock* of recognizing the fully systematic domination of the present. Bernstein, for example, describes the familiar experience of reification: "What purports to be an experience is transformed into the blank stare of the commodity—there only to mirror our projections with an unseemly rapidity possible only because no experience of 'other' is in it."[38] The traditional response of modernist writers would be to celebrate this "other" (use value, phonic excess, polysemy), a privilege that poetry can afford and everyday discourse cannot. The response of today's political writer is to demonstrate *why that "other" is not there* in commodified language use.

If we had to isolate, fetishistically, any one common feature of the language poet's practice, it would be the complex socioaesthetic focus on sentence construction within much of their work—an effect that has been called, albeit far from unequivocally, *the new sentence.*[39] Accordingly, its formal characteristics are described in such a way as to ensure maximum opportunity for reinterpretation. Set within a larger variable structure, like the paragraph, the new sentence is perceived as a flexible coordinate, at once a unit of measure, a relatively autonomous element of syllogistic (dis)continuity, and a wholly autonomous object of cognitive attention. Here are a few examples:

We came to the landing place with buck knives and whale grease for the job. The garbage had yet to be put out. Barges up and down the river intersected long treeless vistas of acquisition. Sugar in the pan was pornography in the minds of men. That intimacy saved for green grass. Your flow. A product said, "Hit me with a club." We were *about* the world, high above apartment houses. You couldn't cross the channel necking on the bridge. After the waldorf salad came virgilian fortitude. I thought I wanted to intend and determine.

Jean Day
"Ticonderoga"

An approximation of love began to haunt him, deny him nothing. Beige afternooons wedged under sky for miles. On the screen gorgeous creatures fly off the handle. Partners time the pauses between gestures. One horizon lowers while the other lifts. He sat next to her in class, trying vainly to control the pseudopod that flowed toward her. They're my hands. The possessive dutifully dispersed over the hayfield.

Bob Perelman
"a.k.a."

The back of the head resting on the pillow was not wasted. We couldn't hear each other speak. The puddle in the bathroom, the sassy one. There were many years between us. I stared the stranger into facing up to Maxine, who had come out of the forest bad from wet nights. I came from an odd bed, a vermillion riot attracted to loud dogs. Nonetheless, I could pay my rent and provide for him. On this occasion she apologized. An arrangement that did not provoke inspection. Outside on the stagnant water was a motto. He more than I perhaps though younger. I sweat at amphibians, managed to get home. The sunlight from the window played up his golden curls and a fist screwed over one eye. Right to left and left to right until the sides of her body were circuits. While dazed and hidden in the room, he sang to himself, severe songs, from a history he knew nothing of. Or should I say malicious? Some rustic gravure soppy but delicate at pause. I wavered, held her up. I tremble, jack him up. . . .

Carla Harryman,
"For She"

374

Andrew Ross

The music is not of my choosing.
The enormous seaminess throws a textbook punch.
But it wasn't the stars that thrilled me.

Alan Bernheimer
"Word of Art"

On the level of traditional poetics, the new sentence has none of the fixed quantitative appeal of its predecessors in the field of prosodic innovation—the move from the foot to the line, to the syllable, and to the breath, marked by a whole series of poetic events such as Pound's *Cathay,* Williams's *Spring and All,* Olson's *The Distances,* and Ginsberg's *Howl.* A more relevant referent would be Gertrude Stein (the Jamesian sentence and the Hemingway sentence are actually fixed ideological qualities rather than experiments in quantitative measure) or the French tradition of the prose poem. The defamiliarizing devices within the sentence, and the syntactical renovation that is worked through between sentences, are part of a process aimed at the consistent decontextualization of the present tense; not the symbolist's infinite present, nor Stein's painstaking exhaustion of the present, but a regeneration of the common diversity of the present through the labor of compositional technique. As a formal medium, the range of aesthetic advantages offered by the new sentence is considerable: multiplicity of points of view, the restricted pleasure of "jump-cutting," narrative experimentation, the capacity to accommodate a limitless variety of information, marked discourses, voice, personality, and so on.

To assess the full rationality of the new sentence, however, it is necessary to step outside poetics and point to the instrumentality of the sentence as a discursive element grounded in social communication. The ability to form and complete sentences is both a class marker and a functional index of practical efficiency in a technocratic world. In the same way the genteel "organic" art-sentence (now largely the discursive preserve of academe) used to betoken a social distance or aloofness from "trade," so now the functionalist sentence is an act of disavowal, not only in its meditated obscurantist ambitions (newspeak—"War Is Peace, Peace Is War"; Marcuse's surrealistic examples of bureaucratic contradiction: "Labor is seeking Missile Harmony"; etc.), but also in its simulation of logical control and classification, behind which lies the largely autonomous reality of the ceaseless circulative capacity of the system. It is at the level of the sentence, then, as the central symbolic form of the social fabric, that meaning is exchanged, which is to say, culturally received, accepted, and consumed by the individual. The decision to work, then, at the level of the sentence rather than at the archaic or "imaginary" level of the nonsyntactical fragment is in many respects the result of a political choice; it represents a decision to meet with the political realities of a shared discursive condition and not to insist on the rarefied rhetorical plane writers are inclined to protectively regard as their inherited polemical turf.

The willfulness of this decision is particularly apparent in Barrett Watten's writing. In contrast to the traditional poetic affection for Anglo-Saxon diction, or to the more recent ludic appeal of etymologizing, much of Watten's language use is singularly Latinate and technologicalist, insisting on the concrete austerity of its object status: "No wires account for / Failure of specific response. / A triangle gives, / circles branch out. Forced / Exposure

375

to limit distorts" ("Position"). Elsewhere, the "sentence-producing" mechanism is foregrounded, its monochromatic rhythms variably transformed:

> *Let no one consider the original noise.*
>
> *Outside there's noise. Time doesn't print.*
>
> *A bar of sulfur lies on a mahogany table. From this point to the frontier is exact.*
>
> *The distance between yourself and what you are intended to see.*
>
> *Steam-driven pilings hold up the bridge like logs under the feet of sunburnt slaves rolling I-beams to their designated resting place on a riverbank in Kansas.*
>
> "Relays"

The flagrant denial of "voice" and "body" here is an internal critique of the *aura* of poetic authenticity. In renouncing this aura, the writing begins to conform to what Benjamin perceived as the radical condition of mass-produced art forms—a capacity to find value in the fact of reproducibility and turn it to popular advantage.

Again, it is not enough to merely celebrate this quality of reproducibility. In some of Watten's work, the automatic rhythm is compressed into more dialectical forms and assumes the density of units of intellectual montage:

> *I*
> *The world is complete.*
> *Books demand limits.*
>
> *II*
> *Things fall down to create drama.*
> *The materials are proof.*
>
> *III*
> *Daylight accumulates in photos.*
> *Bright hands substitute for sun.*
>
> *IV*
> *Crumbling supports undermine houses.*
> *Connoisseurs locate stress.*
>
> "Complete Thought"

Here, repetition has been replaced by the effect of reproducibility taken up in its properly contradictory forms. As Watten puts it, "The train ceaselessly reinvents the station" (with its hint of Saussure's "9:10 Geneva Express"): the practice of *parole* transforms, rather than conforms to, the theoretical shape of *langue*. Above all, however, what is important is that we *recognize* and *accept* the quota of readers' work involved in this kind of poetry. For once, there is the sense that a fair deal has been struck; the labor of composition is somehow equal to the labor of reading, and so the readers share meaning rather than merely responding to the writer's meaning, or else producing their own at will. The result is somewhere between the ease of consumption and the headache of comprehension. Watten's work neither hands out privileges nor jealously guards its own. It *formulates* action.

Andrew Ross

What this last phrase calls to mind, yet again, is that the parameters of conceptual categories like "formalism" have shifted considerably over the past fifty years. If Brecht was correct to insist on the supra-aesthetic dimensions of formalism—"When I read that the autarky of the Third Reich is perfect *on paper,* then I know that this is a case of political formalism"[40]— we no longer share his need to formulate an alternative concept of realism to uphold as a political nostrum. This is not to say that we cannot share his generous and broad-minded conceptual understanding of realism. On the contrary, what I have tried to suggest is that the imperative of political realism no longer means keeping aloof from the dominant political formalism, which is to say, the commodity forms of meaning. Indeed, the realism of writers today is that they can engage this sense of form on its own terms, in order to expose the universality of its codes. Realism, in this sense, is not at odds with a conception of formalism but rather with other, "unrealistic" attempts to construct a subversive space completely outside commodity formalism. Moreover, not only these aesthetic categories of formalism and realism have been displaced, or shifted ground, but so has the very idea of an "aesthetics" itself. As Lyn Hejinian puts it (of William Carlos Williams's position poem), "There will never be another red wheelbarrow, and that very clearly is the type of the fate of any single realism."[41]

Clearly, we are also discussing the fate of Marxist aesthetics, a tradition in which there have only been highly circumscribed roles for poets: the bureaucratic myth of Mayakofskyism, the neo-Byronic freedom fighter, the Maoist/Confucian slogan lyricist. Lukács has almost nothing to say about poetry, and in recent years, Jameson, Macherey, and Eagleton have each, in their own ways, reasserted the traditionally dominant Marxist concern with narrative, and specifically the novel genre. One of the major reasons for this neglect is the ideology of poethood itself and the exclusionary privileges associated with its most resistant quality, that of poetic *license.* Of course, I am not suggesting that in spite of this time-honored conception poets suddenly have the opportunity to be ideological watchdogs. What I argue is that we can interpret the evidence of this serious project undertaken by the language poets as a sign that a certain conception of Marxist aesthetics has perhaps matured, if not wholly come of age, and most significant of all, in America.

To conclude, we should acknowledge, for the last time, the important historical referent of the thirties. Here is Roman Jakobson, stylishly mourning "the generation that squandered its poets": "There are some countries where ladies' hands are kissed, and others where one merely says, 'I kiss your hand.' There are countries where Marxist theory is answered by Leninist practice and countries where the madness of the bold, the bonfire of faith and the Golgotha of the poet are not merely figurative expressions. . . ."[42] It would be polemically apposite to follow this with a different rhetorical challenge written from a different point of view and grounded in the different political-aesthetic realities of today. It is not that I cannot think of at least one or two examples. What makes such a gesture impossible is the fact that rhetoric no longer acts as agent provocateur; it has a different agency and a different object that are just as much internally located as externally projected toward. It is this general shift in the theory and practice of radical writing that I have been examining, and, in the instance of American poetry, I have tried to describe some of the historical, social, and ideological contexts for that shift. There is more than enough evidence today of postmodernist literary and art practices that are seriously politicized. The achievement of these practices is that they are making an art out of the constantly assimilated position in which they find themselves. By contrast, the problem of the intellectual's weary anxiety about co-option persists: How do we tell the real thing from its simulation? The point is, there is no "real thing." Writers and artists have been saying it, and Marxism will have to speak to it.

Notes

1. These lines are from an earlier draft of a chapter in Mary Oppen, *Meaning a Life: An Autobiography* (Santa Barbara: Black Sparrow, 1978), which appeared in *Ironwood*, 5 (1975), p. 58.

2. Interview with Charles Amirkhanian and David Gitin, *Ironwood*, 5 (1975), p. 23.

3. Kenner, of course, has been one of the most successful apologists for Pound. Notwithstanding the consequences of this kind of apology, inasmuch as it coincides with an apology for poetry *tout court*, one might want to begin by asking Hans Magnus Enzensberger's question of all the plaintiffs against poetry: Why is it always poetry *as a whole* that is put on trial? On this point, Plato stands in the same camp as traditional Marxist aestheticians. See Enzensberger's sweeping "Poetry and Politics," *Critical Essays*, ed. Reinhold Grumm and Bruce Armstrong, trans. Michael Roloff (New York: Continuum, 1982).

4. Oppen's answer to Brecht, however, reads as if it might also be the grounds of a response to Enzensberger's question posed above: "The actually forbidden word Brecht, of course, could not write. It would be something like *aesthetic*. But the definition of the good life is necessarily an aesthetic definition, and the mere fact of democracy has not formulated it, nor if it is achieved, will the mere fact of an extension of democracy, though I do not mean of course that restriction would do better." From "The Mind's Own Place," *Kulchur*, 3:10 (Summer 1963), p. 8.

5. Charles Olson, *Charles Olson and Ezra Pound: An Encounter at St. Elizabeth's*, ed. Catherine Seelye (New York: Grossmans/Viking, 1975), p. 53.

6. Oppen, *Meaning a Life*, p. 136.

7. The terms are Althusser's, or are associated primarily with Althusser's critique of Marxist humanism, but the reaction against these tendencies can be traced back through Gramsci, Lukács, and Lenin to Engels's attempts at "revisionism" after Marx's death.

8. See Terry Eagleton's extravagant discussion of Benjamin's description of the *flâneur* as a self-contradictory commodity form in *Walter Benjamin: Or Towards a Revolutionary Criticism* (London: Verso, 1981).

9. "Mayan Letters," *Selected Writings*, ed. Robert Creeley (New York: New Directions, 1966), p. 82.

10. *Prepositions: The Collected Critical Essays of Louis Zukofsky* (Berkeley: University of California Press, 1981), p. 12.

11. Geoffrey Thurley, *The American Moment: American Poetry in the Mid-Century* (London: Edward Arnold, 1977), pp. 184, 36.

12. "Lenin invented . . . a new medium, something between speech and action, which is worth . . . study." Zukofsky quoting Pound in Eric Mottram, "1924-1951: Politics and Form in Zukofsky," *Maps*, 5 (1973), p. 76.

13. Contributor's note to *New Directions in Prose and Poetry*, ed. James Laughlin (New York: New Directions, 1938).

14. Roman Jakobson, "The Generation That Squandered Its Poets," *Literature and Revolution*, ed. Jacques Ehrmann (Boston: Beacon Press, 1970), p. 125.

15. For a concise and evenhanded account of the abandonment of economism, see Raymond Williams, "Base and Superstructure in Marxist Cultural Theory," *Problems in Materialism and Culture* (London: Verso, 1980).

16. Althusser's response to criticism, in *Essays in Self-Criticism*, trans. Graham Lock (London: New Left Books, 1976), includes his famous confession of and apology for "theoreticism."

17 "In the final days of Western Marxism, one can, indeed, speak of a veritable hypertrophy of the aesthetic—which came to be surcharged with all the values that were repressed or denied elsewhere in the atrophy of living socialist politics: utopian images of the future, ethical maxims for the present, were displaced and condensed into vaulting meditations on art with which Adorno or Sartre concluded much of their life's work." Perry Anderson, *In the Tracks of Historical Materialism* (London: Verso, 1983), p. 17.

18 Georg Lukács, *History and Class Consciousness*, trans. Rodney Livingstone (Cambridge: MIT Press, 1971), p. 82.

19 Baudrillard's attack on the concept of "production" can be found in *The Mirror of Production*, trans. Mark Poster (St. Louis: Telos Press, 1975).

20 "The Ecstasy of Communication," *The Anti-Aesthetic: Essays on Postmodern Culture*, ed. Hal Foster (Port Townsend, Wash.: Bay Press, 1983), p. 127.

21 "Towards a Critique of the Political Economy of the Sign," *For a Critique of the Political Economy of the Sign*, trans. Charles Levin (St. Louis: Telos Press, 1981), p. 150. An alternative metaphorical model for the circulation and exchange of information would be Derrida's "postal state"—the product, as he sees it, of the historical development of capitalism and the process of postal rationalization. Derrida's counterprinciple—"a letter can always not reach its destination"—is an appeal to the undecidability of reception/consumption, as opposed to production. See *La carte postale* (Paris: Flammarion, 1980).

22 Marcuse is quoting Stanley Gerr on "the linguistic tendency 'to consider the names of things as being indicative at the same time of their manner of functioning, and the names of properties and processes as symbolical of the apparatus used to detect or produce them.'" From *One-Dimensional Man: Studies in the Ideology of Advanced Industrial Society* (Boston: Beacon Press, 1964), pp. 86-87.

23 To choose two symptomatic manifestations of this debate, Peter Bürger's neglect of contemporary art practices in *Theory of the Avant-Garde*, trans. Michael Shaw (Minneapolis: University of Minnesota Press, 1984), could profitably be balanced against Benjamin Buchlow's incisive review of Burger's book, "Theorizing the Avant-Garde," *Art in America* (Nov. 1984), pp. 19-21. For an argument that considers both sides but leans toward Burger's, see Andreas Huyssen, "The Search for Tradition: Avant-Garde and Postmodernism in the 1970s," *New German Critique*, 22 (Winter 1981), pp. 23-40.

24 Ron Silliman, "The Political Economy of Poetry," $L=A=N=G=U=A=G=E$ (*Open Letter* 5:1), vol. 4, pp. 60-65. For a full-blown analysis of the commercial nepotism that regulates social groupings among American intellectuals, see Richard Kostelanetz's "naming names" exposé of the "New York literary mob" and others in *The End of Intelligent Writing—Literary Politics in America* (New York: Sheed and Ward, 1974).

25 See Jed Rasula's revealing "year by year listing of books of poetry prominently reviewed in the trade press, as derived from the *Book Review Index*." The percentage of reviews devoted to small-press books is, of course, infinitesimal, while writers who have had both trade and small-press publishers have "benefited" or "suffered" respectively from the disparity in the attention paid to their work. Rasula's intention is to show how the representation of Poetry is produced, not to argue that well-known writers are more mediocre than small-press writers. See "The Role of Critics and the Emperor's New Clothes in American Poetry," *Sulfur*, 9 (1984), pp. 149-67.

26 Silliman, "The Political Economy of Poetry."

27 Silliman, for example, comments on the radical difference between the content-specific orientation of minority, oppressed, or gay/lesbian writers, on the one hand, and the "purely aesthetic" schools of white middle-class writers, on the other. He argues that "in fact the aesthetics of those [latter] schools is a direct result of ideological struggle. . . . It is characteristic of the class situation of these schools that this struggle is carried on in other (aesthetic) terms." From "The Political Economy of Poetry," p. 62.

28 Response by Charles Bernstein to Silliman's comments on his "Thought's Measure," $L=A=N=G=U=A=G=E$, vol. 4, p. 22.

29 A representative selection of the early "talks" is in *Hills*, 6, and a later selection has been published as *Writing/Talks*, ed. Bob Perelman (Carbondale: Southern Illinois University Press, 1985). Poet's Theater scripts are published in *Hills*, 9.

30 In the case of the later talks, for example, many of which are subsidized through arts centers in the form of writers' residence grants from the NEA, one has to consider the NEA's erratic decisions in recent years to cut residency grants for artists and to axe critics' grants altogether, while leaving the writers' quota largely intact. The ideological constraints of working under state sponsorship are familiar enough. The NEA, perceived as a national ornament, enjoyed its most prominent period of financial and ideological autonomy under the Nixon administration. The contrast with its impoverished condition under the New Right, which perceives it

as a purely ideological organ, is quite striking. On some recent developments—the political overriding of the "peer-panel" system for grant distribution, the preferential treatment of mid-career as opposed to younger artists—see Catherine Lord, "The President's Man: The Arts Endowment under Frank Hodzoll," *Afterimage*, 10:7 (Feb. 1983).

31   Charles Bernstein, "The Conspiracy of 'Us'," *The L=A=N=G=U=A=G=E Book*, ed. Charles Bernstein and Bruce Andrews (Carbondale: Southern Illinois University Press, 1984), pp. 186-87.

32   Viktor Shklovsky, "The Resurrection of the Word," *Twentieth-Century Studies*, 7/8 (Dec. 1972), p. 41.

33   "If Written Is Writing," *The L=A=N=G=U=A=G=E Book*, p. 29.

34   Quoted by Bill Berkson in "Talk," *Hills*, 6/7 (Spring 1980), p. 19.

35   Ron Silliman, "Disappearance of the Word, Appearance of the World," *The L=A=N=G=U=A=G=E Book*, pp. 121-32.

36   Charles Bernstein, "Writing and Method," *Poetics Journal*, 3 (1983), p. 8.

37   Barrett Watten, "Russian Formalism and the Present," *Hills*, 6/7 (Spring 1980), pp. 50-74.

38   Charles Bernstein, "The Dollar Value of Poetry," *The L=A=N=G=U=A=G=E Book*, p. 140.

39   "1) The paragraph organizes the sentences; 2) The paragraph is a unit of quantity, not logic or argument; 3) Sentence length is a unit of measure; 4) Sentence structure is altered for torque, or increased polysemy/ambiguity; 5) Syllogistic movement is a) limited b) controlled; 6) Primary syllogistic movement is between the preceding and following sentences; 7) Secondary syllogistic movement is toward the paragraph as a whole, or the total work; 8) The limiting of syllogistic movement keeps the reader's attention at or very close to the level of language, that is most often at the sentence level or below." From Ron Silliman, "The New Sentence," *Hills*, 6/7, (Spring 1980), p. 216.

40   Bertold Brecht, "On the Formalistic Character of the Theory of Realism," in Ernst Bloch et al., *Aesthetics and Politics*, ed. Ronald Taylor (London: New Left Books, 1977), p. 72.

41   Quoted from "Footnotes," a collage of comments about realism collected for a public presentation in the catalog for *Eighty, Langton Street Residence Program 1981* (San Francisco, 1982), p. 133.

42   Jakobson, "The Gerneration That Squandered Its Poets," p. 124.

Fred Pfeil

Postmodernism as a "Structure of Feeling"

In a wide range of popular and avant-garde cultural
works, one can see a shift in the subject's relation to
self, language, and difference. This postmodern structure of feeling has its origins in fundamental changes
that have taken place in the family structure of American middle-class life. While the resulting de-Oedipalization has released new sociopolitical forces, these have
been significantly contained by the capitalist hegemony.
Postmodernism foregrounds this inherent irresolution.

This essay is founded in a specific pleasure, a double
bemusement, and perhaps a certain orneriness. The pleasure began when I
discovered New Wave music (at first, Brian Eno and Talking Heads); it was
reformulated in the work of other musicians (The Gang of Four, Philip
Glass), in performance art (Laurie Anderson), and even, to a limited extent,
in prose fiction (Kathy Acker), the rather antiquated and provincial region
of the culture industry in which I myself work. I came to these works halt-
ingly, serendipitously. I behaved as the typical cultural consumer in late
capitalism behaves, operating out of a typically serialized solitude, flying
more or less blind. Only retrospectively, as I tried to analyze and account
for my enjoyment, did I realize that the kind of aesthetic experience they
create and offer—and thus the pleasure I was seeking to understand—had
already been categorized as postmodern.

To this initial bemusement—the perplexity of a new
pleasure, a new name, and the not altogether happy discovery that I had
come to enjoy works that bore a family resemblence to other texts (e.g.,
Ashbery or Sollers) I had long found unsatisfying—was added another: I
soon found a large body of criticism ready to explain not only what these
works were like, how they functioned to produce what effects, but even why
and how these effects might give pleasure. Leaving aside such partial responses as the unrigorous enthusiasm of a Marjorie Perloff,[1] or the blanket
"search-and-destroy" operations carried out by a Hilton Kramer or Gerald
Graff,[2] such criticism falls into two camps, one that finds in postmodernist
art a progressive, subversive, perhaps even potentially revolutionary insight
and impulse; the other that explains its power and attractiveness as the
effect of its stylized (re)presentation of a recent twist in the long dialectic
of capitalist alienation, a freshly extended set of fragmentations and reifications that postmodernist art now invites us to enjoy as the newly beautiful
and true. The stage is thus set for a new version of the old debate over the
possibility of an authentically counterhegemonic artistic production within
late capitalist society—a debate that has been, until now, carried out most
fiercely and fruitfully within the Marxist tradition.[3] Yet—and herein lies my

381

second bemusement, and the orneriness as well—despite the real intelligence that informs discussion of postmodern art from either point of view, I have been dissatisfied with both positions.

Prodded by this blend of pleasure, curiosity, dissatisfaction, and hubris, I want to articulate a rather different understanding both of the postmodern art I have come to enjoy and of its relationship to politics and culture. Such an understanding begins, inevitably, in dialectical self-reflexiveness, in articulating the specific qualities of the enjoyment of postmodernist work I experience as one member of a serially dispersed yet socially distinct group, that is, as a member of a particular *mass audience,* whose emergence constitutes a significant moment in contemporary American culture insofar as it marks a breakdown in the antagonistic yet mutually dependent categories of high culture and mass or "popular" culture. Previously, as Fredric Jameson has noted, the movement of the forms, techniques, and effects of high cultural production into mass culture has been subterranean and anonymous.[4] Schonberg's revolution in musical language, for example, creeps into the scores of countless TV programs and Hollywood films without announcing its name; surrealism is swallowed up and surpassed by each day's crop of smugly self-mocking ads; and the hermetic self-inspection of abstract expressionism is converted into familiarity, even affability, on the walls of corporate lobbies.

Of course, the opposite process also continues to recur, as the motifs of mass culture are "sublimated" and reprocessed into high culture. Until very recently this has been the case in American postmodernism as well. From Warhol through Salle in painting, O'Hara through the L=A=N =G=U=A=G=E group in poetry, Coover, Pynchon, and Barthelme in fiction, the icons and representations of mass culture reappear within forms that we might as well admit are now, by custom and usage, received as ineluctably "high": the so-called quality novel or short story, the volume of poetry, contemporary sculpture, painting, or print. That in this sense "postmodernism" has been until recently only the newest extension of modernism itself is suggested as well, I would submit, by the argument carried out in relatively sterile formalist terms through most of the seventies in such academic-literary journals as *boundary 2, Triquarterly,* and *The Bucknell Review* (and no doubt in various art and music journals as well) over whether such a body of work could even be said to exist as a distinct region within the kingdom of high cultural practices.[5] Now, however, when new work bearing a distinct and undisguised postmodernist stamp "goes gold" in records and sells out concert halls from New York to Portland, Oregon, such arguments and the formalist methodologies on which they rest may reasonably be said to have been resolved and superseded. Postmodernist aesthetic practice, whatever its origins in high culture, is now itself, like Laurie Anderson and Philip Glass, what culture industry specialists call a "crossover" phenomenon. So the question we must ask of it—or rather, of the part of it that is most decisively disengaged from high art—is less where it comes from or how it is made than what pleasures it makes possible for what social groups.

My use of the term "structure of feeling" is intended to indicate precisely such a methodological shift, from the study of fixed and formal internal relations and genealogies to a more fluid, shifting social analysis. The term, of course, is Raymond Williams's attempt to do conceptual justice to any set of circumstances resembling the cultural situation we now face, that is, the unconsolidated emergence of the distinctly new, in both social life in general and aesthetic practice in particular: "For structures of feeling can be defined as social experiences in solution, as distinct from other social semantic formations which have been *precipitated* and are more evidently and more immediately available. . . . Yet this specific solution is never mere flux. It is a structured formation which, because it is *at the very edge of semantic availability,* has many of the characteristics of a pre-formation, until specific articulations—new semantic figures—are discovered in material practice."[6]

I propose that we seek out such work precisely insofar as it speaks to the desire and dread inherent in such a "structure of feeling," of a certain modality of social experience that lies "at the very edge of semantic availability." The origins of this modality lie in part in recent shifts in the processes of the subject's earliest notions of self and other, figure and ground, language and difference.[7] To think of postmodernism as a structure of feeling, however, is to leave the question of its political and/or ideological valence open for as long as possible, until the relationship between this set of aesthetic practices and social reality has been fully theorized and reassembled.

What social groups constitute the mass audience for the postmodernist work of Talking Heads, Laurie Anderson, Philip Glass? What pleasure does this audience seek and find in such work? We may answer the first question fairly summarily; the second will take some time. From my own experience I think it is safe to say this audience is composed primarily of middle-class whites from around eighteen years of age to upward of forty, mostly college-educated, with a greater parity of females to males than has ordinarily been the case in markets for "avant-garde" work. We are speaking, then, of a significant minority within a generation and a half of consumer society, a group that has either lived its childhood or come to maturity through the long crisis and congealment of the sixties and seventies; a generation and a half, moreover, whose social destiny has remained clear: we are to be the switchpoints between capital and labor, the intermediary administrative and reproductive component of a vast apparatus of exploitation and valorization.[8] Our journey has been aided by major transformations in the structure of families and the ideology of parenting, a de-Oedipalizing process both conditioning and conditioned by related developments in the "external" realm of production and typically characterized by the diminution into relative absence of effectual paternal authority in the home and the concomitantly increased, problematic presence of the mother.[9] So far, family and child-rearing practices in both working-class and ruling-class families have proved more autonomous, self-perpetuating, and resistant to change than those of the middle-class American family;[10] but for the offspring of the middle class, de-Oedipalization has had profound effects on the nature of felt experience—a major prerequisite for our mass audience's enjoyment of postmodernist work.

What, then, is the nature of this enjoyment? How is delight produced from the interaction between this audience and a David Byrne intoning:

What is happening to my skin?
Where is the protection that I need?
Air can hurt you too
Air can hurt you too
Some people say not to worry about the air
Some people never had experience with
Air ... Air[11]

or Laurie Anderson's electrically distorted chant, "O Superman—O Judge—O Mom and Dad,"[12] or Lucinda Childs's dispassionate recital of botched quotations and proto-sentences—"I feel the earth move under my feet. I feel tumbling down tumbling down. I feel it Some ostriches are a like into a satchel. Some like them. I went to the window and wanted to draw the earth. So David Cassidy tells you when to go into this one into a meat. So where would a red dress. So this will get some gas. So this could This would be some of all of my great friends. Jay Steve Julia Robyn Rick Kit and Liz. So this would get any energy. So if you know what some like into were. So ... So about one song"[13]—through a musical texture characterized both by its utter harmonic simplicity and repetitiousness and its minute, ceaseless rhythmic transmutations? What common features may we find in such work that enable us to label it "postmodernist" in the first place?

What these works have in common is, first of all, a certain quality or manner of utterance and performance—deadpan, indifferent, depersonalized, effaced—that effectively cancels the possibility of traditional audience identification. The speaker or singer is in no way "expressing" him/herself through his/her performance, inviting us to share and eventually merge our similar yet distinct experience, emotions, and individual sensibilities with his/her own. David Byrne, the main vocalist of Talking Heads, delivers the song's scant melodies in an off-kilter blend of warbles and shouts, a mixture of sudden random enthusiasms and mumbled toss-offs that mock the tropes of expressivity by rendering them "illegible." In *Einstein on the Beach,* the Wilson/Glass "opera," Lucinda Childs and other speakers declaim or recite their texts through the music without a hint of expressive inflection, while the music itself remains similarly centerless. One finds oneself listening less *to* the work than *across* it. As Craig Owens has noted of performance artist Laurie Anderson, "the only access to herself that she allows is through all kinds of technological filters which amplify, distort and multiply her actual voice in such a way that it can no longer be identified as hers."[14]

The result of these techniques is familiar to connoisseurs of "high" postmodernist art: one is confronted not with a unified text, much less by the presence of a distinct personality and sensibility, but by a discontinuous terrain of heterogeneous discourses uttered by anonymous, unplaceable tongues, a chaos different from that of the classic texts of high modernism precisely insofar as it is not recontained or recuperated within an overarching mythic framework. The sense of self (up on the stage or out in the audience) called up and produced by these postmodernist works is a specifically poststructuralist one as well, whose difference from an earlier, more unitary structuralism may be measured by the difference between Lévi-Strauss's "I am the place in which something occurred" and Laurie Anderson's "I am in my body the way most people drive in their cars."[15] The "I" of the Lévi-Strauss quotation, however diverse its determinations, is

384

still single, demarcated, isolable; but the self as aimless driver belongs everywhere and nowhere. Moreover, in this latter view of self and world, whatever passes through the windshield passes through the mind as well; indeed, consciousness may be understood as only that passage, that motion itself.

But a practice that moves away from notions of totalization and singularity and techniques of expressive presence toward new assumptions of decentered dispersion and techniques of absence, depersonalization, and disassembly into a multiplicity of codes immerses us in a fresh and seemingly hopeless dialectic between inside and outside, figure and ground. This dialectic is the second specifically postmodernist constituent of the works I have mentioned, a dialectic that depends on the near-perfect reversibility of the description just formulated above. In presenting us with a shifting, centerless concatenation of codings, postmodernist work from Beckett and Rauschenberg to Laurie Anderson and Talking Heads offers us two opposed alternatives, between which we are free to oscillate indefinitely. We may allow ourselves to drift into that space and accept its mutating babble as the very image of consciousness; or we may confront that same babble, that "scrabble system," as Laurie Anderson calls it,[16] as a distilled representation of the whole antagonistic, voracious world of Otherness, engaged in an endless struggle to engulf, colonize, and devour the self, to scribble its graffiti on our every surface, to precode and appropriate the spot of Being that still permits us to stand. The alternatives, in short, are to disperse ourselves across the codes or take enormous, well-nigh paranoid precautions against them: Laurie Anderson invites us to "Let X = X"; David Byrne warns us to watch out for animals ("They're laughing at us") and "Air."[17] But the result of either point of view is that experience becomes a matter of *pure internality.* Either codes and their unrelenting proliferations are the sole constituents of selfhood, or else they have nothing to do with it except as an overwhelming threat. In either case, the possibility of what we have considered real speech, that is, a meaningful relationship between sign and referent, and of the related distinction between figure and ground has been abandoned.

It follows that such a closed solipsistic universe is fundamentally two-dimensional, lacking depth, perspective, or time. If, through its unbounded dispersion or its incommunicable solitude, there is only the self, then experience itself, in the sense of *events,* is a fiction. Thus the mise-en-scene—or lack thereof—in postmodern art is characterized by shifts in surface rather than development in time. Fredric Jameson has compared this tautological, amnesiac effect with the Lacanian description of schizophrenia: "the only verbal operations available to the schizophrenic are those involved in the contemplation of material signifiers in a present which is unable to hold onto past and present. Each signifier thus becomes a perpetual present, an island or enclave in time, succeeded by a new present which emerges equally in the void, with no links to anything that preceded it, or any project to come."[18]

This description is posed in terms of the view in which the self and the signifier stand distinctly opposed to one another. Yet I believe it could be put in terms of the first view as well, that we could say with equal accuracy that the schizophrenic and/or the postmodernist work finds its Being in this signifier, this discourse; then that one, over there (which, of course, becomes instantly *here*); and so on, ad infinitum. Thus, the lyrics of "O Superman" and the electronically distorted timbres of Laurie Anderson's voice alter abruptly, without transition: first a "Mom" is addressed, among others, in the burbling tones of an amplified mellotron; then a chatty, ordinary voice tells us its owner is not at home and invites us to leave a message; then a third voice or timbre, perhaps a mixture of the first two, says, "Hello? This is your Mother. Are you there? Are you coming home?" Despite these inexplicable shifts in speaker and tone, we may sense the slim possibility of a narrative of sorts; but Anderson is an expert at tempting us with such mirages and then erasing them. The voice will soon change again, and before long another voice—or perhaps one of the earlier ones—will inform us that "neither snow nor rain nor gloom of night shall stay these couriers from the swift completion of their appointed rounds."[19] It is this endless antivista of unrelated presences, surfaces, voices, in an autoreferential succession without consequence, that is suggested by the stammering chorus of Talking Heads's "Heaven" ("Heaven is the place / The place where nothing / Nothing ever happens"),[20] as well as by Edwin Denby's description of the experience of Wilson/Glass's *Einstein on the Beach:* "It isn't symbolism or telling a story—watching it happen, the spacious proportions for looking and seeing make it easy to breathe and stay open and very soon to realize the exalting strength of the music listening to it section by section, a continuous present moment of time for four hours."[21]

Such a schizoid spatialization of time into "sections" is not unambiguously pleasurable, notwithstanding Denby's delight. Just as the vision of the boundlessly dispersed self is caught up with the fear of dissolution, the flip side of the ease of "breathing" and "staying open" is the terror of a contingency from which all possibility of eventful significance has been drained. This is the place, then, to emphasize that each of these three postmodernist "pleasures of the text" contains a countervailing anxiety. Indeed, the experience of this newly constituted mass audience for postmodernist work is most fundamentally this very unstable play between a primal delight and a primal fear, between two simultaneous versions of the primary aggressive impulse, that which seeks to incorporate the world into itself and that which struggles to prevent its own engulfment. This dialectic is the postmodern "structure of feeling." Unlike either previous high culture (with its formal and/or mythic boundaries) or mass culture (with its prepackaged, foretold happy endings), postmodernism immerses us within the desire and dread it evokes without resolving their oscillation on the level of either content or form. It remains to be seen, of course, whether such a practice can continue; how long Laurie Anderson, Talking Heads, Philip Glass, and others like them will keep on producing such decidedly irresolute work before they slide into the ingratiating clichés of mass culture or the formal sublimations of high art.[22] But the fate of such work turns in part on another question, that of the social origins and destiny of the desire and fear, the structure of feeling, called up by this work for its audience.

The question of the social roots of this structure of feeling brings us back to the existence of the two "camps" of cultural criticism cited at the outset. Their explanations of the advent and increasing popularity of postmodernist work follow, of course, from their definitions of its primary functions and effects, and, in one case in particular, more specifically from its internal workings *as art.* Thus, what Rosalind Krauss, Craig Owens, and other members of the *October* editorial group find both essential and progressive about postmodernist work is the extent to which it reveals all experience as already-coded, as so many instances of preexistent codes and discourses at work.[23] The postmodernist project is "to 'de-originate the utterance' ";[24] or, as Charles Russel puts it, "To make discourse evident is the main goal of post-modernist literature and art. To reveal the absolute and intimate connection between ourselves as speakers and listeners and our socially determined patterns of perceiving, thinking, expressing and acting is the function of self-reflexive artworks. Meaning as a system, culture as a set of discourses, individuality as a product of social codes of behavior—these are the themes of our art."[25]

This definition and the claims it entails are obviously not wholly incompatible with my description of the postmodernist work I have enjoyed; indeed, as a description of postmodernist artistic intentions it is substantially correct, especially given the close ties of many postmodernist artists to the institutions of art history and criticism.[26] Yet such a definition does not bring us much closer to an understanding of why large audiences are available for the performance art of Laurie Anderson, the "opera" of Philip Glass and Robert Wilson, the concerts of Talking Heads. Is it possible that these audiences seek and take pleasure in the "de-origination of the utterance," either to liberate themselves from the spell of its codes or to realize themselves as the shifting, uneven product of their proliferation? To ask the question is to answer it; but for the most part, adherents of postmodernism, a progressive cultural practice, do not—and perhaps, given their definition, cannot—face the question at all.[27] The increasing mass appeal of the kind of work they proclaim is less a subject requiring investigation than circumstantial proof that the sub-rosa cultural revolution to free ourselves from the tyranny of enforced signification is indeed under way. So we are invited to assume precisely what seemed to be in question—the political potential and valence of postmodernist work.

That such an aporia is itself the symptom of a systematic contemporary disabling of historical thought is suggested by Jameson's more enlightening account of the postmodernist dynamic. He argues that the emergence of the poststructuralist claim to truth, with its attendant Foucaultian exaltation of free play against the omnipresence of Power, is at one with the postmodernist aesthetic it extols. Both reflect the recent transformation of advanced capitalist society in its ever-increasing repression of the marks of material production, its ever-advancing commodification of culture and language into a meaningless atmosphere of free-floating signifiers, loosed from their signifieds:

> "the autonomization of language" ... is at one with the universal fragmentation, compartmentalization, specialization of all kinds of other areas through late capitalism. However privileged the area of language may seem to be, therefore, from a social perspective it is yet another symptom of the intensified process of reification and commodification, which seeks to colonize ever more remote and archaic enclaves in human experience as well as in the social world, within

the psyche, as well as in Nature itself. (The infrastructural reality of this process ... is what we have seen Mandel [the contemporary Marxist political economist] identify as a new and more totalizing wave of industrialization and mechanization of hitherto unrationalized zones of production.)[28]

Elsewhere, Jameson has proposed the notion of the "linguistic," the concept of a paradigmatic set of literary (and/or more broadly aesthetic) techniques and effects which convey the quintessential "feel" of space and time in a given mode of production. Postmodernism, for Jameson, is just such a "linguistic" or "aesthetic"—one that (re)presents to its audience the alienated, already coded, precommodified "reality" we experience every day in what Debord has called "the society of the spectacle." As such, the workings of postmodernism are at best merely mimetic, at worst habituating, insofar as we learn through it to enjoy the free play of our chains. Jameson does not hold out much hope for those who aim to produce a progressive aesthetic in the present conjuncture: "with the eclipse of culture as an autonomous space or sphere, culture itself falls into the world, with the result that the latter becomes completely acculturated; in the society of the spectacle, the society of the image, media society, everything has become cultural, and this will clearly make for real and new problems about the possibility of any politics, any politics within the cultural sphere proper, since the latter is now virtually coterminous with society as a whole."[29]

Jameson's measured pessimism is a salutary warning to any would-be progressive artists and their proselytizers, including those operating under the banner of the postmodern. And his diagnosis of the postmodernist "linguistic" moment can help us toward a fully social and historical understanding of the structure of feeling I have described. To travel that distance, though, it is necessary to locate those events and processes that may be viewed as prototypical instances of the general phenomena whose hegemonic presence, according to Jameson, is the definitive cultural characteristic of late capitalism: commodification, or the conversion of substance into form, ends and use values into sheer instrumentality; and reification, the materialization into a fantasized concrete of the immaterial, form and the abstract. And we must concentrate on these dialectically interrelated phenomena as they occur in the life cycle of the mass audience whose outlines we have already sketched.

Such instances are not hard to find. Indeed, their presence is obvious in my description of the postmodernist mass audience as the newest generation of consumer society, trained and aimed for positions in what is politely called the "middle strata" of the work force—professionals and managers of the system. That such training involves a protracted "education" in obedience to and enactment of arcane formal procedures, mastery of a specialized instrumentalist vocabulary, and the ability to tolerate both ever-higher levels of abstraction and ever-longer periods of routinized time will be obvious to all who have passed through a non-elite college or university.[30] As good professionals in education, social work, or business, we can all affirm that such preparations are necessary. Our expanded numbers in these fields, the work we do, the forms we fill out and put out, the standards by which we judge and are judged, designate us as both chief agents and most immediate victims of the "bureaucratization of the world," the "adoption of impersonal rules which specify procedure and make possible exact economic calculation."[31] Living out one's working life under "bureaucratic control,"[32] while readministering its rules and norms as our work, we come to inhabit and extend a realm of reification par excellence, a social landscape that, in the words of Jon Schiller, appears "mysterious, omniscient and omnipotent, capricious, pervasive, and seemingly beyond the control of any single individual or group":

> One's experience of such institutions simultaneously feels like an event in nature and a force that is insanely human in its rationality. Unlike the choice of acquiescence or rebellion confronting one in patriarchal [e.g., early capitalist] institutions, the individual now finds himself reduced to adaptation or anomie. It is not surprising that the typical attitudes in relation to bureaucracy repeat those of the pre-oedipal period: helpless dependence and rage; schizoid splits between normal affective experience and the routinization demanded by a peculiar rationality; and paranoid ideation that one is under constant surveillance and control.[33]

Thus the torments of the "bureaucratic soul" in a world from which the visible presence of Power and Authority are gone—torments whose resemblance to both the darkly negative, anxious side of the postmodernist structure of feeling and the Lacanian description of the schizophrenic is far from coincidental. And if we turn from the reified world of production to the spectacular world of consumable objects that confronts this same audience in its leisure time, we will find an equally striking convergence, for the audience for postmodernist work is a subgroup of the most critical and fiercely wooed market sector for consumable commodities. As professionals, managers, administrators, we have a larger share of discretionary income than any class or stratum below us; and we outnumber the ruling class, who in any case cannot be expected to shoulder the enormous "white man's burden" of consumption. The result is that we of the post-World War II baby boom and after who have taken our places in the middle strata of the work force are the primary "target audience" in the society of the spectacle. For us the glossiest magazines are published, from *Mademoiselle* to *Playboy;* for us *Apocalypse Now* and *Kramer vs. Kramer* are made; and for us the cornucopia of advertising pours out its lavish, illusory wealth. In the shorthand of Marxist jargon, we are the "subjects hailed" by the "aestheticization of commodities," well-trained experts in the peculiar art of reading the good sex life into toothpaste or deodorant, the pastoral picnic into the bottle of Gallo chablis:

> We are given two signifiers [in an ad—e.g., Catherine Deneuve and Chanel No. 5], are required to make a "signified" by exchanging them. The fact that we have to *make* this exchange, to do the linking work which is not *done* in the ad, but which is made possible only

389

by its form, draws us into the transformational space between the units of the ad. Its meaning only exists in this space: the field of transaction; and it is here that we operate—*we are this space.*

Now, if the meaning of the ad exists in the transformation of meanings between signs, and if this tranformation takes place in us ... this is placing *us* in the space of the signified.[34]

Once again, here in Williamson's analysis of the interpellation of the reader/viewer/listener as simultaneously subject and signified in the ad, we are confronted with a process that is both a constitutive element of the experience of the emergent mass audience for postmodernist work and a behavior markedly similar to that of our poor schizophrenic. Only this time, we catch him/her on the upswing in his/her prison of internality, at the self-exalting moment of identification across a dispersed field of signifiers. Moreover, as we follow Williamson's Lacanian argument about how we are induced to enter this imaginary space, we encounter another familiar landmark—the pre-Oedipal stage of psychic development and, in particular, the mirror stage. Lacan describes the mirror stage in terms that are simultaneously phenomenological and semiotic/linguistic;[35] it is the crucial intermediary moment between the unformed self's total immersion in the "Imaginary," a state before either "I" or "not I," and the properly Oedipal moment in which the subject receives its name through the access "the Father" gives it to that realm of Law, Authority, and signification Lacan denotes as the "Symbolic." In this unstable stage of development, the child momentarily perceives itself and its reflection or representation as one and the same, a unified "Ideal-Ego"; whereas after its induction into Language and the Symbolic, such a fusion of sign and referent, however longed for, is no longer possible. Yet according to Williamson, advertisements work, that is, persuade us to do the signifying work they require, precisely by promising us that impossible bliss of reunion, an "Ego-Ideal" that tempts us to reach out, then vanishes again:

Ads ... show you a symbol of yourself aimed to attract your desire; they suggest that you can *become* the person in the picture before you. But merging with an "objectified" image of yourself is impossible: the desire for it is simply a channeling of the desire for the pre-Symbolic, Imaginary Ideal-Ego. It is important to remember that the subject *cannot* completely be returned to the mirror as it were, since to understand an advertisement is to comprehend a system of differences that is of the Symbolic order. What they can do is to *misrepresent* the position of the subject, and to misrepresent its relation to him. .... So ads form a symbolic system which appropriates and apparently *represents* the Imaginary; thereby embodying the inherent contradiction of the mirror-phase.[36]

In exposing the way ads feed on our longing for the last moment of pre-Oedipality, when, for better or worse, for bliss or rage, what was

390

outside the unformed self could still be experienced as inside, Williamson's analysis seems to bring us closer still to agreement with Jameson's thesis that postmodernism is the new linguistic for a space-time transformed and degraded by the domination of the processes of reification and commodification. Indeed, if those of us in the middle strata do live fundamentally in, through, and between the pre-Oedipalizing modalities of bureaucracy, on the one hand, and advertising, on the other, then the underlying conclusion of Jameson's Marxist analysis of postmodernism seems inescapable: far from serving any progressive-subversive function, postmodernism merely provides its audience with foregrounded, stylized glimpses of its own alienations, an intensified yet controlled experience of its own unmastered pre-Oedipal quandary. However necessary, in the grand Hegelian dialectic of Marxist becoming, may be the moment it crystallizes, on its way to the proletarianization of the world and the apocalyptic moment of international class struggle, postmodernism today is not revolutionary cultural practice but the newest version of the homeopathic dose.

Yet however suggestive our Marxist analysis may seem to be, it has failed to meditate with sufficient historical self-consciousness on its own terminological instruments—or, more specifically, on the peculiar appropriateness of a distinctly psychoanalytic language to describe public social experience. Moreover, we have failed to mention a third level of description and analysis though which our subject, the mass audience for postmodernist work and the structure of feeling that connects the two, may be investigated: the level of primary socialization, the family, where, as Sartre has said, the subject's "interiorization of the exterior" truly begins.[37] A fully materialist analysis of the postmodernist structure of feeling cannot begin when the members of this mass audience stare at their first commercial or receive their first paychecks; nor can it ignore its own terminological shifts. If the structure of feeling expressed in postmodernist work and its reception is most accurately described in psychoanalytic terms as a pre-Oedipal relationship with the world, if the discourse of class analysis has become infused with (or invaded by) the discourse of psychoanalysis, we must look for an explanation in the de-Oedipalized middle-class home.

A brief review of the basic axioms of post-Freudian psychoanalysis may be in order—in particular, those arising from the work of Melanie Klein. Since Klein's pioneering studies of the mother-child relationship, we have come to understand the Oedipal moment not merely as the rude insertion of the father's power and authority, leading to the child's fear- or envy-ridden compliance, but as a cathexis the child seeks out and desires, since by this means it is able to counter and mitigate the all-enveloping omnipotence of the mother and its attendant, painfully ambivalent—hating and fearing, loving and wanting—relationship with her. Thus, the strength of the Oedipal break may be seen not only as the function of the strength of the father's presence and authority but of both the length and quality of nurturance the child has received from its mother. If the mothering has been marked by relatively severe rearing practices—little touching, say, and/or repeated frustration of oral, anal, and genital drives— the Oedipal break will be less intense than if the same pre-Oedipal period is more indulgent and nurturant.

If these axioms[38] hold, then to understand the de-Oedipalization of the contemporary middle-class family we must examine not only the degree of the father's authority but also the recent history of the practice and ideology of mothering. The social phenomenon of de-Oedipalization is therefore to be read dialectically, as a moment in the history of the American middle-class family characterized both by the father's relative absence and by the onset of more indulgent mothering than that practiced before World War II and Dr. Spock. In other words, de-Oedipalization must also be seen in terms of the increasing strength and intensity of the pre-Oedipal stage of psychic formation. In Schiller's words, "the father's intervention into the [mother-child] dyad became more urgent while his influence was becoming more superficial. Stated in a spatial metaphor, the psychic area occupied by unconscious maternal representations has expanded and the domain of the internalized paternal authority correspondingly diminished."[39]

These interrelated phenomena, in turn, must be understood as effects of wider forces at work in American society. The de-authorization of the middle-class father is an effect created both by the "suburbanization" of American life, the increased real and psychic distance between work site and home, and the replacement at that work site of the "authority of the master"—normally the petit-bourgeois father himself—by the "monotonous power of process,"[40] as he finds his work and status no longer in a bygone kingdom of small business but as a professional member of a bureaucratized state or corporate structure. Likewise, though on a wider historical scale, the postwar changes in mothering are only the most recent extension of a general "softening" of the ideology and practice of child-rearing underway in Western society since around the end of the eighteenth century—a "softening" deeply connected with capitalism's explosive, unrecontainable discovery of the "free individual."[41]

Having reconstructed the concept of the de-Oedipalization of the American middle-class home, it is now possible to reverse field on some of the points contained in the initial Marxist analysis offered earlier: to argue the extent to which the de-authorization of the father combined with the increasing hegemony of the pre-Oedipal mother themselves *enable* the subject to play advertising's elusive Lacanian game, to lose and find itself in the endless corridors of bureaucratic administration and control—and to play something like the same interminable game, with all its pleasures and anxieties, through the experience of postmodernist work. In this way we can account for the necessity of psychoanalytic language, even in what has been so far a Marxist analysis, to describe our structure of feeling. If, as Lacan suggests, the Oedipal moment consitutes the subject's accession through the Father into the realm of the Symbolic, that thenceforth inescapable kingdom of name, signification, and category, and if that accession is incomplete or weak for members of our subject audience, then their experience of the Symbolic will be distinctly toned and to some extent even recaptured by the pre-Oedipal Imaginary. Such a subject may perceive its relationship to Authority not in terms of the Oedipally derived notions of neurosis, repression, and the hysterical symptom, nor within the bounded Symbolic categories of class, but rather in terms of a widely dispersed, elusive yet omnipresent Power before which one either directly acts out a spontaneous rebellion or else caves in, submits, even clings: "Power is everywhere; not because it embraces everything, but because it comes from everywhere. And 'Power,' insofar as it is permanent, repetitious, inert, and self-reproducing, is simply the over-all effect that emerges from all these mobilities, the concatentation that rests on each of them and seeks in turn to arrest their movement."[42] Omnipresent, permanent, repetitious, inert, self-reproducing: the terms of Foucault's notorious definition precisely catalog the full paranoia of entrapment in the pre-Oedipal world. Small wonder that a generation of young American middle-class intellectuals has already come to love it so well and quote it so often; it is the structure of feeling they live.

Our plunge into the family thus seems merely to have strengthened the Marxist case against postmodernism as a potentially progressive cultural movement. Insofar as its structure of feeling can be understood as the product of forces we have tracked back to the capitalist mode of production, our analysis may stand as a Marxist triumph, founded in Marx's original vision of the primacy of production. And insofar as this same structure of feeling proves itself resistant to the fundamental categories of Marxism—the deep ontological reality of forces and relations of production, or that moment of historical becoming inherent in the notion of Class—it shows its own deficiency as an agent of revolutionary change. Yet it is at this point, having set forth a Marxist analysis of postmodernism, that it becomes possible to take the opposite perspective. We may now examine what new light the postmodernist moment throws back on Marxism itself—from a somewhat different yet equally materialist perspective that increasingly offers itself as a point of view and practice superseding Marxism.

I refer, of course, to a specifically feminist materialism whose outlines have begun to appear increasingly distinct in the work of Dorothy Dinnerstein, Nancy Chodorow, Jessica Benjamin, and Isaac Balbus, among others, and whose explanatory power has grown immeasurably over the last ten years or so. It might be possible to argue that feminist-materialist theory today occupies the same relation to the two most visible strains in the American feminist movement that Marx's historical materialism took in relation to the analogous wings of the workers' movement of a century ago: both combating a liberal reformist tendency, on the one hand (social democracy; the "bourgeois" reformist politics of N.O.W.), and an ultra-Left, idealist voluntarism, on the other (anarco-syndicalism; the separatism of "radical" feminists). This analogy is, of course, no proof of the more recent theory's validity, which can only be established by other means. A feminist materialism must be able to demonstrate its self-reflexive understanding of its own historical emergence and enablement out of the postmodernist moment, and the extent to which its method and project constitute a necessary transvaluation of the Marxist perspective on social reality, including the present moment.

We may begin this task by reanalyzing the difference between the old and new conception of power as a specifically *gendered* one. Here, for example, are two quotations, both reasonably well known to their respective audiences, whose somewhat perverse juxtaposition expresses this difference quite well.

Labour is, in the first place, a process in which both Man and Nature participate, and in which Man of his own accord starts, regulates, and	So hold me, Mom, in your long arms. So hold me, Mom, in your long arms.

controls the material reaction between himself and Nature. *He opposes himself to Nature as one of her own forces*, setting in motion arms and legs, head and hands, the natural forces of his body in order to appropriate Nature's production in a form adapted to his wants. By thus acting on the external world and changing it, he at the same time changes his own nature. He develops his slumbering powers and compels them to act in obedience to his sway.[43]

In your automatic arms. Your electronic arms. In your long arms. So hold me, Mom, in your long arms. Your petrochemical arms. Your military arms. In your electronic arms.[44]

    In a very real sense, our evaluation of the postmodernist structure of feeling and our decision for or against a feminist rather than a Marxist materialism both depend on how we interpret the shift in sexual coding these quotes exemplify. The possibility of coding the humanly produced world as maternally feminine clearly arises from the historic explosion of "familialism" in general, and the pre-Oedipal in particular, across the entire cultural map; in its eerie invocation of a military-industrial Mother, so weirdly reminiscent of earlier Romantic appeals to an equally maternal Nature, Laurie Anderson's lines stand as a prototypical illustration of the collapse of the Symbolic back into the Imaginary. Yet the historic moment of de-Oedipalization also makes it possible for us to read into Marx's classic assertion of the ontological primacy of production as the constitutive, defining action of human life a new and startlingly historicized perspective. Suddenly it appears as a neatly compressed account of the very origins of industrial society's obsession with production, objectification, instrumentality, and signification in the Oedipal escape from the Mother, here reprojected as Nature, whose landscape and forces Man becomes Man by learning to dominate.[45]

    By this reading, Marx's grounding of the human project in its form and relations of production is less an unquestionable truth than a projection of a given moment in the long dialectical history of the sex-gender system of the West: a moment that is the very apex of Oedipality itself, given both the ideology and practice of an ever-more indulgent mothering within the newly privatized home, together with the retained-yet-distinct, still-authorized relative presence of the Father. Thus, from the perspective of a feminist materialism, our Marxist argument is at least partly incorrect. It is not true that the postmodernist moment and structure of feeling are distinguished by the fact that "the dominant themes of familialism—including the authority relations identified by psychoanalysis—are pervasive in ideology generally."[46] Rather, such themes are *necessarily dominant* in all societies in which sexuality is socially constructed and arranged.

    One of the chief tasks of a properly materialist feminism—one whose strategies are grounded in the assumption of the ontological priority not of the domination of nature in production but of the domination of women in the family—is a history of the manifold forms and relations of sex-gender systems. Such a history would supply the basis for an account of the Lacanian categories of the Imaginary and the Symbolic, categories left unhistoricized until now.[47] But there is another task for a feminist materialism: the task of accounting for itself. Marx willingly admitted and explained the extent to which his method of historical materialism and its allied utopian vision of communist society was explicitly enabled by the emergence of capitalism: the stripping away of all human relations but the "cash nexus," he argued, permits us to see at last that "the history of all hitherto existing society is the history of class struggles,"[48] just as the historic rise of those two great antagonists, Capital and the massed Proletariat, points the way toward a communist society in which all domination—except of Nature—is only a reminder of the past. How, then, does the feminism of Benjamin, Balbus, and Dinnerstein theorize its own historical enablement out of the crux of the postmodernist moment? Does the de-Oedipalization of contemporary middle-class culture really contain any utopian dimension or revolutionary potential? If so, what is that potential for, and where does it point from here?

The key question in this series is the second, and for Marxists the obvious answer is No. The de-Oedipalization of middle-class life is a capitalist pathology; the postmodernist culture arising from this pathology is a mystification expressing only a very local, representational truth. Revolutionary practices thus must await the moment when the revolutionary subject constitutes itself through a re-Oedipalized entry into the Symbolic, either through full recognition of its name as the Proletariat, master of Nature, vide Jameson, or else through a reconstitution within the family of the authorized Father, as suggested in the recent reactionary work of the Marxist Christopher Lasch.[49] But for a materialist feminism, the answer is Yes. De-Oedipalization opens the way to new, more coherent and complete definitions of domination and Utopia alike. Moreover, insofar as its appearance is itself the perverse dialectical outcome of an earlier hegemony of the Oedipal, with all its associated effects—an emphasis on instrumentality, objectification, the flight from the pre-Oedipal Imaginary into the Symbolic, and the male domination of Nature and women alike—it is a prime example of that very "cunning of History" Marx and Hegel first perceived. Our present confrontation with the social world we have created— a Nature in which we are deeply implicated and from which we derive our being—a social realm now coextensive with what is left of the other nature on which it was built, is the result of a long era of Oedipality and the neurotic domination of Nature.

This problem of Nature and our relationship to it is first and most dramatically experienced by the subject as the problem of that Mother who appears both coextensive and excruciatingly detached from us, who has the power to meet or frustrate our every need.[50] The Oedipal break with the Mother, moreover, serves not to resolve this painful ambiguity of good mommy/bad mommy, inside and outside, but to allow the subject to take flight from it into the Symbolic, where it will be repressed, only to reemerge as the domination of nature and the subjugation of women. The dialectical return of pre-Oedipality closes off this perverse escape route, and the de-Oedipalized subject now must face itself within an ecosystem whose "natural" and "social" elements are inextricably fused. De-Oedipalization makes possible a domination-free conception of political association and action as well. However hostile male leftists and progressives may still be toward women in general and feminism in particular,[51] their origins in de-Oedipalized middle-class homes account in large part for a profound shift in political style, away from vanguardist conceptions and democratic-centralist modes of organization toward grassroots mobilization and conscious decision making.[52]

Such changes are not merely the result of opportunistic thefts or "lessons taken" from the women's movement but are also the result of a deep convergence. This same general process of de-Oedipalization, which loosens the bonds of male domination of women enough to release women and their hitherto repressed social vision of reciprocity and nurturance into the public realm, also dictates that the Oedipal break for the male child more and more closely resembles that incomplete accession to the Symbolic that has been historically characteristic of female psychic development. In Stephanie Engels's terms, "the augmented importance of emotional relatedness, embeddedness, and dependence, and the decline of radical emotional rupture and devastation [i.e., of the Oedipal break] put the contemporary boy in an effective and developmental position that looks much like that traditionally characteristic of little girls."[53]

From a feminist-materialist perspective, then, the de-Oedipalization of American middle-class life releases historically new and progressive social forces into American life—forces that Marxism, with its hypostatization of Oedipality, is essentially incapable of joining or even evaluating at their full worth. Yet these new forces all point to the necessity of a further development within the sex-gender system, for if, as these new materialists maintain, "the character of the relationship between the adult self and its sexual, political and 'natural' others is decisively shaped by the character of the relationship established between the childhood self and its first and most salient, i.e., its parental others,"[54] then the problems for those who participate in the new social movements arising from de-Oedipalization—feminism, the environmental movement, and a host of progressive grassroots coalitions—must be traced back to an unresolved dilemma within the sex-gender system. De-Oedipalization may, for example, determine the subject's reinsertion back into a newly expanded Nature, but it does not supply the material prerequisites for a newly articulated, deliberate yet benign relationship with it. The subject reimmersed in an essentially pre-Oedipal relationship to the world appears more likely to swing from one pole of internality to another, from a rage at all that surrounds and threatens it to a deliriously dispersed self-exaltation across the whole terrain of hollowed-out signifiers. Neither, of course, are the new strategies of consensus and grassroots consciousness raising and mobilization, however salutary these may be compared to their antecedents, presently equipped to deal with internal disagreements or to move from consciousness raising to concrete social action.

Finally, it is clear that the increasing number of de-Oedipalized middle-class male subjects, even ostensibly politically progressive ones, in no way guarantees any decrease in their fear of and hostility toward women. The relative closing off of the Oedipal escape route often seems to have increased that hostility and fear, now that the safety of domination and the flight to the Symbolic is no longer available. Thus, it is possible to return in partial agreement to the Marxist critique of the postmodernist moment in American culture. Lasch's pessimistic depiction of the de-Oedipalized, narcissistic subject's susceptibility to "soft" authoritarianism should not be taken lightly; nor can Jameson's linkage of what he calls "micro-politics" to terrorism, and his judgment of both as politically ineffectual, be dismissed.[55] But from a feminist-materialist standpoint, the solution to such problems lies not in returning to the Symbolic—neither by restoring paternal authority nor by messianic class struggle on a global scale—but in supplanting the false resolution-through-escape offered by Oedipality to the intolerable swings of pre-Oedipality with a genuine passage *through* the pre-Oedipal into a new sense of identity/otherness made possible by the co-equal presence of male and female partners *as mothers*.

A transformation from exclusively female mothering to shared mothering would be revolutionary, then, not only insofar as it would entail wide-ranging transformations in the forms (and, arguably, relations) of production, and in the relation of "public" to "private" life, but inasmuch as the child's subjectivity could for the first time be defined and constituted in a real dialectical interchange between Imaginary and Symbolic realms. This essentially political project could be put in more strictly Hegelian terms, as the transcendence of the antithetical terms of nonidentity/immersion and identity/detachment through a historically new sense of identity as a mutually reciprocal otherness[56]—a sense that would open the way for the development of the new social forces both released and reconstrained by the present hegemony of the de-Oedipal.[57]

I have taken this detour through recent feminist theory in order to lay the ground for an evaluation of the postmodernist structure of feeling, one far different, and far more deeply ambivalent, than either the celebratory fervor of its poststructuralist adherents or the dialectically tempered disapproval of the Marxist camp. The Jamesonian critique of postmodernist cultural practice is correct insofar as it allows us to see the roots of these practices in the de-Oedipalization of middle-class American society. Yet in its privileging of the Oedipal escape into the Symbolic—a privileging inscribed within Marxism's general ontological assumptions—Marxism is unable to discover the historical possibilities of the postmodernist structure of feeling or to specify preconditions for their development. A return to this postmodernist structure of feeling, and more specifically to the experience of those postmodernist works in music and performance art that have recently begun to attract a mass audience, inevitably suggest, from a feminist-materialist perspective, a more dialectical, even ambiguous judgment of that experience—a judgment giving full weight to both the possibilities such work offers us and the constraints it reproduces and distills.

I would like to conclude by trying to describe the experience of postmodernist work from a feminist-materialist standpoint, in something like its full ambiguity and irresolution. I have chosen exemplary moments from three postmodernist works in which there seems to surface, at least for an instant, something like a distinct political or historical reference point. The first moment is the explicit appearance of the figure or image "Einstein" in the Wilson/Glass opera *Einstein on the Beach*. Or perhaps "explicit foregrounding" is the better term, for in a sense the Einstein figure is never absent. In every scene and interlude (or "Knee Play"), performers "dressed 'like Einstein,' as Wilson sees him, in grey pants, suspenders and black tennis shoes," are present on stage.[58] Thus the figure of "Einstein" is decentered, replicated, dispersed across the decelerated, oneiric landscape of the work. Moreover, when an unmistakable representation of Einstein appears—a photograph of the young Einstein flashes on the backdrop, accompanied by the spoken announcement "Berne 1905"; a figure dressed as Einstein, wigged and mustachioed, plays the violin on the forefront of the stage—its presence is immediately folded back into the musical and/or dramatic ground of nonconsequential repetition and succession. In *Einstein on the Beach,* we experience this constant engulfment of the historical figure more or less wholeheartedly as a pleasure; the embedding and scattering of the Symbolic figure, so problematic and disturbing in the range of contradictory meanings its presence calls up (Einstein the socialist and devout pacifist; Einstein the "Father of the Atom Bomb," etc.), defuses the potential force and complication of those meanings by dissolving them in a preverbal Imaginary space. Wilson freely admits how much his dramaturgic practice owes to his observations of the mother-infant relationship;[59] and he describes the goal of his productions as a relationship of Imaginary, preverbal communication-through-identity between spectator and performer: "Ideally, someone in the audience might reach a point of consciouness where he is on the same frequency as one of the performers—where he receives communication directly."[60] Needless to say, this is an impossible ideal, insofar as any communication involves some perception of difference, some relation to that Symbolic realm Wilson wants to efface. Yet the pleasure we are invited to experience is precisely that of an unambiguous, pure, and omnipotent return to life in the Imaginary—to pre-Oedipality as a new, sublime Benign.

Such moments from *Einstein on the Beach,* and the blissful pre-Oedipal immersion they offer us, may be compared with a more troubled moment in the recent work of Wilson's collaborator, composer Philip Glass, in collaboration with filmmaker Godfrey Reggio in his 1982 *Koyaanisqatsi.* As reviewers noted, the film itself is both rather simpleminded and surprisingly incoherent.[61] A narrationless contrast between the steady majestic grace of unspoiled Nature and the brutal, senseless frenzy of contemporary Western industrial society is apparently intended to make us aware that our world is "out of balance" (*Koyaanisqatsi* being a Hopi word for such a world); yet this explicit intent is undercut by the berserk excitement we come to feel during the long montage sequence of speeded-up footage of crowds streaking down stairs, zipping in and out of corporate towers, and of traffic smearing into multicolored veins. The perverse beauty and excitement of this sequence, moreover, are extended and complicated by Glass's music, in which a slowly rising set of choral arpeggios, through ascension, repetition, and crescendo, gradually turn into a nearly intolerable screamfest. In this way—for the music never ceases to be overwhelmingly, repetitiously gorgeous—Glass's score contributes to the film's decoding of the very set of Symbolic categories introduced at its conclusion, when the audience is given a set of Hopi words and proverbs with which, presumably, we are intended to structure and encode the experience we have just been through. The problem is that this literal accession to the Symbolic is rather too much like the Oedipal moment for the American middle-class child, that is, both too weak and too late.

Fred Pfeil

Although the experience of *Koyaanisqatsi* thus proves to be in its own way as much an aesthetic (re)experience of the pre-Oedipal Imaginary as Wilson's *Einstein on the Beach,* here our pleasure in that Imaginary engulfment is more problematically riddled with a pre-Oedipal aggressiveness absent from most of Wilson's work. Such a troubled, delirious, oscillating pleasure is typified in our reaction to the musical sequence just described: so gorgeous, continuous, and overwhelming that we want it never to stop, yet so shatteringly intrusive and monotonous that it is simultaneously a menace to be resisted.

From the critical and political position I have taken here, I would like to say that this latter pleasure seems preferable to the former, not by any criterion of aesthetic "quality" or intensity of feeling, but in terms of the recognitions and affirmations these two different modalities of pleasure call upon us to make. Evidently, both Wilson's dramaturgy and (at least in the sequence discussed) Glass's music invite us to enjoy our fundamentally pre-Oedipal relationship to the world, the reclamation of social experience and historical representation by the Imaginary. Yet whereas in Wilson's work the pleasure induced by that reclamation is a regression to be wished for and enjoyed, in Glass's music it is also experienced as intolerable. Insofar as a modality of pleasure encourages a given attitude toward the structure of feeling it draws on, and so valorizes certain attitudes toward the world, Wilson's work is liable to the charge that it encourages a heedless acceptance and acquiescence on the part of the enjoying subject, while Glass's work more dialectically invites us to enjoy such a pre-Oedipal relationship yet wish for a resolution of its antinomies.

That may be all that the best postmodernist work can do for the mass audience now seeking it out: in this moment—characterized both by the release of new sociopolitical forces through the de-Oedipalization of middle-class American life *and* by the hegemony of this same de-Oedipalized social-sexual structure that tends to block the further development of those social forces—the most progressive postmodernist work can only foreground our inherent irresolution. Thus, postmodernism offers its mass audience the most scandalously ambivalent pleasure possible. Yet as I see and hear these works, there are rare moments that seem to edge slightly past this threshold to hint at the possibility of a genuine passage through the pre-Oedipal into another structure of feeling, another form of life.

Such a moment occurred for me at the end of a performance by Laurie Anderson when, in the characteristically neutral, even empty voice that constitutes a sort of pedal point in her vocal repertoire, she announced "Born—never asked," without inflection. On the screen behind her a series of still images appeared, slide projections of old colored rotogravures depicting various wild animals—leopards, snakes, and so on—in their tropical habitats; meanwhile, a low, percussive cadence of saxophone and taped sound gradually transformed itself into a slowly varying melody, simultaneously blues-y and vaguely "Eastern" in character, familiar from her having performed it on the violin earlier that night. "You were born," she said in the same toneless voice, "and so you're free. Happy Birthday."

The words and pictures offered us a pleasure not so different from that I have just described in connection with Glass's music—a pleasure fundamentally in recognition of our real ambivalence. The covert melancholia of the music, the sense of past time saturating the slides of the old pictures, seemed to hint either that we are inevitably not, after all, so fully, preverbally immersed and/or that perhaps the freedom of such an Imaginary existence was not so free anyway. The very flatness of Anderson's voice both affirmed and retracted its own liberatory announcement. Then the music stopped and the sequence of images concluded with one rotogravure depicting two white men in colonial uniforms astride two elephants, out hunting in what had suddenly become an Empire, a dominated zone. It was an astonishing instant, exhilirating yet perplexing; rather as if, with the entrance of the historical-political into the ambiguous postmodernist pleasure of the pre-Oedipal, I was being hailed by a new sense, a new kind of relationship to the Real, which neither I nor Laurie Anderson nor anyone else in the hall was as yet able to live or name.

My aim in this essay has been not only to articulate the social transformations that have made such a call liminally possible within the most engaged postmodernist work, but to explain this final, most vexing pleasure, and the structure of feeling it might rest on.

Notes

1   Marjorie Perloff, *Frank O'Hara, Poet among Painters* (New York: G. Braziller, 1977), or "Contemporary/Postmodern: The 'New' Poetry," in *Romanticism, Modernism, Postmodernism*, ed. Harry R. Garvin (Lewisburg: Bucknell University Press, 1980), pp. 171-79. In both these writings, Perloff offers interesting insights into the techniques and effects of the poetry she describes but fails to consider the question of what makes such poetry pleasurable to what groups of readers. In other words, her criticism remains enclosed within a formalism that stunts its own best insights.

2   Hilton Kramer's game defense of modernism and high culture in general may be followed in the *New York Times*. Most of Gerald Graff's "pacification" operations to date are collected in *Literature against Itself: Literary Ideas in Modern Society* (Chicago: University of Chicago Press, 1979).

3   For an example of the major arguments and positions involved in the Marxist debate, see Ernst Bloch et al., *Aesthetics and Politics* (London: New Left Books, 1977).

4   See Fredric Jameson, "Reflections in Conclusion," in *Aesthetics and Politics*, pp. 196-213, from which most of my examples of modernist "trickle-down" have been taken, and his equally remarkable "Reification and Utopia in Mass Culture," *Social Text*, 1 (Spring 1979), pp. 130-48.

5   See, for example, the contributions by Ihab Hassan and Wallace Martin in the final section of *Romanticism, Modernism, Postmodernism*, pp. 117-26, 146-54; Ihab Hassan, "Joyce, Beckett, and the Post-modern Imagination," in *Triquarterly*, 34 (Fall 1975), pp. 179-200; and/or David Antin, "Modernism and Postmodernism: Approaching the Present in American Poetry," *boundary 2*, 1, no.1 (Fall 1972), pp. 98-133.

6   Raymond Williams, *Marxism and Literature* (New York: Oxford University Press, 1977), pp. 133-34 (final emphasis mine).

7   In another essay I have explicitly criticized this very concept, and Williams's *Marxism and Literature* as a whole, for its incompatibility with the Marxist-materialist tradition it purports to follow and extend; see Fred Pfeil, "Towards a Portable Marxist Criticism: A Critique and Suggestion," *College English*, 41, no. 7 (Mar. 1980), pp. 753-68. I now wish to alter that criticism, but not retract it. Specifically, it seems to me that Williams's use of concepts like "structure of feeling" and criticisms of such standard Marxist terminology as the familiarly opposed "base" and "superstructure" slide into a proto-idealist abstraction and insubstantiality precisely because his allegiance to the primacy of production blinds him to another at least equally primary process and level of material practice: the acquisition and construction of self, language, and gender, a process that feminists argue is at least as fully constitutive of production in the Marxist sense as it is constituted or determined by the latter. Without the grounding of a feminist theory rooted in the psychosociological history of selfhood, engenderment, and the subject's accession into the universe of signification, Williams's critique of orthodox Marxism rests upon air; and his emphasis on the process of signification appears

as an idealist "invisible man," both swathed and blindfolded by the Marxist wrappings that hold its shape barely in place.

8   See the landmark essay by Barbara and John Ehrenreich, "The Professional-Managerial Class," in *Between Labor and Capital,* ed. Pat Walker (Boston: South End Press, 1979), pp. 5-45.

9   For a vivid social history and analysis of this transformation, see Barbara Ehrenreich and Deirdre English, *For Her Own Good: 150 Years of Experts' Advice to Women* (New York: Doubleday, 1979), pp. 211-324; and for an insightful account of the profound psychological shifts resulting from it, and of their political significance, see Nancy Chodorow, "Oedipal Assymetries and Heterosexual Knots," *Social Problems,* 23 (Apr. 1976), pp. 454-68.

10   On the relative stability of the ruling-class and working-class family structure, see Amy Swerdlow, Renata Bridenthal, Joan Kelly, and Phyllis Vine, *Household and Kin* (Old Westbury, N.Y.: Feminist Press, 1981), pt. 2, pp. 50-105. For a further examination of the life cycle of the contemporary American working-class family, see Lillian Rubin's moving *Worlds of Pain: Life in the Working-Class Family* (New York: Basic Books, 1976).

11   Lyrics from "Air," on Talking Heads, *Fear of Music* (Sire Records, SKR-6076, 1979).

12   Lyrics from "O Superman," on Laurie Anderson, *Big Science* (Warner Bros. Records BSK-3674, 1982).

13   Text by Christopher Knowles, quoted from a booklet accompanying Robert Wilson and Philip Glass, *Einstein on the Beach* (Tomato Records TOM-4-2901, 1979).

14   Craig Owens, "Amplifications: Laurie Anderson," *Art in America,* Mar. 1981, p. 122.

15   The quotation from Lévi-Strauss is the epigraph to Nadine Gordimer, *Burger's Daughter* (New York: Viking, 1979); I do not know its original source. The quotation from Laurie Anderson is in Craig Owens, "The Allegorical Impulse: Towards a Theory of Postmodernism," *October,* 12 (Spring 1980), p. 59.

16   From my notes on her sold-out performance in Portland, Oregon, sponsored by the Portland Center for the Visual Arts, April 24, 1982.

17   "Let X = X" is on Anderson's *Big Science;* "Air" and "Animals" (from which the quotation is taken) are from Talking Heads's *Fear of Music.*

18   Fredric Jameson, "Language and Modes of Production" (unpublished manuscript), pp. 28-29.

19   "O Superman," on Anderson's *Big Science.*

20   "Heaven," on Talking Heads's *Fear of Music.*

21   Back liner notes to Wilson and Glass's *Einstein on the Beach.*

22   In recent works by postmodernist composers Philip Glass and Steve Reich *Glassworks, Variations for Winds, Strings and Keyboard,* 1979, and *Vermont Counterpoint,* 1982—both to my knowledge presently unrecorded—I believe it is possible to hear distinct signs of such harmonies reminiscent of those of Gershwin—signs that may be symptomatic of a movement toward the tropes and satisfactions of mass culture.

23   I should note that, in his recent work, Craig Owens has been concerned to describe and endorse a view of postmodernist cultural production that is simultaneously far more political and more discriminating than the view ascribed to him here; see, for example, "The Discourse of Others," in *The Anti-Aesthetic: Essays on Postmodern Culture,* ed. Hal Foster (New York: Bay Press, 1983). Nonetheless, Owens's main concern remains the politics and intended political effects of specific, politically self-conscious postmodernist works; whereas my aim here, as I hope has now become clear, is to provide a *symptomatic* political reading both of certain internally *un*political, even retrograde postmodern works that have managed to reach a mass audience, and—even more decisively—of the mass audience that consumes them.

24   The phrase is Roland Barthes's, quoted by Rosalind Krauss, "Poststructuralism and the 'Paraliterary'," *October,* 13 (Summer 1980), p. 190.

25   Charles Russel, "The Context of the Concept," in *Romanticism, Modernism, Postmodernism,* p. 190.

26   The members of Talking Heads have New York art school backgrounds, for example, while Laurie Anderson at one time was herself a practicing art historian. In addition to such biographical details, I suspect close relationships inevitably exist as well between the artists and their academic-intellectual publicists.

27   The one exception to this silence that I know of is Rosalind Krauss's suggestion that students' interest in contemporary postmodernist literature—chiefly the work of Barthes and Derrida—follows from their absorption of the modernist tent of self-reflexiveness in both texts and readings; see her "Poststructuralism and the 'Paraliterary'," p. 40. But such an explanation scarcely touches the question of pleasure; rather, it opens up the ground for another round

of the stale argument over whether or not postmodernism is distinct from modernism, a debate I have already suggested we should not have to engage in anymore.

28   Fredric Jameson, "The Concept of the Sixties" (unpublished manuscript), p. 23.

29   Jameson, "Language and Modes of Production," p. 28.

30   Those whose degrees come from community colleges and/or elite schools are invited to investigate the social dynamics of their own educational experience as well. For any such investigation, the most detailed and useful text is, of course, Samuel Bowles and Herb Gintis, *Schooling in Capitalist America* (New York: Basic Books, 1976), especially pp. 201-23.

31   "The bureaucratization of the world" is the title of Henry Jacoby's historical analysis of the rise and spread of bureaucracy (Berkeley: University of California Press, 1973); the second quotation is from Anthony Giddens, *Sociology: A Brief but Critical Introduction* (London: Macmillan, 1982), p. 88.

32   Cf. Richard Edwards's use of this term, as differentiated from either "technical" or "direct" control, in *Contested Terrain: The Transformation of the Workplace in the Twentieth Century* (New York: Basic Books, 1979).

33   Jon Schiller, "The New 'Family Romance'," *Triquarterly*, 52 (Fall 1981), p. 70.

34   Judith Williamson, *Decoding Advertisements: Ideology and Meaning in Advertisements* (Salem: Marion Boyars, 1978), pp. 44-45.

35   See Jacques Lacan, "The Mirror Phase as Formative of the Function of the I," *New Left Review*, 51 (Sept.-Oct. 1968), pp. 71-77.

36   Williamson, p. 65.

37   Jean-Paul Sartre, *Search for a Method*, trans. Hazel Barnes (New York: Knopf, 1963), p. 63.

38   My account here is particularly reductive insofar as it conflates highly significant differences between female and male engenderation and psychic formation in both the pre-Oedipal and Oedipal stages. For a far more comprehensive analysis, see Nancy Chodorow, *The Reproduction of Mothering: Psychoanalysis and the Sociology of Gender* (Berkeley: University of California Press, 1978), especially pp. 57-140; and Isaac Balbus, *Marxism and Domination: A Neo-Hegelian, Feminist, Psychoanalytic Theory of Sexual, Political, and Technological Liberation* (Princeton: Princeton University Press, 1982), pp. 303-22.

39   Schiller, "The New 'Family Romance'," p. 83.

40   Ibid., p.71.

41   A good deal of the concrete historical data necessary for the construction of this argument with regard to American society in particular may be found in Carl Degler, *At Odds: Women and the Family in America from the Revolution to the Present* (New York: Oxford University Press, 1980).

42   Michel Foucault, *The History of Sexuality*, vol. 1, trans. Robert Hurley (New York: Pantheon, 1978), p. 93.

43   Karl Marx, *Capital*, vol. 1 (New York: International Publishers, 1967), p. 177 (my emphasis).

44   "O Superman," on Anderson's *Big Science*.

45   My reading here summarizes and extends that of Balbus in *Marxism and Domination*, pp. 269-78; and of Phyllis Zuckerman, "Nature as Surplus—the Work of the Text in Marx," *the minnesota review*, (n.s.) 20 (Spring 1983), pp. 103-11.

46   Michèle Barrett and Mary McIntosh, "Narcissim and the Family: A Critique of Lasch," *New Left Review*, 135 (Sept.-Oct. 1982), p. 48.

47   See Gayle Rubin, "The Traffic in Women," in *Toward an Anthropology of Women*, ed. Rayna Reiter (New York: Monthly Review Press, 1975), pp. 157-210—probably the first feminist work to lay the grounds for such an undertaking. Isaac Balbus attempts a very brief and inevitably reductive historical sketch of the Western sex/gender system as the determinant of what he calls the "mode of symbolization" in *Marxism and Domination*, pp. 303-52. Of course, much more work needs to be done.
          This is perhaps also the place for a brief word on the peculiar relevance and obstructiveness of Lacanian terminology and analysis in such an undertaking. I suspect, for example, that many Lacanians, perhaps especially Lacanian Marxists, would want to criticize my rough equation of the Lacanian "mirror-stage" with the pre-Oedipal stage as defined by feminist-materialists after Klein. Yet it is this very disengagement of the process of the formation of the self from the mother-child relationship by means of the frankly hypothetical scenario of the child before the mirror that arouses my suspicion. It may be that the importance of Lacanian thought for much recent Marxist theory—for example, in the work of both Jameson and Williamson, cited above—is not only a function of the real value of the concepts of

Fred Pfeil

the Imaginary, the Symbolic, and the Real, for Marxist and feminist work alike, but of the opportunity Lacanian analysis offers Marxism to speak of the constitution of the self in psychoanalytic terms without opening a Pandora's box of the sex/gender system—and thus of sexual politics generally. So, while the categories of the Imaginary and the Symbolic seem to me of fundamental importance for feminist analysis, they must not only be historicized by that analysis but detached as well from any unrevised concept from which the presence of the subject's first and most significant Other and the whole question of engenderation are elided.

48 Karl Marx, "The Communist Manifesto," in *Karl Marx: Selected Writings*, ed. David McLellan (New York: Oxford University Press, 1977), p. 222.

49 The messianic moment of class struggle proper is called up frequently and regularly in Jameson's work. See, for example, the closing pages of his essay "On Interpretation," *The Political Unconscious: Narrative as a Socially Symbolic Act* (Ithaca: Cornell University Press, 1981), pp. 17-102, and the prophecy with which "The Concept of the Sixties" closes: "even if Marxism is . . . not now true, it will become true again as the global development of this new stage of capitalism unfolds before us" (p. 35).

Lasch's more confused and regressive prescriptions may be found in *Haven in a Heartless World: The Family Besieged* (New York: Norton, 1974) and *The Culture of Narcissism: American Life in an Age of Diminishing Expectations* (New York: Norton, 1979). Unfortunately, the undialectical harshness of his judgment of de-Oedipalization infects work that is far more suggestive and interesting than his own. Jon Schiller's "The New 'Family Romance'," for example, is crippled by a reading of de-Oedipalization that owes too much to Lasch and too little to Dinnerstein and Chodorow; thus is he able to conclude that de-Oedipalization leads only to a "rebellious practice" whose "psychology . . . seems to preclude any active political significance" (p. 84).

50 For a fuller exposition of both this point and those that follow, see Dorothy Dinnerstein, *The Mermaid and the Minotaur: Sexual Arrangements and the Human Malaise* (New York: Harper and Row, 1976); and Balbus, *Marxism and Domination*, pp. 303-52.

51 For an insightful analysis of this de-Oedipalized hostility, see Balbus, pp. 384-98, especially p. 393.

52 Unfortunately, the converse seems to be true as well. Insofar as working-class men and women still live and labor within a world in which Oedipality remains supreme, working-class women may continue to find it hard to make common cause with feminism; and working-class men and women alike may find political organizations with one form or another of top-down control—from the Revolutionary Communist party to the local Democratic party machine—most "natural" to them.

53 Stephanie Engels, "Femininity as Tragedy: Re-examining the 'New Narcissism'," *Socialist Review* (Sept.-Oct. 1980), p. 97.

54 Balbus, p. 303.

55 Lasch, "The Concept of the Sixties," pp. 31-35.

56 See Balbus, pp. 279-302. Once again, moreover, it is interesting to compare the de-Oedipalized utopia sketched out by feminist-materialists like Balbus and Dinnerstein with Marx's equally tentative, deliberately sketchy observations on the Utopia at the origin and end of his youthful speculation on communist society in his notes on James Mill; for example, "our products would be like so many mirrors, out of which our essence shone" (*Karl Marx: Selected Writings*, p. 122), appears in light of Lacanian terminology and a feminist-materialist analysis as a flagrant example of the Oedipalized subject's hopeless longing for its pre-Symbolic "Ideal-Ego."

57 I should make clear that of the three major feminist-materialists whose work I have drawn upon here, it is Dinnerstein and Balbus who have argued the case for "co-mothering" along these holistic lines. By contrast, Chodorow calls for co-mothering as a necessary step in the achievement of sexual equality and freedom, that is, for the cause of women's liberation specifically.

58 Susan Flakes, "Robert Wilson's Einstein on the Beach," *The Drama Review*, 72 (Dec. 1976), p. 71.

59 See Calvin Tomkins, *The Scene: Reports on Post-Modern Art* (New York: Viking, 1976), p. 240.

60 Quoted in Tomkins, p. 263.

61 See, for example, Gregory Sandow's review in *The Village Voice*, Oct. 12, 1982, p. 58.

Eugene Holland

Schizoanalysis: The Postmodern Contextualization of Psychoanalysis

The radical cleavage between psychic and social determination no longer exists. Marxist cultural criticism must
dismantle the processes of recoding (bureaucratization,
the nuclear family, and consumerism) that perpetuate
the power of capitalist society and prevent the realization of permanent revolution.

The use of psychoanalysis for marxist cultural analysis
has long presented a serious difficulty: the problem of moving from the
dynamics of the nuclear family in the domestic sphere to questions of economics, politics, and class struggle in the public sphere. Of course, the separation of domestic from public life, as well as the classical form of the
nuclear family, are themselves historical phenomena. And, indeed, Freud
and freudian thought have been readily identified as products of late-nineteenth-century European society, a period in which family life was relatively
autonomous and thus of considerable importance in psychic development.
With the decline of the nuclear family's autonomy in our own, very different
late-twentieth-century society, however, the continuing relevance of orthodox psychoanalysis is far less readily apparent.

In his monumental study of Flaubert, Sartre takes as
his point of departure the autonomous existence and importance of young
Flaubert's family life and then asks how someone with that particular family
background and experience could have become one of the greatest writers
of the age. The crux of Sartre's argument hinges on his answer to the question
What was it about the young Flaubert's neurotogenic childhood that so
perfectly suited him to the objective neurosis of his age? Indeed, how could
Flaubert's art have been "at one and the same time a neurotic response to
a subjective malaise and to the objective malaise of literature?"[1] For the
nineteenth century, then, even a form of psychoanalysis carefully attuned
to the importance of the larger social context proceeds on two parallel tracks:
one psychobiographical, examining Flaubert's family life; the other sociohistorical, examining the culture and society of the Second Empire.

But what happens once the domestic sphere is rein-
tegrated into the fabric of social life? At this point, the status of the family
and the Oedipus complex in psychoanalytic explanation becomes problematic. Even while documenting the decline of the autonomous nuclear family and its permeation by advanced capitalist social relations, for example,
Christopher Lasch nonetheless retains an orthodox freudian emphasis on
the family as prime determinant of psychic life. Yet all the evidence he
presents points in the opposite direction: family life may have been a "haven
from a heartless world" and a predominant influence on the psyche in the
nineteenth century, but the advanced capitalist forms of schooling, government, health care, entertainment, business, and so forth have by now re-

duced the family's role to a minimum.[2] Under these conditions, the old freudian problem of the relatively self-contained nature of family life and childhood may prove less of an obstacle for marxist cultural analysis. There are, moreover, theoretical developments within psychoanalysis itself that may enable us to understand a gamut of important psychic phenomena not derived from oedipal conflict in the nuclear family.

As is so often the case in Freud's works, it is one of his own key discoveries that undermines what otherwise appears to be a basic axiom of freudian theory: the centrality of family life and the Oedipus complex in psychic development. Under the rubric *Nachtraglichkeit,* Freud argues that many psychic disturbances are not the result of a linear determinism based on a traumatic childhood event but rather a dialectical interaction between initially meaningless memory-traces and later experiences that reactivate those traces and endow them with meaning only *"nachtraglich, après coup,"* after the fact. But then these later experiences need not be restricted to the nuclear family: any number of kinds of interaction in any number of social settings may reinvoke childhood memory-traces and endow them with meanings that depend, for one thing, on the existence of a memory-trace but also on the nature of the later experience itself.[3]

Laying heavy emphasis himself on the concept of *Nachtraglichkeit,* Jacques Lacan has further shifted attention away from the nuclear family by rewriting the Oedipus complex as a linguistic rather than a primarily intrafamilial phenomenon. More important than the biological father, in this view, is the function of the "name-of-the-father" in the Symbolic order of language. For Lacan, the structuring of the individual psyche depends on the structure of language, in which the name-of-the-father occupies a central position. Here we have already moved beyond the nuclear family as the determining matrix of psychic life to the quintessentially social instance of language—even if the terms of Lacan's Symbolic order themselves reproduce the structure and dynamic of Freud's original Oedipus complex.

But what if the name-of-the-father functions differently in different societies? This is the question Gilles Deleuze and Felix Gauttari pose in *The Anti-Oedipus,* as they move beyond Lacan to firmly ground individual psychic life in a broadly social rather than strictly familial matrix of determinations.[4] Drawing on a vast range of anthropological and historical data, Deleuze and Guattari show that the name-of-the-father functions in classical oedipal fashion only in certain types of social formation and, moreover, that advanced capitalism is *not* such a social formation. Indeed, they argue that today the Oedipus complex is an anachronism, playing only a marginal—and repressive—role in the hands of the orthodox freudian psychoanalytic establishment.

In order to demonstrate how different the dynamics of the Symbolic order can be in different societies, Deleuze and Guattari present a typology of social forms, drawn from the works of Morgan and Engels but based on the interplay of two categories derived from Nietzsche and Marx: power and economics. The three social formations outlined in *The Anti-Oedipus*—savagery, despotism, and capitalism—are not to be understood as concrete historical stages of social evolution but rather as ideal types, as the logical permutations of basic social organization, shown in Figure 1 as the mapping of a semantic system or *combinatoire.*[5] Savagery, in this scheme, represents "primitive communism," a preclass society where power circu-

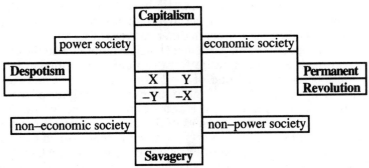

Figure 1.

lates throughout the community and does not accrue to a single group or individual. This is no rousseauistic Utopia, however, since savage society is the one most harshly governed by exacting codes of conduct, belief, and meaning—codes that Deleuze and Guattari consider inherently repressive. And since authentic, unconscious desire is radically indeterminate—or "schizophrenic," in their term, any fixed determination of it, such as that imposed by linguistic and social codes, hence inevitably distorts and misrepresents it.[6]

As much as the Symbolic codes of savage society may irrevocably fix and therefore distort desire, savage coding nonetheless operates in a comparatively egalitarian manner so as to avoid and even actively defuse accumulated power. Under despotism, by contrast, distorting representations are promulgated precisely in order to establish class divisions and hierarchy, as the distortions inherent in all forms of coding are bent to the service of explicit political power and direct social domination. Only here does the name-of-the-father—or, more aptly, the name-of-the-despot—govern the entire Symbolic order; only here are the name-of-the-father and patriarchal domination in the nuclear family homologous with the name-of-the-despot and political domination in society as a whole; only here are all social codes in the Symbolic order subordinated to the all-powerful imperial "overcoding" of the despot. As the privileged source of all "authorized" meaning and true possessor of all social wealth, the despot represents and occupies the fixed center of the Symbolic order in traditional power society.

Under capitalism, by contrast, there is no fixed center of this kind, no transcendental signified, no established authority figure; rather, exchange value and the market ruthlessly undermine and eliminate all traditional meanings and preexisting social codes:[7] the fabric of capitalist society is knit not by concrete, qualitative relations but by abstract, quantitative ones—by the "cash nexus."[8] The basis of capitalist society is not territory, as in savagery, nor the priest, king, or god, as under despotism, but the abstract calculus of capital itself. Capital, as an abstract, quantitative calculus, provides no universal codes capable of organizing and comprehending the whole of social life. In opposition to savage "coding" and despotic "overcoding," then, the semiotic process governing the Symbolic order under capitalism is "decoding," market society's aggressive elimination of all preexisting meanings and codes.[9]

407

According to Deleuze and Guattari, more important than the Oedipus complex in determining the nature of psychic life, given the differing nature of the Symbolic order in different types of society, is the specific *form of semiosis* operative in a particular social formation. And the decoding process, inasmuch as it frees desire from capture and distortion by social coding, must be considered one of the *positive* features of the capitalist Symbolic order: one corollary of the immense productivity of capitalism admired by Marx is the freedom it grants desire to escape fixture in established codes. But the liberating effects of decoding that stem from the economic component of capitalist society are always accompanied by opposing processes of recoding stemming from its power component, which tie freed libidinal energy back onto factitious codes so as to extract and realize privately appropriable surplus value. This opposition between decoding and recoding derives not so much from the classical, nineteenth-century contradiction between outright owners of capital and the dispossessed as from the contradiction between the generally socialized production of surplus value, on the one hand, and its private management, on the other. Capitalism devotes itself to production as an end in itself, to developing the productivity of socialized labor to the utmost; yet due to private investment in the means of production, social labor and life also are restricted to production and consumption which valorize only the already existing capital-stock.

In the third volume of *Capital,* Marx outlines these two moments of capital's ongoing self-expansion.[10] In a first moment, a new, more productive capital-stock transforms the preexisting apparatuses of production and consumption, and this "continual revolution of the means of production" characteristic of capitalism spawns decoding throughout society. But in a second moment, this progressive movement is abruptly stopped and everything is recoded: the evolving apparatuses of production and consumption alike are tied down to now-obsolete capital-stock solely to valorize it and realize profit on previous investment. The decoding process liberates all kinds of creative energies (in consumption as well as in production) at the same time that it revolutionizes and socializes productive forces; but then recoding yokes and stultifies the relations of production and consumption in the service of private surplus appropriation.

In this light, one of the aims of revolution is to eliminate the power component from capitalism so as to enable the decoding process inherent in economic society to free libidinal energy as much as possible from the constraints of social coding. Thus, having disappeared as the basis of despotic society as a whole, the semiotic form of power society nevertheless reappears under capitalism in a host of miniature despotisms, each imposing a factitious code on a domain of human activity whose libidinal energies relentlessly seek to escape it. A marxist cultural criticism wants to target and dismantle the processes of recoding that serve to perpetuate the power component of capitalist society and thus prevent the realization of permanent revolution. This is, in fact, one of the aims of what Deleuze and Guattari call "schizoanalysis," their postmodern transmutation of psychoanalysis. For convenience' sake, we may locate these recoding processes schematically in three domains—the sphere of production, the nuclear family, and the sphere of consumption—according to whether the temporary and local meanings they introduce serve to enable people to perform jobs and administrative functions, induce them to consume certain commodities to realize profit on invested capital, or finally prepare them to accept psychological manipulation in a wide range of oedipal forms.

In the sphere of production, the most pervasive and widely recognized form of recoding is bureaucratization. In bureaucracy, a given domain of human activity is isolated from the warp and woof of social life, stripped of its traditional meanings and practices, and then subjected to the abstract rationality of formal administration. Free human activity is deprived of its spontaneous self-determination and subordinated to the process Max Weber calls "rationalization." But this rationalization takes place in a host of parallel and semiautonomous domains of application linked only by the market; hence, Lukács's concept of reification is more appropriate and revealing. Full-scale capitalist development witnesses the taylorization and technologization of production, the professionalization of knowledge and expertise, the bureaucratization of public administration. Reification in all these domains means that

> artificially isolated partial functions [are] performed in the most rational manner by "specialists," [which] has the effect of making these partial functions autonomous [so that] they develop through their own momentum and in accordance with their own special laws independently of other partial functions of society. . . . All issues are subjected to an increasingly formal and standardized treatment . . . in which there is an ever-increasing remoteness from the qualitative and material essence of the "things" to which [such] bureaucratic activity pertains.[11]

One counterpart to the administrative mode of capitalist recoding exemplified in bureaucracy is the aesthetic of modernism. Although its domain of application is very different, the same form of semiosis applies: cut off from direct communication with its public, the modernist artwork is no longer conceived of as expressing social life itself but rather as presenting the artist's own privileged point of view or mode of perception; reference to the work of art itself replaces reference to social life as the organizing master code of the work. This form of reified recoding appears with particular clarity in architecture of the so-called International Style, especially in the monumental buildings of Mies van der Rohe and the urban plans of Le Corbusier. The office building, referent of high modernist design—the social relations that the signifying systems of architecture and urban planning ultimately refer to—has been banished; and the dense and complex interlocking network of city life has been completely ironed out by Le Corbusier into vacuous parkland punctuated by high-rise towers linked by freeways. *The aesthetic domain is emptied of its conventional, social content and reorganized according to a new and more abstract master code.* All that remains once social reference has been eliminated in these ways is the special meaning these designs are intended to convey, their signified. And what the high modernist monument or cityscape in fact signifies is rationalization itself, the notion of a purely formal or abstract rationality that will solve the problems of the city through systematic simplification and the problems of architectural aesthetics through absolute purification. Thus the decoded, abstract rationality of "form follows function" (the elimination of ornament, the subordination of design to technology, etc.) is reendowed with a positive meaning—recoded "on the spot" or "in place" *(sur place)*, as Deleuze and Guattari would say—with the slogan "less is more."[12]

Because, under capitalism, it is segregated from social production, where decoding operates at full throttle, the nuclear family is a prime locus of recoding.[13] Isolated from society at large, and thus restricted to the family triangle for its objects of desire, the individual psyche takes the full impress of the Oedipus complex; hence the *relative* adequacy of freudian psychoanalysis in describing oedipal desire in the nuclear family under classical or market capitalism, that is, insofar as the nuclear family itself retains a relative autonomy from "external" social forces. But the nuclear family does not long retain even that relative autonomy, as Christopher Lasch has shown, once capitalism moves from the market to the monopoly stage around the turn of the century.

Whereas Lasch considers a renewed Oedipus to be our last hope for psychic health and social stability in the face of rampant pathological narcissism, Deleuze and Guattari see the nuclear family's oedipal inscription of the psyche as a last-ditch effort to repress desire in its authentic, schizophrenic form. Sequestered from the decoding process at work in capitalist society at large, the nuclear family reinscribes the oppressive but now socially obsolete role of the despot in the repressive figure of the father, which the individual then internalizes as the name-of-the-father function of Lacan's Symbolic order. Furthermore, as the nuclear family breaks down and increasingly fails to perform the oedipal reinscription of desire, according to schizoanalysis, it is precisely psychoanalysis that steps in to finish the job. If need be, the psychoanalyst shoulders the mantle of the despot (in the famous "transference") to ensure that no desire at all escapes oedipal triangulation. From the point of view of schizoanalysis, then, the Oedipus is an archaic and reactionary despotism installed at the heart of the nuclear family under capitalism to recontain the free flow of desire unleashed by capitalist decoding in society at large. And the institution of psychoanalysis is the repressive agency of last resort whenever the deteriorating nuclear family fails to ensure complete oedipalization all by itself.

Comparing schizoanalysis with Lasch's perspective is illuminating because both address some of the same material—the disappearance of the autonomous bourgeois ego—but from opposing points of view: the liberation Deleuze and Guattari celebrate under the rubric of schizophrenia, Lasch castigates as a feature of pathological narcissism; Lasch explains the development of what he calls the "culture of narcissism" in terms of the decline of the family, whereas Deleuze and Guattari insist on placing the family in its sociohistorical context and considering culture and society as a whole. Based on the ego psychology of Otto Kernberg and Heinz Kohut, and taking the family as its pivotal determining instance, Lasch's "historical" explanation runs something like this: The autonomous bourgeois family is dissolved by the pervasive administration of monopoly capitalism, with two principal results. First, paternal authority declines, stunting the development of the child's superego; and second, maternal instinct falters, as the mother's ambivalent feelings split the child's self-image into good and bad versions that cannot be synthesized, while the child's inconsistent behavior traumatizes frustration, on the one hand, by inculcating exaggerated expectations that are, on the other hand, systematically denied. The result is a narcissistic personality that will eventually contribute to a narcissistic culture.

The problem with this explanation is not so much that it is wrong—Lasch's work contains valuable insights despite its flaws—but that it retains the centrality of the nuclear family in an orthodox-psychoanalytic interpretation of a culture in which, as Lasch himself documents, the nuclear family plays a less and less decisive role in the formation of the individual psyche. Rather than interpret culture in terms of the vicissistudes of family life, schizoanalysis proposes to understand capitalist culture in terms of capital's basic social processes—decoding and recoding—yet without denying the family unit and the Oedipus complex their particular function within capitalist society.

Schizoanalysis would thus explain the decline of superego functions, and indeed the increase of ego instability itself, not in terms of the demise of the family, as Lasch would have it, but in terms of the decoding of social authority and of experience in general, which takes place (in France, at any rate) during the latter half of the nineteenth century. Schizoanalysis is poststructuralist as well as postmodernist, in that it retains the structuralist axiom that subjectivity is an *effect* of social codes; hence, when they break down, so does the "autonomous" bourgeois subject. The transition from feudal and mercantile despotism to capitalism had already been secured during the period of bourgeois ascendancy through the replacement of authority figures (God, the Sun King, etc.) by the authority of reason. However universal a structure the superego may be, its functions are considerably increased in this first moment of bourgeois cultural revolution, with the internalized conscience of the Protestant spirit and the internalized rationality of the Enlightenment. But as market relations spread throughout society, even this enlightenment reason succumbs to decoding: market society, Marx says, "strips of its halo every profession hitherto regarded with reverence and awe."[14]

In his *Eighteenth Brumaire of Louis-Napoleon,* Marx not only strips bourgeois political philosophy of its halo—by parodying Hegel—but also ruthlessly deflates the social authority of the Second Empire itself, showing why, under democratic conditions, the bourgeoisie had to forfeit its direct political rule and cultural expression in order to maintain its economic rule behind the scenes. And with characteristic accuracy, Marx recognizes that *both* the humiliated bourgeoisie and the defeated proletariat would retreat from the pursuit of their "rational interests" in the public sphere of class struggle into the private sphere of domestic consumption just coming into its own under the Second Empire and which has expanded ever since.

Consumerism is, indeed, the principal vehicle for recoding. Our own experience of the rhythms of fad and fashion in consumer society; the general effects of advertising, mass marketing, public relations, and political propaganda analyzed by Jean Baudrillard, Guy Debord, J. P. Faye, and others; and also accounts of the "successive private religions" of the mod-

411

ernist avant-gardes since the late 1880s offered by Renato Poggioli, Walter Benjamin, and others—all provide ample evidence of the ways in which recoding introduces various local and temporary meanings into the otherwise barren landscape of life under capitalism.[15]

Acknowledging the emergence of consumerism in the latter half of the nineteenth century puts Lasch's decline-of-the-family thesis in a different, somwhat broader perspective: the issue is not just the collapse of paternal authority or maternal instinct but the function of the family in society as a whole. The nuclear family of the late nineteenth century is not some isolated refuge from capitalist competition—indeed, it is no "haven in a heartless world"—but is, rather, the very locus of consumption. Photographs from this period present a telling image, for example, of the bourgeois domestic interior—stuffed full of every last gewgaw and knickknack imaginable.[16] Indeed, if modernist recoding is private religion, then the home is its altar; and its idol, as Walter Benjamin put it,[17] is the fetish called "Commodity." In the garish light of consumerism—which has become blinding and now floods into the public sphere as well (in the form of "recreational shopping," for example), so that the individual body itself has become a temple of narcissistic recoding—narcissistic rage cannot be imagined to be directed against mothers who traumatize frustration by acting inconsistently, but must be understood in relation to an entire society that constantly offers instant and unlimited gratification yet ultimately refuses to "deliver the goods." Consumer society promises everyone satisfaction but can allow no one enough satisfaction . . . to stop consuming.

In the same vein, narcissists' inability to synthesize good and bad is not primarily a result of ambivalent mothering but stems, rather, from the pervasive disjunction under capitalism between the dreary, exploited sphere of work and the glittering rewards of administered leisure and conspicuous consumption. Narcissists may insist that "living well is the best revenge," but no amount of cynical hedonism can bridge the gap between production and consumption—a gap that the expansion of capital steadily reproduces on a larger and larger scale. Thus, narcissistic personality splitting, cynical-defensive disdain for others and for community, and desperate self-absorption are not just the result of absent fathering and bad mothering but a product of the libidinal structure of capitalism itself: narcissism manifests what we might call the "capital-logic" of contemporary culture.

Schizoanalysis provides a means not of simply deriving culture from the logic of capital but of answering Althusser's question regarding how we explain the historical effectivity of a given semiautonomous development.[18] The issue is not whether narcissistic parents are likely to raise narcissistic children (which is all ego psychology by itself can tell us)—of course they are. Nor is the point to deny the family any role whatsoever in perpetrating the culture of narcissism, for Althusser's concept of overdetermination enables us to consider a variety of relations (interdependence or independence, mutual reinforcement or cancellation, etc.) that may obtain between various instances in society. The point here is that nowadays the infantile narcissism fostered by the nuclear family is not *resolved* in adult life but *reinforced and exacerbated* by a social formation in which narcissism resonates wherever the logic of commodities and recoding has penetrated: in bureaucracy, in the professions, in modernist art and architecture—indeed, as Lasch suggests, nearly everywhere.

Now the main thrust of postmodernism—in art as well as theory—and what distinguishes it decisively from modernism, is its refusal of re-coding. In the history of architecture—where its advent is particularly clear-cut and well understood[19]—postmodernism defines itself against modernism by ironically playing with existing architectural codes instead of elaborating new ones of its own, and particularly by playing various codes off against one another. In a public low-income housing project in New Haven, Connecticut, for example, the prominent postmodern architect/urban planner Charles Moore has designed an apartment tower for the elderly in explicit relation to a Knights of Columbus office tower located just across the freeway. The insurance headquarters occupy six or eight glass-walled floors supported on I-beams suspended between massive cylindrical pillars that form the four corners of the building. In the old-age apartment tower, by contrast, the right angles where the four main bare concrete walls would have met have been neatly shaved away, creating a more or less square tower that appears to have no corners at all. Rather than existing independently as a self-contained monument with its own architectural code, Moore's building makes ironic reference to local buildings and architectural codes, thereby highlighting the disparities between the massive stability and presence of the insurance industry and the meager insufficiency and dependency of public housing.

In addition to embedding itself in its specific context in this way, postmodern architecture often borrows from the architectural tradition, unabashedly mixing styles from widely dispersed historical periods or geographic regions. As opposed to modern architecture, and by ironically referring to other buildings and other styles while insisting on relating design to the particular cultural context and physical location, postmodern architecture proclaims not an abstract necessity but its own contingency; not self-contained autonomy but self-confessed relativity; not pure transcendence but particular, historical contextuality. It thereby refuses recoding.[20]

As a postmodern critique and renewal of psychoanalysis, schizoanalysis also refuses recoding, denying privileged status in *The Anti-Oedipus,* for example, to either the marxian or the freudian interpretive code. Instead, it plays the one off against the other, so as to avoid erecting its own master code. Just as the introduction of history into freudian theory relativized the Oedipus complex and politicized psychological analysis, so too is the introduction of the unconscious into economics and politics bound to have far-reaching consequences for marxist political and cultural analysis. Less important for schizoanalysis than so-called rational interests and imputed "class consciousness" are the unconscious dynamics or "forms of semiosis" underlying all kinds of human activity—from the production of value in a factory, for example, to the production of consensus and action in a political group, to the production of meaning in a work of art.

As a form of cultural criticism, schizoanalysis opposes interpretation, for interpretation merely reinforces semiotic despotism by translating one authorized code—that of the author or "creator"—into another authorized code—that of the critic. Rather than reinforce authority by multiplying equivalent codes in this way, postmodernist schizoanalysis produces interference between codes and so acts to undermine their authority. Deconstruction is an important precursor to schizoanalysis, in that Derrida has rendered most forms of interpretation inoperative by demonstrating the inherent instability of the master codes on which interpretation has been based. Yet even though he manages to decode logocentrism, Derrida does so, as he says, strictly from *within* its own parameters. As a discourse of philosophy, deconstruction remains, like modernism, a basically self-referential discourse; so even while heralding the "end of western metaphysics," Derrida remains only on the threshold of postmodernism.

Postmodernist criticism is explicity contextual, and by treating philosophical discourses from Plato to Searle out of context, as so many versions of the same logocentric master code, Derrida inevitably overlooks contextual differences. So, at the limit, deconstructive decoding results merely in dazzling displays of lexical pyrotechnics. Normally, semiotic codes function through the interplay of paradigmatic and syntagmatic relations; but a ("decoded") unstable code cannot impose the constraints on paradigmatic substitution necessary to produce determinate meaning. One result is the so-called textual indeterminacy that has become the trump card of much neo-derridean criticism in the United States—for example, J. Hillis Miller discussing his difficulties interpreting Wallace Stevens's poem "The Rock": "The multiple meanings of the word 'cure,' like the meanings of all key words in 'The Rock,' are incompatible, irreconcilable. They may not be followed, etymologically, to a single root which will unify or explain them, explicate them in a single source. . . . However hard [we try] to fix the word in a single sense it remains indeterminable, uncannily resisting [any] attempts to end its movement."[21] The so-called abyss of the paradigmatic axis of discourse henceforth appears as an unavoidable obstacle to interpretive procedures that would curtail the free play of semiosis and limit paradigmatic substitution according to some law of equivalence (such as cigar "means" penis, money "equals" feces, or whatever).

But discourse always entails syntagmatic relations as well. And whereas the paradigmatic relations of substitution in discourse are *virtual* (hence, "open to interpretation"), the syntagmatic relations of combination in a given discourse are *actual:* a discourse consists precisely of a particular combination of signs that has been *realized.* The hallmark of Foucault's discourse analysis is that it eschews interpretation and concentrates instead on this facticity of actualized discourse. Rather than relate a particular discourse to the entirety of Western metaphysics, Foucault analyzes the specific rules of combination it displays and relates it, along with other discourses displaying these rules, to the specific institutional contexts that form their conditions of existence. Discourse is thus analyzed in its singularity and contingency, instead of being recoded in terms of a personal experience it would express, a period-style it would reflect, or a historical tradition it would transmit and perpetuate. Foucault's sole points of reference are the rules by which a discourse is constituted and the contexts within which it coexists. In refusing the historical master plots of Hegel, Marx, and others, Foucault emphasizes the unexpected, thereby evoking a history that is, by its very constitution, subject to change.

If Foucault's discourse analysis examines the codes operative in specific discursive formations and the effects of power they achieve in particular historical contexts, Deleuze and Guattari's schizoanalysis examines the other side of the coin: the forces at work in discourse and society that challenge the imposed closure of codes and strive to free desire from capture in codified representation. Assuming the effective integration of the classical proletariat into capitalist hegemony—and it is important to be clear on the assumption Deleuze and Guattari are making in a book written in the wake of May 1968 when even the French Communist party sided with the forces of order against the general strike: that there is perhaps not total but, practically speaking, effective integration of the proletariat into the development plan of late capitalism—Deleuze and Guattari assert that the fundamental contradiction in the fully developed capitalist mode of production operates not between discrete social classes but between the socialization of production, on the one hand, and the private appropriation of surplus, on the other. Hence their promotion of schizophrenic decoding as the very movement of permanent revolution, as opposed to the constriction and limitation of social revolution by capitalist recoding.

As a result, schizoanalytic criticism is primarily a *pragmatic* analysis of texts, one that assesses the impact on readers' desire, regardless of content or meaning. A work of art, just as much as a political formation or an economic process, has a form of semiosis that tends either to limit desire to the exigencies of a code or to free desire to pursue its own schizophrenic trajectories.[22] The aims of schizoanalysis are thus to expose strategies of recontainment and closure wherever they operate to recode desire; and, more important, to locate and intensify the "lines of flight" by which, in art as well as politics, desire may avoid and undermine the pervasive recoding of power relations under advanced capitalism.

Notes

1   Jean-Paul Sartre, *L'idiot de la famille* (Paris: Gallimard, 1971-72), vol. 3, pp. 40-41; also cited by Hazel Barnes, *Sartre and Flaubert* (Chicago: University of Chicago Press, 1981), who agrees that "Sartre wants to show that Flaubert became the writer he was in response to two lines of conditioning. . . . One line represents the influence of the family, the other that of society and cultural tradition" (p. 11).

2   See, in particular, Christopher Lasch, *The Culture of Narcissism: American Life in an Age of Diminishing Expectations* (New York: Norton, 1979); see also his earlier study, *Haven in a Heartless World: The Family Beseiged* (New York: Basic Books, 1977).

3   Freud introduces this important concept in "Project for a Scientific Psychology," *Standard Edition*, vol. 1, esp. pp. 356-58; it also figures prominently in his discussion of the "Wolf Man" case, in *Standard Edition*, vol. 17, esp. pp. 37-38.

4   The English version, *Anti-Oedipus: Capitalism and Schizophrenia*, trans. R. Hurley, M. Seem, and H. Lane (New York: Viking, 1977), appeared five years after the French, *L'anti-Oedipe: Capitalisme et schizophrenie* (Paris: Seuil, 1972).

5   For clarity's sake, I present the three social formations Deleuze and Guattari outline in Chapter 3 of *Anti-Oedipus* ("Sauvages, barbares, civilises"), along with the fourth, projected stage (permanent revolution), in a semantic rectangle derived from A. J. Greimas, *Du sens* (Paris: Seuil, 1970).

6   It is crucial to understand that Deleuze and Guattari distinguish absolutely between the *process* of schizophrenia and the clinical entity "the schizophrenic." The latter is a product of psychiatry's forced recoding of the free-flowing libidinal energy characteristic of the process of schizophrenia. Deleuze and Guattari do not condone the institutional production and confinement of "schizophrenics," nor do they idealize their condition.

7   Thus, in a project closely aligned with Deleuze and Guattari's perspective (*Discipline and Punish*, trans. A. Sheridan [1975; New York: Pantheon, 1977]), Foucault distinguishes the centralized form of power characteristic of despotism from the disseminated, quantifying power appropriate to capitalist decoding. The latter is a form of power Foucault himself says is integral to the development of industrial capitalism (in *Power/Knowledge*, ed. Colin Gordon [New York: Pantheon, 1980], p. 105.)

8   That is (using terms Deleuze and Guattari do not), capitalist society is constituted by digital rather than analogous relations: the capitalist "axiomatic" (to revert to their terminology)

joins decoded (digital) flows—of wealth, labor power, knowledge, consumer tastes, and so on—for the sake of extracting a differential surplus from them; whatever local (analogue) codes may temporarily spring up in the process are strictly incidental to capital's basic "axiomatic" process of self-expansion.

9 Some sense of the content of "decoding" may be suggested by recalling how science replaces sense experience with a mathematical calculus, as in lockean psychology where color (henceforth a mere "secondary" quality) is decoded by the calculus of wavelengths ("primary" quality).

10 See Karl Marx, *Capital*, trans. Ernest Untermann, (New York: International Publishers, 1967), vol. 3, pp. 249-50.

11 See Georg Lukács, "Reification and the Consciousness of the Proletariat," *History and Class Consciousness*, trans. Rodney Livingstone, (Cambridge: MIT Press, 1971), especially sec. 1, "The Phenomenon of Reification." I quote from pp. 103, 99.

12 The postmodern critique of modernist city planning and urban "renewal" was initiated in 1961 by Jane Jacob's important book, *The Death and Life of Great American Cities* (New York: Random House/Vintage Press).

13 More properly speaking, the nuclear family for schizoanalysis is the prime locus of "reterritorialization" rather than recoding. Territorialization is the process of fixing desire on an object, whereas coding (and overcoding and recoding) fix desire to representation. Thus, the nuclear family reterritorializes schizophrenic desire by restricting it to certain objects (Mommy and Daddy), while it is actually psychoanalysis that recodes—by providing desire with the socially sanctioned representation of the "Oedipus complex."

14 See Karl Marx, *The Communist Manifesto*, in *Marx and Engels: Basic Writings on Politics and Philosophy*, ed. Lewis Feuer (Garden City: Doubleday, 1959), pp. 6-41, where Marx describes the basis of decoding in this way: "The bourgeoisie has stripped of its halo every occupation hitherto honored and looked up to with reverent awe. It has converted the physician, the lawyer, the priest, the man of science into its paid wage laborers. . . . The bourgeoisie cannot live without constantly revolutionizing the instruments of production, and thereby the relations of production, and with them the whole relations of society. . . . Constant revolutionizing of production, uninterrupted disturbance of all social conditions, everlasting uncertainty and agitation distinguish the bourgeois epoch from all earlier ones. All fixed, fast-frozen relations, with their train of ancient and venerable prejudices and opinions, are swept away, all new-formed ones become antiquated before they can ossify. All that is solid melts into air . . ." (p. 10).

15 See Jean Baudrillard, *Pour une critique de l'economie politique du signe* (Paris: Gallimard, 1972), and *Simulacres et simulation* (Paris: Galilee, 1981); Guy Debord, *La societe du spectacle* (Paris: Buchet-Chastel, 1967); J. P. Faye, *Langages totalitaires* (Paris: Hermann, 1972); Renato Poggioli, *The Theory of the Avant-Garde*, trans. Gerald Fitzgerald, (New York: Harper and Row, 1968); Walter Benjamin, *Charles Baudelaire: Epic Poet in the Era of High Capitalism*, trans. Harry Zohn, (London: NLB, 1973). The term "private religion" has been used by Fredric Jameson to refer to the modernist aesthetic in literature.

16 See, for example, chapter 13 of E. J. Hobsbawn, *The Age of Capital, 1848-1870* (New York: Scribner's Sons, 1975), and the discussion in Rosalyn Williams, *Dream Worlds: Mass Consumption in Late-19th-Century France* (Berkeley: University of California Press, 1982).

17 See Benjamin, *Charles Baudelaire*, especially "Paris, Capital of the 19th Century," sec. 1, 3,4.

18 This is a question posed by Althusser's rewriting the historical problematic in terms of "structural causality" and "overdetermination." See *For Marx*, trans. Ben Brewster (1965; New York: Random House, 1969), specifically: "Contradiction and Overdetermination," pp. 87-128, esp. pp. 119-26; and "On the Materialist Dialectic," pp. 161-218, esp. pp. 200-10.

19 Thanks in large part to the works of Charles Jencks: *The Language of Postmodern Architecture* (New York: Rizzoli, 1977) and *Late-Modern Architecture and Other Essays* (New York: Rizzoli, 1980).

20 For an insightful analysis of postmodern art, see Craig Owens, "The Allegorical Impulse: Toward a Theory of Postmodernism," *October* 12 (1980), pp. 67-86, and 13 (1980), pp. 59-80, esp. pp. 79-80.

21 See J. Hillis Miller in *Georgia Review* (Spring 1976), p. 10.

22 In the *Anti-Oedipus*, the schizoanalysts denied having any political program; but Deleuze and Guattari later actively supported Italian Marxist Toni Negri, to date the most important theoritician of micropolitics. As Michael Ryan puts it in his very suggestive book *Marxism and Deconstruction: A Critical Articulation* (Baltimore: Johns Hopkins University Press, 1982), "we have reached a point in history where the wealth of struggles has outrun the abstractly mediating ["recoding"] form of authority" (p. 217).

Julia Lesage

Women's Rage

Is consciousness-raising sufficient to change women's behavior, including our self-conception and our own colonized minds? We need to promote self-conscious, collectively supported, and politically clear articulations of our anger and rage.

Feminism by itself is not the motor of change. Class, anti-imperialist, and antiracist struggles demand our participation. Yet how, specifically, does women's consciousness change? How do women move into action? How does change occur? What political strategies should feminists pursue? How, in our political work, can we constantly challenge sexual inequality when the very social construction of gender oppresses women?

In 1981 I visited Nicaragua with the goal of finding out how and why change occurred there so quickly in women's lives. "The revolution has given us everything," I was told. "Before the revolution we were totally devalued. We weren't supposed to have a vision beyond home and children." In fact, many Nicaraguan women first achieved a fully human identity within the revolution. Now they are its most enthusiastic supporters. For example, they form over 50 percent of the popular militias, the mainstay of Nicaragua's defense against United States-sponsored invasions from Honduras and Costa Rica. In the block committees, they have virtually eliminated wife and child abuse. Yet in Nicaragua we still see maids, the double standard sexually, dissatisfaction in marriage, and inadequate childcare. Furthermore, all the women I talked to defined their participation in the revolution in terms of an extremely idealized notion of motherhood and could not understand the choice not to reproduce.

I bring up this example of Nicaragua because Nicaraguan women are very conscious of the power of their own revolutionary example. They know they have been influenced by the Vietnamese and Cuban revolutions and are very much shaping how Salvadoran women militants are looking at women's role in the Salvadoran revolution. Because of the urgency and violence of the situation, unity between men and women was and is necessary for their survival, but the women also want to combat, in an organized and self-conscious way, specific aspects of male supremacy in the workplace, politics, and daily life.

Both here and in Nicaragua, women's daily conversation is about the politics of daily life. They talk to each other often, complaining about men and about managing the domestic sphere. Women's talk also encompasses complaints about poor and unstable work conditions, and about the onerous double day. However, here in the United States that conversation usually circulates pessimistically, if supportively, around the same themes and may even serve to reconfirm women's stasis within these

419

unpleasant situations. Here such conversation offers little sense of social change; yet in our recent political history, feminists have used this preexisting social form—women's conversation in the domestic sphere—to create consciousness-raising groups. But to what degree is consciousness raising sufficient to change women's behavior, including our self-conception and our own colonized minds?

We do not live in a revolutionary situation in the United States. There is no leftist political organization here providing leadership and a cohesive strategy, and in particular the struggle against women's oppression is not genuinely integrated into leftist activity and theory. Within such a context, women need to work on another, intermediate level, both to shape our revolutionary consciousness and to empower us to act on our own strategic demands. That is, we need to promote self-conscious, collectively supported, and politically clear articulations of our anger and rage.

Furthermore, we must understand the different structures behind different women's rage. Black women rage against poverty and racism at the same time that they rage against sexism. Lesbians rage against heterosexual privilege, including their denial of civil rights. Nicaraguan women rage against invasions and the aggressive intentions of the United States. If, in our political work, we know this anger and the structures that generate it, we can more genuinely encounter each other and more extensively acknowledge each other's needs, class position, and specific form of oppression. If we do not understand the unique social conditions shaping our sisters' rage, we run the risk of divisiveness, of fragmenting our potential solidarity. Such mutual understanding of the different structures behind different women's anger is the precondition of our finding a way to work together toward common goals.

I think a lot about the phenomenon of the colonized mind. Everything that I am and want has been shaped within a social process marked by male dominance and female submission. How can women come to understand and collectively attack this sexist social order? We all face, and in various ways incorporate into ourselves, sexist representations, sexist modes of thought. Institutionally, such representations are propagated throughout culture, law, medicine, education, and so on. All families come up against and are socially measured by sexist concepts of what is "natural"—that is, the "natural" roles of mother, children, or the family as a whole.

Of particular concern to me is the fact that I have lived with a man for fifteen years while I acutely understand the degree to which heterosexuality itself is socially constructed as sexist. That is, I love someone who has more social privilege than me, and he has that privilege because he is male. As an institution, heterosexuality projects relations of dominance and submission, and it leads to the consequent devaluation of women because of their sex. The institution of heterosexuality is the central shaping factor of many different social practices at many different levels—which range, for example, from the dependence of the mass media on manipulating sexuality to the division of labor, the split between the public and private spheres, and the relations of production under capitalism. Most painfully for women, heterosexuality is a major, a social and psychological mode of organizing, generating, focusing, and institutionalizing desire, both men's and women's. Literally, I am wedded to my own oppression.

Furthermore, the very body of woman is not her own—it has been constructed by medicine, the law, visual culture, fashion, her mother, her household tasks, her reproductive capacity, and what Ti-Grace Atkinson has called "the institution of sexual intercourse." When I look in the mirror, I see my flaws; I evaluate the show I put on to others. How do I break through representations of the female body and gain a more just representation of my body for and of myself?

My social interactions are shaped by nonverbal conventions which we all have learned unconsciously and which are, as it were, the glue of social life. As Nancy Henley describes it in *Body Politics,* women's nonverbal language is characterized by shrinking, by taking up as little space as possible. Woman is accessible to be touched. When she speaks in a mixed group, she is likely to be interrupted or not really listened to seriously, or she may be thought of as merely emotional. And it is clear that not only does the voyeuristic male look shape most film practice, but this male gaze, with all its power, has a social analog in the way eye contact functions to control and threaten women in public space, where women's freedom is constrained by the threat of rape.

We need to articulate these levels of oppression so as to arrive at a collective, shared awareness of these aspects of women's lives. We also need to understand how we can and already do break through barriers between us. In our personal relations, we often overcome inequalities between us and establish intimacy. Originally, within the women's movement we approached the task of coming together both personally and politically through the strategy of the consciousness-raising group, where to articulate our experience as women itself became a collective, transformative experience. But these groups were often composed mostly of middle-class women, sometimes predominantly young, straight, single, and white. Now we need to think more clearly and theoretically about strategies for negotiating the very real power differences between us. It is not so impossible. Parents do this with children, and vice versa; lovers deal with inequalities all the time. The aged want to be in communion with the young, and third-world women have constantly extended themselves to their white sisters. However, when women come together in spite of power differences among them, they feel anxiety and perhaps openly express previously suppressed hostility. Most likely, such a coming together happens when women work together intensively on a mutual project so that there is time for trust to be established.

Yet as we seek mutually to articulate the oppression that constrains us, we have found few conceptual or social structures through which we might authentically express our rage. Women's anger is pervasive, as pervasive as our oppression, but it frequently lurks underground. If we added up all of women's depression—all our compulsive smiling, ego-tending, and sacrifice; all our psychosomatic illness, and all our passivity—we could gauge our rage's unarticulated, negative force. In the sphere of cultural production there are few dominant ideological forms that allow us even to think "women's rage." As ideological constructs, these forms end up containing women.

Women's rage is most often seen in the narratives that surround us. For example: Classically, Medea killed her children because she was betrayed by their father. Now, reverse-slasher movies let the raped woman pick up the gun and kill the male attacker. It is a similar posture of dead-end vengeance. The news showed Patty Hearst standing in a bank with a gun embodying that manufactured concept "terrorist," and then we saw her marrying her FBI bodyguard long after her comrades went up in flames. In melodrama and film noir, as well as in pornography, women's anger is most commonly depicted through displacement onto images of female insanity or perversity, often onto a grotesque, fearful parody of lesbianism. These displacements allow reference to and masking of individual women's rage, and that masked rage is rarely collectively expressed by women or even fully felt.

We have relatively few expressions of women's authentic rage even in women's art. Often on the news we will see a pained expression of injustice or the exploitative use of an image of a third-world woman's grief. Such images are manipulated purely for emotional effect without giving analysis or context. Some great feminist writers and speakers such as Mary Wollstonecraft, Virginia Woolf, Elizabeth Cady Stanton, and Harriet Tubman have provided models by which we can understand ourselves, but too often the very concept of "heroine" means that we hold up these women and their capacity for angry self-expression as the exception rather than the rule.

In Illinois, women chained themselves together in the statehouse when it was clear that the ERA would not pass; the women sought to express our collective anger at our legislators' cowardice and to do so in a conspicuous, public way. But actions such as these often have little effect beyond their own time span. We need to think beyond such forms to more socially effective ones. It is a task open to all our creativity and skill—to tap our anger as a source of energy and to focus it aesthetically and politically. We may have to combine images of anger with something else—say, images of how women can construct the collectivity as a whole. It is here that, by their example, our third-world sisters have often taken the lead. Rosa Parks refusing to sit in the back of the bus, Harriet Tubman leading slaves to the North, an Angolan mother in uniform carrying a baby and a rifle, a Vietnamese farmer tilling and defending her land, Nicaraguan women in their block committees turning in wife abusers to the police—these images let us see that women can gain more for themselves than merely negating the bad that exists. And it is in their constant need to attack both sexism and racism, as well as poverty and imperialist aggression, that third-world feminists now make us all see much more clearly both the urgent need for and the possibility of reconstructing the whole world on new terms.

Artistically, emotionally, and politically women seem to need to glimpse dialectically the transcendence of our struggle against sexism before we can fully express sexism's total negation, that is, our own just rage. Sometimes our suppressed rage feels so immense that the open expression of it threatens to destroy us. So we often do not experience anger directly and consciously, nor do we accurately aim our rage at its appropriate target. To transcend negation and to build on it means that we have to see what is beyond our rage. An example of such transcendence was demonstrated by Nicaraguan mothers of "martyred" soldiers (those killed by U.S.-paid counterrevolutionaries) to Pope John Paul II when he visited Managua in April 1983. They stood in the rows closest to the podium where the Pope spoke and they all bore large photos of their dead children. As the events of the day unfolded, the women created an image that stirred the whole

422

people, one that the Pope could not go beyond or even adequately respond to. Here is what happened: The Pope spoke on and on to the gathered crowd about obeying the hierarchy and not getting involved with the things of this world. In frustration and anger, the women began to shout, "We want peace," and their chant was taken up by the 400,000 others there. The women's rage at personal loss was valorized by the Nicaraguan people as a whole, as the grieving mother became a collective symbol of the demand for peace. The chant, "We want peace," referred simultaneously to national sovereignty, anti-imperialism, religion, and family life. The women spoke for the whole.

This brings me back to my original question about women's political action in the United States today. One of the major areas of investigation and struggle in the women's movement has been the sphere of daily life. This struggle, represented by an early women's movement phrase—"the personal is the political"—derives from women's real material labor in the domestic sphere and in the sphere of social relations as a whole. Women have traditionally done the psychological labor that keeps social relations going. In offices, in neighborhoods, at home, they often seek to make the social environment safe and "better," or more pleasant. That such labor is invisible, particularly that it is ignored within leftist theory and practice, is one of the more precise indices of women's oppression. And it is feminists' sensitivity to and analysis of social process that clarifies for them the sexism on the Left. Often at a leftist conference or political meeting, many men continue to see women and women's concerns as "other," and they do not look at what the Left could gain from feminist theory or from women's subcultural experience or from an analysis of women's labor. Women who come to such an event have already made a commitment to learn and to contribute, so they make an effort to continue along with the group as a whole but are impeded by sexist speakers' intellectual poverty (e.g., use of the generic "he"), macho debating style, and distance from political activism. Furthermore, not only women feel this political invisibility at leftist events. When black labor and black subcultural experience in the United States is not dealt with, nor is imperialism, or when racism is theoretically subsumed under the rubric of "class oppression" and not accorded its specificity, then third-world participants face the same alienation.

To demonstrate this process and analyze what divides us, I will describe an incident that occurred at the Teaching Institute on Marxist Cultural Theory in June 1983. It is worth discussing because it is the kind of incident that happens all too often among us on the Left. Early in that summer session, a coalition of students and the two women faculty members, Gayatri Spivak and me, formed to present a protest statement to the faculty. It was read in every class. Here is what it said:

> The Marxist-Feminist Caucus met on Friday June 17th and concluded that the "limits, frontiers and boundaries" of Marxist cultural theory as articulated by the Teaching Institute excluded and silenced crucial issues of sexism, racism and other forms of domination. We find ourselves reproducing in the classrooms of the Teaching Institute the very structures which are the object of our critique. The Marxist-Feminist Caucus

423

therefore proposes that each class set aside an hour weekly to discuss strategic silences and structural exclusions. A Marxism that does not problematize issues of gender and race, or of class consciousness in its own ranks, cannot hope to be an adequate tool for either social criticism or social transformation.

The institute had a format of having famous Marxist intellectuals lecture, specifically males with job security who have never incorporated a feminist analysis into their theoretical work. Both the format and the content of their lectures enraged some of us, but not others. In a sense, writing a protest statement divided the school's participants between the political ones and the consumers of Marxist theory. This is because critical theory itself has become a pathway for elitist advancement in the humanities and social sciences in universities where these areas are facing huge cutbacks. And the canon of that critical theory is based on Marx and Freud and their contemporary interpretants, Althusser and Lacan. Both at the Teaching Institute and at prestigious universities, young academics could get their quick fix of Marxism, the knowledge of which could help greatly in their academic career.

This is a capitalist mode of consuming knowledge. Too many students, especially career-pressured graduate students, want only a well-conceived lecture, a digest of Marxist theory and social analysis, something that can be written in a notebook, taken home, and quoted from in a future paper or journal article. Furthermore, we intellectuals fall into this capitalist-competitive mode. We feel pressured inside ourselves to be the best. Students are told to buy the best. All the faculty at the Teaching Institute felt that they could not make a mistake, that they had to read and show they had read everything, that they had been challenged on their political practice, accused of being racist or sexist or undemocratic. Our control over the classroom and studied theoretical polish became a kind of professional hysteria and worked against the collective building of Marxist knowledge and theory that we have needed for more effective social change.

Since the early 1970s women have come together in meetings like these, in feminist seminars, caucuses, and workshops, partly in resistance to a certain macho leftist or academic style and partly to build a new body of knowledge and feminist political practice. And we have been successful at doing this but it has meant double or triple work for us. Feminist scholarship does not usually lead to academic promotion for a woman. The knowledge women produce is easily marginalized, as was made painfully obvious at that summer school.

Feminists and third-world students came to the Teaching Institute knowing how much they needed Marxist theory. They understood that abolishing capitalism and imperialism was the precondition for liberation. They came as political participants expecting to learn theoretical tools to use in fighting oppression. But sex and race were too often ignored—I would say stupidly ignored—as social determinants in the theories presented about social change. (Beyond that, students felt intimidated by name-dropping and teachers' and other students' failure to explain terms. They felt they had to give a polished rebuttal or a cohesive "strategic intervention" before they could speak to refute a lecturer's point.) And when students raised issues of sexism or racism, deflection became the all too frequent tactic used by teachers or some of the white male students in response. No wonder that women, with their sex-role socialization, were often too intimidated to speak.

This is a sad analysis, but not an infrequent one in academia. It speaks about political theory and academic sexism and racism, and elitism and class privilege. The incident reveals much of what divides politically progressive people in the United States. These differences must be acknowledged in depth if we are to work together politically in a coalition form. In particular, I understand the texture of women's silence in a forum that demanded a highly rational and developed intervention. Many of the women students at the Teaching Institute already produced feminist theory, but the intimidating nature of this kind of aggressive public speaking made them seem like nonparticipants. And it often happens to me, too. I know that we watch and despair of our own colonized psyches which hold us back in silence precisely when we would choose to be political actors, especially in a Marxist forum.

What we have seen in the 1970s and 1980s in North America and Europe is a supercession of political forms related to developments in radical consciousness. Conditions have evolved in the United States that make it impossible to conceive of a revolutionary organizing strategy that does not embrace a black and minority revolution and a feminist revolution. The lesson of the civil rights/black power movement was that blacks will organize autonomously. Now it is the offspring of that movement, Jesse Jackson's Rainbow Coalition, that has taken the lead in building an anti-imperialist coalition that addresses the specific struggles and organizing forms of blacks, Latinos, women, and gays. Such a coalition relates to the existence of the women's movement, the gay and lesbian movement, the anti-imperialist movement, by supporting these groups' autonomous organizing and granting new respect, not by subsuming or controlling them. Furthermore, at this point in U.S. history, issues of mass culture and mass communication have to be dealt with, so that minority figures such as Jesse Jackson or Harold Washington, Chicago's black major, have developed an ongoing analysis about racism in the press.

As a feminist who has worked both in the cultural sphere and in anti-imperialist work, I have experienced this supercession of forms. In the early 1970s a politically active woman was either "on the Left" or "in the independent women's movement." Some socialist feminists within leftist organizations formed caucuses to try to influence their organizations. In the 1970s I chose to work mostly within the independent women's movement, especially in creating a women's studies program at an urban university. In developing feminist media now within the women's movement, I find many of my sisters addressing broader issues of imperialism, racism, class oppression, and the nuclear threat. Many of us are joining progressive coalitions around these issues. Within these coalitions we must be able openly to declare, "I am a feminist and our feminist position represents the most advanced stand. You men have to join us." Indeed, many men, often younger men, have. As feminists, we are the ones who are building a whole theoretical critique of mass culture and mass communication; we are the ones who are learning how to appropriate all of culture in an oppositional way. And because of our historical position in advanced capitalism, we are one of the first social movements to address cultural issues in such a thorough and complex way.

Many feminists are eager to participate in coalitions, the major political strategy for us in the 1980s. In Chicago, we saw the women's movement and the Left work to elect Harold Washington. In the San Francisco area, gays and lesbians have formed a Central America support group. Both in the United States and abroad, the antinuclear movement contains within it all-women's affinity groups. Latinos in various areas identify and organize as Puerto Rican or Mexican-American according to their ethnic origins and concentration, and also unite in Central American solidarity work. This great diversity of sectoral organizing enriches all of us who are working for social change.

Some of the best aspects of current progressive organizing have, in fact, derived specifically from the development of the contemporary women's movement. I mentioned the consciousness-raising groups earlier. I think the women's movement has introduced into political discourse an open and direct critique of the macho style and political posturing of many male leaders. As feminist activists, we have created among ourselves new forms of discussion and a creative, collective pursuit of knowledge—in contrast to an older, more aggressive, male debating style. Particularly important for me, the women's movement has pursued and validated as politically important cultural and artistic work. In Chicago, where I live, I experience a strong continuum and network among community-based artists and women in the art world. We have built up intellectual ties between academic women and feminist film- and videomakers who have created an analysis of how sexuality is manipulated in the visual culture that surrounds us. As a consequence, feminist film criticism has developed a new theoretical framework for analyzing ideology and the mass media. In fact, I think that our building of a feminist cultural theory has made a key contribution to the Left and to revolutionary movements throughout the world.

When I want to consider how unleashing our anger might capacitate us to act for change, I reconsider Frantz Fanon's essay "Concerning Violence" in *The Wretched of the Earth*. In that essay he describes decolonization, particularly the process by which the native sheds the colonizer's values and the colonizer's ways. I understand that my black and Latina sisters in the United States experience a rage against the economic and racial violence perpetrated every day against them; in a way that is similar to what Fanon describes: this rage knows its resolution lies in a complete change of the economic order in which we live. At the same time, I must ask what kind of rage it would be that would effectively contest women's oppression—given all the levels at which gender inequality and women's oppression is articulated in social and personal life. What Fanon describes to us is a specific historical moment at which mental colonization can be and is surpassed. As I look at women's mental colonization, I see our internalized sense of powerlessness, our articulation into masochistic structures of desire, and our playing out of personae that on the surface seem "passive," "self-defeating," "irrational," "hesitant," "receptively feminine," or even "crazy." Much of this behavior stems from internalized and suppressed rage. Fanon describes such behavior in the colonized and posits active rage, the violent response to violence, as its cure.

426

What would the overturning of male supremacy and women's colonization mean to women? How would it be accomplished? Fanon understands that a whole social structure and a new kind of person must come into being, and that those with privilege know, fear, and resist this. His call to armed struggle, based on the very clear demarcations and abuses of power that the native always sees, signals a survival struggle that does not characterize the war between the sexes. As I read Fanon for what he can teach me about women's resistance to oppression in nonrevolutionary society, I read him as a communist psychiatrist talking about how social movements can change the mentality of the oppressed. When I ask about revolution for women now, minimally I see that our contestation cannot be conducted in the mode of nice girls, of managing the egos of and patiently teaching those who oppress, which is a skill and duty we learned from our mothers in the domestic sphere. If we do so, once again we will be placed in that very role of "helpmate" that we are trying to overcome. Angry contestation may take us the extra step needed to overcome our own colonized behavior and tardy response.

Let me now rewrite for you parts of Fanon's essay to show its power when discussing the relation between psychological and social change. The distance between the violence of colonization and its necessary response in armed struggle, and the emotional rage I am referring to here in combating sexism, marks the distance between the periphery and the center of international capitalism. By using Fanon in this way, I do not wish to co-opt him for the women's movement but to learn from him, just as I learned from the Nicaraguan women's courage and tenacity. If women must learn to be openly angry, we must learn to draw links between ourselves and those who are more oppressed, to learn new methods of struggle and courageous response.

> Combating women's oppression as we know it is a historical process: that is to say, it cannot become intelligible or clear to itself except in the exact measure that we can discern the movements that give it historical form and content. Combating women's oppression is the meeting of two intrinsically opposed forces, which in fact owe this originality to that sort of substantification that results from and is nourished by the social construction of gender. The husband is right when he speaks of knowing "them" well—for it is men who perpetuate the function of wife. Men owe the reproduction of their bodies and psyches to the family.

> Feminist revolution never takes place unnoticed, for it influences individuals and modifies them fundamentally. It transforms passive femininity crushed with inessentiality into privileged agency under the floodlights of history. A new kind of woman brings a new rhythm into existence with a new language and a new humanity; combating women's oppression means the veritable creation of new women who become fully

human by the same process by which they freed themselves.

Feminists who decide to put their program into practice and become its moving force are ready to be constantly enraged. They have collectively learned that this narrow world, strewn with prohibitions, can only be called into question by absolute contestation.

The sex-gender system is a world divided into compartments. And if we examine closely this system of compartments, we will at last be able to reveal the lines of force it implies and to mark out the lines on which a nonoppressive society will be reorganized.

At the level of individuals, anger is a cleansing force. It frees the woman from her inferiority complex and from despair and inaction; it makes her fearless and restores her self-respect.

At this point I will stop citing from and reworking Fanon, deliberately at the point of individual rage. Now is a time when we need to work in coalitions, but we must be very honest about what divides us and what are the preconditions we need before we can work together. I have made the decision to work in leftist and feminist cultural work and in Latin American solidarity work. I think in all our strategies we must analyze the relation of that strategy to feminist, antiracist, and anti-imperialist demands. Women comprise over half the population; any class issues in the United States are intimately tied to the question of racism; we all live off the labor of workers, often underpaid women, in the Third World; and socialist revolution is being waged very near us. Personally, I know that it is by my contact with Nicaraguan women, who insist that men and women must struggle together for our mutual liberation, that I have been politicially and emotionally renewed.

The problems grow more acute. We know that the Right is racist, homophobic, and sexist. We in the women's movement must stop turning our anger against each other and learn the most effective ways to work together for social change. We can focus our anger and harness it, but to do that we must clearly analyze cause and effect. If theory accompanies anger, it will lead to effective solutions to the problems at hand. We have great emotional and social power to unleash when we set loose our all too often suppressed rage, but we may only feel free to do so when we know that we can use our anger in an astute and responsible way.

Michèle Mattelart

Can Industrial Culture Be a Culture of Difference: A Reflection on France's Confrontation with the U.S. Model of Serialized Cultural Production

Translated by Stanley Gray and Nelly Mitchell

The intersection of culture, technology, and economics is an important site of political struggle. The value of the presence of American television series on the world's screens can no longer be estimated by criteria applied in the early seventies. Commercial series are a way of organizing social relations, the penetration of commercial logic into the relations linking the state and civil society.

The Problem: Cultural or Economic?

In France, the need for a cultural policy related to the current strategy of reindustrialization has given a notable urgency to the question of the "American program" or "serialized American production." While the current audiovisual system is passing through a severe production crisis, various new channels of communication are offered to the French through the development of the video market, the opening of a fourth TV channel, the move to the operational stage of direct satellite broadcasting, and the active promotion of cable TV. All this stimulates the urgent need for innovation in the areas of programming and public service. What content should be put in these new containers?

Debates on this question—too rare, we think—falsely revolve around the fear that the creation of new channels will simply open up more welcoming invasion routes for North American programs—a legitimate fear, given the precedent of those countries whose televisual systems have been deregulated. France's problem is no doubt a familiar one. Less familiar is the possibility, a real one since the socialist government's ascension to power on May 10, 1981, that such debate could get somewhere.

The glee of U.S. industrialists would be enough to justify the fear of invasion. A recent issue of *Computerworld* lauded the multiplication of channels and networks in Europe as so many new ways to disseminate American cultural products: "It's good for us!"[1] Our worry is merely the other side of the coin.

The inevitable reference to the North American threat has the advantage of giving one name to various issues at stake while evoking the weight of the several determinants (technical, financial, cultural) that affect communication policy. The North American program becomes the emblem of the mass media model which the logic of capitalism puts into place and generalizes.

What is at stake may be formulated by the following questions: Will the policy favoring technological development, crucial to France's reindustrialization, be able to accommodate a political goal that would seek to prevent the subjection of cultural industries to a single influence, that of the market? Will this policy open the way to the creation of a national programming enterprise, one that would not respond to new challenges by simply copying the transnational production model currently provided by the United States? Will it stimulate the search for alternatives, for original ways of programming and broadcasting? What ratio between equipment and creation will be used in budget allotments? How will commercial logic be aligned with the social logic governing the interests of groups, the widening base of audiovisual production, the participation by citizens in the choice of technologies and the definition of their use? Is a "local" product, one that would permit a particular collectivity to express and to reappropriate its sounds and images, compatible with the international market? Is there an "alternative" product that could be international yet not in the mold of a transnationalized mass culture?

The French observe with fascination the succession of new technologies. They are like the group of shepherds in the Pyrénées village who appear on "La Planète Bleue" ("The Blue Planet," a program designed to popularize science) and are shown to be dazzled by the panoply of new technology displayed before their eyes. Increasingly numerous and euphoric articles in the press celebrate this "advent." We are finally participating in modernity—a modernity we rejected for many years, for reasons that political and cultural anthropology should wish to clarify. Compare France's audiovisual equipmemt with that of the other European countries—television sets in the past; video, today. France is and has always been one of the last to benefit from such goods.

If the signs of technological progress fascinate us so, is it not because they signal modernity par excellence; in other words, American modernity? Few of the media can resist confessing their joy at rejoining the founding myth. It is as though the United States, the first country to have written its history on celluloid, profiting from the combined effects of a liberal economy and the development of the media, had acquired at once and for all time a power and a faculty: the power to anticipate every dream of growth in this world of the image; and the faculty to repeat endlessly with each technological and industrial innovation, "I am your Imaginary."

Dissonant in this echo chamber were the words of the French representative at the UNESCO Conference in Mexico, in July 1982, in a speech decrying the U.S. monopoly of the means and distribution of cultural production and calling for the affirmation of identities and pluralities. The speech inspired a noisy polemic in the French press: cries of indignation against chauvinistic isolationism and jingoism, protesting the suicidal folly of this rebellion against a hegemony seen as natural, hence both fated and justified. The TV page of *Le Monde* took this opportunity to speak of the pusillanimity of "French television and the boredom it exudes." The masses were called upon to exercise their plebiscite, to voice their will regarding the only culture deemed to be theirs in this advanced industrial age.

430

Because of the narrow focus on the harm done to Americano-philia and Atlanticism, an important point of the Mexico speech was almost completely overlooked, though it was as central to this speech as it has been more recently in debates on cultural politics. This was the phrase, or rather watchword, "Economy and Culture, the same struggle," a key phrase designating the true locus of the challenge. In a country like France, which has until recently abhorred such indelicate linking of these two terms and two realities, the phrase has a special force. Malraux's words, "Cinema is an art, but it is also an industry," anticipated the realism of the new watchword, but whether because of the times, Malraux's persona, or the restriction to cinema, his remark was not understood as revolutionary.

The colloquium on "Creation and Development" at the Sorbonne in February 1983, which brought togther 400 intellectuals from all over the world, revealed a general tendency to unbalance the two terms in question: in designing a program for emerging from the crisis, the role of culture was given the most weight; the powerlessness of economy served as reason to belittle it. President François Mitterand said: "Doctrinaire economists give us recipes that don't work anywhere." American economist J. K. Galbraith agreed: "It is the artist who is at the cutting edge of development, not the engineer."[2] It was then generally accepted that one must look to intelligence, innovation, creation, and culture for the salvation of the world. Note that in these verbal jousts, if the words "economy" and "culture" are not always conjoined, their structural tension shows in the personal confrontation of economists and producers of culture.

The views of this colloquium, called by some *l'internationale de l'imaginaire*, were shortlived. Almost immediately, the ministerial reshuffling of March 1983 signaled a return to a more orthodox view. Economists were recalled to their posts; culture took a back seat. The weight of economics was reasserted.

One could foresee that things were not going to be so simple, however. Wherever there is discussion of the future of culture, the shadow of "Dallas" is cast. "Dallas": a ready-made anathema. This is the poverty we want no part of. (A cultural poverty, obviously; in "Dallas" no one is broke!) And yet, while the Sorbonne was excommunicating "Dallas," contracts were being signed to renew programming in France (TF 1, one of the three French television channels, purchased twenty-three more episodes in 1983). While the American writer Susan Sontag was claiming that "American culture is not as important as people say it is,"[3] the great majority of televiewers the world over were preparing to enjoy that Saturday, as usual, J.R.'s latest Machiavellian plots and Sue Ellen's new torments. The contradiction (if it is one) needs analysis because it points to constraints perceived as real in the coupling of economy and culture.

Does Commercial Mean Universal?

One is tempted to explain the success of such TV serials by analyzing their narrative structure or their content, by sticking to the text. Such a media-centric bias would be typical of a certain sociology, one that represses an all-important fact: what is televised is the product of a television system that is in turn the product of a history. The system's organizing mode embodies the characteristics of its genealogy and, beyond that, of its assigned role in the reproduction of the society as a whole, most notably in relation to other socializing systems that express the "general will."

431

Economy and Culture

The equation was settled from the outset in the United States, where the mass media system was developed under the auspices of the commercial. As such the equation served for the conquest of markets and assumed its universalizing role. For this reason it is a serious challenge when France wishes to affirm at once the desire for independence and recognition of the inescapable imperatives of the equation.

Whenever new markets are being conquered, a commercial system has advantages over a system of public service. " 'Merchants have no homeland.' These words are Jefferson's, not mine," said Salvador Allende more than fourteen years ago, explaining to the U.N. General Assembly his government's objections to the actions of foreign firms in Chile. That is to say, business recognizes no frontiers, and markets have no limits. Public services, on the other hand, must obey the logic of national limitation recognized by political states. Commerce is, a fortiori, more favorable to internationalization than public service. Yet it would be a mistake to stop at a juridical definition of public service. This would mask its difference from private service, a radical difference that may be formulated thus: the "audiences" of one are the "citizens" of the other.

It is well known that it took France a long time to see the importance of the technological development of mass culture, and that the role of such technology in the economic and political areas, in the propagation of the country's values and cultural modes abroad, has never had in France the importance it assumed from the start in the United States. Look, for example, at the differences in the way the two countries have used the educational system and the mass media to produce consensus, and at the changes that have brought France to see in the media explosion the main social problem.

It is, in fact, only recently that France has felt the need to imagine a television that would be specifically French and could also compete in the market. In France, the association of television with literature, theater, and cinema has been a telling one, and the production of French cinema seems to have been more often inspired by the creative urge of an author than by the stimulus of commercial competition.[4] If a programming industry has not developed, it is because of the weakness of capital investment in cultural industries, public service in one way or another implying loss of profit. The fact should lead to deeper analysis of the traditional conception of culture in France and its fall-out in today's situation, which is dominated by the imperative to pass to a new stage of serialized productions.[5] This is the kind of discontinuity scorned by those who hold to notions of the "global village" and the "single screen," those who are ready to use the pressure of modern communication to homologize all cultural realities.

If the aim is industrialization, a culture is handicapped when its tradition, emphasizing the cultural connection between creation and the technical capacity to reproduce, dictates that it be seen as a public service. Eloquent on this score was the president of MCA Universal TV, at the last MIP TV in Cannes, April 1983: "In the French products that we see, there is no 'network appeal.' The subjects are generally too national, not commercial enough and also too cultural for the average American viewer. Another thing is that what we are offered are usually mini-series when we are more interested in full-length ones starring actors known to the U.S. public.

432

Michèle Mattelart

For the time being, we aren't buying co-productions. Two years from now we may reconsider, who knows? But I should add that we already have in stock an enormous number of productions. We scarcely need to look for new ones."[6] *Le Film Français* objected that "some U.S. channels buy French series, *HBO* and *PBS*, for example" to which the MCA Universal president replied: "*PBS* has little money and *HBO* aims at a different audience. All well and good, but it isn't for the average American T.V. viewer." (Note the self-complacency, interesting when one remembers that projections of the market for 1990 give the networks only 59 percent of prime-time viewing over the new broadcasting systems. The trend is already confirmed in some large American cities, notably in San Francisco.)

The president of MCA Universal has, in any case, sketched the profile of a product not unlikely to succeed in the game of internationalization: an *average* product aimed at the *average* consumer in the United States, the viewer of American network programs.[7] His criteria are clearly those of the commercial oligopoly that discounts PBS or any kind of programming not aimed at a mass public.

The problem is complicated today by cable networks, which ought to imply segmented markets. Will their productions be fundamentally different from the dominant one? Doubts arise when one hears an independent producer like Lorimar, the producer of "Dallas," speaking at the 1983 Cannes Film Festival: "The films we plan to make for cable will have big budgets and big names. We must keep up the quality, with an eye to international sales."[8] The new systems may well provide new paths to the international market.

The examples of Brazil and Mexico support the thesis that commercial TV is the easiest to internationalize. These countries, alone among outsiders of the industrial group, have succeeded in competing in the international market, particularly Brazil. There are commercial monopolies in both countries: TV Globo in Brazil, and Televisa in Mexico. Both compete internationally using serials in the soap opera mode—*telenovelas* that comprise an overwhelming majority of their dramatic production. The paradox is that in these countries, whose economies are much less independent than those of the large industrialized countries, a commercial monopoly like the television monopoly in Brazil can compete successfully for prime-time hours using programs made at home. Out of the ten most popular programs in Brazil, only two are foreign-made.

In Europe, on the other hand, vulnerability to American series and more generally to the American mode of production has led to a doctrine of privatization, a doctrine with a long history, passing through many phases before yielding the current policy of deregulation. To say simply, as did a French communist deputy at a parliamentary debate, that television is like a "faucet pouring out images made in the U.S." is to overlook this history and to displace the problem by paying more attention to consequences than causes. The success of the American series is only a symptom of dependency on a model in which the standardized series, particularly the American-type series, has a natural place. It is a model that, among the three functions it is supposed to perform—to inform, to educate, to entertain—chooses to emphasize the third, to entertain.

The Concentric Circles of Concentration

It is tempting to explain the strength of North American programs by resorting to the time-honored and undeniably valid arguments that point

433

to high production standards, excellent technical quality, professionalism, the efficiency of the marketing system, the efficacy of block-booking, and so on. Regarding this last practice, it is amusing to remember the petulance with which Boris Vian criticized a comparable practice used in marketing jazz records. In one of his jazz chronicles for *Combat* (October 30, 1947), he wrote:

> This week's gripe is directed specifically at Columbia and to His Master's Voice, two heads of the same hydra. The individuals entrusted with the confection of our favorite black goodies, thinking they were clever, have produced two monstrosities in a very short time: three months ago it was "Whatta You Gonna Do" by Louis Armstrong, with, on the flip side, a horrible thing by Glenn Miller called "Falling Leaves." And now we have a Columbia disc putting Harry James's "I Didn't Mean a Word I Said" on the back of Count Basie's "Lazy Lady Blues." I have to tell these clods that the worst Armstrong is still better than the best Miller, and though I don't want to be nasty to Harry James, this particular number is lousy. I can't believe that Messieurs Columbia and His Master's Voice were unable to come up with other masters of Basie and Armstrong to produce some decent combination. Their abominable act reminds me of rutabaga vendors during the Occupation who would make you buy five kilos of these before they would sell you half a box of "Monstrueux de Carentan."[9] ("Monstrueux de Carentan" are a kind of leeks prized by connoisseurs. Rutabagas were and still are a kind of turnip, as inedible at table as in the moviehouse.) [Translator's note: *Navet*, turnip, is a term used for mediocre films.]

Along with block-booking, we should mention other key components in the American repertoire: mastery of the adventure genre, skill in packaging and balancing scenarios, rhythm, casting, the great tradition of entertainers in the United States, and so on. All these elements attest to the long experience this industry has behind it and its power today as a commercial model of unparalleled entertainment value. It is not only in the form of finished imported products (series and telefilms) that the model operates in our televisual systems, but also and above all in the form of matrices that are, for better or worse, nationalized. Is not all of France invited to quiver with excitement each Sunday at the showing of "Incroyable Mais Vrai" ("Incredible But True"), an exact replica of an American program?[10] Likewise, "Champs Elysees," on Saturday nights, which draws a surprisingly large audience away from "Dallas" on a rival channel, feeds on the kind of musical show perfected in the United States, dishing up a style that almost all our star singers have adopted. Mireille Mathieu, appearing on this program, before a scintillating backdrop of Manhattan, on February 18, 1983, in the company of Patrick Duffy (alias Bobby Ewing of "Dallas"), designated for us in a completely natural fashion that place of ultimate sanction where the box-office value of products like popular songs is determined: *"Et si j'ai su te plaire / C'est à la terre entière / Que je plairai / Mon vieux* New York" ("If I can make it there / I'll make it anywhere," etc.)

All these arguments have weight, centrally or marginally, depending on the case. I would like to try to go deeper and fix several key links in the chain of this American technique.

Reassessing the decision made several years ago by the Cuban Institute of Art and Cinema to devote its resources to the production of a single epic-length, big-budget, historical film, to be coproduced by Spain (and which was to spawn a TV serial), Tomás Gutiérrez Alea, author of *Memorias del Subdesarrollo* and *La Ultima Cena* (among others), drew attention to one of the laws governing the success of an industry: the correlation of quality and quantity. He recalled a moment in the history of the Soviet film industry, reported by the filmmaker Dovjenko:[11]

> Dovjenko says that at a certain moment, the managers of the Soviet film industry realized that, of the let's say 100 films produced so far, only five could be called "excellent" and some twenty "good," whereas there were fifty "mediocre" ones and twenty which were unquestionably "bad." So they decided, with apparent good sense, to produce only "good" and "excellent" films the following year, and they reduced the total number to be produced to twenty-five in which they would invest all the resources and effort it would have taken to make 100. To their surprise it turned out that of these twenty-five films there were only two "excellent" ones and only five "good"; ten were "mediocre" and eight "bad." They decided to limit further the quantity, to concentrate all efforts on very few films and to produce only the number which had been called "good" or "excellent" the year before, judging that if they limited production to seven films they would get seven masterpieces. Result: "Excellent"—0; "Good"— 2, etc.[12]

From another angle, a similar appeal to the correlation of quantity and quality was heard at the beginning of 1983 when the unions of the industry's professionals, artists, and performers voiced their objections to the increase of advertising on TV:

> The intrusion of announcers in programs reduces the amount of "fresh" or original production. Advertising gives us work on a short-term basis but diminishes long-term employment. The law of opinion polls is that films will always get preference over dramatic pieces. "Twelve Angry Men"; people will look at that, so isn't that enough? Announcers aren't interested in programs designed for T.V. in which actors would have an input. No doubt it is dangerous to manipulate cri-

435

teria of quality, but it is well known that it is through a certain *quantity* of original production that the *quality* proper to audio-visual creation will surface. And a management bound by viewer-ratings is not going to take the financial risk entailed by quantity.[13]

Another interesting convergence appears in the conclusions of a study group that met in September 1983 under the auspices of the Coopération Culturelle et Technique Française and the International Council of French-Speaking Radio and Television. The group considered factors working against the effort to reestablish a North-South balance in the exchange of TV programs. Among the conclusions I note the following: "That national production is still weak also explains the fact that programs from the South rarely attain the technical quality required for international diffusion."[14]

Quality/Quantity

The use of pilot programs (only North America can afford them) expresses the cardinal truth of this correlation and reinforces this truth by combining the use of pilots with that of opinion polls. Leaving less to chance, this reduces by a good deal the risk that inevitably plagues the television and film industries.[15]

Underlying both this practice and Dovjenko's demonstration is the obvious question of what is meant by "quality." If any concept is impossible to fix in the absolute it is this one, relative as it must be to international pressure, the definition of needs, aesthetic criteria, and production norms. In the case of the pilot, for example, quality is judged by the appeal of a product to an average viewer and is sanctioned by viewer ratings.

It would require another essay to deal with this complex problem. I will only point out here that in 1981 the three U.S. networks paid for eighty-five pilots that brought forth only twenty-three programs. Since the estimated cost of a pilot hour is some $750,000, the process cost the networks about $63 million in 1981.[16] At NBC the production of pilots has reached a new high. Thirty-one of these were authorized for the 1983-84 season, as compared to twenty-two the preceding season. CBS okayed twenty pilots—thirteen comedies and seven dramas—for 1983-84. These figures belie rumors that the networks are turning away from the production of pilots because of the cost.[17]

Pilot production shows at once the strength and vitality of the North American industry and its remarkable capacity to tap new resources. It also shows the adaptability of a system that can ally a heavily institutionalized organization with an enormous expenditure of creative resources, including marginalized ones, a system that can combine technical perfection and professional finish with experimental forms produced in small, independent studios.

The dialectic operating among the central apparatus and its margins needs exploration. What is concerned is an organic relationship established quite early in the United States among intellectuals, creators, and the cultural industry, and more generally speaking between institutions of knowledge and institutions of industrial research (some might wish to add military research). In France, the relations of large institutions to the creative activities of marginalized sectors (whose marginality tends to shrink like

436

Balzac's *peau de chagrin,* one should add) is only now being theorized, thanks to the current political reversal and the consequent stimulus to restructure. Is it not surprising that the most effective managers of the current restructuring of communication and information industries are, in many European countries, especially in France, veterans of May 1968 or have ties to movements that attacked the functioning of the dominant media? There is no doubt that it would be useful at this point to pursue a historical analysis of the ways in which intellectuals have attained organic or traditional status in each country, and of the way in which their relationship to the machinery of power, that of the media or other, has evolved.

Let me return to the question of quantity, for it raises other points. A first one, frequently made, uses quantity as a trump card by citing the large stockpile of available programs, programs already proven to be profitable on the American market and consequently available to the various national systems at a cost well below that of local production. "A fifty-five minute series costs an average of 1,000,000 FF if it is French, 1/20 of that, or 52,000 FF if it is foreign."[18]

A second point concerns a promising trend of research into the reception of visual messages and an effort to renew our understanding of the image's signifying processes. It is a trend that criticizes by implication the pressure exerted on our notion of image reception by an originary and prevailing code based on the concept of analogy. The new approach locates the significance of the image not just in its impression of reality but in the image's relation to other images within a corpus. What is observed is a complex dialogue of interreferential images producing an effect of exchange and intertextuality.

When Zbigniew Brzezinski said, "The U.S. is the society which is the best at communicating," he no doubt was unaware of the different meanings his sentence might convey. The flow of images in American series constantly rekindles the memory the North American image factory has produced, constantly recalls the image-repertoire from which its images are formed.

There is, in fact, in the United States today, a trend that apparently represents a conscious effort to manipulate this image memory, particularly by reawakening the memory of genres, by playing on the genre-effect: a film like *Raiders of the Lost Ark* is a veritable digest of the adventure film; "Dallas" is positioned at the confluence of the Western, the soap opera, and the family saga. In its time, "Sesame Street" showed the advantage to be gained by a clever recycling of the materials TV provides for the child's image-repertoire each day. It employed these materials as stimuli that could reinforce the effect sought: the dramatization of its educational objectives. It incorporated all the genres and forms that mass culture has popularized among children: cartoons, puppets, sketches, comedies, series, commercials, and so on. The novelty of this prototype of the educational series lay precisely in its synergetic channeling of all the genres and resources of this immense image-bank to create a pedagogical model.[19]

It is as though the process of commercial concentration within the industry itself, evidenced by the rise of conglomerates, had somehow entailed a similar process of concentration in the area of the symbolic. The creation of derivative and of multimedia products is a function of this same movement: the popular TV film is a spin-off of a popular movie; the plaything or the phonograph record continually reawakens a chain of association, definitively blurring the division between infrastructure and superstructure in a vast syndrome of repetition.

Leaving aside the case of the new (as of 1983) Japanese cartoon industry,[20] need I add that the only industrial-cultural complex possessing such a base for cycling and recycling products within the network of commercial goods is the North American one. The new industries of microcomputers and video games eagerly exploit this huge arsenal. French networks would certainly have liked to reproduce this system. Their attempts simply failed.

A New York television director, speaking in Cannes about the opening of the American market to French products, said: "The French must be willing to hedge their bets. They should remember a few essential points: they should study the American market, they should provide a polished product, timed to the minute; they should avoid dubbing or subtitling and produce a version done directly in English; they should conform to the different lengths of American programs (either twenty-two and a half or forty-eight and a half minutes) *leaving time for the commercials which have to be inserted*" (emphasis added).[21]

This last requirement shows how a TV system can maintain its hegemony at a time when, needing more programs than it has in stock, it must accept foreign products. It is well known that the obligation to provide advertising time entails more than the editing of programs—it implies a rhythm; it conditions all of production by creating an imperative to program "technical events." Such constraints are especially troublesome for the French system because it does not tolerate the insertion of commercials into the film itself, and also because it is predisposed by cultural tradition and by the production mode of SFP (Société Française de Production) to make a certain type of film: dramas or historical series. The hiatus, the incongruity that is felt, even if only at the immediate visual level, between the imagery used in historical films and the world of signs used in advertising explains the French resistance to a homogenized televisual discourse. In the televised continuum are juxtaposed "texts" whose discontinuity signals the contradictions existing in society at large, a discontinuity that is a break in the circulation of merchandise. Such contradiction must also filter into the discourse of television in the United States, though communication research rarely takes account of it. This research, when it is critical, is usually dominated by a theory of manipulation. It has not analyzed in any depth how the functioning of political and civil society is articulated in respect to the functioning of this commercial machinery designed to create consensus.

There is, nevertheless, a strong link between the American production of serials and the advertising appeal that governs the mode of production and consumption in all zones of television and perhaps daily life. It is significant, for example, that documentaries are just as affected as other forms by the obsession with speed. A critic of the *Cahiers du Cinema,* summing up a retrospective show of ten years of American television (at the Centre Beaubourg, December 1981) put it this way: "Apparently competition is tough and the T.V. viewer's hand is quick to turn the knob. Every forty-five seconds the documentary changes point of view. A study of the number of changes in angle and scene in American programs would be fascinating. I am sure that if you averaged it out for all programs you would

438

get a BUTT (base unit of television time) of some forty-five seconds."[22] Does this not suggest that the law of competition is operative in every dimension of American TV?

No doubt the principal effect resulting from the intersection of culture and technology is the generation of a temporal mode I will call "spectacular." In a recent study I discovered the pervasiveness of the tempo of advertising in "Sesame Street." This series—the fact needs to be emphasized—remains one of the few examples of a conscious attempt to rethink the problem of the low level of institutionalized mass culture, its correlation of mediocrity and commercial appeal. Wanting to raise the level, its creators could not but obey the commercial laws in place and used advertising appeal to enhance the new pedagogical messages they were sending, primarily, let us not forget, to the children of ethnic minorities who were disadvantaged within the regular school system. On the temporality of the spectacular I wrote:

It is not only the turning to account of "technical events" which characterizes *Sesame Street,* but the inclination to exploit for pedagogical purposes all the stimuli of the world of consumer products, and the standardization of affect wrought by the consumer society in the senses and imaginations of children. Using the seduction of rhythm and variety, *Sesame Street* succeeds above all by recycling the signs available in the vast stockpile of commercial culture and by reintegrating the child in this culture. What triumphs here is a temporal mode determined by industrial culture, a temporality regulated by the artificial, a time unlike that of daily life. It is a time of record times, of the exceptional, of the spectacular. (The creators of *Sesame Street* could not, or did not want to direct their critical thinking to the structuring force commanded by the spectacular.) This mode, geared to technological progress, disqualifies other tempi, other rhythms. Repressed, along with the temporal rhythm of daily life, of reality, and the duration of lived experience, are the rhythms specific to other cultures. The significance of this last is all the more vivid in a series aimed at ethnic minorities, at children coming from cultures other than this highly industrialized one. Fighting against segregation, the series subjects these children to the irreversible progress of modernity. It assimilates, homogenizes, agglutinates them by attuning them to the instantaneity and immediacy inherent in its teaching methods and in the culture of anticipation it promotes. It is legitimate to wonder whether the real educational message of *Sesame Street* does not consist in this initiation to the consumer world with its mass-attuned modalities of time and space.[23]

But the complex reality of commercial television production obliges us to push this analysis further. The merchandising that finds its way into the famous Brazilian *telenovelas,* for example, points, indeed, to a matrix governed by serialized industrial production. But this does not suffice to bring about a total assimulation of the *telenovela* and the North American serial. There is, notably, a different treatment of time and consequently of narrative structure, a treatment responding to the demands of a different mode of audience communication, to an audience subject to a different economy of symbols and a different degree of integration into modernity.[24] The same questions could be raised with respect to the film industry in India and the Middle East, Lebanese television, and so forth.

The notion of time is a central one in the process of the internationalization of televised products. French series are reproached, often by the French themselves, for being too "slow." The stubbornness of this obstacle is expressed in trade negotiations and in articles discussing exchanges or coproductions: "French series drag. French series are a drag." But here, again, it is not easy to determine where the defect or the quality begins or ends.

Culture as an Agency of Planetary Regulation?

In stressing the industrializing role of the North American mass media system, another factor may tend to get slighted. This system has had remarkable service as a nation-builder. At an early date the United States was obliged to create signs that could promote universal alliance, rallying signs to suit the composite nature of the population, made up of immigrants of different races and ethnic origins. The response to this need, compelling since the War of Secession, is provided by the culture of the mass media. The comic book or the Western, series like "Kojak" or "Dallas," contribute importantly to the amalgamation of this national society. What is all too often forgotten is that the first effort to amalgamate took the form of an attack on national society itself. The first test, in fact, of the universal value of North America programs (and of their profitability) is made within the limits of the national territory. The verdict of a sufficiently mixed and representative national public will become a guarantee of universality.[25]

It is interesting that, within the television field, it is the series that tends to prescribe the most universal appeal or the most predictable readings. By increasing the internal constraints of the image and the narrative structure (the recurrence of signs: characters, gestures, scenery, actions), the series rigorously controls the actant-spectator's production of meaning and keeps interpretations from proliferating. The series has a leveling effect that improves its communication with viewers inscribed in different cultural spaces. So the repetition of signs, based on the logic of a mode of production that seeks to minimize costs (an economy of means) also works effectively as communication: by limiting the semantic field it guarantees a more universal readability.

The Italian filmmaker Ettore Scola points to another operation that complements the one I have just described: "The success of a telefilm depends mainly on the specificity of a product which contains in itself its own promotional campaign; each episode stimulates the viewer's desire to reexperience emotions already felt. What counts is not the search for novelty but the confirmation of a habit, and this is true of all aspects, from the program time to the narrative plot to the reappearance of characters and actors. The self-promotion multiplies automatically each week."[26] And the former director of TV Globo says something much like this when explaining why *telenovelas* have had such success on Brazilian networks, particularly TV Globo, where they are shown at seven, eight, and ten o'clock each night: "T.V. is a habit. Whoever can keep the viewer tuning in to the same channel has won the fight for an audience."[27]

This ever-renewed process of amalgamation is seen at another level of ideological communication: American series enter into an incessant dialogue or exchange (though an unequal one) with all the concerns and tensions that agitate civil society, diminishing their contradictions, turning latent problems into already solved ones. Such is the "presence" in them of blacks, women, and ethnic minorities and their problems. All these are oblique means by which these series speak to us, awaken in us their echo.

National Consensus; Worldwide Consensus

Eternally vigilant in plugging any breech in the perfected consensus, stepping up this metabolic vigilance in times of crisis, these series offer us symbolic remedies for our misery in the form of docudramas and family sagas. The medicine they most favor is the return to the family.[28] The force of these fables is today felt the world over.

The value of the presence of American series on the world's screens can no longer be estimated by the criteria applied in the early seventies. The game and the stakes have a different importance and nature. What makes treatment of this theme difficult is in large part the persistence of ready-made judgments and arguments formed under that long militant tradition whose banner reads, "Yankee, go home!" All those who struggled against the Vietnam War shared the view that American preponderance in the field of mass culture was a priori a bad thing and attacked the hegemony of the consumer society. A similarly Manichean view has prospered recently using the slogan, "In the East, nothing new," capitalizing on disappointed hopes or crippled utopias and paralyzing any critical analysis of the two existing antagonistic models. "In any case, its worse on the other side": with this new cliché, free enterprise is equated with freedom itself. The social reality embodying this in its concrete power structure is accepted as the insurpassable horizon of our time. Its stubborn toughness becomes a source of pleasure, something you can play with.

Fascination is the other face of the welfare-recipient complex we suffer as citizens of welfare states born of Keynesianism. It is fed by a marketing policy infatuated with the expensive, extolling the fantastic budgets and the astounding profits made in record time by recent American superproductions.[29] This is the very image of our flabby capitalism, ashamed at having to wait for the state to erect the theater where we could express our inventiveness, our creativity; embarrassed that we can only stage our past history, that we must leave to others the task of nourishing the future's memory.

The advent of the commercial series is also the advent of a commercial mode of organizing social relations, one extending far beyond the organization of cultural production. It is nothing other than the penetration of commercial logic into the relations linking the state and civil society: the state has to resort to advertising in order to mobilize its citizens, using marketing techniques and television to implement its campaigns in the public interest (campigns on contraception, solidarity, promotion of reading skills, etc).

441

National Consensus; Transnational Consensus

This logic, a logic of the privatization of all spheres of collective and intellectual life, responds to the pressure inherent in the model of transnational expansion. Favoring a transnational organization of power, it tends to erode public space and function.

> Whatever obstructs the growing integration of national economies in the world arena and the new international division of labor is apt to become the favored target of this remodeling (i.e., the remodeling of forms of social control recommended by the Trilateral Commission). The primary target is no doubt the Nation-State, its structures and machinery as a whole. Despite their numerous internal contradictions, the structures and organizations of societies labelled "existing democracies" retain genealogically vestigial norms and values which resist the movement towards the transnationalization of economies. Transnational cultural production implies more than a cultural project; it implies a new organization of power. It is probably through the infiltration of cultural merchandise that transnational logic most effectively weakens the various national resistances.[30]

How do things stand with efforts to resist this technological and social mutation? The political crisis it inspires is felt both on the right and on the left, but perhaps more painfully on the left, now that it has—*mirabile dictu*—the chance to exercise power. The national secretary for cultural action of the Socialist party pronounced this indictment in May 1982, at the Cannes Festival: "That the Left, in power, has neither been able nor has wanted to eliminate the influence of the market on the development of cultural industries should surprise no one. But that it should abandon them to the market with enthusiasm, this is a cause for alarm."[31]

The media appear to be subjugated by the dynamics of entertainment, defined, as though by natural fiat, by the American hegemony. In 1984, French Antenne 2 was committed to produce a big family saga in the spirit of "Dallas." "Conceived by two teams of writer-producers, this series of 26 episodes will tell the story of a family which controls an important local daily newspaper."[32] The publishing house Nathan, specializing in pedagogical material, continues to produce software in English for the Thompson microcomputer, following in the wake of Hachette, which has for quite some time now been competing in the American market, and the film company Gaumont, which is stepping up its established operations in the United States and Brazil. As to the well-known fourth channel, promised to be opened soon (as of 1983), the decision to finance it as pay TV seems to put a heavy mortgage on whatever potential it might have had to diversify French programming or to facilitate the intercommunication of small interest groups as part of a wider public service. It seems that pay TV works only for the benefit of the "large public."

Among the effects attributable to this fascination with technology (a fascination leading to a literal transposition into images of the idea of

442

America as the symbol of liberty and democracy), one of the most harmful is surely the perversion of the notion of decentralized, interactive communication. This occurs because the desired virtues are attributed to technology itself, based on the assumption that social revolution is simply a product of technological revolution, even though this latter is usually only a new "interface." One of the important factors affecting the current situation is no doubt the repression of this: that communication, before serving as support or means, is basically a social practice.

Notes

1   Quoted by Herbert Schiller in an interview in *Révolution*, 155 (Feb. 1983).

2   *Le Monde*, Feb. 15, 1983; and *Le Quotidien de Paris*, Feb. 14, 1983.

3   *Le Monde*, Feb. 15, 1983.

4   When he was trying to put togther an encyclopedia of French films to prepare for the advent of video-discs and cassettes, the representative of the audiovisual section of the publisher Seuil noted that quality French film production "has always gone against the grain of the dominant mode of production." Out of 500 titles selected for the catalog (which was compiled with an eye to the international market), only 3 belonged to the firm Gaumont, 40 to Pathé. [Translator's note: i.e., to large firms; the rest were made by small companies.] The representative concluded: "A bad omen for the future of French films, when you consider that today's tendency to concentrate capital does not favor small company production." Interview with Francois Lesterlin, *Sonovision*, Apr. 1979. Quoted in A. and M. Mattelart, "Une culture pour gérer la crise," *Le Monde Diplomatique*, Oct. 1979.

5   It is well known that serial production implies, in one way or another, the death of the individual creator and greatly modifies the status of the scenarist. The financial and commercial director of Antenne 2 explained in the following terms how the status of creation in France could prevent television producers from respecting commercial and international considerations: "The French producer considers himself a creator and hence master of his creation. He does what he pleases and feels. He doesn't think about commercial problems outside his production. He works for his public, and his public is the French public." (Roundtable organized by the Mission pour un Espace Audiovisuel Latin, Paris, Spring 1983.) This could be set alongside the opinion of Jean-Claude Lattes, in 1983 a representative of the publisher Hachette, who said in an interview in *Publishers Weekly*, June 7, 1976: "We have good writers. The problem is that they write for Parisian critics or for their friends rather than for the people who buy books. . . . The tough-minded realism I have discovered in America has meant a lot to me. The French seem to feel ashamed at being involved in business. We have ideas. We are literary. But you, you talk about 'book business.' The difference is fundamental. I want to be an American editor."

6   *Le Film Français*, Feb. 25, 1983. I should note that not all American TV producers prefer regular to mini-series. Some think that the mini-series is the form of the future because, having a lower budget, it makes coproductions advantageous.

7   An opinion confirmed by Woody Allen in an interview for *The Business of Film* at Cannes, May 10, 1983: "America aims most of its production at the middle class, whether it's pop music or automobiles. Europe has always catered to the habits of an aristocratic elite and a poor middle class." And Orson Welles, meeting with the students of the Institut des Hautes Études Cinématographiques de Paris affirmed without hesitation that "French subjects do not interest Americans." These are subjective views, of course, but they show the kind of obstacles to intercultural exchanges.

8   *Le Film Français*, May 11, 1983.

9   Boris Vian, *Autres écrits sur le jazz*, 1 ("Jazz-Hot/Combat"), texts collected, prefaced, and annotated by Claude Remeil (Paris: Christian Bourgeois, 1981).

10   "Incroyable Mais Vrai" is, furthermore, based on paired sequences that show the inventiveness, extraordinary performance, or exploits of all kinds of ordinary people from places like Arizona or the Auvergne. The "local" is transcended through the spectacular. The French host, incidentally, works in collaboration with an American hostess.

11   Alexandr Petrovich Dovjenko, *La palabra y el escritor en el cine* (Montevideo: Ediciones Pueblos Unidos, 1957).

12   Tomás Gutiérrez Alea, "Dramaturgie (cinematográfica) y realidad," document presented to the Séminaire de Dramaturgie Cinématographique held on the occasion of the Fourth Festival of New Latin-American Cinema, Havana, Dec. 2-12, 1982.

13   "Non à l'austérité, le spectacle doit continuer," *Tambour, Télé 7 rouge* (Paris, Winter 1982-83).

14   Document from the Agence de Coopération Culturelle et Technique (Paris, Sept. 1982).

15   A brief comparison will illustrate the risk these industries face. At about the time when the Cuban film industry had its "commercial" failure because it had concentrated all its resources on a single production, United Artists went into bankruptcy because of the failure of an enormously expensive superproduction. It was bought up by MGM.

16   "TV's Drive on Spiralling Costs," *Business Week*, Oct. 26, 1981.

17   Figures given in the Japanese review *Movie/TV Marketing*, 4 (Tokyo, 1983).

18   Claude Degand, "La situation économique du cinéma en Europe," Le Cinéma et l'État, Colloque (Lisbon, June 1978). Quoted in *Filmaction*, special issue on "Les écrans colonisés" (Feb.-Mar., 1982).

19   This matter is explored at length in "Education, télévision et culture de masse. Réflexion sur une industrie des contenus," in A. Mattelart and Y. Stourdzé, *Rapport de la Mission*. Vol. 2: "Technologie, culture et communication" (Paris: La Documentation Française, 1983), pp. 150-78.

20   The cartoon seems to be the TV form most likely to generate by-products. The Japanese cartoon industry (which has taken over dominance in this market, formerly held by North America) is a good example. The cartoon "Dr. Slump," which appeared on Japanese TV screens in May 1981, gave rise, by the end of the same year, to 8,000 different derivative products. Certain Japanese series programmed in France were responsible for 200 such products. See Jacques Mousseau, "Plaidoyer pour une industrie française du dessin animé," *Communication et langage*, 2ᵉ trimestre (1982).

21   *Le Monde*, May 3, 1983.

22   *Cahiers du Cinéma*, Jan. 1982.

23   Michèle Mattelart, "Education, télévision et culture de masse."

24   The incredibly large number of episodes in *telenovelas* is significant. Armand Mattelart and I have published some hypotheses on this subject in *Femmes et industries culturelles* (UNESCO, Document file no. 23, Division of Cultural Development, 1981-82).

25   It has been noticed that the characters of Kojak and Columbo (in the series so named) referred respectively to Eastern Europe and to "Italianness." Thus, these guardians of law and order served admirably as signs of the integration of ethnic minorities into the American nation. The name "Kojak" also seems to answer to the demand for universal appeal by its similarity to one of the most universally known brand names: Kodak. George Eastman, the inventor of celluloid film, decided to name his products "Kodak" because he wanted a worldwide market and the phonemes in this word are pronounced the same in most known languages.
       The move toward the "global film," with as little dialogue as possible, is another symptom. It implies the use of big stars, strong images, and violent action, which do not require subtitles. The French firm Gaumont has moved toward this formula, though rather tamely, in its plans for *La petite bande*, "a charming story without dialogue which will be marketed as a film for children of all languages." *Le Film Français*, May 11, 1983.

26   In "Materiali sul telefilm," 4, *Teleconfronto* (Mostra Internaziale del Telefilm), May 29-June 5, 1983. In *Femmes et industries culturelle*, Armand Mattelart and I examine this question of habit and ritual time in order to correlate the use of daily episodes over a long period of time by telefilms and particularly by *telenovelas* with what we call "feminine temporality," the specific temporal rhythm of feminine subjectivity, which may be found in the lived experience of other oppressed groups.

27   *Brazilian Television in Context* (London: British Film Institute, 1982).

28   Cf. A. and M. Mattelart, *De l'usage des medias en temps de crise* (Paris: Editions Alain Moreau, 1979); in Italian, *I mas media nella crisi* (Editiori Riuniti, 1981), in which this idea is developed at length.

29   Here is how the magazine *VSD* presented Stephen Spielberg's *E.T.* on its front page, when it opened in Paris theaters in December 1982: "*E.T.*, the extra-terrestrial / He makes you laugh, cry, and he earns / 750 million centimes every day / for his producer Stephen Spielberg."

30   A. Mattelart, *Transnationals and the Third World: Struggle for Culture* (South Hadley, Mass.: J. F. Bergin, 1983).

444

Michèle Mattelart

31 Press conference by Didier Motchane, national secretary for cultural action of the Socialist party, Cannes, May 9, 1983.

32 In *Le Film Français*, Feb. 18, 1983. The ad continues: *"Antenne 2* is co-producing this series with a consortium of private companies which, for the occasion, have allied under the name 'Groupment d'Intéret Economique.' Shooting will begin at the end of 1983 and, if the series is successful, another 26 episodes will be prepared. It will be programmed in groups of 13 episodes, shown weekly starting in September, 1983."

Fernando Reyes Matta

The "New Song" and Its Confrontation in Latin America

The context of contemporary Latin America demands that a song move in the spaces created by the culture industry as well as in its own spaces. The resulting alternative distribution channels for popular songs have made it possible to attempt to redeem the products of the electronics industry—the record and the cassette—in order to place them at the service of a revolutionary view of the world.

The Festival de la Nueva Canción Latinoamericana ("New Song") was held in Nicaragua in 1983.[1] The most representative voices of this continental movement were present at this event: Silvio Rodríguez, Noel Nicola, and Vicente Feliú of the Cuban New Troubadours (Nueva Trova) movement; Isabel Parra and Eduardo Carrasco (director of the Quilapayún group) of Chile; Daniel Viglietti from Uruguay; Chico Buarque from Brazil; Mercedes Sosa from Argentina; Aly Primera from Venezuela; Amparo Ochoa from Mexico; and a number of singers and groups from El Salvador, Puerto Rico, Bolivia, Peru, and the U.S. Latin American community. Voices in exile and voices that came from their own countries gathered together to join the mobilizing musical forces of Carlos and Luis Mejía Godoy of Los Palacaguina, and of a dozen or so artists who have participated "with the strength of the guitar" in the struggle to create a new Nicaragua. The festival was organized in solidarity with the Nicaraguan people and as a demonstration of unity in the face of aggressions inflicted upon Central America. But that solidarity held an even deeper meaning, because the artists who joined hands in Nicaragua have earned wide recognition in spite of persecution and boycotts by the industrial system's mass media. Their strength is born of a music that does not shun confrontation but, on the contrary, works to denounce the social and political contradictions of Latin America. This music and poetry are inserted into the popular culture at precisely those points where we find the forms and language of a folklore excluded from the "cultural industry" controlled by the transnational capitalist system.

"Louder, so that the enemy can hear us!" shouted Carlos Mejía Godoy when all the artists were on stage at once to interpret the festival's theme song. These words, which still refer to Central America's circumstances, made evident a very profound perspective: the voices united on a Sunday afternoon in Managua symbolized the presence of a rich and widespread music that for more than twenty years has been capable of providing the impetus for a commitment rooted in the numerous liberation struggles taking place in Latin America.

447

This development, blooming since the mid 1960s, has crystallized into different modes of expression that have contributed, in varying degrees, to the creation of a "new song" or "countersong" for Latin America. These new expressive styles can be found in the Cuban Nueva Trova and the Chilean Nueva Canción movements; in a segment of the Bossa Nova music; in the rescue of Andean chords; and in a variety of other national endeavors for the creation of a new musical culture. As the festival demonstrated, these musicians have been anxious to link their own musical and poetic reality with the instruments and lyrics from other countries that recognize the culture of liberation. Some very significant evidence of this commitment can also be found in the "salsa" music of Rubén Blade and Willie Colón and, since the Malvinas war, in Argentinian rock.

This process is only now beginning to be studied systematically. Growing analysis is centered on the textual and cultural meanings and the sociopolitical determining factors that nourish this music; on specific problems shaping the creative process, including the line between poetry and pamphlet; on questions concerning artists' independence when they have assumed, at the same time, a political and an aesthetic commitment; and on the actual social setting created by the music itself, in view of its extraordinary capacity for expansion. Only now is an attempt being made to compile data and establish a theory to explain this social phenomenon. The research work done by Casa de las Américas in Cuba, the Canto Nuevo Forums promoted by UNESCO, and testimonial investigations carried out by CENECA in Chile and ILET in Mexico make some initial conclusions possible.

There appear to be three essential characteristics of this new music that affect its growth and acceptance:

1. The different manifestations of this new popular song movement, in spite of its meager and wholly insufficient presence in the dominant mass media systems, manage to become widely known and rapidly disseminated from country to country. Thanks to the circulation of tapes, of records passed from hand to hand, of festival registers, and the artists' tours themselves, these songs swiftly cross national frontiers. More than any other expression of the liberation or revolutionary struggle in every country (theater, poetry, novels, films, magazines, etc.), the song being created is distinctively and universally Latin American; moreover, it is ubiquitous.

2. The symbols used by the Canto Nuevo movement apparently appeal successfully to the popular sensibility in all countries, regardless of the actual country of origin of the music itself. Its proposals, both as a social and political commitment and a perspective on the theme of love, are easily adapted to different cultural stages. Thus the Nueva Trova movement has penetrated and expanded in the Chile of Pinochet, just as the creations of the Chilean Nueva Canción movement acquire new meanings among the committed artists of Colombia, Costa Rica, and Mexico. In effect, we are witnessing the development of a *permanent renationalization process* of Canto Nuevo creations. In addition to contributing, then, to the gestation of an alternative and combative Latin American culture, the popular collective memory assumes certain ballads as its own and inscribes them within its particular culture, recognizing a meaning that is historically local and relevant. "Gracias a la Vida" ("Thanks to Life") by Violeta Parra and "Te

Recuerdo, Amanda" ("I Remember You, Amanda") by Víctor Jara are two examples of this process of cultural adoption.

3. The Nueva Canción movement has generated its own independent dynamics to attain social significance, in spite of its being rejected or ignored by the recording transnationals and great regional networks. It has gained a position because its strength is derived elsewhere—from an identification with proposals for truly democratic change. Building on the continuing and reciprocal communication between the minstrels and their public, the movement finds expression in an increasing number of records and cassettes, in a kind of *counterstrategy of dissemination* only made possible through the support of students, workers, poverty-stricken city dwellers, rural workers, and many other grass-roots and base organizations.

Functions and Commitments

In view of previous experience, however, it seems necessary to analyze the *social projections* (or functions) that the Nueva Canción movement has made evident through its different national manifestations.

1. A function of *synthesis* emerges from lyrics, contingent in time and space, and capable of making a powerful appeal to the popular masses and their political vanguards. These texts interpret complex political theories and socioeconomic analyses and disseminate them in an accessible form. A good example is the way the cultural transnational model of consumption is portrayed by Rubén Blade in the "salsa" rhythm: "A plastic girl, rough and close at hand." Pablo Milanés relates the artist to the irrevocable demands of reality: "A poor wretch indeed is the singer of our times / who fears risking his chord / in fear of risking his life." The problem of the exploited rural worker and the struggle for agrarian reform are described in four lines by Daniel Viglietti: "Down with the wire fencing, / down with wires, / the land is mine and yours and theirs, / it belongs to Pedro and María, to Juan and José." Here the overwhelming beauty of the simple but revolutionary idea that the land belongs to everyone is made to encompass the entire universe.

2. A function of *rupture* emerges in that the new music opens possibilities for expression and creates gaps in the dominant discourse where the popular voice is being repressed by political and economic authoritarianism. There is a clear creativity in the construction of language and symbols, beyond the lyrics themselves, that link the identity of the artist and the people in mutual communication. From Chico Buarque's experience in Brazil to the eruption of the Canto Nuevo movement in Chile and the Canto Popular movement born under military dictatorship in Uruguay, there have been countless examples of this opening of gaps for the voice of the neglected masses, for "those who have no voice."

3. A function of *anticipation* emerges in that many expressions of the Canto Nuevo movement work for the construction of a more just and egalitarian society, synthesizing latent hopes. "When the War Is Over, Love" is the Nicaraguan song created under Somoza. Quite simply, but deeply, the social and collective situation is linked to the particular dreams of a couple in love. "Let us step forward, / all our banners flying high, / united in such a way / that loneliness is no more," is Silvio Rodríguez's proposal, in pounding, tropical rhythm. Possibly one of the most universal examples is "We Shall Overcome," created in the thick of the Chilean Popular Unity experience.

449

4. A function of *convocation to meet* emerges in that, for the popular masses, a music that refers to its struggles, hopes, and joys, its understanding of love and solidarity, promotes the possibility of an ardent meeting. One feels closer to those who share in the common struggle. Festivals and special live events pave the way for a symbol whose force and application extend beyond the song itself. Even in the most repressive situations, the song creates a space marked "Here we are." The summons enlarges and deepens the significance of the song. Emotions become collective and a phenomenon is created whereby the whole is greater than the sum of its parts.

5. A function of *denunciation* is essential to the Canto Nuevo movement, provided that the popular masses share interests, struggles, and aspirations. The different creative trends assume the task of denouncing the conditions created both nationally and internationally by the dominant system. From an aesthetic point of view, this is the most dangerous function in the development and existence of the movement. The singer-author walks the razor's edge between poetry and pamphlet at this point. No other fact is as clear to the popular creators: denunciation is not synonymous with coarse language and purile texts. "We mustn't be afraid of pamphlets," says Aly Primera, who mobilizes masses with his music. "He who sees pamphlets in life, will only sing pamphlets in song. But he who sees poetry in life and in the struggle for a better life, will create and sing poetry," declared Silvio Rodríguez in a Mexican interview. Quilapayún has evolved into different (superior?) levels of poetry and music as a result of its European exile; however, when Quilapayún was engaged to sing in Mendoza (an Argentinian city located very close to the Chilean border) at the end of 1983, some 5,000 Chileans in attendance demanded to hear the direct, contingent songs that characterize the history of this musical group and of Chile's political life.

6. A function of *confrontation* emerges in that, although the Canto Nuevo movement and its diversified expressions do not always signify a mass phenomenon (as is generally the case with alternative media expressions in the face of Latin American power situations), such forms of artistic manifestation evidently irritate, disturb, and provoke the hegemonic forces. The strength of the music is especially terrifying. The images it projects achieve greater coincidence with the struggles of the neglected popular masses and their mobilization than those of any other cultural form. This is why the movement is fought against and repressed and, inevitably, situated in a zone of confrontation and defiance. For mass-supported artists, then, the best weapon is an imaginative capacity. Gerardo Vandré, guitar in hand, was banished from Brazil in 1970 for his music; Mercedes Sosa was forbidden radio and TV appearances upon her return to Argentina in 1982 under the military regime. And there are many other examples because the so-called National Security Doctrine, in its unrelenting persecution of the "internal enemy," has always identified the Canto Nuevo movement and its artists with a highly dangerous reality. At the hour of repression, the life of a politician or notorious government official may be pardoned, but never that of a Víctor Jara.

The Canto Nuevo movement fulfills these functions through its social praxis, exemplifying truly democratic alternatives to the transnational capitalist system in force. The artist committed to popular causes needs social organizations to grow and to become a faithful representative, the proper upholder of cultural symbols, a mobilizing agent. Hence the relationship with festivals, labor unions, feminist and student organizations, churches, and a wide variety of institutions that make up the social network the artist strengthens with his or her verses and music. This is the general context to be considered in the following analysis where, in addition to establishing a chronology for the Latin American Nuevo Canción movement's formative process and its significance, an outline of the recording industry's behavior in relation to the movement is provided. Some of the new music's experiences in the construction of its own recording and dissemination networks are also discussed. By linking the movement's technological and artistic extensions, we will be able to better reflect its inquisitive and freedom-seeking nature.

Song and Conflict

Since the end of the sixties a wave of committed and innovative singers and songwriters has grown up in Latin America. Groups of young people and new singing voices have taken the road opened by pioneers like Violeta Parra and Atahualpa Yupanqui, in different circumstances and with different styles. The reality of the continent challenges and creates obligations. The imagination of the song composers was shaken by internal social conflicts; by the progressive and overflowing migration from country to city; by the youth, born at the end of the Second World War, who were searching for their own values; by the Church, which could not avoid committing itself more and more deeply to the necessities of the "people of God"; by the dramatic emergence of the guerrilla army, which left to history the witness and symbol of Che Guevara. All of this involves a generation that made songs into more than objects of transitory entertainment or massive trade.

In Chile, this process came together in the movement that took the name Nueva Canción Chilena. The movement's members broke with so-called neo-folksong, which misrepresents the conflicts in the countryside in descriptions of landscapes and of the aboriginal world viewed through the eyes of the landowners. The songs of Víctor Jara, Angel and Isabel Parra, Rolando Alarcón, Patricio Manns, along with those of groups such as Intillimani and Quilapayún, form part of the current Nueva Canción. They redeem forms and words to create a song that comes from the people and flows back to them. They interweave musical instruments, thereby fulfilling the dream of Latin American integration that neither political nor economic decisions achieve. The *charango* (a small string instrument from the altiplano) and the *cuatro* (a small four-string Mexican guitar) are united with the Andean *quena* (a sort of Indian flute), with the *bombo legüero;* maracas open a space for the *güiro* (a gourd used as an instrument in Cuba) and the claves. The guitars maintain their presence, but in a musical world that is more and more Latin American. This is a new kind of song and lyrics. It is because of this difference that the Nueva Canción Chilena was very influential in the rest of Latin America.

The Chilean song became a source of cultural influence which increased in strength during the three years of the Popular Unity government. At the same time, comparable movements were developing in other places, especially in the very expressive Cuban context, which saw the emer-

451

gence of a new kind of song called the Nueva Trova (*trova* has the same root as "troubador"). Its most famous proponents—Silvio Rodríguez, Pablo Milanés, and Noel Nicola—made their first tour outside Cuba in 1970, in Chile. Three years before, at the Festival of Varadero, it became evident that their music was breaking new and fertile ground. At the beginning, their music was not always understood or accepted in all sectors of Cuban society. However, its richness enabled it to survive, and it came to have a strong influence at the beginning of the 1980s as it was echoed in various parts of the world, especially among Latin American youth.

The period in which the Nueva Canción Chilena and the Nueva Trova were first becoming known was also an epoch in which people became conscious of the contradictions and conflicts inherent in their national situations and began to recognize them as features of a larger phenomenon: underdevelopment and economic and cultural dependency are pressing realities in all of Latin America. This continent has been one of the primary zones of expansion for capitalism in its transnational phase. The phenomenon cuts across the whole of society, affecting its political, social, economic, and cultural dimensions. It invades the process through which societies conceive of their development and define their history.

The sensibilities of the singers are highly responsive to this reality: "If we were Americans," sings Rolando Alarcón;[2] "Song for Latin American Unity" is the contribution of Pablo Milanés; the Uruguayan Daniel Viglietti creates "A Song to My America"; from repressed Brazil emerges Milton Nascimento with "American Heart"; while the Argentinian César Isella invites the American brother to sing, from all of his geographical diversity, in his "Song with Everyone."

This wave of creativity, uniting names of pioneers and new voices, has reshaped and renovated Latin American song. What Yupanqui began in Argentina was followed by the expressive force of Mercedes Sosa, Isella, and many more. In Uruguay, Viglietti is joined by the Olimareños and Alfredo Zitarrosa. In Peru, there is Nicomedes Santa Cruz rediscovering the people's roots, while Tania Libertad begins to follow her own path, as does Amparo Ochoa of Mexico. Soledad Bravo, in Venezuela, erupts with the purity of her voice, which brings the songs of her fellow Latin Americans to levels of extraordinary beauty. Meanwhile, in Cuba, Silvio and Pablo, along with Noel Nicola and Vicente Feliú go back to the hundred-year-old *trova* and bring it to a rebirth in the context of revolutionary history. In Brazil, Chico Buarque, Milton Nascimento, and Gerardo Vandré insist that creativity does not die, even amid the repression and authoritarianism that surrounds them.

All of them and others, too, in one way or another, sowed the seeds of a movement that became an expression of the struggle for social transformation taking place in diverse parts of the continent. For creating both a synthesis and a symbol, these people were persecuted and exiled when the popular movements for social change which nourished the songs were drowned or repressed. Now is the time of ruptures, of silence, and of exile. Yet such Latin American songs continue to live, especially in Europe, and continue the struggles of the 1970s. Its voices clamor for full democracy and for the right to return to sing with their people. This is the case of Mercedes Sosa, the Quilapayún, Viglietti, and the Parras, to name a few. New languages, new geographies, trips and planes, distances and emotions have defined a new chapter, a new sense of living through history, that such songs have to express in order to be themselves. Some doubt that the song of Latin American exile is the real expression of what it is to be Latin American now. Others think the emergence of new currents, what has been called in Chile the Canto Nuevo, characterizes a fertile time in which Latin American heterogeneity searches for convergence. Neither viewpoint is a definite synthesis: these are currents that interweave in a creative continuity, whose meeting creates a collective memory and a basic instinctive resource for the people's sensibility.

As the young Chilean essayist Alvaro Godoy has said, "The *Nueva Canción,* and now the *Canto Nuevo,* are two moments in one movement, with a present and a past, which we would call *popular song,* differentiating it from the *song of the people* which has always existed and which is, without a doubt, its root and its countenance."[3] This inward- and outward-looking song searches for the moment of relevance within different daily realities and a common national direction, creating more than once a dialogue of singer-composers. Some of them advance with the people in the effort to construct new democratic realities. They live in a time of open spaces, in which they can proclaim their commitments, their demands, and their convictions. Others have had to learn to live in semisilence, to use words calculatedly, and at the same time, paradoxically, to give poetry a greater force and suggestiveness. But some are victims of a greater phenomenon: exile, the freedom to sing only at a great distance from the people, as the only alternative to an inner creativity that is close to the self but must maintain a guarded voice amid repression. The cause is the same: the capitalist developmental model which, in its most acute expressions in Latin America, postulates the democracy of consumerism, individualism, atomization, and everything that tears the social fabric in which this song is nourished and defines itself. It is the same capitalism that, joined by the defenders of private interests, is moving against Nicaragua and El Salvador, obstructing a process that aims for the good of the great deprived majorities.

Such reality does not escape the new song. The contributions of Carlos Mejía Godoy and the Palacagüina, like that of the Banda Tepeuani, come from this perception. The former sang of the feats of the Sandinistas against the dictatorship of Somoza; the latter invoked the will to aid the struggle of the Salvadoran people. Song and action. Song, struggle, and poetry. As always. But today the centers of domination have the world communications media structure in their favor; they have philosophers like Milton Friedman to announce that it is the time of "freedom to choose" with money in hand; and they also have their industrially produced symbols, like John Travolta, who sing in their fiberglass environments, under alienating lights, to a youth that has surrendered to an uncommitted wandering in the city, understood as the place where personality dissolves.

Confrontation in the Record Industry

The development of popular song has suffered directly from transnational expansion. Indeed, transnational expansion is simultaneously a political, economic, and cultural phenomenon; thus radio, television, and the recording industry have been practically closed to the expression of commitment to structural change. Obviously, such an attitude is understandable. It is defined by the conflict of interests. And within the boundaries

453

of that confrontation—consciously or not—radio and television stations become instruments of a kind of "transnational culture" that encourages cultural synchronization and moves toward a model of domination of the
world.[4] Advertising, records, imported programs, transnational news agencies, all interweave to create a communications framework that subscribes
to order and coherence.

Within this coherence, popular song is dysfunctional, or else it
is only permitted a degree of presence which does not threaten the dominant
model: "Radio is an auditory medium of communication and its *forte* is
music. It depends, therefore, on recorded materials available to it. The
national recording companies publish almost exclusively foreign recordings
and there are even some companies which only sell imported material. On
the other hand, the public, as it only has that one range of possibilities,
obviously only asks for those songs that are already being delivered to it,"
says the radio/TV announcer Miguel Davagnino in a publication about
Canto Nuevo.[5] In one way, the Mexican Gabino Palomares was saying the
same thing in 1982 when he announced the release of his second album in
five years. He recognized that that was not much but called attention to the
difficulties big industry places before singers like him: "Our music is dismissed by transnational companies. This phenomenon is understandable,
as our themes are in direct conflict with their interests. Fortunately, there
are recording companies that, though small, allow us to record. Our work
recalls that which the minstrels did in their time. There is a lack of truthfulness in the communications media, and we fill the gap. It is arduous
work, above all because we do not have the materials necessary, but the
people's acceptance of our work is what leads us forward."[6]

Another element with a determining influence on the nondistri-
bution of national music, popular song, and folk music is the relationship
between the transnational capitalist recording companies and the disc jockeys and radio programmers. "Making records independently," says Chico
Mario de Souza, the promoter of a musicians' cooperative in Brazil, "we
discovered that the recording companies pay the radio stations to play their
records. Radio becomes a loudspeaker for the recording companies, by means
of bribery. Every month some programmers receive money to play certain
records. They're told: play this piece 20 times a day, this other one 10 times,
and so on. They play very little Brazilian music. Thus the radio stations
keep on playing and making surveys of popularity. They put the music on
the *telenovelas*—because there is bribery there too—and everyone begins to
buy the record, which gives a lot of money to the recording companies."[7]

The situation seems to be similar in the majority of Latin American countries. Mexico, the other giant music market, is a scene of the same
kind of corruption. But in this case the most eloquent testimony, from
someone who saw the murky business from the inside, comes from Jorge
Alvarez, former artistic director of the Capitol label:

> The big record companies have a budget, of course an
> overly high one, to run their public relations, their
> promotion campaigns. There are cases, for example,
> in which payola is not used, that is a check is not given
> so that a certain melody will be programmed by a
> station. But this is made up for by sending the broad-

454

caster on a trip to Europe, or giving him a new car, or sending him to Acapulco. . . . It has been known to happen that artistic directors ask fifty-thousand pesos (US $2000) per month from new small companies, in exchange for promoting their product on a given radio station. The big companies have specialized personnel, known in the radio world, who manage these things. . . . Or else, the record company sends a programmer to a concert in Los Angeles or New York, all expenses paid. In other cases, he or she is invited to Europe on a pleasure trip, on the company's account, of course. . . . Another way to promote records is the one CBS uses: it doesn't give a cent to the artistic directors, but from time to time it gives them a special promotion deal of records to give to the public; it may be a thousand, two thousand, three thousand, five thousand records by the strongest artists: Chicago, or Earth, Wind and Fire.[8]

When music is seen exclusively as a commercial product, and when radio becomes part of a whole system that makes culture an industry and the public a market, all this follows almost inevitably. But there is even more: misrepresentation of the public's taste. "It is said that radio programming is done according to telephone calls. . . . But this too is fixed. I don't know if all of the companies have them, but Capitol does: a few boys and girls contracted to call in by phone and inflate the ratings. Until 1976 when I left Capitol, I never agreed with the method, but it was instituted in 1975."[9]

Pressure, money, fixed programming. All that brings the local system in line with the interests of the big transnational consortia of the record business. If one looks at the heart of the system, the statistics are eloquent. Five companies share 80 percent of the North American market. Warner has 25 percent; CBS, 20 percent; Polydor, 15 percent; RCA, 12 percent; Capitol (EMI), 8 percent.[10] From there, the business expands into the rest of the world, and its growth affects not only small local brands, open to the diffusion of popular song or so-called committed song, but the whole national recording system in countries like Argentina, Venezuela, and Mexico.

The current open market policy has contributed to this pattern by directly affecting local subsidiaries and independent businesses. "Records imported from the United States and Europe, which are sold in the supermarkets, are hurting the national market in general; it is because of this that we music publishers have brought a protest to the corresponding authorities in order that they restrict imports," declared Enrique Márquez in November 1980. Márquez is a well-known Mexican music publisher whose ability to publish Mexican music was seriously affected by the great opening of the market permitted by the government when oil revenues increased.[11] In another oil-producing country, similar complaints were raised two months earlier: "A sharp blow has been received by the Venezuelan recording industry with the decree that permits the free importation of records from this month onwards (September 1980), as one of the hundred products approved by the Venezuelan government. Before, the only records that could be freely imported were of classical music; the new regulations establish that any individual or company can import records, paying only five percent of the value of the product. This is fatal for the national industry," stated a memorandum coming from Caracas, published by the Mexican press.[12]

These examples demonstrate the contradictions generated by the application in the peripheral countries of strategic policies of expanding transnational capitalism. At the same time, there is another factor that determines the conditions for the diffusion of music: the overflowing abundance of cassettes and radio-cassette recorders. A concrete example is given by these Chilean statistics: "The size of national production and its stagnation may be compared to the absolute quantity and the rate of growth of imports. In 1978, the sales figures (of records) of $4.5 million is somewhat higher than the $3.6 million worth of cassettes, both blank and prerecorded, sold during that year. The tendency observed in 1979—a growth of 55%—reveals that already in that year the national market for recordings is supplied principally from the exterior. The competition is mostly from amateur recordings. The $4 million in blank cassettes imported during 1979 indicate that there is a substitute for the consumption of recorded material by the simple home-made copy of that material."[13] In Chile, a country of 11 million inhabitants, it is estimated that there are between 14 and 15 million radio-cassette recorders. It is one of the tools of transnational electronic manufacture that has succeeded in penetrating even the sectors of the population with the least income.

Is this good or bad from the perspective of popular song? Ricardo García, radio announcer and record producer, is recognized as the initial driving force behind the Canto Nuevo in Chile, as he was earlier for the Nueva Canción Chilena. He sees the problem in two facets: industrial and social, from the perspective of the label Alerce, the company that has made available the new voices of Chilean popular song, as well as the creations of Víctor Jara, Violeta Parra, Silvio Rodríguez, and Pablo Milanés. Moreover, his case testifies to the possibility of action even in restricted spaces, when there is the will and tenacity to do so: "The world record market is in crisis, especially in Chile, where the masses' small power to consume is directed towards imported articles. To this problem is added the phenomenon of the radio-cassette, which allows private recording of music. The case of Alerce is more critical, as its public has, in general, scarce resources. However, the real public is much wider. Each Alerce record is heard by more or less large groups, which are particularly interested in folk music or Chilean music, and they re-record on a cassette, which is heard by still more people. This is good for the diffusion of the music, but bad for us."[14]

Alternatives, Force, and Poetry

This situation, in which a song must move in the spaces created by the culture industry as well as in its own spaces, has opened the possibility of alternative distribution channels for popular songs. The record labels that try to create independent distribution systems multiply: labels such as Pueblo, NCL (Nueva Canción Latinamericana), Fotón, Alerce. Behind them is the will to redeem those products of the electronics industry—the record and the cassette—in order to place them at the service of a cultural view of the world that inaugurates new times. Some do not make it, and some only barely do. But they open up vistas to explore that are different from those offered by the transnational capitalist model. An eloquent example was seen in Brazil, where the Musicians' Cooperative of Rio de Janeiro created a department for "alternative records." "The initiator of this was Antonio Adolfo," says Chico Mario de Souza. "He had made several successful recordings and had participated in festivals. But afterwards he began to feel mutilated, unable to produce what he liked. No one wanted to record his music. Then he did it on his own, and then he went out to sell his records from place to place all over Brazil. That way he sold more than 15,000 records and created the consciousness that it was possible to break the boycott of the multinationals. Others followed him: Danilo Caími, Luli and Lucinha. And the secrets of the work were passed to other composers: how to make the cover and credits, what studio to record in, how many records to print, where and how to sell. Thus the movement went on growing."[15]

Though the beginnings of the experiment were modest, they already constitute an important trend. Groups like Barca do Sol and Boca Livre have managed to sell more than 40,000 copies in five months. De Souza's own record, "Raizes," also sold well. For that reason, the press agency EFE reported from Rio de Janeiro, at the beginning of 1981, that

> the Brazilian record market for popular music had in 1980, as a great novelty, the explosion of *independent* producers and the "discovery" of regional markets. . . . "That's enough now" was the rebellious cry of the independent musicians, who triumphed justly. If the list of the *20 best long-playing records of 1980* is analyzed, it is apparent that not less than six were produced independently. . . . The success of the independents is not only due to their intrinsic value, but also to the discovery of the existence of an urban market that likes regional themes. . . . Some dedicated musicians like Dori Gaymmi embraced, or collaborated courageously with, this renovation of musical taste, which, in sum, wishes to escape from the dictates of international fashion in order to submerge itself in the rich sounds, rhythms, and melodies that are closest to the earth and to what is Brazilian.[16]

What can be the force inherent in a popular song that has a mass audience? On the one hand, the answer lies in the vitality and support granted to it by its links to social organizations. Even in very authoritarian situations, as in the Southern Cone, a relationship between song and the social fabric is established. Festivals of solidarity; meetings of students; meetings organized by churches, unions, and other workers' groups; festivals organized by cultural organizations—all create the framework in which popular song finds its ratification and orientation. On the other hand, the inherent force of popular song emerges from its call for commitment to the history of which it is a part and to the destiny of the great deprived majorities. "Today my song is in solidarity with El Salvador and the struggle of its people," said the Mexican Gabino Palomares on presenting his second LP. Eduardo Peralta, a twenty-one-year-old Chilean musician, commented

457

upon returning from Europe and meeting his friends of the Nueva Canción again that "I think about the liberty that clearly shows the inner human, that always transcends systems and schemes. In my songs I want to emphasize the creative potential of the human being." In Uruguay, while talking about the work of almost a hundred artists who perform in theaters and on the stages of sport facilities, the magazine *La Democracia* said in September 1982: "We cannot push aside this cultural manifestation of the historical moment in which we live. . . . Our people need to participate, to find paths, and to do so saying that it is the people who are searching. That is what has given our people the *Canto Popular:* this is the path of their search." Litto Nebbia, with his LP *Creer,* was premonitory when he said of Argentina in 1982: "I believe that in spite of so much melancholy, so much grief and so many wounds, it's only a question of trying to live."

Between 1982 and 1983 a new process began to affect the Latin American reality: *redemocratization.* In Brazil, great opposition figures made their comeback in the political scene by actively participating in state government elections. Leonel Brizola was elected governor of the state of Rio de Janeiro and Darcy Ribeiro was elected deputy governor. The latter is an anthropologist and former minister of education under the Goulart administration deposed in 1964 by the military. Within this context, the Canto Nuevo movement emerges to assume other commitments, standing closer now to the working classes and their struggle for full democracy and total respect for human rights. It is no longer a question of merely recovering the minimum right to say what one thinks, but of breaking off completely with the numerous injustices still in force in Brazil, the most heavily indebted of all third-world countries.

But the situation also calls for progress. The popular "New Song" artists, those in exile and those who strive for liberation in their own countries, have had a chance to meet at the festivals of Sao Paulo and Puerto Alegre. The Cubans Silvio Rodríguez and Pablo Milanés went on a grand tour through Bolivia, while in Chile their music has been gaining steady popularity through cassettes, magazines, and some democratic radio stations. Actually, 1983 marked the beginning of a new stage in the struggle of the Chilean people against the Pinochet dictatorship. The convergence of forces has changed: youth (who were five and ten years old during the coup of 1973) now play a major role and defy the system. No truly massive event could be held without the presence of the new popular song voices, such as Isabel Aldunate, Osvaldo Torres, and many other groups. They sing the irreverent songs of today, the music that demands democracy. And the forbidden songs of fellow artists still in exile are repeated with energy and daring.

Argentina's transformation has brought the forbidden music even closer to the Southern Cone: 1983 found this country exploding with homecomings. Quilapayún traveled a cross-country circuit and reached the outskirts of the Chilean cordillera, while Angel Parra and other important members of the Chilean Nueva Canción movment, still banned from their country, also prepared a grand Argentinian tour. Daniel Viglietti, established in Buenos Aires, is also getting closer to home: Uruguay. He was there in 1983, on the other side of the La Plata River. The Argentinians and many of Viglietti's countrymen, close by, are having the chance to learn of his current thinking: "I don't see myself as a pure musician, or guitar player, or poet.

Fernando Reyes Matta

I rather feel like a man who walks those paths, a human being who is trying to communicate with others, who is trying to receive and transmit some messages in a world organized to destroy them. Capitalism blocks them, manipulates them, changes their meaning. . . . There is a communication war going on, a war in which imperialism destroys news as efficiently as if it were using neutron bombs. Outside appearances are left to remain intact, but truth is being destroyed."[17]

Within this frame of thought and these new political instances—the struggles for recovery or achievement of democracy and a free destiny for Central America—a number of singers met in Varadero, Cuba, on November 27, 1982, at which time the Nueva Canción movement's International Permanent Committee was created. The press release defines this growing commitment and confirms the network constructed by the artists and their creations. Part of the declaration says:

> The artist must not only live and create according to his times; he has a chance to project himself toward the future and to support, through art and life, the continuous clamor for social change demanded by the peoples of all nations. The *Nueva Canción* movement stands side by side of all that which makes man free and guides him along the road toward a better future. It is art without class or country, and its message is that of hope and humanity's highest ideals. We, as participants of the First International *Nueva Canción* Forum, in Varadero, Cuba, celebrate the Tenth Anniversary of the Cuban *Nueva Trova* movement and declare ourselves in favor of nuclear disarmament and world peace, and in favor of the Cuban Revolution, that is building its future in spite of the yankee imperialist blockade and permanent aggressions . . . in favor of solidarity with the popular struggle for total liberation in Latin America and the Caribbean, Africa, Asia, including the industrially developed capitalist countries; against yankee influence in El Salvador and Guatemala and the threat of imperialist intervention in those countries that have decided to determine their own destiny. . . . [18]

The following artists signed on behalf of their respective countries: Brazil, Chico Buarque; Spain, Joan Manuel Serrat; Uruguay, Daniel Viglietti; Chile, Angel Parra; Nicaragua, Carlos Mejía Godoy; Angola, Sam Tocas; German Democratic Republic, Elle Viterhoff; Mexico, Oscar Chávez; Argentina, Armando Tejada Gomez; Cuba, Silvio Rodríguez; and the United States, Pete Seeger. This is the new network created by the "New Song" in Latin America, a message of solidarity and committed struggle that opens its way in the midst of the cultural industry, gaining acknowledgment, especially among youths. It offers hope for those who build the future.

Notes

1   Nueva Canción, Canto Nuevo, Nuevo Cancionero, and so on, are among the different names assumed by a similar process of artistic search and expression within the Latin American

459

struggle for liberation. Consequently, I use these terms (especially the first two) synonymously. Since Nueva Trova, Nueva Canción, and Canto Nuevo refer to specific national movements, they are left in the original Spanish. In any case, all the terms mentioned denote a new popular musical creation, linked to mass organizations and other grass-roots groups and with a problematic relation to the existing economic base. I have defined them collectively as the "new popular song movement."

2   In the context of the "New Song," the term "American" is understood as "Latin American," a projection of Bolivar's conception. It therefore opposes the term "North American," or the more colloquial or pejorative "gringo," commonly used to refer to U.S. citizens.

3   *La Bicicleta* (Santiago de Chile), Apr. 11, 1981.

4   Cees Hamelink, "The Cultural Synchronisation of the World," *WACC Journal*, 11 (1978).

5   *La Bicicleta.*

6   *El Día* (Mexico), Dec. 21, 1980.

7   *Cadernos do Terceiro Mundo* (Rio de Janeiro), June 24, 1980.

8   *Uno más Uno* (Mexico), June 29, 1980.

9   *Uno más Uno.*

10   M. Moskowitz et al., *Everybody's Business* (New York: Harper and Row, 1980).

11   *Excélsior* (Mexico), Nov. 9, 1980.

12   *Excélsior* (Mexico), Sept. 26, 1980.

13   *Poder económico y libertad de expresión*, Diego Portales C., Editorial Nueva Imágen/ILET, 1981, Mexico.

14   *La Bicicleta.*

15   *Cadernos do Terceiro Mundo.*

16   *El Heraldo* (Mexico), Jan. 4, 1980.

17   *Humor* (Buenos Aires), Nov. 1983.

18   *El Día* (Mexico), July 19, 1983.

Simon Frith
Art Ideology and Pop Practice

Historical events and discourses have raised questions
about the meaning of "the popular" and about the nature of "the pleasure" to which recent pop music responds. The practices of pop music produce their own
kinds of low theory, different criteria of political correctness, and different theories of how music can work politically. Current debates begin by accepting the commodity status of music and by defining revolt as style,
politics as gesture.

I want to begin by saying that coming to an American
university from 1983 Britain was a very surreal experience. With a cheer-
leaders' camp and a fraternity weekend in progress, I felt as if I had wandered
onto the set of a satirical film about 1950s American youth culture. In that
setting this conference became a necessary form of security: enter here for
all those comforting words—hegemony, ideology, discourse, and so on. I felt
not so much that we were in an ivory tower as a lighthouse, sending out
beams of theory in the hope that people would see the light, that by illuminating the rocks and eddies of cultural practice we could help them set
their courses more clearly.

In this paper I want, in some respects, to reverse this
process. I have to confess that I spend more time listening to records than
reading theoretical texts, and what interests me are the flashes of light that
come from the cultural marketplace itself. In other words, rather than using
cultural theory to illuminate cultural practice, I want to examine certain
cultural practices and suggest ways in which they can help us refine cultural
theory. This strategy has been forced on me, in part, by necessity. There is
still remarkably little cultural theory, Marxist or otherwise, that makes sense
of the pop and rock process. Adorno remains, after nearly fifty years, the
key referent (think, by contrast, of the development of film theory in the
same period). There are several reasons for the Marxist neglect of popular
music—the organization of the academy and academic disciplines, leftist
assumptions about "the popular" (to which I will return), and so on, but
the effect has been that what theories of pop there are have developed out
of the day-to-day practices of pop itself, out of people's need to bring some
sort of order and justification to the continuing processes of musical evaluation, choice, and commitment—whether such people are musicians, entrepreneurs, or fans.

The practice of pop involves, in short, the practice of
theorizing. Perhaps we should call the results *low theory*—confused, inconsistent, full of hyperbole and silence, but still theory, and theory that is
compelled by necessity to draw key terms and assumptions from high theory,

461

from the more systematic accounts of art, commerce, pleasure, and class that are available. It is this latter process that interests me here. What I want to suggest is that from the mid-1950s (the rock 'n' roll moment) to the end of the 1960s there developed a distinct rock sensibility that had, at its cutting edge, an account of itself that drew on the Marxist critique of mass culture. From the mid-1970s (the punk moment) to the present, by contrast, there has emerged a pop sensibility that has, at its cutting edge, an account of itself that draws on what I am going to call an avant-garde critique of mass culture.

I can best illustrate this rock/pop distinction by example. A recent issue of Dave Marsh's muckraking newsletter *Rock 'n' Roll Confidential* carried a story in praise of Molly Hatchett, the heavy rock band. According to Marsh, when several "radical" new wave/punk bands were asked to play a benefit for a steelworkers' union local in Pittsburgh, they all, for one reason or another, refused. Molly Hatchett agreed immediately and did everything to help make the concert successful—playing for free, contributing their own resources so that other bands could play too, raising a lot of money for the workers. The question this report raised concerned the relationship between Molly Hatchett's music—traditional macho rock—and their politics. A reader asked, Does a correct political act guarantee "good" rock music? Marsh's reply was straightforward: the political importance of rock 'n' roll lies in its articulation of working-class experience. Molly Hatchett had thus shown themselves to be authentic rock 'n' rollers; issues of sexism and racism must be resolved *within* rock 'n' roll conventions. By these criteria new wave, experimental bands are (as the Pittsburgh incident confirmed) elitist and bourgeois—"art" is a way of distancing music from the working class.

This is a useful summary of the politics of the rock sensibility: good music comes from the authentic expression of a (working-class) community's needs and values. In Britain, at about the same time, there took place the annual Glastonbury Festival. This is partly an attempt to preserve the 1960s hippy ethos (it is a drug-centered event, for instance), but it is also, nowadays, a commercial event—you pay to go in and the (considerable) profits go to the Campaign for Nuclear Disarmament. The hippy/CND link is a peace-and-love vibe, and the atmosphere of Glastonbury is usually nonpolitical—the only speech made from the platform this summer, for example, came when one progressive rock band, The Enid, denounced another, Marillion, for signing with EMI.

But then Fun Boy Three appeared. They were at that point a successful commerical pop act (i.e., they had Top Ten hits—they have since split up), both smart and political, but political in a way different from Molly Hatchett. Fun Boy Three's politics came from their management of disparate pop signs. The group—two black men and a white man—was a remnant of Britain's 2-Tone movement (in which punk met ska); their musicians, lined solidly behind them on stage, were all women. Terry Hall, the lead singer, sang entertaining songs without making any attempt to please his audience, to address them, at all. At Glastonbury the group performed a popped-up, contemptuous version of The Doors's "The End," an iconic song of the rock sensibility, and as the song ended Hall dispassionately set fire to the U.S. flag. The political meaning of this gesture (carefully calculated and repeated, to the producer's horror, on a live TV show a couple of days later) was ambiguous. A gesture against Reagan and American imperialism,

462

against Cruise missiles, certainly, but also, equally apparently, a gesture against American music, against rock culture, against the festival itself. Either way, the immediate effect was to jolt the audience's sense of what was happening. Should they cheer or boo? There was a moment of confused hostility; as in avant-garde precedents the audience had to react without knowing how.

The point I want to examine here is not whether Molly Hatchett or Fun Boy Three was, in 1983, more politically correct, but how different criteria of political correctness are produced by different popular sensibilities, by different (low) theories of how music *can* work politically. Rock arguments in the 1960s thus focused on the problem of commercial "co-option," the transformation of culture into commodity, and on rock's relation to certain sorts of organized political struggle, to protest. Rock was thought to be, under certain conditions, and despite the constant process of capital's recuperation, socially subversive. Or at least it could be, and was therefore an important site of struggle. Today, such arguments have lost their force (in Britain that is; in the United States they still have resonance, hence the continued importance of rock heroes like Bruce Springsteen and John Cougar Mellencamp—I will come back to possible reasons for the British/American difference later). As a site of struggle, rock has become too mushy to offer much of a foothold. Those British political rock bands that continue (singing their support of strikers, for example, like the Redskins) seem deliberately, proudly archaic—as if even "authentic" working-class politics is now a matter of style. To quote a British street pamphlet, *The End of Music*, distributed anonymously in Leeds in 1978 but particularly appropriate to this conference setting: "A subversion that was lived directly, active though confused, has been turned into its opposite—consumerism for a passive audience. No longer an incitement to the destruction of the university but an adjunct of the university as Saturday night entertainment, fitting in neatly with the present conformism of students."

This does not mean, however, that music is no longer a site of cultural dispute but, rather, that the terms of the dispute have shifted. Current pop debates start by accepting, celebrating even, music's commodity status, by defining revolt as style, politics as gesture (as with Fun Boy Three's flag burning). This discursive shift is one of the important effects of punk. Punk was the most theorized form of popular music ever, and this was, in part, because it could be used to stand for so many ideas at once. On the one hand, punk was a raw restatement of the rock argument—a challenge to the multinationals' control of mass music, an attempt to seize the technical and commercial means of music production, a rank-and-file youth expression of class solidarity. On the other hand, punk was an art movement, a deliberate attempt by bohemian demimonde of the fashion industry to make a spectacle, to manipulate the media, to con the kids, to make money—"cash from chaos!" in Malcolm McLaren's slogan. At issue in the subsequent squabbles about the meaning of punk were the concepts of authenticity and artifice. Was punk authentic proletarian expression or artificial style? This is, in an important sense, a false dichotomy (which I will come back to), but it marked the division within punk itself, a division subsequently expressed by the freezing of punk proletarianism into the nostalgic gestures of Oi and the emergence of the punk bohemians into the glittery new pop movement. Faced with this choice, British leftist interest in music, stirred

463

by punk, has waned. The role of pop in the era of mass youth unemployment has turned out to be, it seems, "escapism" (just as it was in the 1930s). Adorno lives.

I do not disagree with this conclusion as such, but what I want to examine is the concept of escapism (which is, I suppose, tied into what I mean by the pop sensibility). Escapism is, in cultural practice, not an easy activity, and the problems its poses are precisely the reason why pop debates now turn around the issues of style and artifice rather than class and capital, drawing their terms from avant-garde rather than Marxist models. I am using the term "avant-garde" very loosely here, with the justification that it is a term used loosely (but widely) by pop musicians and audiences themselves; but in general the suggestion is that, whereas rock musicians try to differentiate themselves from the mainstream of pop hackery in the language of authenticity, sincerity, and solidarity, pop musicians define themselves against the cultural mainstream in much more self-consciously formalist terms. Similarly, while the rock tradition depends on a sense of community—musicians speak for as well as to their fans—pop musicians have no desire to represent anyone but themselves, are more concerned with cult and coterie, with establishing difference.

In making such schematic constrasts between rock and pop I should make two points clear. First, I am concentrating here on how these sensibilities differ at their radical edge, but we must note that they also differ in terms of their recuperation. Pop is thus obviously vulnerable to direct commercialism—its criteria of success can be translated into numbers, sales figures, profits, and so on. For Britain's best-selling music magazine, *Smash Hits*, a key exponent of the pop sensibility, to be commercially successful *means* to be culturally significant, and vice versa. The commercial recuperation of rock works differently: the profit motive is concealed by sociology and best-selling records are legitimated in terms of their success at *representing* a mood, a social current, a generation, and so on (think of those 1960s quasi-academic rock books or the general stance of *Rolling Stone*). The recuperation of music in both cases means showing how it *confirms* the social order, but the terms of the confirmation, pop or rock, differ.

Second, the 1970s rock/pop shift was not just the result of some random play of stars and influences. Rock sensibility began to falter (marked by the "crisis" of punk) because of the collapse of the idea—which emerged in the 1950s and gave cultural shape to the 1960s—that "youth" is a community. Orthodox rock history has popular music stagnating until the transformative moment of rock 'n' roll (the central cliché in such history is "the rock revolution"). But we could equally interpret rock 'n' roll as a reactionary cul-de-sac, a futile attempt to deny the logic of mass cultural production in a new folk movement (and folk musicians and folk ideologies, particularly the celebration of "live" performance, were, it should be remembered, central to the development of rock in both Britain and the United States). The new folk was youth, and from this perspective punk was just one more tragic gesture against technological change and capitalist disruption. The fantasy that pop musicians could be some sort of organic intellectuals has been remarkably stubborn, and it was only when the material basis of the fantasy—youth as class—broke down in the 1970s recession that different ways of conceiving of pop politics began to be attractive.

To be a bit more specific, I would like to suggest that the radical version of the pop sensibility draws on three strands of avant-garde thought. The most obvious, but probably least significant, source is avant-garde art music—least significant because even when these musicians are interested in rock devices (electronic amplification, volume, repetition, etc.) they are not much interested in the problem of the rock audience. For example, I went to see the New York composer Glenn Branca conduct one of his symphonies in London. His music is made by a group of musicians playing notes within a minimal range of tones (but a wide range of electronic pitch) over and over again on amplified guitars and homemade electronic keyboards. The music gets louder and louder as the works progress, and the effect, after a while, is of being trapped in a room full of noisy, heavy, relentless machinery—one's ears, by necessity, have to make music, patterns, out of what is, in fact, a din. The performance I went to took place in an arts center before an audience of about thirty people, half, obviously regulars, wearing ear plugs. At the end we all applauded politely. The performance, in short, had no popular cultural significance at all, and I wished that Branca had been playing, instead, as support to Iron Maiden, the heavy metal band that was playing around the corner on the same night. The idea of head-bangers having to make sense of the sheer tedium of Branca's music (which is rather louder than Iron Maiden's as well) is more avant-garde simply because it would have involved the kind of audience challenge (and response) that is no longer possible in the art world itself.

The pop influence of the musical avant-garde has come less from its own particular experiments (New York minimalism, European free improvisation) than from its theoretical argument that people can be made to listen to music that does not confirm their expectations—either because forms are stripped down to their elements and then nothing happens or because (as in free improvisation) all rules as to what is music, what is musical, are suspended. Whatever else is going on, the aim is not to *please* the public. This paradoxical idea—musicians seeking to disrupt their form, to make unpopular music—has obvious resonance for postpunk performers, as does avant-garde formalism, the idea that as music is constructed so it can be deconstructed; taken-for-granted musical meanings are exposed by being placed in "inappropriate" contexts. But although this is certainly an argument developed in art music, its most important source in pop has been, in fact, the technological possibilities of recording and mixing first opened up by black musicians—the dub mixers and toasters of Jamaica, the rappers and scratch mixers of New York City. What they did was change the musical object, the ground of their creativity, from song and performance to the record itself. To make new music out of such finished productions means, quite literally, to deconstruct them. In reggae, anyway, if not in literary criticism, deconstruction is a material practice, one that, among other things, completes the breakdown of the distinction between musician and engineer, artist and technician, record player and record maker.

The most controversial result—Malcolm McLaren's *Duck Rock* LP—is also the most revealing for the argument here. What from a rock perspective was obviously a rip-off (McLaren mixed together African recordings, New York street and radio noise, studio tricks, and claimed the results as his own), was from his own pop art position a political gesture that exposed the national-cultural base of the sound standards we usually take for granted. He suggested, further, that to *conceive* musical meaning was as important an artistic activity as to make music. (And his record's commercial success did indeed help open a space in British charts and dance floors for New York and African sounds.) Think, too, of the way in which records are routinely issued now in a number of mixes (party mix, radio mix, club mix, London mix, seaside mix, etc.). On the one hand, this is an easy way to exploit the fans; on the other hand, it exposes the studio processes and calculations kept hidden when records are presented as "natural," "finished" goods.

This leads to the second set of avant-garde arguments, about the construction of the "authors" of music—the musicians, the performers, the stars. The arguments here partly reflect filtered-down structuralist descriptions of representation but have come into pop most significantly from art schools. The issues can be divided into two.

First, there is the realization that what is involved in pop is not simply music but music as articulated through a performer or, rather, through an image of a performer. Thus we cannot distinguish the meaning of Elvis Presley's music from the meaning of Elvis Presley; and if musical meaning is conventional, not natural, so is our sense of pop personality. We read qualities like sincerity, spontaneity, anger, sexuality, passion, and so on, into performers because of the way they organize the signs of their personality. From this perspective, the basis of performance is not spontaneity (which in ideological terms binds rock to nature) but calculation (which binds pop to culture).

Second, pop works not simply through any old combination of sound, image, and personality, but through their combination as a commercial package. Artistic interest in the making of meaning does not end when the music is made, the record released, the performance over, but is equally invested in the way in which it takes on its public meanings via the media of television, radio, advertisement, the star system, and so on. The new interest in this reflects another technological development—video, which blurs, finally, the distinction between making music and marketing a commodity. Pop groups are now expected to construct their music as its own advertisement, a video spot on MTV.

I want to make two points about these positions. First, they draw, in Britain, on a very long tradition of art school involvement with rock music, which has always placed a premium on style, on the aesthetic combination of sound and look. Presentation (clothes, hair, face, person) has, in this tradition, always been as important as musicianship, personality as careful a construction as everything else—emotions are displayed rather than expressed transparently. British rock stars have rarely been self-effacing, anonymous in the American hairy rock way (except during the "progressive" rock phase of the early 1970s when performers' "musicianship" was guaranteed by their *lack* of pop personality—e.g., Yes, Barclay James Harvest, Supertramp). There has always been a distinct strain of irony running through British pop, an obvious gap between the person and the personality, a detached tone of voice that binds Mick Jagger to Johnny Rotten, Bryan Ferry to Boy George (there is even an art school heavy metal band, Motorhead). These performers present themselves and stand aside; they revel in sexual ambiguity, playing games with the male/female, passive/active conventions that are involved in being sold as a star, in being both an object of desire, a pinup, and its initiator.

It is not enough, though, to explain British pop sensibility by empirical reference to its art school connections. The question is *why* art schools in Britain, unlike the United States, should give shape to popular cultural ambition. This is too wide a question to go into properly here, but it involves contrasting ideologies (and possibilities) of social and geographical mobility. Such ideologies shape mass cultural forms (and explain British youth's peculiar concern with fashion and style) simply because a central task of popular culture in capitalist societies is to handle the problem of individual success and failure. From pop music evidence it seems, then, that in the United States people's opportunities to change their circumstances—to *make* it—are taken for granted (however fallaciously), while in Britain they are not. Successful American musicians have nothing to justify or explain; their wealth and good fortune is not taken to make them any different than their fans (this is most obvious in country music). In Britain, by contrast, pop success is furtive, hedged with guilt, accusations of selling out, justifications of wealth in terms of hard work or good deeds. Rock stars thus justify their position in terms of Romantic ideology, by reference to their *difference* (with which their fans can collude) from "ordinary people"—this is the art school connection. They play down stardom's material consequences, mock their own popularity. It is noticeable that the urban groups in the United States that are least likely to "make it"—blacks and Latins—have the most fashion-conscious youth cultures and the most flamboyant pop personalities (from James Brown to Prince), and something similar to British pop irony can also be found in the proletarian stadium-rock tradition that runs from Alice Cooper through Kiss to Van Halen. But none of these stars has quite the contempt for the mass audience that is essential to the British pop stance. In the United States that only comes from self-consciously bohemian performers—Dylan, Frank Zappa, Jim Morrison, Lou Reed—who did not think of themselves as pop stars in the first place.

In Britain, then, the art school approach to pop has always had an obvious rock presence, but it is only now that it is becoming central to how music is discussed and made sense of. One sign of this is the emergence of David Bowie as a superstar; another is the increasing importance of designers and packagers—Factory Records, for example, became Britain's most successful postpunk independent label with designer Peter Saville as a key member of its staff. But the most direct evidence lies in how pop is now discussed—in magazines and press handouts, in reviews and interviews. Go into the Arts Council bookshop in London's Covent Garden and you can see the new generation of pop culture magazine: *Blitz, Face, ZG,* and *i-D* lie alongside *Art Monthly, Artline,* and *Art Forum* in the same haphazard confusion that they lie next to *No. 1, Smash Hits,* and *Flexipop* in most branches of W. H. Smith. Like the teen weeklies, these new magazines are consumer guides to rock and pop fashion. Like the art glossies, they assume a knowledge of art and design and media form—the terms of modernism, futurism, expressionism, and neoexpressionism are flung about in their attempts to define current styles in music.

These magazines are not, in themselves, radical or even loosely avant-garde, but they do suggest that the processes of pop construction can be analyzed and debated. And so the third strand of avant-garde ideas I want to mention is precisely concerned with politicizing that dispute. The inspiration here was, I suppose, situationism (the reference point of Factory's self-styled "politics," for example), which puts the emphasis on pop as spectacle, situation, event, as something that involves the construction of an audience (and thus returns us to the idea of shocking the public). The pop roots of this argument obviously lie in punk (the Sex Pistols drew directly on situationist theory), but the most significant political music has concerned pop as a sexual event.

Feminist musicians, in particular, have been concerned not simply with the question of rock's musical structure—Is it a patriarchal *form?*—but, more important, with the ways in which performances and events use conventions of masculinity and femininity, situate the audience in certain ways, and define subjectivity. The issue facing women in rock is that, while there have obviously been women's voices, there has also been, far more obviously, a female silence or, to put it more accurately, a female silencing. To speak thus means more than simply to pick up a guitar, to move close to the mike. The first time I saw a feminist rock band perform it took me some time to understand why the event felt so difficult (the women were, at first hearing, using orthodox enough rock musical forms). What I eventually realized was that this was also the first time I had been to a rock concert when I was not, as a man, the subject of the musicians' (male or female) address. The effect was not to be excluded from the event (just as women are not excluded from rock events) but to have no obvious place in it—in an immediate, emotional way I could not make sense of what was happening. And it is precisely this effect that bands concerned with sexual politics, like the Gang of Four and the Au Pairs, have tried to put into play: to confuse an audience and then to use that confusion as the basis for an active process of *making* sense out of conversation, hesitation, the movements in and out of private and public expression.

Again, the rock-despised, "artificial" 1970s genre of disco was important in this context for the questions it raised (in its very use of "formulas") about the pop construction, via dance, of the body. I am thinking not just of the erotic rules written into disco by its gay and non-Wasp connections but also of the importance of the "anonymous" dance floor as a place to pose. Disco offered an alternative to rock 'n' roll's traditional boy-meets-girl party conventions, and Britain's dance floor poseurs, Bowie boys and girls initially, became the New Romantics, a pop movement spawning such ambiguous and even asexual stars as Boy George and Marilyn. If dressing up was, like glam-rock before it, primarily a boys' affair, David Bowie himself was, nevertheless, an important inspiration for girls too (as interviews with both feminist musicians and fans reveal). What mattered was his simple assertion: "I'm different." Sexual politics is about questions, not answers, and Bowie suggested that the most "natural" of rock's meanings, its "raunchiness," was actually just another (and rather dreary) pose.

By this stage of the argument, I am sure that you are wondering about the relevance of such fringe, artistically and politically, self-conscious musicians and consumers to an understanding of how music works as *popular* culture. Before I go on I need to clarify two points in particular.

First, I am not suggesting that pop and rock, as mass cultural forms, have changed in any significant ways. The issues I am talking about, particularly those revolving around creativity and commodity, the artist and the marketplace, are issues deeply enmeshed in the history of capitalism—which accounts, for example, for the continuing importance for rock musicians (and the rock industry, too) of both romantic and modern ideologies. The contradictions of pop, in short, continue, and what I am referring to in describing a shift in sensibility is a shift in the terms people use to make sense of the contradictions and the ways they are positioned by them. To put it simply, the question remains the same—Is commercial success a sign of artistic and/or political failure?—but the terms of the answer change.

Second, I am not suggesting that the word "deconstruction" now trips lightly off record buyers' lips—I do not expect that the average fan of Culture Club, for example, would find this paper of any obvious relevance to their taste. What I am suggesting, rather, is that pop sensibility works as a grid placed over pop practice and pop experience, a framework, a common sense *within* which musicians, record buyers, record producers, disc jockeys, and so on, make sense of what they are doing, account for the choices and judgments they make. Thus, if within the rock discourse an abusive term like "selling out" has wide currency, even though most of its users never stop to think through the assumptions it rests on, so it is now possible to pick up *Smash Hits* and find people using the abusive terms "rockist" without specifying *how* they recognize rockist tendencies (faking sincerity, simulating "community") when they hear them.

I am sure I have been exaggerating the extent to which pop common sense has changed—in reality pop and rock discourses still swirl around together and are not as clearly distinguishable as my schematic approach suggests. Still, there have been changes. I want to end by suggesting a couple of reasons why the sort of pop sensibility I have described has appeared in Britain in conjunction with the rise of Thatcherism, and this goes back to the problem I started with, the meaning of "escapism." To summarize my position, I want to argue, first, that the development of populist discourse in politics, the spread of new sorts of appeal, from the Right to "the People," has raised questions about the meaning of "the popular"; and second, that the development of generalized youth unemployment, the reorganization of youth into a position of dependence, has raised questions about the meaning of "pleasure." The new pop is a response to both sets of questions.

Taking "the popular" first. In a recent paper, Tony Bennett has suggested that the problem of most leftist accounts of the popular is that they use a model of "the people" that refers to an ideal people in the past and/or an ideal people in the future but never real people now (which is why New Right populism has had such an impact—the Left has not been in a strong position to contest it). In terms of popular music, the effect of this has been a convention of analysis that values popular music either as agit-pop (it does things to the people, instructs them, inspires them, etc.) or as folk-pop (it expresses the people, emerges joyously from them). What has not been examined is how music works to construct the people. To put it another way, the description "popular" music is not simply a quantitative description (referring to a number of listeners). It describes, too, a cultural form, part of whose significance is, precisely, that it offers an account of the popular—pop charts, for example, do not just register record sales and airplay but work to give music a particular sort of public presence. Popular music is music that takes up certain spaces in popular memory, that establishes

469

shared codes of musical meaning (most obvious in their shorthand use in advertisements), that works, in other words, to make a particular sort of unity out of the listening public. Subgenres of popular music—rock, disco, reggae, and so on—are engaged in similar processes: they give cultural shape to "taste publics" and in doing so help define what those tastes mean—in terms of identity, commitment, value, and so on. You are what you listen to; you are not what you do not listen to.

There is a lot more to be said about these processes, and in particular, from a Marxist perspective, about their role in defining the petite bourgeoisie, whose identity, so often unstable and ambiguous in material terms, is particularly dependent on symbols of identity and difference. But the point I want to make here is that now, more than ever before, the political work of constructing "the people," and differences among "the people," is visible, as Thatcherism links "the people" to "the nation," reaffirms distinctions of male/female (in the family), black/white (in our "cultural heritage"), employed/unemployed (in the language of enterprise and progress), normal/abnormal (in a reaffirmed moral common sense). And so the idea of the people as "the audience" has become a more self-consciously significant aspect of popular music making, too. The artificiality of "the popular" is, in short, readily apparent, and popular culture reflects the consequent tensions—whether in an aggressively nostalgic reassertion of rock as working-class music, a denunciation of pop elitism, or in the restless new pop attempt to confuse the alliances and divisions on which Thatcherite populism depends, by blurring racial and sexual divisions (like Culture Club), and by making a mockery of the idea of "national" music.

It is thus significant that at the height of the Falklands crisis (when no pop record was, to my knowledge, issued in support of the war) the general move among young white pop musicians was to introduce all sorts of Latin and African elements into their records (and disc jockeys were being similarly eclectic in clubs and discos). Now this was, from one perspective, an echo of British colonialism, making money out of other people's music, but it also contradicted, in musical terms, the nationalist message that was being pumped relentlessly out of every other medium, whether in the crude terms of the tabloid press or in the measured tones with which the BBC absorbed the Task Force into the clichés of 1939-45 war reports. Pop eclecticism can, then, have a cultural effect. It did, that summer, counter the official messages about Latins over there and Britains over here, just as, in 1977, the Sex Pistols's "God Save the Queen" threw its own sort of pall over the official rejoicing at the Silver Jubilee.

As for the problem of pleasure, I have not got much to add to what I say in *Sound Effects*, but the point I want to stress is that just as work can no longer be taken for granted by youth culture, nor, consequently, can leisure, and this, in turn, calls into question the hedonistic routine on which rock and pop have always been based. Thus, though a record like Wham's "Wham Rap!" (a disco-based assertion of the right not to work, to have a good time *all* the time, "You've got soul on the dole!") was a big hit, it clearly worked as fantasy rather than as any sort of explicit political comment. The implications are clear—the fragility of traditional youthful pleasures is now apparent; people have to work at having fun. And the real significance of "Wham Rap!"—that of pop music generally—is that it remains a crucial, perhaps the crucial, source (for youth, at any rate) of unofficial articulations of doubt and need and desire. Pop gives people ways to speak themselves, to think themselves, that can counter (though they often confirm) official ways of saying things. One of the important tasks of populism is to control the ways in which the private becomes public (and vice versa); one of the important tasks of pop is to subvert that control. It is worth noting, in this context, the clear strand of New Right thought in both Britain and the United States which, in the name of high culture, denounces mass culture in general and pop music in particular.

Such attacks are made, as always, in defense of hierarchy and tradition, against ignorance, spurious equality, and so on, but they commonly are placed now within the New Right's celebration of common sense (which is taken to "see off" the "extremism" of trade unions or the "deviance" of feminists). Thus, the danger of current pop music lies less in its mindlessness or triviality (which concerned 1930s mass culture critics) than in its articulation—rock "subverts" common sense. Pop music has become an ideological issue again (the BBC banning records with the same bizarre logic of "offensiveness" as in the mid-1960s) because the problem of leisure and unemployment has arisen just as the leisure *industry* is being acclaimed as the solution to Britain's economic problems. The transformation of electronic goods into consumer goods, the development of cable TV, video recording, home computers, and so on, have put an economic premium on people's leisure tastes (and, in some respects, threatened state and oligopolistic manipulation of those tastes). Pop's leisure significance is thus being fought for again—hence Britain's newest youth subculture, the "casuals," whose aggressive, stylistic celebration of leisure goods and "life-style" conceals both continuing dole queues and continuing "hooliganism"—the street-corner menace now comes from such nice, clean-cut, Tory-looking boys and girls!

The casuals are a suitable symbol of pop politics—elusive, ambiguous, momentary in their cultural effects; signs, in Dick Hebdige's words, of "logic escaping." The problem raised at this conference in the discussion that followed Iain Chambers's paper and mine was how this relates to conventional socialist politics—organized, rational, strategic. Most of the questions revealed a general concern with the *authority* of pop culture and pop criticism. What right had I, as a male/white/bourgeois/academic to interpret the experience of women/blacks/workers/youth? The answer, which I was too nervous to give at the time, is none. Pop meaning is not revealed by experts—whether constituted by good theory or "authentic" experience. Nearly every questioner approached rock and pop in moral terms, as if "good" music gets through despite "bad" people (the industry, superstars, men), as if we can still speak of a "real" popular culture (the culture of the Third World, the oppressed) being "falsified" by capitalist incorporation.

Such an idea of "truth" seems to me an unhelpful starting point. The important question is not whether one piece of music is more authentic than another—Malcolm McLaren versus Afrika Bambaataa, the Thompson Twins versus Holly Near—but why authenticity is an issue in popular culture, why some sorts of *inauthenticity* are more suggestive than others. Pop musicians are not organic intellectuals; they have no authority that matters. It is, rather, their *lack* of authority that enables their effects to happen at the point of consumption. There is an obvious difference (obvious to anyone who has taken pleasure from pop) between meanings grasped "from underneath" and meanings imposed "from on top." However easily we can describe their packaging, their hard sell, it is undeniable that the cultural impact of Elvis Presley or the Beatles, Bob Marley or Michael Jackson, the Sex Pistols or Patti Smith, was not written into their music in advance. The recognitions and resonances they caused in their audiences were unknown until they occurred. Pop music is not revolutionary (or even liberating) as such. It matters because it is an important way in which people, young people in particular, accommodate themselves to capitalism, accommodate themselves, that is, to the contradictions of capitalism. To study pop music is to study a way in which common sense (including our own common sense) is shaped; to discover places, moments, where that common sense breaks down, cannot deal with needs and desires via straightforward consumerism, sets up alternative fantasies and demands.

Pop politics are momentary, operating only in the present (and then as a series of remembered, nostalgic moments). This again confounds the temporal orderliness of socialist politics, the idea of progress and development. From the latter point of view, the so-called ambiguity of pop signs means only an endless process of incorporation. The point, though, is that this (undeniable) process tells us nothing about the "authenticity" of what is incorporated. Pop movements have their effect, their moment, and are then spent, consumed. To give a recent American example: New York's hip-hop scene of graffitists, rappers, scratch dee-jays, and break dancers was a form of self-help that was transformed, almost immediately, from communal activism to Horatio Alger success story. But the latter reading does not invalidate the former, it just reflects a shifting context. The power of the hip-hop community remains an aspect of even its "incorporated" version.

The pleasure of popular cultural forms—whether pop songs, soap operas, or news stories—comes from their play on feelings of recognition and difference, familiarity and novelty, change and stability. The point I want to make finally (and here I differ from Iain Chambers) is that capital's disruption of people's lives is something to resist as well as celebrate. While Thatcherism, for example, is obviously reactionary—*back* to the family, the nation, Victorian enterprise, and so on—it is experienced as radical, as *threatening* taken-for-granted rights—to a job, an education, a hospital bed, an effective trade union. Socialist opposition means looking back as well as forward (and the difficulty for the British Left is precisely how to get the balance right); and keeping a grasp on history is as much a task for popular culture (and for its subversion of official common sense) as is seizing the present. The paradox of pop music, in other words, is that in its endless pursuit of novelty it provides us with moments of delight, partnership, and confidence that are, literally, *recorded*. What most struck me about the conference discussion was the (irrational?) commitment to particular songs, styles, and sounds that was revealed by people's orderly, rational, anxious questions.

Coda 1984: Money Changes Everything

I went to Gothenburg for a meeting of the International Association for the Study of Popular Music. As we waited to take off, Bob Dylan's "Mr. Tambourine Man" (instrumental version) was piped throughout the airplane. Most people at the meeting had been involved, one way or another, in "alternative" popular musics—music for socialism, rock in opposition, independent labels, free radio. I listened to talks on gender and timbre, revolutionary songs in Nicaragua, music while you work, the history of the tango, the new leisure technologies. Everything was connected. During a free afternoon I walked around Gothenburg looking for a record shop. I located the music section in a large department store; it had a rack of "folk music" arranged alphabetically by country. Under "England" I found an LP by Leon Rosselson, the socialist songwriter, and one by Steeleye Span. I bought Victor Jara's *Canto Libre* (on a West German label), Luis Kalaff's *El Rey del Merengue* (Dominican dance music on a French record label), and Black Stalin's *In an Earlier Time* (Trinidadian protest on a New York record label).

One evening we gathered to watch the Eurovision Song Contest; a Stockholm paper was to call for our expert vote and commentary. Some people (like me) were deeply implicated in the aesthetics of Euro-pop; to others, the competition made no musical sense at all. We argued. On screen the Swedish song (performed by a boys-only group, Bucks Fizz) won; it had been performed first, so we had, embarrassingly, missed it. The argument got heated. Should we be involved in the daft commercial process at all? We told the newspaper nothing and agreed that it was good that Sweden won—next year the Swedes could (as in 1975, after Abba) hold an oppositional event.

I returned to England to find a news release from the Labour party: a 2,500-pound prize for a BETTER song for Europe! "A song that reflects the true hopes and concerns of young people in Britain," Eric Heffer said. "We'll be particularly interested in songs about the main themes in the European election campaign—peace, jobs and the waste of resources and human lives in Europe at present." In the *Coventry News* there were details of a forthcoming CND week. On Tuesday, at Barras Green Social Club, Leon Rosselson and Roy Bailey appeared, described in the paper as "well known in disarmament folk circles." On TV the Flying Pickets were being humorous with a pop song, their jokey approach (endemic in left-wing cabaret) conveying an odd mixture of disdain and embarrassment at dealing with pop at all. On the news, National Union of Miners pickets sang new versions of football songs and Neil Kinnock could be seen in Tracy Ullman's video for "My Guy's Mad at Me."

In *New Socialist,* the magazine of the Labour party, Leon Rosselson writes about "the silence at the heart of the labor movement," but his piece is really a description of the "silence" at the heart of popular culture itself. Even the most spontaneous political song must draw on people's musical memories and practices (think of the recurring importance of religious music to protest song), and Rosselson's point is that Britain (or maybe just England?) has no flourishing song culture from and into which political movements can feed. Most people these days sing together only in school assemblies or in well-demarcated rituals—the bus trip, closing time, the terraces (now, apparently, the primary source of picket line and demo songs). Rosselson notes the suggestion that this is "because the mass media and the market place have annexed song, divided people into performers and consumers, turned the song idiom into a package to be purchased for leisure consumption."

All of this serves to rerun the folk/mass/pop culture debate which, despite everything, haunted the Illinois conference on Marxism. To state the obvious again: Not silence but cacophony is at the heart of popular culture; our lives are filled with the sounds of (canned) music—while we work and rest, shop and play. The trouble with the folk argument is that it cannot avoid a tone of heroic regret. I am haunted by the chilling irony of one of Rosselson's images, "women and children in Soweto singing as they were being shot down by the police, singing as they defied the bullets. The power of song."

The power of song. The power of pop. The question is how the latter, which is now our central source of music, can relate to the labor (or any other) movement. Rosselson writes of songs: "They are a way—the most emotionally intense way—of sharing, of feeling less alone and more alive, of making connections between the personal life and the public world. They give hope and heart and at least the glimmer of a vision of a different sort of society. They can help us find our own voices and thus give us back a belief in our own creativity."

A fine description of why pop matters, too—even if it has its effects very differently than in the collective, cooperative, live music-making process Rosselson celebrates. Pop is capitalist culture, not just as a commodity form, but because it is used to make sense of the experience of capitalism (which means something more than the experience of class/age/race/gender). The politics of pop revolves precisely around inauthenticity: pop is about our construction as consumers (of goods, fantasies, imageries); it moves us pleasurably around the marketplace, measures desires in simple cash terms, gives passing shape to the fragmentation of our senses, puts together, on the dance floor, the meaning of the body. Pop is ephemeral and inconsequential, organizes time into an overwhelming *presence*—with the past as nostalgia, the future as daydream. Its manic eclecticism is a perfect expression of the sticky cultural fingers of multinational capital (so that Chilean, English, and Trinidadian political songs reach a Swedish public via American, German, and French record companies on the shelves of a plush bourgeois department store).

Not instructive, not expressive, simply there. How can pop ever be "radical"? It is important not to answer this question by reference to models of nonpop political music. For Rosselson the model is the spontaneous song making of the Wobblies; in Sweden the model was the European alternative rock scene; in Illinois the model was the 1960s movement underpinned by romanticized British youth subcultures. Pop certainly cannot be radical according to these ideals; its politics work differently: *within* the pop process. Pop intentions (the reasons why music is made) matter less than pop effects—segments of Malcolm X's "No Sell Out" careening around the dance floor, people singing along with Special AKA's "Free Nelson Mandela," puzzling out what Elvis Costello is saying in "Peace in Our Time," recognizing the emotional tension of Womack and Womack's "Love Wars." It is easy to dismiss the significance of such bitty, trivial interventions in packaged pleasure, to ridicule, say, Cyndi Lauper's claim to account for female fun, but even at this moment of video-pop, recorded music remains, of all mass media, the most open to the sounds at the bottom of the social heap, the only one in Britain, for example, in which CND support is taken to be the norm, not the exception.

474

Simon Frith

The question remains: How do individual moments of pop consumption relate to socialism, to labor and liberation "movements"? The answer lies in the ways in which pop works to create "the popular," to form communities of style and taste. Remember that pop rarely deals with a "mass" audience as such but, rather, sets up patterns of inclusion and exclusion; and despite the tenacious leftist-folk belief, the possibilities of musical community are not cut off by technological development, by capitalist competition. Black musicians, for example, have gleefully used studio technology, radio, records themselves as tools in a continuous social commentary. The question, then, is how the identities put into play by pop relate to the identities addressed by other media. There are an increasing number of people—advertisers, politicians, knowledge peddlers, designers, clothes makers, disc jockeys, television commentators—telling us who we are; pop feeds into a melee. Its "radical" significance can only be judged by its place—at specific historical moments—in this melee.

Pop offers identities less through shared experience than through shared symbols, a common sense of style. Pop history reveals that radical pop (radical symbolism) makes better sense of some sorts of collectivity than others. The most clear-cut political music, for example, has been rooted in nationalist struggle (as in much black music), in the politics of leisure (as with youth cults or gay disco), or in a combination of the two (as in certain kinds of feminist music). Class consciousness—this is the problem for Marxists—has, by contrast, on the whole not been amenable to pop treatment—pop celebrations of "working classness" have *not* created audiences along politically conscious lines (think of country music or mainstream American "blue-collar rock"). But then the irrelevance of pop to "the labor movement" may reflect the irrelevance of the labor movement (and traditional socialism?) to the ways in which people (including socialists) now define themselves *outside* work. The political meaning of the Labour party's New Song for Europe (which had still not appeared in 1984) will depend not on the ideological correctness of its lyrics but on *how* it is popular. In this debate, that old *Juke Box Jury* question is still the most relevant: Will it be a hit?

Michael Ryan

The Politics of Film: Discourse, Psychoanalysis, Ideology

Social rupture and radical change are not future events. They are permanent possibilities inscribed in the very structure of an inegalitarian society, possibilities confirmed by the sort of ideological operations at work in popular film.

From the mid-1970s through the mid-1980s, Marxist theorizing about film and culture was guided by the work of such path-breaking British theorists as Stephen Heath and Stuart Hall. Heath, working out of an amalgamated paradigm based in the work of French thinkers Roland Barthes, Louis Althusser, Jacques Lacan, Julia Kristeva, and Christian Metz, argued for a theory of "subject positioning" in film. Hall, combining the indigenous cultural studies strain of Richard Hoggart, Raymond Williams, and E. P. Thompson with the Marxist structuralism of Althusser and Pierre Bourdieu, and Antonio Gramsci's recently translated theory of hegemony, argued that culture was a site of domination and resistance. While representatives of these two theories frequently clashed, the two approaches nevertheless shared certain qualities. For example, each in its own way generated pessimistic political conclusions, and neither conceptualized the development of popular-based political strategies. Heath's theory disallowed a politically enabling reading of popular film, while Hall's allegiance to Gramsci's essentially Leninist theory of domination precluded seeing the level of the popular as anything other than a region of resistance to a domination that was given priority, both conceptually and politically. I will be concerned here primarily with film theory, choosing to address the issue of cultural theory elsewhere,[1] although, as I shall argue, the critique of film theory necessarily entails a reconsideration of the concepts of ideology and hegemony operative in cultural studies.

All theories are specific to their society and their time. The recent British theories emerge out of a specific intersection in British intellectual history of a French-influenced, postanalytic philosophical renaissance in literary, social, and philosophical thought, with a resurgent, predominantly Trotskyist-Leninist movement in the 1970s and 1980s. Althusser's notion of ideology and Gramsci's notion of hegemony permitted economism to be superseded in the name of cultural determination, while allowing the retention of the Leninist model of social hierarchy and domination from above. Top-down models of politics have been prevalent on the Left for historical reasons: the undereducation of the masses made management by intellectual elites the only feasible way to carry out reform or revolution. But bottom-up models have also existed—from the Paris Communards to the anarchists, the Wobblies, the Spartacists, and most recently the Italian Autonomists. Although these alternative political forms were always squelched by their opponents, that did not mean their alternative was not valid. In the very real material sense of levels of socialization, education, and cultural development, the world was not ready for them.

British film and cultural theory is aligned with a top down political model that may be appropriate to a society in which the privileging of the popular base is not as strong as in the United States. But, I would argue, the peculiarities of U.S. cultural life, where anti-intellectualism and the critique of social hierarchy are so prevalent that the disfranchised are not likely either to flock to the local cinema to see the latest Straub/Huillet-Oshima double bill or to embrace a new "hegemonic bloc," make necessary slightly different theories of film and culture that would give rise to political models or strategies more suitable to the U.S. context. A first step in that direction would be the replacement of the Leninist or elitist top-down orientation of British theory with an orientation that takes as its point of departure the energies, needs, and desires operative at the popular level and that conceives of those energies as the productive force that generates society. This different conceptual frame necessarily prescribes a more bottom-up political strategy, one that would see the popular base as the primary term in any possible political equation, not as either a mere site of (generally failed) "resistance" or a lower realm of "misrecognition."

Discourse

The study of the relationship between film and society has been split in recent years between the formalist approach (represented by Heath and others) and the sociological approach (represented by Wright, Biskind, *Jump Cut,* and others). But in the light of deconstructive analysis, the formalist/sociological opposition is untenable. The theory of discourse in film formalism must ultimately be a theory of society; and no sociology of film is feasible that is not concerned with discursive and cultural forms.

Film is fundamentally social because it draws on and reproduces social discourses and because it is itself a socially discursive act. Cinematic discourse is inherently social, for even the most formal dimension of film presupposes social codes of perception that allow it to be received and decoded by audiences. Moreover, the external object or referent that film sociology posits for fictional film is always a construct of the semiotic or rhetorical operations of film discourse. Social conventions allow that referent to appear to assume objective or "real" status. The literal referents in film are actors and sets. It is the audience's imagination, schooled in the viewing of fiction, that creates the illusion.[2] In addition, the references to history and society that films generate or presuppose are themselves mediated by other social discourses; at no point do even the most sociological references of film leave the formal dimension of signifying systems and "touch ground." The social ground is itself interwoven with discourses (class, race, sex, ethnicity, nationality, work, personal narrative, etc.). Outside of film representations are other sets of representations, from which the materiality of social life is inseparable. Therefore, formal analysis is inherently social because it is the analysis of representational and perceptual conventions that are collectively held, and sociological analysis is necessarily formal because film enunciates meaning through discursive operations that cannot be deemed secondary to a supposedly pre- or extradiscursive social reality; that reality is itself constituted and mediated by discourses.

I use "discourse" in this broad way to subsume social and cultural systems and activities for a strategic reason. I wish to emphasize that film and the culture and society in which it is produced are not two separate spheres. Film is a subset of social processes (or social discourses). And the strategies of valorization and representation in film are not "fiction" in relationship to a "real" world that is in no way structured by the same sorts of strategies of valorization and representation that one finds in film. The narratives and stories in film are also at work in everyday life, as the stories people tell themselves to make sense of their lives, as the narratives people live out when they perform certain actions (romance), and as the scenarios that script events so that they follow relatively predictable patterns (war, revolution).[3] As social beings, humans inhabit systems of significance; their lives are structured by codes of valorization (aggressive/nonagressive, dominant/nondominant, etc.) that determine the range of their social action. Thus, the concept of discourse allows a deconstruction of the opposition between culture (as a realm of signifying practices) and society (as a realm of experience or life that is supposedly prediscursive, a sort of nature or objectivity that is not shaped by representational codes or mediated by signifying practices).

Films are discourses in part because they are made up of elements (characters, actions, settings, and so on) that already have meanings and values (are encoded) within the existing social systems of significance, the prevailing social discourses or systems of encoded relations whereby each social element takes on meaning by virtue of occupying a certain position in the social system or of being in differential relation to other elements in the system (male/female, rich/poor, white/nonwhite, as well as such things as character types—executive/radical, capitalist/worker, and so on). As each element in language takes on value differentially or relationally, that is, by being marked or not by certain values (inflected/noninflected, etc.), so each social element takes on value through its *difference* from other elements. Each element is encoded by possessing or not possessing certain traits. Films incorporate these elements, recodify them, and give them meanings and values specific to the codes of the film, but the raw material out of which the new values and images are constructed is always already codified by social codes of meaning. For example, the mafia don in *The Godfather* is a negatively valorized figure in the U.S. social code of crime who is revalorized as a heroic figure in the discourse of the film. In other words, the don is a figure who has meaning or who occupies a valorized position in the arrangement of things in U.S. society. His position is encoded in overdetermined ways; that is, it is constituted by certain codes of thought and behavior that prescribe certain articulations of those codes in determinable actions. In addition, his life is made up of a threading together of a number of social discourses (ethnicity, criminality, patriarchy, etc.) that fit into larger chains of social discourses that make up U.S. society at this point in history. Most films rely on such precodified elements, which are incorporated, recodified, and made part of the specifically cinematic discourse of film.

In order to describe the material circuits that connect film discourse to social discourses, I have recourse to the concept of *transcoding*. Film discourse transcodes social discourses. I use the metaphor of "material circuits" to name the real, concrete linkages that conduct ideas, issues, meanings, as well as fears, tensions, and desires, from society into film. The metaphor allows one to circumvent the metaphysical doctrine of representation whereby the referent or object is posited as external to the system of signifiers. The notion of a material circuit implies that there is no exteriority of the referent, no objective ground to the film signifier. Rather, the two are part of one system, or a multiplicity of interconnected systems that relay social ideas and feelings from the extracinematic culture to film and back into the culture, where they circulate further. At no point is the relation between film and society nonmaterial, but it may be incorporeal or unconscious.

Whether or not one uses the concept of "discourse" to describe the film/society relation is ultimately irrelevant. What matters is that the relation be conceived in a way that emphasizes the social character of even the most seemingly formal or aesthetic elements of popular film; that the social world be conceived as a system of valorizations or meanings that are sites of struggle ("contests of representation") between groups for social power; that representation and strategies of representation be seen as essential, rather than secondary, to those valorizations and struggles; and that cinematic representations be linked to those struggles as acts of valorization that privilege one side or the other, one set of values or interests over another. Contemporary film theory that uses the concept of discourse emphasizes the aspect of address by which a film positions its audience to perceive the world in a certain way. The model of discourse is linguistic; the film and the perceiving subject are conceived on the linguistic model of intersubjective communication; and the theory emphasizes the conscious, spontaneous, phenomenal realm of film viewing. By broadening this use of discourse to mean a system of significance, both cognitive and behavioral, that includes cultural forms, social actions, and psychological structures, I wish to emphasize the unconscious, material, nonphenomenal, systematic, and collective character of the film/society intersection.

The "meaning" of popular film, its political and ideological significance, does not reside in the screen-to-subject phenomenology of viewing alone. That dimension is merely one moment in a circuit, one effect of larger chains of determination. Film representations are one subset of wider systems of social representation (images, narratives, beliefs, etc.) that determine how people live and that are closely bound up with the systems of social valorization or differentiation along class, race, and sex lines. Audiences are not univocally "positioned" by films; rather, they either accept or reject cinematic representations of the world, but they do so in accordance with the social codes they inhabit. The specifically cinematic discourse, whereby a film addresses an audience, is determined by broader social discourses, the systems of significance and valorization that determine social subjects as male or female, working class or ruling class, and so on. Thus, I would argue that the psychoanalysis of film cannot be realized fully until it also becomes a sociology of social discourses that permits a more differentiated and situational understanding of how specific films address different audiences and generate different meaning effects in varied contexts.

Psychoanalysis

The broadening of the concept of discourse permits a formulation of the psychoanalytic relation between film and audience that is more social,

480

more oriented toward the interrelation between patterns of conscious, individual identification and unconscious, systematic, and nonphenomenal structures that are transindividual or collective. If films are transcodings of social discourses, and if audiences are not passive receivers but active readers whose reception of film texts is determined in part by social codes in which they live, then both films and audiences are likely to change and be influenced by social transformations. In other words, films do not do one thing at all times to a unidimensional audience, and audiences react in different ways to different film representations depending on the condition of the symbolic codes in which they live, codes that are based in social structures and that change with changes in those structures. Film, film viewing, and film meaning, therefore, are irreducibly historical and social. Film is also, for this reason, irreducibly political, not a positioning of the subject, but a struggle to enlist subjective identification for or against certain values or ideas that are essential to the maintenance or usurpation of social power.

In transcoding social discourses, films offer for identification and internalization either old values or new valorizations (either, say, the independent woman as witch or as admirable and emulatable model); film discourse can help recode the existing social discourses or systems of significance (as, indeed, many films, as a result of transcodings from feminism, recode the prevailing valorization of the independent woman). For example, although the ground of cinematic enunciation must be congruent with the frame of reception, many films seem to enlist audience identification in order, then, to introduce figures or stories or dramatic enactments that shift the frame of reception in some way. Frequently, it is the film forms "closest to home" (melodrama, say) that allow for the greatest leverage in this regard. It is their very formal conservatism that seduces audiences into situations of address that offer new values or shifts in old ones. For this reason, classical genres are frequently characterized by significant shifts in value and ideology (the positing of native Americans in the western, for example, from enemy to object of sympathy [from *Stagecoach* to *Cheyenne Autumn*] or the depiction of independent feminine sexuality in melodrama from anathema to flexible option [from *Peyton Place* to *The Turning Point*]). Thus, film representations enlist audience identification or sympathy with different sides in social debates and social struggles. And the movement of those social struggles in part determines what sorts of representations will appear on screens. Changes in society affect both what sorts of representations appear and how audiences will relate to them.

The emphasis in current film theory on individual perception as subject positioning can be shifted to include collective thought and behavior through this conceptualization of film as an articulation of the broader systems of significance or discourses that make up a society and as an object of collective identification that can help recode prevailing social valorizations. In order to fully describe this process, I will have recourse to what in psychoanalysis is called "object relations theory."[4]

Object relations theory holds that a person's sense of self or identity is constituted through identifications with social objects, images of which are internalized. Such objects can be figures, such as parents, or social values, norms, and institutions, such as the nation, the family, the class, or the ethnic group. Internalization of objects works on even the most "primal" or instinctual levels of the id; consequently, there is nothing in the psyche that is not *social*. All levels of the psyche, including the supposedly presocial realm of instinct, are shaped through relations with social objects. Object relations theory differs from the traditional Freudian libido theory, which understands all social action as manifestations of internal drives or instincts that dominate behavior and must be repressed upon entry into society through the Oedipal passageway. Psychoanalytic film theory, based in the work of the neo-Freudian analyst Jacques Lacan, thus sees sexuality and the problem of sexual difference (essentially, the Oedipal problem) as the focus of film analysis. The theory is concerned with the individual viewer's perceptions or with the positioning of individual subjects rather than with collective social processes, and it privileges as radical those filmmakers who seek to disrupt normal perceptual codes. Popular film is a symptom of regress because it pacifies rather than disturbs, nurtures a narcissistic misapprehension of the real nature of things rather than provokes the audience to question and critique the film's putative status as a realistic representation. Realism is illusory or imaginary because it occludes the difference between film signifiers and their signifieds. Lacanian film theory tends to be pessimistic in regard to the problem of social change on the popular level because instinctual drives, in the traditional Freudian/Lacanian account, are relatively unchanging. All one can hope to do is to rearrange an ineluctable misapprehension through radically discontinuous cinematic strategies of representation.[5]

Object relations theory is different in that it emphasizes collective behavior over individual perception, social institutions and relations over libidinal or exclusively sexual problems, the movement of social change over the stasis of instinct, and the possibility of a politics based in popular desires and needs over a politics based in a counterpopular form of radical film work. An account of the film-society relationship that takes its cue from object relations theory would suggest that in order for a society to remain integral, film images or representations and the symbolic codes that inform them must replicate the objects with which people identify in that society. In other words, film representations must be like the social objects whose images are internalized in the socialization process and who give people a sense of personal and collective identity. All personal identity is therefore social or collective, and people will share certain personality patterns because they share objects of identification: "There are . . . aspects of personality . . . that are shared, and the symbolic codes on which the sharing is based have a controlling influence over the individual in society. In these terms we can understand how a class of individuals experiences, within a believable latitude, similar erotic and aggressive feelings or inhibitions, or how similar frustrations, fears, and anxieties can arise in a group of people faced with the same social conditions."[6] Film representations embody values, portray institutions and norms, and project idealized figures that elicit identifications from audiences that cohere with already socialized or internalized patterns of identification.

Films also can come to represent collectively felt "frustrations, fears, and anxieties." Individual and group anxiety arises when there is a disruption in the symbolic codes or structures of identification that provide meaning and a sense of identity. Such disruption can be produced by crises in the economic, political, or social spheres, since the structures of identification are stitched into those spheres. At times of social crisis or radical change, the images that people identify with (and pay to see) will also change. Social crises upset habitual symbolic codes and patterns of identification, producing a sense of loss, frustration, and anxiety. As a result, people will either regress to more secure objects (authoritarian leaders) or attempt to construct new social situations, symbolic codes, and objects of identification. Film plays a role in this process by providing either regressive or progressive objects of identification, by reasserting old symbolic codes of meaning or by forging new ones, and by depicting either a world in which an unambiguous and secure conservative ideology permits a reconstitution of older patterns of collective identity or one in which more liberal or radical attempts to formulate new values, institutions, and norms are privileged.

Films can thus help create a new social discourse by offering representations of new values, institutions, and modes of behavior for collective identification and internalized modeling. Film discourse and social discourse intertwine as a struggle not only over how reality will be represented but over what that reality will be. Films play a role in the social construction of reality in that they influence collectively held representations or ideas of what society is and should be. They help shape beliefs regarding how people should act, what values should be privileged, what institutions like the family should look like, and so on. Such beliefs are essential to the continued existence of social norms, behavior, and institutions. The patriarchal family would not continue to exist if people did not believe it should exist in that form. Psychological participation is thus required if public values and institutions are to be maintained or changed. And social psychology operates through representations that are collectively held. In this way, reality (the public domain of institutions as well as the beliefs and values people hold regarding what is true or good) is socially constructed. How people perceive the world and what values and institutions of that world they subscribe to are in part determined by representations of that world, which they internalize through the socialization and educational process, one that is reinforced and continued through popular films. That socialization process is also challenged by the representations of alternative values in some films. As a result, popular film is a terrain of contesting representations that articulate a struggle between regressive and alternative models of social institutions and values.

Ideology

The deconstruction of the formalism/sociology opposition through the notion of discourse and the posing of an object-relations-based psychoanalytic alternative to the Lacanian model suggest that the politics of film need not be limited to the creation of avant-garde artifacts. It is possible to imagine a political use of popular film forms that would work to recode the prevailing social discourses. But the existing theory of ideology in film theory legislates against such a possibility. That theory suggests that ideology is a general trait of all popular fictional films, all of which uniformly produce an imaginary misapprehension of real conditions in the audience. Ideology in this sense is an undifferentiated exercise in domination.

The general theory of ideology as domination in British film and cultural studies is nondynamic and nonrelational. The only possible action it allows the oppressed is one of response ("resistance") to a power ("domination," "hegemony") that is conceived as prior, self-sustaining, and unmediated. Fittingly, the only alternative to power, in the cultural theory that derives from this theory of ideology, is another "hegemonic bloc," a replacement of power by power in a top-down approach. There is a necessary relationship between the concept of ideology (furthered by Leninists—Althusser and Gramsci) and the top-down politics of hegemonic blocs or of elite film work that derive from it. The formulation of an alternative bottom-up politics requires a reconceptualization of the notion of ideology.

Rather than conceive of ideology as an exercise in domination that breeds resistance, it might be more accurate to describe ideology as being itself a response to "resistance," as the resistance power groups direct at a force and a potential for revolt that is mistakenly relegated to a secondary or responsive status when it is called "resistance." There can be no ideological domination where there is no "resistance" or where there is no structural threat to the existing order. Ideology in this sense is forced closure, the imposition of harmony on the ever-open possibility of conflict, but the necessity of that force and that imposition itself testifies to something ideology hopes to deny, that is, the primordiality of difference, the structural possibility of a disordering of ideological order that precedes and determines order. Ideology, as the suturing of difference or the representation of unity where there is conflict, is a symptom of an attempt to reduce differences of force that are a necessary structural part of an inegalitarian society to a spurious identity of interests or common desire. Ideology would not be necessary if a potential for resistance or an irreducible and threatening difference did not exist, as a structural possibility of the social system.

For example, the positioning of women in film can be thoroughly ideological, that is, an exercise in domination through representation. But such exercises are always responses to resistances, differences, and desires in society, which, if they were not deflected, channeled, and bound, would result in a radical reconstruction of the order that secures power for dominant racial, sexual, and economic groups. Therefore, ideological films can serve as good barometers of the progressive or radical potentials in a society. They act as registers of the potentially radical energies and forces in a society by reacting against them (deflecting, channeling, and binding).

For example, the representation of women in *Kramer vs. Kramer* is ideological and political because it positions women as objects of eros and power on the part of men and as mirrors for women that reinforce their subjugation through an identification with helplessness and weakness. This exercise in ideological domination is a response to a structural tension or difference of power and position between men and women. It is an exercise in domination, but such an exercise would not be necessary if the subjugated did not threaten (in a structural and permanent way) to break the imposed cohesion and harmony of the system. Women have had to be taught to submit because they would not have done so naturally. The very necessity of "education" of this sort, the promotion of ideology through film, is itself an indication of the unnaturalness of what is taught as being natural. The exercise in domination is also, more specifically, a response to a resistance on the part of women, increasingly since the late 1960s, to the power of men. Such a negative response to the women's movement would not be necessary if that movement were not succeeding in making it possible for women to live and be in ways other than the ones depicted in *Kramer vs.*

Kramer, ways that undermine male power and therefore elicit negative responses.

Films, in consequence, require a double reading. On the one hand, they disclose the contours of ideology, the way desire and fear are channeled to assure the hegemony of white-male-dominated capitalism. On the other hand, they also provide a record of popular energies emerging out of structural differences in society which threaten to disturb hegemony and therefore must be channeled in ways that neutralize them and integrate them to the existing power structure of undifferentiated unity. Hegemonic channeling does not create the energies and differences it manages and administers; rather, it responds to a structural potential for revolt and potentially radical desires. But those differences and energies are not a secondary resistance to a more primordial domination, for it is those energies that build the very social structure that the ruling race, sex, and class control for their own benefit. Hegemony is merely a box encasing social energies that create and maintain the social world, and those energies constitute a real power that hegemonic groups must manage, administer, and control if their rule is not to cease. Hegemony is therefore structurally unstable, a blanket thrown over a tiger rather than a windowless prison.

Social rupture and radical change, in other words, are not future events; they are permanent possibilities inscribed in the very structure of an inegalitarian society, a possibility that is confirmed by the necessity of the sort of ideological operations at work in popular film. To say that film is ideological, therefore, is not simply to say, negatively, that it reinforces the power of the powers that be; it is to say, positively, that there are forces and structural differences in white patriarchal capitalist society that make ideology necessary. Ideology is not domination; it is, rather, the resistance of resistance.

This reformulation of the theory of ideology applies to British cultural theory in general, but it is also meant to address a need specific to the U.S. context for theoretical formulations that tie in with the bottom-up politics that seem the only feasible alternative in U.S. society. The reformulation also applies more specifically to the question of film practice, which includes both the use of film to gain politically enabling knowledge and the use of filmmaking to change minds. It suggests that people interested in carrying out political work through film in the U.S. context might concentrate on popular fictional forms as well as on alternative or avant-garde forms of filmmaking, the value and relevance of which should not be downplayed. And it implies that popular films can be used to read or diagnose the state of mind of those large sectors of society to which popular films appeal. The insights gained from such diagnosis can in turn be used to formulate political programs or policies that would have a popular appeal. Granted, the prevailing subenculturation and undereducation of the popular base in the United States prevents a simple privileging of the popular in ahistorical terms. But the reality of the failure of the U.S. Left to overcome its marginal status, despite its increasing intellectual sophistication, and to attain a popular appeal also makes such a strategy imperative.[7]

Notes

1   See Michael Ryan, *Political Criticism* (forthcoming from MacMillan).

2   See Michael Ryan, "Militant Documentary: *Mai 68 par lui-meme*," *Cinetracts*, 24:3-4 (Fall 1979), pp. 1-21.

3   See Richard Johnson, "What Is Cultural Studies Anyway?" (Mimeograph, Occasional Paper #74, Centre for Contemporary Cultural Studies, Birmingham); and Lisa Gornick, "Turning the Tables: Women Analysts with Men Patients," Ph.D. dissertation, Department of Psychology, Yale University.

4   For a general overview of the theory, see H. Guntrip, *Psychoanalytic Theory, Therapy, and the Self* (New York: Basic Books, 1971).

5   The critique of realism is, of course, carried out in the name of a higher realism or truth— revealing the workings of the cinematic apparatus, destroying the illusion. Like socialist realism, which also criticized fantasy and debunked the personal realm in favor of public duty, the new antisocial realism is critical of the imaginary or self-oriented domain of social life. The problem with raising a formal tactic (displaying the apparatus) to a political principle is that it neutralizes substance or content as a criterion of politics (since content depends on the acceptance of the realist illusion). Some conservative or liberal films—*The Asphalt Jungle* or *Knock On Any Door*, for example—could thus be termed radical because they conclude with a figure of authority addressing the camera and breaking the narrative illusion. Ultimately, of course, content resolves into form, and vice versa. The critique of realism is not that it is bad form but that is has bad political content (ideology). And social content also collapses into a matter of form, for the struggle for social power ultimately comes down to a struggle over the *way* society will be organized, the *form* it will take.

6   G. Platte and F. Weinstein, *Psychoanalytic Sociology* (Baltimore: Johns Hopkins University Press, 1973), p. 23.

7   For a further elaboration of these ideas, see the conclusion to Douglas Kellner and Michael Ryan, *Camera Politica: The Politics and Ideology of Contemporary Hollywood Film* (forthcoming).

**Jack L. Amariglio, Stephen A. Resnick, and
Richard D. Wolff**

Class, Power, and Culture

The concept of overdetermination demands that we reject any essentialist definitions of culture. Thus we cannot explain culture as the result of a single, determining
social process. Indeed, we cannot base our notion of
culture on a single, discursively privileged concept. Art,
music, literature, and history are the result of both economic and political forces, including class processes and
the ordering of social behavior.

Marxist theory is, as always, developing unevenly.
While advances have been made in staking out distinct Marxist positions
in history and epistemology,[1] there does not exist at present a generally
accepted Marxist social theory. Indeed, we do not yet agree about the constitution of those objects that might function as the distinct objects of a
unified Marxist social theoretical discourse. The field of Marxist social theory is made up of numerous concrete "fragments" that can only tenuously
be said to reside in the same theoretical space. Yet we must be wary of
attempts to produce a "grand synthesis" by privileging either certain favored
objects of Marxist discourse or essentialist schemata that reduce the elements of social analysis to the effects of a single element. For us, the fragmentation of Marxist social theory must be viewed as the concrete determination of interacting discursive and nondiscursive processes.

In this paper we want to begin to theorize the speci-
ficity of cultural processes (which we loosely define as processes of the production and circulation of meaning) and their conditions of existence by
focusing on the relation between cultural processes and class. We reject both
the theoretical essentialism that would derive culture from a single determining social process within the social formation and the essentialism that
would derive the *concept* of culture from a single discursively privileged
concept.[2] Hence, we do not aim to treat culture as the necessary effect of a
base-superstructure model that presents cultural processes as the epiphe-
nomena of a social essence. Nor do we advocate the "logical deduction" of
concrete cultural processes from a general concept of social totality.

Overdetermination and the Specificity of Cultural Processes

The question of the specificity of cultural processes
cannot be determined within Marxist discourse independent of the question
of the specific conditions of existence of these processes. Our focus is on
one of these conditions: the concrete class processes that exist alongside the
cultural, political, and natural processes in social formations at a moment
in time. However, the question of specifying cultural processes is not a
secondary question to be resolved by referring it to a *primary* question, that

487

of specifying class processes. In opposition to all such attempts to treat the conceptualization of cultural processes as *complete* or *sufficient* once it is referred to as a *prior* conceptualization of class, we take the following methodological stance: class functions in the social totality, neither as the determinant "in the last instance" of the processes that make up a concrete social formation, nor as the central *concept* of Marxist theory from which all other concepts are derived or to which they must always defer. Instead, following Althusser and Marx,[3] we affirm the overdetermination of *all* social processes, including all concepts (not excepting overdetermination) used to construct these processes in discourse.

The notion of overdetermination means viewing concepts, processes, events, agents, and so on, in terms of their conditions of existence and the effects of their interaction. This concept specifies that every social process is a unique site constituted by the interaction of all other social processes in a social formation. No process can be reduced to the effects of a single process or partial subset of processes. Each uniquely determined social process participates in the overdetermination of all other social processes. An overdetermined social process is not a transparency from which each of the constituent social processes can be simply identified and "read." That is, a social process *does not express* or *represent* any or all of its constituent aspects; rather, it is the product of a *complex process of transformation,* where the determinations emanating from each social process are acted upon and altered as they interact. Overdetermination is a concept that stresses a "decentering" of discourse and history in its rejection of all forms of essentialism.[4]

The logic of overdetermination presents us with a seemingly unsolvable dilemma. If there are no essences or ultimate determinants in Marxist theory, then what is the role of class in that theory? For us, the concept of class serves as an initial position or thesis, the guiding thread from and with which a particularly Marxist knowledge is constructed. Like all concepts, it too is overdetermined and thus its meaning changes as its political, economic, and cultural conditions change. To borrow from Hegel, this initially posed concept or thesis of class is empty. Stripped of its many determinations, it is the abstract idea of class. Its complex meaning is constructed (i.e., it exists) by virtue of its discursive conditions of existence. The ceaseless and mutual interaction between the concepts of class and nonclass processes is precisely how Marxist discourse develops.

One implication of the concept of overdetermination is that cultural processes cannot be completely autonomous or self-reproducing at the level of the social formation. They do not contain their own conditions of existence as their essences. Likewise, the *concept* of cultural processes is not self-contained or self-referential. Cultural processes have no center that manifests itself through the autonomous reproduction of these processes or that stamps every one of the dispersed processes presently termed "cultural" with the mark of the same determination. Cultural processes always emerge and are reproduced in certain locations with specific conditions of existence. As the conditions of existence vary from location to location, cultural processes are dispersed and differentiated. The specific forms in which art, music, literature, and history exist are the combined result of forms of economic processes (including the class processes) and forms of political processes (including the ordering of social behavior). Similarly, the *concept* of culture is equally conditioned, and it emerges as a specific discursive field only by virtue of its overdetermination by concepts of other social processes and by nondiscursive processes. This last point holds as well against the current Marxist reductionism that asserts the primacy of nonclass or non-economic processes (such as signifying or political processes or processes of power) in the determination of social and historical events.[5]

Yet there are a number of theorists who have attacked economic determinism only to replace it with new essences.[6] This tendency is clearly demonstrated in many readings of Michel Foucault's works, in which power relations are seen as the primary or *dominant* constituent of discursive formations, where discursive formations are understood as the predominant constituent of modern cultural processes.

Two similar tendencies have recently emerged from other quarters. The first is crystallized in the American anthropologist Marshall Sahlins's text *Culture and Practical Reason*. Sahlins opposes the Marxist concept of "praxis" as the primary explanation of human culture. Instead, he seeks to find the symbolic or meaningful in all social processes and to enshrine the symbolic "as giving each mode of life the properties that characterize it,"[7] that is, its meaningfulness. Sahlins's symbolic determinism assumes that diverse social processes are essentially marked by the site of their birth in the realm of symbols. Thus Sahlins seeks to demonstrate that exchange is not merely determined by the symbolic but is, at its core, a symbolic event.

A second tendency is the reduction of social relations to "politics," where politics is understood as the interplay of domination and subordination.[8] Such "strategies" assume either that the signifying practices of the cultural sphere *essentially* produce subjects who participate in relations of domination/subordination or that these practices are themselves necessarily inscribed within and bear the imprint of such relations. Similarly, economic relations, including class relations, are seen essentially as relations of exploitation, defined and understood as relations between dominant and dominated.[9]

One of the more subtle examples of this tendency is found in the writings of Barry Hindess and Paul Hirst.[10] They define class relations on the basis of the correspondence between "the separation from/possession of the means of production" and the mode of appropriating surplus labor. Their inclusion of the separation/possession couplet in the definition guarantees that class signifies an underlying "political" relationship, because the couplet is exclusively theorized in terms of rights of exclusion and the forms of domination that derive from these rights. Thus Hindess and Hirst join other Marxists, such as P.-P. Rey[11] and N. Poulantzas,[12] in referring the concept of class to the "deeper" reality of power or exploitation. For these Marxists, class "differentiation" and oppression are *only one form* of the exploitation, oppression, and domination that undergird all social relations. While Foucault is sometimes cited as an authority for this view, we do not agree with this reading of his notions of the relations and exercise of power.

The methodological principle of overdetermination instructs us to refuse each of these tendencies while acknowledging their *partial* truth. Such tendencies always *strictly* deduce the concrete from the general, allowing the concrete to display the sign of its origin. For us, on the other hand, the concrete must be treated as *surface;* there is no "absent" deeper reality manipulating the surface. *Differences* in the constitution of cultural, political, and economic processes cannot be understood unless we specify the relations every distinct process has with its conditions of existence, the other processes that *partly* constitute it. We can now turn to an exploration of the overdetermination of class processes by cultural processes, and vice versa.

Class Processes, Class Positions, and Class Identity

Class processes are the specific social processes that involve the performance/appropriation and distribution of surplus labor.[13] The definition does not designate any *particular* form of performance/appropriation or distribution. Although class processes are partly conditioned by processes of power and culture, no specific form of these processes can be deduced from the general concept of class processes. Similarly, the participation of agents in determinate class processes involves rules of objectification, modes of exclusion, the designation of limits, the stipulation of functions, and so on, on the one hand, and modes of subjectification that allow agents to be inserted into these processes, on the other. However, processes of power and culture do not function as the *primary* constituents of class processes. Rather, the intersection of concrete relations of power, signifying practices, discursive formations, and so on, overdetermines specific class processes of the extraction and distribution of surplus labor.

We differentiate between fundamental class processes (the performance/extraction of surplus labor) and subsumed class processes (the process within which already appropriated surplus labor is distributed to agents).[14] There are different kinds of fundamental class processes (e.g., communal, feudal, capitalist, slave),[15] since there are distinct forms in which surplus labor may be performed/appropriated in a social formation. In addition, each of these fundamental class processes has its subsumed class process. While any concrete social formation may involve different fundamental and subsumed class processes, there is usually one socially prevalent mode of the fundamental class process.[16]

This prevalence does not necessarily entail the economic, political, or cultural domination of the agents who participate in this process in the social formation as a whole. First, it is possible that agents may participate in a prevalent fundamental class process or in any other of the fundamental class processes on both "sides" of the process (as performers *and* extractors of surplus labor). Second, agents may participate in several different fundamental class processes simultaneously (e.g., feudal lords can appropriate rent from peasants and surplus value from agricultural wage laborers; kulak farmers may pay feudal rent to an overlord while they extract surplus labor from wage laborers hired to work their lands; wage earners may produce surplus value for their employers even while they extract corvée labor from their spouses in the household). Third, agents may simultaneously occupy fundamental *and* subsumed class positions (e.g., industrial capitalists can also be financiers or presidents of universities; factory workers can also be owners of the means of production and managers of the production process on the shop floor). Additionally, in some cases (notably, modern corporate capitalism), the direction and control of any fundamental class process may not be in the hands of the agents of that process but may reside instead with occupants of particular subsumed class positions.[17] And finally, the social prevalence of any class process never means that the agents who participate in that process (or the process itself) *essentially* determine the position and status of agents in every other social process. In sum, it is only possible to designate specific class processes at a given historical moment.

One important consequence of this position is that the notion of class is not reducible to the agents who participate in class processes. The notion of class is not a "noun" designating groups of agents who appropriate or distribute surplus labor. Thus, we cannot specify eternal, unambiguously defined groups of agents as *the* ruling or ruled classes. For example, the "working class" and the "capitalist class" of a capitalist social formation are not comprised of permanent residents of singular class positions who represent some permanent class status in and through their every gesture. Class position does not refer to always already constituted class agents. Rather, agents participate and are located in class processes in contradictory ways; they may hold numerous class positions, requiring different and perhaps clashing subjective identities. Similarly, class struggles refer, then, to struggles *over* fundamental and subsumed class processes by agents who occupy different class and nonclass positions; they do not refer to "classes of individuals" struggling. Nor are they either the cause or the result of agents' recognition of their true, essentially determined class positions.[18]

Alliances are frequently formed among agents in different class positions in the course of struggles to reproduce or transform an existing conjuncture of class and nonclass processes.[19] These alliances may change in the course of these struggles, thereby changing the direction and possible outcomes of such struggles. In our view, what comprises a working or capitalist class depends upon the particular alliances that arise at a given moment in the struggle to reproduce or transform the capitalist fundamental and subsumed class processes: only such struggles are *class* struggles. Struggles over nonclass social processes are irreducibly different from class struggles, although they determine class processes and struggles, and vice versa.

The class *identity* of agents is established by the intersection of class and other social processes, most notably cultural processes. It is a multifaceted social constitution that is not reducible to the "experience" of agents in class process. Class identity is the "understanding" agents have of themselves that enables them to participate in *class* processes and, therefore, to occupy particular *class* positions. This "understanding" is differentiated from other forms of "self-knowledge" that enable agents to participate in nonclass processes, although there may be considerable overlap between particular class and nonclass identities.

Class identity is one form of the "subjectification" of social agents. We define processes of subjectification as a subset of cultural processes that constitute agents as *self*-defined and *self*-conscious in relation to "others." They permit the inscription and participation of these "selves" in social processes and subjugate them to the demands, restrictions, rules, and obligations[20] that are enunciated in the processes. Agents are "subjectified" in ways that make it possible for them to occupy numerous, contradictory class positions. The reproduction or transformation of determinate class processes partly depends upon the capacity of class "subjects" to either carry out or subvert the procedures and strategies that comprise the processes. This capacity is not guaranteed by or secured within class processes themselves, nor is it attributable to a reflexive "ideology" that merely mirrors the "objective" class positions. The cultural processes that "subjectify" agents do not uniformly stamp agents with the capacity for *either* subjection or insubordination. They help to produce, in the same set of agents, varying capacities to be subjected and "revolutionized" within different class processes or even within the same class process.

Culture and Ideology

The processes that fundamentally determine the subjectivity of agents in particular class positions are most often labeled "ideological." There is an extensive Marxist literature that deals with the problems of using the concept of ideology to designate particular cultural processes.[21] One frequently mentioned problem is that the concept of ideology is often constructed in relation to a base-superstructure dichotomy. In such a dichotomy, cultural processes are *not* "material" or, if material, are not constituent of the base; instead, they function chiefly to reflect or express a primary material (often economic) reality. Culture is reduced to its function as ideology, and ideology—the realm of "ideas"—always refers to a reality outside of itself. Moreover, ideology reflects that reality in either a "true" or, more often, a mystificatory way. Culture, as ideology, becomes the field of mystified discourse, "falsely" reflecting, even "inverting," the "real" base.

The reduction of culture to its ideological function has two *discursive* functions: first, it establishes a hierarchy of social processes; second, it distinguishes between ideology and science, where science is a true appropriation of the "primary reality" to which it and ideology both refer. When agents misperceive their "real" relations to each other and to their individual experiences, they are under the sway of ideology, which becomes synonymous with "false consciousness." They are inserted into material relations that are objectively harmful to a majority of these agents. In the cultural realm, only science, understood as "revolutionary theoretical practice," is ever completely liberating, although ideology may be historically necessary to achieve partial, strategic gains in actual struggle. The field of culture is limited to the unstable interplay of science and ideology.

Foucault: Discourse, Power, and the Processes of Subjectification

Foucault and Althusser provide two convergent lines of criticism of this view of the relationship between culture and ideology.[22] Foucault, in *The Archaeology of Knowledge,* argues that the relation between ideology and science does function in the constitution of discursive formations but only on a very different basis.[23] Discursive formations are differentiated according to their "regularities"—their rules of object construction, enunciation, formalization, and so on. Such discursive formations are concrete discursive realities whose functioning as either scientific or nonscientific knowledges can never be referred to a silent presence beneath the network of concrete rules and interacting effects that comprise their material existence. The division between science and ideology is not a measure of varying degrees of success in producing truth as opposed to mystification.

For Foucault, science is merely one form of discursive practice. It is never coextensive with what he calls knowledge. The question of the *ideological functioning* of science or any other discursive formation involves the way in which any discourse modifies, articulates, and validates the field of knowledge.[24] For Foucault, to label a discursive formation as nonscientific is to designate a *particular* network of concrete rules of formation that are only partially differentiated from the network of rules that constitute a science. Actual discursive formations are never purely scientific nor "ideological" since there is no center of a discursive formation that guarantees a uniform set of effects or imposes a uniform set of constitutive rules.[25]

Foucault investigates discursive formations for their effects in producing knowledge and power, which are intrinsically interconnected: discursive formations are knowledges that function to permit the operation of power. In some of his formulations, Foucault goes so far as to suggest that the field of discourse is *primarily* constituted by relations of power, while the *primary* effect of knowledge is the exercise of these relations.[26] Discourse is a field of strategies and tactics that creates differentiations placing limits on what can be stated and by whom, and so on.

Discourse also constructs particular modes of objectification (knowledges) through which agents are produced as *subjects* and inscribed within a network of "localized" power relations. For Foucault, the subjectification of agents since the Enlightenment, the historical moment of the emergence of the "subject," is the effect of the emergence of knowledge. Knowledge is the field in which subjects are made the object of discourse, and thus are made ready for the operation of power.[27] For example, Foucault argues that the basis for "disciplines" such as clinical medicine, psychoanalysis, criminology, and political economy is the subject's body as object of knowledge. Thus based, these disciplines permit various nondiscursive interventions into and inflictions on the body, such as imprisonment, surveillance, therapy, enumeration, and "accumulation." The knowledge of subjects in the human sciences thus permits the subjection of agents to the exercise of power in all social processes.

Foucault argues that power has no center, such as the state, from which it extends or derives;[28] rather, it is dispersed throughout the social formation. Although relations of power pervade all social processes, they neither constitute the essence nor the primary determinant of these processes. Relations of power have conditions of existence that are not reducible to these relations. Subjects do not emerge through the interplay of relations of power alone. Foucault says "that the mechanisms of subjectification cannot be studied outside their relation to the mechanisms of exploitation ['which separate individuals from what they produce'] and domination [e.g., ethnic, social, and religious 'forms of domination']. But they do not merely constitute the 'terminal' of more fundamental mechanisms. They entertain complex and circular relations with other forms."[29] Elsewhere, he distinguishes between power relations, relationships of communication, and objective capacities (which are involved in the transformation of the "real" through the application of labor).[30] These "three types of relationships, in fact always overlap one another, support one another reciprocally, and use each other mutually as means to an end."[31] For Foucault, modes of subjectification are not the special province of power but involve the intereffectivity of relations of power with their conditions of existence.

Foucault's acknowledgment of this intereffectivity brings him quite close to the Marxist notion of overdetermination. He is careful not to reduce cultural processes to relations of power, or vice versa. Power is not the essence of "cultural" phenomenon; rather, the discursive formation specifies those aspects of discourse that are in excess of sign systems and that chiefly function in the network of power relations. Meaning is not reduced to power, and power is not reduced to meaning.

Althusser: Subjects and the Materiality of Ideology

A second line of criticism of the reduction of culture and ideology to mystification may be found in Althusser's rejection of the concept of false consciousness and his insistence on the materiality of ideological practice.[32] Ideology is taken from the realm of "ideas" and placed instead within the specific apparatuses that constitute the sites for concrete ideological activities. Furthermore, ideology is defined by those cultural processes whose effect is the constitution of subjects. Subjectification proceeds by concrete cultural processes of "interpellation":[33] naming, identifying, and inscribing subjects within social processes. Since interpellation is never a matter of truth or falsity, ideology exists wherever subjects are created. According to Althusser, ideology represents the "imaginary" relations of individuals to their "real" conditions of existence.[34] Put another way, this discursive content is made up of the naming and narration that construct a view of agents as *subjects* inscribed within and marked by social processes.

Althusser's concept of ideology can be used as a discursive device to investigate the science/ideology opposition. Althusser denies the epistemological basis for the distinction between true (scientific) and mystificatory (ideological) discourses. Rather, the opposition is *partly* a distinction between "objective knowledges" about *theoretically designated* objects and "knowledges" that "function as practical norms governing the attitudes and concrete adoptions of positions of men with respect to the real objects and problems of their social and individual existence, and of their history."[35] Neither of these "knowledges" has an epistemological claim to absolute truth.

Ideological "practices" require particular apparatuses for their performance. Particular class processes are one of the conditions of existence of the reproduction or transformation of these apparatuses, which require the distribution of surplus labor both to themselves and to the agents responsible for their direction and operation. These agents thus occupy subsumed class positions. Conversely, particular forms or modes of subjectification and the apparatuses in which they emerge are conditions of existence for concrete class processes.

Both Foucault and Althusser shift our understanding of the culture-ideology-power conjuncture toward a concern with the specificity of cultural processes and relations of power within which historically determinate subjects are created. We need, however, to distinguish clearly between their theoretical projects. Foucault merely gestures toward class and other social "overdeterminants" of power and culture, while Althusser locates the overdetermination of these social processes at the heart of his project. Foucault substitutes the "juxtaposition" of social processes for the stronger notion of overdetermination. Lecourt has argued that "the weakness in the concept of juxtaposition is precisely that it is *not* a principle of determination."[36]

For Foucault, discursive practices are a primary means and site for the constitution of subjects, although he has recently included nondiscursive practices in the overdetermination of subjects. Althusser, on the

494

other hand, acknowledges from the outset the range and diversity of concrete processes that overdetermine subjects. However, one problem in Althusser's position is his designation of ideological state apparatuses as primary sites within which the subjects of a capitalist social formation are interpellated. This suggests a centering rather than a dispersion of subjectification processes, in contrast to Foucault.

The Overdetermination of Class Processes and Subjectifying Cultural Processes: An Illustration

In the remaining part of this paper we shall examine the inter-effectivity of processes of subjectification and class processes. Since there is no general way to specify the effects of their interaction, we briefly illustrate their overdetermination in a concrete social formation.

We choose as our illustration the interaction of class and nonclass processes in primitive communism. Our choice is informed by both theoretical and political considerations. First, the notion of communism, both primitive and advanced, has a limited but key place in the writings of Marx and Engels. We will reformulate their discussions to "add" that agents may occupy different class (and nonclass) positions in so-called classless societies. This approach permits us to show how struggles over class processes overdetermine and are overdetermined by struggles over cultural processes. Second, this theoretical construct has important political consequences. It suggests that the interaction between class and nonclass processes in a primitive communist social formation may produce struggles over the fundamental class process which set in motion a transitional conjuncture.[37]

In many primitive communal social formations, kinship overdetermines fundamental class processes and is in turn overdetermined by them. Kinship is one way in which agents are constituted as particular kinds of subjects capable of participating in communal class processes. However, kinship is not reducible to its function in creating such subjects. But in this function kinship serves as a condition of existence for the primitive communal fundamental class process.

Kinship is a particular subset of all cultural processes that makes such relations of consanguinity and affinity "meaningful," including forms of address, forms of marriage, modes of descent reckoning, ritual practices, and storytelling. Though they may be predominantly signifying practices, they are not exclusively so. Kinship processes not only produce kin subjects as members of a collective subjectivity (clan or commune), they also position these kin subjects in nonkinship processes, such as class processes, while providing an identity or set of identities for subjects in relation to these nonkinship processes. In many primitive communal social formations, agents enter into fundamental and subsumed class processes as kin or commune members: their class subjectivity is overdetermined by their kin identity, and vice versa.

A primitive communal fundamental class process is one in which the performers of surplus labor are also the extractors of that surplus labor. However, the membership of the commune is never identical with the performers of surplus labor. As Marx forcefully argued in the *Grundrisse*,[38] the commune as such is partly constituted by the intersecting kin/territorial processes that run through the social formation; that is, the commune is in excess of the group of "direct producers." The commune functions as a network of kin/territorial processes to position direct producers within the lineage, commune, and village, so that the extraction of surplus labor is done by the lineage, commune, village. Direct producers, then, both perform and directly appropriate surplus labor through the commune, village, or lineage, but not as an exclusively designated group in opposition to non-surplus-producing members of these social bodies.

Kinship processes distribute agents to class positions in the processes of performing surplus labor. For example, teams of laborers participating in subsistence activities, such as hunting, gathering, agriculture, are often organized along lineage lines. Members of the same lineage, differentiated by age, gender, or proximity to an ancestral totem, may perform different tasks or combine their labor in the performance of surplus labor. To take one specific example, among the seventeenth-century Iroquois, the primary producers of agricultural surplus product were women inscribed in distinct matrilineages. Agricultural plots were chiefly clan holdings worked by members of the same matrilineage—as Iroquois kin rules determined, the women of the clan performing surplus labor as mothers, daughters, and/ or sisters. Women in Iroquois society were, therefore, partly subjectified and inscribed within the communal fundamental class process by kinship designation.

Within the lineage there were further differentiations of tasks that depended upon age, status, and location in relation to ancestral heads of the clan. These differentiations not only distributed agents to different locations in the performance of surplus labor, but also constituted subsumed class positions; some of the clan members, by virtue of their particular kinship status, were either partly or completely freed from the performance of surplus labor. These members received portions of already communally appropriated surplus labor because of their participation in social processes—including those that secured the reproduction of the clans—that served as conditions of existence for the communal fundamental class process.

Among the Iroquois, members of healing societies, sachems (representatives of the clan in communal government), traders, warriors, elders, and so on, all received portions of surplus labor distributed to them by matrons of the clans in their prescribed role as distributors of communally appropriated surplus labor. These subsumed class agents participated in processes that serve to reproduce the conditions of communal surplus labor extraction. For example, sachems were responsible for the recitation of clan legends and for the maintenance of domestic peace according to clan rules. Although the office of clan sachem was held exclusively by Iroquois men, they were elected by the matrons of the clan.

Upon contact with the Europeans, the power of the matrons and sachems to affect tribal decisions and preserve peace was slowly eroded by the growth of certain subsumed classes, such as warriors and traders (mostly comprised of men), who sought to become increasingly independent of the matriclans, whose very independent growth was conditioned on the spread of hostilities, which did much to hasten and even challenge the existing kinship processes. Thus, the transformation of the Iroquois social formation in the seventeenth and eighteenth centuries was determined in part by the alteration in kinship practices and the limitation of the field of their play in affecting the communal fundamental class process. This process was thus displaced in part by the effective destruction of the matrilineal principles and by the ascendancy of occupants of certain subsumed class positions, such as warriors and traders, whose rise was conditioned on *new* modes of subjectification, such as Christianity, individualism, and patriarchal nuclear familial processes.

In Iroquois society, warriors were organized in bands, and their statuses in these bands often depended on their status in the kin hierarchy. In providing protection for the kin-based commune, warriors helped to reproduce the commune and, therefore, the communal fundamental class process. However, as occupants of subsumed class positions, warriors increasingly sought their independence from the clans and struggled to receive larger distributed portions of surplus labor. This struggle to acquire an increased share of surplus labor was affected by the European colonizers who consciously undermined the predominance of the matrilineages through such agents and apparatuses as Jesuit missionaries and the teaching of patriarchal Christianity, and unconsciously undermined matrilineal predominance through the demands of the fur trade (which radically altered the Iroquois' predominant mode of subsistence from agriculture organized on the basis of the matriclan to hunting, which was increasingly less structured by the matriclan). Thus, the introduction of patriarchal nuclear familial relations in the eighteenth century, one of several new modes of subjectivizing warriors (as well as other members of the community) that gradually displaced the matrilineal principles, contributed to warriors gaining greater independence and, thereby, greatly increasing their distributed shares of surplus labor. It should also be noted that these new modes of subjectification inscribed warriors in expanded or newly created noncommunal fundamental and subsumed class processes.

In these communal social formations, where kinship is a primary mode of subjectifying occupants of class positions, these agents do *not* possess unfragmented subject identifications; rather, inclusion in a lineage produces the possibility of insertion in quite different fundamental and subsumed class positions. Among the Iroquois, the same woman might perform and appropriate surplus labor through participation in agricultural clan work teams (thus occupying fundamental class positions), while at the same time holding various "offices" (e.g., as a member of a healing society) or performing other activities (e.g., trading) and, therefore, occupying subsumed class positions. She could also participate in relationships in which no class process occurs; thus, she might occupy no class position. When the same set of kin practices inscribed agents in different class positions, the reproduction of the communal class processes was more easily secured. However, when alternative kin and nonkin modes of subjectification appeared that located agents in class positions, the reproduction of the Iroquois communal fundamental class process was jeopardized.

Kinship is constructed and reproduced in concrete cultural processes through concrete apparatuses. The economic reproduction of agents who play a key part in the emergence, enunciation, transmission, extension, and transformation of kinship signs and procedures is one of the conditions of existence for these processes. The distribution of surplus labor to these agents is necessary for the existence and reproduction of concrete apparatuses where kinship is enunciated and transmitted. For example, particular feast days that celebrate certain ancestral figures or clan totems require a distribution of surplus labor from the producers/appropriators to agents who organize and carry out the ritual symbolic acts of feast/celebration. This is most obviously true for those celebrations where the destruction of wealth (ceremonial offerings) for symbolic purposes takes place. Also, special locations, such as temples or clan lodges, may be created for the performance of acts that entail kin subjectification, such as the recitation and memorization of "founding" myths in which clan totems, ancestors, and current clan members are discursively linked. The existence and reproduction of these locations require the distribution of already communally extracted surplus labor and often are a direct cause for the expansion of the performance of surplus labor.

If the distribution of surplus labor to particular occupants of subsumed class positions is not forthcoming, the existence of the apparatuses in which kinship is formulated and reproduced may be threatened. Not surprisingly, one of the tactics employed by European colonialists in conquering, transforming, and administering diverse primitive communal social formations from the seventeenth to the twentieth centuries was to take control of the agents and/or processes by which communal surplus labor was distributed and redistributed or outlawing such distribution to those rituals and practices designed to reinforce and reproduce the "original" communal kinship structures. As a countertactic, many communal societies ostracized those members who introduced or represented alternative (often European) modes of subjectification within the dominant kinship structure. Ostracism, of course, was a means of cutting off distribution of surplus labor to these agents. As with the Iroquois, clan representatives frequently fought the inroads of Christianity by refusing to permit surplus labor to be directed to institutions or events where Christianity would be taught.

Finally, our illustration reminds us that the agents who secure subjectifying cultural processes must be concerned with the continued distribution of surplus labor to themselves and to the concrete apparatuses of these processes. In addition, their increased demands for shares of surplus labor must come either at the expense of other occupants of subsumed class positions or by increasing the communal surplus labor performed and extracted. These agents may seek alliances that preserve or transform the existing articulation of class processes in order to secure their continued existence in their positions. Of course, these maneuvers have their effects on the very processes they direct.

Although modes of subjectification *do not* mirror the "objective reality" of class processes, certain modes may be judged either useful or problematic at certain historical moments for the emergence, reproduction, or transformation of particular fundamental and subsumed class processes. Struggles between occupants of class positions are partly directed toward upholding, reformulating, or obliterating various subjectifying processes so as to influence the effectivity of these processes on a determinate network of class processes.

Conclusion

In our illustration we have tried to show that struggles over particular cultural processes—the processes of subjectifying agents in kin terms to participate in class processes—overdetermine class struggles. Likewise, we have suggested that struggles over the performance/appropriation and distribution of surplus labor overdetermine these cultural processes. By not reducing culture to power or class, or reducing class to power or culture, we have retained the specificity of diverse social processes while showing that a more thorough understanding of this specificity can be achieved by using a model of overdetermination to examine the intereffectivity of these processes. We have sought to propose a methodolgical guideline to a non-reductionist Marxist analysis of class, power, and culture; in our illustration we work to show how such an analysis can proceed.

Notes

1   We are most interested in the recent attempts to establish antiteleological and antiessentialist Marxist notions. See L. Althusser and E. Balibar, *Reading Capital*, trans. Ben Brewster (London: New Left Books, 1975); L. Althusser, *For Marx*, trans. Ben Brewster (New York: Vintage, 1970); L. Althusser, *Essays in Self-Criticism*, trans. Grahame Lock (London: New Left Books, 1976); B. Hindess and P. Hirst, *Pre-Capitalist Modes of Production* (London: Routledge and Kegan Paul, 1975); B. Hindess and P. Hirst, *Mode of Production and Social Formation* (London: Macmillan, 1977); S. Resnick and R. Wolff, "The Theory of Transitional Conjunctures," *Review of Radical Political Economics* 11:3 (1979); S. Resnick and R. Wolff, "Classes in Marxian Theory," *Review of Radical Political Economics* 13:4 (1982); S. Resnick and R. Wolff, "Marxist Epistemology: The Critique of Economic Determinism," *Social Text* 6:2/3 (Fall 1982); S. Resnick and R. Wolff, *Marxist Theory*, forthcoming.

2   The essentialism we discuss here is what we call essentialism *in* discourse or theory, which we distinguish from epistemological essentialism or essentialism *of* discourse or theory. We reject the epistemological notion that objects of knowledge exist independently of thought and thus can be appropriated in thought. This notion is an essentialism *of* theory. Our antiessentialist position is also incompatible with essentialism *in* theory, which discursively privileges a subset of conceptual statements within theory from which others are logically derived. For further discussion, see Resnick and Wolff, "Marxist Epistemology" and *Marxist Theory*.

3   The concept of overdetermination initially emerged as a concept in the Freudian theory of dream interpretation. To our knowledge, Lukács was the first Marxist to try to appropriate and reformulate this concept for Marxist theory. However, Althusser was the first Marxist both to claim that Marx's own concept of historical causality and epistemology was one of overdetermination. See G. Lukács, "The Tasks of Marxist Philosophy in the New Democracy," quoted in Resnick and Wolff, "Marxist Epistemology"; L. Althusser, "Contradiction and Overdetermination," in *For Marx*, pp. 89–128; Resnick and Wolff, "Marxist Epistemology."

4   Certainly, many noneconomists have rejected the essentialist thought built upon the epistemological positions of empiricism and rationalism. It seems to us they approach but never quite reach the Marxist position of overdetermination. The structural linguistics initiated by Ferdinand de Saussure was an attempt to show the arbitrariness of meaning, decentering the signification of a word into the arbitrary relation of signifier to signified. Similarly, Jacques Derrida's deconstructionist interventions suggest the futility of trying to center a text and find its "given" meaning (its ventriloquist "logos") through a process of interpretation. In place of this logocentrism, Derrida suggests the play and dispersion of textual meanings that are liberated through a process of deconstruction. Richard Rorty's discussion of philosophy as "a mirror of nature" presents a somewhat similar attack on logocentrism, but one restricted to the philosophical dichotomy of thinking/being. Finally, the noted critic of sociobiology, Richard C. Lewontin, has argued that we need to replace mechanistic and reductionist notions of the human organism with a new conception of the organism as an intereffective totality of determinations. For Saussure, see *Course in General Linguistics* (New York: McGraw-Hill, 1966). Our understanding of Derrida is taken from *Writing and Difference*, trans. Alan Bass (Chicago: University of Chicago Press, 1981); and see especially the interview in *Positions* entitled "Positions," in which Derrida discusses his problematic relation to Marxism. For Rorty, see *Philosophy and the Mirror of Nature* (Princeton: Princeton University Press, 1980) and "Philosophy As a Kind of Writing," *New Literary History*, 1978. We are particularly taken with R. C. Lewontin's review of two texts written by the Dialectics of Biology Group. His review, "The Corpse in the Elevator," appears in *The New York Review of Books*, Jan. 20, 1983.

5   In this context, it is interesting to note that Gramsci's well-known opposition to economic determinism does not lead him to accept any form of noneconomic determinism. Instead, he argues that the search for last instance determinisms amounts to the "search for God." See A. Gramsci, *Selections from the Prison Notebooks*, trans. and ed. Q. Hoare and G. N. Smith (New York: International Publishers, 1971), p. 437.

6 Our wording here deliberately echoes that of the Marxist anthropologist Marc Augé. Augé claims that after the initial interest in but consequent rejection of "Althusserianism," Marxism in France was discredited. In its stead, "with the help of history and fashion . . . waves of 'desire' flooded the sociological banks, and a new disembarkation threatened. This was actually a new Holy Alliance (Nietzche, Reich, Bataille, Deleuze) and one for which the Marxists were quite unprepared." Augé clearly recognizes that these newly arisen protagonists wish to reject a "formalist" Marxism only to replace it with a social theory centered once again on the concept of desire. See Marx Augé, *The Anthropological Circle*, trans. Martin Thom (Cambridge: Cambridge University, 1982), p. 66.

7 M. Sahlins, *Culture and Practical Reason* (Chicago: University of Chicago Press, 1976), p. viii; see also pp. 205-21.

8 This tendency shows up quite clearly in contemporary discussions of "sexual politics" and focuses on social "relations" rather than processes that we regard as the operation of a theoretical humanism (an essentialism of the subject).

9 This notion of exploitation should not be confused with Marx's enunciation of the concept of exploitation in *Capital* (New York: International Publishers, 1977). Marx's conception specifies the particular economic *process* of extracting surplus labor or "unpaid labor" and must be differentiated from the more conventional use of the term to express a general relationship between social agents.

10 We restrict our criticisms here to Hindess and Hirst's earlier books, *Pre-Capitalist Modes of Production* and *Mode of Production and Social Formation*.

11 See P.-P. Rey, "The Lineage Mode of Production," *Critique of Anthropology* no. 3 (1975), pp. 27-29.

12 See especially N. Poulantzas, *Classes in Contemporary Capitalism*, trans. David Fernbach (London: Verso, I978), pp. 13-36.

13 For a detailed discussion of the concept of class process and its use in Marxist theory, see Resnick and Wolff, "Classes in Marxian Theory" and *Marxist Theory*.

14 Marx begins to elaborate his notions of fundamental and subsumed class processes in the three volumes of *Capital*. See Resnick and Wolff, "Classes in Marxian Theory."

15 See Marx's brief discussion of these fundamental class processes in *Grundrisse*, trans. Martin Nicolaus (New York: Vintage, I973), pp. 471-514.

16 See Resnick and Wolff, *Marxist Theory*, for an elaboration of the notion of the "social prevalence" of a fundamental class process.

17 Marx, in vol. 3 of *Capital*, focuses on this particular development in the example of advanced capitalism. As Marx sees it, in advanced capitalism managers, owners, financiers of capital often exist separate from industrial capitalists. The direction and control of the capitalist fundamental class process are in the hands of these social groups, but they do not extract (exploit) surplus labor. See in particular chap. 23, pp. 370-90, of *Capital*.

18 For a detailed discussion of the concepts of class position and class struggle, see Resnick and Wolff, *Marxist Theory*.

19 One of Marx's most developed discussions of such "class alliances" can be found in *The 18th Brumaire of Louis Bonaparte* (New York: International Publishers, I968).

20 Our notion of subjectification is clearly related to Foucault's "two meanings of the word subject: subject to someone else by control and dependence, and tied to his own identity by a conscience or self-knowledge"; and also to Althusser's discussion of the "mirror-structure" of the process of subjectification, as agents are "interpellated" simultaneously as subjects and as subjected to a Subject (such as God or the state). See Foucault, "The Subject and Power," which is the afterword to H. Dreyfus and P. Rabinow, *Michel Foucault: Beyond Structuralism and Hermeneutics* (Chicago: University of Chicago Press, I982), p. 212; and Althusser, "Ideology and Ideological State Apparatuses," *Lenin and Philosophy*, trans. Ben Brewster (New York: Monthly Review, I971), pp. 170-83.

21 Three books in which these problems are taken up are R. Williams, *Marxism and Literature* (Oxford: Oxford University Press, I977); R. Coward and J. Ellis, *Language and Materialism* (London: Routledge and Kegan Paul, I977); J. McCarney, *The Real World of Ideology* (Atlantic Highlands: Humanities Press, I980).

22 See also the sections of Gramsci's prison notebooks entitled "The Study of Philosophy" and "Problems of Marxism," pp. 321-472, in *Selections from the Prison Notebooks*. A recent study of Gramsci that places him within the context of an "overdeterminist" conception of culture and ideology is Chantal Mouffe's "Hegemony and Ideology in Gramsci," in C. Mouffe, ed., *Gramsci and Marxist Theory* (London: Routledge and Kegan Paul, I979), pp. 168-204.

Amariglio, Resnick, and Wolff

23 See M. Foucault, *The Archaeology of Knowledge*, trans. A. M. Sheridan Smith (New York: Harper and Row, 1976), pp. 184-86.

24 See Foucault, *The Archaeology of Knowledge*, pp. 178-95.

25 See Foucault, *The Archaeology of Knowledge*, pp. 178-95. See also Lecourt, *Marxism and Epistemology*, trans. Ben Brewster (London: New Left Books, 1975), pp. 199-201.

26 See especially M. Foucault, "Truth and Power," in *Power/Knowledge*, ed. C. Gordon (New York: Pantheon, 1980).

27 See Foucault, "The Subject and Power," p. 208, where he discusses "three modes of objectification which transform human beings into subjects."

28 See Foucault, "Body/Power" and "Truth and Power," in *Power/Knowledge*.

29 See Foucault, "The Subject and Power," p. 213.

30 Foucault, "The Subject and Power," pp. 217-18.

31 Foucault, "The Subject and Power," p. 218.

32 See Althusser, "Ideology and Ideological State Apparatuses," in *Lenin and Philosophy*.

33 "Ideology and Ideological State Apparatuses," pp. 170-77.

34 "Ideology and Ideological State Apparatuses," pp. 162-65.

35 D. Lecourt, *Marxism and Epistemology*, p. 210.

36 D. Lecourt, *Marxism and Epistemology*, p. 204.

37 See J. Amariglio, "'Primitive Communism' and the Economic Development of Iroquios Society," Department of Economics, University of Massachusetts, Amherst, 1983, chap. 3; and Rolf Jensen, "The Transition from Primitive Communism: The Wolof Social Formation of West Africa," *Journal of Economic History* 42:1 (1982), pp. 69-76.

38 See *Grundrisse*, pp. 471-79.

Jean Franco

Beyond Ethnocentrism: Gender, Power, and the Third-World Intelligentsia

Domination has traditionally been semanticized in sexual terms and power has traditionally been associated with masculinity. Recent revolutionary movements have shown us that we have to resemanticize preconstructed gender categories by taking meaning into our own hands and overcoming traditional associations of the feminine with nature and immobility.

Anyone involved in Latin American studies knows what it is to be placed last on the program, when everyone else has left the conference. Latin America (and third-world societies) generally occupy some exceptional and therefore awkward position in mainstream scholarship. Indeed, they are not yet "in" it at all. "British intellectuals: Latin American revolutionaries" was the wording of an ad I once saw in the *New Statesman* in England. It summed up very nicely the separation of intellectual and manual labor along the axis of metropolis and periphery, as well as suggesting the flow of revolutionary action into areas where people know no better than to fight. The conclusion is that the Third World is not much of a place for theory; and if it has to be fitted into theory at all, it can be accounted for as exceptional or regional.

That is why it is worth beginning with Fanon, whose *Black Skins White Masks* and *The Wretched of the Earth* snatched the leadership of revolution away from the first-world proletariat (grown fat on imperialism) and revived the metropolis's paranoid fears of the vengeance that pullulated in the ill-lit streets of the native quarters. For Fanon, the whole colonized world had to be shocked out of its bewitchment. It was a becalmed world whose inhabitants, "wasted by fevers, obsessed by ancestral customs," formed an almost "inorganic background for the innovating dynamism of colonial mercantilism."[1] The colonized fantasies of action had to be converted into revolutionary potential. "The first thing the native learns is to stay in his place and not go beyond certain limits. That is why the dreams of the native are always of muscular prowess; his dreams are of action and of aggression. I dream I am jumping, winning, running, climbing. I dream that I burst out laughing, that I span a river in one stride or that I am followed by a flood of motorcars that never catch up with me."[2] Yet it is within the power of the wretched of the earth, the *fellahin*, to overcome immobility, to turn the relation of colonizer and colonized on its head, to cleanse themselves of inferiority through violence. The native intelligentsia, caught between the ambiguities of folklore and assimilation to the metropolis, will be dragged in the wake of the *fellahin*, forcibly immersed in the struggle.

Clearly, Fanon's blueprint is locked in the same mind/body polarity that separates metropolitan intellect from the sacrificial body of third-world peoples. The white mask woven and painted by the colonizer's discourse can only be broken apart by the confrontation with death. The colonized need recognition in order to know they exist but will only be recognized by the metropolis as a mask or a grinning skull.

From the standpoint of the present, it is easy to see that Fanon's existentialist psychology has its limitations; he understood the alienation of thinking in the foreign tongue of the metropolis but not the pervasive web of discourse in which he was enmeshed. Today, we know much more about the constitution of subjectivities within particular discursive formations; we are aware of the dissolution of the "individual" or the "self" in subjectivities, of the relation between power and knowledge. We can even arrive at a more materialist version of Foucault's theorizing of power by distinguishing between comparatively transient microexercises of power and the perpetuation of knowledge-power through institutions that reproduce both the machinery and the discourse of domination.[3] What makes Fanon's contribution of value is that he recognized that there was something distinct about the colonial struggle, that the separation between manual and mental labor was reproduced in the relationship between the *fellahin* and the intelligentsia, and that this hierarchy had to be destroyed if the revolutionary struggle was to succeed.

This essay attempts to delineate the constitution of the intelligentsia in the Third World, their subordination of manual labor and women, and the consquences of this for the formation of counterhegemonic discourses. I am thus deliberately considering the intelligentsia not as individuals, nor as class fractions, but rather as a systematically constituted group, bound by a common *habitus* (to use Pierre Bourdieu's expression), that is, by common perceptions, dispositions, practices, and institutions that account for the systematized nature of their intellectual production while simultaneously allowing for different discursive strategies within the intellectual field.[4] Since I refer mainly to Latin America, it is necessary to emphasize the crucial and constitutive activity of the *literary* intelligentsia which is empowered by writing. Because it was blocked from making contributions to the development of scientific thought, the intelligentsia was forced into the one area that did not require professional training and the institutionalization of knowledge—that is, into literature. It is here, therefore, that the confrontation between metropolitan discourse and the utopian project of an autonomous society takes place.

Metropolitan discourses on the Third World have generally adopted one of three devices: (1) *exclusion*—the Third World is irrelevant to theory; (2) *discrimination*—the Third World is irrational and thus its knowledge is subordinate to the rational knowledge produced by the metropolis; and (3) *recognition*—the Third World is only seen as the place of the instinctual. In the discourse of exclusion, the Third World exists only as a scenario; it is the stage for the activities of *Nostromo* or worse: consider Werner Herzog, who broke down ancestral customs merely to provide *Fitzcaraldo* with a dramatic movie sequence. (The discourse of metropolitan power refuses to acknowledge the all too human smell of crushed bodies.) In this discourse, the oppressed and exploited are outside civilization and hence constitute its heart of darkness, the negativity against which the metropolitan project must be defined. When the nineteenth-century intelligentsia of Latin America attempted to occupy the first-person position in this discourse, to separate "I," it could do so only by speaking as if the indigenous peoples had ceased to exist, as if they already belonged to the past. This discourse was interrupted and thrown into confusion whenever the masses erupted as subjects of history, as they did during the Mexican Revolution.[5]

A second kind of metropolitan discourse, a discourse of discrimination, was structured as a hierarchy in which an irrational intelligentsia that tried to occupy the subject position in this discourse found itself forced to embody the rich heterogeneity of its own culture and to rationalize it. This was Alfonso Reyes's strategy when he described indigenous culture as red clay that would be washed by the pure waters of Latin culture, or Neruda's strategy when he invoked the dead laborers of the Inca empire and called on them to speak through his lips and mouth.[6] This representative discourse was subverted by some avant-garde writers (especially Vallejo) but was decisively challenged during and just after the Cuban revolution when the intelligentsia, wishing to speak for the masses, was asked to take up the gun and fight with them.

Finally, the discourse of recognition becomes possible when heterogeneity is valorized by the increasingly routinized metropolis. At this moment, the Third World becomes the place of the unconscious, the rich source of fantasy and legend recycled by the intelligentsia, for which heterogeneity is no longer a ghostly, dragging chain but material that can be loosened from any territorial context and juxtaposed in ways that provide a constant frisson of pleasure. The intelligentsia no longer speaks *for* the masses but productively transposes mythic material. But in order to do this, it must distinguish between its properly authorial activity and mere reproduction, between an essentially masculine form of creativity and the feminine reproductive activity. This discourse is only interrupted when the differentiation between male authorship and female reproduction is exposed as a socially constructed position; then women and indigenous peoples can take the production of meaning into their own hands.

Because gender is the last category to be deconstructed in this way, I shall concentrate on this third type of discursive formation. However, some preliminary points need to be made. In the first place, it is important to recognize that in Latin America there is a dislocation between the establishment of a capitalist-dominated economy and the institutionalization of what is generally thought to be its ideology—the work ethic, individualism, an epistemology based on exchange, and so on. That is to say, capitalism in Latin America was articulated with the hacienda and the mine, both of which disciplined the work force not only through direct repression but also by using the paternalistic discourse of the Church. Furthermore, indigenous communes in which symbolic production (artisanry, dance, fiestas), economic production, and reproduction of the labor force were lodged in a single institution, namely, the family, coexisted with plantation and mining enclaves in which the family was often broken up altogether.[7] It is only very recently, with the incorporation of new sectors into the labor force and the instrumental use of the mass media, that there has been a concerted attempt to introduce "modern" values. Thus, the belief systems of the indigenous, blacks, and women were *of necessity* archaic, for no other options were open to them. At the same time, this very anachronism provided them with "regions of refuge," with traditions, moral rights, and spiritual bonds to particular territories (often organized around devotion to saints) that could be explosive when the state encroached on them. In contrast, the intelligentsia was a secular group, empowered by writing and therefore isolated from the culture of the majority of the population. Unlike Samuel Richardson in eighteenth-century England who, according to Terry Eagleton, was "locked into the economic infrastructure of bourgeois England" through his printing firm, which was also "the nub of a whole discursive formation . . . interlocked with every major ideological apparatus of English society,"[8] the Latin American intelligentsia was interlocked only with a ghostly and somewhat abstract "nation." By providing the spiritual webbing of the national spirit, it hoped to soar to immortality.

In the second place, the analogous position of the intelligentsia—which was subordinated to metropolitan discourse at the same time it was constituting the discourse of nationalism—is indivisible from the sexual division of labor. Domination has traditionally been semanticized in sexual terms and power has traditionally been associated with masculinity. Social, political, and economic power are represented through a lexicon that is drawn from sexual relations. Hence the social and the sexual have become intimately connected. In a famous essay published in 1950, Octavio Paz based an analysis of Mexican national character on the contrast between female "openness" (and therefore vulnerability to rape and domination) and male closure (invulnerability). A critique of machismo elevated to the level of a national madness, Paz's Labyrinth of Solitude affirms rather than deconstructs these archetypal differences. Many novels written in the nineteenth and early twentieth centuries were disguised national allegories in which social forces were represented in terms of impotence, castration, domination, and prostitution. In one well-known Puerto Rican story, the protagonist actually castrates himself.[9]

The significance of the semanticization of the social as the sexual has been discussed by Nancy Hartsock in Money, Sex and Power: Towards a Feminist Historical Materialism.[10] This book sets out to show that there is an epistemology of reproduction, just as there is an epistemology of production (Marx) and exchange (capitalism). But there is a serious weakness in an approach that neglects social and discursive formations and the constitution of subjectivity. Ignoring the lesson of Foucault, Hartsock often slips into a history of ideas. Even so, her book shows how the sexual division of labor that subordinated reproduction to the lowest level of human creativity has led to the valorization of intellectual creations "born to the minds of those not contaminated by the concerns or necessities of the body."[11] Hartsock argues that from the Greeks onward public space has belonged to the warrior hero and to the hero-citizen; both have their paradigm in the Greek agonic hero. Intellectual life, too, follows this paradigm, since the search for immortality, conceived as domination within public life, has, since Plato, been associated with the distantiation of intellectual activities from the mortal body, and hence from the "feminine," that have always been associated with the realm of necessity. "Over and over again," Hartsock comments, "the fear of ceasing to exist is played out";[12] and the possibility of fusion, and hence of the death of the self, are found to be at the source of theoretical production and political deeds. This has serious consequences since it subordinates not only the feminine but also all the positive aspects of eros that derive from the experience of reproduction—for instance, connectedness and commmunity.

In the Third World, in which mortality is not only individual but affects entire social movements, which flourish, die, and are forgotten like the ephemeral human body, we should expect this distantiation from the body to be most intense. Indeed, if we take Borges as an example, we find that the quest for immortality (which depends on metropolitan recognition) can only be realized by abstracting the fictional world from any local connotations and turning it into the paradigmatic confrontation of the pursuer and the pursued, the writer and the reader, which often culminates with a male bonding at the point of death.

In Latin America, the subordination of the feminine is aggravated by the rigid confinement of women to private spaces. The terms

| masculine | mobile (active) |
| feminine | immobile (passive) |

were interchangeable with

| masculine | public |
| feminine | private |

primarily because women were traditionally limited to the home, the convent, or the brothel. From the colonial period until recent times, the meanings born by the feminine can thus be illustrated by a simple semiotic diagram (see Figure 1). The central term of the quadrangle is the phallus, which is the bearer of meaning and the active element that determines social reproduction. One term of the semiotic quadrangle is occupied by the mother, who is not a virgin but is the bearer of children and whose space is the home. Here we should keep in mind the privatized and inward-looking Hispanic house and the fact that the virtual confinement of married women to the home had not only been required by the Church but was also intended to ensure the purity of blood that Spanish society had imposed after the wars against the Moors. Thus the mother's immobility is related to racism and to the protection of inheritable property. The opposite term to the mother is the virgin—that is, the nun who is pure and uncontaminated and whose space is the convent. The negation of the mother and the virgin is the whore, whose body is open to all men. For example, in his novel *The Fox Above and the Fox Below,* José María Arguedas describes a brothel in the Peruvian port town of Chimbote where the women sit in small cubicles in the middle of a compound with their legs apart to show their openness.

mother	virgin
phallus	
not virgin not mother (whore)	mother virgin (Mary)

Figure 1.

Yet the compound is also prisonlike; the "public" women are immobile and privatized just as much as the mother or the nun.[13] Finally, there is the impossible other, the mother who is a virgin, the mother of God who is not only the unattainable ideal term but the woman who has given birth to the Creator. (Consider this ironic parallel: Fidel Castro visits Chile, and Mrs. Allende states that the highest task of Chilean women is to give birth to sons who would be like Che Guevara.)

Certainly, what strikes us about this diagram of feminine meanings is the immobility and privacy that it implies. To understand how natural this disposition appears, even to the most sophisticated of the intelligentsia, we have only to read García Márquez's interview in *Playboy*, in which he declares that women "stay at home, run the house, bake animal candies so that men can go off and make wars."[14] Whether this was said in earnest or in jest is beside the point. It is along this axis that social meanings accrue so that the *madre patria* in nationalist discourse is productive or sterile, prostituted or sacred.

Yet in a society scarred by the violence and death that inevitably accompanied capitalist penetration of Latin America, it is not surprising to observe a certain "femininization of values" (to use Terry Eagleton's phrase). Thus, in a poem by Vallejo, the mother's body is depicted as a house, and the womb acquires the configuration of rooms and corridors: "Your archway of astonishment expects me / The tonsured volume of your cares / That have eroded life. The patio expects me / The hallway down below with its indentures and its / feast-day decorations." When the father enters this temple/house, it is on his knees. He has become the subordinate partner in the act of creation. The mother's body, on the other hand, offers the only unchanging territory in an uncertain world: "Between the colonnade of your bones / That cannot be brought down even with lamentations / And into whose side not even Destiny / can place a single finger."

This poem, written before Vallejo joined the Communist party, is in sharp contrast to his Soviet-inspired poems, in which the miners make history through work, or his poems of the Spanish Civil War, where the forging of history is in the hands of the male militia.[15] We also note that the mother can only (literally) *embody* certainty because of her immobility, because she is related to physical territory. Indeed, it was the female territory of the house that allowed private and family memory to be stored; there, archaic values, quite alien to the modern world, continued to flourish.

In the fifties and sixties, for reasons that are too complex to examine here, there was a radical shift in the meanings attached to the feminine. This period was marked by two quite contrary trends. On the one hand, the Cuban revolution aroused hopes that other countries could adopt original versions of socialism. Marxist theory could be Latin Americanized. Yet, during this same period, the struggle for national liberation was countered by a massive onslaught of advanced capitalism. At the very moment Latin America was asserting its difference, the armies of metropolitan corporations—in the form of mass media advertising and consumer goods— were poised, ready to destroy those very structures (urban/rural, commune, plantation) that had for so long been an embarrassment and yet had become the very source of Latin American originality.

The rich heterogeneity that formerly had to be subordinated as irrational began to be proudly displayed by Latin American writers as proof of cultural vitality. Writers like Asturias, Arquedas, Carpentier, Roa Bastos, and Rulfo undertook the recycling of ancient legends, traditional cultures, and archaic ways of life, not as folklore but as literary models of autarkic societies. As the literary intelligentsia discovered the utopian elements in popular culture, it also discovered in that very carnivalesque pluralism the claim on metropolitan attention that had so long eluded it. Thus, when Mario Vargas Llosa, at the outset of his career, declared that the Latin American novel "ceased to be Latin American," he meant that it had finally broken out of the backwater of provincialism and regionalism and had, indeed, become "recognizable."[16] Like Evita Peron, the literary intelligentsia had finally entered into immortality.[17] It was not even necessary for it to follow in Borges's footsteps and abstract plot from all regional and local references so that it could circulate as the agonic confrontation of pursuer and pursued, unencumbered by referentiality. The "new novelists" of the early sixties discovered the shock value of catachresis and juxtaposition in which those once embarrassing heterogenous elements became positive devices for defamiliarization.

This valorization of heterogeneity was accompanied by the reinvention of a myth of authorship, which once again affirmed the difference between natural reproduction and the masculine province of creativity. The slogan of the sixties—liberation through the imagination, immortality through the invention of imaginary worlds or the real autonomous societies like Cuba—was underpinned by the resemanticization of the sexual division of labor:

mother	author
child	creation

In a masculine world dominated by death and violence, the space of the mother had come to seem utopian, the space of a community that does not reproduce agonal relationships. Yet instead of trying to understand what this might mean for the construction of a more humane society and for revolutionary politics, both political leaders and writers during this period felt compelled to reaffirm political and artistic creativity as an exclusively male activity.

Let us take a recent transparent example. In Mario Vargas Llosa's play *La Señorita de Tacna* (1981), the central character is, unusually, a woman. Once the daughter of a prosperous family from Tacna, Mamaé is now senile, poor, and incontinent, kept alive only by her memories of the past. In her youth, during the Peruvian/Chilean war of the 1880s, she had been engaged to a Chilean officer. Learning of his infidelity with a married woman, she decided not to marry him but to become the surrogate mother of her sister's children and the weaver of romantic memories. In a traditional semiotic arrangement, Mamaé might have occupied the position of the nun. In Vargas Llosa's play, however, she is both virgin (that is, she is not caught in the lowly cycle of reproduction) and mother. She thus occupies the position of the Virgin Mary, the one woman who escapes mortality. Mamaé is the source of legend and fantasies that are woven out of her self-denial; nevertheless, she cannot be an author in the true sense. That is why the true protagonist lurks in the wings: Mamaé's grandnephew, Belisario, an apprentice writer who acts as spokesman for this figment of his past and

509

who presents Mamaé to the public. Seated at his desk at the side of the stage, he agonizes over writing, describing himself as "impotent." His impotence is only cured when he allows himself to be seduced by the romantic memories of Mamaé. He watches her, interrogates her on her past, and fills the gaps in her memory with his own inventions. In the final moments of the play, he recognizes that his material comes from Mamaé, that it has been *her* romantic stories that have turned into the "demons" that haunt him as a writer and provide him with *energeia*. The play clearly allegorizes a debate within Vargas Llosa himself, who is drawn to "feminine" material (romance) and needs a surrogate masculine character to launder this material and put it into literary circulation.

Not surprisingly, Mamaé bears a family resemblance to some of the women characters in García Márquez's *One Hundred Years of Solitude* (1967). Here, too, it is a woman, Ursula, who serves as the memory of the Buendia family by weaving lives together in the chain of domesticity. But it is a male, the gypsy Melqúiades, who writes down the epic of the Buendia family in Sanskrit (i.e., a literary language that needs competent deciphering), and it is a male, Aurelino, who discovers how to interpret Melqúiades's manuscript and thus affirms literature as an act of communion between male readers.

What most clearly demonstrates that the old statutes of authorship were problematic, however, was the recurrence in the novels of the sixties and seventies of a topos of monstrous birth and births of monstrosities. Perhaps rather than a topos (i.e., a mere literary commonplace), it would be more appropriate to call the monstrous birth an ideologeme or a collective fantasy. As such, it was intended to resolve the problem of "feminizing values" and criticizing machismo, while at the same time reserving true creativity for the male author. Childbirth was thus depicted as horrendous, more akin to death than life. In Onetti's novel *The Shipyard* (1961), the protagonist, Larsen, is on his way to his death and passes a cabin in which a women he had loved is giving birth: "He saw the semi-naked woman on the bed, bleeding, struggling, her hands clutching her head that was shaking furiously and rhythmically. He saw the astonishing round belly, distinguished the rapid flash of her glazed eyes and her clenched teeth. Finally he understood and could imagine the trap he had just avoided. Trembling with fear and disgust he left the window and began to walk towards the shore." At the end of *One Hundred Years of Solitude*, Amaranta Ursula dies in a massive outpouring of blood, leaving the child of her incestuous love affair "a dry and bloated bag of skin that all the ants in the world were dragging towards their holes along the stone paths in the garden."

In the eyes of these novelists, women can never separate themselves from nature. Fuentes's *Terra Nostra* (1975) opens with a vision of the year 2000 and a collective miracle: "women of all ages, forms, and conditions giving birth" by the banks of the Seine. Among them walks the one-armed writer-hero (one-armed like Cervantes), who imagines them pleading with him to accept the paternity of their children. In José Donoso's *The Obscure Bird of Night* (1979), the entire novel is constructed around the writer's futile attempt to take hold of this archaic power that comes from the creation of life, to steal it from the witches who preside over its secrets and assert their power over it. The recurrence of this ideologeme suggests, therefore, both the writer's ambiguous relation to an unconscious

510

that is defined as feminine and, at the same time, a reaffirmation of women's imprisonment in nature, as if this were the only way that the preservation of authorship as a male activity could be justified.

Yet this was not incompatible with the attribution of new and more positive connotations of the feminine. The very immobility of women, their "territoriality," made them the repository of an underground power that seemed to come from the land itself. In García Márquez's mythic universe, a whole prehistory of Latin America centers on the depiction of primitive matriarchy. We know that this matriarchy already obsessed him even before he became a novelist, for one of his early journalistic pieces is a description of a remote area (rather like Macondo) called La Sierpe.[18] He first heard of La Sierpe when a man from that region of Colombia arrived at a Barranquilla hospital claiming that he was pregnant and about to give birth to a monkey. Thus García Márquez was, even at this early stage, lured by the fantasy of male pregnancy. It led him to a veritable voyage of discovery of La Sierpe, a region whose malaria-ridden inhabitants stubbornly live out their lives in the midst of an impenetrable swamp, connected to the outside world only by trade. What consolidates their proud refusal to be integrated into Colombian society is the myth of the Marquesita, a myth that accounts for their difference, their originality. La Marquesita was a Spanish woman, a virgin who had the power to live as long as she liked but chose to live for 200 years. She accumulated vast wealth in cattle, but before her death she had the cattle trample the land until it became an impenetrable morass. Her treasure was then buried under a tree, access to which was barred by the miraculous swamp.

García Márquez heard this legend from the only person ever to approach the tree under which the Marquesita's treasure was buried; but rather than pursue his journey to the end, this adventurer preferred to return home and tell the story to the world, thus keeping both the legend and the treasure intact. The story can be interpreted as the fantasy of a society of scarcity in a region in which the once bounteous earth had mysteriously become unproductive. By introducing the storyteller and adventurer, however, García Márquez adds another element, for the treasure is associated not only with material wealth but also with the legend itself, indeed with the whole domain of the legendary that both consoles and consolidates the community.

Women could not be storytellers in the age of reason except as witches; as such, they were made into scapegoats. Witches were bearers of the irrational and the archaic, hated and feared since they worshiped a power that was outside the realm of official religion and culture. In contemporary novels such as those of Donoso and Fuentes, witches are the focus of a deep-rooted fear of all that lies outside the male-controlled spectrum of meaning. In García Márquez's legend of La Sierpe, on the other hand, women acquire a different social significance. They are equated with territory and code social meaning as a relationship to the land. These meanings persist long after the material wealth of the land has been exhausted, but they can only be recodified in this new historical stage by male storytellers.

García Márquez elaborates on this myth in interesting ways. In "Mama Grande's Funeral," he describes a territory ruled by a sterile, bloated matriarch who has accumulated vast capital but leaves it in her will to a nun (that is, like the Marquesita, her wealth ceases to circulate after her death). Mama Grande's funeral, which marks the end of the "colonial" epoch, is attended by a spectacular array of dignitaries, circus performers, beauty queens, and relatives and is celebrated by gargantuan feasts. A carnivalesque society whose meanings derive from the body-territory of the matriarch is about to wither away and be replaced by an abstract national state. The story tries to reconstitute a society in which economy, culture, and symbolic production are codified through the matriarchy.

In another version of the matriarchy myth, however, "The Incredible and Sad Story of Erendira and Her Wicked Grandmother," the two women of the title inhabit a desert region between the frontier and the sea (the land is thus no longer a source of wealth). The grandmother accumulates gold ingots by prostituting Erendira because the latter has burned down her house, in other words, has destroyed her territory. Erendira has the hero, Ulises, kill her grandmother, and then she disappears with the gold ingots into the land of legend. Once again myth has been salvaged from the gross material world. In a further stage of this imaginary history, a patriarch (in *The Autumn of the Patriarch*) is the absolute master of a territory that has less and less material reality and is little more than a rhetorical slogan or a sign in a system of exchange controlled by foreign powers.

While García Márquez gives a certain importance to the precapitalist matriarchal society, he still predicates this on a traditional separation between feminine nature and male enterprise. Like other novelists of the sixties and seventies, he upholds utopian values that seem to derive from the sphere that society has designated as "feminine." For instance, in his Nobel prize acceptance speech, he appealed for a Utopia of love to replace the apocalypse of death and destruction of advanced capitalism. Yet in his *Playboy* interview he also showed that he regards politics as an elite activity carried on by a group of representative males—General Torrijos, Fidel Castro, François Mitterand, and him.

This leads me to the connection between the literary intelligentsia of the sixties and the oppositional politics of this same period, a politics dominated by the guerrilla movements and their hero, Che Guevara. No one will deny the heroism of these national liberation movements, many of which ended tragically. Yet the literature they produced, with its ideal of the "new man" activated by nonmaterial incentives, bears out Nancy Hartsock's description of a left-wing theory that is trapped within a negative eros, one that values the violent confrontation with death over community and life. It is only recently that women who participated in these movements have begun to speak of their experiences and to criticize an ideal of the militant that suppressed feelings of weakness. A former Tupamara (of Uruguay) writes: "Feminine sexuality, desire to have children or not to have them, the disposition of our bodies was not taken into account. For instance, maternity was lived by us as an obstacle that prevented us from continuing the struggle, especially the military struggle."[19] Even when a woman managed to become a militant, she was often forced into a traditional gender role and classified as either butch or seductress. Women "were not militants in the true sense."[20] These comments were made by women who admire Che Guevara and neither regret nor reject armed struggle. Yet they are forced to recognize the unbalanced nature of a movement in which one gender constitutes revolutionary meaning and practice.

Before discussing some of the factors that have led to this kind of criticism, let me briefly summarize my argument up to this point. In its confrontation with metropolitan discourses that placed its members in a traditionally female position in the play of power and meaning, the Latin American intelligentsia attempted to speak on behalf of the nonliterate, the indigenous, and women who, through "archaic" institutions and practices, maintained forms of symbolic production that allowed them to deal with and even resist capitalism. In the fifties and sixties this repressed material and the interesting incongruities that had arisen because of the coexistence of different modes of symbolic production led some writers—Asturias, Arguedas, Roa Bastos—to incorporate these subjectivities which were alien to capitalism into their narratives as utopian elements. In other writers, the critique of violence and machismo similarly led to a feminization of values. However, creativity—the active creation of real or imaginary societies that would perpetuate the originality of Latin America beyond the span of mortal life—was still regarded as a masculine province. Women's sole creative function was the lowly task of reproducing the labor force.

Clearly, this state of affairs, in which one sector of the population monopolizes creativity and makes it a quest for immortality, has been seriously challenged in recent years. The reinstallation of military governments and the breakdown of traditional political parties, as well as the establishment of revolutionary governments in Cuba and Nicaragua, has led to serious questioning of the past. Democratic participation has been reevaluated and is no longer regarded as a bourgeois deception but as the only practical basis for socialism. Such participation cannot be developed as long as one gender continues to be subordinate.

At the same time, the violence of military governments in the southern cone, the wars in Central America and the activities of death squads, have all been directed at those places, like the home and the Church, that have harbored "archaic" subjectivities. The murder of the archbishop in El Salvador, of priests and nuns, the attack on the cathedral, the uprooting of indigenous peoples from their homes in Guatemala, the resettlement of working-class populations in Argentina and Chile, the sterilization of Puerto Rican women, the rape of women in front of their husbands and children, all represent ferocious attacks on the family and the Church by the very forces (the military) that rhetorically invoke these institutions. By attacking them and by appealing to more deterritorialized forms of domination— "mass media" and electronic religion or abstract notions of nationhood— the military governments have also unwittingly contributed to the subversion of these formerly "sacred" categories. Moral rights, which formerly had been attached to particular territories or genders, are rapidly undergoing resemanticization, not only by the military, but also by new oppositional forces. The present stage of "deterritorialization," which has separated women from their traditional regions of refuge in the home and the Church, and indigenous peoples from their communities, represents a cultural revolution brought about by imperialism.[21] But this conservative cultural revolution has been so radical that it has also opened up new areas of struggle; as a consequence of these social changes, new types of power, no longer solely identified with masculinity, have become increasingly important.

Let me give one example—the resistance of the "madwomen" of the Plaza de Mayo in Argentina. These women have not only redefined public space by taking over the center of Buenos Aires on one afternoon every week but have also interrupted military discourse (and now the silence of the new government) by publicly displaying the photographs of sons and daughters who have "disappeared." This form of refusing a message of death is obviously quite different from the quest for immortality that has traditionally inspired the writer and the political leader. The women interrupted the military by wrestling meaning away from them and altering the connotations of the word "mother." To the military, they were the mothers of dead subversives, therefore, of monsters. But they have transformed themselves into the "mothers of the Plaza de Mayo," that is, in the words of one of them, into "mothers of all the disappeared," not merely their own children. They have thus torn the term "mother" from its literal meaning as the biological reproducer of children and insisted on social connotations that emphasize community over individuality.

In using the term "mother" in this way, these women show that mothering is not simply tied to anatomy but is a position involving a struggle over meanings and the history of meanings, histories that have been acquired and stored within unofficial institutions. While "mothers of subversives" is univocal, stripped of any connotation but that of reproduction, "mothers of the disappeared" signals an absence, a space that speaks through a lack—the lack of a child—but also a continuing lack within the government of any participatory dialogue, of any answer to the question of how their children disappeared.

The activities of the women of the Plaza de Mayo are symptomatic of many grass-root movements in Latin America, from the *comunidades de base* in Brazil to the popular song movements in Chile and Argentina. These are movements in which the so-called silent sectors of the population are forging politics in ways that no longer subordinate popular culture and women to the traditional view of culture determined by metropolitan discourse. In addition, the postrevolutionary societies of Cuba and Nicaragua have been forced to deal with the participation of women. Nicaragua has, indeed, recognized that creativity is not exclusive to a male elite but is something that is dispersed among the entire population.

In countries under military dictatorship, there is a growing recognition of the importance of cultural politics in the creation of nongendered solidarity groups. To go back to Fanon, this involves transcending the traditional fear of the intelligentsia of immersing its members' individuality in the masses. It also entails realizing that violence, while necessary in self-defense, as in present-day Central America, is not the only way to be revolutionary. That is why an understanding of the socially constructed nature of sexual as well as class and racial divisions is so important, for it enables us to recognize the ethnocentricity of knowledge/power. The fact that the metropolis has always been the place in which knowledge is produced has reinforced the association of domination with masculinity in the Third World and has, therefore, restricted the balanced development of revolutionary movements.

Marx offered an epistemological position that allows us to understand the world *as if* we belonged to the proletariat. Fanon forces us to see the world *as if* we were people of color. One of the lessons of revolutionary movements of the last several years is that we have to resemanticize preconstructed gender categories by taking meaning into our own hands and overcoming the traditional associations of the feminine with nature and the immobile. For those of us living in the metropolis, there is another essential process of defamiliarization. We must step outside the display window of advanced capitalism and look through it from the point of view of societies of scarcity. Then it may appear not only replete but also grotesquely reified. And only then will we understand that the becalmed sea traps not the colonized but the colonizers.

Notes

1   Frantz Fanon, *The Wretched of the Earth* (New York: Grove Press, 1968), p. 51.

2   Fanon, p. 52.

3   For clarification of Foucault's theory and methodology, see "Two Lectures," *Power/Knowledge: Selected Interviews and Other Writings, 1972-77* (New York: Pantheon, 1981).

4   Pierre Bourdieu, *Le sens pratique* (Paris: Les Editions de Minuit, 1980).

5   I am extending the notion of "interruption" as it is developed by David Silverman and Brian Torode, "Interrupting the 'I'," *The Material Word* (London: Routledge and Kegan Paul, 1980), pp. 3-19.

6   Alfonso Reyes, "Discurso por Virgilio," *Antologia de la revista contemporánea* (Mexico, 1973), pp. 163-89. The reference to Neruda is to "Alturas de Macchu Picchu," which is part of *Canto General*.

7   For the relation of this organization to indigenous culture, see Nestor García Canclini, *Las cultura populares en el capitalismo* (Mexico: Nueva Imagen, 1982).

8   Terry Eagleton, *The Rape of Clarissa* (Minneapolis: University of Minnesota Press, 1982), p. 7.

9   René Marques, "En una ciudad llamada San Juan," *En una ciudad llamada San Juan* (Mexico: UNAM, 1960).

10   Nancy Hartsock, *Money, Sex, and Power: Towards a Feminist Historical Materialism* (New York: Longman, 1983).

11   Hartsock, p. 203.

12   Hartsock, p. 253.

13   José María Arguedas, *El zorro de arriba y el zorro de abajo* (Buenos Aires: Losada, 1971).

14   *Playboy Magazine*, 30:2 (1983).

15   "Madre, me voy mañana a Santiago," in *Trilce* (1922), my translation. The Spanish Civil War poems "España, aparta de mi este caliz" ("Spain, Take This Cup from Me") were published posthumously.

16   Mario Vargas Llosa, "Novela primitiva y novela de creación en América Latina," *Revista de la Universidad de México*, 23:10 (1969), p. 31.

17   This refers to a phrase that radio announcers in Argentina repeated daily at the time of Eva Peron's death.

18   Jacques Gilard, ed., *Artículos Costeños*, vol. 1 (Barcelona: Brughera, 1981).

19   Ana Maria Auraujo, *Tupamaras, des femmes de Uruguay* (Paris: des femmes, 1980), p. 163.

20   Auraujo, p. 145.

21   For terms such as "overcoding" and "deterritorialization," I am indebted to Gilles Deleuze and Felix Guattari, *Anti-Oedipus: Capitalism and Schizophrenia* (New York: Viking Press, 1972).

Stanley Aronowitz
The Production of Scientific Knowledge:
Science, Ideology, and Marxism

Science is a socially constituted discourse whose results are linked to a culture's economic, political, and ideological practices. We will never achieve an alternative, critical science until we discard the myths of scientific neutrality and the separation of science and ideology.

My interest in science arose during my years as a representative of the Oil-Chemical and Atomic Workers in the mid-sixties; at the time, this was part of the most technologically advanced production sector in the industrialized world. From 1950 to 1970 two-thirds of the jobs in that industry were abolished because of the shift to continuous flow operation (at the time it was called automation). When I became a teacher in the early 1970s, my earlier experience led me to try to comprehend the relation of Marxism to technology and the problem of advanced industrial societies in which technological transformation seemed to be the fundamental mechanism of capital accumulation, the linchpin of the reorganized labor process, and a most serious problem for the labor movement. My second attempt to deal with this was a paper called "Marx, Braverman and the Logic of Capital."[1] (In 1975 I wrote my doctoral dissertation on *Marx, Science and Technology;* I agreed that the thesis should be left, in the words of the old man, to "the gnawing criticism of the mice," but now the topic keeps popping up as a continuing and growing interest). "Marx, Braverman and the Logic of Capital," my first published work on the technological side of these problems, criticized the one-sided reception of Marx himself in the development of post-Marxian theories of the relation of labor to capital. If we read *Capital* politically, especially the sections from volume 1 on machinery, modern industry, and the labor process, the contradictions in Marx's idea of the proletariat as historical agency leap out of his relentless account of labor and out of his argument that labor degradation is concomitant to accumulation.[2]

Harry Braverman's *Labor and Monopoly Capital,*[3] far from being a supplement to Baran and Sweezy's almost canonical *Monopoly Capital*[4] in recent American Marxism, is also a reading of the lost sixth chapter of Marx's *Capital,* volume 1, "The Result of the Immediate Process of Production." Here Marx shows the dialectic between the accumulation of capital and labor's subordination to it. My critique of Braverman's pathbreaking work—and the similarly important writing in Europe of Andre Gorz,[5] Serge Bologna,[6] and especially Christian Palloix,[7] and others—claims that this reading constitutes a productivist version of the Weberian bureaucratic iron cage. Braverman and Gorz follow Marx in showing not only that capital reconstitutes the character of labor in ways that separate head from hand, design from execution, intellectual from manual labor, but also that "management" is by no means a neutral science. Braverman argues that it is a tool of accumulation designed to reduce the power of the skilled worker by (a) replacing him or her with a machine but, even more important, (b) rationalizing jobs so that the autonomy of the laborer is now transferred to the machine and to a professional manager of capital. We are led inevitably to raise the question of how the domination of capital, not only over the labor process but also over society, may be overturned. Recall that Marx's conception of the working class as historical agency was grounded not only in the centrality of wage labor to the process of production and its separation from ownership and control of the means of production, but also in its capacity to go beyond resistance to capital's initiatives, its ability to achieve self-management of the production process and, by extension, of social relations in their totality.

Although the theorists of the turn-of-the-century Second International took these characteristics for granted, for Marxists after the First World War such optimism was no longer possible. Georg Lukács found the source of the workers' failure to transform a war-torn Europe, despite their mass socialist parties and powerful trade unions, in the power of the commodity form to mask the real relations of society.[8] Lukács's theory holds, with Simmel,[9] that social relations become ensconced as things, but he situates this mystification in capitalist exchange, a conception of technology that grasps that its material form as "progress" disguises a system of social relations based on domination and exploitation. Extrapolating from Lukács's theory of reification, we may infer that the actually existing working class cannot grasp that the scientifically based technologies that have invaded the workplace (and either displaced it or reduced it to impotence) are not part of the natural order but instead are a process of domination. Technological culture, which appears as the natural outgrowth of scientific and social progress, is actually the reified form of labor's economic and social subordination to capital. We enter into relations with computers, for example, perceiving them as valuable tools for calculation, communication, writing, or material production. If Lukács's theory is to be followed, however, this instrumental rationality only prevents us from understanding the degree to which technology constitutes a new culture formed by capital.

Braverman follows a similar line. He regards technological development as an aspect of capital's domination. But rather than focus on the commodity form, that is, on problems of consciousness that arise in the exchange or in cultural relations, Braverman goes directly to the labor process. Here he discovers that "scientific" management and the introduction of new machinery, indeed, the technical division of labor itself, is in the form of domination of capital over labor. Braverman's attack against scientifically based technology as a form of domination retains the basic distinction between "genuine" science and ideology. That is, capitalist "science" becomes the shroud disguising the fact that the main managerial ideology, Taylorism—the separation of design from execution through such devices as the rationalization of tasks into increasingly smaller units, time study, and repetition—is merely capital's weapon of subordination. Braverman's critique leaves natural science alone; he shows, rather, that technology is a social relation and that, in the context of capitalist accumulation, knowledge has political consequences to the extent that it is subsumed under capital as a means to change the traditional labor process in which the knowledgeable worker retained considerable control even though he or she did not own the means of production.

Few of Braverman's commentators have interrogated the distinction between science and ideology retained in his work, even though, after Braverman, the neutrality of technology conceived as a discourse constituted by knowledge separated from its social context is generally regarded as untenable. My concern was to demonstrate that the consequence of Braverman's commentary was to problematize the dialectic of social transformation which in Marxist theory relies on the conscious subject, even if historically constituted. If knowledge has become the major productive force in late capitalism, and its subordination under capital has degraded industrial and clerical labor by rationalizing their skills, then the entire project of historical materialism is thrown into question unless social theory can develop some kind of "new working-class" theory (as Serge Mallet[10] and the earlier Gorz had done). We need not rehearse the bad times on which varieties of this theory have fallen. Suffice it to say that, although capital has subsumed knowledge and those engaged in its production, and the proletarianization of once independent professional strata has increased rapidly in the past twenty years (as new working-class theory predicted), the rationalization of intellectual labor resembles that which afflicted craft workers during the industrialization era. The subordination of knowledge is no less thorough since Taylorism and its variant, Fordism,[11] have imposed themselves universally in the workplace of advanced industrial societies. Although there are differences between manual and intellectual labor, knowledge itself has become fragmented, specialized, and subordinated within specific industrial and commercial configurations. Today, knowledge is subject to a technical division of labor extended both to professionals and to several echelons of management itself. The result, as Gorz argues, is that society's traditional intellectual strata have been transformed into a *technical intelligentsia.*[12]

The technical intelligentsia, ensconced within the technical and social divisions of labor, is no more able to grasp the economic, political, and ideological aspects of its labor than the traditional working class is. Its proletarianization signifies the disappearance of the intellectual as a marginal figure within late capitalism. This development has deep implications for the fate of oppositional social and political practice. As universities, whether "private" or public, become state institutions in the literal meaning, the space for discourse outside the dominant, instrumental, goal-directed mode is significantly narrowed.[13] Increasingly, the professoriate joins the technical intelligentsia, a shift signified by the ubiquity of taxonomies either of a methodological type or of a more conventional disciplinary character. Our entire intellectual life today is marked by its technicalization. Taxonomies not only subordinate knowledge to disciplines that insist on the discrete character of the object of knowledge or methodologies specific to the discipline, but they also construct separate theoretical or literary canons and revered figures around which their specialized discourses revolve. Departure from these models is enough to exclude an individual or a discursive practice from the field.

Taken together, the theses concerning the degradation of labor and the subordination of knowledge and its bearers to capital constitute an important caveat to historical materialism's theory of social transformation, since those developments effectively mediate the formation of the autonomous subject. It is not merely a theoretical question concerning the viability of the notion of historical agency or the subject per se. Such ruminations make interesting disputations, but they are by no means conclusive as a repudiation of the core of Marxism. More interesting are the historical and empirical implications of studies of advanced industrial societies that purport to find a qualitative change in the way social reproduction takes place. The Frankfurt school, Lukács, Braverman, and others who have stressed the so-called counteracting causes to those that endanger the prevailing order (workers' organization, economic crises, wars, social and political instability) have, in different ways, questioned the scientificity of Marxism.[14]

For Marx and, indeed, for the parties of the Second and Third Internationals, such concepts as "total administration," "reification," and "labor degradation" are nothing short of heresy. To focus on the reproductive elements of the social process is to challenge the fundamental premise of historical materialism: the ineluctability of revolt, if not revolution. The profound message of contemporary Marxism is the proposition that the social process reproduces domination, however discontinuous the process may be. Yet the postulate of rupture is inherent in any possible theory of fundamental historical change. And for Marxism there is no automatic procedure: the working-class process, by virtue of its centrality in the production process and its capacity for self-organization, is the means for making history of a different kind. The Frankfurt school (following Lukács) and Braverman (following both Marx and a certain reading of historical evidence) have challenged the most fundamental idea in the entire theory: the proposition that the conjuncture of economic, political, and ideological conditions will constitute a new historical subject. Marxism admits that the question of whether the subject chooses to embark on a definite path of liberation may be indeterminate in the short run, but the theory holds that its ultimate options are limited to those called out by the conjuncture of crisis and self-organization.

These questions raise sharply the status of Marxism as a science of history. Even if it refuses, except in its most orthodox incantations, the eighteenth-century model according to which causality is linear and determination can be specified after a set of limited variables has been named and quantified, Marx's "law of tendency" still forms the heart of the theory. Marxism as a science expects that it can specify a determinate relation between present and future and reads its categories into the past. In short, Marxism claims to be an explanatory and predictive science, one for which the Nietzschean turn of contemporary historiography is entirely reprehensible.[15]

Throughout the twentieth century, one side of the debate concerning Marxism's validity claims has turned on variants of traditional scientific method. Sidney Hook, whose critique is perhaps among the earliest and most prefigurative of later objections, argues that Marxism's claim to scientific validity falls on its lack of "methodological clarity."[16] His criticism is that Marxism looks to experience, not as a test of the validity of its assertions, but only to confirm them. This Popperian view stands on the proposition that theories are true only to the extent that they subject themselves to possible refutation. Further, according to Hook, Marxism has posited the economic as a priori "fundamental in an uninterpreted sense" for determining all other social phenomena. In effect, Marxism fails on its refusal of an experimental turn of mind; its dogmatism, for Hook, marks it as a faith analogous to a religion. And, like a religion, Marxism refuses the "courage to revise" its doctrines in the light of circumstances and instead projects socialism as an absolute from which there is no retreat.

Marxism has been accused of essentialism, especially by poststructuralists. The key term here is the a priori historical subject or the notion of agency on which Marxism pins its theory of revolution. According to Jacques Derrida, whose critiques of Hegel and Husserl may also be interpreted as repudiations of mainstream Marxism, the problem with all efforts to overcome the subject/object splits inherent in classical European philosophy is the persistence of a metaphysical "logocentrism" that inevitably reduces all social, historical, or cognitive phenomena and reverts to traditional canons of scientific explanation.[17] Similarly, Foucault's departure (but not in the double sense) from Marxist historiography consists in his deliberate decision to study marginal social phenomena without imputing overt political significance to what he finds (yet one suspects that the absence of economic and political history among the Foucault school constitutes a new center, just as "history from below" is merely the antinomy of traditional political history).[18] These charges against Marxism are by no means a defense of conventional science. To the contrary, Marxism is accused of scientism, or, to be more exact, is identified with the Enlightenment tradition. Its rationalism is at issue here, not, as Hook claims, its departure from experimental versions of scientific reality.

Habermas charges historical materialism with reductionism, particularly a proclivity for productivism, and thereby argues that Marxism ignores the entire sphere of communicative action.[19] In some ways, Habermas's critique spans those who repudiate Marxism for its nonrational, religious worldview and those who regard Marxism merely as an extension of the Enlightenment, mired in the procedures of empirical science. Habermas wishes to revive philosophical considerations, since he shares the widespread position that the socialist project has been more or less fulfilled by late capitalism, especially if we accept the statist version of the doctrine. Habermas wants to pose the issue of spiritual impoverishment to replace the essentially outmoded problematic of material scarcity. He finds the scientific and technological revolution to have overcome, within and not against the framework of prevailing social relations, most of the complaints of the underlying populations of the nineteenth to early twentieth centuries. Thus the issue is how to complete the unfinished tasks of modernity, not how to challenge modernity itself. These tasks are created by the problems of total administration, by the overbearing power of scientific and technological rationality that solved many problems but suppressed others. For Habermas the unfulfilled promise of the Enlightenment is that our humanity is still incomplete. We are burdened by distorted communication; we are suffering a crisis of meaning; technological rationality has deprived us of communicative competence. Habermas wants to reconstruct historical materialism along the model suggested by speech act theory. Since the crisis of modern

523

life is that social divisions are perpetuated by misunderstandings rising out of the excesses of rational-purposive action (i.e., instrumental rationality), he proposes a culture that permits "context-free communication."[20]

Habermas, however, falls perhaps unwittingly into the de facto acceptance of the two-culture thesis. This is not the thesis of C. P. Snow alone but also the thesis of the natural sciences and the humanities. If one accepts the notion that we live in a scientific culture constituted, as Habermas argues, as "rational purposive" activities, then the major problem for critical theory is to generate a discourse of perfect communication that is, if not ideology-free, at least informed by emancipatory interests. But for Habermas the questions involved in the scientific and technological revolution are more or less taken for granted—or worse, circumvented—as an object of social and cultural inquiry. I wish to advance what should be an unremarkable argument: If what is happening here is the case, it follows that we cannot refuse the proposition that the scientific and technological revolutions today constitute the hegemonic culture of advanced industrial society. The discourses of conservatism and reaction are now heavily dependent on science and technology either to persuade an entire population economically, politically, and ideologically, or to impose themselves as necessary discourses that destroy the possibility of any emancipatory-liberatory politics. We live in a profoundly scientific as well as technological culture. That culture is *the* culture. As abhorrent as that is to Derrideans, the investigation of humanistic culture (indeed, the very notion that forms of social and cultural interaction are a proper object of critical and scientific inquiry) is clearly subordinate to the investigation of nature; in the United States those who study humanistic culture are virtually an oppressed minority. Therefore, the strategy for a counterattack is to interrogate science not only as a form of culture but also as a discourse about truth, which is what I propose to do now.

We are in the midst of a widespread debate concerning the truth claims of science. This debate has been conducted both within Marxism, among philosophers of science, and within organized science itself. It does not (as in the 1930s, with the Social Relations of Science groups both in the United States and in Great Britain) merely speak about the social function of science,[21] about the political and economic influence on the uses of scientific inquiry that still are with us (especially in relation to the anti-thermonuclear war movement); it also addresses whether what we consider ideological discourse also permeates science, and whether the presumed incommensurability of science and ideology, as well as that of science and culture (i.e., general culture) is any longer defensible. It asks whether the unified field of culture now embraces both discourses. This discussion is by no means prompted simply by the generally recognized social uses for which science has been employed. It also reflects what the Marxist literary critic and philosopher Christopher Caudwell called, in the 1930s, the "crisis" in physics, a crucial instance of the crisis in science.[22]

Scientific disputes since the 1920s and 1930s show that inside science itself the concept of unified field theory, which really reduces to the notion of scientific truth as a consensual product (that famous position of Thomas Kuhn and Charles Sanders Peirce, which we are all heir to), is considered contested terrain. The contestation has many different specifications.[23] Consider, from the 1930s, the dispute about wave and particle theory as two alternative explanations for the nature of the physical world. Given the conditions of scientific inquiry, these two are perfectly good explanations for the same object, for the same phenomenon. Of course, along came Niels Bohr, playing the role of rabbi, to declare the theory of complementarity, as demonstrated by the following joke. A husband and wife come to the rabbi's house to seek advice; they're having enormous fights. The rabbi, of course, first asks the man to present his case and invites the woman to leave; the man tells tales of his wife's horrendous behavior, her inability to perform various wifely duties, her abuse of his patrimony and patriarchy, and the rabbi strokes his beard and says to the husband, "You know, you're right." Then the wife comes in and says the husband beats her, is not good to the children, and performs heinous crimes that are virtually unspeakable. The rabbi looks at the woman, strokes his beard with the same gravity, and allows that her case is just. The rabbi's wife is watching this performance and says, "Jake, you are a jelly fish; you are no rabbi, you are basically a compromiser, you are someone who can't make up his mind." He looks at her and he says, "You know, Sadie, you're right."

Niels Bohr tried to make the incommensurable commensurable by declaring that the conditions of scientific inquiry, the experimental method and the whole theoretical apparatus of science, were inadequate to fix on a unified field theory; he also attempted to codify or "authorize" both theories by arguing that they each possessed warranted assertability. Another example: Simultaneously, much to Albert Einstein's chagrin, Werner Heisenberg offered his theory of uncertainty. This revision of physical science drove the "orthodox" Einstein up the wall. He declared that Heisenberg, who was later to write a philosophical reprise of the physical principle declaring the uncertainty of all scientific knowledge, was basically a heathen, or at least a heretic.

The third example is, by now, among historians of contemporary science, a fairly well known understanding of the development of molecular biology. The founding of molecular biology by Francis Crick and James Watson was both an explicit attack on the development of Darwinian evolutionary theory and a fairly self-conscious effort to make a scientific paradigm intrinsically instrumental to technological development and engineering.[24] Gene splicing and other technological innovations are discontinuous not only from the founding of molecular biology of the gene but also from the very project of the foundation of science itself. The molecular biology of the gene declares a radical disjuncture from microbiological historical concerns intrinsic to the discovery and development of evolutionary biology and also from the entire ideal of pure science.

The fourth example, the crisis in Marxism, is but a specific instance of the general crisis of the social sciences. Its first aspect was produced by the apparent breakdown of the certainties of the Stalin era: the primacy of "base over superstructure" (i.e., the determination by the economic of the political, ideological, and cultural spheres). The second major debate within Marxism concerns its status as scientific discourse. I refer to Louis Althusser's effort in the 1960s (heroic as it might be) to endow Marxism with the status of science by showing, in a rather circular way, following Bachelard's notion of the "epistemological break," how Marxism constituted itself through self-critique. In one stroke Althusser performs two extraordinarily difficult, if not contradictory or at least antagonistic, operations. He declares Marxism a science on the basis of its radical break from Hegelian "ideology"; Marxism, he argues, reconstitutes the object of knowledge, transferring it from generic man to the concrete social formation, more specifically to the mode of production. On the other hand, he claims that Marxism announces the radical discontinuity of knowledge itself. So Althusser declares the incommensurability of science and ideology while simultaneously defining Marxist science in terms of its critique of all prior social theory as ideology. Althusser conveniently stops, like E. P. Thompson, at the moment when scientific debate rages most ambiguously, when its status as pristine discourse is in the most difficulty. He simply says that Hegel represents the last possible bourgeois mysticism and that Marxism is constituted as a science by its critique of Hegel, a critique that generates a whole new set of categories. But Althusser then proceeds to act as if Marxism as a science is not problematic. And the only problem, therefore, by logical extrapolation, is of the interpretation of Marxism, not the problem of Marxism itself.[25]

The other effort, in light of the crisis of Marxism, is much more interesting, though not because of its intrinsic value; as a theory, it is inferior to Althusser's. I return to Jurgen Habermas's challenge to the Frankfurt school's theory of science, and I propose to render a brief reprise of the critique by beginning with a discussion of the Frankfurt school's conception of science. The Frankfurt school, in light of the rise of fascism, economic crisis, and the Second World War, which were the constellation of events that generated its interest in science and technology, had by the 1930s and early 1940s developed what amounts to the first thoroughgoing critique of scientific rationality in the late bourgeois epoch. And the fundamental text for cultural theory of science is now celebrating its fortieth publication anniversary. Naturally, I refer to the *Dialectic of Enlightenment,* which appeared originally in German in 1944.[26] Written mostly in the late 1930s and early 1940s, it is an argument about the contradictory character of the Enlightenment and, in the context of the hegemonic discourses of Stalinist versions of Marxism, is clearly understandable as an explicit critique of the Marxist conception of science itself.

The summary arguments are these. Science is the product of the Enlightenment's attempt to elevate reason to an intervention in the social and natural world. But it is divided within itself between its valid and necessary critique of religion and all forms of mysticism, particularly Catholicism, and its attempt to solve humanity's problems by subordinating nature to human ends. This preoccupation with the domination of nature arises from our collective human fear of human emancipation, masked as the fear of the terrors visited upon us by "natural" disasters. The fear of "nature" is really as much the fear of unleashing the possibilities inherent in human reason. According to Horkheimer and Adorno, the domination of nature marches under the flag of reason but is really grounded profoundly in the "irrational," desiring subject. Thus, the Enlightenment elevated empiricism and, later, positivism to the status of a hegemonic ideology that became identical with what we regard as reason and science. Scientific rationality was the instrument of the epistemological break with the essentialism of medieval thought. Nature was deracinated, its substantive character denied; all objects consisted, for the purposes of scientific inquiry at least, in their quantitative, measurable dimensions, and qualities were assigned to the transcendent subject to be endowed on an indifferent "matter."

The scientific enterprise purports to be in the service of human emancipation. But science (and its subordinate, technology) achieve human emancipation through the progressive domination of nature. From its very inception, science is thus an enterprise with an interest, and that interest is the prediction and control of what is considered to be "external" nature. This is separate from considerations of an epistemological character, namely, considerations concerning nature's status (indeed Adorno, following an earlier suggestion of Marx, is later on to understand fully both that nature is historically constituted and that humans are part of natural history).[27] This enterprise of the domination of nature has an unintended consequence. Here we can see the wafts of Weberian theory, namely, that in its attempt to represent the general emancipatory interest through the domination of nature, science also entails the domination of humans. In other words, in order to establish the universal interest, following a very important Marxist view of ideology-free discourse, science purports to separate the domination of nature from human domination and regards *itself* as ideologically neutral. Neutrality here means that science sees itself as having a *universal* interest—that of promoting the discourse of humanity as a whole in its effort to free itself from nature; it does not mean neutral in the absolute sense.

Habermas is not only a product of the eroded soil of postwar German democracy but also partly a product of critical theory itself. In the 1960s, in response to the crisis of the Left, he began his project of trying to construct a new theory of human domination by rejecting Frankfurt theory. "Science and Technology as 'Ideology'," which is a critique of Herbert Marcuse's call for a new science, is a key text. Marcuse insists that the interest of science is not the interest of humanity as a whole. Despite its beneficent features, he claims, science serves the interests of human domination because prediction and control carry over from the domination of nature to the domination of humanity and are implied in class relations. According to Marcuse, there is a possibility for an emancipatory science, based on a genuine conception of the emancipatory interest as human interest. One can see in Marcuse's call for an emancipatory science some elements of what has become the battle cry of the ecological movement. And, however ideological that call may be, at the very least it admits that the interest of emancipation entails a critique, not only of the forms of human domination, but of the domination of nature as well.

Habermas's fundamental move against Marcuse is to argue that science and technology, rather than being interested inquiries in the sense of social antagonism and social domination, are aspects of that sphere of action called "rational-purposive activity." But domination and questions of domination may now be relegated to the realm of communication problems (i.e., problems of interaction). Yet science, technology, and the labor process remain still mystified in his discourse. He makes the radical separation between work and interaction and argues, since he has obliterated class antagonism, that the realm of work and the development of science and technology are in the human interest and that the question of interested inquiry (with respect to the question of domination) has to be confined to areas of interaction—speech acts, communication, and language. What is important here is that there is a curious reversion in Habermas to a relatively old notion of the neutrality of science. And therefore, for Habermas, we cannot critically interrogate science, especially natural science or technology, because those are clearly in the general interest to promote, since he posits an unproblematic relation between humans and nature. Our real task is to move in the direction of talking about intersubjectivity.

Habermas makes a powerful and irrefutable argument against Marcuse's call for a science free of the dominating interest, but only because Marcuse has failed to specify what the contours of such an emancipatory science might be. From this Habermas concludes that there is no possibility for a science other than the one that prevails, since it corresponds to a certain type of universally valid rationality. But, like the legions of scientists, philosophers, and lay persons who have submitted to the ubiquity of science by asserting that its facticity corresponds to the rational, Habermas suffers from the very absence of which Marcuse is accused. He has not looked at science at all, for science itself is rent today. Science is undertaking the same kind of critical self-reflection as that in which neo-Marxist, Derridean, and Foucaultian theory is engaged. Marxism is, of course, stuck in the radical distinction between science and ideology. It rejects the idea of a context-free inquiry, that is, a text whose validity claims may be separated from the interest that gave it life. Yet Marxism hopes to discover truth through the prism of its paradigm, one relative only to the limits to inquiry imposed by the social and historical context. Although Marxism, in principle, admits the partial character of its discoveries, it remains tied to the primacy of the economic (albeit in the last instance), the constitution of a revolutionary subject as an eschatological a priori, and the categorical assertion that knowledge and human interest may be simultaneously linked to the "truth" provided the interest is emancipatory.

My intention is to go beyond the distinction between science and ideology, to "abolish" the category of ideology altogether because it implies its antinomy—a disinterested inquiry which, through both methodological purity and undistorted communication, can achieve something we may call warranted assertibility, truth, validity. Since the object itself is constituted by social interests, as Horkheimer has persuasively argued, our selections are always subject to revision—not only the *ways* we see, but *what* we see.[28] Also, I want to assert, without for the moment engaging in detailed argument, that the traditional distinctions between science and values, emotion and reason, subject and object, are themselves grounded in a kind of modernity that is increasingly doubtful as a methodological presupposition.

Recently, the work of Loren Graham,[29] Paul Feyerabend,[30] and Thomas Kuhn[31] has thrown into question the status of scientific theory, if not scientific practice, as value neutral. Kuhn's argument, which presents itself as an account of how paradigm shifts occur, contains a major caveat in the very means by which its central thesis is explicated. Kuhn explains paradigm shift by reference to the inability of the old paradigm to account for anomalies that appear in the process of performing normal science. As these accumulate, some kind of transformation of quantity into quality occurs. Sooner or later, some elements in the scientific community can no longer tolerate the situation, since among the normative principles of the community remains the ideal of a unified field theory. Kuhn's explanation remains within the extant scientific method: experimentation and the judgment of what Peirce noted as those professionally qualified to determine the truth claims of any new proposition or set of propositions. Although Kuhn acknowledges that the new paradigm bears no necessary relation to the one it replaces—and thereby calls into question realist theories as well as the concept of the history of science as cumulative and continuous—the core of his explanation remains dependent on the sociological arbitrary internal to the process: the activity of the scientific community, especially its normative, a priori propensity to critical and self-reflexive inquiry.

Thus Kuhn's argument for historical disjunction is not rooted in the process of scientific investigation but in the "value" or "ideological" orientation of its (most advanced) practitioners, who have internalized Enlightenment presuppositions concerning reasonable ways of proceeding. Still, the procedures remain unexamined within the confines of even the most critical history and philosophy of science. The point of Feyerabend's *Against Method,* perhaps the most self-consciously radical of the new histories and philosophies of science, is to show that both Newtonian and contemporary physics have no monopoly on the practices considered most radical by scientists. Ptolemaic physics was equally rigorous in experiment, self-reflexive, and open to revision. Moreover, its results, Feyerabend argues, were adequate for explaining the phenomena it investigated. Nevertheless, Feyerabend, Kuhn, and their common mentor, Karl Popper,[32] accept the experimental method as the most rational procedure for achieving scientific validity, especially the injunction to frame questions and answers subject to rules of falsifiability.

Feyerabend wants to argue for the arbitrary character of hegemonic scientific law, and, in turn, to challenge the substantive norms that guide its certification by the scientific community. But while he does not dispute Kuhn's idea that framing scientific paradigms is a matter of establishing truth values independent of social interest, neither does he accept Kuhn's assumption that there is a hierarchy of scientific adequacy. Adequacy is self-referential. If it can be shown that a given paradigm observes the norms of inquiry that correspond to those established by the contemporary scientific community, and its results are valid as types of explanation within those norms, then the whole issue of "truth" disappears. However, both Kuhn and Feyerabend remain bounded by a realist theory of science to the extent that the object of knowledge remains fixed; only understanding varies.

This is, of course, a step backward from Dewey's theory of science, which holds "that the object of knowledge is eventual; that is, it is an outcome of directed experimental operations instead of something in sufficient existence before the act of knowing."[33] Dewey's radical link between the means and the ends of knowledge is strikingly prefigurative of poststructuralist notions of undecidability. Although Kuhn is closer to this perspective, especially emulating Dewey's and Peirce's critique of the method of authority by which knowledge is certified, it seems to me that Dewey has taken the argument further than most contemporary writers. He insists that the notion of disinterested inquiry simply obfuscates the suffering investigator who is infused with intentions: "only operations intentionally performed and attentively *noted in connection* with their products give observed material a positive intellectual value, and this condition is satisfied only by thought; ideas are the perception of this connection."[34] Dewey goes on to argue that "data are selected from total original subject matter which gives the impetus to knowing; they are discriminated for a purpose: that namely, of affording signs or evidence to define or locate a problem, and thus give a clue to its resolution."[35]

We may object that Dewey gives too much weight to intention and seems to contradict his opposite idea that the object is constituted by practice. This apparent logical inconsistency disappears when we take these statements as two moments in a discontinuous process. Although the selection of what he calls "data" expresses interest, and this act has an influence on the constitution of the object, he also removes experimental method from its neutral nest. The "operations" of inquiry, however conventional, are both undecidable in their outcomes and prefigure the form of the result: scientific discovery is framed within discourses that are normatively certified by the prevailing scientific community, but these procedures are no more than tendential. Dewey is straining to argue that scientific action, which appears both rational and purposive, retains its undecidability because the object is not fixed in advance and practice is creative. Nevertheless, the implication is that the notion of value-free inquiry is untenable. Yet, like many others, Dewey assumes that the experimental method, the scientific community, and the enterprise itself, while not value neutral, have a force of ineluctability.

I would like to propose that the weight of recent investigations into the social relations of science, which have in various ways challenged the separation of text from context, the separation of values from facts, and the idea of continuity and progress in scientific development, are all germane to my contention that the Marxist (and conventional scientific) distinction between science and ideology is now quite spurious. For this purpose I want to suggest four categories that bear on this contention, all of which are related both externally and internally to scientific procedures. After discussing these categories, I will undertake a conclusion consisting of metatheoretical reflections.

The four categories are: (1) the problem of the constitution of the object of scientific knowledge (Is the constitution of the object, which is a part of the very inquiry of science itself, ideologically value-free?); (2) questions concerning the status of scientific method (Is experimental method historically and socially constructed, and, moreover, does its historical and social constitution inform the practice of science?); (3) questions concerning the determination of truth claims, the warranted assertabilities of science; and (4) the form and status of the results of science. These issues must be examined. The failure of Marcuse, Althusser, and other critics of scientific culture to deal with the internal constitution of science as a set of practices is perhaps the most problematic aspect of both a Marxist theory of science and of many other theories of science that are informed by radical intentions.

It is by now commonplace in the sociology of science to note that governments and corporations fund certain lines of inquiry and not others. As powerful as this argument may be, in making the argument for the implosion of science and ideology, or at least for their partial implosion, and their problematic separation, I do not want to dwell on the economic and political determination of the object of scientific knowledge. Those issues are much too well known, even if they remain too little theorized. I wish to argue that, in the first place, in social as well as natural scientific inquiry, the division of labor within the scientific community, between physics, chemistry, biology, geology, psychology, sociology, economics, anthro-

530

pology, and political science—a division of labor that is a form of fragmentation with consequences of professionalization—not only influences the results of scientific inquiry but also the very constitution of the inquiry itself.

I am not making pejorative or normative judgments at this time concerning the validity of these moves toward a division of labor based on presumed disciplines. That is a question for another time. What is important to understand is that those divisions, as social scientists, biological scientists, and certainly physicists and chemists have known for a long time, are arbitrary in the sense that sciences are socially and historically constituted by discourses, by professional discourses in particular, and by interest. The object examined is thus inevitably ideological. What goes on when the attempt is made to overcome the ideological character of that inquiry is precisely that, in linking various inquiries, new sciences are created. For example, biochemistry, physical chemistry, physiological psychology, the new developments in sociology, political economy, and so on, show that conventional disciplines, while still with us, have become contested terrain within the development of the scientific community.

The constitution of the scientific object, however, is also intrinsically connected to questions of method. The foundations of scientific method are well known in the ordinary sense but not well known in the critical sense. In the first place, experimentation entails the decontextualization of the object and its insertion into a laboratory situation. As a strategy of inquiry, decontextualization is now the subject of enormous conflict and contestation. When we examine any object separate from its "natural" (i.e., external, social or biological) context, the object is placed in a new controlled environment, one that is oriented to the project of prediction and control. Second, what is entailed by decontextualization, as well as by the division of disciplines and the definitions of scientific objects by the disciplines, is an *intervention;* that is to say, the configuration of the object is itself the result of an interaction between the knower and the known. John Dewey repeatedly makes that point. The constitution of the object itself is not "objective" and detached from the process of inquiry. This is precisely what Heisenberg argues is problematizing all the old categories of physical law. Finally, the abstraction of quality from quantity, the point that is made by Horkheimer and Adorno, not only mathematizes the results but also makes the *character* of the object virtually quantitative. This means that the division of culture into scientific and "humanistic" (or social scientific) cultures is itself defined by the notion that quantity is scientific, whether it be in sociology or in physics, and that quality is poetic or ethical and, consequently, isolated from the framework of science as such.

What the humanities and the social sciences of a critical kind suffer from, in discursive terms, is not their marginalization because they are ideologically oppositional but their marginalization because they are "poetic." And that is given by the character of scientific inquiry, which is, to a large extent, framed by the invocation to prediction and control and by the normative imperative that measurability is the only reliable way of verification and falsification. I repeat: division of labor, the character of science as intervention, decontextualization, the mathematicization of science. On the basis of any inquiry into method, we conclude that the results of investigation are not necessarily untrue, not necessarily devoid of validity.[36] Results are, however, necessarily bound up with certain social and historical norms of inquiry. Science is a discursive field with presuppositions that are themselves problematic.

The forms of the results, the validation of the results of science: I must say that I find all the relevant criticisms of Kuhn and Feyerabend unconvincing. Listen to what must be counted as the most rigorous, as well as the latest, of defenses, not only of the realist theory of science, but also of the correspondence theory of truth, as well as the reflection theory of knowledge, the work of Newton-Smith. I quote from *The Rationality of Science:* "There has been progress in science, this progress is best understood as an improvement in the verisimilitude of our theories. The explanation for the fact that science has been capturing more truth about the world is that we have evolved evidential or epistemic procedures of some success and that the development of science has by and large been determined by scientists acting on the basis of the outcome of the application of these procedures."[37]

This argument against the attempt to implode science and ideology rests finally on two points: the idea that scientific method, scientific procedure, does in fact verify or falsify, whether you are a Popperian or not, and the notion of the rupture with common sense. Newton-Smith is absolutely Gramscian in this sense. He understands fully that science attacks the common sense of immediate perception and tries to unmask immediate perception to achieve theorization. But note in the above quotation the attempt to attack the Kuhnian notion that the scientific community, and, in the case of Feyerabend, its social and ideological influences, is the ultimate court of scientific opinion; and also the response to the notion that this is a socially, not naturally, constituted court. Newton-Smith is constrained to remind us that the progress of science depends on the interpretation by scientists themselves of their own procedures of inquiry. However, the process of inquiry can be shown to be socially and historically constituted, not only with respect to its appearance, but also with respect to its procedures. Thus the notion of scientific truth and scientific progress is at least subject to interrogation, not only on the basis of the assumed a priori validity of the results, but also on the basis of the conditions of scientific inquiry itself. Newton-Smith excoriates Kuhn and Feyerabend for having advanced what amounts to historical relativism, but he fails to show how that conception, the validation of scientific theory, has crept into his own defense of the asocial character of scientific inquiry.

In different ways, Kuhn and Feyerabend argue that normalcy in science is defined by the constitution of the scientific community. Although Feyerabend argues that this constitution is socially constructed, he has nothing to say about the social constitution of science because he is still operating within the discourse of Anglo-American philosophy of science. This absence must be taken as a serious critique of attempts to defend science, not only from an Enlightenment perspective, but also from the Marxist perspective. I contend that there is no longer a normal science, only normal technological research. The concept of normal science is an illusion of philosophers, including Marxist philosophers. Science is precisely characterized by its lack of normalcy; in fact, the notion of normalcy itself, the notion of neutrality, is ideologically reactionary.

Max Black, hardly a Marxist, has made an argument that is ultimately unpersuasive but has a wonderful title, *Science As Metaphor*. Black's argument—that all scientific laws are based on metaphors—may be heretical to those of a literal cast of mind, particularly those who insist that scientific law refers to an external world that is knowable in something like the picture sense described by Wittgenstein or even in the "approximate" connotative sense given to the correspondence theory of truth by Lenin. For theoretical physics, however, the validity of Black's point seems perfectly obvious. The metaphoric character of science suggests an infinite regress of decentering; the hard referent with which scientific law is supposed to be concerned is itself subject to interrogation. The problem is not that of materialism, of a world historically and epistemologically prior to and independent of human cognition, but whether the external world is independent of our practices, including scientific practice. Do the practices of science refer to a pristine *other* which can, in principle, be known through certain kinds of procedures? If our postulate—that science is an intervention rather than an activity of cognition alone—makes sense, then the proposition that scientific law refers to a pristine "other" falls away. Our procedures for knowing the world are, simultaneously, ways of altering it. The metaphoric character of science registers the historicity of science because the metaphors continually change.

I am arguing that the notion of the material object is itself a metaphor that can be historically situated within a specific problematic in the development of the capitalist mode of production—the subsumption of all knowledge under capital and its consequent instrumentalization. (That, of course, is a radical reinterpretation of Marxism, one that will subject me to the charge of relativism, to which I plead guilty.) The certification of the results of scientific investigation, therefore, is not only a matter of concern to the scientific community and its cultural and intellectual norms but also a way of examining the cultural metaphors by which scientists are formed themselves. The notions of precision, quantification, empirical falsification, inference, and other bromides of scientific culture constitute a normative order that can be traced to specific historical roots. But when science digs more deeply into its own foundations, when it begins to ask questions regarding its presuppositions about the natural world, such as whether it can fathom some kind of "ultimate" material building block, it reverts to mysterious and sometimes mystical metaphors. What is the precise meaning of the "black box"? This term testifies to the metaphoricity underlying the concept of precision itself. Theoretical physics is drowning in ambiguity; the more it knows the less does its traditional culture really hold. Heisenberg has remarked that the further up into the level of abstraction physics reaches (or the further down to the level of "reality"), the more ordinary language replaces what is considered in middle-brow culture or "normal" science to be truly rigorous language. And since philosophy proclaimed itself capable only of clearing up the ambiguities of language, of clarifying the meaning of scientific results rather than being capable of discovery, both scientists and philosophers are suffering role confusion. The scientists proliferate tracts, suited for the nonspecialist, that purport to "explain" their bewilderment, and the philosophers become ever more narrow and mathematical in their expression. The scientists are slightly embarrassed that their objects and methods seem to merge with the occult, while the philosophers reaffirm the realist theories as if to hope against hope that by their act of faith everything will be made right again.

If this is true, then among the most important questions for a new politics is the struggle for its autonomy. The "independence of science" demand would not relieve it of social responsibility, for the scientific community would be subject to the same constraints that all citizens suffer, though intellectual freedom would not be impaired. Of course, this question gets fairly tricky when we consider the capital investment needed for inquiry. Nevertheless, I see no particular advantage to the private appropriation of the results of scientific inquiry as opposed to their appropriation by the state: in one case, capital dominates; in the other, a public bureaucracy that may or may not be responsive to popular pressure does. The autonomy of science would not "free" inquiry from the epistemological consequences of social and cultural norms, of the episteme(s) to which scientific knowledge must conform.

Here I wish to distinguish *political* limits from those imposed on knowledge by social life. We can condemn the former but cannot escape the latter. Thus the possibility of an unmediated relation between knowledge and the world to which it putatively refers is bound up with the dream of scientific autonomy that derives, I think, from the political and economic restraints imposed by capitalist and state socialist regimes on all forms of inquiry and expression. Habermas's wish for context-free communication resonates with the desire of art and science for autonomy, but this is not the same as positing its possibility. As long as human life is configured by social relations, nature will be conceived and perceived in the images of the imaginary.

This is, of course, a radical reinterpretation that understands science as a form of social knowledge. Consistent with ecological thinking that has modified our views of nature over the past two decades, this does not imply that the external world is a "projection" of our collective mentality. Its priority to human life is a conclusion of evolutionary theories of the cosmological and the biological kinds, and this axiom constitutes a kind of a priori without which the entire enterprise of historical investigation is really impossible. But the question of priority should not be confused with the autonomy of nature. The Enlightenment project of subsuming nature under "man" runs into difficulty when we consider that nature's rhythms have been altered by human intervention, but not completely. There are still moments of internal autonomy, the violation of which has already produced a revolt of nature against such taken-for-granted assumptions as those underlying industrialization. We have learned survival; we have learned that "atom splitting" is not merely the next conquest but maybe the last; we have learned that the industrialization of space may generate a counterreaction.

Nevertheless, humanity seems to have an almost infinite capacity for forgetting. We all know that, but we deny the metaphoric character of science, on the one hand, and the degree to which science—no less than art or the social sciences—is intimately bound up with social relations, on the other. I am not claiming, as Young and others have done, that science is "merely" a social relation; its procedures, while by no means separate from cultural and social configuration, are, at the same time, specific to the form of inquiry as well as its object.

Stanley Aronowitz

Finally, there is the question of the status of science as truth, including Marxist "science's" truth, questions of warranted assertability based on acceptance of all conditions specified especially in the consensual agreement of the scientific community. I believe that the realist theory of science, while in some sense tenable as a kind of article of faith comparable to Althusser's faith in economic determination in the last instance, has no practical (and I do not mean instrumental) significance with respect to our understanding of scientific inquiry. Therefore, science is a socially constituted discourse whose results are internally linked to the ideological character of its components and are relative to the economic, political, and ideological practices of an episteme or an epoch. We must, of course, go beyond this to specify the conditions for an alternative critical science. But I contend that we will never achieve that alternative critical science until we throw out the myths of the neutrality of science and of the separation of science and ideology.

Notes

1   Stanley Aronowitz, "Marx, Braverman, and the Logic of Capital," *Insurgent Sociologist* (Fall 1978).

2   Karl Marx, *Capital*, vol. 1, especially chaps. 12-15.

3   Harry Braverman, *Labor and Monopoly Capital* (New York: Monthly Review Press, 1974).

4   Paul Baran and Paul Sweezy, *Monopoly Capital* (New York: Monthly Review Press, 1966).

5   Andre Gorz, "The Tyranny of the Factory: Today and Tomorrow," in Andre Gorz, ed., *The Division of Labour: The Labour Process and Class Struggle in Modern Capitalism* (London: Harvester Press, 1976).

6   Serge Bologna, "Class Composition and the Theory of the Party at the Origin of the Workers Councils Movement," in Gorz, ed., *The Division of Labour.*

7   Christian Palloix, "The Labour Process from Fordism to Neo-Fordism," in Gorz, ed., *The Division of Labour.*

8   Georg Lukács, "Reification and the Consciousness of the Proletariat," *History and Class Consciousness* (Cambridge: MIT Press, 1971).

9   Georg Simmel, *The Philosophy of Money* (London: Routledge and Kegan Paul, 1978). Reification for Simmel is a property of an economy in which money dominates all social relations. In contrast, Lukács locates the phenomenon in a specific historical context and a particular social formation, namely, capitalism. It is only when the commodity form penetrates all social relations that reification comes to dominate consciousness, according to Lukács.

10   Serge Mallet, *The New Working Class* (London: Spokesman Books, 1975).

11   According to Palloix, "we must emphasize that Fordism, which still characterizes the labour process today, is not the same as Taylorism; it is a real innovation. . . . Ford took over the essential aspects of Taylorism (separation of design and innovation from execution, division and sub-division of jobs, each movement allowed a specific time) but he also went further in introducing two further principles: a new method of controlling labour-power, the introduction of the flow-line principle (conveyors) in the concrete shape of the assembly line" (in Gorz, ed., *The Division of Labour*, p. 59). The new method of control of labor-power was the day-wage system (in place of piece rates), "thus making it possible to 'regulate' the externally-imposed control of labour-power." This day rate—the famous five-dollar day— "assured capital of an uninterrupted supply of labour" and dampened militancy. It is interesting to note that during the rise of the CIO (1935-41), Ford was the last major automaker to be unionized. The company combined terror with relatively high wages to prevent the self-organization of workers.

12   Andre Gorz, "Technology, Technicians, and the Class Struggle," in Gorz, ed., *The Division of Labour.*

13   See Stanley Aronowitz and Henry Giroux, *Education under Seige* (South Hadley, Mass.: Bergin and Garvey, 1985), especially chap. 8, "Neo-conservative Ideology and the Crisis in Higher Education."

14   See especially Max Horkheimer, *Critical Theory* (New York: Seabury Press, 1972); and Stanley Aronowitz, *The Crisis in Historical Materialism* (South Hadley, Mass.: Bergin and Garvey, 1981).

15   Here we must distinguish Marx, who made this claim once in *The German Ideology*, and the Marxism of the Second and Third Internationals, which never tired of presenting itself in the guise of a natural science, following Engels's suggestion in *Anti-Dühring*. The writings of Lenin and Kautsky are especially important in making the case for Marxism as a "natural science." See V. I. Lenin, *Materialism and Empirical Criticism;* and Karl Kautsky *The Class Struggle* (Ann Arbor: University of Michigan Press, 1975).

16   Sidney Hook, *Reason, Social Myth, and Democracy* (New York: John Day and Co., 1940), p. 107.

17   See Jacques Derrida, *Speech and Phenomena* (Evanston, Ill.: Northwestern University Press, 1970).

18   Michel Foucault, *The Order of Things* (New York: Pantheon Books, 1970).

19   Jürgen Habermas, "Reconstruction of Historical Materialism," *Communication and the Evolution of Society* (Boston: Beacon Press, 1979).

20   Jürgen Habermas, *Theory of Communicative Action* (Boston: Beacon Press, 1984).

21   For an excellent collective study of the British group, see Gary Werskey, *The Visible College* (New York: Holt, Rhinehart and Winston, 1978). No such history exists of the Americans, but a good starting point is Alice Kimball Smith, *A Peril and a Hope: The Scientists' Movement in America* (Cambridge: MIT Press, 1970). The latter volume deals with the postwar effort of some American physicists to respond to the decision of the Truman administration to use the atomic bomb as an instrument of war. Werskey's study deals principally with British Left scientists in the 1930s. See also Ronald Clark, *Haldane* (Oxford: Oxford University Press, 1984). Sadly, this biographer, fundamentally hostile to J. B. S. Haldane's political views, makes little effort to understand his Marxism and the Social Relations of Science movement of which he was a part, although not the most theoretically interesting member. See J. D. Bernal, *The Social Function of Science* (London, 1939), for a fuller explication of the attempt of this fascinating group to comprehend science in social terms.

22   Christopher Caudwell, *The Crisis in Physics* (London: Bodley Head, 1950). This work, originally published in 1939, was perhaps the most sophisticated effort by any English-speaking Marxist to deal with science as a *discourse,* hence subject to ideological influences. That is, as Hyman Levy, one of the leading figures in the Social Relations of Science movement notes in the introduction to the volume, "any scientific theory is necessarily the specialized development of a general social view, even although those who initiate the theory may be profoundly unaware of the connection" (p. viii).

23   See especially Charles Sanders Peirce, "The Fixation of Belief," in Justus Buchler, ed., *The Philosophy of Peirce: Selected Writings* (London: Routledge and Kegan Paul, 1940); and Thomas Kuhn, *The Structure of Scientific Revolutions* (Chicago: University of Chicago Press, 1962).

24   Francis Crick, *Life Itself* (New York: Touchstone Books, 1982).

25   Louis Althusser, *For Marx* (New York: Vintage Books, 1970).

26   Max Horkheimer and Theodor Adorno, *Dialectic of Enlightenment* (New York: Seabury Press, 1973).

27   Theodor Adorno, *Negative Dialectics* (New York: Seabury Press, 1974).

28   Max Horkheimer, *Critical Theory* (New York: Continuum Books, 1972).

29   Loren Graham, *Between Science and Values* (New York: Columbia University Press, 1981).

30   Paul Feyerabend, *Against Method* (London: New Left Books, 1970).

31   Thomas Kuhn, *Structure of Scientific Revolutions* (2d ed.; Chicago: University of Chicago Press, 1970); and, more recently, *The Essential Tension* (Chicago: University of Chicago Press, 1979).

32   Karl Popper, *The Logic of Scientific Discovery* (London: Hutchinson, 1961).

33   John Dewey, "Quest for Certainty," in *John Dewey: The Later Works,* vol. 4, ed. J. Ann Boyleston (Carbondale: Southern Illinois University Press, 1984), p. 136.

34   Dewey, "Quest for Certainty," p. 142.

35   Dewey, "Quest for Certainty," p. 142.

36   Ludwig Fleck, *The Genesis of a Scientific Fact* (Chicago: University of Chicago Press, 1979). See also Bruno Latour and Steve Woolgar, *Laboratory Life* (Los Angeles: Sage Publications, 1980); and Arthur Koestler, *The Case of the Midwife Toad* (New York: Vintage Books, 1973).

Stanley Aronowitz

All of these writers, in quite different ways, show the social constitution of what counts as scientific knowledge. In particular, these works demonstrate the power of the scientific community in determining the truth value of the experimental and theoretical work itself. One could also add the controversy surrounding the observations and theories of Immanuel Velikovsky for evidence that Peirce was right: truth is defined by those professionally certified to name it.

37 W. Newton-Smith, *The Rationality of Science* (London: Routledge and Kegan Paul, 1981). Newton-Smith has made the most serious defense of the realist theory of science in many years. His polemic against the relativism of Popper, Kuhn, and Feyerabend is ably argued. Yet this work, an internalist theory of scientific progress, remains unreflective about the way in which scientific method is constituted socially. The charge that the Popperian school is an irrationalist theory simply stacks the deck against every nonrationalist effort to challenge the truth claims of science. As I have indicated above, this school remains, for the most part, rationalist even if it does not accept a realist account.

Question

Since Husserl, European philosophy of science has recognized the social and historical constitution of the objects, methods, and communities of scientific inquiry. Even in Anglo-American philosophy of science, at least in the current postempiricist phase, these claims are no longer controversial. The question is, what follows from this? Does it follow that we cannot distinguish between scientifically warranted assertions and ideological ones? Second, what do you mean by ideology here? Third, how would you constitute scientific inquiry so that it is not oriented to prediction and control?

Aronowitz

Let me start by saying that we have a different perception of both Anglo-American philosophy of science and Marxist attempts to analyze the question of scientific method. I have not encountered one critique of scientific method as socially and historically constituted by activities that themselves may be construed ideologically. Although Feyerabend studied the constitution of the scientific object and the plurality of theories, Kuhn studied the constitution of scientific communities, and Black studied the form of scientific results, they all ultimately defend the neutrality of science by appealing to the status of scientific method. I would argue that scientific method—a method characterized by decontextualization and by the separation of quality from quantity—is itself a social activity. Furthermore, the issue of intervention, which is an epistemological as well as a historical issue, has not been addressed systematically. Finally, although European philosophy of science is concerned with the effects of rationality, it does not challenge the nature of that rationality. What we have are piecemeal defenses of plurality. For example, Feyerabend ultimately accepts the scientific method and shows that two theories, incommensurable with respect to their results, nevertheless refer rigorously to the same object by means of their procedure. That procedure is held to be historically correct because he never challenges the Popperian view of falsifiability, a view grounded in the project of prediction and control.

Your second question addresses the concept of ideology. I mean to suggest that there is a hegemonic discourse that is socially and historically constituted. This ideology refers to its own conditions of discursive competence, on the one side, and to a prevailing set of practices, on the other. The validity of science, grounded in a theory of correspondence, depends upon the ability of scientific discourse to appear in a relation of verisimilitude with its own practices. Even the Kuhnian theory of paradigm shifts never questions the relation between scientific practices and what science calls the "real."

Your third question is how to reconstitute the object of scientific knowledge. One example would be Ernesto Laclau's attempt to reconstitute society as a set of discourses. A second example is Althusser's insistence that Marx transferred the focus of scientific inquiry from people to society and the mode of production. Once we recognize that we are constituting a counterhegemonic discourse whose relation to the real is forever problematic and linked to our own political, social, and cultural practices, then we are free to do genuinely ecological science, to do genuinely social science. Then the integration of linguistic theory, or for that matter discourse theory, with the ongoing social practices of a putatively radical movement can actually take place. As long as we insist on the closed system of scientific inquiry, one in which both the object of knowledge and the methods by which we know the world are fixed, we can never evolve into a critical science. Thus the first task is a deconstruction that is ruthless, pitiless, and thoroughgoing, including a deconstruction of our own scientific paradigm, which we call Marxism.

Question

Gramsci's *Prison Notebooks*—particularly the tenth and eleventh—deal with the question of science by responding to Vico's notion of scientific certainty. What place does Gramsci's work have in your definition of science?

Stanley Aronowitz

Aronowitz

I have attempted to avoid defining either science or ideology because I think that such definitions become problematic by fixing the limits of this kind of discourse. This refusal is a methodological, not a rhetorical, move. The attempt to define them involves an infinite regress of the relationship between specific hegemonic discourses and historically evolving social interests. We define as certain those discourses that fix particular relations of the so-called natural and social worlds and achieve thereby a kind of aesthetic elegance: as Christine Delphy suggests in her paper, both scientific philosophy and science seek the utmost simplicity and the greatest scope in the explanation of the world.

In this context, let me invoke Dewey, since, although I'm interested in international Marxist and post-Marxist discussions, I want us to get used to thinking and working with Americans. Otherwise we aren't going to make any political progress in this country. John Dewey's *Quest for Certainty* discusses the Gramscian point about hegemonic discourses and the relation between thought and action. (I realize many people would think pragmatism old-fashioned. But wait another five years and analytic philosophy of language will be relegated to the dust bin temporarily because Rorty is raising questions about the role of warranted assertability and pragmatic relations in the constitution of scientific discourse.) The "quest for certainty" is always linked, particularly as a definition of science, to moments of crisis. Certainty, as distinct from the actual practice of science, becomes a kind of religiosity scientists invoke to put Humpty Dumpty back together again. But Humpty Dumpty is rent; he will be put together again only temporarily. Our temporary certainties will present themselves as science, when, in fact, they will be hegemonic ideologies for a particular era.

This has important implications for reconstituting a critical science, which must confront the necessity to understand itself and which can only produce temporary certainties. In the old Frankfurt dialogue this is called "reflexivity," not deconstruction: practices reflect upon and continually modify themselves in recognition of their relativity and historicity in relation to social discourses and social struggles.

Question

You are not denying—or are you—the claim of realism in the last instance, that there is a moment that belongs to the world, a moment that is being interrogated by scientific practices?

Aronowitz

I'm arguing something entirely different. It is evident that there is a natural history prior to human development. It is evident that both physical and biological states or levels of reality have an existence prior to the appearance of human beings. Realism as a theory refers to the status of the referent and of knowledge about the referent. I am arguing that the world of things, our world of referents, is constituted by the practices and discourses of social life. This is no different from Marx's notion of the humanization of nature and the naturalization of "man." This applies not only to the world of everyday life, culture, and work, but also to the world of the natural sciences. Most scientists and philosophers of science do not accept this notion—that the referent is itself the product of historically constituted activity. Once this becomes the new common sense, we can turn our attention toward the new critical science I am talking about, a science devoted to constructing a world out of utopian discourses.

Question

Would a critical science counteract the intrusion of techno-logic into the moral-practical sphere of society?

539

Aronowitz

The project of critical science is informed by the interests of a counterhegemonic discourse. But the first task is to reduce the privileged space that scientific and technological discourses occupy within social affairs. We need to reintroduce ethical and moral considerations into social and discursive practices. As long as science presents itself as anormative (outside the realm of ethical judgment), we are caught in a circle of having to validate Marxism, feminism, or other oppositional practices in the terms set by the Enlightenment; that is, they are outside rationality, even nonrational, with less claim than science to speak of the real. Science presents itself as a neutral discourse, yet it is a mechanism of subordination; it subordinates women, working people, black people.

There is, however, an antagonism within science. This moment of difference is, as Laclau has argued, produced by the confrontation between two blocks of scientific discourse. Too many Marxists have apparently decided that we need not struggle to produce this second, counterhegemonic science because they have assumed that there is only one science. That's Habermas's argument.

Now let's talk about the technological element of this conflict. Technology is a system of reifications and discourses, one that hides a broad range of ideological interests, including those of science. Marxists have always wanted to separate the scientific from the technological in order to preserve the former and appropriate it for themselves. That cannot be done. One has to make a thoroughgoing, fundamental critique of the presuppositions of both, to show that the Greek notion of *techne* as human practice has been radically disjoined from the notion of technology. Technology, in turn, has become a new religion.

Comment (Ernesto Laclau)

I would like to comment on the Habermasian view of technologic implicit in the question. I don't think that everything that happens in society is the superstructural effect of an underlying technological reality. Such an assumption is merely the return of a base/superstructure model. It assumes that everything that is complex in society is so because we are only looking at the surface of social life; but if we go to the ultimate ground or core of society, which in this case would be technology, then we could reconstruct all surface diversity in terms of a system of mediation. I don't think that either society or technology operates in such a way. Technology itself is a discursive ensemble that depends on particular social and historical conditions for its development. There are conditions of possibility of technology itself. The very idea of technology is a scientific abstraction, an analytic abstraction, that combines many phenomena of a very different nature. I am not saying that such abstractions are necessarily wrong. But I don't know whether subsuming these very different discursive practices under the term "technology" and concluding that this hypostatization produces a unique domain of effects provides a sound analysis. This is not to deny that these technological processes have a tendency to autonomize themselves, to constitute a *point de capiton,* a nodal point in society from which a plurality of effects with vast repercussions flow. But this does not make technology an underlying mechanism of determination.

Question (Christine Delphy)

Our preoccupations seem to run along very similar lines. I too am concerned with claims for scientific neutrality. I am particularly concerned with the tendency for Marxists and radicals to take up this idea of the neutrality of science for themselves, appropriating it and claiming they are the scientists. Would you agree that one of the negative effects of Althusser's rereading of Marx in terms of the epistemological break in his thought is that Marxism took the place of "bourgeois" science by claiming its own scientific detachment from social practices? This denies one of the basic findings (I prefer this term to "tenet," which has religious overtones) of what I will call materialism, rather than Marxism, namely, that ideas are socially situated. We cannot found a radical science on the claim that we are not socially situated. This would contradict what a radical science would discover about the world. Consequently, we must avoid assuming that it would be a good thing if science were not socially situated.

Aronowitz

I would agree. Althusser's fundamental strategy for establishing the neutrality of science was the attempt to establish its objectivity, commensurable with the objective status of any other possible science. One can also see science as a secular activity. This would certainly not exempt it from the critique of secularity from the perspective of historicity. That is the major move we have to make, in which case we never make the claim that we are appropriating scientificity in the old sense. At the same time I do not want to lose the word "science." What I want to do is talk about a critical, interested, ideologically and ethically grounded science that speaks for more than itself; it speaks for an emancipatory moment. (This obviously raises questions of representation.) This is a different kind of epistemological break because we are not in the Enlightenment problematic. Then we can talk about a new emancipation. But before we actually start to be technicistic about it, we'd better ask what Habermas does of Marcuse: Show me your science. Don't ask me to have a critical science unless you can show it to me. We need a Bacon before we can have a Copernicus, and I don't mean this in terms of individuals. I mean this now in terms of a whole new collective project.

Sue Golding

The Concept of the Philosophy of Praxis in the *Quaderni* of Antonio Gramsci

By arguing that the philosophy of praxis is itself the science of historical process, Gramsci was able to give new depth and power to our notions of politics. Indeed, he emphasized that people create, in the context of a dynamic history, not only what it is to be human but also what it ought to be. The realm of revolutionary possibility thereby becomes achievable.

That Gramsci chose to refer to marxism as the "philosophy of praxis" rather than continually use the more colloquial expressions "dialectical materialism" or "historical materialism"—or even the term "marxism" itself—usually has been attributed to one of two reasons, sometimes both. The more common of the two dismisses the phrase as a strategic camouflage necessary to divert the censorial gaze of the prison guards whose duty it was—should they find proof that Gramsci's mind was still working in any way, but particularly in an antifascist, pro-left way—to end, and end abruptly, that mental activity.[1] The other reason cited, almost as frequently and often in conjunction with the first, is that for Gramsci, whose intellectual background was in classical German and Italian philosophy, marxism could best be represented as a philosophy of "action" and, more specifically, a philosophy whose improvement was bound up with revitalizing (in a slightly refurbished form) its idealist and speculative roots. Hence, on the one hand, we have long testimonials to the difficulty of reading the "real" meanings behind his strategically placed metaphor; and on the other, whole debates are erupting over how "marxist" or "hegelian" (or crocean, gentilean, bergsonian, sorelian, even kantian) was the "real" philosophy of the Gramsci prison notebooks.[2]

But there is another way of grasping the fullness of that expression, and that is to accept that when Gramsci tendered lengthy or fragmented explanations of what he meant by the "philosophy of praxis"— as he did repeatedly by way of direct or inferential comment—he meant what he wrote. We shall discover that if we accept the development of his arguments, which begin by dismissing notions of "man-in-general" and go on to reformulate "science," "creativity," and "movement," we will be able to understand more fully what makes the philosophy of praxis peculiarly gramscian; and, more to the point, why that particular rendering is such a vital contribution toward the notion of "progress" or, indeed, of "politics" itself. It will be argued that what makes the philosophy of praxis so peculiarly gramscian is not simply the fact that Gramsci relied on, or indeed found refuge among, an entire set of philosophical inquiries that were partly at odds with each other's systematic assumptions. Nor it is simply the fact

543

that his prison work included a vague form of shadowboxing with the great novelists, artists, and political militants of the time. What makes Gramsci's analysis "gramscian" is the kind of systematic answer he attempted to give to a very basic question: what does it really mean—philosophically and politically—to build a better society, as such, and for whom?

If we take that question as a starting point and read his fragmented commentaries not as a set of literal (and seemingly contradictory) prescriptions about tactics or strategy, but rather as a discursive intervention that attempts to address the problem from a variety of angles, we will find that Gramsci's analyses detailing "reality" and "man's" place in it stand as a crossroads, a transitional point as it were, to the more contemporary (and no less controversial) debates erupting on the left today, debates that encompass, by way of Foucault, on the one hand, or Derrida, on the other, movements of resistance, liberation, or change.

The Meaning of the "Political"

For Gramsci that discursive intervention begins, in part, by raising two rather old philosophical debates. The first had more to do with the question of objectivity: that is, "can one write philosophy *outside* history," can it be autonomous from history, can there be a "general philosophy" about philosophy—can it be objective? The second, while following closely on the heels of the first, had a more particular focus: how does one reconcile, or better, resolve once and for all, the age-old opposition between "man" and nature, posed also as that between "man" and society, and now, in twentieth-century terms, posed as an opposition between "man" and science. It was in the context of attempting to determine what a "better" society would (or ought to) be that the whole weight of philosophical tradition tended to rely on these seemingly self-evident paired oppositions, which sought "objectively" to grant to the Homo sapien a generalized essence, distinct from and therefore focused around, God, the market, and, later, science. Hence it was in this context, too, that when Gramsci asked, "In what sense can one identify politics with history and hence all life with politics?" he was searching for a way to end that continual philosophical quest for the "objectivity" of the "external world"[3] which had brought with it all those fossilized or preset conceptions around the so-called nature of "man."[4]

But if, as Gramsci rhetorically proposed, there could be no politics outside history, and hence no human activity outside politics—including creating the human itself—how could this systematically be proposed without appearing simply as a self-evident "truth" gleaned from Marx's eleven *Theses on Feuerbach?* In attempting to answer that question, Gramsci turned to, among others, the philosophical proposals of Vico and Croce regarding their systematizing of "knowledge," "science," and the "aesthetic." And in attempting to "cleanse" these systems of their metaphysical and idealist content,[5] Gramsci used them to make more precise the conceptualizations proposed by Labriola and Marx: that history was no more less than the practical-political activity of "man"; that philosophy was no more nor less than the historical methodology of that practical-political activity.[6]

Like Croce, Gramsci took two points from Vico's *New Science:* the first regarding "man's" ability to produce and comprehend knowledge, encapsulated in Vico's well-known expression *verum ipsum factum* ("the truth is what is done"); the second regarding Vico's argument that human knowledge could only approach Truth, not equal truth per se.[7] To put it another way, "truth" or "law" was something *relative*, always created, rather than something static, dogmatic, or "carved in stone." In this context, Gramsci agreed with Croce that Vico's *New Science* broke with the "self-confidence," as Croce called it, of cartesian philosophy, replacing Descartes's ahistorical identity "I think therefore I am"[8] with the controversial "history is equal to science."[9]

However, Gramsci was attracted both to Croce's accent on philosophy and science as that which incorporated Vico's *verum ipsum factum* (philosophy, as a scientific methodology of the Real), as well as his insistence against an "abstract" or "generalized" Philosophy, against, that is to say, a philosophy without history, against a so-called neutral weltanschauung.[10] But what Gramsci found useful from Croce's work, in fact what he found *crucial* for a philosophy of praxis, can be narrowed to three points: (1) the concept of immanence/becoming (that is to say, creativity) as central to "concrete" progress, which Gramsci linked to a democratic ideology;[11] (2) the concept of the "will" as a *rational* expression; that is, as a practical expression of theoretical intellectual activity; and (3) Croce's insistence on the ethical-political as the site of struggle, the point of arrival for progress and change.[12]

But in order to accept that there could be no such thing as a "neutral" law or science or philosophy without raising the spectre of a dual reality or lapsing into some sort of subjectivist idealism, these "borrowed" arguments would have to be placed in their proper context.[13] For Gramsci, that proper context was the realm of the *political,* where politics would be understood not as the final moment of Spirit but as the point of departure, the "first" moment, as it were, in the making of history.[14] It meant giving *real* (i.e., objectively concrete) substance to political activity which had thus far been hypostasized by crocean idealism as the point of arrival in the unfolding of a "scientific" and "rational" (read: predictable) history. It meant incorporating into a notion of politics the by-now clichéd, machiavellian insight that politics meant "the act of the possible"—strategically understanding and implementing progress and development. In short, it meant breathing a *dynamic,* active—using Gramsci's specifically hegelian term, *immanent*—conception of politics into history and one of history into politics, while maintaining their equivalence at the level of an "identity-in-distinction."[15]

More important, though, it meant that the very notion of progress or development was dynamic rather than static; it did not have, ipso facto, a set definition or prescription but rather involved a struggle, a *political* struggle, to determine precisely what would be considered a "betterment" of society, "progress" as such and for whom.[16] In other words, what actually constituted development or progress for Gramsci was not simply to be conceived in terms of a logical (and linear) attribution of philosophical reason; nor was it to be conceived simply in terms of a technological or scientific "advance," or even as a "result" of technical and bureaucratic foresight.[17] Rather, the meaning of "progress" was constituted as an active elaboration and reconstruction of our theoretical and practical activity; or to put it in Gramsci's words, an elaboration precisely *mediated* by, and as a *result* of, politics.[18]

The converse held true for Gramsci as well: not only that history and philosophy must be placed in this proper context of the "political," but that any and all philosophical/historical discourse entailed or expressed political discourse—not a fixed or immutable politics, but a discourse arising from specific circumstances borne out of specific relations between people living in and acting on a particular society. So that in Machiavelli's *Discourses* and *The Prince,* for example, we would find, following this line of reasoning, not "abstract" suppositions about a "general" people and a society, but a particular historical and political position regarding the rising bourgeois classes and the formation of a new (in this case, liberal) society.[19] The same could be said of Hegel, of Croce, even of Voltaire: their philosophical and literary works, taken as a whole, elaborated a specific, though not unitary or homogeneous, conception of humanity and society, as well as specific theoretical and practical suppositions regarding progress and change.[20]

Gramsci would emphasize a similar point throughout his *Quaderni:* that the work of Marx and Engels, also that of Labriola (and to a lesser extent Bergson and Sorel), initiated, or at least contributed to, a different—and specific—theoretical and practical discourse concerning people and society, progress and development. Gramsci contended that this "different and specific" theoretical and practical discourse provided both a philosophical and a political avenue, not only to disengage the notions of progress and development, the will, and the ethical-political from Croce's speculative (and, some would argue, liberal) logic, but also to acknowledge them as central features of a "philosophy of praxis."

Gramsci was able to forward this argument about the centrality of these notions precisely because of this deliberate conceptual slippage around the notion of "the political" as being, at one and the same time, creativity, immanence, mediation, and strategy. That is, he was able to develop the argument on the basis of what he considered to be Marx's "real dialectic," one that was based on "objective *possibilities,*" one that counterposed philosophy with history to bear as its fruit political struggle.[21] Using Croce's language but Marx's dialectic, Gramsci arrived at what might first appear an ingrown tautology: politics became the first, the last, *and* the mediating moment of the Real.[22]

That very conception of politics, slippery though it might be and imbued as it was with speculative and idealist logic, committed the philosophy of praxis to a theoretical and practical discourse distinct from—but having been produced out of—its idealist, transcendentalist (one also could say positivist) predecessors. If we turn now to the prison notebooks and guide our attention by two further questions, we shall see how Gramsci drew on Marx and Engels, less so on Labriola, Bergson, and Sorel, to detail what has come to be known in contemporary debates on the philosophy of praxis as the "specificity of the political,"[23] and how that specificity marked the conceptualizations of the "will," the ethical-political and historical movement or progress as *marxist* expressions. The two questions are simply these: What is science or the word "scientific"? What is the meaning of this so-called real dialectic?

Sue Golding
What Is Science/Scientific?

For Croce, science above all meant methodology, a "rational"—that is, distinct and predictable—methodology capable of underwriting the logic inherent in "pure" or "objectively" concrete Reality, outside of which there could be no meaningful concept or knowledge. He named that methodology Philosophy, the science of all pure expression, with the logical proviso that his philosophy did not mean a "philosophy-in-general"—or, for that matter, a "science-in-general"—but always entailed the specificity of the (pure) historical moment. Indeed, speculative philosophy was precisely its "expression." But as Gramsci had recognized, this was a mechanical teleology of prediction and evolution, which presented as ethical-political an always already made "progress" neatly unfolding in history.

And yet Gramsci was not adverse to the point Croce was attempting to make and resolve "from the speculative point of view": that the concept of progress or development was something "rational" and hence understandable; something "scientific" and therefore in some way both predictable and within the realm of possibility, that is, "obtainable."[24] The question of science and scientific methodology was not an idle question divorced from leftist political philosophy or practical politics. On the contrary, debates around the concept of science had long since crystallized on the left between the so-called scientific marxists, on the one hand, and the utopian socialists, on the other.[25] Indeed, the former brandished the all too familiar "economic science" (reminiscent of the Second International) which, as Gramsci would argue in his prison notes, conflated the "natural" sciences with that of the "social" and thereby gave credence to the somewhat unfortunate mixed metaphor of the economy as the "anatomy" or "backbone" of society.[26] This led to the equally unfortunate political analysis that not only did society split rigidly along two "scientifically determined" class axes, but also that the strategies to overcome, or better, overthrow, that persistent split could best be calculated "with the precision of the natural sciences"; that is, according to carefully outlined predictions regarding the immanent collapse of capital exchange, circulation, and its addendum, "bourgeois decadent" life-style.[27]

On the other hand, the utopian socialists—Proudhon, Owen, and others (and one might include among this number the latter-day social democrats)—were not ignorant of, nor antagonistic to, the ongoing debates around "science" and its relation to leftist political practice. Indeed, it was Marx who pointed out that the essential flaw in their "utopianism" lay precisely in having conflated the concept of science with that of the Absolute, that is to say, "value-free" Truth.[28] This equating of an absolute knowledge with an absolute science committed the twin errors of regenerating in more contemporary language the pre-vichean, or at best neo-kantian, assumptions around the appropriation of a knowledge existing outside of history, while at the same time it advanced as "progressive" the argument that a value-free society (i.e., one based on "scientific certainty" devoid of any historical specificity or "bias") could exist—in fact *ought* to exist—as the aim of democratic struggle.[29] In this context, and in the name of scientific and technological objectivity, the rigid class reductionism of "scientific marxism" was exchanged, mixed metaphors and all, for the empty abstraction of a philosophical science and society sui generis.

Finally, there was one other appropriation of science that Gramsci criticized thoroughly and dismissed as "vulgar sociology," namely, the

547

scientism best represented by Bukharin's *Popular Manual:*[30] the attempt to pose society as a system, system as science, and science as the search for laws of causality (i.e., for the "eternal truths") or the single ultimate cause— the age-old "search for God."[31] On a theoretical level, the assumptions of the *Manual* lead to separating, and posing as distinctly opposite poles, philosophical materialism which Bukharin described as the only "true philosophy"—and the philosophy of praxis, or as Bukharin was inclined to call it, "subjectivist sociology."[32] For Gramsci, this meant that the worst aspects of "scientific" and "utopian" marxism had been exhumed and recombined for popular consumption, once again in the name of science, so that now the "iron-clad laws" of historical movement found their raison d'être with the absolute truth of formal, positivistic logic. Decrying this mixture, Gramsci pointed to the major flaw in Bukharin's philosophical assumptions: the conflation of "revolution" with "evolution,"[33] or, more to the point, the impossibility of revolutionary praxis, indeed, the impossibility of politics: "The philosophy implicit in the *Popular Manual* could be called positivistic Aristotelianism, an adaption of formal logic to the methods of physical and natural science. The historical dialectic is replaced by the law of causality and the search for regularity, normality and uniformity. But how can one derive from this way of seeing things, the overcoming, the 'overthrow' of praxis? In mechanical terms, the effect can never transcend the cause or the system of causes, and therefore can have no development other than the flat vulgar development of evolutionism."[34]

Gramsci then comes directly to the point: conceived as a way to "predict" future events, or as a "logic" necessary to illuminate as fixed or causal the chain of human history, or even as a "technology" promising a value-free future, the concept of science has little to do with science properly speaking.

> The situating of the problem as a search for laws and for constant, regular, and uniform lines is connected to a need, conceived in a somewhat puerile and ingenuous way, to resolve in a peremptory fashion, the practical problem of the predictability of historical events. Since it "appears," by strange inversion of the perspectives, that the natural sciences provide us with the ability to foresee the evolution of natural processes, historical methodology is "scientifically" conceived [it is thought] only if, and in so far as, it permits one "abstractly" to foresee the future of society. Hence the search for essential causes, indeed for the "first" cause, for the "cause of causes." But the *Theses on Feuerbach* had already criticized in advance this simplistic conception. In reality, one can "scientifically" foresee only the struggle, but note the concrete moments of the struggle, which cannot but be the result of opposing forces in continuous movement. . . . In reality one can "foresee" to the extent that one acts, to the extent that one applies a voluntary effort and therefore contributes to creating the result "foreseen."

... [Consequently] it is necessary to pose in exact terms the problem of predictability of historical events in order to be able to criticize exhaustively the conception of mechanical causalism, to rid it of any scientific prestige and reduce it to a pure myth which perhaps was useful in the past in a backward period of development of certain subaltern social groups.

But it is the concept itself of "science," as it emerges from the *Popular Manual,* which requires to be critically destroyed. It is taken root and branch from the natural sciences, as if these were the only sciences or *science par excellence....* [But] to think that one can advance the progress of a work of scientific research by applying to it a standard method to which it was naturally suited, is a strange delusion which has little to do with science.[35]

Gramsci's conception of science and, more important, his emphasis on "scientific method" as the fundamental method for a philosophy of praxis, at first glance, may not have appeared altogether different from the positions he was challenging, for it, too, focused on logic, predictability, "laws" of historical movement, "economic science," even "truth." The difference, of course, lay in the manner in which he reinterpreted Hegel's posing of the "rational" and "real" and the dialectic of that unity. That is, the difference lay precisely in the way Gramsci posed the unity of logic, truth, economics, law, and movement as the dialectic between history, philosophy, and politics; a unity he named "science" (rather than Spirit) or, to use the phrase Gramsci borrowed from Vico, "the *new science.*"[36] However, this apparent self-defining (and hence seemingly transparent) definition of scientific method = philosophy/history/politics = science[37] actually encompassed a rather specific and meaningful content, for Gramsci had reconstructed the "rational" and the "real."

On the one hand, the "rational" appropriately entailed "theoretical activity." Indeed, it entailed both "intuitive" or commonsensical and intellectual reasoning, closely related to what Gramsci often suggested was Ricardo's methodological approach: the method of logical deduction based on the premise of "supposing that."[38] On the other hand, the "real" entailed "practical activity," that is, the "sensuous, objective *[gegenstandliche]* activity" embodied in the first *Theses on Feuerbach.*[39] It was this "real" activity that Gramsci would elaborate upon as "necessary,"[40] useful,[41] created out of human will;[42] indeed, as an expression of "life" itself.[43] In this context, the "rational" gave way to science (i.e., science as reason and/or method); whereas the "real" implied all human action, that is, history. But this "rational" activity, although distinct from the "real," was the logical premise without which the "real" had no "concrete" meaning. That is to say, the rational and the real were not negations of each other, nor were they opposites. Rather, they were *distincts;* the distincts of "science and life,"[44] of "philosophy and history,"[45] where that active unity of "the rational and real becomes one," where that unity forms a "historic bloc," that is, entails a specific, necessary history, "necessary" precisely because it is created out of the relation between the "thoughts and actions" of humankind *and* our environment.[46] Relying on the third *Theses on Feuerbach,* Gramsci concluded: "The unity of science and life is precisely an active unity, in which alone liberty of thought can be realized; it is a master-pupil relationship, one between the philosopher and the cultural environment. ... In other words, it is the relationship between philosophy and history."[47]

This active unity of theoretical and practical knowledge is what Gramsci named "science." But he was referring to "science"—indeed, to politics as well—in two different senses: "science" as discovery (i.e., "creation") and "science" as methodology (i.e., as traditional philosophy):

> Is not science itself "political activity" and political thought, in as much as it transforms men and makes them different than what they were before? If everything is "politics," then it is necessary—in order to avoid lapsing into a wearisome and tautological catalogue of platitudes—to distinguish by means of new concepts between, on the one hand, the politics which corresponds to that science which is traditionally called "philosophy" and, on the other, the politics which is called political science in the strict sense. If science is the "discovery" of formerly unknown reality, is this reality not conceived of, in a certain sense, as transcendent? And is it not thought that there still exists something "unknown" and hence transcendent? And does the concept of science as "creation" not then mean that it too is "politics"? Everything depends on seeing whether the creation involved is "arbitrary," or whether it is rational—i.e., "useful," to men in that it enlarges their concept of life, and develops life itself to a higher level.[48]

In this context, there is no longer a "science-in-general," nor even the "science" of crocean speculative history-philosophy. It is the science of a specific history and politics, a politics-as-science, as it were, a "political science," the methodology of philosophical-political activity or, more precisely, of "praxis."[49] It is out of this unity, in other words, that a philosophy of praxis emerges.

But it is in Gramsci's readdressing and reposing of the problem of "scientific truth" that he consolidated the complexity (and importance) of having recouped as fundamental to the concept of a philosophy of praxis this active unity of the rational and the real. In the briefly sketched criticisms around the uses of science in terms of philosophical method and political practice, Gramsci already had pointed out that "scientific truth" often is taken to mean three separate things: (1) "orthodoxy," meaning that which is or should entail a philosophically systematic "purity"; (2) "objectivity," meaning that which is cleansed of historical "bias" or, to apply Gramsci's term borrowed (again) from Croce, something free from "error"; and (3) "prediction," meaning, in this context, a rational interpretation of a present or future practical activity according to the laws of historical movement. Yet, although Gramsci's conception of "scientific truth" within a philosophy of praxis included these three elements, their meanings were altered radically by incorporating the "rational" and the "real" in the way outlined above.

Thus, as marxist theory had as its origin "the three cultural movements" of French materialism, German idealism and English political economy—indeed, since it had emerged as the *synthesis* of these movements and could be called the "coronation of modern culture"[50]—orthodoxy, as applied to marxist theory and understood in this "pure" sense, could only produce a contradiction in terms. Developing his position in part from Labriola's arguments around the "scientificity and autonomy" of the philosophy of praxis, Gramsci considered "orthodoxy" to mean philosophic "totality," "self-sufficiency," that is, a *break* from traditional culture, without which a theory could not be revolutionary.

> Orthodoxy is not to be looked for in this or that adherent of the philosophy of praxis, or in this or that tendency connected with currents extraneous to the original doctrine, but in the fundamental concept that the philosophy of praxis is "sufficient unto itself," that it contains in itself all the fundamental elements needed to construct a total and integral conception of the world, a total philosophy and theory of natural science, and not only that but everything that is needed to give life to an integral practical organization of society; that is, to become a total civilization.
>
> This concept of orthodoxy, thus renewed, helps to give a better definition to the attribute "revolutionary. . . ."[51]

Consequently, "orthodox" as applied to the philosophy of praxis means not only that its origins are "impure" but also that if it indeed produces a new weltanschauung, a new world outlook, that outlook can never be "pure" or "neutral" or "general." It always entails error, namely, historical specificity.

So, although this orthodoxy is presented as an autonomous or totalizing rupture from tradition, it is not meant as a break from history. Gramsci's conception of "objectivity" or "objective truth"—meaning that which can *only* be "humanly objective"[52]—put into question the attempts to find refuge in pure systems, pure philosophies, or pure technologies, indeed, pure "truths" devoid of specificity or error.[53] What makes "truth" real, that is, what gives it any meaning, is its subjectivity to history—a point Marx clearly outlined in his *Preface* and one to which Gramsci continually referred: "'My investigation,' to quote Marx, 'led to the result that legal relations as well as forms of state are to be grasped neither from themselves nor from the so-called development of the human mind, but rather have their roots in the material conditions of life.'. . ."[54] And so, relying here on Vico's *verum ipsum factum,* insisting on the importance of Croce's theory of distincts, denying the kantian supposition of an external objectivity to reality, and grounding "objectivity" itself in the unity of the theoretical and practical activity (i.e., the "rational" and the "real") as expressed in both the *Preface* and *Theses on Feuerbach,* Gramsci argued that truth is never "pure," never devoid of (or negated by) error, and never exists outside of historical, that is to say, *human,* construction:

Objective always means "humanly objective." . . . [for] what would North-South or East-West mean without man? . . . Obviously East and West are arbitrary and conventional, that is, historical, constructions, since outside history every point on earth is East and West at the same time. . . . And yet these references are real; they correspond to real facts, they allow one to travel by land and by sea, to arrive where they have decided to arrive, to "foresee" the future, to objectivize reality, to understand the objectivity of the external world. Rational and real become one.

Without having understood this relationship [of objective identified with universal subjective, rational identified with real], it seems one cannot understand the philosophy of praxis, its position in comparison with idealism and mechanical materialism. . . . [55]

Because we can only "know" reality, can only "know" what exists (otherwise we would return to some form of transcendentalism or mysticism), the argument that "objective truth" entails historic specificity also bears on Gramsci's concept of "prediction": it can never be "scientific"; it can never be an act of knowledge as such. "And how could prediction be an act of knowledge?" Gramsci remarked rhetorically; "one knows only what has been and what is, not what will be, which is something 'nonexistent' and therefore unknowable by definition."[56] In Gramsci's estimation, "prediction" has been confused with "science" precisely because the concept "law," and more particularly "law of historical movement," has been rigidified, itself confused with "permanency" and "automatism" and equated to formal logic. But, if we again follow Vico on this point, law can be nothing other than tendency, probability, regularity. Indeed, it is with Ricardo's scientific discoveries in the field of political economy that this connection between law and history is made more specific; that is, in the "concept and fact of determined market: i.e., the scientific discovery that specific and permanent forces have risen historically and that the operation of these forces presents itself with a certain 'automatism'. . . ."[57]

But the question for Gramsci is not one, as he puts it, "of 'discovering' a metaphysical law of 'determinism', or even establishing a 'general' law of causality."[58] The question is precisely *how* relatively permanent forces are constituted and maintained in history. This is where "prediction" reenters. Prediction, if not an act of knowledge, was for Gramsci a "practical act," the practical politics of creating consensus, of creating the result "foreseen"; the practical politics of establishing a collective will, of creating virtue as both "vital impulse" and "fortuna."[59] In other words, it is the practical political activity of creating "what ought to be," of creating the realm of possibilities. In this sense prediction is a part of the ethical-political moment, indeed, a part of progress.[60] Moreover, because prediction is practical activity (i.e., "real," and not a metaphysical event), it is connected to the law of tendency, necessity, even change. But the more complex answer to the question of how prediction constitutes (at least in part) development, praxis—

indeed, what is meant by this notion of change and progress—was detailed by Gramsci through the concept of immanence and by what he called the "real" dialectic.

The "Real" Dialectic

Gramsci reasoned that science means both creative discovery and the methodology of that creation (i.e., the methodology of history in the making). Thus he proceeded with a notion of science that operates on two levels: as theoretical or practical activity,[61] and as the unified *expression* of that activity—as the "organic unity of history, politics and economics" or the unified expression of the "rational and real," outside of which there is no meaningful concept or knowledge. Accordingly, because Gramsci situated—as did others before him—the rational and real within history, as a part of history, as well as an expression of history itself, that theoretical-practical activity is always "man-made" necessary, rational.[62] This led Gramsci to conclude that there can be no omnipotent truth devoid of human activity or historical specificity, nor can there be an underlying, arbitrary, or general logic to knowledge or scientific methodology. Indeed, it allowed him to argue that there can be no "science-in-general" and that, in this context, scienza (science/knowledge) is "political."[63]

But to reason as Gramsci did—that is, to acknowledge and emphasize as continuous this "organic unity" while developing these arguments about science and philosophy in terms of a creativity and method "rooted" in history—is not what divorces Gramsci's philosophy of praxis from the difficulties encountered either in Vico's dualist development of truth and certainty as science or from the transcendental metaphysics of the kantian categories of knowledge. Nor is it that emphasis which divorces the philosophy of praxis from the speculative "history" of Croce's idealist Spirit, or even from the "vulgar evolutionism" of mechanistic or reductionist materialism. Finally, it is not simply this emphasis on science as history or politics that prevents the subsequent equivalences of history, politics, science, and philosophy from becoming an indistinguishable swamp of conceptual identity. What separates the philosophy of praxis from these so-called philosophical errors and, moreover, what prevents it from lapsing into simple tautological reasoning is the way in which the "historical" in "historical materialism" is understood.[64]

For Gramsci, this "knowing how" meant not only conceptualizing history as an *active unity* of theoretical and practical activity, or as the *synthesis* of the rational and real, or even as an *expression* of *movement,* but also conceptualizing concretely what the terms "active unity," "synthesis," expression," and "movement" actually mean in the philosophy of praxis. It is thus the full comprehension of what it means to "take" the hegelian dialectic and "stand it on its feet"; the full comprehension of *how* the "real" dialectic is conceptualized in the philosophy of praxis, what it means to say that it is the heir of German philosophy, French cultural politics, and English political economy, and why that conception removes it from its transcendentalist, materialist, idealist, even positivist roots—namely, why it is "orthodox," totalizing, a break from tradition. In short, knowing how the "historical" of historical materialism is conceptualized is precisely knowing the meaning of *immanence* or *becoming,* and why Gramsci often emphasized that *that* is the central conception in the philosophy of praxis or, indeed, is the philosophy of praxis itself.[65]

Gramsci wrote in a fragment called *Speculative Immanence and Historicist or Realist Immanence,*

> it is affirmed that the philosophy of praxis was born on the terrain of the highest development of culture in the first half of the nineteenth century, this culture being represented by classical German philosophy, English classical economics and French political literature and politics.... But in what sense is the affirmation to be understood? That each of these movements has contributed respectively to the elaboration of the philosophy, the economics, and the politics of the philosophy of praxis? Or that the philosophy of praxis has synthesized the three movements, that is, the entire culture of the age, and that in the new synthesis, whichever "moment" one is examining, the theoretical, the economic, or the political, one will find each of these three movements present as a preparatory "moment"? This seems to me to be the case. And it seems to me that the unitary "moment" of synthesis is to be identified in the concept of immanence, which has been translated from the speculative form, as put forward by classical German philosophy, into an historicized form with the aid of French politics and English classical economics.[66]

This "unitary" moment, this so-called synthesis, conditioned as it were by its distinct "preparatory moments," is not a starting point of investigation or knowledge; it is not a "point of departure."[67] Nor is it unitary in the sense of an indivisible, static, or eternal subjectivity, a "thing-in-itself." Rather, it is a unitary moment in the sense of representing the epoch or bloc of a "history in the making," where that historical epoch, bloc, spirit, or culture of the age is precisely and always an expression of our theoretical and practical creativity or, to use Gramsci's phrase, an expression of absolute historicized immanence.[68]

But for the fuller, more developed meaning of this "arrival," this so-called absolute historicized immanence, Gramsci directed our attention, once again, to the *Theses on Feuerbach.* He commented that, in the first thesis, the unity of the theoretical and practical activity referred to by Marx is precisely the dialectical unity of matter and "man," where matter is understood to mean the material forces of production, the "economic elements,"[69] whereas "man" is understood to mean "the complex social relations" or, "more exactly, the process of his actions."[70] But as we have seen, since Gramsci acknowledged that for the philosophy of praxis there is no such thing as an objective truth free from error, no truth outside history, no thing-in-itself, this suggests that the meaning of both matter and "man" is constructed in and by reality and that, consequently, there neither exists a general or pure economic science nor a natural "man" or "man-in-general." In other words, the meaning of "what is man" is always subject to history; it is historically created, "changes with changes in the circumstances," is the "synthesized" unitary moment of our theoretical and practical activity.

It is a meaning that Gramsci argued is always, consequently, in the process of becoming.[71] This led him to conclude, as well, that not only is the meaning of "what is man" a historical creation, but that meaning itself is a historical creation.[72] Meaning is also, in other words, the synthesized unitary expression of our creation, our theoretical and practical activity. It implies discovery, possibility, change—but not of an arbitrary kind, that is, not of a kind without foundation in the distinct preparatory moments of the rational and real. Meaning, which changes continually with changes in the circumstances, is constructed out of both the realm of necessity *and* the realm of possibility, where necessity is not opposed to possibility. Rather, necessity is the condition without which the realm of possibility could not exist; or, more to the point, meaning is always an expression of historicized immanence, of becoming.

By rendering Vico's *verum ipsum factum* into the "real" dialectic, meaning was, for Gramsci (as he claimed it was for Marx), rational, necessary, the "universal-subjective," always in relation to (and created out of) this process of change, this *process* called history.[73] Science, then, is the methodology of this "coherent unitary expression" of the rational and the real; it becomes linked with the notions of regularity, law of tendency, necessity, certainty. Even humanity itself is this coherent unitary expression (or synthesis) of a people acting in, acting on, and creating anew, not only themselves, but "the inherited living nightmares of the dead," or, in a word, society. This coherent unitary expression, this active unitary or process, was Gramsci's historicized immanence, his "absolute humanism," his "becoming," the "critical act," making the rational and real more "coherent"; in short, a return to the terrain of *politics.*

But it is a politics that includes on its terrain not only a historicized rationality and necessity but the realm of the possible, where possibility is connected to necessity. If, as Marx concluded in the *Theses on Feuerbach,* the "critical act" is the politics of creating from the unity of theoretical and practical activity "changes in the circumstances," then politics is also, to quote Gramsci's reference to Machiavelli and sleight-of-hand to Croce, "the art of the possible." It is this politics as the art of the possible— or the dialectic it implies—that became for Gramsci the cornerstone of his attack against Bukharin's "flat, vulgar evolutionism" of mechanical materialism and the "pure historical movement/progress" of Croce's "scientific-utopianism." Scorning the fact that both Bukharin and Croce (he included here the "actual idealists" as well as other "scientific" and "orthodox" marxists) acknowledged that material conditions change with changes in the circumstances, they did so by "forgetting" that it is *people* who change circumstances; and they did so neither out of arbitrary speculation nor out of carefully developed predictions around the iron-clad laws of historical development. "The uneducated and crude environment has dominated the educator," conceded a sarcastic Gramsci, "rather than the other way around. If the environment is the educator, it too must be educated, but the *Manual* does not understand this revolutionary dialectic."[74]

What is so revolutionary about the real dialectic is precisely this point about becoming and change as not only linked to necessity, the rational and real (i.e., history) but as linked to possibility, to freedom; as a result, the realm of possibility is not simply conceivable, it is obtainable.[75] Moreover, in so historicizing immanence, Gramsci was able to reemphasize that the power to overcome or overthrow, change or make society better, does not materialize out of the air but is born from the old society itself—from human activity, knowledge, science, in all its impure senses. That "no new society ever emerges without the seeds of its development having first been planted in the old" means precisely that the old is the *necessary* condition without which the new cannot be realized, and that the *passage* from necessity to freedom is always a *political*—or critical—act, the synthetic unity of theory and praxis.

But it also means that the struggle to create society, and what it means to talk about, develop, and maintain a better one, a progressive society as such and for whom, is also and always a political struggle, a struggle of becoming, a struggle around potentiality, a struggle to unite the "preparatory moments" of the rational and real into a "unitary moment," one that is never permanent, static, or arbitrary but forms instead a "historic bloc." It is a struggle that involves making more coherent both concrete will (as the first moment of our practical-political activity) and the ethical morality appropriate to it, that is, the articulating of and/or creating anew the ethical assumptions underlying any conception of the world. And that making "more coherent" the synthetic unitary moment—which, as we have seen, is always actively political and one not divorced from history—marks the "passage" or "catharsis" from the old society to the new. Its realization is precisely what Gramsci called "ethico-political hegemony": the political battle to transform society.

> The proposition contained in the "Preface to a Contribution to the Critique of Political Economy" . . . should be considered as an affirmation of *epistemological* and not simply of psychological and moral value. From this, it follows that the theoretical-practical principle of hegemony has also *gnoseological* significance, and here it is that Illich's greatest theoretical contribution to the philosophy of praxis should be sought. . . . The realization of a hegemonic apparatus, in so far as it creates a new ideological terrain, determines a reform of consciousness and of methods of knowledge: it is a fact of knowledge, a philosophical fact. In Crocean terms: when one succeeds in introducing a new morality in conformity with a new conception of the world, one finishes by introducing the conception as well; in other words one determines a reform of the whole of philosophy.

> [Moreover] structure and superstructures form an "historical bloc," that is to say the complex, contradictory and discordant *ensemble* of the superstructures in the reflection of the ensemble of social relations of production. . . . that is, that the "rational" is actively and actually real. This reasoning is based on the necessary reciprocity between structure and superstructure, a reciprocity which is nothing other than the real dialectical process.[76]

[Finally it can be said that] the term "catharsis" can be employed to indicate the passage from the purely economic (egoistic-passional) to the ethico-political moment. . . . This also means the passage from "objective to subjective" and from "necessity to freedom." Structure ceases to be an external force which crushes man, assimilates him to itself and makes him passive; and it is transformed into a means of freedom, an instrument to create a new ethico-political form and new sources of initiatives. To establish the "cathartic" moment becomes, therefore, it seems to me, the starting point for all the philosophy of praxis, and the cathartic process coincides with the chain of syntheses which have resulted from the evolution of the dialectic.[77]

Gramsci himself did not, because he could not, develop a theoretical framework for detailing the cathartic moment, for while able to redress the problems of reductionism and dogmatic orthodoxy by incorporating into the marxist dialectic a notion of science as philosophy of praxis, he did so, in the end, by reintroducing a teleological notion of the economic moment. Thus, while emphasizing people's participation in creating permanency and change, while emphasizing that we create, in the context of that dynamic history, not only the very notion of what it is to be human but also what it ought to be, as such and for whom, his analytic discussion could not readily account for *why* certain popular movements might emerge (or the forms they might take) without having to reintroduce a self-contained, homogeneously defined economic notion of class. It is as if, by posing this double entendre of science as both creativity and law, Gramsci was able to take us to a precipice over which he himself could not leap, namely, the entire rethinking of politics. But the leap he could not make was the very terrain of what, in contemporary terms, has been labeled "discourse theory"—that is to say, the very terrain of reanalyzing the microprocesses of how the political may be constructed; how *meaning* is established, made permanent, or changed.

To put it slightly differently, Gramsci's concept of the philosophy of praxis provides the necessary—but not sufficient—conditions for analyzing and intervening in the processes of social construction. Unlike the work of Foucault, Gramsci's framework cannot explain the movement of how, perhaps even why, for example, societal norms became "medicalized" or even how the advent of changing sexual attitudes resulted in the emergence of various sexual categories and laws regulating their proliferation. Only in the most general terms can Gramsci's nonreductionist notion of the political account for the wide range of social movements that have been named "liberation" movements—the women's movement, the black civil rights movement, or even the gay movement.

This gap, as it were, in Gramsci's work should not blind us to the importance of his insights, particularly for the contemporary debates erupting on the left around notions of science, indeed, politics itself. By arguing that the *concept* of the philosophy of praxis is itself the "science" of the absolute historicized dialectic, Gramsci was able to begin to reemphasize and relocate all the various manifestations of the political. It becomes a complete denial of a dual reality, the complete historicization of the rational and the real, the posing as "active" of the synthesis of their unity, an activity that is nothing less than politics. And therewith comes the complete recognition that it is people, and people alone, who possess the ability to intervene in and change that process called history.

Notes

1 This is not to imply that censorship or, indeed, prison life itself did not take an exacting toll on Gramsci's ability to think, let alone write. But it is to suggest that some scholars writing on Gramsci's *Quaderni* have been somewhat sidetracked by the fact as well as the brutality of his imprisonment, so that it becomes an explanatory feature of his code names for Lenin [Illich] or Trotsky [Bronstein]; indeed, it becomes an explanatory feature in which unfamiliar concepts are attributed as, at least in part, code names. See, for example, "General Introduction," in *Selections from the Prison Notebooks of Antonio Gramsci*, trans. and ed. Quintin Hoare and Geoffrey Nowell-Smith (New York: International Publishers, 1971), pp. xxi-xxv. References to the official Italian edition, *Quaderni del carcere: Edizone dell' Instituto Gramsci*, ed. Valentino Gerrantana, 4 vols. (Torino: Einaudi, 1977), are by volume number (roman), notebook (QC) number, section, page numbers, and cross-reference (cr.) or further citation to the earlier or later versions by Gramsci himself.

2 The attempts to "uncover" the "real" Gramsci are scattered throughout the literature. The well-known attempts to explain the *Quaderni* as leninism par excellence are by the Italian Communist Party (PCI). Less bold but equally sympathetic to the leninist interpretations are, for example, Palmiro Togliatti, *On Gramsci and Other Writings*, ed. Donald Sassoon (London: Lawrence and Wishart, 1979); Christine Buci-Glucksmann, *Gramsci and the State*, trans. David Fernbach (London: Lawrence and Wishart, 1975). In the backlash against official translations of the PCI, and in part to recuperate the complex meaning obscured by those translations, several articles appeared that replaced the various forms of leninism with various forms of idealism. See, for example, Maurice A. Finachiaro, "Gramsci's Crocean Marxism," *Telos*, 41 (1979), pp. 7-32; Paul Piccone, "Gramsci's Hegelian-Marxism," *Political Theory*, 2:1 (1974), pp. 32-45.

3 *Quaderni* III, QC 13 [10], p. 1569; *Prison Notebooks*, p. 137, for first quote; *Quaderni* II, QC 10 [40], pp. 1290-91; *Prison Notebooks*, pp. 367-68.

4 Gramsci argued in the philosophical fragments of the *Quaderni* that the "answer" to the question "What is man?" always carries with it historically constructed assumptions on the nature of humankind. But the question for Gramsci was not "What is man?" Rather, the question was "What can man become?" This implies a notion of potentiality and possibility, not only for every individual, but for society as well—the "terrain" on which our "becoming" is realized. In short, it implies a notion of politics that deals with the "art of the possible." Although this point is central and will be elaborated further in the second part of this essay, cf. *Quaderni* II, QC 10 [54] and *Prison Notebooks*, pp. 351, 354-57.

5 "Cleanse" is precisely the word Gramsci used when referring to a resystematizing of idealist—even transcendental and positivist—philosophy for use in a philosophy of praxis. Cf. *Quaderni* II, QC ii [301], p. 1443 and *Prison Notebooks*, p. 466.

6 See, for example, *Quaderni* II, QC, 7 [33], "Posizone del problema," p. 881, and QC 11 [70], "Antonio Labriola," pp. 1507-9; *Quaderni* III, QC 16 [2], "Quistioni di metodo," pp. 1840-44; cr. *Prison Notebooks*, pp. 361, 386-88, 382-86, respectively.

7 Vico's most well known work, *The New Science*, went through several editions where major changes occurred in the logic. The most profound break was the difference between his 1725 version and that of 1730 (later merely updated in 1744). For his earlier dualist formulation dividing knowledge between that of "man" and that of God, see excerpts contained in Vico, *Selected Writings*, ed. and trans. Leon Pompa (Cambridge: Cambridge University Press, 1982), pp. 81-158. His later formulations are collected from the (1744) third edition, *The New Science of Giambattista Vico*, trans. Thomas G. Bergen and Max H. Fisch (New York: Cornell University Press, 1948), hereafter referred to as *The New Science* (III). Cf. *Quaderni* II, QC 11 [54], p. 1482; earlier version, QC 8 [199], "Unita della teoria e della practica," p. 1060; cr. *Prison Notebooks*, p. 364.

8 Croce, *The Philosophy of Giambattista Vico*, trans. R. G. Collingwood, (London: Howard Latimer, 1913), pp. 2, 5.

9 Croce, pp. 32, 33-35; see also Alfonsina A. Grimaldi, *The Universal Humanity of Giambattista Vico* (New York: S. F. Vanni, 1958), pp. 247-53.

558

Sue Golding

10   It should be pointed out here, of course, that Gramsci was not strictly relying on Croce's (or even Vico's) debating points about science, a point I will clarify shortly. Suffice it to quote Gramsci himself on his reference to Lenin (Illich) and Marx: "Statement of the problem: Production of new *Weltanschauugen* to fertilize and nourish the culture of a historical epoch, and philosophically directed production according to the original *Weltanschauugen*. Marx is the creator of a *Weltanschauug*. But what is Illich's position? Is it purely subordinate and subaltern? The explanation is to be found in Marxism itself as both science and action. The passage from utopia to science and from science to action. The foundation of a directive class [*classe dirigente*] (i.e. of a state) is equivalent to the creation of a *Weltanschauung*." *Prison Notebooks*, p. 381; cr. *Quaderni* II, QC 7 [33], p. 881.

11   Although this point will be clarified directly, I refer the reader to *Quaderni* II, QC 10 [48.11], pp. 1335-36, and QC 10 [40], pp. 1290-91; cr. *Prison Notebooks*, pp. 357-58, 367-68, for a general indication of the direction the argument will follow.

12   Cf. *Quaderni* II, QC [6], pp. 1244-45.

13   *Quaderni* II, QC 11 [59], p. 1486; cr. *Prison Notebooks*, p. 346.

14   *Quaderni* III, QC 13 [10], pp. 1568-69; cr. *Prison Notebooks*, p. 137.

15   The precise meaning of "immanence" as Gramsci used it will be developed more fully later. But for the general outline of the argument, see "Immanence and the Philosophy of Praxis," *Prison Notebooks*, pp. 449-52. Cr. *Quaderni* II, QC 11 [28], pp. 1438-39; cf. QC 11 [24], "Il linguaggio e le metafore," pp. 1426-28; QC 11 [22.IV], pp. 1424-26; cr. *Prison Notebooks*, "The Dialectic," pp. 434-36. For a brief reference to "distincts" (universal concepts that hold their separate identities when originally developed by Croce to refute Hegel's positioning around dialectical synthesis), see *Quaderni* III, QC 13 [10], pp. 1568-70; cr. *Prison Notebooks*, pp. 137-38.

16   See in particular *Quaderni* II, QC 10 [48.11], pp. 1335-38; cr. *Prison Notebooks*, "Progress and Becoming," pp. 350-57. See also Gramsci's "Che cosa e l'uomo?" QC 10 [54], pp. 1343-46; cr. *Prison Notebooks*, pp. 357-60.

17   A brief but concise statement can be found in *Quaderni* II, QC 6 [135], "Pasato e presente. Il fordismo," pp. 799-800.

18   This a complex point which draws on Croce's usage of "concordia discors" as well as on the *Theses on Feuerbach* regarding practical and theoretical activity and their dialectical unity. It forms a basis upon which the notion of organic intellectual and ethical-political hegemony can be further articulated. For an indication of the direction in which Gramsci developed it in terms of "organic intellectuals" and hegemony, see *Quaderni* II, QC 11 [12], nota 1, pp. 1385-87; cr. *Prison Notebooks*, pp. 334-35. For a general comment on the theory praxis nexus and its relation to science, see *Quaderni* II, QC 8 [199], p. 1060; updated version QC 11 [54], p. 1482; cr. *Prison Notebooks*. For Croce's development of "concordia discors" in relation to practical activity, cf. *What Is Living and What Is Dead in the Philosophy of Hegel*, trans. Douglas Ainslie (London: Macmillan, 1915), pp. 15-17; and *The Philosophy of Spirit*, vol. 1: *Aesthetic in Science of Expression*, trans. D. Ainslie (London: Macmillan, 1909), pp. 220-22.

19   In general, this is a point clearly articulated and elaborated upon in the work of C. B. Macpherson. For his well-known arguments regarding the specificity of the assumptions in theories of liberalism, see *The Theory of Possessive Individualism: From Hobbes to Locke* (Oxford: Oxford University Press, 1962), esp. "The Roots of Liberal-Democratic Theory," pp. 1-8, and pp. 166-67, 192-93 regarding (in brief) the assumptions of Machiavelli.

20   For example, cf. *Quaderni* III, QC 20 [4], "Azione Cattolica, ecc.," pp. 2101-3; also cf. *Quaderni* I, QC 5 [141], "Cattolici integrali, gesuiti, modernisti," p. 672.

21   *Quaderni* II, QC 10 [48.II], p. 1338; cr. *Prison Notebooks*, "Progress and Becoming," p. 360.

22   This is to point out the following: (1) that Gramsci argued for a conception of politics as "practical activity," which he equated with "will" and deposited as the first moment or basis of philosophy (e.g., cf. *Quaderni* II, QC II [59], p. 1485; cr. *Prison Notebooks*, p. 345); (2) that history/philosophy has not only its basis as political activity but activity produces "politics" (e.g., QC 11 [12], nota II-IV, pp. 1376-80; cr. *Prison Notebooks*, pp. 324-27; see also Gramsci's arguments concerning the "realm of possibility" and "prediction" as political, in *Quaderni* II, QC 10 [48.11], p. 1338; cf. *Prison Notebooks*, p. 36; and QC 11 [15], pp. 1404-5; cf. *Prison Notebooks*, pp. 438-39); and (3) that the unity of philosophy-history (included in the identity is also "economics") as that which is mediated (or "assured") by politics. This allowed Gramsci to argue later that not only is the "realm of necessity" and the "realm of freedom" political-philosophical activity, but that the very passage from the realm of necessity to the realm of freedom involves struggle, is political, indeed, is the very basis of ethical-political hegemony (see *Quaderni* II, QC, p. 1383; cr. *Prison Notebooks*, p. 331; and QC 8 , *Egemonia e democrazia*," *p. 1056*). *See also* Quaderni II, QC 8 [195],

"La proposizone che 'la societa non si pone problemi per la cui soluzione non esistano gia le premesse materiali,' " pp. 1057-58.

23   The term "specificity of the political" is taken directly from Laclau's intervention in the Poulantzas-Miliband debates. See in particular "The Specificity of the Political," *Politics and Ideology in Marxist Theory: Capitalism-Fascism-Populism* (London: New Left Books, 1977), pp. 51-80.

24   *Quaderni* II, QC 11 [15], pp. 1403-6; QC 10 [48.11], pp. 1335-38; QC 11 [59], pp. 1485-86; cr. *Prison Notebooks*, "The Concept of Science," "What Is Man," and "'Creative' Philosophy," pp. 437-40, 357-60, 345-46.

25   See, in particular, Frederick Engels, "Socialism: Utopian and Scientific," *MESW*, vol. 3, pp. 95-151. Aside from the familiar targets (Dühring, Owen, and, one could include among this number, the nonsocialist Proudhon), Gramsci's arguments around science, political practice, and the debates that ensued also engaged the work of Bornstein, Kautsky, Plekhanov, even Loria, since these theorists represented, albeit in different ways, the interpretation of historical materialism as reducible to an "economic science" (cf. *Quaderni* II, QC 10 [26], pp. 1264-65; *Quaderni* III, QC 15 [74], pp. 1833-34; QC 17 [40], p. 1942; Letter #42 in *Prison Letters*, p. 163 and its addendum note). But an additional point must be made concerning Gramsci's attack on Plekhanov's *Fundamental Principles of Marxism*. Although the point concerning Plakhanov's notion of science as that which is "pure" demands longer attention, it raises an interesting point in the debates between scientific and utopian marxism: the tendencies that fight against Plakhanov's assumptions (notably in the work of Otto Bauer) end by posing a utopian view of science itself. That is to say, the debate no longer becomes one between either/or points but is moved onto the terrain of "science" as the value-free rationalized attempt to construct a more democratic society. To some extent, but from equally different assumptions, the work of Sorel and Bergson, even that of Gentile, tends to cling to a notion of science that allows a reading of activity as that which ought to be more "scientific" (read: rational/progressive). This point will not be addressed here in greater detail given the constraints of space, but since much of Gramsci's subsequent analysis drew on these various posings of "science," it is important to give an initial indication of the variety of positions that were produced in the debates on science and political practice. For an initial reference to Gramsci's criticisms regarding, in particular, Plekhanov and the way in which he used the work of Antonio Labriola to refute it, see *Quaderni* II, QC 11 [70], pp. 1506-9; cr. *Prison Notebooks*, pp. 386-88.

26   *Quaderni* II, QC 11 [50], "Storia della terminologia e della metafore," pp. 1473-76; see also QC 10 [27], "Punti di meditazione per lo studio dell'economia. A proposito del cost detto *homo oeconomicus*," p. 1265. In the *Prison Notebooks*, see, for example, p. 400, n.39.

27   This is particularly in reference to A. Loria, who wrote, accordingly, "For if, as the new apostles of force contend, the proletariat masses can at any moment annihilate the prevailing economic order, why do they not rise against the capitalism they detest, and replace it with the long cooperative commonwealth for which they long? Why is it that after so much noisy organization, the utmost they are able to do is tear up a few yards of railway track or to smash a street lamp? Do we not find here an irrefragable demonstration that force is not realizable at any given moment, but only in the historic hour when evolution shall have prepared the inevitable fall of the dominant economic system?" In *Karl Marx*, trans. E. Paul and C. Paul (London: George Allen and Unwin, 1920), pp. 88-89.

28   Karl Marx, *The Poverty of Philosophy: Answer to the "Philosophy of Poverty" by M. Proudhon* (Moscow: Progress Publishers, 1975), particularly pp. 96-118.

29   D. Suvin, "On Two Notions of 'Science' in Marxism," in *Brave New Universe*, ed. Ron Henighan (Ottawa: Tecumseh Press, 1980), pp. 27-43.

30   *Popular Manual* (Saggio popolare) was the abbreviated title used by Gramsci in the *Quaderni*; its full title cited in the *Prison Notebooks* is *Theory of Historical Materialism: A Popular Manual of Marxist Sociology*. The authorized English translation from the third Russian edition notes the title as *Historical Materialism: A System of Sociology* (New York: Progress Publishers, 1925). All subsequent references will use Gramsci's annotated title.

31   *Quaderni* II, QC 11 [3l], "La causa ultima," p. 1445; cr. *Prison Notebooks*, "On Metaphysics," p. 437. See *Quaderni* II, QC 9 [59], "Nozioni enciclopediche. Empirisimo," p. 1131, for an assault on "empiricism" as a category of truth. Criticizing Bukharin directly, Gramsci wrote that his "vulgar contention is that science must absolutely mean 'system', and consequently systems of all sorts are built up which have only the mechanical exteriority of a system and not its necessary coherence" ("Science and System," in *Prison Notebooks*, p. 434; cr. *Quaderni* II, QC 11 [22.IV], "Quistioni generali," p. 1424).

32   *Quaderni* II, QC 11 [17], p. 1412; cr. *Prison Notebooks*, "The So-Called 'Reality of the External World,'" pp. 441-42.

Sue Golding

33 *Quaderni* II, QC 11 [14], "Sulla Metafisica''; cr. *Prison Notebooks,* "On Metaphysics,'' p. 437. Clearly Gramsci was referring not only to Marx's *Poverty of Philosophy* but to the "Theses on Feuerbach'' as well.

34 *Quaderni* II, QC 11 [14].

35 *Quaderni* II, QC 11 [15], pp. 1403-5; cr. *Prison Notebooks,* pp. 437-39.

36 *Quaderni* II, QC 8 [176], "La 'nuova' scienza,'' pp. 1047-48; see also QC 11 [36.III], "La scienza e le ideologie scientifiche,'' pp. 1451-55; cr. Antonio Gramsci, "Science and 'Scientific' Ideologies,'' trans. Maurice A. Finocchiaro, *Telos,* 39(1979), pp. 151-55.

37 *Quaderni* II, QC 10 [2], "Identita di storia e filosofia,'' pp. 1241-42. Gramsci stated that while this claim seems similar to Croce's identity of philosophy and history, for the philosophy of praxis it is "mutilated'' if it does not also include the identity of history with politics and therefore make that identity "also equal to the identity of politics and philosophy'' (p. 1241). He argued that this is what (in part) differentiated his claim of equivalences from that of Croce. See also *Quaderni* I, QC 11 [12], "Alcuni punti preliminari di riferimento,'' pp. 1375-95; cr. *Prison Notebooks,* pp. 323-43.

38 *Quaderni* II, QC 11 [52], p. 1479; cr. *Prison Notebooks,* p. 412.

39 Marx, "Theses on Feuerbach,'' *MESW,* 1:1, p. 13.

40 "History and Anti-History,'' *Prison Notebooks,* p. 369; cr. *Quaderni* II, QC 10 [II 28.11], p. 1266.

41 Useful meaning "practical'' (as in "efficient''). See *Prison Notebooks,* p. 365; cr. *Quaderni* III, QC 15 [22], "Introduzione allo studio della filosofia,'' p. 1780.

42 *Quaderni* II, QC 7 [35], "Materialismo e materialismo storico,'' p. 886.

43 *Quaderni* II, QC 11 [62], pp. 1488-89; cr. *Prison Notebooks,* pp. 406-7.

44 *Quaderni* II, QC 10[44], "Introduzione allo studio della filosofia,'' p. 1332; cr. *Prison Notebook,* pp. 350-51. For the connection to the notion of "distincts'' the reader is referred to *Quaderni* III, QC 13 [10], pp. 1568-70; cr. *Prison Notebooks,* "Politics as an autonomous science,'' pp. 136-38.

45 *Quaderni* II, QC 10 [44], p. 1332; cr. *Prison Notebooks,* p. 351.

46 *Quaderni* II, QC 11 [20], "Oggettivita e realta del mondo esterno,'' p. 1420. The emphasis on the unity of (and identity with) "the real and the rational'' is not meant to bring Hegel through the back door, as Gramsci wrote: "Without having understood this relationship [that the "rational and real become one''] it seems that one cannot understand the philosophy of praxis, its position in comparison with idealism and with mechanical materialism, the importance and significance of the doctrine of the superstructures. It is not exact, as Croce maintains, to say that in the philosophy of praxis the Hegelian 'idea' has been replaced by the 'concept' of structure. The Hegelian 'idea' has been resolved both in the structure and in the superstructures and the whole way of conceiving philosophy has been 'historicized,' that is to say, a whole new way of philosophizing which is more concrete and historical than went before it has begun to come into existence'' (cr. *Prison Notebooks,* p. 448). The concept of "historic bloc'' was developed in the work of Sorel. It suffices to note at this point *Quaderni* II, QC 8 [182], pp. 1051-52; cr. *Prison Notebooks,* "Structure and Superstructure,'' pp. 365-66.

47 *Prison Notebooks,* pp. 350-51; cr. *Quaderni* II, QC 10 [44], p. 1332.

48 *Quaderni* III, QC 15 (II) [10], pp. 1765-66; *Prison Notebooks,* pp. 244-45, translation slightly altered.

49 *Quaderni* II, QC 7 [35], pp. 883-86; QC 11 [14], pp. 1401-3; QC 11 [15], pp. 1403-6; cr. *Prison Notebooks,* pp. 354-57, 436-37, 437-40.

50 *Quaderni* II, QC 10 [II] [9], p. 1246; cr. *Prison Notebooks,* p. 399; see also *Quaderni* III, QC 16 [9], p. 1855; cr. *Prison Notebooks,* p. 388.

51 *Quaderni* II, QC 11 [27], p. 1434; *Prison Notebooks,* "Concept of Orthodoxy,'' p. 463; see also *Quaderni* II, QC 11 [70], pp. 1507-9.

52 *Quaderni* II, QC 11 [17], pp. 1415-16; cr. *Prison Notebooks,* p. 445.

53 The problem, or rather the importance, of error is one to which Gramsci continually referred. Often he used it as a play on the idealist notion of "pure'' knowledge or truth(s). He inflated Croce's own use of "error'' or falsity in itself to argue, for example, that life can never be only and totally "life'' but must consist of both life and death. The same could be said of Being (being and nothing constituting Being, etc.). Error in this sense comes to mean "specificity,'' even "history,'' where history is all life itself in all its "impure'' activity. In that sense the philosophy of praxis becomes precisely the "philosophy of act (praxis, development), but not of the 'pure' act, but rather to the real 'impure' act, in the most profane and worldly sense of the word'' (*Prison Notebooks,* "'Objectivity' of Knowledge,'' p. 372; *Quaderni* IA, QC 11 [64], p. 1492).

561

The use of "error" by Gramsci was also an attack on Gentile's attempts to revise the Crocean "practical activity" as a "pure act" devoid of intellectual/theoretical activity. Cf. Gentile, *The Theory of Mind as Pure Act*, trans. Wildon Carr (London: Macmillan, 1922); also cited in *Prison Notebooks*, p. 372, n. 66. See also *Quaderni* III, QC 13 [10], pp. 1568-70; cr. *Prison Notebooks*, pp. 136-38.

54 "Preface to *A Contribution to the Critique of Political Economy*," *MESW*, 502-3; cf. *Quaderni* II, QC 10 (II) [12], pp. 1249-50; QC 11 [29], p. 1439; *Quaderni* III, QC 13 [10], p. 1570; cr. *Prison Notebooks*, pp. 365, 458, 138.

55 *Quaderni* II, QC 11 [17], p. 1415; QC 11 [20], pp. 1419-20; cr. *Prison Notebooks* , pp. 445, 447-48.

56 *Quaderni* II, QC 11 [15], p. 1404; cr. *Prison Notebooks*, 438.

57 See further *Quaderni* II, QC 11 [52], p. 1477; cr. *Prison Notebooks*, p. 410.

58 *Quaderni* II, QC 11 [52], p. 1479; *Prison Notebooks*, p. 412.

59 *Quaderni* III, QC 13 [1], pp. 1555-61; cf. *Prison Notebooks*, pp. 125-33; see also QC 11 [52], pp. 1480-81; cr. *Prison Notebooks*, pp. 413-14.

60 Although this point will be developed later, the reader is referred to Gramsci's arguments on progress/development and "becoming," outlined in *Quaderni* II, QC 10 [48.11], pp. 1335-38; cr. *Prison Notebooks*, pp. 357-60.

61 *Quaderni* II, QC 11 [301], pp. 1442-45; cr. *Prison Notebooks*, "Matter," pp. 465-68.

62 An argument developed in part of Gramsci's attack on the equating of history with "natural" history. See, for example, *Quaderni* I, QC 3 [33], "Alcune cause d'errore," pp. 310-11.

63 See also *Quaderni* I, QC 4 [41], "La scienza," pp. 466-67; cr. QC 11 [37], pp. 1455-56.

64 Gramsci writes, "It has been forgotten that in the case of a very common expression [historical materialism] one should put the accent on the first term—'historical'—and not on the second, which is metaphysical in origin. The philosophy of praxis is absolute 'historicism,' the absolute secularisation and earthliness of thought, an absolute humanism of history. It is along this line that one must trace the thread of the new conception of the world" (*Prison Notebooks*, "Concept of Orthodoxy," p. 465; cr. *Quaderni* II, QC 11 [27], p. 1437).

65 Cf. *Quaderni* II, QC 10 [14], pp. 1401-3; cr. *Prison Notebooks*, pp. 436-37.

66 *Prison Notebooks*, "Speculative Immanence and Historicist or Realist Immanence," pp. 399-400; cr. *Quaderni* II, QC 10 II [9], pp. 1246-47.

67 "What the idealists call 'spirit' is not a point of departure but a point of arrival; it is the ensemble of the superstructures moving towards concrete and objectively universal unification and it is not a unitary presupposition" (*Prison Notebooks*, pp. 445-46; cr. *Quaderni* II, QC 11 [17], p. 1416).

68 *Quaderni* II, QC 10 II [17], pp. 1255-56; cr. *Prison Notebooks*, pp. 344-45; see also *Quaderni* II, QC 11 [27], p. 1437; cr. *Prison Notebooks*, p. 465.

69 Cf. Gramsci's fragment on "matter," *Quaderni* II, QC 11 [30], pp. 1442-45; cr. *Prison Notebooks*, pp. 465-68.

70 Cf. *Quaderni* II, QC 10 [54], "Introduzione allo studio della filosofia. Che cosa e l'uomo?," pp. 1343-46; QC 7 [35], pp. 883-86. These fragments are two of the most powerful developments by Gramsci of Marx's sixth thesis on Feuerbach. They present the argument that not only is "man" a historical product, created by "man" himself, but it is "man" alone who determines "what we are and what we can become, whether we really are, and if so to what extent, 'makers of our own selves,' of our own life and our destiny." Cr. *Prison Notebooks*, pp. 351-57.

71 *Prison Notebooks*, p. 355; cr. *Quaderni* II, QC 7, [35] p. 884 (altered slightly from the English translation).

72 For a brief reference, cf. *Quaderni* II, QC 11 [28], "L'immanenza e le filosofia della praxis," pp. 1438-39; QC 11 [24], "Il linguaggio e le metafore," pp. 1426-28; cr. *Prison Notebooks*, "Immanence and the Philosophy of Praxis," pp. 449-52.

73 Cf. *Quaderni* II, QC 11 [16], "Quistioni di nomenclatura e di contenuto," p. 1411; cr. *Prison Notebooks*, pp. 456-57.

74 *Prison Notebooks*, "The Dialectic," p. 436; cr. *Quaderni* II, QC 11 [22.IV], "Quistioni generali," p. 1424.

75 In his "Progresso e divenire," Gramsci connected the concept of "progress" with becoming and the concept of "freedom" with possibility (*Prison Notebooks*, p. 360; cr. *Quaderni* II, QC 10 [48.11], p. 1338).

76 The first quoted passage is from *Quaderni* II, QC 10 [12], pp. 1249-50; cr. *Prison Notebooks*, pp. 365-66 (translation slightly modified). The second passage is from QC 8 [182], "Struttura e superstrutture," pp. 1051-52; cr. *Prison Notebooks*, p. 366.

77 *Qaderni* II, QC 10 II [6.1], "Il termine di *'catarsi,'*" p. 1244; cr. *Prison Notebooks*, pp. 366-67.

Richard Schacht

Marxism, Normative Theory, and Alienation

Marx generally argues that existing moral ideas are
linked inseparably to specific social systems, class interests, and antagonisms. Yet Marx's thought also has a
genuinely normative character, which it needs if it is to
serve as a guide to revolutionary praxis.

For many years, in English-speaking countries, ethical
theory and moral philosophy have consisted chiefly in the kind of inquiry
that has come to be called "meta-ethics." In keeping with the basic spirit
of analytic philosophy more generally, our moral philosophers in the postwar generation seem to have decided that their proper primary task was to
analyze the nature of moral language and moral concepts as people ordinarily use them, rather than to assess them critically, develop and defend
improvements upon them, and apply such revised ethical principles and
norms to general social and concrete interpersonal situations and issues. In
recent years, however, many moral philosophers have once again become
interested in *normative* ethics, venturing to undertake such tasks as these.
This may be at least in part because they have become increasingly aware
of the problematic character of conventional moral concepts and beliefs,
and also of the inability of meta-ethics to contribute significantly to the
resolution of real and pressing problems in personal and social life. The
same remarks also apply with respect to social philosophy and value theory,
which likewise have begun again among us to have a genuinely normative
rather than a merely analytic-descriptive character.

Few of these philosophers are at all well acquainted
with Marxian philosophy. Many of them are aware, however, that Marx's
thought has what at least appears to be a strongly normative character; and
some have actually been moved to wonder whether in fact it has any relevance to their concerns. This is a question, however, to which it is difficult
to give a simple answer. In some sense Marx obviously had normative
pretentions. On the other hand, it is far from clear what these pretentions
actually come to, and even how seriously they are to be taken. Thus, in
recent years a number of important and influential books have appeared,
by writers such as Louis Althusser and Bertell Ollman, in which it is argued
that there is not and cannot be anything like a genuinely Marxian ethics or
normative theory, on the grounds that the thought of the mature Marx
precludes the possibility of this sort of philosophical inquiry.

So, for example, Althusser allows that the early Marx
did subscribe first to a Kantian-Fichtean outlook and then a Feuerbachian
way of thinking, each "humanistic" and with a strong ethical component
based upon a "philosophy of man" appealing to a notion of our "essence."
He contends, however, that Marx broke radically with all such views and

notions around 1845 and henceforth rejected any "recourse to ethics" and every "humanistic ideology," relegating all ethical and valuational schemata entirely to the realm of "ideology," which became for him merely an object of scientific analysis and an instrument of social organization rather than a component of Marxian theory itself. According to Althusser, the mature Marx radically distinguished his form of ("scientific") theory from—and opposed it to—"ideology" generally, inclusive of any sort of ethics, allowing only that "ideology (as a system of mass representations) is indispensable in any society if men are to be formed, transformed and equipped to respond to the demands of their conditions of existence."[1]

Althusser maintains that for the mature Marx the only "real problems" encountered in such human contexts "are organizational problems of the forms of economic life, political life and individual life," which are given a merely "imaginary treatment" when a "recourse to ethics" is made in dealing with them.[2] "Historical materialism cannot conceive that even a communist society could ever do without ideology, be it ethics, art, or 'world outlook'," he writes.[3] But that, for Althusser, still leaves no place whatever for normative ethical theory in Marxist theory proper.

Ollman similarly contends that " 'Marxian ethics' is clearly a misnomer in so far as it refers to Marx,"[4] even though he grants that Marx "expresses feelings of approval and disapproval in his works," is "motivated . . . by some idea of the 'good',"[5] and "sided with the proletariat and incited them to overthrow the system."[6] "I prefer to say that Marx did not have an ethical theory," Ollman writes;[7] for in his view, Marx not only does not do any of the things one must do to qualify as having or elaborating such a theory,[8] but moreover excludes the possibility of doing so through his adoption of a "philosophy of internal relations" in which there is no room for anything of the sort. Ollman tells us, "In this perspective, what is called the fact-value distinction appears as a form of self-deception"; and "judgments can never be severed, neither practically nor logically, from their contexts. . . ."[9]

Like Althusser, Ollman argues that we not only will be disappointed but also misguided if we look for anything like a normative ethical theory in Marx (or continue the search after we have read and learned our lesson from him). In a curious way, the two thus join hands with such less-sympathetic interpreters of Marx as Robert Tucker and Eugene Kamenka, who also deny that Marx has anything of the sort to offer. Rather, Tucker suggests that Marx was "a moralist of the religious kind" in whose thought ethical inquiry had no place.[10] And Kamenka contends that Marxism "has left behind it a legacy of 'reminders' rather than a foundation for moral philosophy or a key to the solution of ethical disputes," going on to observe that "the importance of these reminders at any particular time is directly proportionate to the social *naiveté* and lack of historical sense of these who write about ethics."[11]

I shall attempt to contribute to the clarification of this issue by distinguishing between some of the different things that a Marxian ethical and normative theory might involve and, in my opinion, *does* involve in Marxian thought. I shall argue that there is at least *one* sense in which Marx undeniably has such a theory, which is interestingly similar in certain important respects to the analytic meta-ethics that was long the fashion in Anglo-American philosophical circles, even if different in the particular manner of the analysis given. I shall also suggest, however, that it is a kind of theory that is no more helpful and satisfactory in the treatment of normative issues than is meta-ethics. And I shall further argue that while Marx seems to have *operated* with a further kind of normative theory, and perhaps assumed that yet another kind is possible and desirable, his right to do so is far from clear. This circumstance, I shall contend, raises serious problems that must receive better solutions than they have so far if Marxian thought is to make good its apparent claim to have genuine normative significance, both as critical social theory and as a theory relevant to the way we live our lives and deal with each other.

One of the things that might be meant by a Marxian ethics or moral philosophy is the elaboration of an account of the sort Marx suggests of the way in which *existing moralities* are to be conceived and understood, together with the undertaking of the indicated type of analysis of such moralities as they are to be found in human societies past and present. This *would* be a kind of theory of morality or ethics and a kind of genuine and useful philosophical inquiry, bearing a resemblance to Hegel's approach to ethics as well as to analytic meta-ethics. And this is something Marx clearly envisions and calls for, perhaps inspired by Hegel, but also going beyond him (or at any rate diverging from him).

Here I have in mind Marx's contention that moralities, along with religions, philosophies, and other such products of human thought, are to be conceived as parts of the ideological outgrowths and machinery of social systems, reflecting their structures and the interests of the classes dominant in them. Engendered as devices by means of which these systems are sustained, they serve to induce their members to act in a manner conducive to the systems' functioning and preservation (and thereby to the promotion of the interests of the classes in question). So Marx writes that "religion, family, state, morality, science, art, etc. are only *particular* modes of production, and fall under its general law."[12] They are but "the ideological reflexes and echoes" of the "real-life process" of "definite individuals who are productively active in a definite way" and who therefore "enter into [corresponding] definite social and political relations."[13] Marx continues: "Morality, religion, metaphysics, all the rest of ideology and their forms of consciousness thus no longer retain their semblance of independence. They have no history, no development [of their own]; but men, developing their material production and their material intercourse, alter along with their real existence, their thinking and the products of their thinking."[14]

Marx grants that, owing to the "division of material and mental labor" and the complexity of subsequent developments, it may happen that "theory, theology, philosophy, ethics, etc. come into contradiction with the existing social relations"; but he contends that "this can occur only because existing social relations have come into contradiction with existing forces of production."[15] In this way he proposes "to explain all the different theoretical products and forms of consciousness, religion, philosophy, ethics, etc., etc. and trace their origins and growth from that basis," as well as to take account of "the reciprocal action of these various sides on one another."[16] Nearly always, when Marx speaks of ethics or morality, it is as part of the same litany and to the same effect: the reality of "religious, moral, philosophical and juridical ideas" is granted but linked inseparably to specific social systems, class interests, and class antagonisms.[17] Moral/ethical "ideas" are treated simply as elements of "ideologies" and analyzed accordingly, in broad strokes and with no tentativeness or qualifications.

> Does it require deep intuition to comprehend that man's ideas, views and conceptions, in one word, man's consciousness, changes with every change in the conditions of material existence, in his social relations and social life?
> What else does the history of ideas prove, than that the intellectual production changes its character in proportion as material production is changed? The ruling ideas of each age have ever been the ideas of its ruling class.
> When people speak of ideas that revolutionize society, they do but express the fact, that within the old society, the elements of a new one have been created, and that the dissolution of the old ideas keeps even pace with the dissolution of the old conditions of existence.[18]

The burden of Marx's repeated assertions to this effect and assimilation of existing moralities to ideologies so conceived is that we must learn to view and understand them within this very human, practical, historically variable but always specific context, rather than as though they are or could be "pure" or absolute or of universal and unconditional validity. They are real enough; but their reality is that of historical phenomena constituting contingent and conditioned elements of specific social totalities to be analyzed and reckoned with theoretically and practically, rather than assessed in terms of their general justifiability and normative force. (This task and approach may remind one of Nietzsche's "genealogy of morals" even more than of the Hegelian treatment of ethics to which it has some affinity.)[19] It is undeniable that we may learn a good deal when we think about and analyze existing moralities in this way, and we have much difficult and delicate work to do if we are to do it properly.[20]

As in the case of Nietzsche, however, Marx does not stop with this. He further engages in a kind of normative discourse to which this view of morality cannot coherently be applied (and is not *meant* to apply), when he undertakes not merely to analyze but also to evaluate and pass critical judgment upon the kind of society with which he found himself confronted, to call for its radical transformation, and to argue for the establishment of a different set of social, economic, and political arrangements. The critical social theory of the mature as well as the early Marx has a strongly and strikingly normative dimension that cannot be ignored or eliminated without depriving his entire enterprise of what was to him its supreme purpose and significance for human life. It is reflected in his use of moral language, which owes much more to Kant than to Hegel, as when, for example, in an early essay, having asserted that "the criticism of religion ends with the doctrine that man is the supreme being for man," he writes: "It ends, therefore, with the *categorical imperative* to overthrow all those conditions in which man is an abased, enslaved, contemptible being."[21]

The normative character of Marx's thought is no less clearly evident in his later writings, from the *Manifesto* to the final volume of *Kapital*. From the eleventh thesis on Feuerbach ("The philosophers have only interpreted the world in various ways; the point, however, is to *change* it"),[22] to the appeal at the conclusion of the *Manifesto* ("The proletarians have nothing to lose but their chains. They have a world to win. Working men of all countries, unite!"),[23] to his invocation in the third volume of *Kapital* of the prospect of "the true realm of freedom" in which "begins the development of human energy which is an end in itself" (and which is said to have "the shortening of the working day" as "its basic prerequisite"),[24] Marx makes no secret about his normative concerns. He thus declared, in 1872, that "all the rest of my life will be, as have been all my efforts of the past, dedicated to the triumph of the social ideas which—you may be assured!—will lead to the world domination by the proletariat."[25] He considered "a revolution" to be not only historically inevitable but also "necessary"—"not only because the ruling class cannot be overthrown in any other way," but also because the class overthrowing it can only in a revolution succeed in ridding itself of all the muck of the ages and become fitted to found society anew."[26]

Marxian thought *must* have a genuinely normative character if it is to serve as an impetus and guide to revolutionary praxis. And its normative dimension cannot be conceived as amounting to nothing more than another particular morality of the sort his analytic moral theory relegates to the status of an element of the ideology attendant upon and subservient to the functioning of some specific existing socioeconomic system, without depriving it of its social-critical and revolutionary significance. It would hardly seem, for example, that this is all Marx meant to express in writing, "only in community [with others has each] individual the means of cultivating his gifts in all directions; only in the community, therefore, is personal freedom possible"; that "in a real community the individuals obtain their freedom in and through their association";[27] and that "the proletarians, if they are to assert themselves as individuals, will have to abolish the very condition of their existence hitherto" and "must overthrow the State."[28]

Similarly, Marx concludes the second part of the *Manifesto* by saying: "In place of the old bourgeois society, with its classes and class antagonisms, we shall have an association in which the free development of each is the condition for the free development of all."[29] Thus, it is not only in his early writings that Marx evinces normative concerns, even though in his later writings he seldom approaches the rhetorical level of such earlier passages as the following panegyric to the final stage of communism, depicted as "the complete return of man to himself as a *social* (i.e., human) being—a return become conscious, and accomplished within the entire wealth of previous development. This communism, as fully-developed naturalism, equals humanism, and as fully-developed humanism equals naturalism; it is the genuine resolution of the conflict between man and nature and between man and man—the true resolution of the strife between existence and essence, between objectification and self-confirmation, between freedom and necessity, between the individual and the species. Communism is the riddle of history solved, and it knows itself to be the solution."[30]

Here, then, we find a second type of ethical or normative theory in Marx's thought, very different from the first and of major importance. The question that must be answered, however, is not only what the normative principles are that Marx embraces and employs in this connection, but what *justification* he is able to give for selecting and employing these principles in this way. After all, it is not enough in philosophy or social theory merely to have and affirm and act upon such principles; it is also necessary to make a coherent and convincing case for adopting them. Marxian theory therefore has the task of any normative rather than merely analytic or meta-ethical theory of establishing such a case.

Marx himself actually does very little along these lines. He would appear to *accept* principles that have a certain appeal and have had their philosophical champions (e.g., Kant, Schiller, and Hegel); but he does not have their *right* to them, since he does not subscribe to their grounds for holding them. Yet, he does very little by way of establishing his *own* right to them in any other way. By omission, he left this task to those who came after him; but this task remains largely to be accomplished—if indeed it can be. And he made its accomplishment difficult, at the very least, by advancing a general philosophical position containing very little upon which the sort of case required might be built, and by ruling out traditional ways of doing so. The most promising possibility would seem to be that offered by the conception he tentatively suggests here and there of our fundamental human nature and potentialities. It is far from clear, however, whether this conception will emerge from critical assessment—including his own criticisms of the notions of "man" and the "human essence" in his later writings—rich and substantial enough to support normative principles of the sort his critical and revolutionary social theory would seem to require.

For example, Marx subscribes to and valorizes notions of human freedom, dignity, community, activity, and development that make it possible for him to distinguish between "dehumanized" and "genuinely human" forms of life. These notions enable him to identify practices and social arrangements conducive and detrimental to both; and he draws upon them in detailing the damage wrought by capitalism and bourgeois society, and in targeting certain of their basic features as the focus of revolutionary change. But he wants and needs to be able to do more than show what the contours of different forms of human life are and may be expected to be under different social and economic conditions, or to argue that some are more beset by contradictions and therefore more unstable than others, or to observe that survival is possible under some and not under others, or to suggest (or appeal to the purported fact) that some do or would tend to make people more miserable or more happy than others.

Marx is concerned above all with the *quality* of human life under different actual and actually attainable social and economic conditions. However, he rejects all appeals to religious or metaphysical considerations, which might be invoked either to privilege some forms of it over others or to justify the attribution to human beings of an essential nature that would do so, and insists that human nature takes differing shapes in differing historical circumstances. This, it would seem, leaves only a general consideration of the fundamental characteristics of human existence and their capacity for development (in ways setting human beings increasingly apart from other merely natural creatures and from their own kind on a level of

570

mere subsistence) as a possible basis for a normative theory capable of generating the sorts of qualitative distinctions Marx draws. While he seems to take for granted the possibility of a "philosophy of man" or philosophical anthropology sufficing for this purpose in his early writings, invoking suitably naturalistic notions of "man" and our human "essence" quite freely, he is so critical of the use of such expressions in his later writings that it is far from clear whether he remains committed to any conception of a general human nature sufficient to do more than demarcate our species from others. It is not possible to pursue this question here; but it would seem that it is a question that must be pursued, and that the manner in which it is answered will be crucial to the issue of what is to be made of the normative features of Marx's social theory.

There is yet a third important kind of notion that might be meant by a Marxian ethics or moral philosophy and that might constitute another part of a full Marxian ethical theory. Unfortunately, so much attention has been given to the first two notions I have distinguished that it has been largely neglected. It is crucial, however, not only to the development of Marxian humanism, but also to the extension of the relevance of Marxian philosophy to concrete human life as we now live it and as it might be lived after the kind of transformation of human social life Marx sought. It is this sort of thing that philosophers generally have in mind when they speak of normative ethics. Here the focus is not upon the critical assessment of social systems and the revolutionary praxis needed to transform them but rather upon our conduct and interactions as particular human beings, as we lead our daily lives and face the kinds of personal and interpersonal problems that call for decisions and choices.

Marx was not content, as Hegel had been, to refer all questions of this sort to the established norms prevailing in the society in which one lives. There are many respects in which he found the norms people generally have come to live by to be wanting. This pertains both to how people treat each other and also to what they do with their own lives. So, for example, Marx is repeatedly critical of "the egoistic man . . . , an individual separated from the community, withdrawn into himself, wholly preoccupied with private interest and acting in accordance with his private caprice."[31] It may be that this is the norm in bourgeois society, that those who act in this way do so with a good conscience owing to the way their conscience has been educated, and that Marx accordingly does not see fit to criticize them for doing so, since under the circumstances they could hardly be expected to do otherwise. But this does not lead him to conclude that their manner of acting is unobjectionable. "Human emancipation will only be complete," he writes, "when as an individual man, in his everday life, in his work, and in his relationships, he has become a *species-being.*"[32]

There is something fundamentally amiss, Marx holds, when "within the relationship of estranged labor each man views the other in accordance with the standard and position in which he finds himself as a worker."[33] Even if, according to prevailing standards, we live our lives and relate to others in a morally acceptable or prescribed manner, we are "isolated" from "*human* morality," and "*human* activity, *human* enjoyment, *human* nature" as well.[34] "Real community" is lacking; and it is only in such "community" with others, as has been observed, that Marx considers the individual to be able to "cultivate his gifts in all directions" and even to achieve "personal freedom."[35] The depersonalization, antagonism, brutal competition, and callous exploitation so characteristic of human relationships in bourgeois society, countenanced and even encouraged by bourgeois morality, never ceased to distress Marx; and they are among the central features of bourgeois society upon which he seizes in criticizing it and calling for its revolutionary transformation.

What is at issue here, however, is not merely his stance in relation to prevailing modes of morality on the personal and interpersonal level but, rather, whether there is anything of the sort with which he would have them replaced. It would be a great failing of Marxian theory if it simply had nothing to say along these lines; and it would be absurd if it were to be suggested that on this level what each of us ought to do in any situation, according to Marx, is simply to consult either conventional wisdom or the dictates of conscience or sheer self-interest to discover what the right thing to do might be.

It is perhaps conceivable that a significant Marxian ethic might be developed through an extension and elaboration of the kind of general normative principles that would be needed to render Marx's critical social theory viable, if they could be justified (e.g., on the basis of a sufficiently rich Marxian philosophical anthropology). Marx would seem to have taken for granted the validity and superiority of something like Kantian morality, however, to the defense of which such a strategy would not seem to lend itself at all readily, since it presupposes a picture of our nature very different indeed from Marx's. Here again, however, he neither has Kant's *right* to this morality nor undertakes to establish his own. His polemic against exploitation, for example, echoes and concretely expresses the "supreme practical principle" Kant takes to be one of the ways of stating the "categorical imperative" of morality: namely, "act in such a way that you always treat humanity, whether in your own person or in the person of any other, never simply as a means, but always at the same time as an end." But for Kant "the ground of this principle is: *Rational nature* exists as an end in itself."[36] And that is a "ground" to which Marx nowhere indicates that he is prepared to subscribe, or for which there would even appear to be room in his scheme of things.

This conception of our essentially rational nature, transcending and contrasting with our mundane nature and possessing intrinsic value, likewise underlies many of the other notions that figure prominently in Kant's ethics—for example, dignity, autonomy, self-legislation, the idea and ideal of "a kingdom of ends" as "a systematic union of different rational beings under common laws" of their own making, and their essential equality and equal worth[37]—and that reappear in Marx as the heart of the sort of ethics to which he appears to be committed. But Marx neither undertakes to supply anything along the lines of the "Metaphysic of Morals" Kant provides (in the work cited) in order to render his use of them coherent and justifiable, nor would he seem to have any way of doing so. In his early writings Marx makes some remarks that appear to be intended to indicate the way in which he proposes to go about establishing a naturalistic basis for a normative ethics of the sort he favors. So, for example, he asserts that "the direct, natural, and necessary relation of person to person is the *relation of man to woman*"—by which he appears to mean love—and goes on to contend that "one can therefore judge man's whole level of development"

572

by reference to this paradigmatic type of "relationship," discerning in this way "the extent to which man's *natural* behavior has become *human* . . .; the extent to which, therefore, the *other* person as a person has become for him a need—the extent to which he in his individual existence is at the same time a social being."[38]

Clearly, however, the paradigm Marx appeals to is both problematic and incapable of bearing the burden he assigns to it. The same also applies to his direct appeal to the notion of the "human" itself, as when he writes: "Assume *man* to be *man* and his relationship to the world to be a human one: then you can exchange love only for love, trust for trust."[39] Marx seems to have thought that the idea of a "return of man . . . to his *human*, i.e., *social* mode of existence," resulting in "the positive transcendence of all estrangement,"[40] can also be turned around, enabling one to ground a conception of social existence with normative import for our manner of relating to other people in the underlying conception of our true human nature. But again, this places more weight on the notion of the social character of human life than can be borne by the general meaning Marx gives it in introducing it; and it is far from clear how one might go about extracting from it or adding to it what he would need to be able to justify his rather Kantian ethical views by reference to it.

It must be admitted that, with the exception of a few such inadequate gestures in his early writings, Marx has little to say with respect to the way in which one might go about fleshing out and justifying a morality of a sort that would transcend those associated with previous and present forms of social organization and class interest and that would be more appropriate to our humanity. His proposed interpretation and analysis of existing moralities, along the lines of the first sort of ethical theory identified above, is of no help in this connection, even though it may be granted to constitute an important and illuminating form of inquiry, for the suggestion of which Marx deserves considerable credit and praise. If normative thinking for us is ever to be more than the sort of thing to which that sort of analysis is entirely appropriate, it may be necessary for us first to learn to see and understand existing moralities—our own inherited morality included—in that manner.

If we cannot find our way to a kind of normative thinking with respect to both social formations and personal conduct that does go beyond this sort of thing *and* beyond its analysis, however, then Nietzsche may well have been right in his proclamation of the advent of nihilism. Or a least, if one cannot do so within the context of Marxian philosophy (in the event that it turns out to afford no way of justifying the aims of human emancipation, community, and the free and full development of each and all that Marx espouses, and of establishing and elaborating moral principles), one will have no effective reply to make to interpreters like Althusser, Ollman, Tucker, and Kamenka. And there will be nothing to say to philosophical outsiders who wonder whether Marxian philosophy has anything to offer along normative-ethical lines that they have not heard before and from which they might profit.

It thus may be that, in the end, the only real service of Marxian philosophy in this context is to help break the grip of traditional and prevailing ideologically motivated moralities, thereby perhaps clearing a space (as it were) in which we then—not as Marxian philosophers but simply as philosophers and human beings—may proceed to rethink the whole matter of personal and interpersonal morality, inventing or resolving upon other forms of morality to live by. It would be premature to conclude from the preoccupation of Marx and others with different matters that Marxian thought is *incapable* of engendering a significant moral theory on this level, for which a case might be made that would enable it to lay claim to our philosophical acceptance and personal adherence. But it is far from obvious that it can do so.

One point that can be made in Marx's defense (or at any rate in mitigation of his reticence on this topic), and that is also of no little interest and relevance in this connection, is suggested by Engels in *Anti-Dühring*. After observing that "morality has always been class morality," whether feudal, bourgeois, or even "proletarian," he remarks, "A really human morality which stands above class antagonisms and above any recollection of them becomes possible only at a stage of society which has not only overcome class antagonisms, but has even forgotten them in practical life."[41] This suggests that, while it is meaningful to speak of such a morality in connection with Marxian theory, and while Marxian theory is a least capable of saying something about the conditions under which such a morality would be possible and might be expected to emerge, it is *too soon* to be able to say what it would be like and what it would involve.

Here, again, Marxian moral theory (as far as it goes) would seem to echo that of Kant in taking a significant sort of freedom not enjoyed by human beings as long as they are ensnared in the toils of natural/historical necessity to be a fundamental condition of the possibility of a genuine morality that would be more than a reflection and subtle device of such necessity. And it is of no little interest and significance for the understanding of Marx's thought that he would seem to have envisioned the dawning of a "realm of freedom" under altered social conditions in which the character of human existence itself would be fundamentally transformed, thereby bringing about a state of affairs representing a naturalistic approximation to Kant's attribution to human beings of an essential nature transcending the natural order.[42] But it still would seem to lack any content that would enable one to derive moral principles of any sort from it, by which human conduct might be guided even after this envisioned ultimate emancipation of humanity were to be reached, let alone at the present time.

Indeed, an injunction to act as though one were a member of such a human community would be not only rather meaningless to us at this juncture of human development but also misguided, even if somehow provided with appropriate content, for Marx would appear to consider human beings at present to be so constituted as to be largely incapable of responding in the manner called for and exposed to the likelihood of disastrous consequences if they were to do so. Such a morality, he might well say, could it be elaborated, would not be at all well suited to the conditions under which we live and to the necessity of bringing about their transformation. So he might consider the only sort of personal morality deserving of serious commendation at present to be one subordinated and adjusted to the requirements of a program of revolutionary praxis aimed at the transformation of society along the lines he took to be necessary. This, however, would doubtless be disappointing to most moral philosophers, who would find it a very unsatisfactory substitute for a normative ethic.

Richard Schacht

My conclusion is not that this is the end of the matter. It may well be that one can do more than this, for example, by seeking to extract principles with normative import for interpersonal relations—which might be meaningfully applicable to human life under present as well as future conditions—from Marx's conception of a "species-being," or from his notion of a classless society, or from his idea of "an association in which the free development of each is the condition of the free development of all."[43] And one might be able to construct an argument of some sort for doing so that would be persuasive enough to render this line of thinking convincing. But it remains to be seen whether anything of the sort can be done. My intention here is to issue a challenge and an appeal to Marxian philosophers who have not already cast their lot with dogmatic or orthodox and neo-orthodox Marxism or social scientism, to place normative theory high on their philosophical agenda, ceasing merely to pledge allegiance to the normative commitments expressed in Marx's writings, and undertaking to see whether a viable normative theory in the spirit of Marx can be developed and defended.

I now wish to turn briefly to the implications of what I have had to say up to this point for alienation theory in Marxian thought. A moment's reflection should suffice to make clear that these implications are significant, at least for the possibility of preserving the strong link between alienation theory and normative theory that is evident in Marx's early writings and that continues to characterize a good deal of the literature in the Marxian tradition.[44] It may be that the concept of alienation is sufficiently flexible that it can be given a place and meaning of some sort in any kind of Marxian theory, even if that theory is developed in such a way that all normative theorizing is entirely excluded from it, and that the only type of ethical theory countenanced is of the analytic-interpretive variety I first identified. It should be obvious, however, that the meaning and practical significance of the concept will be greatly affected by the way in which these larger issues are resolved and the theoretical context in which the concept of alienation is situated.

If follows very straightforwardly, for example, that in any version of Marxian theory in which *all* normative theorizing is excluded, the concept of alienation can have no normative import and thus its applicability cannot be taken to warrant any conclusions of a practical nature. It would not matter that it is commonly taken to convey the idea that something has gone wrong in human relations to which it is applicable. If the concept is to have a legitimate place and role in the context of a theory within which no normative principles are permitted or can be justified, the price of its appropriation and use is the disavowal of any such implication and a steadfast refusal to be seduced into making unwarranted evaluative judgments by its extratheoretical associations and connotations.

This point may be illustrated more concretely. Suppose that it is decided to employ the concept of alienation in connection with the occurrence of one of the kinds of separation to which it is often applied, namely, that which consists in a relation of indifference to or rejection of prevailing standards of acceptable social behavior on the part of a nominal member of society. Just as one may analytically identify these standards and what constitutes departures from them, and may even speak of "ethical norms" in this connection, one may also speak of "deviant behavior" in relation

575

to them and may characterize the disposition to engage in such behavior in terms of "alienation" from them. If the only sort of ethical or normative theory one is prepared to countenance or is able to justify consists in the ascertainment of whatever these norms happen to be in any given society and their interpretation as elements of the ideological apparatus of that (type of) society, one is in no position to pass any judgment upon those who do or do not conform to them. One likewise is in no position to pass any judgment upon the society itself, in light of the relative incidence of behavior and dispositions of one kind or the other. Normative criteria are required in order to pass judgments of either sort. Without such criteria, one may identify and interpret the kinds of judgments passed by members of the society, internal to it; but one cannot proceed to any critical evaluation of them.

If such things as the relative incidence of the sort of alienation and related forms of unhappiness in question are to have not only analytic-theoretical but also practical social-critical interest, a different and richer type of Marxian theory with an explicit normative dimension is required. And if the idea expressed by Marx in the eleventh thesis on Feuerbach (to the effect that whereas philosophers previously have only *interpreted* the world, the point is to *change* it) conveys something essential to Marxian thought, then such a richer type of Marxian theory would indeed seem to be called for. Otherwise the eleventh thesis is turned on its head, and the concept of alienation along with the rest of the Marxian conceptual arsenal is completely defused, contrary to Marx's clear intentions.

We have, however, here identified *one* possible conception of alienation that *may* be elaborated and given a place and use in connection with one Marxian way of thinking about ethics and norms. And however inadequate this conception and this approach may be for Marx and many Marxian theorists (along with many other philosophers), they need not and should not be rejected for this reason—especially since it may turn out in the end that there is no satisfactory way of coming up with anything more along both lines within the context of Marxian theory (or even more generally). Here alienation may be construed very generally as a relation of indifference to or rejection of the *ethical-normative order* prevailing in some society on the part of people who are otherwise to be reckoned members of that society. The applicability of this conception, once again, is evaluatively neutral, at least within the context of the first form of ethical-normative theory. If it is possible to identify something that might be considered the ethical-normative order prevailing in a society, and if it is also possible to distinguish between embracing and living in accordance with it and not doing so, then it is possible and appropriate to speak of this sort of alienation in the latter connection and to mean and convey and imply nothing more. And this, it would seem, is exactly as some Marxian theorists and their analytic-philosophical counterparts would have it.

Suppose, however, that it turns out to be possible to do what many other Marxian philosophers seem to be committed to trying to do, namely, develop a normative theory rich enough to ground a critical social theory enabling them to bring forms of society, social institutions, and social practices before the bar of evaluative assessment and to justify the advocacy of modifications of or alternatives to them. In this context an importantly different conception of alienation could be framed and elaborated, the applicability of which would have significant normative and practical implications—as it does in the hands of Marx, most clearly in his early writings.

This conception could have derivative applications to such things as one's labor and one's sensuous and communal life; but its fundamental focus would be upon the quality of the life one lives. It would have the basic significance of *self-alienation,* construed in terms of a disparity between the character of one's life as it is shaped and structured by the social system in which one lives and a kind of human life that is not only alternative but also arguably superior to it. One's relation to the ethical-normative order prevailing in one's society, which is decisive for obtaining the first sort of alienation distinguished, might still be of relevance here; but if so, this would only be to the extent that one's relation (of either alienation or unity) to that particular ethical-normative order, and the relation to the particular social system it mediates, affects whether one is thereby rendered either more or less able to live the kind of human life envisioned and valorized.

If alienation is so conceived, a certain form of society might be considered "alienating" precisely to the extent that its socialization mechanisms were successful in keeping the incidence of the first sort of alienation distinguished *low*—if, that is, the kind of life people were thereby brought to lead was radically at variance with the kind of life held to be preferable. Of course, if the kind of life people are enabled to lead by embracing the existing ethical-normative order and participating fully in the social system with which it is associated comes closer to this valorized kind of life than any other they might actually lead by doing otherwise, then as Hegel long ago suggested, their alienation of the first sort would have the significance of the kind of self-alienation presently under consideration and so would require them to overcome it through the transformation of their relation to that order.[45] Such self-alienation, however it might be concretely conceived, is in the nature of the case lamentable if it is acknowledged to be a possibility at all. It thus differs in this respect from alienation of the first sort, which (as has been observed) may turn out to be either a bad thing or a good thing or merely an evaluatively indifferent human possibility, depending upon what if anything of an evaluative nature one adds to its conceptualization.

There is yet another conception of alienation that might also be usefully conceived in this general connection and must be distinguished from both of those identified above. It may be introduced and elaborated in the context of the form of normative-ethical theory which focuses upon concrete human conduct and undertakes to work out normative principles appropriate to one's manner of relating to other people. Let it be supposed that one reaches the conclusion that there are some such principles, constitutive of a philosophically defensible interpersonal morality. (Their status, it may be noted, would thus be different from and superior to that of the established rules of various existing normative-ethical orders as such.) Alienation here might then be conceived as a certain sort of interpersonal estrangement, consisting in one's encountering and dealing with others as though that morality had no application to one's relations with them.

This conception of alienation is obviously linked to the idea of immorality. It is not simply synonymous with the latter, however, for its focus is not upon the particular content of this morality (whatever that might be) but rather upon one's relation to other human beings, whom one treats other than as deserving to be brought within the compass of moral consideration. It is, of course, quite possible that the idea of such a morality will turn out to be an empty human and philosophical ideal, akin to and as untenable as the metaphysical and theological schemata criticized and repudiated by Marx, Nietzsche, and others. If the tenability of something of the sort is established or supposed, however, then it would make good and interesting sense to differentiate between interpersonal relations that are and are not mediated and informed by the associated moral sensibility. Here one could be conceived to be alienated from others in a special and particularly profound way if one fails to accord them the respect and treatment due them as beings to whom one is related morally. This way of thinking would seem to be reflected in the Marxian polemic against exploitation of some human beings by others. To regard and treat other human beings as but so much exploitable material (whether as laborers or as consumers), and nothing more, would seem to be one of the cardinal sins of Marxian morality, if there is any such thing. And it likewise is singled out by Marx and many Marxian theorists as a relation constituting one of the most acute and lamentable forms of alienation in need of being identified and overcome.

Three different forms of alienation have thus come to light, associated with the three varieties of Marxian ethical and normative theory I have distinguished. One need not choose among them, since they are one and all available to Marxian theorists, and to others as well. But each has its theoretical presuppositions and contexts, and one is entitled to any of them only if one is willing and able to supply them with the theoretical contexts and underpinnings appropriate to them. Doing so may or may not prove to be possible, as was earlier observed. The exploration of this possibility is one of the main tasks falling alike to Marxian theory, and to philosophy more generally at the present time. The outcome of this exploration will have a great deal to do not only with the future course of alienation theory, ethical-normative theory, and Marxian theory but also with future approaches to the entire matter of the way in which human conduct, practices, and institutional arrangements are to be reckoned with. The jury is still out on Marx's eleventh thesis on Feuerbach.

It must be allowed that these are by no means the only uses that have been and may be found for the concept of alienation in Marxian theory and in other theoretical contexts. Others are familiar and possible, independent of any connection with any sort of Marxian (or other) ethical and normative theory.[46] It seems to me, however, that notwithstanding their limitations and the problematic character of at least several of them, these are among the most interesting and potentially significant. Alienation theory and ethical-normative theory can both benefit if pursued in more explicit association than is common, at least in many philosophical circles.

Marxian philosophy, as carried on by at least some of those who conceive of themselves as proceeding in the spirit of Marx, has long been something of an exception to this general rule; and so it is of particular interest in this connection—for which reason I have paid particular attention to it here. In it, both many of the problems and much of the promise associated with a number of important lines of inquiry come to light and admit of being brought into clearer focus. I earlier suggested that the future of Marxian theory is at stake as long as these problems remain unresolved. I would now suggest that the same is true where alienation theory is con-

Richard Schacht

cerned. The two may not stand or fall together; but the fate of each, and the future course of ethical and normative theory as well, undoubtedly can and should be significantly influenced by inquiry relating to the other. And such inquiry must come to terms with the issues to which I have sought to draw attention.

Notes

1   Louis Althusser, *For Marx*, trans. Ben Brewster (London: New Left Books, 1977), p. 235.

2   Althusser, p. 247.

3   Althusser, p. 232.

4   Bertell Ollman, *Alienation: Marx's Conception of Man in Capitalist Society* (Cambridge: Cambridge University Press, 1971), p. 5l.

5   Ollman, p. 44.

6   Ollman, p. 47.

7   Ollman, p. 47.

8   Ollman, p. 46.

9   Ollman, p. 48.

10   Robert C. Tucker, *Philosophy and Myth in Karl Marx*, 2d ed. (Cambridge: Cambridge University Press, 1972), p. 21.

11   Eugene Kamenka, *Marxism and Ethics* (New York: St. Martin's Press, 1969), p. 3.

12   Karl Marx, "Economic and Philosophical Manuscripts of 1844," *The Marx-Engels Reader*, 2d ed., ed. Robert C. Tucker (New York: W. W. Norton, 1978), p. 85.

13   Marx, "The German Ideology," *The Marx-Engels Reader*, p. 154.

14   Marx, "The German Ideology," pp. 154-55.

15   Marx, "The German Ideology," p. 159.

16   Marx, "The German Ideology," p. 164.

17   Marx, "Manifesto of the Communist Party," *The Marx-Engels Reader*, p. 489.

18   Marx, "Manifesto of the Communist Party," p. 489.

19   Cf. Friedrich Nietzsche, *On the Geneology of Morals*, trans. Walter Kaufmann and R. J. Nottingdale (New York: Vintage, 1967), esp. the first and second essays; and G. W. F. Hegel, *Philosophy of Right*, trans. T. M. Knox (Oxford: Clarendon Press, 1942), esp. the preface and the third part. For an extended discussion of Nietzsche in this connection, see Richard Schacht, *Nietzsche* (London: Routledge and Kegan Paul, 1983), chap. 7. On Hegel, see W. H. Walsh, *Hegelian Ethics* (London: Macmillan, 1969).

20   Cf. Alan Wood, *Karl Marx* (London: Routledge and Kegan Paul, 1981), chap. 10, "Morality and Ideology."

21   Marx, "Contribution to the Critique of Hegel's *Philosophy of Right*," *The Marx-Engels Reader*, p. 60.

22   Marx, "Theses on Feuerbach," *The Marx-Engels Reader*, p. 145.

23   Marx, "Manifesto," *The Marx-Engels Reader*, p. 500.

24   Marx, "Capital," vol. 3, *The Marx-Engels Reader*, p. 441.

25   Marx, speech delivered in Amsterdam, *The Marx-Engels Reader*.

26   Marx, "The German Ideology," *The Marx-Engels Reader*, p. 193.

27   Marx, "The German Ideology," p. 197.

28   Marx, "The German Ideology," p. 200.

29   Marx, "Manifesto," p. 491.

30   Marx, "Manuscripts of 1844," p. 84.

31   Marx, "On the Jewish Question," *The Marx-Engels Reader*, p. 43.

32   Marx, "On the Jewish Question," p. 46.

33   Marx, "Manuscripts of 1844," p. 97.

34   Marx, critical marginal notes on the article "The King of Prussia and Social Reform," *The Marx-Engels Reader*, p. 131.

35   Marx, "The German Ideology," p. 197.

36   Immanuel Kant, *The Moral Law (Groundwork of the Metaphysic of Morals)*, trans. H. J. Paton (New York: Barnes and Noble, 1961), p. 96.

37   Kant, pp. 98ff.

38   Marx, "Manuscripts of 1844," pp. 83-84.

39   Marx, "Manuscripts of 1844," p. 105.

40   Marx, "Manuscripts of 1844," p. 85.

41   Friedrich Engels, "Anti-Dühring," *The Marx-Engels Reader*, p. 727.

42   Cf. Marx, "Capital," *The Marx-Engels Reader*, p. 441.

43   Marx, "Manifesto," *The Marx-Engels Reader*, p. 49l.

44   Cf. Adam Schaff, *Marxism and the Human Individual*, trans. Olgierd Wojtasiewicz, ed. Robert S. Alen (New York: McGraw Hill, 1970); Gajo Petrović, *Marx in the Mid-Twentieth Century* (Garden City, N.Y.: Doubleday Anchor, 1967); Leszek Kolakowski, *Main Currents of Marxism: The Founders*, trans. P. S. Falla (Oxford: Clarendon Press, 1978); also Richard Schacht, *Alienation* (Garden City, N.Y.: Doubleday Anchor, 1971).

45   Cf. Schacht, *Alienation*, esp. chap. 2.

46   Schacht, *Alienation*, chap. 7.

Armand Mattelart

Communications in Socialist France: The Difficulty of Matching Technology with Democracy

Translated by Andrew Ross

If we are to understand and intervene in the contentious state of the relation between communication and democracy, we must rethink science and technology as functions of a new set of relations among the diverse components of civil society. The right to communicate, defined as the right to be informed, has largely prevailed over the right, which should be just as inalienable, to produce one's own information.

This study is an attempt to lay out the contradictions faced by the French socialist government in its plan for a "strategy of communication" within the reality of advanced capitalism, where "technological choice" has become a major question of "democratic choice." Communications, or rather the communications industry, is now central to any plans for reindustrialization. Big industrial powers like France see the new communications technologies (the hardware and software industries, respectively producing systems and programs) as a potential means of recovery from the economic crisis. They are also viewed as a possible way out of the political crisis, through restoring the "consensus" (cf. the Nora-Minc Report). The plans for reindustrialization are increasingly becoming society's way of reconstituting power relations between nations, between classes and social groups, and among individuals. Within the solution offered by high technology, the logic of industry is often at odds with the logic of the socius, a fact that emphasizes the importance of any discussion about public participation in "technological choices" to be made in this domain. Such a debate is part of the larger problematic of examining the transformation of the state and its relation to civil society, the fragile balance between public and private sectors, and the specific growth of the private sector, both commercial and noncommercial. It is also a debate that revives certain questions that have long lain dormant in leftist thinking.

Conflicting Lines of Action

In various ways, whether in the shape of simple vows of faith or as a sign of new emergent realities, the question of the relation between democracy and the new communications and information technologies has been the subject of numerous discussions, proposals, and plans, both official and unofficial, ever since the socialist victory in the elections of 1981. "Democratize information" rather than "inform society," as Pres-

581

ident Mitterand announced in the fall of 1981, in contrast to the policy of the previous administration. By developing new research and new communications services, we would no longer be subject to the determinism of *technological supply;* the electronic directory would no longer be imposed upon everyone but would be *proposed;* users would be allowed telematics choices; workers could be assured that the introduction of new technologies into the workplace would be to their benefit. In short, we were to rediscover that "in order to thrive, technology must have a favourable social environment."[1]

In a more concrete way, the national colloquium for research and technology, a widespread consultation of the scientific community that took place before the legal direction and planning of research and technological growth had been worked out, was calling for a "renewed alliance between science and democracy." [2] Between November 1981 and the end of January 1982, thirty-one regional groups across the country each hosted one day of this national colloquium in accord with the principle that "consultation before action is a procedure proper not only to the scientific method but also to the very spirit of democracy itself. . . ."[3] The thousands of contributions made by research groups, universities, trade unions, and professional organizations created a reflective mood unprecedented in the history of French research and helped to work up a state of conscientiousness as much on the part of those who work in scientific technology as those who actually use or could use it. By opting to draw upon all those who effectively have a share in technological choices, the colloquium was trying to make technological research and development into "a national issue about which everyone feels concerned."

The relations between science, technology, and the other great spheres of social activity cannot remain the sole province of those specialists who assume responsibility for its development. Obviously, scientists are in the best position to know about the most promising lines of research, and this is no less the case when it comes to judging how knowledge should be applied in the industrial and commercial fields. Any dialogue between specialists and non-specialists, however, must observe two conditions. The first is to clarify the controversies which spring up internally within the sciences and technologies. For it is clearly there that possible alternatives appear and are discussed; it is there that we must begin by properly establishing an initial form of democratic expression—on the question of scientific and technical ideas and plans. The second condition is to allow neither the scientists nor the engineers the exclusive role of making major decisions which could affect the future of the country. The Government, Parliament, regional bodies, trade unions, associations—the list is not inclusive—must, each according to its responsibilities, be provided with access to the information they require in order to participate in an enlightened manner. In fact, the idea that the

582

entire national community, through its qualified representatives, should be put in "charge" of these decisions, is predicated upon a populace fully informed of the implications of each choice.[4]

Let us say this much at the outset. Such a point of view, which defines the democracy/technology relation in terms of the appropriation of the new technological tools by the whole of society, has not always been included in those discussions or plans that have focused, in other institutional contexts, on the new tools of information and communications. This problematic, for example, is hardly even considered in the report by the Commission on the Future of Audiovisuals (the MOINOT Report), published in mid-October 1981.[5] Although its proposals do point toward a decentralization of the audiovisual media, and are full of vague references to more democratic access to the airways, the general assumption of the report is that of the right to communicate, a right based too unilaterally upon the inalienable right of professionals to communicate and thus to improve their efficiency. Professionalist ideology seems to have fixed the discursive limits for the "democratization" of information.

Clearly, the great poles of the debate about research—the need to rethink science and technology as functions of a new set of relations among the diverse components of civil society—have little or no place in the first official report on audiovisuals. The right to communicate, defined as the right to be informed, has largely prevailed over the right, which should be just as inalienable, to produce one's own information. Moreover, there is scarcely any evidence in the report of thinking about the multiple experiences of video and cinema, which, outside of the big commercial or monopoly circuits of radio/television, have advanced other ways of defining the communication/democracy relation over the last fifteen years, even if they have taken an irregular and often contradictory path. There is no sign in the report of anything equivalent to the "right to social research" claimed by certain sectors—though not all, unfortunately—at the time of the national colloquium: a right that would deny specialized professional circles the privilege of regarding research as their exclusive prerogative; a right that would allow different social groups to instigate research on their own social and material environment or on social equalities, with the choice of deciding for themselves whether or not to take on the services offered by the professionals.[6]

The parliamentary debates on the new audiovisual legislation that took place in May/June 1982 failed to do away with this corporatist logic. The real questions were ignored at the cost of a completely institutional and legalistic debate, one that was clearly necessary but hardly conducive to addressing the essential question under discussion. In privileging interventions about the independence of information from the Right and Left alike, the forum was reduced to dealing with the democracy/communication problem only in terms of the short-term political issues and consequently glossed over the cultural issues, namely, the effects of a communications model upon the very forms of society. Indeed, this unquestioned assumption of the independence of the professionals has put the parliamentary socialists on the defensive and allowed the amnesiacs of the Right to designate and impose their own terrain as the exclusive ground for all discussion. In seeking refuge under the aegis of freedom (the journalist's sanctuary), equality was sacrificed. And, as a result of insisting solely on the need to preserve the independence of the media professionals with respect to political power, the idea of their independence with respect to social relations earned a certain credibility. All of this followed from the assumption that, if the political pressures exerted on journalists were eased, then information and journalistic practice would become transparent. By the same token, all other issues became superfluous: the basic question, for example, of determining how a relation to reality (a relation to the totality of the social body, if not a specific conception of legislating the world of each and every one) is reproduced through social practices, professionally codified within a particular mode of producing information.[7] What is more serious for us is that the result of confining discussion about communication to the corporate sphere or the ideology of journalism, the result of reinstating the golden rule of facts and transparent meanings, is not only to advance the idea of the neutrality of "journalistic technique" but also to sanction an approach to communications technology that points in the same technocratic direction.

These introductory notes are not designed to lose us in conjecture over the issue of the politics (whether categorical or not) of using communications in France right now. We are so used to the idea of giving up, having played Cassandra's part so often. On the contrary, I have tried to give some preliminary idea of the contentious state of the relation between communication and democracy, a state that cannot be ignored if we are to examine the realities of communication and information and thereby develop a fully theoretical reflection on the research topic—communication/democracy. To achieve this, we must be prepared to question a number of received ideas about what constitutes the field of observation proper to communication as a scientific discipline. This is no small task. Like it or not, the polyvalence of new networks of communication and information demands not only interdisciplinary approaches but also multisector analysis.

Democracy and Industrial Planning

It would be fatal to resort to economism as a way of escaping the culturalism of the prophets of the new electronic marketplace or of a democracy on line *(sur console)* that does not give a fig for democracy at all. However, it must not be forgotten that a necessary condition (though certainly not the only one) of the effective functioning of democracy is the state of its economy. By this I mean the way in which a nation manages its heritage of material and symbolic production, the cumulative result of which has been lived and struggled for by individuals, groups, and classes; the way in which a national "community," affected by antagonistic social planning, attempts to recover its needful heritage by constructing or reconstructing it; the way in which this "community" employs the creativity, innovativeness, and inventiveness of its diverse constituent groups as part of a social plan.

To further describe such a national plan involves venturing into unresearched areas like that of national culture and its dialectical relation to the process of transnationalization. These days, when national culture or identity has a global tendency to be transformed into one of those poles of discourse associated with projects that are most antithetical to its existence, it is important to rethink this concept within the concrete context of the power relations responsible for the construction and reconstruction of national culture. It is unfortunate, nonetheless, that "nationalism" or national independence, more often than not, only becomes an operational term of reference whenever popular sentiment needs to be whipped up against an enemy or aggressor (whether commercial or military). At such moments, the terms become symbols of more than just group unity, and consequently class conflict is played down. Obviously it is not my intention here to delve too far into what ought to turn into an important field of critical research.

So far, I have suggested that if we are to speak about democracy, it is difficult to avoid examining the way in which a country mobilizes its energies around an industrial plan for restoring its technological independence. With the political changes of May 1981 and the subsequent nationalizations, this plan has been at the forefront. Can France, along with Europe, maintain its autonomy in the face of transnationals emerging from America and Japan? In pointing to the international competition for leadership in scientific and technological know-how, the steering group responsible for the colloquium on research echoed the words of then presidential candidate François Mitterand on the major elements of the politics of research and technology he promised to implement after the election: "The question to be asked now is a simple one: What is the place of France in this international competition? At the front or at the back? In fifth place, after the U.S., U.S.S.R., Japan, and West Germany, or in first place? Hireling or pioneer? My choice is made. Over the next seven years I want France to be a front runner in the scientific field."[8]

Rather than wonder what response these claims would elicit from a Brazilian, Chinese, or Indian scientist who did not share this Western view of the world, let us content ourselves with pointing out how industrial planning is overestimating its technological potential in order to bring an end to the crisis. Thus, the cutting-edge technologies of information processing, communication, semiconductors, robots, and biotechnology are taken up as a way out of the crisis, a way, given the requisite political will, that would sanction a concerted development of the world economy. What is at stake in this crisis is the redefinition of economic and political relations among different nations and the redistribution of power relations at the international and domestic level. In his report on *Technology, Employment, and Growth* presented at the Versailles summit in June 1982, the French president was confident: "Where is technical progress today, and what effect will it have, in the coming decade, on the crisis we are going through? . . . Not only do we need to look for common solutions to the problems posed by the crisis, and to do that we must agree about its nature and its causes, but we must also look toward those wide open fields which can still be explored together. Science and technology is one of those fields, and its rapid growth will hasten on the upheaval of our societies, and threaten to turn against man himself unless he has established firm control over its development."[9] The same leitmotif was in evidence at the national colloquium on research: "To rely on scientific research and technological progress as the *dynamic components of recovery,* means not only employing them against the direct effects of the crisis, but also assigning them a far-reaching mission, that of providing the bases for another model of social development, one capable of accommodating existing models in making knowledge and its rational deployment the privileged instruments of renewal."[10]

One could easily feel uncomfortable with this way of looking at things and prefer to fall back on the results of the struggles of those various movements, peoples, or individuals who, throughout the industrialized or developing world, object to this vision of a "new model of development"; those who think that the only way of reorganizing the planet is to attack radically the assumptions of *growth* and *needs* and to bring an end to the equation of technical progress with social progress. It is this alternative experience, after all, that keeps the social body running, whether overtly or indirectly. But would this not mean giving short shrift to, or even ignoring, a debate that is much more complicated than simply disembarking while the big guns are trained on those who submit to the constraints of this growth (the constraints of the expansion of capital)? To follow such a course would be to neglect any political discussion on the subject and the opportunity to compare opposing judgments on power relations; we would then risk repeating what has happened, for example, with the nuclear question generally. When one goes to law, one should know how the law is made up, and this is not always so easy.

As the French minister for research and technology observed, "the objective at this point in time is not socialism." Obliged to defend himself against those who accused him of turning socialism into a vague and distant point of reference, he added: "For socialists of any stamp, I ask only one thing: that they are judged by their actions. Socialism lights our way; it is the complete ideal of democracy; it is self-management; democracy spread widely over all areas of life, politics, and economics. We cannot, however, expect it to be achieved in one day, and more to the point, in one country isolated from the rest of the world. Consequently, we have to consider the problem of the development of the other powers and of international relations over the next decade. We must prove that a government of the Left constitutes a response to the crisis, and then allow for changes to be made elsewhere, in other countries."[11] The important thing here is not so much to judge the merits of the philosophy of development and progress that sustains the explicit objectives of the socialist regime as *to go on and iron out the contradictions that pass through them.*

Electronics as a Technology Base

Although this topic has scarcely been the subject of considerable public debate, it is clearly on the question of industrial planning in the electronics field that we have been able to see how the coming recovery in the shape of a technology politics will be governed by tensions and tactical limits. I shall lay out a few points of reference, culled from the proposals contained in the report on the "Electronics Industries Network"[12]—the FARNOUX Report, prepared for the Ministry of Research and Technology in March 1982 and published in May 1982.

1. Electronics has become a technology base. No domain of economic activity is untouched by it. It is integral to all planned products, from military defense systems to communications systems. The control of these products will, in short, determine the future of technological independence as an essential element of national independence. Electronics is all the more strategic because of the very nature of the material it processes and chan-

nels—information. It is bound up in a cultural model that "will either be our own model or else one determined by foreign penetration in the electronics field."

2. Unless self-sufficiency is proclaimed, and France is cut off from technological changes elsewhere, a massive diffusion of electronics products, services, and systems throughout the economy is inevitable. The outcome of this, however, is difficult to predict. "The *real choice* for our country, in actual fact, is between a future that *would only enjoy a portion of the benefits of the development of the Network (Filière) and all of its faults*—because it would be content with consumption, allowing the inevitable rise in imports to lower national employment—and a future in which *we would draw in the maximum of positive returns*—as a result of our will to produce."[13]

3. All of the electronics sectors are interdependent, from the hardware and software systems (including data banks), office equipment, telecommunications and robotics, to large-scale public products. The electronics network thus constitutes a whole and must be examined globally. This synergetic trend will only get bigger; the unity of the electronics network will only get stronger. "This unity," claims the report, "is, and increasingly will be, a technical one: expansion will regularize processed information and homogenize components: borders between software, telecommunications, telematics, office equipment, and public electronics, will be abolished, all of which will lead to the emergence of a vast communications sector. At the heart of this network, complementary links will be strengthened between large-scale technology—like big computers or satellites—and smaller units—like personal computers or private telephone systems; software will circulate through the entire network, increasing its relative worth. This unity also has its industrial side, since companies will expand or diversify their field of activity."[14]

4. Insofar as this unified network is concerned, France will not benefit from a siege politics. A global plan for its reestablishment is required, one that relies on the two pillars of the electronics industry (professional hardware, including arms systems, and telecommunications along with telematics), where France has already succeeded in capturing a share of the world market in recent years.

Reviving the unreliable sectors—components, for example—requires the development of a large public sphere of electronics: "Public electronics is the natural market for producers of components. Unless there is a national public electronics industry of some proportions, French components producers will have no real competitive power."[15] France devotes twenty-five times less funds than Japan to the research and development of public electronics products.

Recommending an integrated plan will not, of course, mean a "free for all. A clear conscience about the *important technological sites,* the present state of the French network, and the potential effects of training, will enable us to concentrate on the 'problem areas' where an extra effort is needed."[16]

(Table 1 presents market and business figures for the electronics networks of the United States, Japan, Western Europe, and the rest of the world in 1980.)

5. The industrial plan proposed by France for the "electronics network" involves a strategy for liberating research and industry which, as

Table 1.

Country	Production[a]	Market[a]	Commercial Sales[a]	Share of Network in GNP (%)
United States	668 (46%)	648 (45%)	+20	3.5
Japan	228 (16%)	164 (11%)	+64	3.7
Western Europe	379 (26%)	409 (28%)	−30	
West Germany	113 (8%)	113 (8%)	−	3.3
France	83 (6%)	82 (6%)	− 1	3.0
Great Britain	74 (5%)	75 (5%)	− 1	3.8
Others[b]	175 (12%)	229 (16%)	−54	
World[b]	1450 (100%)	1450 (100%)		

[a]*Figures are in millions of francs; five francs = one dollar.*
[b]*Excluding COMECON and China.*

Source: DIEHL-FIEE-FARNOUX Report.

the American journal *Business Week* (May 31, 1982) notes, draws its lessons from the experience of rivals, especially Japan. With nationalization, public companies now account for 49 percent of the network, while the private French companies, including small and medium-sized outfits, represent 21 percent, and foreign groups 30 percent (13 percent for IBM and 7 percent for Philips). The laboratories and national research centers are completely public. Ninety percent of the research, study, and development of the electronics network is therefore under state control today.

One major aspect of this liberationary plan is a new scheme for relations between private and nationalized industry, between industries of the same sector (to avoid domestic rivalry), between local industry and academe, and also between designers and users. The launching of flexible national products proves that there is a commitment to ensuring the fluency of the horizontal transfers of technology by bringing together teams of public and private researchers, both industrial and user-oriented, in order to promote new products. All this serves to foreground the need to integrate notions of industrialization and commercialization within the very conception of a new product.

The Redistribution of Transnational Economy

This industrial plan implies that the siting of French companies and their optimum markets should be reconsidered. Because of the size of its market (half of the world, and ten times larger than that of France) and its technological wealth, the United States is a priority site for the internationalization of French firms. Since the European market constitutes close to a third of the world market, economic recovery by way of high technology can only come about in a Europe that is technologically united. Hence the need for a dynamic of alliances and cooperation to aid the development of new products, especially those in the large public domain. On the other hand, the potential for automating the process of production of electronics products "favors the siting, or even the re-siting, of network production in the most developed countries."[17]

Surely there is enough here for us to acknowledge that any discussion of the relation between democracy and communications technology should involve an examination of the logic of redistribution in the international economy, a logic that appears to be inherent in the recovery model offered by high technology. What are the long-term consequences of this twofold movement of relocalizing—a strengthening of industrial ties with the United States and a predictable falling-off of relations with the underdeveloped countries—for the state of the north/south balance? Does the structure of industrial alliances (which follows the lines of the Atlantic military alliances) not reduce to a bare minimum the space for economic negotiation with the Third World? The attitudes of the Western powers in the wake of recent world events (since the Falklands war, for example) tend to prove that Europe as a whole still believes, perhaps wrongly, that the principal contradictions are aligned on an east/west axis, whereas the third-world countries think that they are already aligned, and each day increasingly so, on a north/south axis, and that it is precisely the reorientation of the east/west axis that is really at stake. The case is far from closed. The growing commercial rivalry between the Common Market and the United States is quite capable of causing another fracture in a bloc that is thought of as too good to be true.

There is another question: What could be the impact of the industrial planning of several European countries on an independent French industrial plan that did not tally with their individual ideas about what constitutes a national plan for reindustrialization? The rapid growth of neoliberal economic models in countries like Great Britain has pushed it to the European forefront. Is such a model of development based on the transnational logic not likely to interfere with the unfolding of a national strategy aimed, across numerous contradictions, at circumventing the Japanese and American empires? The rapidity with which the new communication technologies can be installed (Great Britain will be the first in Europe, for example, to have a private telecommunications system run on optical fibers, in direct competition with the nationalized network) should warrant further reflection upon the new deals that determine the concrete structure for forming and shaping technical advances in Europe. One sign, among others, of the leading role played by Great Britain is in its *transborder data flows:* 66 percent of all data flows from Western Europe to the United States come out of Great Britain. Transatlantic data flows, in fact, account for two-thirds of the transborder data flows of that country, against an average of 10 percent for all the other Western European countries.[18]

Moreover, in 1977-78 the large electronics firms chose as their priority target for launching the home video recorders in Europe, Great Britain and then West Germany. Several reasons, insufficiently analyzed in my opinion, led them to act in this way. These reasons drew as much on the patterns and modalities of audiovisual consumption (the importance, for example, of a network of sited installations in Great Britain compared to the French equivalent) as on the structure of the industry of televisual production (in the two chosen countries, an extremely disparate national industry that fell further apart when the video recorder arrived); reasons that were similarly related to the nature of the televisual system in each of these countries. In short, to be able to describe the factors that have had some bearing upon the case of the video recorder, we would need access to a comparative history, which scarcely exists, of the communications systems of Europe; a history that ought to help explain why Great Britain has outstripped the rest of Europe in introducing audiovisual technology ever since the advent of the radio. A comparative study of this kind would be obligatory for anyone who wants to answer this essential question: Why in 1962 did France have one of the smallest television audiences in Europe?—27 percent of all French homes had a television aerial against 29 percent in Italy, 37 percent in Belgium, 41 percent in Germany, 50 percent in the Netherlands, and 82 percent in Great Britain. Another question should be addressed in the same way: Why is there such a disparity today among the European countries in the ownership of video recorders?—in 1982, 2.5 percent of French homes against 10 percent in British homes. Unless we rest easy with a unilateral, mechanistic response that would be a throwback to an analysis of income range, a much more complex study must be taken up.

Some Poles of Cultural Production?

In one way or another, certain problematic features of French planning regarding what are called the "hardware industries" appear again in their own specific way when it comes to drawing up plans for the "software industries." This is unavoidable, since the latter are equally bound up within a similar kind of unifying movement. This movement no longer must be proved, either in the field of information merchandising, where the logic of the interdependent chain of electronics services works toward integrating the various participants (gatherers-producers-carriers), or in the leisure field, which is often confused with the former (multimedia conglomerates, etc.). The factors involved in programming, software, and network planning are at once economic, industrial, social, and cultural.

Although it is relatively easy to sketch the outlines of a plan for developing the electronics technologies—even if they are only in an embryonic phase—it is much more difficult to isolate the features of a corresponding plan for cultural production.

It is clear that this problem arises out of the need to name various partners in order to provoke a national response in the face of the hegemony of transnational productions (television series, video games, videocassettes, etc.). The real differences emerge, however, when those partners have to be identified. Listen to the director in charge of new projects at Hachette, the fifth largest publishing company in the world:

> Because of its position, Hachette has been among the first to be implicated in a process of change that involves all the participants in the cultural sector. The handicaps of French audiovisual production and distribution, compared to that of the U.S., are such that the challenge is posed not so much in terms of the competition between French publishers or producers, as in terms of their solidarity and complementarity. This is one of the active issues which we are addressing. With a view to establishing the bases of a politics of publishing in this area (particularly its legal aspects), we hope that an allied commitment on the part of the principal French groups in audiovisual production can be developed and extended to other groups, and other publishers.[19]

However, the obstacles in the path of effectively building up this understanding between different publishers or producers are much more complex in the case of electronics. There is no evidence of any kind of understanding between a public sector heavily involved in audiovisuals and the big private groups. Not only do these private groups have a very limited experience of televisual production because of public sector domination, but, more to the point, their relations with the state are often at loggerheads. There are quite definite reasons for this, and I will come back to them, reasons suggested here by A. Lefébure, the director for the development of new technologies at Havas, the large, partially state-controlled multimedia group:

> Everything which is not in the public sector suffers in France from a real lack of symbolic legitimacy wherever audiovisuals are involved. So it is no surprise that negotiations between the State and private enterprise, or even a mixed economy, are so fraught with conflict when it comes to managing audiovisual affairs. Since they are accused of only being interested in commercial growth inasmuch as it is linked to a market logic (a familiar danger in itself in this domain), the French communications groups are unable to declare their real ambitions. The field is therefore left open for other transnational groups to establish their publishing interests before going on to tackle the audiovisual market by using processes of deregulation that are becoming so familiar in a number of countries in Europe.[20]

According to the same Havas executive, who is clearly speaking in a personal capacity, the search for a new legitimacy in the affairs of audiovisual broadcasting outside of the public sector "can only take place through a reasoned and voluntary act of support for the creative opportunities that exist in France in this field." This kind of diagnosis points toward the constitution of a new socioindustrial substructure; it advocates relying on some of the complementary poles of creation and production (Hachette, Havas, Sofirad, local radio and public television networks) to promote growth capable of competing closely for international audiences and using these poles to create new relations between multiple partners.[21]

A. Lefébure points to some of the other groups with a potential to be involved: "For well-known reasons, there are many difficulties involved in the development of small, ambitious, and innovative audiovisual structures. There is no shortage of designers, journalists eager to shape the future of the press, technicians capable of important innovations (software, high frequency systems, hi-fi, video), all of them hoping for a chance to realize their potential. Clearly it is up to the State, along with the big companies in the field, to give this kind of initiative a chance, since it is likely to bring commercial success, and will also be a privileged way of winning legitimacy in the public mind, all too easily impressed by events in this domain."[22]

Similar proposals ventured on behalf of the television channels point in the same direction, and thanks to new rulings on audiovisuals, they are hoping to find other partners: "I also hope," declared the programming head of Channel One (TF1), "with the help of various partners, to be able to create an offshoot committed to producing alternatives and thus increasing our audience potential. The channel should make its presence felt in all of the markets of audiovisual creation (teledistribution, video-cassettes, etc.) through direct contact with the manufacturers."[23]

The future of this set of alliances (big/small, national/local, central/provincial apparatus, private/public, commercial/associated sector) will be crucial, since it will determine the form of power relations between partners of unequal strength who do not necessarily have the same idea of national independence, let alone the same idea of democracy as it applies to the field!

The State in All of Its States

Poor state! So much is asked of it and in the form of demands that are difficult to reconcile: it is required not only to set itself up as an arbiter, by coming to the rescue of the big shots, so to speak, the large companies in a bad way, but also to concern itself with the whole base of the pyramid, all of the small-fry responsible for winning credibility for the new solidarity. Perhaps the time has come to question the function of the state, for that is precisely where we shall find the essentials regarding the relation between technology, communication, and democracy.

For those who cared, the socialist victory in many ways represented an opportunity to deliver France from the logics at work in the majority of the large advanced capitalist countries. To work its transformation into the whole restructuring of the world economy, a socialist France would bracket off those fundamental movements that continue to affect its neighbors or its partners. For example, it would not have to face up to those painful questions that plague neo-liberals in England and the United States as part of their obligation to take on the role of "thinkers of the state." France would be concerned only with those logics of privatization that paved the way for a welfare state, given its second wind under the socialist plan.

A simple electoral victory has not put an end to these logics; for those who believe it has, nothing could be further from the truth. These logics continue to shape French society, using the appropriate channels to reintroduce familiar problematics.

1. In the field of communications, there are numerous signs that the redistribution of modes of administrating the public/private relation was stepped up during the late seventies. To make up for its loss of legitimacy, the state, and its administrative logics, sought the kind of support provided by procedures at work in the private sector. By contrast, the private sector was rethinking the "social" and thus taking up where the state had left off. To check the crisis of the state, which is also the crisis of an image, management was called upon to provide the state with a means of rationalizing itself, a way of avoiding wasteful expenditure, while marketing techniques were recruited to cater to other areas of public relations. As a result, we experienced the explosion of "public communication." The total state expenditure for advertising space in the media rose from 39.7 million francs in 1977 to 62.3 million in 1979, of which half was borne solely by the Ministry of Labor and Industrial Relations. In comparing these figures we must take into account the lowering of tariffs granted to campaigns certified

as being in the public interest (for television time, the administrations only paid a quarter of the commercial rate.) This sum would thus correspond to a budget of 128 million francs, a figure much closer to that of the two or three biggest private advertisers: L'Oreal, Colgate-Palmolive, or Unilever.[24]

The second clear evidence was the telematics campaign, scheduled to take off in 1976. With the general head of telecommunications at the Ministry of PTT as its director, this campaign clearly represented a major intervention in state administration at the level of managerial planning. The commercial logic that accompanied the promotion of the new technologies had made its effects felt as much in the advance of the domestic market as in the fundamental movements of the international markets (especially in the large Latin American countries). As there has been very little analysis of the transformation of state practices from this point of view, it is difficult to properly place the malfunctions and asynchronies that are unfailingly produced within one section of the state apparatus—in this case, the Ministry of PTT—by the modernization of some of its branches. It would be incorrect to think that what is rightfully the process of commodifying administrative action infiltrates the state apparatus in a uniform fashion. Resistances of every sort crop up (from those that spring up in the defense of public service to those that prevail in professional or institutional corporatism, not to mention the *terra incognita* of users) and frequently give rise to conflict and dislocation.

Another example of change in the management of the public/ private relation is what seemed to be the first large move in France to bring together a hardware producer (the electronics firm Matra) and a producer of programs (Hachette). We cannot, however, fully appreciate this merger at the end of 1980 without knowing about the subtle pressures that were involved as a result of a spontaneous act on the part of the government of Giscard d'Estaing in its anxiety to redefine the alliance between the state and the large multimedia groups as the new technologies were being ushered in.

Finally, and on a more global level, the ideological debate around the role of the intellectuals (and their relation with the media) has also, in its own way, provided evidence of an epistemological rupture. As part of the transitory epiphenomenon of the "new philosphers," and their inseparability from a media image, a new mode of disseminating (and thus of producing) knowledge made its appearance just as the law of value was stepping up its influence on the intellectual scene. Aside from rumors, this was the first concrete sign of the necessary redefinition of relations between the petit bourgeoisie, the bureaucrats of knowledge (whose diversity has not been examined closely enough because our concept of them—an all too quickly hallowed concept—was narrow and ill-adapted to the new historical conditions of the intellectual), the state apparatus, and the logic of the market.[25]

2. Similarly, in the late seventies the legitimacy of the state was put to the test by other forces in a shake-up not only of relations between the state and civil society but also of the different modes of action of various elements of civil society. The forms of state legitimacy are crumbling fast, from the center outward. The defense of decentralization has become an issue marked by social confrontations and, consequently, much ambiguity. In "decentralizing" themselves, some sectors hoped to find new forms of

legitimizing the center by working from the edges; others saw this return to the local as a special way of broadening the dimensions of democracy in the sense of real power sharing. Any number of struggles, not to mention fantasies, about the democractic virtues per se of the whole structure of decentralization, revolve around this issue of the "local."[26] One very relevant example in this context is the "free-radio" movement and its equivalent in the movements for reclaiming alternative forms of expression, less well advertised because they do not involve the new technology.

In the face of this interrogation of the workings of civil society, a monolithic and manipulatory conception of the state collapses. The state is no longer perceived as a site for the endless reproduction of power but as the site of the production of power: a site marked by power relations between groups, classes, and social projects, where the affirmation of a hegemony coexists with strategies of evasion and deviation. Also on trial in this inquiry are our ways of conceiving party action and its relation to party militants.

The Private/Public Relation

What is the state of the fundamental movements under the socialist government? The tendency to entrust the advertising sector with large public interest campaigns has been borne out, for example, in the first campaign to promote reading. In addition to short broadcasts entitled "Reading: the Roads to Freedom," programed over two months of television time, the campaign has been pursued through posters in bookshops. The cost of backing these campaigns has increased considerably: in 1982 it rose to an estimated 150-160 million francs, compared to 62 million in 1979. There is every reason to ask, as Bernard Miege does, whether "public communications lends itself to the process of manipulating public opinion, a process all the more dangerous inasmuch as it takes the place of democratic channels of debate."[27] Perhaps in the course of asking too much of marketing, one forgets to expect civil society to provide the requisite ethic for instilling in each citizen a degree of conscientiousness about such issues as reading, contraception, solidarity, and so on. As it is, the marketability of a technique (in this case, for the launching of a supposedly social product) seems to have already been established prior to any serious questioning of the vertical forms of social relation that it perpetuates. This is one more item to be added to the catalog of technical perversions.

The debate about the state and the public/private relation in the field of communication is, however, more complicated now than it was before May 1981. The statements from Hachette and, in particular, from Havas seem to suggest this much. And for those faced everyday with the more concrete search for democratic alternatives, the ways of living out the public/private relation have become less straightforward. One thing at least can never be overstated: there exists in France a true "public culture," lived as a legitimate culture of excellence within certain sectors, especially those whose upward mobility depends on the statist or parastatist apparatus. This culture, which has its repressed underside—a genuine repugnance for the private—is no mean obstacle to the rethinking of the alliance of science, research, and industry as it was formulated by the national colloquium— all the more so since it is constructed on a paradox. Because of this "public culture," the relation to the state is lived on a sadomasochistic level. We expect the state to act as protector and arbiter, and then we rush to accuse it of conditioning with a venom that matches our level of indebtedness. In the domain of symbolic production, the chances of any critical discussion of the question of a rapprochement between public and private are even rarer, for this "public culture" is curiously distinguished by its hyper-individualized and aestheticized idea of creation—manifest in some as a constitutional mistrust of anything that could give rise to an industrially reproducible matrix. It is not easy, moreover, to decide between the positive and negative sides of this show of reticence, no more so in the case of the actual process of internationalizing the culture industries than in the deployment of mechanisms of resistance to the normalization of ways of living, thinking, and creating.

That some of the large multimedia groups have made tacit demands on the question of official political support testifies clearly to developments in relations between the state and private enterprise. This only makes sense, however, if we see it in the much larger context of a change in relations between private enterprise and the whole of society, and especially in the domain that interests us, with its vital resources of social creativity and innovation. So how do we interpret the "open letter to the innovators" from Matra-Hachette, published on one whole page of *Le Monde* on February 17, 1982, and addressed to "all innovators, designers of hardware and software in each sector: personal computers, video games, business organization, office equipment, telecommunications, or scientific instruments"? The letter continues:

> The development of privately-accessed information on a large public scale is irrevocable. The economic, cultural, and social stakes are very high. In spite of current foreign pressure, France has the resources to play a leading role in this sector. This will only come about if the development of this public market is governed by clearly defined plans, and is dependent upon tried and tested industrial and commercial structures. The plans have been drawn up. The structures exist. Through its mastery of leading technologies—from components to telecommunications—Matra is building up the technical and industrial potential needed for the development of the personal computer on a large public level in France.
>
> Through its experience in the domain of publishing and broadcasting, Hachette is supplying its share of the conditions necessary to the success of this project.
>
> That is why Matra and Hachette have jointly decided to create a group for research, development, and distribution in the field of this large circulation personal computer.
>
> This group has an "open" structure: open to all those—individuals or companies—with a creative, imaginative spirit, who can and want to help put

France in the top ranks of the international competition for this field.

For those faced with the promotional problem of simply acquiring creative individuals, there is a lot here to think about. As I have noted recently elsewhere, in an attempt to generalize from observations made about other national situations:

> If the question of the relation between the so-called culture industries and the rest of society (institutions, associations, groups, individuals) as a source of creativity for nurturing production has always occupied an important place in the operations of various sectors of this industry, then it goes without saying that the increasing intervention of capital, through information systems, in the most diverse spheres of the everyday life of collectivities and individuals, risks making the industry/civil society into a dominant global issue. The prospective social use of the new information technologies acutely exposes the connexions between the "information industry" and the sites of social innovation, and it does so in political and economic terms qualitatively different from those hitherto recognised. New sets of relations between industrial and non-industrial partners that are being formed, reflect in each case specific relations of force.[28]

The ways in which the transnationals are trying everywhere to circumvent resistance from national education apparatuses is already very revealing on the subject. Given this, we should feel uneasy about the glaring contrast between the extraordinary flexibility of the transnationals in their "open-door" plans for experimentation and the extreme rigidity of the institutional structures.

Clearly we need to to examine the particular way each national corporation organizes and takes advantage of cultural innovations (or resists them), using them as a passport to the new age of electronics. Recently, the head of programming at Channel One was bemoaning the lack of thought given to problems of technical growth: "The engineers and technicians have taken an unparalleled lead over the programming people, and we spoil ourselves on cable and satellite without understanding that the new media must be matched by new programming. Few countries have brought forward a political prospectus in this area, and we are suffering now from a real lack of imagination."[29] This lack of imagination should not be confused with a lack of creative resources. A country can easily be abundant in ideas and yet fail to provide opportunities for realizing them.[30] This reflects the specific national history of forms assumed by the expansion of capital in the cultural sphere as well as the history of modalities of articulation between designers and the totality of structures of cultural production (either public or private).

Social Demand and Social Research

One of the preoccupations of the research colloquium was over the vaguely defined concept of social demand. There was talk of a "social lag in research" and even braver talk of the distance between research and the demand of popular sectors. The following extract from the report of the first commission is especially relevant:

> It is still imperative that the objects to which our scientific efforts will be devoted are chosen in a pertinent fashion. The State will name its priorities, starting with the most obvious, which is to help our country recover from the crisis. Industry, better equipped with new experience and know-how, will reveal new needs. The scientists themselves will find new solutions, new experimental fields, and new theoretical paradigms, each in keeping with the logic of their own disciplines. These three activities, however—and they should be more closely related—come nowhere near to meeting the entire social demand in a sufficiently satisfactory way.
>
> The fact is that the unions, associations, and social movements (ecology, feminism, consumer groups, etc.,) are still poorly equipped, and do not possess, at this point, either the power or the resources to be able to present new demands to the scientific institutions, or to develop their own research—but their needs must be recognized all the same. The fact is that any future committment to decentralization, with the establishment of new centers of decision-making, will give rise to the emergence of new demands that ought to be satisfied, even anticipated. The fact is that we still lack sufficiently scientific studies of large areas of social life: the problems of everyday life, the awkward social integration of youth, procrastination in finding a new pedagogical balance, labor conditions constantly being transformed by the new technologies, urban growth, those arts which foster new scientific interests, etc. We will have to support research on such areas, even if it involves major institutional reorganization. The fact is that there is a large—if not excessive—gap between the given wisdom of political affairs and the knowledge accumulated by the social sciences, and this in spite of the potential lessons that the latter could offer the former. In general, the fact is that research is only doing a small part of what it could do.
>
> It is therefore important to bridge this gap by any means: by privileging new breakthroughs, by encouraging the analysis of latent needs on the part of the scientific institutions themselves, by widening our contacts and experiences, by establishing social communications between diverse public demands and agencies specializing in research. In short, by trying to speed up the social retardation of research.
>
> This ambitious call for new research to answer to new demands will undoubtedly be hampered

597

by errors, failures, and undue caution. Two victories, however, are sure to come of it: a victory *on the part* of science, through its surveying at least a part of this unknown field, and a victory *for* science inasmuch as it will provide society as a whole with new proof of its social usefulness.[31]

Communication sciences in France are not set up in such a way as to be immune to the tropism encountered by other social sciences. Certain research problems are accorded a status out of all proportion, while others are neglected; and this occurs in a context in which the study of communication occupies a negligible position in the hierarchy of political, economic, and social sciences. The list of deficiencies with respect to this idea of "social demand" would be a long one. Here are some examples (in each case, all or nearly all of them have still to be examined):

—A lack of relations between semiological research and the genuine latent demand for discourse analysis on the part of journalists looking for a redefinition of their practices; this gap contrasts with the fluid exchange between semiology and the advertising industry.
—A lack of any detailed understanding of the modes of reappropriating media discourse on the part of the various social categories that constitute the "grand public."
—A lack of any analysis of the strategies of evasion and deviation directed by multiple social agents against the apparatuses of power.
—A lack of any study on the articulation, in a dialectical model of analysis, of the so-called experiments in social intervention (cinema, video, radio) and the functioning of the central apparatuses, the academic experiments with audiovisuals and their practical results. I am thinking, for example, of the importance of scientific film (through the work of Painleve) in the growth of the French cinematographic avant-garde.
—A lack of any dialectical analysis of exchange, or absence of exchange, between university research on cultural production and the field of criticism (newspapers, reviews, magazines, etc.). In many apparently unrelated fields, it is the references and accomplishments of academic research that, one way or another, fix the limits of tolerance for any discourse. Vulgar discourse, or at least one version of it, is no longer acceptable in the analysis of film, while it is still looked on as the dominant mode of analyzing popular music. The notable absence of research in this field (there are only one or two serious French studies of the musical culture industry and even they are inspired by an anthropological vision of the phenomenon of popular music) means that credence is given there to the most idealizing and mystificatory discourses to be found in the whole range of media reporting. Similarly, if one considers the low symbolic legitimacy enjoyed in France by the private (marketing) research circles embarrassed by their relation to profit, do academic references come to be powerful tools of legitimation and exoneration with respect to the logic of the market?
—A lack, so to speak, of any research on the role of inventors, their relation to the culture industries, and to civil society.
—And, above all, the lack of a critical account of the manifold experiments in alternative communication that have been socially active

for more than fifteen years now.

These lacks, which are often read as a resistance to research, are difficult to explain without taking account of the institutional obstacles that have segregated research but also, and more specifically, the great currents of material thinking that have affected, if not governed, any kind of relation to society as a whole.

Social Experimentation

Where the need for an industrial dynamic for developing the new technologies intersects with the need to involve hitherto excluded social partners in the application of these technologies, the concept of social experimentation makes its appearance, with its mission of catering to "social demand" in the field of communications. As the minister for research and technology recalled at the time that the campaign "Technology, Culture, and Communication" was being launched: "Any number of failures have resulted from the past practice of not giving precedence to the distribution of new products over research on their social and cultural impact: prototypes have not got beyond the laboratory stage, and technical experiments have not been absorbed into the social fabric."[32] To test out the sociocultural reception of new technologies entails adjusting technological supply to public demand, trying to bypass the "logic of economic production" and striving to establish some kind of social and democratic control over the tools of technology. It also involves a commitment to eliminating holdups or delays in the socialization of the new by the market.

Clearly, if social experimentation is not to embark once again upon strategies of commercialization, such as the creation of needs through marketing, or be reduced to providing social protection for showcase technology, if it is to have any credibility as a strategy for social change, then it must involve itself in the polemical process of redefining the state. In this regard the essential question is, Which social partners are involved? This leads to others: How is a social demand inaugurated? How is it produced? And how is it picked up? Surely not at the instigation of the great state institutions. Surely not as a result of the market's need to expand, or at least not exclusively. It is here that we should find the limits of the debate about the public/private (state/private) enterprise. The only way beyond these limits is to examine a third pole—private and noncommercial—that some already call the "third sector," while others prefer to stick with the expression "civil society" (without taking stock, from time to time, of the new logics that throw the state into confusion). This new sector should put a check on both the reproduction of "good Samaritan attitudes" fostered by the welfare state and the ascendancy of capitalist valorization.

According to a proposal that went with the grain of the emergent preoccupations of the colloquium,

> In spite of the introduction of new systems of mediation, and in spite of the fact that the majority of current socialist leaders appear to have thrown off the old centralist conceptions about fashioning change in accordance with pre-established ideological models, there is still a grave risk that the "raisons d'Etat," translated

into the sluggishness of the apparatus will lead to the same bureaucratic neutralization of ideas for managing social change by the interested parties themselves, and also to the strengthening of collective attitudes about dependence on the Welfare State. . . . The "third sector" will continue to be marginalized and denied any role as an agent of change, unless it succeeds in establishing an *institutional market,* inserted between the capitalist market and the State-controlled systems—a market of the sort that can be tested and controlled by other systems of valorizing human affairs, other ideas about the ends of social production.[33]

In another document, the problem of technological and social innovation is posed in a more precise way: "Both the policies of the government and the big parties have to recognize the classic erosion of power and *novelty.* This process, which could lead to the total exhaustion of social measures, will only be checked by encouraging the free expression of new propositions, and by setting aside a space for innovation and information-sharing among different social groups. If this does not happen, we will see an increasing decline in the legitimacy of the State, an erosion caused by the growing distance between technostructure and citizen in all of the major sectors: industry, administration, unions, media, etc. The only way to stop this rot is to take the risk of basing the social consensus on the recognition and expression of multiplicities."[34]

For those who clearly do not share the mythical vision of this "third sector," conceived as a sanctuary for values, these observations point to a profound analysis of the complexity and contradictions of the social fabric and its associated structures. Although it is the object of frequent appeals, there is seldom any common agreement about the content of this diverse fabric, for without abstracting it from the long history of the formation of French civil society, the tendency is to accept that the old chartered, almost parapublic companies are as visible in the pattern of this fabric as the new organizations that have risen from recent social struggles outside the workplace and even those, like some groups of parent or family associations, that have recently launched their own critique of the media from outside all the recognized circuits.

At the risk of prolonging a discussion that should be taken up elsewhere, but is rarely posed in these terms, we should not underestimate the vogue for "social experimentation." The current debate in France about this subject, rightly or wrongly, and despite the in vitro connotations of the very term "experimentation," has established itself as one of the major stakes in the democratic redefinition of communication research (among others). It is to this way of perceiving science and its relation to social movements that the researcher must now be committed.

So, too, does this idea deliver us from the narrow-mindedness of the exclusive claim for independence from "all forms of power" that is often confused—as in the case of the journalist—with a belief in the independence of research into social relations: all those acts of faith that win researchers immunity (often for life) from questions about the conditions of productions of their investigations, their reasons for choosing one topic rather than another, and the consequences of their research—in short, the ethics of their practical function. From this point of view, we need only contrast the trajectory of the communication sciences in France with this notion of "social demand" to reveal how much the vast majority of research only pays lip service to the willful demands of power.[35]

Whether one accepts the concepts of social demand and social experimentation or prefers to substitute "social intervention" for the latter, it is clear that there are open-ended issues at stake here. Either they will lead, through new plans for encouraging and soliciting social and technological innovation, to a real democratic surplus in a society that perceives and accepts communication technology as an integral part of social relations and general benefits, or they will give rise to the creation of a body of experts in social engineering and systems theory, which would be the very opposite of what social science should be, in its true anti-elitist colors. The stakes are high, since it is difficult to divorce this issue from the more general question of the redistribution of power among the various classes and social groups that make up French society; for it is in the context of political recovery from the crisis that the professional technician classes (some will call them the new petit bourgeoisie) have expressed increasingly hegemonic aspirations on the subject of the management of society as a whole.

Restoring to Social Experimentation Its Contradictions

The following notes are a contribution to the burgeoning debate on the need to "antagonize" the notion of social demand and all that it entails.

1. Any political project that is no longer content merely to proclaim the prophylactic virtues intrinsic to technology, but elects instead to examine the relation between technology and democracy, or technology and social demand, must, in the context of the current politics of recovery chosen by the socialist regime, contend with powerful internal tensions. It must attempt to reconcile two logics, or injunctions, that seem to be irreconcilable. On the one hand, this means allowing industries to win a market, a plan that actually involves increasing the interfaces between people and machines while encouraging the electrification of the modes of communication between individuals; on the other hand, it means accepting that the expansion of this market is ultimately contained by a social demand, namely, the expression of needs that cannot easily be satisfied by a mode of communication based on electronics. In short, the industrial keynote—or, to recall the words of the president of the French Republic at the Versailles summit, *"the mainstay of the demand* for encouraging the development of markets for new consumer goods and services that make use of technological advances"[36]—risks running up against the imperative of democracy itself.

What this reveals are the true motives and potential drawbacks of a certain conception of social experimentation, for not all social logics necessarily lead to technological solutions. The introduction of technology to social experimentation already involves a reclassification of reality.[37] In effect, we must face up to the basic question, Do people really need technology?

To gauge social demand in this way means reevaluating those experiments in alternative communication carried out through technical means (video, radio, telematics systems), for the side-effects of those experiments are not necessarily technological ones (or at least not in the technological mode that has been privileged from the start): the extension of community television to community radio in Quebec, or the movement from video experiments in selected urban areas to original methods of pedagogical practice with audiovisuals in the *lycees*.[38] These are new ways of estimating the effects of social interventions that tend, when they run aground, to be jettisoned according to the theory of the fatal recuperation of social (so-called marginal or alternative) innovations by the Establishment. One scarcely needs to add that this interpretive schema, inasmuch as it only views social innovation in a regulatory or transitory capacity, frequently crops up in the nick of time for the various national or local powers. The result of treating these alternative experiments as nothing but failures—without even questioning the nature of the failure or the social agents at fault—is to strengthen the cause of all the enemies of a democratic decentralization, not only of the networks of distribution, but also of those that subtend the production of communication and culture. In such a situation, caught between innovation and integration or recuperation (by either the administrative or classical market circuits), there is no room for the debate about the real possibility of the democratic redefinition of civil society mentioned earlier. It is a good thing that our society harbors pockets of resistance outside the purview of these manipulatory, "dualist" concepts of power.

2. A few final observations about the danger of "autonomizing" the current debate on new communication technology in France, and especially the risk of dismissing as redundant any discussion about the nature of democracy:

a. The obsession with technology—inspired by its endemic neopositivism—is a dangerous phenomenon, one that can even bring on fresh symptoms of the technical perversions. The universe of "communication" becomes a privileged space for neutralizing all politics, a specious universe devoid of conflicting interests, power relations, and sociological separatism or resistance. In his study on the introduction of audiovisuals to the bookstore, J. C. Passeron appropriately invokes

> a discretionary expedient, in order to avoid the usual lapse into deception: thinking twice before banking everything on the trump card of a *distributionist optimism*. We are used to seeing the latest thing in technological progress serving to puff up the the scientistic hope that an *increase in cultural goods or in their accessibility will magically bring about the "cultural salvation" of the masses*. No technological innovation, by the simple fact of its medium, has ever justified the cultural inequalities repeatedly produced by the well-worn game of social structures and hierarchies: the technical characteristics of a means of communication never predetermine its social effects to the extent of excluding any effect bound up with the social relations that govern the application of the technical knowledge.[39]

In certain circles, it is as if the mere fact of being in power, of no longer belonging to an eternal opposition, had come to represent the triumph of a good technological conscience, or, rather, a technological legitimacy. The reasons for this obsession are deeply rooted in a history at once old and new. To begin with the old: the forces of the Left never actually came to terms with the instrumentalist conception of technology and have essentially revalidated their belief that the political questions addressed to technology were resolved at the level of the relative efficiency of the tools offered by technical progress. Given this, it is difficult to stage a properly critical inquiry about the relation, for example, between technical knowledge and the reproduction of social divisions in the workplace, the segregation of owners of knowledge/information from the others. Now this inquiry would be particularly strategic at a time when France must respond to a technological challenge closely linked to the political challenge of restructuring the relations of power between groups and classes; at a time when information, the potential to produce it and control its means of application, is increasingly becoming central to both the reorganization of all forms of power and the deepening of social divisions.

As for the new history, one hardly needs to point out that there is no effective way of accounting for the asylum offered by technology without putting it into a global context: a crisis of legitimacy among the great traditional movements that have determined their logics of domination ever since the organization of the working class, and a crisis of the great social ideas (including the very idea of equality). These are both elements of a profound crisis of "politics," of the ways of practicing politics—a crisis that an electoral victory can only displace and that returns with all the more force since it was believed in some circles that the heady nights of the Bastille were back for good.

b. One technology follows hard on the heels of another, and the law of obsolescence is the law of a certain technological progress. What we risk losing as a result of this technological obsession is the long and cumulative history of former practices of resistance in the field of communications, a history that risks being wiped out by the latest gadget simply because the logic of the market only operates from moment to moment. This amnesia works on two levels: time (each new technology is a return to zero hour) and space (we lose even the memory of a position of solidarity built up out of multiple and interacting social practices).

By ignoring the accomplishments and failures of previous experiments, by not reevaluating these failures and finding links among them all, we are passing up the chance of constructing a theory of communication that could absorb the lessons of other research, other disciplines, and other experiments that have been studied in different fields. I am thinking, for example, of those communicologues who turn up their noses at everyone: from researchers on social reproduction in the schools and those who approach the politics of democratization through cultural activity and campaigning, to the pioneers in planning urban space, to those coming from anthropology, literature, and history who have tried to embrace the field of popular culture, past and present.

c. It is in this global context that we find another obsession at work—an obsession with the local. Tired of the great grinding machines of specificity and particularity, the local has, in certain sectors, and for quite some time now, come to be defined as synonymous with a nostalgia for intimacy and communality. Now that the watchword of decentralization has been officially implemented, the local has been reappraised as an important site for redefining the state, a site of confrontation, hitherto unimaginable, for outright contradictory projects.[40]

Clearly, the question of decentralization falls between the acceleration of the process of elimination and dispersal in the face of a tele-centered power and the introduction of new forms and new structures of solidarity. Just as we were beginning to feel less strongly about the need for a debate on the national/transnational question with a view to formulating a politics of independence and reconstruction of national identity, now we are faced with the new urgency of the local/national question and the need to formulate a politics of the redistribution of power. It is here that the idea of "kinship networks" becomes useful when trying to avoid the localist traps.[41]

Notes

1 J. P. Chevènement (minister for research and technology), in *Le Monde*, Sept. 23, 1981, p.1.

2 Ministry for Research and Technology, *Recherches et technologie, Actes du colloque national, 13-16 janvier 1982* (Paris: La Documentation Française, 1982), p. 7.

3 *Recherches et technologie*, p. 7.

4 "Annexe 1: Note d'orientation," *Recherches et technologie*, p. 41.

5 MOINOT Report, published by La Documentation Française, 1982.

6 See F. Guattari, "Note concernant un projet de fondation pour les initiatives locales, les innovations institutionelles, la recherche en science sociale, l'animation et la creation culturelles," Paris, Feb. 1982, mss. In the same spirit of incorporating local collectives, associations, and unions within this "research action," see the interview with Philippe Barret (representative for the social sciences at the Ministry for Research and Technology), "Les sciences de l'homme et de la société," *Revue NON! (Repères pour le socialisme)*, 12 (1982), pp. 114-22.

7 On this point, see my A. Mattelart, *Mass Media, Ideologies and the Revolutionary Movement* (Atlantic Highlands, N.J.: Humanities Press, 1980).

8 Mitterand, in *Recherches et technologie*, p. 15.

9 *Technologie, emploi, et croissance* (report by President Mitterand at the summit meeting of the industrial powers), Versailles, June 5, 1982. See *Le Monde*, June 6-7, 1982.

10 *Recherches et technologie*, p. 39.

11 J. P. Chevènement, in *Témoignage chrétien*, Paris, June 14-20, 1982.

12 *Mission Filière Électronique*. In French, the term *filière électronique* has recently begun to be used for all eleven sectors of industrial electronics production: components, products for the general public, computers, automated office equipment, software and data banks, robotics, medical electronics, scientific instruments, telecommunications, professional electronics (civil and miltary), space technology.

13 Ministry for Research and Technology, *Extraits du rapport de synthese de la mission filière électronique*, Paris, mimeo, Mar. 1982, annexe 7, p. 3.

14 *Extraits*, annexe 5, p. 12.

15 *Extraits*, annexe 4, pp. 7-8.

16 *Extraits*, annexe 4, pp. 7-8.

17 *Extraits*, annexe 5, p. 12. Let us recall some of the aims of the manifesto for technological growth advanced by F. Mitterand at the Versailles summit: "Priority action for technological co-operation between private and public companies, and between nations . . . ; the progressive creation of a world market for technology (standards, patents); a joint initiative to

Armand Mattelart

assure that the Southern nations master the new technologies." See *Technologie, emploi, et croissance.*

18 United Nations, *Transnational Corporations and Transborder Data Flows: A Technical Paper* (New York: U.N. Center on Transnational Corporations, 1982).

19 In *Livres-Hebdo,* Paris, Sept. 22, 1981.

20 A. Lefébure, "Mass media, groupes de communication et société," a personal contribution to the commission on "Technologie, diffusion de la culture et communication," June 1982.

21 Here are some figures to help gauge the internationalization of the French culture industries. In 1980, the sale of French films abroad was only a tenth of book sales and a half of the number of records sold. The sale of television programs itself was only one-fifth of film sales, and the foreign television market represented almost a third of that purchased from abroad. In addition, exports for the publishing industry for the same year were less than 20 percent of its turnover and were concentrated on the Francophone countries, which accounted for 80 percent of this export flow (see J. Rigaud, *Les relations culturelles extérieures,* [Paris: La Documentation Française, 1980]). In 1980, the French television network (TF1, A2, FR3, INA—commercial sale, SFP—loss of franchise) had foreign sales of 5,596 program-hours, against 1,567 in 1978. Also in 1980, 6,000 program-hours were delivered as part of cultural aid to twenty-nine countries, fifteen of which were in North Africa (3,500 hours) and the rest to Mahgreb, Haiti, and several Arabophone and Anglophone nations. The number of coproductions in 1980 rose to 94 hours for TF1 and 36 hours for A2 (for the period 1979-80, an estimated 60 hours were coproduced for FR3). Otherwise, the coproducers were still the traditional partners (Francophones and RFA), with the exception of FR3 (Japan, Mexico) (figures taken from a report by the study group "Action internationale" on the MOINOT Commission, August, 1981).

22 A. Lefébure, "Mass media, groupes de communication et société."

23 Interview with André Harris, "Le déficit de l'imagination," *Le Monde,* May 27, 1982.

24 On the crisis of the image of the state, see the several contributions to the colloquium "Where Is Public Management Going?" (May 28-30, 1980), organized by the University of Paris-Dauphine and the Center for Higher Education in Business Studies (CESA), especially those by J. Lendrevie and R. Laufer. Also see J. L. Albert et al., *Production de la ville et aménagement du discours,* Grenoble III, GRESEC, Jan. 1980, mimeo.

25 See Régis Debray, *Teachers, Writers, Celebrities: The Intellectuals of Modern France* (London: New Left Books, 1982); F. Aubral and X. Delcourt, *Contre la nouvelle philosophie* (Paris: Gallimard, 1977).

26 See *L'objet local: colloque dirigé par Lucien Sfez* (Paris: collection 10/18, 1977).

27 B. Miege, "Le pouvoir et les systèmes d'information: S'interroger sur les enjeux fondamentaux," paper delivered at the Third French Congress on Communication and Information Sciences, May 1982, mimeo.

28 A. Mattelart, " Introduction," *Communication and Class Struggle* (New York: International General, 1983), vol. 2, pp. 17-67.

29 Interview with André Harris, *Le Monde,* May 27, 1982.

30 One can think what one wants about programs like "Ulysses 31" as models of television for children, but the history of its production is, from an industrial point of view, quite instructive. Conceived by a Frenchman, the series was not taken up in France, and after many ups and downs, like the majority of animated cartoon series, was produced in Japan thanks to a coproduction agreement. The study group on the politics of the image set up by the prime minister has noted that in this case, as in many others, all of the necessary elements for its production were there, albeit scattered throughout university laboratories and the electronics industry, but the "horizontal" relation between technology and individual talent was sadly lacking. Convinced, then, that the state should not itself create an animated cartoon industry but only develop the conditions for it to expand and flourish, the director for children's broadcasts at TF1 wrote: "We have thousands of professionals with the talent and the capacity to properly establish animated French cartoons in the world of modern television, if only they were salvaged from their working isolation, encouraged and supported by management with experience in the affairs of the new industry, and above all, if their own enthusiasm were rewarded by concrete measures." (J. Mousseau, "Plaidoyer pour une industrie française du dessin animé," *Communication et langages,* no. 52 [1982])

31 "Commission no. 1. L'apport culturel de la recherche scientifique et technologique" (reporter: Robert Fossaert), *Recherches et technologie,* pp. 92-93.

32 Letter from J. P. Chevènement to the presidents of the commission on "Technologie, diffusion de la culture et communication" (A. Mattelart and Y. Stourdze), Mar. 1982, in *Technologie, communication et culture* (Paris: La Documentation Française, 1982).

605

33   F. Guattari, "Note," pp. 114-22.

34   M. J. Carrieu-Costa and M. Callon, *Projet d'un centre de recherche et de formation sur les innovations technologiques et sociales*, Mar. 1982, mimeo.

35   See, for example, the dossier "Pour un autre television," *NON! (repères pour le socialisme)* (1982), with contributions from A. Spire and D. Goldschmidt; Y. de La Haye and B. Miege, "Les socialistes français aux prises avec la question des media," *Raison présente*, Paris, Winter 1982; P. Flichy, "Pour une politique de l'innovation sociale en audiovisuel," *Le monde diplomatique*, May 1982.

36   President Mitterand, Versailles summit.

37   See C. Collin, "Villeneuve; de la vidéogazette au centre de ressources," *Sonovision* (1978). The Italian experiment with free radio and television deserves a special mention here, not so much in itself, but inasmuch as it fosters a number of myths sustained by the enemies of the democratization of communication. How many times here in France have we seen those who support restricted democracy in the media block a whole discussion by invoking the situation in Italy as one characterized by audiovisual "anarchy."

38   The study group for social experimentation on the MOINOT Commission noted quite correctly, in July/August 1981, that it was possible to adopt two different experimental approaches: "The first, *beginning with the technological system*, involves the desire to test and observe the way in which an environment adopts, rejects, or transforms the system. If it is necessary for an organism vital to the future of communications to keep itself informed about these experiments, even to be in some way associated or intimate with their ways, then we should ask ourselves how the question could be turned around in order to accommodate different forms of experimentation; instead of starting with technique and then examining its applicability, *starting with innovative social practices* and then examining what kind of technical response can be brought to the material needs of communication. New means can certainly be utilized but only inasmuch as they would appear to respond better than the current media, and eventually, in conjunction with these media, to the needs articulated by the users. Such experiments could be carried out by using the existing networks and would not have to wait for the installation of new ones."

39   J. C. Passeron, *Images en bibliothèque, images de bibliothèque* (Paris: Documents du Gides, 1982), pp. 46-47.

40   On the "local" question, see A. Mattelart and J. M. Piemme, *Télévision: Enjeux sans frontières* (Presses universitaires de Grenoble, 1980); in English by the same authors, see "New Means of Communication: New Questions for the Left," *Media, Culture, and Society*, no. 2 (1980), pp. 321-38; J. P. Garnier, "De la crise d'une gestion à la gestion d'une crise ou le charme discret de la décentralisation," *Cahiers Secteur Public* (Paris, 1982).

41   This is where some reflection on experiments like that of the ANTELIM network, which has steadily established radio links between the families of sailors, might provide ballast for the boundless enthusiasm for local radio that has been officially inspired by the plan for decentralizing the public monopoly of radio-television.

Iain Chambers

Contamination, Coincidence, and Collusion: Pop Music, Urban Culture, and the Avant-Garde

In the contemporary city, the traditional distance between the avant-garde and daily urban life has collapsed. A new politics based on their interaction may now be possible.

It is necessary to take seriously the hypothesis according to which only an excess of imagination seizes the profundity of the real. . . .
Henri Lefebvre

What might Lefebvre's statement, made in the context of a discussion of surrealism, mean in the context of the triad pop music, popular culture, and the avant-garde? In seeking an answer, I will be talking about the relationship between an excess of imagination and popular cultural tastes. I want to identify where the project of the historical avant-garde and important tendencies in contemporary urban popular culture meet, as it were, at the periphery of an existing cultural hegemony or cultural block. This involves looking at the struggle for the sense and direction of urban culture that takes place in the "dailyness" of routines, habits, and the subconsciously exercised expectations of common sense in order to see how an excess of imagination is translated into a practical jolting of common sense, which permits previously mute areas and relations to begin to speak.

To think more concretely about this potentiality, we need to consider the spaces in which diverse social forces are brought together—forces that are gendered, racial, and further differentiated in both major and microscopic fashion. This will render, one hopes, slightly more articulate what is quite clearly a long-standing critical silence in discussions about both pop music and contemporary urban popular culture. While I will be referring here to realities found in advanced capitalist societies, I would also suggest that these tendencies have effects in urban centers throughout the world. The effects are different, but they are, in a very complex way, related to developments within advanced capitalist urban culture.

In *The Art of Noises,* published in 1916, the Italian futurist Luigi Russolo drew attention to the "voluptuous" sonorities of the new metropolitan environment: an infinite combination of sirens and horns, crowds and trams, engines and machinery. He proposed a new music to be produced by specially constructed machines, considered himself to be a "noise tuner," and wrote compositions for these instruments bearing such titles as "A City Wakes Up" and "A Conference for Cars and Planes."[1] This futurist provocation usefully serves to isolate a set of significant themes: the machine, mechanical reproduction, and what Antonio Gramsci once called the "directive function" of the city in national life.

The avant-garde's "explosion of dissent" (André Breton) in the early decades of the twentieth century signaled a divide between a contemplative attitude toward art *(l'art pour l'art)* and a radical activism that sought to overcome the "divorce between action and dream" (Breton). Futurism's frantic embrace of modernity and the "machine epoch," Dada's direct refusal of "art" and its proclamation of the victory of daily life over aesthetics, and the surrealist project to give free rein to the unconscious through the liberty of "automatic writing," profoundly undermined the traditional demand for artistic "authenticity." This had now become a false request, an irrelevancy; not, as Adorno was fond of repeating, because the world had grown "false," but because the conditions of perception, reception, and artistic production had irreversibly changed. It was now the epoch of the photograph, the gramophone, the radio, and the cinema: the epoch of mechanical reproduction.

As though to drive this last point home, several tendencies in the avant-garde, particularly in the visual arts, borrowed humble objects from everyday life and simply copied them, or, more provocatively still, presented them unchanged to the public. Marcel Duchamp takes a bicycle wheel and signs it as his own "work." Half a century later, Andy Warhol updates this gesture with his silk-screen reproductions of Coca-Cola bottles and Elvis Presley, Campbell's soup cans and Marilyn Monroe. In both cases, ironic queries were raised about the status of "art" and about the nature of its cultural reproduction in the context of the contemporary urban world.

Cigarette ends, newspaper clippings, and "spilt" paint coalesce on a canvas; Russolo's "noise machines"; Duchamp's "ready-mades"; the whole manifesto of pop art: all form part of a twentieth-century collage suggested and sustained by the metropolis. The mutual "contamination" of the ruptural perception of the avant-garde and the expansion of daily urban culture steadily grows. It touches its logical conclusion when subway graffiti enters the art gallery and the pop video reactivates the surrealist cinema (i.e., David Bowie's "Ashes to Ashes" video, 1980). There are no longer any fixed "sources," no "pure" sounds, no untainted "aura" (Walter Benjamin) against which to evaluate the continual combination, reproduction, and transmission of sounds, images, and objects that circulate in the heterogeneous flux of the modern city.[2] The distance between the gestures of the different artistic avant-gardes and the street blast of a passing portable cassette player balanced on a T-shirted shoulder is today actually a lot smaller than we might think.

The portable cassette player, like the electric guitar, the programmed synthesizer, and the drum machine, but, above all, the record, underscores the importance of mechanical transformation (machines) and reproduction in the formation of pop music. Pop music is "designed for reproducibility" (Walter Benjamin), and one of its possible histories is a history of the development and effects of its technical reproduction.

Toward the end of 1948, recording tape was introduced; until then, recording music had involved registering the acoustic sound directly onto a lacquer-coated disc. This extremely rigid system—for instance, an error in the musical execution meant discarding the disc and starting again—

608

certainly did not encourage the exploration of the sonorial extensions potentially available in the recording situation. But with the introduction of tape, music could be completely constructed inside the studio. By editing, cutting, and splicing, a final sound could be built up from fragments of recording. A fifty-second demo-tape could be turned into a record lasting more than two minutes: this is how Little Richard's "Keep A-Knockin'" was produced. The result was that "recording tape shifted the record from the status of a frozen snapshot to that of a musical montage."[3]

Recording tape represented the first major innovation in postwar recording procedures. The second, occurring in the late 1960s, involved the introduction of multitrack recording facilities. The use of echo and double-tracking in the 1950s and early 1960s in order to "beef up" the sound had already pointed in this direction. But with the introduction of stereo records and then, in rapid succession, four-, eight-, sixteen-, twenty-four-, and thirty-two-track recording, the sonorial framework was vastly extended. Adding recorded track to track, piling up diverse sounds, a four-person group, for example, could produce eight or sixteen "voices" to be simultaneously mixed in the final recorded form.

Multitrack recording permits many musical directions, some seemingly diametrically opposed. While the "artistic" aspiration of parts of "progressive music" now found the space for their rock operas and suites, in the very different reality of reggae, "dub" was able to phase instruments and voices in and out, suspend the pulse and then intensify it, chop up the sound and then enrich it with further effects, while stretching the whole swirling pattern across a stuttering "roots" bass-drum "ridim."

Technology has been central to pop from its beginnings. It is impossible to discuss the music without referring to it: whether it is Elvis working on his sound in the tiny Sun studio in the early 1950s, or the mesmerizing dance floor success of disco twenty years later. Pop music has never existed apart from technological intervention; this only draws further attention to the daily tensions involved at the technological "interface where the economies of capital and libido interlock."[4]

The fact that the recording studio, with its technology and accompanying financial requirements, is the central site of pop's sonorial production by no means implies a simple technological determinism. The history of pop reveals other, often unsuspected tendencies, among them the story of a continual appropriation of pop's technology and reproductive capacities. This has resulted in diversified cultural investments, involving different fractions of white metropolitan youth taking up guitars and synthesizers and adopting various imported sounds, as well as black youth "resignifying" the use of the microphone and the turntable (the deejay's "toast" and "rap") and studio console ("dub"). Both maintain the fruitful paradox of subordinated, frequently oral-centered cultures mastering and extending the electronic medium of pop and, in the process, re-presenting their "selves" in the heartlands of contemporary urban life.

In the exclusive reality of the historical avant-garde, the attempt was undertaken to produce new languages that subtracted themselves from the dulled continuity of past acceptance and present expectation. An analogous case might be made for pop: rock 'n' roll and punk are both obvious occasions when particular musical proposals tore apart an earlier syntax and associated cultural attitudes.

609

I want to add to these stark examples the suggestion that what such eruptive symptoms expose has its daily currency in mechanical reproduction, in its ingression into the web of sonorial reality where records, borrowing an expression from Susan Sontag, "democratize all experiences by translating them" into sounds.[5] Today, we no longer confront "organic" expressions but a cultural "cut-up," a series of fragments—New York rap, London punk, Nigerian "juju," soul, country-and-western ballads, white funk. We subsequently select from these sounds a meaningful bricolage, an environment of sense. The fragmentation of the eye and ear, so self-consciously pursued by the avant-garde in its desire to liberate new experiences, new horizons, is overtaken by the permissive circulation of possibilities permitted by radio, film, television, records, cassettes, video.

This situation both augments and, in an important sense, disrupts the more obvious connections between pop and the recent musical avant-garde. From the late 1960s onward, the music of Frank Zappa, of such German groups as Can, Amon Duul II, and Tangerine Dream, and in England Henry Cow, Brian Eno, and even David Bowie, can be linked to the experiments in serial composition, repetition, and incidental "noise" found in the work of Varèse, Stockhausen, Cage, Riley, LaMonte Young, Glass, and others. But the 1970s were also characterized by an increasing attention to pop's own internal languages and the subsequent basis for a self-generated pop avant-gardism. The elements of this second tendency can be found in the whimsical musical bric-a-brac of Roxy Music, the neurotic funk experiments of David Bowie, and the studied ruptural aesthetics of such postpunk groups as Public Image Ltd and the Gang of Four. In particular, it was punk and its aftermath that clarified the possibility of reassessing pop's existing musical languages and suggested a sonorial collage in which the joins were left exposed as the signifiers of "noise" and "sound" or "din" and "music," were shifted back and forth along the cultural reception of the acoustic spectrum.

The most interesting reflection to be made here is the one I hinted at above—of how mechanical reproduction sweeps away the separate status of the historical avant-garde (which also explains my use of the adjective "historical" up to this point). The previous distance between the avant-garde and daily urban culture is overcome as the former becomes enveloped by the visual and sonorial languages of the latter. Inside the metropolitan plasma of today, the concentrated moment of attention that once accompanied the response to both traditional and subversive art is replaced by Benjamin's concept of "distracted reception." The fabric of tradition is absentmindedly unstitched and a deritualized culture, invaded by the profanity of diverse tastes; it is gradually mastered "by habit under the guidance of tactile appropriation."[6]

In the case of pop music, tactile appropriation—the physical reception of the tangible—is concentrated in the differentiated presence and signification of the body. Let me explain. While the apparently nebulous zone of romance is the privileged domain in pop's emotional empire—and I am referring not only to that usually associated with juvenile girls building fantasies around the pin-ups and records of male stars but, in particular, to the dominant male romanticism of an imaginary street life—it is the body that is its principal focus and carrier.

Iain Chambers

The musical languages of pop—the wrenched sentiments of soul, the exuberance of rock 'n' roll, the verbal contortions of rap, the screeched angst of punk—all tend to propel the body through the sensorial "grain" (Roland Barthes) of the music to the center of the stage. There, in dancing and the immediacy of performance, it is this physical sense of the musical "now" that is pivotal, for it "is the body that ultimately makes, receives and responds to music; and it is the body that connects sounds, dance, fashion and style to the subconscious anchorage of sexuality and eroticism."[7] It being here, where romance and "reality" are fused together, that common sense is often taunted, twisted, and torn apart.

So, my concluding suggestion is that the avant-garde project of purposefully mismatching perception and the taken-for-granted in order to release perspectives from the fetish of common sense tends to find a contemporary realization in the daily culture of the metropolis. Here, the once-researched shock of the historical avant-garde, the transitory immediacy of perpetual sonorial and visual reproduction, and the "'dense and concrete' life" of subordinated cultures—"a life whose main stress is on the intimate, the sensory, the detailed and the personal"—are indiscriminately mixed together.[8]

Further, this urban complexity forces into an extensive, if still frequently unsuspected, dialogue the once-separated episodes of the avant-garde, of popular culture, and a politics based on the detailed possibilities of the everyday: on its class, racial, sexual, local and national construction, variation, peculiarity. As these trajectories cross each other's path and dissolve in the fervent flux of metropolitan life, they increasingly gesture toward a new project. Whatever its eventual shape, that project will need to interrogate existing cultural hegemony and subtract itself from the tired logic of the predictable if it is to challenge successfully existing definitions of daily life. But to do this it will have to be constructed *inside* this present complexity.

Notes

1   Luigi Russolo, *L'arte dei rumori* (Milan: Edizioni Futuriste di "Poesia," 1916). Republished as a supplement in *Alfabeta*, no. 43, Milan, Dec. 1982.

2   Walter Benjamin, "The Work of Art in the Age of Mechanical Reproduction," *Illuminations*, trans. Harry Zohn (London: Fontana, 1973). All references to the essay are to this edition.

3   Iain Chambers, *Urban Rhythms* (London: Macmillan, 1984), p. 14.

4   Peter Wollen, *Readings and Writings* (London: Verso, 1982), p. 176. It is worthwhile recalling a note of Benjamin's on the relation between film and technology: "In the case of films, mechanical reproduction is not, as with literature and painting, an external condition for mass distribution. Mechanical reproduction is inherent in the very technique of film production. This technique not only permits in the most direct way but virtually causes mass distribution" (Benjamin, p. 246). The same can be said for the contemporary production of pop music.

5   The context of this quotation is, "The subsequent industrialisation of camera technology only carried out a promise inherent in photography from its very beginnings: to democratise all experiences by translating them into images" (Susan Sontag, *On Photography* [Harmondsworth: Penguin, 1979], p. 7). The history of recorded music, where we all have the possibility of indulging our tastes and becoming "experts," leads toward similar conclusions.

6   Benjamin, p. 242.

7   Chambers, p. 210.

8   Richard Hoggart, *The Uses of Literacy* (Harmondsworth: Penguin, 1958), p. 81.

Comment (Dick Hebdige)

In your paper I hear a displaced, fragmented, overdetermined discourse, a discourse undermined by libido. I hear description in the sense of de-scription, a talking out. I hear logic escaping, limits acknowledged, transgressed, and reinscribed.

Chambers

Perhaps the best way to begin responding to your suggestive metaphors is to lay out what I see as some of the premises of my work. The closer we move to the different experiences of pop music and popular culture, the more we are forced to acknowledge certain *limits*. There is a limit in being English and white and writing about black music; there is a limit to what *I* can say about a female experience of rock music. This is not necessarily an impoverishment. The recognition of limits is also the recognition of differences, of heterogeneity: the recognition of voices that were previously unheard, unacknowledged. As you have put it: "a reflexive awareness of the knowledge/power relation." The presence of these voices, these relations, these possibilities, these powers, registers a series of tensions that have to be worked into a "sense" where previously there was silence.

Taking urban culture as my referent and mechanical reproduction as its privileged mode of cultural production, I have tried to provide a framework—which extends well beyond the physical environs of the actual city—in which the presence and specificity of popular musics and cultures could be discussed. Obviously, details were overlooked, there were many gaps, but I would like to think that the outline of a suggestive project managed to come through.

Comment

Rock has been defined as a blanket modality that rips off, incorporates, and cannibalizes many other styles, the styles of other cultures. One of the things it does is to eliminate many of the differences that have been socially constructed in those other cultures. Perhaps one of the reasons why some of the Latin music, specifically Salsa, which is also a global style, hasn't had a major impact on rock is because there is little awareness that 25 million Latino people live in the United States. I would argue that rock, as a phenomenon created in the metropolitan centers of the world—the United States, England—has a function of eliminating difference and inscribing indifference imperialistically throughout the world.

Chambers

Let me take the example of Hispanic culture in the United States, of Latin musics in the context of U.S. rock music. This gives me an opportunity to say something more about the idea that the details and differences of particular cultures, musics, and minority tastes come to be systematically cancelled in the logic of present-day urban culture, come, to use an expression, to be "co-opted." The argument runs like this: subaltern cultures, alternative and oppositional forces, are progressively sucked into the hungry urban machine where, their original powers and identities now nullified, they are reproduced among the vacuous choices of metropolitan taste.

It's neat, but beyond its linear simplicity and a suspect romanticism—the "corruption" of "origins," the corruption of the city—it reduces cultural differences to a series of simple antagonisms: "non-co-opted"/"co-opted," "original"/"false." As Ernesto Laclau pointed out, it is a form of reasoning that is forced to treat "meaning" as fixed; "society" as a stable, conceptual "totality"; and "power" as the exercise of a unilateral, direct domination. Naturally, the co-optation thesis can acquire a flexible tone; I wouldn't deny that. But the way it is generally used does suggest that an underlying conceptual rigidity prevents it from acknowledging the real complexity that can be recognized in the cities, in the sights, sounds, and sense of popular urban culture.

Iain Chambers

Question

I want to build on the last question and redirect it to questions about gender, sexuality, and the body. In Latino culture, for example, one immediately notices a concern about the body and what it signifies. Indeed, I think cultural differences involve kinesic differences, including styles of dance and movement. Moreover, on the issue of the body, I thought it strange that disco was not mentioned. One of my students argued that in rock music the body that is being expressed and activated has to do with genitality, but in disco the heartbeat is at the center. In any case, the materiality of the body in its modalities in rock 'n' roll does create different significations. Finally, I wonder if we don't have to examine the ways the body in rock 'n' roll works in a gender-specific manner.

Chambers

I made the body one of the central themes in my talk because I think it is a central semantic zone in pop or rock music. It is, if you like, the site of the senses: of the sexual as well as the more obviously social, of the cultural as well as the corporeal. It is a space—a critical one, a material one—crisscrossed by many forces, including race, gender, and class experience. I tried in passing to suggest some of these, but others were not mentioned. So the criticisms made about the gaps in my paper—the absence of Hispanic music and culture; of gendered subjectivities and rock music; of disco music, which, I thoroughly agree, is *the* music of the 1970s to be considered when talking about musical languages organized around the body—are right.

The discussion of all these aspects could certainly be taken further. It can be argued, for instance, that disco's repetitive cycle and pulse disrupts the ubiquitous sequential logic of rock music and its progression toward climax. Richard Dyer, discussing the importance of disco music in gay culture, has argued that disco breaks down phallocentricity; that is, it celebrates the whole body rather than restricting its attention to genital satisfaction. This possibility, if initially based on formal musical distinctions, acquires conviction as it is related and connected back to the effects and presence of disco in the repertoire of pop, to its history on the dance floor, to its place in gay culture, to its presence as a possibility in contemporary urban culture.

Finally, I think we must come to terms with the specificity of the feminine experience, which has been largely silenced, hidden beneath the dominant ways of talking about pop music and the dominant ways in which pop music is experienced. That is why I wanted to emphasize that the major romantic mode in pop music is that of a masculine, imaginary street life.

Comment

One of the things that really interested me in your paper is how much it depended on what I would take to be a specifically modernist project. You began by quoting the futurist exhaltation of the "voluptuous" sonorities of the new urban environment. It seems to me that one of the things we might do is to look at words like "voluptuous" when they appear in a futurist or modernist project and think about what kind of landscape they codify. From that point of view, the constant appropriation and bricolage that you talked of appear less as a liberatory space and more as a symptom of the immense "tedium of ownership" in a highly developed society and of its need to incorporate and then obliterate difference. In the Hungarian film *Time Stands Still*, kids use music to make open spaces for themselves, but only in the context of a larger defeat. And I would maintain that in the case of people of color, colonized people, and women, the meanings and the liberational spaces are real, but only within a larger structure of oppression.

Chambers

A significant part of that complexity to which I have just referred arises in the transitory, mobile, expansive urban culture in which we all live. Puerto Ricans in New York City, like West Indians in Birmingham, England, have *their* culture. But *this* culture is not a sealed testament. It echoes with everyday experience; it comes out of living your presence in the present; it comes out of New York, out of Birmingham. . . . *This* culture also exists as a part of this city, this time, these conditions. Such proximities have indeed usually heightened racial and cultural identities rather than reduced them.

Question
I want to question your apparent assumption about the liberating potential of rock as a source of meaning to youth subcultures. Personally, I'm just a little bit fearful, and not at all celebratory, about the energizing potential of what is perhaps a rather nihilistic form of music and social energy.

Comment
I'd like to respond to that before Iain does. I think there are differences between the music and the people who are listening to it, and these differences may enable us to understand some of these questions about the effects of the music in the Third World—about the homogenization of culture. It seems true that this music is used as an imperialistic form of culture, but it can also be used by the people who listen to it as an element of youth rebelliousness. I want to defend rock 'n' roll against charges of nihilism and retreat. There are points where rock 'n' roll serves as a focal point for young people's rebelliousness, mixed up with all their ideas of conscience. And in some cases this inchoate rebelliousness may take active political dimensions.

Chambers
What I have been trying to suggest is that cultural powers, arising through differences, choice, heterogeneity—whether Jamaican, Hispanic, or of a more local variety—are reproduced in new forms in the expanding, increasingly electronic context of contemporary urban culture. It is the powers and possibilities of these new forms, where the "meanings" are by no means fixed, where there is still a confusing "order," that is important. If we are not willing to accept this reality— and its particular forms of power, of knowledge—then we are left out in the cold, facing a very grim scenario. On the defensive, desperately seeking to preserve ourselves and our choices from "co-optation," critical intelligence is concentrated in the doomed task of delaying the inevitable: the moment when we pass into the Langian citizenship of *Metropolis*.

Question
On the issue of art and politics, and particularly the politics of rock 'n' roll, I thought you made some very provocative remarks at the very end of your talk. You suggested that there is a conjuncture in advanced capitalist cities between some of the demands of the Left and some of the demands of youth culture to change life, to restructure society. Could you elaborate on this?

Chambers
I think it is very important to begin thinking through, in the here and now, the full implications of this expanded, urban culture; that is, to construct a project that can effectively meet its terms. That is why I insist on its rich complexity. It is all very well to say, "We just gotta live it"—everybody is already doing that! The problem is how to live it most effectively, how to grasp the potential that is already in play, how to *widen the political project without reducing the possible*. This is the Gramscian task, although one might want to say post-Gramscian, of creating a "hegemony" adequate to the present. That, for me, is the real question.

To conclude, I would also insist on a very wide sense of the term "politics." I am not simply talking about the relationship between the political party and culture. I'm referring to the heterogeneous and different possibilities that presently circulate within urban culture. These are frequently not commensurable. There is, as Ernesto Laclau suggested, a "surplus of meaning," an "open" discourse where differences, distinctions, and particulars do not necessarily find an equivalence. But it is there, and not in an assumed conceptual order, that the everday struggle for recognition, meaning, direction, prospects, hegemony, occurs. As Larry Grossberg said, discussing the analysis of pleasure and rock music, something is always left over, left out. I think that "left over" has to do with the threshold, the limits, of analysis. There is something left out of the stilled order of writing, analysis, and its conceptual frames. But it is important that this "left-over" is recognized, is inscribed, in the re-presentation, in the analysis, for what it signals are precisely those trans-formatory powers that threaten to make our present analysis redundant by producing something new: a new reality.

Terry Eagleton
The Critic as Clown

Is there an implicit cultural politics in William Empson's effort to negotiate between intellectual activity and the wisdom of everyday life? Can Marxism recover anything of use from Empson's way of understanding concepts like "pastoral" and "ambiguity"?

All propaganda or popularization involves a putting of the complex into the simple, but such a move is instantly deconstructive, for if the complex *can* be put into the simple, then it is not as complex as it seemed in the first place; and if the simple can be an adequate medium of such complexity, then it cannot, after all, be as simple as all that. A mutual transference of qualities between simple and complex takes place, forcing us to revise our initial estimate of both terms and to ponder the possibility that a translation of the one into the other was made possible only by virtue of a secret complicity between them. If one has a cultural form in which simple characters are made to voice highly wrought rhetorical discourse, or sophisticated figures to articulate simple feelings, then the political effects of the form are likely to be ambiguous. On the one hand, it will obviously enact a certain class collaborationism: how reassuring that aristocrats have common human emotions (how much more real and credible it makes them seem) and, conversely, how complimentary to ruling-class discourse that even peasants, once gripped by fundamental passions, can rise spontaneously to such eloquence. On the other hand, the class structure is momentarily destabilized by such dialogism: if the simple can discourse refinedly without detriment to their simplicity, then they are equal to aristocrats in their sophistication—not as simple as we thought—and superior to them in what simplicity they do have. And if the refined speak a language of simple feeling, then their suavity elevates such common passions at the same time as its ironic excess of them threatens to render it redundant. You cannot really have this dialogic situation other than ironically, since we know that Cockneys do not actually speak like Etonians, but the irony, once more, is a politically unstable one. For the very self-conscious artifice that allows us to bracket all this as a charming fiction also threatens to spread over into, and put in question, the artifice of upper-class discourse itself, which is estranged by its earthy contents at precisely the moment it seeks to defuse and appropriate them. The strange, solemn children of Ivy Compton-Burnett's novels speak exactly the grave, measured, juridical discourse of their elders and betters, which at once confirms that language's authority—even the children speak it!—and threatens to discredit it—even a child can speak it!

The name of the cultural form I am describing is of course "pastoral"; and William Empson's classic study, *Some Versions of*

Pastoral, culminates precisely with a chapter on the child (Lewis Carroll's Alice). Children are a type of critic in all kinds of ways: because of their incessant questioning; because they are parasitically dependent on a language they nonetheless find baffling and alien; because, being outsiders, they can see both more and less than insiders; because they are isolated "intellectuals" not fully conversant with common practices of feeling yet also more emotionally sensitive than most; because their social marginality is the source at once of their blindness and insight. Pastoral is Empson's way of coming to terms with the fraught relations between critic and text, intellectual and society; its ironic interchanges of refinement and simplicity are an allegory of the critic's own dilemma. This is evident enough in Empson's literary style, a version of pastoral all its own. His airy, flattened, colloquial prose, with subclause slung casually onto subclause, at once reproduces a distinctively English ruling-class tone—brisk but genially subdued, cavalierly unbuttoned, the garrulous, gossipy, faintly facetious discourse of throwaway brilliance appropriate to an Oxbridge High Table—and at the same time subverts in its insistent ordinariness the belletristic preciosities or metaphysical solemnities of orthodox critical writing. The racy, underplayed speech of the patrician, in a familiar English paradox, makes implicit alliance with the tongue of the "people" over the heads of a linguistically pretentious bourgeoisie. Reading Empson, one is meant to gather the impression that he understands you rather as the daredevil landlord understands the poacher, as opposed to the petit-bourgeois farm bailiff; the Etonian (or in this case the Wykehamist) is not, after all, so remote from the Cockney. In a characteristically English way, Empson's style enforces its own brilliance by casually disowning it, only occasionally betraying itself by a too studiously placed quip or epigram; his writing is strikingly depthless, plucking insight after insight from a text in an inexhaustible metonymic movement but notably nervous of metaphoric density. He is like us in everything except that he is more clever, but even the cleverness is of the *kind* we could aspire to; and there is perhaps an ironic implication, shadowing the prose, that he is clever because he is like us only more thoroughly so, more shrewdly versed in our common wisdom than we are ourselves.

If there is a "pastoral" irony between critic and reader, the same can be said of the relationship between critic and text. Empson's outrageously rationalistic paraphrases of sacred literary documents, which I distill here by parody, are intended in one sense to parade the grotesque disparity between literary and critical discourses in a flamboyant gesture of dissociation:

> *Oh go not to the war, my love,*
> *For you will ne'er return.*

The sense is: "I am telling you not to have your head turned by military glory, you little idiot, not because you will take my advice, since the fact that I have to plead with you in the first place reveals just the insensitivity which will deafen you to it, but because if I do not advise you thus you will impute to me just the kind of indifference I am asking you not to impute to yourself, and so give yourself an excuse for denying your own finer instincts, which you have anyway done by putting me in this humiliating situation in the first place." (There is probably some sort of smack here at Puritanism).

The interplay between poetic statement and critical commentary forms a kind of pastoral indeterminacy in which the question of which party has the upper hand is left deliberately ambiguous. In one sense the prose commentary humbly flattens itself before the poetry, caricaturing in its breezy colloquiality its helpless incapacity to adequate it, wryly acknowledging an unsurpassable rift between the two registers. In another sense the commentary is considerably more elaborate than the text, tempting us by its commonsensical tone to believe that its own subtle turns are merely derivative of the poem in the very act of outdoing it in intricacy. The two discourses seem at once continuous and incommensurate: the literary text is both enriched and demystified by the criticism; left poorer but more honest in one sense, but impressively complicated in another. A pastoral transference of qualities has been effected: "If my criticism can have something of the subtlety of the text, then the text may have something of the straightforwardness of my criticism, in which case neither piece of writing is exactly what we thought it was." The critics are both richer and poorer than the poem, something of the jester in their heavy-footed cavortings before the majesty of the literary yet also superfluously cerebral and refined in contrast with the simple, passionate spontaneity they analyze.

All cultural critics for Empson are pastoralists, since they cannot escape the occasionally farcical irony of being fine, delicate, and excessively complex about a writing whose power lies ultimately in its embodiment of a "common humanity." The critics are continually haunted by the irony that the very instruments that give them access to those powers also threaten to cut them off from them. This, for Empson, is a permanent rather than a historical condition: *Some Versions of Pastoral* opens with a chapter on proletarian literature which denies the real possibility of the genre since "the artist never is at one with any public." But this liberal-romantic mystification (What exactly is meant here by "at one"?) is surely undercut by a glance at the social history that produced the early Empson. *Seven Types of Ambiguity* was published between the Wall Street crash of 1929 and the financial collapse of Austria and Germany, when British unemployment stood at around two million; *Some Versions of Pastoral* appeared in 1935, the year of the Italian invasion of Ethiopia, the formation of a national government in Britain, and the founding of the Left Book Club. It is not difficult, in this situation, to see why the literary intellectual might have felt somewhat less than at one with the public, or why one fascinated by the verbal cavillings of minor seventeenth-century poets might have experienced some slight need to justify his or her enterprise. Thus, pastoral is, in a sense, Empson's political self-apologia, a form that exposes the ironic contradictions of intellectual sophistication and common wisdom; it is an implicit reflection on the dazzling pyrotechnics of *Seven Types of Ambiguity* in a darkening political scene. The real swains, now, are the hunger marchers. Insofar as the pastoral form is generously capacious, good-humoredly *containing* the conflicts it dramatizes, it is, of course, as Raymond Williams has protested, a flagrant mystification.[1] But what Williams fails to see (understandably enough, for one from the rural proletariat) is that this spurious harmonization of class struggle is the heavy political price Empson momentarily has to pay for a politically well intentioned aesthetic which, in the epoch of wars and revolutions, seeks to return the increasingly fine-drawn analyses of literary critics to their roots in a practical social wisdom. Empson's life-long guerilla campaign against the whole portentous gamut of formalisms and symbolisms, his brusque dismissal of all metaphysical poetics, is the fruit of a profoundly sociable theory of language, which grasps the literary text as discourse rather than langue, refusing purely textual (or "organically contextual") notions of meaning for an insistence that meanings are inscribed in practical social life before they come to be distilled into poetry. The literary text for Empson is no organicistic mystery but a social enunciation capable of rational paraphrase, open to the routine sympathies and engagements of its readers, turning around terms that crystallize whole social grammars or practical logics of sense.

The Empsonian reader is always an active interpreter: ambiguity itself is defined as any verbal nuance that "gives room for alternative reactions to the same piece of language,"[2] and the act of reading depends upon certain tacit social understandings, certain "vague rich intimate" apprehensions carried in collective social practice. Interpretation rests upon the humanist-rationalist assumption that the human mind, however baffled, complex, and divided, is essentially "sane"; to interpret is to make as large-minded, generous allowance as one can for the way a particular mind, however self-broodingly idiosyncratic, is striving to work through and encompass its own conflicts, which can never be wholly inscrutable precisely because they inhere in a shared social medium—language itself—inherently patient of public intelligibility. If criticism is a mug's game, it is because such conflicts, "life" being the multiple, amorphous affair it is, will never endure definitive formulation, never submit to the boundaries of a single sense. But this "pastoral" sense of the loose, incongruous character of history dignifies, rather than tragically defeats, human reason, providing it with the most recalcitrant materials on which to exercise its powers and arrive at the most fulfilling type of (in)adequation. The "aristocratic" refinements of complex analysis, that is to say, are at once at odds with and enhanced by the basic, unfinished stuff on which critical acumen goes to work—just as that "common" stuff at once ironizes the critical gesture itself and, in being revealed by it as in truth inexhaustibly subtle, comes to be on terms with it. Empson, like the Freud by whom he is nervously fascinated, is the kind of rationalist who constantly allows reason to press up against its own stringent limits without for a moment ceasing to trust in its force. In this sense he fits awkwardly into the straw-target category of rationalism ideologically requisite for the fashionable irrationalisms of our own time.

Responding to a question about his attitude toward Leavis and New Criticism, Raymond Williams makes an acute comment on the politics of English criticism:

> I said to people here at Cambridge: in the thirties you were passing severely limiting judgments on Milton and relatively favorable judgments on the metaphysical poets, which in effect redrew the map of 17th-century literature in England. Now you were, of course,

making literary judgments—your supporting quotations and analysis prove it, but you were also asking about ways of living through a political and cultural crisis of national dimensions. On the one side, you have a man who totally committed himself to a particular side and cause, who temporarily suspended what you call literature, but in fact not writing, in that conflict. On the other, you have a kind of writing which is highly intelligent and elaborate, that is a way of holding divergent attitudes toward struggle or toward experience together in the mind at the same time. These are two possibilities for any highly conscious person in a period of crisis—a kind of commitment which involves certain difficulties, certain naiveties, certain styles; and another kind of consciousness, whose complexities are a way of living with the crisis without being openly part of it. I said that when you were making your judgments about these poets, you were not only arguing about their literary practice, you were arguing about your own at that time.[3]

The dilemma outlined by Williams here—one between a highly specialized mode of critical intelligence, which in foregrounding ironic complexity evades certain necessarily univocal social commitments, and a plainer, committed writing that is prepared to sacrifice such ambivalences in the cause of political responsibility—is a modern version of the contradictions which, as I have argued elsewhere, fissure the English critical institution throughout much of its history.[4] Criticism has lurched between a "professional" sophistication that sequesters it from collective social life and a political intervention into the life that, at its best (as with Milton), lends it a substantive function, and at its worst (as with Arnold) degenerates into an ineffectually "amateur" liberal humanism.

Williams, one suspects, would place Empson's work firmly on the second side of his antithesis, and there is much truth in such a judgment. But this would overlook the ironies of pastoral, which, while conscious of the socially determined distance between the language of developed consciousness and a common *Lebenswelt*, nevertheless seeks a basis of dialogue between them. If Empson's pastoral model is transferred, as it would seem to ask to be, from the anodyne artifice of a courtly drama to the problem of the critical intellectual in modern bourgeois society, it can be made to yield up significances akin rather than alien to Williams's own political case. The author of *Seven Types of Ambiguity,* that supposed classic of New Criticism, is also the author of *Milton's God,* a work quite prepared to negotiate its way in most un-Eliotic or un-Leavisian fashion through the twists and turns of Milton's religious ideology, powered as it is by a ferociously debunking Voltairean humanism but steadfast in its acknowledgment of Milton's magnificence. One can trace, indeed, in the radically divided character of *Paradise Lost*—its rational humanism and religious transcendentalism—a veritable allegory of Empson's own critical battles with literary reaction. Empson the ironist and ambiguist is, after all, the critic who writes in *Milton's God* that he feels he can well understand the God

623

Lost from the inside, having been a propaganda specialist himself during the Second World War. The insult is directed against the Christian God, not against propaganda or political rhetoric.

Empson's criticism, that is to say, offers a partial deconstruction of Williams's polarity. That the deconstruction is only partial is surely plain: he is obviously not a "committed" critic in the style of a Milton or a Williams. But those features of his critical approach that look most lemon-squeezingly Wimsattian are in fact nothing of the sort; his relentless un-raveling of finer and finer shades of verbal meaning is no aridly evasive enterprise of the kind Williams is right to denounce, but is itself a political position, inscribed by a whole range of militantly humanistic beliefs—trust in the intelligibility and sense-making capacities of the mind even at its most divided; a dogged refusal of symbolistic mystifications; a recognition of conflicts and indeterminacies—which are a necessary, if not sufficient, condition of any more politically radical criticism. Christopher Norris, in his excellent study of Empson, describes his pastoral as "lift[ing] the sub-tleties of poetic argument into a larger, essentially social air";[5] but while this is true, "ambiguities" for Empson were in a way this all along, not sealed structures of New Critical ambivalence but interpretative struggles and enigmas consequent upon language's ineradicable sociality and correl-ative roughness, its multipurpose functioning in practical life, its intrinsic openness to alternative social histories and tonalities. Poetry is not, for Empson, as for New Criticism and some contemporary deconstruction, the privileged locus of ambiguity or indeterminacy; *all* language is indetermi-nate, and this, precisely, is how it is fruitful and productive. Empson's Cambridge is also the Cambridge of Wittgenstein, who reminds us in the *Blue and Brown Books* that "we are unable clearly to circumscribe the con-cepts we use; not because we don't know their real definition, but because there is no 'real' definition to them."[6] Those who seem suddenly to have discovered that the essence of "literary" language lies in its indeterminacy have obviously not been listening for some years to how the people around them actually talk.

Empson's ambiguities, moreover, have never been purely rhe-torical affairs. They root down into conflicts of impulse and allegiance, in what seems to him the mixed, contradictory character of social being itself, in the friction of competing ideologies and social valuations. Paul de Man is not wrong to claim that Empson's work thus manifests a "deep division of Being itself"; he is mistaken, rather, in appearing to assimilate Empson's category of "contradictory meanings" (the seventh type of ambiguity) to his own model of semantic deadlock (Empson, in fact, writes breezily that "any contradiction is likely to have some sensible interpretations")[7] and in ap-propriating the English critic's esentially *social* notions of conflict to his own ontologizing impulse. Summarizing Empson's famous account of Mar-vell's *The Garden,* in which the mind, having first discovered a delightful unity with Nature, then moves to transcend and annihilate it, de Man in-forms us with enviable authority that "the pastoral theme is, in fact, the only poetic theme, that it is poetry itself."[8] What he means is that pastoral enacts just that ironic dissociation of consciousness from its objects, which is for him the properly demystified condition of all literature. Pastoral as-suages de Man's early-Sartrean horror of "inauthenticity" and "bad faith," that dismal state in which the *être pour soi* cravenly congeals into the *être en soi.* "What is the pastoral convention, then," he asks, "if not the eternal separation between the mind that distinguishes, negates, legislates, and the originary simplicity of the natural?" To which the only answer, even on de Man's own account, is: a good deal more. A few lines earlier de Man notes that in Marvell's poem the thought that annihilates Nature is *"green";* in the very act of dissociation, an equable correspondence between consciousness and the world is ironically reintroduced by this softly intrusive modifier, along with the sense, in Empson's words, of a "humble, permanent, undeveloped nature which sustains everything, and to which everything must return." De Man actually quotes this phrase, but he does not allow it to qualify his own Sartrean dogma of eternal alienation; he seizes the moment of pastoral that best fits his own denial of all productive interchange between consciousness and its surroundings and then redefines the whole *genre*— and, for good measure, poetry itself—solely in these terms.

It is amusingly typical of de Man that he should find even pastoral depressing, and for reasons quite other than Williams's. Marvell, himself, as Empson sees, has no such puritanical inhibitions: the wit and courage of his poem here lie in its refusal to absolutize even the moment of the mind's annihilating transcendence, confident and humorous enough in its own fictions to be able to reinvoke and indulge the notion of harmonious liaison between Nature and mind even at this point of mystical fading and dissolution of the real. De Man's attempt to appropriate both Marvell and Empson, in short, presses him into self-contradiction: he acknowledges the greenness of the thought but then instantly erases its significance, for pastoral is not *only* a demonstration of the division between mind and Nature but also, across that acknowledged rift, a continuous sportive interplay in which each puts the other into question. Fulfilling correspondences between both terms can be delightedly pursued once the myth of any *full* identity between them has been dismantled. De Man's doctrine of eternal separation, for him the absolute truth of the human condition, is for the pastoralist no more than one truth among several, an ironic reminder not to take one's own fictions too seriously, which then therapeutically clears the way for a fruitful alliance with the sensuous world. It is Empson, or Marvell, who is the deconstructionist here, and de Man is the full-blown metaphysician.

De Man's puritanical fear of entanglement in the world of material process, so different from Marvell's deliciously masochistic yearning to be chained by brambles and nailed through by briars, finds a paradoxical echo in the very Marxism de Man (as we shall see in a moment) is out to worst. Few words have rung more ominously in Marxist ears than "natural," and we have all long since learned to rehearse the proper objections to it with Pavlovian precision. Having learned that lesson, however, it is surely time to move on rather than remain, like de Man, fixated in the moment of bleak recognition that aardvarks are not people, repeating that traumatic moment compulsively. Once the consolations of identity have been unmasked as mythical (and pastoral, wrenched by a certain reading, can contribute to that end), we are liberated to inquire what fertile pacts and allegiances between Nature and humanity might in fact be generated, as the ecology movement has for some time been inquiring. The work of Sebastiano Timpanaro, Raymond Williams, and Norman Geras, not to speak of the drama and prefaces of Edward Bond,[9] does not cancel the important caveats of historicist Marxism on this score, but at its best takes us through and beyond them, to the point where the concepts of Nature and human nature are not merely to be dismissed as ideological fictions but are to be theoretically reconstructed. Pastoral asserts that some conditions and styles of feeling are more natural than others, and provided we do not absolutize the term, there is no reason why it should not remain, as it has long traditionally been, an integral part of radical social criticism. There seems something strangely self-thwarting about a culturalist or historicist Marxism that sternly forbids itself to describe as "unnatural" a wholly reclusive life or a society that finds sunshine disgusting.

The political implications of de Man's misreading of Empson are ominous: if the ironies of pastoral are allegorical of the critic's relation to society, or indeed of the relation of all intellectual to manual labor, then it is the uncrossable gulf between them that de Man wishes to reaffirm. This is one reason why his reflections on Empson culminate abruptly, though not wholly unpredictably, in an assault on Marxism, which is, of course, for de Man (if not for 90 percent of Marxists) a poetic dream of utter reconciliation between world and mind. Insofar as Empson himself criticizes this drive as "premature" in his chapter on proletarian literature, he has laid himself wide open to such enlistment; but one cannot imagine that he would support the tragic philosophy that is de Man's only alternative to the loss of the impossible. "The problem of separation," de Man writes, "inheres in Being, which means that social forms of separation derive from ontological and metaphysical attitudes. For poetry, the divide exists forever."[10] It is very hard to see why, if the idea of some total identity between Nature and society is plainly absurd, the absence of it should be considered somehow tragic. Many human beings would quite like to live forever, but not all of them find it tragic that they will not. Some people feel repulsed and alienated by staring at the roots of trees, while others just sit down and have a picnic. The nonidentity of consciousness and being is a fact, which may be construed tragically or not depending on how far you are still secretly in thrall with a vision of unity. The sharpest difference between de Man and Empson on this point is that for Empson the noncoincidence of mind and world, the sophisticated and the simple, is not in itself tragic at all, though it may from time to time involve tragedy. It is true that, in his remark that the poet is never at one with his or her public, Empson suggests a transhistorical estrangement upon which de Man can then pounce, turning the point for good measure against the early Marxian Barthes; but for Empson, the writer's lack of identity with an audience is simply a fact, not the basis of some melancholic ontology. For de Man it is an unquestioned good that consciousness should keep free of its objects, that the critic refuse all definitive identifications; for Empson, the typically pastoral attitude is a more ambiguous one: "I (the artist/critic/intellectual) am in one way better (than the worker/peasant), in another way not as good." Or, as he puts it more accurately elsewhere: "Some people are more delicate and complex than others, and . . . if such people can keep this distinction from doing harm it is a good thing, though a small thing by comparison with our common humanity."[11]

The fact that in a given society some individuals have the means and opportunity to be more cultured than others is not to be guiltily repressed; this, indeed, would be the Sartrean bad faith or false identification whereby intellectuals seek to empty themselves into the *être en soi* of the masses. Part of the implicit courage of *Some Versions of Pastoral,* one feels, is exactly its ironic resistance to the romantic versions of this thirties-style thesis, which was powerfully in the political air and from which the opening chapter on proletarian literature immediately takes its distance. But this is not to leave oneself with no option but romantic alienation, endorsing the eternal isolation of the refined critic and the unchangeable lowliness of the common people. *Some Versions of Pastoral* begins with a brilliant critique of Gray's *Elegy,* which demonstrates just how the poem's imagery tries to trick us into accepting the obscurity of the rural poor as somehow inevitable. Though distinctions of sophistication and simplicity exist, Empson's crucial, most un–de Manian point is that they are a poor thing in contrast with our "common humanity." Pastoral, in manifesting such distinctions, is more than a ruling-class conspiracy because it also reveals them as continually ironized and encompassed by a wider ambience, a general sustaining Nature as it were, which transcends them in its importance. What makes us uniquely different individuals, as Derek Parfit argues in his *Reasons and Persons,* is just not important enough a basis on which to build an ethics—or, one might add, a politics.[12] Pastoral knows a moment of (potentially tragic) separation of mind from world, the cultivated from the simple, self-reflexivity from spontaneity; but it includes this moment within a richer, more complex relationship in which it is recognized that the intellectual must be taught by the masses, that the mind is, after all, a *part* of Nature and not just its other, that the rich are poorer as well as richer than the common people, and that even the intellectuals—hard though it sometimes is to credit them—share a common humanity with others, which ultimately overrides whatever demarcates the two. The critic who recognizes all this is the critic as clown, and one of his several names in our time is William Empson. Paul de Man, for his part, inherits from Nietzsche a notion of action as *mindless* spontaneity (practice as "pure forgetting"), which however qualified (de Man goes on to deconstruct that "pure") puts it eternally at odds with the complexities of theory.[13] It is a nineteenth-century irrationalist current that emerges at its most disreputable in such writers as Conrad and leaves its mark on the work of Althusser.

De Man's epistemology of dissociated spirit most certainly entails a politics of intellectual elitism. Among the objects of consciousness are, of course, mass movements and political commitments, and modern bourgeois-liberal critics can attain some negative authenticity only in that ironic gesture by which, in separating themselves from such empirical engagements, they name them all as ineradicably inauthentic. "The ironic language splits the subject into an empirical self that exists in a state of inauthenticity and a self that exists only in the form of a language that asserts the knowledge of this inauthenticity."[14] In one sense, the intellectual has been discredited: he or she can no longer speak an authentic discourse to a society that has no particular desire to know about Holderlin. In another sense, such an intellectual retains much of his or her traditional authority—retains, indeed, much of the classical *form* of relationship between liberal intelligentsia and society as a whole, and so is able to deliver an authoritative message. That message, however, is now wholly empty and negative: it consists of the ceaseless act of naming the inauthenticity of all empirical engagements. In a way, the form of the intellectual's relation to modern society—the act of rigorous self-separation—has become the content of the enunciation. That the intellectual should still be honored but should really have nothing to say is the material basis of de Man's metaphysical dislocation of mind and being. It is not difficult to see how this doctrine grew up in the United States of America. The intellectual's own discourse is inevitably contaminated by inauthenticity (even Yale is situated in New Haven), constantly threatening to congeal into the reified beliefs of the unreflexive masses and constantly recovering itself only in the blank space it keeps establishing between itself and such entanglements. Thus, when the intellectual's own discourse speaks, it is untrue; and when it is true it must be silent. Meaning and being are ceaselessly at odds, and it is easy to see why this Lacanian doctrine has an appeal when one is trying to teach Kleist in Reagan's America. But if the intellectual's own discourse is inauthentic, it is also because his or her ideological interests are, on the whole, at one with the very society his or her ironic self-distancing seeks to shut out. Only by the *form* of the intellectual's statements can such interests be momentarily transcended; "irony" is the device whereby the modern bourgeois critic can at once collude with and privately disown the ideological imperatives of the modern state.

This is not the case with Empson's mode of irony. Whereas de Man is the patrician who ironizes the ideological *doxa* of the peasant, Empson views the matter in a kind of Bakhtinian reversal: it is the canny sense of the peasant that must keep the ideologizing clerk in check. In a deeply Wittgensteinian gesture, the intellectual's fatal penchant to ride hobbyhorses (a saddening feature, it must be confessed, of the later Empson himself) must be prised open to the therapeutic influence of how language is practically used, exposed to the resources of that collective social wisdom crystallized in its key terms ("complex words"). It is, as it were, the common people, or at least common readers, who live ambiguously, innately suspicious of ideological formalisms that would prematurely synthesize such inconclusiveness; and Empson, as critic, is the spokesperson of this "good sense." Pastoral is a form of the people not because it is written or read by them, or because it figures them other than in absurdly or offensively stylized ways, but because it has about it a kind of "productive looseness" (Christopher Norris), which is the structural mark of this state of ideological conflict and division. The phrase "productive looseness" has a Brechtian ring to it, and the connection seems less surprising once we remember the two men's fascination with John Gay's *Beggar's Opera*. "Putting the complex into the simple" is, after all, a snap enough definition of Brecht's *plumpes Denken*. Looked at in one light, Empson's liberal humanism, his constant striving to give what credit he can to beliefs (such as Milton's) that are deeply repugnant to him, involves an ironic provisionality of attitude not far from de Man's. Both critics can, in this sense, plausibly be construed as baffled, somewhat self-agonizing bourgeois liberals. But there is also a sense in which Empson's ironies carry him to a point closer to the sensibility of a Brecht, for whom irony denotes the necessarily unfinished, processual, contradictory nature of historical affairs, a fact usually more obvious to the ruled than the rulers. There is even a possible link through to Brecht in what Empson learned from his Far Eastern experience: what he reads as the tolerant, ironic magnanimity of the Buddha is very close to the "Chinese" Brecht's sense of the need to maintain a kind of cheerful impassive equipoise in the difficult business of negotiating contradictions.

Terry Eagleton

Contradictions for Brecht were not only sometimes intolerable but also, as he once said with reference to Hegel, a "joke." The jokiness of both Brecht and Empson—the one self-consciously plebeian, the other iconoclastically English—strikes a quite different social tone from the high European humorlessness of de Man. Empson writes in *Some Versions of Pastoral* of a Soviet performance of *Hamlet* (that most de Manian of dramas) that the audience spontaneously decided was a farce. Such people, Empson reflects, "may well hold out against the melancholy of old Russia, and for them there may be dangerous implications in any tragedy, which other people do not see."[15] I think Christopher Norris is right to suggest that Empson may well have approved of such a response to the play. Tragedy, for Empson, is a heroic mode associated with aristocratic absolutism and ascetic self-renunciation, deeply at odds with his own ironic humanism; and in this humanistic suspicion of tragedy he is again very close to Brecht. Like Brecht, the alternative form Empson offers is not some crass triumphalism but, as Norris argues of the quality of his "complex words" ("fool," "dog," "honest," and so on), "a down-to-earth quality of healthy scepticism which . . . permits their users to build up a trust in human nature on a shared knowledge of its needs and attendant weaknesses."[16] This, too, is a pastoral mode of feeling: you must love and admire the "high" human qualities of truth, beauty, virtue, and courage, but you must not be too downcast if people fail to live up to them, or terrorize them with these ideals to a point that makes their weaknesses painful to them. Tragedy moves within the high-minded terrorism of such ideals; however "deep," it is arguably narrower, more violent in its implacable expectations than the large-minded plebeian wisdom that, without a breath of cynicism (the mere flip side of such idealism) knows when not to ask too much of others. Empson's own companionable literary style is antiheroic in this sense, designed not to intimidate a reader; *Milton's God* pushes raciness and iconoclasm to the very brink of academic indecorousness. Brecht's antitragic awareness that there are always other possibilities parallels Empson's reading of the "Metaphysical" poets as constantly entertaining further possible levels of meaning, ironically including within a poem its acts of exclusion. Brecht's belief that an effective play ought always to convey a sense of the (potentially contradictory) meanings it excludes, the pressure of a further possible productivity, is classically Empsonian.

The fact that there is always more productivity where that came from should not be confused with the infinite regress of a certain mode of deconstruction. For Empson, interpretation is certainly, in principle, inexhaustible, and the limitation of the various types of ambiguity to a mere seven is more a joke at the expense of magical numbers than a serious taxonomy. That there is some continuity between Empson the liberal humanist and the antihumanist deconstructionist is signaled in Norris's summary of his critical "method": "He seems constantly on the verge of defining the complex implications, verbal or generic, which might satisfy, by somehow pinning down, his sense of the poem's richness. Yet he constantly relegates this purpose, detecting behind these provisional structures a series of ironies and 'placing' attitudes which prevent their treatment as an integrating function of form."[17] This could clearly be said of Derrida or de Man; indeed, the affinity is well enough mapped in Christopher Norris's own evolution from a sympathetic critic of Empson to an exponent of deconstruction. Yet such a trajectory tends also to impoverish Empson's work, isolating him as the author of *Seven Types of Ambiguity* and pruning away (or conveniently repressing) the more "sociable," proto-political later writing.

The shift from *Seven Types of Ambiguity* to *The Structure of Complex Words*, from "Metaphysical" to "Augustan," "wit" to "sense," reflects a growing recognition on Empson's part that wit and ambiguity, however idiosyncratically "brilliant," are nurtured by collective contexts of tacit significances, as in that Popean "good sense" that marks the inscription of social logics within individual "wit." All discourse for Empson is inscribed by such social rationalities, however much it may disrupt and transgress them; and this is why he turns in *Complex Words* to a period (the eighteenth century) in which the inherent sociableness of language, for all its normative violence, is more clearly apparent than in the seventeenth-century of New Criticism. His appeal here is to "common sense," but though his work is shot through with the limitations of this most English of vices (it lacks, for example, almost any concept of ideology); it also goes some way toward refurbishing the concept. "Common sense" in Empson is often enough his airy impatience with theory, a brisk plain-minded reliance on "what the author probably meant"; if he is one of the few English critics to have taken the pressure of Freud, he does so with notable unease and discomfort. Yet at its best his writing demonstrates just how thin a line there can be between such anemic commonsensicality and the richer Gramscian idea of proletarian "good sense," the routine practical wisdom of those who, more intimate with the material world than their rulers, are less likely to be mystified by high-sounding rhetoric. When Empson declares his pastoral faith that "the most refined desires are inherent in the plainest, and would be false if they weren't,"[18] he is very close to a kind of Bakhtinian populism; indeed, the remark is made in the context of discussing one of Shakespeare's clowns. For Empson, it is Swift who presses this deconstruction of body and spirit, savagery and sophistication, to an extreme limit—significantly enough, a limit to which Empson cannot quite follow him. Empson the rationalistic humanist really does feel that Swift is "blasphemous," rattled as he is by this virulent insistence that every generous human motivation can be rewritten in terms of a degrading vulgarity. For "Swift," here, one might well read "Freud." To attempt to "refunction" the works of Empson in Brechtian spirit cannot be to overlook his egregious limits. Empson is a self-ironizing upper-class liberal rationalist with an exasperatingly commonsensical stance, trapped in a largely tedious form of nineteenth-century atheism and sometimes dangerously sanguine, in typically English style, about human decency. His trust in a "common human nature" can be ideological in the most negative sense of the term and needs to be carefully distinguished from the more positive, materialist senses of that concept to which Marxism has recently begun to turn. What can be retrieved for socialism from Empson's work by a certain tendentious reading must be retrieved against the grain of these evident blindnesses.

To contrast Empson with a later middle-class critic like de Man is, most crucially, to compare a prefascist liberal intellectual with a postfascist one. Two of Empson's most seminal works were written before the full fury of European fascism had been unleashed; and we might well wonder whether his belief in the essential sanity and generosity of the "human mind" is not in part dependent on that chronology. De Man, as I have argued elsewhere, is most interestingly viewed in the light of a bitter "postideological" scepticism belonging to the postfascist epoch;[19] and Empson's buoyant Enlightenment rationality is just what he is out to embarrass. If Marxism cannot accept either position as it stands, it remains true that Empson poses for us the more serious challenge, at least in this sense: that he reminds us forcibly, with what he himself might call a "pastoral flatness," of just what complexity and ambiguity any program of social transformation must encompass, without regarding that transformative end as in any sense unworthy. At the same time it is part of Empson's courage, and evidence of the seeds of socialism that can be detected in his work, that he finally refuses the liberal fetishizing of difference and ambivalence that still serves the cause of liberal oppression. To paraphrase his own version of pastoral, with a materialist sense of "common humanity" in mind: some people are more delicate and complex than others, and this need not matter; indeed, it is a positive enrichment, provided such distinctions do no social harm. But the most seductive subtleties, the most dazzling displays of heroism, virtue, and intelligence, are a poor thing compared to our shared humanity; and whenever we are forced to choose, it is always better to choose the latter.

Notes

1   Raymond Williams, *The Country and the City* (London: Oxford University Press, 1973), p. 21.

2   William Empson, *Seven Types of Ambiguity* (New York: New Directions, 1947), p. 1.

3   Raymond Williams, *Politics and Letters* (New York: Schocken, 1979), p. 335.

4   See Terry Eagleton, *The Function of Criticism* (New York: Schocken, 1984).

5   Christopher Norris, *William Empson and the Philosophy of Literary Criticism* (Atlantic Highlands, N.J.: Humanities Press, 1978), p. 64.

6   Ludwig Wittgenstein, *The Blue and Brown Books* (New York: Harper and Row), p. 25.

7   Empson, *Seven Types of Ambiguity*, p. 197.

8   Paul de Man, *Blindness and Insight* (Minneapolis: University of Minnesota Press, 1983), p. 239.

9   See in particular Sebastiano Timpanaro, *On Materialism* (New York: Schocken, 1980), chap. 1; Norman Geras, *Marx and Human Nature* (New York: Schocken, 1983). See also Terry Eagleton, "Nature and Violence: The Prefaces of Edward Bond," *Critical Quarterly* 26:1-2 (1984). Perry Anderson has remarked that the question of Nature is one Marxism must confront in the future; see *In the Tracks of Historical Materialism* (Chicago: University of Chicago Press, 1984), pp. 56-84.

10   de Man, p. 240.

11   William Empson, *Some Versions of Pastoral* (New York: New Directions, 1960), p. 23.

12   See Derek Parfit, *Reasons and Persons* (Oxford: Oxford University Press, 1984).

13   See Paul de Man, "Literary History and Literary Modernity," in *Blindness and Insight*.

14   de Man, p. 214.

15   Empson, *Some Versions of Pastoral*, p. 13.

16   Norris, p. 86.

17   Norris, pp. 46-47.

18   Empson, *Some Versions of Pastoral*, p. 114.

19   Eagleton, *The Function of Criticism*, p. 101.

Michel Pêcheux

Discourse: Structure or Event?

Translated by Warren Montag, with Marie-Germaine
Pêcheux and Denise Guback

The status and significance of a historical event—like
the 1981 Socialist victory in France—is inseparable from
the equivocal discourses that traverse it. Thus, we must
reject both Marxism's scientism and structuralism's
theoreticism, for events like the Socialist victory are not
systems of "things-to-be-known." We need, instead, to
learn to listen to the often silent speech of the masses.

I can think of several quite different ways to open this
paper. One way would be to take a sentence as a theme and to work on it:
for instance, *On a gagné* ("We won"), as it spread over France on May 10,
1981, a few minutes after 8 P.M., marking the event in which memory and
topicality meet. Another way, perhaps more classical—but what is classicism
today?—would be to begin with a philosophical question: for instance, the
relationship between Marx and Aristotle apropos the idea of a science of
structure. But I am soon threatened by a multiplicity of disciplines looming
from the horizons of philosophy and the human and social sciences. They
remind me that I am not a specialist in Marx or in Aristotle or in the history
of philosophy, and that I do not have before me a specially constructed path
into the boundless archive about May 10, 1981, one that has been growing
daily.

What then? Would it not be wise—a third possible
way—to remain in the field of specialization in which I am now trying to
find my bearings: the field of discourse analysis in the French tradition.[1]
For instance, I could take up, within the set of theoretical and procedural
problems with which the discipline is now confronted, the relationship between analysis as description and analysis as interpretation. But if I take
refuge in this tactic of intervention, how do I escape a long list of prerequisites for a minimal adjustment or "tuning" of what I wish to say to what
will be heard of it? Today, a mode of work cannot be fixed merely by calling
forth some proper names (Saussure, Wittgenstein, Althusser, Foucault, Lacan) or by mentioning areas of the real (history, language, the unconscious).
Will I not be compelled to begin with a series of points to be defined in
order to ensure that they will not function throughout the discussion as
opaque signs of recognition or as theoretical fetishes? Or should I be your
guide on a visit—an ultra-quick one, necessarily—to a construction site that
displays the tools and technical procedures proper to discourse analysis?
Or, further, should I present you with the results of these procedures, in an
attempt to convince you of how pertinent and interesting they are? Yet,

ongoing research tends to set new problems rather than to illustrate the supposed quality of the "answers."

We say in France that someone does not need four ways to go directly to the essential point. But in these circumstances, what would this magic way to the main point be? Agreeing that such a way is nothing but a religious myth, I think it better to go on crisscrossing among the three ways I have just indicated (the event, the structure, and the tension between description and interpretation within the field of discourse analysis). Thus, each way will be improved through the partial intervention of the other two.

"We Won"

Paris, May 10, 1981, 8 P.M. local time. Simplified and recomposed through electronic devices, the face of the future president of the French Republic appears on the television screen. Everyone is amazed, whether through delight or dread: it is the figure of François Mitterand. At the same time, commentators report voting estimates provided by several institutions that specialize in election information processing: they all declare Mitterand the winner. A "special election" program begins: tables of percentages, first reactions of politicians, piping-hot remarks by political experts. All of these (the new fact, the statistics, the first statements) begin to "shape" the event in its immediate context and in the field of memory the event invokes and has already begun to reorganize: French socialism from Guesde to Jaures, the Congress of Tours, the Popular Front, the Liberation. The event on the "front page" of the great TV machinery, the final score of a political Super Bowl or World Series (Mitterand wins the French championship), the major news item refers to a sociopolitical context that is at the same time perfectly transparent (the verdict of numerals, the outcome of a score) and deeply opaque.

The discursive struggle over the naming of the unlikely event began long before May 10 through the tremendous work of formulations (reported, shifted, turned over from one side to the other of the political field), constituting a discursive prefiguration of the event, shaping and fashioning it, with the secret hopes of hurrying or hindering it. This process goes on, marked by the novelty of May 10, but this novelty does not rule out the opacity of the event, inscribed in the oblique play of its denominations. None of these sentences is a paraphrase of the other—François Mitterand is elected president of the French Republic. The French Left wins the day in the presidential elections. Socio-communist coalition takes hold of France. They refer *(bedeuten)* to the same event, but they do not construct the same significations *(sinne):* the discursive struggle goes on through the event.

In the midst of this circulation-confrontation of formulations that does not cease to unfold across the television screen throughout the entire night, a news flash appears that is both a report and a call: all Parisians for whom this event is a victory are to gather on the Place de la Bastille to shout for joy. The others will not be there on such a night. The same will happen in many other French towns. Among the cries of victory, there is one that was taken up with a particular intensity: *On a gagné!*—"We won!"—repeated endlessly, as an inexhaustible echo of the event. The discursive materiality of this collective utterance is most peculiar: neither its content nor its shape nor its enunciative structure are those of a slogan at a demonstration or a political meeting.[2] *On a gagné,* sung with a determinate rhythm and melody (*on-a-ga-gne*/do-do-sol-do), constitutes the deployment, in the field of political events, of the collective chant of fans at a game when their team has just won. When that chant fills the stadium, the passive participation of the audience is reconverted into a collective motor and vocal activity, materializing the celebration of the team's victory the more intensely as it was the more unlikely.[3]

May 1981 was the first time that sport offered itself as the popular metaphor most adequate to the French political field. Such an event requires an elaborate critical study of the links between the mode of functioning of the media, on the one hand, and of professional politicians, on the other, especially since the 1970s.[4] What may be said, in any case, is that the metaphoric play around the utterance "We won" overdetermined the event in underscoring its equivocation. The obviousness of sports results is supported by their presentation in logical tables (team X defeated team Y and is therefore qualified to play team Z, etc.). The results of the game will, of course, become the object of strategic commentaries and reflections by team captains and sports commentators, since there are always other games on the horizon. But all the same, the result as such appears within a discursive universe that is logically stabilized; that is, it is based on relatively limited sets of arguments, predicates, and relations, and it can be comprehensively described through a series of univocal responses to factual questions (the main one of which is, of course, As a matter of fact, who won, X or Y?).

Questions such as Who *actually* won, really, beyond appearances, in the eyes of history? are irrelevant and even absurd when asked about the results of a game. This may be explained by the fact that what is at stake in a game is logically defined as being contained in its result: "team A won" means "team A defeated team B in a game that took place at such and such a site," and no more. Symbolic marks and objects that may be associated with that victory (and therefore may be appropriated by supporters who identify with the team) are only secondary consequences of the result. It is not certain that what has been won by the winners may be shown or described.

Electoral results, when considered according to the way they are displayed by the media, show the same logical univocation. The universe of percentages, provided with rules to determine victory, is all the same a set of predicates, arguments, and relations. From this point of view, we may say that on May 10, 1981, after 8 P.M., the proposition "François Mitterand has been elected president of the French Republic" became true, and no more. But at the same time, the statement *On a gagné* is deeply opaque: its lexicosyntactic materiality (an indefinite pronoun as the subject, the tense and aspectual markers of perfective form, the verbal lexical morpheme "win," and the absence of any object) immerses the utterance in a network of implicit associative relations—paraphrases, implications, commentaries, allusions, and so on—that is, in a heterogeneous series of statements, functioning at various discursive levels, with a variable logical stability.[5]

It follows that the conflation of politics and sport described above functions as a stabilized proposition (indicating an event localized as a point in an area of logical disjunctions) only if we do not ask what the subject of the verb "win" refers to, or what the missing objects refer to.[6] By 1983, the question can no longer be excluded from political debate. *On a gagné!*—we rejoiced in the same way at each victory of the Left: May 1936, Liberation, and so on. Others before us shouted the same words. And every time it has been an "experience" that did not last long. Willingness and enthusiasm wasted; a sudden blaze, but a flash in the pan: the fall, the bog, and the accepted defeat.

"On A Gagné': What Has Been Won, How, and for Whom?"[7]

Concerning the Subject of the Statement: Who Won?

French syntax permits, through the use of the indefinite pronoun *on,* the omission of the subject utterance in "who wins." Is it "we," rank-and-file members of a leftist party? Or the people of the Left? Or those who always supported the perspectives of the Common Program? Or those who first supported it and then suddenly gave up? Or those who, quite at sea in the Left/Right categorization in Parliament, nevertheless felt sudden release through the departure of Giscard d'Estaing and all he represents? Or those who never had anything to do with politics and are amazed and enthusiastic because at last things are changing?

The effacement of the agent induces a complex feedback, intermingling different forms of activism with the passive participation of the electoral spectator, reluctant and skeptical up to the last minute ... when the incredible happens: the critical touchdown is scored and the supporter rushes to the aid of victory. The statement *On a gagné* brings together "those who still believed in it" and "those who no longer believed."[8]

Concerning the Objects of the Statement: What Is Won, How, and for Whom?

Let us consult the dictionary about the verb "to win," *gagner.* We see it can be constructed:

a. with a live subject (an agent endowed with will, feeling, intention, etc.)—to earn one's living, to earn so much per month; to win a competition, to be the winner; to win a game of chance, to win the first prize; to overtake (on land, in space or time) an opponent; to be promoted; to reach a place; to win someone's sympathy, (men, allies, friends); or

b. with a lifeless subject (a thing, a process without any proper will, feeling, or intention.) These "agents" become objects: heat, cold, enthusiam, sleep, illness, joy, sadness overtake us (take hold of me, of him, of us.)

What part did each of these lexicosyntactic ways of functioning play in the equivocal unity of the reverberated chant? "We won": joy of victory is enunciated without an object, but objects are not far away—we won the match, the game, the first set (before legislative elections); but at the same time (see above), we won by chance, as the first prize is won when no one dared to hope for it, and, of course, ground is gained over the opponent, with the anticipation of places to be filled, above all the place from which France is governed, the place of governmental and state power. "The Left takes power in France" is a plausible paraphrase of the formula-statement "We won" as an extension of the event. Assuming power: at last something that may be shown as the object of the verb "to win."

Michel Pêcheux

It is not at all certain that the verb "to win, to take power" may be explained univocally.[9] "Power" may in a way be considered as an acquired object, the deserved fruits of a long effort, or as unexpected good fortune; in any case, the symbolic first prize to be managed for the good of everyone. In another way "power" may be seen as a resistant space to be conquered in an ongoing struggle against the bastions of capitalism (which did its best to prevent it and continues to resist). In still another way, power is a performative act to be upheld (to do what was promised) or even a new set of social relations to be constructed.

On a gagné: for two years, the equivocation of this formula has troubled leftists in government posts as well as other layers of the population; it troubles those who believe in it as well as those who do not, those who are waiting for a large popular movement and those who are resigned to a generalized apoliticism, officeholders and ordinary people. Therefore, there are two distinct temptations: (1) to deny the ambiguity of the event of May 10, for instance, by bringing it down to the logically stabilized level of political institutions (Yes or no, is the French Left in or not? If yes, then let us be consistent with the will of the people.); (2) to deny the event as such, by behaving as if the problems were the same as if the right wing were in power (Nothing really happened. What has been won?).[10] Yielding to either of these temptations would ultimately divide the two Lefts from each other and surrender both to the opponent. If the right wing were to come back into power in France, one would see—too late—what one has lost.

My intention in taking the event of May 10, 1981, as an example has been to raise the question of the status of the discursivities that traverse an event, interweaving propositions that seem logically stabilized and therefore may be univocally responded to (yes or no, X or Y) with those formulations that are irredeemably equivocal. Discursive objects that seem to be stable, that seem privileged by a relative logical independence in relation to statements produced about them, exchange their trajectories with other kinds of objects whose mode of existence is governed by the very way they are spoken about. Is one type of object more "real" than another? Is there an underlying space common to the deployment of such dissimilar objects?

Science, Structure, and Scholasticism

To suppose that, in certain circumstances at least, an object is independent in relation to any discourse about that object is equally to suppose that, in the interior of what appears to be the physical-human universe (things, living beings, persons, events, processes), "there is something of the real." That is, there are points of impossibility determining what cannot fail to be thus. The real is (the) impossibility . . . that things could be otherwise. Therefore, one does not discover the real; one bumps into it, meets it, finds it.

Thus, the domain of mathematics and the natural sciences has to do with the real, insofar as one can say of a mathematician or of a physicist that he or she has found the solution to a problem that had remained up to that point unsolved. Also, we say that a student, facing math or physics homework, has solved such and such part of the problem, that he or she is "right" *(il "a bon")* on such and such a question, while as far as the rest is concerned he or she is "lost" *(il sèche).*

A very great number of material technologies that produce physical or biophysical transformations "have to do with" the real, in opposition

637

to the techniques of divination and interpretation. The point is to find, with or without the aid of the natural sciences, the means of obtaining a result in the most effective possible fashion, while taking into account the exhaustibility of nature: the means to use natural processes, to instrumentalize them, to direct them toward the sought-for effects. To this series is added a multiplicity of techniques of the social management of individuals: they are marked, identified, classified, compared, placed in order, in ranks and tables. They are reassembled and separated according to defined criteria in order to put them to work, to teach them, to give them dreams or hallucinations, to protect them and maintain surveillance over them, to lead them to war, to induce them to have children.

This administrative (juridical, economic, and political) space presents the appearance of a disjunctive logical constraint. It is "impossible" that one is both a bachelor and married, that one has a diploma and does not have a diploma, that one works and is unemployed, that one earns less than x dollars per month and more than that sum, that one is both a civilian and in the military, that one is elected to such and such a function and is not, and so on. These spaces, through which the possessors of knowledge are placed, the specialists and officials of diverse existing orders (all of them functioning as agents and guarantors of these multiple operations), have a very specific property: they essentially forbid interpretation. This interdiction is implied by the ordered usage of logical propositions (true or false) with disjunctive interrogations (Is the state of affairs A or not A?). Correlatively, this interdiction implies the refusal of certain marks of discursive distance,[11] such as "in a sense," "if you like," "we might say," "to an extreme degree," "properly speaking." In particular, these spaces imply the refusal of all quotation marks of an interpretative nature that would displace the categorization. For example, the statement "Such and such a person is very military in civilian life" is prohibited, even though this statement, of course, makes perfect sense.

In the discursive spaces designated above as logically stabilized, a given speaking subject is supposed to know what is being talked about; every statement produced in these spaces reflects structural properties that are independent of the enunciation of the statement. These properties are transparently inscribed in an adequate description of the universe, such that this universe is discursively grasped in the spaces. The apparent unifying factor of these discursive spaces is a series of logical-practical evidences at a very general level, such as: the same object X cannot be at the same time in two different places; the same object X cannot have at the same time property P and property not P; the same event E cannot at the same time have occurred and not have occurred; and so on. The logical homogeneity that conditions the logically representable as a set of propositions capable of being true or false is traversed by a series of equivocities (in particular concerning such terms as Law, Rigor, Order, Principle, etc.), which covers at the same time, like a patchwork, the domains of the exact sciences, technologies, and public services.[12]

This "logical" cover *(couverture)* of the heterogeneous regions of the real is too massive and systematic a phenomenon to be seen simply as a deception, constructed piecemeal by some mystifying Prince: before this false semblance *(faux-semblant)* of a natural and sociohistorical real, covered by a network of logical propositions, everything happens as if it were not in anyone's power totally to escape, even—and perhaps especially—those who believe themselves not to be duped by it *("non-dupes"),* as if this inevitable inclusion would come to be realized in one way or another.

If we put aside all explanations that are not explanations, insofar as they are only the commentaries of this inclusion itself, there is perhaps a crucial point to consider from the direction of the multiple exigencies of everyday life. But to call this point into question supposes the suspension of the position of the universal spectator as the source of logical homogeneity; it necessitates the interrogation of the "pragmatic" subject in the Kantian sense, as well as in the contemporary sense.[13] The idea that these logically stablilized spaces could be imposed from the exterior, like the constraints placed on the pragmatic subject, through the sole power of people of science, specialists, and administrators, becomes, once it is seriously considered, indefensible.

The pragmatic subject—that is to say, ordinary people faced with the diverse exigencies of their lives—has itself an imperative need for logical homogeneity, marked by the existence of a multiplicity of small, portable, logical systems: from the management of everyday existence (for example, in our civilization, wallet, keys, schedules, calendars, papers), to the great decisions of social and private life (I decide to do such and such and not something else, to respond to X and not to Y), to the whole sociotechnical environment of household appliances (the series of objects that we acquire, that we learn how to work, that we throw away or use, that we break or repair or replace). In this space of equivocal necessity, in which are intermingled things and persons, technical processes and moral decisions, instructions for use and political choices, any conversation (from the simplest request for information to discussions, debates, and confrontations) is capable of putting into play a logical bipolarization of statable propositions— with, from time to time, the insidious impression of a univocal simplification, which could eventually be deadly for oneself and/or for others.

It does no good to deny this need (or desire) for the appearance of homogeneity bearing logical disjunctions and categorizations: the universal need for a "semantically normal (i.e., normalized) world" begins with the relation that we each maintain with our own body and our immediate environment (beginning with the distribution of good and bad objects, archaically figured by the disjunction between food and excrement). Nor does it do any good to deny that this need for boundaries coincides with the construction of links between multiple "things to be known" *(choses à savoir):* we say "things to be known" and "things of knowledge"; we say "things of beauty." These "things to be known" can be considered as reserves of accumulated knowledge that we depend on,[14] machines of knowledge against threats of any kind: the state and institutions functioning most often—at least in our societies—as privileged poles of response to this need or demand.

Thus, such "things to be known" stand for things that might be lacking for the happiness (and ultimately for the simple biological survival) of the pragmatic subject; that is, anything that threatens him or her by the very fact that it exists (the fact that it is part of the real, whatever grasp the subject in question has of the structure of the real). It is not necessary to have a phenomenological intuition, a hermeneutic grasp, or a spontaneous apprehension of the essence of typhus to be affected by this malady;[15] in fact, it is quite the contrary: there are "things to be known" (knowledges to be socially managed and transmitted), that is, descriptions of situations, symptoms, and acts (to be performed or avoided) associated with the multiple threats of the real for which ignorance of the law is no excuse—because the real is without pity.

The project of a knowledge that would unify this multiplicity of "things to be known" into a homogeneous representable structure, the idea of a possible *science of the structure* of the real, capable of making it explicit, outside of any false semblance, and of assuring the control over this real without the risks of interpretation (therefore a scientific self-reading of the real, without fault or lack)—this project obviously corresponds to an urgency so vivid, so universally "human," tied (knotted) so well (around the same stake of domination/resistance) to the interests of successive masters of this world, as well as to those of the wretched of the earth, that the phantasm of such an effective, manageable, and transmissible knowledge could not fail historically to use any means to make itself materialize.

The promise of a royal science as conceptually rigorous as mathematics, as concretely effective as material technologies, as omnipresent as philosophy and politics—how could humanity resist such a godsend?

—There was the moment of Aristotelian scholasticism that marked the beginning of the deployment of the categories that structure language and thought, fashioning the model and organon of any systematization: disjunctive questions *en utrum* ("either ... or") considering divinity, the sex of angels, celestial and terrestrial bodies, plants and animals, all things known and unknown. . . . How many catechisms have been structured by the networks of such scholastic questions and responses?

—There is the modern-contemporary moment of positive rigor which has appeared in the historical context of the constitution of physics, chemistry, and biology as sciences, a moment associated with the emergence of a new form of Law (organized into a set of propositions), as well as with a rebirth of mathematical thought. The result is a new organon, constructed in opposition to Aristotelianism and based on a reference to the exact sciences, beginning in its turn to homogenize the real, from mathematical logic to social and administrative spaces, from the experimental hypothetical-deductive method to the "techniques of the proof."

—And, last but not least, there is the moment of marxist ontology, pretending for itself to produce the dialectical laws of history and matter; another organon, partially resembling the two preceding organa and in any case sharing with them the desire for omnipotence: "the theory of Marx is all powerful because it is true" (Lenin). As a whole, the workers' movements have visibly been unable to resist this extraordinary gift of a new unified philosophy capable of institutionalizing itself efficiently as a critical/organizational component of the state (whether the existing state or the state to come). And the basic apparatus of marxist dialectical ontology (with *Capital* as the absolute weapon: "the most powerful missile ever thrown at the head of the bourgeoisie") has shown itself to be capable—like all knowledges of this unified and homogeneous appearance—of justifying anything in the name of urgency.[16]

Neo-positivism and marxism thus form the major episteme of our time, entangled in a partially contradictory manner around the stake of the human and social sciences, with the question of history at the center, that is, the question of the possible forms of existence of a science of history.

The point here is not to decide whether or not *Capital* and the research that has derived from *Capital* have produced what I have called "things to be known." Even for the fiercest adversaries of marxism, the process of capitalist exploitation, for example, incontestably constitutes a "thing to be known," and the owners of capital have learned to use it as much as, and perhaps better than, those they exploit.[17] The same goes for class struggle and several other "things to be known." The question is, rather, to determine if the "things to be known" that have emerged from marxism are capable or not of being organized into a coherent scientific space, integrated into a systematic montage of concepts, such as the productive forces, relations of production, social-economic formations, social formations, infrastructure and ideological, juridical and political superstructures, state power, and so on, in the sense that, for example, the Galilean discovery was capable of constituting the coherent scientific matrix of physics, in the current sense of the term.[18]

The moment of the Galilean rupture opened the possibility of a construction of the physical real as a process, following the track of the impossible proper to this real through the ordered relations combining the construction of conceptual writings and experimental devices (thus employing a part of the register of material technologies evoked above). Accordingly, the first instruments (inclined planes, winches, etc.) used by Galilean physics were inevitably imported from pre-Galilean technological spaces; and it is in the development itself of physics that the aforementioned instruments were transformed, in order to be adapted to the intrinsic necessities of Galilean physics, with, as a retroactive effect, the indefinitely enlarged production of industrialized technical objects associated with a new technical-social division of labor ("scientists," engineers, and technicians), which made physics appear also as a "social science."[19]

The intellectual consequences of the Galilean discontinuity are marked by the fact that for no physicist today is Aristotle a colleague or even the first physicist: Aristotle is simply a great philosopher. Another mark of this discontinuity is that Galilean and post-Galilean physics do not interpret the real—even if, of course, the movement they initiate, the construction of the physical real as process, incessantly becomes the object of multiple interpretations.

The question I am posing here is that of knowing if Marx may or may not be considered the Galileo of the "continent of history."[20] Is there an impossible specific to history, marking structurally that which constitutes the real? Is there an ordered relationship between the formulation of concepts and the construction of instruments capable of grasping the real? And can we discern, with the emergence of Marx's thought, a discontinuity such that the historical real ceases to be the object of divergent interpretations in order to be constituted in its turn as a process (for example, a "process without subject or end[s]," according to the famous formula of Althusser)?

The fact of the "crisis of marxism" is today sufficiently acknowledged. I can be brief and say that everything leads us to think that the epistemological discontinuity associated with Marx's discovery has become extremely precarious and problematic. Marx is neither the first historian nor the first economist, in the sense that Galileo could be the first physicist:

Thucydides, who is apparently not a colleague for the contemporary practitioners of historiography,[21] is without doubt a historian before as well as
after Marx. All we can suppose is that eventually Thucydides would not be
read in the same manner, according to whether or not the reading takes
into account the work of Marx (that is to say, in fact, such and such a
reading of such and such a text signed by Marx, or by Marx and Engels,
etc.). But can we not say exactly the same thing about any great thought
that has emerged out of history? Failing to be the founder of a science of
history, let us say that Marx would be a very great philosopher, as important
as Aristotle.

What would have (and to a certain extent has) happened is that
Marx would be considered the first marxist theoretician, in spite of the
famous phrase with which he rejected the categorizing adjective derived
from his proper name that certain of his contemporaries had already coined
in his lifetime. And the fact that Marx thus refused to recognize himself in
the initial effects associated with the social-historical "reception" of his work
has almost always been understood as a denegation, signifying, in fact, "I,
Karl Marx, am effectively a marxist, but not in the sense in which it is
commonly understood." It seems to me that the aristocratic thematic of the
"good" reading as opposed to "bad" (banal or fallacious) readings, of the
correct interpretation always held in reserve under erroneous interpretations, of the truth as a telos of a potentially infinite process of rectification,
begins at this precise point.

The scholastic effects of the division of reading (exoteric/esoteric
reading, Marx read by X/Marx read by Y, etc.), of which marxism had been
the site from the very beginning, with a quasi-indefinite postponement of
the moment of the decisive experience would not be especially surprising.
The impossible proper to the structure of the historical real—that is, the
specific real considered by marxist theory—is probably literally ungraspable
in the "applications" of the aforementioned theory. The same aporetic point
appears in another way: the question of "instruments." If we consider (as
was the case for a century for a not-negligible part of humanity) marxism
as the science of history put into practice by the proletariat, we must admit
that the practitioners of the science in question were constrained to "borrow" from the existing (and therefore pre-marxist) social-historical world a
whole series of instruments (institutions, or "apparatuses," forms of organization and practices, etc.) in order for this science-practice to be constituted simultaneously as a space of knowledge and a means of intervening
in history.

Insofar as it is a question of intervening in history by obeying
its law (which incidentally presupposes that the "things to be known" concerning history, society, and politics have the structure of laws of the sci-
entific-Galilean type), it is clear that, like the inclined planes and winches
of Galileo, the first "instruments" utilized have been, up to this point,
dissimilar to their new "scientific" goals, inadequate to their transformational function, in a word, crude (only inveterate utopians can believe that
it is possible to construct ex nihilo such social-political instruments by mag-
ically denying the weight of the past). But the crucial problem is that the
development of the applications of marxism as a science-practice, the new
instruments or apparatuses constructed under its scientific auspices, continue to resemble, *grosso modo,* earlier structures—sometimes with aggra-

vations that are more than accidental: in particular, the same patchwork, the same false appearance of logical homogeneity, telescoping the discursive stability proper to the natural sciences, to the material technologies and to procedures of administrative management and control, has not ceased to dominate the different variants of marxism. In other words, to speak brutally, the instruments have not followed theory in its "applications," which can also be understood as an indication that the science-practice in question has not (yet?) been correctly applied.

To speak this way is, again, to suppose a "true" marxism in reserve, a marxism *introuvable*,[22] that is, basically, to repeat Marx's own denegation of the interpretation of his work; it is to be identified with Marx's gesture, in what is most defensive about it. So, let us stop protecting Marx and protecting ourselves through him. Let us stop supposing that the "things to be known" concerning the social-historical real form a structural system, analogous to the conceptual-experimental coherence of the Galilean system.[23] And let us try to comprehend what this systematic phantasm implies as a kind of link to "specialists" of all kinds and to the institutions and state apparatuses that employ them, not in order to place ourselves out of play, or out of state (!), but so we may think the problem outside of a marxist denial of interpretation, that is, by facing the fact that history is a discipline of interpretation and not a physics of a new type.

To Read, To Describe, To Interpret

To raise the question of the existence of a real specific to the disciplines of interpretation requires that the non-logically stable not be considered a priori as a lack, or simple hole, in the real. This assumes that—"the real" understood in various ways—there could exist a real other than that already evoked, as well as another kind of knowledge that is not reducible to the order of "things to be known" or to a network of such things. Thus, we have a real that is constitutively foreign to logical univocation and a knowledge that is not transmitted, learned, or taught but nevertheless exists in the production of effects.

The intellectual movement that was named "structuralism" (as it developed, in particular, in France in the sixties, around linguistics, anthropology, philosophy, politics, and psychoanalysis) may be considered, from this point of view, an antipositivist attempt to take into account the real that thought "bumps into" at the intersection of language and history. New reading practices (symptomatic, archaeological, etc.) applied to textual monuments, and initially to the Great Texts (cf. *Reading Capital*), have emerged from this movement. The principle on which these readings are based consists, as we know, in disengaging what is being said "here" (at a precise place in a text)—said in such a way and no other—from what is being said elsewhere and in another way, in order to be able to "hear" the presence of the "unsaid" within what is said.

Assuming that "any fact is already an interpretation" (an antipositivist reference to Nietzsche), structuralist approaches made it a point to describe the textual discursive constructions in their material imbrication. And paradoxically, they, in this manner, set aside the production of interpretations (of representations of contents, of *Vorstellungen*) in favor of description per se *(Darstellung)* of these constructions. It was in this way that structuralist approaches expressed their refusal to be constituted as a "royal science" of the structure of the real. Nonetheless, we will see in a moment how they were able, in their turn, to be seduced by this phantasm, only to end up appearing as a new "royal science." But first it is necessary to stress the fact that in the names of Marx, Freud, and Saussure a new theoretical foundation, politically heterogeneous, took shape, leading to a critical construction that shattered the literary evidence of "lived" authenticity, as well as the "scientific" certitudes of positivist functionalism.

I recall how, at the beginning of *Reading Capital,* Althusser marked the encounter of these three fields: "Only since Freud have we begun to suspect what listening and hence what speaking (and keeping silence) means *(veut dire);* that this 'meaning' *(vouloir-dire)* of speaking and listening discloses, beneath the innocence of speech and hearing, the specifiable depth of a hidden level, the 'meaning' of the discourse of unconscious—that level whose effects and formal conditions are thought by modern linguistics."[24] The subversive effect of the trilogy Marx-Freud-Saussure was an intellectual challenge that held out the promise of a cultural revolution that would call into question the evidence of the human order as a strictly biosocial order.

To restore something of the specific work of the letter, the symbol, and the trace was to begin to open up a fault within the compact block of pedagogies, industrial and biomedical technologies, and moralizing humanisms or religions. It was to call into question the direct articulation of the biological and the social (an articulation that excluded the symbolic and the signifier from the real). It was an attack on the individual and the collective narcissism of human consciousness (cf. Spinoza in his time), an attack on the eternal negotiation of the "self" (as master/slave of its action, speech, and thought) in its relation to the other self. In a word, the structuralist cultural revolution never ceased to attack the psychological register (and the psychologies—of the "self," of "consciousness," of "behavior," or of the "epistemic" subject). This attack was not engendered by the hatred of humanity that was often attributed to structuralism. It was only the consequence of the recognition of a structural fact proper to the human order: that of symbolic castration.

But at the same time, this antinarcissistic movement (whose political and cultural effects have obviously not been exhausted) turned toward a new form of theoretical narcissism—a narcissism of structure. This theoretical narcissism may be marked in the structuralist tendency to reinscribe its "readings" in the unified space of a conceptual logic. Thus, the suspension of interpretation (associated with the descriptive gestures of the reading of textual constructions) topples over into a sort of structural overinterpretation of the montage as the effect of the whole: this overinterpretation used the "theoretical" level as a kind of metalanguage, organized in a network of paradigms. Structuralist overinterpretation then functions as a translating device, transposing "common empirical statements" into "conceptual structural statements." The mode of functioning of structural analysis (and in particular of what could be called structural materialism or political structuralism) remains secretly governed by the general model of interpretative equivalence. To schematize this, take the empirical statement P1 (for example, "The face of existing socialism is distorted"): ... P1, in fact, means nothing else but ... theoretically comes to say that ... in other words ... that is to say ... the theoretical statement P2 (for example, "Bourgeois ideology dominates marxist theory"). It is above all this state of theoretical

Michel Pêcheux

overhang, the allure of a discourse without a subject simulating mathematical processes, that conferred on structuralist approaches the appearance of a new "royal science," denying, as usual, its own interpretative position.

The paradox of the early 1980s is that the bogging down of French political structuralism, its breakdown as a "royal science" (that nevertheless continues to produce effects, notably in Latin America), coincides with the growing acknowledgment of the works of Lévi-Strauss, Lacan, Barthes, Derrida, and Foucault in the Anglo-Saxon countries—in England, West Germany, as well as in the United States. By a strange seesaw effect, at the precise moment that America discovers structuralism, the French intelligentsia "turns the page" by developing a massive *ressentiment* of the theories suspected of having spoken in the name of the masses, while producing a long series of inefficient symbolic acts and unhappy political performatives. This *ressentiment* is the effect of a profound movement "from below," a sort of ideological backlash necessitating reflection, and must not be confused with the cowardly relief of many French intellectuals who react by discovering retroactively that "theory" has "intimidated" them.

The biggest strength of this critical reexamination is that it calls into question the theoretical "heights" of political structuralism, the ambition to construct a relation to the state (eventually, its identification with the state—and especially with the party-state of the revolution). This backlash has forced us to look toward what is happening "below," in the infra-ecstatic space that constitutes the ordinary of the masses, especially in a period of crisis. It is becoming increasingly obvious that—in history, sociology, and literary studies—we must learn to listen to this often silent speech enclosed within the urgency of survival. We must do more than read (or reread) the Great Works (of science, law, and the state). We must hear the articulations embedded in the "ordinary way" of meaning.[25] But at the same time, the risks of this movement are quite clear, especially the risk of following the greatest ideological slope, of conceiving the "ordinary way of meaning" as a natural psychobiological process inscribed in a logically stabilized discursivity. Hence, the risk of a tremendous regression toward positivism and the philosophies of consciousness.

A meeting such as this could be an opportunity to evade some of these risks, if we can determine the stakes involved and situate the major points of encounter. As far as I am concerned (but I am expressing a point of view here that is not mine alone: it is a working position that is developing in France today), I will point out the strong interest of a theoretical and procedural rapprochement between practices of "ordinary language analysis" (within the antipositivistic perspective that may be drawn from Wittgenstein's work) and "reading" practices derived from structuralist approaches.[26] Taken seriously (i.e., other than as a mere "cultural exchange"), this rapprochement involves, in a concrete manner, ways of working on the discursive materialities implied in ideological rituals, philosophical discourses, political statements, and aesthetic and cultural forms, through their relations to everday life, to "the ordinary" of meaning. This project can only become consistent if it prudently avoids any present or future "royal science" (either positivism or marxist ontologies).

This work pattern imposes a certain number of necessities that must be explained in detail and that I can only mention briefly in closing. The first necessity consists in giving priority to *descriptions* of discursive materialities. According to this perspective, description is not a phenomenological or hermeneutical apprehension in which it indiscernibly becomes interpretation; such a conception of description implies, on the contrary, the recognition of the specific real on which it leans: the real of langue (cf. J. C. Milner, especially in *L'amour de la langue*). And I say *la langue*, that is, neither language, speech, discourse, text, nor conversational interaction but rather what has been put forward by linguists as the condition for existence (in principle), in the form of the existence of the Symbolic as Jakobson and Lacan understood it.

Certain recent tendencies in linguistics are rather encouraging from this point of view. Beyond Harrisian distributionalism and Chomskyan generativism, trends have emerged that question the primacy of logical proposition as well as the limitations imposed on linguistic analysis as sentence analysis. Thus, linguistic research might begin to free itself from its obsession with ambiguity (meant as the logic of "either . . . or") in order to reach what is proper to langue through the role of equivocity, ellipsis, lack, and so on. This play of differences, alternations, and contradictions cannot be seen as the softening of some logical hard core: the equivocation, the "constitutive heterogeneity" (J. Authier) of langue corresponds to Milner's "declarations of faith"[27]: "Nothing of poetry is foreign to *Langue*"; and "No language can be completely thought out without integrating the possibility of its poetry." This imposes on linguistic research the construction of procedures (the modes of questioning facts and the forms of reasoning) capable of explicitly approaching the linguistic fact of equivocity as a structural fact implied by the symbolic order; that is, the necessity of working up to the point at which logical representations (inscribed in the "normal world") cease to be consistent. This is also the argument François Gadet and I developed in *La langue introuvable*.

The object of linguistics, that which is proper to langue, thus appears to be traversed by a discursive division between two spaces: that of the manipulation of stabilized significations, normalized by a pedagogical hygiene of thought, and that of the transformation of meaning escaping from all a priori assignable norms, the work of meaning on meaning, grasped in an indefinite "rebirth" of interpretations. The frontier between the two fields is difficult to determine in that there exists a whole intermediate zone of discursive processes (related to the juridical, to the administrative, and to the conventions of daily life) oscillating around it. And it is in this intermediary discursive region that the logical properties of objects cease to function: objects both have and do not have such and such a property; events both have and have not occurred according to the discursive constructions within which the statements that support these objects and events are found to be inscribed.[28] The fluctuating and paradoxical character of the ordinary register of meaning appears to have almost completely escaped the philosophical perception of the structuralist movement. This register has been the object of a theoretical aversion that has enclosed it globally in the inferno of the dominant ideology and practical empiricism. It has been considered as the blind point of a pure reproduction of meaning.[29]

In doing so, the structuralists were giving credence to the idea that the process of transformation internal to symbolic and ideological spaces is an *exceptional* process: the solitary, heroic moment of theory and poetry (Marx-Mallarmé) as the "extraordinary" work of the signifier. This aristo-

cratic conception, giving itself, de facto, a monopoly on the second field
(that of logically nonstabilized discursivities), remained the prisoner—even
in its "proletarian" reversal—of the old elitist certitude that the dominated
masses never invent anything because they are too absorbed in the logic of
everyday life. Ultimately, the proletariat, the masses, the people, have such
a vital need for logically stabilized universes that the play of the symbolic
order does not concern them at all! On this precise point, the theoretical-
poetic position of the structuralist movement is insupportable.[30] And in
failing to discern how humor and poetry are not the "Sunday of thought,"
but belong to the fundamental elasticity of political and theoretical intelligence, this movement had already given in to the populist argument of
urgency, since it implicitly shared its essential presupposition: the proletariat
has no (time for the luxury of the) unconscious!

From what precedes, it follows that any description (it does not
change anything whether it is a description of objects or events, or a description of a discursive-textual construction, as long as we hold firmly that
"there is no metalanguage") is intrinsically exposed to the equivocity of
langue: any utterance is intrinsically able to become other than itself, to
split discursively from its meaning, to be diverted toward another (except
if the prohibition of interpretation proper to the logically stable is applied
to it). Any utterance or sequence of utterances is thus linguistically describable as a series (lexico-syntactically determined) of possible points of diversion, leaving room for interpretation. It is in this space that discourse
analysis claims to work.

It is here that one finds, once again, the matter of disciplines of
interpretation: because there is something of the "other" in societies and in
history, a link (identification or transference) corresponding to this "other"
proper to discursivity is possible, that is, a relation that opens up the possibility of interpretation. And it is because this link exists that historical
filiation can be organized into memories and social relations into networks
of signifiers. Hence the fact that the "things to be known" mentioned before
are never visible from above like the historical transcendentals of the episteme in Foucault's sense. They are always entangled in memory networks
that lead to identificatory filiations and never to a learning through interaction: the transference is in no way an "interaction," and the historical
filiations in which individuals are inscribed are by no means "learning machines."

From this perspective, the main point is to determine in the
practice of discourse analysis the place and time of interpretation in relation
to description. To say it is not a question of two successive phases, but
rather of an alternation or a pulsation, does not imply that description and
interpretation are condemned to lose themselves in the indescernible. On
the other hand, to say that any description opens onto interpretation is not
necessarily to assume that it opens onto "anything." The description of an
utterance or a sequence necessarily involves (through the detection of empty
syntactical places, ellipses, initiation of negations and interrogation, of various forms of indirect discourse) some "other" discourse as the virtual space
of a reading of the utterance or sequence. And it is this discursive otherness
as virtual presence within the describable materiality of the sequence that
marks from within this materiality the insistence of the other as the law of
social space and historical memory, and thus as the very principle of the

social-historical real, a fact that justifies the use of the term "discipline of interpretation" a propos of disciplines working within this register.

The crucial point is that, within the transferential spaces of identification, constituting a contradictory plurality of historical filiations (through speech, images, stories, discourses, texts, etc.), the "things to be known" coexist with objects about which no one can be sure of "knowing what one is talking about" for the very good reason that these objects inscribed within a filiation are by no means the products of learning—and this happens in the secrecy of the private sphere of the family as well as at the "public" level of institutions and state apparatuses. The phantasm of "royal science" is precisely what comes to deny—at all levels—this equivocity by giving the illusion that one may always know what one is talking about—that is, if you understand what I mean—by denying the act of interpretation at the very moment it occurs.

This point leads to the final question of discursivity as structure or event. From what precedes, one may say that the act that consists in inscribing a given discourse in a series, in incorporating it in a corpus, always risks absorbing the event of this discourse into the structure of the series insofar as this series tends to function as a historical transcendental reading grid or anticipatory memory of the discourse in question. The notion of "discursive formation" borrowed from Foucault has too often drifted toward the ideas of a discursive machine of subjection fitted with an internal semiotic structure and therefore bound to be repetitive. At the limit, this structural conception of discursivity would lead to an obliteration of the event through its absorption in anticipatory overinterpretation.

One should not pretend that any discourse would be a miraculous aerolite, independent of networks of memory and the social trajectories within which it erupts. But the fact that should be stressed here is that a discourse, by its very existence, marks the possibility of a destructuring-restructuring of these networks and trajectories. Any given discourse is the potential sign of a movement within the sociohistorical filiations of identification, inasmuch as it constitutes, at the same time, a result of these filiations and the work (more or less conscious, deliberate, and constructed or not, but all the same traversed by unconscious determination) of displacement within their space: there is no completely "successful" identification; that is, there is no sociohistorical link that is not affected in any way by an "infelicity" in the performative sense of the term—in these circumstances, by a "tragic error" about the other as object of identification. This may even be one of the reasons why such things as societies and history exist instead of merely a chaotic juxtaposition (or a perfect supra-organic integration) of human animals in interaction.

The working position that I evoke here in reference to discourse analysis by no means implies the possibility of some calculation of the displacements of filiation or of the conditions of factual felicity or infelicity. It merely supposes that, through ordered descriptions of discursive constructions, it is possible to detect moments of interpretation as acts that emerge in the form of explicit viewpoints recognized as such; that is, as effects of identifications that are assumed and not denied. Before boundless interpretations in which the interpreter acts as an absolute point, without any other or real, it is for me a matter of ethics and politics: a question of responsibility.

Michel Pêcheux

1   This tradition is represented in a series of publications, in particular in the review *Langages* and the recent collection *Matérialités discursives* (Lille: Presses Universitaires de Lille, 1981).

2   This is in contrast to the classical political chants of the sixties and seventies which were based on a marching rhythm: *Ce n'est / qu'un debut / continuons le / combat!* ("It's just a start, let's keep on fighting!"); or *Nous voulons / nous aurons / sa / tisfaction!* ("We want, we will have satisfaction!).

3   In spite of the cheers, the music, and the fanfare that accompany the action of the players, the direct nonparticipation of the spectators in this action remains the condition of the sports event.

4   It is, above all, a question of political stardom which, voluntarily or not, is determined by the mass-media, electoral bipolarization of parliamentary confrontations: the psychologizing of conflicts through the rhetoric of disputation, suspense, and reconciliation goes hand in hand with the fact that constituencies receive information more rapidly through the television channel than through the hierarchical internal channels of their political or trade union organizations. All of this must be placed within the context of a profound crisis of the Left, of which the crisis of marxism is only one echo. From the "New Philosophy" to the attitude of "it's all over" that appeared in 1978, there emerged a subjective and objective derision of "the political" which opened the way to its carnivalisation: for example, the role of the popular comedian Coluche, who announced his candidacy in the presidential elections of 1981, with the ironic and despairing support of a section of the intelligentsia.
    There were several stages in the evolution of the French High Intelligentsia. Intellectuals in the sixties were engaged in their work in the way that one engages in war (ultimately, a civil war). Gradually, the central metaphor shifted from "political" struggle to that of wrestling with the angel in the solitary space of *écriture*. Today we think in terms of "performance" (most often solo, rarely in a team). To the athletic sense of "performance" is added the connotation of entertainment, of the spectacle. Such an evolution will not improve the rather uneasy relation that a substantial part of the American intelligentsia has traditionally maintained with those "incomprehensible" French intellectual productions, a relation marked by an equivocal oscillation between a reverence for the high priests of the intellect and a fascination with the comedy (deliberate or not) of the clowns of culture.

5   The object of discourse analysis, as it actually developed on the basis described above, is precisely to explain and describe the construction and sociohistorical ordering of constellations of utterances.

6   We may observe here the implicit effect of a paraphrastic translation of "Mitterand elected president" as "We won!" *(On a gagné).* In passing, the "we" is identified with Mitterand.

7   Jacques Mandrin, *Le socialisme et la France* (Paris: Le Sycomore, 1983), p. 19.

8   In the celebration of the birth of the event of May 10, 1981, there was (among other strange gifts) the paradox of the involuntary role of facilitator played by the leadership of the PCF, as if in unleashing a sudden polemic against the Socialist party, the Communist leadership accentuated its own loss of influence (as well as its ability to mobilize), thereby liberating the Left from the hypothesis of a seizure of power dominated by a more or less openly avowed pro-sovietism (a reference to the "positive global balance sheet" of the "actually existing socialism"). What follows is a government of the Left that engages in an audacious politics of deep structural reforms but without the mobilizations that *should* (according to classical marxist politics) support and control the implementation of these reforms—as if the PCF and the CGT had largely lost their historical capacity for mobilization; and as if other organizations and movements of the Left were unable to take over this function. As a result, in France today it is largely the Right that is mobilizing.

9   Mandrin, *Le socialisme et la France,* p. 19.

10   I leave to the side the positions of the Right, amply illustrated in Jean Baudrillard's writings on the "socialist trance." *On a gagné* is interpreted as "We are treating ourselves to the Left" (for a laugh) and then as "We are overcome by the Left" (as by a disease): "it is a monstrous protuberance which expends, which destroys," exactly like the monster in *Alien.* See *In the Shadow of the Silent Majorities* (New York: Semiotext[e], 1983), p. 80.

11   I refer here to the notion of "distance markers," which has been the object of recent research. In particular, cf. Jacqueline Authier, *"Paroles tenues à distance,"* in *Matérialités discursives.* Cf. also Dan Sperber's analysis of the notions of reproduction, description, and interpretation in *Les savoirs des anthropologues* (Paris: Hermann, 1982).

12   The natural sciences grasp the real through the impossible that emerges at the intersection of regulated conceptual writing and technically verified experimental construction. From this point of view, it is trivial to recall that mathematics is also an experimental science whose

constructions are found to be writing itself. The real of the material technologies partially overlaps with the real of the natural sciences insofar as these technologies constitute an indispensable element in experimentation. At the same time, the massive use of technical objects surpasses the real of natural science: the relation to logical disjunction turns away from magical gestures (with their rites, taboos, and prohibitions). Concerning the real of the managerial sciences, which often presents itself as a technical real of a particular type (the "social technologies"), it is fundamentally a prohibition even if it is based, especially in industrialized societies, on the real of the technologies, as well as that of the sciences of nature, finding there the means to manage both the immense register of production and the register of destruction.

13   "The practical law, derived from the motive of happiness, I call pragmatical (rule of prudence)" (Kant, *Critique of Pure Reason*).

14   For work on the art of memory, cf. F. Yates, *The Art of Memory* (London, 1966).

15   Once the barn is set on fire, the conflagration spreads according to the structure of the building and its openings, according to the nature and disposition of the objects and materials that the building contains, to the direction of the wind, and so on, not according to the desire of the arsonist (for revenge, etc.).

16   "To justify" is not the same things as "to produce." Scholasticism did not produce the Inquisition; marxism did not engender the Gulag; neo-positivism did not invent voluntary servitude or the desire for universal scientific domination. But the capacity of such philosophical systems for justification is incontestible.

17   It little matters, in passing, that these knowledges are denied: everyone takes them into account, just as a pedestrian crossing the street takes the cars into account in order to avoid being hit, even if he or she is a professed philosophical idealist!

18   Cf. the discontinuist perspective inaugurated by the work of Alexandre Koyre in opposition to the continuism of Duhem.

19   Jean-Marc Levy-Leblond, *L'esprit de sel* (Paris: Fayard, 1981).

20   This question received an explicitly affirmative response in the framework of "historical structuralism" from Althusser's early work, which posed historical materialism as "the science of history."

21   I am alluding here to a recent article by historian Nicole Loraux, "*Thucydide n'est pas un collègue,*" *Quaderni di storia* 12, 1980, pp. 51-81.

22   This expression takes up the title of a book by D. Lindenberg, *Le marxisme introuvable* (Paris, 1975), which surveys some of the historical avatars of this game of hide-and-seek between the "scientific marxism" of the university and "vulgar marxism" (which produces catechisms for mass consumption). What is called "Anglo-American neo-marxism" is largely, in its present state, an academic phenomenon (linked in large part to the collapse of European political structuralism), that is, a marxism "without organs," except intellectual organs—which is not to say that with the help of the "pragmatic" spirit of Anglo-American culture, this phenomenon will be without repercussions in the cultural, ideological, and political fields, and that it does not hold some surprises for those who are celebrating "the end of marxism!"

23   An expression like "the logic of capital" refers to a real about which there are "things to be known." But is it conceivable to respond with a "yes" or "no" to total questions such as, Is the current French government attacking the logic of capital? or even, Have we in the exact sense of the term "seized power"? See Jacques Mandrin, *Le socialisme et la France*.

24   L. Althusser, *Reading Capital* (London: New Left Books, 1979), p. 16.

25   Cf. Michel de Certeau, *L'invention du quotidien* (Paris: 10/18, UGE, 1980).

26   For more on current developments in discourse analysis in France, see the review *Mots* (4:6) and the collection *Matérialités discoursives* (in particular, J. J. Courtine and J.-M. Maradin, "*Quel objet pour l'analyse de discours,*" and A. Lecomte, "*La frontiere absente*").

27   Jean-Claude Milner, *Ordre et raisons de langue* (Paris: Seuil, 1983), p. 336.

28   Cf. earlier remarks concerning the possible associable referents of the statement *On a gagné*. We might develop similar remarks about such expressions as "the will of the people," "freedom" (of thought or of the market), "austerity" versus "rigor," and so on.

29   This problem constitutes one of the weak points of the Althusserian reflection on the ideological state apparatus, as well as of the initial applications of this reflection in the domain of discourse analysis in France.

30   A hatred of the ordinary gives rise to an anti-intellectual cult of this same ordinary: a certain esoteric structuralism nourished the hatred of philosophy expressed, for example, in the sociology of Pierre Bourdieu.

Hugo Achugar

The Book of Poems as a Social Act: Notes toward an Interpretation of Contemporary Hispanic American Poetry

Translated by George Yúdice and María Díaz de Achugar

Both as a physical object and as a discursive project, a book of poems is intricately articulated to the social and historical conditions of its production. Yet, at certain moments in history, a book of poems can also destabilize the hegemonic discourses of its time.

The present essay has several goals. First, it offers a theoretical position and some critical-analytic tools that together provide for a more adequate approach to the social dimensions of contemporary poetic discourse in Hispanic America. The aim here is to credit the social constitution and power of this poetry while avoiding a reductive method that merely paraphrases poetic content. Second, it offers a general description of what can be called the "enlightened" or "learned" system of Hispanic American poetry after the fifties, as well as of the mediations through which this system operates on the social meaning of the book of poems.[1] While the connection between the two parts of this essay is not necessarily organic, I hope that each part will complement and clarify the other.

Poetry has not yet received much attention from those who study the relations between literature and society in Hispanic America. Moreover, both critically and theoretically the question of poetic production has been set, almost without exception, at the level of the individual poem, without taking into account its articulation within the book of poems. Limited to content paraphrases of individual poems, criticism has ignored the political force of the book itself as a meaningful unit. Consequently, criticism has been unable either to describe or analyze the social meaning of poetry.[2]

I should point out that I am concerned only with the consciously articulated book of poems that, at least in Hispanic America, was rarely produced as such before the nineteenth century. Although this has not yet been proven, it is worth hypothesizing that its emergence is linked to the developing capitalist market. The book of poems distinguishes itself from the mere gathering together of individual poems into a book. Moreover, it breaks with the closed world in which author and readers were members of a limited, named circle. The *Academia Antártica,* articulated among the many coteries and in the court or palace of colonial Peru at the beginning of the seventeenth century, is a good example of an earlier form of poetic communication; there, the "happy few" ruled a largely illiterate population.[3] The book of poems of modernity, by contrast, imagines its reader as an anonymous human being who must be seduced, conquered, and convinced. It even takes for granted the existence of a system shaped by other books of poems also searching for a place in the market. But this mercantile metaphor does not imply a reduction to problems of distribution and consumption; on the contrary, it points to the dynamics of a society in which the book of poems aims to persuade, seduce, or indoctrinate.

As an ideological form, the book of poems is marked in its very discourse by the process and the conditions of production. Thus, these do not operate as simple external forces acting on a book of poetry. The analysis of the relation between poetry and society must presuppose that all elements of the book of poems are ideologically and aesthetically pertinent at more than simply the level of content.

The textual totality of the book of poems is comprised not only of the poems themselves, as has been traditionally maintained, but also of those elements—such as title, epigraph, date, place of publication, visual design and choice of typography, illustrations, and printer's mark—that literary hermeneutics has typically ignored or despised. For instance, the first edition of *España, aparta de mí este cáliz*, illustrated by Pablo Picasso's drawings, was done—as its cover states—by "soldiers of the republic [who] manufactured its paper, composed the text and operated the machines" for "literary editions of the Commisariat, Army of the East," during the "Independence War in the Year of 1939." The historical enunciating situation, or *situation d'énonciation*, verbalized on the cover is an important element in our understanding of a book's meaning.[4] Rather than emphasize its publication as an artistic event, marked by the presence of Picasso's illustrations, the text on the cover foregrounds the book as an attempt to continue "the political war by other means," by opposing other poetic formalizations. This struggle or dialogue between formalizations is a fundamental part of the scene of aesthetic and ideological enunciation that determines the social meaning of the book of poems.

At this point, two different approaches must be distinguished. One position would lead us to think that we can reconstruct the process and the conditions of production of poetic discourse simply with the support of internal textual elements. In other words, internal evidence is sufficient to establish the social and historical situation within which and out of which the book of poems is uttered. By comparison, my own approach—in addition to attempting to avoid the reductive emphasis on content that overlooks the semantic function of the totality of elements constitutive of the book of poems—considers verbal and social contexts external to the book itself. Thus, when Pablo Neruda's *Canto general* is issued in Mexico in 1950, it becomes part of an enunciating situation set in motion the year before with Octavio Paz's *Libertad bajo palabra,* a situation in turn shaped by Neruda's own *Residencia en la tierra,* by Gorostiza's exquisite *Poesie pure,* by Jorge Guillen's writings, and by the black poetry of Nicolas Guillen. The book of poems, in short, enters an enunciating and reading situation that cannot be understood exclusively in terms of its internal poetic specificity. Moreover, within both modernity and contemporaneity, neither authors (nor, in effect, their books) are themselves necessarily naive about their social relations, though books enact those relations whether their authors wish them to or not.

Hugo Achugar

The first edition of *España, aparta de mí este cáliz*, published by the soldiers of the republic, is an example that history seems to have tailor-made for us. In this case, reading the book independently of its editorial presentation implies silencing the aesthetic and ideological project that it performs. As we accumulate a whole critical tradition of such silences, we end by silencing the entire history of efforts to shape the impact of books and the corollary effort to influence future practices. Of course, especially in examples less obvious than Vallejo's book of poems, there is a risk of overemphasizing the material presentation of poetic discourse. Nevertheless, to ignore these elements is to continue a critical tradition that fails to recognize the way modern poetry communicates and consequently blurs distinctions between modernity and the past.

At the time of its appearance, *España, aparta de mí este cáliz* was immediately inserted into a marginal system of circulation and, more important, an articulated poetic system of aesthetic and ideological conventions and propositions that located it in social life. Thus the book was separated from the "destiny" dreamed for it by its author. The cover and printer's marks function as elements marked by the sociohistorical process and conditions of production. They are at once tied to the ideological and aesthetic project of the book of poems and socially articulated to its time. These marks—eloquent even in their infelicity—are part of the formalization of an explicit project, but they could also correspond to an *implied* project in conflict with the intentions of the real author. This makes it particularly risky to limit an analysis to overt thematic content (which may more closely match an author's intentions), as we may see later when we consider Roque Dalton's book of poems.

The book of poems is a unity whose motive is indivisibly articulated with social processes. It has a syntax that draws together poems, epigraph, dedications, and so on, overdetermining and sometimes resemanticizing them. Thus it proposes a particular reading of the *whole,* and the isolated poem should be read in such a way that its integration into the whole of the book changes its meaning. This syntax, violated each time we read the book at random, disregarding the proposed organization, is a formalization of voice. This basic speaker's voice[5] is shaped for this syntax and is informed by an aesthetic-ideological perspective. We can consider both the syntax and the perspective as the products of a process by which a textually made and executed choice points to its own existence.[6] The canonic version of this syntax would be the linear movement—from left to right—that confers a fundamental meaning on the order of the poems. By visualizing the dialogic structure constituting the poetry book, we can, at least in part, describe its formalized project.[7] The description of the book's syntax is, in a way, the description of a perspective on and within the sociohistorical process.[8] The choices implied in the book's syntax presuppose its articulation to an enunciating situation constituted by a dynamic of other perspectives. It is this dynamic that poetically formalizes the sociohistorical process.

Inserting the book of poems into an ideological cultural system makes visible its existence as a social act. Precisely as a social act, the book of poems constitutes a response and a proposition vis-à-vis the *enunciating situation* in which it is developed. The meaning of the book of poems is fully realized in the totality configured by the system of answers and propositions uttered at precise historical stages of the development of a society where the author and reader are unknown to one another. This totality mediates the relation between the book of poems and society. Thus the book of poems, because it is in a dialogic relation with other books of poems or even groups of books of poems, becomes an element of what we call a *poetic system*. In this system, the book of poems works as a social act—both a critique of the social and a proposal for a different universe. The book of poems is an utterance that constitutes a social act; the utterance itself is a social act.

The book of poems is a fact, finished in itself, which simultaneously refers to the entire social and historical process.[9] The ideological universe proposed can be seen as a *representation* or complex *imago* of the sociohistorical processes in which the enunciation of the book of poems is produced. This poetic formalization of a cultural and ideological universe is implicitly a reevaluation of a system of values and representations, whether dominant or potential. This interaction of present and absent elements suggests a way of constituting the symbolic character of poetic discourse as a *nonabsolute totality*. The book's reference to the extratextual universe is partially processed by the universe it shapes. This does not imply that its actual constitution as a partial, selective, and thus nonabsolute totality forbids it from being ideologically uttered or presented as *the* whole.

These social effects function independently of the will of the real author, and, for that reason, they are necessarily involved in relations with the rest of the signs uttered by a society. This does not depend on the receiver being conscious of the process. Indeed, the presence of the poetic system is usually perceived in a very confused way in everyday life. This allows us to understand, for instance, the inclination to portray the literary world as merely an indecisive and indefinite movement within the historical development of a society, for it confuses the world of perception with reality itself.

The necessary relationship between the artistic sign and other similar signs in force at the moment of its publication forms the poetic system. Such a system implies a critical structuration of the relationship between books, permitting them to acquire a particular meaning or value because of their situation at a definite moment in literary production. The poetic system is, of course, nothing but an abstraction resulting from synchronic consideration of a historical process, and its transformation is never independent of the total process of social production. Yet each poetic system acts out its particular perspective on literary value and also presupposes its own notion of what is literary.

The coherence of a book of poems is often not absolute, and the heterogeneity of projects supporting a particular performance is related to the presence of implicit projects that may be in conflict with both the explicit project and the textual formalization. It is in the dialogic situation of the poetic system that this heterogeneity is resolved through struggles that silence particular characteristics of discourse.

The description of a book (or group of books) of poems related to a precise poetic system can only be valid if the total system of artistic production in which it is performed is taken into account. Two prefatory remarks need to be made. First, I assume, even though I will not carry it

654

out, that the description of a poetic system presupposes the description of the syntax of the book of poems and its aesthetic and ideological characterization. Second, my concern is with the "learned" poetic system. I am thus ignoring the popular poetic system and its relations with the former.[10]

The learned Hispanic American poetry that emerged at the beginning of the fifties can be understood as a poetic system constituted by two basic and rather different trends: first, the universalist claims of the avant-garde, which minimize the natural and the regional, and, second, a poetic system that centers its discourse in a local reality underwritten by history, whether national, continental, or racial. Both systems were already present at the end of the nineteenth century and continued to hold sway until the beginnings of "contemporaneity": Pablo Neruda's *Canto general* is from 1950 and Octavio Paz's *Libertad bajo palabra* from 1949. In the following decades the picture does not seem to have varied substantially, although it appears that Hispanic American poetry has become almost schizophrenically polarized: the enumerating delirium of *Canto general* does not shy away from the accidents of geographic, urban, social, and political reality. By contrast, Paz's questions regarding manhood, the earth, and everyday life are based on a referential austerity within which sensual observation designates a culturally interchangeable space operating in every nook and cranny of both the dream and waking states.

Even though all attempts to organize a diverse literary production risk oversimplification, I believe these broad trends provide a valid model for understanding contemporary Hispanic American poetry. The ideological formalization of these projects can be briefly characterized as follows:

1. Books of poems within the universalizing trend typically show (a) playful language and the decisive presence of metaphor; (b) an ahistoric introspection into the anguish generated by urban modernity and the sudden attack of technology; (c) the assumption that the quotidian reveals dimensions of permanent essence; and (d) the use of irony as a reflection on language. All these characteristics maintain the hegemony of the definition of the "poetic" that survives from the preceding period.

2. By contrast, the emerging trend in this struggle for hegemony proposes (a) the "novelization" of lyric discourse; (b) the socialization of those experiences that produce solidarity with local or world liberatory struggles; (c) a tendency toward the linguistic quotidian (i.e., colloquialism) and to everyday experience without projecting their transcendence; and (d) the use of irony to demystify elements of the prestigious-poetic, the historic-canonic, and the devalued-sentimental.

There are those, mechanically following Hugo Friedrich, who argue that it is the first of these trends that embodies modernity: "the dissonant tension" is its touchstone. It is tempting to see this as the hegemonic position that battled for a historic avant-garde during the twenties. In that sense, as E. Sanguinetti has suggested, "every artistic product, sooner or later, will find its precise museum" or its precise canonization.[11] Thus, the historic avant-garde of the twenties, in its universalizing trend, functions as the canonic form of learned poetry from the forties on. Furthermore, we might point to the importance and power held by groups and magazines such as *Sur* and *Poesía Buenos Aires* in Argentina, *Vuelta* in Mexico, *Sardio* in Venezuela, and *Orígenes* in Cuba, as well as the larger number of studies, articles, and Ph.D. theses that consolidated the hegemonic position of this kind of poetry in Europe and the United States. This description of the learned poetic system presupposes that the universalizing trend is canonic, at least for the Garden of Academus, while the second trend represents the opposition or heterodoxy.

If we think of the whole poetic production of a society, however, we must distinguish not only the canonic and the heterodox but the official as well. Of course, literary production, and poetic production as part of it, constitute only one of several kinds of production. They do not exclude class considerations. Thus, the same notions of canon and heterodoxy can be related ideologically and socially. We shall have as many canons and heterodoxies as there are class-conscious social groups acting in the historical process. (In this way, handbooks, anthologies, and histories of literature operate as canons defining, for a determining class or class fraction, the valid aesthetic-ideological system.)

This offical canon, as Alaistair Fowler points out, "is institutionalized through education, maecenas and journalism" and, it might be added, through the publishing industry as well as other ideological state apparatuses.[12] In the total authoritarianism of extreme dictatorship, or the hardest moments of Pinochetism, ideological coherence becomes absolute in the aesthetic realm as well. If there are opposed or underground norms—Marta Traba speaks of a "cultural resistance"—the hegemony of the ruling norm is the only one that can circulate publicly and officially within society.[13] Yet at certain historical moments the multiplication of proposed norms and canons is a verifiable fact. Then it becomes evident that literary production is not entirely fixed by a social class and that power is shared, or at least disputed. These canons or norms acquire their value, to some extent, by virtue of their placement and configuration but mainly because of the absence of alternatives. Anthologies "ignoring" certain authors or the production of a particular sector of society (e.g., songs or the mislabeled "social" or "protest" poetry) make "evident" a canon in agreement with Friedrich's ideal or, in its Hispanic American version, with the canon of modernity proposed by Octavio Paz and Guillermo Sucre. We must, then, speak of a poetic system in someone's interest.

This poetic system does not correspond to the total literary production nor to what has been called the *potential canon* as "the literary canon, which in a wide sense comprehends the entire corpus of what has been written, together with the surviving oral literature."[14] In fact, it has nothing to do with the potential canon but with the accessible canon, because it is difficult, if not impossible, to have access to material controlled by the Hispanic American ruling class. The distinction between the potential and the accessible canons points to a problem of particular relevance in the study of poetic production, that of perishable or discarded or nonofficial material: the lack of institutionalized critical editions of marginal works and their very reduced circulation are perpetuated by those who build the canon. For instance, to what extent can we read the anarchist or socialist poetry of the last century in Latin America? We are not talking about the production, accepted willingly or unwillingly, by the ruling class, but of the invisibility of books the literary historian and anthologist have discarded because they were not considered literature or belles lettres; that is, they were discarded because the aesthetic-ideological horizon of the hegemonic system of values made their inclusion impossible.

Hugo Achugar

The recent edition of a *Plaquette—Poemas de la cárcel*—is really exceptional in this regard. Issued by the Convención Nacional de Trabajadores, C.N.T. (in exile) from Uruguay, it evidently does not exist for the anthologists, critics, and historians, whether official or canonical, whether from Uruguay or the rest of the continent. The problem is not merely political; it implies an aesthetic and ideological choice most often couched in the euphemistic "bad faith" of the slogan "This is not poetry." So it seems that in the Hispanic American case through the end of the fifties, the poetic production that engaged its social milieu represented the learned opposition to the canonic or universalizing tendency. Yet its development brought a growing inclusion of heterodox materials traditionally marginalized. Here it is worthwhile to compare the anthology *Poesía en movimiento* (1966), sponsored by Octavio Paz, and the later *Omnibus de poesía Mexicana* (1971) by Gabriel Zaid. We observe, in this case for a single country, Mexico, how the aesthetic-ideological hegemony operates by proposing what poetry is and can be.

The system of learned poetry changed in the sixties and an alternative to the hegemonic system emerged. It aimed to share power by transforming the conditions of book production and distribution in Hispanic America. Prior to this, poetry that engaged both its social context and the poetics of naming history represented the opposition; while it included such relevant personalities as Neruda, it was an opposition poetry nonetheless. It was during the fifties and especially after the Cuban Revolution that such poetic projects developed—the Pan Duro group in Argentina (including Juan Gelman), the *antipoesía* of Nicanor Parra, the *exteriorismo* of Coronel Urtecho and Ernesto Cardenal, and the poetry of Fernández Retamar, Benedetti, and A. Cisneros. The ascendance of this trend was proportional to the revolutionary process in Cuba and, later, Nicaragua.

In the last three decades the enunciating situation has changed so that both trends function as hegemonic, if we think in terms of the continent and of the relation between the ruling social and cultural forces in different countries. In fact, what has happened is a qualitative transformation operating on the pragmatic level of the publishing industry. This is, nonetheless, only a variation in the correlation of forces that bestow power in the cultural field.

Before World War II the Hispanic American publishing industry had three centers: one, based in the Iberian Peninsula, made the Civil War into a recognized landmark; another was divided between Mexico and Buenos Aires;[15] and one was in Santiago. The printing of books of poems, leaving aside political sponsorship and vanity press publication, was supported, at the continental level, by a few publishing houses and magazines[16] which assumed the function of readers and selectors of Hispanic American poetic discourse. The aesthetic and ideological filters of these publishers and magazines defined, in part, which poetic trends were granted value. Sometimes small areas conceded to poetry became hegemonic, thanks to the publishing industry. During the period between the wars and up to the forties, the publication, centered in Spain, of the work of the republican Spanish publishers in Hispanic America was concentrated in Buenos Aires and Mexico. In this period the Argentinian publishers had an undeniable preponderance, with 50 percent of the Hispanic American market.[17]

This particular Hispanic-Argentinian-Mexican predominance, as well as the relocation of Spanish republicans in Hispanic America, suggests publishers' support for a certain poetry, which ranged from Girondo to Neruda.[18] (That is, from a poetic affiliated to the Hispanic American avant-garde or the Peninsular Generation of 1927 to the explicit "social" expressions at the other end of the spectrum.) In any case, the broad popular front of the forties had its expression within an aesthetic-ideological pluralism within the poetic system.[19] This did not, however, entail a critique of the hegemonic power of a certain poetic trend.

After the fifties and the consolidation of the Cuban Revolution, the picture shifted substantially: the creation of Casa de las Americas in La Habana, with its literary prizes, and the proliferation of new magazines and publishers.[20] This was also the period in which already existing means for the publication of poetry that engaged its sociohistorical context reached its apogee. These new formations functioned to bestow prestige and to dispute the hegemony of the former trend. The literature provoked by the Cuban Revolution on a global level reinforces what was said before: more anthologies and translations of the so-called revolutionary poetry were being published by publishing houses and magazines that belonged to the traditional centers of power. It is also true that, since the beginning of the seventies, this set of phenomena has not maintained the strength it showed in the sixties.

Nevertheless, changes in the enunciating situation around the end of the fifties transformed the way in which books of poems have been inscribed in the Hispanic American learned poetic system. It even altered the meaning of several books of poetry whose public reception began then. In Neruda's *Odas elementales* (1954), for instance, his earlier poetics, necessary to *Residencias en la tierra,* is exchanged for an explicit, socially oriented, didactic project. Indeed, the poetic system can impose *its* polarizations and thereby silence the heterogeneity of particular books. In José Emilio Pacheco's *No me preguntes como pasa el tiempo* (1967), conflicting ideological aesthetic projects allow either a strong or a weak political reading, depending on which elements are foregrounded.

Roque Dalton's *Las historias prohibidas del Pulgarcito* (1975) offers a rather different case. Its inclusion of historical texts and references prevents us from pretending that poetry is exclusively self-referential. Dalton's book of poems—as well as those by Pachecos, Gelman, Fernández Retamar, Cardenal, and others—struggles against a system of values that limits poetry to a linguistic adventure with no historical function beyond the development of the imagination. A somewhat more detailed consideration of Dalton's book of poems and its syntax will illustrate my argument.

The *historias prohibidas* are both histories and stories and thus play with the relation of literature and society. Dalton's book attempts to shape a history of El Salvador that might work as an alternative to the official history of the country. To accomplish this, the book is organized as a collage that mixes up history and fiction. Indeed, the historicity of the discourse does not emerge only from the historical texts or from texts whose narrativity contributes to the development of the book, since the book gathers indigenous songs, lists of names, proverbs, and other similar texts, where the narrative function is minimal or absent. The historicity of the discourse emerges from the overall syntax of the book, which has numerous elements.

For example, the book of poems has a historical order: it starts with the Spanish conquest and arrives at the 1969 war against Honduras. On another level, the numbering in *Antología de poetas Salvadorenos,* worked into the text, establishes an implicitly temporal sequence. More broadly, the book evokes many different aspects of culture and life and inserts them into the historical and social development of El Salvador.

History in *Las historias prohibidas del Pulgarcito* is obviously a thematic element. But it also exists in the form of what the book proposes as a new history of discourse. By the end of the book, we have participated in a certain epic dramatization of poetic discourse itself. The reader integrates the book—whether encountering a poem, proverb, popular song or *bomba,* essay, elegy, song, story, dialogue, or letter—into a whole, blurring by this its fragmentary nature and including each element in a sequence that then becomes a plot and a story, one that dramatizes the transformation of discourses into a critical totality. The reader who, after the first text—where a fragmentary version of the sixteenth-century Spanish conquest is counterpointed against a report from the current (1983) major-general of El Salvador—reads the proverb "Ideas want war," discovers a relation that is both ideological and aesthetic. In pointing to the ideological nature of the preceding texts and their function in masking reality (as well as in justifying repressive action), the proverb carries the contrast to other levels: popular knowledge versus authoritarian rhetoric; the transparency of popular discourse versus the masking opacity of authoritarian discourse. This relationship becomes even more apparent when one continues reading and comes upon the third text—a fragment from 1576—that purports to describe Salvadorean nature and the evil depths of the earth!

Discourse in this book of poems is dramatized from a class perspective, that of class struggle. Indeed, the book of poems assumes that discourse from the Salvadorean ruling class also implies a linguistic and poetic domination. For that very reason the book performs a polyphonic desacralization and linguistic disassembling of the hegemonic discourse. In the best subversive tradition, a number of different verbal elements are juxtaposed: humor, celebrations of the linguistically dominated stratum, narrativity, variations in syntax, and colloquial diction in many of the poems. This collage effect—when confronted intertextually by fragments from the dominant or hegemonic discourse—creates a critical cacophony of voices. These voices are themselves a material part of the class struggle within Salvadorean society.

The deconstructive effects of this polyphony, sometimes sardonic, help to explain the very mixed tone of the book. For example the speaker in the *Bibliografía,* which closes the book, after mentioning a list of books and authors, writes: "Aside from the texts and original poems, three other texts have been modified in order to achieve the effects intended by the author; and two texts, which apparently have been taken from other publications, are apocryphal; they, too, were originally written by the author. It is up to the readers to find them" (p. 232). Playfully, the book states, at a certain level, that the author is not responsible for his work, that he is not an individual but a collective author. Thus the ironic tone does not serve to minimize the book's scope. On the contrary, it constitutes a curious counterpoint to the sometimes tragic history the book narrates. The mixed character of the book's project is, in fact, implied in the surrealist politics

659

of the epigraph by Gabriela Mistral: "El Salvador, Tom Thumb of America...." From the first poem, *"Guerra de guerrillas en El Salvador (Contrapunto)"* (Guerrilla warfare in El Salvador [Counterpoint]), to the last, *"Ya te aviso ..."* ("I'll keep you posted ..."), the book in fact relates a history of El Salvador, though one whose chronology is partly unconventional.

The book's ironic questioning of hegemonic discourse includes a rejection of the dominiant class's notion of poetry. *"Poemita con foto simbólica, dedicado al núcleo de la clase interna lacayo-dominante, que incluye una apreciacíon nada personal sobre lo que cabe esperar de su amo, a juzgar por los vientos que soplan"* ("Little poem with symbolic photo, dedicated to the internal servant-ruling class, that includes as per the veering winds, a not at all personal appreciation about what is expected from its master") is a good example:

Oh	*Oh*
ligarchy	*ligarquía*
step	*ma*
mother	*drasta*
with a murderer husband	*con marido asesino*
dressed in cotton	*vestida de piqué*
as a vulturess	*como una buitra*
lying in wait on the branches	*acechante in las ramas*
of the tangle of History	*del enredo en la Historia*
ridiculous like everything evil	*ridícula como todo lo malo*
we must do away with the fat lady	*hay que acabar contigo gorda*

The exclamatory "Oh," extracted from "oligarchy," satirizes not only the ruling class but also a kind of poetic discourse inherent to that class. Furthermore, it satirizes the image of poetry as a sentimental, self-expressive, and individualistic expression of a spiritual vision of the world. The fact that the poem is placed between a text evoking the 1932 slaughter and "Two portraits of the fatherland" means that its grotesque nature is not a fictional product; it arises from bringing together what is real and unreal. The class struggle within the society is also the poetic, linguistic, and ideological struggle in the book of poems. *Las historias prohibidas del Pulgarcito*, as a book of poems, appears within a discursive situation constituted by two levels—one, the most obvious political, social, and economic conditions of El Salvador and of Central America generally, and, two, the situation of Latin American poetic discourse since the 1950s; both help construct the social meaning of the book of poems.

Despite the eventual evidence of *Las historias prohibidas del Pulgarcito*, it would be possible to try to explain the changes that began to take place in the learned poetic system during the fifties as an autonomous literary evolution, one that, when considered autonomously, seems to have led to a certain chaotic diversity.[21] This chaos, in fact, emerged out of a new reality: the social subject as the wielder of the enunciating power of poetry was not unique in its dispersion. Yet the book of poems, despite its social utterance by aesthetically and ideologically differentiated and polarized subjects, is nonetheless located within the hegemony of enunciation. Thus, the conflict between the two ideological projects in contemporary Hispanic

American poetry reinserts itself into the aesthetic hegemony. This joint social enunciation of projects, in either its explicit or implicit versions, in the last three decades has provoked a resemanticization of books of poems. Consequently, the aesthetic-ideological norm to which it responds (and which is proposed to the Hispanic American reader) acquires a rigidity and coherence more orthodox than what seems to occur in isolated books.

The contemporary Hispanic American book of poems seduces, convinces, indoctrinates, and conquers anonymous readers through an articulation of the poetic system that does not always succeed in foregrounding the peculiarities of heterogeneous discourses. In this sense, the book of poems does not succeed in escaping the sociohistorical enunciating situation. Yet this failure reveals it to be a social act within the real (i.e., not symbolic) struggle for what Marti has called "Nuestra America."

Notes

1   I use "book of poems" as a translation for the Spanish word *poemario*, which emphasizes the notion of wholeness.

2   I could also mention other than Hispanic American authors who have written on poetic production, such as Heidegger, Pfeiffer, Cohen, Della Volpe, Thompson, Adorno, Friedrich, Riffaterre, and Easthope. These authors and the Spanish Americans Reyes and Portuondo speak at two levels: (1) considering the *poem* as a self-sufficient or independent entity, and (2) at the level of the general poetic discourse (i.e., a precise poet's complete work or the poetic language), as different from the colloquial, narrative, or scientific language.

3   See Raquel Chang Rodriguez, "Epístola inédita de Pedro Carvajal, poeta de la Academia Antártica," *Revista de crítica literaria Latinoamericana*, 3 (1976).

4   The term is from Volosinov's *Il linguaggio come pratica sociale* (Bari: Dedali Libri, 1980), in which he uses the notion of *situazione di enonziazione*. For a more complete discussion of the notion of "situation," see Claude Germain, *The Concept of Situation in Linguistics* (Ottawa: University of Ottawa Press, 1979).

5   I have used the term "basic speaker" *(hablante básico)* before, in *Ideologías y estructuras narrativas en José Donoso: 1950-70* (Caracas: Celarg, 1979). At that time, I referred to Booth's "implied author" and to similar notions proposed by Jan Mukarovsky and Miroslav Cervenka. In Latin America the same notion has been used by Antonio Cornejo Polar, Nelson Osorio, and lately by Javier Lasarte, who has proposed the use of "basic enunciator" *(enunciador básico).*

6   It could also be said, considering the heterogeneity of a discourse or its polyphony, that the book of poems offers a multiplicity of not always coincidental perspectives.

7   Even the chronological organization, apparently innocent and naive, of the book of poems is a special case of syntax and never its denial. In the event of *poesia permutante* (permutating poetry), which Cortazar includes in *Ultimo round*, we might talk about a heterodox syntax. Its own condition of "violation of pattern" syntax allows us to discover a peculiar syntactic project. See *Ultimo round* (Mexico: Siglo XXI, 1972), pp. 272-73.

8   It is this syntactic order, for instance, that bestows a special significance on the introductory poem or group of poems and becomes a sort of "reading art." Whether its function is to train the reader or to design a particular cultural-ideological unit, this syntactic order will function within the book of poems as the "rule" to be developed or deconstructed. In this view we could even talk about "catalytic poems," borrowing Barthes's terminology, perhaps drawing attention to the function of the final poem or group of poems, which often provide a syntactic closure to the book of poems.

9   See Umberto Eco, *Trattato generale di semiotica* (Milano: Bompiani, 1975); Thomas Lewis, "Notes toward a Theory of Literary Referent," *PMLA*, 94:3 (1979), pp. 459-75.

10   Although it is not explicitly described, this work does take into account the characteristics of a popular poetic system (e.g., songs, children's literature, rural traditions, and workers' poems) where it proposes notions of poetry effective within the social totality of the enunciating situation in which the learned system makes itself.

11   Cf. Edoardo Sanguinetti, *Vanguardia, ideología y lenguaje* (Caracas: Monte Avila, 1969), p. 13.

661

12   Alaistair Fowler, "Genre and the Literary Canon," *NLH*, 11:1 (1979), p. 98.

13   Marta Traba, "La cultura de la Resistencia," *Literatura y praxis en América Latina* (Caracas: Monte Avila, 1974).

14   Fowler, p. 98.

15   This situation was not free from the particular developments of the productive apparatuses of the nations as well as of their national literatures.

16   One could mention *Atlántida, Claridad, Revista de Occidente, Porrúa, Espasa Calpe, Sur, Emecé, Zig-Zag, Tor, Nascimento y Ercilla. Losada* deserves to be pointed out as particularly open-minded, in both ideological and aesthetic terms.

17   The statistical data place the hegemonic period of the Argentinian publishing houses in the forties. During 1950, 50 percent of the Latin American market was supported by Argentina, a status that would drastically change by 1972 "when its participation becomes 15%." See *Argentina, Brasil, México* (Bogota: Cerlal—UNESCO, 1980), pp. 7-8.

18   The importance of the publishing work in this period becomes evident in the fact that publishers held conferences in 1946 (Santiago, Chile), 1948 (Buenos Aires), and 1964 (Mexico) to create cohesion and organization in support of the "principle of copyright of books in the Spanish language for countries that speak that language" (*Argentina, Brasil, México*, p. 35). While this was an anti-imperialist defense, it was brought about by a kind of Hispanic "Monroe doctrine" of culture that eliminated transnational competition. Competition remained relative since some of the major publishers, such as Espasa-Calpe, had parent companies in Madrid, Buenos Aires, and Mexico.

19   The surrealist axis, Buenos Aires-Mexico-Santiago, also had its part, though less important.

20   I could also mention Arca, La Rosa Blindada, Galerna, Joaquín Mortiz, Techo de la Ballena, and *Marcha* from Montevideo.

21   Santiago Luppoli asserts that "the systematic study of the current poets becomes more difficult every time, since the logical task—ranging them according to their stylistic, ideological, and renewal patterns—is almost unapproachable." See *Handbook of Latin American Studies: Humanities*, no. 36 (Gainsville: University of Florida Press, 1974), p. 411.

Darko Suvin

Can People Be (Re)Presented in Fiction?: Toward a Theory of Narrative Agents and a Materialist Critique beyond Technocracy or Reductionism

People—in the bourgeois individualist sense—cannot be represented in fiction. They become, on the one hand, exempla and, on the other, shifting nodes of narration. Nonetheless, pertinent and crucial relationships among people can be represented, allowing the reader to rearticulate human relationships to the world of people and things.

I believe that fiction is differentiated from other types of social discourse (journalism, scientific texts, philosophy, etc.) by the presence of two necessary and sufficient formal factors: *narrative space/time* (so far best analyzed by Bakhtin's chronotope), which is a transposition and reelaboration of preceding—largely extraliterary—concepts of space and/or time; and *narrative agents,* which are a reelaboration and transposition of—largely extraliterary—concepts about people. These two factors are perhaps two faces of the same coin; they are certainly, to a great degree, consubstantial. For a first approach to an already very complicated matter, I shall in this essay reluctantly but entirely forget about the chronotope and concentrate on agents as fictional simulacra of people.[1]

The Lay of the Land: the Political Stakes

1.1

Before getting into the inevitably somewhat specialized arguments, I want to discuss their intertext, which I suggest in my title by way of the possibilities lurking within both "people" and "(re)present." This intertext, or practical context, is situated at the interface between fictional and other ways of viewing, interpreting, and constructing reality.

1.2

"People" *(gens, Leute)* means, of course, something like women plus men plus children; it does not denote THE people *(le peuple, das Volk)*. This essay will focus on the *images of people* rather than on the *interests of the people* that can be found (re)presented in fiction. Nonetheless, these overlapping connotations are an important signal, for the way people are presented in literature will intimately codetermine what interests that literature might re-present. The stakes, therefore, are very high—both for Marxian critics dealing with culture and for the fate of fiction itself. This subject is a privileged way of entering into and indicating an answer to these radical democratic and socialist questions: Is fiction more than opium for (the) people? Is it also—as this usually truncated text of Marx continues—the heart of a heartless world? Is fiction only ideology or also Utopia and/or cognition? Is there, then, a cognitive (and thus politically usable and ethically justifiable) reason for a radical critic to investigate fiction—be it Shakespeare or "Dallas," Homer or science fiction, Proust or Piercy, comic strips or Brecht—especially when that will involve a halfway conscientious critic in the indispensable mediations of the meta-meta-discourses of modern criticism, thus leaving less time for more direct radical action?

Many radicals throughout the years have come, with reluctance or enthusiasm, to share with pragmatists and philistines the conclusion that there is NO such reason, that a radical cultural critic is an oxymoron of the order of fiery ice or planned disorder. Nikolai Chernyshevsky, the leader of Russian revolutionary populism, said somewhere (the image was to recur in the Soviet debates) that sausages came before Shakespeare. From a vulgar materialist (bourgeois as well as "socialist") point of view, this is undeniable: people cannot exist without eating; they can exist without fiction.

Yet, can they? In the depths of the 1930s depression, did not Hollywood thrive on perverting the pennies of millions of jobless people into profits from soap-opera movies? Does not every halfway intelligent regime in economic-political difficulties buttress itself through the most popular forms of fiction at the same time (if not before) it tries political solutions? The genres vary: in Elizabethan times it was theater, street ballads, or preachings (even technically speaking these are largely fictional); in the nineteenth century, popular novels; today, TV. The orientation remains constant. The biblical author had better food imagery than Chernyshevsky: not by bread alone but also by fictional images—which explain why bread is or is not there, why pie in the sky will come by and by—liveth man and woman.

Thus, to continue with examples from revolutionary leaders, it was not only Che Guevara who might have thought that machine guns were more important than speeches, nor only Mao Tse-tung that working in peoples' actions (in the sense that a sculptor works in marble) was more important than working in poems. Many pragmatists with less flair for insurrection or liberating politics take such an attitude unthinkingly. Let me call this operative attitude (or gesture, in Brecht's sense of *Gestus*) by the name of, arguably, the greatest nineteenth-century poet, also a Communard, who very early on abandoned poem writing for gunrunning: it is the *Rimbaud Syndrome*. I do not maintain that Che or Mao took the wrong decisions *for themselves*—that would be ignorant and presumptuous. But I do maintain that when the Rimbaud Syndrome is adopted as a norm imposed on all possible future Rimbauds, it is pernicious. All of us who have worked within movements aspiring to radical democracy and economic justice, including movements claiming Marxist ascendancies, remember well how our eccentric involvement with not immediately operative sign systems—in particular with fiction—met in general with two responses: either with hostility, or, in the case of our most well meaning and shrewd comrades outside the cultural (wordsmithing, picture making, and similar) trades, with the pitying smile of forbearance for childish pursuits. (Indeed, I seem to detect some echoes of the Rimbaud Syndrome in this conference, where according to my count one can find one and one-third session out of thirteen, or 10 percent, devoted to fictional communication.)

Darko Suvin

Yet *kulturshchiks* (the Russian term from such debates) have a good deal of historical irony to fall back upon. Thus, Chernyshevsky's main positive influence was not in his failed revolutionary action but in his writings, in particular in a fictional text called *What Is to Be Done?* (1865), which forty years later inspired a young man called Volodya Ulyanov to write a nonfictional text of the same title, setting out the theory of a future Leninist party (hardly an ineffective text). Ten years after the second *What Is to Be Done?* its author, then already V. I. Lenin, would interrupt his possibly most important and certainly most utopian piece of wordsmithing (called *The State and the Revolution*) with a concluding statement that it is better to make a revolution than write about it. What I am arguing is not that he was wrong but that he was (necessarily) oversimplifying: that without Chernyshevsky's fiction as well as Chernyshevsky's organizational tradition (which led to Ulyanov's elder brother being executed by tsarism) many central features of the united theory and practice of Leninism would not have existed in the same form. And one thing a good look at fiction and art in general—which fuses conceptualization with sensuality—can teach us is that phenomena only exist in given forms: *not to exist in a given way means not to exist.*

Let me go on with the historical record, to Che Guevara and Mao Zedong. I cannot even hint at the richness of their lives' work, but I wish to isolate one important lesson to be drawn from them: what survives after a generation. A large part of what survives from such lives are narrative images, agents with actions. Che is in this domain surviving as something like a Marxist version of an Arthurian or Spenserian Knight of Justice, giving his life for the cause, a revolutionary Christ-like intercessor for the oppressed. This image is so potent that even Hollywood felt compelled to attempt co-opting and neutralizing it. Similarly, Mao is increasingly becoming a twofold narrative agent: the writer of certain kinds of texts and an imaginary type within global political discourse (the leader of the Long March, the speaker at Yenan, the swimmer in the Yangtze, etc.). It is not that the practice or praxis of fiction is better than, but merely that it is indispensable for and indispensably allied with, the praxis of revolutionary change. Indeed, fiction or narrative (in the wide sense of telling a story with agents and space/time, which englobes equally what the old theories called epic, lyric, and dramatic fiction) is inextricably enmeshed with all social practice. If any ideology or movement pretends to kick narrative and images borrowed from fiction out the front door, they will return by the cellar window. Surely it would be better to do knowingly what you have to do anyway; for only thus, as Hegel said, do you truly do that. Furthermore, only thus can what you do be consciously controlled and corrected.

1.3

This is not to deny that the Rimbaud Syndrome remains a very important and open, particular historical (as different from general theoretical) question. But it, too, is an important question because, before the gunrunning, Rimbaud had an unsurpassed way with words, in his case organized into verse images and narratives.

It might have become apparent that my title conceals some basic choices. Along with the connotational resonance between people (plural) and the people (collective singular), another, more polarized choice is whether

665

either is being—is to be—"*re*-presented" or "represented," or indeed simply "presented."

Re-presenting I take to refer to a supposed copying from or reflection of a supposedly otherwise known external reality. Two minutes' thought suffices to render this untenable in any literal form, so it is quickly provided with a codicil to the effect that a subjective prism is interposed between the objective reality and the image of (the) people. Then it turns out that a norm for the rightness of that prismatic refraction must be found in order to obviate the possible multiplicity of prisms (say, avant-gardist or mystical as against "realistic") and that the normative prism is that of the ruling ideology—be it socialist-realism or the awful capitalist-realism we can see in the halls of any U.S. university in the form of paintings of presidents and board chairmen. This, in short, is a static, conformist, Philistine theory of artistic mimesis, banal and without much interest.

However, if people are represented in fiction as a selection, condensation, and displacement of surface empirical events and the ruling ideological way of seeing them, if they are seen as in a partially steerable daydream, then representation or mimesis is not to be understood as simple copying. No doubt, any thinking is based on models. But representation in fiction is then a process of taking model images of people from nonfictional ways of understanding and of reconstructing social reality into a process that (in ideal cases) develops roughly as follows: The new images go about subverting the heretofore received fictional norms of agential structuring, but as this is happening, the images themselves are in turn modified in and by some autonomous principles of fictional structuring. All of this together enables the resulting views of relationships among people, elaborated by the restructured piece of fiction, to return into our understanding of reality or ideology *with a cognitive increment*. This better understanding permits what Brecht called interventionary, effective, or engaged thinking (in the technical sense of meshing or being in gear). For Brecht, an image or model of a person can be drawn up, into which might be inserted attitudes that the person observed might not have found by him/herself: "but these imputed ways of behavior do not remain the observer's illusions; they turn to realities: the image has become productive, it can change the person modelled, it contains (realizable) proposals. To make such an image means to love" (Brecht, 20:170). The great Brechtian, and indeed Marxian, theme of a productive or creative eros has been formulated before and better than in all the privatized *jouissances*.

Indeed, at this point the mimetic ambiguity of "representing" (which dominates present-day views) should probably be abandoned for the more productive and communicative two-way duplicity of "presenting": presenting images taken from outside fiction as propositions or formative hypotheses for a narrative, but also presenting images transmogrified within fiction as proposals to the pragmatic world. Even in the best case of "realism," representing suggests standing in for something that already exists, as a democratic binding mandate represents the opinions of the mandate-givers. Presenting may in the best, Brechtian case suggest instead erotic increment and plasticity. The roundabout route of art and fiction could thus hide a long-range operativity, intervention, or use value after all. That it does so, and that a horizon can be indicated within which it does so, is the argument of my essay. For if it does not, if people *cannot* be represented

666

in fiction, a great part of the humanist and radical passion that is inalienably allied to a need of changing people's lives, of modifying the relationships among people, would be irrelevant to fiction, and fiction would indeed be irrelevant to it. To expand a remark of Brecht's about drama: if people do not fit (let me add what Brecht presupposed: in however autonomous ways) into the worlds of fiction, then fiction does not fit into the world of people.

1.4

Perhaps I could cap my introductory argument by two axioms and their respective corollaries.

First axiom: We need a *materialist approach.* Our matter is in this case social discourse provisionally fixed in texts that interact with frames of acceptance and nonacceptance (ideologies). Therefore, *any hypothesis to be tried out has to be verifiable through ensembles of texts in interaction with "reading" frames.* This verifiability implies (a) that there exists both a possibility of falsification and a need for a readiness to alter the hypothesis; and (b) (an application of Occam's razor) that the explainability of the text by means of the initial hypothesis is either equal or superior to the explainability by means of any previous, insufficiently materialist hypothesis. In short, hypotheses and text-ensembles-cum-reading-frames are partners or use values.

First corollary: An anecdote has it that Matisse once showed a painting of his to a visitor, who exclaimed he/she had never seen a woman like that, to which the painter answered: "It is not a woman, it is a picture." The material pertinent to re-presenting people in fiction (and all texts) is not people but words, sentences, and what they imply in interaction with reading frames. More particularly, this material is (some equivalent of) a nominal syntagma with a given place in the story—just as the pertinent materials in Matisse's painting are colors and lines with a place inside a frame. Paradoxically, all the lessons of Russian formalism, without which we cannot begin making sense of fiction, belong here under the heading of materialism (albeit a partial and inconsistent, not yet a dialectical one). Formalism is the *A* and *B* of any integrally materialist approach to art, from which we should then proceed to *C, D,* and so on.

Second axiom: We need a *dialectical approach.* If social discourse is provisionally fixed in texts that interact with reading frames or ideologies, then all texts are incomplete products that freeze an ongoing intertextual process. Such textual and metatextual dialogues form unceasing strategies of discourse between large human groups within a society. Therefore, *no text can be even correctly read* without filling in the concavities it designs by its own convexity, *without taking into account the significant presuppositions present within the textual positions.* In matters pertinent to the re-presentation of people in fiction, these presuppositions are attitudes toward people that are possible at the historical moment of the text's freezing. In the first axiom and corollary, materialism means the central position of a material consisting of words and propositions combined in "transphrastic" (more than sentence-length) text-ensembles; in this second axiom dialectic means socially, ideologically precise historical differentiation.

Second corollary: The narrative agents of fiction (to be defined more closely in part 3) will be re-creations not of actual or imaginary people but of given historically possible *attitudes toward* animate and active entities. Just as in painting, where such attitudes are subject to the possibilities of color, line, and their disposition in two-dimensional space pretending to a third dimension, so in fiction the transposition of extraliterary attitudes will be shaped not only by given ideological interests but also by *longue durée* rules of language material, textual coherence, as well as fictional and general ideological conventions. *Longue durée* does not mean ahistorical: it just complicates our materialist analysis with welcome historical dialectics of culture. In strange and imperfectly understood ways, Homer's sun still shines on us. Paradoxically, images of people can be modified out of all empirical or naked-eye recognition—for example, into gods, talking animals, allegorical notions or disembodied narrative voices—yet still remain fabular transpositions and re-creations of possible relationships between people. These image clusters or agential constellations can be both decoded and transposed back into relationships between historical people (in significant cases, with an increment in understanding and a possibility of intervening into them).

1.5

In order to pass to my argument about a theory of narrative agents, I shall attempt to draw some conclusions from this first part. It seems to me that we are faced with two main alternatives for envisaging the presentation of people. *Individualist atomism* talks about the individual's mysterious essence, by definition not to be further analyzed; it is a competitive mystification. *Structuralist collectivism* talks about abolishing personality and substituting for it a camera eye; it is a static mystification. The first, or subject-bound, mystification implies the liberalism of the "free-enterprise" market; the second, or object-bound, mystification implies the technocracy of state-capitalist intervention and multinational corporations. Both finally see society as a stable, vertical class system, this layered stability being its fundamental condition and supreme value ("law and order"). If we instead posit the historical and axiological priority of a dynamic and open horizontal system (which can then accommodate dynamic stability and of which even temporary closures are special cases), a system in which meaning is not preexistent and located either in individual(ist) atoms or in the nodes of a structural(ist) grid but constituted in the interaction of the general and the singular—then we can begin instituting a materialist and dialectical discourse about narrative agents.

It seems necessary, therefore, to proceed along two lines. First, we must induce from historical evidence the possible forms of narrative agents and therefore of agential analysis. This means we must reconsider at least two approaches that have pioneered a sophisticated analysis of fictional agents: (a) the biblical and the Lukácsian notions of types; (b) the Greimasian notion of actants. I shall here be able only briefly to discuss Greimas's and Lukács's approaches. Second, we must put these analytic tools into practice and see whether they illuminate it. In the following argument, drama will be used as an example of all narrative. However, in principle most descriptions and discussions in this essay (e.g., the summarizing table in sect. 3.1) should be applicable to the theory of nondramatic narrations, too.

1.6

I shall conclude this first, introductory part with an operative definition and a division of my further argument. Narrative agents can be in a first approximation defined as *all nouns or nominal syntagmas that can be imagined as independent entities potentially able* (in contrast to the objects) *to carry out independent action in a narrative's imaginary universe or possible world.* However many central questions this still begs, its mixture of intuitive and verifiable elements seems sufficient for a first approach. The necessary linguistic and semiotic elements in this definition function within a "possible world" whose structures are largely borrowed from practical life. In other words, when not modified by new propositions, the presuppositions of dominant ideological ways of understanding everyday reality are retained in narratives. Narrative agents therefore both derive their traits from adjectivized cultural commonplaces and value judgments (such as brave, miserly, amorous) and structure the traits differently from empirical practice for the purposes of a better cognitive overview.

The study of narrative agents is seriously underdeveloped and labors under two grave disadvantages. First, it is still largely naively impressionistic and positivistic. In the 1920s the very well informed Bakhtin noted bitterly that this field was in "a complete chaos": "character, type, *personnage,* story hero, the famed classification of scenic *emplois:* the lover (lyrical, dramatical), the reasoner, the simpleton, etc.—all such classifications and determinations of the *geroi* [Bakhtin's term for something like a narrative agent] are given no common basis or common denominator, nor is there a unified principle extant for their reasoned ordering. Usually the classifications are uncritically contaminated to boot. . . ." More than half a century later, Chatman's synthetic survey of structuralist narrative analysis quotes with approval a lament about the scandalous blanks in even a theory of surface-level agents (the characters), a lament that maintains that the latest advance in this field was E. M. Forster's distinctions from 1928, notably between round and flat characters.[2] Indeed, the illusionistic confusion of narrative agents and people from everyday life is still very much with us.

Second, in the last twenty-five years there has appeared a symmetrical obverse of positivistic empiricism, the abstract apriorism of deducing agents from eternal psychobiological structures sundered from social history. Given that among the most interesting developments in cultural studies today is a sociohistorical semiotics, in parts 2 and 3 I sketch a critique of both ahistorical semiotics and asemiotic history and offer my own proposals for a socioformal theory of agential analysis centered on the key category of "type," as well as for some possibilities of its application to textual agents in general, including in part 4 characters (principally in drama). This might lead, in part 5, to some provisional answers to the question posed in my title.

2. For a Sociohistorical Semiotics of Narrative Agents: A Critique

> What does anyone tell me by saying "Now I see it as. . ."? What consequences has this information? What can I do with it?
> L. Wittgenstein
> *Philosophical Investigations*

2.1

Barthes defined apophantic semiotics as a semiotics that denies the necessity and possibility of "attributing to the sign positive, fixed, a-historical, a-corporeal, in brief: scientific characteristics." Though the rest of part 2 may explain his skepticism toward certain kinds of "science," I would prefer to his sweeping farewell to scientism and metalanguage a more nuanced approach, which would still keep those terms *on condition* that they were subverted from within in order to approach the horizon he desires—that is, on condition that the apophantic science and metalanguage acknowledge and respect their own sociohistorical constitution, in the double sense of sociohistorical coming into being and sociohistorical functioning. This condition could reconcile our technical needs, involving metalevels and formalized analysis, and Barthes's salutary warning that "all relationships of exteriority between one language and another are, *a la longue,* untenable. . . ."[3] Respecting the intimately sociohistorical character of all semiotics means acknowledging that in language any meaning of a term is a matter of historical semantics and pragmatics, and in nonverbal communication it is another variant of, as Eco put it, a "cultural unit." In agential analysis this means returning to the Aristotelian-Proppian orientation and inducing from what Marc Angenot calls "such historical ideal-types as are the genres and the discursive traditions [within] the general economy of social discourse." To indulge instead in supposedly pure deduction and ahistorical universalism leads to a glossocracy that offers little result and that, moreover, is homologous to the technocracies of contemporary monopoly capitalism and monopoly pseudosocialism. Adapting Lévi-Strauss, it can be said that simply to understand the meaning of a term one must permutate it in the context of *all* the discourses pertinent to it.[4] The sociohistorical discourses constitute at the very least one large pertinent group; freezing them out of the permutating process produces an impoverishment of great ideological significance but no scholarly justification.

As I noted in a study written in 1980 (to which I refer the reader for a fuller discussion of all matters in part 2), the analysis of narrative agents was relatively little developed by structuralism and the *structuralisant* semiotics and narratology.[5] Apart from the forgotten Bakhtin, systematic work in agential analysis began only in the wake of Lévi-Strauss, with the works of Greimas and the *Communications* authors. It is their problems that will be considered in this section, and I shall limit myself to the dilemmas and aporias of their basic ideological premise, glossocratic universalism, only in the domain of *the number and nature of agential levels* in narratology (including dramaturgy). Since this was most authoritatively developed by A. J. Greimas, I shall concentrate on the part of his work that provides a generally recognized framework for most later structuralism dealing with narrative agents. I shall first briefly argue for a different articulation of the deepest level of narrative functions (the actants) and then at greater length for a different, "pragmatic" nature and hierarchy of the other levels.

2.2

Aristotle and Propp had, in their different ways, both distinguished two levels of agents (*ethos* vs. *pratton,* or *dramatis persona* vs. *function,* respectively). The first of them is to be read off immediately from the surface elements of the text; the second is not but is to be found by further analysis (it is usually called metatextual). They also stressed that this second, more general and abstract level was the strategically more important one. Propp concentrated in his functions on actions, which only secondarily define six or seven "spheres of action" by as many main agents: hero, villain, donor or provider, helper, sought-for person (and her father), dispatcher or mandator, false hero. Obviously, this is both too much and too little: false hero and villain are both antagonists, the term "hero" contaminates narrative function and ethical approval (e.g., Tartuffe is the narrative but not at all the axiological "hero" of Molière's play), the "sought-for" agent can instead of a princess be any value (e.g., the Grail), and so on. Just as interestingly, though discussing the opposite pole of individualist dramaturgy of the last four centuries in Paris, Souriau worked out six "dramaturgic functions." Somewhat confusingly he identified them with astrological signs, which he fortunately disambiguated by adding clear definitions and persuasive examples. His six functions were the Thematic Force, the Value or Wished-for Good, the Beneficiary (of that Good), the Adversary, the Arbiter (who attributes the Good), and the Helper, who is always a "redoubling" of one of the first five functions. Both Propp and Souriau were also perfectly clear about the possibility of distributing participation in metatextual agents among several textual ones, as well as about the obverse possibility: thus, whether the magical object given to a hero be one horse or a ring out of which issue three youths, this will always represent the Helper's "sphere of action" (Propp, pp. 19-20, 79); the Adversary may be single or divided into eight, as in Molière's *Les Facheux* (Souriau, pp. 95-100). Greimas's first attempt in *Semantique structurale* did not go much beyond reactualizing (be it said in his praise) the multilevel agential analysis of Propp and Souriau into the two levels of *actants* and *acteurs*.

It should be clear that Propp's *Morphology of the Folktale* is not a synthesis but a halfway house between his scrupulous and brilliant historical induction and a pioneering formalizing deduction. (Propp's later works then established a more convincing balance, unfortunately not explicitly applied to narrative agents.) The attendant weaknesses were noted by Lévi-Strauss and Greimas, who rightly attempted a more consistent formalization. But in the process, Greimas, at least, lost sight of Propp's strengths based in historical feedback and misused him by transferring the debate onto the domain of universalist syntax, a dubious advantage. Greimas proposed a basic scheme of agential functions applicable to all narratives, which he divided into Subject, Object, Addressor, Addressee, Helper, and Opponent *(sujet, objet, destinateur, destinataire, adjuvant, opposant)*. His pseudosyntactic terminology and organization of this deepest level of agential functions "offers little evidence how this model [of actants] would work in practice . . ." (Culler, p. 234). The most useful course is, then, a return to a nonindividualist widening and grounding of Souriau's narrative functions. I propose to translate his articulation into the more historical and theater-based vocabulary of the independent functions of Protagonist, Antagonist, Value, Mandator, Beneficiary, and the dependent function of Satellite.[6]

Greimas's breakthrough came in his essay "La structure des actants du recit."[7] The existence and narratological status of the two levels he called *actant* and *acteur* are from that time on generally accepted in agential theory (so that this essay will take them for granted, while not treating exhaustively their outstanding problems, from ontological basis to predicative articulation). In between them, he tentatively and without systematic explanation added a third level called *roles,* defined as "elementary actantial units which correspond to coherent functional fields" ("unites actantielles elementaires correspondant aux champs fonctionnels coherents")—for example, *pere* or *pretre.*[8] Greimas's final refinement on the agential theory came in the essay "Les actants, les acteurs et les figures," where he worked out eight *roles actantiels.* I have analyzed in great detail (Suvin, "Per una teoria," pp. 91-92) the resulting unclear oscillation between binary and ternary typologies, culminating in the Greimas-Courtes attempt to systematize such contradictions.[9] Greimas's first approach had in 1966 been accompanied by engaging modesty-bearing disclaimers such as "Cette interpretation vaut ce qu'ele vaut" (This interpretation is given for what it's worth). He also acknowledged that his actants were "extrapolated from French Syntax," which fifty pages later became "extrapolated from the syntactic structure" ("extra-polees en partant de la syntaxe francaise"—"l'extrapolation de la structure syntaxique," *Semantique structurale,* pp. 134, 185). In his essay from *Semantique narrative et textuelle,* this had already advanced to "a structure . . . that appears more and more able to account for the organization of the human imagination . . ." ("La structure actantielle apparait de plus en plus comme etant susceptible de rendre compte de l'organisation de l'imaginaire humain . . .")! His latter ending—and that of many followers—forgets the beginning.

What is the basis of such hesitations and contradictions? It would be both ungracious and silly to seek it in personal incompetence: Lévi-Strauss, too, hesitates between affirming with equal imperturbability two opposite and contradictory positions. On the one hand, he says, there exist some "universal laws which make up the unconscious activity of the mind," while on the other hand, "the physical universe [is a] projection of the social universe": as far as the linguistic model in general is concerned, the error of formalism lies in forgetting "that there is no language whose vocabulary can be deduced from the syntax." Perhaps Lévi-Strauss's corollary that "to tackle first the grammar and to leave the vocabulary for later means to condemn oneself never to create anything but an anemic grammar and a vocabulary that used anecdotes in place of definitions" should be subject to some clarification of the level of analysis envisaged; nonetheless, I would agree with the particular application he then proceeds to make, namely, this interlocking is indissoluble in narrative entities such as myths and tales, where grammar and vocabulary do not even operate on distinct levels (as he acknowledges they do in language) but "adhere to each other on their whole surface and completely overlap," so that in narrative texts everything is simultaneously both syntax and vocabulary.[10] It is, at any rate, obvious that overarching ideological causes must be sought for such fundamental epistemological oscillations in such leading theoreticians.

2.3

In order to get at such causes, a metatheoretical detour is unavoidable, for it is only the ideologies of technocracy that believe they can formalize their own truth, can lift themselves up by their own bootstraps without paying the price of a dependence on a hierarchically superior system or context (an epistemological version of their belief in quick economic-political fixes that take into account neither transcendental values nor the deeper demands of practice).[11] This is the meaning of Greimas's agnostic stance, that whether we think the semantic organization of meaning(s) is inscribed into social reality, or whether we postulate such an organization for heuristic purposes, the practical consequences will be the same (". . . soit qu'il existe une structure semantique organisant l'univers du sens, soit qu'une telle structure est postulee en vue de l'investigation de l'univers semantique. . . . Les consequences pratiques seront les memes. . . ."). This allows him to conclude that, in any case, the investigator will find given "universes" for investigation. Even in that essay, dealing with the relation of semiotics and natural sciences, Greimas systematically avoids committing himself as to whether such a "universe of meaning" is one of discourse only or of other practices too—for example, it is unclear whether "semantic" in this passage, as in his whole essay, refers to natural or formal languages. It is at this price that Greimas's investigation proceeds to construct formal models supposedly in conformity with such an unexplained "preexisting structure" (*Du sens*, p. 39). This is not a stance that necessarily arises from semiotics: Peirce, who thought that both our interests and our experience of objects were extrasemiotic, would have denied it.

Since all happens within language anyway, Greimas is implying that the "world of meaning" is going to be linguistic—here, "semantic"—in any case. Yet this is a technocratic blanking out of some fundamentals of his model-discipline, for nowhere is the existence of hierarchical levels of analysis clearer than in linguistics, where the formal or syntactic meaning of any element (e.g., a phoneme) is its function as an integral meaning of a superior level (e.g., a morpheme). By that token, then, the question immediately arises, What is the hierarchically superior level to the uppermost linguistic level, that of the sentence? When they do not refuse to answer, most linguists concede this is the (or a) pragmatic level of extralinguistic reality.[12] Only the semantic-pragmatic meaning is usable and to be used in the sense that is current outside of specialized linguistic usage. Greimas's famous title, *Du sens (On Meaning)*, plays with this ambiguity. So far as I can see, he never explicitly argues that syntactic meaning is to be substituted for semantic meaning beyond the sentence—that is, in narratives. However, his whole proceeding presupposes this hidden theoretical claim, which necessarily turns out to be untenable in practice.

It may be becoming apparent, then, that the root of the Greimasian contradictions is to be found in the orthodox structuralist glossocracy, best expressed by his reliance on the very peculiar Hjelmslevian linguistics as his epistemology. Greimas takes Hjelmslev as his authority for founding the actantial model in *the* syntactic structure of natural languages, equated with *the* organization of human imagination.[13] This is cognitively improper, in the above bad sense of an ideological sleight-of-hand, for a formal system is defined by its signs not having any independent meaning outside the system, so that in order to speak about anything it must be in a second moment interpreted in the sense of finding a meaning for its signs. If the system then claims to be "wholly independent of any prior theory, it is in fact constructed *ad hoc*. Thus, if the logician subsequently pretends to search for its interpretation, he is as one who is asked a riddle for which he already knows the answer, and who delights in feigning ignorance!"[14] Greimas's typical proceeding is a structuralist bricolage in fundamentals, followed by a relentless scientistic and combinatory logic in consequences:

a proceeding vaunted by his followers as elasticity and broadmindedness. The other way around, firm foundations and elastic applications, would have been much more sympathetic. Yet whenever he is analyzing actual narrative texts, Greimas finds—to my mind not too surprisingly—that deductive and universalist syntax is an insufficient fundament, and he hastens to supplement it with semantics: a crack through which the social history of peoples' relationships with each other and with the world of things, kicked out of the main door, partially and inconsistently oozes back by a cellar window. In his first book, Greimas started out by hesitating between what he then called the "syntactic actants proper" and "semantic actants," even connecting the actants with a Freudian investment of desire. In *Du sens,* his analyses of a group of Lithuanian folktales required a Proppian recourse to the specific social semantics and, indeed, pragmatics of authority. And in his final development of actants, while allotting them an entirely syntactic nature, he stressed the semantic (or at least mixed) nature of the *acteurs* and the *roles thematiques.*[15]

Thus, the ideological horizon of glossocracy contradicts actual scholarly necessity. I believe this obscurely felt contradiction is the key to Greimas's shifting, overlapping, uneconomic, and often confusing categories, which becloud his undoubted flair for spotting strategic Gordian knots and his pioneering boldness (only in view of which are further attempts—such as this critique—becoming possible). It seems, therefore, imperative to say, today, that if we are to have a viable agential theory, the hesitation between universalist syntax and shamefaced semantics-cum-pragmatics is to be resolved in favor of sociohistorical contextuality and intertextuality in (say) Bakhtin's and Mukarovsky's, and sometimes Lévi-Strauss's and Barthes's, "marxist" sense of a dialogic tension between the worldviews of specific societal groups. It is high time to recognize Hjelmslev's rigidly deductive approach as simply a misleading analogy and to depose it from the narratological hegemony it has illicitly enjoyed.[16] While the conceptual rigor of linguistics is an admirable example, when sundered from social verisimilitude and historical semantics, it easily leads to "a rigorous irrelevance" (Culler, p. 257).

2.4

One witty way of clinching the necessity of an integration of formalized linguistics or semiotics with investigation into socialized actions might be to note that the integration has become increasingly recognized as unavoidable in linguistics itself. It has taken the name of *pragmatics,* defined already by Charles Morris as the domain of relationships between the signs and their interpreters, which clarifies the conditions under which something is taken as a sign. From Peirce, G. H. Mead, and Karl Buhler, through Bakhtin/Voloshinov, Morris, Carnap, and the Warsaw school, to (say) R. M. Martin, Leo Apostel, and John R. Searle, pragmatics has slowly been growing into an independent discipline on a par with syntactics (the domain of relationships between the signs and their formally possible combinations) and semantics (in this sense, the domain of relations between the signs and the entities they designate). Moreover, there are, since the late 1950s, strong arguments that pragmatics is a constitutive and indeed englobing complement of both semantics and syntactics. The basic—and, to any materialist, unexceptionable—argument for it has been suggested in

674

section 2.3: an object or event (word, text, shape, color, change, etc.) becomes a sign only in a *signifying situation;* it has no "natural" meaning outside of it. This situation is constituted by the relation between signs and their users. A user can take something to be a sign only as it is spatiotemporally concrete and localized and as it relates to the user's disposition toward potential action; both the concrete localization and the user's disposition are always sociohistorical. Furthermore, they postulate a reality organized not only around signs but also around subjects, in the double sense of a psychophysical personality and a socialized, collectively representative subject. The entry of potentially acting subjects reintroduces acceptance and choice, temporal genesis and mutation, and a possibility of dialectical negation into the frozen constraints of syntax (in fact, by the most orthodox structuralist standards, only such dynamics can make the—temporary—stability of any structure meaningful). It also regrounds semantics: even in language, "one cannot tell the meaning of most words without observing how the word is used, and what effects it seems to have on our behavior." All words have a pragmatic value based on an implicit classification "that follows the kind of interest which they evoke [in the subject], the advantages or inconveniences, pleasures or sufferings, which they suggest."[17] Thus, each and every semantic presupposition is also a pragmatic one (though the contrary does not obtain).

The signifying situation as the basic cell of pragmatics is clearly the theoretical locus of the hierarchically superior system that must finally allot significations and validate all other investigations into signs (including natural languages). Or, at the very least, pragmatics is the mediation between semiotics and an even more general theory of action or practice. Only pragmatics is able to take into account the situation of the text producers and its social addresses,[18] as well as the whole spread of their relationships within given cognitive (epistemological and ideological) presuppositions, conventions, economical and institutional frames, and so on. And only a semantic-pragmatic decision about pertinent presuppositions and levels of reading can make sense of an at-all-complex text (from, say, a proverb or parable), whose presuppositions, levels, and connotations would otherwise be practically infinite. Realizing much of this, the early Lévi-Strauss (structuralism with a somewhat uneasy conscience) claimed his method could exhaust all the pertinent presuppositions because his texts—the myths—came from a supposedly less complex, "cold" (tribal) society in which the presuppositions were presumed to be frozen and finite (which I doubt, too). These pragmatic presuppositions about the signs' possible uses by their users, then, necessarily inscribe historical reality, as understood by the users, between the lines of any text (in the widest sense). Semiotics is either informed by an open historicity or it is, on its own methodical terms, truncated.

Equally, the sciences are, no doubt, texts (though not purely verbal ones), but the book of science is also—for all its partial autonomy—an interpretation of the book of nature, which is the presupposition of all scientific propositions. Furthermore, what exactly are the pertinent categories that constitute any object of investigation (in the widest sense, including a whole discipline) in the first place? This delimitation, which constitutes not only the cognizable domain but also the possible ways of envisaging and cognizing it, cannot be established from the object alone but only from its interaction with the social subject whose pragmatic point of view or approach is defining the pertinence and by that token constructing the object's cognitive identity.[19] To return to the terms of logics, linguistics cannot be its own epistemology, because no natural language can be wholly formalized without incurring semantic contradictions—as Greimas inevitably does, on a theoretical level, when he is not being fuzzy. Therefore, linguistics cannot and does not provide the criteria valid for every type of cognition but, on the contrary, needs itself to be justified by an epistemology external to it.

Thus, for any pursuit of systematic knowledge, as semiotics, the formal logic of syntax is clearly indispensable. But it is not sufficient, for if the analysis of a text must be begun, it cannot be concluded by an understanding of its syntax. This does not mean that for given, clearly delimited exercises syntactic rules could not be treated as an autonomous object of cognition. But it means that "a well definable (autonomous) syntax is only the syntax of syntactic categories as a purely formal syntax."[20] A syntactically valid analytic system cannot be used to prove anything about an empirical object unless and until the system is related to a semantic interpretation and a pragmatic situation, as was demonstrated in the case of Greimas's actants used to explain narration.

2.5

In conclusion, then, if (and insofar as) Greimas's system of actants is taken as a claim for full interpretative validity with a solid epistemological basis, one would have to apply to it Piaget's evaluation of the philosophical school that (through Hjelmslev) underpins it: logical positivism. "Logical Positivism has committed the imprudence of transforming method into doctrine, in other words of wanting to codify formalizing analysis and of making it co-responsible for a dogmatism . . ." (Piaget, p. 84). I would not go quite so far—as do a number of critics, for example, Timpanaro—as to call Greimas's method objective idealism, since it does not quite claim that the categories of the given sign-system determine *what* there is but "only *how* anything is." I would, rather, call it a medium-rare semiotic idealism—a cross between agnosticism and thoroughgoing idealism.[21] Of course, no idealism or—to give it a historically suggestive name—medieval realism can account for changes in our cognition of the world (never mind changes in an external world). Greimas's attempt is simply one of the most developed—and the dominant one in agential analysis—to investigate the meanings of a text by means of a text "linguistics," "grammar," or "syntax" (all of which are, in fact, shamefacedly founded on the quite exceptional digital model of phonetics). This seems to me, in all cases, a dangerously ambiguous metaphor, and in the worst case it is a positive guarantee of wrong theorizing. The only safe course is to avoid both the thing and the name.[22]

Nonetheless, I have suggested the presence of some undoubtedly stimulating aspects in Greimas—mainly those taking off from Propp. Greimas addressed the crucial dilemma in studying narratives, namely, into which system a text must be integrated in order to become meaningful (i.e., such that an interpreter may explain it). Positivism had answered this by putting its object simply into a quantitatively larger set of texts (an author's opus, a genre tradition, etc.). Structuralism was right to react against this in the direction of qualitatively different levels of analysis, but structuralism

676

was wrong—as is all scholastic realism—in radically sundering deductive and formal cognition (a self-sufficient, closed system of signs) from experiential cognition based on reference to the extrasignific reality of social bodies.[23] In cultural studies, structuralism's answer—to apply to the investigated text a "grammar of narration"—explains texts in terms of a universal structure of the human (or, in Greimas, Indo-European?) mind, as evidenced in language. In a nicely sterile Hegelian antithesis, both positivism and structuralism bypass the actual historical situations in culture, its *pragmatic hierarchy*. Cultural texts may be analyzed into cognitive levels only by seeing how those levels are intimately molded by precise societal values and tensions.

Greimas's multilevel schema of agents should, therefore, be separated out of his unacceptable system and then reworked in a way that incorporates the semantic and pragmatic dimension, namely, societal history and mutability. It should then become possible to use this reworked form within the epistemic axioms of my part 1, within a need for observing material practice as well as the dialectical interrelations that obtain between the synchronic and the diachronic, structure and history, subject and object. True, no historical situation is *fully* formalizable, but it can (and I believe must) be investigated through a series of formalizations open to practice and focusing on strategic stages frozen for synchronic investigation. Thus, I will present a sketch of such a sociohistorical semiotics of narrative agents: a study of sign, necessarily, but signs given meaning by choices within societal histories. No doubt, the sociohistorical concreteness of my proposed new system will have to be inversely proportional to the area it is designed to cover. But it will use semiotics in the proper epistemological hierarchy dominated by relationships of people in signifying situations and not by glossocracy: "It is essential that one does not confuse the *systematic* order in semiotics: syntactics—semantics—pragmatics, with the *epistemological* order of the dimensions of semiosis: pragmatic—semantic—syntactic dimension. The pragmatic dimension of semiosis is epistemologically of primary importance. . . . the pragmatic aspects always appear *at the beginning and at the end* of the study of semiosis."[24]

3. For Sociohistorical Semiotics of Narrative Agents: A Proposal (with Types as the Key Level)

> After all, Kafka is a realist!
> (reputed exclamation by Lukács when he
> saw the Romanian castle where he was
> being interned in 1956)

3.1

I cannot provide here a lengthy inventory of extant narratological contributions to a clear definition and delimitation of the third, intermediate level of agential analysis. Besides Aristotle, Propp, Souriau, Bakhtin, and Lévi-Strauss, one should reevaluate the use of agents in the Marxian tradition, from *The Eighteenth Brumaire* to Brecht and Benjamin.[25] One should also sift and integrate the contributions of structuralists (Barthes, Todorov, Greimas, Rastier, Hamon, Chatman, etc.) and of some other precursors. The structuralists are perhaps best represented by Alexandrescu's book on Faulkner, situating between *personnages* and *actants* a level of *roles*: in

Faulkner's opus (itself a concrete refashioning of a historical and history-oriented genre), Alexandrescu found the *roles* of Indian, black, mulatto, farmer, aristocrat, Yankee, businessman, and intellectual (and I think other "roles" could be found, too). However, since my present concern is to help build a theory of narrative agents, I cannot here give a detailed overview of work in this field. I shall content myself with acknowledging that I used hints from the older authors mentioned in part 2, as well as from those in the preceding two paragraphs, and also from Simmel, the Russian formalists (Eikhenbaum, Balukhatii, etc.), Ubersfeld, and Doutrepont, in order to propose Table 1.[26]

I should stress that the agential levels are cumulative and not exclusive. The two basic ones—actants and types—are to be found in every fictional text, while the uppermost one—characters—may or may not be present in any given text (this depends on the historical epoch and literary genre). Where characters are present, "each is a type but also at the same time a definite individual, a 'this one,' as old man Hegel expresses it. . . ."[27] This points to the key function of the second, or intermediate, level of *types*, on which I shall now focus.

I suggested in part 2 that different scholars have used various, sometimes confusing terms: figure, role, and *emploi* in Vol'kenshtein; *role* or *role pur* in Souriau; "basic characters" in Eco's discussion of James Bond (p. 85); *role* and *role actantiel* in Greimas (if I have understood him and when he uses them); *role* in Alexandrescu and (much less usefully) in Bremond; *role formel* in Rastier; *emploi* in Hamon (p. 106); *role* and *personnage-type* in Ubersfeld (pp. 113-14, 131, 150). Perhaps the actual term used is not of *primary* importance if the level is clearly delimited and articulated, but it is of *some* importance: language speaks us as much as we speak it. Thus, I would not favor "role" in French or English because it invites confusion both with an actor's role in the theater and with the sociological theory of role playing.[28] "Type," however, is both suitably Anglo-French and able to draw sustenance from a confrontation with its wide use in literary criticism and in the theater tradition, which (in English more than in French) draws on such associations as "type of role," "typecast," "stock types," and so on.

3.2

It seems necessary to confront here Lukács's pioneering use, symmetrically inverse to the formalists and structuralists, of terms such as "typical character." I have sufficient space here only for a first sketch of the splendors and miseries in his approach to narrative agents. I shall use for that purpose mainly his early *Theory of the Novel,* the essay on "intellectual physiognomy," and, as his crowning achievement, *The Historical Novel* and the essays on Balzac.[29]

The *Theory of the Novel* may not be thought fair game, since Lukács himself declares in his 1962 preface that its writer's worldview "tended toward a fusion of 'left-wing' ethics and 'right-wing' gnoseology (ontology etc.)" (p. 16). I would add to this a right-wing or bourgeois aesthetics fixated on eighteenth- and nineteenth-century "realism," from Cervantes to Thomas Mann, and evident in his lifelong, sincere hatred of Dada, photomontage, Brechtian dramaturgy, and so on. A deep interest in Baroque drama or novel, as in Benjamin and Bakhtin, is beyond Lukács's ken—not to mention

Table 1.

Agential level	Predicative articulation	Narratological locus	Verbal status and deep structure	Visualizing status	Definition	Historical duration
3 CHARACTER (*personnage* or *personnage-personne*; "round"); not obligatory	A great (though theoretically not unlimited) number of possibly conflicting predicates/traits	Always textual and a dramatis persona (when it exists)	*Proper name*; d.s. = illusion of large number of not fully fixed attributes, only imperfectly to be reconstituted from text + all the contexts	Necessarily figurative (depictable); necessarily individual	Individuality as presupposed by bourgeois practice (e.g., economics) and ideology (e.g., psychology)	Almost point-like—changeable for each different ensemble of spectators
2 TYPE (*type* or *personnage-type*; "flat"), e.g., Vice, Pantalone, Miser, Father, Soubrette; obligatory	A small number—usually 2-6—of compatible predicates/traits	Metatextual or textual—according to whether level 3 exists or not	*Common or generic noun*, can be proper name raised to that status; d.s. = noun + one or a few attributes, or nominal syntagma	Necessarily figurative; not necessarily individual	Societal type (by age + sex + profession, and/or social group, and/or temperament, etc.)	*Courte durée* generations or centuries
1 ACTANT (substitute for Greimas's syntactic terms those of Protagonist, Antagonist, Value, Mandator, Beneficiary, and Satellite; obligatory	One predicate as common denominator of a bundle of semic predicates	Always metatextual; no discrete appearance as dramatis persona	*Common noun*; d.s. = surface (= "force which does what is indicated by the noun")	Not necessarily figurative; necessarily not individual	Function in dramaturgic action	*Longue durée*—epochs or millennia

farther times, places, and less canonic genres (as Shelley's poem of allegorical satire used against him by Brecht). Thus, for all ideological changes, I think his basic stance is in some ways not altered from this phase until the end of his opus.

The "left" ethics are here, as always in Lukács, unexceptionable. They identify, first, the novel's form as "the mirror image of a world out of joint" (p. 12), as the form that expresses a "lost utopian home" (p. 92), a "transcendental homelessness" that comports "the homelessness of the soul in the mandatory order of the supra-personal value-system" (p. 59): "Thus, this first great novel of world literature [i.e., *Don Quixote*] stands at the beginning of the age where the God of Christianity is beginning to leave the world; where Man is becoming lonely and may find meaning and substance only in his soul which is nowhere at home; where the world has been cast loose from its paradoxical moorings in a present Other World and given over to its immanent meaninglessness; where the might of the existing . . . grows to unheard-of proportions . . ." (p. 103). As opposed to the Greeks, and to the Middle Ages, empirical life under the bourgeoisie has split off from the absolute necessity *(Sollen)*, or Essence *(Wesen)*, which united all figures of Hellenic tragedy or epic. The modern novel must painfully "dig up and build up the hidden totality of life." Therefore, the protagonists of the novel "are seekers . . . [to whom] neither goals nor ways can be immediately supplied . . ." (pp. 57-58); "the hero of the novel grows out of this alienness to the outer world" (p. 64). An allegorical struggle results, a psychomachia in which a "problematic individual" is opposed to but also conditional upon a "contingent world" (p. 76). So far, so good— except for the idealization of prebourgeois times, a reasonable though insufficient polemic strategy.[30] Indeed, the realization that in all significant senses there were no individuals in classical epic and tragedy—that isolated individualities only come about when the context for the dramatis personae is reduced to "a hierarchical competition" (p. 39)—is a major breakthrough. It was in fact first, and better, explained in his 1908 long essay "On the Sociology of Modern Drama" (not yet fully available in English) and later best summarized by Arnold Hauser's still indispensable *Social History of Art [and Literature].* It remains, in my opinion, the basis for historical typologies of the last 700 years of European (and later global) culture.

However, when Lukács comes to speak not of overall historical typology (his forte) but of what I here call "narrative agents"—that is, of the actual texture of any novel—the hydra heads of the "right-wing" ontology and aesthetics rear up again. The novel form is correlative to "the epoch of perfect sinfulness" (p. 157)—which is why Dostoevsky, who does not presuppose such an epoch anymore, is not a novel writer! If so, then Man's "soul"—Lukács's main agential term—does not fit into its epoch any more: "the soul is either narrower or wider than the external world, which is given unto it as the stage and substratum of its deeds" (p. 96)—one sees why Thomas Mann portrayed Lukács as the Jesuit Naphta in *The Magic Mountain.* From Cervantes to Dickens and Balzac, one main current of the novel presupposes the "narrowing down of the soul" (p. 111). Another current in the nineteenth century evidences a soul wider than the fate empirical life offers it, so that the novel grows lyrical and actionless (Flaubert, Goncharov). It is not only that the philosophy of history has almost completely smothered feedback from particular novel analyses. Regardless of quite thinkable par-

680

ticular objections, Lukács's terms would not *allow* anybody who might wish to apply or supplement his historiosophy to distinguish between people in everyday life and novel protagonists or other narrative agents. The abundant use of the term "form" remains quite metaphysical, situated within a kind of scholastic vitalism. Lukács is, in fact, entirely innocent of the signific nature of narratives. Just like his great model Hegel, in *Aesthetics* (and like the neo-Kantians), he still uses the crude idealist ontology of form versus content. Finally, his Feuerbachian lay religiosity shows through this unmitigated discourse in capitals, about Man and the World, poles apart from any societal or materialist (i.e., class-oriented) historicity. "Man" is here a "left-ethical" version of Hegel's Absolute Spirit, fallen from classical Eden into the bad times of bourgeois competition. If one compares this to the praise of the bourgeoisie's achievement in *The Communist Manifesto,* the incompatibility between early Lukács and Marxism becomes palpable.

What *The Theory of the Novel* calls "soul" becomes in the 1930s "The Intellectual Physiognomy in Characterization." Lukács's militant development toward Marxism and his involvement first in the German and then in the Soviet ideological debates have, no doubt, given him some further tools and cleaned out the overtly religious terminology. Yet from Hegel to Goncharov, the continuities of this orientation are striking. The vitalist confusion of life and art, allied with some Soviet cultural factions' slogan of "the living man" to be represented in literature, lead him to posit that "the intellectual physiognomy . . . is the chief factor in creating living personality" (p. 150). Having come out of the Exile from Eden, we are now back at a Genesis whose Adam is created by a reader of Hegel. The major advance is, however, represented by the insistence that the creative approach hinges on the writer's relating the individual to the universal. Lukács was certainly one of the philosophically best trained major critics of our century. Nonetheless, he retains the "right-wing epistemology"—the short-circuiting of empirical and aesthetic phenomena, of people and their fictionally displaced and condensed simulacra. The fusion of individual and typical is explained in the old confusion of domains: "Universal, typical phenomena should emerge out of the particular actions and passions of specific individuals" (p. 154). Furthermore (here the Soviet scientistic context may be strong), "typical" is defined as what relates to "the objective general problems of the age" (p. 154). "Typical characters" such as Don Quixote arise out of the writer's having correctly defined "the basic issues and movements of his time" (p. 158)—at best, an ahistorical extrapolation from the necessities of the Russian experiment in the 1930s. It is also necessary to put the characters into extremely intensified (i.e., again typical) *situations*—though I am not sure whether this is a second requirement or the reformulation of the first one in line with Engels's famous letter on "typical characters in typical circumstances" from which the term seems to stem.[31] Goncharov's protagonist Oblomov is thus not an " 'average' man" but an intensified "social type," and it is very suggestively noted that this is obtained "through the intensification of a particular character trait," namely, sloth (p. 165)— how one wishes Lukács had met Propp! In fact, both the average Philistine and the abstractly extreme superman are types divorced from significant social conflicts (pp. 168-69). But such hints are not followed up. It is never explained, first, whether "typical" is to "character" as "universal" is to "particular," or whether the typicality is the result of a successful fusion between the universal and the particular; second, what are the criteria for the successful fusion of typical and characteristic (i.e., for defining the basic issues and movements of one's time) beyond the messianic assumption from *History and Class Consciousness* (and, more important, from Stalin's era) that the workers' party necessarily knows this. It may not have been Lukács's fault that formal systematizations were taboo at that time, but neither is it ours that we cannot do without them today.

The *Historical Novel* may well turn out to be Lukács's masterpiece in cultural analysis, like *History and Class Consciousness* in political philosophy. Both works contain bad mistakes—the latter, the theory of the party, and the former, the Hegelian definition of drama. Nonetheless, having worked in its domain and used the book for a quarter-century, I find it still fundamental: for example, though Scott critics have added other aspects, nobody has bettered Lukács's chapter and his theory of Scott's "average protagonist" as a nationally typical character. Lukács here manages to cap his tortured development from Hegel and Dilthey to Engels and Lenin with a populist class analysis in the creative spirit of the antifascist Popular Front. Thus, he can relate the protagonist (e.g., Frank Osbaldistone in *Rob Roy*) to the general outline of the plot, including the fictionally peripheral "extreme" agent or great historical personality (Rob Roy himself). Laws of literary constellation having to do with historical forces but operating by specific fictional transposition and condensation (what Freud called *Verdichtung und Verschiebung*), thus come to the fore in some chapters and are energetically developed, if never systematized, across the book as a whole. True, Lukács was more comfortable with condensation or intensification—"that is, the singling out of the significant factors from the entire complex of reality, their concentration, and the creation out of their connexions of an image of life upon a heightened level" (p. 147)—than with anamorphic transpositions, where "factors from reality" might be so coded that one would have to take into account the signific reality of the coding, too. He can therefore still say that "the great historical figure, as a minor character, is able to live himself out to the full as human being . . ." (p. 47)—the fuzziness of the agential terms (figure, character, and human being) making this sentence almost unreadable today. But elsewhere Lukács talks of "the relation of the agent's individuality to the universality of the problem" (p. 125), or of the lower-class protagonists in a number of plays from Calderon to Hebbel as having "within themselves that combination of individual passion and social substance which characterizes the 'world-historical individuals'" (p. 120). His best pages in *Balzac and French Realism* and in some other postwar writings then carry on in more detail and on a better known corpus the insights arrived at with these tools: the discussion of the two protagonists in *Lost Illusions* repeats the pattern of inversion arrived at for Scott (Frank versus Rob Roy). In some formulations (e.g., in the preface), he even begins to dissociate type from character and to explain their—necessarily societal—interaction. Only the lack of necessary formalization in the direction of multilevel analysis separates these results from Table 1.

I should hope, therefore, that a properly developed theory of types would accept Lukács's "left" ethical passion, philosophical depth, and historical richness, while rejecting his frequent "right" ontology, epistemology, and aesthetics resulting in instrumental oversimplification—symmetrical to the structuralists' overcomplication. For Marxian literary and cultural critics Lukács is a Great Ancestor. But piety apart, we must sorrowfully note that, though parts of his work remain classical, much of it—in particular the theoretical skeleton—needs large-scale refunctioning.

3.3

Type itself is, then, perhaps best defined as in Whewell: "A type is *an example of any class,* for instance, a species of a genus, *which is considered as eminently possessing the characters of the class.*"[32] This means that such a typicality gains its authority from the specific sociohistorical intertext with its ideological premises. It can and must be based on *any* categorization that has been taken in cultural history (right or wrong from a present-day point of view) to classify people or agents. It will, then, include as important historical cases biblical and other theological typologies as well as Lukács's political-economic one, but it will certainly embrace a larger domain. Thus, types can be and have been classified by sex-cum-age, nationality, profession, social estate or class, physiology, and moral philosophy (Aristotle's *ethos;* the Galenic "temperaments" or "humors"), often by what we would feel are combinations of these categories (Diderot's *conditions,* e.g., Father or Judge, seem to contaminate profession, class, and social role), and so on.

In that light, the very useful term *emploi,* or (more clumsily) "stock character," "stock figure," or "line (of business)"—for example, ingenue, *jeune premier, pere noble, raisonneur,* villain, heavy, walking gentleman—is a particular though historically crucial case of my "type": a type with supplementary theatrical-historical codification, one that has largely survived the rise of my third agential level—the character—though at the price of retreat from textual surface.

To give just two series of examples:

1. A hypothetical Morality (or *Roman de la Rose*) dramatis persona called True Love has two traits: lovingness and its qualitative place in the courtesy system; Shakespeare's Rosalind, in *As You Like It,* is not at all exhausted by half a dozen ideologically compatible predicates or traits such as young, female, well-born—she is also capricious or coquettish, cruel, and so on; as different from both of these extremes, the type and *Maschera* of "amorosa" can be exhausted by half a dozen traits, for example, "young, female, beautiful, not too shrewd, amorous." This is not only a property of the *Commedia dell'arte:* the soubrette is exhausted by something like "female, young, vivacious, lower-class," whereas the ingenue is "girl (i.e., female plus still younger), pure, middle-to-upper class." Of course, all traits such as well-born, pure, vivacious, and so on, are culturally (i.e., socio-ideologically) coded, much as the Noh mask of "the somewhat sad young woman" or "the red-faced *sake* drunkard."

2. The agential semantic field of "warrior/warring" may be articulated as an ideal (but also largely historical) sequence traversing the scale of predicative complexity indicated by the second column in Table 1. At its lower end would be found a mythological personification of War or Ares in Antiquity, or an analogous agent in theater outside Europe (e.g., the Peking Opera), or an allegorical personification such as the medieval Ira (Wrath). All such agents are predicatively poor (though not at all necessarily ineffective) *types,* since they have, I think, two traits only: the warlike char-

acteristic (wrathfulness, aggressiveness) and the relational position or *Stellenwert* in the system of polytheism, cardinal sins, or something similar. The *Commedia dell'arte Maschera* of "Capitano" has already about half a dozen traits: say, officer, middle-aged, braggart, coward, indigent, and Spanish (though the ethnic trait varies according to local history and prejudice). It seems to me to be constitutive of any type that it possess a relatively small number of traits (I have not found more than half a dozen in any so far examined, but this field remains to be further investigated) that are all *culturally congruent or compatible.* This compatibility should be explainable in every particular historical case as the result of a feedback interaction between the social definition of reality from which the traits are taken and the criteria of verisimilitude shared by the audience for which the dramaturgic narration is intended.

A whole historical typology of narrative agents and their various levels could be done on the basis of the hypothesis tabulated above. If fruitful, it could serve as a beacon for research into narratological agents in general, from mythological tales through the individualist novel to the present.

3.4

Some other lines of reasoning also speak in favor of finding types in all fictional narrative—on the textual surface or underneath the characters of individualism. Northrop Frye puts this succinctly and stimulatingly: "All lifelike characters, whether in drama or fiction, owe their consistency to the appropriateness of the stock type which belongs to their dramatic function. That stock type is not the character but it is as necessary to the character as a skeleton is to the actor who plays it" (p. 172). Other postindividualistic critics of diverse persuasions have noted that in any given culture there exist mental stereotypes, what Kant called "schematisms," for given concepts-cum-images represented in art (and, generally, used in social practice). In Auden's poem "The Truest Poetry Is the Most Feigning," the problem of the poet-lover oscillating between empirical reality and fiction meant for a reading frame is, I think, addressed very realistically (italics mine):

> *The living girl's* your *business (some odd sorts*
> *Have been an inspiration to men's thoughts):*
> . . . .
> We *cannot love your love till she take on,*
> *Through you, the wonders of a paragon.* . . . .

These mental schemes are most palpably demonstrable in painting, and they have been persuasively demonstrated by Ernst Gombrich. All painting, he argues, comports the interaction of such schemata in the painter's mind with the possible innovations (which go from zero in, say, ancient Egypt to the continuous care about strengthening the impression of mimetism in the nineteenth century). All thinking passes necessarily through "sorting, classifying; all perceiving relates to expectations and therefore to comparisons."[33] A useful philosophical collocation for such classifications is to say, in the medieval tradition, that they partake of *universalia* such as the Young Man, the Temptress, and so on. In more modern language, we could say that these are agential perceptions and social constructions of reality; a portrait is the "construction of a relational model [which] can be constructed to any required degree of accuracy [in accordance with] its purpose and the requirements of society in which the given visual language gains currency."[34]

In this view, no painterly motif can be truly seen—that is, not only optically registered on the retina but also made into a culturally comprehensible unit—"unless one has learned how to classify and catch it within the network of a schematic form."[35] The motif is not necessarily—is usually not—*exhausted* by being subsumed under a class of generic stereotypes, but unless this first identification is effected to begin with, the motif as motif will simply not exist for an audience, which will then see merely unrelated figures or, indeed, blotches of paint. Even the notoriously "realistic" Dutch genre-painting "created from a limited number of *types and gestures*, much as the apparent realism of the picaresque novel or of Restoration comedy still applies and modifies *stock figures* which can be traced back for centuries. . . . The artist . . . needs a vocabulary before he can embark on a 'copy' of reality" (Gombrich, p. 87; cf. p. 140). Thus, to envisage agents (also) in terms of *universalia*, in terms of cultural units or classifications which then provide a basis for comparison for any new agents, leads to the agential unit and analytic level of *stock figures* or *types*. Even the individualized character, if and when present in a narrative, will gain its full significance when seen as arising out of a more general level of types. As Culler notes, ". . . our cultural codes contain models [of various stock figures]: . . . the *senex iratus* or heavy father, the *miles gloriosus* or braggart, the fop or coxcomb, the pedant. . . . these models guide the perception and creation of characters, enabling us to . . . attribute to each an intelligible role" (Culler, p. 236).

This is, of course, quite consonant with the basic approach of semiotics (unfortunately, as yet little applied in its practice), for in semiotic theory all imaginatively visualized elements of narration, including textual agents, do not signify their supposed mimetic equivalents from life: for example, characters do not signify people from the street. Instead, an agent signifies the *class of entities* of which it is a member: not an "essential" class, of course, as implied by Frye and sometimes even by Gombrich, but an "existential" one within a given sociohistorical paradigm. As holds for any semiotic entity, the *primary* condition of a narrative agent is to be "representative of its class, so that the audience is able to infer from it the presence of another member of the same class . . . in the [imagined narrative] world."[36] This also explains all the "mimetically" unexplainable "non-literal signifiers" in the agential domain, such as the two-dimensional cutouts in Piscator's *Schweyk*, the dishonest statesman in Chinese theater signified by the blue *mang* robe he wears, or any sufficiently non-mimetically presented (e.g., masked) agents. Thus, the upper-class characters in Brecht's *Caucasian Chalk Circle* performance do not represent people who in medieval Transcaucasia went around masked; they signify instead the *typical* quality of that class, the "suppression of their human face" or impulse (e.g., motherliness) under the sway of the power and splendor inscribed in the masks.[37]

Semiotically considered, a dramaturgic agent is always within "quotation marks" (Elam, p. 89): it stands for or signifies a *type*—on which further traits are then grafted in the case of characters. This connects, evidently, with Brecht's theory of estrangement *(Verfremdung)*, as well as with his theory of the unit of dramaturgic semiosis, the gestural kinesic set-cum-attitude he called *Gestus*. Brecht defined *Gestus* as being "sociohistorically significant (typical)," as partaking of some basic "social relationship prevailing between people of a given period" (Brecht, 16:86, 139; see also Elam, p. 76ff.). In dramatic and other narrative this is always a transposition of typical "features of social movement . . . heightened or exaggerated, so as to increase their very 'sociability'" (Elam, p. 78). Semiotics today is confirming that Brecht's basic theories, such as that of *Gestus*, have "only" the huge merit of explaining perennial dramaturgic practice. The stage figure and *Gestus* of Galileo, for example, does not centrally stand for either the historical or any other imaginatively modified individual who had such-and-such a biography but for a parabolic type one can perhaps call "the great but socially flawed scientist." In parables and similar allegorical or quasi-allegorical genres—that is, in almost all the literary and art genres before the rise of individualism—the particular, surface vehicle always intimately interacts with the universal, depth tenor. This holds also for their agents: types are always at or near their surface.

In sum, as a general philosophical proposition, any "unrepeatably individual" feature can only be recognized and analyzed within some net of general concepts and categories. The "individual" phenomenon "in art does not testify to the lack of a system but to the intersection of several diverse systems in one single point."[38] A character can only be understood in dialectical interrelationship with historical concepts and categories of types, which shape the norms of verisimilitude shared by the author and his/her social addressee.

4. Some Indications for Situating "Character"

4.1

I can only briefly suggest here a program of at least book-length research needed to verify the usefulness of a historical-cultural theory of narrative agents. If the hypothesis developed earlier is correct, the answer to the question, Which agential level is to be found on the surface of a text and which is to be found in the presuppositions or depths of a text (i.e., what is textual and what is metatextual)? is neither single nor eternal. It is not given once and for all by the structure of the human brain or unconscious[39] and/or by a universal syntax; on the contrary, it is a *changing* answer, based on dominant aspects of sociohistorical relationships among people—both the relationships of which and to which that text speaks. Such changes happen, no doubt, within a *longue durée* measured in epochs, yet they are nonetheless part of the major "geological" shifts in human relations. One clear instance of such a wholly new (in principle) narrative level is the rise of the individualist *character* in the period between Boccaccio, Shakespeare, Cervantes, and Molière, in whose works its coming into being can be palpably traced.

Of course, this does not mean that agents with conflicting and sufficiently numerous traits (i.e., characters) cannot be found before or outside the European fourteenth or sixteenth century. Basic epistemological shifts in a culture and in social practice come neither overnight nor out of nowhere. If we knew more about different cultures, we could speak with more confidence about controversial matters such as a possible antique or Hellenic individualism arising somewhere between Aeschylus and Euripides. I shall have to leave this aside, as it is for my theoretical purposes indifferent whether to postulate the rise and coming into existence of bourgeois individualism only or of several individualisms that came and went (though I would be inclined to argue with Aristotle that in most Hellenic plays there is no character, only *ethos*, a Hellenic variant of type under the sign of constant categories from moral philosophy, physiology, etc.).[40] I shall similarly leave aside the non-European cultures—though I am again hard put to find characters in the dramaturgies of Noh, the Peking Opera, the Javanese *wayang-topeng* (where the principal actors cannot even speak), or the classical Chinese novel.[41] But in European art, from the Middle Ages on, it seems clear that the deviation from *universalia* toward individuality "is a comparatively recent development."[42] Character in the individualist sense was born together with the bourgeoisie, capitalist money economy, economic rationality, atomization, quantification, and reification of human relationships, including equality before the law, and the whole well-known historical cluster accompanying the rise of this new episteme. Character is the fictional equivalent of private property in the process of production and circulation, of independent individuals in the market "who are the possessors of commodities [and who] place themselves in relation to one another as persons whose will resides in these objects."[43]

Historical semantics can prove that this is precisely the time when the modern meanings of key terms such as *individual, personality* or *character*, and *subject* arose. In English, "individual" originally meant the opposite of what it does after the sixteenth-seventeenth-century watershed, namely, an *indivisible* unity or community in multiplicity (e.g., the Christian Trinity), or "the individual Catholicke Church" (as Milton was still writing at this late date). The singular noun "individual" emancipated itself from explicit and subordinate relation "to the group of which it was, so to say, the ultimate indivisible division" only in the late eighteenth century—a characteristic example of the new usage being in Adam Smith's political economy! The fully fledged ideology of "individualism" emerged, then, in the nineteenth century and was recorded in the English translation of Tocqueville, who characterizes it as "a novel expression, to which a novel idea has given birth." Similarly, the use of "character" for fictional agents dates from the mid-eighteenth century; earlier, if applied to people at all, it had meant their more or less fixed nature, their reputation, or the fixed type and literary genre popularized by Theophrastus, La Bruyère, and Overbury. Finally, "subjective" also changed into its opposite: for the Schoolmen it meant "as things are in themselves," that is, according to their substance. It is "especially from Descartes" that "subject" came to mean the opposite, that is, the thinking, isolated self. Correspondingly, "objective" metamorphosed from the meaning "as things are not in themselves" to "as things are in themselves," beheld by but deduced as independent of the thinking self. In English, the use of "subject" in grammar came in the seventeenth century, and of "object" in the eighteenth century. The modern philosophical distinction "subject-object" (tacitly imported into the earlier syntactic use by Greimas et al.) developed, of course, in and after classical German philosophy.[44]

To verify this in terms of dramaturgic agents (see Table 1): the *kind or category of behavior*—though not necessarily the concrete behavior itself—of a type (as explained in part 3, e.g., a *miles gloriosus* or a La Bruyère *caractere*) is wholly predictable. As different from type, a *character* must possess more than, say, half a dozen traits, of which at least two are eventually found to be contradictory or otherwise incompatible. Thus, in a character even the kind of behavior is *not* wholly predictable. In that sense, this character or *personnage-personne* is an upstart and newfangled kind of agent. It is limited not only by epoch but also by genre[45]—for example, the psychological novel and *piece bien faite* as against fairy tale, paraliterature, and most of the avant-garde of the last century (which in this hypothesis is the beginning of the postindividualist epoch).

I should make clear that none of my arguments have spoken to the historical necessity or value of the rise of individualistic character. My provisional opinion—on a huge subject that requires more investigation willing to admit and, if warranted, compensate for its initial ideological bias—is that the rise of the character as an agential level (just as the rise of its economic and social analogues and bearers, the market and the bourgeoisie) has brought both great advantages and great limitations. The advantages were principally apparent during the ascending historical phase, in Europe, say, up to Balzac, George Eliot, and Tolstoy. In that phase, the character was the agential formulation of the freedom to break through the consensual constraints of hierarchically frozen social types and dogmatic normative systems—connected with despotic monarchism and a stagnant subsistence economy—toward larger horizons of life. The multiplication of traits and their conflictuality, the illusion of agential "roundness" and "three-dimensionality," connoted that human agents and actions were not explained, foreseen, and fixed. Their richness allowed these freshly conceived agents to slip through the insufficient—clumsy and restrictive—net of old *universalia*. In particular, the highly significant chronotopic analogues to this new structure of agents should also be investigated: where the types were timeless and set against a fixed background, so that they pretended to eternal and ubiquitous validity, a character can and does evolve in time and environment. But all such aspects turn into their contraries with the contraction and exhaustion of individualism in our century. On the one hand, the price of its particular kind of freedom begins to weigh more heavily than its achievements as the bourgeoisie shifts from personal competition to fictitious corporative "individualities"; on the other hand, this shift, as well as the failure (so far) of radical alternatives to bourgeois rule, threatens all freedom (in the sense of enlarging possibilities of life), bringing about new monopolistic and stereotype-producing networks—the Leviathans of states, corporations, armies, culture industry, and so on.[46]

4.2

Let me then take, at the end, the trajectory of one typologically and probably historically coherent sequence, whose extreme ends would be the allegorical figure of Avarice (in a hypothetical morality play) and a realistic miser, say Balzac's Gobseck. The two traits of Avarice (the homonymous predicate and its *Stellenwert* in the system of sins) expand in a Renaissance or post-Renaissance type into roughly half a dozen: the type Pantalone can be characterized by the traits "merchant," "old," "male,"

"Venetian," "amorous," and "miserly." Without that last predicate and trait, there would be no Pantalone; that is what dooms his amorous ventures to failure and makes him a permanent butt. Equally, however, it is the new fusion of this trait with the unambiguous class identification of Venetian merchant that makes for both a recognizable and a popular hyperbole of "a precise historical function, as a representative of an industrious bourgeoisie"—"the satire of commercial power" (together with homologous satires of the military power in the Capitano and of sterile learning in the Dottore).[47] The biological age of Pantalone is highly significative: the fact that there is no type of the *young* merchant before bourgeois drama (though well-known in everyday life, and even in prose fiction from the *Novellino* and Boccaccio on) shows that the physical coding is an ideological hyperbole, a plebeian (and possibly also aristocratic) adverse judgment on the vitality of a new class, episteme, way of behaving—in short, of a new *type*. One step further and we are at Molière's Harpagon, who has a similar ideological profile but is already part of the way from type to character (though not quite a contradictory character), probably by way of contamination of several types. The watershed toward character is passed in Shylock, precisely in his speech "Hath not a Jew eyes? . . ." (III.i): there is no type, I think, that can see itself simultaneously through the eyes of antagonists and through its own interiority, since this provides a union of contradictory traits par excellence. Though Shylock may for long stretches be a type, he is no longer only or primarily such (the same would hold for Richard III as against the Medieval Vice). Finally, the usurers and misers of realism, such as Gobseck, draw their strength from the interplay of characterological richness and the steel backbone of the old type, never totally buried under the surface of individualistic character.

Indeed, it is remarkable that characters—verbally bound up with a proper name—can revert to social type and turn their name into a common or generic noun simply by adding an article or a suffix. Molière's Tartuffe became "les Tartuffes" in his first *placet* to the King (August 1664); Don Juan turns into "donjuanism" or *Les Don Juans de village* (title of a play) as readily as Tartuffe does into "a tartuffe" or into *"tartufferie."*[48] This measures the oftentimes small distance between the character and type levels in much literature since Molière: in dramaturgy, it is enough to mention the melodrama (that matrix of all romantic plays), the vaudeville, or even the boulevard comedy whose art consists precisely in pasting the newest traits of the marketplace on the good old masks—a *Commedia dell'arte* inverted, so to speak. As for modern drama, say from Jarry and Chekhov to Brecht and Genet, one could show that part of its strength consists in ironically violating those same type expectations hidden behind the characters (e.g., in Brecht's *Mutter Courage und ihre Kinder* the *miles gloriosus* for Eilif, the ingenue for Kattrin, the niais, benet, or simpleton for Swiss Cheese, and, of course, the miserly merchant for Courage herself).

5. In Lieu of Conclusion

In parts 2-4 of this essay I have argued two points. First, that to understand narrative agents it is necessary to take into account the interaction within each dramatis persona between the three levels of *actantial function,* sociohistorical way of categorizing people or *type,* and often also the particular—individual but no less sociohistorical—*characterization*. In this "spatial-form" (i.e., paradigmatic) textual interaction, hegemonies will shift between the three levels according to given historical periods (as well as given analytic goals).[49] Second, I have argued that the most formalizing analysis can become precise, instead of formalistic, if and only if it enters into a feedback relation to the sociohistorical actuality of the field under scrutiny. That is why, instead of a "pure" technocratic and idealistic birth of agential theory (or, indeed, semiotics) from the spirit of syntax, I pleaded in part 2 for this relation. To speak from within semiotics, such a feedback is, after all, built into its foundations—in Aristotle, in Propp, and at least theoretically even in Lévi-Strauss, as well as in the best practitioners such as the latter Barthes and Eco. This could add the dialectics of historic mutability to the mechanistic atomism of the formalists or the computerized statics of the structuralists and neutralize their respective metaphysics.

However, there is more than a particular (much less fashionable) method of narrative and cultural analysis at stake here. As I argued in part 1, the reply to my title question is hugely important, and I hope my argumentation may lead toward two complementary conclusions: First, empirical individuals, *people* in the bourgeois individualist sense, *cannot* be represented in fiction; they necessarily become, on the one hand, *exempla* (Auden's paragons) and, on the other hand, shifting nodes of narration. Second, pertinent and crucial *relationships among people*—not atomic or pointlike but as a rule dyadic or differential—nonetheless *can* be represented in fiction; in fact, fiction *consists* in their representation and reformulation, which allows the reader to pleasurably verify old and dream up new alternative relationships, to *re-articulate* (in both senses of the word) human relationships to the world of people and things. As Aristotle argued in *Politics* (I.2), humans necessarily live in communities *(polis);* they are "political animals." Thus, all central human relations are, in this widest sense, political, and significant fictional re-presentation of relations among people rearticulates our political relationships.

Notes

1 I trust the current cultural theories discussed in this part of the essay are readily identifiable. Therefore, I will use as few references as possible for the general intertext, here and elsewhere. Indispensible titles and quotes will be footnoted at the first mention and after that referred to by author's name and page number in parenthesis within the body of the essay. In another essay, "On Metaphoricity and Narrativity in Fiction," *Sub-Stance* 48(1986): 51-67, I argue that the chronotope is, in fact, specific only to narrative texts as opposed to metaphorical ones. For part 1, the classical discussion of re-presentation is in Henri Wallon, *De l'acte a la pensee* (Paris: Flammarion, 1970), especially pp. 162-67; I am also abundantly using Bertolt Brecht, *Gesammelte Werke*, vols. 15-20 (Frankfurt: Suhrkamp, 1973). I am bound to note that the Social Sciences and Humanities Research Council of Canada has, from 1981 to 1984, consistently refused to fund research connected with this paper.

2 Mikhail M. Bakhtin, "Avtor i geroi v esteticheskoi deiatelnosti," in *Estetika slovesnogo tvorchestva* (Moscow: Iskusstvo, 1979), pp. 10-11; Seymour Chatman, *Story and Discourse* (Ithaca, N.Y.: Cornell University Press, 1978), pp. 107-8, where three other laments ranging from 1936 to 1966 are also quoted; E. M. Forster, *Aspects of the Novel* (1928; Harmondsworth, U.K.: Penguin, 1962). Translations from Bakhtin (as from all other non-English texts, unless they are cited from English titles) are mine.

3 Roland Barthes, *Lecon inaugurale* (Paris: College de France, 1977), pp. 35-36. The other quotes in this paragraph are from Umberto Eco, *A Theory of Semiotics* (Bloomington: Indiana Universtiy Press, 1977), pp. 66-68 passim; Marc Angenot, "La notion d'actant comme categorie genologique," paper presented at CSRA meeting, Montreal, May 1980. I am deeply indebted to discussions with Angenot, as well as to remarks, indications, and objec-

Darko Suvin

tions of William Dodd, Irwin Gopnik, Cary Nelson, Maria-Luisa Nunes, Patrick Parrinder, Patrice Pavis, and Maria Vittoria Tessitore.

4 Claude Lévi-Strauss, "La structure et la forme," in *Anthropologie structurale deux* (Paris: Plon, 1973), p. 162, trans. by C. Jacobson and B. G. Schoepf as *Structural Anthropology* (New York: Basic Books, 1976).

5 Darko Suvin, "Per una teoria dell'analisi agenziale," *Versus* 30(1981): 87-109, in particular pp. 87-94. Cf. Achim Eschbach and Wendelin Rader, *Semiotik-Bibliographie I* (Frankfurt: Antoren-und Verlagsgesellschaft Syndikat, 1976), and Jonathan Culler's judgment in *Structuralist Poetics* (Ithaca, N.Y.: Cornell University Press, 1975), p. 230. True, as always we can refer to Aristotle (*Poetics*, 1449b-1450a, 1451b, in the edition by L. Golden and O. B. Hardison, Jr. [Englewood Cliffs, N.J.: Prentice-Hall, 1968]; and cf. his *Ethics* and *Rhetorics*); to Vladimir Propp, *Morphology of the Folktale* (Austin: University of Texas Press, 1974), chaps., 2, 6; and to Brecht (see note 1). See also Etienne Souriau, *Les deux cent mille situations dramatiques* (Paris: Flammarion, 1950), pp. 65-81; and for some hints in Vol'kenshtein, Bogatyrev, and Frye, see note 8.

6 A major problem here is the initiating, overarching, or "transcendental" actant that Greimas calls *destinateur* (see the critique by Culler, pp. 233-34) and Souriau calls *balance* (=Arbiter); the Proppian denomination of Mandator seems to work better than either of these but has to be verified by further inductive analyses.

7 The four main works on actants by Greimas to be focused upon are: "Reflexions sur les modeles actantiels," in *Semantique structurale* (Paris: Larousse, 1966); "La structure des actants du recit," in *Du sens* (Paris: Editions du Seuil, 1970)—cf. for agents especially pp, 254ff.; "Les actants, les acteurs et les figures," in Claude Chabrol, ed., *Semiotique narrative et textuelle* (Paris: Larousse, 1973); and, with Joseph Courtes, *Semiotique* (Paris: Hachette, 1979). For other works of his, see notes 9 and 22.

8 Greimas had already, in *Semantique structurale* (p. 188), hinted at a third agential category and level in his account of psychocriticism (e.g., Baudelaire's *porteur de chimere*). Possibly, he based the introduction of this third level on a few hints in Souriau's *role* and *role pur* (pp. 69, 71), but more probably on analytic necessity. Cf. also a few hints about such a possible level, called respectively figure and *emploi*, type, and stock type, in Vladimir Vol'kenshtein, *Dramaturgiia* (1923, Moskva: Sovetskii pisatel', 1960), pp. 106, 111-12, 124-25; Petr Bogatyrev, "Les signes du theatre," *Poetique* 5(1971): 524 (first published in 1938); and Northrop Frye, *Anatomy of Criticism* (Princeton, N.J.: Princeton University Press, 1957), pp. 172ff.

9 Cf. for the two incompatible types of *roles actantiels* the Greimas essay in Chabrol, pp. 165-66, 167, and for *roles thematiques*, pp. 171-75; for agents assigned to *discours* versus *recit* in *Du sens*, pp. 255-56; and for Greimas-Courtes (e.g., entries for *actant, acteur, role thematique*). The differentiations between collective and individual as well as paradigmatic and syntagmatic actant in Greimas's *Semiotique et sciences sociales* (Paris: Editions du Seuil, 1976) do not seem either illuminating or pertinent to the present essay. Claude Bremond, *Logique du recit* (Paris: Editions due Seuil, 1973) attempted to inventory all the principal "narrative roles" into eternal agents, such as *protecteur* and *frustrateur*, or patients, such as *beneficiaire* and *victime*.

10 First quote by Lévi-Strauss, *Anthropologie structurale* (Paris: Plon, 1958), p. 75; quotes in following sentences: ibid., p. 201, and *Anthropologie structurale deux*, pp. 168-69, 172.

11 I will summarize and apply in the following two sections only some of the most basic and pertinent issues of extremely complex and largely unfinished epistemological debates. The handiest brief discussions of preconditions for knowledge may be found in Jean Piaget, ed., *Logique et connaissance scientifique* (Paris, 1967), in particular the essays by Piaget, Jean-Blaise Grize, Leo Apostel, and Jean Ladriere. Since Greimas claims for his approach the authority of a formal *system*, one could also apply to him the strictures of Kurt Godel, "Ueber formal unenthscheidbare Satze . . . ," *Monatshefte f. Mathematik u. Physik* 38(1931): 173-98 (in English: *On Formally Undecidable Propositions of Principia Mathematica and Related Systems* [Edinburgh: Oliver and Boyd, 1962]); and of Alfred Tarski, "Der Wahrheitsbegriff in den formalisierten Sprachen," *Studia philosophica* 1(1935): 261-405; "On Undecidable Statements in Enlarged Systems of Logic and the Concept of Truth," *Journal of Symbolic Logic* 4(1939); and *Introduction to Logic and to the Methodology of Deductive Sciences* (New York: Oxford University Press, 1949), that such a system can only be validated by another, higher and more potent system (in Marxism: practice). I will here simplify by giving Greimas the benefit of the doubt that his approach may rather be used as a *model;* but if so, claims made for it have to be scaled down sharply.

12 Cf., e.g., Emile Benveniste, "Les niveaux de l'analyse linguistique," *Proceedings of the Ninth International Congress of Linguistics* (Cambridge: Cambridge University Press, 1962), pp. 266-93. The followers of "text linguistics" would deny this, but I do not think they have proved their case.

691

13   See *Semantique structurale*, pp. 133, 185, and *Du sens*, pp. 162 passim. Cf., however, even from the standpoint of Brondal's linguistic philosophy, the critique of Greimas's tacit transmogrification of the concept of actant in Svend Erik Larsen, "Le concept d'actant: Greimas et Brondal," *Journal Canadien de Recherche Semiotique* 3(1975): 16-35, esp. pp. 24-26.

14   Grize, "Historique," in Piaget, p. 169.

15   Greimas, *Semantique structurale*, pp. 130, 185ff.; *Du sens*, p. 257; "Les actants, les acteurs et les figures," pp. 169-76. Similar hesitations can be found in many others, not excluding the interesting François Rastier, *Essais de semiotique discursive* (Tours: Mame, 1973), pp. 95-96, 173, 214, or even Barthes. Culler, pp. 76-94, is, I believe, getting at the same problem in his persuasive critique of Greimas's "structural semantics"; further on (pp. 213-14, 233-34) Culler is justly severe about Greimas's arbitrary classifications and tentative speculations elevated into methodology. Cf. also the critique of Greimas's inconsistent syntactic-cum-semantic terminology in K. Bartoszynski, "O badaniach ukladow fabularnych," in H. Markiewicz and J. Slawinski, eds., *Problemy metodologiczne wspolczesnego literaturoznawstwa* (Krakow: Wydawn. Literackie, 1976), p. 181, and of Greimas's "occultation of the enunciating subject" in Timothy J. Reiss, "Semiology and Its Discontents: Saussure and Greimas," *Canadian Journal of Research in Semiotics* 5(1977): 85-97. A general critique of the ahistorical structuralist "syntacticism" is in Paul Ricoeur, *Le conflit des interpretations* (Paris: Editions du Seuil 1969), pp. 31-63; and cf. Ricoeur, "La grammaire generative de Greimas," *Documents [de recherche du groupe de linguistique]* 15(1980); and two further sociohistorically oriented critiques in Henri Lefebvre's beautiful *L'ideologie structuraliste* (Paris: Editions du Seuil, 1975) and Pierre Bourdieu's *Outline of a Theory of Practice* (Cambridge: Cambridge University Press, 1977). Let me not fail to note that an engaging bricolage-type modesty coexists strangely in Greimas with blind Hjelmslevian dogmatism in fundamentals, on which I unfortunately have to focus.

16   Cesare Segre, *Semiotics and Literary Criticism*, trans. J. Meddemmen (The Hague: Mouton, 1973), p. 67, puts it more politely: "Clearly Hjelmslev's highly suggestive scheme is not up to the complexity of literary models"; he notes that valid semiotic criticism should not be limited to a mere defining of matrices. Segre passes the same judgments on Greimas's actants in his entry "Narrazione/narrativita," in *Enciclopedia Einaudi*, vol. 9 (Torino, 1980), p. 696. But Hjelmslev's dichotomy between "pure form" and social substance is very dubious within linguistics itself. Perhaps the most famous critique in that discipline is by Andre Martinet, "Au sujet des *Fondements de theorie linguistique* de L. Hjelmslev," *Bulletin de la Société de Linguistique de Paris* 42, fasc. 1(1946): 19-43; it has been often repeated in French linguistics. Prieto notes that Hjelmslev's abstract formalization is an "illusion symmetrical and inverse" to naive empiricism (*Pertinence* [see note 19], p. 125; cf. pp. 66-69, 122-26). Claude Chabrol discusses incisively Hjelmslev's "dizzying failure" in "De la semiotique en question," in Claude Chabrol and Louis Marin, eds., *Le recit evangelique* (Paris: Aubier Montaigne, 1974), pp. 193-200, 205-9; he notes also that Hjelmslev's claim about the translatability of all other "languages" into natural language was based on unclear concepts and has since been falsified by all attempts to find linguistic forms in music, body gesture and movement, fine arts, and so on. For a general argument on the cognate universalism in analytical philosophy and Whorfian linguistics, see Ferruccio Rossi-Landi, *Semiotica e ideologia* (Milano: V. Bompiani, 1972), pp. 154ff.; and for objections more directly pertinent to Greimas's domain, see Barthes's critiques of the basic syntactic dyad subject-predicate and the "logic" of actions if taken outside the cultural conditions in *S/Z* (Paris, 1970), pp. 82-83, 88-89, 209-10 passim, as well as critiques of Bremond and Greimas in Culler, pp. 208-11 and note 15, and in Rastier, pp. 218-21.

17   First quote: John C. Condon, *Semantics and Communication* (New York: Macmillan, 1975), p. 3; second quote: Albert Carnoy, *La science du mot* (Louvain: Editions Universitas, 1927), p. 43. One of the great pioneers of pragmatics is Bakhtin, for whom *situation* implies the space and time as well as the object or theme of utterance and the evaluative relation of the interlocutors to that utterance and its context—cf., e.g., Bakhtin/Voloshinov's "Stylistics of Artistic Discourse" (1930), forthcoming in Wlad Godzich, ed., *Writings of the Circle of Bakhtin* (University of Minnesota Press); and also *Marxism and the Philosophy of Language* (New York: Seminar Press, 1973) and *Estetika* (see note 2).

18   On that concept see Darko Suvin, "The Social Addresses of Victorian Fiction," *Literature and History* 1(1982): 11-40, with large bibliography.

19   I am following here the fundamental approach by Luis J. Prieto. Cf. "Entwurf einer allgemeinen Semiologie," *Ztschr. f. Semiotik* 1(1970): 261, and *Pertinence et pratique* (Paris: Editions de Minuit, 1975), pp. 147-50 passim, attempting to pursue the epistemological implications of Marx's *Theses on Feuerbach* (though I disagree with some points in Prieto, e.g., his stark Althusserian break between natural and human sciences, between subject and object of cognition).

20   Janos Petofi, cited in Achim Eschbach, *Pragmasemiotik und Theater* (Tubingen: Narr, 1979), p. 69.

Darko Suvin

21   Sebastiano Timpanaro, "Structuralism and Its Successors," in *On Materialism* (London: NLB, 1975); cf. also the general argument of David Savan, "Towards a Refutation of Semiotic Idealism," *Semiotic Inquiry* 3(1983): 6.

22   I cannot enter here into Greimas's evolution after the peak of his actantial theory in the 1970s. I should mention that parallel to the development of linguistic pragmatics he has been attempting to somewhat mend his fences but without basically changing his approach. In his study of a "passion" ("De la colere," *Documents [du groupe de recherches semio-linguistiques de 1'E.H.E.S.S.*] 27(1981), the subtitle of "semantique lexicale" seems to me crucial. To paraphrase calif Omar, it raises a dilemma in both of whose horns it is untenable. Either the "lexical" is contained in semantics, since in a way all meanings of words are *also* lexical, and it is redundant; or it is not so contained, and it is an oxymoron on the order of Brecht's "planned disorder," where the adjective purports to redefine the noun, so that meanings of words are henceforth to be understood *only* as lexical and not also as referential, extrasemiotic in Peirce's sense. Thus, the familiar oscillation between agnosticism and idealism is retained and applied to new domains. Similar is Greimas's interest in the per se not uninteresting attempts at the study of modalities, which amount to a recuperation of ideological studies in a dehistoricized fashion; cf. the latest propositions I know of in his interview with Hans-George Ruprecht, "Ouvertures metasemiotiques," *Semiotic Inquiry* 4(1984): 1-23. His conclusion is that pragmatics, and even "somatic passions," might perhaps be admitted if it stays within (his kind of) semiotics.

23   One of structuralism's most important epistemological precursors and shapers (by way of logical positivism) is Ernst Mach. If my argument about the usable versus useless faces of structuralism is correct, then—for all of Mach's lack of clarity and sometimes sheer agnosticism—Lenin overreacted in *Materialism and Empiriocriticism* (and especially, in the heat of what was centrally a political battle, against Bogdanov, a thinker to be reevaluated). Today, in view of both political and ideological developments during the intervening eighty years, it is impossible to bypass the clarifications of epistemology from Mach and Russell on. However, as my critique indicates, I think these can be accepted only on condition that (as Lenin also insisted) they be refunctioned within a materialist and dialectical horizon. I have approached this huge problem, attempting to use Gramsci, Bloch, Timpanaro, and Habermas, in "On Two Notions of 'Science' in Marxism," in Tom Henighan, ed., *Brave New Universe* (Ottawa, 1980), pp. 27-43. For developed epistemological considerations, cf. Piaget, especially his brilliant essay "Les methodes de l'epistemologie."

24   Doede Nauta, *The Meaning of Information* (The Hague: Mouton, 1970), p. 42.

25   For this different and unduly neglected tradition, which seems to begin with Marx's *Eighteenth Brumaire*, see Hans Gerth and C. Wright Mills, *Character and Social Structure* (New York: Harcourt Brace, 1953); Jutta Matzner, "Der Begriff der Charaktermaske bei Karl Marx," *Soziale Welt* 15(1964): 130ff.; Eduard Urbanek, "Roles, Masks and Characters," in Peter Berger, ed., *Marxism and Sociology* (New York: Appleton-Century-Crofts, 1969); and the essays by John Coombes and Stanley Mitchell in Francis Barker et. al., eds., *Literature, Society, and the Sociology of Literature: 1848* (Colchester: University of Essex, 1977).

26   See notes 5, 8, 15, 16, 48; see also Georg Simmel, *Soziologie* (Munchen: Duncker and Humblot, 1923); Sorin Alexandrescu, *Logique du personnage;* Roland Barthes, "Introduction a l'analyse structurale des recits," *Communications* 8(1966; Paris: Editions du Seuil, 1981): 7-33, and *S/Z;* Philippe Hamon, "Pour un statut semiologique du personnage," *Litterature* 6(1972): 86-110; Tzvetan Todorov, "Personnage," in Oswald Ducrot and Tzvetan Todorov, eds., *Dictionnaire encyclopedique des sciences du langage* (Paris: Editions du Seuil, 1972), pp. 286-92, and *Poetique de la prose* (Paris: Editions du Seuil, 1971); Anne Ubersfeld, *Lire le theatre* (Paris, 1977). Cf. Umberto Eco, "James Bond: Une combinatoire narrative," *Communications* 8 (1966): 83-99.

27   Friedrich Engels, letter to Minna Kautsky, Nov. 26, 1885, in Karl Marx and Friedrich Engels, *Ueber Kunst und Literatur* ([East] Berlin: Henschelverlag, 1953), p. 120. Cf. Lidiia Ginzburg, "O strukture literaturnogo personazha," in *Iskusstvo slova* [Festschrift D. D. Blagoi] (Moskva, 1973), pp. 376-88, and *O psikhologicheskoi proze* (Leningrad: VKP, 1971), for the most sophisticated approach to the relations between type and character that I have found (unfortunately, too late for this study). After my hypothesis of the three agential levels had been given as a lecture at several conferences and universities, Patrice Pavis kindly sent me proofs of his *Dictionnaire du theatre* (Paris: Editions Sociales, 1980), where he (s.v. "actantiel [modele]") briefly indicates his own "Theorie des niveaux d'existence du personnage." Pavis postulates the existence of four agential levels, the two middle ones being actants and characters; between them, he somewhat tentatively but very interestingly postulates a "niveau intermediaire" of *roles* defined as "entites figuratives, animees, mais generales et exemplaires (ex: le fanaron, le pere noble, le traitre)." I am delighted with this convergence—it recurs apropos our evaluation of Brecht's key theoretical concept of *Gestus*, which Pavis deals with at more length in "On Brecht's Notion of *Gestus*," *Languages of the Stage* (New York, 1982), pp. 39-49—and only wish he would develop this insight at more length and into a full analytic level having the same rights as his other two. Pavis's deepest level of

693

"structures elementaires de la signification" seems to me an unnecessary reverence toward Greimas; his fourth level pertains to staging, which seems to me another metalanguage altogether.

28   However, a developed narratological theory of agents will have to seriously confront this theory, both to point out its serious deficiencies and to see what elements may still be usable. Its principal sources are Ralph Linton, *The Cultural Background of Personality* (New York: D.-Appleton-Century, 1945) and *The Study of Man* (New York: Appleton-Century-Crofts, 1964); G. H. Mead, *Mind, Self and Society* (Chicago: University of Chicago Press, 1934); Jacob L. Moreno, *Who Shall Survive?* (Beacon, N.Y.: Beacon House, 1953); and Georg Simmel (see note 26). Cf. also Michael Banton, *Roles* (London: Tavistock, 1965); Erving Goffman, *Encounters* (Indianapolis: Bobbs-Merrill, 1961) and other titles to *Frame Analysis* (New York: Harper and Row, 1974); Georges Gurvitch, ed., *La vocation actuelle de la sociologie*, vol. 1 (Paris: Presses Universitaires de France, 1957); Marcel Mauss, *Sociologie et anthropologie* (Paris: Presses Universitaires de France, 1950); J. Milton Yinger, *Toward a Field Theory of Behavior* (New York: McGraw-Hill, 1965). See also Bruce J. Biddle and Edwin J. Thomas, eds., *Role Theory* (New York: Wiley, 1966); Hans Joas, *Die gegenwartige Lage der soziologischen Rollentheorie* (Frankfurt: Athenaum-Verlag, 1973); and Anne-Marie Rocheblave-Spenle, *La notion de role en psychologie sociale* (Paris: Presses Universitaires de France, 1962). For interesting critiques, cf. Dieter Claessens, *Rolle und Macht* (Munchen: Juventa-Verlag, 1970); Uta Gerhardt, "Toward a Critical Analysis of Role," *Social Problems* 27(1980): 556-67; and Frigga Haug, *Kritik der Rollentheorie* (Frankfurt: Fischer Taschenbuch Verlag, 1972). I am grateful to my master's student Hanneke van Schaik for bringing some of these titles to my attention.
   For attempts at bridging social and theater roles, see much of the Burns book; see also Jean Duvignaud, *L'Acteur* (Paris: Gallimard, 1965), pp. 12-20; Anne-Marie Gourdon, "Role social et role theatral," *Travail theatral* 10(1973): 76-86; Uri Rapp, *Handeln und Zuschauen* (Neuwied, 1973); and Bruce Wilshire, *Role Playing and Identity* (Bloomington: Indiana University Press, 1982).
   Another whole field to be surveyed is that of an analytic philosophy of action; cf. for a first introduction Robert W. Binkley et. al., eds., *Agent, Action and Reason* (Oxford: Oxford University Press, 1971), with an extensive bibliography on pp. 169-99; and R. Tanaka, "Action and Meaning in Literary Theory," *Journal of Literary Semantics* 1(1972): 41-56.

29   Georg Lukács, *Die Theorie des Romans* (Neuwied: Luchterhand, 1965); "The Intellectual Physiognomy in Characterization," in *Writer and Critic and Other Essays*, ed. Arthur D. Kahn (New York: Grosset and Dunlap, 1971); *The Historical Novel* (Harmondsworth, U.K.: Penguin, 1969); *Balzac und der franzosische Realismus* (Berlin: Aufbau-Verlag, 1952); cf. also the splendid "Zur Soziologie des modernen Dramas," *Archiv f. Sozialwiss. u. Sozialpol.* 38(1914): 303ff., so far as I know not yet fully published in English. The title of *The Specificity of Aesthetics* testifies to Lukács's interesting attempts at delving deeper into that crucial subject, though I think still on the same "right" ontological basis of subject versus object, form versus content, and so on.

30   Cf. Darko Suvin, "Looking Backward at Lukács," *To Brecht and Beyond* (Brighton and Totowa, N.J., 1984), pp. 75-79.

31   Draft of Engels's letter to Miss Harkness of Apr. 1888, in Karl Marx and Friedrich Engels, *Ueber Kunst und Literatur*, ed. Michael Lifschitz (Berlin: Henschelverlag, 1953), p. 122. However, I believe that at the back of Lukács's mind is Simmel's discussion of all individuals being also types (e.g., *Soziologie*, pp. 24-28), and probably some Russian nineteenth-century criticism (for this last point I am indebted to discussions with Regine Robin, *Le realisme socialiste*, forthcoming from Payot, Paris).

32   William Whewell, *The Philosophy of Inductive Sciences* (London: J. W. Parker, 1840), I:476-77, quoted approvingly in T. H. Huxley, *Man's Place in Nature, and Other Essays* (London, 1906), p. 272; emphasis is mine. Appropriately, it was Whewell who coined the typifying term "scientist." Very similar is Balzac's definition in his preface to *Une tenebreuse affaire*: "Un type . . . est un personnage qui resume en lui-meme les traits caracteristiques de tous ceux qui lui ressemblent plus ou moins, il est le modele du genre" (paraphrased in present-day terms: A type is a narrative agent who blends characteristic traits of all characters of the same category; he is the model of his *genus*).

33   E. H. Gombrich, *Art and Illusion*, Bollingen Series XXV-5 (Princeton, N.J.: Princeton University Press, 1972), p. 301.

34   Gombrich, p. 90; see also the psychological theories of Bruner and Postman as summarized by Floyd H. Allport, *Theories of Perception and the Concept of Structure* (New York and London, 1955), pp. 376ff., and with further bibliography; also the well-known works of Jean Piaget and S. L. Vygotsky on perception.

35   Gombrich, p. 73. When applied to dramatis personae, any such approach necessarily issues in discussions of typification as allegory; cf. the stimulating remarks of Fredric Jameson,

694

Darko Suvin

Marxism and Form (Princeton, N.J.: Princeton University Press, 1971), pp. 398-400, and *The Political Unconscious* (Ithaca, N.Y.: Cornell University Press 1981), pp. 160-64 passim.

36   Keir Elam, *The Semiotics of Theatre and Drama* (London: Methuen, 1980), p. 8.

37   This whole matter of masks and masking warrants special investigation as, I think, a theoretically crucial point in agential analysis.

38   Ju. M. Lotman and B. A. Uspenskij, "Introduzione," in *Ricerche semiotiche* (Torino, 1973), p. xxvi.

39   As Lévi-Strauss often also seems to believe; cf., e.g., *Anthropologie structurale*, pp. 67, 106—not to speak of Chomsky's approving reference to the "assumption that linguistic and mental processes are virtually identical" in *Cartesian Linguistics* (New York: Harper and Row, 1966), p. 31.

40   Aristotle, *Poetics* (see note 5, also the editor's comments on pp. 124-26, 202); cf. also *Rhetorics* II.12-17 on types by age and status, and *Politics* I.2 on the *polis* versus the single person, as well as Chatman, pp. 108-9, and Gombrich, p. 142 , on types in Greek art.

41   Cf. Darko Suvin, "On Fiction as Anthropology: Agential Analysis, Types, and the Classical Chinese Novel," in J. Hall, ed., *Proceedings of the 1983 Conference on Literature and Anthropology*, University of Hong Kong Press (forthcoming).

42   Gombrich, p. 148, and esp. pp. 148-52. V. M. Zhirmunskii, *Sravnitel'noe literaturovedenie— Vostok i Zapad* (Leningrad: Nauka, 1979), is one of the latest major scholars who notes how in both medieval and oral literature "the typical dominates . . . over the individual" as creativity is enclosed within literary genres that are bearers "not of an individual and idiosyncratic but of a socially typical world view and style" (pp. 161-62). The protagonist's behavior, too, is here determined by norms of *etat*, mundane ritual, etiquette (p. 170).

43   Karl Marx, *Capital*, vol. 1 (New York: Vintage, 1977), p. 178. See Marx's whole key argument on commodity fetishism, in which—very interestingly for further discussion of relations between agents and objects in fiction—he adds that reification of human relations is the obverse of a personification of things. Cf. also Lukács, *History and Class Consciousness* (Cambridge, Mass.: Harvard University Press, 1971).

44   All the examples and quotes of historical semantics in this paragraph come from Raymond Williams, *Keywords* (London: NLB, 1976), s.v. "Individual," "Personality" (for references to "character"), and "Subjective." See also on the (bourgeois) legal framework as enforcing individuality instead of a "person-in-role" or of "role-slices," Goffman, *Encounters*, p. 142; and for the opinion that the subject/object division has been imported into linguistic theory from formal logic, the inventor of the term "actant" himself, Lucien Tesniere, *Elements de syntaxe structurale* (Paris: C. Klincksieck, 1959), pp. 103-5.

45   Barthes, "Introduction," p. 16: "une forme purement historique, restreinte a certains genres (il est vrai les mieux connus de nous) . . ."; cf. also the longer discussions in *S/Z*, pp. 141-42, 153-54, 183-84. Propp has some very similar hints. On character requiring a number of possibly contradictory traits, I am expanding from Chatman, pp. 121-22, who is indebted to Forster (whose discussions derive in turn—just as Lukács's do—from Hegel's *Aesthetics*, perhaps *the* major source on individuality in art). Some of the most fascinating discussions on the sense of the Self before individualism (both in tribal societies and in the Latin concepts of *res* and *persona*) are to be found in Mauss, pp. 232-79, 337-62.

46   On culture industry, the pioneering text is Theodor Adorno and Max Horkheimer's vigorous (if one-sided) *Dialectics of Enlightenment* (London: Continuum, 1979); see in particular, for the evacuation of individuality, pp. 154-56, 84-86, 144.

47   Vito Pandolfi, *Il teatro del Rinascimento e la Commedia dell'Arte* (Roma: Lerici, 1969), pp. 176, 180. Pantalone is, of course, a *Commedia dell'arte Maschera*, and as such a type by theatrical convention physically overcoded into a narrow range of looks and behaviors. Finally, in the eighteenth century the bourgeoisie hit back and changed the nature of dramaturgic agents: "In the *Commedia dell'arte* poor Pantalone was [ridiculed and deluded]; but in my character Comedies I restored the reputation of this good figure, who represents an honest Merchant of my Nation," reported Goldoni; he therefore changed a *dell'arte* scenario with a "libertine, stupid, and ridiculous" Pantalone into "a moral comedy . . . instructive for those who are seduced by interest or friendship to entrust their capital to suspect persons . . . called *The Bankruptcy*"; Carlo Goldoni, *Il teatro comico—Memorie italiane* (Milano: Marsilio, 1982), pp. 189, 218.

48   My discussion of the onomastics of type uses the naive but rich work by Georges Doutrepont, *Les types populaires de la litterature française* (Bruxelles, s.a.). I am indebted to John Ripley and Charles Shattuck for counsels on English "stock characters" or theater types. It should be noted that *naming* is a privileged point of entry into discussions about individualistic fiction, too; see, e.g., Barthes *S/Z*, pp. 74-75, 101-2, 196-97; Todorov, "Personnage," with further bibliography; Ju. M. Lotman and B. A. Uspenskij, "Myth—Name—Culture," in Daniel P.

Lucid, ed., *Soviet Semiotics* (Baltimore, Md.: Johns Hopkins University Press, 1977), pp. 233-52; and the disagreements a propos the eighteenth century between Ian Watt, *The Rise of the Novel* (London: Chatto and Windus, 1957), pp. 18ff., and Joan Rockwell, *Fact in Fiction* (London: Routledge and Kegan Paul, 1974), pp. 105ff., as well as Wolfgang Iser's discussions of Fielding in *Der implizite Leser* (Munich: W. Fink, 1972) and "Die Wirklichkeit der Fiktion," in Rainer Warning, ed., *Rezeptionsasthetik* (Munich: W. Fink, 1975), pp. 308ff.

49 Furthermore, when our understanding wishes, as is proper, to embrace the temporally variable agential system of any text or macrotext (ensemble of texts), agential hegemonies will shift not only paradigmatically but also syntagmatically. In this essay I do not discuss syntagmatic interaction, which is both more frequently studied then and yet logically posterior to the paradigmatic interaction, and which can best be shown *in estenso* by applications to particular texts.

Michèle Barrett

The Place of Aesthetics in Marxist Criticism

Marxist theoretical and critical work typically reduces culture either to ideology and meaning or to an antihumanist concern for the production of meaning. In either case, examinations of the nature of aesthetic experience and questions of aesthetic value are ignored. This has serious political consequences, in part because it fails to engage popular conceptions of art.

Aesthetic questions have never been particularly prominent in Marxist approaches to culture, but they are increasingly relegated to an extremely marginal position in both theoretical and critical debates. Even the very broad title of the conference on which this volume is based—Marxism and the Interpretation of Culture—was apparently not broad enough to include considerations of the aesthetic, rather than the sociological and ideological, dimensions of culture. It is not that Marxism has failed to develop a tradition of work on aesthetics but rather that such concerns are currently out of fashion and, indeed, are often seen as politically reprehensible.

If this description is correct, the situation poses major theoretical and political problems because it has left Marxists unable to engage with bourgeois criticism, dominant educational practices, and popular sentiment. By evading the questions of aesthetic pleasure and value, Marxist criticism and radical cultural intervention place themselves in a relatively weak position. For this reason, I think it is necessary to reconsider the question of a materialist aesthetics and the strengths and dangers inherent in such a project. I shall elaborate on this in the second half of this essay through a critical consideration of the work of the art critic Max Raphael.

Aesthetic Value and Pleasure in Marxist Theory

"Aesthetic" is commonly given three definitions or meanings: (1) received by the senses; (2) referring to beauty; (3) superior taste. The last need not concern us here since sociological approaches have forcefully demonstrated the historical vulnerability of "taste."[1] We can usefully translate the other two meanings into the questions of pleasure and value. When someone says that a piece of music or a poem makes their hair stand on end, or when Cézanne records in his diary that he feels his eyes bleeding as he looks at what he is painting, they refer to sensations that might be called an "aesthetic mode of feeling." A possible equivalent to these heightened sensory perceptions is sexual pleasure, and, indeed, certain "pleasurable" features of art (abundance, extravagance of expression, the tension and resolution characteristic of much Western classical music, for example) can readily be interpreted in more directly sexual analogies. In general, however, the advocates of an aesthetic mode of sensation see it as a separate faculty. The object in this mode of perception is not necessarily identical to "beauty," since a work of art could be recognized to have "great value" without being tied to a particular definition of beauty.

The questions raised by the term "aesthetic" are, briefly: Can we say that there is a distinctive "aesthetic" faculty or mode of perception, and, if so, what is the nature of the pleasure it affords? Can we identify objects or works to which universal aesthetic value adheres? It is difficult to formulate these questions in a noncircular way, and the history of attempts to come to grips with them is, perhaps surprisingly, very sparse. Aesthetics, as a minor subfield of philosophy, considers the questions in the abstract (e.g., What is beauty?) rather than in respect to the claims of particular instances. Art history, the place where one would expect to see aesthetic matters considered, is startlingly silent, often preferring to trace influences or to delight in obscure attributions. Art criticism tends to emphasize the formal properties of the work in question rather than address more general questions of aesthetic pleasure and value. This situation seems curious, since art and literary history and criticism are not reticent to assess and grade their objects of study. However, in a large number of instances the ranking of the works depends upon criteria that are not *aesthetic* (a work is stoical, uplifting, cathartic, illuminating, or whatever). What is often *not shown* is how and why the particular formal properties of the work (situated in an understanding of the different dimensions of particular art forms) can account for the value assigned.

The question might be looked at another way by saying that the aesthetic properties of a work can be differentiated from its meaning. Unfortunately, this works in two ways. Poetry, for instance, is often characterized by a condensation of language (in a non-Freudian sense): a multiplicity of meanings arise from one signifier. Many regard this surplus of meaning as distinctively aesthetic. Yet the reverse is also held: that the aesthetic is precisely constituted in the excess of the signifier over the signified. As Terry Eagleton puts it, "If you approach me at a bus stop and murmur 'Thou still unravished bride of quietness,' then I am instantly aware that I am in the presence of the literary. I know this because the texture, rhythm and resonance of your words are in excess of their abstractable meaning."[2] Further, formulations of this kind do not necessarily help in that they are equally applicable to situations in which no question of the aesthetic arises. Many of Oscar Wilde's epigrams can be said to generate surplus meaning without being regarded as an instantiation of "the literary" or of aesthetic value. Many conference papers flaunt a "texture, rhythm and resonance of [language] in excess of their abstractable meaning," but they are not deemed to be works of "literature." The unresolved relationship between the categories of meaning and the aesthetic underlies the vexed position of the latter in Marxist criticism today.

In fact, neither of the two major critical and theoretical approaches currently applied to the analysis of cultural products adequately addresses the questions of aesthetic pleasure and value. The first theoretical tendency that blocks serious consideration of aesthetic questions has been the dominant influence of the concept of ideology in critical studies. The ghost of Lukács has yet to be laid to rest. While this critical tradition may have rejected class reductionism, it has been content to argue about whether a given work is *really* about class conflict or gender difference, for instance. Criticism of many classic texts often takes the form of an eternal procession of "readings" that claim to have uncovered the essential ideological message of the text. That such readings, whether by Marxists or bourgeois critics, are children of their time has been demonstrated by Ronald Frankenberg in his history of Marxist criticism of *Wuthering Heights*.[3]

Works of art and literature are still seen as the passive and innocent terrain on which ideological armies go about their usual battles. This is not wrong, but it is limited. Of course, works of art do encode ideological positions, but we do not exhaust their significance by decoding their ideological content; nor do we explain how the reception and consumption of works sharing comparable ideological ground may vary dramatically over a period of time. Moreover, this "art-as-ideology" perspective tends to consider aesthetic value only insofar as it can be attributed to supposedly "progressive" texts. The problems of this tortured relationship need not detain us here, although they are legion. The point is that an *exclusive* emphasis on ideology necessarily denies the aesthetic dimensions of the text. As Terry Lovell suggests, it involves treating the cognitive/ideological axis in the work as primary when this should be seen as secondary in imaginative works.[4]

The second major tendency I want to discuss is the very broad one of structuralism, poststructuralism, and deconstructionism. The break with classical theories of representation that are exclusively concerned with a pregiven signified has rightly led to a reconsideration of the means of representation. A theory of signification that emphasizes the text's internal powers of meaning construction, and stresses the multiplicity of readings available in consumption, has both strengths and weaknesses. One major strength of the approach is that it enables us to transcend the boundaries of bourgeois categories: high art and mass culture, literature and popular fiction, the various academic disciplines. To subject the objects and texts of the categories of Art and Literature to the same processes of examination that are applied to those relegated to the sphere of Popular Culture is to deconstruct the categories themselves. This basic egalitarianism, this refusal to categorize according to a supposed attribute of aesthetic status, gives structuralist approaches their subversiveness. However, this radical and democratizing challenge to the definition of art necessarily has its own consequences. If we apply the same conceptual tools to a cartoon or a postcard as we do to a Picasso, we must, by definition, concentrate on their common features (those that our concepts *can* address) rather than on those that differentiate them. Although this is in itself iconoclastic, it inevitably leaves a range of important questions connected with cultural and aesthetic *experience* to the unchallenged pronouncements of bourgeois cultural pundits and critics.

Structuralism's rejection of the salience of aesthetic value is an integral part of its project, and its political thrust depends upon its deconstruction of the pretensions of "the aesthetic" as a separate realm. But there is another reason for its rejection of the question of aesthetics: the intransigent antihumanism of structuralist discourse. The idea of a human aesthetic faculty or mode of sensation is in fact more problematic for a structuralist perspective than the question of aesthetic value itself.

699

This can be seen by looking at the respective fortunes of the notions of aesthetic value and pleasure in contemporary cultural studies and Marxist criticism. "Value" may be out, but "pleasure" is definitely in. This body of work has attempted to construct an antihumanist discourse of pleasure comparable to Roland Barthes's project in *The Pleasure of the Text*. It is the deconstruction of the human subject that underlies the reconstruction of the text as subject: "The text you write must prove to me *that it desires me.*"[5] This notion of the desiring text is built upon a rejection of the subjectivism—seen in this discourse as the product of an essentialist theory of the subject—characteristic of most accounts of the experience of aesthetic pleasure. The desire to avoid formulations that smack of vulgar humanism leads to the extraordinarily cerebral and skeletal character of "the body" in these new theories of pleasure. Fredric Jameson, for instance, reluctantly defines pleasure in physical terms: "Pleasure is finally the consent of life in the body, the reconciliation—momentary as it may be—with the necessity of physical existence in a physical world."[6] This is a curiously grudging description (consent, reconciliation, necessity) that makes one wonder what would constitute un-pleasure.

Claire Pajaczkowska, in an extremely interesting article on semiotic and psychoanalytic theories of art, argues that the psychoanalytic development of linguistic theory facilitates a consideration of the text in its relation to the reader. Although much of what Pajaczkowska has to say concerns visual forms and the analysis of processes such as color, her conclusion makes it clear that art must be understood in psychic rather than aesthetic terms. What is interesting about the following passage is that it clarifies the necessary marginality of pleasure within a deconstructionist theory of the subject: "Or in other words the function of the work of art is to represent the dialectic of the subject, split and triangulated through the exigencies of the incest taboo, to represent and contain this splitting; to represent it as a doubling which is the process of negotiating an imaginary identity, the ego. This process of identification requires the negotiation of sexual difference, it is perhaps the most important function, and *pleasure and meaning (the two tenents of bourgeois concepts of art) are simply by-products* of this socially prescribed and biologically inscribed process of the organization of energy"[7] (emphasis added).

This psychoanalytic conception of art and its "functions" is less mystifying than the Barthesian emphasis on the text as subject. But it is methodologically analogous to sociological readings of art that exclude aesthetic aspects in favor of the social content or determinants of the work in question. And just as sociological accounts can cope best with representations of manifestly social themes, so this approach tends to analyze figurative representations of obvious psychic interest—for example, the madonna and child image. (In this respect, the antihumanist appropriation of psychoanalysis is surprisingly similar to the belligerently humanist Kleinian approach taken in the work of Peter Fuller. Here, works are reconstructed from the point of view of their psychic functions—the negotiation of reparation with the mother in the case of the *Venus de Milo,* for example—and aesthetic considerations are subordinated to explanations in terms of the viewer's needs.[8])

I mention these debates simply to draw attention to the way in which questions about aesthetic sensation, experience, pleasure, and value

Michèle Barrett

have been defined as irretrievably contaminated by "bourgeois humanism." Yet the question of a Marxist humanism is not closed, and the claims of humanism persist most strongly in the area of culture. There is a widely held popular assumption that the dividing line between animals and human beings is marked by "civilization," by considerations beyond those of mere survival, by an appreciation of the realm of the aesthetic. It may well be that such beliefs are historically explicable and/or wrong, but their prevalence cannot be doubted. So, at the very least, we should expect some engagement with them rather than a distanced dismissal of the problem. For those of us who do not recoil with horror from humanism, the fact that questions of aesthetic pleasure and value can only be posed within a humanistic perspective does not render them illegitimate or irrelevant.

It seems to me that much of what is known as "cultural studies" and much of what is seen as Marxist or radical criticism operates within these two tendencies. The major legacy from Marxism is the concept of ideology, and the major legacy from structuralism is the rejection of the subject. These two traditions, incompatible as they undoubtedly are in some respects, have been immensely influential on contemporary work in the general field of culture. Singly or jointly, they account for the marginalization of aesthetic questions in the interpretation of culture.

The rejection of aesthetic questions is one that criticism shares, in fact, with many practitioners and art educators. The notion of serving an apprenticeship in order to acquire skill in an art form has been abandoned in favor of criteria that are, by and large, nonaesthetic. For instance, the judges in a recent poetry competition, filmed as they worked, articulated the notion of "truth to experience" as the main criterion for the winning poem. "Social relevance" is an equally influential basis of judgment. The lack of interest in aesthetic training is surprisingly marked among professionals. The assessment criteria they use, in public examinations, for instance, are often reduced to vague formulations about relevance and conviction.

Although I have said that aesthetic questions are often ignored, it should be emphasized that this must be seen as a rejection rather than an evasion. A principled relativism of the aesthetic is an often argued, and now hegemonic, stance of the Left. Nevertheless, while taking for granted the reasons why this relativism has developed, and fully accepting the spirit of the critique of bourgeois criticism, we cannot afford this relativism because it carries with it serious political and theoretical problems.

First, this relativism is simply unconvincing; it leaves the more plausible position—that we can say a Rembrandt is "better" than an Angelica Kaufmann—to popular and reactionary ideologues. Although we rightly protest the (undoubted) class, race, and gender bias of much criticism and of the definitions of whose work shall be studied and on what assumptions, this does not close the issue. Is it really only because of male dominance in art history that we consider Rembrandt the better painter? Is the limerick I compose on the back of my cigarette packet indistinguishable from one of Shakespeare's plays in terms of its value? We need to engage with the widely held belief that one work is "better" than another and produce convincing arguments either about why this is not so or about what it is based upon.

701

Second, the denial of the aesthetic ignores the fact that the works analyzed in radical criticism are works of the imagination; they are fictional. I do not mean to suggest that this gives them any form of historical or social transcendence, but it does mean that they do not reflect, mediate, or encode in any direct way the content and position frequently attributed to them by virtue of their social origin. This makes the conflation of author and ideology, so common in the content analysis type of radical literary criticism, particularly fraught with dangers. And this leads to a third problem: that this imaginative element and the ambiguity of aesthetic codes allow considerable play in the meaning of the work. Meaning is not immanent; it is constructed in the consumption of the work. Hence, no text can be inherently progressive or reactionary; it becomes so in the act of consumption. There may be an authorial "preferred reading" but the effects may be different from, even opposite to, those intended. Whatever the formal properties of a work, its ideological content, its "political" implications, are not *given*. They depend upon the construction that takes place at the level of consumption.

Perhaps the most important theoretical-political danger of ignoring questions of aesthetic pleasure and value is that we give up ground to a mystificatory view of art. It is precisely the mystique of art, the separation between art and work in our society, that demands that we abandon the rational criteria we apply to all other forms of social production. In this we reproduce the traditional bourgeois ideology of art. In what other work would we deny or evade the question of skill? These attitudes aid a transcendent and nonmaterialist understanding of art. As Max Raphael says: "I might also point out that inspiration is nothing but an illusion on the part of the most barren class in modern society, an illusion which rests upon the distinction that arose in the nineteenth century between socially mechanized production of material goods and individual craft production of spiritual goods. It is a petit-bourgeois fiction which has degraded art to a substitute for religion."[9] Paradoxically, it is through a consideration of skill, technique, and formal properties of art that we can escape mystical and mystificatory assumptions about art and move toward a more democratic understanding. In this context an emphasis on aesthetic skills is, in fact, democratizing rather than elitist. After all, skills may be *acquired,* whereas the notion of an artistic "genius" forbids the aspirations of anyone outside a small and specialized group. This is true even if we accept different degrees of individual aptitude.[10]

Few critics, Marxist or otherwise, have closely attended to the detailed formal and technical issues that develop in their interpretations of works of art. By and large a gulf has been created between those who interpret a work in terms of its "background," the "life" of its creator, or its "conditions of production," and those who stick to close textual analysis. The latter tend to argue—as does, for example, the doyen of "internal" analyses of artworks, Heinrich Wolfflin—that external considerations are irrelevant.[11] Marxists have traditionally rejected the internal approach, seeing the ideological character of a work as demanding that it be socially and historically situated. And Marxist structuralist critics tend to analyze the text to the exclusion of the consumer. There is, however, a minority tradition in European Marxist cultural thought, represented in Adorno's work on music, Della Volpe's work on poetry, and Max Raphael's work on art. Raphael's efforts to combine detailed analyses of the composition of specific works with a broader Marxist interpretation offer us an opportunity to assess the project and judge its strengths and difficulties.[12]

Max Raphael's Aesthetics

Before looking at his analyses of specific paintings, I need to recapitulate some of the central assumptions of Raphael's approach to artworks as aesthetic compositions. This will include his definitions of key terms, his method, his concept of aesthetic value, and his theory of viewing.

Raphael understands the aesthetic as a human faculty, and his bold efforts to define the work of art and the criteria of aesthetic excellence are built on that assumption. *Aesthetic feeling* is regarded as a process in which individual sense perceptions are exteriorized. Feeling becomes relatively independent of individual emotional experience and is assimilated to more universal categories through which the world is appropriated. Art is thus produced by a union of faculties, rather than one faculty. The *aesthetic attitude* is more general than specific aesthetic feelings: "It is not important how the particular part of the world looks that releases our aesthetic vision. What is important is to see it whole, in such a way that we extinguish all our momentary, individual concerns as well as the facticity of things outside us. We may find ourselves in harmony or disharmony with the world, we may feel the sublimity of the cosmos in relation to our tragic finitude or the ridiculous pettiness of our individual selves. Such an experience gratifies and purges us because in it our conflicts, whether with ourselves or with the world, are resolved" (*DA*, p. 190).

Within this framework of aesthetic perception, Raphael argues that aesthetic feeling has a historical and normative aspect, particularly in that the ways in which people constitute a relationship to the world will depend, for instance, on epochs of religious belief or romantic humanism. In this insistence on the historical character of aesthetic feeling, Raphael concurs with his former teacher, Wölfflin, who writes that "beholding is not just a mirror which always remains the same, but a living power of apprehension which has its own inward history and has passed through many stages."[13]

According to Raphael, a *work of art* connects a sensual appropriation of the world to an ideational or cognitive model of apprehension: a "work of art is reality enhanced, which engages the sense both as a whole and in every one of its details and is yet a symbol of nonsensory meanings which extend down to still deeper layers without ever ceasing to appeal to our senses" (*DA*, p. 191). *Artistic excellence* is characterized, on the one hand, by an engagement of the senses and the intellect and, on the other, by a fusion of materials and imagination. Raphael illustrates the first in saying, "The place in history of such unities as the Gothic cathedral or the Doric temple proves that the richest artistic sensibility was achieved not in periods of pure sensualism, but in periods in which sense perceptions were most readily combined with the other human faculties of cognition—the body, the intellect, and Reason" (*DA*, p. 216). Quoting Goethe's view that "that artist will be the most excellent in his genre whose inventiveness and imagination are, so to speak, directly fused with the material in which he has to work" (*DA*, p. 215), Raphael also emphasizes that artistic materials are not contingent or extraneous but are the necessary condition of artistic existence.

Raphael's view of the purpose of art history entails a historical and relativist understanding of judgments of taste. The task of art history is to show the extent to which assignations of artistic value, and the normative status attributed to particular works, are historically bounded. With characteristic confidence he declares that "norms of this type are simply the mistakes an epoch makes about itself, in as much as relative, period factors are usually absolutized along with others. Art history demonstrates this by showing to what extent such predilections vary, and the sociology of art, which shows the economic and social causes that account for each given selection, confirms it."[14]

Raphael's insistence on a historical approach leads him to argue that Marx's thesis on art—as ultimately (though not solely) determined by economic factors—is fruitful not as a universal thesis but in given historical contexts: "It is disclosed only in the course of a specific analysis" (*PMP*, p. 77). Raphael re-poses Marx's famous question about Greek art (Why do we still like it when its foundations are a dead mode of production?) because, he argues, it cannot be answered as it is too general: "Let us formulate the problem concretely: Why could Greek art repeatedly take a normative significance at various epochs of Christian art?" (*PMP*, p. 105).

Raphael's method is encapsulated in the remark he quotes from Rodin: "If you want to write a good book about me, just study one of my sculptures. All that matters is my method. A work that never came off will suit your purposes better than a good one, for it will show the limitations of my method. Should you be unable to discover my method from study of a single work, then you'll never write a decent book either about me or about art. Of course, art critics write about everything under the sun except art" (*DA*, p. 22). Raphael believes that the first task involves describing a work though the closest possible examination. Such a description is a *conceptual reconstitution* of the work involving the following considerations, each of which represents the artistic method as concrete phenomenon (*DA*, p. 198).

1. The constitution of the individual form in terms of material and space.

2. The constitution of the work as a whole—externally (format, immanent structural lines, lines of orientation) and internally (mode of reality, individual idea, aesthetic feeling, motif, etc.).

3. The constitution of the relations between individual forms within the work (internal and external composition, logic of the structure, etc.).

4. The realization of the individual forms as well as of the configuration as a whole.

Raphael is most clear about the first of these considerations—the constitution of individual form. *Materials* (paint, wood, and so on) are translated into the *mean of representation* (in the visual arts: color, light/shadow, line), which in turn are transformed into *means of figuration* through the unique way in which they are blended or contrasted. In adddition to considering means of representation, "reconstitutive description" also explores the artistic form as a spatial structure, examining the number of planes and the tensions generated among them. Raphael's discussion of composition and realization is more diffuse and less clear than his elaboration of the earlier stages of artistic production because he is concerned now with *meaning;* he uses concepts of expressive value, psychic content, worldview, mode of reality, mode of life. It is here, in the reconciliation of formal and historical-ideological considerations, that his theory of aesthetic value begins, and it is to this that I now turn.

Although Raphael rejects mystificatory views of art as inspiration, he develops a view of artistic originality (understood etymologically as "getting to the root") and argues for universal aesthetic value. He believes that value lies in the artist's ability to create a form appropriate to the content, to express a reality in the only possible representational form, which requires that the work be *organic* and *dialectical.* By "organic" Raphael means that the configuration could not be constructed differently: "We speak of an organic or quasi-organic configuration when every individual form is determined by all the others and serves a specific purpose in relation to the whole (Poussin, Leonardo, Houdon, etc.). Such a configuration is self-contained, self-sufficient, speaks for itself—in order to understand it we need not refer to nature or to the artist's personal experiences. It is autonomous, more accurately, has become autonomous as a result of the process of artistic creation" (*DA,* p. 232).

The dialectical dimension of great works of art can be approached in terms of their ambiguity. According to Raphael, "Art frees us from enslavement to words, concepts and false moral values by showing us that life knows differentiations that cannot be reduced to concepts as well as situations which cannot be judged by accepted moral standards" (*DA,* p. 201). This dialectical aspect is crystallized in art's ability to "enhance reality" and extend its meaning. The world of things is undone and a new world is constituted through the construction of the world of values; the more the artist can accomplish this—the more symbolic the work—the greater that work is. Value lies, therefore, in the work that can encompass polarization and harmony, determination and playfulness, diversity and unity, tension within a logical structure. Raphael posits a scale of *relative* values that does not place absolute (perfect) value on the agenda (*DA,* p. 196-97). His own judgments are often quite sweeping, and he argues that these desiderata enable us to distinguish between "facetious and true works of art" (*PMP,* p. 84). Before turning to these contentious claims, I want to consider Raphael's theory of the artist-viewer relation and to look at some illustrations of his method.

It is this theory and its connection to Raphael's formal analysis that locates his greatest contribution to Marxist aesthetics. Raphael instantiates my earlier point about the paradoxically democratizing effects of an emphasis on artistic skill and argues that it is through the *reconstitutive description* articulated by the art critic but experienced by each viewer that the energy in the work is released. The viewer shares the work of the artist insofar as he or she reconstructs the work, which is why Raphael emphasizes that "art leads us from the work to the process of creation": "We see how form is constituted by a specific artistic method and how form follows necessarily upon form. That is what I meant when I said that art leads us from the work to the process of creation. The icy crust of mere presence has melted away and we experience the creative process itself in the new, enhanced reality which both appeals to our senses and suggests an infinite wealth of meanings" (*DA,* p. 191).

The artist must compel the viewer to recreate the process by which the form of the work was made effective; if not, the viewer passes over the work. Raphael argues, "The extent of the viewer's participation in the work varies. In the case of works that do achieve effective form, we are impelled to view them over and over, re-creating them each time; the process may go on indefinitely. In the case of an inferior work, we feel no such urge. This is how the artist gives a finished work the quality of continuing life: he gives the finite the character of infinity, activating the viewer's own infinite aspirations, awakening them and keeping them awake by certain features present in the actual form itself: tensions between opposites and their resolution" (*DA*, p. 224). Hence, the artistic energy locked in the work is only released by this reconstitution in consumption.

Raphael is not only espousing a theory of the *active* viewer (re-conciling aesthetic production and consumption) but also rejecting a re-flectionist theory of art in favor of a more active, somewhat Brechtian view:

> Whatever the deficiencies in Marx's theoretical atti-tude toward art may have been, he was perfectly aware that after the economic, social, and political revolution the most difficult revolution would still remain to be made—the cultural one. Nowhere did he ever exclude art, as he excluded religion, on the ground that there would be no place for it in a classless society. The pseudo-Marxists who put art on the same footing with religion do not see that religion sets limits to man's creative capacities, diverts him from the things of this world, and reconciles class antagonisms by obviously imaginary and frequently hypocritical theories of love, whereas art is an ever-renewed creative act, the active dialogue between spirit and matter; the work of art holds man's creative powers in a crystalline suspen-sion from which it can again be transformed into living energies. Consequently, art by its very nature is no opiate; it is a weapon. Art may have narcotic effects, but only if used for specific reactionary purposes; and from this we may infer only that attempts are made to blunt it for the very reason that it is feared as a weapon. (*DA*, p. 187)

While this passage defines Raphael's position as a Marxist aesthetician, it is only in his substantive analyses that we can test the validity of his method.

Raphael's approach is best illustrated in his comparison of two different treatments of the subject of the Last Supper. He shows that the artists differed in both their ideas of the meaning of the subject and their representation of it. What they share, however, is that each painter found a visual form that in itself expressed the meaning the subject had for him. Leonardo da Vinci expressed degradation, betrayal, and collapse in the drop-ping of the table below the line of vision and in the clustering of the apostles in confused groups. For Tintoretto, the dominant meaning of the subject is not betrayal but the doctrine of transubstantiation that emerges from the Last Supper. To express this movement between the terrestrial and other-

706

worldly spheres, Tintoretto uses a table placed along a wall that stretches into infinity, with light and shadow playing along its length. His discovery of this most appropriate artistic form is all the more striking in that, as Raphael shows, he spent fifty years painting the subject in different ways before finding the particular form that matched his understanding of the theme. Raphael's point is that these artists used figuration (including means of representation) in different ways to render their idea in a material form.

The Demands of Art largely consists of detailed analyses of individual paintings. All I can do here is to sketch out, for purposes of discussion, some examples of Raphael's "reconstitution" of specific works. Raphael greatly admires Cézanne's *Mont Sainte-Victoire* of 1904-6, which he claims is the only one of the seven treatments of this subject by Cézanne that balances tension and arrives at true greatness. He stresses its radical rejection of the conventions of perspective in painting: instead of representing empty space receding to infinite depth, Cézanne gives us filled space with the back of the picture tightly closed. Raphael sees the painting primarily in terms of its use of planes: the back/top plane is pushing forward and inward into the picture; the bottom/front plane is pushing outward to the back of the picture; and the tension is balanced, held in check by the middle plane. Raphael explains in detail how the use and juxtaposition of color contributes to this division of the picture into planes.

Although it is widely known that Cézanne's theme is taken from the countryside around Aix-en-Provence (and, indeed, people visit Mont Sainte-Victoire to "see the original"), the picture is not based on any one viewpoint. No photograph can correspond to what is shown in the painting, since (in Raphael's words) Cézanne has subordinated visual perception to pictorial figuration. This, according to Raphael, is Cézanne's greatest achievement: he uses some aspects of natural appearance but not others. The painting is not a landscape, but nature has provided a model, and Cézanne has "refashioned the classical and given nature a classical solidity."

Raphael's analysis of Picasso's *Guernica* concludes that the primary effect of the painting is shock and that it conveys the "destructiveness of a disintegrating society with a power no other artist has equalled." He describes its figuration as constituted by the use of black and white, rather than color, and by line. The former expresses the most ultimate and general while the latter exemplifies individual emotion. But, Raphael argues, the real world is composed of objects, nature, society, and history; it does not operate with these extremes of abstraction and individuality. Picasso's exclusive reliance on black and white and on line restrict the painting to the category of a private allegory; hence, the understandable confusion among critics as to what, for example, the bull stands for. The pictorial vocabulary is limited and the codes used (e.g., triangles and angles referring back to earlier representational conventions) are not universally accessible.

Raphael argues that the content of *Guernica*—a world without hope, humankind reduced to a scream—is not expressed or achieved *in* the figuration but remains a private intellectual and emotional motivation of the painter that can be seen *through* the figuration. There is, therefore, an arbitrary rather than a necessary relation between form and content in this work. It offers no progression, development, or resolution and has no reference point in its ordering of space. Hence, although Raphael recognizes the power of the painting in terms of *shock,* he concludes that it is an outright failure as a picture since Picasso could find no figuration suited to his idea and had to resort to allegory.

Raphael's view that the formal characteristics of a painting can be linked to social or sociological considerations is illustrated in his discussion of a painting with a more straightforward social content, *The Peasant Family,* by the seventeenth-century painter Le Nain.[15] This, he argues is a "materialist text" in that it views the ruled class from its own point of view, by its representation of *both* oppression and resistance. John Tagg's summary of Raphael's interpretation conveys most clearly this dialectical dimension of the painting:

> The first feature of Le Nain's painting to which Raphael draws attention is the eye level, denoting the height from which the spectator views the scene. He observes that it runs through the eyes of almost all the sitting and standing figures in the picture, just a little below the upper edge of the canvas. The spectator, therefore, sees everything from above looking downwards, so that one's descending glance seems to depress the human figures; an effect which is reinforced by the sensation of weight in the clothing, especially of the two principal women. Not only, therefore, are the figures hemmed in at the top by an invisible frontier, but one's very way of seeing "binds them to the ground like a chain, and this condition of being bound on all sides, this narrow dependence, is more than just a sign of their poverty: it strikes us as its inescapable cause."
>
> Yet the picture Le Nain gives of the plight of the peasants is not one sided. In their very abject state, one sees the peasants' strength and their struggle for existence. One sees, too, that the formal and sensory means by which this strength is expressed are closely linked with the means used to convey their poverty. Whereas the viewer's line of sight depresses them, each of the figures seems to rise up from the hips, as if protesting against its repression. Each individual is constituted by a double and conflicting force: a sinking down and a rising up which embodies that unity of poverty and strength, exploitation and will for freedom which no present-day work has been able to show. "Only by expressing this unity," Raphael declares, "is it possible to avoid the one-sidedness of sentimental pictures about the poor on the one hand, and of falsely heroic, hero-worshipping pictures about workers on the other."[16]

As this example shows, Raphael's primary concern is with the ways in which an artist finds a pictorial form that inherently and inevitably expresses the idea or content of the work. This integral relation of form and meaning is the necessary condition of artistic excellence and aesthetic value. Yet this

708

Michèle Barrett

approach to the analysis of art has significant difficulties, some of which I now want to discuss.

Raphael claims that his method amounts to a science of art in which laws could be formulated. The appendix to *The Demands of Art* starts with a bold declaration: "This work sets itself the task of making art an object of scientific cognition." Raphael describes his theory as "empirical" because it is based on a study of works from all periods and nations. He goes so far as to make the extraordinary statement that "I am convinced that mathematics, which has travelled a long way since Euclid, will someday provide us with the means of formulating the results of such a study in mathematical terms" (*DA*, p. 207). Yet, as with so many art critics, many of Raphael's *interpretative* comments are entirely devoid of qualitative justification, let alone scientific validation. Many of the examples he uses, particularly when illustrating passing points, are ideological readings rather than formal analyses; indeed, this slippage is part of his method. There is a difference between uncontentious observations (e.g., that line is dominant in *Guernica*, or that *Mont Sainte-Victoire* is composed of more than one plane) and statements such as the following: "In *The Virgin and Child with St. Anne* Leonardo da Vinci embodies an idealistic conception of Reason in sensory qualities, which are most fully expressed in the shoulder line" (*DA*, p. 217). Indeed, it is not self-evident that da Vinci's dropping of the table in *The Last Supper* expresses collapse or degradation, or that the raising of the line of vision in Le Nain's *The Peasant Family* inevitably conveys poverty. Such judgments veer perilously toward the reefs on which much bourgeois art history and criticism often founder—the claim that such-and-such a feature inevitably expresses stability or resignation or whatever the critic reads into it. Yet, Raphael insists that these judgments, based on technical observation, must be neutral and impersonal. The question of *value* should only be considered at the *end* of the analysis (*DA*, p. 198). However, he himself does not accomplish this, although in my view his technical analyses provide some openings for a less ideological art criticism.

The underlying reason for Raphael's failure to achieve more neutral and objective positions is an unresolved conflict in his theoretical framework between an emphasis on artistic *production* (in the spirit of Walter Benjamin) and a profoundly Lukácsian subsumption of art to the category of ideology. Raphael is an early exponent of the "relative autonomy" approach to art. At times he categorizes art as a subset *within* ideology and sees types of artistic work (expressive, dogmatic, skeptical, etc.) as ideological. By and large he regards art as a battleground of ideological struggle, although he tries to insist that (to put it crudely) the ideological content is less important than the extent to which the artist can find an appropriate form in which to express it: "what matters in a work of art is not this specific 'something' contributed by the subject matter but the intensity with which the over-all meaning is conveyed by the figuration and for the sake of which whatever might create discrepancy between meaning and content is eliminated" (*DA*, p. 196).

Raphael's position on the classic problem of the economic determination of the cultural is unclear and contradictory. Although, as quoted earlier, he describes cultural revolution as the most difficult of revolutions, he concludes *The Demands of Art* with the following rather orthodox view: "Creative instinct manifests itself with greater freedom in art than in any other domain. A creative, active study of art is therefore indispensable to awaken creative powers, to assert them against the dead weight of tradition, and to mobilize them in the struggle for a social order in which everyone will have the fullest opportunity to develop his creative capacities. The details of this social order cannot be anticipated without falling into utopian dreams. We can and we must be satisfied with the awareness that art helps us to achieve the truly just order. The decisive battles, however, will be fought at another level" (*DA*, p. 204).

In addition to this general orientation, Raphael's interpretations are often based on specific Lukácsian concepts, of which the most important is *totality*. Raphael's understanding of dialectic is rooted in the Lukácsian balance between particularity and totality and in the notion of the historically typical individual: "I believe that it would not destroy but enlarge scientific method in the domain of art to pair the concept of particularity with the concept of totality—a totality which combines the same factors of form, content, and method at a higher level" (*DA*, p. 208).

As I have already suggested, it is uncertain that Raphael's judgments of aesthetic value really do wait, as he demands, for the end of the analysis. In fact, although I have glossed his specific analyses in such a way as to minimize it, much of his interpretation is grounded in the familiar and tedious rhetoric of support for realism and hostility to modernism that vitiates so much of Lukács's own work. To illustrate this I now turn to the "value" element of Raphael's analysis of Cézanne and Picasso.

It is characteristic of Raphael's originality that, although a Marxist aesthetician, he can regard a Cézanne landscape as one of the greatest artworks ever produced and castigate *Guernica,* for decades a symbol of antifascism, as "ineffective propaganda." The substance of Raphael's case is that allegorical painting (of which *Guernica* is an example) is always inferior to painting in which the content is realized in the form,[17] a demand that is tied closely to a realist aesthetics such as Lukács's. Raphael's strictures on Monet's paintings echo, often in detail, those of Lukács on writers such as Joyce or Eliot. Raphael writes that "for all their lyricism they remain bound up with the description of a localized atmosphere. In their contents the here-and-now takes precedence over the universal, the momentary over the enduring. Reason and the human body are alike eliminated as cognitive faculties; the intellect serves only to analyze and differentiate sharpened sense perception, and the feeling accompanying it is vague" (*DA*, p. 232).[18]

Raphael's unstinting praise for Cézanne and his unswerving criticism of Picasso are difficult to comprehend, especially when some of the very features under discussion are shared. Both, Raphael agrees, reject the conventions of perspective and render space as filled rather than empty. It is almost as though a little bit of modernism is acceptable as long as it is compatible with pictorial coherence. Raphael does not engage with the argument that Cézanne and Picasso were engaged in comparable challenges to representational conventions.[19]

The classic position of any realist aesthetics is that the *means* of representation must be concealed, and the Brechtian and modernist challenge to realism is principally concerned with this desideratum. Raphael's insistence that meaning must be realized in form goes hand in hand with the orthodox realist view. His approval of the Le Nain painting mentioned earlier rests partly on the fact that the composition of the work is "concealed and made as far as possible invisible, so as not to interfere with an impression of easy and accidental naturalness."[20]

Insofar as such realist precepts inform Raphael's *reconstitution* of the work, as well as his final evaluation, his criticism elevates a particular aesthetic to universal status. Many Marxist aestheticians have claimed that realism is the natural companion to historical materialism, but the case is far from made. Terry Lovell's *Pictures of Reality* argues that, although Marxist thought is based on a realist epistemology, there are no grounds for assuming that Marxist aesthetics should support realism. Such an assumption confuses the goals of art with those of knowledge.[21] Raphael, for all his insistence that the work of art be apprehended in aesthetic terms, tends to concur with Lukács that "great art" embodies the truths of historical materialism.

Raphael's objection to *Guernica* is that it only shocks and does not point to any resolution. Yet Marxism is not a theory that resembles the eighteenth-century ideal of balance, stability, and the inevitably resolved chord. Nor is its politics that of the "realist" happy ending—waiting for history to make a revolution. Insofar as Marxism is an active theory and politics, calling upon us to make our own struggle, it requires a less dogmatic and complacent aesthetic.

Nonetheless, however unsatisfactory Raphael's interpretations of particular works may be, his method exposes some problems that we need to confront. His precept, drawn from Rodin, of "study the work" and the theory he elaborates of the "active" viewer's role in the reconstitution of the work are useful. But they are limited by the degree to which they exclude social and historical considerations. Raphael does not recognize that meaning is, at least partially, constructed in the history of a work's reception; we cannot view a Rodin sculpture with an eye that is innocent of all knowledge of Rodin's place in a "canon" of works. Raphael does not really acknowledge the social constitution of the body of work he scrutinizes; he does not add to his detailed visual descriptions an adequate description of the class, gender, and race factors that structure the status of the works he chooses to study. And just as each work is located in a cultural-historical context, so our modes of apprehension are specific to the concerns of a particular conjuncture. Although Raphael recognizes the fact of "vision having a history," he tends to relate it to epochal characteristics such as religious belief and to ignore its more local purchase. Raphael's interpretations show the weaknesses of ignoring the social dimensions of reception. He rules by fiat that *Guernica* is ineffective propaganda when as a matter of fact the absence of an allegorical key to the painting has not hindered the polemical manipulation of this powerful work in a propaganda campaign against fascism. Indeed, many would argue that the subject of *Guernica* is treated more effectively through ambiguous and allegorical means than it ever could have been in a realist mode.

Raphael's main difficulty is that he tries to tie form and meaning too closely together. We do not have to espouse a totally relativist position of meaning (which would say that any given work is completely open to the construction of an infinite range of meanings) to argue that the meaning of a work cannot be contained by simple formulae such as meaning should be realized in form, or that reconciliation and synthesis are an essential element of aesthetic value. Raphael's theory of the active viewer tends to see the only possible appropriation of the work as a recreation of the author's

711

work and ties meaning too closely to the question of authorial intention and imagination.

Raphael's work has, for us, a certain methodological innocence. He fails to see that definitions of beauty and aesthetic value are constructed from theoretical tools that have a history, just as vision and modes of aesthetic apprehension have histories. Yet this does not render his work uninteresting. The concepts we use and the subjects we scrutinize are also historically constituted, and we need to beware of assuming that our own methodologies are somehow purer than the old ones. Terry Eagleton points to this by putting a sting in the tail of his characterization of "the aesthetic" as an ideology fostered by psychic fragmentation (and, we could add, the separation of art from work in capitalism). He comments that psychoanalysis, too, is a symptom of psychic fragmentation: "The very analytic instruments we deploy are in this sense ideologically guilty."[22] My point is that we should avoid the assumption that there are historically specific categories such as "the aesthetic" which are reactionary and bourgeois, while our new categories, such as "signification" and "pleasure," are in some way purged of these limitations.

Raphael's usefulness, in my view, lies in the fact that he tries to explore the ways in which meaning is connected both to aesthetic form and to the senses. This project is difficult, and one that few contemporary writers address in its complexity; it is not currently considered very important. The dominant interest in cultural studies at the moment is in a conception of meaning stripped of traditional aesthetic questions, one that does not engage with the issue of the senses. The very definition of "culture" that is effective tends to be exclusively concerned with meaning. The fact that signification theory—the analysis of the meanings constructed in systems of signs—is now a consensual position in various debates is further evidence of this. The insistence that culture is a field of production and that its product is meaning was radical at a time when we were trying to wrest the definition of culture from the grip of reflection theory. That battle, however, is now over, and the exclusive emphasis on meaning in the analysis of culture needs further thought.

Insofar as Raphael tries to explore the connections between meaning and the senses, and between meaning and aesthetic form, his work should be of current interest. Although his interpretations of particular works are often dogmatic or contentious, this does not make his overall project any less important. If we are to continue to try to understand cultural experience as well as signifying practice—if we are to move beyond the often remarked polarization of "culturalism and structuralism"—we must question this reduction of culture to meaning. This reduction has provided a definitional basis for agreement between adherents of very divergent theoretical positions, and for this reason we are perhaps too cautious in stepping out from its protection.

Notes

I would like to thank Cora Kaplan and Mary McIntosh for their help with this paper; also John Tagg for his work in making more of Max Raphael's writings available in English.

Michèle Barrett

1   Janet Wolff, *Aesthetics and the Sociology of Art* (London: Allen and Unwin, 1983), pp. 18-19.

2   Terry Eagleton, *Literary Theory* (Oxford: Blackwell, 1983), p. 2.

3   Ronald Frankenberg, "Styles of Marxism; Styles of Criticism. *Wuthering Heights*: A Case Study," *Sociological Review Monograph*, no. 26 (1978).

4   Terry Lovell, *Pictures of Reality: Aesthetics, Politics, Pleasure* (London: British Film Institute, 1980).

5   Roland Barthes, *The Pleasure of the Text*, trans. Richard Miller (London: Cape, 1976).

6   Fredric Jameson, "Pleasure: A Political Issue," *Formations of Pleasure* (London: Routledge and Kegan Paul, 1983).

7   Claire Pajaczkowska, "Structure and Pleasure," *Block*, no. 9 (1983), p. 13.

8   Peter Fuller, *Art and Psychoanalysis* (London: Writers and Readers Publishing Cooperative, 1980).

9   Max Raphael, *The Demands of Art*, trans. Norbert Guterman (London: Routledge and Kegan Paul, 1968), p. 207. Hereafter cited in the text as *DA*.

10 I discuss this in "Feminism and the Definition of Cultural Politics," in *Feminism, Culture and Politics*, ed. R. Brunt and C. Rowan (London: Lawrence and Wishart, 1983).

11 See, for example, Heinrich Wolfflin, *Classic Art* (Oxford: Phaidon, 1980): "There is a conception of art-history which sees nothing more in art than a 'translation of life' (Taire) into pictorial terms, and which attempts to interpret every style as an expression of the prevailing mood of the age. Who would wish to deny that this is a fruitful way of looking at the matter? Yet it takes us only so far—as far, one might say, as the point at which art begins" (p. 287).

12 Max Raphael was born in Prussia in 1889 and educated in Germany. He lived in various cities, including Paris, and in 1941 settled in New York, dying there in 1952. Much of his work has been published posthumously and some of it is still not available in English. The major works available are *The Demands of Art; Proudhon, Marx, Picasso: Three Studies in the Sociology of Art* (trans. Inge Marcuse, ed. John Tagg [London: Lawrence and Wishart, 1980; New York: Humanities, 1980]). The latter contains a bibliography of Raphael's published and unpublished work, compiled by John Tagg. My exposition is drawn largely from *The Demands of Art*, which deals principally with aesthetic questions. *Proudhon, Marx, Picasso* is more theoretical and sociological in its focus.

13 Heinrich Wolfflin, *Principles of Art History* (New York: Dover, 1950), p. 226.

14 Raphael, *Proudhon, Marx, Picasso*, p. 83. Hereafter cited in the text as *PMP*.

15 An English translation of the relevant part of Raphael's *Arbeiter, Kunst und Kunstler* (Frankfurt: Fischer Verlag, 1975) by Anna Bostock appears under the title "Workers and the Historical Heritage of Art," in *On Art and Society*, a supplement of *Women and Art*, Summer/Fall 1972 (New York).

16 John Tagg, "The Method of Criticism and Its Object in Max Raphael's Theory of Art," *Block*, no. 2 (Spring 1980).

17 Raphael writes in *The Demands of Art*, "Were Picasso to provide an allegorical key to *Guernica*, it would still be true that what he produced is ineffectual as propaganda and dubious as a work of art" (p. 153).

18 Lukács's view that in modernism "man is reduced to a sequence of unrelated experiential fragments" is summarized in "The Ideology of Modernism," *The Meaning of Contemporary Realism* (London: Merlin, 1972).

19 See, for example, Anton Ehrenzweig, *The Psycho-analysis of Artistic Vision and Hearing* (New York: Braziller, 1965). Ehrenzweig compares Cézanne's challenge to the convention of constant peripheral vision with Picasso's challenge to that of constant localization.

20 Quoted in Tagg, "The Method of Criticism," p. 6.

21 Lovell, *Pictures of Reality*, chaps. 4, 5.

22 Terry Eagleton, "Poetry, Pleasure and Politics," *Formations of Pleasure* (London: Routledge and Kegan Paul, 1983), p. 64

Fengzhen Wang
Marxist Literary Criticism in China

Chinese literary criticism has come to recognize that literature need not only conform to our political philosophy but also serve the spiritual needs of the masses. This is not possible without emphasizing formal and aesthetic criteria.

In the past thirty years and more, since the founding of the new China, literary criticism in China has accomplished a great deal, but it has also encountered many problems. The main difficulty was brought about by slogans like "Political criteria first, artistic criteria second," which launched political movements in literary circles from the mid-fifties to the mid-seventies. These aimed to apply the demands of a mass political movement directly to literary art, requiring the latter to be a tool or weapon of the class struggle; they denied that literature and art have their own aesthetic rules and thus ignored the exploration of form, style, and technique. More important, these movements refused to recognize that the broad masses in fact have various spiritual needs, to which art can respond. As a result, the full range of necessary standards in literary criticism were reduced to only one—political—and artistic criteria became at best a subordinate factor. When evaluating a concrete literary work, the political content was the only important element. If it was politically acceptable, it was considered a good work; otherwise, no matter how artistically valuable it might be, it was treated as inferior. Politics essentially replaced art or made it invisible, which led critical writing into oversimplified and formalized generalizations that verged on propaganda.

How did such a situation arise? The first reason, I think, was the widespread misunderstanding of Mao Zedong's speech at the Yanan Forum on Literature and Art in 1942. "Politics cannot be equated with art," he said. "Each class in every class society has its own political and artistic criteria. But all classes in all class societies invariably put the political criterion first and the artistic criterion second."[1] Perhaps what he said was appropriate for that historical moment, but later practice has proved that it is neither so easy nor necessarily appropriate to say which criterion is first and which is second. In any case, the attempt to set these priorities provoked a general misunderstanding of art; and problems in criticism inevitably followed. It is important to remember that Mao also said, "What we demand is the unity of politics and art, the unity of content and form, the unity of revolutionary political content and the highest possible perfection of artistic form. . . . Therefore, we oppose both works of art with an incorrect political view-point and the tendency toward the 'poster and slogan' which is correct in political view-point but lacking in artistic power."[2] While this seems to reject a flat reduction of art to politics, the importance Mao gave

715

to politics in his speech probably made it impossible to avoid these reductive influences on criticism.

The second factor seems to me to have been the influence of Soviet literary criticism, especially the theories of Plekhanov and Zhdanov. In his preface to the *Twenty-Year Essays,* Plekhanov insisted that the first task of criticism was to transfer the thought of the work from an artistic to a social language so as to find the social equivalent for literary phenomena; the second task was to make judgments about the aesthetic value of the work. It is clear that he meant to place political thought before and above questions of artistry and aesthetics. Zhdanov followed Lenin's remark that "literature must become Party literature" in his address to the First Soviet Writers Congress of 1934 and defended such reductionism by saying that "our Soviet literature is not afraid of the charge of being 'tendentious.' " Literature, he argued, must become "a small cog" in the social-democratic mechanism. Clearly he meant that literature belonged to the Communist party, hence to politics. Both Plekhanov and Zhdanov had a strong influence on Chinese critics: their theories were first introduced into China in the thirties, and by the fifties most Chinese critics followed them; and they also had an impact on the younger generations of critics in China. Thus it is not untrue to say that literary criticism in China was, for over thirty years, mainly defined by Zhdanovism and the so-called orthodox school of Marxism.

Since the end of the cultural revolution there has been an energetic and continuing series of discussions on the criteria that should govern literary criticism. The prevailing viewpoint has been to replace the orthodoxy defined by the statment "Literature is subordinate to and must serve politics" with a less reductionist position, namely, "Literature serves the people and socialism." This change is not only a matter of theory but also of practice. While it is the result of theoretical arguments on the relations between literary art and politics, it also sums up the historical experiences of the past thirty years. The change in these slogans is based as well on a Marxist view of historical materialism and dialectics. According to Marx, "In the social production of their existence, men inevitably enter into definite relations, which are independent of their will, namely relations of production appropriate to a given stage in the development of their material forces of production. The totality of these relations of production constitutes the economic structure of society, the real foundation, on which arises a legal and political superstructure, and to which correspond definite forms of social consciousness. The mode of production of material life conditions the general process of social, political, and intellectual life."[3] In other words, the legal, political superstructure and the corresponding forms of social consciousness (including literature) are autonomous; politics and literature cannot be subordinated to the substructure of the social relations of production. Considering current Chinese conditions, this has two implications: (1) Literature has a variety of functions and can serve people of different societies and meet different political contingencies; for instance, Chinese classic poems, Shakespeare's plays, and Balzac's novels were not only good for the people of their own time but also can be beneficial to people at the present time in all countries. (2) Literature and politics also influence each other; moreover, though literature can serve politics in certain social conditions, as happened in China and the Soviet Union, it cannot be limited or reduced to this role.

The change in slogans is, therefore, fundamentally significant for the Chinese people. As a result, Chinese critics are using a dialectical method to rethink and reestablish the criteria appropriate to literary criticism. Engels said in his letter to Lassalle in 1859, "You see I judge your work from an aesthetic and historical point of view, a high criterion, maybe the highest, and only by this gauge can I raise some disagreements, which is the best proof that I admire this work of yours."[4] In fact, in an earlier comment on Karl Grun, Engels said, "We have never criticized Goethe from a moral or a partisan point of view, but from an aesthetic and historical point of view; we do not judge him by the moral, political and human scale."[5] Most critics in China now see Marxist literary criticism as including two perspectives: the aesthetic and the historical. What is the Marxist aesthetic viewpoint? What is the Marxist historical viewpoint? What is their relation? These are the questions that have been and continue to be addressed.

Careful study of the works of Marx and Engels shows that their aesthetic principles are truthfulness and typification. In a comment on Eugene Sue, Marx said that writers should "describe human relations truthfully." When he explained why Greek art had permanent force, the first thing he mentioned was truthfulness. He treated ancient Greece as an early, formative stage of humankind and thought Greek art represented that stage truthfully. Truthfulness, however, is not to be identified with naturalism's attempt to reflect the social world "photographically." Truthfulness transcends such particular conventions; it can be established in (and can ground the evaluation of) such diverse work as Greek epic and myth, the literature of the Middle Ages, Shakespeare, Goethe, and Balzac.

Artistic truthfulness is different from the surface reality of the world. It is the product of a dialectical relation between social life and its essence. In our world, there is both a given reality of events and visual surfaces and some order or rule that governs such events—the essence of things, the soul of existing reality. Literature should not merely copy or imitate the surface reality but try to show its essence by the way it describes concrete matters. Thus, literature differs from philosophy, for it depicts the essence of reality through a description of the events of social life and thereby suggests the relationship between essences and phenomena, whereas philosophical explanations tend to leap immediately from observed phenomena to their essential nature. As Lukács said, "Balzac's greatness lies precisely in the fact that in spite of all his political and ideological prejudices he yet observed with incorruptible eyes all contradictions as they arose, and faithfully described them."[6]

Some people may take this position to be nothing more than traditional or even nineteenth-century realism. But one should not forget that modernism is not so modern as it seems; it is at least 200 years old. There is a direct continuum from the realists who tried to make narrative meaningful to modern critics who define themselves by their separation from realism and even from narrativity itself. The nineteenth-century realist novelists were aware of the possibilities of indeterminate meaning and solipsism, but they wrote against the very indeterminacy they tended to reveal. Their narratives do not acquiesce to the conventions of order they inherited but struggle to reconstruct a coherent world out of a world being decon-

717

structed all around them, like modernist texts. With remarkable regularity, these realist novelists were alert to the arbitrariness of the reconstructed order and believed that their fictions could bring us at least a little closer to recognizing what is not true to ourselves and not in our best interest, and not merely bring us closer to language. For instance, both Balzac and Dickens viewed bourgeois society as overwhelming and inescapable, and their novels presented visions of the fate of subjectivity in that world. Balzac, in the 1842 preface to *La comédie humaine,* saw his effort as a panoramic history portraying a few thousand character types with their passions embedded in everyday life. Each novel in the series focuses on an aspect of that world, whether provincial or Parisian, upper or lower class. Balzac emphasized the interrelations within that world by having some characters appear and reappear in different novels. Dickens, by contrast, in his social novels of the 1850s, saw a schism between human nature and contemporary social life. For him, human beings were like orphans in an urban, industrialized society, one that was hostile and confused, that reduced human beings to stereotypes. Dickens enhanced his somber picture by using certain recurrent symbols, such as the "fog" in *Bleak House,* the "fact" in *Hard Times,* and the "prison" in *Little Dorrit.* Balzac's characters are driven by monomaniacal passions; the world is an object of their desire. Dickens's characters are metaphysical personae for worldly values. Both authors have been charged with creating fixed and one-dimensional characters, but it is more appropriate to say that they portrayed the reduction of subjectivity by the material forces of bourgeois society.

In literature, typification has a direct connection with truthfulness. The notion of typification, or typicality, may be thought old-fashioned in Western literary theory and criticism, but it still has an important place among Chinese critics and writers. As I understand it, it is a means of representing the process of development from essence to phenomena with concrete, vivid, and sensible images. Marx said in his letter to Lassalle that he felt sorry he could not see any "particular" description of characters. (The concept of "particularity," one of Hegel's significant aesthetic conceptions, is very important in Marxist literary thought.) Engels expressed similar concerns in his letter to Minna Kautsky: "As for the characters in those two situations, I think you created them with your usual vivid characteristic description; each is typical and individual . . . and it should be so."[7] Marx and Engels stressed that the general is implied in the individual while the typical individual is the centralized expression of the general. That is why Engels said, "It seems to me that the meaning of realism, except for the details of the reality, is the representation of the typical character in typical situations." According to Engels, typification is different than Horace's typology, than Zola's photographic realism, than Schiller's dissolution of character into abstract rules.

Typification is a whole, consisting of general and special features of time, society, and humankind. It is also a shift of focus from the large to the small, from the general to the particular, but it does not stay at that reduced scale. Lukács said that typification weaves the social, moral, intellectual, and spiritual contradictions into a vivid body. Don Quixote's madness is not capricious but corresponds to a reality in the outside world. Therefore, typical characters stand for something larger and more meaningful than themselves, than their isolated individual destinies: they are concrete individualities that at the same time maintain a relationship with some more general or collective human substance. Hamlet's most obvious characteristic is hesitation and delay; he knows his responsibility is to make a vital change, but he does not know how to accomplish it. Don Quixote is the opposite. He sees his illusion as truth, tries every unrealistic way to realize it, and finally experiences strange disasters. Lukács's writings on Goethe and Balzac, on Schiller and Hegel, and on the rise of the historical novel, are classic critiques of realism and show clearly how important typification is in literary works.

Marxist aesthetics also stress the importance of the unity of form and content. Artistic form is the means to express content, and content must be represented through artistic form; form is useless without content and content is not apprehensible without form—the two cannot be separated. Content includes theme, characters, settings, and situations, while form includes genre, language, structure, rhythm, tone, and color. For a social theory of literature, the problem of form is a problem of the relations between social modes and historical theory, based on the materiality of language and the related materiality of cultural production. It is a problem of the description of these variable relations within specifiable material practices. Form depends on its perception as well as its creation. In the past, as a result of the primary commitment to politics, Chinese critics have given too much attention to content. But now they have taken up the dialectical viewpoint in their critical practice. As a Chinese critic once said, "Literature is like a river. The form is the river-bed and the content is the water. If the river-bed is deep and solid, it can hold more water and make it clear; but there cannot be any real river without water." Good literary works unite content and form in a perfect whole.

Marxist literary criticism must also take a historical point of view. Accordingly, literary criticism should be based on the reality described in concrete works: if the work is about life in the eighteenth century, it should not be criticized according to life in the nineteenth or twentieth century; if the work is about some events in England, it should not be criticized on the basis of events in other countries. In their criticism of Lassalle's *Franz Von Sickingen,* Marx and Engels stated that the critique of the work, whether it is judged to be good or bad, deep or shallow, should be grounded in sixteenth-century German life, for the work represents the revolt led by Sickingen at the beginning of that century. When criticizing Paul Ernst, who believed that the life of the urban petite bourgeoisie expressed in Ibsen's works was the life of that class everywhere, Engels pointed out that he imposed his perception of the German urban petit bourgeoisie on that in Norway. Similarly, Greek myth is a source of Greek art; and the Egyptian myth can never be the "mother's womb" of Greek art. The heroes in Greek myth can only live in that ancient time.

Marx said, "Just as our opinion of an individual is not based on what he thinks of himself, so we cannot judge such a period of transformation by its own consciousness; on the contrary, this consciousness must be explained rather from the contradictions of material life, from the existing conflict between the social productive forces and the relations of production."[8] If we apply this to literary criticism, our judgments of a literary work must be based on the content expressed in the work. We must analyze the work in terms of the time, social life, and situation of the work itself, as Engels did in analyzing the *City Girl* on the basis of the movement of the working class in England in the 1880s. In examining historical reality, we must not forget the historical context. History is a continuum; no event in history is independent. Literature as a whole has the task of depicting social determination, of suggesting the basis of transition, and of pointing to tendencies toward change, whether it does so consciously or unconsciously. Cao Zueqin's *Dreams of the Red Chamber*, which shows the demise of Chinese feudal society through the description of a large family, must be understood in its social context; otherwise, its significance is completely lost.

The history of humankind is a history of class society over the past several thousand years. Even today, although there are countries that no longer have such class distinctions, the reflection of different classes in thought and ideology still exists. Thus, Marxist literary criticism must still include the question of class viewpoints. Marx said that "the human essence is no abstraction inherent in each single individual; in reality, it is the ensemble of the social relations."[9] And class relations are the most basic and pertinent relation in class society, one of the decisive factors for human nature. All people who live in a class society bear the stamp of their own class. As Lu Xun once said, "In *Dreams of the Red Chamber* Jiao Da in Jia's mansion can never fall in love with sister Lin. Jiao Da is a servant while sister Lin is the daughter of a high ranking official and the granddaughter of Grandma Jia, the oldest in Jia's family. They belong to different classes and their thoughts, ideals, language and manners, their ways of living ... all are different. There is no common ground for their falling in love." In his criticism of Sickingen, Engels argued that the play is faulty because the intellectual flaw Lassalle stressed is not the real cause of Sickingen's downfall. The real cause is not a moral but a social one: Sickingen could never have had the support of the revolutionary peasants because his basic social aim was utterly different from theirs, focused not on liberating the land but on reestablishing the petty nobility, which itself suffered from the domination of the great princes and the church. For Marx and Engels, Sickingen does not typify the real historical dilemma; the situation of the play does not give a genuine picture of that period. Sickingen's failure comes from his class position: he has no common interests with the peasants and thus is doomed to failure. Marx and Engels saw the play from a historical class viewpoint. Though there are no longer class distinctions in China, people recognize that different class thoughts and ideologies still exist. The traditional class viewpoint of Marxism is thus still an important and necessary part of Chinese literary criticism.

In recent years, Chinese critics have tried to enlarge and develop their study and interpretation of Marxist doctrines. They have broken the limits of the old criteria and begun to pay attention to the interior, psychological realities of literature. A recent essay on Wang Meng, for example, argues that Wang Meng's stories have a large proportion of psychological description. Psychology has become an important focus for literary criticism, while characters' actions, narrative events, and the outer world have become the background. Deviating considerably from traditional realism, some of Wang Meng's stories include characters that undergo physical metamorphosis; in "Mixed Colour," for example, a horse and a man become one character. Although Wang Meng's stories have transcended traditional time and space and moved in a new direction, somewhat like stream-of-consciousness, they are quite different from pure descriptions of self-conscious or sub-conscious mental processes, which tend to disregard the reader's sensations and experience. Wang Meng treats feelings and descriptions almost like notes and rhythm in a musical composition; they are certainly as important as plot in some of his work. Now that his attempt to develop his own style of realism has attracted critical attention, the critics may develop an expanded conception of realism.

Not long ago there were some debates on "cloudy poems" (poems using an impressionistic technique); these were, in fact, debates on realism. Some said that such poems were an experimental effort to express interior reality; others said they were bad literature and definitely antirealistic. I would like to quote two poems by Gu Cheng, a leading cloudy poet, to give some sense of the typical form.

A Feeling
The Sky is a gray color,
The Road is gray-colored,
The Buildings are gray color,
The rain is gray-colored,
Within a strip of deadly gray,
Two children walk by,
One is bright red,
One is bright green.

Far and Near
You,
In a little while look at me,
In a little while look at the cloud.
I feel that
When you look at me, you are very far;
When you look at the cloud, you are very near.

These poems certainly have moved away from traditional conceptions of realism. Though most critics have severely criticized them, they have stimulated others to reconsider the notion of realism.

Generally speaking, however, realistic modes of representation still prevail in Chinese literature. It is thought that the basic truths of life can be told through the vehicle of individual stories and individual plots. But in the modern Western world, realism has become relatively rare; life is experienced as a kind of waiting without end. The only reality of human experience seems to be the blind routine and drudgery of daily work. People become a part of the social machine. Thus, it is natural that there are differences in how Marxism is applied "according to different concrete conditions." The present approach in China is to restore a Marxist aesthetic and historical viewpoint as both suitable and workable.

Notes

1   *Selected Works of Mao Zedong* (Beijing: People's Press, 1968), p. 871.

2   Ibid.

3   Marx, "Preface," *A Contribution to the Critique of Political Economy* (1859).

4   Marx, Engels, Lenin, and Stalin, *On Literature and Art* (Beijing: People's Literature Publishing House, 1980), p. 101.

5   Ibid., p. 40.

6   Lukács, *Studies in European Realism* (New York: Grosset and Dunlap, 1964), p. 21.

7   Marx et al., *On Literature and Art*, p. 130.

8   Marx, "Preface," p. 390.

9   Marx, *Theses on Feuerbach*.

Hugo Achugar

Hugo Achugar was born in Montevideo, Uruguay, in 1944, and received a Ph.D. in Latin American literature from the University of Pittsburgh. He has taught at the Catholic University of Andreas Vello (Venezuela), the Central University of Venezuela, and is currently at Northwestern University. He is the author of more than ten books, including *Textos para decir maria* (1976) and *Los mariposas tropicales* (1985).

Jack L. Amariglio

Jack L. Amariglio was born in Brooklyn, New York, in 1951. For many years he was involved in community organizing in the working-class, ethnically diverse neighborhood in which he grew up. He received his B.A. in history from the City College of New York in 1973, his Ph.D. in economics from the University of Massachusetts in 1984, and is currently teaching economics at Franklin and Marshall College in Lancaster, Pennsylvania. He has published on the philosophy and methodology of economics, economic history, economic anthropology, and Marxist social theory, and is presently writing a book on different historical forms of "primitive communism" in the pre-twentieth-century United States.

Perry Anderson

Perry Anderson was born Francis Rory Peregrine Anderson in London in 1938 and was educated at Eton College and Oxford University, where he received a B.A. in French and Russian literature. After serving for almost twenty years as the editor of *New Left Review,* he remains the primary voice on the editorial committee. He has done research and taught at the Maison des Sciences de L'Homme (Paris), the University of Manchester, and the Central University of Venezuela. His books include *Passages from Antiquity to Feudalism* (1974), *Lineages of the Absolutist State* (1974), *Considerations on Western Marxism* (1976), *Arguments within English Marxism* (1980), and *In the Tracks of Historical Materialism* (1984). His many essays include several important ones published in *NLR:* "Components of the National Culture," "The Antinomies of Antonio Gramsci," and "Trotsky's Interpretation of Stalinism."

Stanley Aronowitz

Stanley Aronowitz was born in New York City in 1933 and received his Ph.D. from the Union Graduate School. In the sixties he was a labor and community organizer and coedited *Studies in the Left;* in the seventies he co-founded the New American Movement (NAM). He is the author of many books, including *False Promises: The Shaping of American Working-Class Consciousness* (1973), *The Crisis in Historical Materialism* (1981), and *Working-Class Hero: A New Strategy for Labor* (1983). His articles have appeared in *The Nation, Village Voice,* and the *Los Angeles Times,* as well as numerous academic journals. He is currently professor of sociology at the Graduate Center of the City University of New York and the Center for Worker Education and is coeditor of *Social Text.*

Étienne Balibar

Étienne Balibar was born in Avallon (Yonne), France, in 1942 and studied at the École Normale Supérieure and the Sorbonne (with Jean Hyppolite and Georges Canguilhem). He worked with Louis Althusser for many years, coauthoring *Reading Capital,* and has taught at the University of Algiers, the Sorbonne, and presently at the University of Paris; he has also taught in the Netherlands, Cuba, and Mexico. After coorganizing the movement Pour L'union dans les Luttes from 1978 to 1981, he was excluded from the Communist party for criticizing its position on the question of immigrant workers in France. He has published numerous books and articles, including *Sur la dictature du proletariat* (1976) and, most recently, *Spinoza, philosophie politique* (1985).

Michèle Barrett

Michèle Barrett was born near London in 1949 and studied sociology at the Universities of Durham and Sussex. She coedited *Ideology and Cultural Production* (1979), edited *Virginia Woolf: Women and Writing* (1980), authored *Women's Oppression Today* (1980), and coauthored *The Anti-Social Family* (1982). Since 1977 she has taught sociology at the City University of London. She is a member of the editorial collective of *Feminist Review*.

Iain Chambers

Iain Chambers was born near Manchester, England, in 1949, and brought up near Bristol. He studied history and American studies at the University of Keele and did research at the Centre for Contemporary Cultural Studies of the University of Birmingham. He is the author of *Urban Rhythms* (1985) and *Popular Culture: The Metropolitan Experience* (1986) and currently teaches at the University of Naples and publishes widely in both English and Italian.

Christine Delphy

Christine Delphy is a research fellow at the Centre National de la Recherche Scientifique. She was a cofounder, with Simone de Beauvoir, of the journal *Questions Feministes* and remains an editor of *Nouvelles Questions Feministes*. Her publications include *The Main Enemy* (1977) and *Close to Home: A Materialist Analysis of Women's Oppression* (1984).

Terry Eagleton

Terry Eagleton was born in Salford, England, in 1943. Educated at Cambridge University, he currently teaches at Wadham College, Oxford. He is the author of nine books, including *Myths of Power: A Marxist Study of the Brontës* (1976), *Criticism and Ideology* (1976), *Walter Benjamin, Or Towards a Revolutionary Criticism* (1981), and *Literary Theory* (1983). Most recently some of his essays have been collected in *Against the Grain* (1986).

A. Belden Fields

A. Belden Fields was born in Chicago in 1937 and attended the University of Illinois (A.B., 1960) and Yale University (M.A., Ph.D.). He teaches political science at the University of Illinois at Urbana-Champaign. His books include *Student Politics in France: A Study of the Union Nationale des Étudiants de France* (1970) and *Trotskyism and Maoism: Studies of Theory and Practice in France and the United States* (1983).

Jean Franco

Jean Franco was born in Durkinfield, England, in 1924 and teaches in the department of Spanish and Portuguese at Columbia University. She received a B.A. and M.A. in history from the University of Manchester and a second B.A. and a Ph.D. in Spanish from the University of London. She has taught at London, Essex, and Stanford universities and is a founding editor of *Tabloid* and a member of the editorial collective of *Social Text*. She has published numerous articles and books, including *The Modern Culture of Latin America: Society and the Artist* (1967) and *Cesar Vallejo: The Dialectics of Poetry and Silence* (1976). She is currently working on a book on the relations between high, mass, and popular culture in Latin America.

Simon Frith

Simon Frith was born in England in 1946 and received his B.A. from Oxford University and his M.A. and Ph.D. in sociology from the University of California at Berkeley. A leading scholar on popular music, he teaches at Warwick University. He is also a leading rock critic, frequently writing for *Rolling Stone, Village Voice, New Society,* and other popular magazines. He served for four years as rock critic for the *Sunday Times* (London) and is currently writing for *The Guardian.* A founding member and for many years the chair of the British branch of the International Association for the Study of Popular Music, his books on pop music include *The Sociology of Rock* (1978) and *Sound Effects* (1981). He is currently working on a book on the "art school connection" in British popular music.

Sue Golding
Sue Golding was born in New York in 1954 and has studied at the University of Maryland (B.A.), Cambridge University, and the University of Essex. She is completing her Ph.D. in politics at the University of Toronto and has written on the concept of democracy in Gramsci's *Prison Notebooks.* She teaches political science at Trent University and is a longtime activist in gay and feminist politics, especially in struggles for sexual freedom.

Lawrence Grossberg
Lawrence Grossberg was born in New York City in 1947 and attended the University of Rochester, the Centre for Contemporary Cultural Studies of the University of Birmingham, and the University of Illinois at Urbana-Champaign, from which he received his Ph.D. in communications in 1976. He spent a number of years traveling and performing in Europe in an itinerant anarchist theater commune. The author of many articles in the areas of contemporary philosophy and literary theory, cultural studies, philosophy of communication, and popular music, he has served as assistant director of the Unit for Criticism and Interpretive Theory at the University of Illinois and was the assistant director of the summer program Marxism and the Interpretation of Culture. He is currently completing a book with Stuart Hall and Jennifer Daryl Slack entitled *Cultural Studies* and is also working on a book about postmodernism, cultural studies, and popular culture called *Another Boring Day in Paradise.*

Stuart Hall
Stuart Hall was born in Kingston, Jamaica, in 1932 and attended Oxford University as both a Rhodes Scholar and a Jamaica Scholar. A founding member of the New Left Club and the first editor of *New Left Review,* he also helped shape the Centre for Contemporary Cultural Studies at the University of Birmingham, as a research associate and, from 1969 to 1979, as its director, and is currently professor of sociology at the Open University. He has been active in a variety of political struggles and is regarded by many as a leading spokesperson for the British Left. Coeditor of many volumes of the Centre's research (e.g., *Culture, Media, Language* [1980]), numerous Open University readers (e.g., *Politics and Ideology* [1986]), and a number of books on the New Right and the state of the Left (e.g., *The Politics of Thatcherism* [1983]), he also coauthored *The Popular Arts* (1964), *Policing the Crisis: Mugging, the State, and Law and Order* (1978), and *Cultural Studies* (forthcoming). His essays are currently being collected in a number of volumes, including *Reproducing Ideologies.*

Eugene W. Holland
Eugene W. Holland was born in Princeton, N.J., in 1953 and received his Ph.D. in French from the University of California at San Diego. He has taught at Rice University, the University of Iowa, and currently in the departments of romance languages and humanities at Ohio State University. He has written articles on nineteenth-century French literature and critical theory, including "The Suppression of Politics in the Institution of Psychoanalysis" and "Narcissism from Baudelaire to Sartre."

Fredric Jameson

Fredric Jameson was born in 1934 and has come to be regarded as perhaps the leading Marxist literary critic in the United States. Since receiving his B.A. from Haverford College and his Ph.D. in French from Yale University, he has taught at Harvard and Yale universities, the University of California at San Diego and at Santa Cruz, and currently at Duke University. He is coeditor of *Social Text* and the author of many articles and books, including *Sartre: The Origins of a Style* (1961), *Marxism and Form* (1971), *The Prison-House of Language* (1972), *Fables of Aggression* (1979), and *The Political Unconscious* (1981).

Ernesto Laclau

Ernesto Laclau was born in Argentina in 1935 and was educated at the University of Buenos Aires and Oxford University. He teaches in the department of government of the University of Essex and in the department of history at the University of Chicago. He is the author of *Politics and Ideology in Marxist Theory* (1977) and coauthor, with Chantal Mouffe, of *Hegemony and Socialist Strategy: Towards a Radical Democratic Politics* (1985).

Henri Lefebvre

Henri Lefebvre was born in 1901 in Hegetman, Gascony, and studied with Maurice Blondel at the university in Aix-en-Provence and with Leon Brunschvicg at the Sorbonne. He was, and remains, one of the most influential figures in modern French Marxist theory. In the twenties, he cofounded the Philosophies Group, which was initially closely allied with the surrealists. After joining the PCF in 1928, the group began publishing *La Revue Marxiste*, which is often described as the first serious French journal of Marxist theory. In the thirties, he cotranslated the first selections of Marx's 1844 Manuscripts into French. He served in the Resistance during the Second World War, and as a leading member of the anti-Stalinist group within the PCF, he published an internal dissident journal, *Voies Nouvelles*. In 1958 he was expelled from the party and became the moving force behind the dissident Marxist journal *Arguments*. He has taught at the universities of Strasbourg, Paris at Nanterre, and the École Pratique des Hautes Études and has published many books, ranging from his early readings of the more humanistic Marx (e.g., *Dialectical Materialism* [1968], to his analysis of the events of 1968 (*The Explosion* [1969]), to his highly influential *Everyday Life in the Modern World* (1971). Lefebvre currently lives in Paris and continues to write.

Julia Lesage

Julia Lesage is cofounder and editor of *Jump Cut: A Review of Contemporary Cinema*, as well as the author of *A Research Guide to Jean-Luc Godard* (1979). She has taught film theory, criticism, and production at many universities, including Northwestern, the University of Illinois at Chicago, Indiana University, and the Pontifical Catholic University (Lima, Peru). She has lectured and published widely on a broad range of topics in contemporary cinematic theory and practice, Marxism, and feminism.

Catharine MacKinnon

Catharine MacKinnon was born in 1947, attended Smith College, and received her M.Phil. and J.D. (1977) from Yale University. She has been active, as a scholar and lawyer, in many key court battles around issues of gender, particularly in the areas of sex discrimination, sexual harassment, and pornography. Her first book, *Sexual Harassment of Working Women: A Case of Sex Discrimination* (1979), helped to establish and define sexual harassment as a legal injury. More recently, she has been a visible leader and spokesperson for the anti-pornography movement. In addition, she has published a number of articles in feminist theory (e.g., "Feminism, Marxism, Method and the State") which have

726

placed her at the center of current theoretical debates. Her new book, *Feminism Unmodified,* will be published shortly. She has taught at the law schools of the University of Minnesota and Harvard and Yale universities and is currently a visiting scholar at Stanford University Law School.

Armand Mattelart

Armand Mattelart was born in Belgium in 1936 and received his doctorate in law and political economy from the University of Louvain. From 1962 to 1973 he taught at the university in Santiago, Chile, where he worked closely with the Allende government in the attempt to create new initiatives in popular communication. Between 1975 and 1983 he was a professor at the University of Paris, VII and VIII. He has carried out frequent missions for the governments of France, Belgium, and Mozambique, and for the United Nations, in the area of communications policy. Founder and coeditor of the journal, *Comunicacion y Cultura,* which moved from Chile to Argentina and then to Mexico (in 1977), he is currently professor of information sciences and communication and head of the department at the University of Upper Brittany (Rennes II). He is the author of many articles and books, including (with Ariel Dorfman) *How to Read Donald Duck* (1975), *Multinational Corporations and the Control of Culture* (1979), *Mass Media, Ideologies and the Revolutionary Movement* (1980), *Transnationals and the Third World: The Struggle for Culture* (1983), and *Communication and Information Technologies: Freedom of Choice for Latin America?* (1984).

Michèle Mattelart

Michèle Mattelart was born in France in 1941 and studied at the Sorbonne and the University of Paris. She is presently doing research at the Centre National de la Recherche Scientifique in Paris. From 1963 to 1973 she lived in Chile, teaching at the Catholic University of Chile and helping to found a center for national study. During Allende's rule she was involved with both the national television service and publishing for youth. Frequent trips and official missions since then have maintained her close ties with Latin America. She has written many articles and books, including *La cultura de la opresion femenina* (1977), *Women and the Cultural Industries* (1981), and (with A. Mattelart and X. Delcourt) *La culture contre la democratie?* (1985).

Franco Moretti

Franco Moretti was born in Italy in 1949 and is professor of English literature at the University of Salerno. He is editor of the journals *Calibano* and *Quaderni Piacentini,* has edited an anthology of criticism on T. S. Eliot (1975), and has written a study of English left-wing intellectuals in the thirties (1976). His book, *Signs Taken for Wonder,* was published in 1983.

Chantal Mouffe

Chantal Mouffe was born in 1943 in Baulet, Belgium, and attended the Catholic University of Louvain (B.A.), the University of Paris, and the University of Essex (M.A.). She has taught at the National University of Colombia and City University of London and is currently teaching at Westfield College of the University of London and writing for various popular periodicals (e.g., *The Guardian, New Statesman, El Pais*). She has written extensively on problems of ideology and hegemony and has edited a collection of essays, *Gramsci and Marxist Theory* (1979). Most recently, she coauthored *Hegemony and Socialist Strategy: Towards a Radical Democratic Politics* (1985).

Oskar Negt

Oskar Negt was born in Königsberg (now Kaliningrad) in 1934. He has studied and taught at the Universitat Frankfurt am Main, where he was closely associated with the Frankfurt school of critical theory. He is currently professor of sociology at the University of Hannover and has published numerous articles and books, including *Struckturbeziehungen Zwischen den Gesellschaftslehren Comtes und Hegel* (1964), *Universitat und Arbeiterbewegung* (1968), and (with Alexander Kluge) *Offentlichket und Erfarhrung zur Organisationsanalyse* (1972).

Cary Nelson

Cary Nelson was born in Philadelphia in 1946. Educated at Antioch College and the University of Rochester, he is currently professor of English and founding director of the Unit for Criticism and Interpretive Theory at the University of Illinois at Urbana-Champaign. The author of *The Incarnate Word: Literature as Verbal Space* (1973) and *Our Last First Poets: Vision and History in Contemporary American Poetry* (1981) and the editor of several books, including *Theory in the Classroom* (1986), he is presently completing *Reading Criticism: The Literary and Institutional Status of Critical Discourse*, chapters of which have appeared in numerous books and journals, and *Modern American Poetry and Literary History*.

Paul Patton

Paul Patton was born in Australia in 1950 and studied philosophy at the University of Sydney, where he participated in the struggle for the introduction of a women's studies course, which eventually led to the splitting in two of the philosophy department. After receiving an M.A., he completed a Doctorat d'Université at the University of Paris at Vincennes in 1979. Since returning to Australia he has taught social theory, epistemology, and the philosophy of science at Macquarie and Griffith universities and the University of Sydney and is currently at the University of New South Wales. A member of the Intervention Collective, he has published essays and edited collections on, as well as translating, the work of various contemporary French theorists, especially Foucault, Deleuze, and Baudrillard.

Michel Pêcheux

Michel Pêcheux was born in France in 1938 and studied philosophy under Louis Althusser at the École Normale Supérieure, participating in Althusser's famous course for scientists (1967-68), out of which came *Sur l'histoire des sciences*. His later works, including *Language, Semantics and Ideology* (1982) and *La langue introuvable*, critically extend the theory of ideology in light of recent developments in linguistic, psychoanalytic, and Marxist theory. Until his death in 1983 he was research director at the Centre National de Recherche Scientifique.

Gajo Petrović

Gajo Petrović has long had a prominent place in philosophy in Yugoslavia and in the development of a humanistic "neo-Marxist" alternative to orthodox Marxism in Eastern Europe. Born in the town of Karlovac in 1927, he was educated at the University of Zagreb (Ph.D. 1956), where he subsequently was appointed to the philosophy faculty and for many years has been professor of philosophy. The course of his philosophical development and career is reflected in the changing nature of the books he has written. His first book, a study of the thought of the orthodox Marxist Russian philosopher Plekhanov (*The Philosophical Views of G. V. Plekhanov*, 1957), was followed seven years later by two books on matters central to the Western analytic tradition (*From Locke to Ayer* and *Logic*, both 1964). Petrović then began publishing a series of books reinterpreting Marx's thought along humanistic lines, departing markedly from the orthodox ("Stalinist") tradition: *Philosophy and Marxism* (1965), *Why Praxis?* (1972), and *Philosophy and Revolution* (1979). These books and other writings from the mid-1960s onward brought him to the attention of philosophers in the West and established him as an important contemporary interpreter of Marx. He also served as editor-in-chief of the journal *Praxis,* in which a remarkable group of like-minded Yugoslav philosophers found their voice and gained wide attention through their vigorous and bold contributions to a new human-centered understanding of Marxism. During the first part of this period, Petrović and his colleagues focused their criticisms on the theory and practice of Stalinist Marxism, valorized the Yugoslav alternative, and enjoyed the favor of the political authorities in Yugoslavia. As they became disenchanted with and increasingly critical of Yugoslav institutions and practices, however, they lost this favor and eventually became the target of harsh political criticism and repressive measures. At various times they were forbidden to teach and publish in Yugoslavia; the regime also sought to deprive them of their academic positons and to bring about their exile. Petrović led the resistance to these pressures, and he and his colleagues somehow managed to weather the storm, refusing either to abandon their philosophical and critical course or to quit their positions and their country. His and their position remains a difficult and tenuous one; but, with his colleagues, Petrović continues to teach and write in Yugoslavia and to contribute to the further development of Marxist philosophy.

Fred Pfeil

Fred Pfeil was born in 1949 in Port Allegany, Pennsylvania, "a white rural factory town." He "escaped to Amherst College, there to receive equal doses of Civilization and Snobbery" and to work with Tillie Olsen, his first mentor as a fiction writer. While working on a master's degree in creative writing at Stanford University, he labored in a variety of "mainly bottom-line jobs" and was employed by the Navy to teach sailors aboard the USS *Agerholm* in the Pacific. He has taught English at Stephens College in Missouri and currently teaches in the departments of English and twentieth-century studies at Oregon State University at Corvallis. He was a member of NAM and is currently active in Central America solidarity work and the construction of the Rainbow Coalition. Since 1982 he has been coeditor of *The Minnesota Review,* a "journal of committed writing." He has written a number of essays on literature, criticism, and music, in addition to a large body of fictional work. His novel, *Goodman 2020,* was published in 1986, and a collection of his short stories is due out shortly. He is presently working on a documentary novel about the relationships between patterns of masculinity and corporate capitalism in late-nineteenth-century America.

Stephen A. Resnick

Stephen A. Resnick was born in 1938 and received his Ph.D. in economics from M.I.T. in 1964. He has taught at Yale University and City College of New York and currently teaches economics at the University of Massachusetts at Amherst. He has published on such topics as imperialism, international trade and the European Common Market, and economic history. A cofounder, in 1983, of the Association for Economic and Social Analysis, his books include *Colonial Development: An Econometric Study* (with Thomas Birnberg, 1975) and *Marxist Theory: Epistemology, Class, Enterprise and State* (with Richard Wolff, forthcoming). He has also coedited *Rethinking Marxism: Struggles in Marxist Theory* (1986).

Fernando Reyes Matta

Fernando Reyes Matta is a journalist and director of the Division of Communication and Development of the Instituto Latinoamericano de Estudios Transnacionales (ILET). He was professor of broadcasting at the Catholic University of Chile and has taught at Stanford University. He serves as an consultant to numerous international organizations, including UNESCO and the MacBride Commission, and has published many articles and books on Latin American affairs and communication policy, including *Communication and the New Order: The Economic-Technological Crossroads* (1983), *The Concept of Peace and the Influence of*

729

Mass Media upon It: A Latin American Perspective (1977), and *Cuba: Diez anos de revolucion* (1969).

Andrew T. I. Ross
Andrew T. I. Ross was born in 1956 and educated in Scotland, where he spent some time working in the North Sea oil fields. After doing doctoral research at the University of Kent, Indiana University, and the University of California at Berkeley (receiving his Ph.D. in English and American literature from the University of Kent at Canterbury), he worked at Illinois State University and is currently teaching English at Princeton University. A member of the editorial collective of *Social Text*, he has published on a wide range of topics, including cultural theory, sexual politics, psychoanalysis, television, modern literature, and literary criticism. The author of *The Failure of Modernism: Symptoms of American Poetry* (1986), he is also the cotranslator of Jacques Aumont's *Montage Eisenstein* (1986) and is currently working on a study of intellectuals and mass culture.

Michael Ryan
Michael Ryan was born in Ireland in 1951 and received a B.A., M.A., and Ph.D. from the University of Iowa. He has taught at the University of Virginia and currently at Northeastern University and is the author of *Marxism and Deconstruction: A Critical Articulation* (1982) and coauthor (with Douglas Kellner) of *The Politics and Ideology of Contemporary American Film*. He is also the cotranslator of Antonio Negri's *Marx beyond Marx* (1984).

Richard Schacht
Richard Schacht was born in Racine, Wisconsin, in 1941, and received a B.A. from Harvard University, an M.A. and Ph.D. in philosophy from Princeton University, and did postgraduate work at Tübingen University. He is currently professor and chair of the philosophy department at the University of Illinois at Urbana-Champaign and has published widely in European philosophy since Kant, philosophical anthropology, social theory, value theory, and the philosophy of art. His books include *Alienation* (1970), *Hegel and After: Studies in Continental Philosophy between Kant and Sartre* (1975), *Nietzsche* (1983), and *Classical Modern Philosophers: Descartes to Kant* (1984). He is currently working on a book on human nature.

Gayatri Chakravorty Spivak
Gayatri Chakravorty Spivak was born in Calcutta, India, in 1942 and received a B.A. in English from the University of Calcutta in 1959. She came to the United States in 1961 and received a Ph.D. in comparative literature from Cornell University in 1967, under the supervision of Paul de Man. She spent 1963-64 as a research student at Girton College, Cambridge, and taught at the University of Iowa from 1965 to 1978, serving as chair of the comparative literature department from 1975 to 1977. She was professor of English at the University of Texas at Austin from 1978 to 1984, Longstreet Professor of English at Emory University until 1986, and is currently at the University of Pittsburgh. She has published extensively on topics relating to deconstruction, the critique of imperialism, and feminist-Marxism in Asia, Africa, Australia, Eastern and Western Europe, and the United States. In 1974 she published *Myself Must I Remake: Life and Poetry of W. B. Yeats* "in a deliberate response to a certain challenge articulated by the U.S. undergraduate movement in the sixties." In 1976 she published "what by many is considered a text of the other extreme": a translation with critical introduction of Jacques Derrida's *De la grammatologie*. Her most recent book is *In Other Worlds: Essays in Cultural Politics* (1987).

730

Darko R. Suvin

Darko R. Suvin was born in 1930 in Zagreb, Yugosalvia, and studied at the University of Bristol, the Sorbonne, and Yale University, in addition to receiving a B.A., M.S., and Ph.D. from Zagreb University. He is extremely active in many organizations concerned with both theater and science fiction (e.g., he served as coeditor of *Science Fiction Studies* from 1973 to 1981) and is currently professor of English and comparative literature at McGill University and vice-president of the International Brecht Society. He has edited numerous volumes on Brecht and science fiction, and in addition to his many academic contributions he writes theater criticism. He has published many books on a diverse range of topics, most recently *Metamorphoses of Science Fiction: On the Poetics and History of a Literary Genre* (1979), *Victorian Science Fiction in the U.K.: The Discourses of Knowledge and of Power* (1983), and *To Brecht and Beyond: Soundings in Modern Dramaturgy* (1984).

Fengzhen Wang

Fengzhen Wang, an editor, critic, and translator, was born in 1942 to a farmer's family in north China. His early schooling, "directed in accordance with the mottos 'carefully read and write, do physical exercises every morning,'" included studies at Lincheng High School and Peking University. Wang's talent for literature was exhibited in high school when he won the local award for poetry in 1958. From 1968 to 1977 he worked as a businessman and interpreter in a foreign trade company in Beijing. Since 1978 he has been an editor of *World Literature,* a leading magazine in China for translations of foreign literary works and critical essays, and a lecturer at the Institute of Foreign Literature of the Chinese Academy of Social Sciences. "During the Cultural Revolution I was sent to a farm to do physical labor for a year, which enriched my experience of life. With the difficulties facing intellectuals at that time, I managed to get some science fiction books to read and later became a well-known critic in that field." Since the end of the Cultural Revolution he has written essays on foreign writers such as John Keats, Thomas Hardy, Joseph Conrad, and Nathaniel Hawthorne, as well as on the practice of Western literary criticism. He has translated the works of Rene Wellek, Northrop Frye, Erskine Caldwell, John Wain, and others, and has compiled a number of anthologies of English and American stories and critical essays. He has been a visiting scholar at UCLA and is now working on a book about his visit to the United States, as well as on a brief history of Western literary criticism.

Cornel West

Cornel West was born in 1953 and received a B.A. from Harvard University and an M.A. and Ph.D. (1980) in philosophy from Princeton University. He has taught at the Union Theological Seminary and is currently teaching the philosophy of religion at the Divinity School of Yale University. He is a member of the editorial collective of *Social Text* and has been involved for many years in Afro-American and socialist politics. The author of *Prophesy Deliverance! An Afro-American Revolutionary Christianity* (1982), he has written extensively on the relations of Afro-American experience, theology, and Marxism, as well as on contemporary hermeneutic and Marxist philosophy.

Richard D. Wolff

Richard D. Wolff was born in 1942 and attended Harvard University and Stanford University, receiving his Ph.D. in economics from Yale University in 1969. He has taught at Yale University and City College of New York and currently teaches economics at the University of Massachusetts at Amherst. He has published widely on such topics as colonialism in Africa, imperialism, and the theory of economic crises. He has also been active in the U.S. labor movement and socialist community organizations since the 1960s. In 1974 he published *The Eco-*

nomics of Colonialism: Britain and Kenya, 1870-1930. His recent work with coauthor Stephen Resnick on certain basic theoretical problems in the Marxist tradition culminated in the forthcoming *Marxist Theory: Epistemology, Class, Enterprise and State.* He has also coedited *Rethinking Marxism: Struggles in Marxist Theory* (1976) and was a cofounder of the Association for Economic and Social Analysis.